D1327678

CHESS
SUTTON COLDFIELD
ENGLAND
WORLD CHESS
SPECIALISTS

II ENCIKLOPEDIJA ŠAHOVSKIH OTVARANJA II
II ЭНЦИКЛОПЕДИЯ ШАХМАТНЫХ ДЕБЮТОВ II
II ENCYCLOPEDIA OF CHESS OPENINGS II
II ENZYKLOPÄDIE DER SCHACH-ERÖFFNUNGEN II
II ENCYCLOPEDIE DES OUVERTURES D'ECHECS II
II ENCICLOPEDIA DE APERTURAS DE AJEDREZ II
II ENCICLOPEDIA DELLE APERTURE NEGLI SCACCHI II
II ENCYKLOPEDI ÖVER SPELÖPPNINGAR I SCHACK II

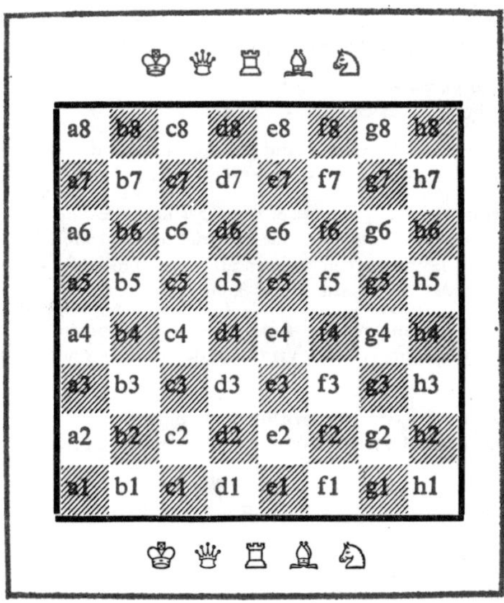

ŠAHOVSKI INFORMATOR • ШАХМАТНЫЙ ИНФОРМАТОР • CHESS INFORMANT • SCHACH-INFORMATOR • INFORMATEUR D'ECHECS • INFORMADOR AJEDRECISTICO • INFORMATORE SCACCHISTICO • SCHACK-INFORMATOR

FIDE • FIDE • FIDE • FIDE • FIDE • FIDE • FIDE • FIDE • FIDE • FIDE
FIDE • FIDE • FIDE • FIDE • FIDE • FIDE • FIDE • FIDE • FIDE • FIDE
FIDE • FIDE • FIDE • FIDE • FIDE • FIDE • FIDE • FIDE • FIDE • FIDE

SISTEM ZNAKOVA • СИСТЕМА ЗНАКОВ • CODE SYSTEM • ZEICHENERKLÄRUNG • SYSTEME DE SIGNES • SISTEMA DE SIGNOS • SPIEGAZIONE DEI SIGNI • TECKENFÖRKLARING

⩲ beli stoji nešto bolje • белые стоят немного лучше • white stands slightly better • weiss steht etwas besser • les blancs ont jeu un peu meilleur • el blanco està algo mejor • il bianco sta un po' meglio • vit står något bättre

⩱ crni stoji nešto bolje • черные стоят немного лучше • black stands slightly better • schwarz steht etwas besser • les noirs ont jeu un peu meilleur • el negro està algo mejor • il nero sta un po' meglio • svart står något bättre

± beli stoji bolje • белые стоят лучше • white has the upper hand • weiss steht besser • les blancs ont le meilleur jeu • el blanco està mejor • il bianco sta meglio • vit står bättre

∓ crni stoji bolje • черные стоят лучше • black has upper hand • schwarz steht besser • les noirs ont le meilleur jeu • el negro està mejor • il nero sta meglio • svart står bättre

+ — beli ima odlučujuću prednost • белые имеют решающее преимущество • white has a decisive advantage • weiss hat entscheidenden vorteil • les blancs ont un avantage décisif • el blanco tiene una ventaja decisiva • il bianco é in vantaggio decisivo • vit har avgörande fördel

— + crni ima odlučujuću prednost • черные имеют решающее преимущество • black has a decisive advantage • schwarz hat entscheidenden vorteil • les noirs ont un avantage décisif • el negro tiene una ventaja decisiva • il nero é in vantaggio decisivo • svart har avgörande fördel

= igra je jednaka • игра равна • the game is even • das spiel ist ausgeglichen • le jeu est égal • el juego està equilibrado • gioco pari • lika spel

∞ igra je neizvesna • неясная позиция • the position is unclear • das spiel ist unklar • le jeu est incertain • la posicion no es clara • gioco poco chiaro • ställningen är oklar

=∞ sa kompenzacijom za materijalnu prednost protivnika • компенсация за материально преимущество противника • with compesation for the material • mit kompesation für das material • avec compensation pour matérriel • con compensatión por el material • con compenso contro il vantaggio di materiale dell' avversario • med kompensation för underlägsenhet materialet

⟳ preimućstvo u razvoju • преимущество в развитии • development advantage • entwicklungsvorsprung • avance de développement • ventaja de desarrollo • vantaggio di sviluppe • utvecklingsförsprång

○ vlada većim prostranstvom • контролируя большое пространство • greater board room • beherrscht mehr raum • grand avantage d'espace • ventaja de ejpacio • maggior vantaggio spaziale • terrängfördel

→ sa napadom • с атакой • with attack • mit angriff • avec attaque • con ataque • con attacco • med angrepp

↑ sa inicijativom • с инициативой • with initiative • mit initiative • avec initiative • con iniciative • con iniziativa • med initiativ

⇆ sa kontraigrom • с контригрой • with counter-play • mit gegenspiel • avec contre-jeu • con contra-ataque • con controgioco • med motspel

⊙ iznudnica • цуг цванг • zug zwang • zugzwang • zug zwang • zug zvang • dragtvang

\# mat • мат • mate • matt • mat • mate • matto • matt

♔ ♕ ♖ ♗ ♘

! vrlo dobar potez • очень хороший ход • a very good move • ein sehr guter zug • un tres bon coup • jugada muy buena • buona mossa • ett bra drag

!! odličan potez • отличный ход • an excellent move • ein ausgezeichneter zug • un excellent coup • jugada excelente • mossa ottima • ett utmärkt drag

? slab potez • плохой ход • a mistake • ein schwacher zug • un coup faible • mala jugada • mossa debole • ett dåligt drag

?? gruba greška • грубая ошибка • a blunder • ein grober fehler • une grave erreur • gran error • grave errore • ett grovt fel

!? potez zaslužuje pažnju • ход, заслуживающий внимания • a move deserving attention • ein beachtenswerter zug • un coup qui mérite l'attention • jugada que merece atención • mossa degna di considerazione • ett drag som förtjönar uppmärksamhet

?! potez sumnjive vrednosti • ход, имеющий сомнительную ценность • a dubious move • ein zug von zweifelhaftem wert • un coup d'une valeur douteuse • jugada de dudoso valor • mossa dubbia • ett tvivelaktigt drag

△ sa idejom... • с идеей... • with the idea... • mit der idee... • avec l'idée... • con idea... • con l'idea.... • med idén...

□ jedini potez • единственный ход • only move • einziger zug • le seul coup • unica jugada • unica mossa • enda draget

⌓ bolje je • лучше было бы • better is • besser ist • est meilleur • es mejor • e' meglio • bättre är

♔ ♕ ♖ ♗ ♘

⇔ linija • линия • file • linie • colonne • linea • fila • linje

⇗ dijagonala • диагональ • diagonals • diagonale • diagonales • diagonales • diagonali • diagonaler

⊞ centar • центр • centre • zentrum • centre • centro • centro • centrum

» kraljevo krilo • королевский фланг • king's side • königsflügel • aile roi • flanco de rey • lato di R • kungsflygen

« damino krilo • ферзевый фланг • queen's side • damenflügel • aile dame • flanco de dama • lato di D • damflygeln

× slaba tačka • слабый пункт • weak point • schwacher punkt • point faible • punto débil • punto debole • svaghet

⊥ završnica • эндшпиль • ending • endspiel • finale • final • finale • slutspel

⧉ lovački par • преимущество двух слонов • pair of bishops • läuferpaar • une paire de fous • par de alfiles • la coppia degli alfieri • löpar par

♔ ♕ ♖ ♗ ♘

(ch) šampionat • чемпионат • championship • meisterschaft • championnat • campeonato • campionato • masterskap

(izt) međuzonski turnir • межзональный турнир • interzonal tournament • interzonen-turnier • tornoi interzonal • torneo interzonal • torneo interzonale • interzonturnering

(ct) turnir kandidata • турнир претендентов • candidates' tournament • kandidaten-turnier • tornoi de candidats • torneo de candidatos • torneo dei candidati • kandidatturnering

(m) meč • матч • match • match • match • encuentro • match • match

(ol) olimpijada • олимпиада • olympiad • olympiade • l'olympiade • olimpiada • l'olimpiade • olympiad

corr. dopisna partija • партия по переписке • correspondence game • fernpartie • partie par correspondence • partida por correspondencia • la partita per corrispondenza • korrespondensparti

7/113, 8/241.. šahovski informator • шахматный информатор • chess informant • schach-informator • informateur d'echecs • informador ajedrecistico • informatore scacchistico • schack-informator

R razni potezi • разные ходы • various moves • verschiedene züge • differents coups • diferentes movidas • mosse varie • olika drag

∟ sa • с • with • mit • avec • con • con • med

┘ bez • без • without • ohne • sans • sin • senza • utan

‖ itd • и.т.д. • etc • usw • etc • etc • ecc • o.s.v.

— vidi • смотри • see • siehe • voir • ved • vedi • se

ENCIKLOPEDIJA ŠAHOVSKIH OTVARANJA U 5 TOMOVA
ЭНЦИКЛОПЕДИЯ ШАХМАТНЫХ ДЕБЮТОВ В 5 ТОМАХ
ENCYCLOPEDIA OF CHESS OPENINGS IN 5 VOLUMES
ENZYKLOPÄDIE DER SCHACH-ERÖFFNUNGEN IN 5 BÄNDEN
ENCYCLOPEDIE DES OUVERTURES D'ECHECS EN 5 TOMES
ENCICLOPEDIA DE APERTURAS DE AJEDREZ EN 5 TOMES
ENCICLOPEDIA DELLE APERTURE NEGLI SCACCHI IN 5 VOLUMI
ENCYKLOPEDI ÖVER SPELÖPPNINGAR I SCHACK I 5 DELAR

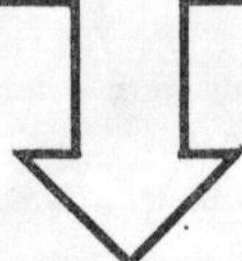

A	— 1. R ⌟ 1. e4, 1. d4 — 1. d4 R ⌟ 1... d5, 1... ♘f6 — 1. d4 ♘f6 2. R ⌟ 2. c4 — 1. d4 ♘f6 2. c4 R ⌟ 2... e6, 2... g6	**V**
B	— 1. e4 R ⌟ 1... c5, 1... e6, 1... e5 — 1. e4 c5	**II**
C	— 1. e4 e6 — 1. e4 e5	**I**
D	— 1. d4 d5 — 1. d4 ♘f6 2. c4 g6 ∟ d7–d5	**III**
E	— 1. d4 ♘f6 2. c4 e6 — 1. d4 ♘f6 2. c4 g6 ⌟ d7–d5	**IV**

II ENCIKLOPEDIJA ŠAHOVSKIH OTVARANJA II
II ЭНЦИКЛОПЕДИЯ ШАХМАТНЫХ ДЕБЮТОВ II
II ENCYCLOPEDIA OF CHESS OPENINGS II
II ENZYKLOPÄDIE DER SCHACH-ERÖFFNUNGEN II
II ENCYCLOPEDIE DES OUVERTURES D'ECHECS II
II ENCICLOPEDIA DE APERTURAS DE AJEDREZ II
II ENCICLOPEDIA DELLE APERTURE NEGLI SCACCHI II
II ENCYKLOPEDI ÖVER SPELÖPPNINGAR I SCHACK II

B

1. e4 R ⌋ 1... c5, 1... e6, 1... e5
1. e4 c5

First published 1975

ISBN 0 7134 3013 3
Printed and bound in Yugoslavia — Beograd
Representative of the Chess Informant with exclusive sales rights for the Encyclopedia of Chess Openings, volume II for West Europe and Commonwealth (except Canada)
B.T. Batsford Limited
4, Fitzhardinge Street, London W1H OAH

Autori sistema enciklopedije • Авторы система энциклопедии • The Inventors of the Encyclopedia Systems • Die Autoren des Systems der Enzyklopädie der Schach-Eröffnungen • Les auteurs des sistemes de l'encyclopédie • Autores del sistema enciclopédico • Autori dei sistemi esposti nell' Enciclopedia • Författarna till Encyklopediens system

A. Matanović, B. Rabar, M. Molerović

Odgovorni urednik • Главный редактор • Editor in-chief • Chefredakteur • Rédacteur responsable • Redactor en jefe • Redattore Capo • Ansvarig utgivare

Aleksandar Matanović

Autor klasifikacije • Автор классификации • Author of the classification • Urheber der Klassifizierung • Auteur de la classification • Autor de la Clasification • Autore della classificazione • Klassifikationsförfattare

Braslav Rabar

Zamenik odgovornog urednika • Заместитель главного редактора • Assistant of the Editor-in-chief • Assistent des Chefredakteurs • Assistant du Rédacteur en Chef • Vice-Redactor • Vice Redattore • Vice Chefredaktör

Dragan Ugrinović

Redakcija • Редакционная коллегия • Editorial board • Redaktion • Collège de rédaction • Colegio de redacción • Collegio Redazionale • Redaktion

Božić Aleksandar, Cvetković Srđan, Judovič Mihail, Krnić Zdenko, Matanović Aleksandar, Molerović Milivoje, Parma Bruno, Ugrinović Dragan

Saradnici-recenzenti • Сотрудники-рецензенты • Assistants-reviewers • Mitarbeiter-Rezensenten • Collaborateurs-recenseurs • Colaboradores-recensionistas • Collaboratori-recensori • Medarbetere-recenscenter

A. Gipslis, E. Gufeljd, M. Filip, S. Marjanović, N. Minev, J. Přibyl, V. Sokolov, D. Šahović, V. Zak

Korice • Переплёт • Cover • Pärm • Couverture • Cubiertas • Copertina • Pärmar

Miloš Majstorović

Direktor edicije • Директор эдиции • Director of the edition • Herstellungsleiter • Directeur de l'edition • Director de la edicion • Direttore editoriale • Produktionschef

Milivoje Molerović

Izdavač • Издатель • Editor • Herausgeber • Editeur • Editorial • Editore • Utgivare

Centar za unapređivanje šaha
Beograd, 7 jula 30 P. Box 739

Štampa: Grafičko preduzeće »PROSVETA« Beograd, Đure Đakovića 21

AUTORI-SARADNICI • АВТОРЫ-СОТРУДНИКИ • AUTHORS-ASSISTANTS • AUTOREN-MITARBEITER • AUTEURS-COLLABORATEURS • AUTORES-COLABORADORES • AUTORI-COLLABORATORI • FÖRFATTARNA-MEDARBETARE

BOTVINIK MIHAIL	(SSSR)
EUWE MAX	(Nederland)
FILIP MIROSLAV	(ČSSR)
GELER EFIM	(SSSR)
GIPSLIS AJVAR	(SSSR)
HORT VLASTIMIL	(ČSSR)
KERES PAUL	(SSSR)
KORČNOJ VIKTOR	(SSSR)
LARSEN BENT	(Danmark)
MATANOVIĆ ALEKSANDAR	(Jugoslavija)
PARMA BRUNO	(Jugoslavija)
POLUGAJEVSKI LEV	(SSSR)
SUETIN ALEKSEJ	(SSSR)
TAJMANOV MARK	(SSSR)
TALJ MIHAIL	(SSSR)
TRIFUNOVIĆ PETAR	(Jugoslavija)
UGRINOVIĆ DRAGAN	(Jugoslavija)
UHLMANN WOLFGANG	(DDR)
VELIMIROVIĆ DRAGOLJUB	(Jugoslavija)

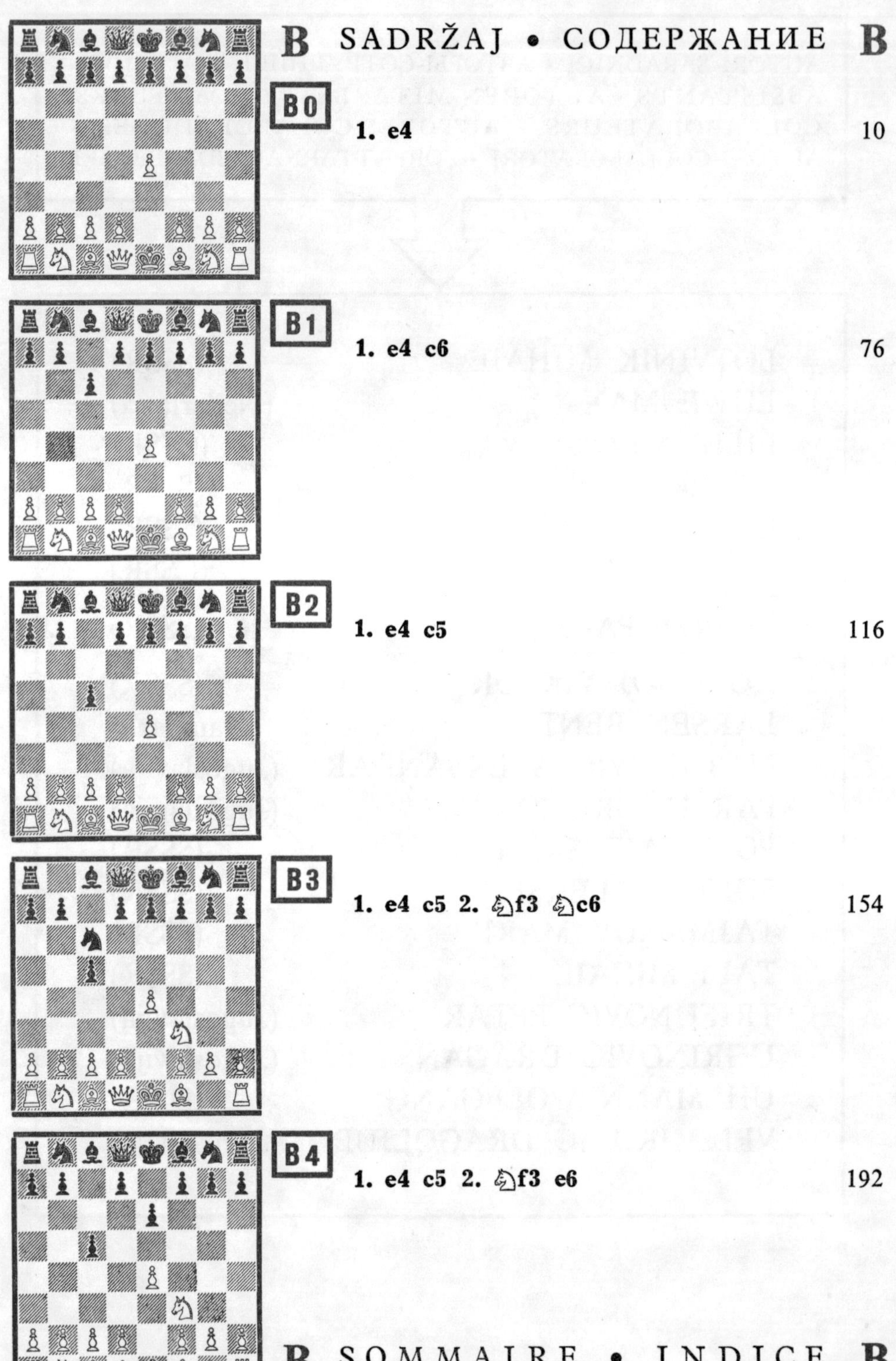

B SADRŽAJ • СОДЕРЖАНИЕ B

B SOMMAIRE • INDICE B

B CONTENTS • INHALT B

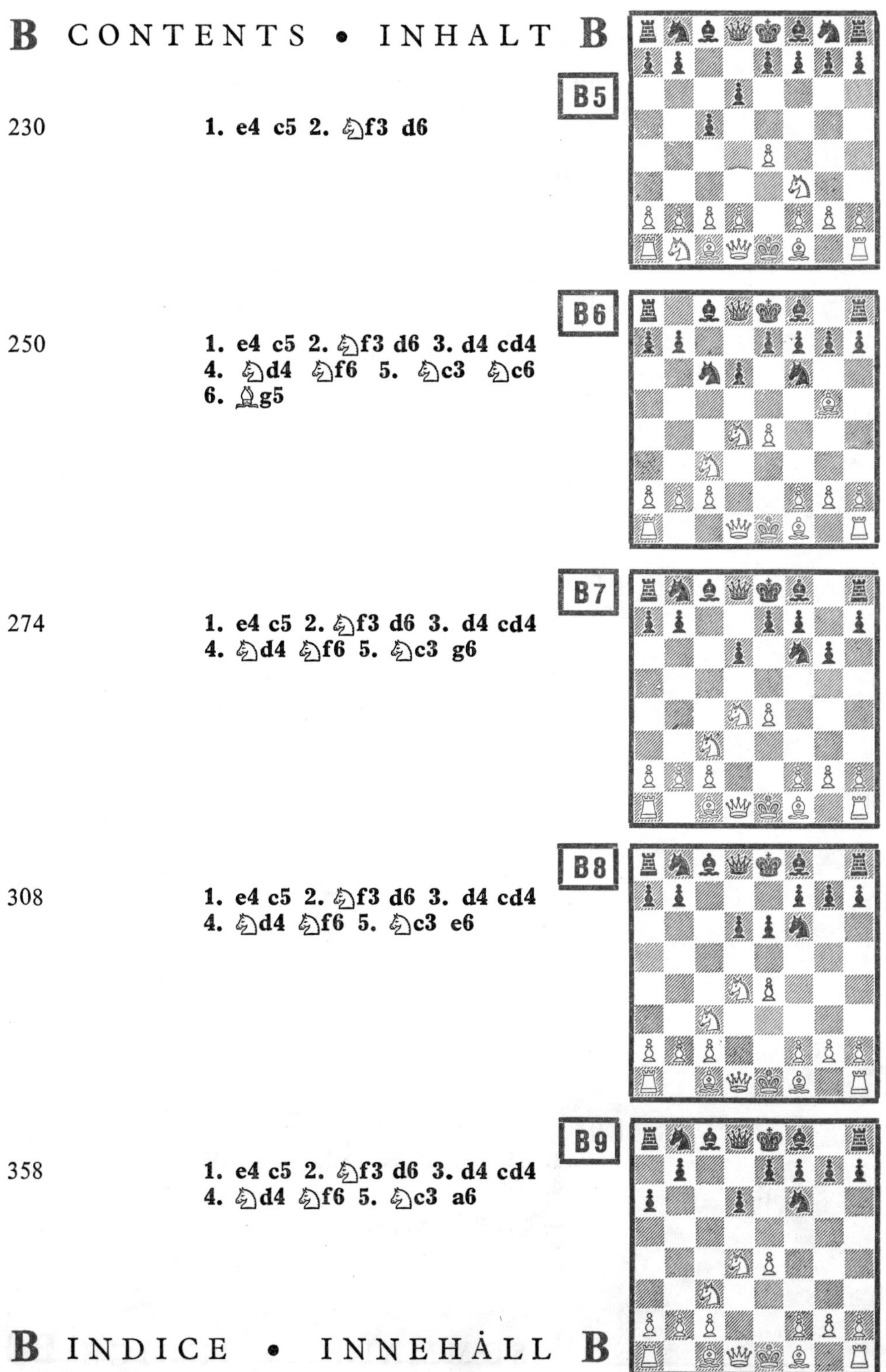

B INDICE • INNEHÅLL B

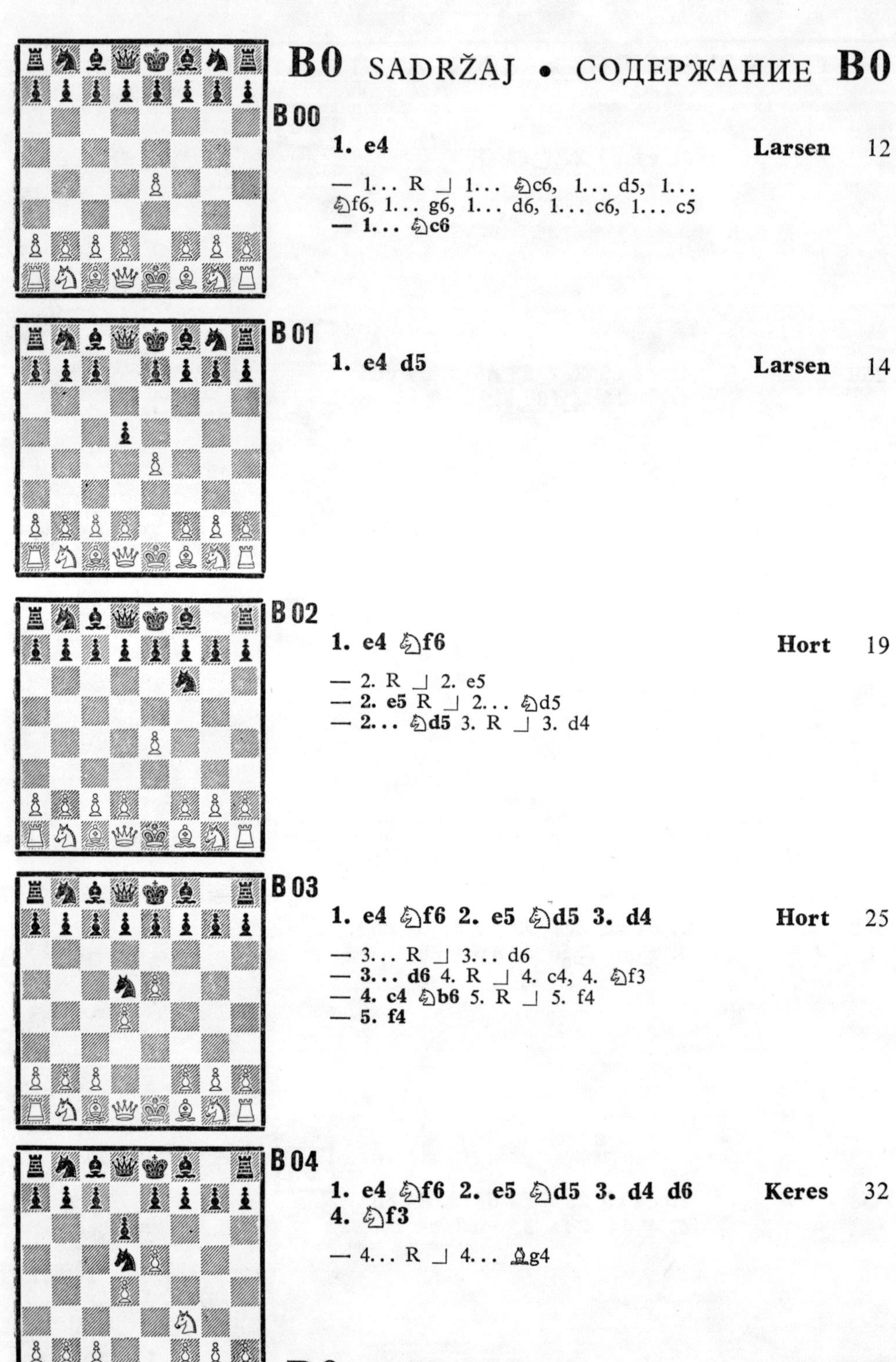

B0 SADRŽAJ • СОДЕРЖАНИЕ B0

B0 SOMMAIRE • INDICE B0

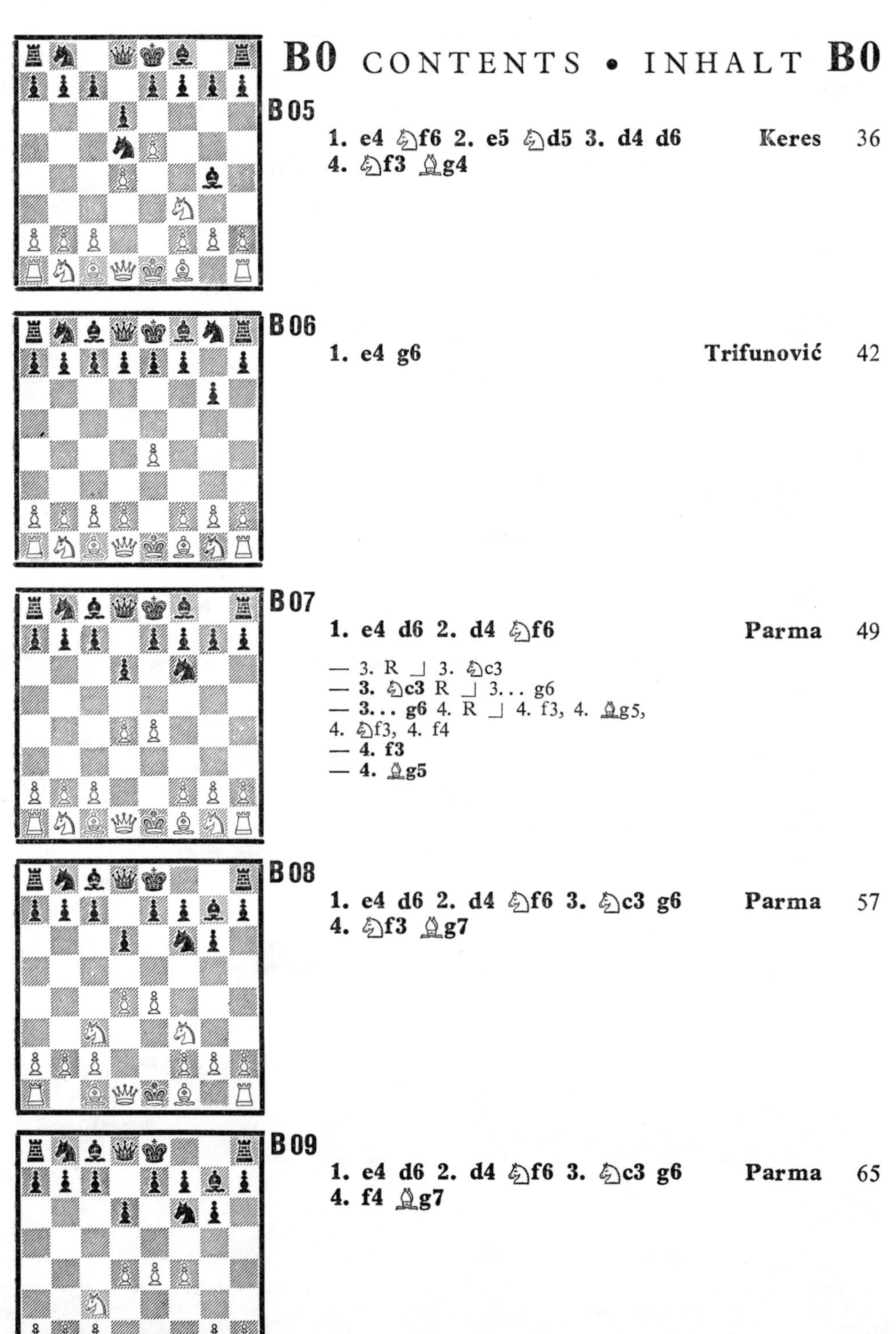

B0 CONTENTS • INHALT B0

B0 INDICE • INNEHÅLL B0

B 00

1. e4

	1	2	3	4	5	6	7	8	9	
1	. . . b6[1]	d4 ♗b7	♗d3[2] f5[3]	f3[4] e6[5]	♘c3[6] fe4	fe4 ♘f6	♘f3 d5	♗g5 ♗e7	♕e2!	±

1. e4 ♘c6 2. d4[7]

	2	3	4	5	6	7	8	9	10	
2	. . . d6[8]	♘f3 ♗g4	♗b5[9] a6[10]	♗a4[11] ♘f6[12]	c4! ♘d7[13]	♗e3 e5	d5 ♗f3	♕f3 ♘e7	♘c3 ♘g6[14]	±
3	. . . . . .	d5 ♘b8[15]	♘e2 e5[16]	de6 ♗e6	♘bc3 ♘c6	♘f4 ♕d7	♗e2 ♘f6	0—0 0-0-0	♘fd5 ♗e7[17]	±
4	. . . e5	de5[18] ♘e5	♘f3[19] ♕f6[20]	♘e5[21] ♕e5	♗d3 ♗c5[22]	♕e2 d6	♘c3 ♘f6	h3![23]		±
5	. . . . . .	d5 ♘ce7	♗d3[24] ♘g6	♗e3 ♘f6[25]	h4 h5	f3 ♗e7	♕d2 d6	c4 c5	♘c3 a6[26]	±

1. e4 ♘c6 2. d4 d5

	3	4	5	6	7	8	9	10	11	
6	ed5 ♕d5	♘f3[27] ♗g4	♗e2 0-0-0	♘c3 ♕a5	♗e3 ♘f6	♘d2 ♗e2	♕e2 ♕f5	♘b3 e5![28]	0-0-0 ed4[29]	=
7	e5 f6[30]	♘f3 ♗g4	♗e2 e6	ef6 ♘f6	c3[31] ♗d6	♘bd2 0—0	0—0 ♕e8[32]			=
8	. . . . . .	f4 ♗f5[33]	♘e2[34] e6[35]	♘g3 fe5	fe5 ♕d7[36]	♘f5 ef5	♗b5 a6	♗e2 g6	0—0 ♗h6[37]	±
9	. . . ♗f5	♘e2 e6[38]	♘g3 ♗g6	h4[39] f6	h5 ♗f7	f4 ♕d7	c3 0-0-0	♗e3 ♔b8	♘d2 ♘h6[40]	=
10	♘c3! de4[41]	d5 ♘b8[42]	♗c4[43] ♘f6	♗f4[44] a6[45]	♕e2[46] b5	♗b3 c5	dc6 ♘c6	♖d1 ♕a5	♗d2 ♘d4[47]	±

[1] **1... f5**? 2. ef5 ♘f6 3. d4 d5 4. ♗d3±; **1... f6**? 2. d4 e6 3. c4! [3. ♗d3?! ♘e7 4. ♗e3?! d5 5. ♘c3 de4 6. ♘e4 ♘d5 7. ♘h3 ♗e7 8. ♕h5 g6 9. ♕h6 ♗f8 10. ♕h4 ♗g7∞ Morphy—Barnes, London 1858] ♘e7 [3... g6 4. ♘c3 ♗g7 5. h4±↑] 4. ♘c3 d5 5. ♘f3±; **1... d6** 2. d4 [2. g3 e5 3. ♗g2 ♘c6 4. ♘e2 g6 5. d4 ♗g4 6. f3 ♗d7 7. ♗e3 ♗g7 8. d5 ♘ce7 9. c4 f5 10. ♘c3 ♘f6= Trifunović—Matanović, Jugoslavija (ch) 1951] e5 3. de5 de5 4. ♕d8 ♔d8 5. ♘c3 c6 6. f4 ♘d7 7. ♘f3 ♗d6 8. ♗c4 f6 9. f5 ♘e7 10. g4± Fuderer—Udovčić, Jugoslavija (ch) 1952; 2... g6 — B 06

[2] **3. f3**?! e6 4. c4 d5 5. cd5 ed5 6. ed5 ♗d5 7. ♘c3 ♘f6 = Donner—Cardoso, Nice (ol) 1974; **3. ♘c3** e6 4. ♘f3 ♗b4 [4... d5? 5. ♗b5 c6 6. ♗d3 ♘f6 7. e5 ♘fd7 8. ♘g5! ♗e7 9. ♕g4!± Aljehin—Rozanov, Moskva 1908; 4... ♘f6? 5. e5 ♘d5 6. ♘d5 ♗d5 7. ♗d3△ c4, 0—0, ♕e2±] 5. ♗d3 d6 △♘d7, ♘e7± Aljehin

[3] 3... e6 4. ♘f3 c5 5. c3 d6?! 6. 0—0 ♘d7 7. ♖e1 ♘e7 8. ♗g5 ♕c7 9. ♘a3 ♘g6 10. h4!±↑ Mattison—Tartakower, Karlovy Vary 1929; 5... ♘f6!?

[4] **4. ef5** ♗g2 5. ♕h5 g6 6. fg6 ♗g7 7. gh7 ♔f8 8. hg8♕ ♔g8 9. ♕g4 ♗h1 10. h4 [10. ♘c3 ♕f8 11. ♗e3 ♕f6 12. h3 ♕h4 13. ♕g6 ♘c6∓ Lombardy—Regan, USA 1974] ♗d5! [10... e6? 11. h5+−] 11. h5 ♗e6 12. ♕g2 ♖h5! [12... c6? 13. h6+−] 13. ♕a8 ♗d5 14. ♕a7 ♘c6 15. ♕a4 ♖h1=∞ Šmit—Vitolinš, SSSR 1969 — 8/97; **4. ♘c3** ♘f6 5. ♕e2±

[5] 4... e5!?

[6] 5. ef5?! ♕h4 6. g3 ♕d4 7. fe6 ♗c5 8. ♕e2 de6 9. ♘h3 ♘d7∞

[7] **2. ♗c4** ♘f6 3. ♘c3 e6 4. d3 d5 = Mjagmarsuren—Keres, Tallinn 1971 — 11/94; **2. ♘f3** g6 [2... ♘f6?! 3. e5 ♘d5 4. c4 ♘b6 5. d4 d6 — B 04; 2... d5?! 3. ed5 ♕d5 4. ♘c3 ♕h5? 5. ♘b5±; 4... ♕a5 — B 01;

2... d6 3. d4 — 2. d4; 2... e6 3. d4 d5 4. Sc3 — C 10] 3. d4 ♗g7 4. d5 ♘b8±

8 2... e6 **3. ♘c3** ♗b4! [3... d5 — C 10] 4. ♘ge2 [4. ♘f3 d6 5. ♗f4 ♘ge7 6. ♗e2 ♗c3 7. bc3 0–0 8. 0–0 ♘g6 9. ♗e3 ♕e7∓ Maroczy–Nimzowitsch, San Remo 1930] d6! [4... d5 5. e5 h5 6. ♘f4! g6 7. ♗e3 ♗c3 8. bc3 ♘a5 9. ♗d3 ♘e7 10. ♘h3!± Kmoch–Nimzowitsch, Niendorf 1927] 5. ♗e3 ♘ge7 6. a3 ♗c3 7. ♘c3 0–0 8. ♗e2 f5!=; **3. f4** d5? 4. e5±; 3... ♘f6!∞; **3. c3**!?±∆ 3... d5 4. e5 f6 5. ♗d3

9 **4. ♘c3** ♘f6 [4... a6 5. ♗e3 e5 6. d5 ♘ce7 7. h3 ♗f3 8. ♕f3 ♕d7 9. g4±○⊞ Suetin–A. Zajcev, Berlin 1968] 5. d5 [5. ♗e3 e5 6. d5 ♘b8 7. h3 ♗h5 8. ♗e2 ♗g6! 9. ♕d3 ♘bd7∞ Saharov] ♘b8 6. ♗e2 g6 7. ♗g5 ♗g7 8. ♘d2 ♗e2 9. ♕e2 c6 10. 0–0 0–0 11. ♖ad1 ♕b6 12. ♘b3 ♘bd7= Averbah–Lutikov, SSSR 1969; 5. ♗b5!±; **4. ♗e3** ♘f6 5. ♘bd2 e5 6. d5 ♘e7 7. h3± Olafsson–Castro, Nice (ol) 1974 — 17/145

10 4... ♘f6 5. c4! a6 6. ♗a4 — 4... a6

11 5. ♗c6? bc6 6. 0–0 g6 7. h3 ♗d7∓

12 5... b5 6. ♗b3 ♘f6 7. c3 e6 8. ♕e2 ♗e7 9. 0–0 0–0 10. ♘bd2 ♗h5 11. a4± Fine–Mikenas 1938

13 6... ♘e4?? 7. d5+–

14 11. h4 ♗e7 [R. Byrne–Dominguez, Mar del Plata 1961] 12. g3!±○⊞

15 3... ♘e5?! 4. ♘c3 c5? 5. f4 ♘d7 6. ♘f3 g6 7. e5! ♗g7 8. e6 fe6 9. de6 ♘b8 10. f5! ♘f6 11. ♘g5 gf5 12. ♗d3 ♘c6 13. ♘d5 ♘e5 14. ♗f5+– Bogdanović–S. Nikolić, Jugoslavija 1965

16 3... g6!?

17 11. b4!±→« König–Mieses, Bournemouth 1939

18 3. c3? d5 4. ♗b5 de4 5. d5 a6 6. ♗a4 b5 7. dc6 ba4 8. ♕a4 f5 9. ♘e2 ♕d3∓ Abramov–Mikenas, SSSR 1942

19 **4. f4**?! ♘g6 5. ♗e3?! ♗b4 6. ♘d2 [6. c3 ♗a5 7. ♕f3 d5! 8. ed5 ♘f6 9. ♗c4 0–0 ∓↑] ♘f6 7. c3 ♗a5 8. ♗d3 ♕e7 9. ♕f3 d5 10. e5 ♘g4 11. ♘b3 ♘e3 12. ♘a5 ♘h4!∓↑; **4. ♘c3** ♗c5 [4... ♗b4 5. ♕d4!±] 5. f4 ♘g6 6. ♘f3 d6 7. ♗c4 ♗e6 8. ♕e2 ♗c4 9. ♕c4 ♕d7 10. f5 ♘6e7 11. ♗g5 f6 12. ♗f4 ♘c6 13. 0-0-0 0-0-0 14. g4± Keres–Mikenas, SSSR 1964

20 4... ♘f3? 5. ♕f3 ♕f6 6. ♕g3 ♕g6 [6... ♕c6 7. ♗d3±⟳↑] 7. ♕c7 ♕e4 8. ♗e3 ±⟳↑ Lombardy–Calvo, Siegen (ol) 1970 — 10/141

21 5. ♗e2 ♘f3 [5... ♗b4 6. c3 ♗c5 7. 0–0 ♘e7 8. ♘bd2 d6 9. ♘b3 ♗b6 10. ♔h1 ♘f3 11. ♗f3 0–0 = Tarve–Keres, Tallinn 1969 — 7/111; 6. ♘bd2! ♘f3 7. ♗f3 ♘e7 8. 0–0 0–0 9. ♘b3 ♘c6 10. g3 ♖e8 11. ♗g2 ♗f8 12. c3 d6 13. f4± Keres–Kevitz, SSSR–USA 1954] 6. ♗f3 ♗c5 7. ♘c3 ♘e7±

22 6... ♗b4 7. ♘d2! ♘f6 8. 0–0 d6 9. ♘c4 ♕e7 10. c3 ♗c5 11. b4 ♗b6 12. a4± Planinc–Lutikov, Jugoslavija–SSSR 1969 — 7/113

23 **9. ♗d2**?! ♘g4! 10. f4? ♕e7∓ Planinc–Lutikov, Jugoslavija–SSSR 1969 — 7/112; 10. ♘d1=; **9. h3**!∆ 9... 0–0 10. ♗d2 ♖e8 11. 0-0-0±

24 4. g3!? ♘f6 5. ♘c3 ♘g6 6. ♗g2 ♗b4 7. ♘e2 d6 8. a3 ♗a5 9. b4 ♗b6 10. ♘a4± Ljubojević–Emma, Skopje (ol) 1972 — 14/156

25 **5... ♗b4** 6. Sd2 ♗a5 7. c4 ♘f6 8. a3! ♗d2 9. ♗d2 d6 10. ♘e2 ♘h5 11. g3± Polugajevski–Rossetto, Mar del Plata 1962; **5... ♗e7**!?

26 11. a3 ♗d7 12. g3 ♕c8 13. b4 b6 14. ♘ge2 0–0 15. ♖b1± Szabo–Rossetto, Buenos Aires 1960

27 4. ♗e3 e6?! 5. ♗e2? ♕g2 6. ♗f3 ♕g6 7. ♘e2 ♘b4 8. ♘a3 ♘d5 9. ♘c4 [9. ♘b5 (Lasker) ♘e3 10. fe3 ♗d6∓] ♕f6 10. ♘g3 ♕d8 11. ♕d2 ♘gf6∓ Brinckmann–Nimzowitsch, Berlin 1927; 4... e5!

28 10... e6? 11. a3 ♗d6 12. 0-0-0± Duras–Spielmann, Wien 1907

29 12. ♘d4 ♘d4 13. ♗d4 ♗c5=

30 3... e6? 4. ♘f3 b6 5. c3 ♘ce7 6. ♗d3 a5 7. ♕e2 ♘f5 8. h4 h5 9. ♘g5 g6 10. ♘d2! ♘ge7 [10... ♘h4? 11. ♗b5+–] 11. ♘f1 c5 12. f3± Spielmann–Nimzowitsch, New York 1927

31 7. ♗f4!?

32 **9... ♘e7**? [= Tartakower] 10. ♘g5!±; **9... ♕e8**=

33 4... ♘h6?! 5. c3 ♗g4 6. ♘f3 ♘f5 7. ♕d3 ♕d7 8. ♘bd2 0-0-0 9. b4 g5 10. ♘b3 ♗f3? 11. ♘c5!+– Kestler-van Geet, Hamburg 1965

34 **5. ♘f3** e6 6. ♗d3 ♗e4! 7. c3 ♕d7 8. 0–0 ♘h6 9. ♕e2 f5 10. ♗e3 ♗e7 11. ♘bd2 0–0 = Nimzowitsch; **5. ♗b5** e6 6. ♘f3 ♕d7 [6... ♘ge7!?] 7. ♗e3 a6 8. ♗e2 ♘ge7 9. 0–0 h5 10. c3 h4 = Coudari–Larsen, Canada 1970 — 10/140; **5. c3** e6 6. ♘f3 ♕d7 7. ♗d3 ♗e4 8. ♕e2 f5 9. ♗e3 ♘h6 10. ♘bd2 ♗e7 11. h3 0–0 12. ♘b3 ♘f7?! 13. g4 ♔h8 14. ♖g1± Duras–Nimzowitsch, Ostende 1907

35 5... fe5!?∆ 6. fe5 e6 7. ♘g3 ♕h4

36 7... ♗g6 8. h4!±

37 12. ♗h6 ♘h6 13. ♕d2 [Kolste–Nimzowitsch, Baden-Baden 1925] ♘f7±

38 4... ♘b4 5. ♘a3 e6 6. ♘g3 ♗g6 7. c3 ♘c6 8. ♘c2 ∆ ♘e3±

39 6. c3 ♕d7 7. ♗d3 0-0-0 8. h4?! ♗d3 9. ♕d3 h5! 10. ♘d2 ♘ge7=; 7. ♗b5!?

40 **12. ♗d3** ♘e7 13. ♕e2 ♘ef5 [Šašin–Vinogradov, SSSR 1967 — 4/131] 14. ♘f5 ef5=; **12. ♗b5**!?△ 12... a6 13. ♗d3

41 3... e6 — C 10

42 4... ♘e5 5. ♗f4!? [5. f3 ef3? 6. ♘f3 ♘f3 7. ♕f3 ♘f6 8. ♗f4 a6 9. h3 g6 10. g4 ♗g7 11. 0-0-0 ♗d7 12. ♕g3±→ Milner Barry–Mieses, Margate 1935; 5... e6! 6. ♕d4 ♘c6 7. ♕e4 ♘f6=] ♘g6 6. ♗g3 f5!? [6... a6 7. f3? f5! 8. fe4 f4 9. ♗f2 e5∓ Wendel–Nimzowitsch, Stockholm 1920; 7. ♗c4 ♘f6 8. ♕e2 ♗f5 9. 0-0-0∞̄⟳↑ Boleslavski] 7. h4 e5!∞ Larsen; 5. ♕d4±

43 **5. ♕d4** e6=; **5. ♘e4** e6=; **5. f3** ef3? 6. ♕f3 ♘f6 7. ♗f4 a6 8. h3△ 0-0-0±→; 5... e6!=

44 6. ♗g5 h6 7. ♗f4 a6 8. a4? e6 9. de6 ♗e6 10. ♗e6 fe6 11. ♕d8 ♔d8 12. 0-0-0 ♔c8 13. f3 ef3 14. ♘f3 ♗c5∓ Jimenez–Larsen, La Habana (ol) 1966 — 2/116; 8. ♕e2!±; 8. f3!?↑

45 **6... g6** 7. ♕e2 ♗f5 8. 0-0-0 ♗g7 9. f3 ef3 10. ♘f3±↑; **6... c6** 7. ♘ge2 cd5 8. ♘d5 ♘d5 9. ♗d5 e6 10. ♗e4 ♕d1 11. ♖d1±⊥⟳↑ Boleslavski

46 7. f3!? ef3 8. ♕f3 g6 9. h3 ♗g7 10. 0-0-0 0–0 11. ♕e3 b5 12. ♗b3 ♘bd7 13. ♘f3 ♗b7 14. ♖he1∞̄ Čeremisin–Mjasnikov, SSSR 1960

47 12. ♘e4 ♕d8 13. ♕e3 ♘e4 14. ♗b4 e5 15. ♗f8 ♔f8 16. ♕e4 ♗f5 17. ♕e5 ♕e8 18. ♕e8 ♖e8 19. ♔d2 h5 [Keres–Larsen, Stockholm 1966/67 — 3/118] 20. c3! ♘b3 21. ab3 ♗e6 22. ♘f3! ♗b3 23. ♖a1△ ♘d4±⊥ Euwe

B01 — 1. e4 d5

	2	3	4	5	6	7	8	9	10	
1	ed5[1]	♘f3[3]	♗e2	0–0	d4	♖e1	♘c3	♘b5	♘d6	=
	♕d5[2]	♗g4[4]	♘f6[5]	e6	♗d6	♘c6	♕h5	0-0-0	♖d6[6]	
2	...	♘c3	d4	♗c4[9]	♘ge2[11]	♗g5	♕d2	f3[12]	g4	±
	...	♕d8[7]	♘f6[8]	♗g4[10]	e6	♗e7	♘bd7	♗f5	♗g6[13]	
3	...	...	...	♗f4[14]	♕d2![16]	0-0-0	♗e5	h4	♘ge2[19]	±
	...	...	g6	♗g7[15]	♘f6[17]	♘d5[18]	0–0	h5		

1. e4 d5 2. ed5 ♕d5 3. ♘c3 ♕a5

	4	5	6	7	8	9	10	11	12	
4	b4?![20]	♖b1	♘f3	d4	♗c4[24]	0–0	♖e1	♗b3	♗g5	∓
	♕b4[21]	♕d6[22]	♘f6	a6[23]	e6	♗e7	b5	♗b7	♘bd7[25]	
5	♘f3	♗b5![27]	0–0	d4	♕d3	bc3	♗c4	♖ab1	♘g5!	±
	♘c6[26]	♗d7	e6	♗b4	♗c3	a6[28]	♘ge7	♖b8[29]	♕f5[30]	
6	...	♗e2[31]	0–0	d3	♗f4					=
	♘f6	♘c6![32]	♗g4	e6	0-0-0[33]					
7	d4	de5[35]	♘f3[37]	♗d2[38]	a3	♗e2	gf3	0–0[39]	bc3	=
	e5[34]	♗b4[36]	♗g4	♘c6	♘d4!	♗f3	0-0-0	♗c3	♘e6[40]	
8	...	♘f3	♗b5[42]	♗e2	0–0	♗f3	de5	♗d2	♖e1[43]	±
	...	♗g4[41]	c6	♗b4	♗f3	♘e7	0–0	♕e5		
9	...	♘f3[44]	h3[46]	♕f3	♗d2[48]	0-0-0	♗c4[49]	♖he1	♗b3[50]	±
	♘f6	♗g4[45]	♗f3[47]	c6	♘bd7	e6	♕c7	0-0-0		

1. e4 d5 2. ed5 ♘f6

	3	4	5	6	7	8	9	10	11	
10	c4[51]	dc6[53]	d3	♘c3[54]	♘f3	♗e2	de4![57]	♔d1	♔c2	∞
	c6[52]	♘c6	e5	♗f5[55]	♗b4!?[56]	e4	♕d1	0-0-0		
11	♗b5	♗e2[59]	d4	♘f3	0–0	c4[61]	♘a3	♕b3[63]	♖d1	=
	♗d7[58]	♘d5	♗f5[60]	e6	♗e7	♘b4[62]	0–0	a5	c6[64]	

	3	4	5	6	7	8	9	10	11	
12	...	♗c4	f3	♘c3[66]	♕e2[68]	♗b3	d6!	a4	d3	⩲
	...	♗g4[65]	♗f5	♘bd7[67]	♘b6	♕d7	cd6[69]	a5	♗e6[70]	
13	...	...	...	♘c3	♘ge2[71]	♗b3[72]	d4	♘c3	0–0	∞
	...	...	♗c8	♘bd7	♘b6	♘bd5	♘c3[73]	e6	a5!?[74]	
14	...	c4[75]	♗d7	d3	♕e2[77]	dc4	dc6	♘f3	♘a3	∞
	♘bd7	a6	♕d7	b5[76]	bc4	c6	♕c6	♗b7	0-0-0[78]	

1. e4 d5 2. ed5 ♘f6 3. d4 ♘d5

	4	5	6	7	8	9	10	11	12	
15	♘f3	h3[80]	g4	♘e5	♘g6	♗g2	c4	♕e2	♗e3[81]	±
	♗g4[79]	♗h5	♗g6	♘d7	hg6	c6	♘5b6	♘f6	e6[82]	
16	c4	♘f3[84]	♗e2	♗e3	♘c3	0–0	♘e5	♕e2	f4[85]	±
	♘f6[83]	♗g4	e6	♗e7	c6	0–0	♗e2	♘bd7		
17	...	...	♘c3	h3[86]	♗e3[87]	♕d2	♗e2	♖d1[88]	0–0	±
	...	g6	♗g7	0–0	♘bd71	c6	♖e8	♕a5?!	a6[89]	
18	...	♘c3[90]	♘f3[91]	♗e2	♗f3	0–0[92]	♖e1	♗g5	♗h5	=
	♘b6	e5!	♗g4	♗f3!	ed4	dc3	♗e7	f6	g6[93]	
19	...	♘f3	♘c3[94]	h3![95]	♗e3	♕d2	d5	g4!	0-0-0	±
	...	g6	♗g7	0–0	♘c6	e5[96]	♘e7	f5	fg4[97]	
20	...	...	♗e2[98]	0–0	b3[100]	♗f3	♗b7	♗e3[101]	♕d4	⩲
	...	♗g4	e6[99]	♘c6	♗f3	♘d4	♖b8	♖b7	♕d4[102]	

[1] **2. e5**? ♗f5 [2... c5 3. c3 e6 4. d4 — C 02; 2... d4!?] 3. d4 e6∓; **2. ♘c3** ♘f6 — B 02

[2] **2... e6**? 3. de6 ♗e6 4. ♘f3±; **2... c6** 3. dc6 ♘c6 [3... e5 4. cb7 ♗b7 5. d3 ♗c5 6. ♘c3±] 4. ♘f3 ♗g4 5. ♗e2 e5 6. d3 ♗c5 7. 0–0±

[3] 3. d4 e5!=

[4] 3... ♘c6 4. ♗e2 [4. d4= — B 00] ♗f5 5. 0–0 0-0-0 6. ♘c3 ♕d7= Janowski–Mieses, Karlovy Vary 1907

[5] **4... c6**?! 5. 0–0 e6 6. h3 ♗f3 7. ♗f3 ♕a5 8. d4 [Platonov–Peljc, SSSR 1968 — 5/108] ♘f6±; **4... ♘c6**!?

[6] 11. ♗e3 e5 12. c3 ♘d5 13. h3 [13. ♘d2? (Jacob–Duras, Ostende 1907) ♗e2 14. ♕e2 ♕e2 15. ♖e2 ed4∓⊥] ♗f3 [13... ♗h3? 14. ♘e5+–] 14. ♗f3 ♕g6=

[7] **3... ♕e5** 4. ♗e2 ♗g4 5. d4 ♗e2 6. ♘ge2 ♕h5 7. ♗f4±⟳; **3... ♕d6** 4. d4 ♘f6 5. ♗g5 c6 6. ♗c4 ♗g4 7. f3 ♗f5 8. ♘ge2 e6 9. ♕d2 ♗e7 [Turiščev–Gubnicki, SSSR 1968 — 5/109] 10. 0-0-0±; 10. 0–0±

[8] 4... c6 5. ♘f3 [5. ♗c4 ♘f6 — 4... ♘f6] ♗g4 6. ♗e2 ♗f3?! 7. ♗f3 e6 8. 0–0 ♘f6 9. ♖e1± Teichmann–Lee (m) 1901

[9] **5. ♘f3** ♗g4 6. ♗e2 e6 7. ♘e5!? ♗e2 8. ♕e2 c6 9. 0–0 ♕d4 10. ♖d1 ♕b6 11. ♗e3 ♕c7 12. ♗f4≅⟳↑ Alexander–Germek, Beograd 1952; **5. ♗e3** c6 6. ♗d3 g6! [6... ♗g4 7. ♘ge2 e6 8. ♕d2 ♗d6 9. ♘g3 ♕c7 10. h3! ♗g3 11. hg4±□⇔ Tarrasch–Pillsbury, Monte Carlo 1903] 7. ♘f3 ♗f5±

[10] **5... e6** 6. ♘f3 ♗e7 7. 0–0 0–0 8. ♕e2 ♘bd7 9. ♖e1 ♘b6 10. ♗b3± Aljehin–Schlechter, Karlovy Vary 1911; **5... c6** 6. ♘f3 e6 7. 0–0 ♗d6 8. ♗g5 ♕c7 9. ♗f6 gf6 10. ♘e4 ♗e7 11. ♕d2± Ljubimov–Bobrov, Moskva 1901; **5... ♗f5** 6. ♕f3! ♕c8 7. ♗g5 ♗c2 8. ♖c1 ♗g6 9. ♘ge2 ♘bd7 10. 0–0 e6 11. ♗f6 gf6 12. d5!± Fischer–Addison, Palma de Mallorca (izt) 1970 — 10/146

[11] **6. f3**?! ♗c8 7. ♗g5 e6 8. f4 [Fuderer–Bronštejn, Jugoslavija–SSSR 1957] ♗e7 9. ♘f3 0–0 10. 0–0 c5∞ Boleslavski; **6. ♘f3** e6 7. h3 ♗h5 8. ♕d3 ♗e7 9. ♘e5 0–0 10. g4 [10. f4? ♘c6! 11. ♘c6 bc6 12. 0–0 ♗g6∓ Karaklajić–Puc, Beograd 1952] ♗g6 11. ♘g6 hg6 12. ♗e3± Minev

[12] 9. ♘g3!? ♘h5!?

[13] 11. h4 h6 12. ♗f4± Andrić–Germek, Beograd 1952

[14] **5. ♗c4** ♗g7 6. ♘f3 ♘f6 [6... ♘h6 7. ♘e4 ♘f5 8. c3 ♘d6 9. ♗d3 0–0 10. 0–0± Boleslavski] 7. 0–0 0–0 8. h3 ♘c6 9. ♖e1 ♘d7 10. ♗g5 h6 11. ♗e3 ♘b6 12. ♗f1 ♗e6 13. ♘e4± Keres–Lutikov, SSSR (ch) 1959; **5. ♘f3** ♗g7 6. h3 ♘h6? 7. g4!± Sokolski; 6... ♘f6!? Fischer

[15] 5... ♘h6 6. ♗e5! f6 7. ♗f4± Fischer

16 **6. ♘b5** ♘a6 7. ♘f3 ♘f6 8. c4 c6 9. ♘c3 ♗g4 10. ♗e2 0–0 11. 0–0 ♘d7 12. ♗e3 e5= Bronštejn–Holmov, SSSR (ch) 1959; **6. ♗c4** ♘f6 [6... e6? 7. ♘b5! ♘a6 8. ♕f3 ♘e7 9. 0-0-0 0–0 10. h4± Duras–Bleykmans, Coburg II 1904] 7. ♘f3 0–0 8. h3 c6±; **6. ♘f3** ♘h6! [6... ♗g4? 7. ♗c4! e6□ 8. h3 ♗f3 9. ♕f3 ♘c6 10. 0-0-0 ± Ravinski–Bebčuk, SSSR 1964] 7. ♕d2 ♘f5 8. 0-0-0 0–0±

17 **6... ♗d4** 7. 0-0-0 ♘c6 8. ♗b5 ♗d7 9. ♘d5! e5 10. ♘f3±; **6... ♕d4** 7. ♕d4 ♗d4 8. ♘b5 ♗b6 9. ♘c7 ♗c7 10. ♗c7±⊥⊡ Fischer

18 7... c6 8. ♗h6 0–0 9. h4 ♕a5 10. h5! gh5 11. ♗d3 ♘bd7 12. ♘ge2 ♖d8 13. g4! ♘f8 [13... ♘g4 14. ♖dg1+–] 14. gh5 ♘e6 15. ♖dg1+–→⟫ Fischer–Robatsch, Varna (ol) 1962; 8... ♗h6!? 9. ♕h6 ♗f5△ 0-0-0 Fischer

19 Fischer

20 **4. ♗c4** ♘c6! [4... ♘f6 5. d3 ♘c6?! 6. ♗d2 ♘d4? 7. ♘b5 ♕b6 8. ♘d4 ♕d4 9. ♘f3 ♕d6 10. ♕e2 ±⟳ Schlechter–Mieses, Praha 1908; 6... ♕e5 7. ♘ge2 ♗e6 8. f4 ♕d6 9. ♘b5 ♕d7 10. ♗e6 fe6 11. a4 a6 12. ♘a3 e5± Griffit, Saunders–Mieses 1913; 11. ♗c3!± Euwe] 5. d3 ♗d7 6. ♗d2 ♕f5 7. ♘ge2 ♘f6 8. ♘g3 ♕g4= Collijn; **4. h3**!? Tartakower

21 4... ♕e5 5. ♗e2 c6 6. ♘f3 ♕c7 7. 0–0±⟳ Breyer–Englund, Scheveningen 1913

22 5... ♕a5?! 6. ♘f3 [6. ♖b5 ♕a6∞ Tartakower] ♘f6 7. ♗c4 ♗g4?! [7... c6∞] 8. ♖b7± Stoltz–Loven, Helsinki 1933

23 7... c6?! 8. ♗d3 b6 9. 0–0 e6 10. ♕e2 ♗e7 11. ♘e4! ♘e4 12. ♕e4 ♕d5 13. ♕g4 ♗f6 14. c4 ♕d8 15. ♗a3=∞→ Leonhardt–Mieses, Praha 1908

24 8. ♗d3!?

25 Thomas-du Mont, Tunbridge Wells 1912

26 4... ♗g4 5. b4!? ♕b4 6. ♖b1△ ♖b7±

27 **5. ♗c4** ♗g4!=; **5. d4**!?

28 9... ♘ge7 10. ♗d2 a6 11. c4!± Tartakower

29 11... 0-0-0? 12. ♘g5 ♖fd8 13. ♘e4△ ♘c5±→⟪ Tartakower

30 13. ♕g3! ♕c2 14. ♗d3 ♕a2 [14... ♕c3 15. ♘f7! ♘f5 16. ♗f5 ♕g3 17. fg3 0–0 (Reti-Rubinstein, Teplice Šanov 1922) 18. d5! ef5 19. dc6 ♗c6 20. ♘e5+– Grünfeld] 15. ♘e4±

31 5. d4 — 4. d4

32 **5... e5**? 6. 0–0 ♗d6 7. d4 0– 9. ♘d6 cd6 10. ♕d4 ♗f5 11. ♗g5±⊡×d6 Fuderer–Popel, Saarbrücken 1953; **5... ♗g4** 6. d4! — 4. d4

33 Barendregt–Larsen, Copenhagen 1960

34 **4... c6** 5. ♘f3 ♘f6 — 4... ♘f6; **4... ♗f5** 5. ♘f3 ♘f6 — 4... ♘f6

35 **5. ♕h5**? ♘c6! 6. ♗b5 ♗d7 7. ♗c6 ♗c6 8. d5 ♗b4 9. dc6 ♗c3 10. ♔f1 ♗d4 11. ♘e2 ♘f6∓ Olsson–Collijn, Stockholm 1920; 5. ♕e2? ♘c6 6. d5 [6. de5 ♗b4 7. ♗d2 ♗f5∓] ♗b4! 7. ♗d2 ♗c3 8. ♗c3 ♕d5 9. f4 ♗f5!∓ Collijn

36 5... ♕e5? 6. ♗e2 ♗b4 7. ♘f3!? [7. ♗d2±] ♗c3 8. bc3 ♕c3 9. ♗d2 ♕c5 10. ♖b1 ♘c6 11. 0–0 ♘f6 12. ♗f4 0–0 [Morphy–Anderssen (m) 1858] 13. ♖b5 ♕e7 14. ♖e1△ ♗d3±→

37 6. ♗d2 ♘c6 7. a3 [7. f4 f6!=∞⟳] ♘d4 8. ♗d3 [8. ab4? ♕a1–+] ♕e5 9. ♘ge2 ♘e2 10. ♕e2 [Puigros–Michel, Bodas del Plata 1941] ♕e2 11. ♗e2 ♗e7=

38 **7. h3** ♗f3 8. ♕f3 ♕e5 9. ♗e2 ♘c6 10. ♗f4∞ Flores–Michel, Mar del Plata 1949; **7. ♗e2** ♘c6 8. 0–0 ♘ge7 [8... ♗c3? 9. bc3 ♖d8 10. ♕e1 ♘ge7 11. ♗g5± Yates–Spielmann, Pistyan 1912] 9. ♗f4 0–0△ ♖ad8, ♘g6 = Tartakower

39 11. ab4? ♕a1 12. ♕a1 ♘c2 13. ♔d1 ♘a1 14. ♗c4 ♘h6 15. ♔c1 ♖d4!∓

40 13. f4 ♘f4 14. ♗g4 ♘e6 15. ♕e2= Asztalos–Kostić, Jugoslavija (ch) 1935

41 **5... e4** 6. ♘g5 ♗f5 7. ♗c4 ♗g6 8. 0–0±; **5... ed4** 6. ♕e2! [6. ♘d4 ♗b4 7. ♗d2 ♕e5 8. ♕e2 ♕e2 9. ♗e2 c6? 10. ♘e4! ♗d2 11. ♔d2±⊥ Sergeant–Mieses, London 1934] ♗e7 7. ♘d4 ♘f6 [7... c6 8. ♗f4 ♘a6 9. 0-0-0± Ritov–Skuja ,SSSR 1971 — 12/124] 8. ♕b5 ♕b5 9. ♘db5 ♘a6 10. ♗f4± Gipslis; **5... ♗b4** 6. ♗d2 ♗g4 7. a3!? [Tartakower; 7. ♗e2 ♘c6 8. a3!± Tarrasch; 7... ed4 8. ♘d4 ♕e5 9. ♘cb5 ♗e2 10. ♕e2 ♗d2 11. ♔d2 ♕e2 12. ♔e2 ♘a6?! 13. ♖he1 0-0-0 14. ♘a7 ♔b8 15. ♘ac6 bc6 16. ♘c6 ♔c8 17. ♘d8 ♔d8 18. ♖ad1± Tarrasch–Mieses, Göteborg 1920; 12... ♔d8±] ♗d6 8. ♗c4±

42 **6. ♗d2** ed4 7. ♕e2 ♘e7 8. ♘b6 ♕b6 9. ♕e5 ♘a6 10. a4± Boleslavski; **6. h3** ed4 7. ♕d4! ♗f3 8. gf3 ♘c6 9. ♕e4 ♕e5 10. ♗b5±⊥⟳ Tartakower

43 Liskov–Persic, SSSR 1957

44 **5. ♗d3** ♘c6 6. ♘ge2 [6. ♗d2 ♘d4 7. ♘b5 ♕b6 8. ♘d4 ♕d4 9. ♘e2 ♕c5 10. 0–0 e6 11. ♘g3 ♗d6∓ Metger–Duras, Ostende 1907] ♗g4 7. f3 ♗h5 8. ♗d2 e5! 9. 0–0 0-0-0∓↑ Olland–Mieses, Karlovy Vary 1907; **5. ♗c4**!? ♘c6 [5... ♗g4? 6. f3 ♗f5 7. ♘ge2 ♘bd7 8. g4 ♗g6 9. h4 h6 10. ♘f4± Kavalek–Larsen, Beverwijk 1967] 6. d5 ♘e5 7. ♗b3 c6 [7... ♗g4 8. f3 ♗f5 9. ♕e2 ♘ed7 10. g4 ♗g6 11. ♗d2± Aronin–Klaman, SSSR 1956] 8. ♕e2 ♘ed7 9. ♗d2 cd5 10. ♘d5 ♕d8± Aronin

45 **5... ♘c6** 6. ♗b5! [6. ♗d2 ♗g4!] ♗d7 [6... ♗g4 7. h3!] 7. d5 ♘e5 8. ♘e5 ♗b5 9. ♗d2!△ ♕f3, 0-0-0±; **5... ♗f5** 6. ♘e5 c6 7. g4! [7. ♗c4?! e6 8. g4 ♗g6 9. h4 ♘bd7 10. ♘d7 ♘d7∞ Suetin–Švedčikov, SSSR

1971 — 12/123] ♗g6 8. h4 — 5... ♗g4; 7... ♗e6!?; **5... c6** 6. ♗c4 [6. ♘e5 ♘bd7 7. ♘c4 ♕d8 8. ♗e2 e6 9. 0—0± Kostić—Puc, Jugoslavija (ch) 1946] ♗g4 7. h3 ♗h5 [7... ♗f3 8. ♕f3 ♘bd7 9. ♗d2△ 0-0-0, g4±] 8. g4 ♗g6 9. ♘e5 ♘bd7 10. ♘g6 hg6 11. ♗d2 e6 12 ♕e2± Boleslavski

46 6. ♗e2 ♘c6 7. ♗e3 0-0-0 8. ♘d2 ♗e2 9. ♕e2 ♕f5 10. ♘b3 e5! [10... e6 11. a3 ♗d6 12. 0-0-0 ♘d5?! 13. ♘a4 e5 14. de5 ♗e5 15. ♘ac5± Duras—Spielmann, Wien 1907] 11. 0-0-0 ed4 12. ♘d4 ♘d4 13. ♗d4 ♗c5=

47 6... ♗h5 7. g4 ♗g6 8. ♘e5 c6 [8... ♘bd7? 9. ♘c4 ♕a6 10. ♗d3 ♕e6 11. ♘e3 0-0-0 12. d5 ♕b6 13. ♘c4 ♕b4 14. a3 ♕c5 15. ♗e3 1 : 0 Aljehin—Schröder, New York 1924] 9. h4 [9. ♘c4 ♕c7 10. ♕f3! ♗c2 11. ♗f4 ♕d8 12. ♕e2± Horowitz—Kibbermann, Warszawa (ol) 1935] ♘bd7 10. ♘c4 ♕c7 11. h5 ♗e4 12. ♘e4 ♘e4 13. ♕f3△ 14. ♗f4± Lasker

48 8. ♗c4!? e6 9. 0—0 ♘bd7 10. ♗f4 ♗e7 11. ♖fe1 0—0 12. a3 ♖fe8 13. ♗g3 ♕b6 14. ♕d3 ♖ad8 15 b4± Botvinik—Konstantinopoljski, SSSR (ch) 1952

49 10. g4!? ♘d5±

50 Rubinstein—Bernstein, San Sebastian 1911

51 3. ♘c3 ♘d5 — B 02

52 3... c5? 4. ♘f3 [4. d4 cd4 5. ♕d4 e6 6. ♘c3 ♘c6 7. ♕d1 ed5 8. cd5 ♘b4∞] e6 5. de6 ♗e6 6. d4±

53 4. d4 cd5 — B 13

54 6. ♘f3?! e4 7. de4 [7. ♘g5? ♗b4 8. ♘c3 ♗g4 9. ♕c2 (9. f3 ef3 10. ♘f3 0—0 11. ♗e2 ♕b6∓⟳→; 9. ♗e2 ♗e2 10. ♕e2 ♕d3∓) ♘d4 10. ♕d2 (10. ♕a4 ♗d7 11. ♕d1 ♕e7 12. ♗e2 0—0∓⟳→) ♕a5 11. ♘ge4 0-0-0∓] ♕d1∞

55 6... ♗c5?! 7. ♗e3 ♘d4! 8. ♗e2 0—0 9. ♘f3 ♖e8± Sotirovski—Marić, Jugoslavija 1950

56 **7... ♗c5** 8. ♗e3 ♗e3 9. fe3 ♕b6 10. ♕d2 ♗e6 11. e4 ♖d8 12. ♘d5± Lasker; **7... e4** 8. ♘h4 ♗g4 9. ♗e2 ♗e2 10. ♕e2 ♕d3 11. ♕d3 ed3 12. 0—0 0-0-0 13. ♗g5±; **7... ♕d7** 8. ♗e2 ♖d8 9. 0—0 ♗d3 10. ♗d3 ♕d3 11. ♕a4!± Lasker

57 9. ♘h4 ♗e6 10. 0—0 ed3 11. ♗d3 ♗c3 12. bc3 ♘e5 13. ♗e2 ♕d1 14. ♖d1 ♖c8∓ Boleslavski

58 3... c6!? 4. dc6 bc6 5. ♗c4 e5 6. d3 ♗c5 7. ♘f3! [7. ♗e3 ♗e3 8. fe3 ♕b6 9. ♕c1 ♘g4 10. ♔e2 ♘e3? 11. ♕e3 ♕b2 12. ♘f3 ♕a1 13. ♘e5 0—0 14. ♖f1± Mieses—Tartakower, Karlovy Vary 1907; 10... 0—0=∞↑] ♘g4 [7... e4 8. ♕e2] 8. 0—0± Tartakower

59 4. ♗d7 ♕d7 5. c4?! c6 6. dc6 ♘c6 **7.** ♘f3 e5 8. 0—0 ♗c5 9. d3 0-0-0 10. ♘c3 ♕d3∓

60 **5... g6**? 6. c4 [6. ♘f3 ♗g7 7. 0—0 0—0 8. c3 ♘c6 9. ♘a3!± Matulović—Zichichi, Venezia 1969 — 7/117] ♘b6 7. ♘c3 ♗g7 8. c5! ♘c8 9. d5 c6 10. ♕b3 b6 11. ♗f3 0—0 [11... bc5? 12. ♕b7 ♘b6 13. dc6 ♗c8 14. c7!+—] 12. ♗e3 cd5 13. ♗d5± Bronštejn—Lutikov, SSSR (ch) 1960; **5... e6**!?△ c5

61 8. a3?! 0—0 [8... ♘c6 9. c4 ♘b6 10. ♘c3 ♗g4 11. d5± Savon—Džindžihašvili, SSSR (ch) 1971] 9. c4 ♘b6 [9... ♘f6 10. ♘c3 ♘e4= Gurgenidze—Kuznjecov, SSSR 1960] 10. ♘c3 ♗f6 11. ♗e3 ♘c6 12. b4 ♕d7∓↑⊞ Casa—Marić, Monte Carlo 1969

62 **8...** ♘b6 9. ♘c3 ♘c6 10. d5 ed5 11. cd5 ♘b4 12. ♘d4 ♗c8 13. ♗f3 0—0 [13... ♘6d5 14. ♘d5 ♘d5 15. ♖e1±] 14. ♘c2 ♗f5 15. ♘b4 ♗b4 16. ♕d4 ± Matanović—Karaklajić, Beograd 1954

63 10. ♗e3 ♘8c6 11. ♕b3 a5 12. ♖fd1 a4! [12... ♗f6? 13. ♖d2! a4 14. ♕d1!± Honfi—Dely, Hungary (ch) 1973 — 16/107] 13. ♕c3 ♗f6=

64 12. ♗f4 ♘d7 13. ♘e1 ♘f6= Kuprejčik—Didiško, SSSR 1969

65 **4... c6** 5. dc6 ♘c6 6. ♘f3 [6. d4 e5! 7. de5 ♘e5 8. ♕e2 ♗b4 9. c3 0—0∞ Kolodzejcik] e5 7. d3 ♗c5 8. ♘c3±; **4... b5** 5. ♗e2 [5. ♗b3 ♗g4 6. f3 (6. ♘f3 ♘d5 7. ♘c3 ♘c3 8. ♗f7? ♔f7 9. ♘e5 ♔g8! 10. ♕g4 ♕d5 —+; 8. ♘e5 ♕d4 9. ♕g4 ♕e5 10. ♔f1 f5 11. ♕f3 ♘e4 12. d3 c5 13. de4 c4 14. ef5 ♕d6! ∞) ♗c8 7. ♕e2 a6 8. a4 b4 9. ♕c4 ♕d6 10. d3 e6 11. ♗f4 e5 12. ♗g5 ♗b7∞ Keres—Lutikov, Tallinn 1964; 7. a4 b4 8. ♘e2 ♘d5 9. c4 ♘f6 10. d4 a5 11. 0—0 e6 12. ♗e3 ♗b7± Žuravljev—Hribovšek, corr. 1966] ♘d5 6. d4 e6 7. ♘f3 ♗d6 8. 0—0 ♗c6 9. a4! b4 10. c4 bc3 11. bc3 0—0 12. c4 ♘f4 13. ♗f4 ♗f4 14. ♘c3 ♕f6 15. ♗d3 ♘d7 16. ♗e4± Matulović—Bronštejn, Hamburg 1965

66 **6. g4** ♗c8! [6... ♗g6? 7. ♘c3 c6 8. f4! h5 9. f5 ♗h7 10. g5 ♘d5 11. ♕h5+— Šagalovič—Veresov, SSSR 1961] 7. ♘c3 a6! [7... ♘bd7? 8. g5 ♘b6 9. ♗b5 ♘fd7 10. f4± Fischer—Bergraser, Monte Carlo 1967 — 3/124; 7... c6!? 8. dc6 ♘c6=∞ Euwe] 8. a4 ♘bd7 [8... c6!?] 9. ♗a2 ♘b6 10. ♘ge2 ♘bd5 11. g5 ♘c3 12. ♘c3 ♘h5 13. d4 g6 14. ♗e3 ♗g7∞ Suetin—Mikenas, SSSR 1964; **6. ♘e2** ♘d5 7. ♘g3 ♗g6 8. 0—0 e6 9. f4 ♘e7! [9... ♘b6 10. ♗b3 ♗c5 11. ♔h1 0—0 12. ♘c3 ♘c6 13. ♘ce4± Mieses—Marshall, Karlovy Vary 1907] 10. d4 h5!∞ Rabar

67 6... c6 7. dc6 ♘c6 8. d3 e5 9. ♗e3± Larsen

68 7. ♘ge2 ♘b6 8. d3 [8. ♗b3 ♘bd5 9. ♘d5 ♘d5 10. ♘g3 ♗g6 11. 0—0 e6 12. f4 ♘e7! 13. d4 h5!∞ Ćirić—Tot, Jugoslavija (ch) 1956] ♘bd5 9. ♘d5 ♘d5 10. ♘g3 ♕d7 11.

0–0 h5 12. d4 0-0-0∞ Spaski–Banks, Canada (ch open) 1971 — 12/125; 10... g6!?= Boleslavski

69 **9... ♕d6** 10. ♘b5 ♕d7 11. ♕e5 0-0-0 12. ♘a7 ♔b8 13. ♘b5 ♘fd5 14. a4 f6 15. ♕e2 ♘f4 16. ♕f2 e5 17. ♘e2± Šagalovič–Rojzman, SSSR 1961; **9... c6** 10. de7 ♗e7 11. d3 0–0 12. ♕f2 c5 [12... ♖fe8!? Marić] 13. ♘ge2 ♖ac8 14. 0–0± Holmov–Goldenov, SSSR 1961

70 **11... d5**? 12. ♕e5 e6 13. ♘b5 ♖c8 14. ♗d2±; **11... ♗e6**! 12. ♗e6 ♕e6 13. ♕e6 fe6 14. ♘b5 ♔d7± Gawlikowski

71 7. ♕e2?! ♘b6 [7... a6 8. a4 ♘b6 9. ♕d3 g6 10. g4 ♗g7 11. ♘ge2 h5!∓ Paar–Božić, Beverwijk 1968 — 5/110] 8. ♕d3 g6 9. ♘ge2 ♗g7 10. ♘g3 0–0 11. b3 a6 12. 0–0 ♘c4 13. bc4 b5 14. ♖b1 bc4 15. ♕c4 e6! 16. de6 ♗e6 17. ♕a4 ♘d5=∞ Belov–Žilin, SSSR 1961

72 8. d3 ♘fd5 9. ♘d5 ♘d5 10. 0–0 g6 11. ♘g3 ♗g7 12. f4 e6 13. ♕f3 c6 14. c3 0–0= Muhin–Boleslavski, SSSR 1964

73 9... e6? 10. ♘e4! ♗e7 11. c4 ♘b6 12. 0–0 0–0 13. ♗e3± Hultquist–Balogh, corr. 1968 — 5/111

74 **11... ♗e7** 12. ♘e4 0–0 13. c4±; **11... a5**!? 12. a3 ♗e7 13. ♘e4 a4 14. ♗a2 0–0 15. c4 ♘e4 16. fe4 e5∞

75 4. ♘c3 a6 5. ♗d7 ♕d7 6. ♕f3 b5 7. d6 ♖a7 8. de7 ♗e7 9. ♘ge2 ♗b7 10. ♕e3 c5 11. 0–0 b4 12. ♘d1 0–0=∞⇗↑ Vajnger–Reško, SSSR 1966

76 6... c6!? 7. dc6 ♕c6 8. ♘f3 [8. ♕f3?! ♕c7 9. ♘e2 ♗g4 10. ♕g3 e5 ∞ Fuderer–Bogoljubov, Beograd 1952] ♗g4 9. 0–0±

77 7. ♘f3!?

78 12. ♘c2 e5 13. 0–0 ♗d6 [Šumaher–Evdokimov, corr. 1955] 14. ♗g5∞

79 **4... g6** 5. ♗e2 ♗g7 6. 0–0 0–0 7. h3! c6 8. ♖e1 ♘d7?! 9. ♗f1 ♖e8 10. c4 ♘c7 11. ♘c3± Geler–Marić, Skopje–Ohrid 1968 — 6/163; **4... ♗f5** 5. ♗d3 ♗d3 6. ♕d3 ♘c6 [6... e6!?] 7. c4 ♘db4 8. ♕b3 e5 9. 0–0 ♘d4 10. ♘d4 ♕d4 11. ♘c3 ♕b6 12. c5!±→ Talj–Korčnoj, SSSR (ch) 1962

80 **5. ♗e2** ♘c6 6. 0–0 e6 7. c3 [7. ♘c3 ♗e7 8. ♘e4 0–0 9. ♘g3 ♘f6 10. c3 ♘h5 11. ♘h5 ♗h5 12. ♗f4 ♗d6= Yates–Bogoljubov, Karlovy Vary 1923] ♗d6 8. ♘bd2 ♘f4 9. ♘e4 ♘e2 10. ♕e2 0–0= Zinser–Karaklajić, Monte Carlo 1967 — 3/125; **5. c4** — 4. c4

81 12. g5!? ♘h5 13. d5!? Razuvajev

82 13. ♘c3± Razuvajev–Gipslis, SSSR 1973 — 16/108

83 4... ♘b4? 5. ♕a4! [5. ♗d2?! e5! 6. a3 ♘4c6 7. de5 ♘e5 8. ♘c3 ♘bc6 9. ♗e3= Šapošnikov–Evdokimov, corr. 1953; 5. a3 ♘4c6 6. d5 ♘e5 7. ♘f3 ♘f3 8. ♕f3 e6 (Aratovski–Evdokimov, corr. 1955) 9. ♘c3 ed5 10. ♘d5 ♗d6 11. ♗e3 0–0 12. 0-0-0± Boleslavski] ♘8c6 6. a3! [6. d5? b5! 7. ♕b5 ♘c2 8. ♔d2 ♗d7! 9. dc6 ♗f5! 10. ♕d5 ♘b4!∓ Rode–Zitzewitz 1910; 8. ♔d1 ♗d7 9. dc6 ♗g4!∓] ♘a6 7. ♗e3 [7. ♘f3± Tartakower–Marshall, Karlovy Vary 1911] ♗d7 8. ♕c2±○⊞

84 5. ♘c3 ♗g4 [5... e5!? 6. de5 ♕d1 7. ♘d1 ♘g4 8. f4 ♘c6 9. h3 ♘h6 10. ♘e3 ♗e6 11. ♗d2 0-0-0 12. 0-0-0 ♗c5=∞ Duras–Tartakower, Wien 1908] 6. ♗e2 ♗e2 7. ♘ge2 e6 8. 0–0 ♗e7= Kinnmark–Keres, Stockholm 1966

85 Sokolski–Štremer, SSSR 1940

86 7. ♗e2 0–0 8. 0–0 ♘bd7 9. ♗f4 c6 10. ♕d2 ♖e8 11. ♘e5 ♘e5 12. ♗e5± Zagorjanski–Marić, Le Havre 1966

87 8. ♗e2 ♘c6 9. ♗e3 e5 10. d5 ♘e7 11. 0–0 h6 12. ♕d2 ♘f5 13. c5 ♘e3 14. fe3 ♘d7 15. b4 a5∞ Talj–Gurgenidze, SSSR (ch) 1959

88 11. 0–0? e5! 12. de5 ♘e5 13. ♕d8 ♘f3 14. ♗f3 ♖d8 15. ♖ad1 ♗e6= Zuidema–Marić, Le Havre 1966

89 13. a3 ♕d8 14. ♕c1 b6 15. ♘e5 ♗b7 16. c5± Talj–Bronštejn, Moskva 1967 — 4/133

90 5. ♗e3?! e5! 6. de5 [6. ♘f3 ♗g4!] ♕d1 7. ♔d1 ♘c6 8. ♘f3 [8. f4 ♗f5 9. ♘f3 0-0-0 10. ♘bd2 ♘a4=∞↑ Tringov–Mečkarov, Bulgaria 1952] ♗g4 9. ♔c2 [9. ♘d2? 0-0-0 10. ♔c2 ♗f5 11. ♔c3 ♘a4 12. ♔b3 ♘c5 13. ♔c3 ♘d3∓ Markov–Mečkarov, Bulgaria (ch) 1952] ♗f3 10. gf3 ♘e5 11. ♘d2 [G. Popov–Bergraser, corr. 1970 — 11/100] 0-0-0∞

91 **6. de5**?! ♕d1 7. ♘d1 ♘c6 8. f4 ♗e6 [8... f6!? 9. ef6 ♗b4 10. ♔f2 gf6 11. ♗e3 ♗e6 12. ♖c1 0-0-0 13. ♘f3 ♖he8=∞↑ Rubinstein–Walter, Moravska Ostrava 1923] 9. b3 0-0-0 10. ♘e3 [10. ♘f3 ♘b4 11. ♘e3 ♗c5∓ Padevski–Karaklajić, Ljubljana 1955] ♗c5 11. a3 ♖he8 12. ♘f3 f6∓ Treybal–Bogoljubov, Pistyan 1922; **6. ♕e2** ♕d4 7. ♘f3 ♕c5 [7... Dd8!?] 8. ♘e5 ♗e6 9. f4 ♗e7 [9... ♘c6 10. ♗e3 ♕e7 11. ♘c6 bc6 12. 0-0-0∞ Pilnik–Karaklajić, Beograd 1952] 10. ♗e3 ♕a5∓ Karaklajić; **6. d5** ♗b4! 7. ♗d2 [7. ♘e2 ♗g4] c6∓ Karaklajić, Marić

92 9. ♕e2 ♗e7 10. c5 dc3 11. ♗b7 ♘8d7 12. cb6 ♖b8 13. ♗f3 ♖b6∓ Honfi–Braun, Kienbaum 1958

93 13. ♗f6 0–0 14. ♗e7 ♕d1 15. ♗d1 cb2 16. ♖b1 ♖e8 17. ♗b3 ♘c6 18. ♗f6 ♘a5= Puc–Karaklajić, Jugoslavija (ch) 1951

94 **6. ♗e2** ♗g4 7. 0–0 ♘c6 8. d5 ♗f3 9. ♗f3 ♘e5 10. ♗e2 ♗g7 11. ♘c3 c6 12. ♕b3 0–0 13. ♖d1 cd5 [Geler–Tan, Petropolis (izt) 1973 — 16/109] 14. cd5± Geler; **6. h3**!?

95 7. ♗e3 0–0 8. ♕d2 ♗g4 9. 0-0-0 ♘c6 10. h3 ♗f3 11. gf3 e5 12. d5 ♘d4 13. f4 [Bobekov–Mečkarov, Bulgaria (ch) 1952] c5!∞

96 9... ♖e8 10. 0-0-0 e5 11. d5 ♘e7 12. g4!± Boleslavski

97 13. ♘g5±→» Gipslis–Marić, SSSR–Jugoslavija 1971 — 12/126

98 **6. ♘c3** e5! 7. c5 ed4 [7... ♘6d7!?] 8. ♘e4 ♘6d7 9. ♕d4 ♕e7 10. ♗b5 ♘c6 11. ♗c6 bc6 12. 0–0 ♗f3 13. gf3 0-0-0 14. ♕a4 ♘e5∞ Lasker–Aljehin, S. Peterburg 1914; **6. c5** ♘6d7! [6... ♘d5? 7. ♕b3 b6? 8. ♘e5 1 : 0 Timman–Bakkali, Nice (ol) 1974; 7... ♗f3 8. ♕b7 ♘e3 9. ♕f3 ♘c2 10. ♔d1±; 6... ♗f3 7. ♕f3 ♘d5 8. ♕b3! b6 9. ♗g5! ♕d7 10. ♘c3 e6 11. ♘d5 ♕d5 12. ♕d5 ed5 13. c6!± Suetin–Šamkovič, SSSR (ch) 1964] 7. h3 ♗h5 8. ♕b3 ♘c6 9. d5 ♗f3 10. ♕f3 ♘d4 11. ♕e4 e5! 12. de6 ♘e6 [Klovan–Gutman, SSSR 1972 — 13/135] 13. c6 ♘f6∞

99 6... ♘c6 7. d5! [7. ♗e3 ♗f3 8. ♗f3 ♘c4 9. ♗c6 bc6 10. ♕a4 ♘b6 11. ♕c6 ♕d7= Teichmann–Mieses, Berlin 1914] ♗f3 8. ♗f3 ♘e5 9. b3! [9. ♗e2 c6 10. ♕d4? ♘g6 11. 0–0 e5!∓ Kuprejanov–Karaklajić, Jugoslavija (ch) 1962] g6 [9... c6 10. dc6 ♕d1 11. ♗d1 (Sabkov–Nenčev, Bulgaria 1967 — 3/126) ♘c6 12. ♗b2±] 10. ♗b2 ♗g7 11. ♘c3± Spielmann–Mieses, Mannheim 1914

100 8. ♗e3 ♗f3 9. ♗f3 ♘c4 10. ♕a4 ♘b6 11. ♗c6 bc6 12. ♕c6 ♕d7=

101 11. ♗e4 ♗e7 12. ♗b2 ♗f6 13. ♗c3∓

102 13. ♗d4 c5 14. ♗e3 ♗e7 15. ♘c3 0–0 [15... ♗f6 16. ♘e4!] 16. ♖ad1 ♖c8 17. ♖d3 ±⊥ Dely–Karaklajić, Beograd 1965

B 02

1. e4 ♘f6[1]

	2	3	4	5	6	7	8	9	10	
1	d3[2] e5[3]	f4[4] ♘c6[5]	♘f3[6] d5[7]	ed5[8] ♘d5	fe5 ♗g4	♗e2 ♗f3	♗f3 ♕h4	g3[9] ♕d4	♕e2 0-0-0[10]	=
2	... d5	e5[11] ♘fd7	f4[12] c5	♘f3 e6	g3[13] ♘c6	♗g2 ♗e7	0–0 0–0[14]	c4 ♘b6		=

1. e4 ♘f6 2. ♘c3 d5[15]

	3	4	5	6	7	8	9	10	11	
3	e5 ♘fd7[16]	e6[17] fe6[18]	d4 c5[19]	dc5[20] ♘c6!	♘f3 g6[21]	♗e3[22] ♗g7	♕d2 ♕a5	♘b5! ♕d2	♗d2 ♔d8[23]	±
4	... ...	... ...	... ♘f6	♘f3 g6[24]	♘e5[25] ♗g7	h4 c5	h5 cd4	h6 dc3	hg7 ♖g8[26]	∓
5	... ...	f4 e6	♘f3[27] c5	g3 ♘c6	♗g2[28] ♗e7	0–0 0–0	d3 f6![29]			∓
6	... ...	♘d5 ♘e5	♘e3[30] c5[31]	f4[32] ♘ec6[33]	♘f3[34] ♕c7	g3 e6	b3 ♗e7	♗b2 0–0	♗g2 ♘d7[35]	=
7	... d4	ef6[36] dc3	fg7[37] cd2	♕d2[38] ♕d2	♗d2 ♗g7	0-0-0 0–0[39]				=
8	ed5 ♘d5	♗c4[40] ♘b6[41]	♗b3 c5[42]	♕h5 e6[43]	d3 ♘c6	♗g5![44] ♗e7	♗e7 ♕e7	♘e4 ♘d7[45]	♗a4 ♘d4[46]	±
9	... ...	... e6	♘f3[47] ♗e7	0–0 0–0	d4 b6[48]	♘e4 ♗b7	♕e2 ♘d7	♖d1 c5	dc5[49] ♘c5	=

1. e4 ♘f6 2. e5 ♘d5[50]

	3	4	5	6	7	8	9	10	11	
10	♗c4 ♘b6	♗b3[51] c5![52]	♕e2[53] ♘c6	♘f3 d5	ed6 e6	♘c3 ♗d6	♘e4 ♗e7	d3 ♘d5[54]		∓
11	♘c3 e6[55]	♘d5[56] ed5	d4[57] d6	♘f3 ♘c6	♗e2[58] ♗e7	♗f4 0–0	0–0 f6	ef6 ♗f6[59]		=

	3	4	5	6	7	8	9	10	11	
12	. . .	d4	♘e4[60]	♘f3	de5	c3[61]	♕c2	♗f4	♖d1!	∞
	. . .	d6	♘c6	de5	♗e7	♘b6	♕d5	♘d7	♕a2[62]	
13	. . .	dc3	♗c4[64]	♘f3	♕d8[66]	♘e5	♘d3	0—0	♗b3	∓
	♘c3	d6[63]	♘c6[65]	de5	♘d8	f6	e5	♗e6	♗d6[67]	
14	. . .	. . .	♘f3	♕d8	♘e5	♗c4[69]	♗e3[70]	♘d3	0-0-0	=
	. . .	. . .	de5[68]	♔d8	♔e8	e6	♗d6[71]	♗d7!?	♗c6[72]	
15	. . .	bc3	d4[74]	♘f3	♗e2[76]	0—0	♘h4	♘f5	♖b1	±
	. . .	d5[73]	c5[75]	♘c6	c4[77]	♗f5	e6	ef5	♕d7[78]	
16	. . .	. . .	f4[80]	♘f3	d4	♗d3	0—0	♕e1[81]	ed6	±
	. . .	b6[79]	♗b7	e6	d6	♗e7	♘c6	♕d7	♕d6[82]	
17	. . .	. . .	f4	♘f3	d4[85]	♗d3	♕d3	♖b1		=
	. . .	d6	♗f5[83]	e6[84]	♗e7	♗d3	♕d7[86]	♕c6[87]		
18	. . .	. . .	f4	♘f3	d4	♗e2	0—0	fe5	♗f4	∓
	. . .	c5!?	d6[88]	g6![89]	♗g7	0—0	de5	♘c6	♗g4[90]	
19	c4	c5[91]	♘c3	dc3	♗c4[94]	♕d5	♗d5	♗e4		±
	♘b6	♘d5	♘c3[92]	d6[93]	d5	♕d5	e6	♗c5[95]		
20	. . .	. . .	. . .	♘d5[96]	d4	cd6	♘f3[98]	♗e2	de5	=
	. . .	. . .	e6	ed5	d6[97]	cd6	♘c6	de5[99]	♗b4[100]	
21	. . .	. . .	♗c4	d4[102]	cd6	♕e2[103]	de5	♘f3	♗d5[105]	=
	. . .	. . .	e6[101]	d6	cd6	de5[104]	♘c6	♘a5	♕d5[106]	
22	. . .	. . .	. . .	♘c3	dc3[108]	♗f4	cb6[111]	♘f3	0—0	±
	. . .	. . .	. . .	♘c3[107]	♘c6[109]	b6[110]	ab6	♗e7	0—0[112]	
23	. . .	. . .	. . .	. . .	♗d5[113]	d4[114]	♕g4	♘f3	♕g3	∞
	. . .	. . .	. . .	♗c5	ed5	♗b4	♔f8[115]	d6	♘c6[116]	

1 Aljehin

2 **2. ♗c4** ♘e4! [2... b5 3. ♗b3 ♗b7 4. d3 e6 5. a4 b4 6. ♘e2 c5 7. c3 ♘c6= Deschaver—Laaber, corr. 1914; 2... e5 — C 24] 3. ♗f7 ♔f7 4. ♕h5 ♔g8! [4... ♔f6? 5. ♕f3 ♔e5 6. d4+—; 4... g6 5. ♕d5 e6 6. ♕e4 ♗g7 7. ♕f4 ♗f6?! 8. ♘c3 d5 9. ♘f3 ♖f8 10. d4± Meštrović—Vukić, Jugoslavija (ch) 1975; 7... ♔e8!∓] 5. ♕d5 e6 6. ♕e4 d5 7. ♕e2 c5∓ Euwe; **2. ♕e2** e5=

3 2... c5 3. ♘f3 — B 29

4 3. ♘f3 — C 42

5 3... ♗c5 4. fe5 ♘e4? 5. ♕g4!+— Wolf

6 4. fe5 ♘e5 5. ♘f3 ♘f3 6. ♕f3 d5 7. e5 ♕e7 8. d4 ♘e4 9. ♗d3 ♕h4 10. g3 ♕g4 11. ♘d2 ♕f3 12. ♘f3= Nimzowitsch—Aljehin, New York 1927; 6. gf3∞ Lasker

7 4... d6 5. ♘c3 ♗e7 6. ♗e2 ♗g4 7. 0—0 0—0 8. ♔h1 ♖e8±○ Rabinovič

8 5. fe5 de4 6. ef6 ef3 7. ♕f3 ♘d4! 8. ♕e4 ♗e6∓↻ Aljehin

9 9. ♔f1? 0-0-0 10. ♘c3 ♗c5 11. ♘e4 ♘e3 12. ♗e3 ♗e3 13. ♕e1 ♕h6 14. ♘g3 ♘d4∓→ Maroczy—Aljehin, New York 1924

10 11. c3 ♕e5 12. 0—0 ♕e2 13. ♗e2 ♗e7!= Euwe

11 3. ♘d2 e5 [3... e6 — C 00; 3... g6 4. ♘gf3 ♗g7 5. g3 0—0 6. ♗g2 c5 7. 0—0 ♘c6 8. ♖e1 b6 9. c3 ♗b7= Hort—Bagirov, Budva 1963] 4. ♘gf3 ♘c6 5. ♗e2 ♗c5 6. 0—0 0—0 7. c3 a5= Gusev—Vasjukov, SSSR 1969 — 7/120

12 4. d4? e6∓

13 6. c3 ♘c6 7. ♘a3 a6 8. ♘c2= Wolf—Oskam, 1922

14 **8... b6**?! 9. c4! dc4 10. dc4 ♗b7 11. ♘c3 0—0 12. b3 ♕b8 13. ♗b2 ♖d8 14. ♕e2 a6 15. ♘e4 ♘f8 16. ♘f6!±→ Halilbeili—Mikenas, SSSR 1965; **8... b5**!?∞

15 **2... ♘c6**? 3. d4 e5 4. de5 ♘e5 5. f4 ♘g6 6. e5 ♘g8 7. ♗c4±↻ Euwe—Breyer, Wien 1921; **2... e5** — C 26

16 3... ♘e4? 4. ♘ce2 [4. d4? ♘c3 5. bc3 e6= Heidenfeld—Hecht, Nice (ol) 1974 — 17/147] d4 5. c3!+— Šahović—Gliksman, Jugoslavija 1973

17 Spielmann; 4. d4 e6 — C 11

18 4... ♘f6 5. ef7 ♔f7 6. ♘f3 ♗f5 7. ♘e5 ♔e8 9. g4±↻ Tartakower—Nilsson 1932

19 **5... e5**? 6. de5 e6 7. f4 [7. ♗d3?! ♘e5! 8. ♕h5 ♘f7∓] ♗e7 8. ♗d3 ♔f7 9. ♘h3 ♘c5 10. 0–0 g6 11. f5±→ Tot–Vidmar jr., Jugoslavija (ch) 1947; **5... g6** 6. h4 ♗g7! [6... ♘f6 7. h5 gh5? 8. ♗e2 ♕d6 9. ♗h5 ♔d8 10. ♘f3 ♘bd7 11. ♘g5+– Voellmy–Staehelin, Schweiz 1938; 7... ♘h5!? 8. ♖h5 gh5 9. ♕h5 ♔d7 10. ♘f3 ♗g7 11. ♗h6 ♗f6 12. g4=∞] 7. h5 ♘f8 8. ♗d3?! ♘c6 9. hg6 hg6 10. ♖h8 ♗h8 11. ♗e3 e5∓ Bobkov–Sokolov, corr. 1960; 8. ♘f3!=∞ Hort, Přibyl; 6. ♘f3!? Tartakower

20 6. ♗d3 ♘f6 7. dc5 ♘c6 8. a3 e5 9. b4 e4 10. ♗b5 e5 11. ♗g5 ♗e6 12. ♕e2 ♔f7 13. ♗c6 bc6 14. ♖d1 ♕b8 15. f3 [Kuindži–Palatnik, SSSR 1967] e3!∞ Palatnik; 9... a6!∓

21 **7... ♘c5**? 8. ♗b5 ♕d6 9. 0–0 g6 10. ♕d4 ♖g8 11. ♗f4 ♗d7 12. ♗d6 ♘d4 13. ♗d7+– Florian–Šajtar, Beograd 1948; **7... ♘f6** 8. ♗b5 ♗d7 9. 0–0 g6 [9... ♕c7 10. ♖e1 h6? 11. ♗c6 bc6 12. ♘e5 g5 13. ♕d3 ♖g8 14. b4 ♗g7 15. ♕g6+– Spielmann–Landau (m) 1933] 10. ♖e1 ♗g7 11. ♗c6 bc6 12. ♘d4 0–0 13. ♗g5 h6 14. ♗h4 e5 15. ♖e5± Spielmann–Domenech, Sitges 1934; **7... a6**!? (Kopilov) 8. ♗e3 ♘f6 9. ♗g5 ♕c7 10. ♗f6? ef6 11. ♕e2 ♔f7∓ Perez–Ljubojević, Lanzarote 1973; 10. a3!±

22 8. **♘d4** ♘f6 [8... ♘c5? 9. ♘c6 bc6 10. ♕d4+–] 9. ♗b5 ♕c7 10. 0–0 ♗d7 [10... e5 11. ♘c6 bc6 12. ♘d5 ♘d5 13. ♕d5+–] 11. ♗c6 bc6 12. f4 ♗g7 13. ♖e1 0–0!= Kuindži–Alburt, SSSR 1974 — 18/126; **8. h4** ♘f6 [8... ♗g7?! 9. h5 gh5 10. ♖h5?! (Kiffmeyer–Schmid, BRD 1972 — 12/127) ♗c3!? 11. bc3 ♘f6△ ♕a5∓; 10. ♗e2! ♕a5 11. ♘g5 ♗c3 12. bc3 ♘f6 13. ♗h5 ♔d7 14. 0–0±→ Šašin–Schmid, Erevan 1965] 9. h5!? [9. ♗b5 ♗g7 10. ♗f4 0–0 11. ♗c6 bc6 12. ♗e5 ♕a5 13. h5?! ♘h5 14. ♗g7 ♘g7 15. ♕d2 e5! 16. ♘e5 ♕c5 17. ♘d3 ♕d6 18. 0-0-0 ♗a6 19. ♕h6 ♘h5 20. g4 ♗d3∓ Izvozčikov–Bagirov, SSSR 1968; 13. ♕d4!±; 11... ♘e4!? 12. ♗e5 ♗e5 13. ♘e4 ♗g7 14. ♗b5 de4 15. ♕d8 ♖d8 16. ♘g5 ♗b2 17. ♖d1 ♖d1 18. ♔d1 e5 19. ♗c4 ♔g7 20. ♘e4 ♗f5∓ Lublinski–Mikenas, SSSR (ch) 1949] gh5 [9... ♘h5? 10. ♖h5 gh5 14. ♘g5±] 10. ♗e2 e5 11. ♘g5 ♗g4 12. ♗g4 hg4 13. ♘e6 ♕d7 14. ♘d5 ♘d5 15. ♕d5 ♕d5 16. ♘c7 ♔f7 17. ♘d5 e6 18. ♘e3± Hort, Přibyl

23 12. ♘g5 ♘de5 13. f4 h6 14. fe5 hg5 15. ♗g5 ♘e5 16. 0-0-0± Zinn–Bagirov, Batumi 1966

24 6... c5 — 5... c5

25 7. ♗f4!? Hort, Přibyl

26 12. ♕d4 ♘bd7 13. ♗b5 ♕b6∓ Suttles–Mecking, Sousse (izt) 1967 — 4/134

27 5. d4 — C 11

28 7. ♗h3!? a6 8. 0–0 ♗e7 9. d3 b5 10. ♘e2 d4 11. a3 ♗b7 12. ♕e1 (Fedorov–Kuprejčik, SSSR 1968) g6!∓

29 **9... ♘b6**?! 10. ♘e2 d4 11. g4 f6 12. ef6 gf6 13. ♘g3 ♘d5 14. ♕e2± Nimzowitsch–Aljehin, Semmering 1926; **9... f6**!∓ Hort, Přibyl

30 5. ♘c3 c5 6. ♘f3 ♘f3 7. ♕f3 ♘c6= Přibyl

31 5... ♘bc6 6. ♘f3 [6. ♗b5? a6 7. ♗a4 b5 8. ♗b3 e6∓↑ Kirov–Vasjukov, Varna 1971; 6. b3 g5 7. ♗b2 ♗g7 8. d4 ♘g6 9. ♗b5 ♕d6 10. ♕d2 ♗d7 11. 0-0-0 0-0-0 12. ♘e2± Tartakower–Colle, Nice 1930; 6... ♘g4 7. ♗b5!±; 6... g6 7. ♗b2 ♗g7 8. d4 ♘d7 9. ♗b5 ♘cb8!? △ c5= Palatnik] ♘f3 7. ♕f3 ♕d6 [7... g6 8. ♗b5 ♗d7 9. d4 ♗g7 10. c3=] 8. ♗b5 ♗d7 9. 0–0 e6 10. c3 ♕e5 11. ♕e2= Aljehin

32 **6. b4**?! ♘ec6! 7. bc5 e5 8. ♗b2 ♗c5∓ van Geet–Marović, Amsterdam 1972 — 13/137; **6. ♘f3** ♘f3! [6... ♘ec6 7. ♗c4 e6 8. c3 ♘d7 9. d4±⟳ Polovodin–Mikenas, SSSR 1971] 7. ♕f3 ♘c6 8. ♗b5 ♗d7 9. ♕g3 ♘d4∓ Yates–Reti, Bad Kissingen 1928; **6. b3** ♘bc6 [6... g6?! 7. ♗b2 ♗g7 8. ♘c4 ♘bc6 9. f4 ♘c4 10. ♗g7 ♖g8 11. ♗c3 ♘b6 12. ♗b5± Romanovski–Toluš, SSSR (ch) 1945] 7. ♗b2 e6 8. f4 ♘g6 9. g3 ♗e7!? 10. ♗g7 ♖g8 11. ♗c3? ♘f4! 12. ♗b5 ♘d5∓↑; 11. ♗b2∞

33 **6... ♘ed7** 7. ♘f3 e6 8. d4 ♘f6= Schwarz; **6... ♘g6** 7. g3 e5= Tartakower

34 7. ♗c4!? g6 8. ♘f3 ♗g7 9. 0–0 ♘d4 10. c3 ♘f3 [10... ♘f5? 11. d4!± Brinckmann–Takacs, Rogaška Slatina 1929] 11. ♕f3∞ Euwe

35 12. 0–0 ♗f6= Tartakower–Landau, 1930

36 4. ♘ce2 ♘g4 5. f4 h5 6. ♘f3 ♘c6 7. ♘g3 h4 8. ♘e4 ♗f5 9. ♗d3 e6 10. h3 ♘h6 11. a3 a5 12. b3 ♗e7 13. ♗b2 ♕d7 14. ♕e2± Hort, Přibyl; 6... c5!?∞

37 **5. fe7** cd2 6. ♕d2 ♕d2 7. ♗d2 ♗e7 8. 0-0-0 ♗e6= Sköld–Asmundsson, Lugano (ol) 1968; **5. bc3** ef6 6. ♘f3 ♗d6 7. d4 0–0 8. ♗d3?! ♖e8 9. ♗e3 c6 10. 0-0-0 ♗g4= Corden–Williams, England 1970; 9... ♗f4!?; 8. ♗e2!?

38 6. ♗d2 ♗g7 7. ♕f3 [7. ♕h5 ♕d6 8. ♘f3 ♕g6 9. ♕g6= Udovčić–Trifunović, Jugoslavija 1951; 7... ♗b2? 8. ♕b5+–; 9. ♕c5!?△ 0-0-0] ♗b2!? 8. ♖d1 ♕d4 9. ♘e2 ♕g4 10. ♕b3 ♗f6 [10... ♗e5? 11. ♗c3 ♗c3 12. ♕c3 0–0 13. ♖d3+–; 10... ♗g7 11. ♗c3? ♘c6 12. ♖d3 ♗c3 13. ♕c3 ♕b4∓; 11. ♘f4∞] 11. ♘f4 ♘c6 12. ♗e2 ♕f5 13. ♘d5 ♗e5 14. ♗c3∞ Balašov–Alburt, SSSR (ch) 1974 — 18/127; 14. f4!? Bronštejn

39 **8... ♗f5**?! 9. ♘e2!? [9. ♘f3 ♘d7= Dueball–Jansson, Raach 1969] ♘d7 10. ♘g3 ♗g6 11. h4 h5 12. f4 e6 13. f5!±; **8... ♘c6** 9. ♗b5! [9. ♗c4 0–0 10. ♘e2 ♘e5 11.

♗b3 c5 12. f4 c4 13. fe5 cb3 14. ab3 ♗e5 15. ♘g3 ♗g4∓ Haag–Bilek, Hungary 1964] ♗d7 10. ♘e2 a6 11. ♗a4 0-0-0 12. ♗c3 ♗c3 13. ♘c3±; **8... 0–0**=

40 **4. ♘d5** ♕d5 5. d4 ♘c6 6. ♘f3 ♗g4 7. ♗e2 0-0-0 8. c3 e5= Alburt–Vasjukov, SSSR (ch) 1967 — 5/114; **4. ♘f3** ♘c3 5. bc3 g6 6. d4 ♗g7 7. ♗e3 c5 8. ♕d2 ♕a5 9. ♗c4 ♘c6= Mosionžik–Bagirov, SSSR 1962; **4. ♘ge2** ♗g4? 5. h3 ♘c3 6. bc3 ♗f5 7. ♖b1 ♕d5? 8. ♘g3 ♗c8 9. c4±↻ Keres–Mikenas, Riga 1968 — 6/164; 7... e6!?; 4... ♘c6=; **4. g3** ♘c3 [4... b6 5. ♗g2 ♗b7 6. ♘f3 e6 7. 0–0 ♗e7 8. ♖e1 0–0 9. ♘e4 ♘d7= Westerinen–Timman, Tallinn 1973; 4... ♗f5 5. ♗g2 c6 6. ♘f3 h6 7. 0–0 e6 8. ♖e1 ♗e7= Ignjatijev–Knežević, Kislovodsk 1968; 4... e5 — C 26] 5. bc3 ♕d5 6. ♘f3 ♕e4 7. ♗e2 ♗h3 8. ♖g1 ♗g4 9. d3 ♕c6 10. c4 e6 11. ♖b1 ♗e7= Benkö–Martz, USA (ch) 1972 — 13/136

41 **4... ♘c3** 5. ♕f3 e6 6. ♕c3 ♘c6 7. ♘f3 ♕f6 8. ♕f6 gf6 9. d4± Schultz–Prokeš, Bardov 1926; **4... ♗e6** 5. ♕f3 c6 6. ♘ge2 ♘c7± Gundersson–Hloušek, Graz 1972 — 15/133

42 5... ♘c6!? Euwe

43 6... c4? 7. ♗c4+−

44 **8. ♘ge2** ♗e7 9. 0–0 0–0 10. ♘e4 ♘d4 11. ♘d4 cd4 12. ♗d2 ♘d5= Tarrasch–Grünfeld, Karlovy Vary 1923; **8. ♘f3**!? g6!?∞ Bagirov

45 10... ♘d5 11. ♘e2 g6 12. ♕h6 ♗d7 13. ♕g7! ♖f8 [13... 0-0-0? 14. ♕f7+−] 14. ♗d5 ed5 15. ♘f6 ♔d8 16. ♘d5 ♕d6 17. 0–0+− Balašov–Mikenas, SSSR (ch) 1970 — 10/147; 11... 0–0!? Talj

46 12. c3 ♘f5 13. g4 g6 14. ♕h3 a6±

47 5. ♕f3!? ♘b4 6. ♗b3 ♘8c6 7. ♘ge2 ♘a5 8. ♗a4 ♗d7 9. a3 ♘d5 10. ♘d5 ♗a4 [10... ed5 11. ♕d5 ♗a4 12. ♕e4±] 11. ♘e3 ♗c6 12. ♕h5 b6 13. b4 ♕f6 14. ♖b1 ♘b7 15. ♗b2 ♕g6 16. ♕h4 ♗d6 17. ♘f4 ♗f4 18. ♕f4 ♘d6 19. d3 0–0?! 20. h4 f6 21. h5 ♕f7 22. h6∞ Simagin–Bagirov, SSSR 1968 — 5/113; 19... f6!△ e5=

48 7... ♘c3 8. bc3 ♘d7= Keres

49 11. ♗b5?! cd4 12. ♘d4 ♕c7 13. c4 ♘5f6 14. ♘f6 ♘f6 15. ♗e3 ♖ac8∓ Bisguier–Keres, Tallinn 1971 — 11/101

50 2... ♘g8 3. d4 d5 [3... d6 4. ♘f3 de5 5. ♘e5 ♘d7 6. ♕f3 ♘gf6 7. ♘c3 e6 8. ♗g5± Spielmann–Flor, Praha 1930; 4... ♗g4 5. h3 ♗f5 6. ♗d3 ♕d7 7. ed6 ed6 8. ♗f5 ♕f5 9. 0–0 ♗e7 10. ♖e1± Smejkal–Vesely, ČSSR 1968 — 5/112; 4... g6 5. ♘c3 ♗g7 6. ♗c4 c6 7. h3 d5 8. ♗b3 b6 9. 0–0 e6 10. ♖e1 ♗a6 11. ♘e2 ♘e7 12. ♘f4 h6 13. c3= Boleslavski–Petrosjan, SSSR 1966] 4. ♗d3 c5 5. c3 ♘c6 6. ♘e2 ♗g4 7. f3 ♗d7 8. 0–0 ♕b6 9. ♔h1 e6 10. ♗c2 ♖c8± Damski–Lejn, SSSR 1958

51 4. ♗e2?! d6 5. ♘f3 de5 6. ♘e5 ♘8d7 7. d4 ♘e5 8. de5 ♗f5∓ Ebralidze–Bagirov, SSSR 1953

52 **4... d6**? 5. ♘f3 d5 6. d4 ♗g4 7. h3 ♗f3 8. ♕f3 e6 9. 0–0 c5 10. dc5 ♘6d7 11. c4! ♘e5 12. ♕e2±≪ Romanišin–Mikadze, SSSR 1968; **4... d5** 5. d4 ♘c6 6. c3 ♗f5 7. ♘e2 e6 8. 0–0 f6 9. ef6 ♕f6= Raškovski–Bronštejn, SSSR (ch) 1973

53 5. d3!? ♘c6 6. ♘f3 e6 7. ♘c3 d6 8. ed6 ♗d6 9. ♘e4 ♗e7 10. ♗e3± Kmoch; 10... ♘d5!∓ Hort, Přibyl

54 Yates–Rubinstein, Dresden 1926

55 3... c6!?

56 **4. g3** d6 5. ed6 ♗d6 6. ♗g2 ♘c3 7. bc3 0–0 8. ♘e2 c5 9. 0–0 ♕c7 10. ♖b1 ♘c6 11. d3 b6 12. f4 ♗b7= Romanovski–Levenfiš, SSSR 1924; **4. ♘f3** d6 5. d4 — 4. d4

57 **5. f4**? d6 6. ♘f3 ♗g4 7. ♗e2 ♗f3 8. ♗f3 de5 9. fe5 ♘c6 10. 0–0 ♗c5 11. ♔h1 0–0 12. c3 ♘e5 13. d4 ♘f3∓ Ciocaltea–Sjuja, Romania 1956; **5. ♕f3** c6 6. ♕g3 [6. d4 d6 7. ♗d3 ♘d7 8. ♕g3 de5 9. de5 ♘c5= Grünfeld] d6 7. d4 ♗f5 8. c3 de5 [8... ♘d7 9. f4?! de5 10. fe5 f6 11. ♘f3 ♗e4 12. ♗e2= Nagy–Vuković, Györ 1924] 9. de5 ♘d7 10. ♘f3 ♘c5? 11. ♘d4 ♗g6 12. h4± Dückstein–Lahti, Raach 1969; 10... ♕b6!= Hort, Přibyl

58 **7. ♗f4** ♗e7 [7... de5 8. de5 ♗c5 9. ♕d2 ♘e7 10. 0-0-0 c6 11. ♗e3! ♕b6 12. ♗c5 ♕c5 13. ♗d3 h6 14. ♖he1 ♗e6 15. ♔b1 0-0-0 16. c3± R. Byrne–Jansson, Skopje (ol) 1972 — 14/161] 8. ♗b5?! 0–0 9. 0–0 ♗g4 10. ♗e2= Sax–Cafferty, Teesside 1972; **7. ♗g5**!? Đurašević

59 Sämisch–Aljehin, Budapest 1921

60 5. ♘f3 ♘c3 [5... ♘c6 6. ♗b5 ♘c3 7. bc3 de5?! 8. ♘e5 ♗d7 9. ♘d7 ♕d7 10. 0–0 ♗e7 11. ♕g4±⊞ Bivšev–Aronin, SSSR 1956; 7... ♗d7 Bagirov; 6. ♘e4!± Hort] 6. bc3 de5 7. ♘e5 ♘d7 8. ♗f4 [8. ♘f3 c5 9. ♗d3 ♕c7 10. 0–0 c4 11. ♗e2 ♗d6 12. ♖e1 0–0 13. ♗f1 b6 14. a4 ♗b7∓ R. Byrne–Olafsson, Lugano 1970] c5 [8... ♗e7 9. ♗d3 ♘e5 10. ♗e5 ♗f6 11. ♕e2 ♗d7 12. 0–0 ♗c6 13. f4± Andersson–Kraidman, Siegen (ol) 1970 — 10/149] 9. ♘c4 ♘b6= Boleslavski

61 8. a3 ♘b6 9. ♗d3 h6 10. ♗e3? ♘d7∓ Nikolić–Knežević, Kislovodsk 1968

62 **12. ♗b5**?! ♕a5 13. ♗c6 bc6 14. 0–0 c5∓ Rustambejli–Pavlenko, SSSR 1966; **12. ♗e2** △ 0–0, ♖a1=/∞

63 4... d5?! 5. c4! [5. ♘f3?! c5 6. ♗f4 ♘c6 7. ♕d2 ♗g4 8. 0-0-0 e6 9. h3? ♗f3 10. gf3 ♕c7∓ Yates–Capablanca, Moskva 1925; 5. f4!? c5 6. ♗e3 e6 7. ♘f3 ♘c6 8. ♗d3 ♗e7 9. 0–0 ♗d7± Knaak–Espig, Görlitz 1972; 9... 0–0=; 5. ♗e3 c6? 6. f4 ♗f5 7. ♗d3± Haag–Lengyel, Hungary 1972 — 12/128; 5... ♗f5 6. ♗d3 ♗d3! 7. ♕d3 e6△ c5= Florian] d4 6. f4 ♗f5 7. ♘e2! ♘c6 8. ♘g3 e6 9. ♘f5 ef5 10. ♗d3 g6 11. a3 a5 12. ♕f3± Ghizdavu–Torre, Niš 1972

64 **5. ed6**? ♕d6 6. ♕d6 cd6∓⊥ Maroczy–Euwe, Karlovy Vary 1929; **5. ♗g5**?! ♘c6 6. ♗b5 ♗d7 7. ♘f3 ♘e5 8. ♘e5 de5 9. ♕e2 c6 10. ♗c4 f6∓ Andersson–Jansa, Sombor 1970; 5... de5!?; **5. ♗f4**!? ♘c6 [5... g6 6. ♕e2!? ♗g7 7. 0-0-0 0–0 8. h4∞ Filipowicz–Jansa, Zinnowitz 1971 — 13/138] 6. ♗b5 ♗d7 7. ♕e2 a6 8. ♗c4 e6 9. ♘f3 de5 10. ♗e5 ♗d6 11. ♗g7 ♖g8 12. ♗e5 ♘e5 13. ♘e5 ♗e5 14. ♕e5 ♖g2 15. ♗d5? ♖g5∓ Šamkovič–Bronštejn, SSSR 1961; 15. 0-0-0∓

65 **5... g6**?! 6. ♘f3 [6. ♗f4!? ♗g7 7. ♕d2 ♘c6 8. 0-0-0 ♗g4 9. ed6 cd6 10. ♗e2 ♗e2 11. ♘e2 ♕a5 12. a3 0–0 13. ♗h6± Banik–Korčnoj, SSSR (ch) 1954] ♘c6 7. ♗f4 ♗g7! [7... e6? 8. ed6 cd6 9. ♕e2 ♗e7 10. 0-0-0 a6 11. h4±→ Keres–Westerinen, Tallinn 1971 — 11/103] 8. ♘g5 [8. ed6!? cd6 9. ♕d2△ 0-0-0, ♗h6, h4↑± Hort, Přibyl] de5 9. ♗f7 ♔f8 10. ♕f3 ef4 11. ♖d1 ♕d1 12. ♕d1 h6 13. ♗b3! [13. ♗g6 hg5 14. ♕d5 e6 15. ♕g5 e5 16. 0–0 ♗e6 17. ♖d1 ♘e7 18. ♗h5 ♖h6∓ Peirhuber–Ligtering, Stockholm 1969] hg5 14. ♕d5 e6 15. ♕g5 e5 16. ♕g6 ♘d8 17. 0–0±; **5... e6** 6. ♘f3 ♘c6 7. ♕e2 ♗e7?! 8. ♗f4! 0–0 9. 0-0-0 d5 10. h4!± Cvetković–Marangunić, Jugoslavija 1970 — 9/109; 6... de5!?

66 7. ♕e2?! f6 [7... e6 8. ♘e5 ♘e5 9. ♕e5 ♗d7 10. ♕g3 ♕f6 11. ♗f4 ♕g6 12. ♕f3 0-0-0 13. ♗a6 c6 14. ♗d3 f5 15. 0-0-0± Basman–Smislov, Lugano (ol) 1968; 15. ♕e3!±] 8. ♗e3 [8. ♗d2 e6 9. 0-0-0 ♗d6 10. ♘h4 ♕e7 11. g3 ♗d7∓ Arnaudov–Jansa, Harrachov 1967] e6 9. ♘h4 g6 10. f4 ♗d6 11. 0–0 ♕e7 12. fe5 ♘e5∓ Green–Williams, England 1970

67 12. ♖d1 g5 13. ♗e3 ♔f7∓ Nežmetdinov–Spaski, SSSR (ch) 1959

68 5... ♘c6 6. ♗b5 ♗d7 7. ♕e2 ♘e5 8. ♘e5 de5 9. ♕e5 f6 [9... c6 10. ♗c4 ♕b8 11. ♕e4 e6 12. ♗g5! h6 13. ♗h4 ♗d6 14. 0-0-0 ♕c7 15. ♕d4 ♗e5 16. ♕c5± Keres–Schmid, Zürich 1961] 10. ♕h5 [10. ♕e2 e5 11. ♗e3 ♗d6 12. 0-0-0 0–0 13. ♗c5 ♗e6 14. ♗c4 ♕e7 15. ♗d6 cd6 16. ♕e4 ♖f7= Kuprejčik–Bagirov, SSSR 1965] g6 11. ♕e2 e5 12. ♗e3 ♗d6 13. 0-0-0 b6 14. f4! 0–0 15. fe5 ♗b5 16. ♕b5 fe5± Markland–Korčnoj, Hastings 1971/72

69 8. ♗e3!? ♘d7 [8... f6!? 9. ♘f3 e5 10. ♘d2 ♗e6 11. f4 ♘d7 12. 0-0-0 ♗d6?! 13. ♘e4 ♔e7 14. ♘d6 cd6 15. g3 ♖ac8 16. ♗g2 b6± Hübner–Ghizdavu, Graz 1972 — 14/159; 12... ♗e7 13. ♗d3△ f5±; 9. ♘d3 ♘c6?! 10. f4 e6 11. 0-0-0 b6 12. c4 ♗b7 13. c5 b5 14. ♗e2 ♗e7 15. ♖he1 ♔f7 16. ♘f2 a6 17. ♗f3 ♖hd8 18. b4± Radulov–Smejkal, Siegen (ol) 1970 — 10/150; 9... e5!?] 9. ♘f3 [9. ♘c4 ♘b6 10. 0-0-0 e6 11. ♘b6? ab6 12. ♗b5 c6 13. ♗b6?? cb5 14. ♖d8 ♔e7 15. ♖hd1 f6 0 : 1 Balašov–Židkov, SSSR (ch) 1972; 11. ♘a5!?; 10... ♘c4=] e5 10. 0-0-0 f6 11. ♘d2 ♗c5 12. ♗c5 ♘c5 13. ♗c4 ♗g4 [13... c6?! 14. f4 b5 15. ♗e2!± Listengarten–Bagirov, SSSR 1974 — 18/128] 14. f3 ♗h5 15. g4 ♗f7= Bagirov

70 **9. f4** ♘d7 10. ♘d7 ♗d7 11. ♗e3 ♗d6 12. 0–0 ♔e7 13. ♖ae1 ♖he8 14. ♗d3 f5∓⊥ Sarapu–Hort, Sousse (izt) 1967; **9. ♗f4** ♗d6 10. 0-0-0 ♘d7 11. ♘d3 ♗f4 12. ♘f4 ♘f6 13. ♖he1 ♗d7 14. ♘d5?! ♘d5 15. ♗d5 c6∓ Lechtynsky–Hloušek, Luhačovice 1971; **9. 0–0** ♗d6 10. ♖e1 ♘d7 11. ♘f3 a6= Nikitin–Bagirov, SSSR (ch) 1969

71 9... ♘d7 10. ♘d3 ♗d6 11. 0-0-0 ♔e7? 12. ♖he1 b6 13. ♗g5 ♘f6 14. f4 ♖e8 15. ♗d5 ♖b8 16. ♘e5 ♔f8 17. ♗c6± Radulov–Westerinen, Helsinki 1972 — 14/158

72 12. f3 ♘d7 13. ♘b4 ♘b6 14. ♗e2 ♗d7 15. a3 a5 16. ♘d3 ♔e7 17. ♘c5 ♗c6 18. c4 ♘d7 19. ♘d7 ♗d7 20. c5± Radulov–Jansa, Örebro 1966; 18... ♗e5!?; 14... ♘d5!?=

73 4... e6 5. f4 d5!? 6. ♘f3 c5 7. d4 ♕a5 8. ♗d2 c4 [8... ♘c6 9. dc5!±] 9. ♗e2 ♗e7 10. 0–0 h5±» Sax–Vukić, Hungary–Jugoslavija 1972

74 5. ♗a3!? b6! [5... c6? 6. f4 ♕a5 7. ♕c1 ♗f5 8. ♘f3 ♘d7 9. ♖b1 ♕c7 10. ♘d4 e6 11. ♗e2? c5!= Tabor–Bagirov, Baja 1971 — 11/104; 11. ♗f8! ♘f8 12. ♕b2 0-0-0 13. ♕a3±→«] 6. f4 c5 7. d4 e6 8. ♘f3 ♕d7 9. ♖b1 ♗a6 10. ♗a6 ♘a6 11. 0–0 g6 12. ♕e2 ♕a4∓ Haik–Torre, Athens 1971

75 5... ♗f5 6. ♘e2 e6 7. ♘g3 ♗g6 8. ♗d3 c5 9. ♖b1 ♕c7 10. 0–0 ♘c6 11. ♗e3 0-0-0 12. f4± Ubilava

76 **7. ♗d3** ♗g4 8. h3 ♗f3 9. ♕f3 e6 10. ♖b1 ♕c7 11. 0–0 c4 12. ♗e2 h5 13. a4 ♗e7 14. g3 ♕d7 15. ♕e3 0-0-0 16. f4 ♖dg8 17. ♕f3 f5= Mecking–Bobocov, Palma de Mallorca 1969; **7. h3** e6 8. ♗d3 cd4 9. cd4 ♘b4 10. 0–0 ♘d3 11. ♕d3 ♗d7= I. Zajcev–Vasjukov, SSSR 1969

77 7... ♗g4!?

78 12. g4 ♘e7 13. gf5!? [13. ♗a3?! f4∞ Goldin–Kopilov, SSSR 1947] ♘f5 14. ♗g4 g6 15. ♕f3±

79 Larsen

80 5. ♕f3?! ♘c6 6. e6 (Larsen) fe6 7. ♗d3 g6? 8. h4!±; 7... d5!∞

81 10. ♕e2 ♕d7 11. ed6 ♕d6 12. ♘e5 0–0 13. a4 ♘e5 14. fe5 ♕d5 15. ♖f4? c5 16.

♗e3 ♖ac8 17. ♖af1 cd4 18. cd4 ♖c3 19. ♗e4 ♕d7 20. ♗h7 ♔h7 21. ♕h5 ♔g8 1/2 : 1/2 Padevski—Larsen, Lugano (ol) 1968 — 6/171; 15. ♖f3!?→; 12. ♘g5!±

82 12. ♘g5! h6 13. ♘e4 ♕d7 14. f5 0-0-0 15. fe6 ♕e6? 16. ♕f2! (△ ♘c5) ♘d4? 17. ♘g3!!+— R. Byrne—Larsen, Monte Carlo 1968 — 5/115; 15... fe6!±

83 **5... g6**!? (Mikenas) 6. ♘f3 ♗g7 7. d4 0—0 8. ♗c4 [8. ♗d3 c5 9. 0—0 de5 10. fe5?! ♘c6 11. ♗e3 ♗g4 12. ♗e4 ♕a5 13. ♕e1 ♖ad8∓ Padevski—Vuković, Smederevska Palanka 1971 — 12/129; 10. de5 ♘c6 11. ♗e3 b6 12. ♗e4 ♕c7∞] c5 9. 0—0 cd4 10. cd4 ♗g4 11. ♗b3 ♘c6 12. ♗e3 de5 13. fe5 e6 14. ♕d2 ♕a5?!± Stanciu—Maciejewski, Bucuresti 1974 — 17/149; 14... ♘a5±; **5... de5** 6. fe5 ♗f5!? [6... ♕d5 7. ♘f3 c5 8. d4 ♘c6 9. ♗e2 cd4 10. cd4 ♗g4 11. 0—0 0-0-0 12. c3 f6 13. ♕a4± Dückstein—Kavalek, Sarajevo 1967; 11... e6 12. ♖b1 ♕d7 13. ♘g5!±↻ Talj—Podgajec, SSSR 1970 — 10/148; 7... ♘c6 8. d4 ♗g4 9. ♗e2 e6 10. 0—0 ♗e7 11. ♘g5 ♗e2 12. ♕e2 0—0 13. ♕h5 ♗g5 14. ♕g5 ♕e4 15. ♗a3± Bilek—Larsen, Sousse (izt) 1967 — 4/135] 7. ♕f3 ♕c8 8. ♗d3 ♗d3 9. cd3 e6 10. ♕g3 c5 11. ♘f3 ♕d7 12. ♘g5 ♗e7 13. ♘e4 ♘c6∞ Tajmanov—Toluš, SSSR 1948

84 6.. de5 7. fe5 ♕d5 8. ♗e2! [8. d4?! ♕e4 9. ♗e2 e6 10. ♕d3 ♕d3=] ♘c6 9. 0—0 ♘e5 10. ♘e5 ♕e5 11. d4 ♕a5 12. ♖b1 e6 13. ♖b7 ±↻ Lisicin—Toluš, SSSR 1948

85 7. ♗e2 ♘d7? 8. 0—0 d5? 9. ♘d4 ♗g6 10. f5 ef5 11. e6±→ Ćirić—Marović, Amsterdam 1968 — 6/169; 7... c5=

86 9... c5!?

87 Bohosjan—Přibyl, Stary Smokovec 1973

88 5... g6!? 6. ♘f3 ♗g7 7. d4 f6∞ Sokolski—Mikenas, SSSR (ch) 1944

89 6... ♘c6 7. ♗c4 [7. ♗b5 a6 8. ♗c6 bc6 9. 0—0 g6 10. d4 cd4 11. cd4 ♗g7= Ciocaltea—Mikenas, Sofia 1962] e6 8. 0—0 ♗e7 9. d4 ♕c7 10. cd6 ♕d6= Haag—Gipslis, Tallinn 1969 — 7/121

90 12. h3 ♗f3 13. ♗f3 cd4 14. ♗c6 bc6 15. cd4 ♕d5 16. c3 c5 17. ♕b3 ♖fd8 18. ♗e3 cd4 19. cd4 f6!∓ Hennings—Gipslis, La Habana 1971

91 4. b3 d6 [4... c5 5. ♗b2 ♘c6 6. ♘f3 d5 7. ed6 ♕d6 8. d4 cd4 9. ♘d4 ♘d4 10. ♕d4 ♕d4 11. ♗d4 ♗f5! 12. ♘c3 e5!? 13. ♗e5 0-0-0⩱] 5. ed6 [5. ♗b2? de5 6. ♗e5 ♘c6 7. ♗b2 e5 8. ♘c3 ♗f5∓↻ Spielmann—Landau (m) 1933] ♕d6 6. d4 ♘c6 7. ♗e3 [7. ♗b2 ♗f5 8. ♘f3 ♘b4 9. ♘a3 ♕e6∓] ♕g6=

92 5... c6!? Rabar

93 6... e6? 7. ♕g4 ♘c6 8. ♘f3 b6 9. ♗g5 ♘e7 10. c6! dc6 11. ♖d1 ♗d7 12. ♗a6 h6 13. ♗h4 ♖b8 14. ♗e2 g5 15. ♗g3 ♘f5 16. h4± Utjacki—Bagirov, SSSR 1971 — 12/130

94 **7. ♗g5** f6 [7... de5 8. ♕b3 ♕d7 9. ♖d1 ♕f5 10. ♗c4 ♘c6 11. ♗d5 h6 12. ♕b5 ♕g6 13. ♘f3 a6 14. ♕a4 ♗d7 15. ♗e3 e6 16. ♗e4 ♕f6 17. ♕b3⩱ Poletajev—Rochno, corr. 1948; 10... h6!? Bagirov] 8. ♕b3 [8. ♗h4 de5 9. ♕b3 e6 10. ♖d1 ♕e7∓ Bagirov] fg5 9. ♗c4 e6 10. ♗e6 ♗e6 11. ♕e6 ♗e7△ ♕d7∓; **7. cd6**!? ed6 8. ♗c4 [8. ♘f3 ♗e7 9. ♗c4 de5 10. ♕d8 ♗d8 11. ♘e5 0—0= Estrin—Bagirov, SSSR 1960] ♗e7 9. ♗f4! (Bagirov) de5 10. ♗e5 0—0 11. ♕d8 ♗d8 12. ♘f3 ♗g4 13. 0-0-0 ♘d7 14. ♗f4 ♘b6 15. ♗b3±

95 Aljchin—Fine, Pasadena 1932

96 **6. d4** d6 7. cd6 cd6 8. ♘f3 ♘c6 9. ed6 [9. ♘d5 ed5 — 6. ♘d5] ♗d6 10. ♗d3 ♘f4 11. ♗f4 ♗f4 12. 0—0 [12. ♕e2 ♘d4?! 13. ♘d4 ♕d4 14. g3 ♗c7 15. ♗b5 ♔e7 16. 0—0 a6 17. ♖ac1± Damjanović—Buljovčić, Jugoslavija 1966 — 1/84; 12... ♘b4 13. ♗b1 ♘d5∞] 0—0 13. ♖e1 g6 14. ♗f1 ♗h6= Ozsvath—Csom, Hungary 1967 — 3/128; 10... ♗e7!? Panov; **6. ♕g4** h5=; **6. ♗c4** — 5. ♗c4

97 7... b6 8. ♗e3 [8. cb6 ab6 9. ♘f3 ♗e7 10. ♗d3 ♗a6 11. 0—0 0—0 12. ♖e1 ♗d3 13. ♕d3 ♘a6 14. ♗d2 c6∓ Filipowicz—Smejkal, Bucuresti 1970] bc5 9. dc5 c6 10. ♗d3 [10. b4 ♗a6 11. ♗a6?! ♘a6 12. a3 ♘c7 13. ♘e2 g6 14. 0—0 ♗g7 15. f4∞ Hennings—Jansa, Polanica Zdroj 1969] ♘a6 [10... ♗a6 11. b4! ♕h4 12. ♖b1 ♗d3 13. ♕d3 ♕g4 14. ♘e2 ♕g6 15. ♘f4± Hennings—Jansa, Bucuresti 1971; 11... ♗d3 12. ♕d3 a5 13. b5 cb5 14. ♕b5±] 11. ♖c1 ♕a5 12. ♗d2 [12. ♕d2 ♕a2 13. ♘f3 ♖b8 14. ♗d4 ♘c7 15. 0—0 ♘e6 16. ♖a1 ♕b3 17. ♖a7 ♗c5 18. ♗c5 ♘c5 19. ♗c2 ♕b6?!∞ Hennings—Honfi, Hungary 1970 — 9/108; 19... ♕b2! 20. ♖b1 ♕b1!—+] ♕a2 13. ♖a1 ♕b2 14. ♗a6 ♗a6 15. ♖a6 ♕e5 16. ♘e2 ♗c5 17. 0—0 0—0 18. ♘f4 ♗b6 [18... ♕f5!?] 19. ♖e1 ♕f5 20. ♕e2 h6 21. ♖a3 ♖fe8 22. ♕e8∞ Hennings—Smejkal, Kapfenberg 1970 — 9/107; 19. ♖a3! ±→》 Franzen—Smejkal, ČSSR (ch) 1972

98 9. f4? de5 10. de5 ♗c5∓

99 10... ♗e7!? 11. 0—0 0—0 12. ♗f4 [12. ♖e1 ♗f5 13. ♗f4 ♖c8 14. ♖c1 ♕d7 15. ♕b3 de5 16. de5 d4= Westerinen—Hecht Helsinki 1972] ♗g4 13. ♕d2 ♖e8 14. ♖fd1 ♖c8 15. ♖ac1 a6= Ničevski—Vasjukov, Jugoslavija—SSSR 1969 — 7/125

100 **11... ♗e7** 12. 0—0 0—0 13. ♕b3 ♖b8 14. ♗f4 ♗e6 15. ♖fd1 ♕a5 16. ♖ac1 h6 17. ♕b5± Franzen—Kupka, ČSSR (ch) 1972; **11... ♗b4** 12. ♗d2 ♕a5 13. a3 [13. ♗b4 ♕b4 14. ♕d2 ♕d2 15. ♔d2 ♗g4 16. ♖ac1

♔e7=] ♗d2 14. ♕d2 ♕d2 15. ♔d2 ♗g4= Siaperas—Flatow, Lugano (ol) 1968

101 5... c6 6. ♘c3 d6 7. cd6 [7. ♕f3 ♘d7= Rabar] ed6 8. ♕b3 de5 9. ♘d5 cd5 10. ♗d5 ♕c7= Dubinin—Kopilov, SSSR 1946

102 6. ♕g4 ♘c6=; 6... h5!?

103 8. ♘f3 ♘b6 9. ♗d3 ♘c6 10. 0—0 ♘b4=

104 8... ♘c6!? 9. ♘f3 ♗e7 10. 0—0 0—0 11. ed6 ♕d6 12. ♘c3 ♘c3 13. bc3 b6= Browne—Hort, Venezia 1971 — 12/132

105 11. ♗d3 ♘b4 12. ♗e4 b6! 13. ♗a8 ♗a6 14. ♕d2 ♕a8∓⫽ h1-a8 Boleslavski

106 12. 0—0 ♕c4 13. ♕d1 [13. ♕d2 ♘c6 14. ♕g5 h6 15. ♕g3 ♘e7 16. ♘a3 ♕d3 17. ♗e3 ♘f5 18. ♕f4 g5 19. ♕c4 ♕c4= Gurgenidze—Mikenas, SSSR 1968 — 6/165] ♗d7 14. ♗d2 ♘c6 15. ♗c3 ♖d8 16. ♘bd2 ♕d5 17. ♖e1 ♗e7 18. ♖e4 0—0 19. ♖g4 b5∞ Gurgenidze—Ciocaltea, Tbilisi 1970 — 9/104

107 **6... ♘f4**? 7. d4 ♘g2 8. ♔f1 ♘h4 9. ♘f3± Ozsvath—Prelovski 1962; **6... d6**!? 7. ♘d5 ed5 8. ♗d5 c6 9. ♗f7 ♔f7 10. cd6 ♕e8 11. ♕f3 ♔g8 12. ♕e3 ♗e6 13. ♘e2 ♘d7 14. 0—0 ♘e5 15. ♕e5 ♗c4 16. ♕e8 ♖e8 17. d3 ♗d3 18. ♖d1 ♗e2 19. d7 ♖d8 20. ♗g5 ♗d1 21. ♖d1 ♗e7 22. ♗e7 ♔f7= Vasjukov—Spaski, SSSR (ch) 1959; 14. f4!?± Holmov

108 7. bc3 d6 [7... ♗c5 8. ♕g4 ♔f8 9. d4±→] 8. cd6 cd6 9. ed6 ♗d6 10. d4 0—0 11. ♘f3 ♕c7= Sergeant—Tartakower, Hastings 1946

109 **7... ♗c5**?! 8. ♕g4 ♔f8 9. ♗f4 d5 10. 0-0-0 ♗d7 11. ♗d3 ♗e7 12. h4± Ravinski—Fridštejn, SSSR 1947; **7... d5** 8. cd6 cd6 9. ed6 ♗d6 10. ♕g4 0—0 11. ♗g5± Weeramantry—Hecht, England 1972 — 13/139; 9... ♕d6!? Gligorić

110 **8... ♕h4**!? 9. g3 ♕e7 10. ♘f3 h6 11. ♗e3 g5 12. ♗b5 ♗g7 13. ♗c6 dc6 14. ♕d4 ♕d7 15. ♕g4± Ubilava—Adamski, Tbilisi 1972; 10... ♕c5!?; **8... ♗c5** 9. ♕g4 g5 10. ♗g5 [10. ♕g5? ♕g5 11. ♗g5 ♘e5! 12. ♗f6 ♘c4 13. ♗h8 ♘b2∓ Kirov—Orev, Bulgaria 1962] ♖g8 11. ♘h3 [11. ♗d8 ♖g4 12. ♗e2 ♖g2 13. ♗c7 ♗f2 14. ♔f1 ♖g1 15. ♔f2 ♖a1 16. ♖a1±; 13... b6 14. b4 ♗f2 15. ♔f1 ♖g1 16. ♔f2 ♖g6 17. ♖hg1 ♗b7 18. ♗h5 ♘e7 19. ♗g6 hg6 1/2 : 1/2 Trapl—Neckař, Hradec Kralové 1972] ♗e7 12. f4 ♘e5 13. fe5 ♗g5 14. ♕h5 ♖g7 15. 0—0 h6 [15... b6? 16. ♖f7!!+— Erler—Espig, DDR 1971 — 12/131] 16. ♖f3!±→»

111 9. ♕g4 ♗b7 10. ♘f3 ♘e7 11. ♗g5?! h6 12. ♕h5 g6 13. ♕h4 ♗g7∓ Polgar—Hort, Örebro 1966; 11. ♖d1∞

112 12. ♕e2 f5 13. ef6 ♗f6 14. ♖fd1± Markland—Ghizdavu, Reggio Emilia 1972/73 — 15/134

113 **7. ♕g4** 0—0 8. d4 f5∓ Augustin—Popov, Leningrad 1960; **7. ♘d5** ed5 8. ♗d5 ♕h4 9. ♕e2 ♘c6 10. ♘f3 ♕e7= Boleslavski

114 8. ♘d5 d6 9. d4 ♗b6= Boleslavski

115 9... ♕e7?! 10. ♕g7 ♕f8±

116 **12. ♗g5**?! ♕d7 13. 0—0 ♗c3 14. bc3 ♕g4∓ Bagirov; **12. 0—0** ♗e6∞

B 03

1. e4 ♘f6 2. e5 ♘d5 3. d4

	3	4	5	6	7	8	9	10	11	
1	... ♘b6[1]	a4[2] a5	♗b5!?[3] c6[4]	♗d3 d5	♗g5! g6	h4 h6	♗e3 ♗g7	♘d2 ♘a6	c3 ♗e6[5]	±
2	... d6	♗c4[6] ♘b6[7]	♗b3 de5[8]	♕h5[9] e6	de5 a5[10]	a4[11] ♘a6	♘f3 ♘c5	♗a2 ♘ba4[12]		=∞
3	... ...	c4 ♘b6	ed6[13] ed6[14]	♘c3 ♗e7[15]	h3[16] 0—0	♘f3 ♗f6[17]	♗e2 ♖e8	0—0 ♘c6	♗f4[18] ♗f5[19]	=

1. e4 ♘f6 2. e5 ♘d5 3. d4 d6 4. c4 ♘b6 5. f4

	5	6	7	8	9	10	11	12	13	
4	... g6[20]	♘c3[21] de5[22]	fe5 ♗g7	♗e3 0—0	♘f3[23] c5[24]	dc5[25] ♘6d7	e6 fe6	♕c2[26] ♕a5	♗e2[27]	∞
5	... ...	... ...	... ...	♘f3 ♗g4[28]	c5 ♘d5	♗c4 e6	0—0 ♘c3	bc3 0—0[29]		±
6	... ♗f5[30]	♘c3[31] e6	♗e3 ♗e7[32]	♘f3 0—0[33]	♗d3[34] ♗d3[35]	♕d3 d5	b3 dc4	bc4 ♘c6	0—0 ♘a5[36]	±

	5	6	7	8	9	10	11	12	13	
7	...	...	...	ed6![38]	♘f3	♗e2	♖c1[39]	b3[40]		±
	...	...	♘a6[37]	cd6	♗e7	0–0	♖c8			
8	...	fe5	d5[41]	♘c3[42]	cd5	♘f3[45]	♕d4[47]	gf3	♗c4[49]	±
	de5	c5	e6	ed5[43]	c4[44]	♗g4[46]	♗f3	♗b4[48]	0–0[50]	
9	...	...	♘c3	♘f3	♗e3[51]	♗e2[52]	0–0	♘d4	♗d4	=
	...	♗f5	e6	♗b4	c5	♘c6	cd4[53]	♘d4	♗c2[54]	
10	...	...	...	...	♗d3!	0–0	c5	bc3	♕e1	±
	...	...	...	...	♗g4[55]	♘c6[56]	♗c3[57]	♘d5	♘de7[58]	
11	...	...	...	...	♗e2[59]	0–0	♗e3[61]	♘e5	♘f3	=
	...	...	...	♗e7	0–0	f6[60]	fe5	♘8d7	c6[62]	
12	...	...	♘f3	e6!?[64]	c5[65]	♗b5	0–0[67]	♕a4[68]	♖f3	∓
	...	♘c6	♗g4[63]	fe6	♘d5![66]	♕d7	g6	♗f3	♗g7[69]	

1. e4 ♘f6 2. e5 ♘d5 3. d4 d6 4. c4 ♘b6 5. f4 de5 6. fe5 ♘c6 7. ♗e3 ♗f5 8. ♘c3[70] e6

	9	10	11	12	13	14	15	16	17	
13	♘f3[71]	♗e2[72]	0–0	bc3	♘d2	♖f4[75]	♕f1	h4![76]		±
	♗b4	0–0[73]	♗c3	♘a5	♕d7[74]	♗g6	c5			
14	...	♕d2[77]	0-0-0[79]	h3[81]	g4	h4	♕f2	gh5	♗e2[82]	∞
	♗g4	♗e7[78]	a5[80]	♗h5	♗g6	♘b4	h5	♖h5		
15	...	♗e2	gf3	♗f2	c5[84]	♘d5	♕d2[85]			±
	...	♗f3[83]	♕h4	♕f4	♘d5	ed5				
16	...	♗e2[86]	0–0	ef6[88]	d5	♘e5	a4!	a5	♕b3	±
	♕d7	0-0-0[87]	f6	gf6	♘e5[89]	fe5	♔b8[90]	♘c8	ed5[91]	
17	...	...	...	c5![92]	♘d5	♘g5[94]	♕e2	♗d4	♔h1	±
	...	...	♗g4	♘d5[93]	♕d5	♗e2	♘d4	♕d4	♕d2[95]	
18	...	♖c1	♗e2[96]	0–0[98]	dc5[100]	a3	b4	♘e5	♘b5	±
	♘b4	c5	♗e7[97]	0–0[99]	♘d7	♘c6	♘de5	♘e5	♗g5[101]	

1. e4 ♘f6 2. e5 ♘d5 3. d4 d6 4. c4 ♘b6 5. f4 de5 6. fe5 ♘c6 7. ♗e3 ♗f5 8. ♘c3 e6 9. ♘f3 ♗e7

	10	11	12	13	14	15	16	17	18	
19	♗e2	0–0	ef6[102]	♕d2[103]	♖ad1	♕c1[105]	♔h1[107]	h3	♗g1[108]	=
	0–0	f6	♗f6	♕e7[104]	♖ad8	h6[106]	♔h8	♗h7	♖fe8[109]	
20	d5	cd5	♘d4	e6[112]	de6	♕g4[113]	g3	0-0-0	gh4[117]	±
	ed5?![110]	♘b4	♗d7[111]	fe6	♗c6	♗h4[114]	♗h1[115]	♕f6[116]		
21	...	♘d4	a3	♘e6[120]	ab4	♘a4[122]	♘b6	♖a8	d6	=∞
	♘b4	♗g6[118]	c5[119]	fe6	cb4[121]	0–0[123]	ab6	♕a8	♗d8[124]	
22	...	♖c1	a3	ab4	♗d4	♕d4[127]	c5	♗b5	♗d7[128]	±
	...	ed5[125]	c5[126]	d4	cd4	♗b4	♘d5	♗d7	♕d7[129]	

1 3... c5? 4. c4 ♘c7 5. d5 d6 6. e6!? fe6 7. ♗d3±→ Keres–Danielsson, Tallinn 1935; 6. f4!?; 6. ♘f3±

2 4. ♘c3 d5 5. ♗f4 ♗f5 6. g4 ♗e6 [6... ♗g6 7. h4 h5±] 7. h3 g6 8. ♘f3 h5 9. ♘g5 ♕d7 10. gh5 ♖h5 11. ♗e2 ♖h8 12. ♕d2 ♗f5 13. 0-0-0 ♘c6 [13... e6 14. h4△ h5±] 14. e6 [14. h4? f6∓] fe6 15. ♗d3 e5! 16. de5 e6=⇆ Štejn–Lutikov, SSSR (ch) 1969 — 8/100; **4. c4** — 3... d6

3 5. ♘f3 d5 6. ed6 cd6? 7. d5! e5 8. de6 ♗e6 9. ♗b5 ♘c6 10. ♘g5± Židkov–Mikadze, SSSR 1972 — 13/140; 6... ed6=

4 5... ♘c6 6. ♘c3± Petrosjan

5 Talj–Lutikov, SSSR (ch) 1969 — 8/101

6 **4. ♗g5** de5 [4... h6 5. ♗h4 de5 6. de5 c6 7. ♘d2 ♗f5 8. ♘b3 ♕c7 9. ♘f3 e6= Šofman–Mikenas, SSSR 1965] 5. de5 ♘c6 6. ♗b5 [6. ♘f3 ♗g4 7. ♗b5 h6 8. ♗d2 e6 9. 0–0 ♘e7 10. h3 ♗h5 11. ♖e1 a6 12. ♗e2 ♕d7= Lutikov–Kopilov, corr. 1968] ♗f5 7. ♘f3 ♘b4! 8. ♘a3 ♕d1 9. ♖d1 ♘c2 10. ♘c2 ♗c2 [Steiner–Aljehin, Budapest 1921] 11. ♗c6=∞; **4. f4** de5 [4... ♗f5 5. ♘f3 e6 6. ♗d3 ♗d3 7. ♕d3 ♗e7!= Ničevski–Papler, Jugoslavija (ch) 1974 — 17/148] 5. fe5 ♘c6 6. c3 ♗f5 7. ♗d3 ♕d7 8. ♘e2 ♗d3 9. ♕d3 e6= Stahlberg–Liliental, Moskva 1935; **4. ed6** ♕d6 5. ♘f3 ♗g4 6. ♗e2 ♘c6 7. 0–0 [7. ♘c3?! 0-0-0 8. ♘d5 ♕d5 9. ♗e3 e5∓↑ Iljin-Ženevski–Reti, Moskva 1925] 0-0-0 8. c3! ♘f4 9. ♗f4 ♕f4 10. b4 e6= Bagirov; 4... ed6=

7 4... e6!? 5. ♘f3 ♗e7 6. 0–0 0–0 7. ♖e1 ♘c6 8. ♘c3 ♘c3 9. bc3 d5 10. ♗d3 ♘a5 11. ♘d2 c5 12. dc5 ♗c5 13. ♕h5± Canal–Grünfeld, Karlovy Vary 1929; 9... b6!?

8 **5... ♘c6**?! 6. e6! fe6 7. ♘f3 g6 8. ♘g5!? [8. h4?! ♗g7 9. h5 e5 10. ♘g5 d5 11. ♕f3 ♗f5 12. hg6 ♘d4–+ Tukmakov–Štejn, SSSR 1962] ♗g7 9. ♗e6 ♖f8 10. d5 ♘d4 11. c3 ♘e6 12. de6± Sax–Hazai, Hungary (ch) 1973 — 16/110; 11. h4!?±; 10. c3!?±; **5... e6**!? 6. ♘f3 ♗e7 7. ♕e2 ♘c6 8. c3 0–0 9. 0–0 a5 10. a4 ♘d5? 11. ♖d1± Diez del Corral–Kraidman, Skopje (ol) 1972; 7... ♗d7!?

9 6. ♕f3?! e6 7. de5 a5! 8. c3 a4 9. ♗c2 ♗d7 10. ♕g3 ♗b5! 11. ♗g5 ♕d5 12. ♘d2 [12. ♘a3 ♗a3 13. ♖d1 ♗b2∓] ♘c6 13. f4 ♘c4∓ Gufeljd–Vasjukov, Kislovodsk 1968 — 6/167

10 7... ♘c6 8. ♘f3 ♘d4 [8... g6? 9. ♕g4 h6 10. ♘c3 ♗g7 11. ♗f4 ♕e7 12. 0–0 0–0 13. ♕g3 a5 14. a4 ♕b4 15. ♖fe1± Sax–Hecht, Amsterdam 1972 — 13/141] 9. ♘d4 ♕d4 10. ♘c3 ♘c4? 11. ♕e2! ♘e5 12. ♘b5± Kučera–Přibyl, corr. 1974

11 8. a3?! a4 9. ♗a2 ♘c6△ ♖a5∓

12 10... ♗d7?! 11. ♘c3 ♘ba4 12. ♗g5 ♗e7 13. ♘a4 ♘a4 14. ♖d1 ♘c5 [14... ♘b2 15. ♗e6+–] 15. ♗e3 0–0 16. c3 ♕e8 17. ♗c5 ♗c5 18. ♘g5 h6 19. ♘e4 ♗e7 20. ♘f6!! ♗f6 [20... gf6 21. ♕h6△ ♖d3+–] 21. ef6 ♖a6 22. fg7 ♔g7 23. ♕e5± Sax–Ghinda, Bath 1973 — 16/111

13 5. ♘f3 g6 — B 04; 5... ♗g4 — B 05

14 5... cd6 6. ♘f3 g6 — B 04

15 6... g6 7. ♘f3 — B 04

16 **7. ♗e3** ♘c6 8. ♗d3 0–0 9. ♘ge2 ♘b4 [9... ♗g4 10. 0–0 ♗f6 11. f3 ♗h5=] 10. 0–0 ♘d3 11. ♕d3 d5 12. c5 ♘c4=; **7. ♗e2** 0–0 8. ♘f3 ♘c6 [8... ♗g4 9. b3?! c5 10. ♗e3 ♘c6 11. ♖c1 f5 12. dc5 dc5= Minić–Smislov, Palma de Mallorca (izt) 1970 — 10/151; 9. 0–0!?] 9. ♗e3 ♗g4 — B 05

17 8... ♘c6 9. ♗e2 ♗f5 10. 0–0 ♗g6 11. b3 ♗f6 12. ♗e3 a5 13. ♖c1 a4 14. ♘a4 ♘a4 15. ba4 ♖e8 16. ♖e1 ♕d7 17. ♕b3 ♗e4=∞ Ničevski–Hort, Athens 1969

18 11. b3 ♗f5 12. ♗e3 d5?! 13. c5 ♘c8 14. ♕d2 ♗e4 15. ♘h2± Sigurjonsson–Rogoff, Haifa 1970; 12... h6=

19 **12. b3** ♗e4 13. ♘e4 ♖e4 14. ♗e3 d5 15. c5 ♘d7 16. ♗d3 ♖e8= Ostojić–Schmid, Monte Carlo 1969; **12. ♖c1** h6 13. b3 ♖e7?! 14. ♕d2 ♕d7 15. ♖fd1! ♖ae8 16. ♗f1 g5 17. ♗g3 ♗e4 18. ♘e4 ♖e4 19. ♗d3± Matanović–Larsen, Palma de Mallorca 1968 — 6/174; 13... ♗e4!?=

20 5... g5? 6. ed6 gf4 7. dc7 [7. ♗f4?! cd6 8. ♘c3 ♗g7 9. ♘f3 ♗g4 10. ♖c1 ♘c6 11. d5 ♘d4 12. ♕d3 ♘f3 13. gf3 ♗h5 14. ♖g1 ♗g6 15. ♕e3 0–0∓ Levčenkov–K. Grigorjan, SSSR 1971] ♕c7 8. ♘c3! e5!? [8... e6 9. c5!±] 9. de5 ♗e6 10. ♗f4 ♘c6 11. ♘e4! ♗b4 12. ♔f2 ♘c4 13. ♗c4 ♗c4 14. ♘f3± Tringov–Planinc, Varna 1970 — 9/114

21 6. ed6 cd6 7. ♘f3 ♗g7 8. ♗e2 0–0 9. 0–0= Cobo–Schmid, Leipzig (ol) 1960

22 6... ♗g7 7. ♗e3 [7. ♘f3 de5 8. fe5 — 6... de5] 0–0 [7... de5 8. fe5 c5 9. dc5 ♘6d7 10. e6 fe6 11. ♘f3 ♕a5 12. ♖c1 ♘c5? 13. ♘d4± Sämisch–Rellstab, Swinemünde 1931; 12... ♘c6∞; 8. de5!±] 8. ♘f3 de5 [8... ♗e6 9. b3±] 9. de5 c6 [9... ♘c6? 10. c5 ♘d7 11. ♗c4 e6 12. 0–0±○ Kupper–Schmid, Zürich 1956] 10. ♕b3 ♗g4 11. ♗e2 ♗f3 12. ♗f3 ♕d3 13. ♘e4 ♕b3 14. ab3± Matanović–Darga, Bordeaux 1964

23 9. h4!? f6? 10. h5 fe5 11. d5 e6 12. hg6 hg6 13. ♗d3 e4 14. ♗e4 ♘c4 [14... ed5 15. ♗g6 ♗f5 16. ♕h5±→] 15. ♕e2 ♘e3 16. ♕e3± Estrin–Pytel, Polanica Zdroj 1971 — 12/136; 9... h5!?∞

24 **9... c6** 10. ♗e2 f6 11. ef6 ef6 12. 0–0 ♖e8 13. ♕d2 ♗e6 14. b3 ♗f7 15. ♖ad1 ♘8d7 = Parniani–Sobi, Varna (ol) 1962; **9... ♗g4** 10. ♗e2 c5 11. dc5 ♘6d7 12. 0–0 ♘c6∞ Quinones–Darga, Amsterdam (izt) 1964

25 10. d5 ♗g4 11. ♗c5 ♘8d7∓

26 12. ♘g5 ♕a5∓

27 **13. h4**?! ♘c5 14. h5 e5 15. hg6 ♗f5∓; **13. ♗e2**!∞

28 8... c5?! 9. d5 ♗g4 10. ♗f4±

29 Parma–Schiffer, Berlin 1971

30 Trifunović

31 6. ♗d3 ♗d3 7. ♕d3 de5 8. fe5 c5 [8... ♘c6? 9. ♘f3 e6 10. a3 ♕d7 11. b4 ♖d8 12. ♗e3 ♗e7 13. ♘c3 0–0 14. ♘e4± Euwe–Colle (m) 1928] 9. ♘f3 [9. d5? e6 10. ♘c3 ♕h4∓ Mikenas] cd4 [9... e6 10. 0–0 ♘c6 11. ♘c3 ♘d4 12. ♗g5⩱ Platonov–Efimov, SSSR 1966] 10. 0–0 ♘c6 11. e6 fe6 12. ♘g5⩱ Mihajlov–Sokolov, SSSR 1969

32 7... de5 8. fe5 — 5... de5

33 **8... d5**? 9. c5 ♘c4?! 10. ♗c4 dc4 11. ♕a4±; **8... ♘c6**?! 9. d5 ♘b4 10. ♘d4 de5 11. ♘f5±

34 **9. ed6** cd6 10. b3 d5 11. c5 ♘6d7 12. ♗d3 ♗d3 13. ♕d3 b6 14. cb6 ♕b6 15. 0–0 ♕a6= Ujtumen–Fischer, Palma de Mallorca (izt) 1970; **9. ♕b3** de5 10. ♘e5 a5 11. a3 ♘8d7 12. ♗e2 a4 13. ♕d1 c5 14. ♘d7 ♘d7 15. ♘a4 cd4 16. ♗d4 ♕c7 17. 0–0 b5 18. ♘c3 bc4 19. g4± Ljubojević–Marović, Jugoslavija 1971 — 11/105

35 9... d5?! 10. ♗f5 ef5 [10... ♘c4? 11. ♗b1 ♘e3 12. ♕d3 ♘f5 13. g4+–] 11. c5 ♘c4 12. ♗f2 [12. ♗c1 b6 13. b3 ♘a5 14. cb6 ab6 15. 0–0 c6 16. ♗b2 ♘a6 17. h3 ♘c7 18. ♔h1 ♘e6 19. ♘d2 g6 20. g4± Ceškovski–Golonišev, SSSR 1966] ♘b2 13. ♕b1 ♘c4 14. ♕b7± Štejn–Mikenas, SSSR (ch) 1962

36 14. ♘d2 ♕d7 15. f5± Fridsche–Caunas, Lipsko 1962

37 Trifunović

38 8. ♘f3 c5 9. dc5 [9. ♖c1? de5 10. fe5 cd4 11. ♘d4 ♗c5∓ Medina–Trifunović, Mar del Plata 1953; 9. d5 ♘b4 10. ♖c1 de5 11. ♘e5 f6!∓ Trifunović; 9. ♗e2 ♗e7 10. 0–0=] dc5 10. a3 ♕d1 11. ♖d1 ♗e7 12. ♗e2± Joppen–Trifunović, Beograd 1954

39 11. 0–0 ♖c8 12. b3 ♘d5!∓ Wade–Trifunović, England 1951

40 ±○ Euwe

41 7. dc5? ♕d1 8. ♔d1 ♘a4! [8... ♘6d7∓ Havin–Toluš, SSSR 1945] 9. b4 a5 10. a3 ab4 11. ab4 ♘c3∓

42 8. d6? ♕h4 9. g3 ♕e4 10. ♕e2 ♕h1 11. ♘f3 ♘c6! [11... ♘c4? 12. ♘bd2! ♘d2 13. ♔d2 g6 14. ♔c2 ♘c6 15. ♗g2 ♘b4 16. ♔b3+–] 12. ♘bd2 ♘d7! [12... ♘d4 13. ♘d4 cd4 14. ♘f3 ♘c4 15. ♔f2 ♘e3 16. ♗e3 de3 17. ♕e3 ♗d7 18. ♖c1 ♖c8 19. ♖c8 ♗c8 20. ♕a7 ♗d6 21. ♗b5+– Bagirov] 13. ♔f2 ♘de5! 14. ♘e5 ♕h2 15. ♗g2 ♘d4 16. ♕d1 ♗d6 17. ♘f1 ♕g2 18. ♔g2 ♗e5–+

43 8... ♕h4 9. g3 ♕d4 10. ♗d2 [10. ♕d4 cd4 11. ♘b5 ♘a6 12. d6 f6!∓; 10. ♘f3 ♕d1 11. ♔d1 ed5 12. cd5 ♗g4 13. ♗e2 ♘8d7 14. ♗f4 h6! 15. h4 0-0-0∓; 10. ♕e2 ed5 11. ♘b5 ♕c4 12. ♕c4 ♘c4 13. ♗c4 dc4 14. ♘c7 ♔d8 15. ♘a8∞ Vesely; 10. ♕e2 a6 11. ♘f3 ♕g4 12. ♗f4 ed5 13. ed5 ♗e7 14. ♗g2± Kostro–Levy, Polanica Zdroj 1969] ♕e5 11. ♗e2 ed5 12. ♘f3 ♕d6 [12... ♕e6 13. 0–0 ♗e7 14. ♖e1 0–0 15. cd5+–] 13. ♗f4 ♕d8 14. 0–0±

44 9... ♕h4 10. g3 ♕d4 11. ♗b5! [11. ♕d4 cd4 12. ♘b5 ♘d5 13. ♗c4! ♘b6! 14. ♗b3 ♘a6 15. ♘f3 ♗d7 16. ♘fd4! ♗c5 17. ♘d6 ♗d6 18. ed6 ♘c5±; 11. ♗f4 g5 12. ♗g5 ♕e5 13. ♕e2 ♗g7 14. 0-0-0 ♕e2 15. ♘ge2 ♗g4 16. ♗g2 0–0 17. h3! ♗e2 18. ♘e2± Werber–Segal, Harrachov 1967; 13... ♕e2 14. ♘ge2 ♗g4 15. ♗g2 ♗g7 16. h3! ♗e2 17. ♔e2 ♘c4 18. ♔d3± Kamišov–Aronin, SSSR 1946] ♗d7 12. ♕e2 ♘d5 [12... a6 13. e6 fe6 14. ♕e6 ♗e7 15. ♗g5 ♘c8 16. ♗d7+– Konovalov–Ignatenko, corr. 1948] 13. e6! fe6 [13... ♗b5 14. ♘b5 ♕b4 15. ♗d2 ♕b2 16. ef7 ♔f7 17. ♕h5 ♔e6 18. ♘f3 ♕a1 19. ♔f2! +– Panov] 14. ♕e6 ♘e7 15. ♘f3 ♕f6 16. ♕e2 ♗b5 [16... ♘c6 17. ♘e4+– Ljubojević–Moses, Dresden 1969] 17. ♘b5 ♘a6 18. ♗g5 ♕b6 19. 0-0-0 ♖d8 20. ♖d8 ♔d8 21. ♖d1 ♔c8 22. ♗f4 1 : 0 Balašov–K. Grigorjan, SSSR 1967

45 **10. ♕d4**? ♘c6 11. ♕e4 ♘b4 12. d6 g6∓; **10. ♗f4** ♗b4 11. ♗c4 ♘c4 12. ♕a4 ♘c6 13. dc6 ♘b2∓; **10. a3**∞ Estrin

46 10... ♗b4 11. ♗c4 ♘c4 12. ♕a4 ♘c6 13. dc6 ♗c3 14. bc3 b5 15. ♕b4! a5 16. ♕c5 ♕d3 17. ♗g5± Boleslavski

47 **11. ♗c4** ♘c4 12. ♕a4 ♘d7 13. ♕c4 ♗f3 14. gf3 ♘e5 15. ♕e4 [15. ♕e2!? ♕e7 16. ♗e3 ♘c4= Sydor–Mikenas, Polska 1968] ♕h4! 16. ♔e2 [16. ♕h4 ♘f3 17. ♔f1 ♘h4 18. ♗g5 ♘f3!∓] ♕e4 17. fe4=; **11. ♗e2**!? ♗b4 12. 0–0 ♗c3 13. bc3 ♕d5 [13... 0–0? 14. ♕d4 ♕c8 15. e6 ♗f3 16. ♖f3 fe6 17. ♗h6!+– Silva–Korostensky, Nice (ol) 1974] 14. ♕d5 ♘d5 15. ♗c4 ♘b6 16. ♗b3±

48 12... ♘c6 13. ♕e4 ♘b4 14. e6± Sokolov

49 13. ♕g4? ♘d5 14. ♕g7 ♖f8∓ Hecht–Dresen, Solingen 1970

50 14. ♖g1 g6 [14... ♕c7? 15. e6 f6 16. ♗h6 ♕c4 17. ♖g7 ♔h8 18. ♖g8! ♔g8 19. ♕g1 1 : 0 Ljubojević–Honfi, Čačak 1970 — 11/106] 15. ♗g5 [15. ♗h6? ♘c6 16. ♕e4 ♘e5 17. ♗f8 ♕f8 18. ♗b5 ♕c5–+ Gibbs–Steward, England 1972] ♕c7 16. ♗b3 ♗c5 17. ♕f4 ♖e8 [17... ♗g1? 18. ♔e2? ♕c5–+ Gheorghiu–Ljubojević, Manila 1973 — 16/118; 18. d6 ♕c8 19. ♔e2? ♗c5? 20. ♘e4!+– Bronštejn– Ljubojević, Petropolis (izt) 1973 — 16/117; 19... ♕c5! 20. e6 ♘8d7!!∓; 19. 0-0-0! ♗c5 20. e6 fe6 21. ♕e5 ♘d5 22. d7!+– Bronštejn] 18. ♗f6 ♘8d7 19. ♘e4! [19. d6 ♘e5! 20. ♔f1 ♗d6 21. ♘b5 ♕c6 22. ♘d6 ♕d6 23. ♖d1 ♕c6 24. ♗e5 ♕b5= I. Zajcev] ♖e5! [19... ♘e5 20. ♖g6!!+– Marjanović–Filipović, Jugoslavija 1974] 20. ♗e5 ♘e5 21. ♔e2!±

51 9. ♕b3 c5 10. ♗g5 ♕c7 11. 0-0-0 ♗c3 12. ♕c3 ♘a6 13. ♕a5 0–0 14. ♗e3 ♖ac8∞ Estrin–Schmidt, Polanica Zdroj 1971 — 12/143; 14... ♕c6!?

52 **10. ♕b3**?! ♕e7 [10... cd4 11. ♘d4 ♕h4 12. g3?! ♕e4 13. ♔f2 ♗c3 14. ♗g2 ♕d4!∓ Marjan–Suba, Novi Sad 1974 — 18/129; 12. ♗f2!?] 11. a3 cd4 12. ♘d4 ♗c5 13. ♘f5 ef5 14. ♗c5 ♕e5 15. ♗e2 ♕c5∓ Suetin–Štejn, Kislovodsk 1972 — 14/164; **10. a3** ♗c3 [10... cd4 11. ♗d4?! ♗c3 12. ♗c3 ♕d1 13. ♖d1 ♘a4 14. ♖c1 ♘c6 15. ♗e2 ♔e7∓⊥ Alexandrescu–Ghizdavu, Timisoara 1972; 11. ♕d4! ♕d4 12. ♗d4 ♗c3 13. ♗c3 ♘a4 14. ♗b4!?∞ Ostojić–Marović, Jugoslavija (ch) 1972] 11. bc3 ♘c6 12. ♗e2 0–0 13. 0–0 ♘a5 14. ♘d2 ♗g6!? 15. ♖f4 [15. ♕e1 ♖c8 16. ♖c1 ♕e7 17. h4 h5 18. ♗g5±↑ Bielczyk–Vaisman, Polska 1972; 17... h6∞] ♖c8 16. h4 h6 17. h5 ♗h7 18. ♕f1 [18. ♖c1 ♕e7△ cd4, ♕a3] ♕c7 [Mesing–Ghizdavu, Timisoara 1972] 19. ♖c1 cd4 20. cd4 ♘d5 21. ♖f3 ♘e3 22. ♖e3 b5∞

53 11... ♗c3?! 12. bc3 0–0 13. ♕e1 ♗g6 14. ♖d1 cd4 15. cd4 ♘e7±⊞ Parma–Hecht, Berlin 1971 — 12/137

54 14. ♕d2 ♖c8 15. ♔h1 0–0 16. b3 ♗c5 17. ♘b5 ♗d4 18. ♘d4 [18. ♕d4 ♕d4 19. ♘d4 ♗e4!=⊥ Keene] ♗g6 [18... a6? 19. ♗f3! ♖b8 20. c5± Urzica–Ghizdavu, Romania 1972] 19. ♗f3 ♖c7 20. ♕e3= Pritchett–Williams, Caorle 1972

55 **9... ♗d3**?! 10. ♕d3 c5 11. 0–0! cd4 12. ♘e4 ♘c6 [12... ♘6d7 13. ♘fg5 ♘e5 14. ♕g3 ♘bd7 15. ♗f4 ♕b6 16. ♗e5 f6 17. ♗d6 fg5 18. ♗b4+– Ivkov–Timman, Amsterdam 1974 — 18/130] 13. c5 ♘c8 14. ♘fg5+– Andrejev–Dranov, SSSR 1972; **9... ♗g6**?! 10. 0–0 ♗c3 11. bc3 ♘8d7 12. ♗g6 hg6 13. ♘g5 ♖f8 14. ♘h7±△ ♕f3 Mesing–Popov, Jugoslavija 1972; **9... c5**!? 10. ♗f5 ef5 11. d5 ♘c4 12. 0–0 0–0 13. ♗g5 [13. ♕d3?!= Padevski–Spiridonov, Varna 1973] ♕d7 14. ♕e2 ♗c3 15. ♕c4 ♗b2 16. ♖ab1 ♗d4 17. ♘d4 cd4 18. e6! fe6 19. de6 ♕c6 20. ♕b3± Ghizdavu, Spasov

56 10... ♗f3? 11. ♕f3 ♕d4 12. ♗e3 ♕d7 13. ♖ad1±↑

57 11... ♘d5 12. ♘e2△ a3+–

58 **13... 0—0**? 14. ♗g5 ♕d7 15. ♗h7!±; **13... ♘de7** 14. ♖b1 ♖b8 15. ♘g5 ♗f5 16. ♗f5 ♘f5 17. ♕e4 ♕d7 18. d5±→ Velimirović –Martz, Vrnjačka Banja 1973 — 15/137

59 **9. ♗e3** 0–0? 10. ♗d3 ♗g4 [10... ♗d3 11. ♕d3±] 11. 0–0 ♘c6 12. h3! ♗f3 [12... ♗h5 13. ♗h7 ♔h7 14. ♘g5 ♗g5 15. ♕h5 ♗h6 16. ♖f6+–] 13. ♕f3 ♘e5 14. ♗h7 ♔h7 15. de5 ♕d3 16. ♖ad1 ♕g6 [16... ♕c4 17. ♖d4 ♕c6 18. ♕h5 ♔g8 19. ♖f6!+–] 17. ♖d4±→« Velimirović – Marović, Jugoslavija (ch) 1972 — 13/148; 9... ♘c6 — 6... ♘c6; **9. ♗d3** ♗g4!? [9... ♗d3 10. ♕d3 ♘c6 11. ♗e3 0–0 12. ♖d1 f6 13. ef6 ♗f6 14. 0–0 ♕e8 15. b3 ♖d8 16. ♕e4!± Velimirović – Hloušek, Kapfenberg 1970 — 9/113] 10. ♗e4 ♘c6 11. ♗c6 bc6 12. 0–0 ♘c4? 13. ♕a4 ♗f3 14. ♖f3 ♕d4 15. ♗e3+–; 12... 0–0= Boleslavski

60 10... ♘c6 11. ♗e3 — 6... ♘c6

61 **11. ♗f4**?! ♘c6 12. ef6 ♗f6 13. d5 ♘a5 14. ♘e5 ♗e5 15. ♗e5 ♘ac4 16. ♗c4 ♘c4 17. ♗g7 ♘e3 18. ♕e2 ♘f1 19. ♗f8 ♘h2 20. ♗c5 ♘g4 21. de6 ♕h4∓↑ Geler – Korčnoj, SSSR (ch) 1960; **11. ef6** ♗f6 12. ♗e3= Bagirov

62 **13... h6**!? 14. c5 ♘d5 15. ♘d5 ed5 16. ♕b3 ♘f6 17. ♘e5 ♕c8 18. ♖ae1 c6= Suetin – Mikenas, SSSR 1961; 17. ♕b7!?; **13... c6** 14. ♕d2 ♕e8 15. ♖ae1 ♖d8 16. ♕c1 ♘f6 17. h3 h6 18. ♘e5 ♘fd7 19. ♘d7 ♘d7 20. ♗f4 ♕g6= Šijanovski – Smislov, SSSR (ch) 1961

63 7... ♗f5? 8. d5 ♘b4 9. ♘d4±

64 Iljin-Ženevski; 8. ♗e3 ♗f3 [8... e6?! 9. ♘bd2±] 9. gf3 e6 10. ♘c3 ♕h4 11. ♗f2 ♕f4∓

65 9. ♗e2 ♕d7! [Euwe; 9... e5 10. d5 ♗f3 11. ♗f3 ♘d4 12. ♗e4 g6 13. 0–0±; 9... ♗f3 10. ♗f3 ♘c4∞] 10. c5 ♘d5 11. 0–0 g6 [11... 0-0-0 12. ♘g5 ♗e2 13. ♕e2 ♘d4 14. ♕f2±] 12. ♘g5 ♗e2 13. ♕e2 ♘d4 14. ♕e5 ♘f6 15. ♘c3$\overline{\overline{\infty}}$; 11... e5!∓

66 **9... ♘c8**? 10. ♗b5 ♗f3 11. ♕f3 ♕d5 12. ♘d2 g6 13. 0–0 ♕f3 14. ♘f3 ♗g7 15. ♗e3±; **9... ♘d7** 10. ♗c4 [10. ♗e2 e5 11. 0–0 ed4 12. ♘g5! ♗e2 13. ♕e2 ♘de5 14. ♘e6 ♕d7 15. ♕h5 g6 16. ♕h7 ♕e6 17. ♕h8 ♘d7±] ♗f3 11. gf3 e5 12. ♕b3± Levenfiš; **9... e5** 10. cb6 e4 11. d5! [11. h3?! ♗h5 12. g4 ef3 13. gh5 e5 14. ♕f3 ♕h4 15. ♔d1 ♕d4 16. ♗d3 0-0-0!∓] ef3 12. gf3 ♗h5 13. bc7 ♕c7 14. dc6 ♕c6 15. ♗e2 ♖d8 16. ♗d2±; 12. ♕a4± Szabo – Cvetkov, Hilversum 1947; **9... ♗f3**!? 10. ♕f3 ♘d4 11. ♕f2 ♘a4 12. ♗e3 ♕d5 13. ♘c3 ♘c3 14. bc3 ♘f5∓ Kopilov

67 11. ♘bd2?! g6 12. ♕a4 ♗g7 13. ♘e5? ♗e5 14. de5 ♘e3 15. ♕e4 0–0!! 16. ♗c6 [16. ♕e3 ♘b4 17. ♕e4 ♕b5–+ Kiley – Hewit, corr. 1960] ♕d4! 17. ♗b7 ♘c2 18. ♕c2 ♕f2#

68 12. ♘bd2 ♗g7 13. ♕a4 ♗f3! [13... 0–0 14. ♘e5 ♗e5 15. de5 ♗f5 16. ♘f3 a6 17. ♗c6 ♕c6 18. ♕c6 bc6 19. ♗h6$\overline{\overline{\infty}}$ Winiwalter – Hort, Krems 1967] 14. ♘f3 0–0 15. ♘e5 ♗e5 16. de5 a6∓

69 14. ♔h1 ♖f8 15. ♖f8 ♔f8 16. ♘c3 a6 17. ♗d2 ♖b8 18. ♖f1 ♔g8 19. ♗c6 ♕c6 20. ♕c6 bc6∓ Boleslavski

70 **8. e6**? fe6 [8... ♗e6 9. d5 ♘d5 10. cd5 ♕d5 11. ♘c3±] 9. ♘c3 e5 10. d5 ♘b4 11. ♖c1 e6 12. a3 ed5∓; **8. a3** e6 9. ♘f3 [9. b4? ♗e7 10. ♘f3 f6! 11. b5 ♘a5 12. ♘bd2 0–0 13. ♕c1 ♘d7 14. ef6 ♗f6 15. ♗e2 ♖c8 16. 0–0 c5∓ Steiner – Tartakower,

Ujpest 1934] ♗e7 [9... ♕d7?! 10. ♗e2 0-0-0 11. 0–0 f6 12. ♘bd2 ♗g4?! 13. b4 fe5 14. de5 ♗f3 15. ♘f3± Dankert – Scheller, corr. 1929] 10. ♘c3 f6=

71 9. ♗e2 ♗e7 10. ♘f3 — 9. ♘f3

72 10. ♗d3?! ♗g4 11. ♗e2 ♗f3 12. gf3 ♕h4 13. ♗f2 ♕f4 14. ♖g1 0-0-0 15. ♖g4 ♕h2 16. ♖h4 ♕g2 17. ♗f1 ♕g5∓ Lasker – Tarrasch, Moravska Ostrava 1923

73 10... ♘a5!?

74 12... ♗g6!?±

75 14. ♖f3 ♕a4 15. ♕f1 c5? 16. d5 ♘d7 17. ♖f5 ef5 18. ♕f5±→ Lebedev – Bješejn, SSSR 1965; 15... ♗g6△ c5∞ Hecht, Bagirov

76 **16. ♘b3** ♕a4 17. dc5?! ♘d7∞ Zuidema – Hecht, Amsterdam 1971 — 12/138; 17. ♘c5 ±; **16. h4**!±

77 10. c5? ♘d5 11. ♘d5 ♕d5 12. ♗e2 0-0-0 13. 0–0 ♕e4∓

78 10... ♘a5!? 11. b3 ♗b4∞ Konstantinopoljski

79 11. ♗e2?! ♗f3 12. gf3 ♗h4 13. ♔f1 f6 14. f4 fe5 [14... 0–0 15. ♔g2 ♕e8 16. c5 ♕g6 17. ♔h3 ♕h6 18. ♔g2 fe5 19. de5 ♖ad8 20. ♕c2 ♘d5∓ Mišta – Přibyl, Olomouc 1972; 19. fe5 ♖f2!–+] 15. fe5 0–0 16. ♔g2 ♕e8 17. ♕c2 ♖f5 [17... ♘e7?! 18. ♕e4 ♘f5 19. ♖hf1∞ Ermenkov – Přibyl, Polanica Zdroj 1973] 18. ♖hg1 ♗g5∓

80 **11... 0–0**?! 12. h3 ♗h5 13. g4 ♗g6 14. h4 ♘b4 15. h5 ♗c2 16. ♖e1± Šijanovski – Spaski, SSSR 1959; **11... ♕d7** 12. h3 ♗f3 13. gf3 0-0-0 14. f4 ♗b4 15. ♕c2 ♔b8 16. a3 ♗c3 17. ♕c3 ♘e7 18. ♗g2? ♕a4!∓ Durao – Bobocov, Praja de Rocha 1969; 18. ♗d3!∞

81 12. ♘e4 ♗f5 13. ♘c5 0–0 14. b3 ♘d7 15. ♗d3 ♗c5 16. dc5 ♘de5 17. ♗f5 ♕d2 18. ♗d2 ef5 19. ♘e5 ♘e5 20. ♘c3 ♖fe8∓ Bronštejn – Kopilov, SSSR (ch) 1951

82 Hora – Přibyl, corr. 1972

83 10... ♗b4? 11. 0–0 ♗c3 12. bc3 0–0 13. ♘g5±→

84 13. ♕c1? ♕c1 14. ♖c1 0-0-0 15. ♖d1 ♗b4 16. a3 ♗c3 17. bc3 ♘a5 18. c5 ♘d5 19. ♔d2 f6= Prins – Tartakower, Hastings 1945/46

85 Bogdanović – Vukić, Jugoslavija 1973

86 **10. d5**? ed5 11. cd5 ♘b4 12. ♘d4 ♘6d5! 13. ♘d5 ♘d5 [13... ♕d5? 14. ♘f5 ♕e5 15. ♖c1 ♕f5 16. ♖c7 ♕e6 17. ♗b5 ♘c6 18. 0–0 ♗e7 19. ♖e1+– Tarman – Benkö, corr. 1948] 14. ♘f5 ♗b4 15. ♗d2 ♕f5 16. ♕a4 c6 17. ♗b4 ♕e4–+; **10. ♕d2**?! ♘b4 [10... ♗e7 11. ♗e2 f6 12. ef6 ♗f6 13. 0–0 0-0-0= Padevski – Martz, Vrnjačka Banja 1973 — 15/136] 11. ♖d1 [11. ♖c1 c5!∓] 0-0-0 12. ♗e2 ♘c2 13. ♔f2 f6∓ Bakulin – Aronin, SSSR 1961

87 10... ♖d8 11. 0–0 ♗g4 12. ♘g5?! ♘c4 13. ♗f2 ♗e2 14. ♕e2 ♗e7 15. ♕h5=∞ Estrin – Okly, corr. 1966; 12. c5!±

88 12. d5!? ♘e5 13. ♘e5 fe5 14. a4!± Mikenas

89 **13... ♕g7** 14. ♕b3!? ♖g8 15. ♖f2 ed5 16. cd5 ♘b4 17. ♘d4 ♗h3 18. ♘e6 ♗e6 19. de6± Hecht – Cafferty, Teesside 1972; 15... ♘e5!?; **13... ed5** 14. ♗b6 cb6 15. cd5 ♗c5 16. ♔h1 ♘e7 17. ♘h4 ♗g6 18. ♖f6± Euwe

90 15... a5 16. ♘b5 ♗b4 17. d6! c5 18. ♗d2!? ♕d6? 19. ♘d6 ♖d6 20. ♗b4! ♖d1 21. ♖fd1±⊥

91 18. cd5 ♘d6 19. ♘b5±→ Boleslavski

92 12. b3 ♗f3 13. ♖f3 ♘d4 14. ♗d4 ♕d4 15. ♕d4 ♖d4 16. ♖f7 ♖d7= Euwe

93 12... ♗f3?! 13. cb6 ♗e2 14. ba7! ♘a7 15. ♕e2±→ Euwe

94 **14. ♕e1** ♗e7 15. ♘d1 f6 16. ♕c3 fe5∓ Robatsch – Hecht, Forssa – Helsinki 1972; **14. b4** ♕e4 15. ♕b3 ♘d4 16. ♘d4 ♗e2 17. ♖f4 [17. ♘e2? ♖d3–+] ♕e5 18. ♖e1 g5 19. ♖f2 ♗h5 20. ♖d2 ♗g7∞ Platonov – Kuprejčik, SSSR (ch) 1969 — 8/105; **14. ♖e1**!?∞ Martz

95 **17... ♕b4**? 18. ♘f7 ♖d2 19. ♖ad1! +–; **17... ♖d5** 18. ♖ad1 ♕c5 19. ♖d5 ed5 20. ♘f7 ♖g8 21. ♕g4 ♔b8 22. ♕e6+– Ghizdavu; **17... ♕d2** 18. ♕d2 ♖d2 19. ♖f7 ♗c5 20. ♘e6 ♗d4 21. ♘d4 ♖d4 22. ♖g7! [22. ♖af1? ♖d7 23. ♖d7 ♔d7 24. ♖f7 ♔e6 25. ♖c7 ♖d8 1/2 : 1/2 Honfi – Ghizdavu, Bucuresti 1973 — 15/135] ♖e4 23. ♖c1 c6 24. ♖f1 ♖e5 25. g4△ ♖ff7±

96 **11. d5**?! ed5 12. cd5 ♘4d5 13. ♗g5 ♗e7 14. ♗b5 ♔f8!∓ Euwe; **11. ♗g5** f6 [11... ♗e7? 12. ♗e7 ♕e7 13. d5±] 12. ef6 gf6 13. ♗h4 ♗e7 14. dc5 ♕d1 15. ♖d1 ♘d7= Pachman; **11. a3**!? cd4 12. ♘d4 [12. ♗g5? dc3! 13. ♗d8 ♖d8 14. ♕b3 cb2 15. ♕b2 ♘a4 16. ♕a1 ♘c2∓↑ Znosko-Borovski – Aljehin, Paris 1925] ♘c6 13. ♘c6 ♕d1 [13... bc6 14. ♕f3±] 14. ♖d1 bc6 15. ♗e2 ♗e7 16. 0–0 ♘d7! [16... 0–0 17. c5! ♘d5 18. ♘d5 cd5 19. ♗a6△ b4±] 17. g4 ♗g6 18. ♗f4 a5 19. ♗f3 ♖c8 20. ♘e4 ♗e4 21. ♗e4 ♘c5 22. ♗f3 a4 23. ♗d2± Tringov – Hecht, Teesside 1972

97 **11... cd4** 12. ♘d4 ♘c6 [12... ♗g6 13. a3 ♘c6 14. ♘c6 bc6 15. ♕d8 ♔d8 16. ♗b6 ab6 17. ♗f3 ♖c8 18. ♘e4±⊥ Negyessy – Lokvenc, Wien 1925] 13. ♘f5 ♕d1 14. ♖d1 ef5 15. 0–0 ♗e7 16. ♖f5 g6 17. ♖f4 ♘e5 18. ♖e4± Bronštejn – Mikenas, SSSR (ch) 1949; **11... ♗g4**!? (Aronin) 12. ♗g5 ♗e7 13. ♗e7 ♕e7 14. ♘e4 0–0 15. dc5 [15. ♘c5 ♘a2∞] ♘d7 16. a3 ♘c6 17. ♕d6 ♗f3 18. ♗f3 ♘de5±

98 12. a3 cd4 13. ♘d4 ♘c6 14. ♘f5 [14. ♘c6 bc6 15. ♗f3 0–0!∓] ef5 15. 0–0 ♘e5 16. ♖f5 ♕d1 17. ♘d1! ♘bd7 18. ♘c3 g6 19. ♖ff1±⊥ Tartakower – Colle 1926

99 12... cd4 13. ♘d4 ♗g6 14. a3 [14. ♘db5 ♘d3? 15. ♗d3 ♗d3 16. ♖f4±⟳ Spaski—Kopilov, SSSR 1959; 14... 0—0∞] ♘c6 15. ♘c6 bc6 16. ♕d8 ♖d8 [16... ♔d8 17. b4±] 17. ♖fd1! [17. ♗f3?! 0—0 18. ♘e4 ♘a4= Parma—Mecking, Palma de Mallorca 1969] 0—0 18. b4 ♘d7 19. ♗f4 c5 20. b5±⊥ Penrose—Mecking, Palma de Mallorca 1969 — 8/106

100 13. a3 cd4 14. ♘d4 ♘c6 15. ♘f5 [15. ♘c6? bc6 16. ♕d8 ♖fd8=] ef5 16. ♖f5 g6 17. ♖f1 [17. ♕d8 ♖fd8 18. ♖ff1 ♘e5 19. ♘b5 ♘d3= Boleslavski] ♗g5 [17... ♘e5 18. ♕d8 ♖ad8 19. ♗b6 ab6 20. ♘d5 ♖d7 21. b4 ♗d8±⊥] 18. ♗c5 ♖e8 [18... ♗c1 19. ♕c1 ♖e8 20. ♘e4 ♖e5 21. ♘f6 ♔g7 22. ♘g4 ♕g5 23. ♘e5 ♕e5 24. ♗e3 ♖e8 25. ♗h6±↑] 19. ♕d8 [19. ♘e4?! ♖e5 20. ♘g5 ♕g5 21. ♗d6 ♕e3 22. ♖f2 ♖f5 23. ♗f3 ♘d4∓→ Estrin—Kopilov, corr. 1971] ♖ad8 20. ♖cd1 ♘e5 21. ♘e4 ♖d1 22. ♖d1 [22. ♗d1 ♗e7 23. b3 ♗c5 24. ♘c5 ♖e7 25. ♗c2 f5= Keres—Šajtar, Praha 1943] ♗e7 23. ♗e7 ♖e7 24. c5±⊥

101 18. ♘c3!± Hort—Knežević, Slnčev Brjag 1974

102 **12. d5**? ed5! [12... ♘e5?! 13. ♘e5 fe5 14. g4 ♗g6 15. de6∞ Siliki—Popov, Varna 1958] 13. cd5 ♘e5∓; **12. ♘h4?** fe5 13. ♘f5 ef5 14. d5 ♘d4! 15. ♗d4 ed4 16. ♕d4 ♘d7! 17. ♔h1 [17. ♘a4 b5 18. cb5 ♗d6 19. ♖ae1∞ Spielmann—Colle, Dortmund 1928; 17... b6∓] ♗d6 18. ♖f3 ♕g5 19. ♖af1 ♖ae8 20. ♕d1 ♘e5∓ Pietzsch— Hort, Harrachov 1967; **12. ♕e1**!? ♘b4 13. ♖d1 ♘c2 14. ♕f2 ♘e3 15. ♕e3 [L. Steiner—Takacs, Wien 1927] c6!?∞ Bagirov

103 13. h3 ♕e8 14. g4 ♕g6 15. ♔h1 ♗e4 16. ♘e4 ♕e4∓ Kitajev—Sokolov, corr. 1964

104 **13... ♕e8**?! 14. ♗g5! [14. ♖ad1 ♖d8 15. ♕c1 ♕g6 16. ♔h1 ♖d7!∞] ♖d8 [14... ♗g5 15. ♕g5 ♖d8 16. ♖ad1± Šapošnikov—Čerepkov, SSSR 1951] 15. ♗f6 ♖f6 16. ♖ad1 [16. ♕e3!?± Ljubojević—Jakovljevski, Jugoslavija 1969 — 7/129] ♗g4 17. ♘e4 ♖f5 18. ♕e3 ♗f3 19. ♖f3 ♖f3 20. gf3 ♕g6 21. ♔h1 ♕h6 22. f4±→ Ignatjev—Larsen, Moskva 1962; **13... ♖f7** (Mikenas) 14. ♖ad1 ♖d7 15. c5! ♘d5 16. ♘d5 ed5 [16... ♖d5 17. ♗c4±] 17. ♘e5! ♗e5 18. ♖f5 ♗f6 19. ♗g4± Lutikov—Bagirov, SSSR (ch) 1960; **13... ♕d7**!? 14. ♖ad1 ♖ad8 15. h3 ♕e8 16. ♕e1 ♖d7 17. ♕g3 ♕g6 18. ♕g6 ♗g6= Matanović—Allan, Lugano (ol) 1968; 15. ♕e1!? Matanović

105 15. c5? ♘d5 16. ♘d5 ed5 17. b4 ♖de8∓↑ Steiner—Takacs, Kecskemet 1928

106 **15... e5**?! 16. d5! [16. de5?! ♘e5 17. ♘e5 ♖d1 18. ♗d1 ♗e5= Gipslis—Mikenas, SSSR (ch) 1970] ♘d4 17. ♘d4 ed4 18. ♗d4 ♗g5 19. ♕a1 c6 20. b3 cd5 21. c5± Boleslavski; **15... ♖d7** 16. h3 ♖fd8 17. g4! ♗g6 18. c5 ♘c8 [18... ♘d5? 19. g5+—] 19. ♗b5± Matanović—Klundt, Siegen (ol) 1970 — 10/154; 16... h6!?; **15... ♗g6** 16. ♔h1 ♖d7 17. d5 ed5 18. ♘d5 ♘d5 19. cd5△ ♗c5± Bronštejn—Rudakovski, SSSR 1945; **15... ♖fe8**!? 16. ♖f2 ♗g6 17. b3 e5? 18. d5 e4 19. ♘g5! ♘d4! 20. ♗g4! [20. ♖d4? ♗d4 21 ♗d4 e3—+] c5 21. ♗e6± Štejn—Podgajec, SSSR 1971 — 11/112; 17... h6!?

107 16. d5? ed5 17. cd5 [17. ♘d5 ♘d5 18. cd5 ♗b2!∓] ♗c3 18. bc3 ♘d5 19. ♗c4 ♗e6∓

108 18. ♖fe1 ♕f7 19. b3 ♖fe8 20. ♗g1 [20. ♖f1?! ♕e7 21. ♖fe1 ♖d7 22. d5?! ♘b4! 23. ♘d4 ed5 24. ♗h5 ♘d3 25. ♖d3 ♗d3 26. ♗f2 ♗d4!∓ Medina—Smislov, Hastings 1970 — 9/110] ♖e7! 21. ♖f1 ♕e8 22. ♕f4 e5∓ Filipowicz—Jansa, Budapest 1970

109 19. ♖fe1 ♕f7 20. c5 ♘d5 21. ♗b5 ♘db4 22. a3 a6 23. ab4 ab5 24. ♘b5 ♘b4 25. ♕c4 ♘c6 26. ♗h2 ♖d7= Hecht—Timman, Wijk aan Zee 1971

110 10... ♘b8? 11. ♗d3 ♗d3 12. ♕d3 ♘a6 13. 0-0-0 ♕d7 14. ♘g5±○ Hecht—Thorvaldsson, Helsinki 1972; 14. d6!±

111 **12... ♕d7** 13. ♗b5! [13. a3?! ♘4d5 14. ♘f5 ♕f5 15. ♘d5 ♕e5 16. ♘c7 ♕c7 17. ♗b5 ♔f8 18. 0—0∞ Pachman] c6 14. 0—0 ♗g6 15. dc6 bc6 16. ♘c6! ♘c6 17. ♗b6 ab6 18. ♕d7 ♔d7 19. ♖ad1 ♔c7 20. ♘d5 ♔b8 21. ♗c6±⊥ Kopilov—Toluš, SSSR 1948; **12... ♗g6** 13. ♗b5 ♔f8 14. 0—0 ♔g8 15. ♘f5 ♗f5 16. ♖f5 [16. ♗b6 ♗g6 17. ♗f2 ♗g5 18. ♕f3 a6 19. ♗c4 b5 20. ♗e2 h6 21. ♖ad1 ♔h7 22. a3±] ♘6d5 [16... ♘4d5 17. ♗b6 ♘b6 18. ♕b3 ♗c5 19. ♔h1 ♕e7 20. ♘a4!+— Stanciu—Partos, Romania 1971 — 11/111] 17. ♕b3 c6 18. a3 ♘a6 19. ♘d5 cd5 20. ♗a6 ba6 21. ♖af1±; **12... ♗c8** 13. ♗b5 [13. d6!? cd6 14. ♗b5 ♗d7 15. e6±; 14... ♔f8!? 15. 0—0 de5 16. ♕f3 f6∞ Ghizdavu] c6 [13... ♔f8? 14. 0—0 ♘4d5 15. ♕f3 f6 16. ♖ad1± Judovič] 14. dc6 0—0 15. 0—0 a6 [15... ♕c7 16. e6! bc6 17. ef7 ♔h8 18. ♗d3 ♘d3 19. ♕d3 ♗f6 20. ♘e4!± Judovič—Ignatjev, SSSR 1974 — 17/153; 16... ♗e6 17. ♘e6 fe6 18. cb7 ♕b7 19. ♕g4±; 16... fe6 17. ♖f8 ♗f8 18. cb7 ♕b7 19. ♕b3± Judovič] 16. cb7 ♗b7 17. ♗e2 ♘4d5 18. ♗f2! ♗g5 [18... ♘c3 19. bc3 ♘d5 20. ♕b3 ♖b8 21. ♗f3+—] 19. ♘f5 ♗c6 20. ♘e4 ♘f4 21. ♗f3± Ghizdavu—Suta, Romania 1970—10/153

112 13. ♕f3 c5 14. dc6 bc6 15. a3 ♘4d5 16. ♘d5 ♘d5 17. ♗c4 ♕a5! 18. ♗d2 ♕c5 19. ♗d5 ♕d5 20. ♕d5 cd5 21. ♖c1 a5= Ljubojević—Hartston, Las Palmas 1974 — 17/154

113 15. ♕h5? g6 16. ♗e2 ♗f6! 17. ♕c5 ♘4d5∓

114 15... 0—0 16. 0-0-0 ♕e8 17. ♘f5±○ Judovič—Germanovič, SSSR 1952

115 **16... ♘6d5** 17. ♗h6!!+—; **16... ♗f6**?! 17. ♘c6? ♘c2! 18. ♔e2 bc6 19. ♗g2 0—0

20. ♗c5 ♘a1 21. ♗f8 ♕f8 22. ♖a1 ♕c5 23. ♗e4 ♗c3 24. bc3 ♕c3 25. ♗h7 1/2 : 1/2 Nikolau – Cafferty, Wijk ann Zee 1971; 17. 0-0-0!±

116 17... ♗f6? 18. ♘f5! ♘6d5 19. ♘g7 ♗g7 20. ♕h5 ♔e7 21. ♗c5 ♔e6 22. ♗h3 1 : 0 Williams – Cafferty, England 1971 — 12/139

117 18... 0–0 19. ♗e2 [19. ♗g5 ♕f1 20. e7?! ♘a2!∓ Kuprejčik – Alburt, SSSR 1974 — 18/132] ♗c6 20. ♗g5 ♕f2 21. ♗h6 ♕f6 22. ♘f5±→ Hort, Přibyl

118 11... ♗g5? 12. ♘f5 ef5 13. ♗d4± Judovič jr. – Mikenas, SSSR 1954

119 12... ♘a6? 13. de6 fe6 14. ♕g4±

120 **13. dc6** ♘c6 14. ♘c6 bc6 15. ♕d8 ♖d8 16. ♗e2 0–0∓⊥; **13. ab4**?! cd4 14. ♕d4 [14. ♗d4 ♗b4 15. ♗e2 0–0 16. 0–0 ed5 17. cd5 ♗c3 18. bc3 ♕d5∓ Judovič] ♗b4 15. de6 0–0 16. ef7 ♗f7 17. ♕d8 ♖fd8 18. ♔f2 ♘c4= Ujtumen – Jansa, La Habana 1967

121 14... 0–0? 15. bc5 ♘d7 16. de6 ♗c5 17. ♕d5+– Kokkoris – Marović (m) 1970

122 15. ♘b5?! 0–0 16. d6 ♗g5 17. ♗d4 ♗e3! 18. ♗e3 ♕h4 19. ♔d2 ♖f1 20. ♖f1 ♘c4–+ Kokkoris – Marović, (m) 1970 — 9/112

123 15... ♘d7?! 16. ♕d4 ♕a5 [16... 0–0 17. de6 ♘b6 18. ♕d8 ♖fd8 19. ♘c5±] 17. d6 ♗d8 18. c5 b5 19. b3 0–0 20. ♘b6 ♕a1 21. ♕a1 ab6 22. ♕b2 [22. ♕c1 bc5 23. ♗b5 ♘e5 24. ♖f1±] ♘e5 32. ♕e5! [23. cb6? ♗h4! 24. ♔d1 ♘g4∓ Kuprejčik – Gipslis, SSSR 1972 — 13/145] ♗f6 24. ♕e6! ♔h8 25. c6 ♖ae8 26. ♕e8 ♖e8 27. ♔f2+– Gipslis

124 19. ♗e2 ♗e4 [19... ♕a2!? 20. ♗d4 b5∞] 20. ♖f1 ♗g2 21. ♖f8 ♔f8 22. ♔f2 =∞

125 **11... 0–0**?! 12. a3 ♘a6 13. ♗d3 ♗c5 14. ♗c5 ♘c5 15. ♗f5 ef5 16. b4 ♘e4 17. ♕d4±↻ Parma – Mihaljčišin, Sarajevo 1971; **11... f6** 12. a3 ♘a6 13. g4! (Velimirović) ♗g4 14. ♖g1 f5 [14... ♗h5 15. ♗e2 fe5 16. ♘g5 ♗e2 17. ♕e2 ♗g5 18. ♖g5 0–0 19. ♕g4 ♕e7 20. de6 c6 21. ♘e4± Majstorović – Cafferty, corr. 1973 — 16/115; 16. ♘e5 ♗e2 17. ♕e2 0–0 18. ♕g4 ♗f6 19. ♕e6 ♔h8 20. ♘e4!± Salceanu – Cafferty, corr. 1974 — 18/133] 15. h3 ♗f3 [15... ♗h4 16. ♔d2 ♗h5 17. ♖g7 ed5 18. cd5 ♘d5 19. ♕a4 c6 20. ♕h4 ♗f3 21. ♗g5 ♕a5 22. b4 1 : 0 Tringov – Rodriguez, La Habana 1971 — 11/110] 16. ♕f3 0–0 17. ♖c2! ♕d7 18. ♖d2 ♖ae8 19. d6 cd6 20. ♕h5±→ Velimirović – Gipslis, La Habana 1971 — 11/109

126 **12... ♘a6** 13. cd5 0–0 [13... ♘c5? 14. b4 ♘e4 15. ♗b5± Denker – Šagivalev, SSSR 1973] 14. ♗a6 [14. ♗e2 ♘c5 15. 0–0 ♘e4 16. ♘d4 ♘c3 17. bc3 ♗g6 18. c4 ♗a3∞ Gergely – Mikenas, SSSR 1971] ba6 15. ♕d4!±; **12... ♘c4**!? 13. ♗c4 dc4 14. ab4 ♕d1 15. ♖d1 ♗b4 16. 0–0 ♗d3 17. ♖fe1 0–0 18. ♗f2 ♖fe8 19. ♘d4 c6= Kostro – Hloušek, Luhačovice 1971; 17. ♖f2±

127 15. ♘d4 ♕b8 [15... ♗g6 16. c5 ♗g5 (16... ♘d5 17. ♗b5 ♔f8 18. 0–0+–) 17. ♖a1! (17. ♗b5 ♘d7 18. e6 0–0 19. ed7 ♗c1 20. 0–0 ♗b2∓ Haik – A. Petrosjan, Schilde 1971) ♘d7 18. ♘f3 ♗h5 19. ♗b5± Veselovski – A. Petrosjan, SSSR 1971 — 12/142; 16... 0–0!? Timman] 16. ♕e2 [16. ♘f5 ♕e5 17. ♗e2 ♕f5 18. c5 ♘d7 19. ♕d5 ♕f4 20. ♖d1 0-0-0∞⇆ Krogius] ♗g6 17. c5 [17. h4?! ♕d8!∓ Štejnberg – A. Petrosjan, SSSR 1971] ♘d7 18. e6 ♘e5 [18... ♘f6 19. ef7 ♔f7 20. ♕e6 ♔f8 21. ♗c4+–] 19. ♕b5 ♔f8 20. ef7 a6! [20... ♗f7? 21. ♗e2+– Konikowski – Schultz, Polska 1972] 21. ♕e8 ♕e8 22. fe8♕ ♖e8 23. ♗e2 ♘d3 24. ♗d3 ♗d3 25. ♔d2 ♗c4!∞ Nunn – A. Mihaljčišin, France 1973 — 16/114

128 18. ♕d5?! ♗b5 19. ♕b7 ♖b8 20. ♕e4 a5∓ Timman – Marović, Banja Luka 1974

129 19. 0–0±

B 04 — 1. e4 ♘f6 2. e5 ♘d5 3. d4 d6 4. ♘f3

	4	5	6	7	8	9	10	11	12	
1	...	♗d3[1]	0–0	c4[4]	♕d3	ed6	♖e1	d5	♕e2	±
	♗f5	♕d7[2]	♘c6[3]	♗d3	♘b6	ed6	♗e7[5]	♘b8		
2	...	a4[7]	♗b5[9]	♗e2	♘bd2	♘g5	♗g4	♘e4	♘d6	±
	♘b6[6]	a5[8]	c6	♗g4	♘8d7	e6	♕g5	♕g6	♗d6[10]	
3	...	c4[11]	e6!?	h4![12]	d5	♘d4	♕d4[15]	♗e2	de6	±
	♘c6	♘b6	fe6	e5[13]	♘d4[14]	ed4	♕d7[16]	e5	♕e6[17]	
4	...	♘e5	♘f7[20]	♕h5	c4![21]	d5	♕f7![23]	♘c3[25]	♗f4	±
	de5[18]	♘d7[19]	♔f7	♔e6	♘5f6[22]	♔d6	♘b6[24]	♕e8	♔d7[26]	
5	...	♘g5	c4[28]	e6![29]	d5	a4	h4!	♖h4	de6	±
	g6	f6[27]	♘b6	fg5	♗g7	a5	gh4	♗e6	♘c6[30]	

	4	5	6	7	8	9	10	11	12	
6	...	...	♗c4[31]	♕e2	0—0	de5	♘f3	♘bd2	h3	=
	...	c6!	♗g7	0—0[32]	de5[33]	h6	♗g4	♕c7	♗f3[34]	
7	...	♗c4	0—0[35]	ed6[36]	♖e1[37]	♗g5	♘bd2[39]	♗b3	♗h4	±
	...	c6	♗g7	♕d6	0—0	♗g4[38]	♖e8	h6	♘d7[40]	
8	...	...	♗b3	♘g5[42]	f4[43]	♘f3	♗e3	♘bd2	0—0	∞
	...	♘b6	♗g7[41]	d5	f6[44]	♘c6[45]	♗g4	♕d7	0-0-0[46]	
9	...	...	...	a4[47]	0—0	h3[48]	♕e2	♘c3	♗f4	±
	...	...	...	a5	0—0	♘c6	d5[49]	♗e6	♕d7[50]	

1. e4 ♘f6 2. e5 ♘d5 3. d4 d6 4. ♘f3 g6 5. c4 ♘b6 6. ed6 cd6 7. ♗e2[51] ♗g7 8. 0—0[52] 0—0

	9	10	11	12	13	14	15	16	17	
10	h3[53]	♘c3	♗f4[55]	♗e3[57]	b3	bc4	♖c1	c5	♗f4	=
	♘c6	♗f5[54]	h6![56]	d5	dc4	♖c8![58]	♘a5	♘bc4	g5[59]	
11	...	...	♗e3	c5[60]	♗c4![61]	♕a4[62]	♖fd1	♕a5	b3[64]	=
	...	...	d5	♘c4	dc4	♗d3	♕a5![63]	♘a5	♗c2[65]	
12	♗e3	♘bd2	c5	♕b3[67]	de5[68]	♘e5	♖fd1	♗g4	f3	±
	♘c6	d5[66]	♘d7	e5	♘de5	♘e5	♘g4[69]	♗g4	♗e6[70]	
13	...	♘c3	b3[71]	c5	b4![73]	♖b1[74]	a4	♗f3	b5	±
	...	♗g4	d5[72]	♘c8	a6	e6	♗f3	♘8e7	ab5[75]	

[1] **5. c4** ♘b6 6. ♘c3 e6± Lipnicki—Panov, SSSR 1950; **5. ♘h4** ♗c8 6. f4 e6 7. ♘f3 ♗e7 [Steiner—Grünfeld, Budapest 1926] 8. c4±

[2] 5... ♗g6? 6. c4 ♘b6? 7. ♗g6 hg6 8. e6!± Bogoljubov—Tarrasch, Breslau 1925; 6... ♗d3!? Bagirov

[3] 6... ♘b4 7. ♗f5 ♕f5 8. c3 ♘c2 9. ♘h4 ♕e4 10. ♘d2 ♕d3 11. ♖b1 de5 12. ♘df3! ♘b4 [Kavalek—Ljubojević, Lanzarote 1973 — 15/145] 13. ♕a4 ♘4c6 14. ♘e5!± Matanović

[4] **7. ♗f5** ♕f5 8. c4 ♘b6 9. ed6 ed6 10. ♖e1 ±○ Timman—Ljubojević, Hilversum 1973 — 15/144; **7. ed6**!?

[5] 10... ♘e7 11. a4± Becker—Grünfeld, Wien 1927

[6] L. Schmid

[7] **5. ♗d3** g6 6. ♗f4 ♗g7 7. 0—0 0—0 8. ♖e1 ♘c6 9. c3 ♗g4 10. h3 ♗f3 11. ♕f3 de5 12. de5 ♘d7= Penrose—Cafferty, England 1964; **5. ♗e2** g6 [5... ♘c6 6. ed6 cd6 7. d5 ♘e5 8. 0—0 g6 9. ♘c3 ♗g7 10. ♘d4±○ Mednis—Saidy, USA (ch) 1970 — 9/118] 6. 0—0 ♗g7 7. ♗f4 [7. b3 ♘c6 8. ♗b2 de5 9. ♘e5! ♘e5 10. de5± Smislov—Schmid, Amsterdam (ol) 1954] ♘c6 8. c3 0—0 9. ♘bd2 ♗f5 10. ♖e1 ♕d7 11. ♗f1±○ Kuijpers—Schmid 1967; **5. ed6** cd6 6. d5 ♘8d7 7. ♗g5 ♘f6 8. ♘c3 g6 9. a4 a5 10. ♗b5 ♗d7 11. ♗f6 ef6 12. ♗d7 ♘d7 13. 0—0±↑ Tukmakov—K. Grigorjan, SSSR (ch) 1973; **5. ♘c3** g6 6. ♗f4 ♗g7 7. ♕d2! ♗g4 8. ♗h6 0—0?! 9. h4 ♗f3 10. h5!±→ I. Zajcev—Zinser, Moskva 1968 — 5/117

[8] 5... ♗g4 6. a5 ♘6d7 7. h3 [7. ed6?! cd6 8. h3 ♗h5 9. ♗e2 e6 10. c3 ♗e7 11. 0—0 0—0= Matanović—Ljubojević, Jugoslavija (ch) 1975] ♗h5 8. g4 ♗g6 9. e6!± Ljubojević

[9] **6. ♗d3** g6 7. h3 ♗g7 8. 0—0 ♘c6 9. ♖e1± Schmid—Dreyer 1958; **6. ♘c3** ♗g4?! 7. h3! ♗f3 [7... ♗h5 8. g4 ♗g6 9. e6! fe6 10. ♘g5±] 8. ♕f3 d5 9. e6! fe6 10. ♕h5 ♔d7 11. ♗f4± Bellin—Hecht, Amsterdam 1973 — 16/119; 6... g6!? Hecht

[10] 13. ed6 ♘c4 14. 0—0±⧉ Dueball—Ogaard, Ribe 1973

[11] **5. ♗b5** a6 6. ♗c6 [6. ♗a4 ♘b6!] bc6 7. 0—0 e6 [6... g6?! 7. ♖e1 ♗g7 8. c4 ♘b6 9. ♗g5!±] 8. ♘bd2 ♗e7 9. ♘c4 a5 10. ♖e1 a4 11. ♗d2 ♗d7= Šamkovič—Larsen, Moskva 1962; **5. ♗e2** de5 6. ♘e5 [6. de5 ♗f5 7. a3 e6 8. 0—0 ♗e7= Bagirov] ♘e5 7. de5 ♗f5 8. c4 ♘b6 9. 0—0 e6 10. ♗e3 ♕d1 11. ♖d1 ♘d7 12. ♘c3 a6 13. f4 0-0-0= Minić—Larsen, Beograd 1964

[12] **7. ♘c3** e5 [7... ♘d7!? 8. ♗d3 ♘f6 9. ♗e3 g6 10. h4 ♗g7 11. ♘g5 e5 12. d5 ♘d4 13. h5 gh5 14. ♗d4 ed4 15. ♘e2 c6!⇆ Vogt—Cibulka, Trenčanske Teplice 1974 — 18/136; 15. ♘ce4!? ♗g4□ 16. ♕c2± Plachetka] 8. d5 ♘d4 9. ♘d4 ed4 10. ♕d4 e5= Honfi—Csom, Hungary 1965; **7. ♗d3** ♘b4 [7...

g6 8. h4!± Moles– Tate, Groningen 1968; 7... e5 8. d5 ♘b4 9. ♘g5 ♘d3 10. ♕d3 e6 11. ♘h7 ♕e7∞ Letelier–Penrose, Moskva (ol) 1956] 8. ♘g5 ♘d3 9. ♕d3 ♕d7 [9... c5 10. ♕f3 ♕c7 11. ♕f7 ♔d8 12. ♕f4 ♔e8 13. d5! e5 14. ♕f7 ♔d8 15. ♘h7+– Murej–Moldavski, SSSR 1968] 10. ♘h7 ♕c6 11. ♕g6 ♔d7∞ Lehmann–Bogoljubov, BRD 1950; **7. ♘g5** e5 [7... ♕d7 8. ♗d3 g6 9. ♘h7 ♖h7 10. ♗g6 ♖f7 11. ♗f7 ♔f7 12. ♕h5 ♔g8 13. h4+– Rošalj–Bujakin, SSSR 1959; 8. ♗e3 e5 9. d5 ♘d8 10. ♗e2 c6 11. ♕c2 ♕c7 12. ♘h7 cd5 13. ♕g6 ♔d7 14. ♗g4+– Makaričev–Kurašov, SSSR 1964] 8. ♗d3 [8. d5 ♘d4 9. ♗e3=] ♘d4 9. ♗h7! [9. ♘h7 ♗e6 10. 0–0 ♕d7∓ Šiškin–Muratov, SSSR 1966] ♖h7 10. ♘h7 ♗f5 11. ♘a3 ♗h7 [11... ♕d7 12. ♘f8 ♕c6 13. 0–0 0-0-0 14. ♗e3± Ćirić–Zuidema, Beograd 1964] 12. ♕h5 ♔d7 13. ♕h7 e6±

13 7... ♘d7!? 8. ♘g5 ♘f6 9. d5 ed5 10. cd5 ♘e5 11. f4 ♘eg4 12. ♗d3 c6∓ Christoffel –Larsen, Zürich 1961; 8. ♗d3!?; 8. h5!± Larsen

14 8... ♘b8 9. ♘g5 e6 10. ♗d3 ♕f6 11. ♘h7±

15 10. ♗d3 ♕d7 11. ♗g5 h6 12. ♗d2 ♕g4 13. ♗e2 ♕e4 14. 0–0 ♗f5∞ Talj–Larsen, Eersel (mct) 1969 — 7/133

16 10... e5 11. ♕d1!± Boleslavski

17 13. ♖h3±↑ Nej–Honfi, Zalaegerszeg 1970 — 8/107

18 Larsen

19 **5... e6** 6. ♕f3 [6. ♕h5 g6 7. ♕f3 ♕e7 8. ♘c3 ♘d7 9. ♗c4 ♘c3 10. ♘d7 ♕d7 11. bc3 ♗g7= Ivkov–Larsen, Bled (mct) 1965] ♕f6 7. ♕g3 h6 8. ♘c3 ♘b4 9. ♗b5 c6 10. ♗a4 ♘d7 [Talj–Larsen, Bled (mct) 1965] 11. ♘e4! ♕f5 12. f3 ♘e5 13. de5±↑ Talj; **5... g6** 6. ♗c4 ♗e6 7. ♘c3! [7. ♗b3 ♗g7 8. 0–0 0–0 9. ♕e2 a5 10. ♘c3 c6 11. ♘d5 cd5 12. a4? ♘c6∓ Jimenez–Larsen, Palma de Mallorca 1967 — 4/138; 8. c3!? Gaprindašvili–Kušnir, Tbilisi (m) 1969 — 7/131] ♗g7 [7... ♘c3? 8. ♗e6!+–] 8. ♘e4 ♗e5 [8... 0–0 9. ♘g5! ±] 9. de5 ♘c6 10. ♘c5 ♘e3! [10... ♘e5? 11. ♘b7 ♕d7 12. ♘c5 ♕c6 13. ♘e6 fe6± Yanofsky–Larsen, Winnipeg 1967 — 5/116] 11. ♗e3 ♗c4 12. b3 b6= Larsen; 6. g3!?± Boleslavski

20 6. ♗c4 e6 7. ♕g4 h5 8. ♕e2 ♘e5 9. de5 ♗d7 10. 0–0 [Talj–Larsen, Bled (mct) 1965] ♕h4!= Larsen

21 8. g3 b5! [8... ♘7f6 9. ♗h3 ♔d6 10. ♕e5 ♔c6 11. ♗g2±→ Utkin–Grants, corr. 1971 — 11/113] 9. a4 c6 10. ab5 g6 11. ♕e2 ♔f7 12. bc6 ♘7b6$\overline{\overline{\infty}}$

22 8... ♘7f6 9. cd5 ♕d5 10. ♕d1±↑

23 **10. c5** ♘c5 11. ♗f4 ♔d7 12. ♗b5 c6 13. dc6 bc6 14. ♕c5 ♕b6= Šamkovič; **10. ♕h3** ♘c5! 11. ♕a3 e5 12. ♗e3 b6 13. ♘c3 ♔e7 14. b4 ♘cd7∞

24 **10... ♘e5** 11. ♗f4 c5 12. ♘c3! a6 13. b4! [13. 0-0-0 g6! 14. ♗e5 ♔e5 15. d6 ♗h6 16. ♔b1 ♕f8!∓] b6 [13... cb4 14. c5 ♔c5 15. ♘a4 ♔d6 16. ♘b2±] 14. ♖b1! g6 15. bc5 bc5 16. ♖b7!+–→; **10... ♘b8** 11. c5! [11. ♗f4 e5 12. c5 ♔c5 13 b4 ♔d6 14. ♗e3 b6 15. ♗c5 bc5 16. bc5 ♔c5 17. d6 ♕e8!–+ Kupper–Popov, Enschede 1963] ♔c5 12. ♗e3 ♔d6 13. ♘a3! a6 14. ♘c4 ♔d7 15. d6!+–→ Kapengut

25 11. c5 ♔c5 12. ♗e3 ♔d6 13. ♘c3 ♘bd5 14. ♘d5 ♘d5 15. ♕d5 ♔d5 16. 0-0-0 ♔c6 17. ♖d8 b6∞

26 13. ♕e6 ♔d8 14. ♕e5 ♕d7 15. 0-0-0±↑

27 **5... h6?** 6. ♘f7! ♔f7 7. ♕f3 ♘f6 [7... ♔e6 8. c4!+–] 8. ef6 ef6 9. ♗c4 ♔g7 Mihaljčišin–Fox, Bognor Regis 1967 — 3/131; **5... de5** 6. de5 ♗g7 [6... h6? 7. ♗c4? c6 8. ♘f3 ♗g7 9. ♘c3 ♗e6 10. 0–0 ♘c3 11. ♕d8 ♔d8 12. ♗e6 ♘e2–+ Kalinovski–Bagirov, Adelaide 1960; 7. ♘f7! ♔f7 8. c4± Stoltz–Rellstab, Stockholm 1930; 6.. ♘c6 7. ♗b5! ♕d7 8. ♕f3 e6 9. 0–0 ♗h6 10. c4 ♘b6 11. ♘e4 ♗g7 12. ♖d1± Janošević –Castaldi, Beograd 1950] 7. ♗c4 [7. e6?! ♗e6 8. ♘e6 fe6 9. ♗e2 ♘c6 10. c3 ♕d6 11. 0–0 0-0-0∓ Janošević–Trifunović, Jugoslavija 1953] c6 8. ♘c3 [8. ♕f3?! 0–0 9. ♘c3 h6 10. ♘ge4 ♘d7 11. ♗b3 ♘e5 12. ♕g3 ♗f5 13. ♗d2 ♘c3 14. ♘c3 ♕d4!∓ Bogdanović–Fuderer, Jugoslavija (ch) 1953] h6 9. ♘f3 ♘c3∓; 8. ♕e2!±

28 **6. ef6** ef6 7. ♗c4 ♕e7 8. ♔d2 ♗h6 9. ♗d5 ♗g5 10. ♔c3 ♔d8∞ Boleslavski; **6. ♗c4** fg5 [6... de5 7. de5 c6 8. ♘f3 ♗g7 9. ef6 ef6 10. 0–0 0–0 11. ♘c3± Bagirov; 6... c6 7. ef6 ef6 8. ♘e4 f5 9. ♗d5 cd5 10. ♘ec3 ♕e7 11. ♗e3 ♕f7 12. 0–0 f4 13. ♗c1 ♘c6 14. ♖e1 ♔d8 15. ♘a3 g5∞ Kuprejčik–Lutikov, SSSR (ch) 1969 — 8/108; 12. ♕f3△ ♘e2, ♘bc3, ♘f4± Bagirov] 7. ♗d5 e6 8. ♗e4 de5 9. de5 ♕d1 10. ♔d1 ♗g7 11. ♗g5 ♗e5 12. ♘c3± Bagirov

29 7. ef6 ef6 8. ♘f3 ♗g4 9. ♗e2 ♗g7= Krogius–Korčnoj, Soči 1958

30 13. ♕g4 ♕c8 14. ♖a3 ♘d4 15. ♖e3!±→ O'Kelly–Golombek, Amsterdam 1950

31 **6. ♕f3** f6 7. e6?! ♕a5 8. ♗d2 ♕b6∓; **6. ♕e2** h6 7. ♘f3 [7. ♘e4 ♗g7 8. f4 0–0 9. ♘bc3 ♘c3 10. ♘c3 c5 11. d5 e6! 12. ♗e3 ed5 13. ♘d5 ♘c6∓ Bogdanović–Kavalek, Sarajevo 1967 — 3/130] ♗g7 8. c4 ♘c7 9. ♗f4 ♘e6!∓ Sanguinetti–Panno, Portorož (izt) 1958; **6. c4** ♘c7 7. ♕f3 f6 8. ef6 ef6= Jansa–Jacobson, Helsinki 1961

32 **7... h6!?** Bagirov

33 8... e6? 9. ♘c3 ♘c3 10. bc3 d5 11. ♗d3 c5 12. ♕g4!± Vasjukov–Larsen, Moskva 1959

34 13. ♘f3 e6= Bagirov

35 6. **♗d5**!? cd5 7. ♗f4± Vuković: **6. h3** ♗g7 7. 0–0 — 6. 0–0

36 7. h3 0–0 8. ♕e2 ♗f5 9. ♖e1 de5 10. de5 ♘d7? 11. ♗d5! cd5 12. ♘c3± Šamkovič–Podgajec, SSSR 1971 — 11/114; 10... ♘b6!? Šamkovič

37 **8. h3** 0–0 9. ♗b3 ♗f5 10. ♖e1 ♕d8 11. ♘bd2?!= Kavalek–Kupka, ČSSR 1969 — 6/179; 11. c4± Hort; **8. ♘bd2** 0–0 9. h3 [9. ♘e4 ♕c7 10. c3 ♘d7 11. ♖e1 h6 12. ♗d2 ♘7f6= Radojčić–Vidmar jr., Jugoslavija (ch) 1947] ♘d7 10. ♗b3 ♕c7 11. ♖e1±↑ Kavalek–Ljubojević, Las Palmas 1973 — 15/143

38 9... ♗e6 10. ♗b3 ♘a6 11. c4 ♘f6 12. ♘c3 ♘c7 13. ♕d2±○ Smislov–Hort, Moskva 1966

39 10. ♗d5 ♕d5 11. ♗e7 ♖e8∞

40 13. c4±↑ Talj–Ljubojević, Wijk aan Zee 1973 — 15/139

41 6... a5 7. a4 d5 8. 0–0 ♗g7 9. ♗f4 0–0 10. ♘bd2± Ciocaltea–Ogaard, Reykjavik 1974 — 17/156

42 **7. ♘bd2**?! 0–0 8. h3? a5! 9. a4? de5 10. de5 ♘a6! 10. 0–0 ♘c5∓ Spaski–Fischer, Reykjavik (m) 1972 — 14/165; 9. c3∓ Gligorić; **7. 0–0** de5?! 8. ♘e5 0–0 9. ♗f4 ♘8d7 10. ♕f3 ♕e8 11. ♕e3 ♘f6 12. ♘c3 c6 13. ♖fe1± Kostro–Přibyl, ČSSR 1973 — 15/142; 7... 0–0!?; **7. ♕e2** ♘c6 [7... d5?! 8. 0–0 0–0 9. ♗f4 ♗g4 10. ♘bd2 ♘c6? 11. ♕e3± Geler–Ghinda, Bath 1973 — 16/120] 8. c3 de5 9. ♘e5 ♘e5 10. de5 ♗f5= Ivkov–Korčnoj, Jugoslavija–SSSR 1958

43 8. 0–0 0–0 9. ♖e1 ♘c6 10. c3 f6 11. ef6 ef6 12. ♘e6 ♗e6 13. ♖e6 ♕d7= Parma–Gheorghiu, Skopje 1968

44 **8... ♘c6** 9. c3 f6 10. ♘f3 ♗f5 11. 0–0 ♕d7 12. ♘bd2 fe5 13. fe5± Karpov–Torre, Leningrad (izt) 1973 — 15/141; **8... 0–0** 9. 0–0 f6 10. ♘f3 ♘c6 11. c3 fe5 12. fe5 ♗g4 13. ♖f2 e6 14. ♘bd2 ♘a5 15. ♗c2 c5 16. h3 ♗f5 17. ♗f5 gf5 18. ♘f1 cd4 19. cd4 ♘c6 20. ♘g3± Alburt–Kakageldijev, SSSR 1974 — 18/135

45 9... 0–0 10. 0–0 a5 11. c3 ♗f5 12. ♘bd2 a4 [12... ♘c6?! 13. ♘h4 fe5 14. ♘f5 ♖f5 15. fe5 ♖f1 16. ♘f1 ♕d7 17. ♗c2 ♖f8 18. h4± Lukin–Šusterman, SSSR 1974] 13. ♗c2 ♗c2 14. ♕c2 f5±

46 Matulović–Ljubojević, Jugoslavija 1972 — 13/149

47 Keres

48 9. ed6 cd6 10. ♘c3 ♗g4 11. ♘b5 ♘c6 12. c3 [Keres–Jansa, Budapest 1970 — 9/116] d5!=

49 10... de5 11. de5 ♘d4 12. ♘d4 ♕d4 13. ♖e1 e6 14. ♘d2±

50 13. ♖ad1± Keres–Kupka, Kapfenberg 1970 — 9/117

51 **7. h3** ♗g7 8. ♘c3 0–0 9. ♗e3 ♘c6 10. ♖c1 d5 [10... ♗f5? 11. d5!± Pytel–Liebert, Debrecen 1970 — 8/110] 11. c5 ♘c4 12. ♗c4 dc4 13. 0–0 ♗f5 Pytel–Gipslis, Lublin 1970 — 8/109; 14. b3!±; **7. ♗e3** ♗g7 — 7. ♗e2

52 **8. ♗e3** 0–0 9. ♘c3 ♗g4 10. h3 ♗f3 11. ♗f3 ♘c6 12. b3 a6 13. a4±↑ Hort–Hartston, Nice (ol) 1974 — 17/150; **8. h3** 0–0 — 8. 0–0

53 **9. b3** ♘c6 10. ♗b2 ♗g4 11. ♕d2 e6 13. ♘a3 d5 13. ♖fd1 dc4 14. ♘c4 ♘c4 15. bc4 ♕b6= Karpov–Vaganjan, SSSR 1969; **9. ♘c3** ♘c6 10. h3 — 9. h3

54 **10... d5** 11. c5 ♘c4 12. b3 ♘4a5 13. ♗e3 b6 14. cb6 ab6 15. ♖c1± Averbah–Korčnoj, SSSR 1960; **10... e5** 11. ♗g5 ♗f6 [11... ♕d7 12. de5 de5 13. ♕d7 ♘d7 14. ♖ad1 f5 15. ♗e3± Ščerbakov–Korčnoj, SSSR 1953] 12. ♗e3 ed4 13. ♘d4 ♘d4 14. ♗d4 ♗e6 15. ♘e4± Timman–Cafferty, corr. 1963

55 Karpov; **11. d5**? ♘a5 12. ♘d2 ♖c8∓ Bagirov; **11. b3**? d5 12. c5 [12. ♗e3!?] ♘d7 [12... ♘c8? 13. ♗f4 b6 14. ♗b5 ♕d7 15. ♖c1± Dementjev–Karpov, SSSR 1971] 13. ♗b2 [13. ♗e3 ♘c5 14. ♘d5 ♘e6 15. ♘c3 ♘ed4 16. ♖c1 ♘e2 17. ♘e2 ♕a5∓ Pelitov–Bobocov, Bulgaria 1968] ♗e4 14. ♘a4 e5!∓ Minev–Bobocov, Varna 1968

56 11... d5 12. c5 ♘c4 13. b3! ♘4a5 14. ♖c1 b6 15. cb6 ab6 16. ♕d2 ♘b7 17. ♘b5±↑ Karpov–McKay, Stockholm 1969

57 12. ♖c1?! e5 13. ♗e3 e4 14. ♘d2 ♖e8 15. ♘b3 d5 16. cd5 ♘b4∓ Karpov–Vaganjan, SSSR 1969 — 7/130

58 14... ♘a5 15. c5 ♘bc4 [15... ♘d5 16. ♘d5 ♕d5 17. ♕d2 ♘c6 18. ♖fd1±] 16. ♗f4 g5 17. ♗g3 ♕d7 18. ♖e1± Karpov–Neckař, Stockholm 1969

59 **17... e5**!= Boleslavski; **17... g5** 18. ♗g3 ♕d7 [18... b6 19. ♗c4 ♘c4 20. ♕e2? bc5!∓ Karpov–A. Petrosjan, SSSR 1971; 20. cb6=] 19. ♗c4 ♘c4 20. ♕e2 ♕e6! 21. ♖fe1 ♕e2 22. ♖e2 e6= Karpov–Vaganjan, SSSR 1969

60 12. cd5 ♘d5 13. ♘d5 ♕d5 14. ♕a4 ♕d6∓ ×d4 Garcia–Jansa, Moskva 1968

61 **13. ♗c1** b6 14. g4 ♗c8 15. b3 bc5 16. bc4 cd4 17. ♘d5 d3!∓ Janošević–Hort, Skopje 1968 — 6/180; **13. ♕b3** ♘6a5 14. ♕b4 b6!∓ Mihaljčišin–Bobocov, Athens 1968

62 14. d5 ♘b4 15. ♗d4 ♗d3! 16. ♗g7 ♔g7 17. ♖e1 ♖c8 [17... ♘c2? 18. ♖c1 ♘e1 19. ♘e1±] 18. ♕d2 ♘c2 19. d6 ed6 20. ♘d5 dc5 21. ♕c3 f6 22. ♘f4 ♖c6!∓ Pelitov–Orev, Bulgaria 1962

63 **15... ♘d4**? 16. ♘d4 ♗d4 17. ♖d3!±; **15... e5** 16. d5 [16. de5 ♘e5 17. ♘e5 ♗e5 18. ♖c1 (Fuchs–Radovici, Berlin 1969) ♕e8!=] ♘e7 17. d6 ♘f5 18. ♘e1!± Osnos–Suetin, SSSR (ch) 1965; **15... f5** 16. d5 ♘e5 [16... f4 17. dc6 fe3 18. cb7? ef2 19. ♔h1 ♖b8 20. c6 e5!∓; 17. ♗f4! ♘d4 18. ♘d4 ♗d4 19. ♖d3 ♖f4 20. ♖d4! ♖d4 21. ♖d1 ♖d1 22. ♕d1 ♕a5 23. ♕d4± Maeder–Eales, corr. 1969; 20. ♘e2!?] 17. ♘e1! [17. ♘d4 f4 18. ♗f4 ♖f4 19. ♘e6 ♕b8 20. ♘f4 ♘f3 21. gf3 ♕f4 22. ♖d3! ♕g5 23. ♔f1 cd3 24. ♕c4 (Zuidema–Timman, Amsterdam 1969) ♕f5!∞ Boleslavski] f4 18. ♗d4 ♕c8 19. ♘d3 cd3 20. ♗e5 ♗e5 21. ♕c4± Boleslavski

64 **17. b4** ♘c6 18. b5 ♘b4∞; **17. ♘e1** ♗f5 18. ♖ac1 ♘c6 19. g4 ♗d7 20. d5 ♘b4= Dvorecki–Bagirov, SSSR (ch) 1973 — 16/112

65 18. ♖d2 cb3 19. ab3 ♘b3 20. ♖c2 ♘a1 21. ♖a2 ♘b3 22. ♖a3 ♘c5 23. dc5 ♖fd8= Euwe

66 **10... ♗f5** 11. d5 ♘b4 12. ♗d4 ♗h6 13. ♗c3 ♗c2 14. ♕c1 ♗d3 15. ♗d3 [15. ♖e1 a5∞ Gipslis–Vasjukov, SSSR 1968] ♘d3 16. ♕c2±; **10... ♗g4** 11. d5! ♘e5 12. ♘e5 ♗e2 13. ♕e2 ♗e5 14. ♘f3 ♗g7 15. ♖ad1 ♘d7 16. b3±○ Bronštejn–Bagirov, SSSR 1964; **10... e5** 11. de5 de5 12. ♗c5 ♖e8 13. ♘e4± Klovan–Ovanesjan, SSSR 1968

67 12. ♘b3 e5 13. de5 ♘de5=

68 13. ♕d5 ed4 14. ♘d4 ♘d4 15. ♗d4 ♘c5!=

69 15... d4!?

70 18. ♕b7± Ničevski–Jansa, Athens 1969 — 8/103

71 11. d5 ♗f3 12. ♗f3 ♘e5=

72 **11... e5** 12. d5! ♘e7 13. ♖c1±; **11... e6** 12. ♕d2 d5 13. c5 ♘d7 14. ♖ac1 [14. ♖ab1 ♘f6 15. ♘e5 ♗e2 16. ♘c6 bc6 17. ♕e2 ♘d7= Rossolimo–Tartakower 1951] ♗f3 15. ♗f3 f5 [Ozsvath–Honfi, Hungary 1953] 16. ♘e2!△ b4±

73 13. h3 ♗f3 14. ♗f3 e6 15. ♕d2 [15. b4 a6 16. b5 ab5 17. ♘b5 ♘8e7= Toran–Korčnoj, Uppsala 1956] ♘8e7 16. ♘b5? ♘f5!∓ ×d4 Browne–Fischer, Rovinj-Zagreb 1970 — 10/155; 16. ♘e2!=

74 **14. ♕b3** e6 15. ♖fd1 ♘8e7 16. b5 ♘a5 17. ♕b4 ab5 18. ♘b5 ♘ec6∓ Zuidema–Hort, Örebro 1966; **14. ♕d2** e6 15. ♖fd1 ♘8e7 16. ♘e1 ♗e2 17. ♘e2 ♘f5∓ Westerinen–Hort, Leningrad 1967 — 3/129

75 18. ab5 ♘a5 19. ♗e2 [19. ♗g5 h6 20. ♗e7 ♕e7 21. ♕d3 ♕g5∞ Janošević–Gheorghiu, Skopje 1968] ♘f5 20. ♕d2! h6 21. ♖fd1 ♖e8 22. b6 e5 23. ♘b5 ♘d4 [23... ed4 24. ♗f4 ♗e5 25. ♗e5 ♖e5 26. ♘c7 ♖c8 27. ♕a5 ♖e2 28. ♕b5 ♖c2 29. ♖bc1±; 24... ♘c4 25. ♕c2 ♘a3 26. ♘a3 ♖a3 27. ♗c7 ♕g5 28. ♗b5 ♖c3 29. ♕a2 ♘h4 30. ♗g3 ♖c8 31. c6!± Boleslavski] 24. ♗d4! ed4 25. ♘c7 ♘c4 26. ♗c4±

B 05 1. e4 ♘f6 2. e5 ♘d5 3. d4 d6 4. ♘f3 ♗g4

	5	6	7	8	9	10	11	12	13	
1	h3[1]	♕f3	de5	♗c4[4]	♕e4	♗e3[7]	0–0	♕h4		=
	♗f3[2]	de5[3]	e6	♘c6[5]	♘de7[6]	♘f5	♕h4[8]	♘h4		
2	...	...	...	♗d2	♕g3	♘c3	♗c3	♕e3	♕c3	=
	...	...	...	♘d7![9]	♘c5	♘c3	♘e4	♘c3	♕d5[10]	
3	c4[11]	♗e2	c5[13]	cb6[15]	♗f3	♕f3	0–0[17]	♕b7	♗e3	=
	♘b6	de5[12]	e4[14]	ef3	♗f3	♘c6![16]	♘d4[18]	ab6	♖b8[19]	
4	♗e2	♘e5	♕e2	0–0[22]	c4	♗g5	♘c3	♖ad1	♖d3[23]	±
	de5[20]	♗e2	c6[21]	e6	♘f6	♗e7	0–0	♘bd7		
5	...	0–0[25]	♗f3	de5	♕e2[27]	♖e1[29]	♗d2	c4	♗c3	∞
	c6[24]	♗f3[26]	de5	e6	♘d7[28]	♕c7	♗c5	♘e7	a5[30]	
6	...	♘g5	e6![31]	g4[33]	♗d3[34]	♕d3	0–0[35]	♘e6	♕e2	±
	...	♗f5	fe6[32]	♗g6	♗d3	g6	♗h6[36]	♕d7	♗c1[37]	
7	...	...	♕e2	de5	0–0	f4[39]	♘e4	♘bd2[41]	♘c5	±
	...	♗e2	de5	e6	♘d7[38]	♗e7	♘c5[40]	♘b4[42]	♗c5[43]	

1. e4 ♘f6 2. e5 ♘d5 3. d4 d6 4. ♘f3 ♗g4 5. ♗e2 ♘c6

	6	7	8	9	10	11	12	13	14	
8	c4[44]	ed6[45]	0—0[47]	♘c3[48]	b3	♗e3	c5	h3[51]	b4[53]	=
	♘b6	ed6[46]	♗e7	0—0	♗f6[49]	d5[50]	♘c8	♗e6[52]	a6![54]	
9	0—0	a4![56]	a5	♘g5	♕e2	♖d1	a6	c4	d5	±
	♘b6[55]	de5	e4[57]	♗e2	♘d5	g6	b6	♘f6	♘e5[58]	

1. e4 ♘f6 2. e5 ♘d5 3. d4 d6 4. ♘f3 ♗g4 5. ♗e2 e6

	6	7	8	9	10	11	12	13	14	
10	0—0[59]	c4	ed6[61]	d5![62]	cd5	gf3![63]	♗b5	♕d4	♖e1[64]	±
	♘c6[60]	♘b6	cd6	ed5	♗f3	♘e5	♘ed7	♕f6	♔d8[65]	
11	...	...	ed6![66]	♘c3[67]	♗f3	d5	♗f4	♗g3	♗e2[69]	±
	...	♘de7	♕d6	♗f3[68]	0-0-0	♘e5	♘7g6	♕b4		

1. e4 ♘f6 2. e5 ♘d5 3. d4 d6 4. ♘f3 ♗g4 5. ♗e2 e6 6. 0—0 ♗e7 7. c4 ♘b6

	8	9	10	11	12	13	14	15	16	
12	ed6[70]	b3	♘c3[72]	♗e3[74]	c5	b4	♖b1[78]	a4[79]	b5	∞
	cd6	♘c6[71]	0—0[73]	d5[75]	♘c8[76]	a6[77]	♗f6	♘8e7	♘a5[80]	
13	...	...	♗b2	♘bd2	c5[82]	a3[83]	b4	♖e1	♖a2[84]	⩲
	...	...	0—0[81]	d5	♘d7	♗f6	a6	b6		
14	...	♘c3	♗e3	d5!	♗f3	de6[87]	♗g4	♗e6	♗b6[89]	⩲
	...	0—0	♘c6[85]	♗f3[86]	♘e5	fe6	♘ec4[88]	♔h8	♘b6[90]	
15	...	...	...	c5	♗f3[91]	♗f4[92]	b3	♖c1[94]	♘a4![95]	⩲
	...	...	d5	♗f3	♘c4	♘c6[93]	♘4a5	b6		
16	h3	ed6	♘bd2[96]	b3	♗b2	c5	a3	b4	♖e1	⩲
	♗h5	cd6	♘c6	0—0	d5	♘d7	f6!?[97]	a6	♗f7[98]	
17	...	♘c3	♗e3[100]	c5	♗f3	♗f4[103]	b3	♖c1[105]	dc5	∞
	...	0—0[99]	d5[101]	♗f3![102]	♘c4	b6![104]	♘a5	bc5	♘ac6[106]	
18	...	...	...	...	...	b4	♖c1	♗e2	♗c4	⩲
	...	...	...	...	...	b6	c6[107]	a5	ab4[108]	
19	...	...	...	...	gf3	b4	f4	♗d3	♕h5[111]	±
	...	...	...	...	♘c8[109]	f5[110]	♔h8	g5		
20	♘c3	♗e3[112]	c5	gf3[113]	b4	f4	fe5	♗d3	♕g4[115]	±
	0—0	d5	♗f3	♘c8	f6[114]	fe5	♕e8	♗d8		

[1] Panov; 5. ♗c4? e6 6. h3 ♗h5 7. ♕e2 ♘b6 8. ♗b3 ♘c6 9. g4 ♗g6 10. ♘c3 de5 11. de5 ♘d4 12. ♘d4 ♕d4 13. ♗e3 ♕d7 14. ♖d1 ♕c6 15. f3 ♗b4∓ Akopjan—Alburt, SSSR 1970

[2] 5... ♗h5? 6. e6!±; 6. g4 ♗g6 7. e6!±

[3] 6... c6 7. ♗c4 de5 8. de5 e6 9. 0—0 ♘d7 10. ♕e2 ♕c7 11. ♖e1⩲○ Ćirić—Cuderman, Jugoslavija (ch) 1961

[4] **8. ♗d3**? ♘c6 9. ♕g3 ♘db4! 10. ♗e4 ♕d4∓; **8. g3** ♘c6 9. ♗b5 ♕d7 10. ♕e4 ♗c5∓ Rubinstein—Spielmann, Moskva 1925; **8. ♕g3** ♘d7 9. ♗e2 c6 10. ♘a3 ♕a5 [10... ♘e7 11. ♘c4! ♘f5 12. ♕c3⩲ Boleslavski] 11. ♗d2 ♗b4 12. c3 ♗a3 13. ba3 ♘e7∓ Bagirov; **8. ♕e4** ♘d7 9. ♗c4 ♘c5! [9... c6 10. 0—0 ♕c7 11. ♖e1±○ Popov—Buljovčić, Jugoslavija 1966 — 2/117] 10. ♕e2 ♘b6 11. ♗b3 a5 12. a3 ♘b3 13. cb3 ♗e7∓ Boleslavski; **8. a3** ♘d7 [8... ♘c6? 9. ♗b5±; 8... c6 9. ♘d2 ♘d7 10. ♕g3 ♘e7!= L. Steiner—Koblenc 1937] 9. ♕g3 [9. c4 ♘e7 10. ♕b7 c6! 11. b4 a5 12. ♗b2 ♘c5!∓ Hačaturov—Mikenas, SSSR 1943] h5! [9... f6 10. ef6 ♕f6 11. ♕g5 ♕f7 12. ♗e2 ♗e7= Asztalos—Vuković, Debrecen 1925] 10. ♗e2! [10. ♘d2!? h4 11. ♕b3 ♖h5 12. ♘f3

♘e5∓ Panov–Mikenas, SSSR 1943] h4 11. ♕b3 ♖b8 12. 0–0 ♘e5 13. c4 ♘b6 14. ♗e3 ♘c6 15. ♖d1 ♕f6 16. ♘c3=∞ Nemet–Segal, SSSR 1967

5 8... ♘b4? 9. 0–0! ♘c2 10. ♕b7 ♘d7 11. ♗b5!±

6 9... ♘b6 10. ♗b5 ♕d5 11. ♘c3 ♕e4 12. ♘e4 0-0-0 13. ♗c6 bc6 14. b3± Suetin–Mikenas, SSSR (ch) 1965

7 10. c3 ♘g6 11. ♗f4 ♘f4 12. ♕f4 g5! 13. ♕e3 [13. ♕f6 ♖g8 14. ♘d2 ♗g7∓ Öim–Mikenas, SSSR 1965] ♗g7 14. ♗b5 ♕d5∓ Gipslis–Mikenas, SSSR 1953; 11. ♗b5=

8 11... ♘e3 12. fe3 ♗c5 13. ♕f4 0–0 14. ♘c3 ♕d2 15. ♖ae1±→ Panov

9 8... ♘c6?! 9. ♗b5 ♕d7 10. ♘c3 a6 11. ♗a4 b5 12. ♘d5 ♕d5 13. ♕d5 ed5 14. ♗b3± Halilbejli–Bagirov, SSSR 1959

10 = Mikenas

11 Aljehin

12 6... e6 — 5. ♗e2

13 7. ♘e5 ♗e2 8. ♕e2 ♕d4 9. 0–0 ♘8d7 10. ♘d7 ♕d7 [10... ♘d7? 11. ♘c3 c6 12. ♗e3 ♕e5 13. ♖ad1 e6 14. ♕f3!± Aljehin–Reshevsky, Kemery 1937] 11. a4! [11. ♘c3 e6 12. ♗e3 ♗e7 13. ♖ad1 ♕c6 14. ♕g4 0–0∓ Thomas–Flor, Antverpen 1932] ♕c6 12. ♘a3 e6 13. a5 ♘d7 14. ♘b5=∞ Aljehin; 9. ♘a3!? Aljehin

14 7... ♘6d7 8. ♘e5 ♗e2 9. ♕e2 ♘e5 10. de5 ♘c6 11. ♗f4 ♕d4 12. ♗g3 e6=; 10... e6!?

15 8. ♘g5 ♗e2 9. ♕e2 ♘d5 10. 0–0 [10. ♕b5 ♘c6 11. ♘c3 e6 12. ♘ge4 ♗e7=] ♘c6 11. ♖d1= Aljehin

16 10... ab6 11. ♕b7 ♘d7 12. ♗f4 e5 13. ♗e5 ♘e5 14. de5 ♗b4 15. ♘c3 ♗c3 16. bc3 0–0± Aljehin–Euwe (m) 1937

17 11. bc7 ♕c7 12. ♗e3 ♖d8 13. ♕d1? e5∓ Ciocaltea–Bagirov, Baku 1966

18 11... e6 12. ♘c3 ab6 13. d5! ed5 14. ♘d5 ♖a5 15. ♖e1±↑ Ciocaltea–Sutiman, Bucuresti 1952

19 14. ♕e4 ♘b5! 15. ♕a4 ♕d7 16. ♖d1 ♘d6= Fine

20 **5... g6** 6. ♘g5 [6. h3 ♗f3 7. ♗f3 c6 8. ed6±] ♗e2 7. ♕e2 h6 [7... ♗g7? 8. ♕f3! +–] 8. ♘f7! ♔f7 9. ♕f3 ♔e6 10. ♕g4 [10. c4 ♘b6 11. d5 ♔d7 12. ♕g4± Klovan–Vojtkevič, SSSR 1962] ♔f7 11. e6 ♔g7 12. ♕f3 ♘f6 13. ♕b7 c6 14. ♘c3± Uusi–Vooremaa, SSSR 1962; 11... ♔f6!?; **5... ♘d7** 6. h3 ♗h5 7. ♘g5 [7. e6!? fe6 8. ♘g5 ♗f7 9. ♗g4 ♘7f6 10. c4± König–Türn, München (ol) 1936] ♗g6 [7... ♗e2 8. e6!±] 8. e6! ♘7f6 9. ♗d3 ♕c8 10. ♗g6 fg6 11. 0–0 c6 12. ♕d3 ♕c7 13. c4± Maroczy–Vuković, London (ol) 1927; 6... ♗f3 7. ♗f3 c6 8. ed6 ed6 9. ♗d5!±; **5... ♗f3** 6. ♗f3 c6 7. ed6 ♕d6 8. 0–0±

21 7... ♘b6 8. 0–0 ♘8d7 [8... ♕d4? 9. ♖d1 ♕h4 10. ♗g5! ♕g5 11. ♖d8+–] 9. ♖d1± Euwe

22 8. ♕f3!?

23 Bastrikov–Hasin, SSSR 1957

24 Flor

25 6. c4 ♘b6 7. ♘bd2 de5 8. ♘e5 ♗e2 9. ♕e2 ♕d4 10. ♘df3∞ Levenfiš; 9... e6!?; 7. ed6!? Euwe

26 6... de5 7. ♘e5 ♗e2 8. ♕e2 ♘d7 [8... e6 9. b3 ♘d7 10. c4 ♘5f6 11. ♘c3± Aljehin] 9. f4 e6 10. c4 ♘5b6 11. ♗e3 ♗e7 12. ♘c3±○ Botvinik–Flor, Moskva 1936

27 9. c4 ♘e7 10. ♕d8 ♔d8 11. ♗f4 ♘d7 13. ♖e1 ♔c7= Zurahov–Kopilov, SSSR 1955

28 9... ♕c7 10. c4 ♘e7 11. ♗g4 [11. ♗d2 ♘d7 12. ♗c3 g5!∓ Matanović–Knežević, Jugoslavija 1965] ♘d7 12. f4 h5! 13. ♗h3 0-0-0 [13... ♘f5 14. ♗f5 ef5 15. e6?! ♘c5!∓ Gajduk–Čujčev, SSSR 1950] 14. ♗e3 ♘f5 15. ♗f5 ef5∓ Botvinik–Flor, Nottingham 1936; 10. ♖e1 ♘d7 — 9... ♘d7

29 **10. c4** ♘e7 11. ♗f4 ♘g6 [11... h6? 12. ♘c3 g5 13. ♘e4 ♘f5 14. ♖ad1 ♕a5 15. ♗d2± Janošević–Knežević, Skopje 1966] 12. ♗g3 ♕c7 13. ♖e1 ♗b4 14. ♘c3 ♗c3 15. bc3 0-0-0 16. h4 [16. ♗e4 ♘c5 17. ♗c2 ♖d7 18. ♕e3 ♕a5∓ Čehover–Kopilov, SSSR 1954] ♘c5 17. ♖ad1 ♕a5 18. ♕e3 ♘e7∓ Aronin–Furman, SSSR 1952; **10. b3** ♕c7 11. ♗b2 ♘f4 12. ♕e4 ♘g6 13. ♖e1 0-0-0∞ Kuznjecov–Kopilov, SSSR 1964

30 **13... ♘g6** 14. ♘d2±; **13... a5** 14. a3 ♘g6 15. g3 ♗a7∞ Matanović–Knežević, Jugoslavija 1973

31 **7. ♗g4**!? ♗g4 8. ♕g4 de5 9. de5 e6 10. 0–0 ♘d7 11. c4 ♘b4 12. ♕e2±○ Ciocaltea–Westerinen, Bucuresti 1974; **7. ♗d3** ♗d3 8. ♕d3 de5 9. de5 [9. ♕f5!? ♘f6 10. de5 g6 11. ♕f4 h6 12. ♘f7 ♔f7 13. ♘c3± Baranov; 9... f6 10. ♘h7 ed4 11. 0–0! e5 12. c4 ♘c7 13. f4 (Bagirov–Vasjukov, SSSR (ch) 1972 — 14/167) ♕d7!∞] h6 10. ♘f3 [10. ♘e4 e6 11. 0–0 ♘d7 12. f4 ♘c5=] e6 11. 0–0 ♘d7 12. ♖d1 ♕c7 13. c4 ♘5b6 [13... ♘e7 14. ♗f4 ♘g6 15. ♗g3 0-0-0 16. ♘c3 ♗b4!∓ Euwe; 14. ♘c3! ♘g6 15. ♘e4! ♘de5 16. ♘e5 ♘e5 17. ♕g3!±↑ Böök] 14. ♕e2± Böök–Reshevsky, Kemery 1937

32 7... ♗e6 8. ♘e6 fe6 9. ♗g4 ♘c7 10. 0–0 ♘d7 11. ♖e1 e5 12. ♗d7 ♕d7 13. de5± Pachman–Seimeanu, Bucuresti 1954

33 8. ♗d3 ♘a6 9. 0–0 ♘ac7 10. c4 ♘f6 11. ♘c3 g6 12. ♖e1 ♗g7 13. ♗f5 ef5 14. ♕b3 [Gufeljd–Bagirov, SSSR 1971 — 12/146] ♖b8!∓

34 9. ♘e6 ♕d7 10. ♘f4 ♗f7 11. c4 ♘b6 12. b3 e5 13. de5 de5 14. ♘d3 ♕c7∓ Türn–Keres, SSSR 1945

35 11. ♘e6 ♕d7=

36 **11... ♘c7** 12. ♕f3!±; **11... ♕d7** 12. ♖e1 ♘a6 [12... e5 13. ♕f3! ♘f6 14. de5±] 13. ♕f3 ♘f6 14. ♘e6± Euwe

37 14. ♖c1 ♘c7 15. ♘c7 ♕c7 16. ♖e1± Euwe

38 9... ♗e7 10. ♘e4 0–0 11. c4 ♘b6 12. b3 c5 13. ♗b2 ♘c6 14. ♘bd2± Boleslavski–Smislov, SSSR 1943

39 10. c4 ♘e7 11. ♘c3 [11. f4 ♘f5 12. ♘e4 ♕b6 13. ♔h1 h5= Koch–Alster 1955] ♘f5 12. ♘f3 [12. ♗f4 ♗e7 13. ♘ge4 g5 14. ♗g31 h5∓ Sajgin–Furman, SSSR 1952; 12. ♖d1 ♗e7 13. ♘ce4 c5 14. ♕h5? g6 15. ♕f3 h6∓ Kirilov–Kopilov, SSSR 1947] ♕c7 13. ♖e1 ♗b4 14. ♗d2 a5 15. a3 ♗c3 16. ♗c3 0–0 17. ♖ed1±○ Unzicker–Schmid, BRD (ch) 1959; 14... 0–0!=

40 **11... 0–0** 12. c4 ♘5b6 13. ♖d1±; **11... b5**!? Müller

41 12. ♘bc3 0–0 13. ♔h1 ♕b6 14. ♘d5 cd5 15. ♘c5 ♗c5∓ Akopjan–Kopilov, corr. 1965

42 12... ♕c7!?

43 14. ♔h1 0–0 15. ♘e4 ♗e7 16. a3± Milev–Dittmann, Kienbaum 1958

44 **6. e6** fe6 7. ♘g5 ♗e2 8. ♕e2 ♘d4 [8... e5 9. ♕c4!±] 9. ♕d1 [9. ♕e4 c5!∓] h6 10. ♘e6 ♘e6 11. ♕d5 ♕c8 12. ♕h5 ♔d8 13. 0–0 g5∓ Muhin–Kaunas, SSSR 1968; **6. h3** ♗f3 7. ♗f3 de5 8. de5 e6 9. 0–0 ♘db4!= Bondarevski–Mikenas, SSSR 1942

45 **7. e6** fe6 8. ♘c3 g6 9. ♘g5 ♗e2 10. ♘e2 ♕d7∓ Simagin–Fridštejn, SSSR 1947; **7. ♘c3** de5 8. d5!? ♗f3 9. ♗f3 ♘d4 10. c5 ♘d7 11. ♗e3 ♘c5 12. 0–0 e6∞↑ Gligorić–Penrose, Leipzig (ol) 1960

46 7... cd6 8. d5! ♗f3 9. ♗f3 ♘e5 10. ♗e2 g6 [10... ♖c8 11. b3 g6 12. ♗b2 ♗g7 13. ♕d2 ♖c4?! 14. bc4 ♘ec4 15. ♗g7! ♘d2 16. ♗h8± Klavin–Karasev, SSSR 1961] 11. ♗e3 ♗g7 12. ♘d2 0–0 13. 0–0± Unzicker–van Scheltinga, England 1951

47 8. d5 ♗f3 9. ♗f3 ♘e5 10. ♗e2 ♗e7 [10... g6 11. 0–0 ♗g7 12. ♘d2 0–0 13. ♖b1= Kinnmark–Cafferty, corr. 1964] 11. 0–0 0–0 12. ♘d2= Koc–Štejnberg, SSSR 1958

48 **9. ♘bd2** 0–0 10. d5 ♗f3 11. ♘f3 ♘e5 12. ♘e5 de5 13. ♗e3 ♘d7= Štejn–Mikenas, SSSR 1962; **9. ♗e3** 0–0 10. b3 f5! 11. ♘c3 [11. ♕d2 f4!∓] f4 12. ♗d2 ♗f6= Kavalek–Larsen, Solingen 1970

49 10... d5? 11. c5 ♘c8 12. h3 ♗e6? 13. ♗b5 ♘a5 [13... ♗f6 14. ♗c6 bc6 15. ♗f4± Matulović–Minić, Jugoslavija (ch) 1966 — 3/133] 14. ♘e5 f6 15. ♘d3 g5 16. ♖e1± Šmit–Mikenas, SSSR 1968 — 6/173

50 **11... ♖e8** 12. h3 ♗h5 13. ♕d2 d5 14. c5 ♘c8 15. ♖ad1± Smislov–Spaski, SSSR 1960; **11... ♘e7** 12. h3 ♗f3 13. ♗f3 c6 14. ♗g4! g6 15. ♗h6 ♗g7 16. ♕d2±

51 **13. b4**!? ♘8e7 [13... a6!? 14. ♖b1 ♘8e7 15. a4 ♘f5 16. h3 ♗f3 17. ♗f3 ♗d4 18. ♘d5 ♗e3 19. ♘e3 ♘e3 20. fe3 ♕g5∓ Vasjukov–Knežević, Kislovodsk 1968 — 6/172] 14. b5 [14. h3 ♗f3 15. ♗f3 ♘b4 16. ♖b1 ♘a6 17. ♖b7 ♘c5!∓] ♘a5 15. h3 [15. ♘e5!?] ♗f3 16. ♗f3 c6 17. ♕d3 ♘c4 18. ♗f4 ♘g6∓ Gipslis–Larsen, Sousse (izt) 1967 — 4/136; **13. ♖b1** ♘8e7 14. h3 ♗f3 15. ♗f3 ♘f5 16. ♘d5 ♗d4= Butnoris–Mikenas, SSSR 1967 — 3/127

52 **13... ♗f5** 14. ♕d2 h6 15. ♖ad1 ♘8e7?! 16. g4 ♗h7 17. h4±→ Kurajica–Hort, Sombor 1968 — 6/183; **13... ♗f3** 14. ♗f3 ♘8e7 15. ♖c1 [15. g4 g6 16. ♖e1 b6 17. cb6 ab6? 18. ♖c1± Kurajica–Minić, Jugoslavija 1969; 17... cb6!=; 17. ♘a4!?; 16. ♖c1!±; 15. ♕d3 g6 16. ♖ad1± Boleslavski] ♖e8 16. g4 g6 17. a3 ♗g7 18. b4 h6 19. ♘e2± Tatai–Ciocaltea, Reggio Emilia 1968

53 **14. ♕d2** h6 [14... ♘6e7 15. g4 g6 16. ♘e1 ♗g7 17. f4 f5 18. g5± Boleslavski] 15. ♘h2 ♘8e7 16. ♘g4 ♘f5 17. ♘f6 ♕f6= Sigurjonsson–Olafsson, Reykjavik 1970; **14. ♘e1** ♘8e7 15. g4 ♘g6 16. f4± Kurajica; 15... g6!∞ Knežević

54 **14... ♘b4**? 15. ♖b1 ♘a6 16. ♗a6 ba6 17. ♕a4±; **14... a6**! 15. ♖b1 [15. b5 ab5 16. ♘b5 ♘a5! 17. ♗f4 c6 18. ♘d6 ♘d6 19. ♗d6 ♖e8=; 15. ♕d2 ♘8e7 16. ♖fb1 ♘f5 17. b5 ab5 18. ♖b5 ♗c8 19. ♖b2 g6= Matulović–Knežević, Jugoslavija 1968] ♘8e7 16. a4 [16. g4 h6 17. ♘e1 g5 18. ♘g2 ♘g6∓ Estrin–Gik, Dubna 1968; 17. ♗d3 g5! 18. a4 ♗g7 19. b5 ab5 20. ab5 ♘a5∓ Pedersen–Jansa, Athens 1970 — 8/111; 18. ♘e2!? (Boleslavski) ♗g7!△ f5∞] ♘f5 17. b5 ab5 18. ab5 ♘e3 19. fe3 ♘e7=

55 **6... g6**? 7. e6!± Zita–Vidmar, jr. Karlovy Vary – Marianske Lazni 1948; **6... ♗f3** 7. ♗f3 de5 8. de5 e6 9. c4 ♘de7 10. ♕a4 ♕d4 11. ♗g5!± Kirilov–Žuhovicki, SSSR 1946; **6... de5** 7. ♘e5 ♗e2 8. ♕e2 ♘e5 9. de5± Brinckmann–Schönmann, BRD 1927

56 7. h3 ♗f3 8. ♗f3 de5 [8... e6 9. ed6 ♗d6 10. ♗c6 bc6 11. ♘c3± Listengarten–Mikenas, SSSR 1962; 9... ♕d6 10. c3△ ♘d2, ♘e4±] 9. de5 ♕d1 10. ♖d1 e6 11. b3 ♘e5 [11... ♗e7 12. ♗b2±] 12. ♗b7 ♖b8 13. ♗a6 ♘d5 14. ♗b2 ♗d6 15. ♗f1 f6 16. c4 ♘b4 17. ♘c3± Novopašin–Mikenas, SSSR (ch) 1962

57 8... ♘d7 9. a6 b6 10. de5 ♘de5 11. ♘e5 ♕d1 12. ♗d1 ♘e5 13. ♗f4± Matanović

58 15. ♘e4± Bogdanović—Kneževič, Jugoslavija (ch) 1967 — 3/132

59 6. h3 ♗f3 7. ♗f3 c6 8. c4 ♘b6=; 6... ♗h5!?

60 6... de5 7. ♘e5 ♗e2 8. ♕e2 ♘d7 9. c4 ♘5b6 10. ♘f3 ♗e7 11. ♘c3 0—0 12. ♖e1 ±○ Lutikov—Kuprejčik, SSSR 1970; 9. ♖d1!±

61 8. b3 ♗e7 9. ♗b2 0—0 10. ♘c3 de5 11. ♘e5 ♗e2 12. ♘e2= Agejčenko—Bagirov, SSSR 1969

62 9. ♗e3 d5 10. c5 ♗f3 11. ♗f3 ♘c4∓ Hecht

63 11. ♗f3 ♘e5 12. ♗e2 [12. ♗e4 ♗e7 13. ♘c3 0—0 14. f4!±] ♗e7 13. a4 0—0 14. ♖a3 f5 15. f4 ♘g6± Yates—Colle, Scarborough 1930

64 14. ♕f6 gf6 15. ♘c3 0-0-0 16. f4 f5!= Boleslavski—Bagirov, SSSR 1956

65 **14... ♗e7** 15. ♕f6 gf6 16. ♘c3 ♔d8 [16... a6 17. ♗e2 ♘e5 18. f4± Vogt—Heidenfeld, Skopje (ol) 1972] 17. f4 f5 18. ♗d3± Boleslavski; **14... ♔d8** 15. ♕d1 ♕f5 16. ♘c3 ♘e5 17. f4 ♕g4 18. ♕g4 ♘g4 19. ♘a4!± Boleslavski

66 8. ♕a4 ♕d7 [8... d5 9. ♘c3 ♕d7± Banik—Mikenas, SSSR 1951] 9. ed6 cd6 10. ♖d1 d5 11. ♘c3 dc4 12. ♕c4! [12. d5 ♘d5 13. ♘d5 ed5 14. ♗c4 ♗e6 15. ♗f4 a6!∞ Kopajev—Mikenas, SSSR 1949] ♘d5 13. ♘e5 ♘e5 14. de5 ♗e2 15. ♕e2 ♘c3 16. bc3 ♕c6 17. ♗g5!±

67 9. ♗e3 ♘f5 10. ♘c3 0-0-0 11. c5 ♕e7 12. ♕a4 ♗f3 13. ♗f3 [Brinckmann—Grünfeld, Kecskemet 1927] ♘cd4!∓ Takacs

68 9... ♘g6 10. d5! ed5 11. cd5 ♗f3 12. gf3! ♘ce5 13. ♘b5 ♕d7 14. f4± Aronin—Mikenas, SSSR 1951

69 Unzicker—Pomar, Bad Pyrmont 1951

70 8. b3 ♘c6 9. ♗b2 de5 10. ♘e5 ♗e2 11. ♕e2 ♘e5 12. de5± Rossetto—Sumar, Mar del Plata 1958

71 9... 0—0 10. ♗e3 [10. a4 a5 11. ♘c3 d5 12. c5 ♘6d7 13. ♘b5 b6! 14. cb6 ♕b6∓ Donner—Trifunović 1951] ♘6d7 11. ♘c3 ♘f6 12. ♕d2 d5 13. c5 ♘c6 14. ♕b2 ♗f3 15. ♗f3 e5= Fuderer—Trifunović, Jugoslavija 1951; 10. ♗b2±

72 10. h3 ♗f3 11. ♗f3 ♗f6 12. ♗e3 d5 13. c5 ♘d7 14. ♘a3 0—0∓ Witkowski—Mikenas 1960

73 10... ♗f6 11. ♗e3 [11. ♗b2 d5 12. c5 ♘d7 13. ♘b5 ♘c5 14. dc5 ♗b2 15. ♘d6 ♔f8 16. ♖b1 ♗f3 17. ♗f3 ♗e5∓ Alexander] d5 12. c5 ♘d7 13. b4! [13. ♖c1 0—0 14. a3 ♘c5! 15. dc5 ♗f3 16. ♗f3 d4 17. ♗c6 bc6 18. ♗d2 dc3= Boleslavski—Mikenas, SSSR 1944; 14. ♕d2 ♘c5 15. ♘d5 ♘e4= Panov—Mikenas, SSSR 1943] ♘b4 14. ♖b1 ♘c6 15. ♖b7 ♗f3 [15... ♘c5? 16. dc5 ♗c3 17. ♕a4 ♕c8 18. ♗b5!+—] 16. ♗f3 0—0! [16... ♘c5 17. ♘d5!± Nedeljković—Janošević, Jugoslavija (ch) 1948] 17. ♕a4 ♕c8± Mikenas

74 11. ♗b2 d5 12. c5 ♗f3 13. ♗f3 ♘d7 14. ♕d2 ♗f6 15. ♘a4 ♖e8∓ Nyholm—Grünfeld 1927

75 **11... ♖e8** 12. h3 ♗h5 13. d5!±; **11... ♗f6** 12. ♖c1 d5 13. c5 ♘c8 14. b4 ♘b4 15. ♕b3 ♘c6 16. ♕b7 ♘8e7= Bednarski—Bagirov, Budva 1963; 12. ♘e4!±

76 12... ♘d7 13. b4 [13. ♕d2 f5? 14. ♘g5 ♖f6 15. f3 ♗h5 16. ♘h3± Bely—Šefc 1956; 13... h6!∞] f5 [13... a6 14. ♖b1 ♘f6 15. h3 ♗h5 16. ♘e5! ♗e2 17. ♘c6 bc6 18. ♕e2 ♘d7 19. f4± Tartakower—Takacs, Budapest 1926; 13... ♘b4 14. ♖b1 ♘c6 15. ♖b7 ♖b8 16. ♖b8 ♘db8 17. h3± Talj—Vasjukov, SSSR (ch) 1967 — 5/119; 15... ♘a5 16. ♖b5 a6 17. ♖b1 ♗f6 18. ♘a4± Česnauskas—Bagirov, SSSR 1962; 15... ♗f3 16. ♗f3 ♗f6 17. ♕a4 ♕c8 18. ♖b5 a6 19. ♖b2 ♖a7 20. ♖fb1± Barštatis—Višomirskis, SSSR 1955] 14. b5 ♘a5 15. ♘d2 ♗e2 16. ♘e2 g5!∞ Pogacs—Gereben, Hungary 1953

77 13... ♗f6 14. b5 ♘a5 15. ♘d2 [15. ♗f4 ♘e7 16. ♘e5 ♗e2 17. ♘e2 ♗e5 18. ♗e5 ♘c4= Parma—Still, Lugano (ol) 1968] ♗e2 16. ♘e2 ♘e7 17. ♕a4 a6= Šamkovič—Aronin, SSSR 1953; 17. a4!?

78 14. ♘e5?! ♘e5 15. de5 ♗f5 16. f4 ♗g6∞ Robatsch—Hort, Venezia 1969 — 7/135

79 15. b5 ab5 16. ♖b5 ♗f3 17. ♗f3 b6= Romanišin—Bagirov, SSSR 1968

80 17. ♗f4 ♘f5 18. ♘e5∞ Minić—Hort, Zagreb 1969 — 7/136

81 10... d5 11. c5 ♘d7 12. a3 0—0 13. b4 a6 14. ♘bd2 ♗f6 15. h3 ♗h5 16. ♖e1 b6± Durao—Hecht, Malaga 1972 — 13/154

82 12. ♖c1 dc4 13. bc4 ♖c8 14. h3 ♗f5 15. ♕b3± Smislov—Bagirov, SSSR 1960; 12... ♗f6!?

83 13. ♖e1 b6 14. ♗b5 ♕c7 15. b4 a6= Averbah—Bagirov, SSSR 1959

84 Damjanović—Timman (m) 1969

85 10... ♘8d7 11. b3 ♘f6 12. ♖c1 h6 13. ♘d2 ♗e2 14. ♕e2 ♘bd7 15. ♕f3± Hasin—Mikenas, SSSR (ch) 1957

86 11... ed5 12. ♘d5 [12. cd5 ♗f3 13. ♗f3 ♘e5=; 12. ♗b6 ♕b6 13. ♘d5 ♕b2∞] ♘d5 13. ♕d5 ♗f6 [13... ♕c7 14. ♖ad1± Gipslis—Marović, SSSR—Jugoslavija 1971 — 12/148;

13... ♗e6!? 14. ♕d2±] 14. ♖fd1 [14. ♖ab1 ♗e6 15. ♕b5 d5 16. ♖bd1 d4 17. ♕b7 ♕d6 18. ♕a6 ♕c5 19. ♕b5± Matanović–Ghizdavu, Bath 1973 — 17/159] ♕c8 15. ♖d2± Lejn–Smislov, SSSR (ch) 1967

87 13. b3 ♘f3 14. ♕f3 e5 15. g4! f5 16. gf5 g6 17. f6± Boleslavski–Bagirov, SSSR 1963

88 14... ♖f6 15. b3 ♘g4 16. ♕g4± Matanović–Bagirov, Wijk aan Zee 1965

89 16. ♗d4 ♘b2 17. ♕c2 ♗f6!∞ Bihovski–Bagirov, SSSR 1967

90 17. ♕b3 ♗f6 18. ♖ad1 ♗c3 19. ♕c3± Timman–Bagirov, Tbilisi 1971 — 12/149; 18... ♕e7!?±

91 12. gf3!? ♘c8 13. b4 ♘c6 14. b5 ♘a5 15. ♕a4 b6 16. ♖ac1 ♗f6∞ Georgadze–Alburt, Lublin 1972 — 14/169; 14. ♖b1!?

92 13. ♗c1 ♘c6 14. b3 ♘4a5 15. ♗e3 b6 16. ♘a4 [16. cb6 ♕b6 17. ♘a4 ♕b4= Minić–Bagirov, Batumi 1966] ♖b8 17. ♖c1 [Karpov–Bagirov, SSSR (ch) 1968] b5! 18. ♘c3 ♗g5 19. ♕d2 ♗e3 20. fe3 f5= Boleslavski

93 13... ♘b2? 14. ♕b1±

94 15. ♖b1 ♗f6 16. ♗e3 b6= Geler–Korčnoj, Stockholm (izt) 1962

95 Sax–Hecht, Wijk aan Zee 1973 — 15/151

96 **10. a4** 0–0 11. a5 ♘6d7 12. ♗e3 f5? 13. ♘c3± Evans–Martz, USA (ch) 1972 — 13/156; 12... ♘c6!±; 10... a5!?; **10. ♘c3** 0–0 11. ♗e3 ♘c6 [11... ♗f6? 12. ♘e4 ♗e7 13. ♖c1 ♘c6 14. ♘g3± Ivkov–Nievergelt, Beograd 1954; 11... ♘8d7 12. b3 ♘f6 13. ♖c1 ♖c8 14. ♖e1 a6 15. ♗f1± Kapengut–Smislov, SSSR (ch) 1971] 12. d5! ed5 [12... ♗f3 13. ♗f3 ♘e5 14. de6 fe6 15. ♗g4±] 13. ♘d5 ♘d5 14. ♕d5 ♗g6±

97 14... ♗f6 15. b4 a5 16. ♖c1! b6 17. cb6 ♕b6 18. ♕a4± Torre–Schmid, Nice (ol) 1974 — 17/163

98 17. ♘f1 b6! [17... e5? 18. ♘e3 e4 19. ♘d2 ♗e6 20. ♘e4!± Ribli–Hecht, Wijk aan Zee 1972 — 13/153] 18. ♘e3 ♕c7 19. ♕d2 ♖fd8± Medina–Hecht, Malaga 1972 — 13/155

99 **9... ♘c6**? 10. ed6 cd6 11. d5 ed5 12. ♘d5±; **9... de5** 10. ♘e5 ♗e2 11. ♕e2 ♕d4 12. ♖d1± Euwe; **9... ♘8d7** 10. ed6 cd6 11. b3 0–0 12. a4 a5 [12... ♘f6 13. a5 ♘bd7 14. a6 b6 15. ♗a3± Gipslis] 13. ♗f4 ♘b8 14. ♖e1± Boleslavski–Bronštejn (m) 1950; 12. ♗f4!? Vuković

100 10. ♗f4 d5?! 11. c5 ♘6d7 [11... ♗f3 12. ♗f3± Geler] 12. b4± Gufeljd–Vasjukov, SSSR 1972; 10... de5=

101 10... a5 11. b3 d5 12. c5 ♘6d7 13. ♕d2 ♗f3 14. ♗f3 b6 15. cb6 c5?! 16. dc5 ♗c5 17. ♘a4!± Gipslis–Alburt, SSSR 1974 — 18/142; 15... cb6± Gipslis

102 11... ♘6d7?! 12. ♖c1!? [12. b4 b6 13. ♖c1 c6 14. ♘a4 ♗f3 15. ♗f3 a5 16. a3 ab4 17. ab4 b5 18. ♘b2 f6 19. ♘d3± Evans–Martz, USA 1973; 14... a5? 15. g4 ♗g6 16. b5!± Kavalek–Martz, USA (ch) 1973 — 16/123; 14... f6!?; 13... a5! 14. a3 ab4 15. ab4 bc5 16. bc5 ♘c6± Kavalek] b6 13. c6!± Evans

103 13. b3 ♘e3 14. fe3 b6 [14... ♘c6!? Petrosjan] 15. e4 c6 16. b4 bc5 17. bc5 ♕a5 18. ♘d5 [18. ♕d3 ♘a6∞] ♗g5 19. ♗h5∞ Spaski–Fischer (m) 1972 — 14/168; 19. ♕d3!?

104 13... ♘c6 14. b3 ♘4a5 15. ♖c1! [15. ♕d2 b6 16. ♖ac1 bc5 17. dc5 (Geler–Hecht, Budapest 1970) ♖b8!∞] b6 16. ♘a4 b5?! 17. ♘c3 b4 18. ♘e2± Geler–Bronštejn, Petropolis (izt) 1973 — 16/124

105 15. ♘a4 ♘d7 16. ♕d2 c6= Ciocaltea–Williams, Nice (ol) 1974 — 17/161

106 **16... ♘d7**? 17. b4 ♘c6 18. ♘d5!+– Adorjan–Přibyl, Luhačovice 1973; **16... ♘ac6** 17. ♖e1! [17. ♕d2 ♘d7 18. ♖fe1 ♖b8 19. ♘a4 ♖b4∓ Schmid] ♗g5 [17... ♘d7!? 18. ♘d5 ed5 19. ♗d5 ♘db8 20. b4 a6 21. ♖c4 ♖a7 22. ♕f3 ♕e8∞ Gufeljd–Palatnik, SSSR 1973] 18. ♘d5 [18. ♕d2 h6 19. ♗g5 hg5 20. ♖cd1?! ♘d7 21. ♘d5? ed5 22. ♗d5 ♘de5!∓ Rossmann–Grünberg, DDR (ch) 1974] ed5 19. ♗g5 ♕g5 20. ♗d5 ♔h8∞ Kavalek–Schmid, Nice (ol) 1974 — 17/162

107 14... a5 15. ♘d5 ed5 16. ♖c4± Gipslis

108 **16... dc4** 17. b5 bc5 18. ♕f3 cd4 19. ♖fd1 ♘d7 20. ♖d4± Beljavski–Palatnik, SSSR 1974 — 18/144; **16... ab4** 17. ♘a4 dc4 18. ♘b6 ♖a2 19. ♖c4 ♘a6 20. ♕b3 ♖a5± Gipslis

109 12... ♘c4 13. ♗c4 dc4 14. ♕a4±

110 13... ♗h4!?

111 ± R. Byrne

112 9. b3 de5 10. ♘e5 ♗e2 11. ♘e2 c5 12. ♗b2 ♕c7= Lasker–Flor, Moskva 1936

113 11. ♗f3 ♘c4 12. ♗f4 [12. ♗c1 b6 13. b3 ♘a5 14. ♘a4?! ♘b7!= Matanović–Vukić, Jugoslavija (ch) 1972 — 13/157; 12. b4!?] ♘c6 13. b3 ♘4a5 14. ♕d2 [14. ♖c1 f6! 15. ♖e1 ♕d7 16. ♕d2 ♖ae8∞ Matanović–Vukić, Jugoslavija 1974] b6 15. ♘a4 f6! 16. ♖fe1 ♕d7 17. ♗g4 ♖ae8 18. ♖ac1 fe5= Pavlov–Vukić, Jugoslavija 1973 — 17/160; 17. ♖ac1!?

114 12... f5?! 13. f4±○ Matanović–Vukić, Jugoslavija 1973

115 Matanović–Vukić, Jugoslavija (ch) 1975

B 06 **1. e4 g6**

	2	3	4	5	6	7	8	9	10	
1	f4[1]	♘f3	e5	d4	dc5[5]	♘c3	♘e4	♗d3	h3	∞
	♗g7[2]	d5[3]	c5	♗g4[4]	♘c6	d4	♕d5	f6	♗f5[6]	
2	d4	♗c4[8]	♕e2	♘f3	♗b5	c3	d5	h3	♕f3	=
	d6[7]	♘f6	♘c6!?[9]	♗g4	♘d7	e5	♘cb8	♗f3	♗e7![10]	
3	...	h4	♗g5	c3	♘d2	♘e4	♘f6	♗e3	♗d3	±
	...	h5[11]	♗g7	d5	de4	♘f6[12]	ef6	0–0	♘c6[13]	
4	...	f4[14]	♘f3	♗d3[17]	0–0	e5![19]	♕e1[20]	♕g3	♕h3	±
	♗g7	d6[15]	♘f6[16]	0–0[18]	♘bd7	♘e8	e6[21]	♘b6	f6[22]	
5	...	...	...	dc5[23]	♗d2[24]	♘c3	♗d3	♕e2	♗e3	=
	...	...	c5	♕a5	♕c5	♘f6	0–0	♘c6	♕a5[25]	
6	...	...	c3[26]	cd4	♘f3	e5[29]	♘c3	d5	a3	∓
	...	c5	cd4[27]	♕b6[28]	♘c6	♘h6	0–0	♘b4	♘a6[30]	

1. e4 g6 2. d4 ♗g7 3. c3

	3	4	5	6	7	8	9	10	11	
7	...	♘d2[32]	♘e4	♗c4	♘g5[35]	♘1f3	♘e4	♘c5[36]	0–0	±
	d5[31]	de4[33]	♘d7	♘df6[34]	♘d5	h6	♘gf6	0–0	b6[37]	
8	...	ed5!	♘f3	♗e3[39]	cd4	♘c3	♗b5	0–0	d5	±
	...	♕d5	c5[38]	cd4	♘c6	♕d8	e6[40]	♘e7	♘d5[41]	
9	...	...	♗e2!	♘f3	♘e2	cd4	0–0	♘bc3	♗f4!	±
	...	...	c5[42]	♕e6[43]	cd4	♘f6[44]	0–0	♕b6	♗d7[45]	
10	...	♗e3[46]	♗c4	f3[48]	♗b3	♘e2	0–0	a4	♘d2	=
	d6	♘d7[47]	♘gf6	0–0[49]	c5	♕c7	b6	a6	♗b7[50]	
11	...	♘f3	e5[52]	♘e5	♗c4	0–0[54]	de5	♕d8	f4[56]	=
	...	♘f6[51]	de5	0–0[53]	♘bd7	♘e5[55]	♘g4	♖d8		

1. e4 g6 2. d4 ♗g7 3. c3 d6 4. f4

	4	5	6	7	8	9	10	11	12	
12	...	de5[58]	g3	ed6[59]	♕e2	♘e2![60]	♘a3![61]	♘b5	f5!	±
	e5[57]	♕h4	♕e7	♕e4	♕e2	cd6	♗e6	♔d7	gf5[62]	
13	...	♗d3	♘f3	fe5	♗g5	♗h4	♗f2	cd4	♘bd2	∞
	♘f6	e5![63]	♗g4	de5	h6	g5	ed4	♘c6	♘h5![64]	
14	...	e5	♘f3	♗c4	♗b3	fe5	dc5[67]	♔d1	e6	=∞
	...	♘d5	0–0	♘b6[65]	de5[66]	c5	♕d1	♘6d7	♘c5[68]	
15	...	...	...	♗d3	♗e4	dc5	♕d8	♘e5![71]	fe5	±
	...	...	...	c5	♘c7[69]	de5[70]	♖d8	♗e5	♘d7[72]	
16	...	...	fe5	♘f3	♗c4	0–0[74]	cd4[75]	♘c3	♗b3[76]	=
	...	de5	♘d5	0–0	c5![73]	cd4	♘c6	♗e6	h6![77]	

1. e4 g6 2. d4 ♗g7 3. ♘c3 c6[78]

	4	5	6	7	8	9	10	11	12	
17	♗c4[79]	♗b3	♘ce2[81]	e5	a3	♖a3	f4	♘f3	0–0	±
	b5[80]	b4	♘f6[82]	♘d5	ba3	0–0	d6	♘d7	♘7b6[83]	

	4	5	6	7	8	9	10	11	12	
18	f4 d5	e5 h5	♘f3[84] ♗g4	h3 ♗f3	♕f3 e6[85]	g3[86] ♕b6	♕f2 ♘e7	♗d3 ♘d7	♘e2 0-0-0[87]	=
19	. . . . . .	. . . . . .	♗e3 ♘h6	♘f3[88] ♗g4	♗e2 e6[89]	♕d2[90] ♘d7	g3[91] ♘f5	♗f2 b5	h3 ♗f3[92]	±

1. e4 g6 2. d4 ♗g7 3. ♘c3 d6

	4	5	6	7	8	9	10	11	12	
20	♘ge2[93] ♘d7[94]	g3[95] e5	♗g2 ♘e7	0—0 0—0	a4 ♘c6	♗e3[96] ed4	♘d4 ♘de5	♘de2 ♗g4	h3 ♗f3[97]	±
21	♗e3 a6[98]	♕d2[99] b5	f3 ♘d7	♘h3[100] ♗b7	♘f2 c5	♗e2 cd4	♗d4 ♘gf6	g4[101] h6	a3 ♘e5[102]	±
22	. . . c6	♕d2[103] b5[104]	h4[105] h5	♘h3[106] a6	♗d3 ♘d7	♘e2 ♘gf6	f3 ♗b7	0—0 e5	c3 0—0[107]	=
23	. . . . . .	. . . . . .	0-0-0 ♘d7[108]	♔b1[109] ♘b6[110]	♗d3 a5	h4 h5	♘h3 b4	♘e2 ♗h3	♖h3 e6[111]	±
24	f4 a6[112]	♘f3 b5[113]	♗d3[114] ♗b7	♕e2[115] ♘d7[116]	e5 e6[117]	a4 b4	♘e4 d5	♘f2 c5	dc5 ♘c5[118]	±
25	. . . ♘c6	♗e3[119] ♘f6	h3[120] 0—0	g4 e5	de5 de5	f5 gf5[121]	gf5 ♘d4	♘f3 c5	♗g5! ♕b6[122]	±
26	. . . c6	♘f3[123] ♗g4[124]	♗e3[125] ♕b6[126]	♕d3[127] ♘f6![128]	0-0-0 d5	e5 ♘e4	♘e2 ♘a6	♕a3 ♗f8	h3 ♗d7[129]	±

1. e4 g6 2. d4 ♗g7 3. ♘f3 d6

	4	5	6	7	8	9	10	11	12	
27	♘c3 c6[130]	♗e2[131] ♘d7[132]	a4[133] a5[134]	0—0 ♕c7	♗e3 ♘gf6	♘d2 d5	ed5[135] ♘d5	♘d5 cd5	♘b1[136]	±
28	. . . ♗g4	♗e3[137] ♘c6[138]	♗b5[139] a6	♗c6 bc6	h3 ♗f3	♕f3 e6[140]	e5 ♘e7	♘e4 ♘d5	♗g5 ♕b8[141]	±
29	♗c4[142] ♘f6[143]	♕e2[144] 0—0[145]	0—0[146] c6[147]	♗b3 ♗g4[148]	♘bd2 a5[149]	a4 d5	c3[150] ♘a6	h3 ♗f3	♕f3	±
30	. . . . . .	. . . ♘c6	c3[151] 0—0	0—0 ♘h5[152]	d5 ♘b8	♗e3 e5[153]	de6 fe6	♗g5 ♕e8	♕e3 ♘c6[154]	±

1 **2. h4** h5 3. d4 c6 4. ♗d3 ♗g7 5. ♘e2 d6 [5... d5!? 6. e5 ♘h5∞] 6. ♗g5 [6. ♘c3!?] ♕b6 7. c3 ♕b2! [7... e5? 8. ♘d2 ♗e6 9. de5 de5 10. ♗c4!± Velimirović—Bohosjan, Kapfenberg 1970 — 9/122] 8. ♘d2 ♕b6∞ Velimirović; **2. ♗c4** ♗g7 3. c3 c6 4. ♗b3 d5 5. ed5 cd5 6. d4 ♘f6 7. ♘f3 0—0 8. 0—0 ♘c6∞ Kinnmark—Planinc, Nice (ol) 1974 — 17/146

2 2... c5 — B 21

3 **3... d6** 4. c3 c5 5. ♗b5 ♗d7 6. ♗d7 ♕d7 7. 0—0 ♘c6 8. d4 0-0-0 9. d5 ♘a5 10. ♕c2! ♔b8 11. c4± Botvinik—Kotov, SSSR 1967 — 3/135; 7... ♘h6!?; 4... ♘f6! 5. e5 ♘d5 6. d4 — 2. d4; **3... c5** 4. c3 d5 5. e5 ♘h6 6. ♗b5 ♗d7 7. ♗d7 ♕d7 8. d4 cd4 9. cd4 0—0 10. ♘c3 ♘c6 11. h3 f6 12. ♕b3 fe5 13. de5 e6 14. ♘e2± Bronštejn—Padevski, Zagreb 1965

4 **5... cd4** 6. ♘d4 ♘c6 7. ♘c3±; **5... ♘c6**!?

5 6. c3 cd4 7. cd4 h5 8. ♗e2 ♘h6±; 7... ♘c6!△ ♗f3∓

6 **11. ef6** ♘f6 12. ♘f6 ♗f6! 13. ♗f5 gf5∓; **11. ♕e2** fe5 12. ♘fg5 ♘f6 13. ♗c4 ♕d7 14. g4 ♗e4 15. ♘e4 ♘d5∞ Minev—Planinc, Novi Sad 1972

7 **2... e6**? 3. ♘f3 [3. ♗d3 ♗g7 4. ♗e3 c5 5. c3 cd4 6. cd4 ♕b6 7. ♘e2 ♕b2 8. ♘bc3 ♕b6 9. ♖c1 ♘a6 10. ♘b5 ♗f8 11. 0—0 d6 12. d5 ♕a5 (Anderssen—Staunton, London

1851) 13. de6±→] ♘c6 4. d5 ♘e7 5. de6 de6 6. ♕d8 ♔d8 7. ♘c3 ♘c6 8. ♗f4 f6 9. 0-0-0 ♗d7 10. ♗b5± Steinitz–Bird (m) 1866; **2... b6** 3. ♘c3 ♗g7 — 2... ♗g7

8 3. f4 c5? 4. dc5! ♕a5 5. ♘c3 ♕c5 6. ♘d5! ♗g7 7. b4 ♕d4 8. ♕d4 ♗d4 9. c3 ♗g7 10. ♗b2 ♔d8 11. 0-0-0±↑ Matulović–Timman, Sombor 1972 — 14/170; 3... ♗g7! — 2... ♗g7

9 4... ♗g7 5. ♘f3 — 2... ♗g7

10 △ ♗g5= Talj–Matulović, Skopje (ol) 1972 — 14/172

11 **3... ♗g7** 4. h5 c5 [4... ♘f6 5. h6! ♗f8 6. ♘c3±] 5. d5 gh5 6. ♘c3 ♗c3 7. bc3 ♘f6 8. f3 ♖g8 9. ♘e2 ♕a5 10. a4± Spaski–Ufimcev, SSSR 1958; **3... ♘f6**! 4. ♘c3 — B 07

12 7... ♘d7!?

13 11. ♘e2 ♘e7 12. ♕d2 ♗f5 13. ♗c4± Hort–Keene, Reykjavik 1972 — 13/159

14 3. ♗c4 d6 [3... c5? 4. dc5 ♕a5 5. c3 ♕c5 6. ♕b3! e6 7. ♗e3 ♕c7 8. ♘a3 a6 9. ♗b6 ± Nikolau–E. Bilek, Beograd 1967 — 3/122] 4. ♘e2 ♘f6 5. f3 0–0 6. ♘bc3 c6 7. ♗g5 b5 8. ♗b3 ♘bd7= Calvo–Ivkov, Palma de Mallorca 1967 — 4/145; 4. ♘f3± — 3. ♘f3; 3... c6 4. ♘c3 — 3. ♘c3

15 **3... c6** 4. ♘f3 d5 5. e5 h5 6. ♗e2 ♘h6 7. ♘bd2 b6 8. ♘f1 e6 9. ♘e3 ♗a6 10. b3 ♗f8 11. c4 ♘g4 12. 0–0± Polgar–Vadasz, Hungary 1969 — 8/98; **3... d5** 4. e5 ♗f5 5. ♘e2! e6 6. ♘g3 ♘e7 7. ♗e2 c5 8. dc5 ♕a5 9. c3 ♕c5 10. ♘d2 ♘bc6 11. ♘b3 ♕b6 12. ♘f5 ♘f5 13. ♕d3 h5 14. ♗d2 0-0-0 15. 0-0-0± Čistjakov–Kremenecki, SSSR 1968

16 **4... ♗g4** 5. ♗c4 [5. c3 ♘d7 6. ♗c4 e6 7. h3 ♗f3 8. ♕f3± Loman–Albin, Dresden 1892] ♗f3 6. ♕f3 ♘c6 7. c3 e6 8. 0–0 ♘ge7 9. f5!± Gereben–H. Müller, Beverwijk 1965; **4... c6** 5. ♗d3 ♘d7 6. 0–0 ♕b6 7. c3 e5 8. fe5 de5 9. ♘a3! ed4 10. ♘c4 ♕c7 11. e5!±→ Zilbert–Liberzon, SSSR 1968 — 6/187

17 5. e5 de5! [5... ♘fd7 6. ♗c4 ♘b6 7. ♗b3 ♘a6 8. 0–0 c5 9. c3 0–0 10. ♘g5± Karaklajić–Robatsch, Smederevska Palanka 1956] 6. fe5 ♘d5 7. c4 [7. ♗d3!?; 7. ♗e2!?] ♘b6 8. ♘c3 ♗g4!? [8... 0–0?! 9. ♗e3 ♗e6 10. d5 ♗g4 11. ♕d4 ♗f3 12. gf3 c6 13. 0-0-0± Antošin–Nežmetdinov, SSSR 1953] 9. ♗e3 c5 10. dc5 ♘6d7∞ Fridštejn

18 5... c5 6. dc5 ♕a5 7. ♘c3 — B 09

19 **7. ♘c3** e5=; **7. c3** c5 8. ♔h1 ♕c7 9. ♕e2 e5 10. ♘a3± Menvielle–Bilek, La Habana (ol) 1966 — 2/119

20 8. ♘g5!?± Parma

21 8... c5 9. f5!? [9. c3±] de5 10. fg6 hg6 11. ♕h4 ed4 12. ♗h6 ♘ef6 13. ♘g5 ♕b6 [13... ♘e5? 14. ♖f6+– Bisguier–Larsen, Zagreb 1965] 14. ♘d2±→»

22 11. ♘c3 ♕e7 12. ♗d2 ♘d5 13. ♘e4± Ebrahimi–van Setters, Bruxelles 1968

23 **5. d5** ♗g4 6. ♗e2 ♘f6 7. ♘c3 0–0 8. 0–0 ♗f3 9. ♗f3 ♘fd7 10. ♔h1 ♘a6 11. ♗e2 ♘c7∞ Drimer–Štejn, Berlin 1962; **5. ♗b5**!? ♘c6!?△ 6. d5 a6∞

24 **6. c3** ♕c5 7. ♗d3 ♘f6 8. ♕e2 0–0 9. ♘bd2 e5! 10. fe5 de5 11. ♘c4 b5 12. ♘a5 a6 13. ♘b3 ♕c7 14. 0–0 ♘bd7∓ Bogdanović–Kotov, Sarajevo 1966 — 1/93; **6. ♘bd2** ♕c5 7. ♘b3 ♕b4 8. ♘fd2 ♘f6 9. ♕f3 0–0 10. ♗d3 ♕b6 11. ♘c4 ♕c7 12. 0–0 ♗g4 13. ♕g3 ♗d7 14. ♘e3 a5 [Suetin–Polugajevski, SSSR (ch) 1963] 15. ♘d2△ 15... a4 16. a3∞ Suetin

25 11. 0–0 ♗g4 [McCormick–Benkö, USA 1967 — 3/123] 12. h3=

26 **4. ♘f3**?! cd4 5. ♘d4 ♘c6!; **4. d5**!? d6 5. c4 — E; **4. dc5**!?

27 4... d5!? 5. e5 [5. ♗b5 ♘c6! 6. ♕a4 cd4! 7. ♗c6 bc6 8. ♕c6 ♗d7 9. ♕d5 dc3 10. ♘c3 ♗c3! 11. bc3 ♘f6 12. ♕e5 0–0=∞⟳↑ Bouaziz–Ivkov, Sousse (izt) 1967 — 4/132] f6 6. ef6 ♘f6 7. dc5 0–0∞ Ivkov

28 **5... d5** 6. e5 ♘c6 7. ♗e3 ♘h6 8. ♘c3 0–0 9. ♘f3 ♗g4 10. ♗e2 e6= Store–Richardson, corr. 1971; **5... d6**!? Keene

29 7. ♘c3!? ♘d4?! 8. ♘d5 ♘f3 9. gf3! ♕d8 10. ♕c2!=∞↑; 7... ♘h6! Keene

30 **11. d6**? ed6 12. ♕d6 ♕d6 13. ed6 ♖e8△ ♘f5-♘d6∓ Keene; **11. ♗d3** d6 12. ♕e2 ♘c5 13. ♗c4 ♗g4∓ Caro–Keene, Camaguey 1974 — 17/164; **11. ♗c4**!?

31 **3... b6** 4. f4 [4. ♗d3 c5 5. ♘e2 ♘c6 6. ♗e3 cd4 7. cd4 ♗b7 8. ♘c3 ♘f6 9. f3 0–0 10. ♖c1 e5 11. d5 ♘b4 12. ♗b1 ♘e8! 13. ♘b5 ♗h6!= Buhman–Kotov, SSSR 1968] ♗b7 5. ♗d3 ♘f6 6. ♕e2 c5 7. d5±↑⊞; **3... c6** 4. ♘f3 d5 5. e5 c5 6. dc5! ♘c6 7. ♗b5 ♗g4 8. ♘bd2 ♕c7 9. 0–0 ♘h6 10. h3 ♗d7 11. ♗c6 bc6 12. ♘b3± Matulović–Rakić, Jugoslavija 1969 — 7/116; 5... f6!?

32 4. e5 c5! 5. f4 cd4 6. cd4 ♘c6 [6... ♘h6?! 7. ♗e2 0–0 8. ♘c3 ♘c6 9. ♗e3 f6 10. ♘f3 ♘f5 11. ♗f2 fe5 12. de5! d4 13. ♕b3 ♔h8 14. 0-0-0± Minić–Rakić, Beograd 1968 — 6/161] 7. ♘c3 h5 8. ♗b5 ♗g4 9. ♘ge2 e6 10. ♗e3 ♘ge7 11. ♕d2 a6 12. ♗d3 ♗f5!= Suetin–Spiridonov, Tbilisi 1970

33 **4... ♘f6** 5. ♗d3 0–0 6. ♘gf3 c5 7. 0–0 cd4 8. e5! ♘e8 9. cd4 ♘c6 10. h3 ♘c7 11. ♘b3 ♘e6 12. ♗e3± Šmit–Alburt, SSSR 1970; **4... ♘h6** 5. ♘gf3 0–0 6. ed5 ♘f5 7. ♗d3 ♕d5 8. 0–0 c5?! 9. ♗e4 ♕d6 10. d5 ♖d8 11. ♖e1 ♕c7 12. ♘c4± Scholl–Kurajica, Beverwijk 1969; 8... ♕d8±; **4... c5** 5. dc5 ♘f6 6. ed5 [6. ♗b5 ♗d7 7. ♕a4 de4!∓ Bakulin–Razuvajev, SSSR 1963] ♕d5 7. ♘b3! [7. ♘gf3 ♕c5 8. ♗e2 0–0 = Hennings–

Guljko, SSSR 1966 — 6/158] ♕d1 8. ♔d1 ±⊥; **4... c6** — B 12

34 6... ♘gf6? 7. ♗f7! ♔f7 8. ♘g5+−

35 7. ♘f6 ♘f6 [7... ef6 8. ♕b3 ♕e7 9. ♗e3±] 8. ♘f3 0−0 9. 0−0±

36 10. ♘f6 ef6! 11. 0−0 0−0 12 ♖e1 c6 13. ♗b3 ♗e6= Talj−Gufeljd, SSSR 1970 — 10/142

37 12. ♘d3⩲× e5

38 **5... ♗g4**? 6. ♘bd2 ♘c6 7. ♗c4 ♕f5 8. ♕b3± Zander−Carls, Hamburg 1921; **5... ♘h6**? 6. ♘bd2 0−0 7. ♗c4 ♕d8 8. ♕e2 ♘c6 9. ♘e4 ♘f5 10. 0−0 ♘d6 11. ♗b3 ±↑⊞ Adorjan−Spiridonov, Polanica Zdroj 1970 — 10/144

39 6. dc5?! ♕d1 7. ♔d1 ♘f6 8. ♗e3 0−0 9. ♘bd2 ♘g4∞̄ Nilsson−Gaprindašvili, Göteborg 1968 — 5/107

40 9... ♗d7? 10. 0−0 a6 11. ♗e2! ♗g4 [11... e6 12. d5!±] 12. d5! ♗f3 13. ♗f3 ♘e5 14. d6!± Suetin−Arnaudov, Albena 1970 — 10/143

41 12. ♘d5 ♕d5 13. ♕a4± Suetin

42 5... ♕g2?? 6. ♗f3+−

43 6... ♕d6 7. dc5! [7. d5 e6 8. c4⩲ Marić; 7. ♘e2!?] ♕c5 8. ♘e2±⟳↑

44 8... ♕b6 9. 0−0 ♘c6 10. ♘bc3!±⟳↑

45 **11... ♕b2**? 12. ♖b1 ♕a3 13. ♘b5+−; **11... ♘a6** 12. ♖c1±; **11... ♗d7** 12. ♖c1 ♘a6 13. ♗e5 ♖fd8 14. ♘f4 ♗c6 15. d5! ♗e8 16. ♕e2± Benkö−Ciocaltea, Malaga 1971 — 11/97

46 **4. ♗d3 e5** 5. ♘e2! ♘c6 6. 0−0 ♘ge7 7. f4! ed4 8. f5!∞̄→ Pomar−Ivkov, Palma de Mallorca 1966 — 2/118; 5... ♘f6!? 6. 0−0 0−0 7. f4 c6; **4... c6**! 5. f4 e5! 6. de5 [6. ♘f3 ♗g4 7. ♗e3 ♕b6! 8. ♕b3 ♗f3 9. ♕b6 ab6 10. gf3 ed4 11. cd4 ♘a6 12. ♘c3 ♘c7 13. a3 ♘f6 14. ♔f2 ♗h6!∓ Czerniak−Andersson, Göteborg 1971] de5 7. fe5 [Suetin−Csom, Berlin 1968 — 6/190] ♕h4! 8. g3 ♕e7 9. ♘f3 ♗g4= Uhlmann

47 4... e5 5. de5 ♗e5 6. ♘f3 [6. f4?! ♗g7 7. ♗c4 ♕e7 8. ♘d2 ♘f6 9. ♕c2 d5∓ Fritz−Winawer, Nürnberg 1883] ♗g7 7. ♗c4⩲

48 6. ♘bd2 e5 7. d5 0−0 8. h4 ♘b6 9. ♗e2 ♘e8 10. h5 f5 11. hg6 hg6 12. f3 f4 13. ♗f2 ♗f6!∓ Marco−Bardeleben, Hastings 1895

49 6... d5!? 7. ed5 [7. ♗d3 e5 8. ♘d2 0−0∓ Török−Adorjan, Hungary 1971; 7. ♗d5 ♘d5 8. ed5 ♘f6 9. c4 b5!∞̄] ♘b6△ ♘bd5=

50 12. ♗a2 b5 13. b4 c4= Kovačević−Meštrović, Jugoslavija (ch) 1967 — 3/137

51 **4... e6**?! 5. ♗d3 ♘e7 6. a4! ♘d7 7. 0−0 a5 8. ♘a3 0−0 9. ♘b5 e5 10. de5 de5 11. ♗e3±↑⟪ Benkö−Planinc, Novi Sad 1972 — 14/171; **4... b6** 5. ♗e3 ♗b7 6. ♘bd2 e5?! 7. de5 de5 8. ♗c4 ♘e7 9. ♕e2 0−0 10. h4! ♘d7 11. h5 ♘f6 12. hg6 ♘g6 13. 0-0-0± Steinitz−Mongredien, London 1863; **4... c6** 5. ♗g5 ♕a5 6. ♘bd2 ♘d7 7. ♗e2 ♘gf6 8. 0−0 ♘f8 9. ♖e1 ♘e6 10. ♗h4 ± Holmov−Csom, Budapest 1970 — 9/121; **4... ♘d7** 5. ♗d3 e5 6. 0−0 ♘gf6 7. a4 a5 8. ♖e1 0−0 9. h3 ♖e8 10. ♘a3 h6= Kozomara−Ivkov, Sarajevo 1968 — 5/120

52 **5. ♕c2** 0−0 6. ♗g5 c6 7. ♘bd2 h6 [7... b5? 8. a4! ba4 9. ♖a4 ♘bd7 10. b4 ♗b7 11. ♗a6!± Bronštejn−Perez, Amsterdam (izt) 1964] 8. ♗h4 [8. ♗e3 ♘bd7=] g5 9. ♗g3 ♘h5=; **5. ♘bd2** — B 07

53 6... ♘bd7!?

54 8. ♕b3? ♘e5 9. de5 ♘e4 10. e6 fe6 11. ♗e3 ♔h8 12. ♘d2 ♘d2 13. ♗d2 ♖f2!∓ Klaman−Ufimcev, SSSR (ch) 1947

55 8... c5?! 9. ♕b3±

56 Ufimcev

57 **4... c5**? 5. dc5 ♘f6 [5... dc5 6. ♕d8 ♔d8 6. e5±⊥] 6. cd6 ed6 7. e5! de5 8. ♕d8 ♔d8 9. fe5 ♖e8 10. ♘f3 ♘c6 11. ♗b5 ♗d7 12. ♗c6 ♗c6 13. 0−0 ♘g4 14. ♗g5 ♔c8 15. ♘bd2± Štejn−Suttles, Sousse (izt) 1967 — 4/142; **4... ♘d7** 5. ♘f3 e5 6. ♗c4 ♕e7 7. 0−0 ♘gf6 8. fe5 de5 9. b3! 0−0 10. ♗a3 c5 11. ♘bd2 b6 12. ♕e1 ♗b7 13. ♕h4± Hübner−Suttles, Palma de Mallorca (izt) 1970

58 5. ♘f3 ♗g4! [5... ed4?! 6. cd4 ♗g4 7. ♗e2 c6 8. 0−0 ♕b6 9. ♘bd2 ♗f3 10. ♖f3 ♕d4 11. ♔h1 ♘f6 12. ♖d3 ♘g4 13. ♖d4 ♘f2 14. ♔g1 ♘d1 15. ♖d6± Cejtlin−Nikolajevski, SSSR (ch) 1971 — 12/151] 6. de5 ♗f3 7. ♕f3 de5 8. ♗c4 ♘d7! 9. 0−0 ♘gf6 10. f5 ♕e7= Pogats−Budinszky, Hungary 1969 — 8/116

59 7. ♘f3? de5 8. ♘e5 ♘d7! 9. ♘d7 ♕e4 10. ♕e2 ♕e2 11. ♗e2 ♗d7∓ Veres−Adorjan, Hungary 1969 — 8/115

60 9. ♗e2 cd6 10. ♘a3 ♘c6 [10... ♗e6 11. ♘b5 ♔d7 12. f5 ♗d5! 13. ♗f3 ♗c6 14. ♘d4 ♗d4! 15. cd4 ♘e7= Portisch−Lahti, Raach 1969] 11. ♗e3 ♘f6 12. ♘b5 ♔e7 13. 0-0-0 ♘g4! 14. ♗g4 ♗g4 15. ♖d2 b6! 16. ♘e2 ♖hd8= Mednis−Forintos, Siegen (ol) 1970

61 10. ♗g2 ♘c6 11. ♘a3 ♗g4 12. ♘c4 0-0-0 13. ♘e3 ♗e6 14. 0−0 ♘ge7= Portisch−Yanofsky, Lugano (ol) 1968 — 6/186

62 13. ♗f4 ♘f6 14. ♘d6 ♘d5 15. 0-0-0 ♔e7 16. ♗g2± Portisch−Suttles, Siegen (ol) 1970

63 5... 0−0 6. ♘f3 c5 7. dc5 dc5 8. 0−0 ♘c6 9. e5 ♘d5 10. ♗e4± Ree−van Baarle, Nederland 1971 — 13/158

64 13. ♗b5 ♘f4 14. 0—0 0—0 ∞ Spaski—Olafsson, Moskva 1971 — 12/166

65 **7... e6**?! 8. 0—0 a6 9. a4 [9. ♕e1 ♘c6 10. ed6 ♕d6 11. ♘bd2! ♘ce7 12. ♘e4 ♕d8 13. ♗d2 b6 14. ♖d1 ♗b7 15. ♗b3± Larsen—Ujtelky, Copenhagen 1965] ♘c6 10. ♕e2 ♘ce7 11. ♗d3 ♗d7 12. a5±○ Bukić—Ujtelky, Beograd 1968 — 6/188; **7... c6** 8. a4 ♘a6 [8... a5 9. 0—0 ♘a6 10. ♕e2 ♘ac7 11. ♘a3 ♔h8 12. ♗d3 f6 13. ♘c4 ♗h6 (Bogdanović—Kotov, Soči 1967) 14. ♕e1!△ 14... ♘f4 15. ♗f4 ♗f4 16. ♕h4±] 9. 0—0 ♘ac7 10. ♕e1! f6 11. ♕h4 ♗e6 12. ♘a3 ♕d7 13. ♗d2 b5 14. ♗d3 ♘b6 15. ab5 cb5 16. ♖ae1 [Smejkal—Smislov, Hastings 1968/69 — 7/139] de5 17. fe5 a6± Gligorić

66 **8... ♘a6** 9. ♕e2 c5 10. e6 f5 11. d5 c4 12. ♗c4 ♘c7 13. 0—0 ♘bd5 Bogdanović—Ivkov, Jugoslavija (ch) 1967 — 3/121; 14. ♗b3±; **8... c5** 9. dc5 [9. 0—0 cd4 10. cd4 ♘c6 11. h3 ♘a5 12. ♗c2 ♘d5 13. ♕e1 b6∞ Kinnmark—Andersson, Göteborg 1971] dc5 10. ♕d8 ♖d8 11. ♗e3± Fridštejn

67 10. 0—0 cd4 11. cd4 ♘c6 12. ♘c3 ♗g4∓ van den Berg—Ivkov, Wijk aan Zee 1971 — 11/117

68 13. ef7 ♔h8 14. ♗c4 ♘c6=/∞ Ivkov

69 8... ♘b6 9. dc5 dc5 10. ♕d8±⊥ Ivkov

70 9... dc5 10. ♕d8 ♖d8 11. ♗e3±⊥; 10. 0—0!?

71 11. fe5? ♘d7 12. c6 bc6 13. ♗c6 ♖b8=/∞ Lehmann—Ivkov, Palma de Mallorca 1968 — 6/189

72 13. c6 bc6 14. ♗c6 ♖b8 15. ♗d7 ♖d7 16. 0—0±

73 8... ♗g4 9. 0—0 e6 10. ♕b3 ♗f3 11. ♖f3 ♘b6 12. ♗e2 ♕d5?! 13. ♗e3 ♕b3 14. ab3± Bronštejn—Nikolajevski, SSSR (ch) 1966/67 — 3/136; 12... ♘8d7!?△ c5 Petrosjan

74 **9. ♕b3**? ♘b6 10. dc5 ♘c4 11. ♕c4 ♗f5! 12. ♘d4 ♘c6!∓ Pytel—Balcerowski, Polska 1970 — 9/120; **9. dc5** ♗e6! [9... ♘c7? 10. ♕d8 ♖d8 11. ♘g5±] 10. ♘g5 [10. 0—0 ♕c7!△ 11. ♗d5 ♕c5∓; 10. ♗d5 ♕d5 11. 0—0 ♕c5 12. ♕d4 ♘a6∓⊕ Teschner—Keene, Berlin 1971 — 12/152] ♘c6! 11. 0—0 ♘e5 12. ♘e6 fe6 13. ♖f8 ♗f8∓; 10. ♕d4!?△ ♕h4 Keene

75 10. ♕d4 e6 11. ♗g5 ♘c6! 12. ♗d8 ♘d4 13. cd4 ♖d8= Konstantinopoljski—Kotov, SSSR 1967

76 **12. ♘g5**? ♘c3 13. ♘e6 ♘d1 14. ♘d8 ♖ad8 15. ♖d1 ♘d4—+; **12. ♗d3** ♖c8 13. ♘e2 ♕b6∓↑⊞ Scholl—Gaprindašvili, Wijk aan Zee 1969

77 **12... ♘a5**? 13. ♘g5 ♘b3 14. ♘e6 ♘c3 15. bc3 fe6 16. ♖f8 ♗f8 17. ab3± Nej—Saidy, Tallinn 1973 — 15/154; **12... h6**= Keres

78 **3... b6** 4. ♗e3 ♗b7 5. ♗d3 e6 6. ♕d2 d6 7. ♘ge2 ♘d7 8. 0—0 ♘e7 9. f4 0—0 10. f5± Steinitz—Blackburne, London 1862; **3... e6** 4. ♗e3 [4. f4 ♘e7 5. ♗e3 a6 6. ♘f3 b5 7. ♗d3 f5 8. e5 ♗b7 9. 0—0 Scholl—Ujtelky, Wijk aan Zee 1969 — 7/114; 9... 0—0±] d5 5. ♕d2 h6 6. 0-0-0 ♘e7 7. f3 a6 8. h4 b5 9. ♘ge2 ♗b7 10. ed5 ed5 11. h5 g5 [Kurajica—Ujtelky, Wijk aan Zee 1969 — 7/115] 12. g4±

79 4. ♘f3 d5 — B 15

80 **4... d5** 5. ed5 b5 6. ♗b3 b4 7. ♘ce2 [7. dc6? bc3 8. c7 ♕c7 9. ♕f3 ♘f6! 10. ♕a8 0—0 11. ♕f3 ♗b7 12. ♕c3 ♕c3 13. bc3 ♗g2 14. f3 ♗h1 15. ♔f2 e5!∓ Džindžihašvili—Gurgenidze, Tbilisi 1965; 7. ♘e4 cd5 8. ♘c5± Fridštejn] cd5 8. ♘f3± Ljubojević; **4... d6** 5. ♕f3 e6 6. ♘ge2 ♘d7 7. a4 a5 8. h4 ♘gf6 9. ♗a2 h5 10. ♗g5 [Ljubojević—Ciocaltea, Vršac 1971 — 12/165] ♕b6!?±; 10... ♕c7±; 5. ♘f3 ♘f6 — B 08

81 6. ♘a4 d6 7. ♘f3 ♘f6 8. e5 ♘d5 9. 0—0 0—0 10. h3± Ljubojević—Cardoso, Nice (ol) 1974 — 17/174

82 6... d5 7. ed5 [7. e5 a5!? 8. c3 ♕b6 9. ♘f3 ♗g4 10. ♘f4 e6 11. 0—0 ♘e7 12. h3 ♗f3 13. ♕f3 ♘d7 14. ♘d3!± Döry—Ermenkov, Bulgaria 1970] cd5 8. ♘f3± Ljubojević

83 13. h3 ♕c7 14. ♔h1 ♗b7 15. f5!± Georgadze—Radev, Tbilisi 1971 — 12/122

84 6. ♗d3 ♘h6 7. ♘f3 ♗f5 8. 0—0 ♘d7 9. ♘h4 e6 10. ♘f5 ♘f5 11. ♘e2 ♗f8 12. c3 c5 13. ♔h1± Krogius—Bronštejn, SSSR (ch) 1966/67 — 3/120; 7... ♗g4!=

85 8... h4 9. f5!±

86 9. ♗e3 ♕b6! [9... h4? 10. ♗d3 ♘e7 11. 0—0 ♘d7 12. ♗f2 ♘f5 13. ♘e2 ♕e7 14. b3 0-0-0 15. c4± Liberzon—Smislov, SSSR (ch) 1966/67] 10. 0-0-0 h4∓

87 13. c3 f6= Fischer—Petrosjan, Beograd 1970 — 9/154

88 7. ♕d2?! ♘g4 8. ♘f3 ♘e3 9. ♕e3 ♗g4 10. 0-0-0 e6 11. g3 ♘d7 12. h3 ♗f3 13. ♕f3 ♕b6 14. g4 0-0-0= Savon—Gurgenidze, Gori 1971 — 11/96

89 8... ♗f3? 9. ♗f3 e6 10. g3 ♘f5 11. ♗f2 ♘d7 12. ♕d2± Radulov—Bohosjan, Bulgaria (ch) 1971 — 11/161

90 **9. g3** ♘f5 10. ♗f2 h4! 11. ♖g1 ♗f8 12. ♘g5 ♗e2 13. ♘e2 hg3 14. hg3 [Radulov—Arnaudov, Bulgaria (ch) 1971 — 11/163] c5!∞; **9. 0—0** ♗f8 10. h3 ♘f5 11. ♗f2 ♗f3 12. ♗f3 h4 13. ♘e2 ♘d7 14. ♔h2 ♗e7 15. ♘g1 ♔f8= Klovan—Podgajec, SSSR 1974

91 10. 0-0-0? b5 11. h3 ♗f3 12. ♗f3 h4 13. ♘e2 ♘f5 15. ♔b1 ♘b6∓ Honfi—Gurgenidze, Kislovodsk 1968 — 6/159

92 13. ♗f3 ♗f8 [13... ♘b6 14. b3!; 13... h4 14. g4 ♘g3 15. ♖g1±] 14. ♘e2

♘b6 15. b3 a5 16. ♔f1 ♗e7 17. ♔g2± Radulov–Velikov, Bulgaria (ch) 1971 — 11/162

93 **4. ♗c4** ♘c6! 5. ♗e3 ♘f6 6. f3 0–0 7. ♘ge2 e6 8. ♗b3 b6 9. ♕d2 ♗a6 [Kristiansson–Keene, Reykjavik 1972 — 13/180] 10. h4∞ Keene; **4. ♗g5** h6 5. ♗h4 ♘c6 6. ♗b5 ♗d7 7. ♘f3 ♘f6 8. 0–0 0–0 9. e5 de5 10. de5 ♘g4 11. ♖e1 a6 12. ♗c6 ♗c6 13. ♗g3 h5= Zajcev–Guljko, SSSR 1974

94 **4... a6**?! 5. a4 ♘d7 6. g3 c5?! 7. dc5 ♘c5 8. ♗g2 ♘f6 9. 0–0 ♗d7 10. ♗e3± Buljovčić–Ivkov, Sombor 1968 — 6/198; **4... c6** 5. g3 e5 6. ♗g2 ♘e7 7. 0–0 0–0 8. a4!± Matulović–Czerniak, Bucuresti 1966 — 1/99; **4... ♘f6** — B 07

95 **5. ♘g3**!? e5 6. d5 ♘e7?! 7. ♗e2 0–0 8. h4± Matulović–Wibet, La Habana (ol) 1966 — 2/125; 6... ♘gf6!?∞; **5. ♗e3** e5 6. d5 ♘e7 7. g4! f5 8. gf5 gf5 9. ♖g1 0–0 [9... f4? 10. ♘f4!± Hetenyi–Glatt, Hungary (ch) 1972 — 13/176] 10. ♗h6 ♖f7∞ Florian

96 9. d5 ♘e7△ f5⇆»

97 13. ♗f3 ♘f3 14. ♔g2 ♘fe5 15. b3 ♖e8 16. ♕d2± Guljko–Muratov, SSSR 1974

98 **4... ♘c6** 5. d5 ♘b8 6. ♕d2 c5 7. ♗e2 a6 8. a4 ♕b6 9. ♖a2 ♕b4 10. f3 ♗c3 11. ♕c3 ♕c3 12. bc3±⊥ Volovič–Kotov, SSSR 1969 — 7/149; **4... e5** 5. de5 [5. ♘ge2 ♘f6 6. f3 ed4 7. ♘d4 0—0 8. ♗c4 a6 9. a4 ♘c6± Mohrlok–Lengyel, Varna (ol) 1962] ♗e5 [5... de5 6. ♕d8±⊥] 6. ♗d4±

99 **5. ♗e2** ♘d7 6. h4 h5 7. ♘h3 b5 8. ♕d2 ♗b7 9. f3 ♖c8 10. 0-0-0 c5 11. dc5 ♘c5 12. ♔b1 ♕c7 13. ♗d4 ♗d4 14. ♕d4 ♘f6= Espig–Ivkov, Raach 1969; **5. a4**!?

100 **7. a4** b4 8. ♘d1 ♖b8 9. a5! e5 10. d5 f5 11. ♖a4 b3 12. cb3 ♘gf6 [Balinas–Ivkov, Lugano (ol) 1968 — 6/203] 13. ♕c2!± Ivkov; **7. d5**!? Keene

101 11. a3 0–0 12. h4!? [12. 0–0?! ♕c7 13. ♖ac1 ♘b6∓ Jimenez–Keene, Camaguey 1974 — 17/175] ♘b6 13. h5 e5 14. ♗e3 d5 15. ed5 ♘bd5 16. ♗c5 ♘f4!∞ Cardoso–Keene, Nice (ol) 1974 — 17/176

102 13. ♘d5 ♘d5 14. ed5 0–0 15. f4 ♘d7 16. ♗g7 ♔g7 17. h4± Ciocaltea–Botterill, Hastings 1971/72 — 13/173

103 5. a4!?

104 5... ♘d7 6. a4!? [6. h4 h5 7. ♘h3 ♘h6 8. f3 e6 9. ♘f4 e5 10. de5 de5 11. ♘d3± Bogdanović–Milić, Jugoslavija (ch) 1955] f5 7. 0-0-0 ♕a5 8. ef5 gf5 9. ♗c4 b5 10. ab5 ♕a1 11. ♘b1± Westerinen–Suttles, Sombor 1970 — 10/167

105 **6. a4** b4 7. ♘a2 [7. ♘d1 a5 8. c3 bc3 9. bc3 ♘d7 10. ♖b1 ♘gf6 11. f3 0–0 12. c4 ♗a6∓ Augustin–Filip, ČSSR (ch) 1968] a5 8. ♗d3 ♗a6 9. ♘e2 ♘f6 10. ♗h6 0–0 11. ♗g7 ♔g7 12. 0–0 ♕b6 13. c3 c5= Klovan–Nikolajevski, SSSR 1967; **6. ♗d3** a5 [6... ♘d7 7. ♘f3 ♗b7 8. ♘e2 ♕c7 9. c3 e5= Toluš–Botvinik, SSSR 1965] 7. a3 ♗a6 8. ♘f3 ♘d7= Dueball–Hübner, BRD 1971 — 11/128; **6. f3** ♘d7 7. ♘h3 ♘b6 8. ♘f2 h5 [8... a5 9. ♗e2 ♘c4? 10. ♗c4 bc4 11. 0–0 h5 12. ♖ae1 ♖b8 13. d5 c5 14. e5!± Geler–Benkö, Lugano (ol) 1968] 9. ♗e2 a5 10. a4 b4 11. ♘d1 ♗e6 12. b3 [Ciocaltea–Suttles, Siegen (ol) 1970 — 10/170] ♘f6=

106 7. f3 ♘d7 8. ♘h3 ♘b6 9. b3 [9. ♘f2 a5 10. ♗d3 ♖b8 11. b3 ♗d7 12. ♘e2 a4∓ Mjagmarsuren–Suttles, Sousse (izt) 1967] ♕c7 10. ♗d3 a6 11. ♖d1 ♘f6 12. ♘g5 0–0 13. 0–0 c5 14. dc5 dc5 15. ♕f2∞ Radulov–Gurgenidze, Tbilisi 1965

107 **12... d5** 13. ♘g5 0–0∞ Radulov–Nikolajevski, Varna 1968 — 6/202; **12... 0—0** 13. ♗h6 ♕b6=

108 6... ♘f6!? 7. f3 ♕a5 — B 07

109 **7. ♘ge2**?! ♕a5!△ b4∓; **7. f3** ♘b6 8. h4 h5 9. ♘h3 a5 10. ♘f2 b4 11. ♘b1 ♖b8∞ Evans–Suttles, San Antonio 1972 — 14/181; **7. e5**!? d5 [7... de5 8. d5!] 8. h4 ♘b6 9. h5 gh5 10. ♘h3 f6 11. ♘f4 ♗g4 12. f3△ ♘h5± Kuprejčik–Pedersen, Teesside 1974; 7... b4!?∞

110 7... ♕a5!?

111 13. f3 ♘f6 14. ♗g5 ♕c7 15. ♖hh1± Štejn–Bronštejn, SSSR 1961

112 **4... c5** 5. dc5 ♗c3 6. bc3 dc5 7. ♕d8 ♔d8 8. ♗c4 e6 9. ♘f3 ♘f6 10. f5! ♘e4 11. ♘g5 ♘d6 12. fg6 hg6 13. ♗f4 ♖h4 14. ♗d6 ♖c4 15. ♘f7± Selivanovski–Gruzman, SSSR 1964; **4... ♘a6** 5. ♘f3 ♗g4 6. ♗e3 c6 7. h3 ♗f3 8. ♕f3 ♘c7 9. 0-0-0 d5 10. e5 ♕d7 11. g4± Gligorić–Ljubojević, Teesside 1972 — 13/175; **4... ♘f6** — B 09

113 5... ♘d7 6. ♗c4 e6 [6... b5? 7. ♗f7 +–] 7. a4 ♘e7 8. 0–0 0–0 9. ♗e3 d5 10. ♗d3± Honfi–Sandor, Wijk aan Zee 1969 — 7/150

114 6. a3 ♗b7 7. ♗e3 ♘d7 8. ♗d3 c5 9. e5!? cd4 10. ♗d4 ♗f3 11. ♕f3 de5 12. fe5 ♗e5 13. 0-0-0!=∞↑ Levy–Friedgood, Johannesburg 1972 — 13/178

115 **7. ♗e3** b4 8. ♘b1 ♘f6 9. ♘bd2 ♘bd7 10. h3 0–0 11. 0–0 c5= Dückstein–Ivkov, Bamberg 1968 — 5/132; **7. 0—0** ♘d7 8. e5 e6 [8... c5? 9. ♘g5! ♘h6 10. f5 cd4 11. fg6! dc3 12. gf7 +– I. Zajcev–Adamski, Polanica Zdroj 1970 — 10/165] 9. a4 b4 10. ♘e4 [Scholl–Keene, Nederland 1970 — 10/164] ♗e4 11. ♗e4 d5 12. ♗d3 ♘e7±; **7. a4** b4 8. ♘e2 ♘d7 9. c3 bc3 10. bc3 c5 11. ♖b1 ♖b8 12. 0–0 e6 13. f5± Ljubojević–Day, Canada (ch open) 1974; 8... ♘f6!?

116 **7... c5** 8. dc5 dc5 9. e5! ♘c6 10. ♗e3! ♘d4 11. ♘d4 cd4 12. 0-0-0± Talj–Szabo, Soči 1973 — 16/133; 12. ♖d1!± Talj; **7...**

♘f6 8. e5 de5 9. fe5 ♘d5 10. ♘g5!± Ljubojević—Panno, Palma de Mallorca 1972 — 14/201

117 8... c5? 9. ♘g5!△ e6±

118 13. ♗e3± Jansa—Vogt, Leipzig 1973 — 17/172

119 **5. ♘f3** ♗g4 6. ♗e3 ♗f3 7. gf3 d5 8. e5 e6 9. ♕d2 ♘ge7∓ Talžanov—Ufimcev, SSSR 1965; 6... e5!? Euwe; **5. d5** ♘d4 6. ♗e3 c5 7. dc6 ♘c6=

120 6. ♗e2 0—0 7. ♘f3 ♗g4 8. 0—0 ♘d7 9. h3 ♗f3 10. ♖f3 e5 11. de5 de5 12. f5 ♘d4 13. ♖f2± Kuijpers—Kotov, Amsterdam 1968 — 6/191; 9. e5!?

121 9... ♕d1 10. ♖d1±⊥○

122 13. ♗f6! ♕f6 14. ♘d5 ♘f3 [14... ♕d6 15. ♘d4 ed4 16. ♕g4!±] 15. ♕f3 ♕h4 16. ♔e2± Fischer—Udovčić, Rovinj-Zagreb 1970 — 9/127

123 **5. ♗e3** ♕b6 6. ♖b1 f5! 7. ♘f3 ♘d7 8. ef5 gf5 9. ♗d3 ♘df6 10. ♕e2 ♘h6 11. h3 [11. d5 c5 12. b4 ♘fg4!∓] ♗d7 12. 0—0 ♕c7 13. ♘g5 d5!∓ Judovič—Botvinik, SSSR 1966 — 1/92; **5. ♗c4**!? b5 6. ♗b3 b4 7. ♘a4 ♘f6 8. e5 ♘d5 9. ♘f3 ♘b6?! 10. 0—0 ♘a4 11. ♗a4 0—0 12. a3± Bronštejn—Juhtman, SSSR (ch) 1959; 9... 0—0±

124 5... ♘d7?! 6. ♗e2 e5 7. 0—0 ed4 8. ♘d4 ♕b6 9. ♗e3! ♕b2 10. ♕d2± Judovič—Borisenko, corr. 1964/65

125 6. ♗e2 ♕b6 [6... d5 7. ♗e3 de4 8. ♘e4 ♘d7 9. ♘e5 ♗e2 10. ♕e2 ♘gf6= Donner—Petrosjan, Bled 1961] 7. e5 ♘h6 8. ♘e4 0—0 9. c3 ♗f5 10. ♘f2 c5∓ Terentjev—Šapošnikov, SSSR 1961

126 **6... ♘d7** 7. h3 ♗f3 8. ♕f3 ♕a5 9. e5 d5 10. ♗d3± Fichtl—Czerniak, Bucuresti 1967; **6... d5** 7. e5 e6 8. h3 ♗f3 9. ♕f3± Matanović—Korčnoj, Erevan 1965

127 **7. ♕d2** ♗f3 8. gf3 ♘d7 9. ♗c4 [9. 0-0-0 ♕a5 10. ♔b1 b5 11. h4 ♘b6 12. b3 ♘f6 13. ♗h3 e6 14. ♕d3 ♖b8∓ Pavlov—Czerniak, Bucuresti 1966 — 1/91; 14. e5!?] e6 10. ♗b3 d5 11. ♘e2 ♕a6 12. f5 gf5 13. ef5 e5!∓ Murej—Alekseev, SSSR 1965; **7. ♖b1**!? ♗f3 8. ♕f3 ♗d4 9. ♘a4 ♕a5 10. b4 ♕a4 11. ♗d4=∞ Honfi—Vasjukov, Kislovodsk 1968 — 6/199

128 7... ♗f3 8. gf3 ♘d7 9. 0-0-0 ♕a5 [9... 0-0-0 10. ♗h3 ♔b8 11. f5± Hartoch—Czerniak, Amsterdam 1968] 10. ♔b1 b5 11. h4 b4 12. ♘e2 ♘gf6 13. ♘g3 0—0 14. h5 ±→» Ostojić—Kaplan, Sao Paulo 1973 — 16/132

129 13. ♘d2 e6 [13... f5 14. ♘e4 fe4 15. ♘c3 e6 16. ♕b3±⊥ Suetin—Gufeljd, Tbilisi 1969 — 8/125] 14. ♕b3 ♘d2 15. ♖d2 c5 16. ♕b6 ab4 17. g4±

130 **4... b6** 5. ♗c4 [5. ♗d3 ♗b7 6. ♗e3 e6 7. ♕d2 ♘d7 8. 0-0-0 ♘e7 9. h4 h5 10. ♘g5± Steinitz—de Vere, London 1866] e6 6. 0—0 ♘e7 7. a4 a6 8. ♖e1 h6 9. ♘e2 ♘d7 10. c3 0—0 11. ♘g3 ♗b7 12. ♗f4± Bednarski—Wibe, Skopje (ol) 1972 — 14/179; **4... ♘d7** 5. ♗c4 ♘b6 6. ♗b3 c6 7. a4 a5 8. ♘g5 ♘h6 9. ♕f3 0—0 10. h4!±→» Reshevsky—Yanofsky, Lugano (ol) 1968 — 6/201; 5... e6!?; **4... ♘c6** 5. h3 e5 6. d5 ♘ce7 7. g4!± Langeweg—Hübner, Wijk aan Zee 1971 — 11/126; **4... ♘f6** — B 08

131 **5. ♗g5** ♕b6 6. ♕d2 ♕b2 7. ♖b1 ♕a3 8. ♗c4 ♕a5 9. 0—0 e6 10. ♖fe1 a6 11. ♗f4± Talj—Tringov, Amsterdam (izt) 1964; 5... ♘f6 — B 08; **5. g3** ♗g4 6. ♗g2 ♕b6 7. d5 ♕b4 8. 0—0!± Feldman—Cejtlin, SSSR 1971 — 11/129; 7. ♘e2!? ♘f6 8. h3 Kotov

132 **5... b5** 6. a3 a6 7. 0—0 ♕c7 8. ♗e3 ♘d7 9. ♕d2 ♘b6 10. e5 d5 11. b3± Uusi—Gurgenidze, SSSR 1965; **5... ♗g4** — 4... ♗g4

133 6. 0—0 ♘h6 7. h3 0—0 8. ♗e3 f6 9. ♕d2 ♘f7 10. d5 f5 11. ef5 gf5 12. ♘d4± Benkö—Suttles 1964; 6... b5±

134 6... ♘h6 7. 0—0 0—0 8. ♖e1 ♔h8? 9. ♗f1 e5 10. h3 ♕c7 11. b3 ♖d8 12. a5 ♘f8 13. d5 c5 14. a6! b6 15. ♗b5± Matulović—Suttles, Palma de Mallorca 1970 — 10/171; 8... e5!?

135 10. e5 ♘g8 11. f4 ♘f8 12. g4 h5!∞ Benkö—Kurajica, Malaga 1970 — 9/125

136 12. ♘b1△ ♘c3± Kurajica

137 5. ♗e2 c6 6. h3 ♗f3 7. ♗f3 ♕b6 8. ♘e2 ♘f6 9. 0—0 ♘bd7 Meštrović—Benkö, Sarajevo 1967 — 3/139; 10. g3±⊞; 6. a4!?

138 5... c6 6. h3 ♗f3 7. ♕f3 ♕a5 8. 0-0-0 ♘d7 9. g4 ♘gf6 10. h4 h6 11. g5 ♘h5 12. e5 de5 13. ♗c4 e6 14. ♘e4 ♕c7 15. gh6 ♗h6 16. ♗h6 ♖h6 17. ♕e3 ♖h8 18. de5± Polugajevski—Bronštejn, SSSR (ch) 1959

139 6. ♗e2 e5! [6... e6 7. ♕d2!△ 0-0-0±] 7. d5 ♘ce7 8. ♘g1!± Tajmanov

140 9... ♖b8 [Gligorić—Robatsch, Moskva (ol) 1956] 10. e5! de5 11. de5△ 11... ♗e5 12. ♖d1±

141 13. 0—0 h6 14. ♗f6 ♗f6 15. ef6 ♕b2 16. c4 ♕d4 17. cd5 cd5 18. ♘c3± Smislov—Timman, Wijk aan Zee 1972

142 4. ♗e2 e6 5. c3 ♘d7 6. 0—0 ♘e7 7. ♘bd2 b6 8. a4 a6 9. ♖e1 ♗b7 10. ♗d3 0—0 11. ♘c4± Petrosjan—Spaski (m) 1966 — 1/86

143 **4... c5** 5. dc5! ♕a5 6. c3 ♕c5 7. ♕b3 e6 8. ♗e3 ♕c7 9. ♘a3 ♗d7 10. ♗f4 ♘e7 11. ♖d1 ♘c8 12. ♘d4± Euwe—Penrose, München (ol) 1958; **4... a6** 5. 0—0 e6 6. a4! ♘e7 7. ♗e3 0—0 8. ♕d2 d5 9. ♗d3± Trajković—Rakić, Jugoslavija 1968 — 5/124; **4... ♘c6** 5. 0—0 ♘f6 6. d5 ♘b8 7. e5 de5 8. ♘e5 0—0 9. ♘c3 ♘bd7 10. ♘f3 ♘e8 11. ♖e1± Hübner—Keene, Wien 1972 — 14/185; **4... e6** 5. ♗b3 d5 6. ♘bd2 ♘e7 7. 0—0 0—0 8. ♖e1

♘d7 9. c3 c5 10. e5 b5 11. ♘f1 a5 12. ♗c2 b4 13. h4!± Spaski–Ujtelky, Soči 1967 — 4/146; **4... c6** 5. ♗b3 b5 6. 0–0 ♘a6 7. c3 ♘f6 8. e5 ♘d5 9. ed6 ♕d6 10. ♘bd2 ♗f5 11. ♖e1 0–0 12. ♘e4 ♗e4 13. ♖e4± Ostojić–Smislov, Monte Carlo 1969 — 7/141; 5... ♘f6 6. ♕e2± — 4... ♘f6

144 **5. e5** de5 6. ♘e5 0–0 7. 0–0 [7. c3 ♘bd7!] ♘bd7 8. ♕e2 ♘e5 9. de5 ♘d5 10. ♘d2 c6 11. ♘f3 ♕c7 12. ♖e1 e6= Rauzer–Goldberg, SSSR (ch) 1940; **5. ♘bd2** 0–0 6. 0–0 ♘c6 7. e5 [Parma–Portisch, Skopje–Ohrid 1968 — 6/192] de5 8. de5 ♘d5= Portisch

145 **5... d5** 6. ed5! ♘d5 7. 0–0 ♘c6 [7... 0–0 8. ♗g5 ♘c6 9. c3± Jansa–Darga, Lugano (ol) 1968] 8. ♖d1 ♗g4 9. h3 ♗f3 10. ♕f3 e6 11. c3± Ribli–Forintos, Hungary (ch) 1971 — 12/153; **5... c6** 6. ♗b3 0–0 7. e5 [7. ♗g5 h6! 8. ♗h4 e5 9. de5 de5 10. ♘bd2 ♕c7 11. ♘c4 ♘h5 12. ♗g3 ♘f4∞ Matulović–Botvinik, Beograd 1970 — 9/123] de5 8. de5 ♘d5 9. 0–0 ♗g4 10. ♘bd2 ♘d7 11. h3 ♗f5 12. ♖e1 [Talj–Timman, Skopje (ol) 1972 — 14/183] ♘c5!? [Talj] 13. ♘c4 ♘b3 14. ab3±

146 **6. e5** de5 7. de5 ♘d5 8. 0–0 ♗g4 9. ♖d1 c6 10. ♘bd2 ♘d7 11. h3 ♗f5 12. ♘b3 ♘7b6 13. ♗d3 ♗d3 14. ♖d3 ♕c8= Ostojić–Benkö, Orense 1974; **6. h3** c5! 7. e5 ♘e8 8. c3 cd4 9. cd4 [Quinteros–Robatsch, Nice (ol) 1974 — 17/165] ♘c6 10. 0–0 de5 11. de5 ♘d4!= Quinteros; **6. ♘bd2** ♘c6 7. c3 e5 8. de5 ♘h5! [Jansa–Adorjan, Sombor 1972 — 14/173] 9. 0–0 de5 10. ♖d1= Adorjan

147 **6... ♗g4** 7. e5 ♘e8 [7... de5 8. de5 ♘fd7 9. e6 ♘e5 10. ef7 ♔h8 11. ♕e5! ♗e5 12. ♘e5 ♗f5 13. ♗d2!± Jansa–Gaprindašvili, Göteborg 1968 — 5/123] 8. ♖d1 ♘c6 9. ♗d5 ♕d7 10. ♗f4± Adorjan–Hort, Budapest 1973 — 15/156; **6... ♘fd7** 7. ♗g5! ♘c6 8. c3 ♕e8 9. ♘a3 a6 10. ♖ad1 e5 11. ♘c2 ♘b6 12. ♗b3± Židkov–Tringov, Varna 1973 — 15/157

148 **7... ♕c7** 8. e5 de5 9. de5 ♘d5 10. ♖e1 ♘a6 11. c3 ♘c5 12. ♗c2 b6 13. a3 a5 14. c4 ♗a6 15. ♘bd2 ♘f4 16. ♕e3± Talj–Gufeljd, Moskva 1972 — 13/161; **7... d5** 8. ♘bd2 b6 9. ed5! cd5 10. ♖e1 e6 11. ♘e5 ♘e8 12. ♘df3± Gufeljd–Planinc, Skopje 1971 — 12/155; **7... ♘a6** 8. ♖d1 ♘c7 9. e5 ♘fd5 [Ćirić–Hort, Krems 1967] 10. ♘bd2±

149 8... d5?! 9. c3 ♘bd7 10. e5 ♘e8 11. h3 ♗f3 12. ♘f3 ♘c7 13. h4!± Savon–Šamkovič, SSSR (ch) 1971 — 12/154

150 10. e5 ♘fd7 11. h3 ♗f3 12. ♘f3 e6 13. c4 [13. ♗g5 ♕b6 14. ♖a3 c5∓ Gipslis–Botvinik, SSSR 1963] ♘a6 14. ♗g5 ♕b6 15. ♗a2 ♘b4∓ Matanović–Botvinik, Beograd 1969 — 8/119

151 **6. 0–0** ♗g4! 7. c3 e5 8. ♗b5 ed4 9. cd4 0–0 10. ♗c6 bc6 11. h3 ♗d7 12. ♘c3 ♖e8 13. e5 ♘d5∓ Bihovski–Fedorov, SSSR 1974; **6. e5**!? de5 [6... ♘d7? 7. ♗f7! ♔f7 8. ♘g5 ♔e8 9. ♘e6 ♘d4 10. ♘g7 ♔f7 11. ♕c4±] 7. de5 ♘g4 8. ♗b5?! ♗d7 9. ♗f4 0–0 10. ♘c3 a6 11. ♗c4 b5!∓ Vasjukov–Ribli, Wijk aan Zee 1973 — 15/155; 8. e6!?∞; **6. h3** 0–0 7. ♘c3 e5 8. de5 de5 9. ♗e3 ♘d4! [9... ♕e7? 10. 0-0-0± Aljehin–Konsultanti, Montreal 1923] 10. ♗d4 ed4 11. 0-0-0 c5 12. e5 ♘e8 13. ♘e4 ♕c7∓; 10. ♕d3=

152 **7... e5** 8. de5 ♘e5 9. ♘e5 de5 10. ♗g5! ±; **7... ♗g4** 8. h3 ♗f3 9. ♕f3 e5 10. ♗b5 ed4 11. ♗c6 bc6 12. cd4 ♖e8 13. ♘c3±; 8. ♘bd2!?

153 9... c6 10. ♘bd2 cd5 11. ed5 ♘d7 12. ♗b3△ ♘d4, f4± Velimirović

154 13. ♘bd2 ♘a5 14. e5!± Rukavina–Adorjan, Sombor 1972 — 14/174; 13... ♗d7±; 13... ♔h8!?△ e5, ♘f4

B 07 — 1. e4 d6 2. d4 ♘f6

	3	4	5	6	7	8	9	10	11	
1	♘d2[1]	♘gf3	♗c4[2]	0–0[3]	c3[5]	de5	♘e5	♕e2	b4	=
	g6	♗g7	0–0	♘c6[4]	e5[6]	♘e5[7]	de5	♕e7	♘e8[8]	
2	...	...	♗e2	c3	0–0	♖e1[11]	de5[12]	♘e5	f3[13]	=
	...	...	0–0	♘c6[9]	♖e8[10]	e5	♘e5	♖e5		
3	♘c3	♗e3[15]	a4[17]	♕d2	f3	h4	de5	0-0-0		∞
	g6[14]	c6[16]	♗g7	0–0[18]	♘bd7	e5	♘e5	d5[19]		
4	...	♗c4	♕e2[20]	e5	♗d2	♗b3[23]	a4	de5	♘f3	∞
	...	♗g7	c6[21]	♘d5[22]	0–0	a5	de5	♘a6	♘c5[24]	
5	...	g3	♗g2	♘ge2[25]	0–0	de5[28]	♗g5[29]	♘d5	ed5	±
	...	♗g7	0–0	e5[26]	♘c6[27]	de5	♗e6[30]	♗d5	♘e7[31]	

1. e4 d6 2. d4 ♘f6 3. ♘c3 g6 4. ♗e2 ♗g7 5. h4[32]

	5	6	7	8	9	10	11	12	13	
6	. . . c5[33]	d5 0—0[34]	h5 b5	♗b5[35] ♘e4[36]	♘e4 ♕a5	♘c3 ♗c3	bc3 ♕b5	♗h6[37] ♖e8	hg6 fg6[38]	=
7	. . . . . .	dc5 ♕a5	♔f1[39] ♕c5	♗e3 ♕a5[40]	h5[41] gh5[42]	f3[43] ♘c6	♘h3 ♗h3	♖h3 0-0-0	♖g3 ♖hg8[44]	±
8	. . . ♘c6	h5[45] gh5[46]	♗e3[47] ♘g4	♖h5 ♘e3	fe3 e6	♕d2 ♗d7	0-0-0 ♕e7	♘f3 0-0-0	♖dh1 h6[48]	=

1. e4 d6 2. d4 ♘f6 3. ♘c3 g6 4. f3

	4	5	6	7	8	9	10	11	12	
9	. . . c6	♗e3 ♕b6[49]	♕c1[50] ♗g7[51]	♗d3[52] 0—0	♘ge2 ♕c7[53]	g4[54] e5	de5 de5	♘g3 b5[55]		∞
10	. . . . . .	. . . ♘bd7	♕d2 b5[56]	♘ge2[57] ♘b6[58]	b3 ♕c7[59]	g4 e5	♗g2 b4	♘d1 a5	0—0 c5[60]	=
11	. . . . . .	. . . . . .	. . . . . .	♘h3 ♗b7[61]	♗e2[62] e5[63]	0—0 a6	♖ad1 ♗g7	♘f2 0—0	de5 de5[64]	=
12	. . . ♗g7	♗e3[65] 0—0[66]	♕d2 ♘c6[67]	0-0-0 e5	d5 ♘d4[68]	♘ge2 c5	dc6 bc6	♘d4 ed4	♗d4 ♗e6[69]	±
13	. . . . . .	. . . . . .	. . . c6	h4[70] ♘bd7	♗h6 e5	de5 de5	0-0-0 ♕e7	h5 ♘h5	g4 ♘f4[71]	±

1. e4 d6 2. d4 ♘f6 3. ♘c3 g6 4. f3 ♗g7 5. ♗e3 c6 6. ♕d2

	6	7	8	9	10	11	12	13	14	
14	. . . ♕a5	♘ge2[72] ♘bd7[73]	♗h6 ♗h6	♕h6 b5	♘c1[74] ♕b6	♘b3 a5	a4 b4	♘d1 ♗a6	♘e3[75] ♖c8[76]	±
15	. . . . . .	. . . . . .	♘c1 b5	♘b3[77] ♕c7	♗h6![78] 0—0	h4 e5	h5 ♗h6	♕h6 ♘b6[79]		±
16	. . . ♘bd7	♘h3[80] ♕a5	♘f2 b5	♗e2 a6	0—0 ♗b7[81]	♗h6 0—0	♗g7 ♔g7	f4 ♖ad8	♔h1 e5[82]	±
17	. . . . . .	. . . b5	♘f2[83] a6	♗e2 ♕c7	0—0 0—0	♗h6[84] c5[85]	♗g7 ♔g7	d5 ♗b7	a4 b4[86]	=
18	. . . . . .	g4 h6[87]	♘ge2 b5	♘g3 ♘b6	b3 a5	a4 b4	♘ce2 ♗a6	♖d1 ♕c7	h4 e6[88]	±
19	. . . b5	0-0-0[89] ♕a5[90]	♔b1[91] ♘bd7[92]	♗h6 ♗h6	♕h6 ♘b6[93]	♘h3[94] ♗h3[95]	♕h3 ♘a4[96]	♘a4[97] ba4	♕h6 a3[98]	=
20	. . . . . .	♘ge2 ♘bd7	♘c1[99] ♘b6	♗h6 0—0	♗g7 ♔g7	a4 b4	♘d1 a5	♘e3 c5	dc5 dc5[100]	=
21	. . . . . .	♗d3 ♘bd7	♘ge2[101] a6[102]	a4 ♗b7	0—0 0—0	♔h1 ♕c7	♘g3 e5	de5 de5	♕f2 ♖fe8[103]	=
22	. . . . . .	♗h6 ♗h6	♕h6 ♘bd7[104]	♗d3[105] e5[106]	de5 de5	0-0-0 ♕e7	♘ge2 a6	♔b1 ♗b7	♘c1 ♘c5[107]	=

	1. e4 d6 2. d4 ♘f6 3. ♘c3 g6 4. ♗g5								
	4	5	6	7	8	9	10	11	12	
23	. . . h6	♗e3[108] c6[109]	f3 ♗g7	♕d2 ♕a5	♘ge2[110] b5	g3 ♘bd7	♗g2 ♗b7	0—0 a6	a3 ♕c7[111]	±
24	. . . c6	♕d2[112] b5[113]	♗d3 h6[114]	♗e3 ♘g4	♗f4 e5	de5 de5	♗g3 h5	♘f3 h4[115]	♗e5 ♘e5[116]	±
25	. . . ♘bd7	f4 h6[117]	♗h4 ♘h5	f5[118] ♗g7	fg6[119] fg6	♗c4 c5	♘ge2 ♘b6	♗b5 ♗d7	0—0 ♗b5[120]	∞
26	. . . ♗g7	♕e2 h6[121]	♗h4 c6	0-0-0 ♘h5[122]	♕f3 ♕c7	♔b1 ♘d7	g4 ♘hf6	g5 hg5	♗g5 ♘b6[123]	=
27	. . . . . .	e5 ♘fd7[124]	f4[125] f6[126]	ef6 ef6	♗h4 0—0	♗c4 ♔h8	♘ge2 ♘c6	0—0 ♘b6	♗b3 d5![127]	=
28	. . . . . .	f4 h6[128]	♗h4 c5	e5 ♘h5	dc5[129] ♘f4[130]	ed6 g5	♗f2 0—0	g3[131] ♘g6	♕d2 ed6[132]	∞
29	. . . . . .	♕d2 h6[133]	♗e3[134] ♘g4	♗f4 e5[135]	de5 ♘e5	0-0-0 ♘bc6	h3[136] g5[137]	♗e3 f5	f4 gf4[138]	=
30	. . . . . .	. . . . . .	♗f4 g5[139]	♗g3[140] ♘h5	0-0-0[141] c6[142]	♗c4 ♕a5	♗b3 b5	♔b1 ♘d7	f4[143]	±
31	. . . . . .	. . . c6	f4[144] 0—0[145]	♘f3[146] b5	♗d3[147] ♗g4[148]	f5 b4	♘e2 ♘bd7	0—0 c5	c3 bc3[149]	∞

¹ **3. f3** ♘bd7 [3. . . e5? 4. de5 de5 5. ♕d8 ♔d8 6. ♗c4± Ivkov—Donner, Wijk aan Zee 1968; 3. . . c5 4. d5 g6 5. c4 b5∞ Korčnoj—Parma, Palma de Mallorca 1969; 4. c3! ♘bd7 5. ♗e3 e6 6. ♗d3 ♗e7 7. ♘e2± Spaski—Jansson, Göteborg 1971 — 13/179] 4. c4△ ♘c3 — E; **3. ♗d3** e5 [3. . . g6 4. ♘f3 ♗g7 5. 0—0 0—0 6. c3 ♘c6 7. ♘a3 ♖e8?! 8. ♗g5± Andersson—Jansson, Sverige 1969; 4. f4 ♗g7 5. ♘f3 0—0 6. 0—0 (Bisguier—Larsen, Zagreb 1965) ♘c6 7. c3△ e5±] 4. c3 g6 5. f4 — B 06

² 5. c3 0—0 6. ♗d3 [6. h3 b6 7. ♗c4 e6 8. 0—0 ♗b7 9. ♕e2 c5 10. dc5 bc5= Simagin—Bronštejn, SSSR 1967] ♘c6 [6. . . ♘bd7 7. 0—0 e5 8. ♖e1 c6 9. a4 a5 10. ♕c2 ♕c7 11. b3± Karpov—Kirilov, SSSR 1971] 7. 0—0 e5?! 8. de5 ♘e5 9. ♘e5 de5 10. ♘c4! [10. ♕e2 ♗h6= Andersson—Hartston, Hastings 1972/73 — 15/161] ♘d7 [10. . . ♘h5!?] 11. b4 ♖e8 12. ♗c2= Benkö—Jansa, Siegen (ol) 1970 — 10/158; 7. . . ♘d7!=

³ 6. ♕e2 ♘c6 [6. . . c6 7. ♗b3 ♗g4 8. e5 de5 9. de5 ♘d5 10. 0—0 ♘d7 11. h3 ♗f5 12. ♖e1 Talj—Timman, Skopje (ol) 1972 — 14/183; 12. . . ♘c5=] 7. c3 e5 8. de5 ♘h5! 9. g3 ♘e5 10. ♘e5 ♗e5 11. ♘f3 ♗g7 12. ♗g5 ♕e8 13. ♘d2 a6∓ Jansa—Adorjan, Sombor 1972 — 14/173; 9. 0—0 de5 10. ♖d1=

⁴ 6. . . c6 7. ♗b3 d5 [7. . . ♘bd7 8. ♖e1 e5 9. ♘c4± Smejkal—Sznapik, Polanica Zdroj 1972 — 15/160; 7. . . ♕c7 8. e5 de5 9. de5 ♘d5 10. ♖e1 ♘a6 11. a3 ♘c5 12. ♗a2 ♖d8 13. ♕e2 b5 14. ♘e4± Talj—Kärner, Tallinn 1973 — 16/126; 7. . . ♘a6 8. c3 ♘c7 9. e5 ♘fd5 10. ♖e1 b5 (Minić—Hort, Vinkovci 1968 — 6/204) 11. h3±; 7. . . ♗g4 8. ♕e2 d5 9. c3 ♘bd7 10. e5 ♘e8 11. h3± Savon—Šamkovič, SSSR 1971 — 12/154] 8. ♕e2 [8. e5 ♘e8 9. ♖e1 ♘c7 10. ♘f1 f6 11. ef6 ef6 12. ♗f4 ♘ba6= Smejkal—Popov, Smederevska Palanka 1971] a5 [8. . . b6 9. ed5 cd5 10. ♖e1 e6 11. ♘e5± Gufeljd—Planinc, Skopje 1971 — 12/155] 9. c3 ♘a6 10. ♖e1 e6 11. e5± Šabanov—Lejn, SSSR 1973

⁵ 7. e5 [Parma—Portisch, Skopje 1968 — 6/192] de5 8. de5 ♘d5=

⁶ 7. . . ♗g4 8. ♖e1 e5 9. h3 ♗f3 10. ♘f3 ed4 11. ♘d4 ♘e4 12. ♖e4 d5 13. ♗g5! ♕g5 14. ♘f3± Hort—Larsen, Copenhagen 1965

⁷ 8. . . de5 9. ♕c2 [9. ♖e1 a6 10. a4 ♘h5 11. ♘f1 ♕d1 12. ♖d1 ♗g4 (Trifunović—Botvinik, Nordwijk 1965) 13. ♘e3 ♗f3 14. gf3 ♘f4 15. ♘d5=] ♕e7 10. a4 ♘h5 11. b4 ♘d8 12. b5 ♕f6∞ Adžemjan—Raškovski, SSSR 1963

⁸ 12. a4 ♘d6 13. ♗b3 ♗e6= Kirov—Bılek, Varna 1970

⁹ **6. . . ♗g4** 7. 0—0 e6 8. ♕b3 ♕c8 9. h3 ♗f3 10. ♗f3 ♘c6 11. e5± Gipslis—Gufeljd, SSSR 1970; **6. . . c6** 7. 0—0 ♗g4 [7. . . ♘bd7 8. ♖e1 ♕c7 9. ♗f1 b5 10. a4± Gipslis—Barczay, La Habana 1971; 9. . . e5 10. a4 ♖e8 11. a5 ♖b8 12. ♘c4± Geler—Ree, Wijk aan Zee

1969 — 7/152; 10... d5 11. de5 ♘e5 12. ♘e5 ♕e5 13. ed5 ♕d5 14. ♗c4 ♕a5 15. ♘b3 ♕c7 16. ♕f3± Karpov—Vogt, Stockholm 1969] 8. a4 ♘bd7 9. h3 ♗f3 10. ♗f3 ♕c7 11. ♖e1 ♖fe8 12. ♘c4 d5 13. ed5 cd5 14. ♘e5± Ree—Benkö, Canada 1971; **6... ♘bd7** 7. 0—0 e5 8. ♖e1 [8. de5 de5 9. ♖e1 b6 10. ♗f1 ♗b7 11. ♕c2 ♖e8 12. b4± Tatai—Ivkov, Venezia 1969; 8... ♘e5 — 6... ♘c6] ♖e8 9. ♗f1 b6 10. a4 [10. ♗b5 ♗b7 11. de5± Gipslis—Planinc, SSSR — Jugoslavija 1972] a5 11. ♗b5± Torre—Suttles, Skopje (ol) 1972 — 14/184; **6... c5** 7. dc5 dc5 8. 0—0 b6 [8... ♘c6 9. ♕c2 b6 10. ♘c4 ♗b7 11. a4 ♕c7 12. ♖e1 ♘a5 13. ♗f1 ♘c4 14. ♗c4± Petrosjan—Mecking, Palma de Mallorca 1969 — 8/114] 9. ♕c2 ♗b7 10. ♖e1 ♘bd7 11. a4 ♕c7 12. h3 ♖ad8 13. ♗c4 ♘h5 14. ♘f1 ♘e5= Benkö—Westerinen, Netanya 1971; **6... b6** 7. 0—0 e6 [7... ♗b7 8. ♕c2 c5 9. d5 ♘bd7 10. ♖e1 ♘e5 11. ♘e5 de5 12. a4± Benkö—Lehmann, Las Palmas 1972] 8. ♖e1 ♗b7 9. ♗d3 c5= Filip—Bronštejn, Moskva 1967 — 3/142

10 **7... e5** 8. de5 [8. ♖e1 h6? 9. de5 de5 10. b3 ♖e8 11. ♕c2 b6 12. a4± Gipslis—Ozsvath, Lublin 1969 — 8/128; 8... ♖e8 — 7... ♖e8] ♘e5 9. ♘e5 de5 10. ♕c2 [10. a4 a5 11. ♖e1 b6 12. b3 ♗b7 13. ♗a3 ♖e8 14. ♗b5± Kärner—Talj, SSSR 1972 — 14/182; 11... ♗h6] ♗h6 [10... ♗e6 11. ♘f3 ♘d7 12. ♘g5± Larsen—Quinteros, Las Palmas 1974] 11. ♖d1 ♕e7 12. ♘c4 ♗c1 13. ♖ac1 b6 14. ♖d2 ♗b7 15. ♗f3 ♖fd8= Fuchs—Matulović, Kapfenberg 1970; **7... ♘d7** 8. a4 [8. b4!?] e5 9. de5 ♘ce5 10. ♘e5 ♘e5 11. ♘c4 ♖e8= Furman—Petrosjan, SSSR (ch) 1969

11 8. e5!? Šamkovič

12 **9. ♗f1** ed4 10. ♘d4 [10. cd4 ♗g4∓] ♘d4 11. cd4 c5 12. d5 a6 13. a4 ♗d7∓ Cobo—Ghizdavu, Timisoara 1972 — 13/160; **9. d5** ♘b8 10. ♗f1 c6 11. dc6 ♘c6 12. ♗c4 [12. ♘c4!?] h6 13. h3 [Geler—Parma, Siegen (ol) 1970 — 10/172] ♗e6∓

13 **11. f4** ♖e7! 12. ♗f3 ♕e8∓ Joita—Ghinda, Romania 1970; **11. f3**=

14 **3... c6** 4. ♘f3 [4. f4!?] ♗g4 5. h3 ♗h5 6. ♗e2± Foltys—Puc, Wien 1949; **3... e5** 4. de5±

15 **4. ♗f4** ♗g7 [4... c6 5. ♘f3 ♗g7 6. ♕d2 b5?! 7. ♗d3 ♗g4 8. ♗h6 ♗h6 9. ♕h6± Beniš—Kubiček, Olomouc 1973; 6... ♕a5!?△ ♘bd7] 5. ♕d2 0—0 [5... ♘c6 6. d5 e5 7. dc6 ef4 8. ♗b5 0—0 9. ♘ge2 a6∓ Schmid—Botvinik, Hamburg 1965; 6. 0-0-0!?] 6. 0-0-0 ♘c6 7. ♗b5 ♘a5 8. ♗e2 [8. h4!?] ♘g4 9. ♗g4 ♗g4 10. f3 ♗d7 11. h4 ♘c4∓ Grabczewski—Smislov, Polanica Zdroj 1968 — 6/205; **4. ♘ge2** ♗g7 5. ♘g3 0—0△ c5∞; **4. h4** ♗g7 5. ♗e2 — 4. ♗e2

16 4... ♗g7 5. ♕d2 ♘g4 6. ♗g5 h6 7. ♗h4 c6 8. 0-0-0 0—0 9. f4 b5 10. ♔b1 b4 11. ♘ce2 ♘a6 12. e5± Svešnikov—Guljko, SSSR 1972

17 **5. ♕d2** b5 6. ♗d3 ♘bd7 7. ♗h6 ♗h6 8. ♕h6 ♗b7 9. ♘f3 e5! [9... ♕c7?! 10. 0—0± Planinc—Parma, Jugoslavija (ch) 1969] 10. 0—0 a6 11. ♖ad1 ♕e7 12. ♖fe1 ♘g4= Corden—Botterill, England 1970/71; **5. f3** — 4. f3

18 6... ♘g4 7. ♗g5 h6 8. ♗h4 a5 9. ♗c4 ♘f6 10. f3 g5 11. ♗f2 d5∞ Westerinen—Timman, Amsterdam 1970; 8... ♕b6!?

19 Westerinen—Parma, Netanya 1971 — 11/132

20 **5. f4** — B 09; **5. ♘f3** — B 08

21 **5... ♘c6** 6. e5 [6. ♗e3 ♘e4=] ♘d4 7. ef6!?±; **5... e5** 6. de5 de5 7. ♗g5 0—0!∞

22 6... de5 7. de5 ♘d5 8. ♘f3 ♗g4 9. 0—0 0—0 10. ♕e4 ♗f3 11. ♕f3 e6 12. ♖e1 ♘d7 13. ♕g3 ♕c7= Klovski—Gufeljd, SSSR 1968 — 6/207; 8. ♗d2!△ 0-0-0±

23 8. 0-0-0!?

24 12. ♗d5 cd5 13. ♗e3 ♘e4∞ Tan—Smislov, Petropolis (izt) 1973

25 6. ♘f3 ♘bd7 7. 0—0 e5 8. h3 b6 [8... c6 9. ♖e1 ♕c7 10. ♗e3 b5 11. a3 a6 12. ♔h2 ♗b7∓ Pfleger—Ljubojević, Olot 1972; 9. a4 a5 10. ♖e1 ♕c7 11. ♗g5 h6 12. ♗e3 ♖e8 13. ♕d2 ♔h7 14. ♖ad1± Pollak—Platzak, BRD 1967 — 4/143] 9. de5 de5 10. ♕c2 c6 11. ♖d1 ♖e8 12. ♗e3 ♗f8= Etruk—Borisenko, SSSR 1966; 6... c5! 7. 0—0 cd4 8. ♘d4 — B 70

26 6... ♘bd7 7. 0—0 c5 [7... c6 8. a4 ♕c7 9. a5 ♖b8 10. ♖e1 b5 11. ab6 ab6 12. d5 e5 13. dc6 ♕c6 14. ♘f4± Bednarski—Saidy, Lublin 1973] 8. dc5 [8. h3 a6 9. ♗e3 ♕c7 10. f4? cd4 11. ♗d4 e5 12. ♗e3 b5∓ Pavlenko—Cejtlin, SSSR 1971; 10. dc5 ♘c5 11. ♘f4±] ♘c5 9. ♗e3 ♗d7 10. a4 ♗c6 11. f3 b6 12. ♕d2 ♕d7 13. b3 ♖fd8 14. ♖ad1 a6 15. ♘f4 e6 16. ♘d3 ♕c7 17. ♗g5± Dely—Ljubojević, Pula 1971

27 7... c6 8. a4 [8. h3 ♘bd7 9. ♗e3 ♖e8 10. f4 ef4 11. ♗f4 ♘b6 12. ♕d3± Fajbisovič—Cejtlin, SSSR 1970] a5 9. h3 ♖e8 [9... ♕c7 10. b3 ♘a6 11. ♗b2 ♖e8 12. ♕d2 ♗d7 13. ♖fe1 ♖ad8 14. ♖ad1 ♗c8 15. ♕c1 ed4 16. ♘d4 ♘c5 17. ♕a1± Kogan—Karasev, SSSR 1969] 10. ♗g5 [10. ♗e3 ♘bd7 11. b3?! ♕c7 12. ♕d2 b6 13. ♖fe1 ♗a6 14. ♖ad1 ♖ac8 15. ♗h6 b5∓ Zichichi—Hort, Venezia 1971 — 12/167; 11. f4!?] ♘bd7 11. ♕d2 ♕c7 12. ♖ad1 ♘b6 13. b3 ed4 14. ♘d4 d5 15. ♗f6± Hübner—Donner, Skopje (ol) 1972

28 8. h3? ed4 9. ♘d4 ♘e4∓ Buljovčić—Matulović, Sombor 1968 — 6/206

29 9. ♕d8?! ♖d8 10. ♗g5 ♗e6 11. ♘d5 [11. f4? ef4 12. ♘f4 ♗c4 13. ♘d3 ♘g4 14. ♗d8 ♖d8⩱ Cobo—Andersson, Camaguey 1974 — 17/178] ♗d5 12. ed5 ♘d4=

30 9... ♕d1 10. ♖ad1 ♗g4 11. h3 ♗e2 12 ♘e2 h6 13. ♗e3±⊥⊡

31 12. c4± Andersson

32 5. g4 c5 6. g5 ♘fd7 7. d5 a6 8. h4 b5 9. h5 ♕a5∓ Katalimov–Etruk, SSSR 1966; 5... ♘c6!?

33 5... h5 [5... ♘bd7 6. ♗e3 e5 7. ♕d2 h5 8. 0-0-0± Gufeljd–Tokarev, SSSR 1959; 5... c6 6. h5 gh5 7. ♗h5 ♘h5 8. ♖h5 ♕b6 9. ♘ge2 ♗g4 10. ♖g5± Nurmamedov–Nikolajevski, SSSR 1965; 6... b5 7. h6±] **6. ♘h3** ♘c6 [6... c5 7. dc5 ♕a5 8. ♘g5±; 6... c6 7. ♘g5 0–0 8. 0–0 e5 9. de5± Bhend–Plater, Moskva (ol) 1956; 6... 0–0 7. ♘g5 ♘c6 8. ♗e3 e5 9. d5 ♘e7 10. ♕d2 c6∞ Nurmamedov–Kärner, SSSR 1969; 9... ♘d4 — 6... ♘c6] 7. ♘g5 [7. ♗e3 0–0 8. ♕d2 e5 9. d5 ♘d4 10. f3 c6∓ Lombard–Keene, Wien 1972] 0–0 8. ♗e3 e5 9. d5 ♘d4∓ Wade–Smislov, La Habana 1965; **6. ♗g5** ♘c6 [6... c6 7. ♕d2 ♕a5 8. ♘h3± Fridštejn; 7... ♕c7!?] 7. ♕d2 a6 [7... ♘h7△ e5!?] 8. 0-0-0 b5 9. e5± Beni–Garcia, Tel Aviv (ol) 1964; **6. ♗e3** ♘c6 — 5... ♘c6

34 6... h5 7. ♗g5 [7. ♘h3 ♘a6 8. ♘g5 ♘c7 9. 0–0 0–0 10. a4 e6 11. de6 ♘e6 12. ♗c4 ♘d4∞ Kapengut–Tukmakov, SSSR 1962; 7... ♘bd7 8. f4?! ♘g4! 9. ♕d3 ♘df6∓ Spaski–Juhtman, SSSR 1959] a6 [7... ♕a5 8. f3 ♘bd7 9. ♘h3 a6 10. a4 ♘e5 11. 0–0 ♕b4∞ Čistjakov–Kremenecki, SSSR 1968] 8. a4 ♕a5 9. ♗d2 ♘bd7 10. ♘h3 ♘e5= Nežmetdinov–Šamkovič, SSSR 1967

35 8. hg6 b4 9. gh7 ♔h8 10. ♘b1 ♘e4∞̄ Wade–N. Littlewood, England 1964

36 8... ♕a5 9. ♗d2 ♘e4 10. ♘e4 ♕b5 11. ♗c3 ♗c3 12. ♘c3 ♕b2 13. ♘ge2 ♗f5∞ Cvetkovič–Črepinšek, Jugoslavija 1970 — 9/128

37 12. ♘h3 ♕c4!∓ Fridštejn

38 14. ♖h4 ♘d7 15. ♘f3 ♖b8 16. ♕d2 ♗a6 17. c4 ♕b4= Mesing–Gipslis, Riga 1968

39 **7. ♗d2** ♕c5 8. h5 0–0 9. ♘h3 ♗h3 10. ♖h3 ♘c6∓ O'Kelly; **7. cd6** ♘e4 8. de7 ♘c3 9. bc3 ♗c3 10. ♔f1 ♗a1?! 11. ♗g5 ♘c6 12. ♕a1∞̄ Dobrev–Tringov, Varna 1970 — 9/129; 9... ♘c6!∓

40 8... **♕b4**? 9. a3 ♕b2 10. ♗d4+–; **8... ♕c7** 9. h5 ♖g8 10. h6 ♗h8 11. ♘h3 a6 12. ♘f4± Trapl–Pachman, ČSSR (ch) 1963

41 9. ♘h3 ♗h3 10. ♖h3 h5∓

42 **9... ♘c6** 10. h6 ♗f8 11. ♘d5± Mikenas–Bivšev, SSSR 1956; **9... 0–0** 10. hg6 hg6 11. ♕d2 ♖e8 12. ♗h6 ♗h8 13. ♕f4 ♗e6 14. ♕h4 ♘bd7 [Meštrović–Matulović, Sarajevo 1969] 15. ♗f8!?±

43 10. ♗h5 ♘c6 11. ♗e2 h5 12. f3 ♗e6 13. ♘h3 d5 14. ed5 ♗d5 15. ♘f4 0-0-0 16. ♕e1 e5∓ Maslov–Koc, SSSR 1962; 11... ♗e6!?△ 0-0-0, d5∓

44 14. ♖g5 ♕c7 15. ♘d5± Mesing–Rukavina, Sarajevo 1971

45 **6. d5** ♘e5△ c6∓; **6. ♗e3 h5** 7. f3 [7. ♕d2 e5 8. d5 ♘d4 9. f3 c5 10. ♘d1 ♗d7 11. c3 ♘e2 12. ♘e2 ♘g8 13. ♘f2 f5 14. ♗g5 ♗f6 15. 0-0-0 f4∞ De Greif–Donner, Cienfuegos 1973] e5 [7... a6? 8. ♘h3 b5 9. ♕d2 ♗d7 10. ♘g5± Banik–Barstatis, SSSR 1962] 8. d5 ♘d4∞; **6... e5** 7. de5 [7. d5 ♘d4 8. ♗d4 ed4 9. ♕d4 0–0 10. ♕d2 ♖e8 11. f3 ♘h5 12. g4 ♘g3 13. ♖h3 ♘e2 14. ♘ge2 c5 15. 0-0-0 ♕a5∓ Keres–Bouwmeester, Hag 1962; 11... c6 12. 0-0-0 cd5 13. ♘d5 ♘d5 14. ♕d5 ♕f6 15. c3 ♗e6∓ Kirov–Pytel, Lublin 1971] ♘e5 8. f3 ♗e6 9. ♕d2 ♘h5 10. ♗f2 0–0 11. 0-0-0 b5∞ Holaszek–Jansson, Siegen (ol) 1970 — 10/173

46 6... ♘h5 7. ♗h5 gh5 8. ♗e3 e5 [8... ♗d7 9. ♘ge2 e6 10. ♖h5 a6 11. ♕d2± Thorbergsson–Jansson, Siegen (ol) 1970] 9. ♘ge2 ed4 10. ♘d4 ♘e5 11. ♖h5 ♗e6 12. ♕e2 ♕d7 13. ♘f5± Klaman–Kotov, SSSR 1956

47 7. f3△ ♘h3!?

48 14. ♘h2 ♖dg8 15. ♗f3 ♕f8 16. ♕f2 ♗e8= Sax–Simić, Vrnjačka Banja 1974 — 17/179

49 5... b5?! 6. e5 b4 [6... ♘fd7 7. f4±] 7. ef6 bc3 8. bc3 ef6 9. ♗d3 ♗g7 10. ♘e2 0–0 11. 0–0 ♖e8 12. ♕d2 d5 13. ♖fe1 ♗e6 14. ♘f4± Lejn–Bastrikov, SSSR 1963

50 **6. a3** ♗g7 7. ♗c4 d5 8. ed5 cd5 9. ♗d5 ♕b2 10. ♘ge2 ♕b6 11. ♗b3 0–0 12. 0–0 ♘c6= Žuhovicki–Gufeljd, SSSR 1970; **6. ♕d2** ♕b2 7. ♖b1 ♕a3 8. ♗c4 ♘bd7 9. ♘ge2 ♗g7 10. 0–0 0–0 11. g4 e5?! [11... d5? 12. ♖b3±] 12. d5∞̄ Albano–Moliger, Ybbs 1968; 11... ♕a5!?∞

51 6... ♘bd7 7. ♗c4 ♕a5?! 8. ♕d2 b5 9. ♗b3 ♗g7 10. ♘ge2 0–0 11. 0–0 ♕c7 12. ♗h6 ♗h6 13. ♕h6 b4 14. ♘d1 c5 15. c3± Kislov–Cejtlin, SSSR 1970

52 7. ♘ge2 0–0 8. ♘f4 ♘fd7!? [8... ♕a5 9. ♗e2 e5 10. de5 de5 11. ♘d3 ♘bd7 12. 0–0 ♖e8 13. a4 ♘f8∓ Lipnicki–Bronštejn, SSSR (ch) 1951] 9. ♘ce2 ♕c7△ e5∓ Boleslavski

53 8... ♘bd7 9. h4 [9. 0–0 ♕a5?! 10. ♕e1 e5 11. ♕f2 ♘h5 12. a3 ed4 13. ♘d4 ♘c5 14. ♗e2 ♕c7 15. ♖ad1± Pilnik–Rossetto, Mar del Plata 1966; 9... ♕c7=; 9. e5 ♘d5 10. ♘d5 cd5 11. ed6 ♕d6 12. 0–0 ♖e8= Jimenez–Addison, Palma de Mallorca 1970] ♖e8 10. e5 [10. g4 c5∞ Boleslavski] ♘d5 11. ♘d5 cd5 12. e6 [12. f4!?] ♘f6∞ Gheorghiu–Benkö, Tel Aviv (ol) 1964

54 9. 0–0 e5 10. ♔h1 ♖e8 11. ♕d2 ♘bd7 12. ♖ad1 b5 13. ♘g3 ♘f8= Jurkov–Tomson, SSSR 1962

55 **12. a3**?! a6 13. h4 c5 14. g5 ♘e8 15. ♘d5 ♕d6 16. b4 ♘d7 17. c4 ♗b7∓ Savon–Dely, Debrecen 1970 — 10/174; **12. h4** b4 13. ♘a4 c5 14. ♗c5 ♖d8∞

56 6... ♗g7 — 4... ♗g7

57 **7. a4** b4 8. ♘d1 a5 9. ♗h6 [9. ♗d3 e5 10. ♘e2 ♗g7 11. 0–0 0–0 12. c3 d5∓ Lebedev–Botvinik, SSSR 1964] ♗h6 10. ♕h6 ♕b6 11. ♘e2 ♗a6 12. ♕d2 0–0 13. ♘e3 [Klovan–Šašin, SSSR 1970] c5∓; **7. ♗d3** ♗b7 8. g4 e5 9. g5 [9. h4!?] ♘h5 10. ♘ce2 ♗g7 11. c3 a6 12. ♘g3 ♘g3 13. hg3 ♕e7 14. ♘e2 d5∓ Hartston–Penrose, England (ch) 1968; **7. g4** ♘b6 8. g5 ♘h5 9. ♗d3 e5 10. a4 b4 11. ♘ce2 a5 12. c3 b3∞ Romanišin–Jansson, Göteborg 1971

58 7... ♕a5 8. g4 [8. ♘c1 ♕c7 9. a4 b4 10. ♘d1 e5 11. c4 bc3 12. ♘c3 ♗g7 13. ♗e2 0–0 14. 0–0 d5∞ Rubinetti–Smislov, Buenos Aires 1970] ♗b7 9. g5 ♘h5 10. ♘g3 e5 11. ♘h5 gh5 12. f4± Espig–Peev, Varna 1973

59 8... a5 9. a4 b4 10. ♘d1 ♘bd7 11. ♘b2 ♗g7 12. ♗h6± Minić–Pirc, Jugoslavija (ch) 1962; 10... ♗a6!?

60 13. d5 h5 14. g5 ♘h7 15. a3 ♗a6= Hennings–Smislov, La Habana 1967

61 **7... a6** 8. ♘f2 e5 9. ♗e2 ♕c7 10. 0–0 ♗g7 11. de5 de5 12. a4 ♗b7 13. ♖fd1 [13. ab5 ab5 14. ♗b5∞] 0–0 14. ♕d6± Geler–Andersson, Hilversum 1973 — 15/164; **7... ♘b6** 8. ♘f2 [8. g4 h5!? 9. g5 ♗h3 10. ♗h3 ♘c4 11. ♕f2 ♘h7 12. f4 e6 13. d5 cd5 14. ed5 e5 15. fe5 ♘e5 16. ♘e4 ♗e7∓ Zinn–Smislov, Kapfenberg 1970 — 9/130; 15. ♘e4!?] ♕c7 9. ♗e2 [9. b3 a6 10. a4 ♗b7 11. ♗e2 ♗g7 12. 0–0 0–0 13. ♘d3± Ciocaltea–Benoit, Monte Carlo 1969 — 7/155] a6 10. 0–0 ♗b7 11. a4 ♗g7 12. ♗h6 0–0 13. b3 b4 14. ♗g7 ♔g7 15. ♘d1 c5 16. d5± Hennings–Lengyel, Debrecen 1970

62 8. 0-0-0 a6 9. ♔b1 ♕c7 10. g4 e5 11. g5 ♘h5 12. ♘f2 ♖d8 13. ♘e2 c5 14. d5 ♗g7 15. ♘g3 ♘f4∞ Torre–Jansson, Siegen (ol) 1970

63 8... ♗g7 — 4... ♗g7

64 13. ♘d3 ♕c7 14. ♘c5 ♖ad8= Jimenez–Botvinik, Palma de Mallorca 1967 — 4/158

65 5. ♗c4 c6 6. ♗b3 b5 7. ♗e3 ♘bd7 8. ♘ge2 a5 9. a3 ♗a6 10. 0–0 0–0 11. ♕d2 ♕c7 12. ♖fd1 ♘b6 13. ♘g3 ♖ab8= Štejn–Parma, Hamburg 1965

66 5... e5? 6. de5 [6. ♘ge2 ♘c6 7. d5 ♘e7 8. ♕d2± Zinn–Besser, Halle 1967 — 3/144] de5 7. ♕d8 ♔d8 8. ♗c4± Hennings–Donner, La Habana 1967

67 **6... b6** 7. ♗h6 c5 8. d5 e5 9. de6 ♗e6 10. ♗g7 ♔g7 11. 0-0-0 ♘c6 12. h4± Ciocaltea–Balcerowski, Tel Aviv (ol) 1964; **6... e5** 7. d5 ♘e8 [7... c6 8. 0-0-0± Klovan–Kampenus, SSSR 1960] 8. g4 ♗f6 9. 0-0-0 c5 10. h4± Zarubin–Toluš, corr. 1967 — 4/157

68 8... ♘e7 9. h4 ♘e8 10. g4 c6 11. h5± Gik–Krjukov, SSSR 1969 — 7/154

69 **13. e5?** de5 14. ♗e5 ♕a5 15. ♖e1 ♗a2∓ Kapeloš–Osnos, SSSR 1972; **13. ♘a4!**±

70 **7. a4?!** ♘bd7 8. ♘ge2 e5 9. g4? d5∓ Basman–Gligorić, Hastings 1973/74; **7. ♗h6** b5 [7... ♕a5 8. g4 b5 9. ♗g7 ♔g7 10. ♘ge2 ♘bd7 11. h4 h5 12. g5 ♘e8 13. f4± Boleslavski] 8. 0-0-0 ♗e6 9. d5 cd5 10. ed5 b4 11. ♗g7 ♔g7 12. ♘e4 ♘d5 13. ♗c4 ♘f6 14. ♗e6 fe6 15. ♘g5=/∞ Šilov–Savon, SSSR 1967; **7. ♘ge2** e5 8. 0-0-0 ♘bd7 [8... ♕a5? 9. h4 b5 10. g4 ♘a6 11. ♗h6 b4 12. ♘b1 ♗e6 13. h5± Rossetto–Matanović, Amsterdam (ol) 1954; 10. ♗h6 b4 11. ♘b1 c5 12. de5 de5 13. ♗g7 ♔g7 14. h5 ♕c7 15. hg6 fg6 16. ♕h6 ♔g8 17. ♘f4 +– Zinn–Czerniak, Polanica Zdroj 1964] 9. ♗h6 ♕a5 10. h4 ♖e8 11. ♗g7 ♔g7 12. h5± Sholl–Donner, Holland (ch) 1969; **7. 0-0-0** b5 8. g4 ♘bd7 9. h4± Evans–Garcia, La Habana (ol) 1966 — 2/126

71 13. ♕h2 ♗h6 14. ♕h6 f6 15. ♗c4 ♔h8 16. ♘h3±→ Muhin–Savon, SSSR 1963

72 7. ♗d3 b5 8. ♘ge2 ♘bd7 9. 0–0 a6 10. ♗h6 0–0 11. ♗g7 ♔g7 12. f4 e5 13. fe5 de5 14. de5 ♘g4= Noskov–Etruk, SSSR 1972

73 7... b5 8. g4?! — 6... b5

74 10. ♕d2 a6 11. ♘c1 0–0 12. ♗e2 ♕b6 13. a4 ♗b7= Privorotski–Etruk, SSSR 1968

75 14. ♗a6? ♕a6 15. ♕e3 0–0= Hartston–N. Littlewood, England (ch) 1968

76 **14... ♗f1** 15. ♖f1 ♕a6 16. 0-0-0 ♖c8 17. ♖fe1 c5 18. e5+– Noskov–Etruk, SSSR 1964; **14... ♖c8** 15. ♘c4± Uusi–Etruk, SSSR 1963

77 9. g4 ♕c7 10. ♘d1?! ♘b6 11. ♘f2 h5 12. h3 a5 13. b3 ♘fd7 14. ♖b1 b4 15. c4 c5∓ Suttles–Matanović, Sousse (izt) 1967

78 10. ♗e2 a6 11. g4 ♘b6 12. h4 h5 13. g5 ♘fd7 14. f4 c5∓ Vasjukov–Etruk, SSSR 1962

79 **14. a4?!** ba4 15. ♘a4 ♗e6 16. de5 de5 17. ♘bc5 ♘h5 18. g4 ♘f6 19. ♕g5± Suetin–Polugajevski, Sarajevo 1965; **14. de5** de5 15. 0-0-0±

80 **7. 0-0-0** ♕a5 8. ♔b1 ♘b6 9. ♗d3 ♗e6 10. ♕e2 ♘a4 11. ♘a4 ♕a4 12. b3± Pirc; 8... b5 — 6... b5; **7. ♘ge2** ♘b6 [7... ♕c7 8. a4 0–0 9. h4 e5 10. 0-0-0 d5 11. ed5 ♘b6 12. de5 ♘c4? 13. ef6+– Kurajica–Rukavina, Jugoslavija 1969 — 7/156; 12... ♘fd5!? 13. ♘d5 ♘d5 14. ♗d4 c5=/∞] 8. ♘c1 ♗e6 9. ♘b3 ♘c4 10. ♗c4 ♗c4 11. ♗h6 ♗h6 12. ♕h6 ♕b6= Milić–Pirc, Beograd 1952; 7... b5 — 6... b5

81 10... 0–0 11. ♗h6 ♕c7 12. ♗g7 ♔g7 13. a4 b4 14. ♘d1 a5 15. ♘e3± Ciocaltea–Domnitz, Tel Aviv (ol) 1964

82 15. fe5 de5 16. de5 ♘e5 17. ♕f4± Geler–Liebert, Kapfenberg 1970 — 9/131

83 8. ♗h6 0–0 9. ♘f2 e5 10. ♗g7 ♔g7 11. 0-0-0 ♕a5 12. ♔b1 ♖e8 13. h4 h5 14. g4 ♘b6∞ Karpov–Gipslis, SSSR 1972 — 13/181

84 11. ♖ad1 e5 12. f4 ♗b7 13. de5 de5 14. f5 ♖ad8 15. a3 c5 16. fg6 hg6= Spaski–Jansson, Stockholm 1969

85 11... e5 12. ♗g7 ♔g7 13. f4 b4 14. ♘d1 ed4 15. ♕d4 c5 16. ♕d3 ♗b7∞ Hennings–Timman, Soči 1973

86 15. ♘d1 e6= Hartston–Rukavina, Vrnjačka Banja 1972

87 **7... e5** 8. 0-0-0 [8. d5 cd5 9. ♘d5 ♘d5 10. ♕d5 ♘b6 11. ♗b5 ♔e7 12. ♕d2 ♗e6 13. ♘e2 ♕c7 14. ♘c3± Akopjan–Karasev, SSSR 1970] 0–0 9. h4 b5 10. de5 de5 11. ♕d6± Šamkovič–Pismeni, SSSR 1964; **7... b5** — 6... b5

88 15. ♔f2± Matanović–Pirc, Beverwijk 1958

89 **7. a3** ♘bd7 8. g4 ♘b6 [8... a6!?] 9. ♗h6 ♗h6 10. ♕h6 ♕c7 11. ♘h3 ♘c4∞ Kurajica–A. Zaharov, Jugoslavija–SSSR 1963; **7. h4** h5 8. ♘h3 ♘bd7 9. ♘g5 ♗b7 [9... a6 10. 0-0-0 ♕c7 11. ♘e2 c5 12. dc5 dc5= Hecht–Torre, Amsterdam 1973] 10. ♗e2 0–0 11. 0–0 a5 12. f4 b4 13. ♘d1 c5 14. d5 ♘g4= Ciocaltea–Razuvajev, Ljubljana 1973 — 15/163; **7. g4** ♕a5 [7... ♘bd7 8. g5 ♘h5 9. f4 ♘b6 10. ♘f3 0–0 11. 0-0-0 ♘c4∓ Svešnikov–Anikajev, SSSR 1969; 9. ♘ge2 b4?! 10. ♘d1 e5 11. ♘f2 0–0 12. 0-0-0± Arbakov–Karasev, SSSR 1971; 7... h5!?] 8. ♘ge2 h5 9. g5 ♘fd7 10. ♘c1 0–0 11. ♗d3 b4∓ Schöneberg–Guljko, Örebro 1966

90 7... b4 8. ♘ce2 a5 9. ♗h6 0–0 10. h4± Malachi–Björnsson, Dresden 1969 — 8/130

91 8. e5 b4 9. ef6 bc3 10. fg7 cd2 11. ♗d2 ♕d2 12. ♖d2 ♖g8 13. h4 h6= Heuer–Etruk, SSSR 1964

92 8... b4 9. ♘ce2 ♗e6 10. ♘c1 ♘bd7 11. g4 ♖b8 12. h4 ♘b6 13. h5 ♘c4 14. ♗c4 ♗c4 15. h6± Šijanovski–Kotov, SSSR 1961

93 10... b4 11. ♘ce2 ♗a6 12. ♘h3 c5 [12... ♘b6 13. ♘g5 ♘a4 14. ♔a1 ♖b8 15. ♘c1 ♘c3 16. ♗a6 ♘d1 17. ♗c4∞̅ Arbakov–Petkevič, SSSR 1971] 13. dc5 ♕c5= Klovan–Karasev, SSSR 1971 — 11/134

94 11. ♘ce2 ♘c4 12. ♘c1 ♖b8 [12... ♕b6 !?] 13. ♘ge2 ♕b6 14. g4 a5 15. ♘g3 a4 16. h4 a3 17. b3 ♘b2= Polugajevski–Gipslis, SSSR 1966

95 **11... ♘c4**? 12. e5 de5 13. ♗c4 bc4 14. de5 ♕e5 15. ♖he1+– Klovan–Etruk, SSSR 1964; **11... ♖b8** 12. ♘f4 ♘c4 13. ♗c4 bc4 14. ♔a1 ♕b6 15. b3 ♕a5 16. ♔b2 ♖g8 17. ♖he1± Seredenko–Ufimcev, SSSR 1965; **11... ♗e6**!? 12. d5 ♗h3 13. gh3 b4 14. ♘e2 cd5 15. ♘d4∞̅ Saharov

96 12... 0–0 13. ♕h6 b4 [13... ♘c4 14. ♘e2 ♔h8 15. h4 ♖g8 16. ♘c1 ♕d8 17. ♘d3 ♕f8± Klovan–Gufeljd, SSSR (ch) 1963; 13... ♘a4 14. ♘a4 ba4 15. ♕d2 ♕b6=] 14. ♘e2 c5 15. g4 c4 [15... e5? 16. ♘g3!+– Platonov–Savon, SSSR 1968 — 5/135] 16. ♘g3 ♔h8∞

97 **13. ♘e2** ♕b4 14. b3 ♕a3∓→; **13. ♖d3** c5∓; 13... 0–0∓

98 **14... ♖ab8**!?; **14... a3** 15. ♕d2 [15. b3? g5–+] ♕d2 16. ♖d2 ab2 17. ♔b2 ♘d7=

99 **8. g4** ♘b6 9. b3 ♕c7 10. h4 h5 11. g5 ♘fd7 12. ♗g2 ♗b7 13. 0–0 b4 14. ♘d1 c5 15. c3∞ Espig–Balašov, Riga 1967; **8. ♗h6** ♗h6 9. ♕h6 ♕c7 10. g4 ♗b7 11. ♘g3 ♘b6 12. 0-0-0 0-0-0 13. g5 ♘fd7 14. f4 ♔b8 15. ♗e2 b4 16. ♘b1 c5= Suetin–Gipslis, SSSR (ch) 1967 — 3/147

100 15. ♕d8 ♖d8 16. ♘b3 ♘fd7 17. ♗b5 ♗a6!? 18. ♗d7 ♘d7 19. ♘a5 ♘b6∞̅ Hartston–Torre, Nice (ol) 1974 — 17/180

101 **8. ♘d1** e5 9. c3 a6 10. ♘e2 0–0 11. 0–0 d5 12. ♘f2 ♗b7 13. a4 ♖e8∓ Hecht–Forintos, Siegen (ol) 1970 — 10/169; **8. ♘h3** 0–0 9. ♘f2 a6 10. 0–0 c5 11. a4 cd4 12. ♗d4 b4= Jimenez–Gufeljd, Leningrad 1967 — 3/145

102 **8... ♗b7** 9. ♗h6 ♗h6 10. ♕h6 ♕b6?! 11. a4 b4 12. a5 ♕c7 13. ♘b1 c5 14. ♘d2± Kuprejčik–Balašov, SSSR 1968; **8... ♘b6** 9. ♗h6 0–0 10. ♗g7 [10. h4 e5 11. h5 ♕e7 12. 0-0-0 b4 13. ♘b1 c5 14. ♗g7 ♔g7 15. dc5 dc5 16. ♘g3 c4△ c3∓ Cejtlin–Kozlov, SSSR 1970] ♔g7 11. 0–0=

103 15. ♖fd1 ♘f8 16. ♘b1 ♘e6 17. ♘d2 ♘d7 18. c3 ♗f8= Geler–Hort, Amsterdam 1970

104 **8... b4** 9. ♘d1 ♘bd7 10. ♘e3 ♕b6 11. 0-0-0 a5 12. ♘h3 a4 13. ♗c4± Klovan–Lamaja, SSSR 1969; **8... ♕a5** 9. ♕d2 ♘bd7 10. ♗d3 ♕b6 11. ♘ge2 e5 12. de5 de5 13. a4 b4 14. ♘d1 a5 15. ♘e3 ♘c5 16. ♘c4 ♕c7 17. ♕e3 ♘fd7 18. 0–0 ♗a6= Tringov–Gheorghiu, Kecskemet 1964

105 **9. 0-0-0** b4 10. ♘ce2 ♕b6 11. ♔b1 a5 12. ♘c1 a4 13. g4 c5 14. dc5 ♘c5 15. ♘ge2 ♗d7 16. ♕e3 0–0∓ Karasev–Averbah, SSSR 1963; **9. ♘h3** b4 [9... ♕a5 10. ♘g5? ♗a6 11. g4 b4 12. ♘d1 b3 13. c3 e5 14. ♗a6 ♕a6 15. de5 ♘e5∓ Ujtumen–Lejn, SSSR 1970; 10. ♕d2=] 10. ♘d1 ♕b6 11. ♕d2 c5 12. dc5 ♘c5 13. ♘f4 a5 14. ♘e3 ♗b7 15. ♗c4 0–0 16. h4 e6∞ Bakulin–Botvinik, SSSR 1964

106 9... ♕a5 10. ♘ge2 ♗a6 11. 0–0 ♖c8? 12. b4!△ a4± Kuprejčik–Murej, SSSR 1969 — 8/131; 11... b4!?

107 15. ♘b3 ♘b3 16. ab3 0-0-0= Kuprejčik–Razuvajev, SSSR 1969

108 **5. ♗f4** ♗g7 6. h3 c5 7. dc5 ♕a5 8. ♕d2 ♕c5 9. ♗e3 ♕a5 10. ♗d3 ♘c6 11. ♘ge2 ♘d7 12. 0–0∞ Holmov–Botvinik, SSSR 1963; **5. ♗h4** ♗g7 6. ♗e2 [6. e5 ♘fd7 7. f4 c5 8. ed6 cd4 9. ♘b5 ♘f6±; 6... de5! 7. de5 ♘g4∞] c5 7. e5 ♘h5 8. dc5 ♘f4 9. ♗g3 de5 10. ♕d8 ♔d8 11. 0-0-0 ♗d7 12. ♗f3 ♘c6= Unzicker–Botvinik, Moskva (ol) 1956; **5. ♗f6** ef6 6. ♕d2

♗g7 7. 0-0-0 c6 8. ♔b1 [8. f4 0–0 9. h3 f5 10. e5 de5 11. de5 ♕d2∓ Kirilov–Rubin, SSSR 1963] 0–0 9. h4 f5 10. ♗d3 fe4 11. ♘e4 d5 12. ♘c3 ♕f6 13. ♘ge2 [Vasjukov–Parma, Suhumi 1966] ♗f5=

109 5... ♘g4 6. ♗f4 ♗g7 7. ♘f3 [7. ♕d2 — 4... ♗g7] ♘c6 8. ♗g3 e5 9. de5 ♘ge5= Juarez–Savon, Mar del Plata 1971; 6. ♗c1!△ f3±

110 8. ♗d3!?

111 13. ♔h1 c5 14. d5± Liberzon–Etruk, SSSR 1968

112 **5. ♕e2** h6 [5... ♗g7 — 4... ♗g7] 6. ♗f6 [6. ♗h4 ♗g7 — 4... ♗g7] ef6 7. 0-0-0 ♗g7 8. f4 0–0 9. g4 b5 10. ♕f3 b4 11. ♘b1 d5 12. ed5 ♕d5∓ Minić–Parma, Zagreb 1965; **5. f4** ♕b6 [5... ♗g7 — 4... ♗g7] 6. ♗c4 ♕b2 7. ♘ge2 ♕b4 8. ♗f6 ef6 9. ♗d3 ♗g7 10. f5∞ Ribeiro–Fuderer, München 1954

113 5... ♕a5 6. f4 ♘bd7 7. ♗d3 ♗g7 8. 0-0-0 [8. ♘f3 h6 9. ♗h4 e5 10. de5 de5 11. 0–0 0–0 (Richardson–Penrose, England 1968) 12. f5±] e5 9. ♘f3 h6 10. ♗h4 0–0 11. de5 de5 12. f5±

114 6... ♘bd7 **7. f4** ♘b6 [7... ♗g7 8. ♘f3 b4 9. ♘d1 0–0 10. ♘f2 c5 11. c3 cd4 12. cd4 ♗b7 13. 0–0 d5 14. e5 ♘e4 15. ♕b4± Novopašin–Zaharov, SSSR (ch) 1963; 8... 0–0 — 5... c6] 8. e5 ♘fd5 9. ♘e4 f6 10. ♗h4 ♗h6 11. ef6 ef6 12. ♘e2± Kuprejčik–Gipslis, SSSR 1969; **7. ♘ge2** ♘b6 8. 0–0 h6 [8... ♗g7!?] 9. ♗f6 ef6 10. d5± Suetin–Parma, Titovo Užice 1966; **7. ♘f3** ♗g7 8. ♗h6 0–0 [8... ♗h6!?] 9. e5 [9. h4 e5 10. ♗g7 ♔g7 11. h5 ♘h5 12. g4 ♕f6∞ Macukevič–Cejtlin, SSSR 1968] ♘e8 10. h4 de5 11. h5±→ Veresov–Gipslis, SSSR 1962

115 11... ♗g7 12. ♗h4 [12. h3 h4 13. hg4 hg3 14. ♖h8 ♗h8 15. ♕h6 gf2 16. ♔e2 ♗f6 17. g5± Talj–Gufeljd, SSSR 1968 — 6/208] f6 [12... ♗f6!?] 13. h3 ♗h6 14. ♕e2 b4 15. ♘a4 g5 16. ♗g3 h4 17. ♗h2± Aronin–Smislov, SSSR 1951

116 13. ♘e5 ♕f6 14. f4 ♗h6 15. ♘e2 ♕e5 16. fe5± Liberzon–Torre, Nice (ol) 1974 — 17/181

117 **5... c6** 6. e5±; **5... ♘b6** 6. a4 a5 7. ♗d3 ♗g7 8. ♘f3 0–0 [8... ♘h5 9. f5± Đurašević–Pirc, Jugoslavija (ch) 1952] 9. 0–0 ♘fd7 10. ♕e1 f6 11. ♗h4 c5 12. d5± Trifunović–Pirc, Jugoslavija (ch) 1952

118 **7. ♕d2** ♘f4 8. ♕f4 g5 9. ♕f2 [9. ♕f3 gh4 10. ♗c4 e6 11. ♗e6 ♘e5∓] gh4 10. ♗c4 e6 11. 0-0-0 ♘b6 12. ♗e2 ♗d7 13. ♘h3 ♕e7∞ Richardson–Keene, England 1969; **7. ♘ge2** g5 8. fg5 e6 [8... e5? 9. ♕d2 ♗e7 10. 0-0-0±] 9. ♕d2 ♗e7∞

119 8. ♗c4 ♘f4 [8... c5!?] 9. ♕f3 g5 10. ♗f2 c5∓ Ostojić–Benkö, Monaco 1969; 9. ♕d2!?

120 13. ♘b5 ♕d7∞ Richardson–Beach, corr. 1970

121 5... c6 6. f4 h6 [6... ♘h5? 7. g4 h6 8. gh5 hg5 9. hg6 ♗d4 10. ♕c4 ♕b6 11. ♕f7 ♔d7 12. 0-0-0+– Suetin–Matulović, Sarajevo 1965; 6... 0–0!?] 7. ♗h4 ♘h5 8. ♕d2 ♘f4∞ Češkovski–Etruk, SSSR 1965;

122 **7... 0–0** 8. e5 de5 9. de5 ♘d5 10. ♕d2 ♗e6 11. f4± Žuravljev–Kärner, SSSR 1968; **7... ♕a5** 8. f4 [8. e5? de5 9. de5 ♘h5 10. ♖e1 ♗e6∓ Canal–Parma, Reggio Emilia 1966] ♘h5 9. ♕f3 ♘f4= Boleslavski

123 Polugajevski–Parma, SSSR–Jugoslavija 1969

124 5... de5 6. de5 **♘g4** 7. ♕d8 ♔d8 8. ♘f3! [8. ♖d1 ♗d7 9. f4 h6 10. ♗h4 g5 11. e6 fe6 12. ♗g3 ♘e3△ ♘f5∓; 11. fg5 hg5 12. ♗g5 ♘h2∓] ♗e6 9. ♗h4 ♘e5 10. ♘g5 ♗d7 11. ♗g3 ♘bc6 12. ♗b5=∞ Raaste–Parma, Nice (ol) 1974; **6... ♕d1** 7. ♖d1 ♘fd7 [7... ♘g4? 8. h3 ♘e5 9. ♘d5+–] 8. ♘d5 ♗e5 9. ♘f3 ♗d6 10. ♗e7 ♗e7 11. ♘c7 ♔d8 12. ♘a8 b6∞ Keene

125 6. ed6 cd6 7. ♘f3 h6 [7... ♘c6?! 8. d5 ♘ce5 9. ♘e5 ♘e5 10. ♗e2 0–0 11. 0–0 a6 12. a4 ♗f5 13. ♖a3± Mikenas–Gipslis, SSSR 1963; 7... 0–0 8. ♗e2 ♘f6∞] 8. ♗e3 [8. ♗h4? f5 9. ♗c4 g5 10. ♗g5 hg5 11. ♘g5 ♘f6 12. ♘f7 ♕c7∓ Vitolinš–Karasev, SSSR 1973] 0–0∞

126 **6... de5** 7. de5 c6 8. ♗c4 ♕a5 9. ♘f3 ♘c5 10. ♗e7+– Kupper–Maier, Wien 1953; **6... 0–0** 7. ♗c4 ♘b6 8. ♗b3 a5 9. a4 ♘a6 10. ♘b5 d5 11. ♘f3 c6 12. ♘d6± Kupper–Udovčić, Opatija 1953; **6... h6** 7. ♗h4 c5 8. ed6 g5 9. fg5 ed6 10. ♘f3 ♕a5 11. ♕e2± Gurevič–Hartman, SSSR 1964

127 **12... ♘a5**? 13. d5±; **12... d5=**

128 **5... c5**? 6. e5 cd4 [6... ♘g4 7. ♗b5+–] 7. ef6 ef6 8. ♕d4 ♕e7 9. ♘ce2!+–; 8... ♘c6!?; **5... 0–0** 6. e5 [6. ♘f3 c5 7. d5 b5 8. ♗b5 ♘e4 9. ♘e4 ♕a5 10. ♘c3 ♗c3 11. bc3 ♕b5 12. ♔f2 f6∓ Milić–Pirc, Jugoslavija 1953; 6. ♗d3 c5 7. dc5 dc5∞ Keene; 6. ♕d2 c5!?] ♘fd7 [6... ♘e8? 7. ♘f3 ♘d7 8. ♗c4 ♘b6 9. ♗b3 d5 10. 0–0± Unzicker–Pirc, Opatija 1953; 8. h4! h6 9. h5=∞→ Nettheim–Hamilton, corr. 1961] 7. ♘f3 c5 8. ed6 cd4 9. ♗e7 ♖e8 10. ♘d4 ♕b6 11. ♘db5± Keene; 6... ♘g4!∞

129 8. ♘d5? cd4 9. ♗b5 ♗d7 10. ♗e7 ♕a5 11. b4 ♕b5!∓ Minev–Kvjatkovski, Bulgaria (ch) 1956

130 8... de5? 8. ♕d8 ♔d8 10. 0-0-0 ♗d7 11. fe5 [11. ♘d5 ♘c6 12. ♘e7±] ♗e5 12. ♘f3 ♗c3 13. bc3 ♘c6 14. ♗c4± Fridštejn

131 11. ♕d2 ♘c6 12. 0-0-0 ♕a5? 13. a3 ed6 14. ♘b5+– R. Byrne–Parma, San Juan 1969 — 8/134; 12... ed6!∞

132 13. 0-0-0 ♕f6 14. cd6 ♗g4 15. ♗d4 ♘e5∞ Mednis—Parma, Noristown 1973

133 **5... 0—0** 6. 0-0-0 c6 7. f3 b5 8. g4 b4 9. ♘ce2 ♕a5 10. ♔b1 ♗e6 11. ♘c1 ♘bd7 12. h4± Jovanić—Pirc, Jugoslavija (ch) 1956; **5... ♘bd7** 6. ♗h6?! ♗h6 7. ♕h6 c5 8. ♘f3 cd4 9. ♘d4 ♘e5= Trifunović—Pirc, Mar del Plata 1950; 6. 0-0-0±

134 6. ♗h4 0—0 [6... c6 7. f3 b5 8. ♗f2 ♘bd7 9. ♘ge2 0—0 10. ♗e3 ♔h7∞ Sajgin—Nikolajevski, SSSR 1962; 7. f4 ♗e6 8. ♘f3 d5 9. ♗d3 de4 10. ♘e4 ♘e4 11. ♗e4 ♗d5 12. ♕e2△0-0-0± Fuderer—Pirc, Opatija 1953] 7. 0-0-0 [7. f4 c5!?] c6 8. f4 [8. e5?! ♘d5 9. f4 ♗f5∓ Panov—Simagin, SSSR 1946] b5 9. e5 b4∞ Radevič—Redkin, SSSR 1960; 6... g5 7. ♗g3 — 6. ♗f4

135 **7... ♘c6** 8. d5 e5 [8... ♘ce5 9. h3 g5 10. hg4 gf4 11. f3 c5 12. ♘h3∞ Kuprejčik—Didiško, SSSR 1972; 9. f3±] 9. ♗g3 ♘e7 [9... ♘d4 10. f3 ♘f6 11. ♘d1 c6 12. c3 ♘b5 13. ♘e3±] 10. f3 ♘f6 11. 0-0-0± Žuravljev—Judovič, corr. 1968/69 — 8/133; **7... ♘d7** 8. ♗e2 e5 9. de5 ♘ge5 10. 0-0-0 ♘b6 11. ♘f3 ♘f3 12. gf3± Ree—Hort, Amsterdam 1970 — 10/175

136 10. ♘d5 ♗e6?! 11. ♗g3 [11. h3 — 10. h3] 0—0 12. f4 ♘d7 13. ♘f3 [Ivlev—Lebedev, SSSR 1963] ♗d5=; 10... f5!∞

137 10... ♗e6?! 11. ♗e3 ♘c4 12. ♗c4 ♗c4 13. ♘f3 [I. Zajcev—Savon, SSSR (ch) 1963] ♕f6△ 0-0-0∞; 11. ♘d5!± Hecht—Parma, Vršac 1973 — 16/137

138 13. ♗f4 ♗e6 14. ef5 ♗f5 15. ♗e2 ♕d7= Lutikov—Parma, Sarajevo 1969

139 **6... ♘bd7** 7. 0-0-0± [7. ♘f3 c5 8. d5 g5 9. ♗g3 ♘h5∞ Kramer—Vidmar, Utrecht 1950]; **6... c6** 7. 0-0-0 [7. f3 b5 8. ♗d3 ♕c7 9. g4 ♘bd7 10. ♘ge2 a6 11. a4 e5∞ Ozsvath—Ribli, Debrecen 1970] b5 [7... ♕a5!?] 8. e5 b4 9. ef6 bc3 10. ♕c3 ♗f6 11. ♘f3 c5 12. ♗e5± Kamenecki—Dubovik, SSSR 1964; **6... ♘c6** 7. 0-0-0 [7. ♗b5 ♘d7 8. ♘f3 a6 9. ♗e2 (Veresov—I. Zajcev, SSSR 1964) e5∞] g5 — 6... g5

140 7. ♗e3 ♘g4 8. 0-0-0 ♘c6 [8... c6 9. h4 ♘e3 10. ♕e3 g4 11. f4 ♕a5 12. e5± Bivšev—Šilov, SSSR 1961] 9. h4 ♘e3 10. fe3 [10. ♕e3!?] g4∓

141 8. ♘ge2 ♘c6 9. d5 ♘a5 10. f4 c6 11. ♘c1 [Kuuskmaa—Toluš, corr. 1967 — 3/148] cd5 12. ed5 ♘f4∞

142 8... ♘c6 9. d5 [9. ♗b5 ♗d7 10. ♘ge2 ♘g3 11. hg3 a6 12. ♗c6 ♗c6 13. f4 e6 14. d5 ♗d7 15. de6 fe6 16. e5± Smislov—Kuzminih, SSSR 1951] ♘e5 10. ♗e2 ♘g3 11. hg3 c5 12. f4 ♘g4 13. e5± Leonidov—Blehcin, SSSR 1969

143 Fischer—Mednis, USA (ch) 1958

144 **6. ♗h6** ♗h6 [6... 0—0 7. h4 e5 8. ♗g7 ♔g7 9. 0-0-0 ♕e7 10. f3± Atanasov—Hort, Leipzig 1973] 7. ♕h6 ♕a5=; **6. f3** ♕a5 [6... b5 7. 0-0-0 b4 8. ♘ce2 ♕b6 9. ♔b1 ♗a6 10. ♘h3 ♘bd7 11. ♘c1 ♗f1 12. ♖hf1 c5∞ Bikov—Kudinov, SSSR 1971] 7. 0-0-0 h6 8. ♗e3 ♘bd7 9. ♔b1 b5 10. ♕e1 ♖b8∞ Damjanović—Etruk, Talin 1969 — 7/157; **6. 0-0-0** h6 7. ♗e3 ♕a5△ b5, ♘bd7∞ Boleslavski

145 6... b5 7. ♗d3 ♕b6 8. ♘f3 ♗g4 9. e5 de5 [Simovič—Volovič, SSSR 1965] 10. fe5! ♘fd7 11. ♗e4±

146 7. 0-0-0 b5 8. e5 [8. ♗d3 Da5 9. ♔b1 b4 10. ♘ce2 ♗a6∓ Keene] b4 9. ef6 ef6 10. ♗h4 bc3 11. ♕c3 ♕b6 12. ♘f3 ♘a6 13. ♗c4 d5∓ Nikitin—Liberzon, SSSR 1963

147 8. e5? b4∓

148 **8... a6** 9. 0-0-0 b4 10. ♘e2 a5 11. f5± Kurajica—Marangunić, Zagreb 1969 — 7/158; **8... h6** 9. ♗h4 b4 10. ♘d1 a5 11. 0—0 ♗a6 12. ♗a6 ♘a6 13. ♕d3 ♕b6 14. ♘e3± Hermlin—Kärner, SSSR 1969; **8... ♘bd7** 9. 0—0 [9. e5 b4 10. ♘e2 de5 11. fe5 ♘d5 12. ♗h6± Bisguier—Tarjan, USA 1973 — 15/165] ♘b6 [9... ♗b7 10. e5 ♘e8 11. ♖ae1 f6 12. ef6 ef6 13. ♗h4 ♗h6 14. d5± Liberzon—Liebert, Luhačovice 1971; 9... b4△ ♕b6!?] 10. e5 [10. ♖ae1 b4 11. ♘d1 c5 12. c3 bc3 13. bc3 cd4 14. cd4 ♗b7 15. f5!± R. Byrne—Gipslis, Sousse (izt) 1967 — 4/159; 14... d5 15. e5 ♘e4 16. ♗e4 de4 17. ♖e4 ♗a6⩱ R. Byrne—Portisch, Hastings 1970/71 — 11/133; 15. ♗f6!?] b4 11. ♘e2 ♘fd5 12. f5 c5 13. ♗h6± Soltis—Botterill, Graz 1972

149 13. bc3 ♕a5 14. ♕f4 cd4 15. cd4 ♕a4∞ Browne—Hort, Madrid 1973

B 08 1. e4 d6 2. d4 ♘f6 3. ♘c3 g6 4. ♘f3 ♗g7

	5	6	7	8	9	10	11	12	13	
1	♗f4[1] 0—0[2]	♕d2 a6[3]	♗h6 b5	♗g7 ♔g7	♗d3 ♗b7	e5 ♘fd7	♗e4 ♗e4	♘e4 de5	de5 ♘b6[4]	±
2	♗g5 c6[5]	♕d2[6] b5[7]	♗d3 ♗g4	♕f4[8] ♗f3	♕f3 ♘bd7	0—0 0—0	♖fe1 ♕c7	♖ad1 a6	♕h3 e5[9]	=

	5	6	7	8	9	10	11	12	13	
3	. . . 0—0	♕d2 d5[10]	♗d3[11] c5[12]	dc5 ♘e4	♘e4 de4	♗e4 ♕d2	♘d2 ♗b2[13]	♖b1 ♗d4		∞
4	♗c4 c6[14]	e5[15] de5[16]	♘e5 0—0	0—0 ♘bd7	♗g5[17] ♘b6[18]	♗b3 a5[19]	a4[20] ♘fd5	♘d5 cd5	♗f4 f6[21]	=
5	. . . . . .	♗b3 0—0[22]	0—0[23] ♗g4[24]	h3 ♗f3	♕f3 ♘bd7	♗e3 e5[25]	♖ad1 ♕e7	♖fe1 ♘h5	de5 de5[26]	±
6	. . . 0—0	♕e2[27] c6[28]	e5[29] ♘d5[30]	0—0[31] ♘c3	bc3 ♗g4	♗f4 ♘d7[32]	ed6[33] ed6	h3[34] ♖e8	♕d3 ♗f3	=
7	. . . . . .	♗b3 ♘c6[35]	h3[36] ♘a5	0—0[37] ♘b3	ab3 ♘d7[38]	♗e3 a6	♕d2 ♖e8	♖ad1 e6	e5 b6[39]	=
8	. . . . . .	0—0 ♘e4[40]	♗f7[41] ♖f7	♘e4 h6	h3 ♘d7[42]	♕d3 ♘f8	♗d2 ♗f5	♕e2 c6	c3 ♕b6[43]	∞
9	. . . . . .	. . . ♗g4	h3 ♗f3	♕f3 ♘c6	♗e3 e5[44]	de5 ♘e5	♕e2 ♘e4	♗f7[45] ♘f7	♘e4 ♖e8[46]	=
10	h3 0—0	♗e3[47] c6[48]	a4[49] ♘bd7[50]	♕d2[51] ♕c7[52]	♗e2 b6	0—0 a6	♗h6 ♗b7	♗g7 ♔g7	♖fe1[53] b5	=

1. e4 d6 2. d4 ♘f6 3. ♘c3 g6 4. ♘f3 ♗g7 5. ♗e2 0—0[54]

	6	7	8	9	10	11	12	13	14	
11	h3[55] e5[56]	0—0 ed4	♘d4 ♖e8	♗f3 ♘bd7	♗g5 h6	♗h4 ♘e5	♗e2 g5	♗g3 ♘g6	♗f3 a5[57]	∞
12	0—0 ♘a6[58]	♖e1[59] c5	e5[60] ♘g4[61]	ed6 ♕d6	♘e4 ♕c7	♗a6 ba6	♘c5 e5	h3 ed4	♘b3 ♘f6[62]	±
13	. . . ♘bd7	e5[63] ♘e8	♗g5[64] f6	ef6 ef6	♗e3 c6	d5 c5	♕d2 ♖f7	♖ae1 ♘f8	h3 ♘c7[65]	±
14	. . . ♘c6	d5[66] ♘b8	h3[67] c6	♗g5[68] ♗d7[69]	a4 a5	♖e1 ♘a6	e5[70] de5	♘e5		±
15	. . . ♗g4	♗g5[71] ♘c6	h3 ♗f3	♗f3 ♘d7[72]	♘e2 h6	♗e3 e5	c3 ♘b6	♕b3[73] ♘a5	♕c2 ♘ac4[74]	=
16	. . . . . .	♗e3 ♘c6[75]	d5[76] ♘b8	♖e1[77] c6	♘d2[78] ♗e2	♕e2 ♘bd7	a4 ♕a5	♘b3 ♕c7	a5 a6[79]	±
17	. . . . . .	. . . . . .	. . . ♗f3	♗f3 ♘e5	♗e2 c6	f4[80] ♘ed7	dc6[81] bc6	♕d2[82] ♘b6[83]	a4 a5[84]	±
18	. . . . . .	. . . . . .	♕d2 e5[85]	de5 de5	♖ad1 ♕c8[86]	♕c1[87] ♖d8	♖d8 ♕d8	♖d1 ♕f8	h3 ♗f3[88]	=
19	. . . . . .	. . . . . .	. . . . . .	d5 ♘e7	♖ad1[89] ♗d7[90]	♗h6[91] ♗h6[92]	♕h6 ♔h8	♘e1 ♘eg8	♕d2 ♕e7[93]	±

1. e4 d6 2. d4 ♘f6 3. ♘c3 g6 4. ♘f3 ♗g7 5. ♗e2 0—0 6. 0—0 c6

	7	8	9	10	11	12	13	14	15	
20	♖e1[94] ♕c7[95]	♗f4[96] ♘bd7[97]	e5 ♘h5	ed6 ed6	♗e3 ♘b6[98]	h3 ♖e8	♕d2 ♘f6	♗d3 ♗e6	♗g5 ♘bd5[99]	=
21	h3 ♘bd7[100]	♗f4[101] ♘h5[102]	♗g5 ♖e8[103]	♕d2 ♕c7	♖fd1 b5	a4 b4	♘b1 ♘hf6	♕e3 ♗b7	♘bd2[104]	±

	7	8	9	10	11	12	13	14	15	
22	a4	e5[106]	ed6	♗f4	♕d2	a5	h3	g4	♕e3	±
	♘bd7[105]	♘e8[107]	♘d6	♘f6	♗f5	♕c7	♖ad8	♗e6	♕c8[108]	
23	...	h3[109]	♗e3[111]	de5	♕d2[112]	♖fd1[113]	♗f1	a5	♗c4	±
	♕c7	♘bd7[110]	e5	de5	♘h5	♘f4	♖e8	♗f8	♘e6[114]	
24	...	h3[115]	♗g5[117]	♗e3	♘d2	ed5	♘d5	c3	♘f3	±
	a5	♘a6[116]	h6	♔h7	d5[168]	♘d5	cd5	♘c7	♘e8[119]	

[1] 5. ♗e3 0—0 [5... c6 6. a4 0—0 7. ♗e2 ♕c7 8. ♘d2 e5 9. d5 cd5 10. ed5 ♘a6 11. 0—0 ♘b4 12. ♘c4± Planinc—Tringov, Ljubljana 1969 — 7/159; 7... ♘bd7!?] 6. ♕d2 [6. ♗e2 ♗g4 7. ♕d2 ♘c6 8. 0-0-0 e5 9. de5 de5 10. h3 ♗f3 11. ♗f3 ♕e7∞ Bajkov—Kimelfeld, SSSR 1974; 6... ♘c6 — 5. ♗e2] e5 [6... ♘bd7 7. ♗h6 e5 8. ♗g7 ♔g7 9. 0-0-0 ♕e7 10. h4± Castillo—Najdorf, Dubrovnik (ol) 1950; 6... c6 7. h3 b5 8. ♗d3 ♕c7 9. ♗h6 b4 10. ♘e2 c5= Szily—Stalda, Stuttgart 1939] 7. de5 de5 8. 0-0-0 ♕e7 9. h3 ♘bd7= Larsen—Penrose, Dundee 1967 — 4/156

[2] **5... ♘bd7** 6. ♕d2 c5 7. dc5 [7. ♗h6 ♗h6 8. ♕h6 cd4 9. ♘d4 ♘e5 10. ♗b5 ♗d7= Rossolimo—Pirc, Dubrovnik (ol) 1950] ♘c5 8. e5±; **5... c6** 6. ♕d2 b5 [6... ♕a5 7. h3 ♘bd7 8. 0-0-0 b5? 9. e5 b4 10. ef6+— Korčnoj—Pirc, SSSR—Jugoslavija 1957; 8... 0—0 !?] 7. ♗d3 ♗g4 8. ♗h6 — 5. ♗g5; **5... ♘c6!** 6. ♕d2 ♗g4 7. d5 ♘b8 8. ♗e2 — 5. ♗e2

[3] **6... ♘bd7** 7. 0-0-0 c6 [7... c5 8. dc5 ♘c5 9. e5 ♘h5 10. ♗h6 ♕a5 11. ♗g7 ♘g7 12. ed6 ed6 13. ♗c4± Pachman—Tikovsky, Praha 1943] 8. e5 ♘e8 9. h4± Darga—Kuijpers, Berlin 1965; **6... ♗g4** 7. ♗e2 0—0 — 5. ♗e2

[4] 14. 0-0-0± Darga—Larsen, Beverwijk 1967

[5] **5... ♘bd7** 6. ♕d2 c5=; 6. e5±; **5... h6** 6. ♗f4 [6. ♗h4 c6 7. ♕d2 g5 8. ♗g3 ♘h5 9. 0-0-0 b5 10. h3 ♘g3 11. fg3 ♕a5∞ Saharov—Podgajec, SSSR 1970; 6. ♗e3 0—0? 7. h3 ♘c6 8. ♕d2 ♔h7 9. 0-0-0 ♘d7 10. d5±; 6... ♘g4 7. ♗f4 ♘c6 8. ♗b5! 0—0 9. ♗c6 bc6 10. h3±; 6... ♘bd7 7. h3 c6 8. ♕d2 b5 9. ♗d3 ♘b6 10. b3 (Bastrikov—Ustinov, SSSR 1959) ♕c7∞] ♘bd7 [6... 0—0 7. ♕d2 ♔h7 8. 0-0-0 a5 9. ♗d3 ♘a6 10. e5 ♘g8 11. h4± Tarrasch—Davidson, Semmering 1926; 6... c6 7. h3 b5 8. ♗d3 a6 9. 0—0 0—0 10. ♕d2 ♔h7 11. e5± Guljko—Kaem, SSSR 1972] 7. ♕d2 [7. h3 c5!?] g5 8. ♗g3 ♘h5 9. ♗c4 g4 10. ♘g1 c5∞ Boleslavski—Bondarevski, SSSR (mch) 1941

[6] 6. e5 de5 7. ♘e5 ♗e6 8. ♕d2 ♘bd7 9. ♘d3 0—0 10. f3 ♖e8 11. ♘f4 ♗f5 12. g4 e5!∓ Bisguier—Gipslis, Zagreb 1965

[7] **6... ♕a5** 7. 0-0-0 b5 8. e5± Helbig—Wojzik, corr. 1967 — 3/149; **6... ♗g4** 7. 0-0-0 [7. ♕f4 ♗f3 8. ♕f3 ♘bd7 9. 0-0-0 ♕a5 10. h4 c5? 11. e5+— Suetin—Korčnoj, SSSR 1962; 10... 0-0-0!∞] h6 8. ♗e3 b5 9. ♗d3 a6 10. ♖de1 ♘fd7 11. e5± Talj—Bronštejn, SSSR 1973 — 15/166; **6... d5** 7. ♗f6!±

[8] 8. ♗h6 ♗h6 9. ♕h6 ♗f3 10. gf3 e5 11. de5 de5 12. 0-0-0± Beneš—Kubiček, Olomouc 1973; 8... 0—0!?∞

[9] Željandinov—Vitolinš, SSSR 1967

[10] **6... c6** 7. ♗h6 [7. ♗d3 ♗g4 8. 0-0-0 b5 9. e5 b4 10. ♘e4 ♘e4 11. ♗e4 d5 12. h3 ♗e6!∞ Talj—Koc, SSSR 1962; 8. h3 ♗f3 9. gf3 b5∞] ♗g4 8. ♗e2 b5 9. a3 ♘bd7 10. ♗g7 ♔g7 11. e5± Szilagyi—Sapi, Hungary (ch) 1968; **6... ♗g4** 7. ♗e2 [7. 0-0-0 ♘bd7 8. ♗h6 e5 9. ♗g7 ♔g7 10. ♗e2± Krasnov—Glotov, SSSR 1966 — 1/96] ♗f3 8. ♗f3 e5 [8... c6 9. h4 e5 10. d5 ♕a5 11. h5± Klaman—Bivšev, SSSR 1958] 9. d5 ♘bd7 10. h4±→⟫ Uusi—Kimelfeld, SSSR 1959

[11] 7. ♗f6 ef6 8. ed5 [8. ♘d5 f5∓] ♖e8 9. ♗e2 ♘d7△ ♘b6=

[12] 7... de4 8. ♘e4 ♗g4∞

[13] 11... ♘a6 12. c6 ♖b8 13. ♗f4 e5 14. ♗e3 bc6∞ Mnacakanjan—Hodos, SSSR (ch) 1963; 12. 0-0-0!±⊥

[14] **5... ♗g4?** 6. e5±; **5... ♘e4?** 6. ♗f7 ♔f7 7. ♘e4 ♖f8 8. h4±

[15] **6. 0—0** d5 [6... 0—0 7. e5 de5 8. de5 ♘g4 9. ♗f4± Lechtynsky—Liebert, Luhačovice 1971 — 11/135; 6... b5 7. ♗d3 b4 8, ♘e2 ♗g4 9. ♘g3 ♘bd7∞ Feller—Keene, Siegen (ol) 1970] 7. ♗d3 [7. ed5 cd5 8. ♗b5 ♗d7 9. ♗d7 ♘bd7 10. ♖e1 0—0 11. ♗f4 ♖c8 12. ♕d3 ♘b6 13. b3 ♕d7 14. ♖ac1 ♕f5∓ Marić—Portisch, Skopje—Ohrid 1968] ♗g4 8. e5 ♘fd7 9. h3 ♗f3 10. ♕f3 e6 11. ♘e2 c5 12. c3 ♘c6∓ van Scheltinga—Botvinik, Wageningen 1958; **6. ♕e2** b5 [6... d5 7. e5!? dc4 8. ef6 ♗f6 9. ♗h6⩱; 6... 0—0 — 5... 0—0] 7. e5 bc4 8. ef6 ♗f6 9. ♗h6 d5 10. h3⩱ Kločko—Volokov, SSSR 1967

[16] 6... ♘d5!? 7. ♗d5 cd5 8. ♘d5 ♕a5 9. ♘c3 de5= Šašin

[17] **9. ♕e2** ♘b6 [9... a5?! 10. a3 ♘b6 11. ♗a2 ♕d4? 12. ♘f7△ ♗e3+—; 11... ♗f5 12. ♖e1 a4 13. ♗e3 ♘fd5 14. ♘d5 ♘d5 15. c4± Padevski—Petrosjan, Tel Aviv (ol) 1964] 10. ♗e3 [10. ♗b3 ♕d4 11. ♖d1 ♕h4 12.

♘f7 ♖f7 13. ♕e7 ♘bd5 14. ♖d5 cd5 15. ♗d5 ♕f2=∞⧉; 11... ♕c5!∓] ♘c4=; **9. f4** ♕c7 10. ♕f3 a6 11. ♖e1 e6 12. ♗b3 c5 13. ♗e3 cd4? 14. ♗d4± Talj—Bilek, Miskolc 1963; 13... b6!∞; **9. h3** ♘b6 10. ♗b3 a5 11. a4 ♘bd5 12. ♖e1 ♗f5 13. ♘d5 cd5= Reshevsky—Ciocaltea, Siegen (ol) 1970 — 10/168

18 **9... ♘e5** 10. de5 ♘g4 11. e6±; **9... c5** 10. ♘d7 ♗d7 11. dc5 ♕c7 12. ♗f6±

19 **10... ♘bd5** 11. ♘d5 cd5 12. c4 ♗e6 13. c5±; **10... ♘fd5** 11. ♘d5 cd5 12. ♗h4 ♗e6= Ničevski—Udovčić, Zagreb 1970

20 11. a3 a4 12. ♗a2 ♘fd5 [12... ♘bd5 13. ♘d5 ♘d5 14. ♗h4 ♗e6 15. ♖e1± Veresov—Malich, DDR 1965] 13. ♘d5 cd5=

21 14. ♘d3 ♖e8 15. ♖e1 ♘c4 16. ♕f3 e6= Perez—Tringov, La Habana 1965

22 **6... b5** 7. e5± I. Zajcev—Lipiridi, SSSR 1967; **6... ♗g4** 7. h3 ♗f3 8. ♕f3 ♘bd7 9. ♘e2 e6 10. ♘g3 d5 11. e5 ♘g8 12. h4± Nikolić—Gurgenidze, Jugoslavija—SSSR 1968; **6... d5** 7. e5 ♘fd7 8. ♗f4 ♘f8 9. h3 ♘e6 10. ♗e3 f6 11. ef6 ef6 12. ♘e2± Bouwmeester—Botvinik, Amsterdam 1963

23 **7. ♕e2** ♗g4 8. h3 9. ♕f3 e6 10. ♗g5 h6 11. ♗h4 ♘bd7 12. 0—0= [12. 0-0-0 ♕a5 13. ♕e2 b5 14. f4 b4 15. ♘b1 d5∓ Medina—Botvinik, Palma de Mallorca 1967]; **7. h3** a5 [7... ♕c7 8. e5 de5 9. de5 ♖d8 10. ♕e2 ♘d5 11. ♘d5 cd5 12. ♗f4± Schmid—Bouwmeester, Varna (ol) 1962] 8. a3 a4 9. ♗a2 ♘bd7 10. 0—0 e5 11. ♗e3 ♕c7= Csom—Uhlmann, Zinnovitz 1967

24 **7... a5** 8. a3 a4 9. ♗a2 ♗g4 [Schöneberg—Lechtynsky, Kapfenberg 1970 — 9/132] 10. h3±; **7... d5** 8. ♖e1 [8. e5 ♘e8 9. ♖e1 ♘c7 10. ♗e3 f6 11. ef6 ef6 12. h3 ♗e6 13. ♕d2± I. Zajcev—Volovič, SSSR 1964] ♗g4 9. ♗g5± Nežmetdinov—Malich, Soči 1965

25 10... e6!?

26 14. ♘e2 ♘hf6 15. c3± Medina—Szabo, Solingen 1968

27 **6. e5** de5 [6... ♘e8 7. 0—0?! c6 8. h3 b5 9. ♗b3 a5 10. a4 b4 11. ♘e4 d5∞ Estrin—Ufimcev, SSSR 1949; 7. ♗g5! ♘c6 8. ♕e2 ♔h8 9. 0-0-0± Antošin—Vasjukov, SSSR 1954] 7. ♘e5 [7. de5? ♕d1 8. ♘d1 ♘g4∓] c5 [7... ♘e8 (Fuchs—Matulović, Polanica Zdroj 1965) 8. ♗f4 ±; 7... ♘bd7 8. 0—0 c5 9. ♗e3 cd4= Malisov—Tarve, SSSR 1968] 8. dc5 ♕a5 [8... ♕d1 9. ♘d1 ♘bd7 10. ♘d3 e5=∞ Cafferty—Sherman, England 1970] 9. 0—0 ♕c5 10. ♕e2 ♘h5 11. ♘g4 ♘c6 12. ♘e4 ♗g4∓ Keres—Košanski, Sarajevo 1972; **6. h3** ♘e4 7. ♗f7 [7. ♘e4 d5 8. ♗d3 de4 9. ♗e4 c5=] ♖f7 8. ♘e4 e6 9. 0—0 ♘d7= Schweber—Matanović, Tel Aviv (ol) 1964; **6. ♗g5** h6 7. ♗f4 ♘e4= Golovko—Murej, SSSR 1963; **6. ♗e3** ♘e4 [6... ♗g4 7. h3 ♗f3 8. ♕f3 ♘c6 9. ♗b5 ♘d7 10. ♖d1 e5 11. ♗c6 bc6 12. 0—0 ♕b8 13. b3 ♕b4=; 9. 0—0 — 6. 0—0] 7. ♗f7 [7. ♘e4 d5 8. ♗d3 de4 9. ♗e4 c5=] ♖f7 8. ♘e4 h6 9. h3 ♘d7△ ♘f8=

28 **6... ♗g4** 7. e5 ♘e8 8. ♗g5△ 0-0-0± Kuznjecov—Šipov, SSSR 1964; **6... ♘c6** 7. h3 e5 8. de5 ♘e5 9. ♘e5 de5 10. ♗g5 c6 11. ♖d1± Kuprejanov—Udovčić, Jugoslavija (ch) 1962

29 7. ♗g5 b5 [7... h6 8. ♗f6 ef6= I. Zajcev—Bondarevski, SSSR 1960] 8. ♗d3 ♕c7 9. e5 de5 10. ♕e5 ♕d8∓ Balog—O'Kelly, corr. 1966

30 7... de5 8. de5 ♘d5 9. ♗d2 [9. h3 ♗e6 10. ♗d2 ♘d7 11. 0—0 ♕c7 12. ♖fe1 ♖ad8 13. ♗b3 ♘c5 1/2 : 1/2 Ničevski—Vasjukov, Jugoslavija—SSSR 1969] ♘c3 10. ♗c3 b5 11. ♗d3 ♕b6∞ Vesely—Maršalek, ČSSR 1960

31 **8. ♗d5** cd5 9. ♗f4 ♗g4 10. ed6 e6∓; **8. h3** ♘c3 9. bc3 c5=

32 10... de5 11. de5 ♕c7 12. ♕e3± Unzicker—Kotov, Hamburg 1960; 11... e6!∞

33 11. e6? d5∓

34 12. ♗d6? ♖e8 13. ♕d3 ♗f5—+

35 6... ♗g4 7. h3 ♗f3 8. ♕f3 ♘c6 9. ♘e2 e5 10. de5 ♘e5 11. ♕e3 ♖e8 12. 0—0 a5 13. ♘c3 ♘ed7 14. ♕f3 ♘c5= Estrin—Kogan, SSSR 1952

36 7. ♗e3 ♗g4 8. h3 ♗f3 9. ♕f3 e5 10. de5 de5 11. ♘e2 [11. ♘d5 ♘d4 12. ♘f6 ♗f6 13. ♕g4 ♔g7 14. c3 ♘b3 15. ab3 ♕d3= Spaski—Kotov, Soči 1967] ♘a5 [11... ♕d6 12. 0—0 ♖ad8 13. ♗g5 ♘d4 14. ♘d4 ed4 15. ♖ae1± Vasjukov—Murej, SSSR 1967; 12... ♕b4!?] 12. ♖d1 ♕e7 13. 0—0 ♘b3 14. ab3 ♖fd8= Boleslavski

37 8. ♗e3 c6 9. 0—0 [9. ♕e2 d5 10. e5 ♘e8 11. ♕d2 f6 12. ♗h6 b5 13. 0-0-0 ♘c4∓ Pelitov—Bronštejn, Szombathely 1966] d5 10. e5 ♘e4 11. ♘e4 de4 12. ♘g5 ♘b3 13. ab3 f5 14. ef6 ef6 15. ♘e4 f5 16. ♗g5± Saharov—Vasjukov, SSSR 1963; 8... ♘b3 9. ab3 b6=

38 9... b6 10. ♖e1 ♗b7 11. ♗g5 h6 12. ♗h4 e6 13. e5 de5 14. de5 ♕d1 15. ♖ad1 ♘d5= Saharov—Parma, SSSR—Jugoslavija 1966

39 Saharov—Gufeljd, SSSR (ch) 1963

40 6... ♘c6 **7. h3** ♘e4 8. ♗f7 ♖f7 9. ♘e4 d5 [9... e5 10. de5 de5 11. ♕d8 ♘d8 12. b3 ♗f5 13. ♖e1 ♘c6= Kirilov—Kampenus, SSSR 1964] 10. ♘c3 [10. ♘eg5 ♖f8 11. ♖e1 ♕d6 12. c4 h6 13. cd5 ♕d5 14. ♘e4 ♕f7∓ Medina—Parma, Tunis 1973; 10. ♘c5 ♕d6 11. ♗e3 e5 12. de5 ♘e5∓ Medina—Larsen, Las Palmas 1972 — 13/162] ♕d6 [10... ♗f5 11. ♗e3 ♕d7 12. ♘g5 ♖ff8 13. f4= Unzicker—Keene, Berlin 1971; 10... h6!?△ g5] 11. ♘b5 ♕d7 12. c3 a6 13. ♘a3 h6 14. ♘c2 ♕d6 15. ♘e3 ♗e6∞ Holmov—Rukavina,

Dubna 1973 — 16/138; **7. ♗e3** a6 [7... ♗g4 — 6... ♗g4] 8. a4 ♘e4 9. ♘e4 d5 10. ♗d3 de4 11. ♗e4 ♕d6 12. c3 ♗f5 14. ♗f5 gf5 15. g3± Filip–Larsen, La Habana 1967; **7. d5** ♘b8 [7... ♘a5!?] 8. e5 [8. h3 c6= Witt–Balcerowski, Tel Aviv (ol) 1964] de5 9. ♘e5 ♘bd7 10. ♘f3 ♘e8 11. ♖e1± Hübner–Keene, Wien 1972 — 14/185

41 7. ♘e4 d5 8. ♗d3 de4 9. ♗e4 c5 10. dc5 [10. ♗e3 cd4 11. ♗d4±; 10... f5!? 11. ♗d3 f4∓] ♕c7 11. c3 ♘d7 12. b4 a5 13. ♖b1 ♘f6 14. ♗c2 ♗e6 15. ♗b2 ♗a2∓ Estrin–Gusev, SSSR 1951

42 9... d5 10. ♘c5 ♘c6 11. c3 ♕f8 12. ♘e5 ♘e5 13. de5 c6 14. f4± Medina–Andersson, Las Palmas 1972

43 14. ♘g3 ♗e6∞ Holmov–Hodos, SSSR (ch) 1962

44 9... ♘d7 10. ♖ad1 [10. ♕d1 ♘b6 11. ♗b5 ♘a5 12. ♕e2 c6 13. ♗d3 d5∓ Horberg–Kotov, Stockholm 1959; 10. ♖fd1 e5 11. de5 ♘ce5 12. ♕e2 ♘c4 13. ♕c4 ♖e8 14. ♗d4 ♘e5 15. ♕f1?! ♗h6= Honfi–Vadasz, Hungary (ch) 1971 — 12/169] e5 11. de5 de5 [11... ♘ce5 12. ♕e2 ♘c4 13. ♕c4 ♘b6 14. ♕b3± Holmov–Gufeljd, SSSR 1966] 12. ♘d5 [12. ♘e2!?] ♘d4 13. ♕g4 ♘e6 14. ♖d2 c6 15. ♘b4 ♕e7 16. ♗e6 ♘f6= Medina–Padevski, Kapfenberg 1970

45 12. ♘e4 ♘c4 13. ♗g5 f6 14. ♕c4 d5= Boleslavski

46 14. ♕d3 ♕e7= Boleslavski

47 **6. ♗g5** c6 7. ♕d2 b5 8. a3 ♗b7 9. ♖d1 a5∓ L. Kovacs–Ivkov, Sombor 1968 — 6/209; **6. ♗d3** ♘c6 7. 0–0 ♘d7 8. ♘e2 e5 9. c3 ♘b6 10. ♗e3 f5∓↑ Balitinov–Štejn, SSSR 1963

48 **6... ♘c6** 7. g3 [7. ♕d2!?± Marić–Ivković, Jugoslavija 1972 — 13/182] e5 8. ♗g2 ♗d7 9. 0–0 ♖e8 10. ♕d2 a6 11. ♖ad1± Kavalek–Vasjukov, Praha–Moskva 1967 — 5/137; **6... ♘bd7**!? 7. ♕d2 c5 8. ♗h6 [8. dc5 ♘c5 9. e5 ♘fe4 10. ♘e4 ♘e4 11. ♕d5 ♘c5= Toran–Pirc, München 1954] cd4 9. ♘d4 ♘c5 10. ♗g7 ♔g7 11. f3 ♕a5 12. a3 ♘e6 13. 0-0-0 ♘d4= Czerniak–Vidmar, Wien 1951; **6... e5**!? Pachman

49 7. ♗d3 ♕c7 8. 0–0 e5 9. ♖e1 ♘bd7 10. a4 ♖e8 11. ♕d2 b6= Furman–Petrosjan, SSSR (ch) 1961

50 7... e5 8. de5 de5 9. ♕d8 ♖d8 10. ♗c4 ♘bd7 11. a5± Haag–Czerniak, Bucuresti 1967 — 3/140

51 8. ♗e2 e5 9. de5 de5 10. ♘d2 ♕e7 11. ♘c4 ♘e8 12. 0–0 ♘c5 13. ♘d6 ♘d6 14. ♗c5 ♖d8 15. a5 ♕h4= Sax–Parma, Nice (ol) 1974

52 **8... ♕a5**? 9. ♗e2 e5 10. 0–0 ed4 11. ♘d4 ♕e5 12. ♗f4 ♕e7 13. ♘f3± Torre–Portisch, Nice (ol) 1974 — 17/186; **8... e5**!?

53 13. ♘h4? b5 14. f4 b4∓ Griffiths–Miles, Birmingham 1974 — 17/185

54 **5... a6** 6. 0–0 b5 7. e5 ♘fd7 8. ♖e1 ♘c6 [Weinstein–Suttles, Chicago 1973] 9. e6±; **5... c5** 6. d5 [6. 0–0?! cd4 7. ♘d4 — B 70; 6. dc5 ♕a5 7. 0–0 dc5 8. e5 ♘g4 9. ♗f4 ♘c6 10. ♖e1± Fridštejn; 7... ♕c5 8. ♗e3 ♕a5 9. ♘d4 0–0 10. ♘b3±] ♘a6 7. 0–0 [7. ♘d2 ♘c7 8. a4 a6 9. a5 ♗d7 10. ♘a4± Donner–Teschner, Wageningen 1957] ♘c7 8. ♖e1 [8. a4 0–0 9. ♗f4 b6 10. h3 ♗b7 11. ♖e1 ♖e8 12. ♗c4 a6 13. ♕d3 ♘d7 14. e5± Kluger–Talj, Kislovodsk 1964; 8... a6 9. ♘d2 ♗d7 10. e5 de5 11. ♘c4 b5 12. ab5 ab5 13. ♖a8 ♕a8 14. ♘e5 b4 15. d6 ed6!∞ Larsen–Szabo, Büsum 1969] 0–0 9. a4 a6 10. ♗g5 h6 11. ♗f4 ♗d7 12. ♕d2 b5 13. e5 de5 14. ♗e5 b4 15. ♗f6± Spaski–Schmid, Varna (ol) 1962

55 **6. ♗g5** c5 [6... ♘bd7 7. ♕d2 c5 8. 0–0 cd4 9. ♘d4 a6 10. ♔h1 ♕c7 11. f4 h6 12. ♗h4 b5= Ceškovski–Usakov, SSSR 1962; 6... ♗g4 7. ♕d2 ♘c6 8. d5 (Ujtumen–Savon, Krakow 1964) ♘b8∞] 7. dc5 ♕a5= Persitz–Gabrovšek, Ljubljana 1955; **6. ♗f4** ♘c6 [6... ♗g4 7. ♘d2 ♗e2 8. ♕e2 ♘c6 9. ♘f3 ♘h5 10. ♗e3± Krasnov–I. Zajcev, SSSR 1962; 6... c6 7. 0–0 ♗g4 8. h3 ♗f3 9. ♗f3 ♘bd7 10. e5± Minev–Gipslis, Bad Liebenstein 1963; 6... ♘bd7!?] 7. 0–0 [7. d5 e5 8. de6 ♗e6 9. 0–0 ♖e8 10. ♖e1 h6 11. h3 g5 12. ♗e3 d5∓ Unzicker–Botvinik, Varna (ol) 1962] ♗g4 8. d5 ♘b8 9. h3 [9. ♕d2 ♘bd7 10. ♗h6 — 6. 0–0] ♗f3 10. ♗f3 c6 11. ♕d2= Lehmann–O'Kelly, Palma de Mallorca 1966; **6. ♗e3** ♗g4 [6... ♘bd7 7. 0–0 e5 8. de5 de5 9. ♘d2 b6 10. b4 ♗b7 11. a4 ♕e7 12. ♕b1 ♖fd8 13. a5± S. Garcia–Gligorić, Hastings 1973/74] 7. ♕d2 ♘c6 8. d5 ♘b8 [8... ♗f3? 9. gf3! ♘e5 10. h4± Planinc–Marangunić, Jugoslavija (ch) 1969] 9. 0–0 — 6. 0–0

56 **6... c6** 7. 0–0 — 6. 0–0; **6... c5** 7. dc5 [7. e5 de5 8. de5 ♕d1 9. ♗d1 ♘e8 10. ♘d5 ♘c6 11. ♗g5 f6∞ Đuraševič–Štejn, Jugoslavija–SSSR 1961; 7. 0–0 cd4 8. ♘d4 — B 70] ♕a5 8. 0–0 ♕c5 9. ♗e3 ♕c7 [9... ♕a5!?] 10. e5 de5 11. ♘b5 ♕c6 12. ♘e5± Kuzmin–Nikolajevski, SSSR 1970; **6... ♘a6** 7. ♗e3 [7. 0–0 — 6. 0–0] c5 8. d5 ♘c7 9. a4 a6 10. ♘d2 ♖b8 11. a5 ♗d7 12. ♘a4 e6∞ Hübner–Keene, Southport 1969; **6... b6**!? 7. e5∞ [7. ♗e3 ♗b7 8. ♗d3 c5∓ Segal–Czerniak, Israel 1971 — 12/171]

57 15. a4 c6∞ Daskalov–Bohosjan, Bulgaria (ch) 1972

58 **6... ♘fd7** 7. ♗e3 c5 8. ♕d2±; **6... c5** 7. dc5 dc5 8. ♕d8 ♖d8 9. ♗e3 b6 10. ♖fd1 ♗d7 11. ♘e5 ♘e8 12. ♘d7 ♘d7 13. f4± Gufeljd–Kutarašvili, SSSR 1971; **6... a6** 7. ♖e1 [7. a4?! b6 8. ♖e1 ♗b7 9. ♗c4 e6 10. ♗f4 ♘bd7 11. ♕d2 b5∞ Kavalek–Suttles, Nice (ol) 1974 — 17/189; 7. ♗f4 b5 8. e5

♘fd7 9. a4 (Najdorf–Stahlberg, Amsterdam 1950) b4±] b5 8. e5 ♘fd7 [8... de5 9. de5 ♕d1 10. ♗d1 ♘e8 11. a4 b4 12. ♘d5 ♘c6 13. ♗g5±; 8... ♘e8 9. a4 b4 10. ♘d5±] 9. e6 fe6 10. ♘g5 ♘f6 11. ♗f3△ ♘e6± Holmov–Gipslis, SSSR (ch) 1963; **6... e5** 7. de5 de5 8. ♕d8 ♖d8 9. ♗g5 [9. ♘e5 ♘e4 10. ♘f7? ♘c3 11. ♗c4 ♖d4–+; 10. ♘e4 ♗e5 11. ♗g5±] ♖e8 10. ♖fd1 ♗g4 [10... h6 11. ♗f6 ♗f6 12. ♘d5 ♗d8 13. ♘e5 ♖e5 14. ♘b6+–] 11. h3 ♗f3 12. ♗f3 ♘c6 13. ♘b5△ c3±; **6... b6** 7. ♖e1 [7. e5 ♘fd7 8. ♖e1 de5 9. de5 ♘c6 10. e6 fe6 11. ♗e3 ♘f6 12. ♗b5 ♘b4∞ Geler–Bilek, Lugano (ol) 1968; 7. ♗e3 ♗b7 8. ♘d2 e5 9. d5 ♘e8 10. ♘c4± Cvetkov–Smislov, Moskva 1947] ♗b7 8. ♗f1 c5 9. d5 ♘a6 10. ♗f4 ♘c7 11. ♕d2 a6 12. ♗h6 b5 13. ♗g7 ♔g7 14. a3 e6 15. de6 ♘e6 16. ♖ad1± Gligorić–Benkö, Beograd 1964

59 7. h3 c5 [7... c6 8. ♖e1 ♘d7 9. ♗g5 b5 10. ♕d2 ♘c7 11. ♖ad1 ♘b6 12. e5± Smislov–Lutikov, SSSR 1966 — 2/130] 8. e5 ♘e8 9. ♗e3 b6 10. ♗c4 ♘ec7 11. ed6 ed6 12. dc5 bc5 13. ♗f4± S. Garcia–Keene, Palma de Mallorca 1971

60 8. ♗a6 cd4 9. ♗b7 ♗b7 10. ♘d4 ♖c8 11. ♘b3 ♖c3 12. bc3 ♘e4 13. ♕d3± Smislov–Larsen, Monte Carlo 1967 — 3/150

61 **8... de5** 9. de5 ♕d1 10. ♖d1 ♘g4 11. ♘d5 ♘e5 12. ♘e5 ♗e5 13. ♗h6±; **8... ♘e8** 9. ♗g5±

62 15. ♘bd4± Geler–Sax, Budapest 1973 — 15/169

63 **7. ♗g5** c5 8. e5 cd4 9. ef6 ef6∓ Kostić–Pirc, Ljubljana 1951; **7. ♗f4** c5 [7... e5 8. de5 de5 9. ♘e5 ♘e4 10. ♘e4 ♘e5 11. ♕d8 ♖d8 12. ♗g5± van Geet–Kersten, Amsterdam 1952] 8. dc5 ♘c5 9. e5±

64 **8. ♖e1** c5 9. ♗g5 h6 10. ♗h4 cd4∞; **8. ♗f4** c6 [8... c5 9. dc5 ♘c5 10. ♕c1 de5 11. ♘e5 (Akulin–Lurganov, SSSR 1968) ♘d6±; 10. ♕d2±; 8... ♘b6 9. h3 c6 — 6... c6] 9. ♖e1 de5? 10. de5 ♘c7 11. ♕c1 ♘e6 12. ♗h6± Gligorić–Robatsch, Hastings 1961/62; 9... ♘b6! — 6... c6

65 Spaski–Hodos, SSSR 1962

66 **7. h3** e5 8. de5 de5 [8... ♘e5 9. ♘e5 de5 10. ♕d8 ♖d8 11. ♗e3 c6 12. ♖ad1 ♖d1 13. ♖d1 ♗e6 1/2 : 1/2 Hort–Bronštejn, Krems 1967; 10. ♗c4 Browne–Mednis, USA (ch) 1973 — 16/140; 10... ♘e7△ ♗e6=] 9. ♗g5 [9. ♕d8 ♖d8 10. ♗g5 ♗e6 11. ♖fd1 h6 12. ♗e3 ♘e8 13. ♘e1 ♘d4∓ Matulović–Botvinik, Beograd 1969 — 8/138] ♗e6=; **7. ♗g5** h6 [7... ♗g4 — 6... ♗g4] 8. ♗f4 [8. ♗h4 ♗g4 — 6... ♗g4] a6 9. a4 ♕e8△ e5= Haag–Gufeljd, Tallinn 1969 — 7/162; **7. ♗e3** ♖e8 [7... ♗g4 — 6... ♗g4] 8. d5 ♘b8 9. ♕d2 ♗g4 10. ♖ad1 ♗f3 11. ♗f3 ♘bd7 12. ♗e2 e6 13. de6 ♖e6 14. f3± Vasjukov – G. Garcia, Camaguey 1974

67 **8. ♖e1** c6 9. ♗f1 ♗g4 10. h3 ♗f3 11. ♕f3 ♘bd7 12. ♗e3 ♕a5 13. a3 ♖ac8 [Kostro–Razuvajev, Moskva 1970 — 10/176] 14. ♗d4 ∞; **8. ♗e3** c6 9. ♘d2 b5 10. dc6 b4 11. c7 ♕c7 12. ♘b5 ♕b7 13. a3 ♗d7 14. ♘d4 ♘c6= Jansa–Forintos, Wijk aan Zee 1971; **8. ♗g5** c6 9. ♘d2 ♘bd7 10. a4 a5 11. ♘b3 ♘e5∞ Lejn–Talj, SSSR (ch) 1972 — 14/186

68 **9. a4** a5 [9... ♘bd7 10. ♖e1 ♘c5 11. ♗f1 e5 12. b4 ♘ce4 13. ♘e4 ♘e4 14. ♖e4 f5 15. ♗g5 ♕e8 16. ♖e1 h6 17. dc6± Furman–Šamkovič, SSSR 1973 — 16/139] 10. ♗e3 [10. ♗g5 — 9. ♗g5] ♘a6 11. ♘d2 ♗d7 12. dc6?! ♗c6∓ Antošin–I. Zajcev, SSSR (ch) 1970; **9. ♖e1** ♘bd7 [9... a5!?] 10. ♗f1 [Tajmanov–Dely, Vrnjačka Banja 1974 — 17/191] cd5 11. ed5 ♘c5±○; **9. ♗f4** ♘bd7 10. ♖e1 ♘c5 11. ♗f1 cd5 12. ed5 ♗f5 13. ♘d4± Ghitescu–Matulović, Reykjavik 1970

69 9... ♘bd7 10. ♖e1 ♖e8 11. ♕d2 a6 12. a4 ♕c7 13. ♗f1 cd5 14. ed5 ♘b6 [Antošin–Gufeljd, SSSR 1969 — 9/135] 15. ♖e3±

70 12. dc6 ♗c6 13. ♗b5 ♘b4 14. ♕e2 h6 15. ♗f4 e5= Karpov–Korčnoj, Leningrad (izt) 1973 — 15/172

71 **7. h3** ♗f3 8. ♗f3 ♘c6 [8... e5 9. de5 de5 10. ♗g5 c6 11. ♕e2± Velimirović–Bukić, Jugoslavija (ch) 1963] 9. ♘e2 [9. ♗e3 — 7. ♗e3] e5 10. c3 ♖e8 11. d5 ♘e7 12. g4 h6 13. ♘g3 c6 14. c4 b5∓ Muhitdinov–Botvinik, SSSR 1967 — 4/163; **7. ♖e1** ♘c6 [7... ♘fd7? 8. ♘g5 ♗e2 9. ♘e2 e6 10. c3 ♘b6 11. a4± Vasjukov–Gurgenidze, SSSR (ch) 1967 — 3/152; 7... c6 — 6... c6] 8. ♗e3 — 7. ♗e3

72 9... h6 10. ♗e3 [10. ♗h4 ♘d7 11. ♘e2 ♕e8 12. ♗g4 Tatai–Boudi, Camaguey 1974, 12... e5=] e5 11. de5 [11. d5!?] de5 12. ♘b5 a6! 13. ♕d8 ♖fd8 14. ♘c7 ♖ac8 15. ♘d5 ♘d5 16. ed5 ♘d4= Polugajevski–Matulović, Lugano (ol) 1968 — 6/213

73 **13. b3** d5∓ Matulović–Botvinik, Beograd 1970 — 9/136; **13. ♕c1**!?

74 15. ♗c1 ed4 16. ♘d4 [Smislov–Timman, Amsterdam 1971 — 12/170] d5=

75 7... ♘bd7 8. a4 c6 9. ♖e1 e5 10. de5 dc5 11. ♘d2± Averbah–Pirc, Beverwijk 1963

76 **8. ♖e1** e5 9. d5 ♘e7 [9... ♗f3 10. ♗f3 ♘e7 11. a4 ♘d7 12. ♗e2 f5 13. f3 ♘f6 14. ♕d3 f4∞ Vasjukov–Johansson, Reykjavik 1968] 10. ♕d2 ♘e8 11. ♖ad1 ♗d7 12. ♗c4 ♔h8∓ Mjagmarsuren–Ivkov, Sousse (izt) 1967 — 4/166; **8. h3** ♗f3 9. ♗f3 ♘d7 [9... e5 10. de5 de5 11. ♘b5 ♕e7 12. c3 h5 13. b4± Ceškovski–Cejtlin, SSSR 1971; 11... a6!=] 10. ♘e2 [10. ♕d2 ♘b6 11. ♗e2 e5 12. de5 de5 13. ♕d8 ♖ad8∓ Ćirić–Botvinik, Wijk aan Zee 1969] e5 11. c3 ♔h8∞ Czerniak–Robatsch, Moskva (ol) 1956; **8. ♘d2** ♗e2 9. ♕e2 e5 10. d5 ♘e7 [10... ♘d4 11. ♕d3 c6 12. ♗g5± Boleslavski; 11... ♘d7 12. **b4**

c5 13. dc6 bc6 14. ♘b3± Butnoris–Guljko, SSSR 1969] 11. ♖fd1 ♕c8 12. f3 ♘h5∞ Keene; **8. a4** ♖e8 [8... e5 9. d5 ♘e7 10. ♕d2 — 8. ♕d2] 9. a5 e5 10. de5 ♘e5 11. a6 b6 12. ♘e5± Averbah–Ghizdavu, Bucuresti 1971 — 11/141

77 **9. ♕d2** ♘bd7 10. ♗h6 ♗f3 11. ♗f3 c6 12. ♗g7 ♔g7 13. ♖fe1 ♕a5= Westerinen–Razuvajev, Vilnus 1969; **9. h3** ♗f3 10. ♗f3 c6 11. ♕d2 ♘bd7 [11... cd5!?] 12. dc6 [12. ♖ad1 ♕c7 13. ♖fe1 a6 14. ♗e2 ♖fe8 15. ♖f1 b5= Teschner–Parma, Hamburg 1965] bc6 13. ♗e2 ♕c7 14. ♖ad1 ♖fd8 15. f4± Janošević–Ivkov, Sarajevo 1968

78 10. ♕d2 cd5 11. ed5 ♗f3 12. ♗f3 ♘bd7 13. ♗d4 ♖e8 14. ♖e2± Szilagyi–Gheorghiu, Tel Aviv (ol) 1964

79 15. h3± Tajmanov–Ivkov, Budva 1967

80 11. a4 ♕c7 12. a5 a6 13. f4 ♘ed7 14. ♗f3 cd5 15. ed5 ♖fc8 16. ♕e2 b5!? [16... ♕c4 17. ♖fe1± Kuzmin–Benkö, Hastings 1973/74] 17. ab6 ♘b6 18. ♖a6 ♖a6 19. ♕a6 ♘c4∞

81 **12. ♗d4** ♕a5 [12... cd5 13. ed5 ♖c8 14. ♔h1 a6 15. ♗f3 b5 16. a4± Holmov–Cejtlin, SSSR (ch) 1960] 13. ♔h1 cd5 14. ed5 ♘b6 15. ♗f3 ♖ac8∓ Saharov–Bronštejn, SSSR 1967 — 4/162; **12. ♗f3** cd5 13. ed5 ♖c8 [13... ♕a5!?] 14. ♖f2 ♘b6 15. ♗d4 ♖c4∞ Jimenez–Matulović, Palma de Mallorca (izt) 1970 — 10/177; **12. ♕d2** cd5 13. ed5 ♕a5 14. ♖ad1 ♖ac8 15. ♗d4 ♘b6 16. ♖fe1 ♘c4∞ Qunones–Keene, Camaguey 1974 — 17/196

82 **13. ♗c4** d5 14. ed5 ♘b6 15. ♗b3 ♘fd5= Janošević–Savon, Skopje 1968; **13. ♗f3** ♘b6 14. ♕e2 d5 15. ♖ad1 e6 16. a4 ♘c4 17. ♗c5± Matulović–Rukavina, Sarajevo 1971

83 13... ♖b8 14. b3 ♕a5 15. ♖ad1± Damjanović–Timman, Sombor 1972

84 15. ♖ad1 ♕c7 16. b3± Janošević–Rukavina, Sarajevo 1971

85 **8... ♗f3** 9. ♗f3 ♘d7 10. ♖fd1 [10. ♖ad1 ♘b6 11. ♗e2 e5 12. d5 ♘e7 13. f3 f5 14. g3 ♘d7 15. ♖f2 ♘f6 16. ♗f1 ♘h5 17. ♘e2 fe4= Portisch–Suttles, San Antonio 1972; 12. de5!?] ♘b6 11. ♗e2 e5 12. de5! de5 13. ♘b5 ♕b8 14. c3± Parma–Keene, Berlin 1971 — 12/174; **8... ♖e8** 9. ♖ad1 [9. ♖fe1 e5 10. d5 ♗f3 11. ♗f3 ♘d4 12. ♗d4 ed4 13. ♘b5 ♖e5 14. ♘d4 ♕e8=∞ Čečeljan–Cejtlin, SSSR 1969; 9. d5 ♗f3 10. ♗f3 ♘e5 11. ♗e2 c6 12. ♗d4 ♕a5 13. ♖ad1= Andersson–Keene, Hastings 1971/72 — 13/184] ♗f3 10. ♗f3 e5 11. de5 ♘e5 12. ♗e2 a6 13. ♗g5± Andersson–Ree, Las Palmas 1973; **8... d5** 9. ed5 ♘d5 10. ♘d5 ♕d5 11. h3 ♗f3 12. ♗f3 ♕d7 13. ♖ad1 ♖ad8 14. c3 e5 15. de5± Cejtlin–Kremenecki, SSSR 1974; **8... ♘d7** 9. d5 [9. ♘g5 ♗e2 10. ♘e2 e5 11. d5 ♘e7 12. f3 h6 13. ♘h3 ♔h7 14. c4±; 10... ♘b6 11. b3 e5 12. d5 ♘d4 13. ♘c1 f6 14. ♘h3 c6∞ Džjuban–Cejtlin, SSSR 1971] ♗f3 10. ♗f3 ♘ce5 11. ♗e2 ♘b6 12. b3 c6 13. f4△ dc6±

86 **10... ♕e7** 11. ♗g5 ♗f3 [11... ♕e6 12. ♗f6 ♕f6 13. ♘d5 ♕d6 14. c3 ♖ad8 15. ♕g5 ♗e6 16. ♗b5± Browne–Kaplan, Skopje (ol) 1972 — 14/187] 12. ♗f3 ♘d4 13. ♘d5 ♕d6 14. c3± Andersson–Mecking, Wijk aan Zee 1971 — 12/173; **10... ♕d2** 11. ♖d2 ♖fd8 12. ♖fd1 ♖d2 13. ♖d2 ♘e8 14. ♘d5 [14. h3 ♗f3 15. ♗f3 ♘d4 16. ♗d1 ♘d6 17. ♖d3 c5 18. f3 f5∞ Reshevsky–Biyiasas, Petropolis (izt) 1973; 14. ♗b5!?] ♗f3 15. gf3 ♘d4 16. ♗d1 ♘e6 17. c3 ♗f8 18. ♗a4 ♔g7 19. ♘b4 ♘c5= Reshevsky–Ivkov, Santa Monica 1966

87 11. ♗g5 ♗f3 12. ♗f3 ♘d4 13. ♕d3 c6= Enklaar–Matulović, Wijk aan Zee 1974 — 17/198

88 15. ♗f3 a6= Timman–Matulović, Wijk aan Zee 1974 — 17/197

89 10. a4 ♗d7 [10... ♗c8 11. ♘e1 ♘d7 12. a5 a6 13. ♘d3 f5 14. f3 ♘f6 15. ♖fb1 ♗d7 16. ♖a3 ♔h8= Vasjukov–Parma, Camaguey 1974 — 17/200; 10... ♘e8 11. a5 a6 12. ♖a3 ♗d7 13. g3 f5 14. ♘g5 h6∞ Benkö–Ostojić, Wijk aan Zee 1969 — 7/161] 11. a5 a6 12. ♘e1 ♘h5 [42... ♘e8 13. f3 f5 14. g3 ♘f6 15. ♘d3 ♖f7∞ Rogoff–Timman, Malaga 1971 — 11/138] 13. ♘d3 f5 14. f3 ♘f6 15. b4 f4 16. ♗f2 g5∓ Geler–Vasjukov, Kislovodsk 1968 — 6/210

90 **10... ♘d7** 11. ♘g5± Spaski–Parma, La Habana (ol) 1966 — 2/129; **10... ♗f3** 11. ♗f3 ♘d7 12. ♗e2 f5 13. g3 ♘f6 14. f3 ♕d7 15. ♗b5△ ♖f2± Spaski–Parma, San Juan 1969 — 8/137

91 11. ♘e1 ♘g4 12. ♗g4 ♗g4 13. f3 ♗d7 14. ♗h6 ♗h6 15. ♕h6 c6∓ Browne–Timman, Stockholm 1971/72 — 13/183

92 11... ♘g4!?

93 15. f4± Planinc–Ree, Wijk aan Zee 1974 — 17/199

94 **7. ♗f4** ♘bd7 [7... ♗g4 8. h3 ♗f3 9. ♗f3 ♘fd7 10. ♗e3 e6 11. ♕d2 d5 12. ♗h6± Gufeljd–Podgajec, SSSR (ch) 1973; 7... ♘h5!?] 8. h3 — 7. h3; **7. ♗g5** ♕c7 [7... h6 8. ♗e3 ♘bd7 9. h3 e5 10. ♕d2 ♔h7 11. ♖ad1± Giterman–Etruk, SSSR 1968; 8... ♘g4 9. ♗f4 e5 10. de5 de5 11. ♕d8 ♖d8 12. ♗g3 ♘d7 13. ♖fd1 ♖e8 14. ♗c4±] 8. ♕d2 e5 9. ♖ad1 ♗g4= Giterman–Juhtman, SSSR 1966

95 **7... ♘bd7** 8. ♗f4 ♘e8 [8... ♕c7 — 7... ♕c7] 9. ♕d2 ♘c7 10. ♖ad1 ♖e8 11. e5± Gufeljd–Ozsvath, Debrecen 1970 — 10/178; **7... ♗g4** 8. ♗g5 [8. h3 ♗f3 9. ♗f3 e5 10. ♗e3 ♘bd7 11. ♕d2 ♖e8 12. ♖ad1 ♕c7= Jimenez–Malich, Harrachov 1966 — 1/98] ♘bd7 [8... h6 9. ♗e3 ♘bd7 10. ♕d2 ♔h7 11. e5± Talj–Levin, SSSR 1970] 9. e5 ♘e8 10. ♕d2 de5 11. de5 ♗f3 12. ♗f3 ♘c7 13. ♖ad1 ♘e6 14. ♕d7 ♘g5 1/2 : 1/2 Geler–Parma, Skopje 1968

96 8. e5 de5 9. ♘e5 ♘bd7 10. ♗f4 ♘e5 11. de5 ♘d5 12. ♘d5 cd5 13. ♕d5 ♖d8 14. ♕b3 ♗e6 15. c4 b5!?∞ Palatnik–Džindžihašvili, SSSR (ch) 1973

97 8... ♘h5 9. ♗e3 e5 [9... ♘d7 10. ♕d2 b5 11. a3 a6 12. ♖ad1 ♘hf6= Vasjukov–Nikolajevski, SSSR (ch) 1967] 10. ♘g5 ♘f6 11. f4 h6= Boleslavski

98 11... ♖e8 12. ♕d2 ♘df6 13. h3± Geler–Vasjukov, SSSR (ch) 1966/67 — 3/151

99 Geler–Adorjan, Budapest 1973 — 15/168

100 **7... e5** 8. de5 de5 9. ♕d8 ♖d8 10. ♘e5 ♘e4 11. ♘e4 ♗e5 12. ♗g5 ♖e8 13. ♖ad1± Keene; **7... ♕c7** 8. ♗f4 ♘h5 [8... ♘bd7!?] 9. ♗e3 e5 10. a4 a5 11. ♕d2 ♘d7 12. ♖ad1 ♘hf6 13. de5 de5 14. ♗c4± Geler–Tukmakov, SSSR (ch) 1973; **7... b5** 8. e5 ♘e8 9. a4 [9. ♗f4 ♗b7 10. ♖e1 ♘d7 11. ♗f1 b4 12. ♘e4 c5 (Smislov–Lange, Dortmund 1961) 13. ed6±] b4 10. ♘e4 ♗f5 [10... f5 11. ♘ed2± Vasjukov–Gurgenidze, SSSR 1962] 11. ♘g3 ♗e6 12. c4 [12. a5 ♘d7∞ Averbah–Kotov, SSSR 1960] bc3 13. bc3 ♗d5 14. ♖e1 ♘d7 [Karpov–Hort, Nice (ol) 1974 — 17/192] 15. ed6 ♘d6 16. ♗f4±

101 **8. ♗g5** h6 9. ♗c3 e5 10. ♕d2 ♔h7 11. de5 [11. ♖fd1 ed4 12. ♗d4 ♖e8 13. ♕f4 ♕e7∓ Vasjukov–Vitolinš, SSSR 1972 — 13/186] de5=; **8. e5** ♘e8 [8... de5 9. de5 ♘d5 10. ♘d5 cd5 11. ♗f4±] 9. ♖e1 [9. ♗f4 ♘b6 10. ♕c1 ♗f5 11. ♗h6 f6 12. ♗g7 ♘g7 13. ♖e1 ♖f7 14. ♗f1 d5 15. a4± Smislov–Petrosjan, SSSR 1964; 10... f6 11. ed6 ed6= Botvinik–Simagin, SSSR 1955] ♘b6 [9... de5 10. de5 ♘c7 11. ♗f4 ♘e6 12. ♗g3± Gligorić–Kotov, Hastings 1962/63] 10. ♗f4 [10. ♗g5 f6 11. ef6 ef6 12. ♗f4 d5= Aronin–Botvinik, SSSR 1965] ♘c7 11. ♗g3 f5 12. ef6 ef6 [Filip–Petrosjan, Curaçao (ct) 1962] 13. d5±; **8. ♗e3** ♕c7 [8... e5 9. de5 de5 10. ♕d6 ♖e8 11. ♗c4 ♕e7 12. ♕e7 ♖e7 13. a4± Marić–Petrosjan, Vinkovci 1970 — 10/179] 9. a4 — 7. a4

102 8... e5 9. de5 de5 10. ♘e5 [10. ♗h2 ♕e7 11. ♖e1 ♘h5= Liberzon–Balcerowski, Moskva 1963] ♘e4 11. ♘e4 ♘e5 [11... ♗e5!?] 12. ♕d8 ♖d8 13. ♗g5±

103 9... h6 10. ♗e3 e5 11. ♕d2 ♔h7 12. ♖fd1 ♕c7 13. a4 ♖e8 14. d5 c5 15. ♘b5 ♕b8 16. a5± Vasjukov–Dončenko, Dubna 1973

104 Vasjukov–Andersson, Camaguey 1974

105 7... ♗g4 **8. ♗g5** ♘bd7 9. ♕d2 ♕c7 10. ♖fd1 e5= Stahlberg–Pirc, Marianske Lazni 1965; **8. ♖e1** d5 9. ed5 [Tajmanov–I. Zajcev, SSSR 1964] ♗f3±; **8. ♗e3** ♘bd7 9. h3 ♗f3 10. ♗f3 ♕c7 [10... e5 11. ♕d2 ♖e8 12. a5 ed4 13. ♗d4 ♘e5 14. ♗e2± Zagorovski–Zaharov, SSSR 1971; 11. b4 ed4 12. ♗d4 ♖e8 13. ♖b1 ♗h6 14. g3± Westerinen–Mecking, Lugano (ol) 1968 — 6/211] 11. ♕d2 [11. b4? a5 12. b5 c5 13. d5 ♘b6 14. ♗e2 ♖fe8 15. ♖a3 e6∓ Westerinen–Benkö, Palma de Mallorca 1968 — 6/212] e5 12. a5±; **8. ♘d2** ♗e2 9. ♕e2 d5 [9... ♘h5 10. ♘f3 e5 11. de5 de5 12. ♖fd1 ♕c8 13. g3± Tatai–Parma, Solingen 1968; 9... ♘fd7 10. ♘b3 ♘a6 11. ♗g5± Haag–Polugajevski, Budapest 1965] 10. e5 ♘e8 11. ♘f3 ♘c7 12. h4 ♘e6 13. h5 ♘a6 [13... c5 14. dc5±] 14. ♗e3 ♘c7 15. ♕d3± Polugajevski–Malich, Sarajevo 1965

106 8. ♖e1 e5 9. a5 [9. ♗f1 a5 10. de5 de5 11. b3 ♖e8 12. ♗a3 ♗f8= Tajmanov–Gipslis, SSSR 1970 — 9/134] ed4 10. ♘d4 ♖e8 11. ♗f1 ♘c5 12. f3 d5= Filip–Bednarski, Tel Aviv (ol) 1964

107 **8... ♘d5** 9. ♘d5 cd5 10. ed6 ed6 [10... e6 11. ♗f4 ♘f6 12. ♕d3 ♘e4 13. ♕a3 ♖e8 14. ♗b5±] 11. c3 ♘f6 12. ♘e1 ♗f5 13. ♗g5± Antošin–Schmid, Venezia 1966 — 1/97; **8... de5** 9. de5 ♘d5 10. ♘d5 cd5 11. ♗f4 ♕c7 12. ♔h1 e6 13. ♖a3± Antošin

108 16. ♘e5± Ćirić–Balcerowski, Jugoslavija 1970 — 10/181

109 **8. ♘d2** e5 9. de5 de5 10. ♘c4 ♖d8 11. ♕e1 ♘a6 12. ♗e3 ♘g4 13. ♗g5 f6∓ Tatai–Evans, Venezia 1967 — 4/165; **8. e5** de5 9. ♘e5 ♗e6 10. ♗f4 ♕c8=; **8. ♗e3** ♘bd7 9. ♘d2 e5 10. d5 cd5 11. ed5 a6 12. a5 b5 13. ab6 ♘b6 14. ♗b6 ♕b6 15. ♘c4 ♕c7∞ Honfi–Tringov, Budapest–Sofia 1971 — 11/140; **8. a5** ♘bd7 9. ♖e1 e5 10. ♗f1 ♖b8 11. b3 b6 12. ab6 ab6 13. ♗b2 b5 14. g3 ♖e8 15. ♗g2 Šamkovič–Tringov, Leningrad 1967 — 4/164; 15... b4△ ed4, c5, ♗b7∞

110 8... e5 **9. de5** [9. ♗e3 ed4 10. ♘d4 ♖e8 11. ♗d3 ♘bd7 12. f4 a6 13. ♘de2 c5 14. ♘g3 d5∓ Wright–Botterill, England 1970/71; 11. ♗f3 ♘bd7 12. ♖e1 a5 13. ♕d2 ♘c5 14. ♗f4 ♘fd7 15. ♖ad1 ♘e5 16. ♗e2 ♕b6∓ Kostro–Smislov, Polanica Zdroj 1968] de5 10. ♗e3 ♘h5 11. ♖e1 [11. a5 ♘d7 12. ♘d2 ♘df6 13. ♖e1 ♘f4 14. ♗f1 ♘e6 15. ♘a4± Simagin–Liberzon, SSSR 1963; 11... ♘f4!=] ♘f4 12. ♗f1∞; **9. ♖e1** ♘bd7 10. ♗f1 ♖e8 [10... ed4!?] 11. d5± Uljanov–Kimelfeld, SSSR 1964

111 9. a5 e5 10. de5 de5 11. ♗e3 **♖d8** 12. ♗c4 [12. ♕c1 ♘f8 13. ♘d2 ♘e6= Hecht–Bilek, Kecskemet 1964] ♘f8 [12... ♘c5 13. ♕e2 ♘ce4 14. ♘e4 ♘e4 15. ♗b6±] 13. ♕e2 ♗e6 14. b4 ♘h5 15. ♖fe1 ♘f4 16. ♕f1± Enklaar–Timman, Wijk aan Zee 1974; **11... ♘h5** 12. ♕d2 [12. ♖e1 ♘f4 13. ♗f1 h6 14. ♘a4 ♖d8 15. ♘d2 ♘f6 16. ♕b1 g5∞ Kostro–Filipowicz, Polska (ch) 1972 — 13/185] ♘f4 13. ♗c4 b5 14. ab6 ♘b6 15. ♗b6± Browne–Donner, Skopje (ol) 1972

112 11. ♕c1 ♖e8= Mecking–Bilek, Sousse (izt) 1967

113 12. ♗c4 ♘b6 13. ♗b3 ♗e6= Matulović–Gurgenidze, SSSR–Jugoslavija 1966

114 **15... ♘c5** 16. ♗f4 ef4 17. e5±; **15... ♘e6** 16. ♘g5 ♘dc5 [16... ♘f6 17. ♘e6 ♗e6 18. ♗e6 ♖e6 19. ♕e2± Geler] 17. b4 ♘g5

18. ♗c5 ♗c5 19. bc5 ♕e7 20. ♕e3± Geler–Szabo, Hilversum 1973 — 15/171

115 8. **♗g5** h6 9. ♗f4 ♘bd7 10. h3 e5= Schweber–Smislov, Buenos Aires 1970; **8. ♖e1** ♘a6 [8... ♘bd7 9. e5 ♘e8 10. ♗f4 (Ćirić–Polugajevski, Jugoslavija–SSSR 1964) ♘b6±] 9. ♗f1 [9. e5 de5 10. ♘e5 ♘b4 11. ♗c4 ♗f5 12. ♗b3 c5 13. g4 c4 14. ♗c4 ♗c2∓ Ree–Hort, Wijk aan Zee 1970 — 9/133; 9. ♗f4 ♘b4 10. h3 ♘h5 11. ♗h2 f5∞ Johansson–Jansson, Sverige (ch) 1969] ♗g4 10. h3 ♗f3 11. ♕f3 ♘d7 12. ♕d1 ♕b6 13. ♘e2 e5 14. de5 ♗e5= Poutiainen–Planinc, Nice (ol) 1974; **8. e5** ♘d5 [8... de5 9. de5 ♘g4 10. ♗f4 ♕d1 11. ♗d1 ♘a6 12. h3 ♘h6 13. ♗e2 ♘b4 14. ♖ac1 ♗f5 15. ♘d4 ♖ad8 16. ♖fd1 c5∓ Langeweg–Smislov, Tel Aviv (ol) 1964; 13. g4! ♘b4 14. ♖ac1 ♗e6 15. ♗e2 ♖ad8 16. ♗e3 f6 17. ♘d4± Langeweg–Bobocov, Beverwijk 1965] 9. ♘d5 [9. ♘e4 de5 10. ♘e5 ♘d7 11. f4 ♘e5 12. fe5 ♗f5 13. ♘g3 ♗e6 14. c3 f6=] cd5 10. ♗f4 de5 11. ♗e5 ♘c6= Boleslavski; **8. ♗e3** ♘g4 [8... ♘a6 9. ♘d2 ♘b4 10. ♘cb1 ♗d7 11. c3 ♘a6 12. ♘a3 ♕c7 13. ♗f4± Tatai–Poutiainen, Nice (ol) 1974 — 17/194; 9... ♕c7 10. f4 d5 11. e5 ♘e8 12. g4 f5 13. h3 e6 14. ♕e1± Bajkov–Volovič, SSSR 1974] 9. ♗g5 h6 10. ♗h4 ♘d7 11. ♘d2 ♘gf6 12. ♘c4 d5 13. ed5 ♘d5∞ Petkevič–Kuindži, SSSR 1973

116 8... ♕c7 9. ♖e1 [9. ♗e3 ♘a6 10. ♕d2 ♖e8 11. ♗h6± Kuzmin–Barreras, Cienfuegos 1973] e5 10. de5 de5 11. ♗c4 ♘a6 12. ♗e3 ♘h5 [12... ♘d7!?] 13. ♕c1 ♘f4 14. ♗f4 ef4 15. e5± Lutikov–Vogt, Leipzig 1973 — 17/184

117 **9. ♖e1** ♘b4 10. ♗f1 e5 11. g3 ♖e8 12. ♗g2 ed4 13. ♘d4 d5 14. e5 ♘e4∓ Haag–Vadasz, Hungary 1970 — 11/139; **9. e5** de5 10. de5 ♕d1 11. ♖d1 ♘d7 12. ♗f4 ♘ac5 13. ♖e1 ♘e6 14. ♗g3 ♘b6 15. ♖ad1 ♗d7 16. ♘e4 ♖fd8 17. b3 ♗e8∞ Dueball–Planinc, Nice (ol) 1974 — 17/193; **9. ♗e3** ♘b4 10. ♕c1 [10. ♕d2 ♕c7 11. ♖ad1 ♖d8 12. ♕c1 ♗d7 13. ♘d2 ♖ac8 14. ♘c4 b5∓ Liljedahl–Hort, Göteborg 1971 — 12/172] ♖e8 11. ♘d2 ♘d7 12. f4 c5 13. d5 f5 14. ♘b5 fe4 15. ♘e4 ♘b6 16. c4 ♗f5 17. ♘g5 e5∞ Matulović–Panno, Palma de Mallorca (izt) 1970 — 10/180; **9. ♗f4** ♘c7 10. ♕c1 ♗d7 11. ♗h6 b5 12. e5 ♘fd5 13. ♘e4 b4 14. c4± Ćirić–Bronštejn, Amsterdam 1968

118 11... e5? 12. de5△ ♘c4±

119 16. ♗f4± Antošin–Ciocaltea, Budapest 1973 — 15/170

B 09

1. e4 d6 2. d4 ♘f6 3. ♘c3 g6 4. f4 ♗g7

	5	6	7	8	9	10	11	12	13	
1	e5	de5[2]	♔d1	♔e1	h3	ef6[5]	g4	♘f3	♗e3	=
	de5[1]	♕d1	♘g4[3]	f6[4]	♘h6	ef6	♗e6	♘c6	0-0-0[6]	
2	♗c4	♗f7	♘e4	♘f3	0–0	c3	♕b3	♘fg5	♗e3	=
	♘e4[7]	♔f7	♖e8	♔g8	♘d7	b6[8]	e6	♘f8	h6[9]	
3	♘f3	♗e3[11]	♗e2[12]	e5[14]	de5	h3	♗f3	0–0[15]		±
	♘c6[10]	0–0	♗g4[13]	de5	♘d7	♗f3	♘b6			
4	...	♗b5[16]	e5[18]	h3[19]	♕d4	♕d5	♘g5	♕b7	bc3	∞
	c5	♗d7[17]	♘g4	cd4	de5[20]	e4	♘h6	♗c3[21]	♗b5[22]	
5	...	...	...	e6	ef7[23]	♘b5[24]	♘c3	♘d4	♕d4[26]	=
	...	...	...	♗b5	♔d7	♕a5	cd4	♗d4[25]	♘c6[27]	
6	...	dc5	♗d3[28]	♕e2	♗e3[30]	0–0	h3	♕f3	♕f2	∞
	...	♕a5	♕c5	0–0[29]	♕c7[31]	♗g4[32]	♗f3	♘bd7	a6[33]	
7	...	...	...	...	...	0–0	♖ad1[35]	♗c4	♗b3[37]	∞
	...	...	...	...	♕a5	♗g4[34]	♘c6[36]	♘h5	♗c3[38]	
8	...	e5	dc5[40]	fe5	e6	♗c4	♕e2	♗e3	♗b3	±
	...	♘fd7[39]	de5	0–0[41]	fe6	♘c5	♘c6	♕b6	♕a5[42]	

1. e4 d6 2. d4 ♘f6 3. ♘c3 g6 4. f4 ♗g7 5. ♘f3 0–0

	6	7	8	9	10	11	12	13	14	
9	♗c4[43]	♗f7	♘e4	0–0	♘g3	♕d3	♗d2	c3		=
	♘e4[44]	♖f7	♖f8	h6	e6	♕f6	♘c6	♗d7[45]		

	6	7	8	9	10	11	12	13	14	
10	♗e2	dc5[47]	♘d2	♘b3	♕d3[49]	♗e3	♕e2	♘d4	h3	=
	c5[46]	♕a5[48]	♕c5	♕b6	♗g4[50]	♗e2	♕c6	♕c8	♘c6[51]	
11	...	...	0—0	♔h1	♕e1[53]	♗d3[55]	♖f3	♖f1	♗e3	±
	...	...	♕c5	♘c6[52]	♗g4[54]	♗f3[56]	♘d4	♕h5[57]	e5[58]	
12	...	...	...	...	♗d3[59]	♕e1	♗e3[60]	♕h4	f5	∞
	...	...	...	♘bd7	a6	b5	♕c7	♗b7	♖fe8[61]	
13	e5	de5	♔d1	♗d3[64]	♔e2	♗e3[66]	♗c4[67]	♖ad1	♗c5	=
	de5[62]	♕d1	♖d8[63]	♘e8[65]	♘c6	♘b4	♘c2	♗g4	♗f8[68]	
14	...	...	...	♔e1	h3[70]	♗e3[72]	♗c4	ef6	♔f2	=
	...	...	♘g4	♘c6[69]	♘h6[71]	f6	♔h8	ef6	♘a5[73]	
15	...	fe5	♗c4[74]	♕e2[76]	♗d5	♘d5	c4	d5	d6	±
	...	♘d5	♗e6[75]	c5[77]	♗d5	♕d5	♕d7	e6	f6[78]	

1. e4 d6 2. d4 ♘f6 3. ♘c3 g6 4. f4 ♗g7 5. ♘f3 0—0 6. e5 ♘fd7

	7	8	9	10	11	12	13	14	15	
16	♗c4[79]	♗b3[81]	♗e3[83]	♕e2	ab3	0—0	h3	♗f2	♖fe1	=
	♘b6[80]	♘c6[82]	♘a5	♘b3	f6	c6	♗e6	♕d7	fe5[84]	
17	h4	e6	h5	dc5[86]	♖h5	♗d3	♖h4	♗e3	♕d3	∞
	c5[85]	fe6	gh5	♘c5[87]	♘bd7	♘f6	♗d7	♘d3	♕e8[88]	
18	...	h5	hg6	gf7	e6[91]	ed7	♗d3[93]	bc3	♖h4	∓
	...	cd4	dc3[89]	♖f7[90]	♖f6[92]	♗d7	h6[94]	♘c6	♕b6[95]	
19	...	...	...	...	♗c4	♘g5[97]	♘f7[99]	♕h5[100]	♗d3	∓
	...	...	...	...	e6[96]	♘f8[98]	♔f7	♔g8	h6[101]	
20	...	...	♕d4	♕f2[102]	♘g5[104]	hg6	♘ce4[105]	♘e4	♕d4	=
	...	...	de5	e4[103]	♘f6	hg6	♘e4	♕d4	♗d4	

1. e4 d6 2. d4 ♘f6 3. ♘c3 g6 4. f4 ♗g7 5. ♘f3 0—0 6. ♗d3

	6	7	8	9	10	11	12	13	14	
21	...	h3	♕f3	♗e3	de5[109]	f5	♕f2	ef5	0—0	±
	♗g4[106]	♗f3	♘c6[107]	e5[108]	de5	♘d4[110]	gf5[111]	b5	c5[112]	
22	...	dc5[113]	♕e2[114]	e5	♘d5	♗e4	c3[116]	0—0	♖d1	±
	c5	dc5	♘c6	♘d5	♕d5	♕d7[115]	b6	♗b7	♕c7[117]	
23	...	e5[118]	♗e3[120]	dc5	♗c5	0—0[121]	♔h1	♕e1	♘d2	±
	♘a6	♘e8[119]	c5	♘c5	dc5	♕a5	♘c7	♕b4	♗e6[122]	
24	...	e5[123]	♘e4[124]	c3	♘ed2[126]	♘c4	cd4	0—0	♘e3	±
	♘bd7	♘e8	c5	♕b6[125]	cd4	♕c6	♘c7	♘b6	♘bd5[127]	
25	...	0—0	fe5[129]	d5[130]	dc6	♔h1	b3	a4	♗a3	±
	...	e5[128]	de5	c6[131]	bc6[132]	♕e7[133]	♘h5	♘f4	c5[134]	
26	...	♗e3[135]	fe5	d5	♕d2[138]	dc6	0—0	♘g5	h3	=
	♘c6	e5[136]	de5	♘e7[137]	c6	♘c6	♗e6	♕d7	♘d4[139]	
27	...	...	♗g1	fe5	d5	h3	♕d2[142]	0-0-0	♗e4	∞
	...	♘g4	e5	de5	♘d4[140]	♘h6[141]	f5	fe4	♘hf5[143]	

1. e4 d6 2. d4 ♘f6 3. ♘c3 g6 4. f4 ♗g7 5. ♘f3 0—0 6. ♗d3 ♘c6

	7	8	9	10	11	12	13	14	15	
28	e5	de5	♗d2[145]	♗e4	h3	♕f3	♕d3	0-0-0	fe5	∞
	de5[144]	♘d5	♗g4[146]	♘b6[147]	♗f3	♘d4	f6	fe5	♘c6[148]	

	7	8	9	10	11	12	13	14	15	
29	...	fe5	♗e4[150]	h3[152]	ef6[153]	♗d5[154]	0–0	♖e1	♘d4	±
	...	♘g4[149]	f6[151]	♘h6	ef6	♔h8	♘f5[155]	♘cd4	♘d4[156]	
30	...	...	♗e2[157]	♗e3	e6[159]	0–0[161]	♘d5	c4	♕b3	=∞
	...	♘h5	♗g4	f6[158]	♘b4[160]	♘d5[162]	♕d5	♕e6		
31	...	...	♘d5	c3	♕e2[164]	0–0[165]	ef6	♗e4		=
	...	♘d5	♕d5	♗e6[163]	♖ad8	f6	ef6	♕c4		
32	0–0	e5[167]	de5	h3[169]	bc3	♗f5[171]	♖d1	♘d4	♗e3	±
	♗g4[166]	de5[168]	♘d5	♘c3[170]	♗f5	♕d1	gf5	♖fd8	♘d4[172]	

1 5... ♘fd7 6. e6 [6. ♗e3 c5 7. ♗b5 0–0 8. ♘f3 cd4 9. ♗d4 de5 10. fe5 a6∓ Gurgenidze–Timman, Tbilisi 1971 — 12/176; 6. ♘e4 0–0 7. ♘f3 c5 8. c3 cd4 9. cd4 ♘b6 10. ♗e2 ♘c6 11. 0–0 ♗e6 12. ♘fg5 ♗d5= Bronštejn–Etruk, SSSR 1962] fe6 7. ♘f3 ♘f6 8. ♘g5 0–0 9. ♗e3 ♘d5 10. ♘d5 ed5 11. ♕d2 c5 12. 0-0-0∞ Rozenberg–Kremenecki, SSSR 1972; 6. ♘f3 0—0 — 5. ♘f3

2 6. fe5 ♘d5 7. ♗c4 [7. ♘e4?! ♘b4△ 8. a3 ♗f5∓] ♘c3 8. bc3 0–0 9. ♘f3 c5=

3 7... ♘fd7 8. ♘d5 ♔d8 9. ♘f3 c6 [9... f6!?] 10. ♘e3 f6 11. ef6 ♗f6 [11... ef6 12. ♘c4 ♘c5 13. ♘d6 ♗e6 14. f5± Adorjan–Vadasz, Hungary 1970] 12. ♘g4± Adorjan–Hartoch, Amsterdam 1971

4 **8... ♘c6** 9. h3 ♘h6 10. ♘d5 ♘d4 11. ♘c7 ♔d8 12. ♘a8 ♘c2 13. ♔f2 ♘a1 14. ♗e3 f6 15. ♘f3 fe5 16. ♗b5+– Lukin–Cejtlin, SSSR 1972; **8... h5** 9. ♘d5 ♔d8 10. ♘f3 c6 11. ♘e3 f6 12. h3 ♘h6 13. ♗d3 ♘f5 14. ♘f5 gf5 15. e6± Poljak–Bondarevski, SSSR 1944; **8... c6** 9. h3 ♘h6 10. g4 f6 11. ef6 ef6 12. ♗c4 ♘f7 13. ♖h2± Bronštejn–Benkö, Monte Carlo 1969 — 7/163

5 10. ♘d5 ♔d8 11. ef6 ef6 12. ♔f2 ♗e6=

6 Tompa–Sapi, Hungary 1970

7 **5... d5** 6. ed5 ♘bd7 7. ♘f3 0–0 8. ♘e5 ♘b6 9. ♗b3 a5 10. a3 a4 [10... ♘bd5 11. ♘d5 ♘d5 12. 0–0 c6 13. c4 ♘c7 14. ♗e3 ♗e6 15. ♖c1± Ljubojević–Hartoch, Amsterdam 1972 — 13/196] 11. ♗a2 ♘bd5 12. ♘d5 ♘d5 13. 0–0 e6 14. ♗d2 ♘f6 15. ♗b4 ♖e8 [Ljubojević–Keene, Palma de Mallorca 1971] 16. c4!±; **5... 0—0** 6. e5 ♘fd7 [6... ♘e8 7. ♘f3 c6 8. ♗e3 a5 9. a4 d5 10. ♗e2± Selivanovski–Judovič, SSSR 1964; 6... de5 7. de5 ♕d1 8. ♔d1 ♘e8 9. ♗e3 ♘c6 10. ♗d5± Ljubojević–Vadasz, Vrnjačka Banja 1971 — 11/147] 7. e6 [7. ♘f3 — 5. ♘f3] fe6 8. ♗e6 ♔h8 9. ♘f3 c5 — 5. ♘f3; **5... c5**! 6. e5 [6. dc5 ♕a5 7. ♗d2 ♕c5 8. ♕e2 0–0 9. 0-0-0 ♗g4∓; 6. d5 0–0 7. ♘ge2 e6 8. de6 ♗e6 9. ♗e6 fe6 10. 0–0 ♘c6 11. h3 d5∓ Ljubojević–Donner, Amsterdam 1972 — 13/195] ♘fd7 7. ♘f3 — 5. ♘f3

8 10... ♘f6 11. ♕b3 d5 12. ♘f2 c6 13. ♖e1 ♕b6 14. ♕a3 ♗f8 15. ♘e5± Ljubojević–Donner, Palma de Mallorca 1971 — 12/177

9 14. ♘f3 ♗b7 15. ♕c2 ♕e7 16. ♖ae1 ♕f7= Ljubojević–Donner, Wijk aan Zee 1972

10 5... ♗g4 6. h3 ♗f3 7. ♕f3 e5 8. de5 de5 9. fe5? ♘fd7 10. e6 fe6 11. ♕g4 0–0∓ Glutman–Varigin, SSSR 1966 — 1/100; 9. f5±

11 6. ♗e2 ♗g4 7. d5 ♘b8 8. e5△ ♘g5± Dückstein–Sigurjonsson, Siegen (ol) 1970 — 10/182; 6... 0–0!?

12 **7. e5** ♘g4 8. ♗g1 de5 9. de5 f6 10. ♗c4 ♔h8 11. ♘b5± Balašov–Rukavina, Soči 1973; **7. ♗b5** a6 8. ♗c6 bc6 9. ♕d2 ♗d7 10. 0–0± Velimirović–Forintos, Vrnjačka Banja 1973

13 **7... ♘g4** 8. ♗g1 e5 9. d5 ♘e7 10. h3 ♘f6 11. fe5 de5 12. ♗h2±; **7... e5** 8. fe5 de5 9. de5 ♘g4 10. ♕d8 ♖d8 11. ♗g5 ♖d7 12. ♘d5±

14 **8. d5** ♘b8 9. h3 ♗f3 10. ♗f3 c6 11. ♕d2 cd5 12. ed5 ♘bd7 13. 0–0 ♖c8 14. ♗d4 ♕a5 15. ♖fe1 ♖fe8 16. a3 ♘b6! [16... a6? 17. ♖ad1± Tringov–Botvinik, Beograd 1969 — 8/143] 17. ♕f2 ♘fd7∓ Tringov–Ivkov, Beograd 1969 — 8/144; **8. 0—0** ♘d7 9. h3 ♗f3 10. ♖f3 e5 11. de5 de5 12. f5± Kuijpers–Kotov, Amsterdam 1968 — 6/191

15 R. Byrne–Keene, Hastings 1971/72 — 13/197

16 6. d5 0–0 7. e5 ♘e8 8. ♗e3 ♗g4 9. ♕d2∞ Belov–Kudinov, SSSR 1971

17 **6... ♘bd7**? 7. e5 ♘g4 8. e6+–; **6... ♔f8** 7. e5 de5 8. fe5 ♘g4 9. h3 ♘h6 10. dc5± Lengyel–Ozsváth, Hungary 1962; **6... ♘fd7** 7. ♗e3 [7. dc5 dc5 8. 0–0± Boleslavski] 0–0 8. ♕d2 a6 9. ♗d7 ♘d7 10. h4± Pupel–Kampenus, SSSR 1958

18 7. ♗d7 ♘fd7 8. d5 ♘a6 9. 0–0 0–0 10. ♕e2 [10. ♗e3 ♘c7 11. ♕d2 b5 12. ♖ae1 ♘b6 13. ♕f2 b4△ f5∓ Žuravlev–Gipslis, SSSR 1969; 10. f5 ♕b6 11. ♔h1 ♘c7 12. ♘e2 c4∓ Savon–Hort, Petropolis (izt) 1973] ♘c7 11. ♖d1 b5∞ Savon–Korčnoj, SSSR (ch) 1973 — 16/145

19 **8. ♘g5** ♗b5 9. ♕g4 ♗d7 10. e6 ♗e6 [10... fe6? 11. ♘h7+– Burger–Suttles, USA (ch) 1965] 11. ♘e6 fe6 12. dc5 ♗c3 [12... ♕d7 13. cd6 ed6 14. ♗d2 ♘c6 15. 0-0-0 0-0-0 16. ♘e4± Estrin–Šašin, SSSR 1968 — 7/167] 13. bc3 ♕a5∓ Lee–Suttles, La Habana (ol)

1966; **8. ♗d7** ♕d7 9. d5 [9. ♘g5 cd4 10. e6 fe6 11. ♕g4 dc3 12. ♘e6 cb2−+ Purdy−R. Byrne, USA 1968 — 5/142] de5 10. h3 e4 11. ♘e4 ♘f6 12. ♘e5 ♕a4= Wittmann−Parma, Graz 1974

20 **9... ♘h6** 10. g4 0−0 11. ♗d7 ♘d7 12. ♗e3 ♕a5 13. 0-0-0 ♘b6 14. ♔b1 ♖ac8 15. ♘d5± Klovan−Cejtlin, SSSR 1973 — 16/144; **9... ♗b5** 10. ♘b5 ♘c6 11. ♕e4 ♕a5 12. ♘c3 ♘h6 13. g4 0-0-0 [13... 0−0!?] 14. ♗d2 f5 [14... de5 15. fe5 ♘e5 16. ♘e5 ♖d2 17. ♔d2 ♗e5 18. ♖ad1± Ljubojević−Benkö, Skopje (ol) 1972 — 14/192; 15... ♘g8 16. 0-0-0 ♘e5 17. ♘e5 ♗e5 18. ♕c4△ ♕f7±] 15. ef6 ef6 16. 0-0-0 ♖he8 [16... d5 17. ♕e6 ♔b8 18. ♖he1 d4 19. ♘e4 ♕d5 20. ♕d5 ♖d5 21. c4±] 17. ♕c4 d5 18. ♕b3 ♕c5 19. ♖he1± Levy−Peev, Cienfuegos 1973 — 16/143

21 12... 0−0? 13. ♕a8 ♗c3 [13... ♕c7 14. ♗d7 ♗c3 15. bc3 ♕c3 16. ♔e2 ♘d7 17. ♕d5+−; 13... ♗b5 14. ♘b5 ♕a5 15. c3 ♕b5 16. ♕e4+− Kurajica−Keene, Wijk aan Zee 1974 — 17/207] 14. bc3 ♗b5 15. ♕a7 ♘f5 16. ♔f2±

22 14. ♕b5 ♕d7 15. ♕d7 ♔d7 16. ♘e4 ♖c8∞ Hartston−Suttles, Nice (ol) 1974 — 17/208

23 9. ♘g5? f5−+

24 10. ♘g5? h5 11. ♘b5 ♕a5 12. ♘c3 cd4 13. ♕e2 dc3−+ Jensen−Keene, Haag 1967

25 12... ♕h5 13. ♘e4 [13. ♕f3 ♘c6 14. ♘de2 ♘h6= Krogius−Polugajevski, SSSR (ch) 1958] ♘c6 [13... ♘h6 14. ♕h5 gh5 15. f5 ♘f7 16. f6 ♗f6 17. ♘f6 ef6 18. 0−0±; 16. ♗e3 ♘c6 17. 0-0-0± Lejn−Kampenus, SSSR 1959] 14. ♘g3 ♕h4 [14... ♕a5 15. ♗d2 ♘e3 16. ♗a5 ♘d1 17. ♘c6 ♘b2 18. ♘e5 de5 19. ♗c3 ♘a4 20. 0-0-0±] 15. ♘f3 ♕f6 16. ♘g5 ♘h6 17. c3±

26 13. ♕g4 ♕f5 14. ♕f3 ♘c6 15. ♘e2 ♕e6∓ Tringov−Benkö, Sarajevo 1967

27 **14. ♕d2** ♖hf8 15. h3 ♘f6= Zuckerman −Benkö, USA (ch) 1966/67 — 3/154; **14. ♕d5** ♕d5 15. ♘d5 ♘d4= Zuidema−Suttles, La Habana (ol) 1966; **14. ♕d1** ♕f5 [14... h5 15. h3 ♘f6 16. 0−0 ♕c5 17. ♖f2 ♖af8 18. ♕f3± Bogdanović−Saidy, Sarajevo 1971; 14... ♘f6 15. 0−0 ♕c5 16. ♔h1 ♖hf8 17. ♕f3 ♖f7 18. ♗e3 ♕h5= Yepez−Sigurjonsson, Caracas 1970; 14... ♕h5 15. ♕f3 ♖hf8 16. ♗d2 ♘f6 =] 15. h3 ♕e6 [15... ♘f6 16. 0−0 ♖hf8 17. ♗e3 h5 18. ♕d2± Karasev−Gipslis, SSSR (ch) 1970] 16. ♕e2 ♕e2= Keres−Benkö, Winnipeg 1967

28 **7. ♗b5** ♗d7 8. ♗d7 [8. ♕e2? ♘e4∓ Klavinš−Kampenus, SSSR 1956] ♘bd7 9. 0−0 ♕c5 10. ♔h1 0−0 [10... ♘g4 11. ♕d3 ♗c3 12. bc3 ♖c8 13. ♗d2 0−0 14. ♖ab1± Černikov−Kuznjecov, SSSR 1963] 11. ♕e2 ♖ac8 12. ♗e3 ♕c4∓ Honfi−Hort, Monaco 1969; **7. ♘d2** ♕c5 8. ♘b3 ♕c7 9. ♗e2 ♘bd7 10. ♗e3 ♘b6= O'Kelly−Farre, Malaga 1961; **7. ♕d3** ♕c5 8. ♗e3 ♕a5 9. ♕b5 [9. ♘d2 0−0! 10. ♘b3 ♕h5 11. ♗e2 ♗g4 12. h3 ♘c6 13. a3 e5∓ Klovan−Vitolinš, SSSR 1971 — 12/179; 9. ♗e2 0−0 10. 0−0 a6 11. ♔h1 ♘bd7 12. a3 ♘c5 13. ♕d2 ♕c7 14. ♗d3 e6 15. ♕e1 ♘g4∓ Geler−Nikolajevski, SSSR 1958] ♕b5 10. ♗b5 ♘c6 11. 0-0-0 a6 12. ♗d3 ♘g4= Radulov−Spaski, Amsterdam 1973 — 17/202

29 8... ♘c6 9. h3 [9. ♗e3 ♕a5 10. 0−0 0−0 — 8... 0−0] ♘h5!?∞

30 9. ♗d2 ♘c6 10. h3 ♘h5 11. ♕f2 ♕f2= Smejkal−Benkö, Lugano (ol) 1968

31 9... ♕b4 10. 0−0 [10. 0-0-0? ♘e4−+; 10. a3 ♕b2 11. ♔d2 ♘e4 12. ♘e4 d5 13. ♖hb1 de4∞ Tolonen−Kirpičnikov, SSSR 1974] ♕b2 11. ♘b5 ♘e8 12. a3 [12. ♘a7 ♘c6 13. ♖ab1 ♕a2 14. ♘c8 ♖c8 15. ♖b7 ♘f6∞ Bitman−Šapošnikov, SSSR 1973] ♕f6 [12... ♕a1 13. ♖a1 ♗a1 14. c3 a6 15. ♘a7± Fridštejn] 13. e5 ♕e6 14. ♗c4 ♕d7 [14... ♕g4 15. h3±; 14... d5 15. ♘g5±] 15. ♘g5± Fridštejn

32 10... ♘bd7 **11. h3** a6 12. a4 [12. ♕f2 b5 13. a3 e5∓ Goldberg−Šapošnikov, SSSR 1972; 13. ♕h4 ♗b7 14. f5 b4 15. ♘e2 d5∓ Rittman−Kaplan, Puerto Rico 1971] b6 13. ♕f2 ♗b7 14. ♕h4 ♘c5 [14... ♗c6 15. f5 b5 16. fg6 hg6 17. ♘g5± Balašov−Cejtlin, SSSR 1971 — 12/180] 15. f5 b5 16. ab5 [Talj−Gufeljd, SSSR 1970 — 10/183] ♘d3=; **11. ♔h1** a6 12. a4 b6 [12... e5 13. a5±] 13. e5 de5 [13... ♘g4 14. e6±] 14. fe5 ♘e5 15. ♗f4 ♘fd7 16. ♖ae1 f6 17. ♗e5 ♘e5 18. ♘d5± Jansa−Nowak, ČSSR 1972 — 13/190

33 14. a4 e6 15. ♕h4 ♖ae8∞ Kuprejčik−Razuvajev, SSSR 1969

34 **10... ♘c6** 11. h3 [11. ♖ad1 ♘g4 12. ♗d2 ♕b6 13. ♔h1 ♕b2 14. ♘b5 a6∓ Doran−Suttles, Canada 1971; 11. ♔h1 ♗g4 12. h3 ♗f3 13. ♕f3 ♖ac8= Parma−Fernandez, La Habana 1971 — 11/142] e5 [11... ♗d7 12. a3 ♖ac8 13. ♕f2 ♕d8 14. ♕h4 e6 15. f5 ♘e8 16. ♗g5 f6 17. fg6 hg6 18. e5+− Velimirović−Tringov, Skopje 1971 — 12/181; 12... ♖fc8 13. ♕f2 ♗e8 14. f5 ♘e5 15. ♘e5± Olafsson−Benkö, Wijk aan Zee 1969 — 7/165] 12. fe5 [12. ♕f2? ef4 13. ♗f4 d5∞ Jansa−Oleksa, ČSSR (ch) 1960] de5 13. ♕f2 ♗e6 14. ♕h4± Hort−Szabo, Leningrad 1967 — 3/153; **10... ♘bd7** 11. h3 a6 12. ♕f2 e5 13. fe5 de5 14. ♕h4 b5 15. ♗h6 ♗b7∞ Ree−Benkö, Wijk aan Zee 1969 — 7/166

35 11. h3 ♗f3 12. ♕f3 ♘c6 13. a3 ♘d7 14. ♗d2 ♕b6 [14... ♕d8 15. ♔h1 ♖c8 16. ♖ab1 ♘b6 17. ♘e2 ♘d4 18. ♘d4 ♗d4 19. e5± Unzicker−Timman, Nice (ol) 1974] 15. ♔h1 ♘c5 16. ♖ab1 [16. b4 (Hort−Suttles, Zagreb 1972 — 14/188) ♘d3 17. ♕d3 ♕d4=] ♘d3 17. cd3 e6 [17... ♕b3? 18. f5 ♖fe8 19. ♗g5 ♖ac8 20. ♘d5± Adorjan−Suttles, Hastings 1973/74 — 17/203] 18. ♗e3 ♕a5 1/2 : 1/2 Spaski−Bronštejn, Tallinn 1973

36 11... ♘bd7 12. h3 ♗f3 13. ♕f3 ♖ac8 14. g4 ♘b6∞ Kuindži−Cejtlin, SSSR 1973

37 13. ♖d5!?△ ♖g5 Spaski

38 14. bc3 ♕c3 15. f5 ♘f6 [15... ♘a5 16. ♗d4 ♘f4 17. ♕f2 ♕f3 18. gf3 ♘h3 19. ♔g2 ♘f2 20. ♖f2±; 16... ♕c7 17. h3 ♘b3∞ Gligorić–Hort, Skopje (ol) 1972] 16. h3 ♗f3 17. ♕f3 ♘a5 18. ♖d3 ♕c7∞ Spaski–Fischer, Reykjavik (m) 1972 — 14/190

39 6... de5 7. ♗b5 [7. de5 ♕d1 8. ♔d1 ♘g4 9. ♔e1 ♘c6 10. ♗b5± Peretz–Domnitz, Netanya 1969 — 7/164] ♘fd7 8. de5 0–0 9. 0–0 a6 10. ♗d3 ♘c6 11. ♗e4±

40 **7. e6** fe6 8. ♘g5 ♗d4 [8... ♘f6 9. dc5 ♘c6 10. ♗d3 dc5 11. 0–0 0–0 12. ♕e1 ♘b4∓ Hartston–Timman, Hastings 1973/74] 9. ♘e6 ♗c3 10. bc3 ♕a5 11. ♗d2 ♘f6∓; **7. ♗c4** cd4 8. ♕d4 0–0 **9.** ♕e4 ♘c6 10. e6 fe6 11. ♗e6 ♔h8 12. ♕e2 ♘c5∓ Ljubojević–Jansa, Skopje (ol) 1972 — 14/193; **7. ed6** 0–0 8. ♗e3 [8. de7 ♕e7 9. ♗e2 cd4 10. ♘d4 ♖e8∞̄; 8. dc5 ♕a5∞] ♕b6 9. de7 ♖e8∞ Matulović–Adorjan, Wijk aan Zee 1974 — 17/204

41 8... ♘c6!?

42 14. 0–0± Bronštejn–Tringov, Reykjavik 1974 — 17/205

43 6. ♗e3 **c6** 7. ♗d3 [7. ♕d2 ♘bd7 8. e5 ♘g4 9. ♗g1 c5∓ Lejn–Savon, SSSR (ch) 1961; 8. ♗d3!?] ♘bd7 8. h3 ♕c7 9. g4 e5 10. de5 de5 11. f5± Hort–Bengtsson, Örebro 1966; **6... ♘bd7** 7. ♕d2 c5 8. 0-0-0 [8. dc5 ♘c5 9. ♗c5△ 0-0-0±] ♕a5 9. ♔b1 ♖e8 10. h3± Capece–Leksander, Ybbs 1968; **6... c5** 7. dc5 ♕a5 8. ♗d3 [8. ♕d2 dc5 9. ♘e5 ♖d8 10. ♗d3 ♗e6 11. ♘b5 ♕b6∓ Hasin–Glotov, SSSR 1967; 9. ♗d3 ♖d8 10. e5 c4= Radulov–Timman, Skopje (ol) 1972 — 14/195] dc5 [8... ♘g4 9. ♗d2 ♕c5 10. ♕e2 ♘c6 11. h3 ♘h6 12. g4± Heilino–Redyemit, corr. 1956] 9. e5 ♘d5 10. ♗d2 ♘c3 [10... ♘b4 11. ♗c4± Radulov–Parma, Montilla 1974] 11. ♗c3± Kurajica–Eising, Wijk aan Zee 1974 — 17/206; **6... ♘c6** 7. ♕d2 [7. ♗d3 — 6. ♗d3 ♘c6 7. ♗e3] ♗g4 8. d5 ♘b8 [Lejn–Gufeljd, SSSR 1966 — 3/156] 9. ♗e2=; **6... b6**!∞

44 **6... c6** 7. ♗b3 ♘a6 8. e5 ♘e8 9. ♗e3± Kavalek–Mednis, USA (ch) 1972 — 13/194; **6... c5** 7. e5 ♘fd7 [7... ♘g4!?] 8. ♗e3 cd4 9. ♗d4 de5 10. fe5 e6∓ Ceškovski–Cejtlin, SSSR 1969; 8. e6 — 6. e5

45 Euwe

46 **6... b6** 7. e5 ♘e8 8. h4 ♘d7 9. h5± Bitman–Šackes, SSSR 1964; **6... c6** 7. 0–0 b5 [7... ♘bd7 8. e5 ♘d5 9. ♘e4 f5 10. ♘eg5 ♘c7 11. ♗c4± Vasjukov–Kofman, SSSR 1953; 8... ♘e8 9. ♗e3 ♕b6 10. ♕d3 ♕a5 (Fischer–Udovčić, Bled 1961) 11. h4±; 7... ♘a6 8. e5 ♘d5 9. ♘d5 cd5 10. c3± O'Kelly–Bouwmeester, Utrecht 1961] 8. e5 ♘e8 [8... de5 9. de5 (Estrin–Makarov, SSSR 1966) ♘fd7 10. ♗e3±; 8... ♘fd7 9. a4 b4 10. ♘e4 ♘b6 11. a5 ♘d5 12. ♕e1±] 9. a4 b4 10. ♘e4± Vasjukov–Gurgenidze, SSSR 1954; **6... ♘a6** 7. 0–0 c5 8. e5 [8. ♔h1 b6 9. ♗d3 ♗b7 10. d5 ♘c7∞ Pedersen–Hort, Athens 1969 — 8/142] ♘e8 9. dc5 [9. d5 ♘ac7 10. ♗e3 b6 11. ♕d2 a6∞ Poutiainen–Torre, Athens 1971] ♘c5 10. ♗e3 b6 11. ♕d2 ♗b7 12. ♖ad1± Levy–Hort, Siegen (ol) 1970; **6... ♘bd7** 7. e5 ♘e8 8. h4± Burn–L. Paulsen, Breslau 1889

47 7. d5 **b5** 8. e5 de5 9. fe5 ♘g4 10. ♗b5 [10. ♗f4 ♘d7∓; 10. d6 ed6 11. ♕d5 ♕b6 12. ♕a8 ♗b7 13. ♘d5 ♕a6 14. ♘c7 ♕b6=] ♘e5 11. ♘e5 ♗e5 12. ♗h6 e6 13. ♗f8 ♕h4 14. ♔f1 ♔f8 15. ♕e1± Čistjakov–Kotov, SSSR 1960; **7... ♘a6** 8. e5 ♘d7∞ Littlewood–Keene, England (ch) 1972; **7... e6** 8. de6 ♗e6 9. 0–0 ♘c6 [9... d5 10. f5 gf5 11. ef5 ♗f5 12. ♘h4 ♗g6∓] 10. f5 gf5 11. ef5 [11. ♗g5 fe4 12. ♘e4 d5∓ Bejlin–Antošin, SSSR 1955] ♗f5 12. ♗g5 h6 13. ♗h4 d5∓

48 7... dc5 8. ♕d8 ♖d8 9. e5 ♘e8 10. ♗e3 b6 11. ♖d1± Boleslavski–Pirc, Helsinki (ol) 1952

49 10. g4 d5 11. ♘d5 ♘d5 12. ♕d5 ♘c6 13. ♕c5 ♘b4 14. ♗d1 ♗e6∞̄ Bednarski–Balcerowski, Polska 1970 — 9/139

50 10... ♘bd7 11. ♗e3 ♕c7 12. 0–0 b6 13. ♗f3 ♗b7= Witkowski–Timman, Wijk aan Zee 1971 — 11/148; 12. g4!?

51 Witkowski–Hartoch, Wijk aan Zee 1971

52 **9... ♕c7** 10. ♕e1 ♘c6 11. ♕h4± Zwaig–Westerinen, Halle 1967 — 3/158; **9... b5** 10. e5 de5 11. fe5 ♘g4 12. ♕d5±; **9... ♘g4** 10. ♘d5 e6 [10... ♘c6 11. c3 a5 12. h3+–; 11... ♕a5 12. ♘d4±] 11. b4 ♕f2 12. ♘e7 ♔h8 13. ♖b1 ♕b6 14. ♘g5 ♘h6 15. f5± Leonidov–Kremenecki, SSSR 1973

53 **10. ♘d2** a5 [10... ♘d4 11. ♘b3 ♘b3 12. ab3±; 10... ♗e6 11. ♘b3 ♗b3 12. ab3 b5∞ Keene] 11. ♘b3 [11. ♘c4 ♘g4 12. ♘d5 ♘f2 13. ♖f2 ♕f2 14. ♗e3 ♕h4 15. g3 ♕h3 16. ♘cb6∞̄ Westerinen–Donner, Bamberg 1968 — 5/143; 11... ♗g4 12. ♗e3 ♕h5! 13. ♗f3 b5 14. ♘b6 ♖ad8∓ Česnauskas–Etruk, Pärnu 1964] ♕b6 12. a4 ♘b4 13. ♖a3 [13. g4 ♗g4 14. ♗g4 ♘g4 15. ♕g4 ♘c2 16. ♘b5 ♘a1 17. ♘a1 ♕c6!∓ Fischer–Korčnoj, Curaçao (ct) 1962; 13. ♗f3 ♗e6 14. ♘d4 ♗c4 15. ♘ce2 e5 16. ♘b5 d5∓ Locov–Šmit, SSSR 1962; 13. f5 d5 14. fg6 hg6 15. ♘d5 ♘fd5 16. ed5 ♗f5∓ Zurahov–Savon, SSSR 1960] ♖d8 14. ♗f3 d5 15. e5 ♘e4 16. ♘d4 f6∞ Pietrusiak–Pacl, ČSSR 1971 — 12/182; **10. ♗d3** ♘b4 [10... e5!? Fridštejn] 11. ♕e1 b6 12. ♘g5± Boleslavski–Ufimcev, SSSR 1951

54 **10... d5** 11. e5 ♘e4 12. ♗d3 ♘c3 13. bc3 f6 14. ♗e3 ♕a3 [Kestler–Donner, Bamberg 1968] 15. ef6 ef6 16. f5±; **10... ♗d7** 11. ♗d3±

55 11. a3? ♗f3 12. ♗f3 ♘d4 13. ♗e3 ♘f3 14. ♖f3 ♕c4∓ Dückstein–Savon, Sarajevo 1967

56 11... ♖fc8 12. ♗e3 ♕h5 13. ♘e2± Dückstein–Donner, Varna (ol) 1962

57 13... b5 14. ♗e3 ♘g4 [14... b4 15. ♘a4 ♘c2 16. ♘c5±] 15. ♗g1 b4 16. ♘d5± Pedersen–Andersen, Copenhagen 1968

58 14... e5 [Rusakov–Bastrikov, SSSR 1963] 15. f5!?±; 15. ♘e2±

59 **10. ♕d3** a6 11. ♗e3 ♕c7∓ Wade–Gipslis, Bucuresti 1968; **10. ♘d2** a6 11. ♗f3 [11. ♘b3 ♕c7 12. ♗f3 ♘b6∓ Wade–Šamkovič, Palma de Mallorca 1967 — 2/134; 11. a4 b6 12. ♕e1 ♗b7 13. ♗f3 e5 14. ♕h4 ♖fe8= Westerinen–Gufeljd, Leningrad 1967] ♖b8 [11... e5 12. f5 b5 13. g4± Zvezev–Kuperman, corr. 1973] 12. ♘b3 ♕c7△ b5∞; **10. ♘e1** b6=

60 12. e5 de5 13. fe5 ♘g4 14. e6 [14. ♕e4 ♘b6∞] ♘de5∞

61 Penrose–Botterill, England (ch) 1973

62 6... ♘e8 **7. ♗c4** c5 8. d5 ♗g4 9. e6 fe6 10. h3 ♗f3 11. ♕f3 e5∓ Razuvajev–Černin, SSSR 1968; **7. ♗d3** c5 8. dc5 de5 9. ♘e5 ♕d4 10. ♕f3 ♗e5 11. ♗e3 ♕b4∞ Gavran–Darzinek, SSSR 1969; **7. ♗e3** c5 [7... ♘d7 8. h4 c5 9. h5 cd4 10. ♗d4 de5 11. fe5 ♘c7 12. hg6 hg6 13. ♕d2 ♘e6 14. 0-0-0 ♕a5∞ Estrin–Krasnov, SSSR 1966; 8. ♗e2 b6 9. h4± Bertok–Plater, Bratislava 1957] 8. dc5 ♘c6 9. ♗e2 [9. ♗c4 ♕a5 10. 0–0 ♗g4∞; 9. ♕d2 ♗g4 10. 0-0-0 ♗f3= Estrin–Černin, SSSR 1968; 9. ed6 ed6 10. ♕d2 ♕a5 11. cd6 ♘d6 12. ♗d3 ♖d8 13. ♘d1 ♘b4=∞ Timoščenko–Karasev, SSSR 1972 — 14/191] ♕a5 10. cd6 ed6 11. ♕d5 ♕d8 [11... ♕b4 12. ♕b5 de5 13. ♕b4 ♘b4 14. 0-0-0± Estrin–Karasev, SSSR 1968 — 6/215] 12. 0-0-0 ♗e6 13. ♕b5 ♕b8∞ Lepeškin–Gufeljd, SSSR (ch) 1966; **7. h4** ♗g4 [7... c5!?] 8. ♗e2 [8. h5 de5 9. hg6 hg6 10. fe5 c5 11. ♖h4 ♗f3 12. ♕f3 ♘c6∓ Žilin–Koskin, SSSR 1963] ♘d7 9. ♘g5± Gipslis–Czerniak, Pecs 1964

63 **8... ♘e8** 9. ♘d5 ♘c6 10. ♗b5 ♗e6 11. ♗c6 ♗d5 12. ♗d5 ♖d8 13. ♔e2 ♖d5 14. c4± Zajcev–Platonov, SSSR (ch) 1969; **8... ♘h5** 9. ♔e1 ♘c6 10. ♗b5 f6 11. ef6 ♘f6 12. ♗c6 bc6 13. ♔f2 ♗f5= Makaričev–Gedevašvili, SSSR 1972

64 **9. ♗d2** ♘e8 [9... ♘d5 10. ♘d5 ♖d5 11. ♗c4 ♖d8 12. ♘g5 e6 13. h4± Letzelter–Sepp, Strasbourg 1972 — 13/188; 9... ♘g4!?; 9... ♘h5!?] 10. ♗c4 ♗g4 11. ♖f1 ♘c6 12. h3 ♗f3 13. ♖f3 ♖d4 14. ♗d3 [Estrin–Kubiček, Olomouc 1972] f6=; **9. ♔e1** ♘d5 10. ♘d5 ♖d5 11. ♗c4 ♖d8 12. ♘g5 [12. ♗e3 ♗f5 13. ♘d4 ♗e4 14. ♔f2 c5= Tolonen–Ceškovski, SSSR 1974] e6 13. ♗e3 [13. ♗e2 ♘c6 14. c3 b6 15. ♗f3 ♗b7 16. ♗e3 ♘a5 17. ♗b7 ♘b7 18. ♔e2± Honfi–Barcza, Hungary 1966] b6 14. ♔f2 [14. ♗d3 ♗b7 15. ♔f2 ♘c6 16. a3 ♘d4 17. ♖ad1 ♘f5 18. ♗e4± Honfi–Padevski, Kecskemet 1966] ♘c6 15. h4 [15. ♗e2 ♗b7 16. ♗f3± Bronštejn–Vasjukov, SSSR (ch) 1966] ♗b7 16. h5± Volčok–Kan, corr. 1967; 9... ♘e8 10. ♗e3 [10. ♗c4 ♗f5 11. ♗e3 ♘c6 12. ♖c1 ♘a5 13. ♗e2 f6∓ Tatai–Keene, Skopje (ol) 1972] ♘c6 11. ♗b5 [Žuravlev–Etruk, SSSR 1967] f6∞

65 9... ♘d5 10. ♘d5 ♖d5 11. ♔e2 ♗f5 12. ♗f5 gf5 13. ♗e3 [13. ♖g1 f6 14. g4 fe5 15. fe5 ♘c6 16. gf5 ♔h8 17. ♗f4 ♖f8 18. ♖ad1± Jansa–Szabo, Luhačovice 1971] ♘c6 14. c3 [14. ♖hg1± Mohrlok–Donner, Büsum 1968 — 5/141] e6 15. ♖hg1 f6 16. ef6 ♗f6 17. g4 ♔f7 18. g5± Cejtlin–Murej, SSSR 1972

66 11. ♗e4 f6 [11... ♗d7 12. ♗e3 f6= Honfi–Hort, Luhačovice 1971] 12. ♗d5 ♔h8 13. ♗e3 ♗g4 1/2 : 1/2 Gligorić–Keene, Hastings 1971/72

67 12. ♗e4 f5 13. ♗d3 ♘d3= Bellin–Keene, England 1969

68 15. ♗b3 b6= Barczay–Parma, Jugoslavija 1971

69 **9... c5** 10. h3 ♘h6 11. ♗e3 b6 12. ♘d5± Ree–Pfleger, Bad Aibling 1968; **9... h5** 10. ♘d5 ♘c6 11. ♗b5 ♗d7 12. h3 ♘h6 13. ♔f2 ♖fd8 14. ♗c6± Velimirović–Tringov, La Habana 1971 — 11/146

70 **10. ♗b5** f6 11. h3 ♘h6 12. ef6 [12. ♘d5? fe5 13. fe5 ♘f7 14. ♘c7 ♖b8∓ Estrin–Kotkov, SSSR 1972 — 13/189] ef6 13. ♗c4 ♔h8 14. ♔f2=; **10. ♗c4** ♘b4 11. ♗b3 ♗e6 12. ♗e6 fe6 13. ♔e2 ♘c2 14. ♖b1 ♖ad8 15. ♘e4 ♘d4 16. ♘d4 ♖d4 17. ♘g5 ♖df4=∞ Šamkovič–Tukmakov, SSSR (ch) 1971

71 10... ♘b4!? Fridštejn

72 11. g4 f6 12. ♘d5 fe5 13. ♘c7 ♖b8 14. ♘e5 ♘e5 15. fe5 ♘f7= Kavalek–Darga, Beverwijk 1967

73 15. ♗e2 b6 16. ♖ad1 ♘f5= Westerinen–Jansson, Stockholm 1970/71

74 **8. ♘d5** ♕d5 9. c4 [9. ♗e2 c5 10. c3 cd4 11. cd4 ♘c6∓ Ozsvath–Sandor, Hungary 1967] ♕e4 10. ♔f2 ♗f5∓ Krabbe–Bouwmeester, Amsterdam 1959; **8. ♘e4** ♗f5 [8... ♘c6 9. ♗e2 f6= Barcza–Androvicki, Hungary 1953] 9. ♘g3 ♗g4 10. c4 [10. ♗e2!?] ♘b6 11. ♗e3 c5 12. dc5 ♘6d7 13. ♗e2 ♘c6∓ Bertok–Sandor, Bratislava 1957

75 8... c6 9. 0–0 a5 10. ♗g5 h6 11. ♗d2 ♗e6 12. ♘d5 ♗d5 13. ♗d5 cd5 14. c3 ♖a6 15. ♘e1± Unzicker–Matanović, Berlin 1971

76 **9. ♗b3** c5 10. dc5 ♘c3 11. ♕d8 ♖d8 12. bc3 ♘d7= Pogats–Sandor, Hungary 1954; **9. ♗d5** ♗d5 10. ♘d5 ♕d5 11. ♕e2 b5 [11... ♕a5 12. ♗d2 ♕b6 13. 0–0 ♕b2 14. ♕c4 ♕b6 15. ♖ab1± Unzicker–Donner, BRD – Nederland 1971; 11... c5 — 9. ♕e2] 12. 0–0 ♘d7= Unzicker–Parma, Palma de Mallorca 1969

77 **9... c6** 10. ♘d5 ♗d5 11. ♗d5±; **9... ♘c3**!?

78 **15. ♗e3** b6 16. ef6 ♗f6= Koch–Richter, corr. 1955; **15. ♗f4** ♘c6 16. 0-0-0± Szily–Sandor, Hungary 1956

79 **7. ♘g5** ♘b6 [7... c5 8. e6 cd4 9. ed7 ♗d7 10. ♘ce4 d5∞ Murej–Gufeljd, SSSR 1968 — 6/216] 8. ♗d3 ♘c6 9. d5 ♘b4 10. e6 ♘d3 11. ♕d3 fe6 12. de6 ♕e8 13. ♕h3 h6 14. ♘f7 ♖f7∓ Eropov–Kärner, SSSR 1969; **7. e6** fe6 8. h4 [8. ♘g5 ♘f6 9. ♗c4 ♘d5∞; 9... d5 10. ♗d3 c5∓ Fridštejn] ♘f6 9. ♗d3

c5 [9... ♘c6 10. h5 gh5 11. a3 ♗d7 12. ♕e2 ♕c8 13. ♘e4 ♗e8∞ Razuvajev—Kremenecki, SSSR 1968] 10. h5 [10. dc5 d5 11. ♘g5 ♘c6 12. h5 gh5 13. ♖h5 h6 14. ♖h1 e5∓ Szell—Petran, Hungary 1971 — 11/145] gh5 11. ♘e4 h6 12. dc5 ♘e4 13. ♗e4 ♕a5 14. ♔f2 ♕c5 15. ♗e3 ♕b4 16. ♕d3 ♘d7∓ Nowak—Baňas, ČSSR 1972 — 13/191

80 **7... de5** 8. de5 ♘b6 9. ♕d8 [9. ♗d3 ♗f5 10. ♗f5 ♕d1 11. ♘d1 gf5 12. ♘e3 e6 (Minev—Padevski, Bulgaria 1966) 13. ♖g1±; 9... c5!?] ♖d8 10. ♗b3 c6 [10... c5 — 7... ♘b6] 11. ♗e3± Havski—Tarasov, SSSR 1957; **7... e6** 8. ♗e3 a6 [Cejtlin—Kremenecki, SSSR 1972 — 13/193] 9. a4∞; **7... c5** 8. e6 fe6 [8... ♘b6 9. ef7 ♔h8 10. ♗e2 cd4 11. ♘d4 ♘c6 12. ♗e3 ♖f7 13. 0—0 ♗d7 14. ♕d2± Holmov—Gipslis, SSSR 1958; 10. h4!? ♗g4 11. h5 gh5 12. ♗e2± Velimirović—Rajković, Skopje 1971 — 12/178] 9. ♗e6 ♔h8 10. d5 ♘a6 11. ♘g5 ♘c7 12. h4 ♘f6 13. h5 gh5 14. ♘h7 ♔h7 15. ♖h5= Šmit—Džindžihašvili, SSSR 1974 — 17/201

81 **8. ♗d3** ♘c6 [8... c5!?] 9. 0—0 [9. ♗e3 f6=] de5 10. de5 ♗f5=; **8. ♗e2** de5 9. fe5 ♘c6 10. 0—0 ♗g4 [10... f6 11. ef6 ef6 12. a4 a5 13. ♘b5± Bertok—Pirc, Zagreb 1955] 11. ♗e3 f6 [11... ♘b4 12. h3 ♗f5 13. ♖c1 (Bogdanović—Pirc, Jugoslavija 1955) ♘6d5=] 12. ef6 ef6 13. a4 ♖e8 [13... ♘a5!?] 14. ♗f2 a5 15. h3 ♗e6= Ribli—Timman, Helsinki 1972

82 **8... c5?** 9. dc5 dc5 10. ♕d8 ♖d8 11. ♗e3 ♘a6 12. a4±; **8... ♘a6** 9. ♘e4 [9. ♗e3!?] ♗f5 10. ♘g3 ♗g4 11. h3 ♗f3 12. ♕f3 de5 13. ♕b7 ef4 14. ♘e2 ♕c8= I. Zajcev—Savon, SSSR (ch) 1970

83 **9. ♘e2** ♘a5 10. c3 ♘b3 11. ab3 f6∓ Padevski—Donner, Amsterdam 1972; **9. 0—0** ♘a5 10. ♕e2 [10. ♘e4 ♘b3 11. ab3 f6∓ Minev—Tringov, Bulgaria 1969 — 8/139] c5= Boleslavski

84 16. fe5 ♘d5∞ Unzicker—Tringov, Ljubljana 1969; 16... d5=

85 7... ♘b6 8. h5 ♗g4 9. hg6 fg6 10. ♗e2 de5 11. ♘g5 ♗f5 12. g4 [12. fe5 h5 13. g4 hg4 (Gipslis—Botvinik, SSSR 1965) 14. ♗e3△ ♕d2±] ed4 13. ♘a4 ♕d5 14. ♗f3 ♕a5 15. ♗d2 ♕a4 16. gf5±

86 10. ♖h5 ♘f6∞

87 10... ♘f6 11. ♗d3 ♘c6 12. a3 h6 13. ♗d2 b6∞ Kristiansen—Botterill, Graz 1972 — 14/189

88 16. 0-0-0 ♕g6∞ Estrin—Sanakojev, corr. 1971 — 12/175

89 9... hg6 10. ♕d4 ♕b6? 11. ♘d5+—; **10... ♖e8?** 11. f5 [11. ♕g1 de5 12. ♕h2 e4 13. f5 ♘f6 14. ♘e5± Rudenski—Koroljev, SSSR 1967 — 2/131] ♘e5 12. ♘e5 ♕a5 13. ♗b5+— Nikolajev—Dragomirecki, SSSR 1969 — 8/141; **10... de5** 11. fe5 [11. ♕f2 e4 12. ♕h4 ♘f6 13. ♘e4 ♖e8 14. ♘eg5 e5 15. fe5 (Gergelj—Kimelfeld, SSSR 1968 — 5/139) ♖e5∞; 12. ♘e5!±] e6 12. ♗g5 ♕b6 13. ♕h4± Eales—Littlewood, England 1967; **10... ♘c6** 11. ♕f2 e6 [11... de5 12. ♕h4 ♘f6 13. fe5 ♘h5 14. g4+— Kaganovski—Makarov, SSSR 1963] 12. ♕g3±

90 10... ♔h8? 11. ♖h7 ♔h7 12. ♘g5 ♔h6 13. ♕d3+—

91 11. ♘g5 cb2 12. ♗c4 [12. ♗b2 ♕a5—+] ♘e5! [12... ba1♕ 13. ♗f7 ♔f8 14. ♘h7 ♔f7 15. ♘g5=] 13. ♕h5 [13. fe5 ♕a5 14. ♗d2 ♕e5—+] ♕a5 14. ♔f1 d5 15. ♗b2 ♖f4 16. ♘f3 dc4—+ Bihovski—Bebčuk, SSSR 1966 — 1/99

92 **11... ♖f5** 12. ed7 cb2 [12... ♕d7 13. b3±; 12... ♗d7 13. ♗c4 e6 14. ♕d3 h6 15. ♘g5±] 13. ♗c4 [13. dc8♕ ♕c8 14. ♗b2 ♗b2∓] ♔f8 14. ♘d4 [14. dc8♕ ♕c8 15. ♗b2 ♗b2 16. ♕d3 ♗a1 17. ♘d4 d5∓] ♗d7 15. ♗b2 ♕a5 16. c3 ♖f4 17. ♖h5∞; 14. ♘g5± Žuravlev; **11... cb2** 12. ef7 ♔f8 [12... ♔h8? 13. ♗d3+—] 13. ♗b2 ♗b2 14. ♗c4 [14. ♖h7 ♕a5 15. ♔f2 ♕c5△ ♘f6∓; 14. ♖b1!?] ♕a5 15. ♔f1 ♘f6 [15... ♗a1? 16. ♕a1 ♘f6 17. ♖h7+—] 16. ♘g5 [16. ♖b1 ♕c3△ ♗g4∓] ♕b4 17. ♕d3 ♗f5∓ Žuravljev—Vitolinš, SSSR 1967 — 3/155

93 13. ♘g5? cb2 14. ♗c4 d5—+ Russ—Judovič, corr. 1969 — 8/140

94 13... cb2 14. ♗b2 ♖e6 15. ♔f1 ♗b2 16. ♖b1 ♗f6 17. ♗c4±→

95 16. g4 ♖af8 17. f5 e6 18. ♔f1 [Karlson—Mučnik, SSSR 1967] ♘e5!∓

96 **11... cb2** 12. ♗f7 ♔f8 13. ♗b2 ♕a5 14. ♔f2 [14. ♕d2 ♕d2 15. ♔d2 ♔f7 16. e6±] de5 15. fe5 ♘c6 16. ♗b3± Norkin—Malisov, SSSR 1963; **11... ♘f8** 12. ♗f7 [12. ♘g5 e6 — 11... e6] ♔f7 13. ♘g5 ♔g8 14. ♕h5 h6! [14... cb2? 15. ♕f7 ♔h8 16. ♗b2 ♕a5 17. c3 ♕a4 18. ♘h7+— Konikowski—Plater, Polska 1968; 14... de5?! 15. ♕f7 ♔h8 16. ♕b3±] 15. ♕f7 [15. ♘f7 ♕a5∓] ♔h8 16. ♕b3 [16. f5 ♕a5∓; 16. ♗e3 cb2 17. ♖d1 ♗g4 18. ♕b3 ♕a5 19. ♗d2 ♕a6 20. ♘f7 1/2 : 1/2 Olexa—Hosnedl, corr. 1971] ♕a5 17. ♘f7=

97 12. f5 ♘e5 13. fe6 ♘f3 14. ♕f3 ♖e7 15. ♕f5 h6 16. ♖h6 ♕e8 17. ♕h7 ♔f8 18. ♕f5 ♔g8 1/2 : 1/2 Filipov—Efremov, SSSR 1970; 13... ♖e7!±

98 12... ♘e5 13. ♕h5 [13. fe5 cb2 14. ♕h5 ♕g5—+] h6 [13... ♕a5 14. fe5 ♕e5 15. ♗e2 ♖f5 16. g4± Sorokin—Dubovik, corr. 1968 — 5/140] 14. fe5 hg5 15. ♕h7 ♔f8 16. ♕h8 ♗h8 17. ♖h8 ♔g7 18. ♖d8 ♘c6∓ Keene

99 **13. f5** cb2—+; **13. ♕h5** ♖f5 14. ♘e6 ♖h5 15. ♘d8 ♗e6—+; 13... ♖c7—+

100 14. f5 cb2 [14... d5? 15. f6± Borda—B. Toth, Hungary 1971 — 11/144; 14... ♕a5 15. fe6 ♔e8 16. ♕h5 ♘g6 17. ed6 cb2± Tarakanov—Kanev, SSSR 1971] 15. fe6 ♗e6 16. ♕h5 [16. ♖f1 ♔g8 17. ♖f8 ♔f8 18. ♕f3 ♕f6!—+ Demičev—Seredenko, SSSR 1966] ♔e7±

101 16. g4 ♗d7 17. g5 ♗e8 18. ♕h3 h5 19. g6 de5 20. ♕h5 ef4∓⇆ Fridštejn

102 **10. fe5**? ♘e5 11. ♕h4 ♗f5 12. hg6 ♘f3 13. gf3 ♗g6 14. ♗d2 e6∓ Šipoš–Liberzon, SSSR 1962; **10. ♕g1** e4 11. ♘e4 ♘f6 12. ♘f6 ef6 13. hg6 ♖e8 [13... ♕e7!? Ghizdavu–Balašov, Riga 1967] 14. ♔f2 hg6 [14... fg6 15. ♕h2 ♕b6 16. ♔g3 h5∞ Gašić–Milić, Vrnjačka Banja 1967 — 2/133] 15. ♕h2 ♘d7 16. ♕h7 ♔f8 17. b3 ♘c5∓ Gašić–Keene, Bognor Regis 1967

103 **10... ef4** 11. hg6 hg6 12. ♗f4 ♘f6 13. ♕h4 ♕a5 14. ♘g5 ♗g4 15. ♗d3 ♘bd7 16. 0–0± Bronštejn–Palmiotto, München (ol) 1958; **10... e6** 11. hg6 fg6 12. ♕g3! ef4 13. ♗f4 ♕a5 14. ♗d2 ♘f6 15. ♗c4± Štejn–Liberzon, SSSR 1965

104 11. ♘e4 ♘f6 12. ♘f6 ef6 13. hg6 ♖e8△ fg6=

105 13. ♕h4 ♕d4 14. ♘b5 ♕b6 15. ♗c4 ♗g4∓ Padevski–Matanović, La Habana (ol) 1966 — 2/132

106 **6... ♘fd7** 7. 0–0 c5 [7... e5 8. de5 de5 9. f5± Fischer–Jovanović, Vinkovci 1968] 8. d5 e6 9. de6 fe6 10. ♘g5 ♘b6 11. a4 ♘c6 12. a5 h6 13. ab6 hg5 14. ♕g4± Fischer–Domnitz, Netanya 1968 — 6/218; **6... c6** 7. 0–0 b5 [7... ♕b6 8. ♔h1 ♗g4 9. e5 ♘e8 10. ♘e2 ♘d7 11. ♕e1± Lechtynsky–Kubiček, ČSSR 1968; 7... ♘bd7 8. ♔h1 ♘b6 9. ♕e1 d5 10. e5± Ed. Lasker–Najdorf, La Habana 1952] 8. e5 [8. a3 a6 9. ♔h1 ♕c7 10. e5 ♘d5 11. ♘g5± Matanović–Tartakower, England 1951] ♘e8 9. ♘e4 a5 10. ♕e1± Boleslavski–Mosionžik, SSSR 1967 — 4/167

107 8... ♘fd7 9. ♗e3 e5 10. fe5 [10. de5 fe5 11. f5±] c5 11. dc5 dc5 12. ♕f2 ♘c6 13. 0–0± Estrin–Zaharov, SSSR 1963

108 9... ♘d7 10. ♕f2 ♘b4 [10... e5 11. de5 de5 12. f5 ♘d4 13. g4± Žuravljev–Kampenus, SSSR 1964] 11. ♗c4 [11. 0-0-0!?] ♘b6 [11... c5 12. dc5 ♘c5 13. ♗c5 dc5 14. e5 ♕d4 15. ♗b3± Kapengut–Etruk, SSSR 1965; 13. 0–0 ♕c8 14. e5± van den Berg–Bobocov, Beverwijk 1965] 12. ♗b3 a5 [12... ♘c6 13. 0–0 ♘a5 14. ♖ad1 ♘bc4 15. ♗c1 c6 16. f5± Penrose–Robatsch, Hastings 1961/62] 13. a4 d5 14. 0–0 de4 15. ♘e4 ♘6d5 [Zinser–Bobocov, Le Havre 1966] 16. ♗d2±

109 10. fe5 de5 11. d5 ♘d4 12. ♕f2 c6 13. dc6 [13. 0—0 cd5 14. ♗g5 de4∓ Zaharjan–Mojsejev, SSSR 1967 — 4/170] bc6 14. 0–0 ♘d7∓ Sarapu–Mecking, Sousse (izt) 1967

110 11... gf5 12. ♕f5 ♘d4 13. ♕f2± Fischer–Benkö, USA (ch) 1964

111 **12... ♘d7** 13. 0–0 c6 14. a4 a5 15. ♗c4± Matanović–Bobocov, Zagreb 1964; **12... c6** 13. g4 ♕b6 14. 0-0-0 gf5 [Klovan–Kärner, SSSR 1968] 15. gf5±; **12... c5** 13. g4 b5 14. g5 c4 15. gf6 ♗f6 16. 0-0-0± Jansa–Pavlik, ČSSR 1966; **12... b5** 13. 0–0 [13. 0-0-0 c5 14. g4 b4 15. ♘d5 ♘d5 16. ed5 e4 17. ♗e4 ♖e8∞ Kunstovič–Kestler, Dortmund 1973] gf5 — 12... gf5; 13... b4!?

112 15. ♘e4!± Bednarski–Kraidman, Tel Aviv (ol) 1964

113 7. d5 e6 8. de6 fe6 [8... ♗e6? 9. f5 ♗c8 10. 0–0 ♘c6 11. ♔h1 ♘g4 12. ♘d5± Matanović–Vidmar, Jugoslavija (ch) 1951] 9. 0–0 ♘c6 10. ♔h1 [10. f5? ef5 11. ef5 ♗f5 12. ♗f5 gf5 13. ♗g5 ♕d7 14. ♘h4 ♘d4 15. ♕d3 ♘e4∓ Rossolimo–Benkö, USA (ch) 1968] d5 11. e5 ♘g4∓

114 **8. 0—0** ♘c6 9. ♗e3 ♘d4= Ed. Lasker–Wade, Hastings 1953; **8. ♗e3** ♕a5 9. ♗d2 ♗g4 10. e5 ♘fd7 11. h3 ♗f3 12. ♕f3 ♘c6 13. h4± Spaski–Garcia, Mar del Plata 1960; **8. e5** ♘d5 9. ♘d5 ♕d5 10. ♕e2 ♘c6 [10... ♗f5 11. ♗f5 gf5 12. ♗e3 ♘c6 13. 0–0 ♖ad8 14. ♖fd1 ♕e4 15. ♘g5 ♕a4 16. ♖d8± Ubilava–Vinkel, SSSR 1971] 11. ♗e4 — 8. ♕e2

115 11... ♕d8 12. ♗e3 ♕a5 13. c3 ♗f5 14. ♗f5 gf5 15. ♕c4 ♖ac8 16. a4± Ivanenko–Gufeljd, SSSR 1963

116 12. ♗e3 b6 13. h4 ♗b7 14. ♖d1 ♕g4 15. h5 ♖ad8 16. ♖h4 ♕e6 17. hg6 hg6 18. ♘g5± Tan–Pirc, Beverwijk 1963; 12... ♕c7!?

117 15. e6! f5 16. ♖d7 ♕c8 17. ♗d5± Levin–Tukmakov, SSSR 1963

118 7. 0–0 c5 8. d5 [8. e5 ♘g4∓ Janošević–Benkö, Beograd 1964; 8. ♗a6 cd4 9. ♘d4 ba6 10. ♘b3 a5 11. ♕f3 ♗b7 12. a4 ♕b6∓ Barczay–Sandor, Hungary 1967 — 5/145] **♘c7** 9. a4 [9. ♕e1 b5? 10. ♗b5+–; 9... e6 10. de6 ♘e6 11. f5 ♘d4 12. ♕h4± Padevski–Sandor, Varna 1969; 9... ♗d7 10. a4 a6 11. a5 ♗b5 12. ♕h4 e6 13. f5± Gligorić–Larsen, Beverwijk 1967 — 3/159] e6 10. de6 fe6 11. ♘g5! [11. ♔h1 ♘fe8 12. ♘g5 ♗h6 13. h4 ♗g5∞ Menvielle–Padevski, La Habana 1967 — 2/136; 11. e5!?] h6 [11... b6 12. ♗d2 a6 13. ♕e2 ♖a7 14. ♖ae1 b5 15. e5± Lejn–Cejtlin, SSSR (ch) 1971] 12. ♘f3 ♘h5 13. g3 e5 14. f5± Guljko–Kremenecki, SSSR 1974; **8... ♘b4**! 9. ♗c4 e6 10. de6 ♗e6 11. ♗e6 fe6 12. a3 ♘c6∓

119 **7... de5** 8. de5 [8. fe5 ♘d5 9. ♘d5 ♕d5 10. c4 ♕d8 11. 0–0 ♗g4 12. ♗e4 c6∞ Bisguier–Benkö, USA (ch) 1964; 10. c3!?± Fridštejn] ♘d5 9. ♘d5 ♕d5 10. ♕e2 ♗f5 11. ♗f5 gf5 12. ♗e3 f6 [12... ♖fd8 13. 0–0 ♘b4 14. a3 ♘c6 15. ♖fd1 ♕e6 16. ♘g5 ♕g6 (Parma–Ree, Titovo Užice 1966) 17. ♕b5±] 13. ef6 ♗f6 14. 0–0 ♕e4 15. c3 ♘c5 16. ♘d2 ♕d3 17. ♕f2 ♘a4 18. ♖ab1 c5 19. ♘f3± Ree–Timman, Nederland 1971 — 13/198; **7... ♘d7** 8. ♘e2 [8. 0–0 c5 9. ♗e3 ♘b4 10. ♗c4 cd4 11. ♗d4 ♘c6∓ De Greiff–Monostori, corr. 1966; 8. ♕e2 c5 9. d5 ♘b4= Pedersen–Sirkia, Siegen (ol) 1970] c5 9. c3± Marović

120 8. 0–0 c5 9. ♗e3 cd4 10. ♗d4 ♘ac7 11. ♕e1 ♗g4 12. ♖d1± Padevski–Gipslis, Zagreb 1965

121 11. ♗e4 ♕a5 12. 0–0 ♘c7 13. ♘d2 ♕b4 14. ♕f3± Klovan–Cejtlin, SSSR 1970

122 15. ♘ce4± Šmit–Karasev, SSSR 1970

123 7. ♕e2 c5 [7... e5? 8. de5 de5 9. fe5 ♘g4 10. ♗g5 ♕e8 11. ♘d5+–] 8. d5 [8. e5 ♘e8 — 7. e5 ♘e8 8. ♕e2; 8... cd4!? Boleslavski] ♘b6 8. a4 [9. 0–0 e6 10. de6 ♗e6 11. f5 ♗d7 12. a4 c4 13. ♗c4 ♘c4 14. ♕c4 ♗c6∞̄] e6 10. de6 [10. a5? ed5∓] ♗e6 11. a5 ♘bd7 12. 0–0 ♖e8 13. ♕f2 c4 14. ♗e2 ♖c8 15. h3 ♘c5 16. ♘g5 [Polugajevski–Gipslis, SSSR (ch) 1963] h6!∞

124 8. ♕e2 c5 9. ♗e3 cd4 10. ♗d4 de5 11. fe5 ♘c7 12. ♗c4 [12. 0-0-0 ♘e6 13. ♗f2 ♕a5 14. ♗g3 ♘b6 15. h4 ♗d7 16. h5 ♖ac8 17. ♕e1 ♘a4= Trofimov–Ivanov, corr. 1967] ♘b6 13. ♗b3 [13. ♗b6 ab6 14. ♖d1 ♕e8 (Quinones–Smislov, Amsterdam 1964) 15. 0–0 =] ♕e8 [13... ♗g4 14. ♕e4 ♗f3 15. gf3 ♘e6= Kuipers–Rocha, Malaga 1965] 14. 0-0-0 ♗e6 15. h4 h5 16. ♘g5 ♕c6!= Witkowski–Balcerowski, Polanica Zdroj 1964; **8. ♘g5** de5! [8... e6 9. h4 h6 10. h5±→; 9... de5 10. de5 ♘c5 11. h5±; 9... c5 10. h5 cd4 11. hg6 hg6 12. ♕g4 (Radčenko–Strebkov, SSSR 1964) ♘ef6 13. ef6 ♘f6 14. ♕h3 dc3 15. bc3 ♖e8 16. ♗b2△ 0-0-0∞̄] 9. fe5 ♘b6 10. ♗e3 c5 11. dc5 ♘d5∞; **8. ♘e2** c5 9. c3 [Blair–Santasiere, USA 1968 — 6/219] cd4 10. cd4 ♕b6∞; **8. h4** c5 9. h5 ♘c7 10. hg6 hg6 11. e6 ♘e6 12. f5 ♘d4 13. fg6 ♘f6∞ Lepeškin–Kremenecki, SSSR 1965

125 9... cd4 10. cd4 ♕b6 11. a4 ♘b8 12. a5 ♕d8 13. 0–0 de5 14. de5 ♘c6 15. ♗e2± Jansa–Tringov, Bucuresti 1968

126 10. ♕e2 cd4 11. cd4 ♘b8! 12. ♗e3 ♘c6 13. ♘c3 ♘b4 14. ♗e4 f5 15. ♗b1 ♘c7 16. a3 ♘bd5= Browne–Parma, Sarajevo 1970

127 15. ♘d5 ♘d5 16. ♕e2± Gligorić–Rocha, Hastings 1964/65

128 7... c5 8. d5 a6 9. a4 ♕c7 10. ♕e2± Rossolimo–Müller, Dubrovnik (ol) 1950

129 8. de5 de5 9. f5 gf5 10. ef5 ♘c5∓ Tsagan–Plater, Ulan Bator 1965; 9... ♘c5!?

130 9. de5 ♘e5 10. ♘e5 ♕d4 11. ♔h1 ♕e5 12. ♕f3 [12. ♗f4 ♕c5 13. ♕f3 ♗e6 14. ♗e3 ♕h5 15. ♕g3 c6∓ Larsen–Bouwmeester, Kopenhagen 1952; 13. ♕d2 ♗e6 14. ♗h6 ♗h6 15. ♕h6 ♘g4∓ Nilsson–Bouwmeester, Göteborg 1952] c6 13. ♗f4 [Gligorić–Kuijpers, Tel Aviv (ol) 1964] ♕c5∓

131 9... ♘e8!? Donner

132 10... ♕b6 11. ♔h1 ♕c6 12. ♕e1△ ♕h4±

133 **11... ♕c7** 12. ♗e3 ♘b6 13. a4 a5 14. ♕e1 ♘fd7 15. ♖d1 ♕d8 16. ♕f2± Matulović–Tringov, Siegen (ol) 1970 — 10/185; **11... ♘h5**!?

134 15. ♗b5 ♘f6 16. ♕e1± Matulović–Portisch, Skopje 1968 — 6/220

135 **7. h3** ♘b4 8. ♗e3 [8. ♗e2 c5 9. dc5 ♘h5∓] b6 9. a3 ♘d3 10. cd3 c5 11. ♕d2 ♗a6∓ Penrose–Keene, England 1971 — 12/183; **7. d5.** ♘b4 [7... ♘b8 8. 0–0 c6 9. ♕e1 cd5 10 ed5 ♘a6 11. ♗a6 ♕b6 12. ♗e3 ♕a6∓ Hasin–Juhtman, SSSR 1964; 9. dc6 ♘c6 Gligorić–Matulović, Jugoslavija (ch) 1965; 10. ♕e1!±] 8. ♗e2 [8. 0–0 c6 9. a3 ♘d3 10. ♕d3 cd5 11. ♘d5 ♘d5 12. ♕d5 ♕b6 13. ♔h1 ♗d7∓ Yanofsky–Botvinik, Tel Aviv (ol) 1964; 9. dc6 bc6 10. h3 ♘d3 11. cd3 ♕b6 12. ♔h2 ♗a6 13. ♖e1 ♘d7∓ Lancaster–Harman, England 1968] a5!? [8... c6 9. a3 ♘a6 10. ♗e3 cd5 11. ed5 ♘c5 12. 0–0 ♗g4 13. ♗d4± Minev–Kolarov, Bulgaria 1965; 10... ♕c7 11. ♘d2 ♗d7 12. 0–0 ♘c5 13. ♗f3 cd5 14. ed5 b5= Bouwmeester–Parma, Amsterdam 1965] 9. a3 ♘a6 10. ♗e3 c6 11. 0–0 ♗d7 12. h3 ♘c5 13. ♘d2 cd5 14. ed5 b5 15. ♘b3 b4∓ Mikenas–Etruk, SSSR 1968; **7. f5** ♘b4 [7... e5? 8. fe6 fe6 9. 0–0 ♕e7 10. ♕e1 ♘d8 11. ♕h4± Hort–Donner, Wijk aan Zee 1972; 7... ♘e8? 8. ♗e3 e5 9. de5 ♘e5 10. ♘e5 ♗e5 11. ♕f3 c6 12. g4 ♕h4 13. ♔d2 ♘f6 14. ♖ag1± Popov–Šamkovič, SSSR 1971] 8. 0–0 [8. fg6 ♘d3 9. ♕d3 hg6 10. ♗g5 d5 11. e5 ♗f5 12. ♕e3 ♘g4 13. ♕d2 f6= Savon–Hort, Moskva 1971 — 12/186; 8... hg6 9. ♗g5 c5!? 10. d5 e6 11. 0–0 ed5 12. ed5 ♕b6 13. ♕d2 ♗g4∓ Tukmakov–Sigurjonsson, Reykjavik 1972] c5 [8... gf5 9. ef5 c5 10. ♗g5 cd4 11. ♗f6 dc3 12. ♗g7 ♔g7 13. f6 ef6 14. bc3± Savon–Timman, Wijk aan Zee 1971; 11... ♗f6!? 12. ♘e4 e5∞] 9. dc5 [9. d5 gf5 10. ef5 ♘d3 11. ♕d3 c4∓ Marjasin–Didiško, SSSR 1972] dc5=

136 7... ♘d7 8. e5 ♘b6 9. 0–0 ♗g4 10. h3 ♗f3 11. ♕f3 e6 12. ♖ad1 ♘b4 13. ♘e4± Bisguier–Udovčić, Tel Aviv (ol) 1964

137 **9... ♘d4** 10. ♘e5 [10. ♘d4 ♘g4 11. ♘f5 gf5 12. ♗c5 ♖e8? 13. ef5 ♘f6 14. 0–0± Štejn–Matanović, SSSR–Jugoslavija 1965; 12... f4 13. ♗f8 ♕h4 14. ♔d2 ♗f8∞̄; 12... fe4△ f5∓] ♘d5 11. ♗d4 ♘f4 12. ♗f1 ♘e6= Baretić–Pirc, Jugoslavija (ch) 1968 — — 5/144; 12. ♘e2 ♘e2 13. ♗e2 ♕e7 [13... ♕h4 14. ♗f2 ♕e4 15. ♘f3 ♖e8 16. ♔f1+– Rubinetti–Mecking, Mar del Plata 1969] 14. ♘g6 [14. ♘f3 ♖d8∓] fg6 15. ♗g7 [15. ♕d3 ♖d8 16. ♕b3 ♗e6 17. ♗c4 ♖d4=] ♕h4 16. g3 ♕e4= Euwe; 12. ♗c4! c5 [12... ♘g2 13. ♔f2 ♕h4 14. ♔g2 ♗h3 15. ♔g1 ♖ad8 16. ♗d5 ♕g5 17. ♔f2 c5 18. ♗c5+– Sutton–Todorčević, Skopje (ol) 1972 — 14/198] 13. ♗c5 ♗e5 14. ♕d8! ♖d8 15. g3±; **9... ♘g4** 10. ♗c5 ♘d4 11. ♗f8 ♕f8 12. h3 ♘e3 13. ♕d2 ♗h6∞̄; 10. ♗g1 — 7... ♘g4

138 10. 0–0 ♘e8 [10... c6!?] 11. ♘b5 a6 [11... f5?! 12. c4 fe4 13. ♗e4 ♘f5 14. ♗g5± Kuijpers–Donner, Beverwijk 1967] 12. ♘a3 ♘d6 13. c4 f5∞

139 15. ♖ad1 ♖ac8 16. ♕f2 a6 17. ♕h4 h5 18. ♘e6 [18. g4?! ♖fe8∓ Lublinski–Toluš, SSSR 1968 — 6/222] ♕e6 19. ♗g5= Suetin

140 10... ♘e7 11. h3 ♘f6 12. ♗h2 ♘ed5 13. ed5 e4 14. 0–0 ed3 15. ♕d3 ♗f5 16. ♕c4± Mecking–Keene, Hastings 1971/72

141 11... ♘f6 12. ♘e5 [12. ♘d4 ed4 13. ♗d4 ♘d5 14. ♗g7 ♕h4 15. ♔d2 ♕g5=] ♘e4 [12... ♘f5 13. ef5 ♖e8 14. ♗h2 ♘d5 15. 0–0 ♗e5 16. fg6+– Pebo–Tamme, SSSR 1972] 13. ♗e4 ♗e5 14. ♗d4 ♕h4 15. ♔e2 ♗d4 16. ♕d4 f5 17. ♖af1± Minić–Pirc, Jugoslavija 1965

142 12. ♗c4 ♗d7 [12... c5 13. dc6 bc6 14. ♗e3± Dückstein–Andersen, Krems 1967] 13. ♕d2 b5 14. ♗d4 ed4 15. ♘b5 ♖e8 16. 0–0 ♖e4 17. ♘bd4 ♕f8∞ Kuzmin–G. Garcia, Cienfuegos 1973; 12... f5!?

143 15. ♕e1 ♘f3 [15... ♕f6 16. ♔b1 ♗d7 17. ♗h2 ♖ae8 18. ♖f1 ♕b6∞ van den Weide–Kuijpers, Nederland 1972] 16. ♗f3 ♘d4 17. ♗e4 ♗f5 [17... c5!?] 18. ♔b1 ♗e4 19. ♕e4 ♕d7 20. ♗h2 ♖ae8 21. ♖he1 b5∞ Savon–Donner, Cienfuegos 1973 — 15/176

144 **7... ♘g4** 8. h3 ♘h6 9. ♗e3 de5 10. fe5 ♘f5 11. ♗f5 ♗f5 12. g4 ♗c8 13. ♕d2 ♘b4 14. 0-0-0 ♘d5 15. ♘e4± Sax–Vadasz, Hungary 1970 — 10/186; **7... ♘d7** 8. ♘e4 ♘b4 9. ♗e2 [9. h4?! ♘d3 10. ♕d3 ♘b6 11. h5 de5 12. fe5 ♗f5∓ Peres–Ortega, Lugano (ol) 1968] ♘b6 10. c3 ♗f5 11. ♘fg5 ♘4d5 12. g4± Boleslavski; **7... ♘e8** 8. ♗e3 ♘b4 9. ♗c4 ♗f5 10. ♖c1 c5 11. d5 ♗g4∞ Kuijpers–Botvinik, Amsterdam 1966 — 2/135

145 9. ♘d5 ♕d5 10. ♕e2 ♗g4 [10... ♗f5 11. ♗f5 gf5 12. ♗e3 ♖ad8 13. 0–0 ♕e4= Zuidema–Balcerowski, Tel Aviv (ol) 1964; 13... ♕e6 14. ♖fe1 1/2 : 1/2 O'Kelly–Donner, La Habana 1967] 11. ♗e4 [11. ♗c4 ♕d7 12. c3 ♘a5 13. ♗b5 c6 14. ♗a4 ♖ad8 15. ♗c2 ♗e6 16. b3 f6= Liberzon–Savon, SSSR (ch) 1967] ♕a5 12. ♗d2 ♕b6= Gufeljd–Polugajevski, SSSR (ch) 1963

146 **9... ♘c3** 10. ♗c3 ♗f5 11. ♗f5 ♕d1 12. ♖d1 gf5 13. ♖d7 [13. h3 ♖ad8 14. ♔e2 e6 15. g4± Szabo–Donner, Amsterdam 1972] ♖ac8 14. h3 f6 15. e6± Hort– Donner, Skopje (ol) 1972 — 14/200; **9... ♘db4** 10. ♗e4 f5 11. ♗c6 ♘c6 12. ♕e2 a6 [12... ♗e6 13. 0-0-0 ♘d4 14. ♘d4 ♕d4 15. ♗e3 ♕b4 16. ♖d4± Kapengut–Didiško, SSSR 1974 — 17/209] 13. 0-0-0 e6 14. ♗e1 ♕e8 15. ♗h4± Gligorić–Matanović, Zagreb 1965; **9... ♘cb4** 10. ♗e4 [10. ♗c4 ♘b6 11. ♗b3 a5∞] c6 [10... ♘b6 11. a3 ♘a6 12. ♕e2 ♘c5 13. 0-0-0 ♘e4 14. ♘e4 c6 15. ♗a5 ♕e8 16. ♕f2 ♘d5 17. ♕h4± Ljubojević–Donner, Wijk aan Zee 1973 — 15/174; 14... ♕d5 15. ♘c3 ♕c4 16. ♕c4 ♘c4 17. ♘d5 ♗g4 18. ♗b4± Parma–Keene, Dortmund 1973 — 15/177] 11. ♘d5 [11. a3 ♘c3 12. ♗c3 ♘d5 13. ♗d5 cd5 14. 0–0 ♗f5 15. ♕e2 ♖c8 16. ♖ad1 ♖c4= Vulfson–Guljko, SSSR 1974; 13. ♗d2 f6 14. c4 ♘b6 15. ♕e2 ♗e6 16. b3 fe5 17. fe5 ♗g4 1/2 : 1/2 Bronštejn–Etruk, SSSR 1971; 11. 0–0!?] cd5 12. ♗b4 de4 13. ♕d8 ♖d8 14. ♘d2 e3 15. ♘b3 ♗f5 16. c3 ♖d7 17. ♗c5± Matulović–Jansa, Sarajevo 1972; **9... ♗e6** 10. ♕e2 ♕d7 11. ♘d5 ♕d5 12. ♗c3 ♗h6 13. ♕e3 ♗f5 14. ♗f5 gf5 15. 0–0 ♖ad8= Matanović–Darga, Winnipeg 1967; **9... ♘b6**!?

147 10... ♘c3 11. ♗c3 ♕d1 12. ♖d1 f6 13. 0–0 fe5 14. fe5 ♗h6 15. ♗d5 ♔h8 16. h3‖+ Matuloivć–Bronštejn, Sarajevo 1971 — 11/150

148 **15... ♘c6** 16. ♕e2 ♕d4∞; **15... c5**!?

149 8... ♘e8 9. ♗c4!±

150 **9. ♘e2** f6 10. ef6 ef6 11. h3 ♘h6 12. c3 ♖e8 13. ♗f4 ♘f5 14. ♕d2 g5∓ Kuijpers–Spaski, Beverwijk 1967 — 3/160; **9. ♗c4** ♘a5△ c5∞; **9. h3** ♘h6 10. ♗c4 [10. ♗e3 f6 11. ♕d2 ♘f7 12. ef6 ef6 13. 0-0-0 ♘e7 14. ♔b1 ♗e6 15. ♖he1 ♘d5= Kuijpers–Hort, Wijk aan Zee 1971; 10. ♗e4 f6 — 9. ♗e4] ♘f5 [10... ♘a5 11. ♗e2 f6 12. 0–0 ♘f5 13. ♘e4± Klovan–Etruk, SSSR 1968; 10... ♔h8!?] 11. ♘e2 ♘a5 12. ♗d3 f6∞ Fridštejn

151 9... f5 10. ♗c6 bc6 11. h3 ♘h6 12. ♗f4 ♘f7 13. ♕d2 ♗e6 14. 0-0-0± Suetin–Donner, La Habana 1969

152 **10. ef6** ♗f6 [10... ef6 11. 0–0 ♔h8 12. ♖e1 ♘h6 13. ♘a4 ♘e7 14. ♘c5± Suetin–Gipslis, Budva 1967; 12... ♘d4! 13. ♘d4 f5 14. ♗d5 (Kapengut–Etruk, SSSR 1969 — 8/146) ♕d6 15. g3 ♕c5∓; 12. h3 ♘h6 13. ♗d5 — 10. h3] 11. ♗c6 [11. h3? ♗h4∓; 11. ♘e2? ♘d4 12. ♘ed4 e5∓ Tratatovici–Ghizdavu, Romania 1970 — 10/188; 11. ♘d5 ♘d4 12. ♘d4 ♗h4 13. g3 ♘f2 14. ♕e2 e6∞ Keene] bc6 12. 0–0 c5 13. dc5 ♗b7=∞ Paoli–Polgar, Kecskemet 1972; **10. ♗d5** ♔h8 11. ef6 [11. h3 — 10. h3] ef6 12. 0–0 f5 13. ♗f4 ♘f6 14. ♗c6 bc6 15. ♖e1 [Suetin–Etruk, SSSR 1972] ♘e4!?∞ Talj

153 **11. ♗h6** ♗h6 12. ♕e2 ♗f4![12... e6 13. ♗c6 bc6 14. ♘e4± Kudrašov–Muratov, SSSR 1970] 13. 0–0 ♘d4 14. ♕c4 ♔h8∓; **11. ♗d5** ♔h8 12. 0–0 ♘f5 13. ♖e1 [13. ♗c6 bc6 14. ♖e1 fe5 15. de5 c5 16. ♕d5 ♕d5 17. ♘d5 c6 18. ♘f4 ♘d4∓ Klavin–Kampenus, SSSR 1960; 16. ♕d8 ♖d8 17. ♗f4 ♘d4∓ Plachetka–Keene, Dresden 1969] ♘fd4 14. ♘d4 ♘d4 15. ♕d4 e6 [15... c6 16. ef6±] 16. ef6 ♗f6 17. ♕c5± Gligorić–Quinteros, Vinkovci 1970 — 10/190; 12... fe5 13. de5 ♘f7 [13... ♘b4 14. ♗g5 ♘f5 15. ♗b3 h6 16. ♕d8 ♖d8 17. ♗f4 g5∓ Plachetka–Vadasz, Hungary 1970 — 9/141; 14. ♗b3! ♕d1 15. ♖d1 ♗f5 16. ♗g5!±] 14. ♗f4 [14. e6 ♘fe5 15. ♘e5 ♖f1 16. ♕f1 ♘e5 17. ♗f4 ♕d6∓] ♘fe5 15. ♘e5 ♘e5 16. ♕e2=∞ Klovan–Etruk, SSSR 1971 — 12/184

154 **12. ♗e3** ♘f5 13. ♗f2 ♗h6= Unzicker–Donner, Bamberg 1968; **12. 0—0** ♘e7 [12... ♘f5 13. ♗c6 bc6 14. ♖e1 ♖e8 15. ♖e8 ♕e8 16. ♗f4± Kagan–Gulbrandsson, Ybbs 1968] 13. ♗f4 g5 [13... c6 14. ♕e2 g5 15. ♗h2 f5∞ Ljubojević–Milovanović, Jugoslavija 1970; 13... ♘hf5 14. ♘b5 c6 15. ♘c7 g5∓ Ivarsson–Jansson, Sverige 1970] 14. ♗e3 f5 15. ♗d3 f4 16. ♗f2 ♘ef5∓ Klovan–Etruk, SSSR 1967 — 4/169; 13. ♘e2 ♘hf5 [13... c6 14.

c3 ♗e6= Kagan–Ghizdavu, Ybbs 1968] 14. c3 c6 15. ♘f4 ♘g3= Gheorghiu–Mecking, Buenos Aires 1970 — 10/189; 13. ♖e1 ♘hf5 [13... ♘f7 14. ♕e2 ♘f5 15. ♕f2 c6 16. d5± Weichert–Vadasz, Graz 1972 — 15/173] 14. ♗f4 g5 15. ♗h2 h5 [Bouwmeester–Keene, England 1969] 16. ♕d3±; 13. ♗d3 ♔h8 14. ♗e3 ♘ef5 [14... c6 15. ♖e1 ♘hf5 16. ♗f2 ♘d5 17. ♘d5 cd5 18. c4± Schmid–Tringov, Lugano (ol) 1968; 14... g5!?] 15. ♗f2 ♖e8 16. ♖e1 ♗d7±; 13. ♗e3!?

155 13... ♖e8 14. ♖e1 ♖e1 15. ♕e1 ♘e7 16. ♗b3± Klovan–Žuravljev, SSSR 1972

156 16. ♕d4 c6 17. ♗f4 cd5 18. ♘d5 ♗f5 19. ♖e7± Golovej–Borisenko, SSSR 1971

157 **9. ♗e4** ♗g4 10. ♗e3 f6 11. ef6 [11. e6 f5 12. ♗d5 f4 13. ♗f2 ♘f6 14. ♗b3 ♘a5∓ Lambshire–Keene, England 1971; 11. ♕e2 fe5 12. ♗c6 bc6 13. ♕c4 e6 14. ♗g5 ♕b8∓ Gligorić–Keene, Berlin 1971 — 12/185] ♘f6 [11... ef6 12. ♕d3 Peretz–Jansson, Siegen (ol) 1970 — 10/187; 12... ♘e7∞; 11... ♗f6 12. ♗c6 ♗h4 13. g3 bc6 14. 0–0 ♗f6=] 12. ♗c6 bc6 13. 0–0 ♘d5 14. ♘d5 ♕d5 [14... cd5 15. h3 ♗f3 16. ♖f3 ♕d6= Kuijpers–Botterill, England 1971 — 13/200] 15. c3 ♖ab8= Kagan–Parma, Netanya 1971 — 11/151; **9. ♗c4** ♗g4 10. ♗e3 ♘a5 [10... ♗f3 11. ♕f3! ♘d4 12. ♕e4 ♘f5 13. g4+– Klovan–Vadasz, SSSR 1972; 10... ♔h8 11. ♕d2 f6 12. ef6 ♗f6 13. 0–0± Karpov–Nikolajevski, SSSR 1971 — 13/199] 11. ♗e2 c5 12. d5 ♗f3 13. ♗f3 ♘c4 14. ♕e2 [14. ♗c1 ♘e5 15. ♗h5 gh5 16. ♕h5 f5∞] ♘e5 15. ♗h5 gh5 16. ♕h5 Sax–Botterill, Graz 1972 — 14/196; 16... f5! ∞; **9. ♘e2** ♗g4 [9... f6!?] 10. c3 ♗f3 11. gf3 e6 12. 0–0 f6∞

158 10... ♕d7!?

159 **11. ef6** ef6 12. 0–0 [12. ♕d2 f5 13. 0-0-0 f4 14. ♗f2 ♕d7∞ Barczay–E. Nagy, Hungary 1973 — 16/146] f5 13. h3 ♗f3 14. ♗f3 [Zuidema–Fuller, Skopje (ol) 1972 — 14/199] f4 15. ♗f2 ♘g3 16. ♖e1 ♘f5=; **11. d5** ♘e5 12. ♘e5 ♗e2 13. ♕e2 fe5 14. 0-0-0 ♕d7 [14... ♘f4!?] 15. ♕b5 ♕g4∞ Browne–Timman, Amsterdam 1971

160 11... f5 12. d5 ♘b4 13. ♗c4 c6 14. d6 ♕d6 15. ♕d6 ed6 16. e7 ♖f7 17. ♗f7 ♔f7 18. 0-0-0±

161 12. ♕d2 ♘d5 13. ♘d5 ♕d5 14. c4 ♕e6 15. d5 ♕d7 16. ♘d4 e5 17. de6 ♗e6= Tringov–Simić, Vrnjačka Banja 1973

162 12... c6 13. ♕d2 ♗e6 [13... ♕c8 14. ♖ae1 ♗e6 15. ♘h4± Kapengut–Parma, Erevan 1971] 14. ♘h4 g5 15. ♗h5 gh4 16. ♘e4 ♘d5 17. ♗h6± Kapengut–Tukmakov, SSSR 1972

163 **10... f6** 11. ♕e2 ♔h8 12. ♗c4 ♕d8 13. ef6 ef6 14. 0–0± Lee–Andersen, La Habana (ol) 1966; **10... ♗g4** 11. 0–0?! 12. ♗e5∞ Boudy–Zwaig, Dresden 1969; 11. h3 ♗f3 12. ♕f3 ♕f3 13. gf3 e6 [13... ♖ad8 14. ♔e2 f6 15. e6± Gheorghiu–Gipslis, Bucuresti 1966; 14... e6 15. ♗e4 ♖d7 (Ribli–Bilek, Debrecen 1970) 16. h4±] 14. ♗e4 ♖ab8 15. h4 [15. ♔e2 ♘e7 16. ♗g5 f6 17. ef6 ♗f6= Tajmanov–Vasjukov, Reykjavik 1968 — 5/147; 16. ♗d2±] ♘e7 [15... h5 16. ♗g5± Gheorghiu–Donner, Wijk aan Zee 1968 — 5/146] 16. h5± Gligorić–Vasjukov, Skopje 1790; 11. ♕e2 ♖ad8 [11... e6 12. ♗e4 ♕d7 13. 0–0 f6 14. ef6 ♗f6 15. h3± Kolker–Glotov, SSSR 1967] 12. ♗e4 ♕d7 13. h3 ♗e6 14. 0–0 ♗d5 [14... f6 15 ♗f4 fe5 16. ♗c6± Jansa–Lanč, ČSSR 1970 — 9/140] 15. ♗d5 ♕d5 16. ♗f4± Fischer–Perez, La Habana 1965

164 11. c4 ♕d7 12. d5 ♘b4 13. ♗b1 ♗g4∞

165 12. ♘g5? ♘d4! 13. cd4 ♕d4 14. ♘e6 fe6 15. ♗c4 ♗e5 16. g3 ♖f2∓ Suetin–Židkov, SSSR 1972 — 14/197

166 7... e5 8. fe5 [8. de5 de5 9. f5 gf5 10. ef5 ♘b4 11. ♗g5 ♘d3 12. ♕d3±; 10... e4!?; 9... ♘b4 10. fg6 hg6 11. ♗g5 ♘d3 12. cd3± Padevski–Udovčić, Zagreb 1965] de5 9. d5 ♘e7 [9... ♘d4!?] 10. ♘e5 ♘fd5 [10... ♘e4 11. ♘g6±] 11. ♘f7 ♘c3 12. bc3! [12. ♘d8 ♘d1 13. ♗c4 ♔h8= Judovič–Lujk, corr. 1967/68 — 4/168; 12. ♕f3 ♕e8 13. ♗c4 ♘cd5 ∞] ♖f7 13. ♖f7 ♔f7 14. ♗c4⩱

167 **8. ♕e1** ♗f3 [8... ♘d7 9. ♘g5 h6 10. d5 (Pomar–Robatsch, Marianske Lazni 1965) 10. ♘d4∞] 9. ♖f3 ♘d4 10. ♖h3 c6 [10... ♘g4 11. ♕h4 h5 12. ♘d5±→ Weksler–Dreyk, USA 1972] 11. f5 ♕b6 12. ♔h1 ♘g4∓ Mironov–Borisov, corr. 1973/74; **8. ♘e2** e5 [8... ♘b4 9. h3 ♘d3= Letzelter–Gheorghiu, Monaco 1968] 9. fe5 de5 10. d5 ♘d4 11. ♗e3 ♘h5 12. ♗d4 ed4 13. h3 ♗f3∓ Toluš–Polugajevski, SSSR 1963; **8. ♗e3** e5 9. de5 [9. fe5 de5 10. d5 ♘d4 11. ♕d2 ♗f3 12. gf3 ♘h5 13. ♕g2= Hort–Bobocov, Nordwijk 1965; 11... ♘f3 12. gf3 ♗h3 13. ♖f2 ♘h5∓ Estrin–Mučnik, SSSR 1967; 9. ♘e2 ed4△ ♖e8∓] de5 10. h3 ef4 11. ♗f4 ♗e6=; **8. ♗b5** ♘d7 9. ♘e2 e5 10. c3 ♕e7= Keres–Westerinen, Bamberg 1968

168 **8... ♗f3** 9. ♖f3 de5 10. de5 ♘d5 11. ♘e4±; **8... ♘e8** 9. ♗e3 ♘b4 10. ♗e2 c6 11. a3 ♘d5 12. ♘d5 cd5 13. h3± Hindle–Gheorghiu, Vrnjačka Banja 1967; **8... ♘d7**!?

169 **10. ♗d2** ♘d4 11. ♗e4 c6 [Padevski–Zwaig, La Habana (ol) 1966 — 2/137] 12. ♔h1=; **10. ♘d5** ♕d5 11. h3 ♗e6 [11... ♗f3 12. ♕f3 ♕f3 13. ♖f3 ♖ad8 14. ♗d2 ♖d7 15. ♗c3 ♘d4= Bagirov–Averbah, SSSR (ch) 1963] 12. ♕e2 [12. ♕e1!?] ♖fd8 13. ♗e4 ♘d4= Markland–Portisch, Hastings 1970/71 — 11/149; 11... ♗f5 — 10. h3

170 10... ♗f5 11. ♘d5 ♕d5 12. ♗f5 ♕d1 [12... ♕c5!?] 13. ♖d1 gf5 14. ♗e3 [Portisch–Vasjukov, Amsterdam 1969 — 8/145] ♖ad8 15. ♔f2 e6 16. g4±

171 12. ♗e3!?

172 16. cd4 e6 17. g4± Parma–G. Garcia, Camaguey 1974

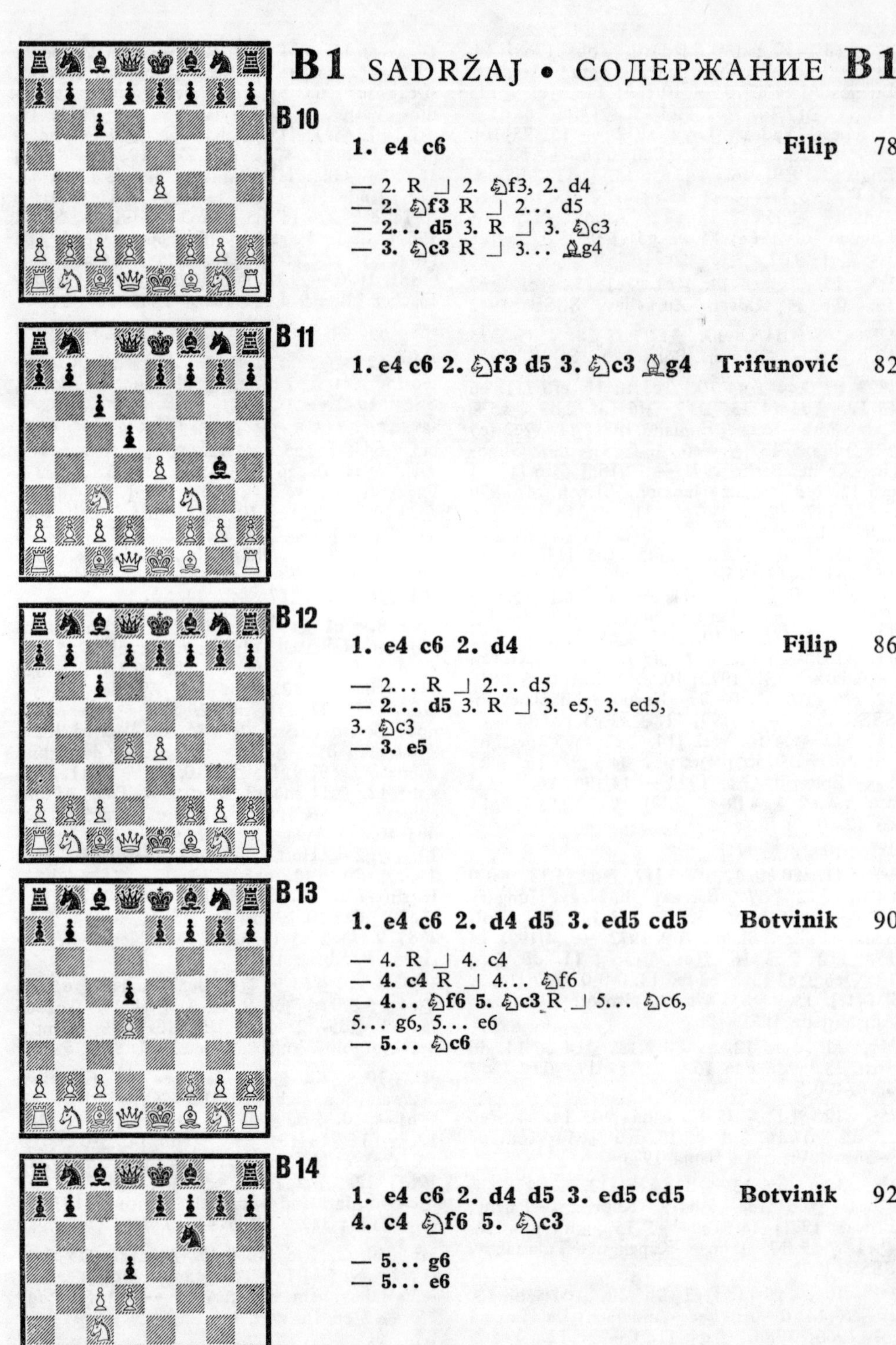

B1 SADRŽAJ • СОДЕРЖАНИЕ B1

B1 SOMMAIRE • INDICE B1

B1 CONTENTS • INHALT B1

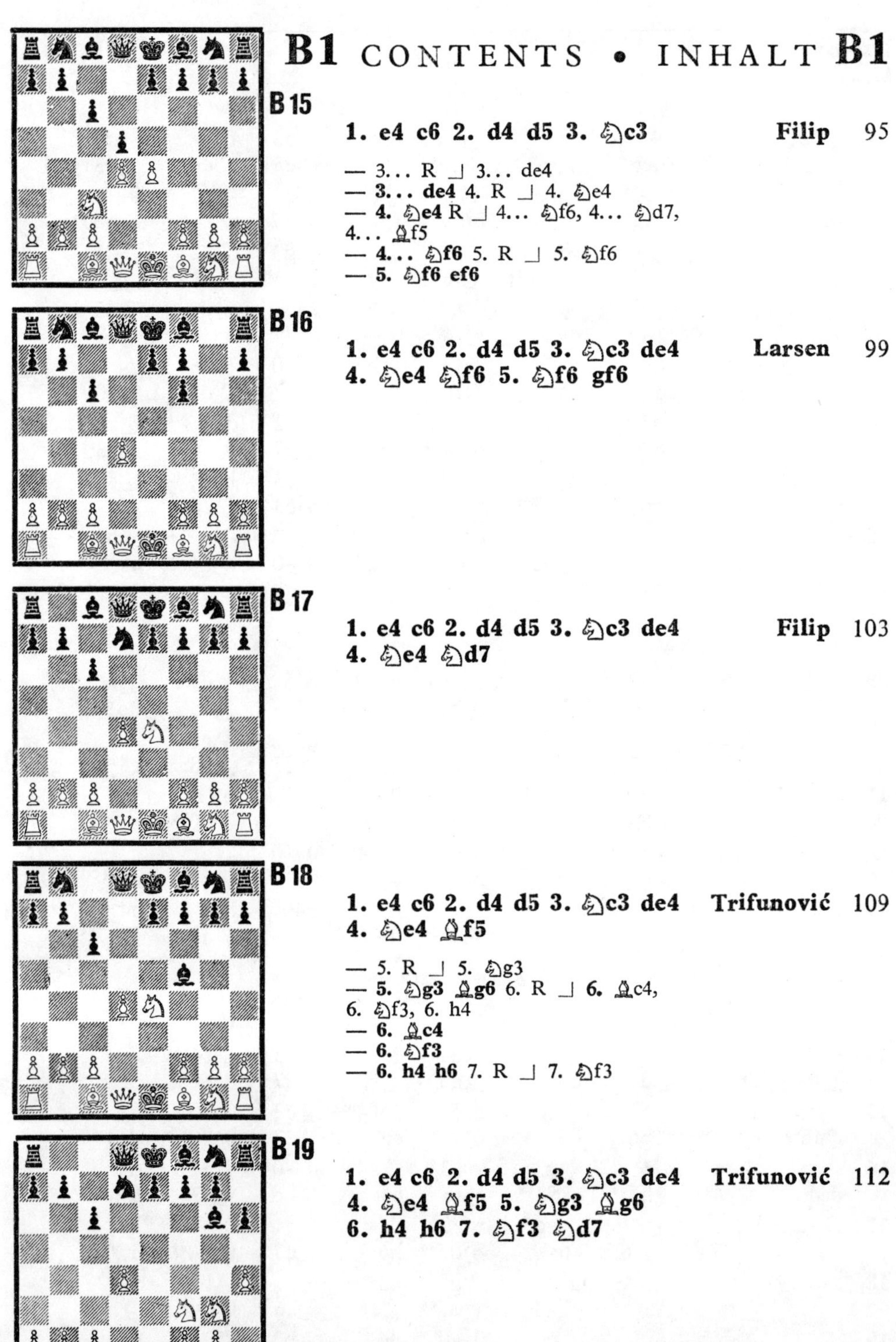

B1 INDICE • INNEHÅLL B1

B 10

1. e4 c6

	2	3	4	5	6	7	8	9	10	
1	♘e2[1]	e5	d4	c3	♘g3	dc5	♗e3	f4	♗d3	∓
	d5[2]	c5	♘c6	♗f5[3]	♗g6[4]	e6	♘e5	♘c6	♗d3[5]	
2	b3	♗b2	♘e2[7]	♘g3	h4	♘c3	h5	♕e2	0-0-0	=
	d5[6]	de4	♗f5[8]	♗g6	h6	♘f6	♗h7	e6	♘bd7[9]	
3	♘c3	♕f3	♘e4	b3[11]	♘f6	♗b2	♕g3	♗e2	♗d1	=
	d5	de4[10]	♘d7	♘df6[12]	♘f6	♗g4	e6	♗f5	♗g6[13]	
4	c4	d4[14]	♗d2	♕d2	♘c3	f4[16]	♘f3	♕d4	♕d2	±
	e5	♗b4[15]	♗d2	d6	♘f6	0—0	ed4	c5	♘c6[17]	
5	. . .	♘c3[18]	cd5	ed5	♘f3	♗b5	0—0	♘e5	d4	±
	e6	d5	ed5	cd5	♘f6	♘c6[19]	♗e7	♗d7	0—0[20]	
6	. . .	ed5	cd5[21]	♘c3	♕a4[23]	g3[24]	♗g2	d4	♘ge2	±
	d5	cd5	a6[22]	♘f6	♘bd7	g6	♗g7	0—0	♘e8[25]	
7	. . .	. . .	. . .	♗b5[26]	♗c4	♗b3[28]	♘c3	bc3	♘f3	=
	. . .	. . .	♘f6	♗d7[27]	♕c7	♘d5	♘c3	♘c6	g6	
8	. . .	. . .	. . .	♕a4	♘c3	g3[30]	♗g2	♘ge2[31]	♕b3	∞
	. . .	. . .	. . .	♘bd7[29]	g6	♗g7	0—0	♘b6[32]	a5[33]	

1. e4 c6 2. d3

	2	3	4	5	6	7	8	9	10	
9	. . .	g3[34]	♗g2	♘d2	♘gf3	0—0	ed5	♖e1	♘f1	=
	e5	♘f6	d5	♗d6[35]	♘bd7	0—0	cd5	♖e8	h6[36]	
10	. . .	♘d2	♘gf3	e5[38]	e6	h3	g4	♘g5	d4	±
	d5	♘f6[37]	♗g4	♘d7	fe6[39]	♗h5	♗f7	♗g8	e5[40]	
11	. . .	. . .	de4[41]	♘gf3	♗e2[44]	0—0	c3	b3		=
	. . .	de4	e5[42]	♗c5[43]	♕e7	♘f6	a5	0—0[45]		
12	. . .	. . .	♘gf3[46]	g3[47]	de4	♗c4[50]	0—0	♖e1	c3[52]	=
	. . .	g6	♗g7	de4[48]	b6[49]	♘f6	0—0	♕c7[51]	e5[53]	
13	. . .	. . .	. . .	. . .	♗g2	0—0	b4[55]	ba5	a4[58]	=
	. . .	. . .	. . .	e5	♘e7[54]	0—0	a5[56]	♕a5[57]	♕c7[59]	

1. e4 c6 2. ♘f3 d5[60]

	3	4	5	6	7	8	9	10	11	
14	e5[61]	d4	c3	♘bd2	dc5	♕a4	♘f3	♗f4[63]		=
	♗g4[62]	e6	♘d7	c5	♗c5	♗f3	♘e7	0—0[64]		
15	♘c3	e5	♘e2[67]	d4	dc5	♘f4[69]	♗e2	0—0	c4	±
	♘f6[65]	♘e4[66]	♕b6	c5	♘c5[68]	e6	♗e7	0—0	dc4[70]	
16	. . .	♘e4	h3[72]	♘g3	♕f3	♗c4[75]	0—0[76]	♖e1	d4	±
	de4	♗g4[71]	♗h5[73]	♗f3[74]	♘f6	e6	♘bd7	♕c7	0-0-0[77]	
17	. . .	. . .	♗c4[78]	♘eg5	♕e2	d4	♘e4	0—0[81]	a4	±
	. . .	♘d7	♘gf6	e6[79]	♘d5[80]	h6	♗e7	0—0[82]	a5[83]	
18	. . .	. . .	♘f6[84]	g3[85]	♗g2	h3[87]	b3	♗b2	♕e2	=
	. . .	♘f6	gf6	♗g4	♕d7[86]	♗e6	♘a6	0-0-0	♗h6[88]	
19	. . .	. . .	. . .	♗c4	0—0	d4	♗b3[91]	♖e1	c4	=
	. . .	. . .	ef6	♗e7[89]	0—0	♗d6[90]	♘d7	♕c7	c5[92]	

1 2. e5 d5 3. ed6 e6 4. b3 ♗d6 5. ♗b2 ♘f6 6. ♘a3 b5 7. c4 a6 8. g3 0–0 9. ♗g2 ♕e7 10. ♘c2 [van Geet–Hort, Beverwijk 1968 — 5/149] e5!∓; **2. f4** d5 3. e5 ♗f5 4. d4 e6 5. ♘f3 c5 6. c3 ♘c6 7. ♗d3 ♘h6∓ Krause–Könecke 1952

2 2... e5 3. d4 d6 4. ♘bc3 ♘f6 5. ♘g3 ♗e7 6. ♗e2= Stoljar–Dubinin, SSSR 1961

3 **5... cd4** 6. cd4 ♗f5 7. ♘bc3 e6 8. a3 ♘ge7 9. ♘g3 ♗g6 10. h4 h6 11. h5 ♗h7 12. ♗e3 ♘c8± Nežmetdinov–Ilivicki, SSSR 1963; **5... ♗g4** 6. f3 ♗d7 7. e6 ♗e6 [7... fe6!?] 8. dc5 ♘f6 9. b4 g6 10. ♗f4 ♗g7 11. ♘d4 0–0 12. ♘c6 bc6 13. ♗e5 ♗h6 14. ♗d3 ♘d7∓ Barendregt–Botvinik, Amsterdam 1966

4 **6... ♗b1** 7. ♖b1 e6 8. a3 c4 9. h4 ♕c7 [9... ♕d7 10. h5 ♘a5 11. ♗g5 h6 12. ♗e3± Zagorovski–Ilivicki, SSSR 1963] 10. h5 0-0-0 11. ♕g4 ♔b8 12. ♗e2± Bronštejn–Simagin, SSSR 1961; **6... ♗d7** 7. dc5 [7. ♗e3!?] e6 8. ♗e3 ♘e5 9. f4 ♘c6 10. ♗d3 ♘f6 11. ♘bd2 g6 12. 0–0 ♗g7∓⊞ Rossetto–Filip, La Habana 1967

5 11. ♕d3 ♘f6 12. ♘bd2 ♗e7 13. 0–0 [Rossetto–Bronštejn, Amsterdam 1964] a5!∓⊞

6 2... e5 3. ♗b2 d6 4. d4 ♘f6 5. ♘d2 ed4 6. ♗d4 d5 7. e5 ♘e4 8. ♘e4 de4 9. ♕d2 ♗a3 10. ♘e2 ♗f5 11. ♘g3 ♗g6 12. ♗e2 0–0 13. h4 h6 14. ♖d1 ♕e7∓ Vasjukov–Furman, SSSR 1964; 7. ed5!?=

7 4. ♘c3 ♘f6 5. ♘ge2 ♗f5 [5... ♕c7 6. ♘g3 ♕f4 7. ♕e2 ♗g4 8. ♕e3 ♕e3 9. fe3 e5 10. ♗e2 ♗e2 11. ♔e2± Vasjukov–Ćirić, 1964] 6. ♘g3 e6 7. ♕e2 ♗b4 8. 0-0-0 ♕e7= Šackes–Goldberg, SSSR 1961

8 **4... f5**?! 5. ♘g3 ♘f6 6. f3 ef3 7. ♕f3 e6∞; **4... ♘f6**!? 5. ♘g3 ♘bd7 6. ♘c3 ♘c5∞

9 11. ♘ge4 [Bokučava–Holmov, SSSR 1967] ♕a5! 12. ♔b1 ♗e7 13. g3 0-0-0 14. ♗g2 ♘d5=

10 **3... ♘f6** 4. e5 ♘fd7 5. d4 e6 6. ♕g3 c5 [6... a6 7. ♗e3 ♕b6 8. 0-0-0±] 7. ♘b5 cd4 8. ♘f3 a6 9. ♘bd4 ♘c6 10. ♗d3 ♕c7 11. ♘c6 bc6 12. 0–0 ♘c5 13. b4 ♘d3 14. cd3± Schmidt–Delander, Berlin 1970; **3... d4** 4. ♗c4 ♘f6 5. e5 dc3 6. ef6 cd2 [6... cb2 7. ♗f7 ♔d7 8. ♗b2 ef6 9. ♘e2 ♔c7 10. 0–0± Šahov–Trudov, SSSR 1964] 7. ♗d2 ef6 8. 0-0-0=∞

11 5. d4 ♘df6! 6. c3 [6. ♗d3 ♕d4∓] ♘e4 7. ♕e4 ♘f6=

12 **5... ♘gf6** 6. ♘g3 e6! [6... g6 7. ♗b2 ♗g7 8. h4 ♕c7 9. 0-0-0 0–0 10. ♖e1 e5 11. h5 a5 12. hg6 hg6 13. ♘e4 ♖e8 14. ♘h3±→ Lombardy–Brinck-Claussen, Krakow 1964] 7. ♗b2 ♕a5=

13 11. ♘f3 ♗d6 12. ♕h4 ♗e7= Csom–Navarovszky, Kecskemet 1969 — 6/223

14 3. ♘f3 d6 4. d4 ♘d7 5. ♘c3 ♘gf6 — A

15 3... d6! 4. ♘f3 ♘d7 5. ♘c3 ♘gf6 — A

16 7. 0-0-0 ♕e7 8. f4 ef4 9. ♕f4 0–0 10. ♗d3 ♘bd7 11. ♘f3± Nej–Böök, Tallinn 1969 — 7/171; 7... ♘bd7!?

17 11. 0-0-0± Talj–Nej, Pärnu 1971 — 12/187

18 3. d4 d5 4. cd5 ed5 [4... cd5 5. e5 — C 02] 5. e5?! ♘a6 [5... ♗f5 6. ♘c3 ♗b4 7. ♘f3 ♘e7 8. ♗d3 0–0 9. a3 ♕a5 10. ♗f5 ♘f5 11. ♕d3 ♘e7 12. 0–0 ♗c3 13. bc3± Čukajev–Zinn, Berlin 1962] 6. ♘c3 ♘c7 7. ♘ge2 ♘e7 8. ♘f4 ♘f5 9. ♗e3 ♘e6 10. ♘e6 ♗e6 11. ♗d3 ♘e3 12. fe3 ♕h4 13. g3 ♕g5∓ Talj–Bisguier, Bled 1961; 5. ed5=

19 7... ♗d7 8. ♕b3 ♗b5 9. ♕b5 ♕d7 10. ♘e5 ♕b5 11. ♘b5 ♘a6 12. d3± Suetin

20 **11. ♗f4**±; **11. ♗g5** ♘e5 12. de5 ♘e4 13. ♗e7 ♘c3 14. ♗d8 ♘d1 15. ♗d7 ♖fd8 16. e6± Hübner–Petrosjan, Sevilla (mct) 1971 — 11/153

21 4. d4 — B 13

22 4... ♕d5? 5. ♘c3 ♕d8 [5... ♕a5 6. ♗c4 ♘f6 7. ♘f3 e6 8. 0–0 ♗e7 9. d4 0–0 10. ♕e2! ♘c6 11. ♗f4 ♗d7 12. ♖fd1± L. Steiner–Carls 1928] 6. d4 e6 7. ♗f4 ♘f6 8. ♘f3 ♘c6 9. ♗c4 ♗e7 10. 0–0 0–0 11. a3 b6 12. b4 ♗b7 13. d5 ed5 14. ♘d5 ♘d5 15. ♗d5 ♖c8 16. ♖c1 ♔h8 17. ♕b3± Keres–Radovici, Leipzig (ol) 1960

23 6. ♕b3 ♘bd7 [6... g6 7. ♘ge2 ♗g7 8. ♘f4 0–0 9. ♗e2 ♘bd7 10. 0–0 b5 (Keres–Vukić, Sarajevo 1972 — 13/201) 11. a4!±] 7. ♗e2 ♘c5!? 8. ♕c4 e6 9. ♗f3 ed5 10. ♘d5 [10. ♗d5∞] ♗e6=∞

24 7. ♘f3 g6 8. d4 ♗g7 9. d6 ed6 10. ♗f4 0–0! 11. ♗e2 ♖e8 12. 0–0 b5= Randvir–Kotov, SSSR 1947; 7... ♖b8!?

25 11. 0–0 ♘d6 12. ♗f4± Dückstein–Müller, Österreich 1966

26 5. ♘c3 ♘d5 6. ♘f3 ♘c6 7. ♗b5 [7. d4 ♗g4 — B13] e6 8. 0–0 ♗e7 9. d4 0–0 10. ♖e1 ♗d7 11. ♘d5 ed5 12. ♗f4 ♗g4 13. ♗c6 bc6 14. ♖c1 ♖e8= Keres–Filip, Moskva 1967

27 5... ♘bd7 6. ♘c3 [6. ♘f3 a6= Pachman] g6 [6... a6 7. ♗d7?! ♕d7 8. ♕b3 ♕g4 9. ♘ge2 b5 10. 0–0 e6 11. d4 ♗d6= Varnusz–Flesch, Hungary 1963; 7. ♗a4?! b5 8. ♗c2 ♘b6 9. ♘f3 ♘bd5 10. d4 e6 11. 0–0 ♗e7 12. ♗g5= Day–Bordonada, Penang 1974 — 18/179; 7. ♕a4 g6 8. ♘f3 ♗g7 9. 0–0 0–0 10. ♗d7 ♗d7 11. ♕b3 ♕c7 12. d4 ♖ad8 13. ♗g5 h6 14. ♗h4 ♗c8 15. ♖fe1± Evdokimov–Gorenštejn, corr. 1962; 7... ♖b8!?] 7. d4 ♗g7 8. d6! e6 [8... ed6 9. ♗f4±] 9. ♘f3 0–0 10. 0–0 a6 11. ♗e2± Sax–Bordonada, Nice (ol) 1974

28 7. ♕b3?? b5–+

29 5... ♗d7!? 6. ♕b3 ♘a6 7. d4 [7. ♕b7? ♘c5 8. ♕b4 e6–+; 7. ♗a6 ba6 8. ♘c3 ♖b8 9. ♕d1 ♗b5∓] ♕b6 [△ ♕b3] 8. ♗c4 ♖c8 9. ♘c3! [9. ♘f3 ♕b4∓; 9. ♘e2 ♕b4 10. ♘d2 b5 11. a3 bc4 12. ♕b4 ♘b4 13. ab4 ♘d5 14. ♖a7 e6 15. ♘e4 ♘b4∓ Szabo–Sliwa, Szcawno Zdroj 1957] ♘b4 [9... ♕d4? 10. ♗a6 ba6 11. ♘ge2±] 10. ♗e2∞

30 **7. g4** ♗g7 8. g5 ♘h5 9. ♘ge2 [9. d4 0–0 10. ♗e3 ♘b6 11. ♕a5 e6 12. de6 ♗e6∓ Adamski–Liliental, Baku 1964] 0–0 10. ♘g3 e6 11. ♘h5 gh5 12. ♕h4 ♘e5 13. ♗g2 ♘g6∓ Gurevič–Ritov, SSSR 1967; **7. h4** ♗g7 8. h5 ♘h5 9. g4 ♘f6 10. g5 ♘g8 11. d4 ♔f8 12. ♗e3 ♘b6 13. ♕b3 ♗f5∓ Littleton–Filip, Praia da Rocha 1969 — 8/148; **7. d6** ed6 8. ♘f3 ♗g7 9. ♗e2 0–0 10. d4 ♘b6 11. ♕d1 ♘bd5 12. 0–0 h6 13. ♘d5 ♘d5 14. ♕b3 ♘e7∓ Matulović–Udovčić, Jugoslavija (ch) 1963

31 9. d4 ♘b6!=

32 9... e6!? 10. ♘f4 [10. de6 ♘c5 11. ef7 ♖f7 12. ♕c4 ♘d3 13. ♔f1 ♗f5∓] ♘b6 11. ♕b3 ed5∓ Musatov–Korčmar, SSSR 1968; 10. d6!=

33 11. ♘f4 a4 12. ♕b5 ♗d7 13. ♕b4 ♖e8 14. 0–0 ♗f8 15. ♕d4 ♗f5 16. ♕e5 ♗g7=∞ Suetin–Gurgenidze, Kislovodsk 1972 — 14/202

34 **3. f4** d5 [3... ef4 4. ♗f4 d5 5. ed5 cd5± Šamkovič] 4. fe5 de4 5. ♘c3 ♗b4! 6. ♗d2 ♗f5 7. e6 [7. ♘e4 ♗e4 8. ♗b4 ♗g2∓] ♘h6 8. ef7 ♘f7=∞ Robatsch–Ortega, La Habana 1963; **3. ♘f3** d6 4. g3 ♘f6 5. ♗g2 ♗e7 6. 0–0 0–0 7. h3 [7. ♘c3 ♕c7 8. a4 a5 9. d4 ♘a6 10. h3 ♖e8= Šamkovič–Barcza, Salgotarjan 1967; 7. ♘bd2 ♘bd7 8. c3 ♖e8 9. ♕c2 ♗f8 10. a4 a5= Tringov–Šamkovič, Varna 1970 — 9/144] ♘bd7 8. ♘bd2 ♖e8 9. a4 ♗f8 10. a5 d5 11. ♕e2 g6 12. ♖d1 ♖b8= Ljubojević–Bilek, Bath 1973; 9... a5!?

35 5... ♗c5 6. ♘gf3 0–0 7. 0–0 [7. ♘e5 ♖e8=] ♖e8 8. c3 ♘bd7 9. b4 ♗f8 10. ♗b2 ♕c7 11. a3 a5 [Štejn–Jimenez, La Habana 1969 — 6/226] 12. ♕c2!±

36 Štejn–Barcza, Tallinn 1971

37 **3... e5** 4. ♘gf3 ♘d7 [4... ♗d6 5. g3 ♘e7 6. ♗g2 0–0 7. 0–0 f5 8. ed5 cd5 9. c4 ♘bc6 10. cd5 ♘d5 11. ♕b3 ♗c7 12. ♘e5+– Savon–Pomar, Wijk aan Zee 1972; 9... dc4 10. ♘c4 ♘bc6 11. ♖e1 ♘g6 12. h4± Ivkov] 5. d4! [5. g3 ♘f6 6. ♗g2 de4 7. de4 ♗e7 8. 0–0 0–0 9. b3 ♕c7 10. ♗b2 ♖fe8 11. a4 b6 12. ♘c4± Platonov–A. Zajcev, SSSR (ch) 1969] de4 [5... ed4 6. ed5 c5 7. ♘c4 ♗e7 8. d6 ♗f6 9. ♗f4 ♘b6 10. ♘b6 ab6 11. ♗b5 ♗d7 12. ♕e2± Šamkovič–Porath, Constanza 1969] 6. ♘e4 ed4 7. ♗c4 [7. ♕d4 ♘gf6 8. ♗g5 ♗e7 9. 0-0-0 0–0 10. ♘d6± Talj–Smislov, Jugoslavija (ct) 1959] ♘df6 8. ♘eg5 [8. ♘fg5 ♗e6? 9. ♘e6 fe6 10. ♘g5 ♕a5 11. ♔f1 ♘d5 12. ♕e2± Kuprejčik–Kapengut, SSSR 1968] ♘h6 9. 0–0 ♗e7 10. ♘d4 0–0 11. c3 ♘f5 12. ♘ge6 ♗e6 13. ♘e6 ♕d1 14. ♖d1 ♖fc8 15. ♗f4± Ljubojević–Marović, Jugoslavija (ch) 1972; **3... ♘d7** 4. ♘gf3 ♕c7 5. ed5 cd5 6. d4 g6 7. ♗d3 ♗g7 8. 0–0 e6 9. ♖e1 ♘e7 10. ♘f1 ♘c6 11. c3 0–0 12. ♗g5± Fischer–Marović, Zagreb-Rovinj 1970

38 5. h3 ♗f3 [5... ♗h5 6. g4 ♗g6 7. e5△ e6±] 6. ♕f3 e6 7. g3 ♘bd7 8. ♗g2 ♗e7 9. 0–0 ♕b6 10. ♕e2± Konstantinopoljski–Sokolski, corr. 1965

39 6... ♗e6 7. ♘d4 ♘f6 8. ♘e6 fe6 9. g3 e5 10. ♗h3 e6 11. ♘f3 ♗d6 12. ♘g5± Bronštejn–Vorotnikov, SSSR 1970 — 9/142

40 11. de5 ♘e5 12. f4 e6 13. ♕e2 ♘bd7 14. ♘b3± Maslovski–Birbrager, SSSR 1973

41 4. ♘e4 ♘d7 5. ♘f3 ♘gf6=

42 4... ♘f6 5. ♘gf3 ♗g4 6. h3 ♗f3 [6... ♗h5 7. e5 ♘d5 8. e6 f6 9. g3 ♗g6 10. ♘d4 ♘c7 11. c3 ♕d5 12. ♕b3! ♕h1 13. ♕b7+– Štejn–Birbrager, SSSR 1966] 7. ♕f3 ♘bd7 8. ♗e2 e6 9. 0–0 ♕c7 10. a4 ♖d8 11. ♘c4 b5 12. ab5 cb5 13. ♗f4!±→ Hort–Pomar, Wijk aan Zee 1972 — 13/204

43 5... ♕c7 6. ♗c4 ♗e7 7. 0–0 ♘f6 8. b3 ♗g4 9. ♗b2 ♘bd7 10. ♖e1 ♖d8 11. h3 ♗h5 12. ♗d3 0–0= Nežmetdinov–Baranov, SSSR 1964

44 **6. ♘e5**? ♗f2∓; **6. ♗d3** ♘f6 7. ♕e2 ♘bd7 8. ♘c4 ♕c7= Kärner–Korčmar, SSSR 1968 — 5/153; **6. ♗c4** ♕e7! [6... ♘f6 7. ♕e2 ♕c7 8. a4 0–0 9. h3 ♘h5 10. g3 ♗e7= Pietzsch–Pachman, Halle 1960; 7. ♘e5! ♗f2 8. ♔e2 ♗e6 9. ♗e6 fe6 10. ♘dc4 ♕d1 11. ♖d1 ♗c5 12. ♗e3 ♘e4 13. ♔f3 ♗e3 14. ♔e4 ♗c5 15. ♖f1± Boleslavski] 7. 0–0 ♘f6=

45 Sax–Markland, Nice (ol) 1974

46 **4. f4** ♘f6 [4... ♗g7 5. e5 c5 6. c3 ♘c6 7. ♘b3 b6 8. ♗e2 e6 9. ♗e3 h5 10. ♘f3 ♘h6 11. ♗f2 ♘f5 12. d4 c4 13. ♘bd2± Petrosjan–Bhend, La Habana (ol) 1966] 5. ♘gf3 ♗g7 6. e5 ♘g4 7. ♘b3 h5 8. ♗e2 ♘h6 9. 0–0 ♕b6 10. d4 ♗g4 11. ♗e3 e6 12. ♗f2 ♘f5∓ Šamkovič–Sokolov, SSSR 1963; **4. g3** ♗g7 5. ♗g2 ♘f6 [5... e5!] 6. e5 ♘g4 7. d4 h5 8. ♘e2 ♘a6 9. c3± Štejn–Hort, Sousse (izt) 1967

47 **5. d4** de4 6. ♘e4 ♗f5 7. ♘c5 b6 8. ♘b3 ♘f6 9. g3 ♕c8 10. h3 0–0 11. ♕e2 a5∓ Malis–Filip, M. Ostrava 1972; **5. e5** c5 6. c3 ♘c6 7. d4 cd4 8. cd4 ♕b6 9. ♘b3 ♗g4 10. ♗e2 ♘h6∓ Robatsch–Portisch, Kecskemet 1962; **5. ♗e2** e5 6. b3 ♘e7 7. ♗b2 ♘d7 8. 0–0 0–0 9. d4 ed4 10. ♗d4 ♘f6 11. ed5 ♘ed5= Florian–Filip, Brno 1974; **5. c3** e5 6. a4 [6. ♗e2 ♘e7 7. h4 h6 8. h5 g5 9. d4 ed4 10. ♘d4 0–0 11. 0–0 c5 12. ♘c2 ♘bc6 13. f4 gf4 14. ♖f4 (Ljubojević–Hort, Madrid 1973 — 16/147) ♘e5!∓] ♘e7 7. a5 0–0 8. ♗e2 h6 9. 0–0 f5 10. b3 ♔h7 11. ♗a3 ♖g8 12. ♖e1 g5⇆∞ Ljubojević–Savon, Petropolis (izt) 1973

48 5... ♘f6 6. ♗g2 0–0 7. 0–0 ♗g4 8. h3 [8. ♖e1 ♘a6 9. e5 ♘d7 10. h3 ♗f3 11. ♘f3

♘c7 12. h4 f5 13. ef6 ef6 14. ♗f4± Bilek—Malich, Skopje (ol) 1972] ♗f3 9. ♕f3 ♘bd7 10. ♕e2 de4 11. de4 ♕c7 12. a4 ♖ad8 13. ♘b3 b6 14. ♗e3 c5 15. a5± Fischer—Ibrahimoglu, Siegen (ol) 1970

49 6... ♘f6 7. ♗g2 0—0 8. 0—0 ♗g4 [8... h6 9. ♕e2 ♘a6 10. ♘c4 ♗e6 11. ♗f4 ♘d7 12. ♖fd1 ♕c8 13. c3 ♖d8 14. h4± Schweber—Pilnik, Zavate 1972] 9. h3 ♗f3 10. ♕f3 ♘bd7 11. ♕e2 e5 12. a4 ♕c7 13. ♘c4± Gufeljd—Kolarov, Odesa 1968 — 6/224

50 7. ♗g2? ♗a6∓

51 9... ♗g4!?

52 10. e5 ♘d5 11. ♘e4 ♖d8∓

53 11. a4 a5 12. b3 ♖d8 13. ♕c2 h6= Nežmetdinov—A. Zajcev, SSSR (ch) 1967 — 5/148

54 6... ♘h6 7. 0—0 0—0 8. ed5 cd5 9. c4 ♘c6 10. cd5 ♕d5 11. ♘c4 ♕e6 12. ♗h6 ♗h6 13. ♘fe5! ♘e5 14. ♖e1 f6 12. f4± Ribli—Barcza, Budapest 1971 — 13/202

55 **8. ♖e1** d4 9. a4 a5! [9... c5? 10. ♘c4 ♘bc6 11. c3 ♗e6 12. cd4 ♗c4 13. dc4 ed4 14. e5± Fischer—Hübner, Palma de Mallorca (izt) 1970 — 10/191] 10. ♘c4 b5 11. ♘a3 ♗a6= Hübner; **8. c3** ♘d7! [8... de4 9. ♘e4!? b6 10. ♖e1 h6 11. ♘ed2 ♕d3 12. ♘e5 ♕d6 13. ♘ec4 ♕c7 14. ♘e4± Planinc—Ćirić, Čačak 1970 — 10/192] 9. b4 b6 10. ♗b2 ♗b7 11. ♖e1 ♖e8= Štejn—Hort, Los Angeles 1968 — 5/152

56 8... ♘d7 9. ♗b2 b6 [9... ♕c7 10. ♖e1 d4 11. c3 dc3 12. ♗c3± Štejn—Golombek, Kecskemet 1968 — 5/151] 10. ♖e1 d4 11. c3 dc3 12. ♗c3 ♗a6 13. ♘b3 ♕c7 14. d4± Bronštejn—Saidy, Tallinn 1973 — 15/179

57 9... ♖a5 10. ♗b2 ♕c7 11. ♕e2 [11. a4 h6 12. ♖e1 d4 13. c3 c5 14. ♖c1 dc3 15. ♗c3 ♖a6= Štejn—Cobo, La Habana 1968 — 6/225] d4 [11... de4!?] 12. c3 dc3 [12... c5!?] 13. ♗c3 ♖a4 14. ♘c4 b5 15. ♕c2 ♗e6 16. ♘ce5 f6 17. ♘c4± Štejn—Haag, Tallinn 1969 — 7/172

58 10. ♗b2 ♘d7 [10... d4 11. ♘c4 ♕c7 12. a4 c5 13. ♘fd2 ♗h6 14. c3 ♘ec6? 15. cd4± Hartoch—Vukić, Banja Luka 1974 — 18/180; 14... dc3! 15. ♗c3 ♘ec6△ ♖d8, ♘a6, ♗e6= Vukić] 11. ♖e1 d4? 12. a4 ♕d8 13. ♘c4 c5 14. c3 b6 15. cd4 cd4 16. ♗a3 ♗a6 17. ♕b3± Zinn—Kolarov, Kapfenberg 1970 — 9/143; 11... ♕c7!=

59 11. ♗b2 d4 12. c3 dc3 [12... c5!? 13. cd4 cd4 14. ♘c4 ♘ec6 15. ♗a3 ♖e8 16. ♗d6 ♕d8 17. ♘fd2 ♗e6= Přibyl—Filip, ČSSR 1974] 13. ♗c3 ♖d8 14. ♘c4 f6 15. d4 ♗e6 16. ♕e2 ed4 17. ♘d4 ♗f7 18. ♗h3± Gufeljd—Sivohin, SSSR 1973; 14... ♘d7!△ c5, ♘c6= Filip

60 **2... d6** 3. d4 ♗g4 4. h3 ♗h5 5. ♗e3 ♘f6 6. ♘bd2 ♘bd7 7. c3 ♗g6? 8. e5 ♘d5 9. e6! fe6 10. ♗e2∞ Bronštejn—Tartakower, Saltsjöbaden (izt) 1948; 7... e6=; 7... e5=; **2... g6** 3. d4 ♗g7 4. ♘c3 d5 — B 15

61 3. ed5 cd5 4. b3 [4. d4 ♘c6△ ♗g4=] ♘f6 5. ♗b2 e6 6. ♗e2 ♗e7=

62 **3... ♗f5** 4. ♗e2 [4. ♘d4? ♗g6 5. e6 ♕b6 6. ♕g4 c5 7. ef7 ♔f7 8. ♘f3 ♘f6∓⟳ Toluš—Kotov, SSSR (ch) 1939] e6 5. 0—0 ♘d7 6. ♖e1 c5 7. d3 ♘e7= Bauer—Starck 1958; **3... c5** 4. d4 ♘c6 5. c3 ♗g4 6. ♗b5 e6 7. ♘bd2 cd4! 8. cd4 ♕b6∓

63 10. ♕g4 ♘g6 11. ♗b5 0—0 12. ♗d7 ♕d7= Toluš—Konstantinopoljski, SSSR (ch) 1939

64 Toluš—Goglidze, SSSR (ch) 1939

65 3... d4 4. ♘e2 c5 5. ♘g3 [5. d3 ♘c6 6. g3 e5 7. ♗g2 ♗e7! 8. 0—0 f5 9. ♘d2 ♘f6 10. ef5 ♗f5 11. ♘c4 ♕c7 12. f4 e4∓ Matanović—Tartakower, Hastings 1953/54; 5. c3 dc3 6. bc3 ♘f6 7. ♘g3 e6 8. d4± Grünfeld] ♘c6 6. ♗c4! e5 7. d3 ♗e7 8. 0—0 ♘f6 9. ♘h4± Keres—Tartakower 1954

66 4... ♘fd7 5. d4 [5. e6!? fe6 6. d4 e5 7. de5 e6 8. ♗f4 ♗e7 9. ♘g5 ♗g5 10. ♕h5± Boleslavski] e6 6. ♘e2 c5 7. c3 ♘c6 8. g3 cd4 9. cd4 ♗b4 10. ♘c3 f6 11. ef6 ♕f6 12. ♗g2 0—0 13. 0—0± Solovjev—Čistjakov, SSSR 1961

67 **5. ♗e2** ♘c3 6. dc3 ♗g4=; **5. ♘e4** de4 6. ♘g5 ♕d5 7. d3 ed3 8. ♗d3∞; **5. ♘b1** ♗f5 6. d3 ♘c5 7. ♗e3 e6 8. ♘bd2 ♗e7 9. ♗e2 0—0 10. 0—0 ♘cd7 11. c4 ♘a6 12. a3 ♘c7 13. b4±

68 7... ♕c5 8. ♘ed4 ♘c6 9. ♗b5! ♗d7 [9... a6 10. ♗c6 bc6 11. 0—0 ♕b6 12. e6 fe6 13. ♘e5± Šabašov—Gedult, Vitel 1972] 10. 0—0 ♘e5 [10... e6 11. ♗e3 ♕b4 12. c4 dc4 13. ♕c2 ♘c5 14. a3 ♕a5 15. ♗c4± Boleslavski] 11. ♘e5 ♗b5 12. ♘b5 ♕b5 13. ♖e1± Nežmetdinov—Kamišov, SSSR 1950

69 8. ♕d5 ♘c6∞

70 12. ♗c4 ♘c6 13. ♕e2±

71 **4... ♗f5** 5. ♘g3 ♗g4! 6. h3! ♗f3 — 4... ♗g4; **4... ♘h6** 5. d4 ♘f5 6. c3 g6 7. h4 ♘d6 8. ♘d6 ♕d6 9. h5 ♗g7 10. ♗e3± Rabar—Matulović, Jugoslavija 1958

72 **5. ♘g3** ♘f6 6. ♗e2 e6 7. ♘e5 ♗e2 8. ♕e2 ♕d5 9. ♘f3 c5= Lasker—Flohr, Zürich 1934; **5. ♗c4** e6 6. c3 ♘d7 7. d4 ♘gf6 8. ♘g3 ♕c7 9. h3 ♗f3 10. ♕f3 ♗d6= Smislov—Makagonov, SSSR (ch) 1939; **5. d4**!? ♗f3 [5... e6 6. ♗d3 ♘f6 7. h3 ♗h5 8. 0—0 ♘e4 9. ♗e4 ♘d7= Spaski—Petrosjan, SSSR 1955] 6. ♕f3 ♕d4 7. ♗d3∞; 7. ♗e3∞ — B 11

73 5... ♗f3 6. ♕f3 ♘d7 7. d4 [7. ♘g5 ♘gf6 8. ♕b3? e6 9. ♕b7 ♘d5!∞ Fischer—Cardoso, Portorož (izt) 1958] ♘gf6 8. ♗d3 e6 9. c3 ♗e7 10. 0—0 ♘e4 11. ♕e4 ♘f6 12. ♕h4 ♘d5 13. ♕g4± Talj—Portisch, Bled (mct) 1965

74 6... ♗g6? 7. h4 h6 8. ♘e5 ♗h7 9. ♕h5 g6 10. ♕f3 [10. ♗c4 e6 11. ♕e2±] ♘f6 11. ♕b3 ♕d5 12. ♕b7+− Lasker−Müller, Zürich 1934

75 8. ♗e2 e6 9. 0−0 ♗d6 10. b4 ♕c7 11. ♖b1 ♘bd7 12. d4 0−0 13. c4 ♖fe8 14. c5 ♗f8 15. ♗c4 e5= Tajmanov−A. Zajcev, SSSR 1969

76 9. c3 ♗d6 10. d4 0−0 11. ♗g5 ♘bd7 12. 0−0 ♕a5 13. h4± Boleslavski−Panov, SSSR 1943

77 12. a4 c5 13. a5 a6 [A. Zajcev−Bronštejn, Moskva 1968 — 5/155] 14. ♗f4! ♗d6 15. ♗d6 ♕d6 16. dc5 ♕c5 17. ♗f1△ b4±

78 5. d4 ♘gf6 — B 17

79 6... ♘d5 7. d4 — B 17

80 **7... ♘b6**? 8. ♘e5+−; **7... h6**? 8. ♘f7+−

81 10. ♗d2!?△ 0-0-0 Gufeljd

82 10... ♕c7 11. ♗b3 0−0 12. c4± Smislov−Golombek, Venezia 1950

83 Ceškovski−Džindžihašvili, SSSR 1972 — 14/211

84 5. ♘g3 c5 [5... h5 6. h3 h4 7. ♘e2 ♗f5 8. d3 ♘bd7 9. ♗g5 ♘e5 10. ♘e5 ♕a5∓ Rovner−Sokolski, SSSR 1948; 6. h4 ♗g4 7. ♗e2 ♘bd7 8. d4 e6=; 6. ♗c4 h4 7. ♘e5 e6 8. ♘e2 ♕a5 9. f4 ♘bd7= Kan−Flor, SSSR 1944] 6. b3 [6. ♗c4 ♘c6 7. 0−0 e6∓; 6. d4 ♘c6 7. dc5 ♕d1 8. ♔d1 ♗g4 9. ♗e2 0-0-0=; 6. ♗b5 ♗d7 7. ♕e2 ♘c6 8. 0−0 e6 9. ♖e1 ♘d4 10. ♘d4 cd4 11. ♘f5 ♕b6 12. ♗d7 ♔d7 13. ♘h4 ♗d6 14. ♘f3 ♖he8∓ Ceškovski−Bronštejn, SSSR 1969; 9. b3!=] ♘c6 7. ♗b2 e6 8. ♗b5 ♗d7 9. 0−0 ♗e7 10. ♕e2 0−0 11. ♗c6 ♗c6 12. ♘e5 ♕c7= Lutikov−Botvinik, SSSR 1966

85 **6. b3** ♖g8 [6... ♗g4 7. ♗e2 ♘d7 8. ♗b2 ♕c7 9. ♘h4 ♗e2 10. ♕e2= Estrin−Konstantinopoljski, SSSR 1949] 7. ♗b2 ♗h6 8. ♕e2 ♗g4 9. 0-0-0 ♘d7= Penrose−Larsen, Hastings 1956; **6. ♗c4** ♖g8 [6... ♕c7!?; 6... ♗g4?! 7. ♘e5! fe5±] 7. 0−0 ♗g4 8. d4 ♕c7! =; **6. d4** — B 16

86 7... e6 8. b3 [8. d4 ♘d7 9. 0−0 ♗g7 10. ♖e1± Konstantinopoljski−Flor, SSSR (ch) 1946] ♘d7 9. ♗b2 ♗g7 10. h3 ♗h5 11. ♕e2± Keres−Pachman, Moskva 1967 — 3/162

87 8. 0−0 ♗h3 9. b3 [9. d4 ♗g2 10. ♔g2 ♘a6 11. ♗e3 h5 12. a4 ♘b4 13. ♖e1 ♕f5 14. ♖e2 0-0-0∓↑ Lisicin−Budo, SSSR (ch) 1937] ♘a6 10. ♗b2 ♗g2 11. ♔g2 0-0-0 12. ♖e1 h5 13. ♕e2 ♘c7= Rauzer−Budo, SSSR (ch) 1937

88 Rauzer−Konstantinopoljski, SSSR (ch) 1937

89 6... ♗d6 7. ♕e2 [7. 0−0 0−0 8. d4 ♗e6 9. ♗e6 fe6 10. ♖e1 ♖e8 11. c4 ♘a6 12. ♗d2 ♕d7 13. ♗c3± Fischer−Panov, Skopje 1967] ♗e7 [7... ♕e7 8. ♕e7 ♔e7 9. 0−0 ♗e6 10. ♖e1! ♔d7 11. ♗e2 a5 12. d4 a4 13. ♗e3 ♘a6 14. c3 ♘c7 15. c4± Klovan−Vistaneckis, SSSR 1964] 8. 0−0 0−0 9. ♖e1 [9. d4 ♗g4 10. c3 ♖e8 11. ♖e1 ♘d7 12. h3 ♗f3 13. ♕f3± Kurajica−Holmov, Skopje 1969 — 7/181] ♗d6 10. d4 ♗g4 11. ♕e4 f5 [11... ♗h5 12. ♘h4± Ragozin−Boleslavski, SSSR 1942] 12. ♕d3 ♗f3 13. ♕f3 ♕h4 14. ♕f5 ♕h2 15. ♔f1 ♕h4 16. ♗e3 c5 17. g3± Novopašin−Kuvaldin, SSSR 1966

90 8... ♗g4 9. c3! [9. ♗f4 ♗d6 10. ♗g3 ♗f3 11. ♕f3 ♗g3 12. hg3 ♕d4 13. b3 ♕c5 14. ♖ad1 b5= Boleslavski−Golombek, SSSR−England 1946] ♗d6 [9... ♖e8 10. ♖e1±] 10. h3 ♗h5 11. g4 ♗g6 12. ♘h4 ♘d7 13. ♕f3 ♖e8 14. ♘g6 hg6 15. h4 ♘f8 16. ♗d2± Boleslavski−Batujev, SSSR 1939

91 9. ♖e1 ♕c7 10. ♕d3 ♖d8 11. ♕e4 ♘d7 12. ♗d2 ♘f8 13. ♗d3 ♘g6 14. c4 c5 15. dc5 ♗c5 16. b4 ♗f8= Suetin−Sokolski, SSSR 1959

92 12. ♗e3 ♖d8 13. ♕c2 b6 14. ♖ad1 ♘f8 15. h3 ♘g6 16. ♖d2 ♗b7= Boleslavski

B 11

1. e4 c6 2. ♘c3 d5 3. ♘f3 ♗g4

	4	5	6	7	8	9	10	11	12	
1	d4[1]	h3	g4[4]	♘e5	♘e4	♗g2	♘d7[6]	♗e4	♗g2	=
	e6[2]	♗h5[3]	♗g6	♗e4	de4	♘d7[5]	♕d7	♘f6	♖d8[7]	
2	h3	ed5[8]	♗b5	g4	♘e5[9]	d4[11]	♘g6	♕d3[12]	♗c6	±
	♗h5	cd5	♘c6	♗g6	♕d6[10]	f6	hg6	0-0-0[13]	♕c6[14]	

1. e4 c6 2. ♘c3 d5 3. ♘f3 ♗g4 4. h3 ♗h5 5. ed5 cd5 6. ♗b5 ♘c6 7. g4 ♗g6 8. ♘e5 ♖c8

	9	10	11	12	13	14	15	16	17	
3	d4[15]	♕e2[17]	h4[19]	0−0[20]	h5	♘e4	c3	♘c4	♘d6	±
	e6[16]	♗b4[18]	♕b6	♘e7[21]	♗e4	de4	♗d6	♕d8	♕d6[22]	

	9	10	11	12	13	14	15	16	17	
4	...	...	...	h5	0—0[23]	♗c6[25]	bc3	♘c6	f3	∞
	...	...	♘e7	♗e4	0—0[24]	♗c3	♘c6	♖c6	♖c3[26]	
5	...	...	...	bc3	♗b2[27]	h5	f3	fe4[28]	0—0[29]	∞
	...	...	♗c3	♕a5	♘e7	♗e4	f6	fe5		

1. e4 c6 2. ♘c3 d5 3. ♘f3 ♗g4 4. h3 ♗f3

	5	6	7	8	9	10	11	12	13	
6	gf3	d4[30]	♗f4[31]	h4[32]	a3[34]	bc3	fe4	♕f3	♖h3	∓
	e6!	♘d7	♗b4	♘gf6[33]	♗c3	de4	♘e4	♕a5		
7	♕f3	♘e4	d4	♘f6	c3	g3	♗g2	0—0	♖e1[35]	±
	de4	♘d7	♘gf6	♘f6	e6	♗e7	0—0	♕b6		
8	...	g3[36]	♘e4	♕e4	♕d5[38]	♗g2	c4	cd5		=
	♘f6	♘e4	de4	♕d5[37]	cd5	e6	♘c6	♘b4[39]		
9	...	♗e2	0—0	♖d1	ed5	♗b5	♘e2	d4		=
	...	e6	♗c5[40]	♗d4	cd5	♘c6	♗c5	♗e7		
10	...	d3	g3[41]	♗d2	♘b1	b3[44]	♗g2	a3	♘d2	∓
	...	e6	♗b4[42]	d4	♕b6[43]	♘bd7	a5	♗d2	♕c5[45]	
11	...	...	a3	g4[47]	d4	♕d3[50]	ed5	♘e2	♗g2	=
	...	...	♗e7[46]	♘fd7[48]	♕b6[49]	e5	ed4	0—0	♘f6[51]	
12	...	d4	♕e3[52]	♘e4	♕e4	♕d3	♗e2	0—0		±
	...	de4	♘bd7[53]	♘e4	♘f6	e6[54]	♗e7	0—0[55]		
13	...	d4[56]	♗d3	e5[59]	♕g3	h4[61]	♘e2	h5	c3	±
	e6	♘f6[57]	♗e7[58]	♘fd7	g6[60]	♕b6[62]	c5[63]	♖g8[64]	♘c6[65]	
14	...	...	♘e4[66]	♗d3[68]	♗e3[70]	0-0-0	♔b1[72]			=∞
	...	de4	♕d4[67]	♘d7[69]	♕d5	♘gf6[71]				

1 4. **ed5** cd5 5. h3 ♗f3 6. ♕f3 e6 7. d4 ♘c6 8. ♘e2 ♘b4 9. ♕b3 ♖c8 10. ♘c3 ♕c7 11. ♗b5 [11. ♗e3 ♘f6 12. ♕a4 ♘c6 13. ♗d3 ♗e7 14. 0—0 0—0 15. ♗d2 a6∓ Macelle—Macskasy, Canada 1951] ♘c6 12. ♘e2=; **4. ♗e2** e6 5. 0—0 ♘f6 6. h3 ♗f3 7. ♗f3 ♗e7 8. d4 0—0 9. e5 [9. ♗f4? ♕b6 10. e5 ♘fd7 11. ♘a4 ♕c7△ c5∓] ♘fd7 10. ♘e2=

2 4... de4? 5. ♘e4 ♗f3?! 6. ♕f3 ♕d4 7. ♗e3! [7. ♗d3 ♘d7 8. ♗e3 ♕d5 9. ♕g3 ♘e5? 10. 0—0 ♘d3 11. cd3 g6 12. ♖fe1 ♗g7 13. ♗a7+— Gligorić—Avirović, Jugoslavija (ch) 1949; 9... ♘gf6!∞] ♕b2 8. ♗c4 ♘f6 [8... ♕a1? 9. ♔e2 ♕h1 10. ♕f7 ♔d7 11. ♗e6 ♔c7 12. ♕f4+—] 9. 0—0 ♘bd7 [9... ♕c2? 10. ♕f5! ♔d8□ 11. ♖fd1 ♘bd7 12. ♗d3 ♕b2 13. ♘g5 ♔e8 14. ♗c4 e6 15. ♗e6 fe6 16. ♕e6+— Motl—Melčak 1940] 10. ♖ab1=∞↑

3 5... ♗f3 6. ♕f3±

4 6. ♗e2 ♘f6=

5 9... f6?! 10. ♘c4=∞

6 10. ♗e4? ♘e5 11. de5 ♕a5∓

7 Planinc—Kurajica, Skopje 1969 — 8/149

8 5. d4 e6 6. ♗e2 ♘f6 7. e5 ♘fd7 8. 0—0 ♗e7 [8... c5? 9. ♗g5! ♕c8 10. ♘b5 h6 11. ♗h4 a6 12. ♘d6 ♗d6 13. ed6 ♗f3 14. ♗f3 cd4 15. ♕d4 0—0 16. c4± Bivšev—Simagin, SSSR 1958] 9. ♘h2 ♗g6 10. f4 f6 11. ♗g4 f5 12. ♗f3 ♘b6= Solontjev—Volovič, SSSR 1961

9 8. d4 e6 9. ♘e5 ♘e7 10. h4 f6 11. ♘g6 hg6 12. ♗e3 ♖c8 13. ♗d3 ♘b4 14. ♗f1 ♔f7 15. a3 ♘bc6 16. ♗d3 [Keres—Filip, Buenos Aires 1964] e5!=

10 **8... ♕b6**? 9. ♘d5+—; **8... ♕c7** 9. d4 e6 10. ♕e2 (△ ♘d5) ♘f6 11. h4 ♗b4 12. h5 ♗e4 13. f3 0—0 14. ♗c6 bc6 15. g5! c5 16. ♗e3 ♗f3 17. ♘f3 ♘e4 18. 0—0 ♘c3 19. bc3 ♗c3 20. ♖ad1 ♖ab8 21. ♖f2 ♖b2 27. h6+— Suetin—Veresov, SSSR 1955

11 △ ♗f4

12 11. ♗e3? e6 12. ♕d2 ♕c7 13. ♗d3 ♔f7 14. h4 ♗b4 15. a3 ♗a5 16. ♔f1 ♕d7∓ Boleslavski—Dubinin, SSSR (ch) 1940

13 11... ♔f7? 12. ♘d5+—

14 13. ♕g6 e5 14. ♕d3! [14. ♗d2 ♘e7 15. ♕d3 e4 16. ♕e2 ♘g6 17. 0-0-0 ♘h4 18. ♘b5 ♕b6 19. c4± Boleslavski—Bondarevski, SSSR

1941; 14. . . e4! 15. ♕f5 ♔b8 16. 0-0-0± Boleslavski] ♗b4 15. ♗d2 e4 16. ♕b5 ♗c3 17. ♕c6 bc6 18. bc3± Keres – Bondarevski, SSSR 1941

15 9. h4 f6 10. ♘g6 hg6 11. d4 e6 — 9. d4

16 9. . . f6? 10. ♘g6 hg6 11. ♕d3 ♔f7 12. ♘d5±

17 10. h4 f6 11. ♘g6 [11. h5 ♗c2 12. ♘c6 bc6 13. ♕c2 cb5 14. ♕e2 b4 15. ♕e6 ♕e7 16. ♕e7 ♘e7 17. ♘e2 ♘c6 18. ♗f4 ♔d7 19. ♔d2 ♗d6= Moses – Kelbeck, Harrachov 1967] hg6 12. ♗e3 [12. ♕d3 ♔f7 13. ♗e3 ♕e5 14. h5 gh5 15. gh5 ♘ge7 16. ♔f1 ♘b4 –+ Usačij – Usov, SSSR 1959; 13. h5 gh5 14. gh5 ♘ge7 15. ♗e3 ♘f5∓ Fischer – Smislov, Jugoslavija (ct) 1959] ♗b4 13. ♔f1 ♗c3 15. bc3 ♘e7 15. ♕e2 a6 16. ♗d3 ♘a5= Liberzon – Smislov, SSSR (ch) 1960

18 **10. . . ♗d6** 11. ♘g6 hg6 12. ♘d5 ♗b8 13. ♘c3 ♕d4 14. ♗e3 ♕b4 15. 0-0-0± Gurgenidze – Liberzon, SSSR (ch) 1960; **10. . . ♗e7** 11. ♗f4 ♔f8 12. ♘c6 bc6 13. ♗a6± Klovan – Tabrosjan, SSSR 1959

19 11. a3 ♗c3 12. bc3 ♘e7 13. h4 ♕a5 14. ♖h3 a6 15. ♗c6 ♘c6 16. ♘c6 ♖c6 17. ♖b1 b5 18. h5 ♗e4 19. ♖b3 h6 20. ♖g3 f6∓ Žilin – Bagirov, SSSR 1962

20 12. a3 ♗c3 13. bc3 ♘e7 14. h5 ♗e4 15. 0 – 0 [15. f3 f6 16. ♘c6 bc6 17. ♗a6 ♗f3 18. ♕f3 ♕a6 19. h6 ♖g8 20. hg7 ♖g7 21. ♕f6 ♖g6 22. ♕h8?! ♔d7 23. ♕h7 c5 24. g5 cd4 25. ♖h6 ♖f8 –+ Gurgenidze – Bagirov, SSSR (ch) 1960; 22. ♕f4 ♕c4 23. ♖h7 ♕c3 24. ♔f1 ♔d7 25. ♕f7 ♕c4= Boleslavski] a6! 16. ♗d3 [16. ♗c6 ♘c6 17. ♘c6 ♕c6 18. f3 ♕c3 19. ♗d2 ♕d4 20. ♗e3 ♖c2 21. fe4 ♖e2 22. ♗d4 ♖e4 –+] ♗d3 17. cd3 ♘e5 18. ♕e5 f6 19. ♕e1 ♔f7∞ Boleslavski

21 **12. . . ♕d4**? 13. ♖d1△ ♘d5+ –; **12. . . a6** 13. ♗c6 bc6 14. h5 ♗e4 15. ♘e4 de4 16. c3 ♗e7 17. f3! ef3 18. ♖f3+ – Klovan – Circenis, SSSR 1960; **12. . . ♘f6** 13. ♘a4 [13. h5? ♗c2 14. ♕c2 ♕d4 15. ♕e2 ♗d6∓ Boleslavski; 13. ♗e3 h6∞] ♕a5 14. h5 ♗e4 15. f3 a6 [15. . . 0 – 0 16. c3 ♘e5 17. de5+ –] 16. ♗c6 bc6 17. b3 ♗c3 18. ♘c3 ♕c3 19. ♗e3 ♕c2 [19. . . ♗c2 20. ♖ac1+ –] 20. ♕a6 0 – 0 21. ♖ac1+ – Boleslavski

22 18. ♕e4±

23 13. f3 a6 14. ♗c6 ♘c6∓

24 13. . . ♗c3 14. bc3 a6 [13. . . h6!? Bagirov] 15. ♘c6 ♘c6 16. ♗c6 ♖c6 17. f3 ♖c3 18. ♗d2 [18. fe4 ♖g3] ♖c2 19. fe4 de4 20. ♖ad1 ♕d4 21. ♗e3 ♕b2 22. ♖d2 ♖d2 23. ♕d2 ♕d2 24. ♗d2 0 – 0 25. g5± Romanišin – Bagirov, SSSR 1974 — 18/181

25 **14. ♘e4** ♘d4; **14. ♘c6** ♘c6 15. ♗c6 ♗c3! 16. ♗b7 ♗d4 17. ♗c8? ♕h4 – +; 16. bc3! ♖c6 — 14. ♗c6

26 **18. fe4**? ♖g3; **18. ♗d2** ♖c2 19. fe4 de4∞ Bagirov

27 **13. 0—0** ♕c3 14. ♗c6 [14. ♗e3 ♘e7 15. h5 ♗e4 16. f3 ♗c2 17. ♖ac1 0 – 0∓] bc6 15. ♕a6 ♘e7 16. ♗a3 ♕d4 17. ♗e7 ♔e7 18. ♕a3 [18. ♕b7 ♔d6∓] c5 19. ♕a7 ♔f8 20. ♕d7 ♖e8△ f6∓; **13. ♖h3** ♘e7 14. h5 ♗e4 15. ♗d2 h6 16. c4 ♕d8∓; **13. ♗d2** ♘e7 14. c4 [14. h5 ♗c2 15. ♖c1 ♗e4! 16. f3 f6 17. ♘c6 bc6 18. ♗a6 ♗f3∓] ♕a3 15. h5 [15. cd5 ed5 16. c3 0 – 0 17. h5 ♗e4 18. f3 ♘e5 19. fe4 ♘f3 20. ♕f3 ♕b2 21. 0 – 0 ♕d2∓] ♗c2 16. 0 – 0 0 – 0 17. ♘c6 ♘c6 18. ♗c6 ♖c6∓

28 16. ♘c6 bc6 17. ♗a6 [17. ♗c6 ♖c6 18. fe4 0 – 0 19. ed5 ♘d5 20. 0 – 0 ♖b8∓] ♖b8 18. 0-0-0 ♗f3 19. ♕f3 ♕a6 20. h6 g6 21. ♕f6 ♖f8 22. ♕e6 ♕a2∓

29 Trifunović, Minev

30 6. d3!?△ f4

31 7. ♗e3!?△ ♕d2, 0-0-0

32 8. a3!? ♗e7 9. ♗g2

33 8. . . ♘e7? 9. h5±↑

34 9. e5? ♘h5 10. ♗g5 ♕a5 11. ♗d2 ♕b6 12. a3 ♗e7 13. ♗e3 g6∓ Talj – Botvinik (m) 1960

35 ±⊞○

36 **6. e5** ♘fd7 7. e6 [7. ♕g3 e6 8. ♗e2 c5 9. f4 ♘c6 10. b3 ♘d4∓; 7. d4 e6 8. ♗f4 c5 9. dc5 ♘c6 10. ♕g3 ♕a5 11. ♗d2 ♕c5 12. f4 g6∓ Sergijevski – Stoljar, SSSR 1960] fe6 8. d4 e5! 9. de5 ♘e5 10. ♕g3 ♘f7 11. ♗f4 ♘d7 12. 0-0-0 e5 13. ♖e1 ♕f6 14. ♗e5 ♘fe5 15. f4 ♗d6 16. fe5 ♘e5∓; **6. g4** ♘e4 7. ♘e4 de4 8. ♕e4 ♘d7 9. ♗g2 [9. c4 ♘c5 10. ♕e3 ♘e6 11. b3 ♘d4 12. ♗d3 g6 13. ♗b2 ♗g7 14. ♗c3 ♕d6 15. b4 0 – 0 16. 0 – 0 ♖ad8∓ Šapošnikov – Simagin, corr. 1965] e6 10. d4 ♗d6△ 0 – 0, e5=

37 8. . . ♘d7 9. ♗g2 e6△ ♗d6=

38 9. ♗g2!? e6 10. 0 – 0

39 Boleslavski

40 7. . . ♗e7 8. ♖d1△ d4

41 **7. ♗d2** ♘bd7 8. g4 ♗b4 [8. . . h6 9. ♗g2?! ♗b4 10. ♕d1 ♕e7 11. a3 ♗a5 12. 0 – 0 de4 13. de4 e5∓ Keres – Yanofsky, Winnipeg 1967 — 5/156; 9. 0-0-0 ♗b4 10. a3 ♗a5 11. h4 ♕e7 12. g5+ – Planinc – Kurajica, Sarajevo 1970 — 9/146; 8. . . g6 9. 0-0-0 ♗g7 10. h4! h5 11. g5 ♘g4 12. ♗h3 ♕b6 13. ♖de1 ♘ge5 14. ♕g3± Darga – Donner, Beverwijk 1964] 9. a3 [9. g5 ♘g8 10. h4 d4 11. ♘b1 ♕b6∓ Suetin – Šamkovič, SSSR 1972 — 14/203] ♗a5 10. g5±; 7. . . ♗b4! 8. a3 ♗d6 9. g4? d4 10. ♘e2 ♕b6∓ Zuckerman – Marović, Malaga 1968 — 5/157; 8. g3 — 7. g3; **7. g4** ♗b4 8. ♗d2 [8. g5 ♕a5 9. ♗d2 d4 10. gf6 dc3 11. bc3 ♗c3∓] ♕a5 9. a3 d4 10. ♘b1 ♗d2 11. ♘d2 h5∓ Boleslavski; **7. ♗e2** ♘bd7 8. ♕g3 g6 9. 0 – 0 [9. h4 h5 10.

0–0 ♕b6 11. ♖b1 ♗h6 12. ♗g5 ♗g5 13. hg5 ♘h7 14. ed5 ed5∓ Gurgenidze–Petrosjan, SSSR 1961] ♗g7 10. ♗f4 ♕b6 11. ♖ab1 0–0= Smislov–Botvinik (m) 1958

42 **7... g6** 8. ♗g2 ♗g7 9. 0–0 0–0 10. ♗g5 ♘bd7 11. ♖ae1 h6 12. ♗c1 b5= Vasiljev–Ilivicki, SSSR 1958; **7... ♗e7** 8. ♗g2 0–0 9. 0–0 ♘a6 10. ♕e2 ♘e8 11. e5 ♘ac7 12. h4 h6 13. ♘d1 ♕d7 14. c4 f5= Averbah–Flor, SSSR (ch) 1951; **7... ♘bd7** 8. ♗g2 ♗c5 9. 0–0 0–0 10. ♕e2 ♗d4 11. ♔h2 ♗c3 12. bc3 de4 13. de4 ♕a5= Smislov–Flor, SSSR (ch) 1950

43 9... ♗d2 10. ♘d2 e5! [10... ♕a5 11. a3 ♘bd7 12. ♕e2 h5 13. h4 ♘g4 14. ♗h3 ♘df6 15. 0–0 0-0-0 16. ♘c4 ♕c7 17. e5 ♘e8 18. a4±→ Boleslavski–Mikenas, SSSR (ch) 1957] 11. ♗g2 c5 12. 0–0 ♘c6 13. ♕e2 ♕e7 14. f4 0-0-0 15. a3 ♘e8! 16. b4 cb4 17. ♘c4 f6 18. fe5 fe5 19. ab4 ♘c7 20. ♘a5 ♘b5 21. ♘c6 bc6∓ Fischer–Petrosjan, Jugoslavija (ct) 1959

44 10. c3 ♗c5 11. ♗c1 ♘bd7 12. ♕e2 [12. ♗g2? ♘e5 13. ♕e2 dc3 14. bc3 ♗f2–+; 12. ♘d2 ♘e5 13. ♕e2 0-0-0 14. c4 g5∓] 0-0-0 13. e5 ♘d5 14. ♗g2 [14. c4 ♘b4 15. a3 ♘d3 16. ♕d3 ♘e5 17. ♕e4 d3 18. ♕e5 ♗f2 19. ♔d2 ♗d4 20. ♕f4 g5 21. ♕g5 ♗b2 22. ♖a2 ♕f2 23. ♔d1 ♕c2–+] ♕c7 15. f4 f6∓

45 14. ♕d1 h5 15. h4! [15. ♘f3 ♕c3 16. ♔e2 ♕c5 17. ♕d2 ♘e5 18. b4 ♘f3 19. ♗f3 ♕e5∓ Fischer–Keres, Jugoslavija (ct) 1959] ♘g4 16. 0–0 ♘de5∓

46 **7... ♘bd7** 8. g4 g6 [8... ♗d6 9. g5 ♘g8 10. h4 ♘e7 11. h5 ♕b6 12. ♗h3 0-0-0 13. a4 a5 14. 0–0± Fischer–Cagan, Netanya 1968 — 6/228] 9. h4 [9. ♗g2 ♗g7 10. 0–0 0–0 11. ♕g3 ♘e8 12. f4 f5 13. e5 ♘c7 14. ♘e2 ♕e7 15. ♔h1 a5 16. ♗e3± Atanasov–Kolarov, Bulgaria 1970 — 10/193; 11... de4!? 12. de4 e5=; 9. ♕g3 ♗c5 10. h4 h5 11. g5 ♘g4 12. ♘d1 de4 13. de4 ♕b6 14. b4 ♗d4∞] h5 10. g5 ♘g4 11. ♗h3± Boleslavski; **7... ♕a5** 8. ♗d2 ♕b6 9. 0-0-0 d4 10. ♘e2 a5 11. g4 ♗c5 12. g5 ♘fd7 13. h4 ♕b5 14. ♘c3! dc3 15. ♗c3 ♕b6 16. ♗g7 ♖g8 17. ♗c3 ♗d4 18. ♗d4 ♕d4 19. c3 ♕b6 20. d4 ♘a6 21. ♗c4⯹ Mučnik –Halilbejli, SSSR 1958; **7... ♗c5**!? 8. ♗e2 [8. g4 0–0 9. h4 ♘bd7 10. g5 ♘e8 11. ♗h3 ♕e7∞] 0–0 9. 0–0 ♘bd7 10. ♕g3 ♗d4 11. ♗h6 ♘e8 12. ♗g5 ♘df6 13. ♗f3 ♕d6 14. ♗f4 ♕c5= Fischer–Larsen, Zürich 1959

47 8. g3 0–0 9. ♗g2 ♘e8 10. 0–0 f5 11. ♕e2 ♘c7 12. ♗d2 ♘d7 13. ♖ae1 ♗f6= Boleslavski–Bagirov, SSSR 1959

48 8... de4 9. de4 ♘fd7 10. ♗e3 ♗g5 11. 0-0-0 ♗e3 12. ♕e3±

49 **9... ♗g5** 10. ♗e3 ♗e3 11. fe3±; **9... ♘f8** 10. ♗e3 ♘g6 11. ♕g3 ♗h4 12. ♕h2 ♘d7 13. 0-0-0± Smislov–Botvinik (m) 1958

50 10. ♗d3?! ♕d4 11. ♗e3 ♕f6∓

51 14. dc6 ♘c6 15. 0–0 ♖ad8=

52 7. ♘e4? ♕d4 8. ♗d3 ♘bd7! 9. ♗e3 ♕d5 10. ♖d1 e6 11. 0–0 ♗e7 12. ♘f6 ♘f6 13. ♕g3 ♗d6 14. ♕h4 ♕e5 15. g3 ♗c5∓ Dubinin–Ilivicki, SSSR 1957

53 **7... ♘d5** 8. ♕e4 ♘c3 9. bc3 ♘d7 10. ♖b1 ♕c8 11. c4 e6 12. ♗d3 ♗e7 13. 0–0± Boleslavski; **7... ♕a5** 8. ♗d2 ♕f5 9. 0-0-0 e6 10. f3 ef3 11. g4 ♕a5 12. ♗c4⯹ Mesing–Nemet, Jugoslavija 1967 — 4/176

54 **10... ♕b6** 11. ♗e2 e6 12. 0–0 ♗e7 13. c4 ♖d8 14. ♗e3 c5 15. ♖fd1 0–0 16. ♕b3± Mesing–Šamkovič, Timisoara 1972 — 13/206; **10... ♕d5** 11. c4 ♕d6 12. ♗e2 e5 13. d5 e4 [13... cd5 14. cd5 ♕d5 15. ♕d5 ♘d5 16. ♗b5 ♔e7 17. 0–0⯹] 14. ♕c2 ♗e7 15. dc6 ♕c6 16. 0–0 0–0 17. ♗e3±↑ Fischer–Keres, Bled 1961

55 ±⌓ Boleslavski

56 **6. ♗e2** ♘f6 7. 0–0 ♘bd7 8. d4 de4 9. ♘e4 ♘e4 [9... ♗e7 10. ♖d1 0–0 11. c4 ♘e4 12. ♕e4 ♗f6 13. ♗e3 ♖e8 14. ♖ab1 ♕c7 15. b4± Bogoljubov–van Scheltinga, England 1951] 10. ♕e4 ♘f6 11. ♕d3 ♕c7 12. c4 ♗e7 13. ♗d2 0–0 14. ♗c3 ♖ad8 15. ♕f3 ♕d7= Milić–Clarke, Moskva (ol) 1956; **6. g3** ♘f6 7. ♗g2 de4 8. ♘e4 ♘e4 [8... ♘bd7 9. d4 ♘e4 10. ♕e4 ♘f6 11. ♕d3 ♗e7 12. 0–0 0–0 13. b3 ♕b6 14. ♗b2 ♖ad8 15. ♖ad1 ♖d7= Alexander–Golombek, England 1951] 9. ♕e4 ♕d5 10. d4 ♘d7 11. 0–0 ♕e4 12. ♗e4 ♘f6 13. ♗f3 0-0-0= Lutikov–Ilivicki, SSSR 1957; **6. a3**!? ♘d7 7. d4 g6 8. ♗e3 ♗g7 9. 0-0-0 ♘e7 10. g4 ♕a5 11. h4 h6 12. ♕g3 0-0-0 13. ♗e2± Panno–Pomar, Palma de Mallorca 1971 — 12/189

57 **6... ♕b6** 7. ♗d3 ♘f6 [7... ♕d4 8. ed5 ed5 9. ♗f4 ♘d7 10. 0-0-0± Keres–Flor, Budapest (ct) 1950] 8. 0–0 de4 9. ♘e4 ♕d4 10. ♘f6 ♕f6 11. ♕g3 ♕e7 12. ♗f4 ♘d7 13. ♖ad1 ♘f6 14. ♗e5 0-0-0 15. ♗e2!± Panov–Kopilov, SSSR 1946; **6... ♗b4** 7. e5 [7. ♕g3 de4 8. ♗d2 ♘e7 9. ♕g7 ♘g6 10. ♘e4 ♗d2 11. ♘d2 ♘d7 12. ♗d3± Keres–Augustsson, Amsterdam (ol) 1954] c5 8. a3 ♕a5 9. ab4! ♕a1 10. ♗b5 ♘c6 11. 0–0 cd4 12. ♘d5 ed5 13. ♕b3 ♘e7 14. ♗g5± Ciocaltea–Soos, Romania 1952; **6... g6** 7. ed5 cd5 8. ♗f4 ♘c6 9. ♗b5 ♗g7 10. 0–0 ♘e7 11. ♗e5 0–0 12. ♗g7 ♔g7 13. ♘e2 a6 14. ♗c6 ♘c6 15. c3 ♕f6= Konstantinopoljski–Kasparjan, SSSR 1952

58 7... de4 8. ♘e4 ♕d4 — 6... de4

59 8. ♗e3 0–0 9. 0–0±

60 9... ♗f8 10. ♘e2 [10. 0–0 ♕b6 11. ♗e3 ♕b2 12. ♘e2 ♕b6 13. c4 ♕a6 14. ♘f4 dc4∞ Toluš–Flor, SSSR (ch) 1950] c5 11. c3 ♘c6 12. 0–0 cd4 13. cd4 ♕b6 14. ♗e3 ♕b2 15. ♖ab1± Bronštejn–Makagonov, SSSR 1947

61 10. ♘e2 c5 11. c3 ♘c6 12. 0–0 ♕b6 13. ♕f4 ♖c8 14. a3 cd4 15. cd4 ♘a5 16. ♗e3 ♘c4= Boleslavski

62 10... h5? 11. ♗g6! ♖g8 12. ♗f7 ♔f7 13. ♕f3 ♔g7 14. ♖h3 ♕e8 15. ♘e2+−

63 11... h5 12. ♗g6 fg6 13. ♕g6 ♔d8 14. ♕e6±→

64 12... c4? 13. hg6 cd3 14. ♖h7 ♖f8 15. gf7 ♔d8 16. ♕d3±

65 14. ♕e3 0-0-0 15. h6± Bronštejn–Makagonov, SSSR (ch) 1951

66 7. ♕e4 ♘f6 8. ♕d3 ♘a6=

67 7... ♘f6 8. ♗d3 ♘bd7 9. c3 [9. 0–0 ♘e4 10. ♗e4 ♘f6 11. ♕d3 ♗d6 12. ♗f3 ♕c7= Gligorić–Pirc, Saltsjöbaden (izt) 1948] ♘e4 10. ♕e4 [10. ♗e4 ♘f6 11. ♗c2 ♕d5 12. ♕d5 ♘d5 13. ♗d2 ♗d6= Wade–Golombek, Opatija 1953] ♘f6 11. ♕e2 ♕d5 12. 0–0 ♕h5 13. ♕h5 ♘h5 14. ♗e3±⊥ Boleslavski–Bronštejn (m) 1950

68 8. c3 ♕d5 [8... ♕b6!?] 9. ♗f4 [9. ♗g5 f5 10. ♖d1 ♕e4 11. ♕e4 fe4 12. ♖d8 ♔f7 13. ♗f4 ♘f6 14. ♖b8 ♖b8 15. ♗b8 ♗a3∓ Monticelli–Euwe, Venezia 1948] f5 10. ♘g5=∞

69 8... ♘f6 9. c3 [9. ♗e3 ♕b2 10. 0–0 ♘e4 11. ♕e4 ♕f6 12. ♖ab1=∞; 9... ♗b4 10. ♔e2 ♕d8 11. ♖hd1 ♘e4 12. ♕e4=∞; 9... ♕d8 10. 0-0-0 ♘bd7 11. ♗c4=∞ Boleslavski–Flor, SSSR (ch) 1950] ♕d8 10. 0–0 ♗e7 11. ♖d1 ♘bd7 12. ♕g3 ♘e4 13. ♗e4 g6 14. ♗f4=∞ Korčnoj–Spaski, SSSR (ch) 1959

70 **9. c3** ♕b6 10. ♕g3 ♘gf6 11. 0–0 0-0-0 12. ♘g5 ♘c5 13. ♗c2 ♗d6∓ Troianescu–Golombek, Budapest 1952; **9. ♗f4** ♘e5 10. ♗e5 ♕e5 11. 0-0-0 ♗e7∞ Pachman

71 **10... f5**? 11. ♘g5 ♕f3 12. gf3±; **10... ♕a2**!?

72 **11. c4** ♕a5 12. ♗d2 ♕a2 13. ♗c3 ♗e7 14. ♖he1 ♘e4 15. ♗e4 ♕c4∓ Milić–Golombek, Opatija 1953; **11. ♔b1**=∞

B 12

1. e4 c6 2. d4

	2	3	4	5	6	7	8	9	10	
1	...	c3[1]	♘f3[2]	♘bd2	♗d3	♘e4	♘f6	0–0	♖e1	±
	g6	♗g7	d5	♘d7	de4	♘gf6	♘f6	0–0	♖e8[3]	
2	...	f3[4]	♗e3[6]	♘c3[8]	♖b1	ed5	♗b5	♘ge2		=
	d5	e6[5]	♘f6[7]	♕b6	c5	ed5	♘c6			
3	...	♘d2	♗d3[10]	c3	♘e4	♘c5	♘b3	♕d3	♘f3	±
	...	g6[9]	♗g7	de4[11]	♗f5	b6	♗d3	♘f6	0–0[12]	
4	...	e5	dc5	♗b5[13]	♘c3	♗e3[14]	♘f3[15]	♘e5	♕h5	±
	...	c5	♘c6	♕a5	e6	♗d7	♘e5[16]	♗b5	g6[17]	
5	...	...	...	♗e3[18]	c3	♗d4	♗d3	♗c5	♗f5	±
	...	...	e6	♘e7[19]	♘f5	♕c7	♗c5	♕c5	ef5[20]	

1. e4 c6 2. d4 d5 3. e5 ♗f5

	4	5	6	7	8	9	10	11	12	
6	g4[21]	f3	h4	♗d3[23]	♕d3	g5				∓
	♗e4[22]	♗g6	h5	♗d3	e6[24]	♘e7				
7	♘f3	♗d3[25]	0–0	c3	♕d3	♖e1	♗e3	♘bd2		=
	e6	♘e7	♘d7	♗d3	♘g6	♗e7	0–0	c5[26]		
8	♘c3	g4	♘ge2	h4[28]	♕d4[30]	♕a4	♘f4	♘h5		∞
	e6	♗g6	c5[27]	cd4[29]	♘c6	h5	♗h7	a6[31]		
9	h4	g4[33]	h5[35]	c3	f4	♘f3	♗h3[36]	0–0	♘a3	=
	h6[32]	♗d7[34]	c5	e6	♕b6	♘c6	0-0-0	♔b8	cd4[37]	
10	...	c4[38]	♘c3	cd5[40]	♗g5	♕d2[41]	♕g5	hg5		=
	h5	e6	♘d7[39]	cd5	♗e7	♗g5	♕g5	a6[42]		
11	♗d3	♕d3[44]	♘c3[46]	♘ge2	♘f4[48]	♘d3	♗e3	f4	♗f2	=
	♗d3[43]	e6[45]	♕b6	♕a6[47]	♕d3	♘d7	♘e7	♘f5	h5[49]	

	4	5	6	7	8	9	10	11	12	
12	c4 e6	♘c3 dc4[50]	♗c4 ♘d7	♘ge2[51] ♘e7	0—0 ♘b6	♗b3 ♕d7[52]	♘g3 ♗g6	♗e3 0-0-0[53]		=
13	♘e2 e6	♘g3[54] ♗g6[55]	h4 h6	h5 ♗h7	♗d3 ♗d3	♕d3[56] c5[57]	c3[58] ♕b6	0—0 ♘c6	♖d1[59] ♖c8[60]	=
14	. . . . . .	. . . . . .	. . . h5	♗e2[61] c5[62]	dc5[63] ♗c5	♘d2[64] ♘c6	♘b3 ♗b6	♗h5 ♘e5	♗g6 ♘g6[65]	=

1 3. **f4** d5 4. e5 ♘a6 5. ♘f3 h5 6. ♘bd2 ♘c7 7. ♗d3 ♘h6 8. ♘f1 ♘f5 9. ♘e3 ♗h6 10. ♘f5 ♗f5 11. ♗f5 gf5 12. 0—0 e6= Padevski—Hort, Varna 1969 — 8/99; **3. ♘c3** ♗g7 [3. . . d5 — B 15] 4. ♗c4 [4. f4 d5 5. e5 — B 15] d5 5. ed5 b5 6. ♗d3 b4 7. ♘ce2 cd5 8. a3 ba3 9. ♖a3± Lukin—Karasev, SSSR 1970; **3. ♘f3** ♗g7 4. ♗e2 d5 5. e5 ♗g4 6. 0—0 ♕c7 7. c4 ♗f3 8. ♗f3 dc4 9. ♘a3± Lutikov—Zinn, Leipzig 1973

2 4. ♗d3 d5 5. ♘d2 [5. ed5 cd5 6. ♘f3 ♘c6 7. ♗f4 ♘h6 8. ♘bd2 0—0 9. 0—0 f6 10. c4± Mecking—Ciocaltea, Vršac 1971 — 12/194] ♘h6 [5. . . de4 6. ♘e4 ♘d7±] 6. ♘gf3 — 2. . . d5

3 11. ♗g5± Adorjan—Vadasz, Hungary 1970 — 9/153

4 Tartakower; 3. ♗d3 de4 4. ♗e4 ♘f6=

5 **3. . . ♘f6** 4. ♘c3 de4 [4. . . e6!?] 5. fe4 e5 6. ♘f3 ed4 7. ♘d4 ♗g4 8. ♕d3 ♘a6? 9. ♘c6± Ozsvath—L. Popov, Bulgaria 1971 — 12/191; 8. . . ♘bd7∞; **3. . . de4** 4. fe4 e5 5. ♘f3 ♗e6! [5. . . ed4 6. ♗c4→; 5. . . ♗g4 6. ♗c4 ♘d7 7. c3±] 6. c3 [6. ♘c3 ♗b4=] ♘f6 7. ♗d3 ♘bd7 8. ♕e2 ♗d6 9. ♘bd2 ♕e7= Kasparjan—Holmov, SSSR 1949

6 **4. ♘d2** de4 5. ♘e4 ♘f6 6. ♗g5 ♘bd7 7. ♕d2 ♗e7 8. ♘f6 ♗f6 9. ♗f6 ♕f6= Jimenez—Barcza, La Habana 1963; **4. ♘c3** ♘f6 [4. . . ♗b4 5. ♗e3 de4 6. a3 ♗c3 7. bc3 ♕a5 8. ♗d2=∞ Tartakower—Flor, Kemeri 1937] 5. e5 [5. ♗g5 ♕b6 6. a3 c5 7. ♗e3 ♗d7 8. e5 ♘g8 9. ♘ge2 f6 10. f4± Lutikov—Gavrilov, SSSR 1972; 5. . . h6! 6. ♗h4 ♕b6 7. a3 c5 8. ♘ge2 ♘c6 9. dc5 ♗c5 10. ♘a4 ♕a5 11. ♘ec3 ♗e7 12. ♗f6 ♗f6 13. ed5 ♘d4=∞ Smislov—Botvinik (m) 1958] ♘fd7 6. f4 c5 — C 11

7 **4. . . de4** 5. ♘d2 ef3 6. ♘gf3! ♘f6 7. ♘c4 ♘d5 8. ♗d2 ♗e7 9. ♗d3=∞ Smislov—Gereben, Budapest 1949; **4. . . ♕b6**!? 5. ♘d2 c5= Gereben

8 **5. ♗d3** c5 6. c3 cd4 7. cd4 de4 8. fe4 ♘e4∓ Tartakower—Sultan Khan, Semmering 1931; **5. ♘d2** ♕b6 6. ♗d3 c5 7. c3 ♘c6 8. dc5 ♗c5 9. ♗c5 ♕c5 10. ♕e2 0—0 11. 0-0-0 e5∓ Kuznjecov—Čistjakov, SSSR 1972

9 3. . . de4 4. ♘e4 — B 15

10 **4. e5** ♗g7 5. ♗d3 c5 6. c3 ♘c6 7. ♘e2 ♕b6 8. 0—0 ♗g4 9. dc5 ♕c5 10. ♘b3 ♕b6 11. e6!? ♗e6 12. ♘f4 ♘f6 13. ♘e6 fe6 14. ♗e3=∞ Geler—Botvinik, SSSR (ch) 1964; **4. c3** ♘f6 5. e5 ♘h5 6. g3 ♘g7 7. h4 h5 8. ♗e2 ♗f5 9. ♘gf3 e6 10. ♘g5 c5= Georgadze—Gurgenidze, Tbilisi 1974; **4. ♘gf3** ♗g7 5. h3 ♘h6 [5. . . de4 6. ♘e4 ♘d7 7. ♗c4 ♘gf6 8. ♘f6 ♘f6 9. 0—0±] 6. ♗d3 0—0 7. 0—0 a5 [7. . . f6 8. ♖e1 ♘f7 9. c4 e6 10. ♘f1 de4 11. ♗e4 c5 12. dc5 ♕d1 13. ♖d1 f5 14. ♗c2 ♘a6 15. ♖b1 ♘c5 16. b4± Vasjukov—Gurgenidze, SSSR 1973] 8. a4 ♘a6 9. ♖e1 c5 10. e5 cd4 11. ♘d4 ♘c5 12. ♘2f3 ♘f5 13. ♗d2 ♘d4 14. ♘d4 f6 15. ♗f4 ♕b6± Tukmakov—Spaski, Moskva 1971 — 12/192

11 5. . . ♘h6 6. ♘gf3 0—0 7. 0—0 f6 8. ♖e1 ♘f7 9. ♗c2! ♘a6 10. ♘f1 e5 11. de5 fe5 12. h4!± Darga—Ciocaltea, BRD—Romania 1971 — 11/98

12 11. 0—0 ♕c7 12. ♖e1 ♖e8 13. ♘e5 ♘bd7 14. ♕f3 ♖ac8 15. ♗f4 ♘e5 16. ♗e5± Geler—Botvinik, SSSR 1967 — 4/177

13 5. ♘f3 ♗g4 6. ♗b5 ♕a5 7. ♘c3 e6 8. ♗e3 ♘e7 9. ♗d2 [9. h3 ♗f3 10. ♕f3 a6 11. ♗a4 ♘g6∓ Boleslavski] ♕c7 10. ♗e2 a6 11. 0—0 ♘g6∓ Spaski—Kotov, SSSR (ch) 1955

14 7. ♕d4 ♘e7 8. b4 ♗d7 9. ba5 ♘d4 10. ♗d7 ♔d7 11. ♖b1∞ Simagin

15 8. ♗c6 ♗c6 9. ♘f3 ♗c5 10. ♗c5 ♕c5 11. ♕d4± Pachman

16 8. . . ♘ge7 9. a3 ♘g6 10. ♗c6 ♗c6 11. ♗d4± Boleslavski

17 11. ♘g6 ♘f6 12. ♕h4 ♘e4 13. ♘f8± Boleslavski

18 **5. ♘c3** ♘c6 6. ♗f4 ♘ge7 7. ♘f3 ♘g6 8. ♗e3?! ♘ge5 9. ♘e5 ♘e5 10. ♕h5 [10. ♕d4!?] ♘c6 11. 0-0-0 ♗e7 12. f4 g6= Talj—Botvinik (m) 1961; **5. ♕g4** ♘d7! [5. . . ♘c6 6. ♘f3 ♕c7 7. ♗b5 ♗d7 8. ♗c6 ♕c6 9. ♗e3 ♘h6 10. ♗h6 gh6 11. ♘bd2 ♕c5 12. c4 0-0-0 13. 0—0 ♔b8 14. ♖fd1 ♕b6 15. ♕h4± Talj—Botvinik (m) 1961] 6. ♘f3 ♘e7 7. ♗g5 h6 8. ♗e7 ♕e7 9. ♘c3 ♕c5 10. 0-0-0 a6 11. ♔b1 ♘b6= Talj—Botvinik (m) 1961; **5. ♘f3** ♗c5 6. ♗d3= Pachman

19 5. . . ♘c6 6. ♗b5 ♕a5 7. ♘c3±

20 11. ♘f3 ♘c6 12. 0–0 0–0 13. ♘bd2± Boleslavski

21 **4. f4** e6 5. ♘f3 ♘h6 6. ♗e2 ♕b6 7. 0–0 c5 8. c3 ♘c6 9. ♔h1 cd4 10. ♘d4 ♗c5 11. ♘f5 ♘f5 12. ♗d3 g6∓ Schiffers–Jurevič, Kiev 1903; **4. c3** e6 5. ♘e2 c5 6. ♗e3 ♘c6 7. f4 c4? 8. ♘g3 ♗g6 9. ♗e2 ♘ge7 10. 0–0 ♘f5 11. ♘f5 ♗f5 12. ♘d2 h5 13. b3± Iljin-Ženevski–Šiponov, SSSR 1929; 7... ♕b6!∓ Iljin-Ženevski

22 **4... ♗g6** 5. h4 h5 [5... h6 6. h5 ♗h7 7. e6 ♘f6∞] 6. e6 fe6 7. ♗d3 ♗d3 8. ♕d3 hg4 9. ♕g6 ♔d7 10. ♕g4 ♘f6 11. ♕h3 ♖h5! 12. ♘f3 [12. ♘e2!?] ♖f5∞ Mieses–Speyer, Scheveningen 1923; **4... ♗d7** 5. c4 [5. b4? a5 6. c3 ab4 7. cb4 e6 8. ♗d2 ♕b6∓; 5. ♗d3 e6 6. c3 c5 7. ♘f3 ♘c6 8. 0–0 cd4 9. cd4 ♕b6∓ Boleslavski] e6 6. ♘c3 ♘e7! 7. c5?! b6 8. b4 a5 9. ♘a4 ♘c8 10. ♖b1 ab4 11. ♖b4 bc5 12. dc5 ♕c7∓ Bronštejn–Petrosjan, SSSR (ch) 1959

23 7. e6? ♕d6 8. ef7 ♗f7∓ Aljehin

24 8... hg4? 9. e6±

25 5. ♗e2 ♘e7 [5... c5 6. 0–0 ♘c6 7. ♘c3 ♗g4∓ Konstantinopoljski] 6. 0–0 ♘d7 7. ♘bd2 ♗g6 8. ♖e1 ♘f5 9. ♘f1 ♗e7 10. c3 0–0 11. ♗d3 c5 12. ♘e3 ♘e3 13. ♗e3 c4∓ Lowgree–Bronštejn, 1958

26 Matanović–Milić, Jugoslavija (ch) 1955

27 **6... h6** 7. h4! [7. ♗e3 ♘d7 8. ♕d2 a6 9. h4 h5 10. ♘f4 ♘e7 11. ♘g6 ♘g6 12. g5 ♘e7 13. ♗h3 g6= Hodžajev–Flor, SSSR 1951] c5 8. h5 ♗h7 9. ♗e3 ♘c6 10. f4±○ Boleslavski; **6... ♕h4** 7. ♗e3 ♘h6 8. ♗h6 gh6 [8... ♕h6 9. h4±] 9. ♘g3 ♗e7 10. f4 f6 11. ♗g2± Blumenfeld–Kasparjan, SSSR 1931; **6... f6**!? 7. ♘f4 [7. f4 fe5 8. fe5 ♕h4 9. ♘g3 h5∓→] ♗f7 8. ♘d3 h5 9. gh5 ♗h5 10. ♗e2 ♗f7= Blumenfeld–Kasparjan, SSSR 1937

28 7. ♗e3 ♘c6 8. h4 cd4 [8... ♕a5 9. h5 ♗e4 10. ♖h3 h6 11. ♗d2 ♗h7 12. ♘e4 ♕c7 13. ♘c5 ♗c5 14. dc5 ♘e5 15. ♗f4 ♘e7 16. ♖e3 ♘7c6 17. ♗e5 ♘e5 18. ♕d4 ♘c4 19. ♕g7 0-0-0∓⟳ Gottstein–Weitz 1955] 9. ♗d4 h6 10. ♕d2 ♗b4 11. a3 ♕a5 12. h5 ♗h7 13. ♗g2 ♘ge7 14. ♖c1 ♗c3 15. ♕c3 ♖c8 16. ♕a5 ♘a5 17. b4 ♘c4∓ Lublinski–Sokolski, SSSR 1949

29 **7... ♘c6**? 8. h5 ♗e4 9. ♘e4 de4 10. c3 cd4 11. ♘d4! [11. cd4 ♗b4 12. ♗d2 (Lublinski–Konstantinopoljski, SSSR 1948) f6!=] ♘d4 [11... ♘e5 12. ♕a4 ♘d7 13. ♗g2 ♘f6 14. g5 ♘d5 15. ♗e4± Boleslavski] 12. cd4 ♗b4 13. ♗d2 ♗d2 14. ♕d2 ♕d5 15. ♕b4± Boleslavski; **7... h6** 8. ♘f4 ♗h7 9. ♗e3 ♘e7 10. dc5 ♘ec6 11. ♗b5 ♘d7 12. ♕e2 ♕c7 13. 0–0 ♕e5 14. ♖ad1 ♗c5 15. ♘fd5 ♗e3 16. ♘e3 ♘b6 17. f4±↑ Korčnoj–Bivšev, SSSR 1951; **7... h5** 8. ♘f4 ♗h7 [8... cd4? 9. ♘g6 hg6 10. ♘b5 ♘c6 11. ♗d3±→] 9. ♘h5 cd4 10. ♕d4 ♘c6 11. ♗b5! ♗c2 12. ♗g5±↑ Boleslavski

30 8. ♘d4 h5⇆

31 △ b5∞ Boleslavski

32 **4... c5** 5. dc5! [5. ♘c3 ♘c6 6. ♗b5 h5 7. ♘ge2 e6 8. ♗g5 ♕c7 9. 0–0± Aronin–Simagin, SSSR 1961] ♕c7 6. ♘c3 ♘c6 7. ♘f3 ♖d8 8. ♘b5 ♕c8 [Talj–Botvinik (m) 1961] 9. c3± Smislov; **4... ♕d7** 5. ♘c3 h6 6. ♗e3 e6 7. g4 ♗h7 8. ♘ge2 ♘a6 9. ♘f4 ♘c7 10. ♕d2 0-0-0 11. 0-0-0 b6 12. ♗g2± Aronin–Šackes, SSSR 1961

33 **5. ♘e2** e6 6. ♘g3 ♘e7 7. ♘c3 ♘d7 8. ♗e3 ♗h7 9. ♗d3 ♗d3 10. cd3 h5! 11. ♘ce2 [Talj–Botvinik (m) 1961] ♘g6= Pachman; **5. ♗d3**!? ♗d3 6. ♕d3 e6 7. h5± Boleslavski

34 **5... ♗h7** 6. e6! fe6 7. ♗d3 ♗d3 8. ♕d3 ♕d6 9. f4 ♘d7 10. ♘f3 0-0-0 11. ♘e5 ♘e5 12. fe5± Gufeljd–Spiridonov, Helsinki 1961; **5... ♗c8** 6. ♘c3 ♕b6 7. ♗h3 e6 8. ♘ge2 c5 9. 0–0 ♘c6 10. ♗e3± Aronin–Bronštejn, SSSR 1961

35 **6. c3** c5 7. ♗g2 e6 8. ♘e2 ♗b5 9. ♘a3 ♗e2 10. ♕e2 cd4 11. cd4 ♗a3 12. ba3 ♘c6∓ Talj–Botvinik (m) 1961; **6. c4** e6! 7. ♘c3 [Bronštejn–Portisch, Moskva 1961] c5! 8. dc5 ♗c5 9. cd5 ed5∓ Pachman; **6. ♗e3** c5 7. c3 ♘c6 8. a3 a5 9. b3 e6 10. h5 b5! 11. ♘f3 ♕b8 12. ♗g2 c4 13. bc4 bc4∞ Bronštejn–Donner, Budapest 1961

36 10. ♘a3 cd4 11. cd4 0-0-0 12. ♘c2 ♔b8 13. ♗d3 ♘ge7= Talj–Pachman, Bled 1961

37 13. cd4 ♖c8= Pachman

38 **5. ♘c3** e6 6. ♘f3 ♗g4 7. ♗e2 c5 8. ♗e3 ♘c6 9. dc5 ♗f3 10. ♗f3 ♘e5= Aronin–Smislov, SSSR 1961; **5. ♘e2** e6 6. ♘g3 ♗g6 — 4. ♘e2

39 6... ♘e7 7. ♗g5!±

40 7. ♘ge2 ♘e7 8. ♘f4 dc4 9. ♗c4 ♘g6 10. ♘h5 ♘de5 11. ♗e2 ♘d3 12. ♗d3 ♗d3∓ Talj–Averbah, SSSR (ch) 1961; 8. ♘g3!?

41 9. ♗e7 ♘e7 10. ♘b5 0–0∓⟳

42 = Boleslavski

43 **4... ♗g6**? 5. e6 ♕d6 6. ef7 ♗f7 7. ♘f3 ♘d7 8. 0–0± Richter–Engels, Wiesbaden 1924; **4... e6** 5. ♗f5 ef5 6. ♘e2 ♘a6 7. 0–0 ♘c7 8. b3 ♘e7 9. ♗a3± Vasiljčuk–Bronštejn, SSSR 1961

44 5. cd3 e6 6. ♘f3 [6. f4 ♘e7 7. ♘f3 ♘f5= Radulov–Kolarov, Bulgaria 1964] ♘d7 7. 0–0 ♘e7 8. ♘c3 ♘f5 9. ♘e2 ♗e7 10. ♗d2 0–0= Ručkin–Babuškin, SSSR 1963

45 5... ♕a5? 6. ♘c3 ♕a6? 7. e6 ♕d3 8. ef7 ♔f7 9. cd3 e6 10. f4± Ufimcev–Ravkin, SSSR 1961; 6... e6!?

46 6. **f4** ♕a5! [6... ♕b6 7. ♘e2! c5 8. c3 ♘c6 9. dc5! ♗c5 10. b4 ♗f2 11. ♔f1 a5 12. b5± Konstantinopoljski] 7. c3 ♕a6 8. ♕d1 [8. ♕a6 ♘a6 9. ♘f3 c5 10. ♗e3 ♘h6∓] c5 9. ♘e2 ♘c6 10. ♘d2 cd4 11. cd4 ♕d3∓ Boleslavski; **6. ♘f3** ♕a5 [6... ♕b6 7. 0–0 ♕a6! 8. ♕b3 ♘d7= Konstantinopoljski] 7. ♘bd2 [7. c3 ♕a6 8. ♕a6 ♘a6 9. ♗e3 ♘e7∓] ♕a6 8. c4 ♘d7 9. 0–0 ♗e7 10. ♘e1 h5 11. cd5 ♕d3 12. ♘d3 cd5= Stoltz–Flor, Saltsjöbaden (izt) 1948; **6. ♘e2** c5 [6... ♕a5 7. ♘bc3 ♕a6 — 6. ♘c3; 6... ♕b6 7. 0–0 ♕a6 8. ♕d1 c5 9. c3 ♘c6 10. ♘d2 cd4 11. cd4 ♕d3∓ Atkins–Capablanca, London 1922] 7. c3 ♘c6 8. 0–0 ♘ge7 9. f4 cd4 10. cd4 h5∓ Vestol–van Scheltinga, Helsinki (ol) 1952

47 7... c5 8. dc5 ♗c5 9. 0–0 ♘e7 10. ♘a4 [10. a3 ♕c6!=] ♕c6 11. ♘c5 ♕c5 12. ♗e3 ♕c7 13. f4 ♘f5 14. ♗f2! [14. c3? ♘c6 15. ♖ad1 g6∓ Nimzowitsch–Capablanca, New York 1927] h5 15. ♖ac1 ♘c6 16. c4± Boleslavski

48 8. ♕h3 ♘e7!∓

49 13. ♔e2 b6 14. b4 a5 15. a3= Boleslavski

50 5... ♘d7 6. cd5 [6. ♘ge2 dc4 7. ♘g3 ♘b6! 8. ♘f5 ef5∓ Pachman] cd5 7. ♘ge2 [7. ♘f3 ♘e7 8. ♗g5 a6 9. ♘h4 ♗g6 10. ♗e2 ♕b6 11. ♕d2 ♘c6 12. ♖d1 ♖c8 13. 0–0 ♗e7= Unzicker–Golombek, München 1954] ♘e7 8. ♘g3 ♗g6 9. ♗d3 [9. ♗g5 ♕b6 10. ♕d2 ♘c6 11. ♖d1 h6= Henkin; 9. h4 h5 10. ♗g5 a6 11. ♗d3 ♗d3 12. ♕d3 ♕b6 13. 0–0 ♘c6 14. ♖ad1 ♗e7= Boleslavski] ♘c6 10. 0–0 ♕h4 11. ♗b5 ♗e7! 12. ♗e3 0–0 13. f4 f5= Stoltz–Golombek, Amsterdam (ol) 1954

51 7. ♘f3 ♘b6 8. ♗b3 ♘e7 9. 0–0 ♘ed5 [9... h6 10. ♕e2 ♘ed5 11. ♘e4 ♗e7 12. ♗d2 a5 13. a3 ♘d7 14. ♖ad1 0–0 15. ♗c1 ♕b6 16. ♗c2 ♖fd8 17. ♘g3 ♗g6! 18. ♗g6 fg6= Kotov–Flor, SSSR (ch) 1955] 10. ♕e2 ♗e7 11. ♘e4 0–0= Johannessen–Porath, Leipzig (ol) 1960

52 9... h6 10. ♘g3 ♗g6 11. ♘ce4 ♘f5? 12. ♘f5 ♗f5 13. ♘g3 ♗g6 14. f4 ♘d5 15. f5± Damjanović–Flor, Balatonfüred 1960; 11... ♗e4±

53 **11... h5**? 12. ♘ge4 ♘ed5 13. ♗g5± Pachman; **11... 0-0-0**!= Konstantinopoljski

54 5. ♘f4 c5! [5... h6? 6. ♗d3 ♗d3 7. ♘d3 ♘d7 8. 0–0 c5 9. dc5 ♘c5 10. ♘c5 ♗c5 11. ♕g4 g6 12. c4± Ćirić–Hočevar, Jugoslavija (ch) 1960; 5... ♗e7 6. ♗d3 ♗d3 7. ♘d3 h5 8. ♘d2 ♘d7 9. 0–0 g6 10. ♘f3 ♘h6 11. ♗h6 ♖h6 12. ♕d2 ♖h7 13. a4± Szabo–Barcza, Budapest 1959] 6. dc5 ♗c5 7. ♗d3 ♘e7 8. 0–0 0–0 9. c3 [9. ♘d2 ♘bc6 10. ♗f5 ♘f5 11. ♘f3 ♗b6 12. ♘d3 f6∓↑ Krogius–Ilivicki, SSSR 1957] ♘d7 10. ♕e2 ♕c7 11. ♖e1 ♖ac8 12. ♘d2 a6= Ciocaltea–Golombek, Moskva 1956

55 5... ♘e7 6. h4 [6. ♗g5 ♕b6 7. b3 ♗g6 8. h4 h6 9. ♗e3 ♘f5 10. ♗d3 ♘g3 11. fg3 ♗d3 12. ♕d3 c5 13. c3 ♕a6∓ Gusev–Goldberg, SSSR 1950; 6. ♘f5 ♘f5 7. c3 c5 8. ♕b3? ♕c7 9. ♗b5 ♘c6 10. 0–0 h5 11. ♗e3 a6 12. ♗c6 bc6∓ O'Donnel–Larsen, USA 1970 — 10/194; 8. ♗d3 g6= Larsen; 6. ♗d3 ♗d3 7. ♕d3 ♕a5 8. c3 ♕a6 9. ♕a6 ♘a6 10. ♗e3 ♘f5 11. ♘f5 ef5△ ♘c7= Simagin–Gufeljd, SSSR (ch) 1960; 6. c4 ♗g6 7. ♘c3 ♘d7 8. h4 h6 9. h5 ♗h7 10. ♕b3 ♕b6= Henkin–Flor, SSSR 1960] h6 [6... c5 7. ♘c3 a6 8. ♗g5 cd4 9. ♘f5 ef5 10. ♕d4 ♘bc6 11. ♕f4 ♕c7 12. 0-0-0±] 7. h5 ♗h7 8. ♗d3 ♗d3 9. ♕d3± Boleslavski

56 9. cd3 ♘e7 [9... ♕b6 10. ♗e3! ♕b2 11. ♘d2 ♗b4? 12. 0–0 ♗d2 13. ♖b1 ♕a2 14. ♗d2 b6 15. ♗b4∞ Kuzmin–Bordonada, Nice (ol) 1974 — 18/183; 11... ♕b6 12. 0–0 ♘e7 13. f4 ♘f5 14. ♘f5 ef5 15. g4± Asaturjan–Hodos, SSSR 1969 — 8/151; 11... ♕c3!? Sokolov; 9... ♘d7 10. ♘c3 ♕b6 11. ♘ce2 c5 12. dc5 ♗c5 13. d4 ♗b4 14. ♔f1 ♖c8 15. ♗e3 ♘f8 16. ♖c1 ♘e7 17 ♖c8 ♘c8= Spaski–Liberzon, SSSR 1960] 10. ♘c3 ♘a6 [10... ♘f5!? Pachman] 11. 0–0 ♕d7 12. ♘ce2 ♘f5 13. ♘h1 [13. ♘f5 ef5 14. f4 g6 15. g4 ♖g8 16. ♔h1 0-0-0∓ Matulović–Pachman, Sarajevo 1961] c5 13. dc5 ♗c5 15. d4 ♗b6 16. g4 ♘e7 17. ♘hg3 0-0-0 18. f4 f6= Pachman

57 9... ♕a5 10. c3 ♕a6 11. ♕a6! ♘a6 12. f4! c5 13. f5 cd4 14. fe6 fe6 15. cd4 ♗b4 16. ♔e2 ♘e7 17. a3 ♗a5 18. ♖f1 ♖c8 19. ♔d3± Arutjunov–Halilbejli, SSSR 1960

58 **10. f4** ♘c6 11. f5?! ♘d4∓; **10. dc5** ♘d7= Konstantinopoljski

59 12. dc5 ♕c7! [12... ♗c5 13. b4 ♗e7 14. ♖e1 a5 15. b5 ♘d8 16. ♗e3 ♗c5 17. ♘d2± Treybal–Engel, Sliač 1932] 13. f4 ♗c5= Pachman

60 13. ♘a3 cd4 14. cd4 ♗a3 15. ba3 ♘a5= Heidenfeld–Pachman, Madrid 1960

61 **7. ♘d2** c5 8. dc5 ♘c6 [8... ♗c5 9. ♘b3 ♕b6 10. ♘c5 ♕c5 11. c3 ♘c6 12. ♗e3 ♕a5= Spaski–Bronštejn, SSSR 1961] 9. ♘f3 ♗c5 10. ♗d3 ♘ge7 11. 0–0 ♗d3 12. cd3 ♘g6∓ Matulović–Minev, Beograd 1961; **7. ♗d3** ♗d3 8. ♕d3 ♕a5 9. c3 ♕a6=

62 7... ♗e7 8. ♗h5 ♗h5 9. ♘h5 g6 10. ♘f4 ♖h4 11. ♖h4 ♗h4 12. ♕g4 ♘h6 13. ♕h3± Pachman

63 **8. ♗h5** ♗h5 9. ♘h5 g6 10. ♗g5 ♗e7 11. ♗e7 ♕e7 12. ♘g3 ♖h4∓ Brzoska–Veresov, Polanica Zdroj 1958; **8. ♘h5** ♗h5 9. ♗h5 g6 10. ♗e2 ♖h4 11. ♖h4 ♕h4 12. ♗e3 ♘c6 13. c3 [Espig–Golz, DDR 1967] ♗h6∓; **8. c3** ♘c6 9. ♗e3=

64 9. ♘c3 ♘c6 10. ♗g5 ♗e7 11. ♕d2 ♘b4 12. ♗b5 [12. ♗d1? ♖c8 13. a3 ♘c6 14. ♗e7 ♘ge7 15. f4 a6 16. ♗e2 ♘a5 17. ♖c1 ♘f5∓ Timman–Vukić, Banja Luka 1974 — 18/182; 12. ♖c1!?△ a3= Vukić] ♔f8 13. ♗a4= Vukić

65 13. ♗g5 ♕d6 14 ♕e2 ♕e5 15. ♕e5 ♘e5 16. f3 f6= Bronštejn–Botvinik, SSSR 1966

1. e4 c6 2. d4 d5 3. ed5 cd5

	4	5	6	7	8	9	10	11	12	
1	♗d3[1]	c3	♘e2[3]	♗f4	♗d6	♘d2	de5	♗b5	♗d7	±
	♘c6	♕c7[2]	e6	♗d6	♕d6	e5[4]	♘e5	♗d7	♕d7[5]	
2	...	...	♘f3	♕b3[7]	♕b7	♕c8	gf3	♗e3	♔e2	±
	...	g6	♗g4[6]	♗f3	♕c8	♖c8	♘d4	♘f3[8]	♘e5	
3	...	...	h3[9]	de5	♘f3[10]	0—0	♘e5	♘d2		=
	...	♘f6	e5	♘e5	♗d6[11]	0—0	♗e5	♗c7		
4	...	...	♗g5	♕b3	♘e2	♘g3	f3	hg3	♗f5	=
	...	...	♗g4[12]	♕d7[13]	e6	♘h5	♘g3	♗f5	ef5[14]	
5	...	...	♗f4	♘f3[15]	♘bd2[16]	♗e3	0—0	♘b3	♖e1	±
	...	...	g6	♗g7	♘h5[17]	0—0[18]	f5	♕d6	f4[19]	
6	...	...	...	♕b3[20]	♕a4	♕c2	♘f3	♘bd2	0—0	±
	...	...	♗g4	♘a5[21]	♗d7	a6[22]	b5	g6	♗g7[23]	
7	...	...	...	...	♘d2	♘gf3[24]	♘e5[25]	♗e5[26]	♕c2	±
	...	...	...	♕c8	e6	♗e7	♘e5	0—0	♗f5[27]	

1. e4 c6 2. d4 d5 3. ed5 cd5 4. c4[28] ♘f6[29] 5. ♘c3 ♘c6

	6	7	8	9	10	11	12	13	14	
8	♘f3[30]	cd5[32]	♕b3[33]	gf3	♕b7	♗b5	♕c6	♕b5[35]	♘d5	±
	♗g4[31]	♘d5	♗f3	e6[34]	♘d4	♘b5	♔e7	♕d7[36]	♕d5[37]	
9	♗g5	♗e2[39]	♘ge2	d5	0—0	♗f4	♕a4	♕c4	♕b3	±
	♗g4[38]	♗e2[40]	dc4[41]	♘e5	h6[42]	♘g6	♕d7	♖c8	e5[43]	
10	...	d5	b4	ab3	b4	♗b5	♘f3			∞
	dc4	♘a5[44]	cb3	b6[45]	♘b7	♗d7				
11	...	♗c4	♕d4	0-0-0	f4	fe5	♘f3	♖he1	♘e4	±
	...	♕d4[46]	♘d4	e5	♗c5	♘g4	♘c6	h6	♗b6[47]	
12	...	cd5	♗e3[49]	de6	ef7[50]	♗c4[52]	♘f3	♗d4	♕e2	±
	♕b6	♘d4[48]	e5	♗c5	♔e7[51]	♖d8[53]	♗g4[54]	♖d4	♔f8[55]	
13	...	♗f6[56]	cd5	♕d2	bc3	♘f3	♗e2	0—0		±
	♕a5	ef6	♗b4	♗c3	♕d5	♗g4[57]	0—0			

[1] **4. ♘c3** ♗f5 5. ♘f3 [5. ♗d3 ♕d7] ♘c6 6. ♗b5 e6 7. ♘e5 ♕c7 8. g4 ♗g6 9. h4 f6 10. ♘g6 ♗g6∞; **4. ♘f3** ♗g4 5. ♗d3 ♘c6 6. c3 e6 7. ♕b3 ♕d7 8. ♘bd2= Spielmann—Stahlberg (m) 1933; **4. c3** ♗f5 [4... ♘c6 5. ♗f4 ♗f5 6. ♘f3 e6 7. ♕b3 ♕c8 8. ♘bd2 ♘f6 9. ♗e2 ♗e7 10. 0—0 ♘e4= Larsen—Spaski, San Juan 1969 — 8/152] 5. ♘f3 [5. ♗d3 ♗d3 6. ♕d3 ♘c6 7. ♘f3 e6=] ♘f6 6. ♗b5 ♘bd7 7. ♘h4 ♗g6 8. ♗f4 e6 9. ♘d2 ♘h5 10. ♘g6 hg6= Fischer—Hort, Vinkovci 1968 — 6/230

[2] 5... e5 6. de5 ♘e5 7. ♕e2 ♕e7 8. ♗b5±

[3] **6. h3** ♘f6 7. ♘f3 g6 8. 0—0 ♗f5∓ Toluš—Flor, SSSR 1944; **6. f4** ♘f6 7. ♘f3 ♗g4 8. 0—0 ♘e4∓

[4] 9... ♘f6 10. ♘f3 0—0 11. 0—0 e5 12. de5 ♘e5 13. ♘e5 ♕e5 14. ♖e1± Mieses—Carls, Baden-Baden 1925

[5] 13. 0—0±

[6] **6... ♗g7** 7. h3 [7. ♗f4 ♘h6 8. ♘bd2 0—0 9. 0—0 f6 10. c4± Mecking—Ciocaltea, Vršac 1971 — 12/134; 8. ♕d2±] ♘h6 8. ♗f4 0—0 9. ♕d2 ♘f5 10. 0—0 f6 11. ♖e1 ♖e8 12. c4 ♘cd4 13. ♘d4 ♘d4 14. cd5± Cejtlin—Savon, SSSR (ch) 1970 — 11/154; **6... ♗f5**!?

[7] 7. h3 ♗f3 8. ♕f3 ♗g7 9. 0—0 e6 10. ♘d2 ♘f6 11. ♕e2 ♕d6 12. ♘f3 ♘d7 13. ♖e1 a6 14. ♗g5 0—0 15. ♕d2 ♖fe8 16. ♗f4 ♕e7 17. ♖e2 b5 18. a3 ♘a5= Mosionžik—Bronštejn, SSSR 1969

8 11... ♘c6 12. ♗b5 e5 13. ♗a7± Rossolimo–Bronštejn, Monte Carlo 1969 — 7/174

9 6. **f4** g6 7. ♘f3 ♗f5∓; 6. **♘e2** e5=; 6. **♘f3** ♗g4 7. 0–0 e6 8. ♕b3 ♕c7 9. ♘bd2 ♗d6 10. ♖e1 0–0∓; 7. h3=

10 8. ♕e2 ♕e7 9. ♗b5 ♗d7 10. ♗d7 ♘fd7∓

11 8... ♘c6 9. 0–0 ♗e7 10. ♗e3 0–0=

12 6... ♘e4 7. ♗e4 de4 8. d5 ♘e5 9. ♕a4 b5 [9... ♕d7 10. ♕e4 ♕b5 11. ♕e5 ♕b2 12. ♕e2 ♕a1 13. ♕c2±] 10. ♕e4 [10. ♕b5 ♗d7 11. ♕e2 ♘d3∓] f6=∞

13 7... **♕b6** 8. ♘d2 e6 9. ♘gf3 ♗d6 10. 0–0 h6 11. ♕b6 ab6 12. ♗e3 0–0 13. ♖fe1± Ragozin–Petrosjan, SSSR 1949; 7... **♘a5** 8. ♕c2±

14 van den Bosch–Capablanca, Budapest 1929

15 7. h3 ♗g7 8. ♘f3 ♗f5 [8... 0–0 9. 0–0 ♘h5 10. ♗h2±] 9. 0–0 [9. ♗f5 gf5 10. ♘h4 e6 11. ♕e2 0–0∓] ♗d3 10. ♕d3 0–0 11. ♘bd2 ♕b6=

16 8. 0–0 ♗g4 9. h3 ♗f3 10. ♕f3 ♕b6∞ Gusev–Bronštejn, SSSR 1947; 9. ♘bd2±

17 8... ♗f5 9. ♗f5 gf5 10. ♘e5 ♕b6∞ Spielmann–Sämisch, Berlin 1920; 10. ♕b3±

18 9... **f5** 10. ♘b3 f4 11. ♗d2 0–0 12. 0–0 ♗g4 13. ♗e2 ♕d6 14. ♘c1 ♘f6 15. ♘d3 ♘e4 16. ♖e1± Hennings–A. Zajcev, Debrecen 1970 — 10/195; 9... **♕c7** 10. 0–0 0–0 11. ♖e1 f5 12. ♘b3 f4 13. ♗d2± Bronštejn–Dominguez, Las Palmas 1972 — 14/204

19 13. ♗d2 ♗g4 14. ♗e2 ♖ae8 15. ♘c1 ♗f3 16. ♗f3 e5∓ Fischer–Czerniak, Netanya 1968 — 6/229; 15. ♘e5±

20 7. **f3** ♗h5 8. ♘e2 e6 9. ♘d2 ♗d6=; 7. **♘e2** ♕d7 8. ♕b3 ♗h5 9. 0–0 ♗g6=; 7. **♘f3** ♕b6 8. ♕b3 ♗f3 9. gf3 e6 10. ♘d2 ♘d7= Milner-Barry–Flor, Hastings 1934/35

21 7... ♕d7 8. ♘d2 e6 9. ♘gf3 a6 [9... ♗f3 10. ♘f3± Tringov–Pomar, Büsum 1968 — 5/158] 10. 0–0 ♗h5 11. ♘e5±

22 9... e6 10. ♘f3 ♕b6 11. a4 [11. ♘bd2 ♗b5= Maroczy–Capablanca, Lake Hopatkong 1926] ♖c8 12. ♘bd2 ♘c6 13. ♕b1± Fischer–Petrosjan, Beograd 1970 — 9/149

23 13. ♖fe1 0–0 14. b4±

24 9. h3?! ♗h5 10. ♘gf3 ♗e7 11. ♘e5 ♘e5= Zinn–Kozma, Kapfenberg 1970 — 9/148

25 10. 0–0 0–0 11. ♘e5 ♗h5 12. ♕c2 ♗g6 13. ♘g6 hg6 14. ♘f3± Browne–Larsen, San Antonio 1972 — 14/205; 11... ♘e5±

26 11. de5 ♘d7 12. 0–0 ♘c5 13. ♗b5 ♔f8= Hübner–Smislov, Hastings 1968/69 — 7/173

27 13. ♗f5 ef5 14. ♕b3 [14. 0–0 g6 15. f3 ♕c6 16. ♕b3 ♘d7= Matulović–Vukić, Jugoslavija 1971 — 11/155] ♕c6 [Nežmetdinov–Šamkovič, SSSR 1970 — 9/147] 15. a4±

28 Panov

29 4... **e5** 5. de5 d4 6. ♘f3 ♘c6 7. ♗d3±; 4... **e6** 5. ♘c3 ♘f6 — B 14; 4... **♘c6** 5. cd5 [5. ♘c3 e5 6. cd5 ♘d4 7. ♗e3 ♘f5= Korn; 5... ♘f6 — 4... ♘f6] ♕d5 6. ♘f3 — B 22; 4... **dc4** 5. ♗c4 ♘f6 6. ♘c3 e6 7. ♘f3 — D

30 6. ♗f4 g6! 7. ♘f3 ♗g7 8. ♕b3 dc4 9. ♗c4 0–0=

31 6... **e6** — B 14; 6... **g6** 7. ♗g5 ♘e4 8. cd5 ♘c3 9. bc3 ♕d5 10. ♕b3±

32 7. **♗e3** e6 8. h3 ♗f3 9. ♕f3 ♕b6 10. 0-0-0 ♗b4 11. c5 ♕a5 12. ♘b5 0–0 13. ♔b1 ♘e4 14. ♕f4 a6 15. ♘d6 ♘d6 16. ♕d6 e5! 17. ♕d5 ed4 18. ♗f4 ♕c5∓ Larsen–Trifunović, Beograd 1964; 7. **♗e2** e6 [7... dc4 8. d5 ♗f3 9. ♗f3 ♘e5 10. 0–0 ♕d7 11. ♕e2 ♘f3 12. ♕f3 0-0-0 13. b3!± Mikenas–Flor, Folkestone (ol) 1933] 8. c5 ♘e4 9. h3 ♗f3 10. ♗f3 ♘c3 11. bc3 ♗e7=

33 8. ♗b5 ♖c8 9. h3 ♗f3 [9... ♗h5 10. 0–0 e6 11. ♖e1 ♗e7 12. ♖e5∞ Hasin–Bagirov, SSSR (ch) 1961] 10. ♕f3 e6 11. 0–0= Krause–Nimzowitsch, corr. 1925

34 9... **♘d4**? 10. ♗b5+–; 9... **♘c3**? 10. ♕b7 ♘d4 11. bc3 ♘c2 12. ♔e2 ♖b8 13. ♕c6 ♕d7 14. ♕d7 ♔d7 15. ♗h3 e6 16. ♗f4 +– Panov; 9... **♘db4** 10. ♗e3 ♘d4 11. ♗d4 ♕d4 12. ♗b5 ♘c6 13. 0–0±; 9... **♘b6** 10. d5 ♘d4 11. ♕d1 e5 12. de6 fe6 13. ♗e3 ♗c5 14. b4 ♕f6 15. bc5 ♘f3 16. ♔e2 0–0 17. cb6 ♕c3 18. ♗g2 ♕c4 19. ♕d3± Žuravljev–Gutman, SSSR 1972 — 13/208

35 13. ♘b5? ♖b8 14. ♘d4 ♕d7 15. ♗e3 ♖b2 16. ♕c4 f6 17. ♖d1 ♔f7 18. ♘b3 ♗e7 19. 0–0 ♖c8–+ Žuravljev–Stecko, SSSR 1971 — 11/156

36 13... ♘c3 14. bc3 ♕d5 [14... ♕d7 15. ♖b1!± Fischer–Euwe, Leipzig (ol) 1960] 15. ♖b1 ♖d8 16. ♗e3 ♕b5 17. ♖b5± Cortlever–Karaklajić, Wijk aan Zee 1972 — 13/207

37 14... **ed5** 15. ♕b4 [15. ♕e2 ♕e6 16. ♗e3 f6 17. ♖c1± Panov–Sergejev, SSSR 1930] ♔e8 16. ♕d4± Fischer; 14... **♕d5** 15. ♕d5 [15. ♕b4 ♔e8 16. ♕a4 ♕d7=] ed5 16. 0–0 ♔e6 17. ♖e1 ♔f5 18. ♗e3 ♗e7= Smejkal–Filip, ČSSR 1968 — 6/231; 16. ♗e3±

38 6... **♗e6** 7. ♗f6 [7. ♘ge2 dc4 8. ♘f4 ♘d4 9. ♘e6 ♘e6 10. ♗c4!=∞ Velimirović–Ćirić, Jugoslavija 1966 — 1/107] ef6 8. c5 ♗e7 [8... g6 9. ♘f3 ♗g7 10. h3 0–0 11. ♗b5± I. Zajcev–Šamkovič, SSSR 1967 — 4/179] 9. ♗b5 0–0 10. ♘ge2 ♕c7 11. 0–0 f5 12. ♕d2 ♗f6 13. ♗c6 bc6 14. b4± Botvinik–Flor, SSSR 1965; 6... **e6**! — B 14

39 7. f3 ♗e6 8. c5 g6 9. ♗f6 ef6 10. ♗b5 ♗h6 11. ♘ge2±

40 7... ♗e6 8. ♗f3±

41 8... e6 9. cd5 ed5 10. ♕b3±

42 **10... g6** 11. d6 ed6 12. ♗f6 ♕f6 13. ♘d5 ♕d8 14. ♕a4±; **10... e6** 11. ♗f6 gf6 12. ♕a4 ♕d7 13. ♘b5 ♖c8 14. de6 fe6 15. ♖ad1±

43 15. de6± Talj–Bronštejn, SSSR (ch) 1971 — 12/195

44 7... ♘e5 8. ♕d4 ♘d3 9. ♗d3 cd3 10. ♘f3 h6 [10... e6?! 11. 0-0-0±; 10... g6 11. ♗f6 ef6 12. 0–0 ♗e7 13. ♖ad1± Botvinik–Flor, (m) 1933; 10... ♗f5 11. 0–0 h6 12. ♗f6 gf6 13. ♕f4± Bobocov–O'Kelly, Zevenaar 1961] 11. ♗f4 [11. ♗h4 g5 12. ♗g3 ♗g7= Nežmetdinov–Mojsejev, SSSR 1970 — 10/197; 11. ♗f6 ef6 12. 0-0-0 ♗d6 13. ♖he1±] g5 12. ♗e5 ♗g7 13. ♕d3±

45 9... ♕b6 10. ♗b5 ♗d7 11. ♗f6 ef6 12. ♗d7 ♔d7 13. ♕g4 ♔d8 14. ♘ge2=∞→

46 **7... a6** 8. ♘f3 b5 9. d5 ♘a5 10. ♗e2 ♗b7 11. ♘b5± Cejtlin–Krutjanski, SSSR 1971 — 11/157; **7... ♘d4** 8. ♘f3 ♘f3 9. ♕f3±

47 15. ♗f4± Paronlek–Lundkvist, corr. 1970 — 10/196

48 7... ♕b2? 8. ♖c1 ♘b4 9. ♘a4 ♕a2 10. ♗c4 ♗g4 11. ♘f3 ♗f3 12. gf3 1 : 0 Botvinik–Spielmann, Moskva 1935

49 **8. ♖c1** e5=; **8. ♘f3** ♘f3 [8... ♕b2 9. ♖c1 ♘f3 10. ♕f3±] 9. ♕f3 ♗d7±; **8. ♘ge2** ♘f5 [8... ♘e2 9. ♗e2 ♕b2? 10. ♘b5 ♘e4 11. ♖b1 ♕a2 12. ♘c7 ♔d8 13. ♘e6!+–] 9. ♕d2 [9. ♘g3∞] h6 [9... ♘d6 10. ♘g3±] 10. ♗f4 [10. ♗f6 ef6 11. ♘g3 ♗d6= Polugajevski–Bagirov, SSSR (ch) 1969 — 7/175] g5 11. ♗e5 ♘g4 12. ♗d4±

50 10. ♕a4 ♔e7 11. b4?! ♗b4 12. ♘e2 ♖d8 13. ♖c1 ♗e6 [13... ♘g4!?] 14. a3 ♗c5∓ Estrin–Bagirov, SSSR 1958; 11. 0-0-0∞ Euwe

51 10... ♔f7 11. ♗c4△ ♘ge2±

52 11. ♘ge2 ♕b2 12. ♖c1 ♖d8 13. ♘d4 ♗d4 14. ♕e2 [14. ♗d4 ♖d4=] ♕e2 15. ♗e2= Muhitdinov–Makagonov, SSSR 1962

53 **11... ♕b2** 12. ♘ge2 ♘c2 13. ♕c2 ♕a1 14. ♗c1 b5 15. ♗b3 ♗b7 16. 0–0 ♖hc8 17. ♗f4± Dely–Sallay, Hungary 1964; **11... ♗g4** 12. ♕c1 [12. ♕g4 ♘c2 13. ♔d1? ♖ad8 –+; 13. ♔f1 ♘g4 14. ♘d5 ♔f8 15. ♘b6 ♘ge3 16. fe3 ♗b6 17. ♖c1 ♘e3 18. ♔e2 ♖c8 19. b3 ♘c4∓] ♗f5 13. ♗d4 ♗d4 14. ♕d2 ♖hc8 15. ♗b3 ♗e6 16. ♘f3± Schardtner–Sallay, Hungary 1969

54 12... ♕b2 13. 0–0! [13. ♕c1 ♘f3 14. gf3 ♕b4 15. ♗c5 ♕c5 16. ♕e3 ♕e3 17. fe3 ♗e6= Žuhovicki–Bagirov, SSSR 1957] ♕c3 14. ♖c1 ♕b2 15. ♖e1 ♔f8 16. ♘d4 ♗d4 [16... ♖d4 17. ♕h5! ♘h5 18. ♗d4 ♕f2 19. ♗f2 ♗f2 20. ♔f2+– Romanov] 17. ♕d3 [Romanov–Flerov, corr. 1963] b6 [17... ♕b6 18. ♗d4 ♖d4 19. ♖e8 ♘e8 20. ♕h7+–] 18. ♖cd1 ♗f5 19. ♕f5 ♗e3 20. fe3 ♖d2 21. ♕f3 ♖ad8 22. ♗b3±

55 15. ♗b3 a5 16. 0–0 a4 [Röthgen–Gelenczei, corr. 1967 — 3/167] 17. ♗d1!± Boleslavski

56 **7. ♕d2** e5 [7... dc4 8. ♗c4 e5 9. d5 ♘d4 10. f4± Keres–Czerniak, Buenos Aires (ol) 1939] 8. ♗f6 gf6 9. ♘d5 ♕d2 10. ♔d2 ♗h6 [Sajtar–Pachman, ČSSR 1944] 11. ♔c3 ed4 12. ♔b3 0–0 13. ♗d3±; **7. ♘f3** ♗g4 [7... ♘e4?! 8. cd5±] 8. ♗f6 [8. ♗e2? dc4 9. ♗f6 ef6 10. d5 ♗f3 11. gf3 0-0-0∓ Heuer–Talj, SSSR 1972 — 14/206] ef6 9. cd5 ♗b4 10. ♕b3 ♗f3 11. dc6 ♗c6 12. ♗c4 ♗a4∓ Alburt–Ruderfer, SSSR 1970 — 10/198

57 11... ♗h3?! 12. gh3 ♕f3 13. ♕e3± Estrin–Onat, Albena 1974 — 18/186

B 14

1. e4 c6 2. d4 d5 3. ed5 cd5 4. c4 ♘f6 5. ♘c3

	5	6	7	8	9	10	11	12	13	
1	... g6	♗g5[1] ♗g7	♘f3[2] ♘e4	cd5 ♘g5	♘g5 0–0	♗c4[3] e5	♘f3 ed4	♘d4 ♕h4	♘ce2 ♗g4[4]	=∞
2	... ...	cd5 ♗g7	♗c4[5] 0–0	♘ge2 ♘bd7	♘f4 ♘b6[6]	♗b3 ♗f5[7]	0–0 ♘c8[8]	♖e1 ♘d6	h3 ♖c8[9]	±
3	... ...	... ♘d5	♕b3[10] ♘b6[11]	♗b5 ♗d7[12]	♘f3 ♗g7	♘e5 0–0	♘d7 ♘8d7	♗e3 ♘f6	0–0 ♘fd5[13]	=

1. e4 c6 2. d4 d5 3. ed5 cd5 4. c4 ♘f6 5. ♘c3 g6 6. ♕b3 ♗g7[14] 7. cd5 0–0

	8	9	10	11	12	13	14	15	16	
4	♗g5[15] ♕a5	♗f6 ef6	0-0-0 ♘d7	♔b1 ♘b6	♗d3 ♗g4	♖c1 ♗h6	♖c2 ♖ad8	h3 ♖fe8	♘ge2 ♗e2[16]	=

	8	9	10	11	12	13	14	15	16	
5	♘ge2 ♖e8	g3[17] e6	de6[18] ♗e6	♕b7 ♘bd7	♗g2 ♖b8	♕a6[19] ♘b6	b3 ♘fd5	0–0 ♘c3	♘c3 ♕d4[20]	=
6	g3 ♘bd7[21]	♗g2 ♘b6[22]	♘ge2 ♗f5	♘f4[23] h6[24]	0–0 g5	♘fe2 ♕d7	f4[25] g4	a4		∞
7	... e6	de6[26] ♘c6	ef7 ♔h8	♘ge2 ♕e7	♗e3 ♘g4	♔d2[27] ♗e6	d5 ♗f7	♗h3 ♘ge5	♖ad1 ♘a5[28]	=∞
8	♗e2 ♘bd7[29]	♗f3[30] ♘b6	♗g5[31] ♗g4[32]	♗f6 ♗f3	♘f3 ♗f6[33]	a4 ♕c7	0–0 ♖fd8	a5 ♕c4	♖a3	±

1. e4 c6 2. d4 d5 3. ed5 cd5 4. c4 ♘f6 5. ♘c3 e6

	6	7	8	9	10	11	12	13	14	
9	♘f3[34] ♘c6[35]	c5 ♗e7[36]	♗b5 0–0	0–0 ♗d7	a3[37]					±
10	... ♗e7	c5[38] 0–0[39]	♗d3[40] b6	b4 a5[41]	♘a4 ♘fd7[42]	h4[43] f5[44]	♘g5 ♕e8	♔f1 ab4	♘e6 ♘c5[45]	∞
11	... ...	♗g5 ♘c6	♖c1[46] 0–0	c5 ♘e4	♗e7 ♕e7	♗e2 ♘c3[47]	♖c3 e5	♘e5 ♘e5	♖e3	±
12	... ...	... 0–0	c5[48] b6	b4 a5	a3 ♘e4	♗e7 ♕e7	♘e4[49] de4	♘e5 ♘d7[50]		=
13	... ...	cd5 ed5[51]	♗b5 ♗d7[52]	♗d7[53] ♘bd7	0–0[54] 0–0	♕b3 ♘b6	♗g5 ♖e8	♖fe1		±

1 6. ♘f3 ♗g7 7. ♗e2 0–0 8. 0–0 ♘c6 9. h3 dc4 10. ♗c4 b6= Burger–Benkö, USA (ch) 1969 — 8/153

2 7. ♗f6 ♗f6 8. ♘d5 ♗g7 9. ♘f3 ♘c6=

3 10. ♕d2 ♘d7 11. ♗c4 a6 12. a4 ♕b6 13. ♘f3 ♕b4 14. ♗e2 ♘b6 15. a5 ♘c4 16. ♗c4 ♕c4∓ Enevoldsen–Karaklajić, Beverwijk 1967 — 3/169

4 14. ♖c1 ♘d7=∞ Bessenay–Marić, France 1971 — 11/159

5 7. ♗b5 ♘bd7 8. d6 0–0 [8... ed6 9. ♕e2 ♔f8 10. ♘f3 h6 (Velimirović–Gliksman, Jugoslavija 1968 — 6/162) 11. 0–0±; 9... ♕e7 10. ♕e7 ♔e7 11. ♘f3±] 9. de7 ♕e7 10. ♘ge2 a6 11. ♗d3 b5 12. 0–0 ♗b7 13. ♗g5 [13.a3 ♖fe8 14. ♗g5 1/2 : 1/2 Minić–Bronštejn, Vinkovci 1970 — 10/200] ♘b6 14. ♕d2 ♖fe8 15. ♘g3 ♕d7 16. ♘ce2 ♘e4 17. ♗e4 ♗e4 18. b3 ♘d5 19. f3 1/2 : 1/2 Bronštejn–Gurgenidze, SSSR 1972

6 9... ♘e8 10. 0–0 ♘d6 11. ♗b3 ♘b6 12. ♗e3 ♗d7 [Padevski–Bilek, Nice (ol) 1974 — 17/215] 13. ♘d3±

7 10... ♕d6 11. 0–0 ♗d7 12. ♖e1 a5 13. a4 ♖fc8 14. h3 h6 15. ♖e5 ♘c4 16. ♕e2± Talj–Wade, Tallinn 1971 — 11/158

8 11... ♕d7 12. ♖e1 a5 13. a4 ♖fd8 14. h4 h5 15. ♕e2± Szabo–Kostro, Luhačovice 1971 — 12/196

9 14. ♗d2 ♘fe4 15. ♘e4 ♘e4 [Cejtlin–Ritov, SSSR 1972 — 13/209] 16. ♗e3±

10 **7. ♗b5** ♗d7 8. ♕b3 ♘b6 9. ♘f3 ♗g7= Degenhardt–Delander, BRD 1967 — 3/171; **7. ♗c4** ♘b6 8. ♗b3 ♗g7 9. ♘f3 [9. ♘ge2 0–0 10. 0–0 ♗f5 11. d5 ♘a6 12. ♗e3 ♘c8= Bisguier–Larsen, Palma de Mallorca 1971 — 12/197] ♘c6 10. a4 ♘d4 11. ♘d4 ♕d4 12. ♕d4 ♗d4 13. a5 ♘d7 14. ♘d5 ♗e5 15. 0–0=∞ Cejtlin–Vorotnikov, SSSR 1973 — 15/181

11 7... ♘c3 8. ♗c4 e6 9. bc3 ♘c6 10. ♘f3 ♗g7 11. ♗a3 ♗f8 12. 0–0 ♗a3 13. ♕a3 ♕e7 14. ♕c1± Talj–Pohla, SSSR 1972 — 14/207

12 8... ♘8d7 9. a4 a5 10. h4 ♗g7 11. h5 0–0 12. hg6 hg6 13. ♘ge2 e5 14. ♘e4± Velimirović–Vukić, Jugoslavija 1970 — 9/150

13 **13... e6**? 14. d5± Mesing–Atanasov, Varna 1973 — 15/183; **13... ♘fd5** 14. ♘d5 ♘d5=

14 6... dc4 7. ♗c4 e6 8. d5 ed5 9. ♘d5 ♘d5 10. ♗d5 ♕e7 11. ♗e3 ♗g7 12. ♘f3 0–0 13. 0–0 ♘c6 14. ♖fe1± Boleslavski

15 **8. ♗d3** ♘a6 9. ♘ge2 ♘c7 10. ♘f4 b6 11. 0–0 ♗b7 12. ♗c4 ♕d6=; **8. ♗f4** ♘bd7

9. d6 ed6 10. ♗d6 ♖e8=; **8. ♗c4** ♘bd7 9. ♘ge2 ♘b6 10. 0–0 ♘c4 11. ♕c4 b6 12. ♗g5 ♗b7 13. ♘f4 ♕d7= Aljehin–Euwe, Bern 1932; **8. ♘f3** ♘bd7 9. ♗g5 ♘b6 10. ♗f6 [10. ♗c4 ♗f5 11. ♖d1 ♘e4 12. 0–0 ♘c3 13. bc3 ♖c8∓ Talj–Bronštejn, SSSR (ch) 1961; 11. ♗f6=] ef6!=

16 Vasjukov–Bronštejn, Kislovodsk 1968 — 6/233

17 **9. ♗g5** e6 10. de6 ♗e6 11. ♕b7 ♘bd7 12. 0-0-0 ♕a5 13. ♕b5 ♕b5 14. ♘b5 ♗a2=; **9. ♘f4**!?

18 **10. d6** ♕d6 11. ♗g2 ♘c6 12. 0–0 ♘d5= Cejtlin–Buhman, SSSR 1973 — 15/182; **10. ♗g2** ed5 11. ♗e3=

19 **13. ♕a7** ♗c4 14. ♗f3 ♘d5 15. ♘d5 [15. ♕a4 ♘7b6∓] ♖e2 16. ♗e2 ♗d5∓; **13. ♕f3** ♗g4 14. ♕f4 ♕a5 15. f3 ♘d5 16. ♕d2 ♘e3∓

20 **17. ♗b2** ♕d2 18. ♖ab1 ♗c3 19. ♖fd1 ♕c2 20. ♖dc1 ♕b2∓; **17. ♗f4** ♕c3 18. ♗b8 ♖b8 19. ♕a7 ♗e5 20. ♖ac1 ♕b4=

21 8... ♘a6 9. ♗g2 ♕b6 10. ♕b6 ab6 11. ♘ge2 ♘b4 12. 0–0 ♖d8 13. d6 ♖d6 [13... ed6 14. ♗g5 ♖e8 15. a3 ♘c6 16. ♖fe1 ♗g4 17. ♗f6 ♗f6 18. ♘d5± Talj–Botvinik, SSSR 1966 — 2/145] 14. ♗f4 ♖d7 15. ♖fd1 ♘bd5 [15... ♘fd5 16. a3 ♘f4 17. ♘f4 ♘c2 18. ♖ac1 ♘d4 19. ♘fd5±] 16. ♗e5± Spaski–Petrosjan (m) 1966 — 1/109

22 9... ♘e8?! 10. ♘ge2 ♘d6 11. ♗f4± Makaričev–Cejtlin, SSSR 1974 — 17/214

23 11. 0–0 ♕d7 12. a4 [12. ♖e1 h6 13. a4 ♖ad8 14. d6 ♕d6 15. ♘b5 ♕d7 16. ♘a7± Fuchs–Bronštejn, Berlin 1968 — 6/234] ♗h3 [12... ♗d3 13. d6 ed6 14. a5 ♗c4 15. ♕b4± Liberzon–Gurgenidze, SSSR (ch) 1969 — 7/176] 13. ♗h3 ♕h3 14. ♘f4±; 11... ♗d3△ ♗c4=

24 11... a5?! 12. 0–0 g5 13. ♘fe2 h6 14. ♖e1 ♖c8 [14... ♗d3 15. a4] 15. h3± Matanović–Vukić, Jugoslavija (ch) 1967 — 3/168

25 14. a4 ♗h3∞

26 9. ♗g2 ♘d5 10. ♘ge2 ♘c6= Gipslis–Seleznev, SSSR 1961

27 13. ♘d5 ♕f7∓

28 **16... b5**?! 17. ♕b5± Gheorghiu–Johannessen, La Habana (ol) 1966 — 2/144; **16... ♘a5**∞̅

29 **8... b6** 9. ♗f3 ♗b7 10. ♘ge2 ♕d7 [10... ♘a6 11. 0–0 ♕d7 12. ♗g5 ♖fd8 13. ♖fe1 ♘d5 14. ♗d5 ♗d5 15. ♕a3± Zinn–Brümmer, DDR (ch) 1964] 11. ♗f4 ♖d8 12. ♖c1 ♘a6 13. ♕a3 ♗f8 14. b4± Boleslavski; **8... ♘a6** 9. ♗f3 [9. ♗g5 ♕b6 10. ♕b6 ab6 11. a3 ♖d8 12. ♗f6 ♗f6 13. ♖d1 ♗f5 14. ♗c4 ♖ac8 15. ♗b3 b5∞̅ Fischer–Yanofsky, Netanya 1968 — 6/232] ♕b6 10. ♕b6 [10. ♕d1 ♖d8 11. ♘ge2 ♘b4=] ab6 11. ♘ge2 [11. ♗f4 ♘b4 12. ♔d2 ♘g4 13. ♗e3 e5 14. de6 ♗e6 15. ♗b7 ♖a7 16. ♗f3 ♖d8 17. ♘ge2±; 12... ♗f5∞] ♘b4 12. 0–0±; **8... ♘e8** 9. ♘f3 ♘d6 10. ♗f4 ♗g4 11. ♖d1 ♗f3 12. ♗f3 ♘d7 13. 0–0 ♘b6 14. ♖fe1± Vasjukov–Doda, Beograd 1964

30 9. ♘h3 ♘b6 10. ♘f4 ♗g4 [10... a5? 11. a4 ♕d6 12. 0–0 (Janošević–Gliksman, Jugoslavija (ch) 1967 — 3/170) ♗g4±] 11. ♗g4 ♘g4 12. h3 ♘f6 13. 0–0 ♕d7=

31 **10. ♘ge2** ♗f5 [10... a5?! 11. ♗f4 ♗f5 12. ♖d1 ♖c8 13. 0–0 ♖c4 14. ♕b5± Pietzsch–Spiridonov, Sofia 1967 — 4/181; 10... ♗g4 11. ♗g4 ♘g4 12. a4 ♘f6 13. ♘f4 ♕d7 14. a5 ♘c8 15. 0–0 ♘d6 16. ♖e1 ♘f5 17. ♖a4± Hort–Hennings, DDR 1972 — 14/208; 16... ♖fe8 17. h3 ♖ad8 18. ♖a4± Hort–Gipslis, Praha 1974 — 18/187; 16... ♖ac8!? Hort] 11. ♘f4 g5 12. ♘h5 [12. ♘fe2 g4 13. ♘g3 ♗g6 14. ♗e2 ♘bd5 15. ♕b7 ♖b8 16. ♕a7 ♘b4∞] ♘h5 13. ♗h5 e6 14. g4 ♗g6 15. de6 ♕d4±; **10. ♗f4** ♗g4 11. ♗g4 ♘g4 12. ♘f3 ♘f6 13. d6±

32 **10... ♗f5** 11. ♖d1 ♕c8 [11... ♕d7 12. h3 h5 13. ♘ge2 ♖ad8 14. d6 ed6 15. 0–0 d5 16. ♘g3± Levenfiš; 11... a5 12. a4 ♖c8 13. ♘ge2 ♖c4 14. ♕a2 ♕d7 15. b3 ♖c7 16. ♗f6 ♗f6 17. ♕d2± Zinn–Spiridonov, Krakow 1964; 11... ♘e8 12. ♘ge2 ♘d6 13. 0–0±] 12. h3 ♕c4 13. ♕c4 ♘c4 14. g4 ♗d7]14... ♗c2? 15. ♖d2!+– Vasjukov–Gurgenidze, SSSR (ch) 1969 — 7/177] 15. ♗c1±; **10... a5** 11. ♗f6 ef6 12. ♘ge2 ♗f5 13. ♕d1 [13. ♕b5? ♘c8 14. 0–0 ♘d6 15. ♕b3 ♗d3 16. ♖fd1 ♗c4 17. ♕c2 f5 18. ♘f4 ♖c8 19. ♗e2 b5∓ Bagirov–Gurgenidze, SSSR (ch) 1969 — 7/178] ♘c4 14. b3 ♘b2 15. ♕d2 ♘d3 16. ♔f1 ♘b4 17. a3 ♘a6 18. h3± Grabczewski–A. Zajcev, Albena 1970 — 10/199

33 12... ef6 13. 0–0 ♕d7 14. ♖ac1±

34 **6. c5** ♗e7 7. ♘f3 — 6. ♘f3; **6. ♗g5** ♘c6 7. c5 [7. cd5 ed5 8. ♗f6 ♕f6 9. ♘d5 ♕d8=; 8. ♗b5 ♗e7 9. ♘ge2 0–0 10. 0–0= Padevski–Filip, Harrachov 1966 — 1/110] ♗e7 8. ♗b5 0–0 9. ♗c6 [9. ♘f3 ♘e4 10. ♗e7 ♕e7 11. ♕c2 ♘g5 12. ♘g5 ♕g5 13. ♗c6 bc6 14. 0–0 e5= Keres–Aljehin, Nederland 1938; 10... ♘e7 11. ♖c1 b6 12. ♘e4 de4 13. ♘e5 bc5 14. ♖c5 f5∓] bc6 10. ♘f3 ♘e4 [10... ♗a6 11. ♘e5 ♕c7 12. ♕a4±] 11. ♗e7 ♕e7 12. 0–0 ♘c3=; 6... ♗e7 7. ♘f3 — 6. ♘f3

35 6... ♗b4 7. cd5 ♘d5 8. ♗d2 0–0 9. ♗d3 b6 [9... ♘c6 10. 0–0 ♘f6 11. ♗g5± Bañas–Navarovszky, Trenčanske Teplice 1974 — 18/188] 10. ♘d5 ♗d2 11. ♘d2 ed5 12. 0–0 ♗a6 13. ♘f3 [13. ♗a6 ♘a6 14. ♕a4 ♘c7 15. ♘f3 ♖e8 16. ♖fc1 ♖e4= Jansa–Spiridonov, Athens 1969 — 8/155] ♗d3 14. ♕d3 ♘c6 15. ♖ac1±

36 7... ♘e4 8. ♕c2 [8. ♗b5 ♕a5 9. ♗d2 ♘c3 10. ♗c6 bc6 11. ♗c3 ♕a6 12. ♘e5 ♗e7 13. ♘d3± Vasjukov–Pfleger, Bucuresti 1967 — 3/172; 8... ♗d7 9. 0–0 ♗e7 10. ♖e1 f5

11. ♗c6 ♗c6 (Bitman–Solovjev, SSSR 1969 — 8/154) 12. ♘e5±; 10... ♘c3 11. bc3 0–0 12. ♗f4 b6 13. cb6 ab6 14. ♗d3 ♖a3 15. ♕d2 ♕a8 16. h4 g6?! 17. h5 ♕a5 18. ♖ec1 ♖a8 19. hg6 hg6 20. ♘e5± Holmov–Milić, Beograd 1967 — 4/184; 16... ♕a5 17. ♖ec1 ♖a8∓] f5 [8... ♘c3 9. ♕c3±] 9. ♗b5 ♗d7 10. 0–0 ♗e7 11. ♗c6 bc6 12. ♗f4 0–0 13. b4± Vasjukov–Padevski, Varna 1971 — 12/198

37 **10. ♖e1** b6 [10... ♖c8 11. ♗f4 b6 12. ♗a6 bc5 13. ♗c8 ♗c8 14. ♖c1± Gheorghiu–van Geet, Wijk aan Zee 1968 — 5/160; 10... a6 11. ♗d3 b6 12. cb6 ♕b6 13. ♘e5 ♖fc8 14. ♘d5 ed5 15. ♘c6 ♖c6 16. ♖e7 ♗e6 17. ♕a4 ♔h8∞ Šamkovič–Hort, Leningrad 1967 — 4/183; 11. ♗c6±] 11. ♗c6 [11. ♕a4 ♕e8=] ♗c6 12. b4 ♘e4 13. ♘e4 de4 14. ♘e5 ♗d5=; **10. a3**± Boleslavski

38 **7. a3** 0–0 8. c5 ♘e4 9. ♕c2 f5 10. ♗e2 ♘c6 11. ♗b5 ♗f6 12. ♗c6 bc6 13. 0–0 g5∓ Keres–Konstantinopoljski, SSSR (ch) 1948; **7. ♗d3** dc4 8. ♗c4 0–0 9. 0–0 ♘c6 [9... ♘bd7 10. ♕e2 ♘b6 11. ♗b3 ♘bd5 12. ♖e1 b6 13. ♘e5 ♗b7= List–Kotov, England–SSSR 1946] 10. ♗b3 a6 11. ♖e1 ♘a5 12. ♗c2 b5∓ Korčnoj–Savon, Moskva 1971 — 12/199; **7. ♗f4** ♘c6 [7... dc4 8. ♗c4 0–0 9. 0–0 ♘c6 10. ♖c1 a6= Ljubojević–Smislov, Petropolis (izt) 1973 — 16/151] 8. a3 0–0 9. ♖c1 ♘e4 10. ♗d3 ♘c3 11. ♖c3 dc4 12. ♖c4 ♕a5 13. ♗d2 ♕d5= Keres–Talj, SSSR (ch) 1957

39 7... b6 8. b4 a5 9. ♘a4 ♘fd7 10. ♗b5 0–0 11. a3 ab4 12. ab4 e5∞

40 8. b4 ♘e4 9. ♕c2 ♘c6 [9... f5 10. ♗d3 ♗f6 11. ♖b1 g5 12. 0–0 g4 13. ♘e5 ♗e5 14. de5 ♘c6 15. f3± Estrin–Ilivicki, SSSR 1964] 10. a3 e5∓

41 9... bc5 10. bc5 ♘c6 11. 0–0 ♗d7 12. h3 ♘e8 13. ♗f4 ♗f6 14. ♗b5 ♘c7 [Fischer–Ivkov, Buenos Aires 1960] 15. ♗c6 ♗c6 16. ♕d3±

42 10... ♘bd7 11. ♗f4 [11. a3 ab4 12. ab4 bc5 13. bc5 e5 14. de5 ♘c5 15. ef6 ♘d3 16. ♕d3 ♗f6 17. ♘d4 ♕e8 18. ♗e3 ♖a4∓; 14. ♘e5 ♗c5 15. 0–0 ♘e5 16. de5 ♘e4=] ♘h5 [11... ab4 12. c6 ♘c5 13. dc5 bc5 14. 0–0 ♕a5 15. ♘b2 ♗a6∞] 12. ♗d2 [12. ♗g3 f5 13. ♘e5 ♘g3 14. ♘c6 ♕e8 15. ♘e7 ♕e7 16. hg3 ab4 17. c6 ♘f6 18. ♘b6 ♖a3∓] ab4 13. c6⩱ Simagin–A. Zajcev, corr. 1966 — 2/147

43 **11. b5** bc5 12. dc5 e5 [12... ♘c5? 13. ♘c5 ♗c5 14. ♗h7 ♔h7 15. ♘g5+–] 13. c6 e4 14. cd7 ♘d7 15. 0–0 ef3 16. ♕f3 ♘e5 17. ♕g3 ♘d3 18. ♕d3 d4= Sokolski–Simagin, corr. 1966; **11. ♕c2** ♘c6 12. b5 ♘b4 13. ♗h7 ♔h8 14. ♕b1 bc5 15. dc5∞ Nejštadt–Černišev, SSSR 1959

44 **11... h6** 12. ♖h3 [12. ♗h6 gh6 13. ♕d2 ♔g7 14. ♖h3 ♖h8 15. ♕f4∞] e5 [12... ab4 13. ♗h6 ♖e8 14. ♖g3 ♗f6 15. ♘g5 gh6 16. ♘h7±] 13. ♗h6 ♗f6 [13... e4!?] 14. ♗e3 [14. ♖g3 e4 15. ♘g5 ♘c6? 16. ♕h5+– Keller–Pomar, Lugano (ol) 1968 — 6/235; 15... ed3!∓] e4 [14... ed4 15. ♗h7 ♔h8 16. ♘g5 g6 17. ♗g6 fg6 18. h5 ♗g5 19. hg6 ♔g8 20. ♖h8 ♔g7 21. ♖h7 ♔g8 22. ♕h5 ♘f6 23. ♗d4 ♕e8 24. ♔f1 ♗a6 25. ♔g1+–] 15. ♘g5 g6 16. ♗b5±; **11... ab4** 12. ♘b6 ♘b6 13. ♗h7±

45 15. ♘ac5 bc5 16. ♘f8 c4 17. ♘h7 cd3 18. ♘g5 ♗a6 19. ♔g1 ♘c6 20. ♕f3∞ Karlsson–Mahlin, corr. 1970 — 9/151

46 8. ♗d3 dc4 9. ♗c4 0–0 10. 0–0 a6=

47 11... ♖d8 12. ♕c2 [12. 0–0 e5=] ♘c3 13. ♕c3 e5 14. ♘e5 [14. 0–0 ed4 15. ♕d2=] ♘e5 15. de5 d4 16. ♕g3 ♗f5 17. 0–0 d3⩱

48 **8. ♖c1** ♘e4=; **8. ♗d3** dc4 9. ♗c4 b6 10. 0–0 ♗a6 11. ♗a6 ♘a6 12. ♘e5 ♘b4 [12... ♖c8 13. ♕a4+–] 13. a3 ♘bd5 14. ♘c6 ♕d7 15. ♘e7 ♕e7 16. ♘d5 ed5 17. ♖e1 ♕d6 18. ♗f6 ♕f6 19. ♖e5± Unzicker–Pomar, Leysin 1967 — 4/187; 9... ♘c6!?; 9... a6=

49 12. ♘a4? ab4 13. ab4 bc5 14. bc5 ♕a7 15. ♗d3 ♕a5 16. ♘d2 ♗d7 17. ♗c2 ♗b5∓ Kan–Makagonov, SSSR (ch) 1939

50 **13... ♖d8** 14. ♗b5 ab4 15. ab4 ♖a1 16. ♕a1 bc5 17. dc5± Hort–Ćirić, Amsterdam 1970 — 10/201; **13... ♘d7**=

51 7... ♘d5± — D

52 8... ♘c6 9. ♘e5 ♗d7 10. 0–0 0–0 11. ♖e1 ♖c8 12. ♗g5 ♗e6 [12... a6!? Pachman] 13. ♗c6 bc6 14. ♘a4 h6 [14... c5 15. dc5 ♗c5 16. ♘c5 ♖c5 17. ♕d4± Pachman–Szabo, Leipzig (ol) 1960] 15. ♗f6 ♗f6 16. ♘c5± Velimirović–Benkö, Vrnjačka Banja 1973 — 15/184; 12. ♗f4±

53 9. ♕b3!?±

54 10. ♗f4±

B15 — 1. e4 c6 2. d4 d5 3. ♘c3

	3	4	5	6	7	8	9	10	11	
1	...	a3[1]	♘e4	♘f6	a4[3]	♗c4	♕e2	♕e7	♘e2	±
	b5	de4	♘f6[2]	ef6	b4	♗d6	♕e7	♔e7	♗e6[4]	
2	...	♘f3	h3	♗f4[6]	♘e4	c3	♗d3	0–0	♖e1[8]	±
	g6	♗g7	♘h6[5]	de4[7]	♘f5	0–0	b6	♗b7		

	3	4	5	6	7	8	9	10	11	
3	...	...	...	♘e4	♗c4[10]	♘f6[11]	0—0	♖e1[12]	♘e5[14]	±
	...	...	de4	♘d7[9]	♘gf6	♘f6	0—0	♗f5[13]	♗e4[15]	
4	...	e5	f4	♗e3[16]	♘f3[17]	♗e2	♕d2[19]	g3	♗f2	±
	...	♗g7	h5	♘h6	♗g4	e6[18]	♘d7	♘f5	b5[20]	
5	...	f3[21]	♘f3	♗c4[23]	0—0	♘e5	♕f3			∓
	de4	ef3[22]	♗f5	e6	♗e7	♗g6	♘f6[24]			
6	...	♘e4	♘f3	♗c4[26]	♘f6	c3[29]	♗h6	♕d2	h4	±
	...	g6[25]	♗g7	♘f6[27]	♗f6[28]	0—0[30]	♗g7[31]	♘d7	♘f6[32]	
7	...	...	♘g3[33]	♘f3	♘d4[35]	♘df5[37]	♔d1	♗c4	♖e1	±
	...	♘f6	e5[34]	ed4	♗e7[36]	♕d1[38]	♗f8	♗e6	♔d7[39]	
8	...	...	...	♘f3	♗d3	dc5	a3	0—0	b4	=
	...	...	c5	e6[40]	♘c6	♗c5	0—0	b6	♗e7[41]	

1. e4 c6 2. d4 d5 3. ♘c3 de4 4. ♘e4 ♘f6 5. ♘f6 ef6

	6	7	8	9	10	11	12	13	14	
9	c3[42]	♗d3	♕c2[44]	♘e2	h4	h5	hg6	♕b3[46]	♕b7	=
	♗d6	0—0[43]	♖e8	g6	♘d7[45]	♘f8	fg6	♗e6	♗d5[47]	
10	♗c4	♕e2	♗b3[50]	ab3	♘e2	♗f4	♘f4	c3[52]	b4	±
	♕e7[48]	♗e6[49]	♗b3[51]	♕e2	♗d6	♗f4	♘a6	0-0-0	♔b8[53]	
11	...	♘e2[54]	0—0	♗b3[56]	♘f4	♖e1	♖e8	♗e3	♕d2	±
	♗e7	0—0	♘d7[55]	♖e8	♘f8	♗d6	♕e8	♕e4	♘g6[57]	
12	...	♘e2[58]	♗e3	♕d2	0-0-0	♗f4	♗d6	♗d3		=
	♗d6	♕c7[59]	0—0	♖e8[60]	♘d7	♘b6[61]	♕d6	♗e6		
13	...	♕e2	♘f3[63]	c3	h3	g4	♘h4	♗b3	♗d2[65]	±
	...	♗e7[62]	♗g4[64]	♘d7	♗h5	♗g6	♘b6	♘d5		
14	...	...	♕e7	♘e2[66]	♗d3[68]	♗f4	♗d6	b3	c4	±
	...	♕e7	♔e7	♗e6[67]	♘d7[69]	♘b6[70]	♔d6	♔c7	♖ad8[71]	

[1] 4. e5 e6 5. a3 a5 6. ♘ce2 ♗a6 7. ♘f4 b4 8. ♗a6 ♘a6 9. ab4 ab4 10. ♘f3 ♗e7 11. h4 h5 12. ♘g5 ♗g5 13. hg5 g6 14. g4 h4 15. ♗e3±↑ I. Zajcev—Gurgenidze, SSSR (ch) 1968

[2] 5... ♗f5 6. ♗d3! ♗e4 [6... ♕d4 7. ♘f3 ♕d5 8. ♕e2±↑ Petrosjan, Suetin] 7. ♗e4 ♘f6 8. ♗d3 ♕d4 [8... e6 9. ♘f3 ♗e7 10. ♕e2 ♘bd7 11. 0—0 0—0 12. ♖e1 ♖e8 13. ♘e5± Talj—Gurgenidze, SSSR (ch) 1968 — 7/179] 9. ♘f3 ♕d5 10. 0—0 e6 11. ♖e1$\overline{\overline{\infty}}$

[3] **7. ♘f3** ♗d6 8. ♗d3 0—0 9. 0—0 ♗g4 10. a4 b4 11. c4 bc3 12. bc3 ♘d7 13. ♗e4 f5 14. ♗c6 ♖c8 15. ♗d7 ♖c3 16. ♗f5 ♗f5$\overline{\overline{\infty}}$ Kuprejčik—Bokučava, Dubna 1970; **7. c3** ♗d6 8. ♗d3 0—0 9. ♕f3 ♗e6 10. ♘e2 ♗d5 11. ♕h3 g6 12. 0—0 ♘d7 13. a4 ba4 14. ♖a4 ♖e8= Šmit—Bronštejn, SSSR 1970 — 10/206

[4] 12. ♗d3 ♘d7 13. 0—0 ♖ac8 14. ♖e1± Klovan—Gurgenidze, SSSR (ch) 1968

[5] 5... ♘f6 6. e5 ♘e4!? [6... ♘fd7 7. ♗f4 e6 8. ♕d2±○ Paoli—Bönsch, Olomouc 1973] 7. ♗d3! [7. ♘e4 de4 8. ♘g5 c5 9. ♗c4 0—0 10. e6 f6 11. ♘e4 b5 12. ♗e2 cd4 13. ♗f3 ♘c6 14. 0—0 ♕b6 15. ♖e1 ♗b7 16. ♗f4 ♖fd8= Spaski—Ceškovski, SSSR 1974 — 18/192; 9. e6 ♗e6 10. ♘e6 fe6 11. dc5 ♕d1 12. ♔d1 0—0 13. ♔e2 ♘a6 14. ♗e3 ♖ac8= Timoščenko—Mačulski, SSSR 1974; 9. dc5 ♕a5 10. ♗d2 ♕c5 11. ♗c3 ♘d7 12. ♗d4 ♕d5 13. e6! ♗d4 14. ♕d4± Karasev—Nebolsin, SSSR 1969 — 8/157; 12... ♕a5!?∞] ♘c3 8. bc3 c5 9. dc5 ♕a5 10. 0—0 0—0 11. ♗e3 ♘d7 12. c4± Gheorghiu—Cardoso, Torremolinos 1974 — 18/191; 9... ♘c6!?

[6] **6. ♗d3** 0—0 7. 0—0 f6 8. ♖e1 ♘f7 9. ♕e2 [9. e5 fe5 10. de5 e6 11. h4 c5∓ Balašov—Lutikov, SSSR 1969; 9. a4 e5 10. de5 fe5 11. b4 ♗e6 12. ♗a3 ♖e8 13. ♗f1 d4= Penrose—Ciocaltea, Nice (ol) 1974] e5 10. ♗e3 f5?! 11. ef5 e4 12. fg6 hg6 13. ♘e4∞ Koc—Lutikov, SSSR 1970 — 10/207; **6. e5** f6 7. ♗f4 0—0 8. ♕d2 ♘f7 9. 0-0-0 b6 10. ♖e1 a5 11. ♗d3±↑ Cejtlin—Buhman, SSSR 1967

[7] **6... f6**? 7. ed5 cd5 8. ♘b5 ♘a6 [8... 0—0 9. c4 g5 10. ♗c7 ♕d7 11. ♗h2± Veli-

mirović—Ciocaltea, Reykjavik 1974] 9. c4 0—0 10. ♕b3 e5∞ Keres—Kärner, Tallinn 1973 — 15/187; 10. cd5!±; **6... ♕b6** 7. ♕d2 de4 8. ♘a4 ♕d8 9. ♗h6 ♗h6 10. ♕h6± Žuravljev—Cejtlin, SSSR 1972; **6... 0—0** 7. ♕d2 de4 8. ♘e4±

8 Ničevski—Notaroš, Jugoslavija 1973 — 16/153

9 **6... ♘f6**?! 7. ♘f6 ♗f6 8. ♗c4 ♕d6 [8... ♗f5 9. 0—0 ♘d7 10. ♖e1 ♘b6 11. ♗b3 h5 12. ♘e5± Najdorf—Rossetto, Argentina 1973 — 16/154] 9. ♕e2 a5 10. 0—0 b5 11. ♗d3 ♗f5 12. a4 b4 13. ♗c4± Vasjukov—Basman, Varna 1971 — 12/201; **6... ♗f5** 7. ♘g3 ♘f6 [7... ♘d7 8. ♗c4 ♘gf6 9. ♕e2 e6 10. ♗b3± Johansson—Botvinik, Varna (ol) 1962] 8. ♘f5 gf5 9. ♗d3 e6 10. ♕e2 c5 [10... 0—0 11. g4±] 11. dc5 [11. ♗f5±] ♕a5 12. c3 [12. ♗d2 ♕c5 13. ♗c3 ♘c6 14. 0-0-0 0-0-0 15. g4 ♘e8= Šahović—Botvinik, Beograd 1969 — 8/158] ♕c5 13. ♗e3±

10 7. ♗d3 ♘gf6 8. ♘f6! [8. 0—0 ♘e4 9. ♗e4 0—0 10. c3 ♕c7 11. ♖e1 c5 12. ♗g5 cd4 13. ♘d4 ♘c5= Estrin—Ceškovski, SSSR 1973] ♘f6 9. 0—0 0—0 10. ♖e1 ♕d6 11. ♗g5 c5 12. ♕e2 e6 13. dc5 ♕c5 14. ♗e3 ♕c7 15. ♗d4 b6 16. a4 ♗b7 17. a5± Kottnauer—Hübner, Hastings 1968/69

11 8. ♕e2 ♘e4 9. ♕e4 ♘b6 [9... ♘f6 10. ♕h4±] 10. ♗b3 a5 11. a4 ♗f5 12. ♕h4 ♕d7 [Keres—Donner, Amsterdam 1971 — 12/200] 13. ♗h6!± ♗h6? 14. ♗f7+— Keres

12 10. ♗f4 b6 11. ♕e2 ♗b7 12. ♖ad1 e6 13. ♘e5 ♕e7 14. ♗a6± Gufeljd—Spiridonov, Tbilisi 1969 — 9/152

13 **10... ♘d5** 11. c3 a5 12. a4 b6 13. ♕e2 ♗f5 14. ♗g5± Browne—Kovačević, Rovinj-Zagreb 1970; **10... b6** 11. ♗g5 ♗b7 12. ♕e2 e6 13. ♘e5 ♕d6 14. ♗b3 h6 15. ♗h4± Ghizdavu—Spiridonov, Bucuresti 1971 — 12/202; **10... e6** 11. ♕e2 [11. ♕d3 b6 12. ♗g5 c5 13. ♘e5 ♗b7 14. dc5 bc5 15. ♕g3 ♕c7∓ Lutikov—Bronštejn, SSSR (ch) 1964] b6 12. ♗g5 ♗b7 13. ♖ad1±

14 11. ♗g5 ♕c7 [11... ♖e8 12. c3 ♕b6 13. ♕c1 ♖ad8 14. ♗b3 ♕c7= Parma—Donner, La Habana 1971] 12. ♕e2 ♖ae8 13. c3 ♘d5 14. ♕d2 ♘f6 15. ♕f4=

15 12. ♗g5 ♗d5 13. ♗d3 ♗e6 14. c3 ♘d7 15. ♘f3± Talj—Kolarov, Kapfenberg 1970 — 10/205

16 **6. ♘f3** ♗g4 7. h3 ♗f3 8. ♕f3 e6 9. g3 [9. ♗e3 h4 10. ♗d3 ♘e7 11. 0—0 ♘d7 12. ♗f2 ♘f5= Liberzon—Smislov, SSSR (ch) 1967] ♕b6 10. ♕f2 ♘e7 11. ♗d3 ♘d7 12. ♘e2 0-0-0 13. c3 f6= Fischer—Petrosjan, Beograd 1970 — 9/154; **6. ♗d3** ♘h6 7. ♘f3 ♗f5 8. 0—0= Krogius—Bronštejn, SSSR (ch) 1967 — 3/120

17 7. ♕d2?! ♘g4 8. ♘f3 ♘e3 9. ♕e3 ♗g4= Savon—Gurgenidze, Gori 1970 — 11/96

18 8... ♗f3?! 9. ♗f3 e6 10. ♗f2 [10. g3 ♘f5 11. ♗f2 ♘d7 12. ♕d2± Radulov—Bohosjan, Bulgaria 1970 — 11/161] ♘d7 11. 0—0 ♕a5 12. a3 ♘f5 13. ♕e2 ♗f8 14. g3 c5 15. b4± Gaprindašvili—Polihroniade, Medellin 1974

19 **9. g3**?! ♘f5 10. ♗f2 h4 11. ♖g1 ♗f8 12. ♘g5 ♗e2 13. ♘e2 hg3 14. hg3 [Radulov—Arnaudov, Bulgaria 1970 — 11/163] c5! 15. c3 cd4= Božić; **9. 0—0** ♗f8 10. h3 ♘f5 11. ♗f2 ♗f3 12. ♗f3 h4 13. ♘e2± Klovan—Podgajec, SSSR 1974 — 18/189

20 12. h3 ♗f3 13. ♗f3± Radulov—Velikov, Bulgaria 1970 — 11/162

21 **4. ♗e3** ♘f6 5. f3 ef3 6. ♕f3 ♗g4 7. ♕f2 e6∓ Gunderam; **4. ♗c4** ♘f6 5. f3 ef3 [5... e3!?; 5... ♗f5 6. ♕e2 ef3 7. ♘f3 e6 8. 0—0 ♗e7 9. ♗g5 ♘bd7 10. ♖ad1 0—0 11. ♔h1 ♕c7∓] 6. ♘f3 e6∓ Pachman

22 **4... e3**!?; **4... e5** 5. de5 ♕d1 6. ♘d1 ef3∓

23 6. ♘e5 ♘d7 7. ♕f3 e6△ ♘e5∓ Gunderam

24 Gunderam

25 **4... e5**? 5. ♘f3! ♗g4 [5... ed4 6. ♕d4±; 6. ♗c4±] 6. ♗c4 [△ ♗f7] ♗h5 7. g4 ♗g6 8. ♘e5 ♗e4 9. ♗f7+—; **4... f5**? 5. ♘c3±; **4... ♘h6**? 5. ♗h6 gh6 6. ♗c4△ ♕h5±

26 **6. ♗e2** ♘d7 [6... ♗g4 7. c3 ♘d7 8. ♘fg5 ♗e2 9. ♕e2 ♘df6 10. ♗f4± Andersson—Benkö, Palma de Mallorca 1971 — 12/203] 7. 0—0 ♘gf6= Parma; **6. h3** — 3... g6

27 6... ♘d7?! 7. ♗f7!?

28 7... ef6 8. 0—0 0—0 9. ♖e1 ♗g4 10. c3± Jansa—Sitiriche, Tel Aviv (ol) 1964

29 8. ♗h6? ♕a5 9. c3 ♕h5 10. ♕d2 ♗h3! 11. ♘e5 ♗e5∓ Agejčenko—Bunatjan, SSSR 1964

30 8... ♗g7!?

31 9... ♖e8 10. ♘g5 e6 11. h4±

32 11. h5± Sherwin—Denker, New York 1968 — 5/164

33 **5. ♕d3** ♘e4 6. ♕e4 ♕d5=; **5. ♘g5** e6 [5... ♗f5!?] 6. f4 ♗d6 7. ♗c4 0—0 8. ♘e2 ♘bd7 9. 0—0 ♘b6 10. ♗b3 c5= Osičanski—Kiričenko, corr. 1968 — 5/165; **5. ♗d3** ♘e4 6. ♗e4 ♗f5=

34 5... h5 6. h4 [6. ♗c4? h4 7. ♘3e2 b5 8. ♗b3 h3 9. ♘h3 ♗h3 10. gh3 ♘bd7 11. ♕d3 e5∓ Pohla—Gerčikov, Tallinn 1965] ♗g4 7. ♗e2 ♗e2 8. ♘1e2 ♘bd7 9. ♕d3± Spielmann—Aljehin, Karlovy Vary 1911

35 7. ♕d4 ♕d4 8. ♘d4 ♗c5 9. ♘df5 0—0 10. ♗e3 ♗e3 11. ♘e3 ♗e6 12. 0-0-0 ♘bd7= Aljehin—Capablanca, New York 1927

36 7... ♗c5? 8. ♕e2 ♗e7 [8... ♕e7 9. ♕e7 ♗e7 10. ♘df5±] 9. ♗e3 c5 10. ♘df5

0—0 11. ♕c4± Aljehin—Tartakower, Kecskemet 1927

37 8. ♗e2 0—0 9. 0—0 ♗c5 10. ♘b3 ♕d1 11. ♖d1 ♗b6=

38 8... ♕a5? 9. ♗d2 ♕e5 10. ♕e2±

39 12. ♗e6 fe6 13. ♘e3± Boleslavski

40 6... ♘c6 7. ♗e3 ♘d5 [7... cd4 8. ♘d4 ♕a5 9. c3 ♗d7= Boleslavski] 8. ♗e2 e6 9. 0—0 ♗e7 10. ♗c1 0—0 11. dc5 ♗c5= Cvetkov—Sokolski, Moskva 1947

41 12. ♗b2 ♗b7= Spielmann—Hönlinger, Wien 1929

42 **6. g3** ♕d5 [6... ♗d6 7. ♗g2 0—0 8. ♘e2 ♗f5 9. 0—0 ♖e8 10. c4 ♘a6 11. ♘c3 ♕d7 12. a3 ♗h3 13. ♗e3± Rauzer—Rabinovič, SSSR (ch) 1933; 6... ♗e6 7. ♗g2 ♗d6 8. ♘e2 0—0 9. 0—0± Boleslavski] 7. ♘f3 ♗d6 [7... ♗g4 8. ♗e2 ♗e7 9. h3 ♗h5 10. 0—0±; 7... ♗f5 8. c3 ♗e7 9. ♕e2± Boleslavski] 8. ♗g2 0—0 9. 0—0 ♕h5 10. c4 ♗g4= Boleslavski; **6. ♘f3** ♗d6 7. ♗d3 [7. ♗c4 0—0 8. 0—0 ♗g4 =] 0—0 8. 0—0 ♗g4 9. ♗e3 ♘d7 10. c4 c5 11. ♗c2 ♕c7 12. h3 ♗h5= Kuijpers—Flor, Amsterdam 1963

43 7... c5 8. ♘e2 ♘c6 9. ♗e3 ♕e7 10. dc5 ♗c5 11. ♗c5 ♕c5 12. ♕c2 ♗e6 13. 0—0± Gurgenidze—Holmov, SSSR (ch) 1967 — 3/176

44 **8. ♘e2** ♘d7 [8... ♕c7? 9. ♕c2 g6 10. h4 ♗e6 11. h5 f5 12. ♗h6 ♖e8 13. 0-0-0 ♘d7 14. hg6 fg6 15. g4±→ Suetin—Andersson, Soči 1973] 9. 0—0 ♖e8 10. ♘g3 ♘f8=; **8. ♕h5** g6 9. ♕h4 c5 [9... ♘d7 10. ♘e2 c5 11. 0—0 ♕b6 12. ♗c4 cd4 13. cd4 f5 14. ♘c3 ♕b4 15. ♗b3 ♗e7 16. ♗g5± Medina—Donner, Beverwijk 1965] 10. ♘e2 ♘c6 11. ♗h6 ♖e8 [11... f5? 12. ♗g5 ♕b6 13. 0—0 cd4 14. cd4 ♖e8 15. ♗c4± Pilnik—Najdorf, Mar del Plata 1942] 12. dc5 ♗c5=

45 10... c5!? 11. h5 f5 12. hg6 hg6 13. ♗e3 [13. g4 ♕c7? 14. ♗g5± Planinc—Puc, Čačak 1969 — 8/159; 13... f4!? 14. ♗g6 ♕f6 15. ♗h7 ♔f8∞ Marić] f4 14. ♗g6 fe3? 15. ♗f7 ♔f7 16. ♖h7+— Zelevinski—Goldberg, SSSR 1961; 14... ♕f6∞

46 13. ♗h6 ♗e6 14. 0-0-0 f5 15. ♔b1 b5 16. ♘c1 ♕f6 17. f4 ♗d5 18. ♖h3 ♘e6∞ Pilnik—Golombek, Amsterdam 1951

47 15. ♔f1 [Szabo—Flor, Groningen 1946] a6 16. c4 ♖b8 17. ♕a6 ♖a8= Boleslavski

48 6... ♗e6 7. ♗e6 fe6 8. ♕h5 g6 9. ♕e2 ♔f7 10. ♘f3 ♗g7 11. 0—0 ♖e8 12. ♖e1 ♘d7 13. ♗e3 ♕c7 14. ♖ad1 ♖ad8 15. ♕c4± Matanović—Lange, Hamburg 1955

49 7... ♗g4 8. f3 ♗e6 9. ♗e6 ♕e6 10. ♗f4 ♗e7 11. ♕e6 fe6 12. ♗b8 ♖b8= Dely—Ribli, Kecskemet 1972 — 13/211; 8. ♕e7±

50 **8. ♗e6** ♕e6 9. ♘h3 g5 10. f4 g4 11. ♘f2 f5 12. h3 g3 13. ♘d3 ♘d7 14. b3 0-0-0 15. ♕e6 fe6 16. ♗b2∞ Matanović—Wade, Skopje (ol) 1972; **8. ♗d3** ♕c7 9. ♕f3 ♗d6 10. ♘e2 0—0 11. ♘g3 ♖e8 12. 0—0 ♘d7 13. ♗d2 c5?! 14. c3 ♖ad8 15. ♖fe1± Lechtynsky—Nowak, Luhačovice 1973 — 13/210; 13... ♗d5∞ Hort

51 8... ♘d7 9. ♗f4 ♘b6 10. 0-0-0 ♘d5 11. ♗d2 b5 12. ♘f3 ♕d7 13. ♘e1± Talj—Bronštejn, SSSR 1974 — 18/193

52 13. 0-0-0 0-0-0 14. ♖he1 ♖he8= Estevez—Lechtynsky, Luhačovice 1973

53 15. ♔d2± Kuijpers—Lechtynsky, Nice (ol) 1974

54 7. ♘f3 0—0 8. 0—0 — B 10

55 8... ♗d6 9. ♗f4 ♖e8 10. ♕d2 ♗e6 11. ♗d3 [11. ♗e6!?] ♗e7 12. c4 ♘d7 [Živodov—Hodos, SSSR 1969 — 8/160] 13. d5±

56 **9. ♘g3** ♘b6 10. ♗b3 ♕c7 11. ♖e1 ♗d6 12. ♕h5 ♘d5 13. ♘e4 ♗d7 14. c4 ♗b4 15. ♖d1 f5 16. ♘g3 ♘f6= Goldenov—Sokolski, SSSR 1963; **9. c3** ♘b6 10. ♗d3 ♖e8 11. ♕c2 g6 12. ♗h6 ♘d5 13. ♖fe1± Bronštejn—Hodos, SSSR 1968 — 7/180; **9. ♗f4** ♖e8 10. ♕d2±; **9. ♖e1** c5 10. c3 cd4 11. cd4 ♗b4 12. ♘c3 ♘b6 13. ♗b3 ♗f5 14. d5± Štejn—Bronštejn, Amsterdam (izt) 1964

57 **14... ♗f4** 15. ♗f4 ♗e6 16. ♖e1 ♕f5 17. c4 ♖d8 18. ♗c2±; **14... ♘g6**! 15. f3 ♕f5 16. ♘g6 hg6 17. c4±

58 **7. ♕f3** 0—0 8. ♘e2 ♘d7 9. 0—0 ♘b6 10. ♗d3 ♘d5 11. c4 ♘e7 12. ♗f4 ♘g6 13. ♗d6 ♕d6 14. ♖fe1 c5 15. ♖ad1 cd4 16. ♗g6 hg6 17. ♘d4 ♕a6= Robatsch—Flor, Amsterdam 1966; **7. ♕h5** 0—0 8. ♘e2 ♘d7 [8... g6 9. ♕f3 ♖e8 10. ♗h6 ♗f5 11. 0-0-0±→ Keres—Mikenas, Buenos Aires 1939] 9. 0—0 c5 10. dc5 ♗c5 11. ♗f4 g6 12. ♕h4 ♘b6 13. ♗b3 ♗e6 14. ♗h6 ♖e8= Gheorghiu—Donner, Hamburg 1965

59 7... 0—0 8. 0—0 ♕c7 [8... ♗e6 9. ♗b3 ♕c7 10. ♘g3 ♖e8 11. c4 c5 12. d5 ♗c8 13. f4 f5 14. ♗c2± Romanovski—Šašin, SSSR 1965] 9. ♘g3 ♘d7 10. ♖e1 [10. ♕h5 c5 11. ♗h6? ♗g3 12. fg3 ♕d6 13. ♖f4 f5 14. ♗g5 h6∓ Tenenbaum—Judovič, SSSR 1962] c5 11. ♘f5!? ♘b6 [11... ♗h2 12. ♔h1 ♘b6 13. ♘e7 ♔h8 14. ♕h5 ♘c4 15. ♖e4 ♗g3 16. fg3+— Kaplan—Donner, San Juan 1969] 12. ♗d3±↑

60 9... ♘d7? 10. ♗f4±

61 11... ♖e2 12. ♗d6 ♖d2 13. ♗c7 ♖f2 14. ♖he1 ♘f8 15. ♖e8 b5 16. ♖de1± Pachman

62 7... ♔f8 8. ♘f3 [8. ♗e3 h5 9. 0-0-0 b5 10. ♗b3 a5 11. a3 ♗a6 12. ♕f3 ♕c7 13. g4 hg4 14. ♕g4± Matulović—Johansson, Halle 1967] h5 9. ♗e3 [9. ♗d2 g6 10. 0-0-0 b5 11. ♗d3 ♔g7 12. ♖de1 ♗e6 13. ♘h4 ♗a2 14. g4 b4 15. ♖hg1± Fichtl—Novak, Stary Smokovec 1972] g6 10. 0-0-0 b5 11. ♗b3 a5 12. a4 ♗a6 13. ♕d2 ba4 14. ♗a4 ♔g7 15. d5 c5 16. ♗f4± Fink—Ždanov, corr. 1961

63 8. ♕d3 0–0 9. ♘e2 ♗d6 10. 0–0 ♕c7 [10... ♘d7 11. ♗f4 ♘b6 12. ♗b3 ♗g4 13. ♗d6 ♗e2 14. ♕e2± Klovan–Seleznev, SSSR 1966] 11. g3 b5 12. ♗b3 c5 13. ♗d5 ♘c6 14. dc5 ♗c5 15. ♕b5 ♘b4 16. ♗a8 ♗a6=∞ Boleslavski; 8. ♕h5 0–0 9. ♘e2 c5 [9... g6 10. ♕h6 ♗e6 11. ♗e6 fe6 12. ♕h3 ♕a5 13. ♗d2 ♕f5 14. ♕b3 b6 15. 0-0-0± Kostić–Tot, Jugoslavija (ch) 1947; 10... ♗f5! 11. ♗b3 c5 12. ♗e3 ♘c6 13. 0-0-0 c4! 14. ♗c4 ♘b4 15. ♗b3 ♖c8=∞ Mnacakanjan–Simagin, SSSR 1965] 10. ♗e3 ♕a5 11. ♗d2 [11. c3? ♘c6 12. dc5 ♘e5∓] ♕c7 12. ♗f4 ♕a5 13. c3 g6 14. ♕h4 cd4 15. ♘d4 ♕c5= Matulović–Kurajica, Skopje 1969 — 8/161

64 8... 0–0 9. 0–0 — B 10

65 Bogoljubov–Aljehin 1942

66 9. ♗d2 ♖d8 10. ♘e2 ♗f5 11. 0-0-0 b5 12. ♗b3 a5 13. a4 ♗e6 14. ♗e6 fe6 15. ♘c3 ♗b4= Doroškevič–Gerčikov, SSSR 1967

67 9... ♖e8 10. 0–0 ♗f5 11. c3 ♔f8 12. ♗f4± Pachman–Dobiaš, Brno 1944; 11... a5 12. ♘g3 ♗g6 13. f4 b5 14. ♗e2 h6 15. f5 ♗h7 16. ♘e4± I. Zajcev–Gerčikov, SSSR 1966

68 10. ♗b3!? ♘d7 11. 0–0 ♖he8 12. ♖e1 ♔f8 13. ♗f4 ♗f4 14. ♘f4 ♗b3 15. ab3 f5 16. f3 ♖e1 17. ♖e1 ♖e8 18. ♖a1± Kurajica–Holmov, Skopje 1969 — 7/182; 12... ♔d8!±

69 **10... c5** 11. ♗e3 c4 12. ♗e4 ♘d7 13. 0-0-0 ♖ab8 14. ♖he1 ♘b6 15. ♘c3 ♗d7 16. ♗f3± Klovan–A. Zajcev, SSSR 1969; **10... ♖d8** 11. 0–0 a5 12. ♖e1 ♘a6 13. a3 h6 14. ♗d2 ♘c7 15. ♘f4 ♗f4 16. ♗f4 ♘b5± Matanović–Bronštejn, Portorož (izt) 1958; 15. c4!?

70 11... b5 12. a4 a6 13. ♗e4 ♗d5 14. ♗d5 cd5 15. ab5 ab5 16. ♔d2± Bihovski–Goldberg, SSSR 1963

71 15. ♔d2 ♖he8 16. ♖ae1 ♘c8 17. ♔c3± Matulović–Smislov, Siegen (ol) 1970 — 10/208

B 16 — 1. e4 c6 2. d4 d5 3. ♘c3 de4 4. ♘e4 ♘f6 5. ♘f6 gf6

	6	7	8	9	10	11	12	13	14	
1	♗c4[1] ♗f5[2]	♘e2[3] e6	♘g3[4] ♗g6	h4[5] h5	♗f4[6] ♗d6	♕d2 ♕c7	♗d6 ♕d6	0-0-0 ♘d7	♖he1 0-0-0	=
2	♗f4 ♗f5[7]	♗c4 e6	♘f3[8] ♖g8[9]	0–0 ♗d6	♗d6 ♕d6	♘h4 ♗g6	f4 f5!	c3 ♘d7	♕e2[10] 0-0-0	=
3	♕d3 ♘d7[11]	♘e2 ♘b6	♘f4[12] e5	de5 fe5	♕e4 ♕e7	♘d3 ♗g7	♗d2 ♗e6[13]	♗b4 ♕g5	h4 ♕f5[14]	=
4	♗e3 ♗f5[15]	♘e2[16] ♘d7	♕d2 ♘b6[17]	♘g3 ♗g6	c4 h5	h4 e6	♗e2 ♗d6	0–0[18] ♗e7	♖ac1 f5[19]	∞
5	♘e2 ♗g4[20]	♕d3[21] ♗h5[22]	♕b3!?[23] ♕c8[24]	♘f4 ♗g6	♗c4 e6	0–0 ♘a6	♖e1 ♗e7	♘e6 fe6	♗e6 ♕c7[25]	±
6	. . . ♗f5	♘g3[26] ♗g6	h4 h6[27]	h5[28] ♗h7	c3[29] e6[30]	♗e3 ♘d7	♕d2 ♕a5	♗e2 0-0-0	♗h6[31] ♗h6[32]	=∞
7	. . . h5	♕d3[33] ♕a5[34]	♗d2 ♕f5	♕b3 ♗h6	0-0-0[35] ♕f2	♗h6 ♖h6	♘c3 e6	♗e2 ♕f4	♔b1 ♕c7[36]	=∞
8	♗e2 ♗f5	♘f3[37] e6	0–0 ♕c7[38]	c4 ♘d7[39]	d5[40] 0-0-0!	dc6[41] bc6	♗e3 ♗c5	♕c1 ♖hg8	♖d1 ♕b6[42]	=
9	. . . ♘a6	♘f3[43] ♗g4	0–0 ♘c7	c4 ♕d7	♗e3[44] ♗g7[45]	♘h4 f5!	h3 ♗e2	♕e2 f4	♗f4 ♘e6[46]	=
10	♘f3 ♗f5[47]	♗d3[48] ♗g6?!	0–0 ♕c7[49]	c4 ♘d7	d5 0-0-0	♗e3 e5	♗e2 ♔b8	♖c1 f5[50]	c5! cd5[51]	±

1. e4 c6 2. d4 d5 3. ♘c3 de4 4. ♘e4 ♘f6 5. ♘f6 gf6 6. ♘f3 ♗g4

	7	8	9	10	11	12	13	14	15	
11	♗e2[52] e6[53]	♗f4[54] ♘d7[55]	0–0 ♘b6	♖e1[56] ♗d6	♗g3 ♗g3	hg3 ♕d5	c3 h5	♕c1 0-0-0	a4 ♗f3[57]	=

	7	8	9	10	11	12	13	14	15	
12	...	h3	0–0	♗e3	c4	d5!	cd5	♗h6	♘d2	±
	...	♗h5	♗d6[58]	♘d7	♗g6[59]	ed5[60]	c5	♕a5	0-0-0[61]	
13	...	0–0[62]	c4[63]	d5[65]	♘h4[66]	♕e2	cd5	♗e3		=
	♕c7	♘d7	♖g8[64]	e5	♗e2	cd5	♘b6	♕c4[67]		
14	...	♗e3	c4[69]	♘d2[70]	♕e2	d5	♗d4	de6	0-0-0	∞
	...	♘d7[68]	e6	♗e2	f5	0-0-0	♖g8	fe6	e5[71]	
15	...	h3	0–0	d5	c4	♗e3	♗b6	♗f3	cd5	±
	...	♗h5[72]	♘d7[73]	♖d8[74]	♘b6	♗f3	ab6	cd5	♗h6[75]	

1. e4 c6 2. d4 d5 3. ♘c3 de4 4. ♘e4 ♘f6 5. ♘f6 gf6 6. c3 ♗f5[76]

	7	8	9	10	11	12	13	14	15	
16	♗c4[77]	♘e2	♘g3	♕e2[80]	f4	♘f1[81]	♘d2	♘f3	♗d2	=
	e6	h5[78]	♗g6[79]	♘d7	f5	h4	♘f6	♗h5	♗d6[82]	
17	♘f3	g3[84]	♗g2	♗f4	♗e3	0–0	♘h4	♕c2	♖ad1	±
	♕c7[83]	e6[85]	♘d7	e5	0-0-0	♔b8	♗e6	♘b6	♘c4[86]	
18	♘e2	h4[88]	♘g3	♗e2	♕e2	0–0	c4	a3[89]	♘e4	=
	h5[87]	♘d7	♗g4	♗e2	♕a5	0-0-0	e6	♗d6[90]	♗b8[91]	
19	...	♘g3	f3[92]	♗d3[93]	♘e2	♗h6	♕d2	♘f4	0–0[95]	±
	...	♗g4	♗e6	♕c7[94]	♗h6	♖h6	♖h8	♕d6		

[1] 6. g3?! ♕d5 7. ♘f3 ♗f5 [7... ♗g4?! 8. ♗g2 ♘d7 9. 0–0 e5 10. h3! ♗f3 11. ♗f3 ♕d4 12. ♕e2 ♘b6 13. ♗e4±↑⧉ Simagin–Jansen, corr. 1968] 8. c3 [8. c4 ♕e4 9. ♕e2 ♘a6 10. a3 0-0-0 11. ♗g2 e5 12. ♕e4 ♗e4 13. de5 ♘c5?! 14. 0–0 ♘b3 15. ♗f4!∞ Lilienthal–Toluš, SSSR (ch) 1945; 13... fe5!∓] ♘d7 9. ♗g2 ♕c4 10. ♗e3 ♘b6 11. ♘d2 ♕a6 12. ♗f1 ♕a5 13. ♗e2 ♘d5= Fletzer–Gligorić, Venezia 1949

[2] 6... ♕c7? 7. ♕h5!± Jamieson–Talj, Nice (ol) 1974 — 17/219

[3] **7. ♗f4** — 6. ♗f4; **7. ♘f3** — 6. ♘f3; **7. c3** — 6. c3

[4] 8. 0–0 h5? 9. ♖e1 ♗d6 10. ♘g3 ♗g6 11. ♘e4 [11. ♕f3!? ♗c2? 12. ♗f4 ♗f4 13. ♕f4 h4 14. ♘f1 ♕e7 15. ♖e2 ♗g6 16. ♖ae1 0–0 17. ♕h6 1 : 0 Ofstad–S. Johannessen, Norge (ch) 1968] ♗e4 12. ♖e4 f5 13. ♖e1 ♕h4 14. h3 ♘d7 15. ♗e6! fe6 16. ♖e6 ♗e7 17. ♔h2!+– Koc–Savon, SSSR 1962; 8... ♗d6! 9. ♘g3 [9. ♖e1 ♕c7!] ♗g6 10. f4 [10. ♖e1 ♕c7! 11. d5?! cd5 12. ♗d5 ♘c6△ 0-0-0∓ Minev] f5=

[5] **9. f4** f5!=; **9. 0–0** ♗d6!= — 8. 0–0

[6] 10. ♗e2? ♗d6 11. ♘h5? ♗h5 12. ♗h5 ♕a5–+

[7] 6... ♕b6!? 7. ♘f3!? ♕b2 8. ♗d3∞ Poulsen–Larsen, Copenhagen 1973

[8] 8. ♕d2 ♗d6 9. ♘e2 [9. ♗g3 ♕c7 10. ♘f3 ♘d7 11. 0-0-0 0-0-0= Krutihin–Voronkov, SSSR 1952] ♕c7 10. 0-0-0 h5 [10... ♘d7 11. ♗d6 ♕d6 12. ♘g3 ♗g6 13. ♕h6!△ h4-h5± Rabar; 10... ♗f4 11. ♘f4 ♘d7 12. ♕e3 0-0-0 13. ♗d3 ♗d3 14. ♖d3 ♔b8 15. ♖hd1± Hübner–Bleimann, Groningen 1964/65] 11. ♖he1 ♘d7=

[9] 8... ♗d6 9. ♗g3 ♕c7 [9... ♕e7!?] 10. ♕e2 ♗g4 11. ♕e4 f5 12. ♗d6 ♕d6 13. ♕e5 ♕e5 14. ♘e5 ♘d7 [Bednarski–Hort, Budva 1963] 15. ♘d3±

[10] 14. a4?! 0-0-0 15. a5 ♘f6 16. a6 b6 17. ♕b3 ♘h5 18. g3 c5!∓↑ Sokolski–Konstantinopoljski, SSSR (ch) 1950

[11] **6... ♗g4**?! 7. ♗e2 [7. ♘e2!± — 6. ♘e2] ♗e2 8. ♘e2 ♘d7 9. ♗e3 ♕a5 10. ♗d2 ♕c7 11. 0-0-0 0-0-0 12. ♕h3 h5? 13. ♔b1 e6 14. c4 c5 15. d5! ed5 16. ♗f4± Kozomara–Sokolov, Sarajevo 1958; **6... ♕b6**?! 7. ♗e2 ♗g7? [⌓ 7... ♘a6] 8. ♕g3! [8. ♘f3 ♗g4 9. 0–0 ♘d7 10. ♗e3 ♕c7 11. ♘h4 ♗e2 12. ♕e2 e6 13. ♕h5 f5= Parma–Lutikov, Jugoslavija–SSSR 1966] ♖g8 9. ♗d3!±; **6... ♘a6** 7. ♗d2 ♘c7 [7... ♕b6? 8. 0-0-0 ♗e6 9. a3 0-0-0 10. ♘f3 ♗d5 11. ♗e3 e6 12. c4! ♗f3 13. gf3 c5 14. d5 ♗d6 15. f4 f5 16. ♗g2±⧉↑⊞ Bakulin–Konstantinopoljski, SSSR 1966] 8. ♘f3 [8. 0-0-0!?] ♗g4 9. ♗e2 ♕d7 10. ♕b3 ♘b5 11. c3 [11. c4? ♗f3 12. cb5 ♗g2 13. ♖g1 ♗d5∓ Šišov–Zagorjanski, SSSR 1953] ♘d6 12. 0-0-0 0-0-0=

[12] 8. ♘g3 h5! 9. h4 ♗g4 10. ♗d2 ♕c7=

[13] 12... f5? 13. ♕e2△ ♗b4, ♗c3±

[14] 15. ♘c5 ♕e4 16. ♘e4 0-0-0= Marić–Sušić, Vrnjačka Banja 1966

15 6... ♕b6!? 7. ♕c1 ♗f5 8. ♘e2 e6 9. ♘g3 ♗g6 10. ♗e2 h5 [10... c5 11. dc5 ♗c5 12. ♗c5 ♕c5 13. ♕f4± Domnitz—Cagan, Netanya 1969 — 7/183] 11. h4 ♗d6!∞ Sokolov

16 7. ♗d3 ♗g6 8. ♘e2 ♘a6 9. ♕d2 [9. ♗a6? ♕a5 10. ♕d2 ♕a6 11. 0—0 e6 12. ♘g3 0-0-0 13. ♕c3 h5∓ Romanovski—Levenfiš, SSSR (ch) 1920] ♘c7 10. 0-0-0 ♘d5∞

17 8... e6 9. ♘g3 ♗g6 10. ♗e2 ♕c7 11. 0-0-0 [11. 0—0? h5! 12. ♖fd1 h4 13. ♘f1 h3 14. g3 0-0-0 15. c4 c5! 16. d5 e5 17. ♖ac1 f5∓ →» Bakulin — Bronštejn, SSSR (ch) 1965] 0-0-0∞

18 13. c5? ♗g3∓

19 15. ♗f3 e5∞ Matanović—Bronštejn, Hastings 1953/54

20 **6... c5** 7. d5±; **6... e5** 7. ♗e3 ♗e6 8. ♘g3±; **6... e6** 7. ♘g3 c5 8. ♗e3 cd4 9. ♕d4 ♕d4 10. ♗d4± e5? 11. ♗e3 ♘c6 12. ♗b5 ♗d7 13. f4± Estrin—Bagirov, SSSR 1951

21 **7. f3** ♗f5 8. ♘g3 ♗g6 9. f4 [9. h4 ♕c7] e6 10. c3 [10. f5? ♗f5 11. ♘f5 ♕a5 12. ♗d2 ♕f5 13. ♗d3 ♕d5∓] ♗d6∓ Euwe—van den Hoek, Nederland 1942; **7. c3** ♘d7 8. ♕b3 ♕b6 9. ♕c2 e5 10. ♗e3 0-0-0 11. ♘g3 ed4 12. ♗d4 ♗c5∓ Westerinen—Bronštejn, Tallinn 1971 — 11/164; **7. h3** ♗h5 8. g4 [8. c3 ♘d7 9. ♕b3 ♕b6=] ♗g6 9. ♘g3 f5!=

22 7... ♘d7?! 8. h3 [8. ♘g3!?] ♗e2 [8... ♗h5!?] 9. ♗e2 ♕c7 10. ♗e3 e6 11. 0—0 ♗d6 12. c4 0-0-0 13. d5!± Browne—Kavalek, USA (ch) 1971

23 8. ♘f4 ♗g6 9. ♘g6 hg6 10. ♗d2 [10. ♗e3 ♘d7 11. 0-0-0 e6 12. ♗e2 ♕a5= S. Vuković—Tot, Jugoslavija (ch) 1957] ♘d7 11. 0-0-0 ♕c7 12. g3 0-0-0 13. h4 e6 14. ♗e2 f5= Bakulin —Suhanov, SSSR 1971

24 **8... ♗e2** 9. ♗e2 ♕c7? 10. ♗h5! ♕a5 11. ♗d2 ♕h5 12. ♕b7+— Marić—Tot, Jugoslavija (ch) 1957; **8... ♕b6** 9. ♕h3! ♗e2 10. ♗e2 ♘d7 11. ♗h5! ♗g7 12. 0—0 ♘f8 13. ♗e3±⟳↑ Marić—Kržišnik, Vukovar 1966 — 2/153

25 15. ♗h6 ♔d8 [Bednarski—Ermenkov, Varna 1972 — 13/213] 16. ♖ad1 ♕b6 17. d5!± Minev

26 7. c3 — 6. c3

27 8... h5!? 9. ♗e2 ♘d7 10. c3 [10. ♔f1!?] ♕a5 11. b4 ♕c7 12. ♘h5 a5 13. ♘f4 ab4 14. ♘g6 fg6 15. ab4 e5 16. ♖b1 0-0-0=∞ Sindik—Kristiansen, France 1974

28 9. c3 e6 10. ♗d3 ♗d3 11. ♕d3 ♕a5 12. ♕f3 ♘d7 13. ♘h5 f5= Iljin-Ženevski—Kan, SSSR (ch) 1931

29 10. ♗f4 ♘d7 11. ♕d2 ♕b6 12. 0-0-0 0-0-0 13. ♗c4 e5∞ Hort—Simagin, Moskva 1960; 10... ♕b6!?

30 **10... ♕b6** 11. ♗c4 ♘d7 12. a4 a5 [12... e6 13. a5 ♕c7 14. ♕f3± Voronkov] 13. ♕f3 e6 14. 0—0 ♗c2 15. ♗f4 ♗b3 16. ♗d3 e5 17. ♗e3 ♗d5 18. ♗e4± Flor—Horowitz, SSSR—USA 1945; **10... ♘d7**!?

31 14. 0—0 e5!∞

32 15. ♕h6 [Mecking—Larsen, San Antonio 1972 — 14/209] e5!=∞↑

33 **7. ♗f4** ♗f5 8. ♘g3 ♗g6 9. h4 ♘d7 10. ♗e2 e5 11. de5 [11. ♗e3 ♕a5 12. c3 0-0-0∓↑⊞] fe5 12. ♗g5 ♕a5 13. c3 f6 14. ♗e3 0-0-0∓↑ Baturinski—Simagin, SSSR 1946; **7. h4** ♗g4 8. c3 ♘d7 9. ♕b3 ♘b6 10. ♗f4 ♕d7 11. 0-0-0 ♗e6 12. ♕c2 a5 13. ♘g3 ♕d5 14. a3 ♕a2 15. ♕b1 ♕b1 16. ♔b1 ♘d5∓ Yanofsky—Larsen, Dallas 1957; **7. ♘c3** ♗g4 8. ♗e2 ♖g8 9. ♗e3 e6 10. h3 ♗e2 11. ♕e2 ♕a5= Kopajev—Bronštejn, SSSR 1947

34 7... h4 8. h3± Zinser—Pachman, Venezia 1967 — 4/190

35 10. ♗h6 ♖h6 11. ♘g3 ♕e6=

36 15. ♘e4 ♕e7 16. ♕e3 ♖h8 17. c4=∞⟳↑ van den Berg—Pachman, Beverwijk 1965

37 7. ♗f3?! ♕a5 8. c3 h5?! 9. ♗h5 ♘d7 10. ♗g4 ♗g4 11. ♕g4 0-0-0=∞ Lasker—Nimzowitsch, Peterburg 1914

38 **8... ♘d7** 9. c4 ♗g6?! 10. d5 e5 11. ♘d2 ♕c7 12. ♘b3 ♗d6 [Kavalek—Bronštejn, Szombathely 1966 — 2/155] 13. dc6 bc6 14. ♗c3 ♖d8 15. ♕e1!±; 9... ♕c7!?; **8... ♗g7** 9. c4 [9. ♖e1 0—0 10. ♗f4 ♕b6 11. ♕c1 ♘d7 12. a4 c5 13. ♗e3 ♕c7= Ciocaltea —Botvinik, Hamburg 1965] 0—0 10. ♗e3 ♘d7 11. d5!± Ivkov—Donner, Santa Monica 1966 — 2/154

39 9... ♗d6 10. d5 c5 11. ♘h4! ♗h2 12. ♔h1 ♗g6 13. de6 fe6 14. ♗g4 f5 15. ♗f5 ef5 16. ♖e1 ♗e5 17. ♗f4± Matulović—Flesch, Jugoslavija—Hungary 1964

40 10. ♗d2 ♗d6 11. ♔h1 ♖g8! 12. c5?! ♗e7 13. ♕c1 ♗e4 14. ♗f4 ♕a5 15. ♗g3 h5∓ →» Kaplan—Larsen, San Antonio 1972 — 14/210

41 11. ♘d4 ♗g6 12. de6 ♘e5!

42 Kavalek—Larsen, Solingen 1970 — 9/155

43 7. c3 ♘c7 8. ♘f3 ♗g4 9. ♘h4 ♗e2 10. ♕e2 ♕d5 11. 0—0 0-0-0 12. ♗e3 ♕e4= Matulović—Ćirić, Jugoslavija (ch) 1964

44 10. ♗f4!?

45 10... h5 11. ♕b3 b6 12. d5 c5 13. ♖ad1 ♕d6 14. ♖fe1 ♗g7 15. ♘h4± Matulović—Hort, Sarajevo 1965

46 15. ♗e3 ♘d4 16. ♕h5 0-0-0= Jangarber—Kopilov, SSSR 1968 — 6/236

47 6... ♗g7 7. ♗e2 [7. ♗d3?! ♗g4 8. c3 ♘d7 9. ♗c2 e6 10. ♗f4 ♕b6 11. ♖b1 0-0-0∓ Santos—Smislov, Lugano (ol) 1968 — 6/237] ♗f5 8. 0—0 e6 — 6. ♗e2

48 **7. ♗c4** ♕c7!? [7... ♖g8?! 8. ♗f4! e6 9. 0–0 ♗d6 10. ♗d6? ♕d6 11. ♘h4 ♗g6 12. f4 f5 13. c3 ♘d7 (Sokolski–Konstantinopoljski, SSSR (ch) 1950) 14. ♕e2 0-0-0 15. ♖ad1 ♘f6∓ Voronkov; 10. ♗g3±; 9. ♗g3!? Boleslavski] 8. ♗e3 ♘d7 9. ♕d2 e6 10. ♗f4 ♗d6 11. ♗d6?! ♕d6 12. 0-0-0 0-0-0= 13. ♘h4 ♗g6 14. h3 ♘b6 15. ♗b3 ♖d7!∓↑⊞ Savage–Larsen, Washington 1972; **7. c3** — 6. c3; **7. ♗e2** — 6. ♗e2

49 8... e6 9. c4 ♗d6 10. d5! ♕c7 11. de6 fe6 12. ♖e1 ♗f7 13. ♗f5 e5 14. ♕d3± Bitman–Rozanov, SSSR 1962

50 13... c5 14. ♘h4 f5 15. f4±

51 **14... ♘c5** 15. ♗c5!+– Radulov–Larsen, Hastings 1972/73 — 15/188; **14... cd5** 15. c6! bc6 16. ♗b5±→

52 **7. g3** e6 8. ♗g2 ♘d7 9. 0–0 ♗g7! [9... ♘b6? 10. ♕d3 ♘d5 11. a3 ♗d6 12. ♖e1 ♘e7 13. b4 a5 14. b5 ♗f5 15. ♕e2 cb5 16. ♘h4 ♕d7 17. d5!±→ Romanovski–Flor, SSSR 1945] 10. ♖e1 0–0 11. ♗e3 ♖e8 12. ♕c1 ♘f8= Konstantinopoljski–Flor, SSSR (ch) 1945; **7. ♗c4** ♖g8 8. 0–0 e6?! 9. ♗f4 ♗d6 10. ♗g3 f5 11. ♕d3 ♗f3 12. ♕f3 ♗g3 13. hg3 ♕d4 14. ♕b3!⩱→ Boleslavski–Havin, SSSR 1940; 8... ♕c7!=

53 7... ♘a6!? — 6. ♗e2

54 **8. c3** ♘d7 9. ♘h4 ♗e2 10. ♕e2 ♕a5 11. 0–0 0-0-0 12. ♗e3 ♖g8 13. a3 f5 14. ♘f3 ♕d5∞ Yanofsky–Szabo, Dallas 1957; **8. 0—0** ♗d6 9. c4 [9. h3 h5!?] ♖g8! 10. ♔h1 ♘d7 [10... f5 11. d5 cd5 12. cd5 e5 13. ♘e5! ♗e5 14. ♖e1± Matanović–Szabo, Portorož (izt) 1958; 10... ♕c7 11. d5!±] 11. d5 ♘c5 [11... cd5 12. cd5 e5 13. ♘d4 ♗e2 14. ♕e2△ ♘f5±] 12. ♘d4 [12. dc6!?] f5 13. ♗g4 ♖g4 14. h3 ♕f6 15. ♘f3 ♖c4 16. dc6 ♘e4 17. cb7 ♖b8∞ Tringov–Smislov, La Habana 1965

55 8... ♗d6 9. ♕d2 [9. ♗g3 ♕c7 10. ♘d2 ♗f5 11. ♘c4 ♗g3 12. hg3 ♘d7 13. ♗d3 ♗d3 14. ♕d3 0-0-0 15. 0-0-0 ♘e5!= Averbah–Simagin, SSSR 1946] ♕c7 10. ♗d6 ♕d6 11. c4 ♘d7 12. 0–0 0–0! [12... 0-0-0 13. ♖fd1 ♖hg8 14. b4±→《 Holaszek–Dückstein, Wien 1972] 13. ♖ad1 ♔h8!∞

56 10. ♕d2 ♘d5 11. h3? ♘f4 12. ♕f4 ♗f5 13. c3 ♗d6∓ Ratner–Flor, SSSR 1945

57 16. ♗f3 ♕g5= Bronštejn–Flor, SSSR 1945

58 9... ♗g7 10. ♗f4 0–0 11. c4±

59 11... ♕c7!?

60 12... cd5 13. cd5 e5 14. ♕b3 b6 15. ♗b5± Tringov

61 16. ♘c4 ♕c7 17. ♕a4±→《 Tringov–Opočensky, Bratislava 1957

62 **8. c3** ♘d7 9. ♕a4 e6 10. ♗d2 [10. 0–0 ♖g8 11. ♗e3 ♘b6△ ♘d5] ♖g8 11. 0-0-0 ♗f5! 12. ♘h4 ♗e4 13. f3 b5! 14. ♕b3 ♗d5∞ Levenfiš–Konstantinopoljski, SSSR 1947; **8. ♘h4** ♗e2 9. ♕e2 ♘d7 10. 0–0 [10. ♕h5 ♕d6 11. 0–0 ♕d5= Natapov–Zelevinski, SSSR 1961] e6 11. c4 0-0-0 [11... ♘b6 12. g3 h5 13. ♗f4 ♕e7 14. ♖fd1± Olafsson–Bhend, Zürich 1959] 12. g3 [12. ♘f3 ♖g8 13. ♗d2 c5 14. ♗e3 ♕c6 15. g3 ♕e4 16. ♘d2 ♕g4= Hecht–Smislov, Hamburg 1965] h5 [12... ♖g8 13. d5! ♕e5 14. ♕f3 cd5 15. ♗f4± Matanović–Ćirić, Jugoslavija (ch) 1962] 13. d5 ♖e8∞ Gurgenidze–Savon, SSSR (ch) 1962; **8. ♕d2** ♘d7 9. ♕f4 ♕f4 10. ♗f4 ♘b6= Arnštejn–Semenov, SSSR 1962

63 **9. h3** h5!; **9. ♘h4** ♗e2 — 8. ♘h4

64 9... 0-0-0 10. ♕a4 ♔b8 11. ♗e3 ♖g8 — 9... ♖g8

65 10. ♗e3 0-0-0 11. ♕a4 ♔b8! [11... e5? 12. ♖fe1! e4 13. ♘h4 ♗d6 14. g3 ♗h3 15. ♗f1 ♗f1 16. ♔f1± Levenfiš–Sokolski, SSSR (ch) 1949] 12. ♖fd1 [12. ♔h1 f5 13. d5 c5 14. b4 e5 15. ♖ab1 f4∓→》 Hudjakov–Zelevinski, SSSR 1965] e6 13. b4 f5 14. d5 c5∞ Goldenov–Konstantinopoljski, SSSR 1937

66 11. dc6!?

67 Matanović–Pachman, Wien 1957

68 8... e6 9. c4 ♗b4 10. ♔f1!?; 9... ♘d7 — 8... ♘d7

69 **9. h3** ♗f5 10. ♘h4 ♗g6 11. ♗c4 e6 12. ♕e2 0-0-0 13. 0-0-0 [Keres–Konstantinopoljski, SSSR (ch) 1952] ♘b6! 14. ♗b3 ♘d5∞; **9. ♕d2** 0-0-0 10. 0-0-0 ♖g8 11. ♗f4 ♕b6 12. ♕d3 ♗e6 13. a3∞ Gufeljd–Bronštejn, SSSR 1959

70 **10. ♕a4** ♖g8 11. h3 ♗h5! [11... ♗f5 12. ♘h4 ♗e4 13. 0-0-0!±] 12. 0–0 ♗d6 13. b4 ♗f4 14. ♕b3 0-0-0 15. a4 f5 16. ♖fb1 ♖g7∓ →⇔ g, Abrošin–Konstantinopoljski, corr. 1955; **10. ♕b3** 0-0-0 11. ♖c1 ♕b6? 12. ♕b6 ab6 13. ♘d2! ♗e2 14. ♔e2 ♗e7 15. ♖hd1± Tajmanov–Flor, SSSR 1948; 11... ♗d6!△ 12. d5 ♘e5∞ Voronkov

71 Tajmanov–Flor, SSSR (ch) 1948

72 8... ♗f5 9. c4 ♘d7 10. 0–0 ♖g8? 11. ♘h4! ♗g6 12. ♘g6 hg6 13. d5± Smislov–Ratner, SSSR (ch) 1945

73 9... e6 10. c4 ♘d7 11. d5±

74 10... 0-0-0 11. ♕d4 c5 12. ♕a4△ ♗f4±

75 16. ♕a4 ♔f8 17. ♖fe1 ♗f4± Smislov–Pachman, Amsterdam (izt) 1964

76 **6... e6** 7. ♘e2 ♘d7 8. ♘g3 ♘b6 9. ♗d3 ♕d5 10. 0–0 h5 11. ♗e4 ♕d8 12. ♘h5 f5 13. ♗f3 ♗d6 14. g3± Bernstein–Flor, Groningen 1946; **6... e5** 7. ♗c4 ed4 8. ♕b3 ♕e7 9. ♘e2 b5 10. ♗d3 ♗e6 11. ♕c2± Nimzowitsch; **6... ♕d5** 7. ♘f3 ♗f5 8. ♗e2△ 0–0, c4±; **6... ♕c7** 7. ♗c4 e6 [7... ♗f5 8. ♕f3 ♕d7 9. ♘e2 ♖g8 10. ♘f4 ♗g4 11. ♕e4 ♕f5

12. f3 ♕e4 13. fe4 e5 14. h3!± Bonč Osmolovski–Konstantinopoljski, SSSR 1949] 8. ♕h5! c5 9. d5 e5 10. ♘e2 ♗d6 11. f4± Kaplan–Rossolimo, Puerto Rico 1967 — 4/191; **6... b6**!? Voronkov

77 **7. ♕f3** e6 8. ♘e2 h5 9. h3 ♕d5 10. ♕d5 cd5∓↑⟪ Wade–Pachman, La Habana 1963; **7. ♗d3** ♗g6 8. h4 ♕d5 9. ♗g6 hg6 10. ♕f3 ♗g7 11. ♗e3 ♘d7 12. ♕d5 cd5∓⊥⊞↑⟪ S. Nedeljković–Bronštejn, Jugoslavija–SSSR 1957; **7. ♕b3** ♕c7 8. ♗c4 [8. ♗f4? ♕f4 9. ♕b7 ♗h6 10. ♘f3 0–0 11. ♕a8 ♕c7 12. d5 ♕b6 13. ♗c4 ♗c8–+ Fuderer–Szabo, Göteborg (izt) 1955] e6 9. ♘f3 ♘d7=; **7. ♗f4**!? ♕b6∞

78 **8... ♗d6**? 9. ♘g3 ♗g6 10. ♗h6!± Ujtumen–Hort, Palma de Mallorca (izt) 1970 — 10/209; **8... ♗e4**? 9. 0–0 ♗d5 10. ♗d3 c5 11. c4 ♗c6 12. d5! ed5 13. cd5 ♕d5 14. ♘f4±→; **8... ♘d7** 9. ♘g3 ♗g6 10. 0–0 [10. h4 h5 11. ♗e2 ♗d6 12. ♘h5 ♕c7△ 0-0-0=∞ Minev] ♕c7 11. f4 [11. a4? 0-0-0 12. ♕e2 h5∓ Pohla–Bronštejn, Pärnu 1971 — 12/205] f5!=

79 9... ♗g4!?

80 10. h4 ♗d6 11. ♗e2 ♕a5 12. b4 ♕c7 13. ♘h5 ♘d7△ 0-0-0, a5=∞

81 12. 0–0!?△ ♗e3, ♘h1-f2-d3-e5

82 **16. ♗d3** ♕c7! 17. ♗f5 ♗f3 18. gf3 0-0-0 19. ♗h3 ♗f4∓ Ciocaltea–Pachman, Moskva 1956; **16. 0–0**! ♕c7 17. ♕e1 ♗f3 [17... ♗f4? 18. ♗f4 ♕f4 19. ♘h4 ♕e4 20. ♘f5! ef5 21. ♖f5!+–] 18. ♖f3 0-0-0=

83 7... e6 8. ♗f4 ♘d7 9. ♗e2 ♘b6 10. 0–0 ♘d5 11. ♗g3 ♗h6 12. c4 ♘f4 13. ♗f4 ♗f4 14. d5!±↑⊞ Boleslavski–Flor, SSSR (ch) 1944

84 **8. ♗c4** e6 9. ♕e2 ♗e7! [9... ♘d7? 10. ♘h4 ♗g6 11. f4 f5 12. ♗e6! fe6 13. ♘g6 hg6 14. ♕e6±; 11... 0-0-0 12. f5! ef5 13. 0–0 ♗d6 14. g3 ♖g8 15. ♘g2± Boleslavski] 10. ♘h4 ♗g6 11. f4 f5!=; **8. ♘h4** ♗g6 9. ♕f3 ♘d7 10. g3 e6 11. ♗g2 f5 12. ♗g5 ♗g7 13. 0–0 0–0= Nejkirh–Bronštejn, Gota 1957

85 8... ♘d7!?

86 16. ♗c1 ed4 17. ♗f4 ♗d6 18. ♖d4 ♗f4 19. ♖f4 ♖d2 20. ♕c1 ♖hd8 21. ♘f3± Đurašević–Hort, Marianske Lazni 1962

87 **7... ♘d7** 8. ♘g3 ♗g6 9. h4 h5 10. ♗e2 [10. ♗d3 ♗d3 11. ♕d3 ♕a5= Pilnik–Bronštejn, Göteborg (izt) 1955] e5 [10... ♕a5!?] 11. ♗h5 ♗h5 12. ♘h5 ed4 [12... ♕a5 13. ♕f3±] 13. 0–0!± Sokolov–Szabo, Balatonfüred 1958; **7... ♗g4**!? 8. f3 ♗f5 9. ♘g3 ♗g6 10. f4 f5 ∞ Liberzon–Hort, Moskva 1963; **7... e6** 8. ♘g3 ♗g6 — 6. ♘e2

88 8. ♘f4?! h4 [8... ♗g4 9. f3 ♗f5 10. ♘h5 ♖h5 11. g4± Kaminski–Vorotnikov, SSSR 1972 — 13/212] 9. ♕f3 [9. ♗d3!?] ♘d7 10. g4 hg3 11. fg3 [11. hg3 ♗g4 12. ♕g2 ♘e5!∓] e5 12. g4 ♗h7 13. ♘e2 ed4 14. cd4 ♗b4 15. ♔f2 ♕e7∓ Bilek–Bronštejn, Budapest 1955

89 14. ♗f4 ♘b6! [14... e5 15. ♗e3±; 14... ♗h6 15. ♗h6 ♖h6 16. d5 cd5 17. cd5 ♕d5 18. ♕e3± Boleslavski] 15. ♖fd1 ♗h6 16. ♗h6 ♖h6 17. ♘e4 ♖g6 18. b4 ♕f5 19. ♘g3 ♕g4∓ Gudmundsson–Bronštejn, Reykjavik 1974

90 14... ♕c7!? 15. c5 [15. ♘h5? c5!] ♗e7△ ♖dg8, ♖g4∞

91 16. c5 f5 17. b4 ♕a6 18. ♘c3 ♕e2 19. ♘e2 [Averbah–Sokolski, SSSR (ch) 1950] ♖dg8! 20. ♗g5 ♖g6=

92 **9. ♗e2** ♗e2 10. ♕e2 ♕d5 11. 0–0 ♘d7 12. ♗e3 [Čistjakov–Konstantinopoljski, SSSR 1954] ♘b6=; **9. ♕b3** ♕b6=

93 10. ♗f4!? Estrin–Stezko, SSSR 1974 — 17/218

94 **10... h4** 11. ♘e2△ ♗f4±; **10... ♕a5**!?

95 Mučnik–Voronkov, SSSR 1957

B 17 1. e4 c6 2. d4 d5 3. ♘c3 de4 4. ♘e4 ♘d7

	5	6	7	8	9	10	11	12	13	
1	♘f3[1]	♘eg5[2]	♗e2[4]	♘f3	0–0	♗g5	c4	d5	cd5[5]	±
	♘df6	♗g4[3]	♗f3	e6	♗d6	♘e7	♘g6	cd5		
2	...	♘c3[6]	♗f4[8]	♗d3	♕d3	0–0	♖fe1	♘g5	♘e4	=
	♘gf6	♘b6[7]	♗f5	♗d3	e6	♗e7	0–0	h6	♘bd5[9]	
3	...	♘g3	♗c4[11]	♗b3	c3[13]	dc5[15]	♕e2	♗c2	♘e5	=
	...	e6[10]	♘b6[12]	c5	♕c7[14]	♘bd7[16]	♘c5	♗e7	0–0[17]	
4	...	...	♗d3	0–0[19]	♕e2[21]	dc5[23]	♗c4	♖d1	♘e5	±
	...	...	♗e7[18]	0–0[20]	c5[22]	♘c5[24]	b6	♕c7	♗b7[25]	
5	...	...	...	0–0	♘d4	♘f3[28]	♕e2[29]	♗f4[31]	♖ad1	=
	...	...	c5	cd4[26]	♗c5[27]	0–0	b6[30]	♗b7	♕c8[32]	

	5	6	7	8	9	10	11	12	13	
6	...	♘f6	♘e5[33]	c3[35]	♘f7[37]	♕f3	g4	gf5	♕e3[39]	±
	...	♘f6	♗f5[34]	♘d7[36]	♔f7	e6[38]	♕f6	♕f5	c5[40]	
7	...	...	...	c3[41]	♗d3	0—0	♕e2	dc5	c6	=
	...	...	♗e6	g6	♗g7	0—0	c5	♕c7	bc6[42]	
8	♗c4	♘g5[44]	♘1f3	c3	h3	♕f3	♗d2	♕e2	♕e4[47]	±
	♘df6[43]	♘h6[45]	♗g4[46]	e6	♗f3	♘d5	♕f6	♘f4		
9	...	♘g5	♘1f3[48]	♘e4	♗b3	♘g3[51]	0—0	♘e5	c4	±
	♘gf6	♘d5	h6[49]	♘7b6[50]	♗f5	♗h7[52]	e6	♘d7[53]	♘5f6[54]	
10	...	...	♘e2	♘f3	0—0	♖e1[57]	♘c3	♗d3	♘e4[59]	=
	...	e6	h6[55]	♗d6[56]	♕c7	0—0	b5[58]	♗b7	♘e4[60]	

1. e4 c6 2. d4 d5 3. ♘c3 de4 4. ♘e4 ♘d7 5. ♗c4 ♘gf6 6. ♘g5 e6 7. ♕e2 ♘b6[61]

	8	9	10	11	12	13	14	15	16	
11	♗b3	♘5f3	a3[64]	♗a2	dc5[66]	♘e5	♘gf3	0—0	♘e5	=
	h6[62]	a5[63]	a4	c5[65]	♗c5	0—0	♘bd7	♘e5	b6[67]	
12	...	...	dc5	c6	♘h3[69]	0—0	♘f4	c4	♘d3	=
	...	c5	♘bd7[68]	bc6	♗e7[70]	♕b6	♗a6	c5	0—0[71]	
13	...	...	♗e3	♘e5	♘gf3	0—0	♘c4	dc5	♗c5	=
	...	...	♕c7	a6[72]	♘bd5	♗d6[73]	♗e7	♗c5	♕c5[74]	
14	...	...	♗f4	♗e5	♘d2[76]	♘gf3[78]	0—0	♘d4	a3	=
	...	...	♘bd5[75]	♕a5	cd4[77]	♗e7	0—0	♗d7	♕c5![79]	
15	♗d3	♘5f3	dc5[82]	♗d2	0-0-0[83]	♘h3	♘hg1[85]	c4	♗c3	∓
	h6[80]	c5[81]	♗c5	♕c7	♘bd7	g5[84]	♖g8	b6	♗b7[86]	
16	...	...	...	♘e5	♘gf3	♘e5	0—0[89]	♖d1[91]	b4[93]	=
	...	...	...	♘bd7[87]	♘e5[88]	0—0	b6[90]	♕e7[92]	♗d6![94]	
17	...	...	...	♘e5[95]	♕e5	♗d2	♘f3[98]	♘e5	♗e2![101]	=
	...	...	♘bd7	♘e5[96]	♕a5[97]	♕c5	♕e5[99]	♗c5[100]	♘e4[102]	

1. e4 c6 2. d4 d5 3. ♘c3 de4 4. ♘e4 ♘d7 5. ♗c4 ♘gf6 6. ♘f6 ♘f6

	7	8	9	10	11	12	13	14	15	
18	c3	♘f3[104]	h3	g4	♘e5	♗f4				∞
	♕c7[103]	♗g4	♗h5[105]	♗g6	e6[106]	♗d6				
19	♘f3	c3[108]	♕e2[109]	h3	♕f3	0—0	♖e1	♗f4	♗g5	=
	♗f5[107]	e6	♗g4	♗f3	♕c7	♗e7	0—0	♗d6	♗e7[110]	
20	...	♘e5	0—0[111]	♕e2	♗g5	♖ad1	♗d3	♘f3	♕d3	=
	...	e6	♗d6[112]	0—0	♕c7	b5	♘d5	♗d3	c5[113]	
21	...	0—0	♗g5[114]	♕e2	♖ad1	h3	♕f3	♗e3![116]		±
	...	e6	♗e7	♗g4	0—0[115]	♗f3	♘d5			
22	...	♕e2	♗g5	0-0-0	h3	♕f3	♗e7	♔b1[118]	♕e4	±
	...	e6	♗e7	♗g4[117]	♗f3	♘d5	♕e7	♖d8	b5[119]	

1 **5. ♕e2** e6 6. ♗f4 [6. ♘f3 ♘gf6 7. ♘f6 ♘f6 8. g3 c5=] ♘df6 7. 0-0-0 ♘e4 8. ♕e4 ♘f6 9. ♕f3 ♕a5=; **5. ♘e2** ♘gf6 6. ♘2g3 e6 7. ♗c4 ♗e7 8. 0—0 ♘e4 9. ♘e4 ♘f6 10. ♘f6 ♗f6 11. c3 0—0= Dementjev—Holmov, SSSR (ch) 1970 — 10/211; **5. ♗d3** ♘gf6 6. ♘g5 [6. ♘f6 ♘f6 7. c3 ♗g4=] e6 7. f4 h6 8. ♘5f3 c5 [8... b6 9. ♘e2 ♗b7 10. 0—0 ♕c7 11. f5±→ Littlewood—Hoen, Tel Aviv (ol) 1964] 9. c3 cd4 10. cd4 ♗b4=

2 **6. ♘c3** ♗g4 7. ♗e2 e6 8. h3 ♗f3 9. ♗f3 ♗d6 10. ♕d2 ♘e7 11. ♘e4 ♘f5 12. c3 ♘h4= Šišov–Kasparjan, SSSR 1956; **6. ♘c5** e6 7. ♘d3 ♗d6 8. ♗f4 ♗f4 9. ♘f4 ♘e7 10. ♘d3 b6 11. ♘de5 ♗b7= Trifunović–Matanović, England 1951; **6. ♘g3** ♗g4 7. ♗e2 e6 8. 0–0 ♘e7 [8... ♗d6 9. ♘e5 ♗e2 10. ♕e2± Kostić –Karaklajić, Jugoslavija (ch) 1949] 9. ♖e1 ♘g6= Rabar–Trifunović, Jugoslavija (ch) 1948

3 **6... h6**? 7. ♘f7 ♔f7 8. ♘e5 ♔e8 9. ♗d3+–; **6... ♗f5** 7. ♘e5 ♘h6 8. ♗c4 e6 9. f3±; **6... e6** 7. ♘e5 ♘h6 8. ♗c4 ♗e7 9. 0–0 0–0 10. ♕d3± Bogdanović–Bilek, Zagreb 1955

4 △ ♘f7; 7. ♗c4 e6 8. ♘f7?! ♗f3 9. ♘d8 ♗d1 10. ♘e6 ♗c2 11. ♘c7 ♔d7 12. ♘a8 ♗d6∓ Milić–Trifunović, Jugoslavija (ch) 1948

5 Gligorić–Rabar, Jugoslavija (ch) 1948

6 **6. ♗d3** ♘e4 7. ♗e4 ♘f6 8. ♗d3 ♗g4 9. c3 e6 10. h3 ♗h5 11. ♗e2 ♗d6 12. ♘e5 ♗e2 13. ♕e2 ♕c7 14. f4 0–0 15. 0–0 c5∓ H. Steiner–Flor, Moskva 1946; **6. ♘ed2** ♘b6 7. c3 ♗f5 8. ♘e5 e6=

7 **6... ♕c7** 7. ♗d3 e6 8. 0–0 ♗d6 9. ♖e1 0–0 10. ♕e2 ♗f4 11. ♘e4 ♗c1 12. ♖ac1 b6 13. ♘e5± Smislov–Füster, Moskva 1949; **6... e6** 7. ♗d3 [7. ♗c4 ♕c7 8. ♕e2 ♗d6 9. ♗g5 0–0 10. 0–0 b6 11. ♖fe1± Konstantinopoljski–Veresov, SSSR 1935] c5 [7... ♗e7 8. 0–0 c5 9. ♕e2 cd4 10. ♘d4 0–0 11. ♗g5 ♘c5 12. ♖ad1 ♘d3 13. ♖d3± Bronštejn–Kotov, SSSR 1946; 8... 0–0!±] 8. ♕e2 cd4 9. ♘d4 ♗c5 10. ♘b3 ♗d6 11. ♗g5 a6 12. 0-0-0 ♕c7 13. ♔b1 0–0 14. ♘e4±→ Talj–Šamkovič, SSSR (ch) 1972 — 14/213; 10... ♗e7!±

8 7. ♗e2 ♗f5 8. 0–0 e6 9. ♖e1 ♗e7 10. h3 ♘bd5= Konstantinopoljski–Flor, SSSR (ch) 1948

9 Antošin–Flor, SSSR (ch) 1955

10 **6... h5** 7. ♗d3! e6 8. ♕e2 c5 9. ♗g5 ♕a5 10. ♗d2 ♕b6 11. 0-0-0 cd4 12. ♖he1 ♗c5 13. c3! dc3 14. ♗c3±→ Gurgenidze –Kopilov, SSSR 1958; **6... g6** 7. h4! h5 8. ♗c4 ♗g7 9. ♕d3 e6 10. ♗g5± Levenfiš–Ravinski, SSSR 1928; **6... c5** 7. ♗c4! [7. d5 ♘b6 8. ♗b5 ♗d7 9. ♗d7 ♕d7 10. c4 ♘c4 11. 0–0 g6 12. ♕c2 ♘d6∓ Talj–Savon, SSSR 1970 — 10/217] b5 8. ♗e2 ♗b7 9. 0–0 c4 10. a4 a6 11. b3 ♗d5 12. ♘e5± Timoščenko–Razuvajev, SSSR 1972; 7... cd4!±

11 7. c3 c5 8. ♗d3 cd4 9. ♘d4 ♗e7 10. 0–0 ♘c5 11. ♗c2 ♗d7= Bronštejn–Petrosjan, Moskva 1967 — 3/180

12 **7... ♗e7** 8. ♕e2 0–0 9. 0–0 c5 10. ♖d1±; **7... c5** 8. dc5 ♗c5 9. 0–0 0–0 10. ♕e2 b6 11. ♘e4 ♗e7 12. ♖d1 ♕c7 13. ♘eg5 ♘c5 14. ♘e5± Boleslavski; **7... ♗d6** 8. 0–0 0–0 9. ♕e2 ♕c7 10. ♘e4 ♗f4 11. ♘f6 ♘f6 12. ♗f4 ♕f4 13. ♖ad1 b6 13. ♘e5± Boleslavski–A. Zajcev, SSSR 1969

13 9. ♕e2 cd4 10. 0–0 d3=

14 9... cd4 10. ♘d4 ♗e7 11. 0–0 0–0 12. ♕f3! [12. ♕e2 ♗d7 13. ♖e1 ♘bd5 14. ♗g5 ♖e8 15. ♖ad1 ♕a5 16. ♗d2 ♗a4= Smislov–Kotov, Groningen 1946] ♕c7 13. ♖e1△ ♗f4±

15 10. 0–0 c4=

16 10... ♗c5 11. 0–0 0–0 12. ♕e2 ♗d7 13. ♗g5±

17 14. 0–0 b6=

18 7... ♗d6 8. 0–0 ♕c7 9. ♖e1 0–0 10. b3 c5 11. dc5 ♘c5 12. ♗c4 b6 13. ♗b2 ♗b7 14. ♗f6 gf6 15. ♘h5±→ Ćirić–Rodriguez, Lugano (ol) 1968

19 8. ♕e2!? 0–0 9. ♗g5 c5 10. 0-0-0 cd4 [10... ♖e8 11. ♔b1 cd4 12. ♗c4 ♕b6 13. ♖d4± Balinas–Filip, Nice (ol) 1974] 11. ♔b1 [11. h4 ♘c5 12. ♘d4 ♕a5! 13. ♔b1 ♗d7∓] ♘c5 12. ♘d4 ♘d3 13. ♖d3± Jovčić–Ćirić, Jugoslavija 1971 — 12/207; 11... Da5!?

20 8... c5 9. ♖e1 b6 10. c4! cd4 11. ♘d4 ♗b7 12. ♘df5±

21 **9. c4** c5 10. b3 b6 11. ♗b2 ♗b7 12. ♕e2 ♖e8 [12... ♗f3 13. ♕f3 cd4 14. ♗d4 ♘c5± Grigorjev–Judovič, SSSR 1934] 13. ♖ad1 ♕c7 14. ♗b1 ♘f8 15. dc5 ♗c5 16. ♘e5 ♘g6 17. ♘e4 ♘e4= Spaski–Ćirić, Soči 1965; **9. c3** c5 10. ♘e5 cd4 11. cd4 ♘b6 12. ♗g5 ♘bd5 13. ♖c1 ♗d7= Becker–Döry, Wien 1918

22 9... b6 10. ♗f4! ♗b7 11. ♖ad1 c5 12. dc5 ♗c5 13. ♘e5±

23 **10. c3** b6 11. ♖e1 [11. ♘e5 ♗b7 12. f4 cd4! 13. cd4 ♘e5 14. de5 ♘g4 15. ♗h7 ♔h7 16. ♕g4 ♕d4 17. ♔h1 ♖ac8∓ Jevsejev–Flor, SSSR 1949] ♗b7 12. ♘e5 cd4 13. cd4 ♘d5= Kashdan–Kotov, USA–SSSR 1946; **10. ♖d1** ♕c7 [10... cd4 11. ♘d4 ♖e8 12. b3 ♕b6 13. ♗b2 ♘f8 14. ♘f3 ♗d7 15. ♘e5± Talj–Filip, Moskva 1967 — 3/179] 11. c4 ♖e8 12. dc5 ♘c5 [12... ♗c5 13. ♘e4 ♘e4 14. ♗e4 ♘f6 15. ♗c2 e5= L. Steiner–Flor, Saltsjöbaden (izt) 1948] 13. ♗c2 ♘cd7 14. ♘e4 b6 15. ♗a4 ♖d8 16. ♘f6 ♗f6 17. ♗g5 ♗b7 18. ♖d7 ♖d7 19. ♗f6 gf6 20. ♗d7 ♕d7= Talj–Ćirić, Budva 1967 — 4/197

24 10... ♗c5 11. ♗f4 b6 12. ♖ad1 ♕e7 13. c3 a5 14. ♘e4±

25 14. ♗f4 ♖fe8? 15. ♘f5! ef5 16. ♗f7 ♔f8 17. ♗e8 ♔e8 18. 18. ♘g6+–; 14... ♕c8!±

26 8... ♗e7 9. c4 cd4 10. ♘d4 ♘e5 11. ♗e2 0–0 12. ♗f4 ♘g6 13. ♗e3 a6 14. a3 ♕c7 15. b4± Spaski–Yanofsky, Winnipeg 1967 — 5/168

27 **9... ♗e7** 10. b3 0–0 11. ♗b2 [11. c4 ♕c7 12. ♗b2 ♖d8 13. ♕e2 ♘f8 14. ♘e4±→ Ivkov–Berger, Amsterdam (izt) 1964] ♘c5 12. ♗c4! ♗d7 13. ♕e2 ♕b6 14. ♖ad1 ♖fe8 15.

♘f3± Bradvarević–Trifunović, Jugoslavija (ch) 1964; **9... ♘c5** 10. ♗b5 ♗d7 11. b4 ♗b5 12. ♘b5 a6 13. ♘d4 ♘cd7 14. a3 [Spaski–Smislov, Amsterdam (izt) 1964] ♘b6! =; 10. ♗c4! ♗e7 11. b3 0–0 12. ♗b2 — 9... ♗e7

28 **10. ♗e3** 0–0 11. ♕e2 ♘d5 12. ♖ad1 ♘e3 13. fe3 g6 14. ♘e4 ♗e7∓ Čerepkov–Petrosjan, SSSR (ch) 1960; **10. ♘b3** ♗b6 11. ♘h5 ♘h5 12. ♕h5 ♘f6 13. ♕h4 ♗d7= Bilek–Smislov, Tel Aviv (ol) 1964; **10. c3** ♗d4 [10... 0–0 11. ♘h5 a6 12. ♖e1 ♗e7 13. ♗g5 ♘h5 15. ♕h5 g6 16. ♗e7± Ivkov–Filip, Beverwijk 1964] 11. cd4 0–0=

29 11. b3 b6 12. ♗b2 ♗b7 13. ♕e2 ♕c7 14. ♘e4 ♘e4= Spaski–Filip, Nice (ol) 1974 — 17/222

30 11... ♕c7 12. ♘e4 ♗e7 13. ♗g5 b6 14. ♖ad1±↑

31 12. ♘e4 ♗b7 13. ♘f6 ♘f6 14. ♗g5 h6 15. ♗h4 ♕d5=

32 **13... ♘d5**? 14. ♗g5 ♕c7 15. ♘h5 ♔h8 16. ♗e4 f6 17. ♗h4 ♗d6 18. c4 ♗a6 19. ♘g7± → Talj–Vasjukov, SSSR (ch) 1965; **13... ♕c8** 14. ♔h1 a6=

33 **7. c3** ♗g4 8. ♗e2 e6 9. h3 [9. 0–0 ♗e7 10. ♗f4 0–0 11. ♖e1 ♘d5 12. ♗g3 ♗f3 13. ♗f3 ♗d6= Boleslavski–Kotov, Saltsjöbaden (izt) 1948] ♗h5 10. ♘e5 ♗e2 11. ♕e2 ♗d6 12. ♗g5 ♕c7 13. 0-0-0 ♘d7= Pilnik–Petrosjan, Amsterdam (ct) 1956; **7. ♗c4** — 5. ♗c4

34 **7... g6** 8. ♗c4 ♘d5 9. 0–0 ♗g7 10. ♕e2 0–0 11. ♗b3 a5 12. a3 ♕b6 13. ♖d1 ♗e6 13. ♗a2± Saharov–Flesch, Varna 1958; **7... ♘d7** 8. ♘d3 [8. ♗f4 ♘e5 9. ♗e5 ♕d5 10. c4 ♕e4 11. ♕e2±] e6 9. ♗f4 ♗e7 10. ♗e2 0–0 11. 0–0 b6 12. ♗f3 ♗b7 13. ♖e1± Kavalek–Bleimann, Netanya 1971 — 11/165

35 8. ♗c4 — 5. ♗c4

36 **8... ♗g6** 9. h4 ♘d7 10. ♘g6 hg6 11. ♗g5 ♘f6 12. ♕c2 e6 13. 0-0-0± Levy–Liverios, Haifa 1971 — 10/214; **8... e6** 9. g4 ♗g6 10. h4 ♗d6 11. ♕e2! c5 [11... ♗e5 12. de5 ♕d5 13. ♖h3 ♘g4 14. ♕g4 ♗f5 15. ♕f3+– Jansa–Flesch, Sombor 1971 — 10/215] 12. ♗g2! [12. h5? ♗e4 13. f3 cd4 14. ♕b5 ♘d7 15 ♘f7 ♗g3 16. ♔e2 d3 17. ♔e3 ♕f6 18. ♔e4 ♕f7 19. ♖h3 a6 20. ♕g5 (Karpov–A. Zajcev, SSSR 1970 — 9/156) e5! 21. ♖g3 ♘c5∓] cd4 13. h5 dc3 14. ♕b5 ♔f8 15. hg6± Ćirić

37 9. ♗f4 e6=

38 10... ♔g6? 11. g4 ♗c2 12. ♕e2+–

39 13. ♕f5 ef5 14. ♗c4 ♔f6 15. ♖g1 ♖e8 16. ♔f1 h6 17. h4 g6 18. ♗f4 ♖e4 19. ♗g3±

40 **13... ♘f6** 14. ♗d3 ♕d5 15. f3 ♗d6 16. ♕e2± Spaski–Donner, San Juan 1969 — 8/163; **13... c5** 14. ♗h3 cd4 15. cd4 ♗b4 16. ♔f1 ♕b5 17. ♔g1 ♖he8 18. ♕b3 ♕b6 19. ♗e3 ♘f8 20. ♗g2± Kavalek–Barcza, Caracas 1971 — 10/216

41 **8. c4** g6! [8... ♘d7 9. ♗f4 ♘e5 10. ♗e5 ♕a5 11. ♕d2 ♕d2 12. ♔d2± Bronštejn–Razuvajev, SSSR (ch) 1972 — 14/214] 9. ♗e2 [9. d5?! cd5 10. cd5 ♕d5 11. ♕a4 ♘d7∓] ♗g7 10. 0–0 0–0 11. ♗e3 ♕c7 12. h3 ♖fd8 13. ♘f3 b5 14. b3 [14. cb5 cb5 15. ♗b5 ♕b7 16. ♕a4 ♗d5∞] bc4 15. bc4 c5 16. d5 ♗f5∓ Gufeljd–Razuvajev, SSSR (ch) 1972 — 14/215; **8. ♗e2** g6 9. c3 ♗g7 10. 0–0 0–0 11. ♗d3 c5 12. ♘f3 cd4= Mecking–Filip, Vršac 1971 — 12/206

42 14. ♖e1 ♖ab8= Timoščenko–Razuvajev, SSSR 1971

43 5... ♘b6 6. ♗b3 ♗f5 [6... ♘f6 7. ♘f6 ef6 8. ♕h5! ♕e7 9. ♘e2 ♗e6 10. 0–0 g6 11. ♕h4± Hamann–Yanofsky, Netanya 1969 — 6/238] 7. ♘g3 ♗g6 8. h4 h6 9. ♘f3 e6 10. ♘e5 ♗h7 11. ♕e2 ♕e7 12. ♗d2 ♘f6 13. 0-0-0± Liberzon–Karasev, SSSR (ch) 1970 — 10/210

44 6. ♘c3 ♗f5=

45 6... ♘d5 7. ♘1f3 ♗f5 8. g4 ♗g6 9. ♘e5 f6 10. ♘g6 hg6 11. ♘e4 e6 12. c3 ♗d6 13. ♕e2± Lutikov–Vasiljev, SSSR 1962

46 **7... e6** 8. c3 ♗e7 9. ♕e2 0–0 10. h4 c5 11. ♗e3 ♘f5 12. 0-0-0 ♘e3 13. fe3 ♕c7 14. ♖df1± Kopilov–Ravinski, SSSR 1953; **7... g6** 8. c3 ♗g7 9. h3 0–0 10. g4 b5 11. ♗b3 ♘d5 12. ♕e2± Šamkovič–Livšin, SSSR 1961

47 Vasjukov–Livšin, SSSR 1956

48 7. ♗b3 h6 8. ♘5f3 ♘7f6 9. ♘e2 ♗f5 10. ♘g3 ♗h7 11. 0–0 e6 12. c4 ♘b6 13. ♗f4 ♗e7 14. ♕e2± Honfi–Reško, Hungary 1961

49 7... g6 8. ♕e2 h6 9. ♘e4 ♕c7 10. ♗d5 [10. 0–0 ♗g7 11. ♗b3 0–0 12. c4 ♘5f6 13. ♘c3 e6± Kozma–Pithart, ČSSR 1956] cd5 11. ♘c3 ♕c4 12. ♕c4 dc4 13. ♘d5± Schmid–Hönlinger, BRD 1955

50 **8... e6** 9. ♕e2 ♕c7 10. 0–0 ♗e7 11. ♗b3 0–0 12. c4± Rooze–Dunkelblum, Belgique 1966; **8... ♘7f6** 9. ♘f6 gf6 [9... ef6 10. 0–0 ♗e7 11. ♗b3±] 10. ♗b3 ♕c7 11. c4± Kavalek–Perez, Tel Aviv (ol) 1964

51 10. ♕e2 e6 11. 0–0 ♗e7 12. ♘e5 0–0 13. ♗d2 ♘d7 14. ♘g3 ♗h7 15. ♖ad1± Dückstein–Bouwmeester, Schweiz 1962

52 10... ♗g4 11. h3 ♗f3 12. ♕f3 g6 13. ♗d2 a5 14. a3 a4 15. ♗a2 ♗g7 16. 0-0-0 0–0 17. h4± Suetin–Bronštejn, SSSR (ch) 1964

53 12... ♕c7 13. c4 ♘f6 14. ♗f4 g5 15. ♗e3 0-0-0 16. ♕e2 ♖g8 17. f4± Lukin–Reško, SSSR 1973

54 **14. ♕e2** ♘e5 15. de5 ♘d7=; **14. ♗f4** ♘e5 15. ♗e5 ♗d6 16. ♕e2 [Fischer–Portisch, Stockholm (izt) 1962] ♗d3!=; 16. ♕f3± Konstantinopoljski

55 7... ♘b6 8. ♗b3 c5 9. c3 ♗e7 10. 0–0 0–0 [10... c4 11. ♗c2 ♗d7 12. ♘f4 g6 13.

♖e1 ♗c6 14. b3 ♘fd5 15. ♘ge6±→ Simagin–Korčnoj, SSSR 1960] 11. ♖e1 ♘bd5 [11... ♗d7?! 12. ♘f4 ♘bd5 13. ♕e2± Samarian–Koppin, corr. 1968 — 5/166] 12. dc5 ♗c5 13. ♘d4 ♕b6 14. ♘gf3 ♖d8 15. ♗g5± Spaski–Lejn, Soči 1965

56 8... b5 9. ♗d3! [9. ♗b3 c5 10. dc5 ♗c5 11. 0–0 0–0 12. ♘ed4 ♕b6= Guljko–Razuvajev, Dubna 1970] ♗b7 10. c3 ♕b6 11. a4 a5 12. ab5 cb5 13. ♘g3 ♗d6 14. ♕e2 0–0 15. ♘e5 ♖fd8 16. f4± Bronštejn–Vasjukov, SSSR (ch) 1965

57 10. ♘c3 b5 11. ♗d3 b4 12. ♘e4 ♘e4 13. ♗e4 ♘f6 14. ♗d3 0–0 15. ♕e2 ♗b7 16. ♗d2 c5 17. dc5 ♕c5∓ Simagin–Smislov, SSSR 1963

58 **11... ♘d5** 12. ♘e4 ♗f4 13. ♗f4 ♕f4 14. ♘g3! [14. ♗f1 b6 15. g3 ♕c7 16. ♗g2 ♗b7 17. c4 ♘5f6 18. ♘f6 ♘f6 19. c5 ♖fd8= Štejn–Pfleger, Tel Aviv (ol) 1964] b6 15. ♘e5 ♘e5 16. ♖e5 ♕h4 17. ♕d2 ♗b7 18. ♖ae1± Boleslavski; **11... a6** 12. ♘e4 b5 13. ♘d6 ♕d6 14. ♗f1 c5 15. dc5 ♕d1 16. ♖d1 ♘c5 17. ♗e3± Geler–Smislov, SSSR 1964

59 **13. a3** a6 14. b4 e5=; **13. ♕e2** b4 14. ♘e4 c5=

60 14. ♗e4 c5=

61 **7... ♗e7**? 8. ♘f7+–; **7... ♘d5** 8. ♘1f3 ♗e7 9. 0–0 h6 10. ♘e4 0–0 11. ♗b3± Tarve–Randvir, SSSR 1961

62 **8... ♕d4**? 9. ♘1f3△ 10. ♘e5±; **8... ♘bd5** 9. ♗d2 a5 10. c4 a4 11. ♗d1 ♘c7 12. ♘1f3 h6 13. ♘e4 ♗e7 14. ♗c2 b5 15. c5± Spaski–Perez, Tel Aviv (ol) 1964; **8... ♗e7** 9. ♘1f3 0–0 10. ♗d2 a5 [Parma–Donner, Beverwijk 1963] 11. c4 a4 12. ♗c2△ 13. ♗c3± **8... c5** 9. ♘1f3 [9. ♗e3 cd4 10. 0-0-0 ± 9... ♕c7! 10. c3 ♗d7 11. 0-0-0 c4 12. ♗c2 ♘bd5= Neukirch–Starck, DDR 1962; 9. dc5 ♗c5 10. ♘1f3 ♗d7 11. ♗d2 h6 12. ♘e4± Pachman] cd4 [9... h6 10. dc5! ♗c5 11. ♘e4 ♘e4 12. ♕e4 0–0 13. ♗d2△ 0-0-0±] 10. 0–0 ♗e7 11. ♖d1±

63 **9... ♗e7** 10. ♗d2 [10. ♘h3 c5 11. ♗e3 ♘bd5 12. 0-0-0 ♘e3 13. fe3 ♕c7 14. ♘e5 a6 15. g4±→ Talj–Benkö, Amsterdam (izt) 1964; 10... g5!?] a5 [10... 0–0 11. 0-0-0△ ♘e5, g4±→] 11. c4 0–0 12. ♘h3 c5 13. dc5 ♗c5 14. 0-0-0 ♕e7 15. ♘e5 ♘bd7 16. f4± Hasin–Livšin, SSSR 1958; **9... ♗d6** 10. ♘e5 ♕e7 11. ♘gf3 ♗d7 [11... c5 12. ♗e3 0–0 13. g4! ♘fd5 14. ♗d2 cd4 15. g5±→ Jurkov–Čistjakov, SSSR 1962] 12. ♗d2 c5 13. dc5 ♗c5 14. 0–0 a6 15. a3 ♖c8 16. c4 ♗c6 17. ♘c6 ♖c6 18. ♗a2 ♗d6 19. b4± Gheorghiu–Pachman, Kecskemet 1964

64 **10. c4** a4 11. ♗c2 ♗b4∓; **10. c3** a4 11. ♗c2 ♕d5∓; **10. a4** c5 11. ♗f4 ♗d6 12. ♗e5 0–0 13. 0-0-0 [13. ♘h3!?] c4 14. ♗c4 ♘a4∞ Talj–Petrosjan, SSSR (ch) 1973 — 16/157

65 11... ♗e7 12. c3 [12. ♗e3 ♘bd5 13. ♘e5 ♘e3 14. fe3 0–0 15. 0-0-0 ♕c7 16. ♘1f3 b5 17. g4 ♘e4 18. c3 c5∓ Krasnov–Volovič, SSSR 1965; 12. ♗d2 c5 13. dc5 ♘bd7 14. ♘e5 ♘c5 15. ♘gf3 ♘ce4 16. ♕b5 ♗d7 17. ♘d7 ♕d7 18. ♕d7 ♘d7 19. ♗e3 ♗c5∓ Maršalek–Smislov, Oberhausen 1961] c5 13. ♗f4 ♗d6 14. ♗g3 ♗g3 15. hg3 cd4 16. ♘d4 0–0 17. ♘gf3 ♕c7 18. 0-0-0± Suetin–Ćirić, Budva 1967 — 4/193

66 12. ♗f4 c4!? 13. ♗c4 ♘c4 14. ♕c4 ♕b6 15. 0-0-0 [15. ♘e2 ♗d7△ ♗b5] ♘d5 16. ♗e5 ♗d7 17. ♕d3 ♗b5 18. ♕d2 ♖c8 19. ♘e2 f6 20. ♗g3 g5 21. h4 g4 22. ♘e1 ♗e2 23. ♕e2 h5△ ♗h6$\overline{\overline{\infty}}$

67 17. ♕f3 ♗a6 18. ♖e1 ♕d4! 19. c3 ♕h4 20. ♗e3= Tukmakov–A. Zajcev, SSSR (ch) 1970

68 10... ♗c5 11. ♗d2 0–0 12. ♘e5 ♘bd5 13. ♘gf3 b6 14. 0-0-0 ♕c7 15. g4 a5 16. g5 hg5 17. ♗g5±→ Trapl–Perez, Oberhausen 1961; 11... ♕c7!? Pachman

69 12. ♗d2 ♕b6 13. ♘h3 ♗a6 14. c4 ♗b4 15. 0–0 ♗d2= Jansa–Filip, Luhačovice 1968

70 12... ♗d6 13. ♗e3 ♕c7 14. 0-0-0 0–0 15. g4 ♘g4 16. ♖hg1 ♘df6 17. ♔b1 e5∞ Ciocaltea–Barcza, Debrecen 1961

71 17. ♘de5 ♖fd8 18. ♗c2 ♗b7 19. b3 ♗f8= Suetin–Petrosjan, SSSR 1959

72 **11... cd4** 12. ♗d4 ♗c5 13. ♘gf3 [13. ♕b5 ♘bd7 14. ♘d7 ♘d7 15. ♗g7? ♖g8 16. ♗h6 ♕e5∓] 0–0 14. 0-0-0 a5 15. a3 a4 16. ♗a2± Spaski–Pfleger, Tallinn 1973; **11... ♗d6** 12. ♘gf3 0–0 13. 0–0 [13. g4 ♘fd7!∞ Kuprejčik–Flesch, Sombor 1970 — 10/212] a5 [13... ♘bd7 14. c3 b6 15. ♖ad1 ♗b7= Spaski–Benkö, Amsterdam (izt) 1964] 14. c4 ♘bd7 15. ♘d7 ♗d7= Štejn–Smislov, SSSR 1964; **11... ♗d7** 12. ♘gf3 ♖c8 13. c4 cd4 14. ♗d4 ♗b4 15. ♔f1 ♗c5 16. ♗c3 ♗c6 17. ♘c6 ♕c6 18. ♘e5 ♕c7! [18... ♕e4? 19. ♗c2 ♕e2 20. ♔e2± Kuprejčik–Petrosjan, SSSR (ch) 1969] 19. ♘g4 ♗e7= Pachman

73 13... cd4? 14. ♗d4 ♗c5? 15. ♗a4 ♔e7 16. ♘c6 bc6 17. ♗c5± Fichtl–Barcza, Berlin 1962

74 17. a4 0–0 18. a5 ♗d7 19. ♘ce5 ♖fd8 20. ♖fd1 ♗e8= Gheorghiu–Filip, Tel Aviv (ol) 1964

75 10... cd4 11. 0-0-0±

76 12. c3? ♘c3 13. ♕d2 ♘fe4–+

77 12... b5 13. c4 bc4 14. ♗c4 cd4 15. ♘f3 ♗e7 16. ♘d4 ♗d7 17. 0–0 0–0 18. a3±

78 13. 0-0-0 b5! [13... ♗e7 14. ♘c4 ♕d8 15. ♘f3±] 14. ♘gf3 [14. ♗f6 ♘f6 15. ♕f3 ♖b8 16. ♘e2 ♕b6∓ Littlewood–Pfleger, Hastings 1964/65] ♘c3! 15. bc3 dc3∓

79 17. c4 ♘f4 18. ♗f4 ♕d4= Suetin—Filip, Soči 1973 — 16/156

80 8... ♕**d4**? 9. ♘1f3 ♕d5 10. 0—0±; **8... c5** 9. dc5 ♗c5 10. ♘1f3 h6 11. ♘e4 ♘e4 12. ♕e4 ♘d5 13. 0—0 ♗d7 14. ♘e5 ♗c6 15. b3± Matulović—Donner, Palma de Mallorca 1967 — 4/196

81 9... ♗e7 10. ♗d2 ♘bd5 11. 0-0-0 ♘d7 12. ♘e5 ♘e5 13. de5 ♕c7 14. f4 ♗d7 15. ♘f3 0-0-0= Kuprejčik—Smislov, SSSR 1972 — 13/214; 12. a3!△ 13. c4±

82 **10. ♗e3** ♘bd5 [10... ♕c7 11. ♘e5 ♗d7 12. ♘gf3 ♖c8 13. c3 c4 14. ♘d7 ♕d7 12. ♗c2 ♗d6 (Korenski—Holmov, Soči 1973) 13. 0—0=] 11. ♘e5 ♘e3 12. fe3 a6! [12... ♗d6? 13. ♘gf3 ♗e5 14. ♘e5 cd4 15. ♗b5± Šamkovič—Donner, Amsterdam 1968 — 6/239] 13. ♘gf3 ♕c7 14. 0-0-0 b5 15. c3 ♗d6 16. ♖hf1 ♗b7∞; 14. 0—0=; **10. ♗f4** ♘bd5 11. ♗e5 cd4 12. 0-0-0 [Brglez—Schulz, corr. 1968 — 5/167] ♕a5∞

83 12. ♘e5? ♗f2 13. ♔f2 ♕e5—+

84 13... a6 14. ♔b1 b5 15. ♗f4 ♕b6 16. ♘e5 ♗b7= Ivkov—Filip, Tel Aviv (ol) 1964

85 14. ♗c3? g4 15. ♘e5 gh3 16. ♘d7 ♗d7 17. ♕f3 hg2 18. ♖hg1 0-0-0! 19. ♗f6 ♗c6 20. ♗d8 ♗f3 21. ♗c7 ♔c7∓

86 ∓ Boleslavski

87 11... 0—0? 12. ♘gf3 ♘bd5 13. a3 b6 [13... ♗d6 14. g4!±] 14. g4 ♗b7 15. ♖g1 ♘d7 16. g5±→ Darga—Filip, Tel Aviv (ol) 1964

88 12... 0—0 13. ♗d2 ♘e5 14. ♘e5 ♗d4 15. 0-0-0 ♕d5! [15... ♕b6 16. ♘c4 ♕c7 17. ♗e3 ♗e3 18. ♕e3 ♗d7= Parma—Filip, La Habana (ol) 1966; 16. c3! ♗c5 17. g4±↑] 16. f4 ♕a2 17. c3 ♗c5 18. g4 ♘d5 19. g5 [Kirpičnikov—Lejn, SSSR 1974 — 18/195] ♗a3! 20. ba3 ♕a3=

89 14. ♗d2 ♕d5 15. 0-0-0!? [15. 0—0 ♗d4 16. ♘c4 ♗d7 17. ♘e3 ♕e5∓ Hennings—Filip, La Habana 1967 — 4/194] ♕a2 16. c3$\overline{\overline{\infty}}$ Hennings—Minev, Cienfuegos 1972 — 13/215

90 14... ♗d6 15. ♗f4 ♕c7 16. ♖fe1 b6 17. ♖ad1 ♗b7 18. c4 ♖fd8= Matulović—Pfleger, Lugano (ol) 1968 — 6/241; 15. f4!△ ♗d2, ♖ae1±

91 **15. ♕f3** ♕c7! [15... ♖b8 16. ♗f4 ♗b7 17. ♕h3±] 16. ♖e1 ♗d6 17. ♕g3 ♘d7 18. ♗f4 ♗b7 19. ♖e3 ♘e5= Jansa—A. Zajcev, Soči 1965; **15. ♗f4** ♗b7 16. ♖ad1 ♕e7 17. ♗g3 ♖fd8 18. c3 ♗d6 19. ♖d2 ♖ac8 20. ♖fd1 ♗b8 21. c4 ♔f8= Kuzmin—Hort, Banja Luka 1974 — 18/194

92 15... ♕c7 16. ♘g4±↑

93 16. ♗f4 ♗b7 17. ♗g3 ♖fd8= Matanović—Pfleger, Tel Aviv (ol) 1964

94 **16... ♗b4**? 17. ♘c6 ♕c5 18. ♘b4 ♕b4 19. ♕f3 ♖b8 20. ♗a3±; **16... ♗d6**! 17. ♗b2 [17. ♘c6 ♕c7 18. b5 (Smislov—Donner, Palma de Mallorca (izt) 1967 — 4/195) ♖e8! 19. ♗b2 e5∓] ♗b7 18. a3 ♖fd8 19. c4 a5! 20. b5 ♖ac8=

95 **11. b4** b6! [11... a5 12. c3 ab4 13. cb4 b6 14. a4 bc5 15. b5 ♘d5∞ Levy—Filip, Praia de Rocha 1969] 12. ♗e4 ♘e4 13. ♕e4 ♗a6 14. cb6 ab6 15. ♘e2 ♖c8$\overline{\overline{\infty}}$ **11. c6** bc6 12. ♗f4 ♕b6 13. c3 ♘d5 14. ♘h3 ♗e7 15. 0—0 ♘f4 16. ♘f4 0—0 17. ♘e5± Ree—Filip, Wijk aan Zee 1970; 12... ♘d5△ ♗f6=

96 11... ♘c5 12. ♗b5±

97 12... ♘d7!? 13. ♕e2 ♘c5 14. ♗b5 ♗d7 15. ♗d2 ♗b6 16. ♕b5 ♕d7 17. ♕e2 ♗d6 18. 0-0-0± Radulov—Onat, Nice (ol) 1974 — 17/221; 17... ♕d5=

98 14. ♕e2 ♗d6 15. ♘f3 ♗d7△ ♗c6=

99 14... ♗d6 15. ♕e2 b6 16. 0-0-0 ♗b7 17. ♗e3 ♕c7 18. ♗b5± Radulov—Sloth, Skopje (ol) 1972 — 14/212

100 15... ♗d6 16. ♘c4 ♗c5 17. f4 b6 18. 0-0-0 0—0 19. ♖he1 ♖d8 20. ♘e5 ♗b7= Radulov—Filip, Skopje (ol) 1972

101 16. ♗b5 ♔e7 17. ♗e2 ♘e4 18. ♘d3 ♗d6 19. ♗e3 ♗d7 20. ♗d4 f6 21. ♗f3 ♗c6 22. 0-0-0 ♖hc8∓ Parma—Smislov, Lugano (ol) 1968 — 6/240

102 17. ♘d3 ♗d6 18. ♗e3 ♗d7=

103 **7... ♗f5** 8. ♕b3 ♘d5 9. ♕b7 ♘b6 10. ♘f3! f6 11. ♗b3 ♕d6 12. ♕a6 g5 13. ♗e3+— Keres—Pfleger, Hastings 1965; **7... e6** 8. ♘f3 ♗e7 9. 0—0 0—0 10. ♕e2 b5 11. ♗d3 ♗b7 12. ♗f4! [12. ♗g5 a6 13. ♘e5 ♘d5 14. ♗d2 c5= Žuhovicki—Smislov, SSSR (ch) 1961] ♕b6 13. ♘e5 ♖ad8 14. a4 a6 15. a5± Štejn—Vasjukov, SSSR (ch) 1964

104 **8. ♗g5** ♘e4 9. ♗e3 ♗f5 10. ♘f3 [10. ♗f7 ♔f7 11. ♕f3 e6 12. g4 g6= A. Zajcev] e6 11. ♕e2 ♗d6 12. ♗d3 ♗g6= Gipslis—A. Zajcev, SSSR 1969; **8. ♕b3** e6 9. ♘f3 ♗d6 10. 0—0 h6 11. ♖e1 0—0= Wade—Richter, Trenčanske Teplice 1949

105 9... ♗f3 10. ♕f3 e6 11. 0—0 ♗d612. ♗g5 ♘d5 13. ♖fe1± Gheorghiu—Pachman, La Habana (ol) 1966 — 2/156

106 11... ♘d7 12. ♗f4 ♘e5 13. ♗e5± Štejn—Filip, Erevan 1965

107 7... g6 8. 0—0 ♗g7 9. ♖e1 0—0 10. c3 ♕d6 11. ♕e2 ♖e8 12. ♗g5 !♗f5 13. ♗h4± Matanović—Ćirić, Jugoslavija (ch) 1969

108 8. ♗f4 e6 9. 0—0 ♗e7 10. c3 0—0 11. ♕b3 ♕b6 12. ♕b6 ab6 13. ♗b3 b5∓ Pietzsch—Smislov, Moskva 1963

109 9. ♗f4 ♗e7 10. ♘e5 ♘d5 11. ♗g3 0—0 12. 0—0 ♖c8 13. ♕e2 b5 14. ♗b3 ♘f6 15. ♗h4 ♕c7 16. ♖fe1 ♗d6 17. ♖ad1 ♘d5 18. ♗g3 ♘b6∓ Lokvenc—Smislov, Leipzig (ol) 1960

110 Mnacakanjan – Filip, Erevan 1965

111 **9. g4 ♗g6!** [9... ♗e4 10. f3 ♗d5 11. ♗d3 ♗d6 12. c4 ♗e5 13. de5 ♘g4 14. ♗f4 g5 15. cd5 gf4 16. fg4 ♕d5 17. 0–0 0-0-0 18. ♖f3 ♖hg8–+ Rauzer – Veresov, SSSR 1934; 11. ♗e2 b5 12. a4 ♗d6 13. ab5 ♗e5 14. de5 ♘g4 15. ♗f4 (Štejn – Ivkov, Amsterdam 1970 — 8/162) ♕b6 16. ♖f1 ♘e3 17. ♗e3 ♕e3 18. ♕d3± Ivkov] 10. h4 ♘d7 11. ♗f4 ♘e5 12. ♗e5 h5∓; **9. c3** ♗d6 10. ♕e2 ♕c7 11. ♗b3 h6= Halilbejli – Lojev, SSSR 1961

112 **9... ♗e7** 10. ♖e1 [10. ♗b3 a5 11. c4 0–0 12. ♗f4 c5 13. dc5 ♗c5 14. ♕e2 ♕d4∓ Gligorić – Smislov, Moskva 1963] h6 [10... ♗e4 11. ♗g5 ♗d5 12. ♗d3±; 10... ♘d7 11. ♗f4 ♘e5 12. ♗e5 0–0 13. c3 b5 14. ♗b3 c5= Matanović – Filip, Erevan 1965; 11. ♘f7!? ♔f7 12. ♕f3∞̄] 11. c3 0–0 12. ♗f4 ♘d5 13. ♗g3 ♗h4 14. ♗b3 ♗g3 15. hg3 ♕e7 16. g4± Ivkov – Pachman, Vrnjačka Banja 1967 — 3/178; **9... ♘d7** 10. ♗f4 ♘e5 11. ♗e5 ♗d6=

113 Spaski – Ilivicki, Soči 1965

114 9. h3 ♗e7 10. ♕e2 0–0 11. ♖d1 ♕c7 12. ♘h4 ♗e4 13. ♗g5 ♗d5 14. ♗d3 b5 15. ♘f3 h6 16. ♗d2 a6= Reshevsky – Smislov, Palma de Mallorca (izt) 1970

115 11... ♕a5 12. ♗f6!? ♗f6 13. d5±↑

116 **14. ♗c1** ♗g5 15. ♗e3 ♕f6 16. ♕f6 ♗f6= Larsen – Filip, Palma de Mallorca (izt) 1970 — 10/213; **14. ♗e3**!± Larsen

117 10... h6 11. ♗h4 ♘e4 12. g4! ♗h7 13. ♗g3 ♘g3 14. fg3 ♕c7 15. ♘e5 ♗d6 16. h4±→ Talj – Füster, Portorož (izt) 1958

118 14. ♖he1 0–0 15. ♔b1 ♖ad8± Matanović – Petrosjan, Jugoslavija – SSSR 1969

119 16. ♗d3 a5 17. c3 ♕d6 18. g3 b4 19. c4± Fischer – Petrosjan, Bled 1961

B 18 — 1. e4 c6 2. d4 d5 3. ♘c3 de4 4. ♘e4 ♗f5

	5	6	7	8	9	10	11	12	13	
1	♗d3[1] ♕d4[2]	♘f3 ♕d8[3]	♕e2 ♘f6[4]	♗d2[5] ♗e4	♗e4 ♘e4	♕e4 e6	0-0-0			∞̄
2	♕f3 e6[6]	♗e3[7] ♕a5	c3[8] ♗a3	b4 ♕d5	♗d3 ♗b2	♖b1 ♗e4	♗e4 ♗c3	♔f1 ♕a2	♘e2	∞̄

1. e4 c6 2. d4 d5 3. ♘c3 de4 4. ♘e4 ♗f5 5. ♘g3 ♗g6

	6	7	8	9	10	11	12	13	14	
3	♘h3[9] ♘f6[10]	♘f4 e5	♘g6[11] hg6	de5 ♕d1	♔d1 ♘g4	♘e4 ♘e5	♗e2 f6[12]	c3 ♘bd7	♗e3 0-0-0[13]	±
4	... e6	♘f4[14] ♗d6[15]	c3[16] ♘f6	h4 ♕c7	h5 ♗f4	♗f4 ♕f4	hg6 fg6	♕d2 ♕d2	♔d2 ♘bd7[17]	=
5	f4 e6[18]	h4[19] h5[20]	♘f3 ♘d7	♗c4[21] ♗e7	0–0 ♕c7[22]	♘e2 0-0-0	c3			=
6	♗c4 ♘d7	♘f3[23] ♘f6	0–0 e6	♕e2[24] ♗e7[25]	♖e1[26] ♘d5[27]	♗b3 0–0[28]	c4[29] ♘b4	a3 ♘d3	♖d1 ♘c1[30]	±
7	... e6	♘1e2[31] ♗d6	h4[32] h6	♘f4 ♗f4[33]	♗f4 ♘f6	h5[34] ♗h7	♕e2[35] ♘bd7	0-0-0 ♘d5	♗d2 ♘7f6[36]	±
8	... ...	... ♘f6	0–0 ♗d6[37]	f4 ♕d7![38]	♗d3[39] ♗d3	♕d3 g6[40]				=
9	... ...	... ...	♘f4 ♘d5	♘g6 hg6	♘e4[41] ♕h4	♕e2 ♗e7[42]	♗d2 ♘d7	0-0-0 ♘7f6	♘g5[43]	±
10	... ...	... ...	... ♗d6	♗b3[44] ♕c7[45]	♕f3 ♘bd7	h4[46] e5[47]	♘g6[48] hg6	♗e3 0-0-0	0-0-0[49] ed4[50]	=
11	♘f3 ♘f6[51]	h4 h6[52]	♘e5 ♗h7	♗c4 e6	♕e2 ♘d5	♗b3 ♘d7	♗d2 ♘7f6	0-0-0[53]		±
12	... ♘d7	♗d3 e6[54]	0–0[55] ♘gf6	♖e1[56] ♗e7	c4[57] 0–0[58]	♗g6 hg6	♗f4 ♖e8	♕c2 c5	♖ad1 cd4[59]	±

	6	7	8	9	10	11	12	13	14	
13	...	...	...	c4	♗g6	♕a4	b4	♕b3	a4	∞
	...	...	♕c7	0-0-0[60]	hg6	♔b8	♘h6	♘f5	e5[61]	
14	h4	♘h3[63]	de5	c3[65]	♗e2	♕b3[67]	♗f4			±
	h6[62]	e5[64]	♕a5	♕e5	♘f6[66]	♕c7	♕b6[68]			
15	...	...	♘f4	♗c4	0—0[69]	♘e6	♗e6	♖e1	♗g8	=
	...	e6	♗h7	♘f6	♗d6	fe6	♘bd7![70]	♕c7	♔f8[71]	
16	...	f4	♘f3	h5	♗d3	♕d3	♗d2	0-0-0	♘e2	=
	...	e6	♘d7[72]	♗h7	♗d3	♕c7	0-0-0[73]	♗d6	♘gf6[74]	

[1] 5. ♘c5 b6 6. ♘b3 e6 7. ♘f3 ♘d7 [7... ♗d6 8. g3 ♘e7 9. ♗g2 h6 10. 0—0 0—0 11. ♕e2± Bronštejn—Petrosjan, SSSR 1966 — 2/115] 8. g3 ♘gf6 9. ♗g2 ♖c8 10. 0—0 ♗d6=

[2] 5... e6 6. ♘f3 [6. ♘e2 ♘f6 7. f3 ♘bd7 8. 0—0= Engels—Kohler, Oyenhausen 1938] ♘d7 7. 0—0 ♗e4 8. ♗e4 ♘gf6 9. ♗d3 ♗d6 10. ♕e2±

[3] 6... ♕d5 7. ♕e2 ♘f6 [7... e6?! 8. ♘h4 ♗g6 9. ♘g6 hg6 10. ♗f4±⟳↑] 8. c4 ♕d8 9. 0—0±

[4] **7... e6** 8. ♗f4 ♘d7 9. 0-0-0 ♘gf6 10. ♘f6 [10. ♘eg5?! ♗d3 11. ♖d3 ♘d5 12. ♖d5 cd5 13. ♘f7 ♕f6 14. ♘h8 ♕f4—+ Persitz—Porath, Israel 1961] ♕f6 11. ♗g5 ♕g6 12. ♗f5 ♕f5 13. ♕d2 ♕d5 14. ♕f4+—; **7... ♗e4** 8. ♗e4 ♘f6 9. 0—0! [9. ♗d3 e6 10. 0—0 ♘bd7 11. ♗g5 ♗e7 12. ♖ad1 ♕a5 13. ♖fe1 (Stökl—Voorvinde 1940) 0-0-0∓] ♘e4 10. ♕e4 e6 11. ♗g5 ♗e7 12. ♖ad1 ♕c7 13. ♖fe1 0—0 14. ♗f4 ♕a5 15. ♗e5∞̄↑

[5] 8. ♘f6 gf6 9. ♗f5 ♕a5 10. ♗d2 ♕f5 11. 0-0-0 ♘d7 [11... ♕e6? 12. ♕d3 ♕a2 13. ♕d8+—] 12. ♗e3 ♕a5 13. ♕c4 e6∓ Fajarowicz—Blümich 1930

[6] **5... ♕d5** 6. ♗d3 ♗e4 7. ♗e4 ♕d4 8. ♘e2∞̄⟳ Kmoch; **5... ♗e4** 6. ♕e4 ♘f6 7. ♕d3 ♘bd7 8. ♘f3 ♕c7 9. ♗e2 e6 10. 0—0 ♗d6= Leonhardt—Lee, Ostende 1907; **5... ♗g6** 6. ♗e3 ♘d7 7. ♗d3 ♘gf6 8. ♘e2 ♘e4 9. ♗e4 ♗e4 10. ♕e4 e6 11. ♘f4 ♘f6 12. ♕d3 ♗d6= Juhtman—Pines 1958

[7] 6. c3 ♘d7 7. ♗f4 ♘df6 8. ♘d2 ♘e7 9. h3 ♘ed5 10. ♗e5 ♗g6 11. ♕g3 ♗e7∓ Spielmann—Kolnhofer, Wien 1933; 11. ♗d3!? Grünfeld

[8] 7. ♗d2 ♕d5 8. ♗d3 ♕d4 9. 0-0-0 ♘d7∓ Felderhof—Euwe, Haag 1933

[9] 6. ♘1e2 e6 [6... e5? 7. de5 ♕d1 8. ♔d1 ♗c5 9. ♘f4! ♗f2 10. ♘g6 hg6 11. ♘e4 ♗d4 12. ♘d6 ♔e7 13. ♗c4 f6 14. ♘f7 ♖h5 15. c3! ♗b6 16. ♗f4 ♔f8 (Prins—Szabo, Venezia 1949) 17. g4± Brinckmann; 6... ♘d7 7. h4 h6 8. ♘f4 ♗h7 9. ♗c4 e5 10. ♕e2 ♕e7 11. de5 ♕e5 12. ♗e3 ♗c5= Talj—Botvinik, (m) 1960; 10. ♘d3! ed4 11. 0—0±→ Talj] 7. h4 h6 [7... ♘f6 8. h5 ♗f5 9. ♘f5 ♕a5 10. c3 ♕f5 11. ♘g3 ♕a5 12. ♗f4± Talj—Bagirov, SSSR 1964] 8. ♘f4 — 6. h4

[10] **6... e5**? 7. de5 ♕a5 [7... ♕d1 8. ♔d1 ♗c5 9. ♘f4! — 6. ♘1e2] 8. c3 ♕e5 9. ♗e2 ♘f6 10. ♗f4 ♕a5 11. ♕b3±; **6... h6**? 7. ♘f4 ♗h7 8. ♗c4 ♘f6 [8... e5 9. de5 ♕a5 10. c3 ♕e5 11. ♘fe2 ♘f6 12. ♗f4 ♕c5 13. ♕b3 ♕e7 14. 0-0-0± Koch—Groschupf, DDR 1954] 9. 0—0 e6 10. ♖e1 ♗e7 11. ♗e6 g5 12. ♗b3! [12. ♘gh5 0—0 13. ♗b3 gf4∞ Prins—Pomar, 1951] gf4 13. ♗f4 ♗g6 14. ♕d2±→; **6... ♘d7** 7. ♗c4 [7. ♘f4 e5! 8. ♘g6 hg6 9. de5 ♘e5=] ♘gf6 [7... e5 8. ♕e2 ♕e7 9. 0—0±; 7... e6 — 6. ♗c4] 8. ♘f4 e5 9. ♘g6! [9. de5 ♕a5 10. ♗d2 ♕e5 11. ♘ge2 ♗c5 12. 0—0 0-0-0 13. ♘g3 ♕d4 14. ♗d3 (Keres—Kasparjan, SSSR (ch) 1952) ♘e5!∓] hg6 10. de5 ♕a5 [10... ♘e5 11. ♕e2 ♕e7 12. ♗b3±] 11. ♗d2 ♕e5 12. ♕e2±□

[11] 8. de5 ♕d1 [8... ♕a5? 9. ♗d2 ♕e5 10. ♗e2 ♕b2 11. ♘g6 hg6 12. ♖b1± Konstantinopoljski] 9. ♔d1 ♘g4 10. ♘g6 — 8. ♘g6

[12] 12... ♗e7 13. ♗e3 0—0 14. g3 ♘bd7 15. c3 ♘f6 16. ♘f6 ♗f6 17. ♔c2± Grečkin

[13] 15. ♔c2 ♘b6 [Fischer—Foguelman, Buenos Aires 1960] 16. a4!±

[14] 7. c3 ♗d6 8. ♗e2 ♘e7 9. 0—0 0—0 10. ♘f4 ♘d7 11. ♘g6 ♘g6 12. ♗d3 ♕h4= Bird, Blackburne—Bardeleben, Weiss, England 1888

[15] **7... ♕h4** 8. ♗e2 [8. ♕e2 ♘d7 9. c3 0-0-0 10. ♘g6 hg6 11. ♘e4 ♕e7 12. ♗g5± Ragozin—Flor, Moskva 1935] ♘d7 9. ♗e3 ♗d6 10. ♕d2 ♕e7 11. ♘g6 hg6 12. ♘e4 ♗c7 13. c4± Novopašin—Furman, SSSR 1963; **7... ♘d7** 8. ♗c4 — 6. ♗c4

[16] 8. ♘g6!? hg6 9. ♗c4 ♕c7 10. ♘e4∞

[17] 15. ♖e1 ♔f7 16. ♗c4 ♖ae8∞̄ Boleslavski—Petrosjan, Zürich (ct) 1953

[18] 6... h5 7. ♘f3 [7. f5? ♗f5 8. ♘f5 ♕a5∓] h4 8. ♘e2 ♘d7 9. ♘e5 ♘e5 10. fe5 e6 11. ♘f4 ♗f5∓; 7. h4 e6 — 6... e6

[19] 7. ♘f3 ♗d6 8. ♗d3 ♘e7 [8... ♘d7 9. ♗g6 hg6 10. ♘e4 ♘df6 11. ♘eg5± Szabo—Müller, Venezia 1949] 9. 0—0 ♘d7 10. ♔h1

♕c7 11. ♘e5 ♖d8 12. ♕e2 ♗d3 13. ♘d3 0–0 14. ♗d2 c5 15. ♘e4 ♘f5 16. dc5 ♘c5∓ ×f4 Marshall–Capablanca, New York 1927

20 7... h6 — 6. h4

21 9. ♘e5? ♘e5 10. fe5 ♗e7∓

22 10... ♗h4? 11. f5! ef5 [11... ♗g3 12. fg6 fg6 13. ♕d3 ♘e7 14. ♘g5+–] 12. ♘h4 ♕h4 13. ♘f5 ♗f5 14. ♖f5 ♘gf6 15. ♕e2 ♔f8 16. ♖f4 ♕g3 17. ♖f3 ♕g4 18. ♗f4 ♖e8 19. ♕f2± Ellerman

23 7. ♘1e2 e5? 8. 0–0±; 8. f4±; 7... e6 — 6... e6

24 9. ♘g5 h6 10. ♘h3 ♗d6 11. ♘f4 ♗f4 12. ♗f4 ♘d5 13. ♗c1 [13. ♗d2 ♕b6!] ♕h4 14. ♗d3 ♗d3= Talj–Petrosjan, SSSR 1961

25 9... ♗d6 10. ♘e5!± 0–0? 11. ♗e6 fe6 12. ♘g6 hg6 13. ♕e6+–

26 10. ♘e5 ♘e5 11. de5 ♘d5 12. ♖d1 ♕c7 13. ♗d3 0-0-0 14. ♗g6 hg6 15. ♗d2 ♖d7= Panov–Ebralidze, SSSR (ch) 1937

27 16... 0–0 11. ♗b3±

28 11... b5 12. a4! b4 13. a5±

29 12. ♗d2 a5 13. a4 ♖e8 14. ♖ad1 ♕c7= Puc–Kozomara, Jugoslavija 1960

30 15. ♖ac1±○

31 7. ♘h3 ♘f6 8. 0–0 ♗d6 9. ♗b3 ♘bd7 10. ♘f4 ♕c7 11. ♕f3 e5 12. ♘g6 hg6 13. c3 [Simagin–Dubinin, corr. 1969 — 7/185] 0–0=

32 8. 0–0 ♘d7 9. f4 ♘e7=; 8... ♘f6 — 7... ♘f6

33 9... ♗h7 10. ♘fh5!±

34 11. ♕d2 ♘bd7 12. 0-0-0 ♘d5 [12... ♘b6!? 13. ♗b3 a5 Geler] 13. ♖de1± Talj–Botvinik (m) 1960

35 12. ♕d2 ♘bd7 13. 0-0-0 ♘d5= Karaklajić–Udovčić, Jugoslavija (ch) 1957

36 15. ♗d3 ♗d3 16. ♕d3 ♕c7 17. ♔b1 0-0-0 18. ♖h4 ♕e7 19. c4±↑ Geler–Bagirov, SSSR (ch) 1959

37 8... ♘bd7!? 9. ♗b3 [9. f4?! ♘b6 10. ♗b3 c5⇆ Dely–Florian, Hungary (ch) 1958] ♘b6 10. ♘f4 ♗d6 11. ♖e1 [Westerinen–Pomar, España 1970 — 9/157] ♕c7=

38 **9... ♘e4** 10. f5 ♗g3 11. ♘g3 ♘g3 12. fg6 ♘f1 13. gf7 ♔f7 14. ♕g4 ♖e8 15. ♗h6!± Keres; **9... ♗f5** 10. ♘f5 ef5 11. ♘g3 g6 12. ♖e1± Altšuler–Zagorovski, corr. 1967 — 3/183; **9... ♕c7** 10. f5! [10. ♔h1 ♘bd7 11. f5 ef5 12. ♘f5 ♗f5 13. ♖f5 0–0± Zajcev–Pavlov, SSSR 1967 — 4/199; 10... ♗f5 11. ♘f5 ef5 12. b3± Westerinen–Cagan, Ybbs 1968 — 6/242] ef5 11. ♘f5 ♗f5 [11... ♗h2? 12. ♔h1 0–0 13. g3! ♗f5 14. ♖f5 ♗g3 15. ♖f6!+– Keres–Golombek, Moskva 1956; 12... ♗f5 13. ♖f5 ♗d6 14. ♗g5 ♘bd7 15. ♘f4±→ Keres] 12. ♖f5 ♘bd7 13. ♘g3 0-0-0 14. ♕f1± Fichtl–Golombek, München (ol) 1958

39 10. f5?! ef5 11. ♗d3 ♘e4∓

40 = Boleslavski

41 10. ♗b3 ♘d7 11. ♗d2 ♕h4 12. c3 ♗d6 13. ♕f3 ♘7f6 14. ♘e2 [14. 0-0-0 ♗f4 15. ♘f1 ♕g4= Gligorić–Ojanen, Varna (ol) 1962] ♕e4 15. ♕e4 ♘e4 16. ♗c1 0-0-0= Polugajevski–Osnos, SSSR (ch) 1965

42 11... ♘f6 12. ♘g5 ♕d4? 13. ♘f7!±

43 ± Boleslavski

44 **9. 0–0** ♘d5! [9... ♕c7 10. ♕f3! 0–0 11. ♗b3 ♘bd7 12. h4 ♗f5 13. ♘f5 ef5 14. ♘h3± Simagin–Flor, SSSR 1967] 10. ♘gh5 0–0 11. ♗b3 ♘d7 12. ♘g6 hg6 13. ♘g3 ♕h4= Talj–Botvinik (m) 1961; **9. ♘g6** hg6 10. ♗g5 ♘bd7 11. 0–0 ♕a5 [Talj–Botvinik (m) 1960] 12. ♕d2=

45 9... ♘d5?! 10. ♘g6 hg6 11. ♘e4 ♗e7 12. 0–0 ♘d7 13. c4 ♘5f6 14. ♘g5 ♘h7 15. ♘f3 ♕c7 16. g3 c5 [16... 0-0-0 17. ♕e2 ♖he8 18. ♗f4 ♗d6 19. ♗e3!△ 20. c5; 20. d5±] 17. d5 e5 18. ♗a4± Korčnoj–Petrosjan, Stockholm (izt) 1962

46 11. 0–0 e5! 12. ♘g6 hg6 13. ♖e1 0-0-0 14. ♗f7 ed4 15. ♗g6 ♘e5 16. ♗f5 ♔b8 17. ♕d1 g6 18. ♗h3 ♘d5=∞↑ Kotov–Antošin, SSSR 1963

47 11... 0-0-0 12. h5 ♗f5 13. ♘f5 ♕a5 14. c3 ♕f5 15. ♕d3 ♕d3 16. ♘d3= Keres–Petrosjan, Los Angeles 1963

48 12. de5? ♘e5 13. ♕e2 0-0-0! 14. h5 ♘eg4! 15. hg6 hg6 16. ♖h8 ♖h8 17. ♕f3 [17. ♕c4 ♕b6 18. ♘d3 ♘f2! 19. ♘f2 ♗g3–+] ♘h2∓

49 14. ♗f7?! ed4 15. ♗d4 ♘e5 16. ♗e6 ♔b8=∞↑

50 15. ♗d4 ♘c5 16. ♗f6 ♗f4 17. =b1 gf6=

51 6... e6? 7. h4 h6 [7... ♘f6 8. h5 ♗e4 9. ♘e4 ♘e4 10. ♗d3 ♘f6 11. ♕e2±] 8. ♘e5 ♗h7 9. ♗c4 ♘d7 10. ♕e2 ♘e5 11. de5 ♗e7 12. ♗d2 ♕b6 [12... ♗c2 13. ♗c3 ♗g6 14. ♖d1 ♕c7 15. h5 ♗h7 16. f4± Zavernjaev–Filipov, SSSR 1962] 13. 0-0-0±

52 7... ♘h5 8. ♘e2! ♘d7 9. g4 ♘hf6 10. h5 ♗e4 11. ♘g3 ♕a5 12. ♗d2 ♕d5 13. ♗g2 ♗f3 14. ♕f3 ♕d4 15. g5 ♘d5 16. 0-0-0± Suetin–Ratner, SSSR 1951

53 Bely–Clarke, Moskva (ol) 1956

54 7... ♗d3 8. ♕d3 e6 9. 0–0 ♘gf6 10. ♗f4 ♗e7 11. ♖fe1 0–0 12. c4 ♖e8 13. ♖ad1 ♕b6 14. ♕c2± Matulović–Milić, Jugoslavija (ch) 1955

55 8. ♗g6 hg6 9. ♕e2 ♘gf6 10. ♗d2 ♕c7 11. 0-0-0 ♗d6 12. ♔b1 0-0-0= Fuderer–Golombek, Beograd 1952

56 **9. b3** ♗e7 10. ♗b2 0–0 11. ♗g6 hg6 12. c4 a5 13. ♕e2 a4 14. ♗c3 ab3 15. ab3 ♕b6= Andrić–Trifunović, Jugoslavija (ch) 1951; **9. c4** ♗d6 10. b3 0–0 11. ♗b2 ♕c7 12. ♗g6 hg6 13. ♕e2 ♖fe8 14. ♘e4 ♘e4 15. ♕e4± Spaski–Karpov, Leningrad (mct) 1974 — 17/224

57 10. ♗g5 ♗d3 11. ♕d3 0–0 12. c4± Gligorić–Darga, Bled 1961

58 10... ♗d3 11. ♕d3 0–0 12. ♗d2 ♕c7 13. ♗c3 ♖fe8 14. ♖ad1 ♖ad8 [14... ♗f8 15. ♘e5 ♖ad8 16. ♕f3 ♘e5 17. de5 ♖d1 18. ♖d1 ♘d7 19. ♘e4± O'Kelly–Pfeiffer, Bled 1950] 15. ♕e2 c5 16. dc5 ♗c5 17. b4 ♗e7 18. ♖c1± Unzicker–Golombek, Stockholm (izt) 1952

59 15. ♘d4 ♗b4 16. ♗d2 ♗d2 17. ♕d2 a6 18. b4± Najdorf–Kotov, Zürich (ct) 1953

60 9... ♘gf6 10. ♗g6 hg6 11. ♕e2 ♗d6 12. ♖d1 0–0 13. ♘e4 ♗f4± Geler–Matulović, SSSR–Jugoslavija 1964

61 15. de5 ♘e5 16. ♘e5 ♕e5 17. ♗b2 ♕c7∞ Dückstein–Petrosjan, Varna (ol) 1962

62 6... h5!? 7. ♘h3 e5 8. de5 ♕a5 9. c3 ♘d7 [Böttger–Wolfensberger, BRD 1967 — 3/184] 10. e6 ♕e5 11. ♗e2 ♕e6 12. ♘f4±

63 7. ♗d3 ♕d4?! 8. ♘f3 ♕d6 9. ♗g6 ♕g6 10. ♕e2 ♕d6 [10... ♘d7 11. h5 ♕d6 12. ♖h4 e6 13. ♖d4 ♕c7 14. ♗f4 ♕a5 (Marić–Sušić, Jugoslavija 1966 — 2/117) 15. ♔f1!±⟳↑] 11. 0–0 e6 12. ♖d1 ♕c7 13. ♖d4 ♘f6 14. ♗f4 ♕a5 15. ♘e5± Minić–Vukić, Vrnjačka Banja 1966 — 2/164; 7... ♗d3 8. ♕d3 e6 9. ♘f3 — 6. ♘f3

64 Capablanca

65 **7. ♗d2** ♕e5 8. ♗e2 ♕b2 9. ♖b1⩱; **7. ♕d2** ♗b4 8. c3 ♕e5 9. ♗e2 ♗c5 10. ♘f4 ♘d7= Panov

66 **10... ♘d7** 11. ♗f4 ♕e6 12. 0–0 0-0-0 13. ♕a4±; **10... ♗c5** 11. ♗f4 ♕d5 [11... ♕e6 12. 0–0 ♘e7 13. ♖e1 0–0 14. b4! ♗b6 15. ♗a6+–] 12. ♕d5 cd5 13. 0–0 ♘e7 14. ♗f3± Pachman

67 11. ♗f4 ♕d5=

68 Kovacsy–Lepsenyi, corr. 1963

69 **10. ♕e2** ♗d6 11. ♗e3 [11. ♗e6 0–0!∓; 11. c3 ♘bd7 12. ♗e6 fe6 13. ♘e6 ♕e7 14. ♘f5 ♗f5 15. ♘g7 ♔f7 16. ♘f5 ♕e2 17. ♔e2 (Keres–Olafsson, Bled 1961) ♗f8=; 11... ♕e7= Pachman] ♘bd7 12. ♘gh5 ♘h5 13. ♘h5 ♖g8! 14. g4 ♕c7 15. g5 ♗g6 16. 0-0-0 0-0-0= Talj–Botvinik (m) 1960; **10. ♗b3** ♗d6 11. ♘fh5 ♖g8 12. ♗f4 ♗f4 13. ♘f4 ♘bd7 14. ♕d2 ♕c7 15. 0-0-0 0-0-0= Ciocaltea–Botvinik, Tel Aviv (ol) 1964

70 12... ♕c7 13. ♖e1 ♘bd7 14. ♗g8 ♔f8 15. ♗h7 ♖h7 16. ♘f5⩱ Talj–Botvinik (m) 1960; 13. ♘h5!±→ Kondratjev

71 15. ♗h7 ♖h7 16. ♘f5 g6! 17. ♗h6 ♔g8 18. ♘d6 ♕d6 19. ♗g5 ♖e7 20. ♕d3 ♔g7= Botvinik, Goldberg

72 8... ♗d6 9. h5 ♗h7 10. ♗d3 ♗d3 11. ♕d3 ♕c7 12. ♘e5 ♘f6 13. ♗d2 ♘a6 14. 0-0-0 0–0–0 15. ♔b1 c5!= Pedersen–Delander 1963

73 12... ♘gf6 13. 0-0-0 [13. ♘e5 ♗d6 14. 0-0-0 0–0 15. ♘e2 c5 16. ♘d7 ♘d7 17. ♔b1 ♖fd8 18. g4± Dückstein–Hort, ČSSR 1968 — 5/170] c5 14. ♕e2 0-0-0 [14... ♗d6 15. ♘f5 ♗f4 16. dc5±] 15. ♘e5± Kavalek–Saidy, Las Palmas 1973 — 16/159

74 15. ♔b1 ♔b8 16. ♕b3 ♕b6 17. ♘e5 ♕b3= Ciocaltea–Golombek, Moskva 1956

B 19

1. e4 c6 2. d4 d5 3. ♘c3 de4 4. ♘e4 ♗f5 5. ♘g3 ♗g6 6. h4 h6 7. ♘f3 ♘d7

	8	9	10	11	12	13	14	15	16	
1	♗d3 ♗d3	♕d3 ♕c7[1]	♗d2 e6	0-0-0 ♘gf6	c4[2] 0-0-0[3]	♗c3[4] ♗d6	♘e4 ♗f4	♔b1 ♘e5	♘e5 ♗e5[5]	=

1. e4 c6 2. d4 d5 3. ♘c3 de4 4. ♘e4 ♗f5 5. ♘g3 ♗g6 6. h4 h6 7. ♘f3 ♘d7 8. ♗d3 ♗d3 9. ♕d3 ♕c7 10. ♗d2 e6 11. 0-0-0 ♘gf6

	12	13	14	15	16	17	18	19	20	
2	♔b1 0-0-0	c4[6] c5[7]	♗c3 cd4[8]	♘d4[9] a6[10]	♘f3[11] ♗c5	♕e2 ♗d6[12]	♘e4 ♗e7[13]	♘f6 ♗f6	♗f6 gf6[14]	=
3	... ...	... ...	♕e2 ♗d6[15]	♘e4 ♘e4	♕e4 ♘f6	♕e2 a6[16]	♗c3 ♖he8	♖he1 cd4	♘d4 ♗c5[17]	=

1. e4 c6 2. d4 d5 3. ♘c3 de4 4. ♘e4 ♗f5 5. ♘g3 ♗g6 6. h4 h6 7. ♘f3 ♘d7 8. h5 ♗h7

	9	10	11	12	13	14	15	16	17	
4	♗c4 e6	♕e2 ♘gf6	♗b3[18] ♗d6	♘d2 ♕c7	♘de4 ♗f4	♗f4[19] ♕f4	♕d2			=
5	♗d3 ♗d3	♕d3 e6[20]	♗d2[21] ♕b6[22]	0-0-0 ♘gf6	♘e5[23] ♗e7	♖he1[24] ♖d8	♕e2[25]			±

1. e4 c6 2. d4 d5 3. ♘c3 de4 4. ♘e4 ♗f5 5. ♘g3 ♗g6 6. h4 h6 7. ♘f3 ♘d7 8. h5 ♗h7 9. ♗d3 ♗d3 10. ♕d3 ♕c7

	11	12	13	14	15	16	17	18	19	
6	♖h4 e6	♗f4 ♗d6	♗d6 ♕d6	♘e4[26] ♕e7[27]	♕a3[28] ♕a3	ba3 ♔e7	♖b1[29] ♖b8[30]	♘c5 ♘c5	dc5 a5[31]	=
7	♗d2 e6	0-0-0 0-0-0	c4[32] ♘gf6[33]	♗c3 ♗d6	♘e4 ♗f4	♔c2 ♘e5	♘e5 ♗e5	♘c5 ♗d6	♘b3[34]	±
8	. . . . . .	. . . ♘gf6	♘e4[35] 0-0-0[36]	g3[37] ♘c5[38]	♘c5 ♗c5	♔b1[39] ♗d6	c4 c5	♗c3[40] a6[41]		=
9	. . . . . .	. . . . . .	♔b1 0-0-0	c4 c5	♗c3[42] cd4	♘d4 a6	♕e2 ♗d6	♘f1[43] ♘c5	♘b3 ♘b3[44]	=
10	. . . . . .	♕e2 ♘gf6[45]	0-0-0 0-0-0[46]	♘e5 ♘e5	de5 ♘d7[47]	f4 ♗e7	♘e4[48] ♘c5	♘c3 f6	ef6 ♗f6[49]	±
11	. . . . . .	. . . . . .	. . . . . .	. . . ♘b6	♗a5[50] ♖d5[51]	♗b6[52] ab6	c4 ♖d8[53]	♘e4 ♘e4[54]	♕e4 ♗d6[55]	±
12	. . . . . .	. . . . . .	c4 ♗d6[56]	♘f5 ♗f4[57]	♗f4 ♕f4	♘e3 ♕c7	0-0-0 b5	cb5 cb5	♔b1 0—0[58]	±

1 **9... e6** 10. ♗f4 ♘gf6 11. 0-0-0 ♘d5 12. ♗d2 b5 [12... ♕c7 13. c4 ♘5f6 14. ♔b1±] 13. ♔b1 ♗d6 [13... ♗e7 14. ♘h5 ♗f6 15. g4 g6 16. ♘f6 ♘5f6 17. g5 hg5 18. ♗g5± Suetin–Kasparjan, SSSR 1952] 14. ♘e4 ♘7f6 15. ♖hg1 ♖b8 16. g4 b4 17. ♘d6 ♕d6 18. g5 ♘d7 19. ♖de1± Matanović–Wade, Opatija 1953; **9... ♘gf6** 10. ♗f4 ♕a5 11. ♗d2 ♕c7 — 9... ♕c7

2 **12. ♘e5?** ♘e5 13. de5 ♕e5 14. ♖he1 ♕c7 15. ♘f5 ♘d5 16. c4 0-0-0 17. cd5 ♖d5 18. ♘d4 ♗c5∓; **12. ♕e2** ♗d6 [12... 0-0-0 13. ♘e5 ♘e5 14. de5 ♘d7 (Rossolimo–Eliskases, Mar del Plata 1949) 15. ♗c3±] 13. ♘e4 ♗f4 14. g3 ♗d2 15. ♘ed2= Averbah–Holmov, SSSR (ch) 1948; **12. ♘e4** 0-0-0 13. g3 ♘c5 [13... ♘e4 14. ♕e4 ♗e7 15. ♔b1 ♖he8 16. ♖he1 ♕b6 17. ♕e2 ♕b5 18. c4 ♕f5 19. ♔a1 ♗d6 20. ♗c3± Matulović–Hort, Sombor 1968 — 6/251] 14. ♘c5 ♗c5 15. ♔b1 ♗d6 16. c4 c5 17. ♗c3 a6△ cd4= Boleslavski, Filip

3 12... b5?! 13. cb5 cb5 14. ♔b1 ♕b7 15. ♖he1 ♗e7 16. ♖c1 a6 17. ♘e5± Kasparjan–Smislov, SSSR (ch) 1947

4 **13. ♕e2** ♗d6 14. ♘e4 ♗f4=; **13. ♘e4** ♘g4!? 14. ♕e2 ♘df6 15. ♘f6 gf6 16. h5 ♖g8 17. ♔b1 ♗e7 18. ♗c1 f5∞ Vukčević–Matanović, Jugoslavija (ch) 1958; **13. ♔b1** — 12. ♔b1

5 17. ♕e3 ♘e4 18. de5 [18. ♕e4 ♗f6 19. ♖d2 ♖d7 20. ♖hd1 ♖hd8 21. g3 ♕b6∓ Hennings–Hort, Harrachov 1967] ♖d1 19. ♖d1 ♖d8= Szabo–Barcza, Leningrad 1967 — 4/203

6 13. ♖he1 c5 14. c3 ♗d6 15. ♘e4 ♘e4 16. ♕e4 ♘f6 17. ♕e2 c4 18. ♗e3 ♔b8∓ Rabinovič–Makagonov, SSSR 1938; 14. c4=

7 13... ♗d6 14. ♘e4 ♘e4 15. ♕e4 ♘f6 16. ♕e2 c5 [16... ♖he8 17. ♗c3 ♕e7 (Pilnik–Golombek, Budapest 1952) 18. ♘e5±] 17. ♗c3 cd4 18. ♘d4 a6 19. ♘f3±

8 14... ♗d6 15. ♘e4 ♘e4 16. ♕e4 ♘f6 17. ♕e2 a6 18. ♘e5± Fine

9 15. ♗d4 ♗c5 16. ♘e4 ♗d4 17. ♕d4 ♔b8=

10 15... ♘c5 16. ♕e2 ♘a4 17. ♘b5 ♘c3 18. ♘c3 ♖d1 19. ♖d1 a6 20. h5± Padevski–Barcza, Kecskemet 1966 — 2/171

11 **16. ♘b3** ♘c5 17. ♕f3 ♗e7 18. ♗a5 ♖d1 19. ♖d1 ♕e5 20. ♗c3 ♕c7= Spaski–Portisch, Budapest 1961; **16. ♕e2** ♗d6 17. ♘e4 ♘e4 18. ♕e4 ♘c5 19. ♕c2 ♗e5 20. ♖he1

♗f6 21. g3 ♖d7= Unzicker–Porath, München (ol) 1958

12 17... ♘g4 18. ♘e4 ♘df6 19. ♘f6 gf6 20. ♘d4 ♖hg8 21. b4 ♕e5= Sokolov–Sušić, Jugoslavija 1965

13 18... ♘e4 19. ♕e4 ♘f6 20. ♕e2 ♕c6 21. ♖de1 ♗c7 22. ♘d4±

14 **20... ♘f6** 21. ♘e5± Spaski–Petrosjan (m) 1966 — 1/119; **20... gf6**△ ♘e5=

15 **14... a6** 15. ♘e5 ♘e5 16. de5 ♘d7 17. f4 ♘b8 18. ♗c3± Parma–Barcza, Kapfenberg 1970 — 9/158; **14... cd4** 15. ♘d4 a6 16. ♘b3 ♗d6 17. c5! ♗g3 18. ♗a5 ♕e5 19. ♕c2 ♖de8 20. c6 ♘b8! 21. cb7 ♔b7 22. fg3± Parma–Vukić, Jugoslavija (ch) 1972 — 13/219

16 17... cd4 18. ♘d4 a6 19. ♗c3 [19. ♘b3!?] ♗c5 20. ♘b3 ♖d1 21. ♖d1 ♖d8 22. ♖d8± Matulović–Kolarov, La Habana (ol) 1966 — 2/172

17 Parma–Ivkov, Jugoslavija 1964

18 **11. ♘e5** ♘e5 12. de5 ♘d7 13. ♗f4 [13. 0–0 ♕h4? 14. ♗b3 g6 15. ♖d1 ♗g7 16. c3 gh5 17. ♖d4 ♕e7 18. ♘h5 ♗f8 19. ♗f4 ♗g6 20. ♘f6+– P. Johner–Kmoch, Debrecen 1925; 13... ♕c7 14. f4 ♗c5 15. ♔h2 ♘b6 16. ♗b3 ♕e7 17. ♕g4 0-0-0∓] ♘b6 14. ♖d1 ♕c7 15. ♗b3 ♘d5 16. ♗c1 0-0-0 17. 0–0 ♗e7= Mnacakanjan–Poljak, SSSR 1957; **11. 0–0** ♗e7 12. ♖e1 ♘d5 13. ♗b3 0–0 14. c4⩲; 11... ♗d6!?=

19 14. ♕f3? ♗c1 15. ♖c1 0-0-0 16. c3 ♘e4 17. ♘e4 e5∓ Keller–Barcza, Zürich 1959

20 10... ♘gf6 11. ♗f4 ♕a5 12. b4!? [12. ♗d2 ♕c7 — 10... ♕c7] ♕b4 13. c3 ♕b5 14. c4 ♕a5 15. ♗d2 ♕a6 16. 0–0 e6 17. ♖fe1 ♗e7 18. ♘f5?! ef5 19. ♖e7 ♔e7 20. ♗b4 ♔d8 21. ♘e5 ♘e4–+ Velimirović–Hort, La Habana 1971 — 11/166; 18. a4!∞̄

21 11. b3 ♘gf6 12. ♗b2 ♕a5 13. ♗c3 [13. c3 ♗a3 14. 0-0-0 ♗b2=] ♗b4 14. ♗b4 ♕b4 15. ♕d2 [15. c3 ♕e7△ c5] ♕d2 16. ♔d2 c5= Spaski–Karpov, Leningrad (mct) 1974 — 17/226

22 11... ♕c7 — 10... ♕c7

23 13. c4?! ♕a6 14. ♔b1 ♗d6 15. ♘e2 ♘g4 16. ♗e1 0-0-0= Tatai–Larsen, Palma de Mallorca 1971 — 12/208

24 14. f4 ♖d8 15. ♕c4 ♘e5 16. de5 ♖d4= Andersson–Larsen, Palma de Mallorca 1971 — 12/209

25 △ ♘f7± Milić

26 14. ♘d2 ♕e7 15. ♖h3 0-0-0 16. 0-0-0 ♘gf6 17. ♘ge4 ♘e4 18. ♘e4 ♘f6 19. ♘c5 ♘d7 20. ♘e4 [20. ♘b3 ♕g5 21. ♔b1 ♘f6=] ♘f6 21. ♕e2 ♘e4 22. ♕e4 ♕f6= Geler–Bukić, Beograd 1969 — 8/166

27 14... ♕b4 15. ♕c3 ♕c3 16. bc3 ♔e7 17. ♘c5 ♘gf6 [17... b6 18. ♘d7 ♔d7 19. ♖g4±; 17... ♘c5 18. dc5±] 18. ♘b7 ♖hc8 19. ♘e5 c5 20. ♘a5 ♖c7 21. 0-0-0± Spaski–Botvinik, Leiden 1970 — 10/219

28 15. 0-0-0 ♘gf6 16. ♘f6 [16. ♘ed2 0-0-0 =] gf6= Gligorić–Petrosjan, Jugoslavija (ct) 1959

29 17. ♘c5 ♘c5! [17... b6 18. ♘d7 ♔d7 19. ♘e5±; 17... ♘gf6 18. ♘b7 ♖hb8 19. ♘a5 ♖b6 20. ♘e5 ♖c8 21. 0-0-0± Perenyi–I. Lörincz, Hungary 1973 — 16/160] 18. dc5 a5 19. ♖b1 — 17. ♖b1

30 17... b6 18. ♘e5 ♘e5 19. de5 f5 20. ♘g3 [20. ♘d6 ♘f6 21. ef6 ♔d6 22. fg7 ♖hg8 23. ♖d1 ♔c7=; 20. ♘c3 ♔f7 21. ♖d4 ♘e7 22. ♖bd1?! ♘d5 23. ♘d5 ed5= Browne–Pomar, Siegen (ol) 1970 — 10/221; 22. ♖d7! ♖hd8 23. ♖bd1 ♔e8 24. ♖7d6± Marić] ♖d8 21. ♖a4 ♖d7 22. ♖d1 ♖d1 23. ♔d1 a5 24. ♖d4 c5 25. ♖d2 ♔f7 26. ♖d8 ♖h7 [Beljavski–Pomar, Las Palmas 1974 — 17/225] 27. ♖b8!±

31 **20. ♖a4** ♘f6 21. ♖a5 ♘d7 ∞̄; **20. ♘e5** ♘f6 21. ♖d4 ♖hc8 22. ♖b3 ♖c7 23. g4 ♖d8 24. ♖b7 ♖d4 25. ♘c6 ♔d7 26. ♘d4 ♖b7 27. c6 ♔c7 28. cb7 ♘g4 29. ♘c6 ♔b7 30. ♘a5 ♔c7= Bellon–Pomar, Olot 1975

32 **13. ♕e2** ♗d6 [13... ♘gf6 — 12. ♕e2] 14. ♘e4 ♗e7 [14... ♗f4!?] 15. c4 ♘gf6 16. ♘c3 ♖he8 17. g3 ♗f8 18. ♔b1 e5!? [18... ♕a5? 19. ♘e5± Spaski–Barcza, Soči 1966 — 2/166] 19. de5 ♘e5 20. ♗f4 ♖d1 21. ♕d1 ♘fd7∞; **13. ♔b1** ♘gf6 — 12... ♘gf6

33 13... ♗d6!? 14. ♗c3!?

34 Bronštejn–Kotov, Amsterdam 1968 — 6/246

35 13. ♘e5? ♘e5 14. de5 ♕e5 15. ♖he1 ♕c7 16. ♘f5 ♘d5 17. c4 0-0-0 18. cd5 ♖d5 19. ♘d4 ♗c5 20. ♘e6 fe6∓ Židkov–Podgajec, SSSR 1968 — 5/171

36 13... ♘e4 14. ♕e4 ♘f6 15. ♕e2 0-0-0 16. g3 ♖d5 17. ♗f4 ♗d6 [17... ♕a5 18. ♔b1 ♖b5 19. ♘e5±; 18... ♘h5 19. ♗d2 ♕a6 20. c4 ♘f6 21. ♘e5±] 18. ♘e5 [18. ♗d6 ♖d6 19. ♘e5 ♖hd8 20. c3 c5= Štejn–Korčnoj, Sousse (izt) 1967] ♗e5 [18... ♘d7 19. c4 ♖a5 20. ♗d2±] 19. ♗e5 ♕a5 20. ♔b1 ♖hd8 21. g4±

37 14. c4 c5 15. ♘f6 ♘f6! [15... gf6 16. d5 ♘b6 17. ♗a5± Radulov–Pomar, Nice (ol) 1974 — 18/196] 16. ♗c3 cd4 17. ♘d4 a6= Minić

38 **14... ♘g4**? 15. ♕e2 ♘df6 16. ♗f4 ♕a5 17. ♘f6 gf6 18. ♘d2 f5 [Geler–Petrosjan, Moskva 1967 — 3/185] 19. f3 ♘f6 20. ♘b3 ♕b5 21. c4△ ♕e5+–; **14... ♘e4** 15. ♕e4 ♗e7! [15... ♗d6 16. c4 c5 17. ♔b1 a6 18. d5 ♘f6 19. ♕c2± Matanović–Marović, Jugoslavija 1967 — 4/588; 17... ♖he8 18. ♗c3 ♘f6 19. ♕e2 ♖e7 20. ♘e5± Gheorghiu–Benkö, Palma de Mallorca 1968 — 6/250] 16.

♔b1 ♖he8 17. c4 c5 18. ♗f4 ♗d6 19. ♘e5 ♘e5 20. de5 ♗f8 21. ♗e3± Geler–Hort, Skopje 1968 — 6/247; 19... ♖e7!= Gheorghiu –Hort, La Habana (ol) 1966

39 **16. ♗f4** ♗d6 17. ♗e5 ♗e5 18. ♘e5 c5 19. ♕c4 ♖d5 20. f4 ♘e4= Belinkov–Podgajec, SSSR 1968; **16. c3** ♗d6 17. ♕e2 ♘d7 18. c4 c5 19. ♗c3 cd4 20. ♘d4 a6 21. ♘b3 ♖hg8 22. ♖d2 ♗e7= Kapengut–Podgajec, SSSR 1970; **16. ♖h4** ♗d6 17. ♕e2 ♖d7 18. ♘e5 ♗e5 19. de5 ♘d5= Suetin–Šamkovič, Tbilisi 1969 — 8/168

40 18. ♖c1 b6 19. ♕e2 ♕b7= I. Zajcev–Petrosjan, SSSR 1968

41 △ cd4=

42 15. ♕e2 ♗d6 16. ♘e4 ♘e4 17. ♕e4 ♗e7! 18. ♗f4 ♗d6 19. ♗d6 ♕d6= Matulović–Hort, Sousse (izt) 1967 — 4/587

43 18. ♘e4 ♘e4 19. ♕e4 ♘f6 20. ♕e2=

44 Reshevsky–Sherwin, USA (ch) 1966/67 — 3/187

45 **12... 0-0-0** 13. ♘e5 ♘b6 [13... ♘e5 14. de5 ♘e7 15. 0-0-0 c5 16. f4 ♘c6 17. c3±] 14. c3 ♘f6 15. 0–0! ♗d6 16. a4 ♖hf8 17. a5 ♘bd7 18. f4 ♘b8 19. b4± Nikitin–Lazarev, SSSR 1966 — 2/167; **12... ♗d6** 13. ♘e4 ♗f4 14. ♘e5! ♗d2 [14... ♘e5 15. ♗f4 ♘d3 16. ♕d3 ♕f4 17. g3 ♕c7 18. ♕a3±; 14... ♗e5 15. de5 ♘e5 16. ♗b4 0-0-0 17. f4 c5 18. fe5 cb4 19. 0–0 ♕e5 20. ♖f7 ♕d4 21. ♘f2 ♘f6 22. ♖d1 ♕b6 23. ♖d8 ♖d8 24. ♖g7 ♖d5 25. g4±] 15. ♘d2 ♘e5 16. de5 0-0-0 17. ♘c4 ♔b8 18. ♘d6 f6 19. f4± Boleslavski

46 **13... c5** 14. ♖h4! [14. ♔b1 0-0-0 15. c4 a6? 16. ♘e5± Vogt–Rukavina, Skopje (ol) 1972 — 14/216; 15... ♗d6!?] ♘b6 [14... 0-0-0 15. dc5± Boleslavski] 15. ♗f4 ♕c6 16. ♘e5 ♕a4 17. ♖e1△ ♘f7± Minić; **13... ♗d6** 13. ♘f5 ♗f4 15. ♘g7 ♔f8 16. ♘e6 fe6 17. ♕e6∞; 15. ♘e3±

47 15... ♘d5 16. f4 c5 17. c4 ♘b4 18. ♗b4 ♖d1 19. ♖d1 cb4 20. ♘e4 ♗e7 21. ♘d6± Spaski–Botvinik, SSSR 1966 — 2/170

48 17. ♗e3 ♕a5 18. ♔b1 ♘c5 19. c3 ♖d1 20. ♖d1 ♖d8 21. ♖d4± Suetin–Pachman, Titovo Užice 1966 — 2/169

49 20. ♕c4 ♕b6 21. b4 ♘a6 22. ♘e4± Spaski–Petrosjan (m) 1966 — 1/118

50 **15. c3** c5 16. ♔b1 ♗d6 17. f4 cd4 18. cd4 ♔b8= Boleslavski; **15. ♖h4** c5 [15... ♗d6 16. ♗a5 ♗e5 17. de5 ♖d1 18. ♔d1 ♘fd7 19. ♖e4 (19. ♖g4!? ♖g8 20. f4∞) ♖d8 20. ♔c1 ♘c5 21. ♖g4! (21. ♖e3 ♖d5 22. ♗d2 ♕d8 23. b3 ♕h4 24. ♖f2 ♘bd7= Holmov–Hort, Leningrad 1967 — 3/186) ♖d5 22. ♖g7 ♘b3 23. ab3 ♖a5 24. c4 ♖e5 25. ♖g8 ♔d7 26. ♕d2 ♔e7 27. ♕h6+– Haag–Flesch, Salgotarjan 1967 — 4/201] 16. ♗a5 ♗d6 17. dc5 ♗e5 18. ♖d8 ♖d8 19. cb6 ♗f4 20. ♔b1 ab6 21. ♗b6 ♕b6 22. ♖f4± Ubilava–Peresipkin, SSSR 1974; 17... ♗c5!? Filip; 16... cd4!? 17. ♖hd4 ♗c5=

51 15... c5 16. c4 ♔b8 [16... ♖d4 17. ♖d4 cd4 18. ♔b1 ♗d6 19. c5+– Haag–Golz, Zinnowitz 1966 — 2/168; 16... cd4 17. ♔b1 ♗d6 18. c5±] 17. dc5 [17. ♔b1!?△ 17... ♗d6 18. dc5 ♗c5 19. f4±] ♗c5 18. f4 ♗d4 19. ♔b1 [19. ♘f7 ♕f7 20. ♖d4 ♖d4 21. ♕e5 ♕c7= Marić–Vukić, Jugoslavija (ch) 1967 — 3/188] ♗e5 20. fe5 ♘fd7 21. ♘e4± Runau–Moghadam, England 1971/72 — 13/216

52 16. b4 ♖a5 17. ba5 ♗a3 18. ♔b1 ♘a4 19. ♕f3! [19. ♕e1 ♘d5∓] ♗b4 20. ♖d3 ♕a5 21. ♘e2 ♘d5 [21... ♖f8± R. Byrne–Saidy, New York 1969 — 8/167] 22. ♖h3 [22. ♕f7 ♘ac3 23. ♘c3 ♗c3 24. ♕e6 ♔b8 25. ♖c3 ♘c3 26. ♔b2 ♘d5 27. ♕d6 ♔a8 28. ♕c5 ♕d2 29. ♘d3 ♖e8∓ Tarnai] f6 23. ♘g6 ♖d8 24. ♘gf4 ♘dc3! 25. ♘c3 ♗c3∓ Schepers–Tarnai, corr. 1972 — 13/217

53 17... ♖a5 18. ♔b1 ♗d6 19. f4 ♖d8 20. ♖d2! [20. ♘e4 ♘e4 21. ♕e4 ♔b8 (21... f6 22. ♘d3 ♕d7 23. g3 ♗f8 24. ♘c1 ♔c7 25. a3 ♕f7 26. ♕e2± Bednarski–Smislov, Palma de Mallorca 1967 — 4/200) 22. b3 (22. g3 b5 23. c5 ♗e5 24. de5? ♖a4 25. ♕e3 ♖d5 26. b3 ♕d7∓ Maeder–Podgajec, Dresden 1969 — 8/165; 24. ♕e5!=) b5 23. c5 ♗e5 24. de5 ♖d5 25. ♖d5 ed5 26. ♕b4= Jansa–Podgajec, Sombor 1970 — 10/220; 20. ♖hf1 ♕e7 21. ♘e4± Widera–Tarnai, corr. 1974 — 18/197] b5 [20... c5 21. ♖hd1±] 21. c5 ♗f8 [21... ♗e5 22. fe5 ♘d5 23. ♘e4±] 22. ♘e4±

54 18... c5? 19. ♘c3 ♗d6 20. ♘b5 ♕e7 21. dc5 ♗c5 22. ♘a7 ♔c7 23. ♘f7+– Tatai–Pomar, Malaga 1968 — 5/172

55 20. f4 f5 21. ♕e2 ♗e5 22. ♕e5 ♕e5 23. de5 ♔c7± Mecking–Pomar, Lugano (ol) 1968 — 6/248; 20. ♘f3 ♖he8 21. ♔b1 ♕e7 22. ♖he1 ♕f6 23. g3 ♗c7 24. a3± Spaski–Pomar, Palma de Mallorca 1968 — 6/249

56 13... 0-0-0 14. ♘e5±

57 14... 0-0-0 15. ♘d6 ♕d6 16. ♗a5 ♖de8 [16... b6 17. ♗c3△ a4, a5± Geler] 17. ♘e5 ♕e7 18. ♗c3 ♖d8± Karpov–Pomar, Nice (ol) 1974 — 12/228; 18. f4± Geler

58 **19... a6**? 20. d5±; **19... 0–0**! 20. g4 ♘e4 21. ♖hg1?! ♘g5 22. ♘g5 hg5∞ Spaski–Karpov, Leningrad (mct) 1974 — 17/227

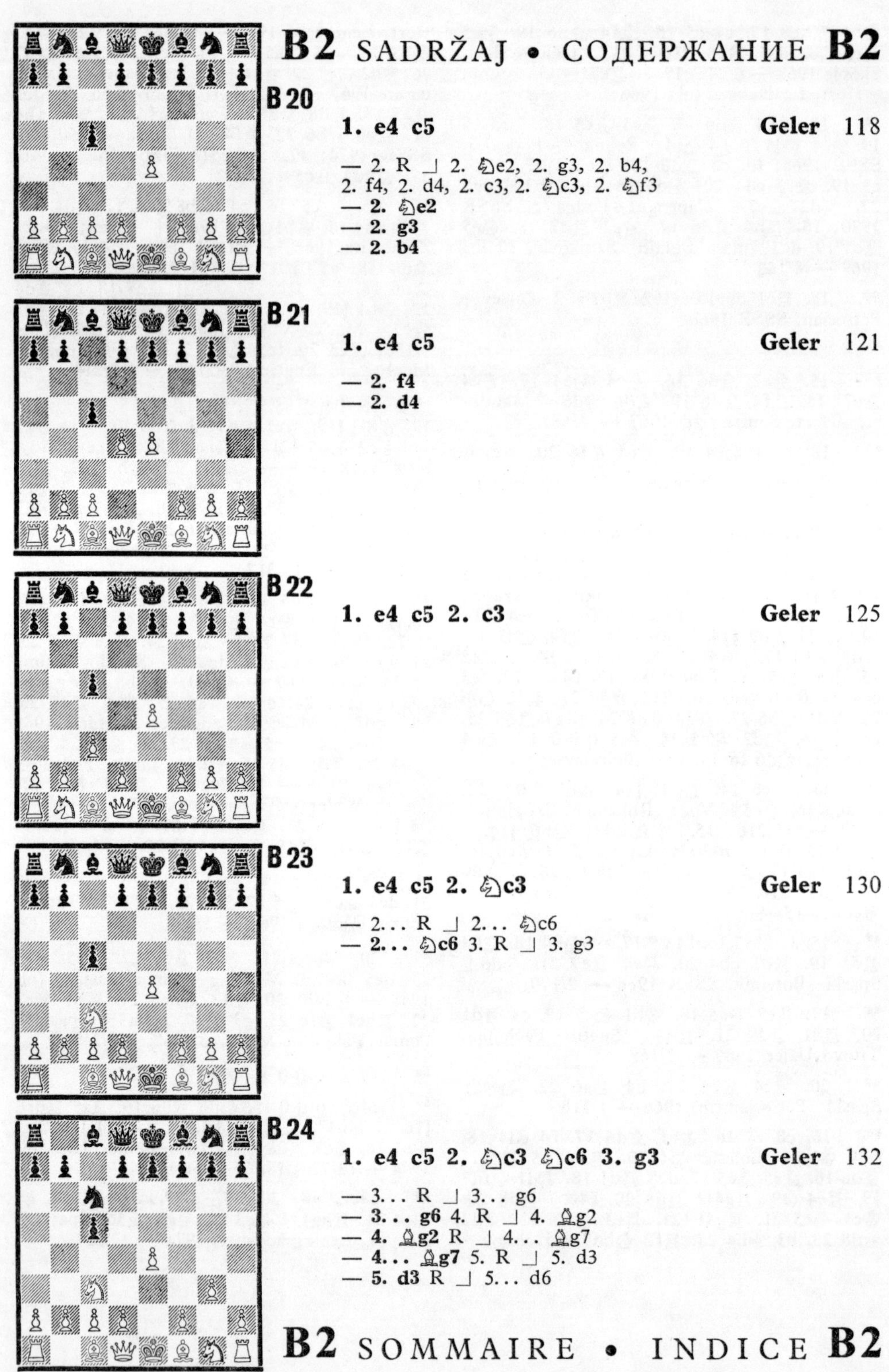

B2 SADRŽAJ • СОДЕРЖАНИЕ B2

B2 SOMMAIRE • INDICE B2

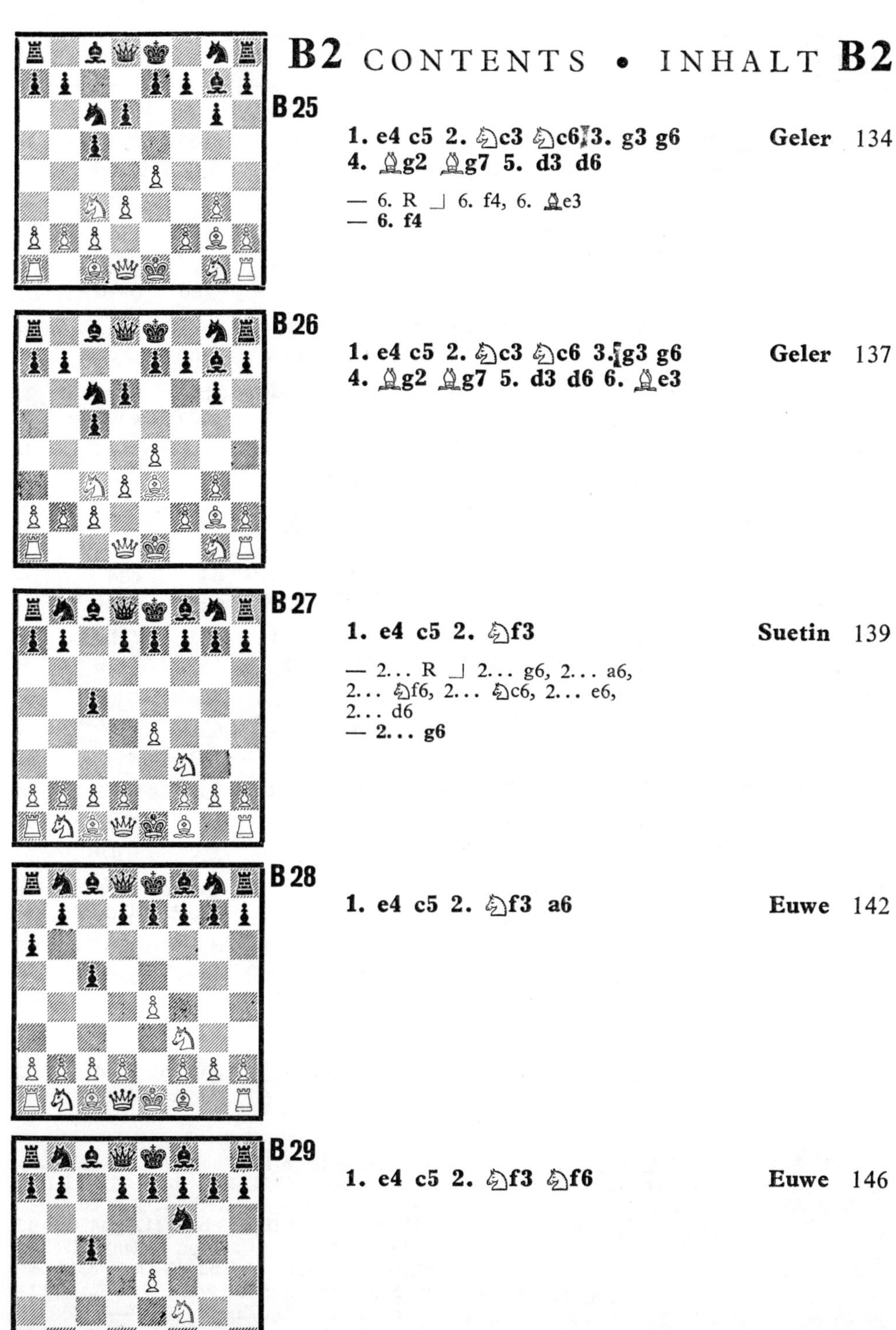

B2 CONTENTS • INHALT B2

B2 INDICE • INNEHÅLL B2

B 20 — 1. e4 c5

	2	3	4	5	6	7	8	9	10	
1	b3[1] e6[2]	♗b2[3] ♘c6[4]	♘f3 ♘f6	♘c3[5] d6	g3[6] ♗e7	♗g2 0–0	d4 cd4	♘d4 ♗d7	0–0 ♘d4[7]	=
2	c4 ♘c6	♘c3[8] e5[9]	g3 h5!	h4 d6	♗g2[10] ♗g4	f3 ♗e6	d3 ♗e7			=
3	♘e2[11] d6[12]	g3[13] ♘c6[14]	♗g2 ♘f6[15]	0–0 e5	c3 ♗e7	d4 ♕c7	dc5 dc5	♘a3 ♗e6	♗g5 0–0[16]	=
4	. . . ♘f6	e5 ♘g4[17]	d4[18] cd4	♕d4[19] d6	ed6 ♘c6	de7[20] ♕e7	♕f4 g6	♘a3 ♗h6	♕g3 ♗c1[21]	=
5	. . . . . .	♘bc3 d5[22]	ed5 ♘d5	♘d5 ♕d5	d4[23] cd4[24]	♕d4 ♕d4	♘d4 a6[25]	♗e3 ♗d7[26]	0-0-0 ♘c6[27]	±
6	. . . . . .	. . . ♘c6	g3 d5!	ed5 ♘d4![28]	♗g2[29] ♗g4	0–0 ♘d5[30]				=
7	g3 e6[31]	♗g2 d5[32]	ed5[33] ed5	d4![34] cd4	♘e2[35] ♘c6	0–0 ♗c5	♘d2 d3	♘f4![36]		±
8	. . . g6	♗g2 ♗g7	♘e2[37] ♘c6[38]	0–0[39] d6	c3 e5[40]	d3[41] ♘ge7	♗e3[42] 0–0	d4 ed4[43]	cd4 ♕b6[44]	=
9	. . . . . .	. . . . . .	. . . . . .	. . . e6	c3 ♘ge7	d4[45] cd4	cd4 d5	ed5 ♘d5	♘bc3 0–0[46]	=
10	. . . d5!	ed5[47] ♕d5	♘f3[48] ♗g4	♗g2[49] ♕e6![50]	♔f1 ♗h3[51]	d4[52] cd4	♘d4 ♕d7[53]	♘c3 ♘c6	♘c6 ♕c6[54]	=
11	b4 cb4[55]	d4[56] d5	ed5[57] ♘f6![58]	♗b5 ♗d7[59]	♗c4 ♗g4	f3 ♗f5	a3[60] ♘d5	ab4 ♘b4	♘a3 e6[61]	∓
12	. . . . . .	♗b2 ♘f6![62]	e5 ♘d5	♘f3[63] e6[64]	d4 b6[65]	a3 ♗b7	ab4 ♗b4	c3 ♗e7	♗d3[66] ♘f4[67]	∓
13	. . . . . .	♘f3 e6[68]	d4 ♘f6[69]	♗d3 ♗e7	0–0 d6[70]	♘bd2 0–0	e5 ♘d5	♘e4 de5[71]	de5 ♘d7[72]	∓
14	. . . . . .	a3 ba3[73]	♘a3[74] d6[75]	d4[76] ♘f6	♗d3 e5[77]	♘f3[78] ♗e7	0–0 ♘c6[79]	d5 ♘b4	♗b5 ♗d7[80]	=∞
15	. . . . . .	. . . e6	ab4 ♗b4[81]	c3 ♗e7	d4 d5[82]	♗d3 ♘f6[83]	e5 ♘e4	♘d2 ♘d2[84]	♗d2 h6[85]	∓
16	. . . . . .	. . . d5!	ed5[86] ♕d5[87]	♘f3![88] e5	ab4 ♗b4	♗a3[89] ♗a3	♘a3[90] ♘c6	♘b5[91] ♕d8	♗c4 ♘f6[92]	∓

[1] **2. ♗c4** e6 3. ♕e2 ♘c6 4. c3 ♗e7 5. d3 d5 6. ♗b3 ♘f6=; **2. ♕e2** e5=; 2... e6 — C 00; **2. d3** ♘c6 3. ♘d2 g6 4. g3 ♗g7 5. ♗g2 e6 6. ♘h3 ♘ge7 [6... h5!?] 7. 0–0 0–0 8. ♖e1! e5!∞ Suttles–Geler, Palma de Mallorca (izt) 1970

[2] **2... ♘f6** 3. e5 ♘d5 4. ♗b2 ♘c6 5. ♘f3 [5. g3 d6 6. ed6 e5 7. ♗g2 ♗e6 8. ♘e2 ♗d6 9. ♘bc3 ♗e7= Czerniak–Rossetto, Beograd 1962] ♘f4 6. g3 ♘e6 7. ♗g2 g6 8. c3 ♗g7 9. d4 cd4 10. cd4 d5 11. 0–0 0–0 12. ♘c3 ♘c7 13. ♕d2 b6 14. ♖ac1±↑ Czerniak–Janošević, Beograd 1954; **2... d6** 3. ♗b2 ♘f6 4. ♘c3 ♘c6 5. f4 a6 6. ♘f3 b5 7. ♗d3 e6 8. 0–0 c4?! 9. ♗e2 cb3 10. ab3 b4?! 11. ♘a4 ♘e4 12. ♘d4!± Czerniak–Hamann, Netanya 1968 — 6/391; **2... ♘c6** 3. ♗b2 d6 [3... d5 4. ed5 ♕d5 5. ♘c3 ♕e5 6. ♕e2! ♕e2 7. ♘ge2± Czerniak–Cebalo, Zagreb 1969 — 7/297] 4. ♗b5 ♗d7 5. c4 e6 6. ♘e2 ♕h4 7. d3 ♘f6 8. g3 ♕h5 9. ♘d2 ♘e5 10. ♗d7△ ♕c2± Orendy–Barcza, Hungary 1961

3 3. ♘f3 d6 4. ♗b2 a6 [4... e5?! 5. ♗c4 ♗e7 6. 0–0 ♘c6 7. ♘c3 ♗g4 8. ♘d5 ♘f6 9. ♖e1± Keres–Tukmakov, SSSR (ch) 1973 — 16/284; 4... ♘f6 5. ♘c3 ♗e7 6. ♗b5 ♘bd7 7. d4 cd4 8. ♕d4 0–0= Holmov–Tukmakov, Moskva 1969 — 8/303; 5. e5 de5 6. ♘e5 ♘bd7 7. ♘d7 ♗d7 8. ♗e2 ♗c6 9. 0–0 ♗e7 10. ♘a3 0–0 11. ♘c4± Westerinen–Schmidt, Forssa–Helsinki 1972] 5. g3 b6 6. d4 ♗b7 7. ♘c3 ♘f6 8. d5 [8. ♕e2!?] ed5 9. ed5 ♘bd7 10. ♕e2 [10. ♗g2? ♕e7!∓ Westerinen–Bellon, Torremolinos 1974 — 17/347] ♕e7 11. 0-0-0∞ Bukić

4 3... ♘f6 4. e5 ♘d5 5. ♘f3 ♗e7 6. c4 ♘c7 [6... ♘b4!?] 7. ♘c3 f6 8. ♘e4 fe5 9. ♘e5 0–0 10. d4 [10. ♕g4?! ♘e8 11. ♗d3 d6 12. ♘f3 e5∓ Westerinen–Kaplan, Skopje (ol) 1972] cd4 11. ♕d4 ♗b4 12. ♗c3! [12. ♔d1?! d6∓ Westerinen–Talj, Tallinn 1973 — 15/322] ♘c6 13. ♘c6 ♗c3 14. ♕c3 bc6± Keres, Nej

5 5. e5 ♘d5 6. ♘c3 ♘c3 7. ♗c3 ♗e7 [7... b6 8. ♗d3 ♗b7 9. ♕e2 ♕c7 10. h4 ♘e7 11. ♗b2 ♘d5 12. g3 ♘b4 13. ♗e4 h6 14. a3 ♗e4 15. ♕e4 ♕c6= Matanović] 8. ♗d3 b6 9. ♕e2 ♗b7 10. h4 ♕c7 11. ♖h3 g6 12. ♘g5 ♘d4 13. ♗d4 cd4 14. f4 h6= Schweber–Mecking, Buenos Aires 1970 — 10/395

6 6. d4 cd4 7. ♘d4 ♗d7 8. ♗e2 ♗e7 9. 0–0 0–0=

7 11. ♕d4 ♕c7 12. a4 a6 13. ♕d3 ♖ac8 14. ♖ac1 ♖fd8= Czerniak–Tatai, Netanya 1973 — 15/305

8 **3. ♘e2** e5 [3... e6 4. g3 g6 5. ♗g2 ♗g7 6. 0–0 ♘ge7 7. d3= Gusev–Baer 1949] 4. d3 g6 5. g3 d6 6. ♗g2 ♗e6 7. ♘bc3 ♕d7= Rellstab; **3. ♘f3** e5 [3... g6 4. d4 cd4 5. ♘d4 — B 36; 3... e6 4. d4 cd4 5. ♘d4 — B 44] 4. ♘c3 d6 5. d3 ♘ge7=

9 **3... ♘f6** 4. f4 [4. d3 e6! 5. f4 d5 6. e5 ♘g8 7. ♘f3 ♘ge7 8. ♗e2 ♘f5 9. 0–0 ♗e7 10. ♕e1 0–0∓ Beni–Talj, München (ol) 1958] d6 5. d3 g6 6. ♗e2 ♗g7 7. ♗e3 0–0 8. ♘f3 ♗g4=; **3... e6** 4. ♘f3 [4. f4 ♘d4?! 5. ♘ce2 e5 6. ♘d4 cd4 7. ♕f3 d6 8. fe5 de5 9. ♕g3± A. Steiner–Reti, Trenčanske Teplice 1928; 4... ♘ge7! 5. ♘f3 d5 6. d3 g6 7. ♗e2 ♗g7 8. 0–0 0–0∓ Carls–Euwe, Göteborg 1920] ♘f6 5. d3?! d5 6. cd5 ed5 7. ♗g5 ♗e7 8. ♗f6 ♗f6 9. ♘d5 ♗b2 10. ♖b1 ♗d4∓ Carls–Becker, Haag 1928; 5. d4 cd4 6. ♘d4 ♗b4 — B 44; **3... g6** 4. d3 ♗g7 5. g3 d6 6. ♗g2 e6 7. ♘ge2 ♘ge7 8. ♗g5 h6 9. ♗e3 ♘d4= Sliwa –Botvinik, Budapest 1952

10 6. ♗h3 ♘f6 7. d3 ♗e7 8. ♗c8 ♖c8 9. ♗g5?! ♘g4! 10. f3 ♗g5 11. fg4 hg4 12. ♕g4 ♘d4 13. ♖h2 g6∓

11 Keres

12 **2... e5** 3. c3 [3. ♘bc3 ♘c6 4. g3 g6 5. ♗g2 ♗g7 6. ♘d5 ♘ge7 7. ♘ec3 ♘d5 8. ♘d5 ♘e7= Kozomara–Bobocov, Sarajevo 1962] ♘c6 4. d4 d5! 5. de5 de4 6. ♕d8 ♔d8 7. ♘g3 ♘e5 8. ♘e4 ♗e7=; **2... d5** 3. ed5 ♘f6 [3... ♕d5 4. ♘bc3△ d4±⟳] 4. ♘bc3 ♘d5=; **2... e6** 3. d3 [3. d4 d5!=] d5 4. ♘d2 ♘c6 5. g3 ♘f6 6. ♗g2 ♗e7 7. 0–0 [7. ed5!?] 0–0 8. ♘f4! de4 9. ♘e4 ♘e4 10. de4 [10. ♗e4?! ♕c7 11. ♖e1 ♗d7 12. c3 ♗d6 13. ♕h5 f5! 14. ♗g2 ♖ae8∓ Cardoso–Lombardy, Manila 1973 — 16/275] ♕c7=

13 3. c4 ♘f6 4. ♘bc3 e5 5. d3 ♘c6 6. h3 ♘d4 7. ♗e3 ♗e7 8. f4 ♗d7 9. ♕d2 ♕a5 10. 0-0-0 b5∓↑ Bidev–Vošpernik, Jugoslavija 1954

14 **3... b5**? 4. ♗g2 ♗b7 5. d4! cd4 6. ♘d4 a6 7. 0–0 ♘f6 8. ♖e1± Keres–Kotov, Pärnu 1947; **3... d5**!? 4. ♗g2 [4. e5] de4 5. ♗e4 ♘f6 6. ♗g2 ♘c6 7. d3 e6 8. ♘d2 ♗d7 9. ♘b3 ♗e7 10. 0–0 0–0 11. ♗e3 b6= O'Kelly–Denker 1946; 8. ♘bc3!? Schwarz; **3... g6**!?

15 4... g6 5. 0–0 ♗g7 — 2. g3

16 11. ♘c2= Obuhovski–Kuncevič, SSSR 1959

17 3... ♘d5!? 4. c3 ♘c6 5. d4 d6 [5... cd4 6. cd4=] 6. ed6 ed6 [6... ♕d6 7. ♘a3±; 7. c4!?] 7. ♘f4 ♘f4 8. ♗f4=

18 4. f4 d5=

19 5. ♗f4? ♘e5! 6. ♗e5 ♕a5∓

20 7. ♕f4 e5∓

21 11. ♖c1 0–0 12. h3 ♘f6 13. ♕e3 ♕b4 14. ♕c3 a5= Lutikov–Bronštejn, SSSR 1971 — 12/318

22 3... d6

23 6. ♘c3?! ♕d8 7. ♗c4 e6 8. 0–0 ♗e7∓× d4 Plater–Botvinik, Moskva 1947

24 **6... e6** 7. ♗e3 cd4 8. ♘d4 a6 9. ♗e2!± Nimzowitsch–Alapin, Riga 1913; **6... e5** 7. de5 [7. ♘c3!? ♕d4 8. ♗b5 ♗d7 9. ♕e2 ♘c6 10. 0–0 0-0-0 11. ♖d1 ♕g4∓ Keres–Filip, Helsinki (ol) 1952; 8. ♗e3 ♕d1 9. ♖d1 ♗e6 10. ♘e4!± Schwarz] ♕e5 8. ♗d2 ♗e7 [8... ♕b2 9. ♘c3!±↑] 9. ♗c3 ♕g5 10. ♘g3 0–0 11. ♗d3±; **6... ♘c6** 7. ♗e3 cd4 8. ♘d4± — B 29

25 **8... e5**?! 9. ♘b5 ♘a6 10. ♗e3 b6 11. 0-0-0±; **8... ♗d7** 9. ♘b5 ♗b5 10. ♗b5 ♘c6 11. ♗e3± Foltys–Szabo, Venezia 1949

26 **9... e5**? 10. ♘b3 ♗f5 11. 0-0-0 ♘d7 12. ♗d3 ♗d3 13. ♖d3 0-0-0 14. ♘a5!+– Keres–R. Byrne, SSSR–USA 1955; **9... e6**!?

27 11. ♘b3 e6 12. ♘c5 0-0-0 13. ♗e2± Keres–Kotov, Moskva 1947

28 5... ♘d5?! 6. ♗g2 ♘c3 7. bc3 e6 8. 0–0 ♗e7 9. ♖b1 0–0 10. c4!± Keres–Foltys, Salzburg 1943

29 6. ♘d4?! cd4 7. ♘b5 e5∓↑

30 Keres

31 2... d6

32 3... ♘c6 4. ♘c3 ♘f6 5. ♘ge2 d5 6. ed5 ed5 7. d4±× d5

33 4. ♘c3 — B 23

34 **5. ♘f3** ♗g4=; **5. ♘c3** — B 23

35 6. ♕d4 ♘c6 [6... ♘f6 7. ♗g5 ♗e7 8. ♘c3 ♘c6 9. ♕a4 0–0= Spielmann–Mieses, Österreich 1910] 7. ♕d5 ♕d5 8. ♗d5 ♘b4=∞

36 **10. cd3** ♘f6 11. ♘b3 ♗b6=; **10. ♘f4**!±↑

37 4. d3 e5 [3... e6△ ♘c6, ♘ge7] 5. ♘e2 h5! [5... ♘e7 6. f4△ 0–0±⊞] 6. h4 a6 7. a4 d6 8. 0–0 ♘c6 9. c3 ♖b8= Kuznjecov–Pervušin, SSSR 1954

38 4... d6 5. c3 ♘c6 6. d4 cd4 7. cd4 ♕b6 8. ♘c3 ♘d4 9. ♘d5 ♕c5 10. ♘d4 ♗d4 11. ♗e3 ♗e3 12. fe3 ♗d7 13. ♖c1 ♕a5 14. b4 ♕a2 15. 0–0±↑ Bialas–Koh, Berlin 1955

39 5. c3 e5! 6. 0–0 [6. ♘a3 ♘ge7 7. 0–0 0–0 8. ♘b5 d6 9. d4 ed4 10. cd4 a6 11. dc5 dc5= Kozomara–Matulović, Jugoslavija 1961] ♘ge7 7. d3 0–0 8. ♗e3 b6 9. c4 d6 10. ♘bc3 ♘d4= Donner–Gligorić, Eersel (m) 1968 — 5/325

40 6... ♘f6?! 7. d4 cd4 8. cd4 0–0 9. ♘bc3 ♗d7 10. h3 ♖c8 11. ♗e3 a6 12. ♖c1±○ Trifunović–Bulat, Jugoslavija (ch) 1953

41 7. d4!?

42 8. a3?! 0–0 9. b4 b6 10. f4!? ef4! 11. gf4 d5 12. e5 ♗g4 13. h3 ♗e2 14. ♕e2 f6 15. b5 ♘a5∓ Keres–Fischer, Curaçao (ct) 1962

43 9... cd4 10. cd4 d5 11. ♘bc3 ed4 12. ♘d4 de4 13. ♘c6 ♘c6 14. ♗c5 ♕d1 [14... ♖e8 15. ♘e4 ♕a5 16. ♕e1! ♗f5 17. ♕a5 ♘a5 18. ♘d6 ♖e2 19. ♖ae1 ♖b2 20. ♗d5 ♗e6 21. ♖e6!+−→ Pachman–Vasjukov, Gota 1957] 15. ♖ad1 ♖d8= Pachman–Lehmann, Marianske Lazni 1960

44 **10... ♗g4** 11. f3 cd4 12. ♘d4 ♗d7! 13. ♘c3 [13. ♕d2!?] ♕b6 [Knežević–Razuvajev, Moskva 1968 — ‿/326] 14. ♘f5 ♕b2 15. ♘e7 ♘e7 16. ♗d4=∞ Judovič; **10... ♕b6** 11. ♘bc3 cd4 12. ♘a4 ♕a6 13. ♘d4 ♘e5= Pachman–Talj, Amsterdam (izt) 1964

45 7. d3 d5 [7... 0–0 8. ♗e3 b6 9. d4 d6 10. f4 cd4 11. cd4 ♗a6= Krstev–Damjanović, Jugoslavija (ch) 1961] 8. ed5 ♘d5 9. ♘d2 0–0 10. ♘b3 b6 11. d4 cd4 12. ♘bd4 ♘d4 13. ♘d4 ♗a6= Robatsch–Ivkov, Beverwijk 1963

46 **10... ♘de7** 11. ♗g5 h6 12. ♗f4± Krstev–Stupica, Jugoslavija (ch) 1961; **10... 0–0** 11. ♘d5 ed5 12. ♗e3 [Botvinik–Gligorić, Hastings 1961/62] ♗g4=

47 **3. ♗g2** de4 4. ♗e4 [4. ♘c3 f5 5. f3 ef3 6. ♘f3 ♘c6 7. 0–0 e5 8. d3 ♗e7 9. ♕e2 (Spielmann–Bogoljubov, Sliač 1932) ♗f6!∓] ♘f6 5. ♗g2 ♗g4 6. ♘e2 ♘c6∓; **3. ♘c3** d4 4. ♘ce2 [4. ♘b1 ♘c6 5. d3 e5 6. ♗g2 ♗d6 7. ♘e2 h5∓↑] e5∓○

48 4. ♕f3!? Lasker

49 5. ♗e2? ♘c6 6. h3 [6. ♘c3 ♕h5 7. d3 ♘f6 8. ♗e3 e6 9. h3 ♖c8 10. ♔d2 ♗f3 11. ♗f3 ♕e5∓ Kopilov–Grečkin, SSSR 1946] ♗d7 7. ♘c3 ♕e6 8. d3 ♘d4 9. ♘d4 cd4∓ Novopašin–Saharov, SSSR 1968 — 6/394

50 **5... ♕e4** 6. ♔f1! ♘c6 7. ♘c3±; **5... ♘c6** 6. h3 [6. ♘c3 ♕d7 7. h3 ♗h5 8. 0–0 ♘f6 9. d3 e6 10. ♘e2 e5= Kuznjecov–Aronin, SSSR 1961] ♗f5 7. 0–0 ♕d7 8. ♔h2 0-0-0 9. d3 e5 10. ♘c3 f6 11. ♗e3 ♘d4 12. a3! ♔b8 13. ♘d2±

51 6... ♘c6?! 7. h3 [7. d3 ♕d7 8. h3 ♗f5 9. ♘c3 e5 10. ♗e3 ♖d8= Trifunović–Petrosjan, Beograd 1956] ♗h5 8. ♘c3 ♘f6 9. ♘e2 ♕d7 10. ♘f4 ♗g6 11. d3 e5 12. ♕e2 ♗d6 13. ♘g6 hg6 14. c4 0-0-0 15. ♘g5± Gurgenidze–Bikov, SSSR 1960

52 7. ♘c3 ♘c6 8. d3 ♕d7 [8... ♘f6? 9. ♗e3! b6 10. ♘g5 ♗g2 11. ♔g2 ♕d7 12. ♕f3±→ Trifunović–Bolbochan, Mar del Plata 1952] 9. ♗e3 ♗g2 10. ♔g2 e6=

53 8... ♕d5 9. ♕f3! ♗g2 10. ♔g2 ♕f3 [10... ♕d4? 11. ♕b7+−] 11. ♔f3±

54 11. ♕d5 ♕d5 12. ♘d5 ♗g2 13. ♔g2 0-0-0= Pachman–Tajmanov, Buenos Aires 1960

55 **2... b6**?! 3. bc5 bc5 4. c3 e5 5. ♘f3 ♘c6 6. ♗b5±; **2... e5**?! 3. bc5 [3. ♘f3 ♘c6 4. b5 ♘d4 5. ♘e5 ♕e7 6. ♘g4 ♕e4 7. ♘e3± Schwarz] ♗c5 4. ♘f3 d6 5. c3±↑⊞; **2... d6** 3. bc5 [3. ♗b5 ♗d7 4. ♗d7 ♕d7 5. a3=; 3. ♘f3 cb4 —B50] dc5 4. ♘c3 ♘f6 5. ♗c4 e6 6. ♘f3 ♗e7 7. 0–0 0–0 8. e5! ♘fd7 9. ♕e2 a6 10. a4± Spielmann–Patay, Meran 1926; **2... e6** 3. bc5 [3. ♘f3!?] ♗c5 4. d4 ♗b4 [4... ♗b6 5. f4±○] 5. c3 ♗a5 [5... ♗e7!?] 6. ♘f3 ♘f6 7. ♗d3 [7. ♗g5 ♕c7=] 0–0 8. 0–0±; **2... d5** 3. ed5 ♕d5 4. ♘c3 ♕e5 5. ♕e2 ♕e2 6. ♗e2 e6 [6... cb4 7. ♘d5±; 6... ♘d7!?] 7. bc5 ♗c5 8. ♘e4 ♗e7 9. ♗b2 f6 [9... ♘f6!?] 10. ♘f3 ♘c6 11. 0–0 ♘h6 12. d4 0–0 13. ♗c4!±

56 3. ♗c4?! e6△ d5∓↑⊞

57 4. e5 ♘c6 5. ♘e2 ♗f5 6. ♘f4 e6 7. ♗e3 h6 8. ♘d2 ♘ge7∓

58 4... ♕d5?! 5. ♘f3 [5. c4 bc3?! 6. ♘c3 ♕a5 7. ♗d2 e6 8. ♘e4 ♕d5 9. ♕c2 ♘c6 10. ♘f3 ♗b4 11. ♗c4 ♗d2 12. ♘ed2 ♘d4 13. ♕b2 ♘f3 14. gf3 ♕g5 15. ♗b5 ♔f8 16. ♘e4 ♕e7 17. ♖d1=∞ Benitez–Euwe, Puerto Rico 1948; 5... ♕a5!?] ♘f6 [5... ♗g4?! 6. ♗e2 ♘c6 7. 0–0 e6 8. c4 bc3 9. ♘c3 ♕d7 10. d5!±→; 5... e6!?] 6. ♗e2 ♘c6 7. 0–0 e6 8. a3 b5 9. c3 a6 10. ab4 ♗e7 11. c4± Bronštejn–Arlatovski, SSSR 1955

59 5... ♘bd7 6. ♘f3=; 6. a3!?

60 8. ♘e2 ♘d5 [8... ♘bd7!?] 9. ♘g3 ♗g6∓

61 11. ♘e2 ♗e7 12. 0–0 0–0 13. c3 ♘d5 14. ♗b3 ♘c6 15. ♘c2! ♖c8 16. ♘e3 ♘e3 17. ♗e3 ♘a5!∓ Ozsvath–Varnusz, Hungary 1973 — 15/304

62 **3. . . ♘c6** 4. d4 d5 5. ed5 ♕d5 6. c4! bc3 7. ♘c3 ♕d8 [7. . . ♕d4? 8. ♘b5!+−] 8. d5 ♘b8 9. ♘f3 ♘f6 10. ♗b5 ♘bd7 11. 0−0± Müller−Aronin, SSSR 1968 — 6/390; **3. . . d5**!?

63 5. ♗c4 ♘b6 6. ♗b3 e6∓

64 5. . . d6 6. ed6 ♕d6 7. a3!?=∞

65 6. . . d6 7. ♗b5 ♗d7 8. ♗d7 ♕d7 9. 0−0=∞

66 10. c4 ♘b4 11. ♘c3 0−0 12. ♗e2 a6∓ Padevski−Tajmanov, 1970

67 11. 0−0 ♘d3 12. ♕d3 0−0 13. ♘bd2 d6∓

68 **3. . . ♘c6** 4. d4 d5 5. ed5 ♕d5 6. c4 bc3 7. ♘c3 ♕a5 8. d5 ♘f6 [8. . . ♕c3 9. ♗d2 ♕f6 10. dc6 bc6 11. ♖c1 ♗d7 12. ♗c4 ♕d6 13. ♕e2 ♘f6 14. 0−0 e6 15. ♘e5±] 9. dc6 ♕c3 10. ♗d2 ♕c6 11. ♖c1 ♕e4 12. ♗e2 e6 13. ♖c4±⟳; **3. . . d5** 4. ed5 ♘f6 5. a3 ♘d5! 6. ab4 ♘b4 7. ♗b2 [7. d4 ♗f5 8. ♘a3 e6 9. ♗b5 ♘8c6 10. c3 a6 11. ♗e2 ♘d5∓ Thomas −Schmid, Hastings 1951/52] ♘8c6 8. ♘a3 ♗f5 9. ♗e2 e6 10. 0−0 ♗d6 11. d4 0−0∓ Thomas−Gligorić, Hastings 1951/52; **3. . . d6** — B 50

69 4. . . d5 5. e5 ♕b6 6. a3 ba3 7. c3 ♘h6 8. ♘a3 ♗e7 9. ♗d3 ♗d7 10. ♗h6 gh6 11. 0−0±

70 6. . . 0−0 7. e5 ♘d5 8. a3=∞

71 9. . . ♘c6!? 10. ed6 ♗d6 11. ♘d6 ♕d6∓

72 11. g3 ♕c7 12. ♗b2 ♖d8 13. ♕e1 b6 14. ♘eg5 ♘f8 15. ♕e4 h6 16. ♘h7 ♘g6 17. h4 ♗b7∓ Šijanovski−Suetin, SSSR 1959

73 **3. . . e5**? 4. ab4 ♗b4 5. c3 ♗c5 6. ♘f3 ♘c6 7. ♗c4 d6 8. d4 ed4 9. cd4 ♗b6 10. 0−0 ♗g4 11. ♕b3± Marshall−Verlinski, Moskva 1925; **3. . . ♘c6**? 4. ab4 ♘b4 [4. . . ♘f6? 5. b5 ♘d4 6. c3 ♘e6 7. e5 ♘d5 8. c4 ♘df4 9. g3 ♘g6 10. f4±→ Marshall−Rogosin, New York 1940] 5. c3 ♘c6 6. d4±; **3. . . ♘f6** 4. e5 ♘d5 5. ab4 ♘b4 6. c3 ♘d5 7. ♘f3 e6 8. d4±

74 4. d4 e6 [4. . . e5? 5. ♗a3 ♗a3 6. ♘a3 ♘f6 7. ♘b5! 0−0 8. de5 ♘e4 9. ♕d5± Spielmann−Colle, Baden Baden 1925] 5. ♗d3 d5 6. e5 ♘c6 7. c3 a6∓

75 4. . . d5 5. ed5 ♕d5 6. ♗b2 ♘c6 7. ♘b5 ♕d8 8. ♕f3 e5 9. ♗c4 ♘f6 10. ♕b3± Spielmann−Sämisch, Karlovy Vary 1923

76 5. ♗b2 ♘f6 6. ♗c4 ♘c6 7. ♕e2 g6 8. ♘f3 ♗g7 9. d4 0−0 10. 0−0=∞ Klaman−Dubinin, SSSR 1946

77 6. . . e6 7. ♘e2 ♗e7 8. 0−0=∞

78 7. ♘e2!? ♗e7 8. 0−0 ♘c6 9. c3 0−0 10. ♘c2 ♕c7 11. ♘e3 b6 12. ♗a3 ♖d8 13. f4=∞ Dorn−Fischer, Österreich 1955

79 8. . . ♘bd7 9. c3 0−0 10. ♘c2=∞

80 11. ♕e2 0−0 12. ♗c4 ♘a6 13. ♘e1 ♘c5 14. f3=∞ Dorn−Simagin, Österreich 1953

81 4. . . d5!?

82 6. . . d6 7. ♘f3 [7. f4 f5 (Tartakower) 8. ♘d2 ♘f6 9. ♗d3 0−0 10. ♘gf3 ♘c6 11. 0−0 (Marshall−Haida, Marianske Lazni 1925) d5!∓] ♘c6 8. ♗e3 b6! 9. ♗b5 ♗d7 10. d5 ed5 11. ed5 ♘a5 12. ♘a3 ♘f6 13. 0−0 0−0 14. ♖e1 ♖e8∓ Marshall−Tarrasch, San Sebastian 1912

83 7. . . de4!?△ ♘f6

84 9. . . f5?! 10. ef6 ♘f6 11. ♘gf3 0−0 12. 0−0=∞

85 11. ♘f3 ♘c6 12. 0−0 0−0∓

86 4. e5 ♘c6 5. d4 ♕b6 [5. . . ♕c7 6. ♘f3 ♗g4 7. ab4 ♘b4 8. c3 ♘c6 9. ♘a3 a6 10. ♗e2 e6 11. 0−0 ♖d8∓ Yates−Berger, London 1926] 6. ♗e3 ♗f5 7. g4 [7. ♗d3 ♗d3 8. ♕d3 e6 9. ab4 ♘b4 10. ♕d1 ♘e7∓ Grünfeld] ♗e4 8. f3 ♗g6 9. e6 fe6 10. ♗d3 ♗d3 11. ♕d3 e5! 12. c3 ed4 13. cd4 e5!∓ Orienter−Grünfeld, Wien 1946

87 4. . . ♘f6!? 5. ab4 ♘d5 6. ♘f3 e6 [6. . . ♘b4!?] 7. ♗b2 ♘d7 8. g3 ♘5f6 9. ♗g2 ♗b4 10. 0−0 0−0= Littlewood−Cafferty, Hastings 1960/61

88 5. ♗b2 e5 6. ♘f3 [6. ab4 ♗b4 7. ♘c3 ♗c3 8. ♗c3 ♘c6 9. ♘f3 ♘ge7 10. ♗e2 0−0 11. 0−0 f6∓ Spielmann−Sämisch, Marianske Lazni 1925] ♘c6 7. c4 ♕e6 8. ♗d3 f6 9. 0−0 ♗c5 10. ♗e4 ♘ge7∓

89 7. ♘a3 ♗a3 [7. . . ♘f6 8. ♘b5 0−0! 9. ♘c7 ♕c5 10. ♘a8 e4 11. ♘g1 ♖e8!△ e3∓→; 9. ♗e2 e4 10. ♘fd4 ♘c6 11. ♘c6 bc6 12. ♗a3 ♗a3 13. ♘a3 ♕g5!∓ Rossetto −Iliesco, Mar del Plata 1944] 8. ♗a3 ♘c6 9. c4 ♕d8 10. ♕b1 ♘ge7∓ Bronštejn−Benkö, Moskva 1949

90 8. ♖a3 ♘c6 9. ♘c3 ♕d6! 10. ♘b5 ♕e7 11. ♕a1 ♘f6! 12. ♗c4 [12. ♘a7? e4 13. ♘g1 0−0∓] 0−0 13. 0−0 ♗g4∓ Podgorny−Pachman, ČSSR (ch) 1953

91 9. ♗c4!?

92 12. 0−0 0−0∓

B 21 — 1. e4 c5

	2	3	4	5	6	7	8	9	10	
1	f4 d5[1]	ed5 ♕d5[2]	♘c3 ♕d8	♘f3 ♘f6	♘e5! e6	♕f3 ♗e7	b3![3] a6[4]	♗b2 ♘bd7	0-0-0 ♕c7[5]	±

	2	3	4	5	6	7	8	9	10	
2	. . . d6	♘f3 a6[6]	a4 ♘c6	♗e2[7] ♘f6	d3 e6[8]	0–0 ♗e7	♘c3 0–0	h3 ♖b8	♗e3 b5[9]	=
3	. . . e6	d3[10] d5	♘d2 ♘c6	♘gf3 ♘f6	c3 ♗e7	a3 a5	g3 b6	e5 ♘g4[11]	♕e2[12] h5[13]	=
4	. . . ♘c6	♘f3[14] e6[15]	♗b5 ♘ge7[16]	0–0 a6[17]	♗e2 g6	d3 ♗g7	c3 0–0[18]	♗e3 d6	d4 cd4[19]	=
5	. . . . . .	. . . g6	d3[20] ♗g7[21]	c3 d6	g3[22] e5	♗g2 ♘ge7	0–0 0–0	♗e3 ♗d7	fe5 ♘e5[23]	=

1. e4 c5 2. d4 cd4[24]

	3	4	5	6	7	8	9	10	11	
6	♘f3[25] ♘f6[26]	e5 ♘e4[27]	♕d4 d5	♘bd2![28] ♘c6	♗b5 ♗f5[29]	0–0 e6[30]	♕a4 ♕c7	♘e4 ♗e4	♘d4[31]	±
7	. . . e5	c3[32] dc3	♘c3[33] ♘c6[34]	♗c4 ♗b4[35]	0–0 ♘f6[36]	♘d5				±
8	c3[37] d3[38]	♗d3[39] ♘c6[40]	c4 ♘f6[41]	♘c3 g6	♘f3[42] d6	h3 ♗g7	0–0 ♘d7	♗e3[43] 0–0[44]	♗e2[45]	±
9	. . . dc3	♘c3[46] e6[47]	♗c4[48] a6[49]	♘f3 b5	♗b3 ♗b7[50]	♕e2 ♗b4	0–0 ♗c3	bc3 ♘e7	♗a3! ♘bc6[51]	±

1. e4 c5 2. d4 cd4 3. c3 dc3 4. ♘c3 ♘c6

	5	6	7	8	9	10	11	12	13	
10	♘f3[52] e6[53]	♗c4[54] ♗b4	0–0 ♘ge7[55]	♕e2 0–0	♖d1 ♗c3	bc3 d5	♗d3 de4	♗e4 ♕a5	♖b1 ♖d8[56]	±
11	. . . g6	♗c4 ♗g7[57]	0–0[58] ♘h6[59]	h3 0–0	♗f4 ♔h8[60]	♕d2 ♘g8	e5!			=/∞
12	. . . d6	♗c4 ♘f6[61]	e5 ♘g4[62]	e6! ♗e6[63]	♗e6 fe6	♘g5 ♘f6	0–0 ♕d7	♖e1 e5	♕b3 d5[64]	±
13	. . . . . .	. . . e6	0–0[65] ♘f6[66]	♕e2 a6	♖d1 ♕a5[67]	♗f4 ♘e5	♘e5 de5	♗d2 ♕c7	♖ac1 ♗e7!?[68]	±
14	. . . . . .	. . . . . .	. . . . . .	. . . ♗e7	♖d1 e5[69]	h3 0–0	♗e3[70] ♗e6	♗e6[71] fe6	♖ac1 ♖c8[72]	=

1 **2... e5?!** 3. ♘f3 ef4 4. ♗c4△ 0–0, d4±; **2... ♘f6** 3. d3 ♘c6 4. ♘f3 d5 5. e5 ♘g8 6. ♗e2 ♗g4 7. 0–0 e6 8. c4 ♘ge7 9. ♘c3 dc4 10. dc4 ♘f5 11. h3! [11. ♕a4 ♘fd4 12. ♘d4 ♕d4 13. ♖f2 ♗e2 14. ♘e2 ♕d3 15. f5 ♗e7!∞ Larsen–Talj, Amsterdam (izt) 1964] ♗f3 12. ♗f3 ♕d4 13. ♕d4 cd4?! 14. ♘e4 ♗e7 15. c5± Bednarski–Larsen, Palma de Mallorca 1967 — 4/372; 13... ♘fd4±; **2... g6**!? 3. d3 ♗g7 4. g3 d5! [4... ♘c6 5. ♗g2 e6 6. ♘d2 ♘ge7 7. ♘h3! d5 8. 0–0 0–0 9. e5± Petrosjan–Pachman, Moskva 1967 — 3/350] 5. ♘d2 de4 9. ♘e4 ♘f6 7. ♘f2 ♕d5 8. ♘f3 ♕e6 9. ♗e2 ♘d5= Lombardy–Čirić, Wijk aan Zee 1969 — 7/298

2 3... ♘f6 4. ♗b5 ♗d7 5. ♗d7 ♕d7 6. c4±

3 8. ♗b5 ♘bd7 9. f5 0–0 10. ♘f7 ♖f7 [10... ♔f7 11. fe6 ♔e6 12. ♗c4+−] 11. fe6 ♖f8 12. ed7 ♘d7∓

4 8... 0–0 9. ♗b2 ♘bd7 10. 0-0-0 ♕c7 11. ♖e1 a6 12. g4 b5 13. ♗g2± Hennings–Polugajevski, Kislovodsk 1972 — 14/307

5 11. ♖e1 ♖b8 12. g4 b5 13. ♗g2 ♗b7 14. ♕e2 ♗g2 15. ♕g2 ♘e5 16. fe5 ♘d7 17. ♘e4± Zinn–Minev, Halle 1967

6 **3... ♘f6** 4. ♘c3 g6 [4... ♘c6 — B 23] 5. ♗b5 ♗d7 6. ♗d7 ♕d7 7. 0–0 ♘c6 8. ♔h1 ♗g7 9. d3 0–0 10. ♗e3= Zinn–Vranešić, Siegen (ol) 1970 — 10/375; **3... ♗g4**!?

7 5. ♗c4?! e6 6. ♘c3 ♘f6! 7. ♕e2 ♗e7 8. d3 d5∓ Trifunović

8 6... ♖b8!?

9 11. ab5 ab5 12. ♕d2 b4 13. ♘d1=

10 3. ♘f3 d5 4. ed5 ed5 5. ♗b5 ♗d7 [5... ♘c6 6. 0—0 ♘f6=] 6. ♗d7 ♘d7 7. 0—0 ♗d6 8. d4=

11 9... ♘d7 10. d4 0—0 11. ♗e2 ♖b8 12. 0—0±

12 10. ♘b1?! h5 11. d4 g6 12. ♗d3 ♗a6 13. ♗a6 ♖a6 14. ♕e2 ♖a8 15. h3 ♘h6∓↑ Levy—R. Byrne, USA 1968 — 6/392

13 11. ♗g2=

14 **3. g3**?! d5 4. ed5 ♕d5∓↑⊞; **3. ♗c4** e6 4. ♘c3 ♘f6 [4... ♘ge7?! 5. ♕h5!±↑] 5. e5 d5 6. ef6 [6. ♗b5 ♘e4! 7. ♗c6 bc6 8. ♘f3∓] dc4 7. fg7 ♗g7 8. ♘f3 ♘d4 9. 0—0 0—0∓; **3. d3** e6 4. ♘f3 ♘f6 5. g3 d5=

15 **3... ♘f6** ♘c3=; **3... d5**!?

16 **4... ♘d4** 5. ♘d4 cd4 6. 0—0±; **4... ♕c7** 5. ♗c6 [5. d4 cd4 6. ♘d4 ♗c5∓] ♕c6 6. d3 d6 7. 0—0 ♘e7 8. ♘c3 g6 9. a4! b6 [9... ♗g7 10. e5! d5 11. ♘b5±] 10. ♕e1 a6 11. ♘g5 ♗b7 12. ♗d2 ♗g7 [Buela—Fernandez, La Habana 1967 — 4/373] 13. ♕g3±

17 5... d5!? Larsen

18 8... d5!? Larsen

19 11. ♘d4 ♘d4 12. ♗d4 e5! 13. fe5 [Larsen—Kavalek, Las Palmas 1974 — 17/339] ♘c6!=

20 4. ♗b5 ♗g7 5. 0—0 ♘f6 6. ♗c6 bc6 7. ♕e2 0—0 8. d3 d6 9. ♘c3 ♖b8 10. ♖b1 ♘e8 11. ♘a4 ♘c7 12. b3 f6 13. ♕f2 e5= Larsen—Evans, Amsterdam (izt) 1964

21 4... d6 5. g3 ♗g7 6. ♗g2 e5 7. 0—0 ♘ge7 8. c3 0—0 9. ♗e3 b6 10. d4 ♖b8 11. ♘a3=

22 **6. ♗e2** e6 7. 0—0 ♘ge7 8. ♕e1 d5!= Trapl—Hort, ČSSR 1972 — 13/330; 8. ♗e3!?; **6. ♗e3**!? ♘f6 7. h3 0—0 8. ♗e2=

23 11. ♘e5 ♗e5 12. d4 cd4 13. cd4 ♗g7=

24 2... g6 3. ♘f3 — B 27

25 3. ♕d4 ♘f6 [3... ♘c6=] 4. ♘f3 g6 5. e5 ♘c6 6. ♕f4 ♘d5 7. ♕e4 ♘c7 8. ♘c3 ♗g7 9. ♗f4 ♘e6 10. ♗c4 ♘f4 11. ♕f4 0—0 12. 0—0 ♕a5=

26 **3... e6**; **3... ♘c6**; **3... d6**

27 **4... ♘d5** 5. ♕d4 — B 29; **4... ♘g8**!?

28 6. ed6 ♘d6 7. ♗f4 ♘c6 8. ♕d2 ♗g4 9. ♗e2 ♘e4 10. ♕e3 ♕a5 11. c3 ♘f6 12. ♘a3 ♘d5 13. ♕c1± Schmid—Alster, Wien 1957

29 7... ♘d2 8. ♗d2 e6 [Smederevac—Puc, Jugoslavija (ch) 1955] 9. ♕g4±

30 8... a6? 9. ♗c6 bc6 10. ♕a4 ♕d7 11. ♘e4 ♗e4 12. e6!△ ♘g5±→ Keres—Schmid, Bamberg 1968 — 5/341

31 ± Ivkov

32 4. ♗c4 ♕c7 5. ♗b3 ♘f6 6. ♘g5 [6. ♘bd2!?] d5 7. ed5 ♗d6 8. c3 h6 9. ♘f3 dc3 10. ♘c3 a6 11. 0—0 0—0 12. h3 ♗f5 13. ♗e3 ♘e4 14. ♖c1 ♘c3 15. ♖c3 ♕e7 16. ♕c1 ♘d7∓

33 5. ♗c4!?

34 5... d6 6. ♗c4 ♗e6 [6... h6? 7. ♗f7 ♔f7 8. ♘e5 ♔e7 9. ♘d5 ♔e6 10. ♕g4+— Krogius—Ojanen, 1951] 7. ♗e6 fe6 8. ♕b3 ♕c8 9. ♘g5±

35 6... d6 7. ♘g5 ♘h6 8. 0—0±

36 7... ♗c3 8. bc3 d6 9. ♗a3 ♗g4 10. ♖b1± Gereben—Salay, Hungary 1954

37 Tartakower, Morra, Matulović

38 **3... ♘f6** 4. e5 ♘d5 — B 22; **3... d5** 4. ed5 ♕d5 — B 22

39 4. c4 ♘c6 5. ♘f3 d6 6. h3 [6. ♗d3 ♘f6 7. 0—0 e6 8. ♘c3 ♗e7 9. ♗f4?! e5 10. ♗g5 ♗g4 11. ♗e2 ♗f3 12. ♗f3 0—0= Gaprindašvili—Kušnir (m) 1965;9. ♗g5!±; 7... ♗g4!?] g6 7. ♗d3 ♗g7 8. 0—0 ♘f6 9. ♘c3±○

40 **4... d5**? 5. ♗b5+—; **4... d6** 5. ♘f3 ♘c6 6. 0—0 ♗g4 7. h3 ♗h5 8. g4 ♗g6 9. ♗e3 ♘f6 10. ♘bd2 ♕c8 11. ♘d4± Matulović—Vasiljević, Jugoslavija 1953; **4... g6** 5. ♘f3 d6 6. 0—0 ♗g7 7. h3 ♘f6 8. c4 0—0 9. ♘c3 b6 10. ♗e3 ♘bd7 11. ♖c1 ♗b7 12. ♗b1 ♖c8 13. ♘d2 ♖e8 14. b4±○ Matulović—Vošpernik, Jugoslavija (ch) 1953

41 **5... e5**?! 6. ♘f3 ♗c5 7. 0—0 d6 8. h3 ♘f6 9. ♘c3 0—0 10. a3 a6 11. b4± Marić—Puc, Vinkovci 1958; **5... g6** 6. ♗d2 ♗g7 7. ♗c3 ♘f6 8. ♘f3 d6 9. h3 0—0 10. 0—0 b6 11. ♘a3 ♗b7 [Marić—Pirc, Jugoslavija (ch) 1956] 12. ♘c2=; 6. ♘f3 d6 7. h3 ♘f6 — 5... ♘f6

42 7. f4 d6 8. ♘f3 ♗g7 9. 0—0 0—0=

43 10. ♘d5 0—0 11. ♖b1 ♘de5 12. ♘e5 de5 13. b4 ♗e6 14. ♗e3 ♘d4 15. f4± Marić—Ivkov, Jugoslavija (ch) 1956

44 10... ♘de5 11. ♖c1 ♕a5 12. ♗e2 ♘f3 13. ♗f3 ♗e6 14. ♗e2 0—0 15. ♕d2 ♖fc8 16. b3 ♖ab8 17. ♖fd1±○ Ivkov—Szabo, Mar del Plata 1955

45 Sokolov—Pirc, Jugoslavija (ch) 1956

46 **4. ♘f3**!? cb2!?△ ♕b6; **4. ♗c4**!? cb2 5. ♗b2 e6 6. ♘f3 ♗b4 7. ♘bd2∞

47 **4... d6** 5. ♘f3 [5. ♗c4!? e6 6. ♘ge2 a6 7. 0—0 ♗e7 8. ♘g3 ♘f6 9. ♕e2 ♘c6 10. ♗e3±] ♘d7 6. ♗c4 e6 7. ♗f4 e5 8. ♕b3 d5 9. ♗d5 ♘c5 10. ♗f7 ♔e7 11. ♗g5 ♘f6 12. ♘d5+—→ Ivkov—Bauza, Mar del Plata 1955; **4... g6** 5. ♘f3 ♘c6 — 4... ♘c6

48 5. ♘f3 ♗b4 6. ♕d4! ♘c6 7. ♕g7 ♕f6 8. ♕f6 ♘f6 9. ♗d2 0—0 10. ♗d3±; 8. ♗h6!?±

49 5... ♗b4 6. ♘e2 a6 7. 0—0 b5 8. ♗b3 ♘c6 [8... ♘f6? 9. e5 ♘g4 10. ♕d4! ♗c3 11. ♘c3±] 9. ♘g3 ♘ge7 10. ♗e3±

50 7... b4 8. ♘d5!±

51 12. ♖fd1 ♕a5 13. ♕b2 ♖d8 14. ♘d4±↑ Matulović–Scocco, Italia 1955

52 5. ♗c4!?

53 5... e5?! 6. ♗c4 d6 7. ♘g5 ♘h6 8. 0–0 ♗g4 9. ♗f7 ♘f7 10. ♕g4 ♘g5 11. ♗g5 ♗e7 12. ♗e7 ♕e7 13. ♘d5!± Bondarevski–Peterson, SSSR 1959

54 6. ♗f4!? a6 [6... d6!? Kotov] 7. ♗c4 [7. e5?! ♘ge7 8. ♗d3 ♘g6 9. ♗g3 ♕c7 10. 0–0 ♗e7?! 11. ♖e1 0–0 12. h4± Ivkov–Fuderer, Zagreb 1955; 10... ♘ge5 11. ♘e5 ♘e5 12. ♖e1 d6∓ Kostić] ♘ge7 8. 0–0 ♘g6 9. ♗g3 ♗e7 10. ♕e2 0–0 11. ♖fd1± Marić–Bertok, Jugoslavija 1955

55 7... a6 8. ♕e2 ♘ge7 9. ♖d1 0–0 10. e5!± Sokolov–Nikolac, Jugoslavija 1954

56 12. ♖d8 ♕d8 13. ♗a3 ♕a5 14. ♗d6± Matulović–Rabar, Ljubljana 1953

57 **6... ♘a5**? 7. ♕d4 f6 8. 0–0 ♘h6 9. e5! ♘f5 10. ef6 ef6 11. ♖e1 ♗e7 12. ♘d5 ♔f8 13. ♖e7 ♕e7 14. ♗h6+– Dubek–Weinstein, USA 1958; **6... d6** 7. ♗g5 ♗g7 8. ♕b3±

58 **7. ♗f4** d6 8. 0–0 ♘f6 9. ♕e2 0–0 10. ♖fd1 ♗g4= Nahlik–Holmov, SSSR 1957; **7. e5** ♕a5 8. 0–0 ♘e5 9. ♘e5 ♗e5 10. ♖e1=∞ Sokolov–Pete, Jugoslavija 1954

59 **7... ♘f6**? 8. e5 ♘g4 9. ♗f7 ♔f7 10. ♘g5 ♔e8 11. ♕g4 ♘e5 12. ♕a4△ ♘e6+– Matulović–Del Pezzo, Italia 1954; **7... d6** 8. h3 ♘f6 9. ♕e2 0–0 10. ♖d1 ♘d7 11. ♗g5 a6 12. a4± Lutikov–Zajcev, SSSR 1958

60 9... ♘a5? 10. ♗e2 ♔h8 11. ♕d2 ♘g8 12. ♖fd1 a6 13. ♖ac1±

61 6... a6 7. ♕e2 [7. e5?! de5? 8. ♕d8! ♘d8 9. ♘d5! ♘e6 10. ♘b6 ♖b8 11. ♘e5 ♘f6 12. ♘f7 ♔f7 13. ♗f4±; 7... e6!∓] ♘f6 8. 0–0 ♗g4 [8... e6!?] 9. ♖d1 ♕c8 [9... e6?! 10. ♗f4±] 10. ♗f4 g6 [10... g5?! 11. ♗g3!±→ Matulović–Sokolov, Italia 1953] 11. ♖ac1 ♗g7 12. ♘d5!± Stöckl–Martin, Wien 1950

62 **7... ♘e5**?? 8. ♘e5 de5 9. ♗f7+–; **7... de5** 8. ♕d8 ♘d8 [8... ♔d8 9. ♘g5! ♔c7 10. ♘f7 ♖g8 11. ♘b5 ♔b8 12. ♘e5+– Matulović–Vincenti, Italia 1954] 9. ♘b5 ♖b8 10. ♘e5 e6 11. ♘c7 ♔e7 12. ♗e3± Kristiansson–Roberts, Harrachov 1967 — 4/383

63 **8... f6** 9. ♗f4 g6 10. ♘d4 ♘ge5 11. ♗e5 de5 12. ♘c6 ♕d1 13. ♖d1 bc6 14. ♘b5! +–; **8... fe6** 9. ♘g5±

64 14. f4 e6 15. fe5 ♗c5 16. ♗e3±

65 7. ♗f4 ♘f6 [7... a6 8. a4?! ♘f6 9. ♕d2 ♗e7 10. ♖d1 ♕a5 11. ♗d6? ♗d6 12. ♕d6 ♘e4–+ Tartakower–Najdorf, Saltsjöbaden (izt) 1948; 11. 0–0∓; 8. ♕e2 ♗e7 9. ♖d1 ♘f6 10. e5 ♘h5 (Reicher–S. Szabo, Bucuresti 1953) 11. ♗e3!± Gligorić, Sokolov] 8. ♕e2 [8. 0–0?! ♗e7 9. ♕e2 e5 10. ♗e3 0–0 11. ♖fd1 ♗g4 12. a3 ♕d7 13. h3 ♗h5 14. ♖d2 a6∓ Matanović–Kotov, Jugoslavija–SSSR 1958] ♘h5 9. ♗e3 ♗e7 10. ♖d1 ♕a5 11. 0–0 ♘f6= Tartakower–Lokvenc, Venezia 1948

66 **7... ♘ge7** 8. ♗g5! [8. ♕e2 ♘g6 9. ♖d1 ♗e7 10. a3 0–0 11. b4 ♗d7∓] a6 [8... ♕d7 9. ♕e2 ♘g6 10. ♖ad1±; 10. ♖fd1!? h6 11. ♗e3 ♗e7 12. ♘d4±↑] 9. ♕e2 [9. a4 h6 10. ♗h4 ♕c7 11. ♕e2 ♘g6 12. ♗g3 ♗e7∓ Gančev–Estrin, Bulgaria 1970 — 10/386; 10. ♗e3 ♘g6 11. ♘d2 ♗e7 12. f4=∞ Cappello–Saidy, Venezia 1969 — 8/295] h6 10. ♗e3 ♘g6 11. ♖ad1 [11. ♖fd1 b5 12. ♗b3 ♗e7 13. ♖ac1 ♗d7 14. ♘d4 ♘d4 15. ♖d4 0–0∓ Mučnik–Estrin, SSSR 1951] ♗d7 12. ♘d4 ♘a5 13. ♗e6! fe6 14. ♕h5 ♔f7 13. f4±→ I. Zajcev–Saharov, SSSR (ch) 1968; **7... ♗e7** 8. ♕e2 a6 9. ♖d1 ♗d7! [9... ♕c7 10. ♗f4 ♘e5 11. ♗e5 de5 12. ♖ac1 ♕b8 13. ♗b5!+– Makles–Paoli, Le Havre 1966 — 1/237] 10. ♗f4± Parma–Eliskases, Mar del Plata 1962

67 **9... ♗d7** 10. ♗f4 b5 11. ♗b3 ♕b8 12. ♖ac1 ♗e7 13. e5 [13. h3?! 0–0 14. e5 de5 15. ♘e5 ♘e5 16. ♗e5 ♕b7∓ Stöckl–Alster, Praha 1949] de5 14. ♘e5 ♘e5 15. ♗e5 ♕b7 16. ♗f6 gf6 17. ♘d5 ed5 18. ♗d5+– Gligorić, Sokolov; **9... ♕c7** 10. ♗f4 [10. ♗g5 ♗e7 11. ♖ac1 0–0 12. ♗b3 h6 13. ♗f4 e5 14. ♗e3 ♕d8 15. ♘d5 ♘d5 16. ♗d5 ♗d7= Fischer–Korčnoj, Buenos Aires 1960] ♘e5 [10... e5 11. ♘d5!±; 10... ♗e7 11. ♖ac1 0–0 12. ♗b3 ♖d8 13. ♘d5!± Matulović–Bradvarević, Jugoslavija (ch) 1957] 11. ♗b3 [11. ♗e5 de5 12. ♖ac1 ♗d7 13. ♗e6 ♗e6 14. ♘d5+–→ Matulović–Segi, Jugoslavija 1953; 12... ♕b8!?±] ♗d7 [11... ♗e7 12. ♖ac1 ♕b8 13. ♘d4 0–0 14. ♗g3!△ f4±↑ Talj–Najbult, 1962] 12. ♖ac1 ♕b8±↑ Gragger–Đurašević, Beograd 1951

68 **13... ♗d7**? 14. ♗a6! ♖a6 15. ♘b5 ♗b5 16. ♕b5 ♖c6 17. ♗a5!+– Graždancev–Žarkov, SSSR 1968 — 5/340; **13... ♗e7**!?±↑

69 9... ♗d7?! 10. ♗g5 0–0 11. ♗f6 gf6 12. ♘b5 ♕b8 13. ♖d3!± Cibulka–Zajic, ČSSR 1966 — 2/321

70 **11. b4** ♗e6 12. ♗e6 fe6 13. ♕c4 ♕c8 14. ♘b5 ♘d4 15. ♕c8 ♘f3 16. gf3 ♖fc8 17. ♗e3 d5∓↑⊞; **11. ♗g5** ♗e6 12. ♗f6 ♗f6 13. ♘b5 ♗e7 14. ♗e6 fe6 15. ♕d3 ♕d7 16. ♖d2 ♖ad8 17. ♖ad1 ♕c8 18. ♕b3 a6 19. ♘d6 ♗d6 20. ♖d6 ♘d4!∓ Lokvenc–Bolbochan, Wien 1950; **11. b3** a6 12. ♗a3 ♕a5 13. ♕b2 ♘b4 14. ♖ac1 b5 15. ♗b4 ♕b4 16. ♘d5 ♘d5 17. ♗d5 ♖a7∓ I. Zajcev–Tajmanov, SSSR (ch) 1969 — 8/296

71 12. ♖ac1 ♗c4 13. ♕c4 ♖c8 14. ♕b5 [14. ♕a4 ♕d7 15. b4 a6 16. b5 ab5 17. ♕b5 ♖a8 18. ♖b1 ♖fb8 19. a4 h6∓ Marić–Karaklajić, Jugoslavija (ch) 1956] b6 15. ♗g5 ♕e8 16. ♗f6 ♗f6 17. ♘d5 ♗d8 18. ♕a6±↑ Emma–Goldenberg, Argentina (ch) 1960; 13... h6∞

72 14. b4! a6 [14... ♘b4 15. ♕b5 d5 16. ♘e5± Marić–Trifunović, Sarajevo 1958] 15. b5= Pokojowczyk–Gligorić, Jugoslavija 1971 — 11/270

B 22

1. e4 c5 2. c3[1]

	2	3	4	5	6	7	8	9	10	
1	. . . ♘f6[2]	e5[3] ♘d5	♘f3[4] ♘c6	♘a3!?[5] g6[6]	g3 ♗g7[7]	♗g2 ♘c7![8]	♕e2 0—0	0—0 d6	d4 cd4[9]	∓
2	. . . . . .	. . . . . .	d4 cd4[10]	♗c4[11] ♕c7[12]	♕e2[13] ♘b6	♗d3[14] ♘c6	♘f3 g6	0—0 dc3	♘c3 ♗g7[15]	$\overline{\infty}$

1. e4 c5 2. c3 ♘f6 3. e5 ♘d5 4. d4 cd4

	5	6	7	8	9	10	11	12	13	
3	♕d4 e6[16]	♗c4 ♘c6	♕e4 d6[17]	♘f3[18] de5[19]	♘e5 ♘e5[20]	♕e5 ♘b6[21]				=
4	. . . . . .	♘f3 ♘c6	♕e4 d6[22]	♘bd2 de5	♘e5 ♘e5![23]	♕e5 ♕d6	♗b5 ♗d7	♗d7 ♕d7	♘f3 ♕c7[24]	=
5	cd4 d6[25]	♗c4 ♘b6[26]	♗b3 de5[27]	♕h5[28] e6	de5 ♘c6	♘f3[29] g6[30]	♕g4 ♗g7	0—0 ♘e5!	♘e5 ♗e5[31]	∓
6	. . . . . .	. . . . . .	♗b5 ♗d7	♕e2 ♗b5	♕b5 ♕d7	♘c3 e6	♗g5 ♕b5	♘b5 ♔d7	♘f3 d5[32]	=
7	. . . . . .	♘f3 ♘c6[33]	♘c3[34] de5[35]	de5[36] ♘db4![37]	♕d8[38] ♔d8	♔d1 ♗f5				∓
8	. . . . . .	. . . . . .	♗e2 g6[39]	0—0 ♗g7	♕b3 de5	de5 0—0[40]	♖d1 e6	♘c3 ♘e5	♘d5 ed5[41]	=
9	. . . . . .	. . . . . .	♗c4 ♘b6[42]	♗b5[43] d5[44]	♘c3 ♗g4	h3 ♗f3[45]	♕f3 e6	0—0 ♗e7[46]	♕g3 ♔f8[47]	∞

1. e4 c5 2. c3 d5 3. ed5 ♕d5[48] 4. d4

	4	5	6	7	8	9	10	11	12	
10	. . . e5[49]	de5[50] ♕e5	♗e3 ♘f6	♘f3 ♕c7	♘a3![51] a6					±
11	. . . ♘c6	♘f3[52] ♗g4[53]	♗e2 cd4[54]	cd4 e6[55]	♘c3 ♕a5[56]	0—0 ♘f6	h3[57] ♗h5	a3 ♗e7[58]	♗e3 0—0[59]	±
12	. . . . . .	. . . . . .	. . . e6	h3![60] ♗h5	c4 ♕d7	d5 ed5	cd5 ♗f3	♗f3 ♘d4	0—0 ♗e7[61]	±
13	. . . . . .	. . . cd4	cd4 ♗g4[62]	♘c3! ♗f3[63]	gf3[64] ♕d4	♕d4 ♘d4	♘b5 e5[65]	♘c7 ♔d7	♘a8 ♗b4[66]	±
14	. . . . . .	. . . . . .	. . . e5	♘c3 ♗b4	♗d2 ♗c3	♗c3 e4![67]	♘e5 ♘e5	de5 ♘e7	♕a4[68] ♗d7[69]	=
15	. . . e6	♘f3 ♘c6[70]	♗d3 ♘f6	0—0 ♗d7[71]	dc5 ♗c5	♕e2 ♕h5	♘bd2 ♗d6	♘c4 ♗c7	♖e1 0-0-0[72]	∓
16	. . . . . .	. . . . . .	♗e2 ♘f6	0—0 cd4	cd4 ♗e7	♘c3 ♕d6[73]	♘b5 ♕d8	♗f4[74] ♘d5	♗g3 0—0[75]	=
17	. . . . . .	. . . . . .	♘a3 ♕d8[76]	♗f4[77] ♘f6	dc5 ♘d5	♗d6 ♗d6	cd6 ♕d6	♗e2[78] 0—0	0—0 ♕e7	=

Alapin

2... **b6** 3. d4 ♗b7 4. ♗d3 e6 5. ♘f3 ♘e7 6. 0—0 ♘g6 7. ♗g5 ♗e7 8. ♗e7 ♕e7 9. ♖e1= Florian—Haag, Gyula 1965; 6. ♘bd2 ±; 4. d5±; **2... g6** 3. d4 [3. ♘f3 ♗g7 4. d4 — B 27] cd4 [3... ♗g7 4. dc5 ♘a6 5. ♗e3 ♕c7 6. ♗a6 ba6 7. ♗d4 ♘f6 8. f3 ♖b8 9. ♕d2 0—0 10. ♘e2 ♖d8 11. 0—0 e5 12. ♗e3 ♗f8∞ Štejn—Nej, SSSR 1960] 4. cd4 d5 5. e5 ♘c6 6. ♘c3 ♗g7 7. ♘f3 ♗g4= Bhend—Bilek, Kecskemet 1964; 7. ♗e2±; **2... ♘c6** 3. ♘f3 [3. d4 d5 4. ed5 ♕d5 — 2... d5] d5 [3... ♘f6 4. e5 ♘d5 — 2... ♘f6] 4. ed5 [4. ♕b3 de4 5. ♘g5 e6 6. ♘e4 ♗e7 7. ♗e2 ♘f6 8. d3 0—0 9. 0—0 b6= Ignatjev—Holmov, SSSR 1955] ♕d5 5. d4 — 2... d5; **2... d6** 3. d4 [3. ♘f3 — B 50] ♘f6 [3... ♘d7 4. f4 e6 5. ♘f3 ♕c7 6. ♗d3 g6 7. 0—0 ♗g7 8. ♘a3 a6 9. ♗e3 ♘e7 10. b4 0—0 11. bc5 dc5 12. ♘c4 b5 13. ♘ce5± Heidenfeld—van Scheltinga, Enschede 1963] 4. ♗d3 [4. dc5 ♘c6 5. ♗c4 ♘e5 6. ♗b5 ♗d7 7. ♗d7 ♕d7 8. ♘f3 ♘f3 9. ♕f3 dc5 10. 0—0 ♕c6= Marić—Udovčić, Jugoslavija (ch) 1953] g6 5. f4 ♗g7 6. ♘f3 — B 06; **2... e6** 3. d4 d5 4. ed5 [4. e5 — C 02] ed5 [4... ♕d5 — 2... d5] 5. ♘f3 ♘c6 [5... ♗d6 6. dc5 ♗c5 7. ♗e2 ♘c6 8. 0—0 ♘ge7 9. ♘bd2= Padevski—Karpov, Skopje (ol) 1972 — 14/324 — C 08] 6. ♗b5 [6. ♗e3 cd4 7. ♘d4 ♘f6 8. ♗e2 ♗d6± Minev—Talj, Sarajevo 1966 — 1/244] ♗d6 7. 0—0 [7. ♗e3 cd4 8. ♘d4 ♘e7=; 8. ♗d4 ♘f6 9. 0—0 0—0 10. ♗f6 ♕f6 11. ♕d5 (Svešnikov—Gufeljd, SSSR 1973 — 15/310) ♗f4!=∞] ♘e7 8. ♘bd2 0—0 9. dc5 ♗c5 10. ♘b3 ♗d6 11. ♘bd4 — C 09

3 **3. ♗d3** ♘c6 4. ♘f3 c4! 5. ♗c2 d5 6. e5 [6. ed5?! ♕d5∓↑⊞] ♘d7 7. ♕e2 e6∞; **3. d3**!?△ ♘d2

4 4. ♗c4 ♘b6 5. ♗b3 d5=

5 Heidenfeld; 5. d4 cd4 6. cd4 d6 — 4. d4

6 **5... e6** 6. g3 ♗e7 7. ♗g2 0—0 8. 0—0 b6 9. c4 ♘db4 10. d4 cd4 11. ♘d4 ♗b7= Wade—Pachman, Buenos Aires 1960; **5... d6** 6. ♗b5 [6. ♘c4?! ♗g4 7. ♗e2?! ♘f4∓ Süer—Hort, Athens 1969 — 8/297; 6. ed6 ♗g4 7. ♗b5 ♕d6 8. 0—0 e6 9. ♘c4 ♕c7 10. ♘ce5 ♗f3 11. ♘f3 ♗d6 12. d4 0—0 13. dc5 ♗c5 14. ♗d3 ♘e5 15. ♘e5 ♕e5= Heidenfeld—Penrose, Madrid 1960; 6... e5 7. ♗b5 ♗d6 8. 0—0 0—0= Heidenfeld—Darga, Enschede 1963] ♗d7 7. ed6 ed6 8. d4 cd4 9. ♘d4 ♗e7 10. 0—0 0—0 11. ♘f5 ♗f5 12. ♕d5 ♗e6 13. ♕f3 d5 14. ♘c2 ♕b6= Heidenfeld—Unzicker, München (ol) 1958

7 6... b6!? 7. ♗g2 ♗a6 8. c4 ♘db4 9. 0—0 ♗g7 10. ♘b5 ♖c8 11. d3 ♗b7 12. a3 ♘a6 13. ♗f4 0—0 14. ♕d2 ♘c7 15. ♘c7 ♖c7= Heidenfeld—Pomar Madrid 1960

8 7... d6 8. ed6 ♕d6 9. 0—0 0—0 10. d4 cd4 11. ♘b5 ♕c5 12. ♘bd4 ♖d8 13. ♘c6 bc6 14. ♕a4 ♖b8 16. ♘d4 ♗d7 17. ♘b3 ♕b6 18. ♕h4 ♗f5= Heidenfeld—Portisch, Madrid 1960

9 11. cd4 ♗g4 12. ♖d1 ♘e6∓↑ Bisguier—Fischer, Stockholm (izt) 1962

10 **4... ♘c6**?! 5. ♗c4 ♘b6 6. ♗f7! ♔f7 7. dc5 ♘c4 8. ♕d5 e6 9. ♕c4 ♘e5 10. ♕e2 ♕f6 11. ♘d2 b6 12. cb6 ♕f5 13. ♘gf3 ♘f3 14. ♘f3 ab6 15. 0—0± Vasjukov—Polugajevski, SSSR 1955; **4... d6**!? 5. ed6 ♕d6 6. ♘f3 ♘c6 7. c4 ♘b6 8. d5 ♘e5 9. ♗e2 g6 10. 0—0 ♗g7 11. ♘c3± Heidenfeld—O'Sullivan, Dublin 1956; **4... e6** 5. c4 ♘c7 6. d5±

11 5. ♘f3!?

12 5... ♘b6 6. ♗b3 d6 [6... d5 7. cd4 ♘c6 8. ♘e2 ♗g4 9. f3 ♗f5 10. ♘bc3 e6 11. 0—0 a6 12. ♘g3 ♗g6 13. f4 ♘e7 14. a4 h5 15. a5 h4 16. f5! ef5 17. ♘ge2 ♘c4 18. ♗a4 ♘c6 19. ♗c6 bc6 20. ♕a4 ♖c8 21. b3+— Rakić—O'Kelly, Bognor Regis 1957; 11... ♖c8 12. ♗e3 ♕d7 13. ♘g3 ♗g6 14. f4 ♘a5 15. f5 ♗f5 16. ♘f5 ef5 17. ♕f3 ♘b3 18. ab3± Matulović—Duraševič, Jugoslavija (ch) 1957; 6... e6 7. ♘f3 d6 8. ♗g5 ♗e7 9. ♗e7 ♕e7 10. cd4 0—0 11. ♘c3±↑⊞; 6... dc3 7. ♘c3 ♘c6 8. ♘f3 d6 9. ed6△ ♘g5±] 7. ed6 [7. cd4 — 5. cd4] ♕d6 8. cd4 ♘c6 [8... ♗f5 9. ♘f3 e6 10. ♘c3 ♗e7 11. 0—0 0—0 12. d5 ed5 13. ♗e3 ♘c6 14. ♗b6 ab6 15. ♘d5± Marić—Udovčić, Jugoslavija (ch) 1956] 9. ♘f3 ♗f5 10. ♘c3 e6 11. 0—0 ♗e7 12. ♗e3 0—0 14. a3 ♖fd8 15. ♕e2 a6 16. ♖fd1 ♘d5 17. ♘d5 ed5= Matulović—Udovčić, Jugoslavija (ch) 1957

13 **6. ♕b3**?! ♕e5 [6... e6?! 7. ♗d5 ♕e5 8. ♘e2 d3 9. ♗e3 ed5 10. ♘f4± Kozomara—Pirc, Jugoslavija (ch) 1957] 7. ♘e2 d3! 8. ♗d3 c6∓; **6. ♕d4**?! ♘b6△ ♘c6

14 7. ♗b3 d3! 8. ♕e4 ♕c6 [8... ♘a6 9. ♗e3 e6 10. ♘f3 d5 11. ed6 ♗d6 12. ♘bd2 ♘c5 13. ♗c5 ♗c5 14. 0—0 ♗e7= Matulović—Janošević, Jugoslavija (ch) 1957] 9. ♕f4 d5! 10. ♘f3 ♕g6 11. 0—0 ♘c6 12. ♘a3 ♗g4∓ Lukić—Rabar, Jugoslavija (ch) 1955

15 11. ♖e1 0—0 12. ♗g5 d5 13. ed6 ♕d6 14. ♖ad1 ♕b4 15. ♗e7 [15. ♕d2? ♖d8 16. ♕c1 ♗e6 17. ♗h6 ♗h8!∓ Miles—Sax, Bath 1973 — 16/277] ♘e7 16. ♕e7 ♗c3 17. bc3 ♕c3 18. ♗b5!=∞ Adorjan, Florian

16 5... ♘c7 6. ♘f3 ♘c6 7. ♕e4 g6 8. ♗c4 ♗g7 9. 0—0 b5 10. ♗b3 ♘a5 11. ♘bd2 ♗b7 12. ♕h4± Marić—Deže, Jugoslavija 1969 — 8/298

17 **7... f5** 8. ♕e2 ♕h4 9. ♘f3 ♕e4 10. ♗d5 ed 11. ♗e3 ♘e5 12. ♘bd2 ♘f3 13. ♘f3± Matulović—Bogdanović, Jugoslavija (ch) 1958; **7... ♘b6** 8. ♗b3 d6 9. ed6 ♗d6 10. ♘f3 ♘d7!? [10... 0—0? 11. ♘g5 g6 12. ♕h4 h5 13. g4±→] 11. 0—0! ♘c5 12. ♕g4! ♘b3 [12... 0—0 13. ♗c2 f5 14. ♕h5 ♕e8 15. ♕e8 ♖e8 16. ♖d1 ♗f8 17. b4!± Marić—Huguet, Monte Carlo II 1969 — 7/309] 13. ♕g7! ♘a1

14. ♕h8 ♔d7 15. ♕h7 ♕f6 16. ♖d1±→ Marić–Coulon, Strasbourg 1973 — 15/312

18 8. ed6 ♘f6 9. ♕e2 ♗d6 10. ♗g5 [10. ♘f3 0–0 11. ♗g5 ♗e7 12. 0–0 ♕c7= Cuartas–Kinnmark, Siegen (ol) 1970 — 10/390] a6 11. **a4** ♘e5 12. ♘d2 ♘c4 13. ♘c4 ♗e7 14. ♘f3 **b6** 15. 0–0 ♕c7 16. ♘fe5 ♗b7= Cortlever–Schmidt, Wijk aan Zee 1972 — 13/337

19 8... ♗e7 9. 0–0 [9. ed6 ♕d6 10. 0–0 0–0 11. ♗g5 ♗g5 12. ♘g5 ♘f6 13. ♕e3 ♕e5! 14. ♕e5 ♘e5 15. ♘d2 ♖d8 16. ♖fd1 ♗d7∓ Matulović–Geler, Beograd 1969] de5 10. ♘e5 ♘e5 11. ♕e5 0–0 12. ♗d5 ♗f6 13. ♕e2 ed5= Kozomara–Šamkovič, Sarajevo 1963

20 **9... ♗d6** 10. ♘c6 bc6 11. 0–0 0–0 12. ♘a3 f5 13. ♕d3∞ Leonidov–Mojsejev, SSSR 1967 — 3/358; **9... ♘f6** 10. ♘c6 ♘e4 11. ♘d8 ♔d8 12. 0–0 1/2 : 1/2 Kozomora–Rabar, Sarajevo 1958

21 Matulović–Polugajevski, Beograd 1969

22 7... f5!? 8. ef6 [8. ♕e2!? ♗e7 9. g3 0–0 10. ♗g2 ♕c7 11. 0–0∞ Vorotnikov–Tajmanov, SSSR 1973] ♘f6 9. ♕h4 ♕c7! [9... d5 10. ♗b5 ♗d6 11. ♗f4 0–0 12. ♗c6 bc6 13. 0–0 ♗f4 14. ♕f4 ♘e4∓ Matulović–Matanović, Jugoslavija (ch) 1958; 10. ♗d3 ♗d6 11. ♗g6! ♔d7 12. ♗c2 ♔c7 13. ♘d4±↑ Alburt–Šmit, SSSR 1970 — 10/389] 10. ♘bd2 [10. ♗d3? ♘b4∓] b6!? [10... ♗e7 11. ♗d3 ♘e5 12. ♘e5 ♕e5 13. ♘e4= Padevski–Tajmanov, Vrnjačka Banja 1974 — 17/345] 11. ♘e4 ♘e4 12. ♕e4 ♗b7 13. ♗f4 ♗d6 14. ♗d6 ♕d6= Padevski–Sax, Vrnjačka Banja 1974

23 **9... ♕c7** 10. ♘c6 bc6 11. ♘c4 g6 12. ♕e5! ♕e5 13. ♘e5 ♗g7 14. f4 g5 15. g3 gf4 16. gf4 ♗h6 17. ♗g2± Lejn–Balašov, SSSR 1969; **9... ♘f6** 10. ♕a4 [10. ♘c6? ♕d2!∓] ♕d5 11. ♘df3 ♗d6 12. ♗f4 ♕e4 13. ♕e4 ♘e4 14. ♗d3± Hort–Polugajevski, Beograd 1970 — 9/277; **9... ♗d6**!? 10. ♗b5 0–0! 11. ♘c6 bc6 12. ♗c6 ♖b8$\overline{\overline{\infty}}$ Schmidt–Kirov, Lublin 1971 — 12/326

24 14. ♕c7 ♘c7 15. c4 ♗c5 16. ♔e2 a5!? 17. ♗f4 ♘a6=⊥ Bronštejn–Hort, Monte Carlo 1969 — 7/308

25 5... e6 6. ♘f3 [6. a3△ ♗d3±] ♘c6 [6... ♗e7 7. ♘c3 ♘c3 8. bc3 d5 9. ed6 ♕d6 10. ♗e2 0–0 11. 0–0 ♘d7 12. a4 ♕c7 13. ♕b3 b6= Nimzowitsch–Vidmar, New York 1927; 9. ♗d3±↑ Aljehin] 7. ♗e2 d6 8. 0–0 ♗e7 9. ♘bd2±↑⊞

26 6... de5 7. de5 e6 8. ♘f3±

27 **7... ♘c6** 8. e6!? fe6 9. ♘f3 g6 10. ♘g5 ♗h6?! 11. ♘f7! [11. ♘e6? ♗e6 12. ♗e6 ♗c1 13. ♕c1 d5! 14. ♕c5! ♕d6 15. ♗h3 0–0 16. ♘c3 ♖f4∓ Marić–Matulović, Skopje–Ohrid 1968 — 6/419] ♔f7 12. ♗h6 ♖e8 13. h4±; 10... ♗g7!? Marić; **7... ♗f5** 8. ♘f3 e6 9. 0–0 d5 10. ♗g5 ♗e7 11. ♗e7 ♕e7 12. ♘c3 0–0= Marić–Rabar, Jugoslavija (ch) 1957

28 8. ♕f3!?

29 10. f4!?

30 10... ♕d3 11. ♘c3 ♘c4! [11... ♗b4!? 12. ♗d2 ♘c4 13. 0-0-0 ♘d2 14. ♖d2 ♕g6 15. ♕g6?! hg6∓ Mihaljčišin–Gufeljd, Debrecen 1969 — 8/299; 15. ♕h3 h5!∞] 12. ♕h4 [12. ♘e2 ♗b4 13. ♔f1 ♘4a5∓↑] ♘4e5 13. ♘e5 ♘e5 14. ♗e3! [14. ♗g5 ♗d7 15. ♖d1 ♕g6! 16. 0–0 ♗e7!∓ Marić–Honfi, Monte Carlo II 1968 — 5/343] ♗d7 15. ♕g3 ♕f5 16. 0-0-0! ♗c6 17. ♗c2 ♕h5 18. ♖he1$\overline{\overline{\infty}}$

31 14. ♖d1 ♗d7 15. ♗h6 ♗b2!∓ Liberzon–Polugajevski, SSSR (ch) 1968/69 — 7/307

32 Minev–Šajtar, Marianske Lazni 1954

33 6... de5 7. de5 ♗g4 8. ♕b3! ♗f3 9. ♕f3 ♘c6 10. ♗c4 e6 11. ♗d5 ed5 12. 0–0 ♗e7 13. ♖e1±↑⊞; 11... ♕d5!?

34 **7. ♗b5**?! ♕a5 8. ♘c3 ♘c3 9. ♗c6 bc6 10. bc3 ♗e6 11. ♗d2 ♕d5 12. ed6 ed6 13. ♕c2 ♗e7 14. ♗e3 0–0∓ Reid–O'Kelly, Dublin 1956; **7. ♕b3** e6 8. ♗b5 [8. ♘c3 ♘c3 9. bc3 de5 10. ♘e5 ♘e5 11. de5 ♗e7 12. ♗a3 0–0 13. ♖d1 ♕c7 14. ♗d6?! ♗d6 15. ed6 ♕c6 16. c4 ♖d8 17. ♕a3 e5∓ Padevski–Tajmanov, Moskva 1956] ♗d7 9. ♘c3 ♘c3 10. bc3 de5 11. ♗c6 ♗c6 12. ♘e5 ♕d5= Minev–Najdorf, Amsterdam (ol) 1954; **7. ed6** ♕d6 8. ♘c3 g6 [8... ♗g4 9. ♗e2 e6 10. 0–0 ♗e7 11. ♕b3 0–0 12. ♘d5 ed5= Unzicker–Geler, Göteborg (izt) 1955; 11. h3 ♗h5 12. ♕b3 0–0 13. ♘d5 ed5 14. ♗e3 f5 15. ♖ac1 f4∓ Teschner–Talj, Riga 1959; 12. ♘b5 ♕d8 13. ♘e5 ♗e2 14. ♕e2=] 9. ♗c4 ♘c3 10. bc3 ♗g7 11. 0–0 0–0= Harlamov–Furman, SSSR 1965

35 **7... ♘c7**?! 8. ed6 ed6 9. d5 ♘b8 10. ♕d4 ♘d7 11. ♗e2± Csom–Quinteros, Siegen (ol) 1970 — 10/388; 8... ♕d6!?; **7... e6** 8. ♘d5 [8. ♗c4!? ♘c3 9. bc3 de5 10. de5 ♕a5 11. 0–0 ♕c3 12. ♕e2 ♕a5 13. ♗f4 ♗e7 14. ♖fd1 0–0 15. h4 ♖d8 16. h5 ♗d7 17. ♖ab1$\overline{\overline{\infty}}$ Ribli–Šahović, Nederland 1972] ed5 9. ♗d3 [9. ♗e2 de5 10. de5 ♗e7 11. 0–0 0–0 12. ♗f4 ♗e6 13. ♘d4 ♕b6 14. ♘b3 ♖fd8= Solovjev–Grigorjan, SSSR 1964] ♗e7 10. h3 de5 11. de5 0–0 12. 0–0 ♗e6 13. ♗f4 ♖c8 14. ♖c1 ♕b6 15. ♕d2± Sanguinetti–Najdorf, Rio de Janeiro 1957; **7... ♘c3** 8. bc3 e6 [8... de5? 9. d5 e4 10. ♘g5!±; 8... ♕a5!?; 8... ♗g4!?] 9. ed6 ♗d6 10. ♗d3± Minev–Korčnoj, Oslo 1954; **7... ♗e6**!?

36 8. ♗b5!?

37 **8... ♘c3** 9. ♕d8 ♔d8 [9... ♘d8 10. bc3 ♗d7 (10... ♘c6 11. ♗b5 ♗d7 12. a4!± Csom–Hohler, Vrnjačka Banja 1972) 11. ♘d4 (11. ♗e3?! g6 12. h4 h6 13. ♗e2 ♗g7 14. 0–0 ♘c6∓ ×e5 Pomar–Polugajevski, Palma de Mallorca 1972) ♖c8 12. ♗e3!± Razuvajev–Šamkovič, SSSR 1967 — 4/386] 10. bc3 h6 [10... ♗g4 11. e6!±↑] 11. ♗b5 e6 12. ♗e3 ♗d7 13. a4 [13. 0–0!? ♔c7 14. **a4**!± Csom–Matulović, Athens 1969 — 8/300] ♔c7 [13...

b6? 14. a5! ba5 15. 0–0 ♔c7 16. ♖fd1± Csom–Hennings, Berlin 1968 — 6/422] 14. a5±; **8... ♗e6**!? 9. ♗d2 [9. ♘b5 ♕b6 10. ♘bd4 0-0-0 11. ♘c6 bc6 12. ♗d2 ♘b4∞ Csom–Rodriguez, Lugano (ol) 1966 — 6/421] ♘db4?! 10. ♘b5 ♗f5 11. ♗b4 ♘b4 12. ♘bd4 ♗d7 13. e6!± Redolfi–Saidy, Varna 1958; 9... ♘c3!?∞

38 9. a3 ♕d1 10. ♔d1 ♘a6∓ Menvielle–Gheorghiu, Las Palmas 1972

39 **7... ♗f5** 8. 0–0 e6 9. ♘c3 ♘c3 10. bc3 d5 11. ♘d2 h6 12. f4 ♗e7= Bogdanović–Janošević, Jugoslavija (ch) 1953; **7... de5** 8. ♘e5 e6 9. 0–0 ♗e7 10. ♘c6 bc6 11. ♘d2 0–0 12. ♘c4 ♗a6= Muhitdinov–Smislov, SSSR 1959

40 10... ♘e5 11. ♘e5 ♗e5 12. ♗b5 ♔f8 13. ♖e1±

41 14. ♖d5 ♘f3 15. ♗f3 ♕c7= Alburt–Sosonko, SSSR 1967 — 5/342

42 **7... e6** 8. 0–0 [8. ♕e2 de5 9. de5 ♗b4 10. ♗d2 ♗d2 11. ♘bd2 ♘a5 12. 0–0 ♘c4 13. ♘c4 0–0 14. ♘d6 ♕b6 15. ♖ad1 ♗d7 16. ♖d4 f5!= Enklaar–Najdorf, Wijk aan Zee 1973; 8. ♗b3 ♗e7 9. 0–0 0–0 10. ♕e2 ♘a5 11. ♗d5 ed5 12. ♘c3 ♗e6 13. ♗f4 ♘c6 14. ♖fd1± Marić–Cuderman, Jugoslavija (ch) 1957] ♗e7 9. ♕e2 [9. ♘bd2 de5 10. de5 ♘b6 11. ♗b3 ♘d4 12. ♘d4 ♕d4 13. ♕e2 ♗d7 14. ♖d1 ♗c6 15. ♘c4 ♕e4= Antošin–Averbah, SSSR (ch) 1956] 0–0 10. ♘c3 ♘c3 11. bc3 de5 12. de5 b6 13. ♕e4 ♗b7 14. ♗d3 g6 15. ♗h6 ♖e8 16. ♖ad1 ♕c7 17. ♕f4±↑» Gašanov–Privorotski, SSSR 1964; **7... de5** 8. ♘e5 [8. de5 ♘db4!] e6 9. 0–0 ♗e7 10. ♘c3 ♘c3 11. bc3 ♘e5 12. de5 0–0= Macijevski–Pytel, Polska 1973

43 8. ♗b3 de5 9. d5 ♘a5 [9... ♘b4?! 10. ♘c3 ♗g4 11. ♗a4± Ketola–Westman, Marianske Lazni 1962] 10. ♘c3 ♘b3 11. ♕b3 11. ♕b3 e6 12. 0–0 ed5 13. ♘e5 ♗e7 14. ♗e3 0–0 15. ♗b6 ab6∓ Moldavski–Gik, SSSR 1968 — 6/420

44 **8... ♗d7** 9. ♘c3 e6 10. 0–0 ♘b4?! 11. ♗g5 ♗e7 12. ♘e4! de5 13. ♘d6 ♔f8 14. ♘b7 ♕c7 15. ♗e7 ♔e7 16. ♕b3 ♘6d5 17. ♗d7± Svešnikov–Mišučkov, SSSR 1972; **8... de5** 9. ♘e5 [9. ♗c6 bc6 10. ♘e5 ♗e6! 11. 0–0 ♗d5= Margulis–Keclah, SSSR 1972] ♗d7 10. ♗c6! [10. ♘d7 ♕d7 11. ♘c3 e6 12. 0–0 a6 13. ♗c6 ♕c6= Žuravljev–Gutman, SSSR 1971] ♗c6 [10... bc6? 11. ♕f3] 11. ♘c6 bc6 12. 0–0!± Rozenberg; **8... e6**!? 9. 0–0 ♗e7 10. ed6 ♕d6 11. ♘c3 0–0 12. ♖e1 ♘d5 13. ♘e4 ♕c7 14. a3 ♗d7 15. ♗d3 ♖ac8 16. b4± Bernhardt–Spanjaard, Krefeld 1967 — 3/357

45 10... ♗h5 11. g4 ♗g6 12. e6! fe6 13. ♗f4±

46 12... ♖c8 13. ♕g4 a6= Levin–Saharov, SSSR 1960

47 14. ♘e2 ♖c8 15. ♗f4∞ Svešnikov–Palatnik, SSSR 1973 — 15/311

48 3... ♘f6?! 4. ♘f3 a6 5. c4 e6 6. de6 ♗e6 7. ♘c3 ♘c6 8. ♗e2 ♘d4 9. d3 ♘e2 10. ♕e2± Olafsson–Bijan, Mar del Plata 1960

49 **4... cd4** 5. cd4 e5 6. ♘f3 [6. ♘c3!? ♕d4 7. ♗e3 ♕d1 8. ♖d1 ♘f6=∞] ed4 7. ♕d4 ♕d4 8. ♘d4 a6 [8... ♘f6?! 9. ♗b5 ♗d7 10. 0–0 ♘c6 11. ♖e1 ♗e7 12. ♗c6 bc6 13. ♘c3 ♘d5 14. ♘d5 cd5 15. ♗f4±⊥ Sokolov–Četković, Jugoslavija 1954] 9. ♘c3 ♘f6 10. ♗e2 ♗c5! 11. ♘b3 ♗b4 12. ♗d2 0–0 13. 0–0 ♘c6 14. a3 ♗e6∞ Marić–Eliskases, Sarajevo 1958; 10. ♗g5!± Sokolov; **4... ♘f6**!?

50 **5. ♗e3**?! cd4 6. cd4 ♘c6! [6... ed4 7. ♘c3 ♕a5 8. ♗d4 ♘c6 9. ♗b5 ♗d7 10. ♕e2! ♘ge7 11. ♘f3 0-0-0 12. 0–0 ♘d4 13. ♘d4± Janošević–Primavera, San Benedetto 1955] 7. ♘c3 ♗b4 8. ♘f3 ♗g4 9. ♗e2 ed4 10. 0–0 ♗c3 11. bc3 d3∓ Livanov–Pivkin, SSSR 1960; **5. ♘f3**!? ed4 [5... e4 6. ♘e5 ♗e6 7. ♗c4 ♕d6 8. ♕b3 ♗c4 9. ♕c4 ♕c7 10. 0–0± Matanović–Udovčić, Jugoslavija (ch) 1953] 6. cd4 cd4 7. ♕d4 — 4... cd4

51 **8. ♗b5** ♗d7 9. ♕a4 ♗e7 10. 0–0 0–0 11. ♘a3 ♘d5 12. ♗d2 a6 13. ♗d7 ♘d7= Kuzmičev–Sokolov, SSSR 1967; **8. ♗e2** ♗d6?! 9. ♘a3± Baxter–Tsagan, Tel Aviv (ol) 1964; 8... ♗e7±

52 **5. ♘a3**?! cd4 6. ♗c4 ♕d6∓; **5. dc5** [Aljehin] ♕c5 [5... ♕d1!? 6. ♔d1 e6∞] 6. ♗e3 ♕a5 7. ♘a3 [7. b4 ♕c7 8. ♘a3 ♘f6 9. ♘b5 ♕b8 10. ♘f3 e5 11. ♗c4 ♗e7 12. ♕b3 0–0 13. ♘g5 ♘d8 14. ♖d1±↑ Canal–Euwe, Zürich 1954; 10... ♘g4△ g6= Euwe] ♘f6 [7... e5?! 8. ♘c4 ♕c7 9. ♕a4 ♗e6 10. ♘f3 f6 11. b4! ♖c8 12. b5 ♗c4 13. ♗c4 ♕a5 14. ♕b3! ♘d8 15. 0–0± Markus–Bebčuk, SSSR 1962] 8. ♘c4 ♕c7=

53 **5... ♘f6**!?; **5... e5**!?

54 5... ♘f6!?; 6... 0-0-0!?

55 7... ♖d8!? 8. ♘c3 ♕a5△ e5 Rozenberg

56 **8... ♗b4** 9. 0–0 ♕a5 10. a3! [10. ♘e4 ♘f6 11. ♘f6 gf6 12. ♗f4 0–0 13. a3 ♗e7 14. ♕b3 ♕b6= Juhtman–Aronson, SSSR 1957] ♘f6? 11. d5! ed5 12. ab4! ♕a1 13. ♘d2! +– Aljehin–Podgorny, Praha 1942; **8... ♕d7** 9. 0–0 ♘f6 10. ♗g5! [10. ♗e3 ♗d6 11. ♕d2 0–0= Perlis–Rubinstein, Wien 1908; 10. ♘e5 ♗e2 11. ♘d7 ♗d1 12. ♘f6 gf6 13. ♖d1 0-0-0 14. ♗e3 ♗b4 15. ♖ac1 ♗c3 16. bc3 ♖d7 17. ♗h6 f5= Matulović–Trifunović, Jugoslavija (ch) 1958; 15. d5!±⊥ Sokolov; 10. h3 ♗f3 11. ♗f3 ♘d4 12. ♗b7! ♖d8 13. ♗e3± Cibulka–Maršalek, ČSSR 1966 — 1/238] ♘d5 [10... ♗e7 11. h3! ♗f3 12. ♗f3 ♘d4 13. ♗b7 ♕b7 14. ♕d4±] 11. h3 ♗h5 12. ♕d2± Marić–Jean, Monte Carlo II 1967 — 3/356

57 10. ♘e5? ♗e2 11. ♘c6 ♕c3! 0 : 1 Perlis–Tartakower, Ostende 1907

58 11... ♖d8 12. g4 ♗g6 13. b4! ♗b4 14. ab4 ♕a1 15. ♕b3 ♖d4 16. ♗a3 ♗c2 17. ♕c2 ♕a3 18. ♘b5+− Capablanca−Czerniak, Buenos Aires (ol) 1939

59 13. b4 ♕d8 14. b5 ♘a5 15. ♕a4 b6 16. ♖fc1± Vasjukov−Toprover, SSSR 1954

60 Aljehin; **7. 0—0** ♘f6 8. ♗e3 cd4 9. ♘d4 ♗e2 10. ♕e2 ♘d4 11. ♗d4 ♗e7 12. ♖d1 [12. ♘d2 0−0 13. ♖fd1 ♖fd8 14. ♗e5 ♕c6 15. ♘b3 ♖d1 16. ♖d1 ♕a4= Thorvaldsson−Canal, Tel Aviv (ol) 1964] ♕c6 13. c4 0−0 14. ♘c3 ♖fd8 15. b3 ♖d7 16. ♖d3 ♖ad8 17. ♖ad1 b6= S. Nikolić−Puc, Jugoslavija (ch) 1965; 8. ♘a3± Sokolov; **7. c4** ♕d7 8. d5 ed5 9. cd5 ♗f3 10. ♗f3 ♘d4 11. 0−0 ♘f6 12. ♘c3 ♗e7 13. ♗e3± Angelov−Hristov, corr. 1961

61 13. ♗e3±

62 6... e6!?

63 **7... ♕a5** 8. d5 ♘e5 [8... 0-0-0 9. ♗d2 ♘e5 10. ♕c1 ♕c7 11. ♘b5+−] 9. ♘e5! ♗d1 10. ♗b5 ♔d8 11. ♘f7 ♔c8 12. ♔d1+− Kirilov−Skuja, SSSR 1965; **7... ♕d6** 8. d5 ♘e5 9. ♗b5 ♗d7 10. ♗f4! ♗b5 11. ♗e5 ♕a6 12. ♘d4± I. Zajcev−Kaufman, SSSR 1968

64 8. ♘d5? ♗d1 9. ♘c7 ♔d7 10. ♘a8 ♗h5∓

65 **10... ♘e6** 11. f4! a6 12. f5 ab5 13. ♗b5 ♔d8 14. fe6 fe6 15. ♗e3+− Kirilov−Salata, SSSR 1964; **10... ♘c2** 11. ♔d1 ♖c8 [11... ♘a1 12. ♘c7 ♔d7 13. ♘a8 e5 14. ♗e3 b6 15. ♗a6+−] 12. ♘a7 ♖c5 13. b4 ♘b4 14. ♗b5 ♘c6 15. ♗e3 ♖d5 16. ♔e2+− Smart−Nordstrom, Budva 1963; **10... 0-0-0** 11. ♘d4 ♖d4 12. ♗e3 ♖d7 [12... ♖b4!? Marić] 13. ♗b5 ♖c7 14. ♗a7 e6 15. ♗b6+− Hennings−Bindrich, DDR 1969 — 7/306

66 **13. ♗d2**?! ♗d2 [13... ♘f3!? Kapengut] 14. ♔d2 ♘e7 15. ♗c4 ♖a8 16. ♗f7 ♖f8 17. ♗h5∞ Šmatkov−Kuncevič, SSSR 1973; **13. ♔d1**!± Rozenberg

67 **9... ♕e4** 10. ♕e2! ♕e2 11. ♗e2 e4 12. d5 ef3 13. ♗f3 ♘ce7 14. ♗g7 ♘g6 15. d6 h6 16. ♗h8 ♘h8 17. 0−0 ♘f6 18. ♖ac1 ♔d8 19. ♖fe1 ♘e8 20. ♖c8! 1 : 0 Kićović−Forintos, Bognor Regis 1956; **9... ed4** 10. ♘d4 ♘ge7!? [10... ♘d4 11. ♕d4 ♕d4 12. ♗d4 ♘f6±⊥⊡] 11. ♘c6 ♕c6 12. ♗g7 ♖g8 13. ♗d4 ♗h3 14. ♖c1 ♕e4 15. ♗e3 ♗g2 16. ♖g1 ♗f1 17. ♖g8 ♘g8 18. ♔f1± Matulović−Ćirić, Jugoslavija (ch) 1956

68 12. e6!?

69 13. ♕a3 ♕e6! [Schlechter; 13... e3?! 14. f3 ♕e6 15. ♖d1± Nimzowitsch−Chajes, Karlovy Vary 1911; 13... ♗b5!? 14. ♖d1 ♗d3 15. ♗d3 ed3 16. 0−0 ♘c6 17. ♕d6?! ♖d8 18. ♕a3 h5!∞ Martz−Kapengut, Ybbs 1968 — 6/418; 17. ♖fe1 0-0-0 18. ♖e3± Boleslavski] 14. ♖d1 [14. ♕b4 ♗c6 15. ♗b5 ♗b5 16. ♕b5 ♕c6 17. ♕e2= Sokolov] 0−0 15. **♖d6**?! **♕f5 16. ♗e2 [16. ♗c4** ♘g6 17. 0−0 ♘h4!∓ Luer−Thorsteinsson, Tel Aviv (ol) 1964] ♗e6! 17. 0−0 ♘g6∓ Marić−Rossolimo, Novi Sad 1972 — 14/317; 15. ♖d2!?= Rossolimo

70 **5... a6** 6. ♗e3 ♘d7 7. c4 ♕c6 8. ♘bd2 ♘gf6 9. ♕c2 ♗e7 10. h3 0−0 11. ♗d3 b6 12. 0-0-0±; **5... ♘f6** 6. ♘a3 [6. ♗e3 ♘c6 7. ♘a3 cd4 8. ♘b5 ♕d7 9. ♘bd4 ♘d5 10. ♗b5 ♘e3 11. fe3 ♕c7= Makaričev−Džindžihašvili, Tbilisi 1973] ♕d8 [6... cd4 7. ♘b5 ♘a6 8. ♕d4 ♗c5 9. ♕d5 ♘d5 10. b4 ♗e7 11. a3 0−0 12. c4 ♘dc7 13. ♘c3 ♗f6 14. ♗b2 ±⊥ Glatman−Bobolovič, SSSR 1964] 7. ♗e2 ♘c6 8. 0−0 cd4 9. ♘b5 ♗e7 10. ♘bd4 ♘d4 11. ♕d4 0−0 12. ♗g5 h6 13. ♗h4 ♕d4 14. ♘d4 g5 15. ♗g3 ♘d5 16. ♗f3 ♘f4= Trifunović−Gligorić, Jugoslavija (ch) 1951

71 7... ♗e7 8. ♗e3 [8. ♗g5? cd4! 9. ♕e2 h6 10. ♗h4 0−0 11. ♖d1 e5∓ Svešnikov−Štejn, SSSR 1973 — 15/309; 8. dc5 ♕c5 9. ♗e3 ♕a5 10. ♘bd2 0−0 11. ♗f4 b6 12. ♘c4 ♕d5 13. ♕e2 ♗a6 14. ♖ad1 ♕h5 15. ♘ce5 ♘e5 16. ♗e5 ♗b7= Banik−Rojzman, SSSR 1963; 8. c4 ♕d8 9. dc5 ♘d7 10. a3 ♘c5 11. ♗c2 ♕d1 12. ♖d1±⊥ Svešnikov−Averkin, SSSR (ch) 1973] cd4 [8... 0−0? 9. dc5 ♗c5 10. ♗h7△ ♕d5, ♗c5±] 9. cd4 ♘b4 [9... 0−0 10. ♘c3 ♕d8 11. ♖c1 ♘b4 12. ♗b1 b6 13. ♘e5 ♗b7 14. ♗g5 ♖c8 15. ♖e1 ♘bd5 16. ♕d3±→» Matohin−Dubinin, SSSR 1963] 10. ♘c3 ♕d8 11. ♗b1 0−0 12. ♘e5 ♗d7 13. ♕f3 ♗c6 14. ♕h3 ♖c8 15. ♖e1 ♖e8 16. ♗g5 g6 17. a3 ♘bd5 18. ♗a2± Gipslis−Baumbach, Bad Liebenstein 1963

72 13. h3 h6 14. a4 g5∓↑» Banik−Suetin, SSSR (ch) 1965

73 **9... ♕a5** 10. ♗b5! [10. ♘e5!? 0−0 11. ♘c6 bc6 12. ♗f3 ♗a6 13. ♖e1 ♖ac8∞ Saharov−Bagirov, SSSR 1964] 0−0 11. ♘e5 ♘b4 12. ♕e2 a6 13. ♗c4 ♕d8 14. a3 ♘bd5 15. ♖d1 ♗d7 16. ♗g5 ♖c8 17. ♗d5± Tartakower−Gligorić, Amsterdam 1950; 17. ♖d3!±→»; **9... ♕d8** 10. ♗g5 0−0 11. ♖c1 b6 12. ♕a4 ♗b7= Marić−S. Vuković, Jugoslavija 1959

74 11. ♘e5 0−0 12. ♘c6 bc6 13. ♘c3 ♖b8 14. ♘a4 ♘d5 15. ♕c2 ♖b4∓↑ Banik−Korčnoj, SSSR (ch) 1960

75 13. ♘c3 b6 14. ♖c1 ♗b7 15. ♗d3 ♖c8= Halilbejli−Tajmanov, SSSR 1963

76 **6... a6** 7. ♘c4 ♕d8 8. ♗e3 b5 9. ♘ce5 ♘e5 10. ♘e5 ♕c7 11. a4 ♖b8 12. ab5 ab5 13. ♕f3 c4 14. ♕c6 ♕c6 15. ♘c6 ♖b7 16. ♖a8+− Stoltz−S. Nedeljković, Beograd 1952; **6... cd4** 7. ♘b5 ♕d8 8. ♗f4! [8. ♘bd4±] g5 9. ♘c7 ♔e7 10. ♗g3! ♖b8 11. ♘d4+− Makarov−Andrejev, Bulgaria (ch) 1951

77 7. ♘c2=

78 **11. ♘b5** ♕e7 12. c4 a6 13. cd5 ed5 14. ♕e2 ab5 15. ♕e7 ♔e7 16. ♗b5 ♔d6∓; **11. ♗c4** ♕e7!∓ Hennings−Korčnoj, Siegen (ol) 1970 — 10/387

B 23 — 1. e4 c5 2. ♘c3

	2	3	4	5	6	7	8	9	10	
1	. . .	d4	♕d4	♗b5![2]	♗c6	♕d8	♗f4	0-0-0	♗e5	±
	g6[1]	cd4	♘f6	♘c6[3]	dc6[4]	♔d8	♗g7	♔e8		
2	. . .	♘f3[5]	♗c4	d3	0–0	a4	h3	♗e3	♘d2	=
	d6	e5[6]	♗e7	♘f6	♘c6	0–0	h6	♗e6	d5[7]	
3	. . .	g3[8]	ed5[10]	♗g2[11]	♘ge2[12]	♘e4	♗e4	d3	♗g2	=
	e6	d5[9]	ed5	♘f6	d4[13]	♘e4	♘d7!	♘f6	♗d6[14]	
4	. . .	♘ge2[15]	g3	ed5	♘d4[18]	♘b5	♘d4	♘b3	f3	=∞
	♘c6	♘f6[16]	d5	♘d4[17]	cd4	a6[19]	e5!	♕d5	h5[20]	
5	. . .	f4	♘f3[22]	♗b5	♘d4[24]	♘e2	♗d3[27]	0–0	e5	∓
	. . .	g6[21]	♗g7	♘d4[23]	cd4[25]	♕b6[26]	♘f6[28]	d5	♘e4!	
6	. . .	. . .	. . .	♗c4	f5	fe6	d3	♗g5	♗h4	∓
	. . .	. . .	. . .	e6[29]	♘ge7[30]	fe6[31]	0–0[32]	h6	g5[33]	
7	. . .	. . .	♘f3	♗b5[35]	♕e2[37]	♘e4	♗c6	b3	♗b2	±
	. . .	e6	d5[34]	♘e7[36]	de4	a6	♘c6	♗e7	0–0[38]	
8	. . .	. . .	. . .	. . .	d3[39]	0–0	♗c6	b3[40]		=
	. . .	. . .	. . .	♘f6	♗e7	0–0	bc6			
9	. . .	. . .	. . .	♗b5[41]	♘d4	♘e2	♗d3	0–0	a3	∓
	. . .	. . .	♘ge7	♘d4[42]	cd4	a6	♘c6[43]	♗c5[44]	0–0[45]	

1 **2... e5**?! 3. ♗c4!△ d3, f4, ♘f3±; **2... a6**!? O'Kelly

2 **5. e5** ♘c6 6. ♕f4 ♘h5 7. ♕e4 d6 8. ed6 ♕d6 9. ♗e3 ♗g7 10. ♘b5 ♕b8 11. c3 0–0 12. ♗e2 a6 13. ♘d4 ♘d4 14. ♗d4 ♗f5 15. ♕e3 ♘f4∓→ Grob–Bronštejn, Helsinki (ol) 1952; **5. ♘d5** ♗g7 6. ♗g5 ♘c6 7. ♕c3 0–0 8. ♗f6 ef6 9. 0-0-0 f5 10. ♕c4 fe4 11. ♕e4 d6∓ Kasparjan–Keres, SSSR (ch) 1947; **5. ♘f3** ♘c6 6. ♕a4 d6 7. e5 ♘g4 8. ♗b5 ♗g7 9. ed6! [9. ♘d4 ♘e5 10. f4 ♘d7 11. ♘c6 bc6 12. ♗c6 ♗c3 13. bc3 ♕c7∓; 11. ♗c6 bc6 12. ♘c6 ♗c3∓] ♕d6 10. ♗f4 ♕c5 11. ♘e4 ♕b6=

3 5... a6 6. e5!?±

4 6... bc6 7. e5 ♘g8 8. ♘f3±

5 **3. ♘ge2** e5?! 4. ♘d5 ♘c6 5. ♘ec3! a6 6. a4 g6 7. ♗c4 ♗g7 8. d3 ♗e6 9. 0–0 ♖b8 10. f4±↑ Schöneberg–Minić, Berlin 1968 — 6/401; 3... g6; 3... ♘c6; **3. f4** g6 [3... ♘c6 — 2... ♘c6] 4. ♘f3 ♗g7 5. ♗b5 ♗d7 6. ♗d7 ♕d7 7. 0–0 ♘c6 8. d3 e6! [8... ♘f6 9. h3 0–0 10. ♗e3 b5 11. ♕d2 b4 12. ♘e2± Padevski–Browne, Amsterdam 1972] 9. ♗e3 [9. f5?! ef5 10. ef5 ♘ge7∓] ♘f6 10. h3 0–0 11. d4 cd4 12. ♘d4 ♘d4 13. ♗d4 ♕c6= Lukin–Gutman, SSSR 1974 — 18/326

6 Nimzowitsch; **3... ♗g4**?! 4. h3 ♗f3 5. ♕f3 ♘c6 5. ♗b5!?±; **3... a6** 4. g3 [4. d3 b5 5. g3 ♗b7 6. ♗g2 e6 7. 0–0 ♗e7 8. b3 ♘c6 9. ♗b2 ♗f6= Medina–Portisch, Palma de Mallorca 1972] ♘c6 5. ♗g2 ♗g4!? 6. h3 ♗f3 7. ♗f3 g6 8. d3 ♗g7= Hort–Fischer, Palma de Mallorca (izt) 1970 — 10/379; **3... ♘f6** 4. e5 — B 50

7 Hort–Portisch, San Antonio 1972

8 **3. ♕e2**?! ♘c6 4. ♘f3 ♘ge7 5. g3 d5 6. ♗g2 d4 7. ♘d1 e5 8. 0–0 f6 9. b3 ♗g4∓ Smislov–Larsen, Hastings 1972/73 — 15/306; **3. f4** d5 4. ♘f3 de4 [4... ♘f6!? Keres] 5. ♘e4 ♘c6 6. ♗b5 ♗d7 7. 0–0 [7. ♕e2 a6 8. ♗c6 ♗c6 9. d3 ♘f6 10. 0–0 ♗e7 11. ♘f6 ♗f6 12. ♗e3 ♕d5∓ Čistjakov–Hasin, SSSR 1957] ♘h6 [7... a6!? Keres] 8. b3 ♘f5 9. ♗b2 ♗e7 10. g4!? ♘fd4 11. ♘d4 ♘d4∓ Přibyl–Nej, Tallinn 1973 — 15/307; **3. ♘ge2** d6 [3... d5; 3... ♘c6] 4. g3 ♘f6 5. ♗g2 ♗e7 6. 0–0 0–0 7. f4 ♘c6 8. d3 ♘d4?! 9. ♘d4 cd4 10. ♘e2± Šamkovič–Tukmakov, SSSR 1970 — 10/380; 8... ♖b8= Šamkovič

9 3... b6?! 4. ♗g2 ♗b7 5. ♘ge2 d6 [5... h5 6. h4 f5? 7. ♘f4 ♘f6 8. d3 fe4 9. de4 ♘c6 10. e5!±→ Rosenthal–Anderssen, Wien 1873] 6. 0–0 ♘d7 7. d4 cd4 8. ♘d4±

10 **4. d3** ♘f6 5. ♗g2 ♗e7 6. ♘ge2 d4 7. ♘b1 ♘c6 8. 0–0 0–0 9. f4 b6 10. ♘d2 ♗b7 11. h3 ♖c8 12. g4± Nowak–Vasjukov, Hungary 1970 — 9/270; 6... de4= Gufeljd; **4. ♗g2** d4?! 5. ♘ce2 ♘c6 6. d3 e5 7. f4 ♗d6 8. ♘f3 ♗g4 9. 0–0 ♘ge7 10. c4 ef4 11. gf4±

Ozsvath–Barczay, Lublin 1969 — 8/288; 4... ♘f6!=

11 5. d4 cd4 6. ♕d4 ♘f6 7. ♗g5 ♗e7 8. ♗g2 ♘c6 9. ♕a4 0–0= Spielmann–Mieses (m) 1910

12 **6. d4**?! cd4 7. ♕d4 ♘c6 8. ♕d1 d4 9. ♘ce2 ♗c5 10. ♘f3 ♗f5 11. 0–0 0–0∓ Suttles–Talj, Hastings 1973/74 — 17/340; **6. d3**!? d4 [6... ♗e7 7. ♘ge2 d4 8. ♘e4 0–0 9. 0–0 ♘c6 10. ♘f4 ♘e5 11. ♘f6 ♗f6 12. ♘d5 ♗g4 13. f3 ♗e6 14. ♘f6 ♕f6 15. f4 ♘c6 16. ♕h5 ♗f5 17. g4 g6 18. ♕h3 ♗d7 19. f5±→ Čigorin–Tarrasch, Ostende 1907] 7. ♘e4 ♘e4 [7... ♗e7 8. ♘f6 ♗f6 9. ♕e2 ♗e7 10. ♘h3 ♘d7 11. 0–0 0–0 12. ♖e1 ♗d6 13. ♗f4 ♘f6 14. ♗d6 ♕d6 15. ♕e7±↑ Guljko–Vladimirov, SSSR 1968 — 6/396] 8. ♗e4 ♗d6 9. ♕h5 ♘d7 10. ♗g5 ♗e7 11. ♘f3 h6 12. h4 ♖g8! 13. ♗f4 ♘f6 14. ♕e5= Smislov–Trifunović, Moskva 1947

13 6... ♘c6 7. 0–0! [7. d4 cd4 8. ♘d4 ♗b4 9. 0–0 0–0 10. ♗g5± Csom–Malich, Berlin 1968 — 7/300; 8... ♗g4 9. ♘c6 bc6 10. ♕d3 ♗e7 11. 0–0 0–0 12. ♗e3 ♖e8 13. ♘a4 ♕a5 14. b3 ♘e4∓ Espig–Vasjukov, Berlin 1968 — 6/400; 9. ♕d3 ♗e7 10. h3 ♗e6 11. ♘e6 fe6 12. 0–0 0–0= Fischer–Bertok, Rovinj-Zagreb 1970 — 9/271] ♗e7 8. d3 0–0 9. ♗g5!± Larsen–Suetin, Copenhagen 1965

14 11. 0–0 0–0 12. ♗f4 ♗g4 13. ♗d6 ♕d6 14. h3 ♗d7 15. ♘f4 ♖fe8 16. ♕d2 ♗c6 17. ♖ae1 ♘d7= Spaski–Korčnoj (m) 1968 — 6/397

15 **3. ♗c4** ♘f6 4. d3 d6 5. ♘ge2 e6 6. ♗g5 ♗e7 7. ♕c1 0–0 8. 0–0 a6= Rossolimo–Talj, Wijk aan Zee 1968 — 5/328; 4... e6!?; **3. ♘f3** e6 [3... e5 4. ♗c4 g6 5. d3 h6 6. 0–0 ♗g7 7. ♘e1! d6 8. f4 ♘f6 9. ♘d5 ♘d5 10. ♗d5 ef4 11. ♗f4±↑ Matulović–Evans, Siegen (ol) 1970 — 10/378] 4. g3 [4. ♗b5 — B 30] d5 5. ♗g2 [5. ed5 ed5 6. ♗g2 d4 7. ♘e2 g6 8. 0–0 ♗g7 9. c4 ♘f6 10. d3 h6= Hug–Polugajevski, Petropolis (izt) 1973 — 16/282; 7... ♘f6 8. d3 ♗d6 9. 0–0 0–0 10. ♘d2 ♗g4 11. h3 ♗d7 12. ♘c4 ♗c7 13. ♗f4 ♖e8 14. ♖e1 ♘h5 15. ♗c7 ♕c7 16. c3!± Hecht–Talj, Skopje (ol) 1972 — 14/310; 8... ♗e7= Talj] d4 6. ♘e2 g6 7. d3 ♗g7 8. 0–0 ♘ge7 9. ♘h4 e5= Spaski–Korčnoj (m) 1968 — 6/398

16 **3... e5**? 4. ♘g3 [4. ♘d5△ ♘ec3, ♗c4, d3, 0–0, f4±↑] g6 5. ♗c4 ♗g7 6. d3 ♘ge7 7. h4 ♘d4 8. ♘d5 b5? 9. ♗g5!± Jurkov–Salov, SSSR 1959; 8... h6!?; **3... e6** 4. g3 ♘ge7 [4... d5 5. ed5 ed5 6. ♗g2 d4 7. ♘d5 ♘f6 8. ♘ef4 ♘d5 9. ♘d5 ♗d6 10. 0–0 0–0 11. d3 ♗e6 12. ♕h5 ♘e5! 13. h3 ♘g6 14. f4! f5 15. c4± Möhring–Antošin, Zinnowitz 1966 — 2/316; 6... ♘f6 7. d4 — 2... e6] 5. ♗g2 ♘d4 6. ♘d4 [6. 0–0 g6?! 7. b4 ♘e2 8. ♘e2 ♗g7 9. ♖b1± Hort–Kuijpers, Halle 1967; 6... ♘ec6=] cd4 7. ♘e2 ♘c6 8. 0–0 ♗e7 9. d3 d6 10. c3= Larsen–Hübner, Palma de Mallorca (izt) 1970 — 10/382

17 5... ♘d5 6. ♗g2 ♘c7 7. 0–0 e5 8. d3 ♗e7 9. f4!? ef4 10. ♗f4 ♗g4? 11. h3 ♗e2 12. ♕e2 0–0 13. ♖ae1 ♗d6 14. ♕h5!± Hort–Kinnmark, Halle 1967 — 3/352; 10... 0–0!?

18 6. ♗g2 ♗g4 7. 0–0 [7. d3? ♘d5 8. ♗d5 ♕d5!–+ Gurgenidze–Kotov, SSSR 1954] ♘f3 8. ♗f3 ♗f3 9. d4 c4 10. ♕d2 ♘d5 11. ♘f4 [Hort–Osnos, Leningrad 1967 — 3/351] e6=

19 7... ♕b6?! 8. c3!±

20 11. c4 ♕c6 12. ♕e2 ♗e6 13. d4 e4∞ Rakić–Nemet, Beograd 1966 — 2/318

21 3... d6 4. ♘f3 ♘f6 5. g3 e6 6. ♗g2 ♗e7 7. 0–0 0–0 8. ♔h1 ♗d7= Aronin–Vajsman, SSSR 1964; 4. ♗b5! ♗d7 5. ♗c6 ♗c6 6. ♘f3 g6 7. d3 ♗g7 8. d3 — 3... g6

22 4. b3 ♗g7 5. ♗b2 d6 6. ♗b5 ♗d7 7. ♘f3 [7. ♘ge2!?=] a6 [7... ♘d4 8. ♗d7 ♕d7 9. 0–0=] 8. ♗c6 ♗c6 9. d3 e6 10. 0–0 ♘e7 11. ♕e1 0–0 12. ♕h4 ♗d7 13. ♘d1 ♘c6 [Nun–Mojsejev, corr. 1971 — 12/320] 14. ♕f2=

23 5... d6 6. 0–0 [6. ♗c6!?] ♗d7 7. ♗c6 [7. d3 ♘d4 8. ♗d7 ♕d7 9. ♘d4 ♗d4?! 10. ♔h1 0-0-0 11. ♕e1 ♗g7 12. ♖b1 ♔b8 13. b4± Bronštejn–Furman, Moskva 1953; 9... cd4 10. ♘e2 f5 11. ef5 gf5 12. ♘g3 ♘f6 13. ♘h5 ♘h5 14. ♕h5 ♔f8=] ♗c6 8. d3 ♘f6 9. ♕e1 b6 [9... 0–0 10. ♗d2 e6 11. ♕h4?! ♘h5!∓ Heidenfeld–Najdorf, La Habana (ol) 1966 — 2/317; 11. e5!?; 10. f5 ♘d7 11. ♕h4±↑ Zinn–Padevski, DDR–Bulgaria 1959] 10. ♔h1 ♕c7 11. ♗d2 e6 12. ♕h4±↑ Pietzsch–O'Kelly, Madrid 1960

24 6. ♗c4 e6 7. e5 [7. ♘d4?! cd4 8. ♘e2 ♘e7 9. d3 0–0 10. ♗b3 d5∓↑ Gurgenidze–Saharov, SSSR 1966] d5 [7... d6!?] 8. ♘d4 cd4 9. ♗b5 ♗d7 10. ♗d7 ♕d7 11. ♘e2 f6 12. ♘d4 fe5 13. fe5 ♗e5 14. ♘f3 ♗g7 15. 0–0 ♘f6 16. ♕e2 0–0 17. d3 ♕d6 18. c3 ♖ae8∓↑ Tarasov–Ilivicki, SSSR 1966

25 6... ♗d4?! 7. ♘e2 ♗g7 8. c3±↑⊞

26 **7... ♘f6** 8. e5 ♘d5 9. c3 0–0 10. ♕b3 ♘c7 11. ♘d4 d6 12. ♘f3 ♘b5 13. ♕b5 de5 14. fe5 f6∞; **7... e6** 8. c3 [8. 0–0 ♘e7 9. d3 0–0 10. ♗a4 d5 11. e5 b5! 12. ♗b5 ♕a5 13. c4 dc3 14. ♘c3 ♖b8 15. ♗a4 ♗a6 16. ♖f2 f6!∓↑ Pietzsch–Udovčić, Dortmund 1961] dc3 [8... ♕b6!? Hort] 9. dc3 a6 10. ♗d3 d5 11. ♗e3 ♘e7 12. ♕b3 0–0 13. 0–0 ♗d7 14. ♗d4 ♕c7 15. ♗g7 ♔g7 16. ♘d4 de4 17. ♗e4 ♘c6= Rossolimo–Hort, Wijk aan Zee 1968 — 5/327

27 8. ♗c4 e6 9. d3 [9. c3 ♘e7 10. ♘d4 ♗d4 11. cd4 ♕d4 12. d3 d5∓↑⊞] d5 10. ed5 ed5 11. ♗b3 ♘e7∓; 8... ♘f6! 9. e5 ♘e4∓; 9. d3 d5∓ Pachman

28 8... d6 9. c3 dc3 10. dc3 ♘f6 11. ♕b3 ♕c5 12. ♕b5 ♕b5 13. ♗b5 ♗d7 14. ♗d7 ♔d7!∓ Bohosjan–Suetin, Albena 1970 — 10/376; 10. bc3!= Suetin

29 5... d6 6. d3! [6. 0–0 e6 7. f5 ef5 8. d3 ♘ge7 9. ♕e1 ♘e5 10. ♘e5 de5 11. ♕f2 0–0 12. ♕c5 f4!∓ Estrin] ♘f6 7. 0–0 0–0 8. f5!? [8. ♕e1 ♘d4 9. ♗b3 ♘b3 10. ab3 ♗d7 11. f5! gf5 12. ♕h4 ♘e8 13. ♘g5±→ Balašov–Cejtlin, SSSR 1969 — 7/299; 12... fe4 13. ♘g5 h6 14. ♘ge4±→ Vorotnikov–Šašin, SSSR 1972 — 13/333] gf5 9. ♕e1 ♘a5 10. ♗d5 fe4 11. ♘g5! e6 12. ♖f6!±→ Bellon–Merino, Orense 1974 — 17/341

30 **6... gf5** 7. d3 ♘ge7 8. 0–0 d5 9. ed5 ed5 10. ♗b3 ♗e6 11. ♘e2 ♕d7 12. c3 0-0-0 13. d4 c4 14. ♗c2±; **6... ef5** 7. d3 ♘ge7 8. 0–0 0–0 9. a3∞; **6... d5**!? 7. ed5 ed5 8. ♘d5 ♗f5 9. d3 ♘ge7 10. ♗g5 0–0 11. 0–0 ♕d6=

31 7... de6 8. d3 ♘a5 [8... h6!?△ g5] 9. 0–0 [9. ♗b5 ♗d7= Boleslavski] 0–0 10. ♕e1 ♘ec6 11. ♗g5 f6 12. ♗e3 ♘c4!? [12... ♘d4 13. ♕f2 ♘c4 14. dc4 ♘f3 15. ♕f3 ♕e7 16. ♖ad1 b6 17. ♗f4! e5 18. ♘d5± Klovski–Korelov, SSSR 1965] 13. dc4 ♕e7 14. ♖d1 b6 15. ♗f4±

32 8... d5 9. ♗b3 0–0 10. 0–0 ♕d6 11. ed5 ed5 12. ♘e4!±

33 11. ♗f2 d5 12. ♗b3 ♘d4 13. ♗d4 cd4 14. ♘e2 ♕b6 15. 0–0? de4 16. ♘d2 ♖f1 17. ♕f1 e3 18. ♘e4 ♘d5 19. h4 gh4∓ Knežević–Smejkal, Smederevska Palanka 1971 — 13/332; 15. ♘g3∓

34 **4... a6** 5. g3 [5. d4; 5. a4!?] d5 [5... b5 6. ♕e2 ♗b7 7. ♗g2 ♕c7 8. d3 ♘d4 9. ♕f2! ♘f3 10. ♗f3 ♘e7?! 11. ♗e3 ♖c8 12. 0–0 g6?! 13. e5!± Meleghegyi–Puschmann, Hungary 1971 — 11/266; 10... d6△ ♗e7, ♘f6= Florian] 6. d3 ♘f6 7. ♗d2 ♗e7 8. ♗g2 b5 9. ♘e5 ♗b7 10. ♘c6 ♗c6= Hug–Bobocov, Skopje (ol) 1972 — 14/311; **4... d6**!?

35 **5. e5**?!∓; **5. ed5**?! ed5 6. d4?! cd4 7. ♘d4 ♗c5∓

36 5... a6 6. ♗c6 bc6 7. d3 ♘f6 8. 0–0 ♗e7 9. ♕e1 0–0 10. b3 ♕c7 11. ♘a4± Portisch–Pomar, Malaga 1961

37 **6. ♘e5**? d4 7. ♗c6 ♘c6 8. ♘c6 bc6 9. ♘b1 d3 10. c4 e5! 11. ♕f3 ef4 12. e5 ♗e7 13. ♕c6 ♗d7 14. ♕f3 ♗h4 15. g3 0–0!∓ Figler–Podgajec, SSSR 1971 — 12/319; **6. ed5** ♘d5! [6... ed5 7. ♕e2 ♕d6 8. ♘e5 ♗d7 9. ♗c6 ♗c6 10. ♘b5 ♕d8 11. 0–0± Rogoff–Tukmakov, Graz 1972 — 14/308; 7... ♗g4 8. ♗c6 bc6 9. 0–0 ♕d6 10. b3± Zinn–Doda, Lugano (ol) 1968 — 6/393] 7. ♘e5 ♗d7 8. ♗c6 ♗c6 9. ♘c6 bc6∓ Smislov–Olafsson, Jugoslavija (ct) 1959

38 11. 0–0± Rossolimo–Zuckerman, USA (ch) 1966/67

39 **6. ♕e2** ♗e7 7. 0–0 0–0 8. ♗c6 bc6 9. d3 [9. b3 c4 10. bc4 ♗a6 11. d3 dc4 12. d4 ♕a5 13. ♗d2 ♗b4 14. ♕e1 ♕a3!∓; 9... a5!?△ ♗a6] c4 10. d4 ♘e4 11. ♘e4 de4 12. ♕e4 ♕d5∓ Bilek–Štejn, Kecskemet 1968; **6. e5** ♘d7 [6... d4?! 7. ♗c6 bc6 8. ef6 dc3 9. fg7 cd2 10. ♕d2 ♕d2 11. ♗d2 ♗g7 12. 0-0-0 ♖b8 13. ♘e5±] 7. ♗c6 bc6 8. 0–0 ♗e7 9. d3 0–0 10. ♕e1 ♖b8 11. b3= Kasparjan–Bronštejn, SSSR (ch) 1947

40 **9. ♗d2**?! ♗a6! 10. e5 ♘d7 11. ♕e1 d4!∓↑ Hug–Gligorić, Skopje (ol) 1972 — 14/309; **9. b3**!= Gligorić, Velimirović

41 **5. d4**?! ♘d4 6. ♘d4 cd4 7. ♕d4 ♘c6 8. ♕f2 d5! [8... ♗b4 9. ♗d3 0–0 10. 0–0 d6 11. ♗e3 b6 12. ♖ad1± Sigurjonsson–Ciocaltea, Caracas 1970 — 10/377] 9. ed5 ed5 10. ♗d3 ♗e7 11. ♗d2 0–0 12. 0-0-0 d4∓ Hug–Smislov, Petropolis (izt) 1973; **5. g3** d5 6. ♗g2 d4 7. ♘e2 d3 8. cd3 ♕d3 9. 0–0 ♕e4 10. d4 ♕d5 11. ♘c3 ♕c4∓ Ozsvath–Witkowski, Lublin 1969 — 8/289; 6. d3!?; **5. ♗e2**!?

42 **5... d6** 6. d4! cd4 7. ♘d4 ♗d7 8. ♘f3±; **5... a6** 6. ♗c6 ♘c6 [6... bc6?! 7. e5±] 7. d4 d5 [7... cd4 8. ♘d4 d6 9. ♘c6 bc6 10. ♕g4±↑] 8. ed5 ed5 9. 0–0 cd4 10. ♖e1 ♗e7∓

43 8... ♕b6!?△ g6, ♗g7

44 9... ♘b4!?

45 11. b4 ♗a7 12. ♕e1 d5 13. e5 f6 14. ♕h4 h6∓ Hennings–Geler, Kislovodsk 1972

B24 — 1. e4 c5 2. ♘c3 ♘c6 3. g3

	3	4	5	6	7	8	9	10	11	
1	...	♗g2	d3	h3[3]	f4	♘ge2	0–0	♔h2	♘d5	±
	d6[1]	g6[2]	h5	e5	♗h6	♗e6	♕d7	0-0-0[4]	f5[5]	
2	...	♗g2[6]	f4[8]	e5[9]	ef6	bc3[11]	♘f3	0–0	♘e5[12]	±
	e6	♘f6[7]	d5	d4[10]	dc3	♕f6	♕d8	♗e7	♘e5[13]	
3	...	d3	♗e3	♕d2	♗g2	♘h3	0–0	♗h6	♖ae1	±
	g6	♗g7	b6[14]	♗b7	d6	e6[15]	♘ge7	0–0	♕d7[16]	

1. e4 c5 2. ♘c3 ♘c6 3. g3 g6 4. ♗g2 ♗g7

	5	6	7	8	9	10	11	12	13	
4	♘ge2[17] e6[18]	d3[19] ♘ge7	♗g5[20] 0–0	♕d2 ♖b8	♗h6 ♗h6	♕h6 b5	h4[21] f6	♕e3 ♕b6	f4 ♘d4[22]	=
5	♘h3 e6[23]	0–0 ♘ge7	d3 0–0	♗e3[24] b6	♕d2 d5	♗h6[25] d4	♗g7 ♔g7	♘e2 e5	f4 f6[26]	=
6	d3 b6[27]	♘h3![28] ♗b7	0–0 d6	f4 h6[29]	f5 ♗c3	bc3 g5	♘f2 ♕c7[30]	♘g4 ♘e5	♘e3 ♘f6[31]	±
7	... e6	♗e3[32] ♘d4[33]	♘ce2 b6[34]	c3 ♘e2	♘e2 ♗b7	♕d2 f5	0–0 ♘e7	♖fe1 0–0	♗g5 ♕e8[35]	=

1 **3... e5**?! 4. ♗g2 g6 [4... ♘f6 5. d3 d6 6. ♘ge2 ♗e7 7. f4± Čigorin–Schiffers (m) 1880] 5. ♘h3!? ♗g7 6. 0–0 d6 7. f4 ♘ge7?! 8. f5! gf5 9. ♕h5 ♘d4 10. ♘g5 ♘g6 11. ef5 ♗f5 12. ♗d5 ♕d7 13. ♘f7+– Tajmanov–Minić, SSSR–Jugoslavija 1965; 7... ♘d4±; **3... ♖b8** 4. f4 [4. ♗g2 b5 5. ♘ge2 e6 6. d4 b4! 7. ♘b1 cd4 8. ♘d4 ♕b6∓; 6. ♘f4 ♘f6 7. 0–0 ♗e7 8. ♖e1 d6= Hasenfuss–Barcza, München 1936] e6 5. ♗g2 b5 6. d3 b4 7. ♘ce2± Schwarz; **3... ♘f6** 4. ♗g2 d5?! 5. ♘d5 [5. ed5 ♘b4 6. ♘ge2 ♘bd5 7. 0–0± Pachman] ♘d5 6. ed5 ♘b4 7. ♘e2 ♘d5 8. d4 e6 9. 0–0 ♗e7 10. dc5 ♗c5 11. c4± Bronštejn–Lisicin, SSSR 1947; 4... e6 — 3... e6

2 **4... h5**?! 5. h3!? g6 6. d3 ♗g7 7. f4 e5 8. ♘f3 ♗e6 9. 0–0 ♕d7 11. ♘g5 h4 12. g4 ef4 12. ♘e2± Bilek–Drimer, Bucuresti 1961; **4... ♗d7** 5. ♘ge2 ♕c8 6. d3 [6. ♘f4 ♗g4 7. f3 ♗d7 8. d3 g6 9. ♘cd5 ♗g7 10. c3 ♖b8 11. 0–0= Tarrasch–Sämisch 1922; 6. h3 g6 7. d3 ♗g7 8. ♗e3 ♘d4 9. ♕d2 ♖b8 10. ♘d1 e5 11. f3 ♘ge7 12. ♘f2± Rellstab–Türn München (ol) 1936] g6 7. 0–0 ♗g7 8. ♘d5 ♖b8 9. c3 ♘f6 10. ♘f6 ♗f6 11. f4 ♗h3 12. f5± Skalička–Winter, Praha (ol) 1931; **4... ♘f6** 5. d3 ♗g4!? 6. ♘ge2 [6. f3 ♗d7 7. f4±] ♘d4 7. h3 [7. 0–0?! ♘f3 8. ♔h1 h5! 9. h3 e5∓ Pachman–Najdorf, Mar del Plata 1955] ♗f3 8. ♗f3 ♘f3 9. ♔f1 e5 10. ♔g2 ♘d4 11. ♗g5± Gligorić, Sokolov

3 6. h4?!=

4 10... ♘ge7 11. ♘d5±

5 12. c3 h4 13. gh4 ♗g7 14. fe5 ♗e5 15. ♘df4± Balašov–Murej, SSSR 1970 — 9/272

6 4. ♘ge2 d5 5. ed5 ed5 — B 23

7 **4... ♘ge7** 5. d3 d5 6. f4 d4 7. ♘ce2 e5 8. f5 f6 9. g4 ♕d6 10. ♘g3 ♗d7 11. g5 0-0-0 12. gf6 gf6 13. ♗f3 ♔b8 14. ♗h5 c4 15. ♘f3 cd3 16. cd3 ♘b4 17. 0–0 ♖c8 18. ♘e1 a5 19. ♗f7± Zagorovski–Ejdlin, SSSR 1969; **4... ♖b8** 5. ♘f3!? [5. f4 — 3... ♖b8] b5 6. 0–0 b4 7. ♘e2 ♘f6 8. d4! ♘e4 [Csom –Flesch, Szombathely 1966 — 2/319] 9. d5! ed5 10. ♘f4 ♘f6 11. ♘d5 ♘d5 12. ♕d5 ♗e7 13. ♗f4 ♖b6 14. ♗d6± Marić

8 **5. ♘ge2** ♗e7 [5... d5 6. ed5 ed5 — B 23; 6. d4!± Šamkovič] 6. 0–0 a6!? 7. d3 [7. d4; 7. f4!? Schwarz] 0–0 8. h3 ♖b8 9. f4 b5 10. g4 b4 11. ♘a4 [11. ♘b1 d5∓] d5 12. e5 ♘d7∓ Larsen–Matulović, Palma de Mallorca (izt) 1970 — 10/381; **5. d3** ♗e7 [5... d5!? Suetin] 6. ♘h3 [6. f4 d5! 7. ♘h3!? d4 8. ♘e2 e5 9. ♘f2 h5!∓↑] d5! 7. 0–0 0–0 8. ♗d2 [8. ♗g5?! d4 9. ♘e2 e5 10. ♗f6 ♗f6 11. f4 c4∓ Suttles–Naranja, Palma de Mallorca (izt) 1970 — 10/383] d4 9. ♘e2 e5=; **5. ♘f3** d5 6. ed5 ed5 7. 0–0 d4=

9 6. ♕e2 d4=

10 **6... ♘d7** 7. ♘f3 ♖b8 8. ♕e2 b5 9. 0–0 b4 10. ♘d1 ♕b6 11. d3 ♗e7 12. f5± Aronin–Estrin, SSSR 1951; **6... ♘g8** 7. ♘f3 ♘h6 [7... ♘ge7 8. g4±] 8. 0–0 ♘f5 9. g4 ♘fd4 10. ♘d4 ♘d4 11. ♘e2 ♘e2 12. ♕e2± Aronin–Bronštejn, SSSR 1966

11 8. fg7 cd2 9. ♗d2 ♗g7 10. c3=

12 **11. d4** 0–0=; **11. c4**!? Keres

13 12. fe5 ♕c7 13. ♕h5 0–0 14. d3 ♗d7?! 15. ♗e4! g6 16. ♕f3 f5 17. ef6± Szabo–Lengyel, Budapest 1970 — 9/273; 14... c4!±

14 **5... ♘d4** 6. ♘ce2±; **5... d6** 6. ♗g2 — B 26

15 8... e5 9. 0–0△ f4±↑

16 12. ♗g7 ♔g7 13. f4± Hort–Toran, Palma de Mallorca 1969 — 8/294

17 Čigorin; **5. f4** d6 [5... ♖b8 6. ♘f3 b5 7. 0–0 d6 8. d3 — B 25] 6. ♘f3 e6 7. ♘e2 ♘f6 8. d3 0–0 9. h3 d5 10. e5 ♘d7 11. c3±; 6... e5; 6... ♗g4!?; 6... ♘h6!?; **5. ♘f3** e5 6. d3 d6 — B 25

18 **5... ♖b8** 6. d3 b5 7. 0–0 b4 8. ♘d5 e6 9. ♘e3 ♘ge7 10. f4 ♗b7 11. c3 d5 12. f5±↑; **5... d6** 6. 0–0 ♘h6!? [6... e5 7. d3 ♘ge7=] 7. d3 0–0 8. h3 f5 9. ♗e3 ♗d7 10. ♕d2 ♘f7 11. f4 ♖b8= Popa–Bondok, Romania 1954

19 6. 0–0!? ♘ge7 7. d3△ ♗g5= Gufeljd

20 7. ♗e3 ♘d4=

21 11. 0–0!?=

22 14. ♕d2 d6 15. h5 ♗d7 16. hg6 hg6 17. ♘d4 [17. ♘d1 ♔g7!△ ♖h8∓ Panov–Nikitin, SSSR 1970] cd4 18. ♘e2=

23 **5... d6** 6. 0–0 ♘f6 7. a3 [7. d3 — B 25] 0–0 8. ♖b1 ♗g4 9. f3 ♗c8 10. ♘f2 d5 11. d3 d4 12. ♘a4 ♘d7 13. c4 a6 14. ♕c2 ♕c7 15. ♗d2 b6 16. f4± Tajmanov–Gurgenidze, Tbilisi 1967 — 3/353; **5... h5** 6. 0–0 d6 7. d3 — B 25

24 8. ♗d2 h6 [8... d5?! 9. ed5△ ♘f4±] 9. a3 ♖b8 10. ♖b1 b5 11. b4 cb4 12. ab4 d6 13. ♘f4 ♗d7 14. ♘ce2 e5 [14... ♘e5∞ Sokolov] 15. ♘d5 ♘d5 16. ed5 ♘e7 17. ♕c1 ♕c7 18. ♖b3 ♖fc8? 19. ♖c3 ♕b7 20. ♗h6± Tajmanov–Matulović, Kislovodsk 1966 — 2/320; 18... ♔h7=

25 10. ed5 ed5 11. ♗f4 ♘d4 12. ♔h1 ♖e8 13. ♘g1 ♗b7 14. ♖ae1 ♕d7= Smislov–Tajmanov, SSSR 1947

26 **14. fe5** ♘e5 15. ♘f2 g5∓ Tajmanov–Štejn, Tbilisi 1967 — 3/354; **14. f5** g5 15. ♗f3 [15. ♘g5 fg5 16. ♕g5 ♔h8 17. f6 ♘g6 –+] ♘g8!= Suttles–Gipslis, Sousse (izt) 1967 — 4/378

27 **5... ♖b8** 6. f4 [6. a4!? a6 7. f4±; 6. h4!? h5!? 7. ♗g5 b5 8. ♕d2 b4 9. ♘d1 d6 10. ♘e2 ♗d7 11. 0–0± Zwaig–Wostin, Skopje (ol) 1972; 6. ♗e3 d6 — B 26] b5 7. a3 a5 8. ♘f3 b4 9. ab4 ab4 10. ♘e2 d6 11. 0–0 ♘h6 12. h3± Tarve–Talj, SSSR 1971 — 12/321; **5... ♘h6**!? 6. ♗d2 f5 7. ♕c1 ♘f7 8. ♘h3 ♘d4 9. f4 d6 10. ♘f2 e6 11. ♘d1 0–0 12. c3 ♘c6 13. 0–0 d5∞ Csom–Velimirović, Hungary–Jugoslavija 1966; 6. ♗e3 d6 — B 26

28 **6. ♘ge2** d6 [6... ♗b7 7. ♗e3△ d4; 7... ♘d4? 8. ♗d4 cd4 9. ♘b5+–] 7. 0–0 ♗b7 8. ♗e3 [8. f4 f5 9. g4?! fg4 10. f5 ♕d7 11. ♘f4 gf5 12. ef5 ♗d4 13. ♔h1 ♗c3∓ Smislov–Botvinik (m) 1954] ♘d4 9. ♗d4 cd4 10. ♘b5 e5 11. a4= Botvinik; **6. f4**!? ♗b7 7. ♘f3 e6 8. 0–0 ♘ge7 9. ♘h4 [9. ♗d2 a6!? 10. ♖b1 b5 11. e5 d5 12. ♘e2 ♕b6 13. c3 b4 14. ♕e1 a5 15. c4± Smislov–Kotov, Moskva 1947] ♘d4?! 10. ♘e2 d5 11. c3 ♘e2 12. ♕e2 0–0 13. f5 ef5 14. ef5 ♘c6 15. fg6 hg6 16. ♘g6! fg6 17. ♕e6 ♔h7 18. ♕h3 ♔g8 19. ♖f8 ♔f8 20. ♕h7+– I. Zajcev; 9... d5±

29 8... ♘f6?! 9. e5±

30 11... ♘f6 12. ♘g4 ♘g4 13. ♕g4△ ♕h5± Portisch

31 14. ♕e2 ♖g8 15. ♘d5 ♗d5 16. ed5 [Smislov–Portisch (m) 1971 — 11/267] ♔f8±

32 **6. f4** ♘ge7 7. ♘f3 d5 8. 0–0 b6!? [8... 0–0 9. ♕e1 d4 10. ♘d1 e5 11. ♘f2 ♕c7 12. ♗d2 ♗d7 13. ♕e2 b5 14. ♘h4± Bakulin–Nikitin, SSSR 1970] 9. ♔h1 ♗a6 10. ♕e2 0–0 11. ♗d2 ♘d4= Ovčinikov–Spaski, Kislovodsk 1960; **6. ♘h3** ♘ge7 7. 0–0 — 5. ♘h3; **6. ♘ge2** h5?! 7. h3 ♘h6 8. ♗e3 ♘d4 9. ♕d2 d6 10. 0–0±; 6... d6 — B 25

33 6... ♕a5 7. ♗d2 [7. ♘e2 ♘d4 8. 0–0 ♘e7 9. ♘c1?! d6 10. ♕d2 ♗d7 11. ♘b3 ♕b6! 12. ♖ae1 h5 13. h4 a5! 14. ♘d1 ♕b4!∓ Biyiasas–Ljubojević, Petropolis (izt) 1973 — 16/276; 9. ♔h1 0–0 10. a3 ♘ec6 11. ♖b1 d6 12. b4 ♕d8∞ Smislov–Boleslavski, SSSR 1945] ♘ge7 8. ♘f3 0–0 9. 0–0 ♘d4 10. ♘d4 cd4 11. ♘e2 ♕b6 12. c3± Pachman–Vaitonis, Stockholm (izt) 1952

34 **7... ♘e2**?! 8. ♘e2 ♗b2 9. ♖b1 ♕a5 10. ♗d2 ♕a2 11. ♖b2 ♖b2 12. ♗c3±; **7... d6** — B 26

35 14. ♘f4 ♘c6= Medina–Mecking, Palma de Mallorca 1969

B 25 — 1. e4 c5 2. ♘c3 ♘c6 3. g3 g6 4. ♗g2 ♗g7 5. d3 d6

	6	7	8	9	10	11	12	13	14	
1	♘h3[1] h5?![2]	0–0[3] h4[4]	g4 ♘f6	f3 ♗d7	♗e3 ♕c8	♕d2 ♘h7	♖ae1 ♘f8	a3[5]		±
2	... ♘f6	0–0 ♗g4[6]	f3 ♗h3	♗h3 0–0	♗e3 ♘e8[7]	♕d2 ♘c7	♖ae1 b6	♘d1 d5	♕e2 e6[8]	=
3	♘f3 e5[9]	0–0 ♘ge7	♗e3[10] 0–0	♕d2 ♘d4	♗h6[11] f6!	♗g7 ♔g7	♘e1[12]			=
4	♘ge2 ♘f6[13]	0–0[14] ♖b8[15]	h3 e5	♘d5 ♘d5	ed5 ♘d4	c3 ♘f5	a3 a5	♖e1 ♗f6	g4 ♘h4[16]	=
5	... e5	0–0[17] ♘ge7	♗e3 0–0	f4 ♘d4	♕d2 ♗e6	♖ae1 ♕d7	♘c1 ♖ad8	♘d1 b6	c3 ♘dc6[18]	=
6	f4 ♖b8[19]	♘f3 b5	0–0 b4[20]	♘d5 e6	♘e3 ♘ge7	a3 a5	ab4 ab4	f5 ef5	ef5 ♗f5[21]	±

	6	7	8	9	10	11	12	13	14	
7	...	♘f3[22]	0—0[24]	♔h1	♗e3	♕e2[25]	♗g1	♘d1	c3	±
	f5	♘f6[23]	0—0	♗d7	♖b8	b5	b4	♘e8	♘c7[26]	
8	...	♘f3	0—0	♘h4[29]	f5	♗g5	♘e2[31]	♕e2	♖ab1	=
	♘f6	0—0[27]	♖b8[28]	♘d4[30]	b5	b4	♘e2	♘d7[32]	♘e5[33]	
9	...	...	...	h3	a3![35]	♗e3	ab4	♘e2	b3![37]	±
	...	...	...	b5[34]	a5	b4	ab4	♗b7[36]	♖a8[38]	
10	...	♘f3	0—0[40]	♗d2[42]	♖b1	a3	a4	♘a4	♘d4	∓
	e6	♘ge7[39]	0—0[41]	♖b8	b5	a5[43]	ba4![44]	♘d4	♗d4[45]	
11	...	...	...	♗e3	♖b1[47]	♘e2	♗f3	c3	d4	±
	...	...	...	♘d4[46]	♖b8[48]	♘f3	b5	a5	cd4[49]	
12	...	♘h3[50]	0—0	♘f4[53]	♘fd5	♘d5	♘f4	c3	a3	=
	e5	♘ge7[51]	ef4[52]	0—0	♘d5	♗e6	♗d7	b5	a5[54]	

1 **6. ♘d5**?!; **6. ♗d2** e5=; **6. ♗g5** ♕a5 7. ♘ge2 [7. ♕d2!?] h6 [7... c4?! 8. ♗d2±↑] 8. ♗e3 e5 9. 0—0 ♘ge7 10. f4 f5 11. ♕d2 0—0 12. ef5= Estrin

2 **6... e5** 7. f4 — 6. f4; **6... e6** 7. ♗e3 — B 26

3 7. f3 e5 [7... h4 8. g4 e5 9. 0—0 ♘ge7 10. f4 f5± Novak—Ozsvath, Tbilisi 1972] 8. ♗e3 ♘d4 9. ♘d5 ♗e6 10. 0—0 ♘e7 11. ♘e7 ♕e7 12. c3 ♘c6 13. ♕d2 h4= Padevski—Velimirović, Vrnjačka Banja 1973 — 15/308; 9. ♘f2± Padevski

4 7... ♘h6 8. f3 ♗d7 9. ♘e2 e5 10. c3 ♕b6 11. ♔h1 0-0-0 12. ♕c2 ♔b8 13. ♗e3 ♕c7 14. ♖fc1± Suttles—Benkö, USA 1965

5 Tajmanov—Ciocaltea, Harrachov 1966

6 7... 0—0!? 8. f4 [8. ♘e2 d5! 9. f3 e5 10. c3 h6 11. ♘f2 ♗e6= Novak—Furman, Harrachov 1966 — 1/233; 8. f3!?] ♗g4 [8... ♖b8 9. ♘f2 ♗d7 10. g4± Graf—Fridman, Subotica 1967] 9. ♕d2 ♘d4 10. ♔h1 ♕d7 11. ♘g1?! ♗e6 12. ♘d1 d5!∓ Medina—Benkö, Malaga 1970 — 9/274; 11. ♘f2=

7 10... ♘d4?! 11. ♗d4 cd4 12. ♘e2△ c3±

8 15. f4 f5 16. ♗c1 ♖f7 17. ♗g2 ♕d7 18. ♘f2 ♖d8 19. c3 b5= Spaski—Petrosjan (m) 1966 — 1/235

9 **6... ♘d4**?! 7. ♘d4 cd4 8. ♘e2 e6 9. c3 dc3 10. ♘c3 ♘e7 11. ♗e3 0—0 12. 0—0 b6 13. ♕d2± Smislov—Čistjakov, Soči 1974; **6... e6** 7. ♗g5 ♘ge7 8. ♕d2 h6 9. ♗e3 e5 10. 0—0 ♗e6 11. ♘e1 ♕d7 12. a3 ♗h3 13. f4 ♘d4 14. ♖b1 ef4 15. ♗f4± Smislov—Kotov, SSSR 1943; **6... ♘f6** 7. 0—0 0—0 8. h3 e5 9. ♔h2 ♘d4 10. ♗e3 b5 11. a3 ♗d7 12. ♘e2 a5 13. c3 ♘e2 14. ♕e2= Smislov—Mojsejev, SSSR 1952

10 **8. h3** h6 9. ♗e3 0—0 10. ♕d2 [10. ♘d5?! f5∓↑] ♔h7 [10... h5 11. ♗h6 ♘d4 12. ♗g7 ♘f3 13. ♗f3 ♔g7 14. ♔h2±] 11. ♘h4 ♗e6 12. f4 f5 13. ♘d5= Estrin; **8. ♘h4**!? Mecking

11 10. ♘e1 f5 11. f4 ♖b8 12. ♘d5 fe4?! 13. ♘e7! [13. de4? ♘d5 14. ed5 ♘f5∓] ♕e7 14. de4 ♗e6 15. c3± Kopilov—Goldberg, SSSR 1949; 12... ♘d5=

12 **12. ♘d4**?! cd4 13. ♘e2 ♗g4 14. f3 ♗e6∓ Mecking—Portisch, Vršac 1971 — 12/324; **12. ♘e1**= Mecking

13 Lasker; **6... ♕d7**?! 7. ♗e3 b6 8. f4 ♗b7 9. 0—0 ♘d4 10. ♕d2 h5 11. h3 f5 12. ♗f2!± Karpov—Schaufelberger, Nederland 1968 — 5/335; **6... ♖b8** 7. 0—0 [7. ♗e3 ♘d4 8. ♕d2 b5 9. f3 e6 10. ♘d1 b4 11. 0—0 ♘e7 12. ♘d4 cd4 13. ♗h6 0—0 14. ♗g7 ♔g7 15. ♘f2 e5= Thomas—Ekström, Zaandam 1946; 7. a4!?] b5 8. a3 [8. ♘d5 e6 9. ♘e3 ♘ge7 10. c3 b4 11. ♗d2 0—0 12. ♕c1 bc3 13. bc3 ♗a6 14. ♕c2 ♕a5∓ Nilsson—Euwe, Haag 1928; 8. f4 b4 9. ♘d5 ♘d4 10. ♘d4 ♗d4 11. ♔h1 e6 12. ♘e3 ♘e7 13. a3! 0—0 14. ab4 cb4 15. ♕e1 ♕c7 16. ♘c4 d5 17. ♗e3± Panov—Tajmanov, SSSR 1952] e6 9. ♗e3 ♘d4 10. ♕d2 ♘e7 11. ♘d1?! 0—0 12. ♖b1 a5∓ Szily—Bilek, Kecskemet 1962; 11. ♗h6!?±; **6... ♗d7**!? 7. 0—0 ♕c8 8. ♘f4 ♘f6 9. a4 0—0 10. h4 ♖e8 11. f3 ♘d4 12. ♗e3 ♗c6 13. g4 e5= Kopilov—Smislov, SSSR 1947; **6... e6** 7. 0—0 [7. ♗e3 ♘d4 — B 26] ♘ge7 8. ♗d2 ♕d7 9. ♕c1 h6 10. ♘d1 b5 11. ♘e3 ♗b7= Calvo—Panno, Palma de Mallorca 1972 — 14/315

14 7. h4 0—0 [7... ♖b8 8. ♗g5 0—0 9. ♕d2 b5 10. 0—0 b4 11. ♘d1 ♘d4! 12. ♘d4 cd4 13. a3 b3 14. c4 ♘d7 15. f3 ♘c5 16. ♘f2 f6 17. ♗h6 e5= Larsen—Geler (m) 1966 — 1/234] 8. ♗g5 [8. ♗e3 — B 26] ♗d7 9. ♕d2 ♘d4 10. ♘d4 cd4 11. ♘e2 ♕b6 12. 0—0 ♖ac8 13. c3 dc3 14. ♘c3 ♗c6= Smislov—Stahlberg, Amsterdam (ol) 1954

15 7... 0–0 8. h3 ♖b8 [8... ♘d4 9. ♗e3 e5 10. ♔h2 ♘e8 11. f4 ♗e6 12. ♕d2 ♖b8 13. ♘d1 f5= Vejnger–Judovič jr., SSSR 1961] 9. ♗e3 b5 10. ♕d2 b4 11. ♘d1 ♕c7 12. f4 ♘d7 13. g4 ♘d4 14. ♘g3 ♗a6= Wibe–Korčnoj, La Habana (ol) 1966

16 Šišov–Polugajevski, SSSR 1972

17 7. ♘d5 ♘ge7 [7... ♘ce7 8. ♘ec3 ♘d5 9. ♘d5 ♗e6 10. c3 ♗d5 11. ed5 ♘e7= Tot–Trifunović, Jugoslavija (ch) 1960] 8. c3?! ♘d5 9. ed5 ♘e7 10. 0–0 0–0 11. f4?! ♗d7 12. h3 ♕c7 13. ♗e3 ♖ae8∓ Smislov–Botvinik (m) 1954; 8. ♘e3!? Karpov

18 Holmov–Talj, SSSR (ch) 1964

19 **6... ♘d4** 7. ♘ce2 ♘h6 8. c3 ♘e2 9. ♘e2 0–0 10. h3 ♕b6 11. g4 ♔h8 12. g5 ♘g8 13. ♘g3± Kuvaldin–Meščerjakov, SSSR 1964 **6... ♘h6** 7. ♘f3 [7. ♘ge2 0–0 8. h3 f5 9. ♗e3 ♗d7 10. 0–0 ♘d4 11. ♗f2 e6 12. ♘d4 cd4 13. ♘e2 e5∓ Sokolov–Kostić, Jugoslavija 1953] 0–0 8. h3 f5 9. 0–0 ♗d7 10. ♗e3 ♘d4 11. ♕d2 ♘f7 12. ♖ae1 ♔h8 [12... e5!? Gligorić, Sokolov] 13. ♘d1 ♕c7 14. ♘h4 ♖ae8 15. c3 ♘c6 16. ef5 gf5 17. d4!± Smederevac–Sokolov, Jugoslavija 1957; **6... b6**!? 7. ♘f3 ♗b7 8. 0–0 ♕d7 9. ♗e3 [9. f5±] f5 10. ♕d2 ♘f6 11. ♔h1 0-0-0 [Bernstein–Fischer, Netanya 1968 — 6/405] 12. a3±

20 8... ♘f6 9. e5! [9. h3 b4 10. ♘d5 ♘d5 11. ed5 ♘d4=] de5 10. fe5 ♘g4 11. e6 ♗e6 [11... 0–0 12. ♗f4 ♖b6 13. ef7 ♖f7 14. ♘g5±] 12. ♘g5 ♕d4 13. ♔h1 ♗d7 14. ♘ce4 ♘ce5 15. ♗f4 ♖c8 16. h3 ♘h6 17. c3 ♕a4 18. ♘c5!± Wade–R. Byrne, Hastings 1971/72 — 11/268

21 15. ♘f5 ♘f5 16. ♘g5 ♘e5 17. ♗d5 0–0 18. ♖a7±→ Kopilov–Belov, SSSR 1963

22 7. ef5 gf5 8. ♕h5 ♔f8 9. ♕d1 ♘f6 10. ♘f3 ♔f7! 11. ♘g5 ♔g6 12. h4?! h5∓ Tarve–Pohla, Pärnu 1971 — 12/322

23 7... e5?! 8. ♘d5±

24 8. ♗e3 ♘g4 9. ♗g1 e5 10. h3 ♘h6=

25 11. ♕d2 b5≠

26 **14... ♘c7** 15. ♖c1± Smislov–Larsen, München (ol) 1958; **14... ♕c8**!?△ ♕a6 Boleslavski

27 **7... ♗d7** 8. h3 h5 9. ♗e3 ♕b6 10. ♕c1 [10. ♖b1 ♘d4±] ♘d4 11. ♘h4 [11. 0–0 ♘f3 12. ♖f3 0–0=] ♗h6 12. ♘d1 ♖g8 13. c3 ♘c6 14. ♕d2 e5 15. fe5 ♗e3 16. ♘e3 ♘e5 17. 0–0± Minev–Dimitrov, Bulgaria 1961; **7... ♖b8** 8. 0–0 ♗d7 9. h3 ♘d4 10. ♗e3 ♘f3 11. ♕f3 0–0 12. ♕f2 ♗c6 13. ♖ad1 ♕c7 14. d4 cd4 15. ♗d4± Bhend–Atard, Kecskemet 1964; **7... a6**!? 8. a4 ♕c7

28 **8... ♘e8** 9. h3 ♘c7 [9... f5!?] 10. ♗e3 b6 11. ♕d2 ♗b7 12. f5 d5 13. ♗h6! ± Smislov–Ilivicki, SSSR 1952; **8... ♗d7** 9. ♗d2 a6 10. a4 ♖b8 11. ♘h4 b5 12. ab5 ab5 13. f5± Estrin; 11. h3!?±

29 9. a4 a6 10. ♘h4 [10. h3 b5 11. ab5 ab5 12. ♗e3 b4] ♗d7 11. f5 b5 12. ab5 ab5 13. ♗g5 b4 14. ♘e2 ♕b6 15. ♕d2 ♖a8 16. ♖ab1 ♘e5 17. ♔h1 ♖a2 18. ♘f4 ♗c6 19. fg6 hg6∞ Fjeldsted–Tajmanov, Reykjavik 1968 — 5/331

30 9... ♗d7 10. f5 b5 11. ♗g5! b4 12. ♘d5 a5 [12... ♘d5 13. ed5 ♘d4 14. ♕d2!±] 13. ♔h1 ♘e5 14. ♕d2 ♗c6 15. ♖ae1± Spaski–Petrosjan (m) 1966 — 1/232

31 12. ♘b1 ♘d7 13. ♘d2 ♘e5 14. ♔h1 a5 15. ♖b1= Spaski–Geler (m) 1968 — 5/334

32 13... ♘e8!? Korčnoj

33 **14... ♖b6**?! 15. ♕d2 ♖a6 16. ♗h6 ♖a2 17. fg6 fg6 [17... hg6? 18. ♗g7 ♔g7 19. ♘f5+– Korčnoj] 19. e5± Medina–Korčnoj, Palma de Mallorca 1968 — 6/410; **14... ♘e5** 15. ♕d2 a5 16. ♗h6 ♗d7 17. ♘f3 ♘f3 [17... ♕b6?! 18. ♘e5 de5 19. ♗e3± Lejn–Saharov, SSSR (ch) 1968 — 7/302] 18. ♖f3 f6= Petrosjan, Suetin

34 9... ♘e8!? 10. ♗d2 b5 11. ♖b1 e6 12. ♕e1 ♘d4 [12... b4!?] 13. ♘d4 cd4 [13... ♗d4!? Matanović] 14. ♘e2 ♕b6 15. a3 e5 16. ♔h2 f5 17. ef5 gf5 18. ♗a5 ♕a6 19. ♗b4± Spaski–Benkö, Palma de Mallorca 1968 — 6/411

35 **10. a4** ba4!△ ♗d7=; **10. g4** b4 [10... c4?! 11. e5!± Gligorić, Sokolov] 11. ♘e2 c4 [11... ♘d7 12. g5 ♘b6 13. ♘h2 ♘d4 14. ♘d4 ♗d4 15. ♔h1 f5 16. gf6 ♗f6 17. ♘g4± Benkö–Aaron, Stockholm (izt) 1962] 12. ♗e3 ♗a6 13. ♘ed4 ♘d4 14. ♗d4 ♕c7 15. ♖f2 ♖fe8 16. f5 [Smislov–Tajmanov, SSSR 1959] ♖bc8±

36 **13... ♗d7** 14. g4 ♘e8 15. ♖b1 ♘c7 16. ♕e1 ♘b5 17. ♕f2 ♖a8 18. f5 ♖a2 19. ♕h4 ♘e5 20. ♘e5 ♗e5 21. ♗h6±→» Lazarev–Šmit, SSSR 1963; **13... ♕c7** 14. b3 ♗b7 15. g4 ♖a8 16. ♖c1 ♖a2 17. ♘g3△ f5±↑» Tarve–Karasev, SSSR 1972; **13... ♘e8** 14. ♖b1 ♘c7 15. f5 ♘b5 16. ♕d2 ♘bd4 17. ♘h4 ♘e2 18. ♕e2 ♘e5 19. ♘f3 ♘f3 20. ♕f3 ♗b7 21. h4± Reshevsky–Korčnoj (m) 1968 — 5/329

37 **14. ♕d2** ♖a8 15. ♖ab1 ♕a5 16. b3 d5! 17. e5 d4= Vorotnikov; **14. g4**!? ♖a8 15. ♖b1 ♖a2 16. ♘c1 ♖a6 17. ♕e1 ♕c7 18. ♘e2 ♖a2 19. ♕h4± Bakulin–Šackes, SSSR 1970

38 15. ♖c1 ♖a2 16. g4 e6 [16... ♕a8 17. ♕e1 ♕a6 18. ♕f2 ♘a7 19. f5 ♘b5 20. fg6 hg6 21. ♘g5 ♘a3 22. ♕h4±→» Spaski–Geler (m) 1968 — 5/336; 18... ♘d7!?; 16... ♘d7!?] 17. ♘g3 ♖e8 18. f5±

39 7... ♖b8 8. 0–0 ♘ge7 9. e5! de5 10. fe5 ♘e5 11. ♗f4 ♘f3 12. ♕f3 ♖a8 13. ♗e3 0–0 14. ♗c5 ♗d4 15. ♗d4 ♕d4 16. ♔h1 ♖b8 17. ♘e4± Bronštejn–Keres, Zürich (ct) 1953

40 8. ♗e3 ♘d4 9. ♕d2 ♕a5 10. 0–0 ♘ec6 11. ♘e1 0–0 12. ♕f2 ♖b8 13. ♘d1 ♗d7= Ozsvath–Navarovszky, Budapest 1965

41 8... d5 9. ♘h4 f5 10. e5 a6 11. ♘e2 ♗d7 12. c3 0–0 13. ♗e3± Knežević–Tot, Jugoslavija (ch) 1960

42 **9. a3** ♗d7 10. ♖b1 ♖c8 11. ♗d2 ♘d4 12. ♘e2 ♗a4! 13. b3 ♗c6 14. c4 ♘f3∓ Spaski–Geler (m) 1968 — 5/333; **9. ♔h1** ♗d7 [9... ♖b8 10. a4 ♘d4 11. ♘h4 f5 12. ♘b1 a6 13. c3 ♘c6 14. ♗e3 b5 15. ab5 ab5 16. ♘d2 ♗d7= Larsen–Pavlov, Halle 1963] 10. ♕e1 ♘d4 11. ♕f2 f5 12. ♗e3 e5 13. ♘d1 fe4 14. de4 ♗c6 15. ♘g5 h6 16. ♘h3 ♕a5∓; **9. ♖b1** ♗d7 10. ♗e3 ♘d4 11. ♘e2 ♘f3 12. ♗f3 ♗c6 13. g4 f5 14. ♘g3 ♕d7∓ Seledkin–Gutman, SSSR 1974; **9. ♘e2** f5 10. c3 ♔h8 11. ♗e3 b6 12. ♖b1 e5 13. b4?! fe4! 14. de4 ♗e6 15. ♕d2 ♕d7∓; 13. ef5!?△ b4

43 11... f5?! 12. ♗e3 ♕c7 13. ♗f2 ♔h8 14. ♖e1 b4 15. ab4 cb4 16. ♘e2 fe4 17. de4 e5 18. ♕d2 ♗e6 19. ♘c1!±↑ Spaski–Larsen (m) 1968 — 5/7

44 12... b4?! 13. ♘b5 d5 14. c4 bc3 15. bc3 c4 16. ♗e3 cd3 17. e5 ♗a6 18. ♕d3± Spaski–Larsen (m) 1968 — 5/3

45 15. ♔h1 ♗d7 16 c3 ♗g7 17. ♕c2 ♕c7∓ Tarve–K. Grigorjan, SSSR 1972

46 9... ♖b8 10. d4 [10. h3 ♘d4 11. ♗d4?! cd4 12. ♘e2 e5 13. c3 dc3 14. bc3 b6!∓ Jović–Minić, Jugoslavija 1974 — 17/343; 11. g4!?∞ Minić] ♕b6 11. dc5 ♕b2 12. ♖b1 ♕c3 13. ♖b3 ♕a5 14. cd6 ♘d5 15. ed5± Sakarello–James, Skopje (ol) 1972

47 **10. ♘h4** ♖b8 11. ♕d2 f5 12. ♖ae1 b5 13. ♘d1 b4 14. c3 bc3 15. bc3 ♘dc6∓ Koh–Judovič, corr. 1972 — 13/334; **10. ♕d2** d5 [10... b6?! 11. ♗d4! cd4 12. ♘b5 ♘c6! 13. e5 de5 14. ♘e5 ♘e5 15. ♗a8 ♗d7 16. ♗e4 ♗b5 17. fe5 ♗e5± Medina–Andersson, Las Palmas 1974 — 17/342; 10... ♖b8 11. g4 f5 12. gf5 gf5 13. ♔h1 ♘g6 14. ♖g1 b5 15. ♖af1 b4 16. ♘d1 ♘f3 17. ♖f3 ♗b7= Wade–Matulović, Skopje 1968; 12... ef5 13. ♖ae1 ♔h8 14. ♔h1 ♘f3 15. ♖f3 b6 16. ♗f2 ♗b7∓ Medina–Smislov, Siegen (ol) 1970 — 10/385; 10... ♘ec6!?] 11. ed5 ed5 12. ♗d4?! cd4∓ Wade–Matanović, Vinkovci 1968 — 6/414; 12. ♗f2∓ Matanović, Parma

48 10... ♘ec6 11. ♘e2△ c3±↑⊞

49 15. cd4 e5 16. ♕d2±

50 7. ♘f3 ♘ge7 8. 0–0 [8. ♗e3 — B 26] 0–0 9. ♗e3 ef4 [9... ♘d4 — B 26] 10. gf4 f5 11. ♕d2 ♖b8 12. a3 b6 13. ♖ae1 h6 14. ♔h1 ♗e6 15. ♖g1 ♕d7 16. ♕f2 d5 17. ed5 ♘d5 18. ♘d5 ♗d5 19. ♕g3 ♔h7 20. c3 ♖be8 21. h4± Spaski–Minić, SSSR–Jugoslavija 1965

51 7... ♘f6?! 8. 0–0 0–0 9. f5±→»

52 8... **0–0**? 9. f5! [9. ♗e3 f5=] gf5 10. ef5 ♗f5 [10... ♘f5 11. ♕h5±→] 11. ♖f5! ♘f5 12. ♗e4 ♘fd4 13. ♕h5 ♖e8 14. ♕h7 ♔f8 15. ♗g5±→» Bilek–Gheorghiu, Bucuresti 1968 — 5/330; **8... ♘d4**!? 9. f5?! gf5 10. ♗g5 f6! 11. ♕h5 ♔d7 12. ef5 ♘c2 13. ♖ac1 ♘d4 14. ♘e4 ♕f8∓ Trapl–Přibyl, ČSSR 1972 — 13/335

53 9. ♗f4!? 0–0 10. ♕d2 Portisch

54 15. ♗e3 ♘e5 16. h3= Bilek–Evans, Lugano (ol) 1968 — 6/409

B 26 1. e4 c5 2. ♘c3 ♘c6 3. g3 g6 4. ♗g2 ♗g7 5. d3 d6 6. ♗e3

	6	7	8	9	10	11	12	13	14	
1	... ♘h6[1]	♕c1[2] ♘g4	♗d2 ♘d4	h3 ♘e5	♘ce2 0–0[3]	f4 ♘ec6	c3 ♘e2	♘e2 f5	0–0[4]	±
2	... ♖b8	♕d2[5] b5	♘f3[6] b4	♘d1 ♘d4[7]	♘h4 e5	f4 ef4	♗f4 ♘e7	0–0[8] h6	♗e3 g5[9]	±
3	... ♘f6	h3[10] 0–0[11]	♕d2[12] ♘d4[13]	♘ce2[14] e5	c3 ♘e6	f4[15]				±
4	... e6	♘h3[16] ♘ge7[17]	0–0 0–0[18]	♕d2 e5[19]	♗h6 f6!	♗g7 ♔g7	f4[20] ♗e6	♘d5 ♕d7[21]		=
5	... ...	♕d2 ♘d4[22]	♘f3[23] e5[24]	h3[25] ♘e7	♘e2 0–0	♘ed4[26] cd4	♗h6 f6	♗g7 ♔g7	0–0 ♗e6[27]	=
6	... ...	... ...	♘ge2 ♘e7	0–0 0–0	f4[28] f5[29]	♖ae1 ♖b8	♘d1 b5	c3 ♘e2	♕e2 b4[30]	=
7	... ...	... ...	♘d1 e5[31]	c3 ♘c6	♘e2 ♗g4	0–0[32] ♘ge7	f4 0–0	♘f2 ♗e6	♘h3 ♕c8[33]	±

	6	7	8	9	10	11	12	13	14	
8	...	...	♘ge2[34]	0–0	♕e2[36]	bc3	♖ab1	♗h6	e5	=∞
	...	♕a5	♘d4	♘e2[35]	♗c3[37]	♕c3	♘e7[38]	♘c6	♘e5[39]	
9	...	♕d2[40]	f4[42]	♘f3	0–0	♗f4	♖f3	♗h6	♗g7	=
	e5	♘ge7[41]	♘d4	0–0[43]	ef4[44]	♘f3	♗e6	♘c6	♔g7[45]	
10	...	...	h4[46]	♘h3	f4	♖h3	♖h1	♕f2	♖f1	∞
	...	...	h5	♘d4	♗h3[47]	♕d7	♖b8	b5	ef4[48]	

1 **6... ♕d7**?!; **6... ♗d7** 7. ♕d2 ♘d4 8. ♘d1 ♗c6 9. c3 ♘f5 10. f4 ♘e3 11. ♘e3 ♘f6 12. ♘f3 0–0 12. 0–0± Ignatjev–Šamkovič, SSSR 1962; **6... ♘d4** 7. ♘ce2 [7. ♕d2 e6 — 6... e6] e6 8. c3 ♘e2 [8... ♘c6 9. d4 cd4 10. ♘d4 ♘d4 11. ♗d4 e5 12. ♗e3 ♘e7 13. ♘e2 0–0 14. 0–0 ♗e6 15. ♕d2± Smislov–Denker, SSSR–USA 1946] 9. ♘e2 ♘e7 10. ♕d2 ♗d7 11. ♗h6 [11. d4 ♕c7 12. 0–0± Smislov–Čistjakov, SSSR 1946] 0–0 12. h4± Ivkov

2 7. h3 f5 8. ♕d2 [8. f4 ♘d4 9. ♕d2 e6 10. ♘f3 0–0 11. 0–0 ♘f7 12. ♖ae1 ♗d7 13. ♘d1 ♘b5! 14. c3 ♖c8 15. ♘f2 ♗c6 16. g4 b6 17. ef5 ef5 18. gf5 gf5 19. ♔h1 d5∓ Konstantinov–Petrosjan, SSSR 1951; 8. ♘ge2 0–0 9. 0–0 ♖b8 10. a4 ♘d4 11. ♕d2 ♘f7 12. f4 ♗d7 13. ♔h2 ♗c6 14. ♖ab1= Smislov–Kopilov, SSSR 1951] ♘f7 9. ef5 gf5 10. ♘ge2 ♘d4 11. ♘f4 0–0 12. ♘h5 ♗h8 13. ♘d5± Klaman–Rubel, SSSR 1956

3 10... ♕b6 11. f4 ♘c2?! 12. ♕c2 ♕b2 13. ♕b2 ♘d3 14. ♔f1 ♗b2 15. ♖b1 ♗e6 16. ♗c3± Smislov–Bronštejn, SSSR (ch) 1951

4 Boleslavski

5 **7. ♘f3** ♘f6 8. h3 b5 9. ♕d2 b4 10. ♘d1 ♗a6= Hecht–Keene, Teesside 1972 — 13/336; **7. a4** e6! [7... a6 8. ♕d2 b5 9. ab5 ab5 10. ♘ge2 b4 11. ♘d1 ♘d4 12. 0–0 e5 13. f4± Čerepkov–Bilek, Budapest 1961] 8. ♕d2 ♘d4 9. ♘f3 ♘e7 10. 0–0 0–0 11. ♗h6 e5 12. ♗g7 ♔g7= Hort–Fischer, Rovinj-Zagreb 1970 — 9/276

6 **8. ♘ge2** b4 9. ♘d1 e5 [9... a5 10. a3 b3!? 11. c3± Medina–Ljubojević, Skopje (ol) 1972 — 14/313] 10. 0–0 ♘ge7 11. ♗h6 [11. f4 ♕c7 12. fe5 ♘e5 13. ♗h6= Kristofel–Petrosjan, Zürich 1961] 0–0 12. ♗g7 ♔g7 13. ♘e3 ♗e6 14. f4± Klatan–Bangiev, SSSR 1972; **8. ♘d1**!? e5 9. c3 b4 10. ♘e2 bc3 11. bc3 ♗d7 12. 0–0±

7 9... ♗g4!? 10. h3 ♗f3 11. ♗f3 ♘f6 12. ♗g2± Smislov–Fischer, Rovinj-Zagreb 1970 — 9/275

8 13. c3!? bc3 14. bc3 ♘e6 15. ♗h6!± Portisch

9 15. ♘f3 ♘f3 16. ♗f3± Smislov–Portisch (m) 1971 — 11/269

10 **7. ♕d2** ♘g4 8. ♗f4 [8. ♗g5 h6 9. h3?! ♘f2! 10. ♗e7 ♘d3∓] e5 9. ♗e3 [9. ♗g5 f6 10. ♗e3 ♘e3 11. fe3 0–0 12. ♘ge2 ♘e7= Nikolić–Smejkal, Varna 1971] Se3 10. fe3 0–0 11. ♘ge2 ♘e7 12. 0-0-0 ♗h6 13. h4 ♗g4 14. ♖df1=; **7. ♕c1** ♘d4 [7... h5 8. h3 ♗d7 9. f4 ♕b6 10. ♘f3 ♘d4 11. ♘h4! ♗c6 12. 0–0 ♘d7 13. ♔h2± Pachman–Ciocaltea, Bucuresti 1952; 8... e5 9. f4 ♗e6 10. ♘f3 ♘d4 11. ♘g5 ♗d7 12. 0–0 0–0 13. ♕d2± Pachman–Toran 1955; 7... 0–0 8. ♗h6 ♘d4 9. ♗g7 ♔g7 10. ♘ce2 ♘e2 11. ♘e2 d5= Pachman–Filip (m) 1954; 10. f4!± Pachman] 8. ♘d1 e5 9. c3 ♘e6 10. ♗h6 0–0 11. ♗g7 ♘g7 12. ♘e2 [Pachman–Olafsson, Portorož (izt) 1958] d5 13. ed5 ♘d5 14. 0–0 ♗e6=

11 **7... ♗d7** 8. ♕d2 h5 9. ♘ge2 ♕c8 10. f4 ♖b8 11. d4 cd4 12. ♘d4 0–0 13. ♘d1±; **7... ♖b8** 8. ♕d2 b5 9. ♗h6 0–0 10. ♗g7± Augustsson–Barcza, Amsterdam (ol) 1954

12 8. ♘ge2 ♘e8 [8... e5 9. 0–0 ♘d4 10. f4 ♘h5 11. f5!±→» Bakony–Kapu, Hungary 1955] 9. ♕d2 ♘d4 10. ♘d1 ♖b8 11. ♘f4?! ♘c7 12. c3?! e5! 13. ♘e2 ♘e2 14. ♕e2 b6 15. 0–0 d5 16. c4 de4 17. de4 f5∓↑ Keres–Najdorf, Zürich (ct) 1953; 11. c3=; 11. 0–0=

13 **8... ♘e8** 9. ♗h6 ♘d4 10. ♗g7 ♔g7 11. h4 h6 12. h5 g5 13. f4± Tenenbaum–Judovič, jr. SSSR 1961; **8... ♖e8**!? (Pachman) 9. ♘ge2 ♗d7 10. 0–0 ♖b8 11. f4 ♕c8 12. g4 b5 13. ♘g3±

14 9. ♘d1 e5 10. c3 ♘e6 11. ♘e2 d5! 12. ♗h6 de4∓ Augustsson–Olafsson, Iceland 1956

15 ± Schwarz

16 **7. ♕c1**?! ♘d4 8. ♘ge2 ♘e7 9. 0–0 0–0 10. h3 [10. f4!?] f5 11. f4 ♘ec6 12. ♕d2 ♖b8 13. a4 a6∓; **7. f4** ♘h6 [7... ♘ge7 8. ♘f3 ♘d4 — B 25] 8. h3 [8. ♘f3 ♘g4 9. ♗g1 ♘d4 =] f5 9. ef5 ♘f5 10. ♗f2 ♘cd4= Estrin; 9. ♘ge2!?; **7. ♘ge2** [△ d4] ♘d4 8. 0–0 [8. ♕d2 — 7. ♕d2] ♘ge7 9. f4 ♖b8 10. ♖b1 ♘ec6 11. a3 ♕a5 12. ♗d2 ♕c7= Smislov–Opočensky, Moskva 1946

17 7... ♕d7 8. ♕d2 b6 9. 0–0 ♗b7 10. a3 ♘d4 11. ♖ae1 ♘e7 12. ♘d1 a5 13. f4 0–0= Medina–Panno, Palma de Mallorca 1971 — 12/325

18 8... b6 9. ♕d2 h6 10. ♖ae1 [10. ♘f4!? ♗b7 11. ♖ab1 ♕d7 12. ♘ce2 e5 13. ♘d5 ♘d5

14. ed5 ♘e7 15. c4 g5? 16. f4!± Augustin–Kavalek, ČSSR 1968 — 6/412; 15... ♘f5∞] ♗b7 11. f4 ♕d7 12. f5 gf5 13. ef5 ♘f5 14. ♖f5 ef5 15. ♗h6=∞ Suttles–Kavalek, Sousse (izt) 1967

19 **9... ♖e8**?! 10. ♖ab1 b6 11. ♗h6 ♗h8 12. f4 ♗d7 13. g4!± Day–Spaski, Canada 1971 — 12/323; **9... ♖b8** 10. ♗h6 b5 11. ♖ae1 ♘d4 12. ♗g7 ♔g7 13. f4 f5 14. ♘d1 ♗d7 15. ♕f2!± Suttles–Padevski, Lugano (ol) 1968 — 6/404; **9... f5**±

20 12. ♖ae1 ♗h3 13. ♗h3 f5=

21 **13... ♗d5**?! 14. ed5 ♘d4!? [14... ♘b4? 15. fe5 de5 16. d4! ed4 17. ♘f4± Hug–Hübner, Skopje (ol) 1972 — 14/314] 15. c3 ♘df5 16. ♕f2!±; **13... ♕d7**=

22 **7... ♘ge7**±; **7... ♖b8**!? Estrin

23 Pachman; 8. f4!? Smislov

24 **8... ♗d7** 9. 0–0 ♕c7 10. ♘e1 h5 11. h3 ♗c6 12. ♘d1±; **8... ♘ge7** 9. 0–0 0–0 10. ♗h6! ♘f3 11. ♗f3 ♘c6 12. ♗g7 ♔g7 13. ♗g2± Pachman

25 9. 0–0 ♗h3!=

26 11. c3 ♘f3 12. ♗f3 ♗e6 13. ♗g2 ♕d7∓

27 15. c3 dc3 16. bc3 d5=

28 10. ♘d1 d5! 11. ♘c1 [11. c3 ♘e2 12. ♕e2 d4∓] e5! 12. c3 ♘e6∓ Bednarski–Korčnoj, Bucuresti 1966 — 1/236

29 10... ♘ec6 11. f5!?△ ♗h6±↑»

30 Kopilov–Petrosjan, SSSR (ch) 1949

31 8... ♘e7 9. c3 ♘c6 10. ♗h6 0–0 11. h4±↑»

32 11. f3 ♗e6=

33 15. ♘g5 ♗d7 16. ♖ac1 f6 17. ♘f3 f5 18. fe5 ♘e5 19. ♘e5 de5 20. d4±↑ Hort–Kurajica, Zagreb 1969 — 7/305

34 **8. ♘d1** ♕d2 9. ♔d2 ♘f6 10. h3 ♗d7 11. f4 e5 12. fe5 ♘e5 13. ♘e2 0–0 14. ♖f1 h6 15. ♘dc3 b5 16. a3 a5 1/2 : 1/2 Keres–Reshevsky, Helsinki (ol) 1952; **8. ♘f3** ♘d4 9. 0–0 ♗d7 10. a3 ♖c8 11. ♖ab1 b6∓ Augustin–D. Byrne, Lugano (ol) 1968 — 6/415; 10. ♘e1=

35 9... ♘e7 10. ♔h1 [10. f4!?±] ♗d7 11. f4 ♖b8 12. g4±↑ Smislov–Kottnauer, Moskva 1947

36 10. ♘e2 ♕d2 11. ♗d2 ♗b2?! 12. ♖b1 ♗g7 13. e5!±↑ Thomas–Kottnauer 1947; 11... ♘e7=

37 10... ♘e7 11. ♗d2±

38 12... ♘f6 13. f4 ♕a5 14. e5±

39 15. ♗b7 ♗b7 16. ♖b7=∞

40 **7. ♘d5**?! ♘ce7 8. ♘e7 ♘e7 9. ♕d2 0–0 10. ♘e2 ♗e6 11. h4 ♕b6 12. c4 h5∓ Smederevac–Ivkov, Jugoslavija (ch) 1955; **7. f4** ♘ge7 8. ♘f3 ♘d4 9. 0–0 0–0 10. ♖b1 ♗g4 11. ♘e2 f5 12. ♗d4 fe4 13. de4 cd4 14. c3 ♕b6= Evard–Polugajevski, SSSR 1959

41 7... ♗e6!? 8. f4 [8. ♘f3 h6 9. 0–0 ♘f6 10. h3 ♕d7 11. ♔h2 g5 12. ♘g1 ♘d4∓ Ignatjev–Bronštejn, SSSR 1962] ♘ge7 9. ♘f3 ♘d4 10. 0–0 0–0 11. ♖ae1 [11. ♖f2!? Hort] ♘f3 12. ♗f3 ♕d7= Hort–Talj, Wijk aan Zee 1968 — 5/339

42 **8. ♗h6** 0–0 9. h4?! ♗h6! [9... f5?! 10. h5 f4 11. ♗g7 ♔g7 12. hg6 ♘g6 13. 0-0-0 ±→» Smederevac–Bobocov, Beograd 1961] 10. ♕h6 f6! 11. ♕d2 ♘d4∓; 9. ♘ge2= Boleslavski; **8. ♘ge2** 0–0 9. 0–0 ♗e6! [Hort–Larsen, Sousse (izt) 1967 — 4/382] 10. f4=

43 9... ♗h3 10. 0–0 ♗g2 11. ♔g2 0–0 12. ♖ae1 ♕d7 13. ♘e2 b6 14. ♘eg1 ♘ec6 15. c3 ♘f3 16. ♘f3 d5= Hort–Johansson, ČSSR 1968 — 5/338

44 10... ♗g4 11. ♘h4 ef4 12. ♗f4 ♕d7 13. ♖ae1 ♖ae8 14. ♖f2 b5 15. ♘d1 ♗d1 16. ♖d1 d5 17. ♗e3 b4= Pachman–Bogdanović, Sarajevo 1963

45 15. ♖af1 ♕e7= Smislov–Talj, Leningrad 1962

46 Hort

47 10... ♗g4 11. 0–0 ef4 12. ♘f4 0–0 13. ♖f2 ♔h7 14. ♖af1 ♕d7 15. ♘cd5± Ćirić

48 **14... b4**?! 15. ♗d4 ed4 16. ♘b1± Ćirić–Kozomara, Sarajevo 1968 — 5/337; **14... ef4**!?∞

B 27 — 1. e4 c5 2. ♘f3

	2	3	4	5	6	7	8	9	10	
1	...	d4	♘d4	♗d3	0–0[2]	♘c3	♕e2	♗b5	♕g4	=
	b6	cd4	♗b7	d6[1]	♘f6	e6	♗e7	♘fd7[3]	0–0[4]	
2	...	...	...	♘c3	♗d3[6]	f4	♘f3	0–0	♕e1	±
	...	...	...	a6[5]	g6[7]	♗g7	d6	♘f6	0–0[8]	
3	...	d4[9]	♘d4	♘c3	f4?![10]	e5[11]	♘cb5[12]	ef6	♘b5	=
	♕c7	cd4	♘f6	a6	b5	b4	ab5	gf6	♕c6[13]	
4	...	c3	e5	d4	♕d4[14]	♗c4	♕e4	♗f4	♗g3	=
	...	♘f6	♘d5	cd4	e6	♘c6[15]	♘de7!?	♘g6	d6	

1. e4 c5 2. ♘f3 g6										
	3	4	5	6	7	8	9	10	11	
5	d4[16] ♗g7	dc5[17] ♕a5[18]	♘c3[19] ♘f6[20]	♘d2[21] ♕c5	♘c4 ♕c6[22]	♘d5[23] ♘d5	ed5 ♕f6	♗d2 0–0	♗c3 ♕f4[24]	∞
6	. . . . . .	♘c3 ♕a5[25]	♗e3[26] ♘f6[27]	♕d2[28] ♘c6[29]	dc5[30] ♘g4	♗c4[31] ♕b4	♗b3 0–0[32]	0–0 ♗c3	bc3 ♕e4[33]	±
7	. . . cd4	♕d4[34] ♘f6[35]	e5 ♘c6	♕a4[36] ♘d5	♕e4[37] ♘db4	♗b5[38] ♕a5	♘c3 d5	♕e2[39] ♗g4	0–0 d4![40]	∓
8	. . . . . .	. . . . . .	♗b5 ♘c6[41]	♗c6 bc6[42]	e5 ♘d5	0–0[43] ♗g7	♕h4 0–0	♗h6[44]		±
9	♗c4 ♗g7	0–0 ♘c6	c3 d6	d4 ♘f6	e5[45] de5	♘e5[46] ♘e5[47]	de5 ♕d1	♖d1 ♘d7	f4	±
10	c3 ♗g7	d4 cd4	cd4 d5	e5 ♗g4[48]	♗b5[49] ♘c6[50]	♘bd2[51] ♕b6	♗c6 ♕c6	0–0 ♖c8	♖e1 ♕c2[52]	=
11	. . . . . .	. . . . . .	. . . . . .	ed5 ♘f6[53]	♗b5 ♘bd7	d6[54] ♕a5	♘c3 ♘e4	0–0 ♘d6	♗a4 0–0[55]	±

1 5... ♘c6 6. ♘c6 ♗c6 7. 0–0 e6 8. ♕e2 ♕h4 9. ♘d2 ♘f6 10. ♘f3 ♕h5 11. ♖e1 ♗c5 12. h3± Geler–Džindžihašvili, SSSR 1971

2 6. c4 ♘f6 7. ♘c3 e6 8. 0–0 ♗e7=

3 9... ♘bd7? 10. ♘c6 ♗c6 11. ♗c6±

4 11. ♗e3 ♘f6 12. ♕h3 a6 13. ♗d3 ♘bd7 14. f3 ♕c7 15. g4= Bakulin–Volovič, SSSR 1964

5 **5... e6**? 6. ♘db5! a6 [6... d6? 7. ♗f4 e5 8. ♘d5! ♘a6 9. ♗e3 ♗e7 10. ♗c4 ♘f6 11. ♘f6 gf6 12. ♕h5 0–0 13. ♘c3! ♘c5 14. ♗h6 ♘e6 15. 0-0-0+– Hecht–Velimirović, Budapest 1973 — 15/314] 7. ♘d6 ♗d6 8. ♕d6 ♘c6 9. ♗e3±; **5... g6**?! 6. ♗c4 ♗g7 7. 0–0 ♘c6 8. ♗e3 ♘a5 9. ♗d3 ♖c8 10. ♕e2 ♘c6 11. ♘c6 dc6 12. f4± Konstantinov–Vasiljčuk, SSSR 1964; **5... ♘c6** 6. ♗e3 ♘f6 7. f3 e6 8. ♕d2 a6 9. ♗e2 ♕c7 10. ♘b3 ♗b4 11. a3 ♗c3 12. ♕c3± Konstantinov–Katalimov, SSSR 1964

6 **6. ♗g5**?! h6 7. ♗h4 ♘c6 8. ♘f5 d6= Nežmetdinov–Katalimov, SSSR 1964; **6. ♗c4** e6 7. 0–0 b5 8. ♗b3 b4? 9. ♘a4 ♗e4 10. ♖e1 ♘f6 11. ♗g5 ♗c6 12. ♕e2 ♕a5 13. ♗f6 gf6 14. ♖ad1± Estrin–Katalimov, SSSR 1969 — 7/310; 8... ♘c6±; 7... ♘c6±

7 6... e6 7. 0–0 ♕c7 8. ♗e3 d6 9. f4 ♘f6 10. ♕f3 ♘bd7 11. ♕g3 h5?! 12. f5!± Abakarov–Anohin, SSSR 1964

8 11. ♕h4 ♘bd7 12. ♗d2 ♖c8 13. ♖ae1 ♘c5 14. f5 gf5 15. ef5 d5 16. ♗e3 b5 17. ♗d4± Vasjukov–Katalimov, SSSR 1966; 12... b5!±

9 **3. c4** e5=; **3. ♘c3** a6 4. a4?! e6 5. ♗c4 [5. d4 cd4 6. ♘d4 ♗b4!∓] ♘c6 6. 0–0 ♗d6 7. d3 ♘ge7 8. ♗e3 b6 9. ♔h1 0–0= Puc–Quinteros, Ljubljana–Portorož 1973 — 15/313; 4. d4 cd4 5. ♘d4 e6 — B 43

10 **6. g3**; **6. ♗d3**; **6. ♗e2**

11 **7. ♗d3** b4 8. ♘d5 [8. ♘ce2 ♗b7 9. ♘g3 h5!∓] ♘d5 9. ed5 ♕c5∞; **7. a3** ♗b7 8. ♗d3 e6=

12 **8. ef6** bc3 9. fe7 ♗e7 10. ♗e2 0–0∞; **8. ♘ce2** ♘e4∞

13 11. ♕d5 ♘a6 12. ♕c6 dc6 13. ♘d4 ♗d7 14. ♗d2 e5 15. fe5 fe5 16. ♘f3 f6 17. ♗c4 ♘c7= Tringov–Quinteros, Čačak 1970 — 10/391

14 6. cd4 d6!=

15 7... ♘b6 8. ♗b3 ♘c6 9. ♕e4 d5 10. ♕e2 ♘d7 11. ♗f4 b6 [11... f6 12. ♗d5±] 12. 0–0 ♘c5 13. ♘a3! ♗a6 14. ♘b5 ♕d7 15. c4± Honfi–Quinteros, Čačak 1970 — 10/392; 9... d6!±

16 3. c4 ♗g7 4. d4 d6 [4... cd4 5. ♘d4 ♘c6 — B 37] 5. ♘c3 ♘c6 6. ♗e3 ♕a5 [6... ♕b6 7. ♘a4 ♕a5 8. ♗d2 ♕c7 9. d5 ♘d4 10. ♘d4 ♗d4 11. ♗c3±; 6... ♗g4 7. dc5 dc5 8. ♕d8 ♖d8 9. ♗c5 ♗f3 10. gf3 ♗d4 11. ♗d4 ♘d4 12. 0-0-0± Euwe] 7. d5 ♗c3 8. bc3 ♘e5 9. ♘e5 ♕c3 10. ♗d2 ♕e5 11. ♗d3∞

17 4. d5 — A

18 4... ♘a6? 5. ♗a6 ♕a5 6. c3 ♕a6 7. ♕e2 ♕c6 8. ♗e3 ♕e4 9. ♘bd2 ♕c6 10. 0–0 ♘f6 11. ♘d4 ♕c7 12. ♘b5 ♕d8 13. ♗f4± Rajna–Nagy, Hungary 1960

19 5. ♗d2 ♕c5 6. ♗c3 ♘f6 7. ♗d3 ♘c6 8. 0–0 d6 9. ♘bd2 0–0 10. ♘b3 ♕b6 11. a4 e5 12. ♖e1 ♕c7 13. ♗c4 ♗e6= Janošević–Szabo, Budapest 1965

20 **5. . . ♕c5** 6. ♘d5!±; **5. . . ♗c3** 6. bc3 ♘f6 [6. . . ♕c3 7. ♕d2?! ♕a1 8. c3 ♘a6!∞; 7. ♗d2! ♕c5 8. ♖b1±] 7. ♗d3 ♘c6 8. 0–0 ♕c5 9. ♖b1 a6 10. ♗e3 ♕h5 11. e5 ♘d5 12. ♗d2! ♘e5 13. ♘e5 ♕e5 14. ♖e1 ♕f6 15. ♕c1± Klovski–Veresov, SSSR 1967

21 6. ♗d3 ♕c5 7. 0–0 d6 8. ♗e3 ♕h5=

22 **7. . . d6** 8. ♗e3 ♕c7 9. e5! de5 10. ♘b5 ♕d8 11. ♕d8 ♔d8 12. 0-0-0±; **7. . . 0–0** 8. e5 ♘g4 9. ♕g4 d5 10. ♗e3! ♕b4 11. ♕h4 dc4 12. 0-0-0 ♘c6 13. ♖d5± Lutikov–Larsen, Beverwijk 1967 — 3/360

23 8. e5? ♘e4 9. ♘d5 e6!=

24 12. ♗g7 ♔g7 13. ♗d3 d6! [13. . . b5 14. ♘e3 ♕b4 15. ♕d2 ♕b2 16. 0–0 d6 17. ♖ab1± Velimirović–Forintos, Budapest 1973 — 15/317] 14. ♕d2 ♕f6∞ Velimirović

25 4. . . cd4 5. ♘d4 ♘c6 — B 34

26 5. d5 — A

27 5. . . ♘c6 6. d5 ♘e5 7. ♘d2 d6 8. ♗e2 a6 9. 0–0 ♘f6 10. h3 0–0 11. f4 ♘ed7 12. ♘c4 ♕c7 13. a4 ♖b8 14. a5± German–Bilek, Stockholm (izt) 1962

28 6. ♘d2 cd4 7. ♘b3 ♕c7 8. ♗d4 0–0 9. e5 ♘e8 10. ♘b5 ♕d8 11. ♘a7 ♘c7 12. ♘b5 ♘b5 13. ♗b5 ♘c6± Bobocov–Bilek, Sarajevo 1962

29 6. . . ♘g4? 7. ♘d5 ♕d8 8. ♗f4 d6 9. dc5 ♗b2 10. cd6 ed6 11. ♖d1 0–0 12. c3 ♗a3 13. h3 ♘f6 14. ♗g5± Alexander–Kotov, Hastings 1963

30 7. d5!? ♘b4 8. e5 ♘g4 9. ♗f4 f6 10. ef6 ♘f6± De Greiff–Haag, La Habana 1962

31 8. ♘d5!?

32 9. . . ♘e3 10. ♕e3! ♘d4 11. 0-0-0 e5 12. ♘d5 ♕c5 13. ♘d4 ed4 14. ♕g5! b6 15. ♘f6 ♔f8 16. ♗d5+–

33 12. ♗d4±

34 4. ♘d4 ♘c6 — B 34

35 4. . . f6? 5. c4±

36 **6. ♕d3**? ♘g4 7. ♕e4 ♘ge5 8. ♘e5 ♕a5–+; **6. ♕c4**? d5 7. ♕f4 ♘g4 8. ♘c3 d4! 9. ♘e4 ♗g7–+; **6. ♕h4** ♘e5!? 7. ♘e5 ♕a5 8. ♘c3 ♕e5 9. ♗e2∓

37 7. c4? ♘c7! 8. ♘c3 ♘e6! 9. ♗d2 ♗g7 10. ♘d5 0–0 11. ♗c3 ♘c5 12. ♕c2 d6∓ Unzicker–Eisinger, BRD 1949

38 8. a3 d5! 9. ♕e2 ♘a6 10. b4 ♘c7 11. ♗b2 ♗g7 12. g3 ♗g4 13. ♘bd2 ♘e6 14. 0-0-0 ♗h6 15. ♕d3 ♕b6 16. h3 ♗f5 17. ♕e2 ♖c8∓ Štejnberg–Židkov, SSSR 1968 — 5/345; 12. ♘bd2∓

39 10. ed6 ♗f5 11. ♕e5 ♘c2 12. ♔e2 0-0-0 13. ♕h8 ♘a1∓

40 **11. . . a6**? 12. ♗a4 b5 13. a3+–; **11. . . 0-0-0** 12. a3 ♘d4 [12. . . ♗f3 13. ♕f3 ♘e5 (13. . . ♘c2 14. ♗c6 bc6 15. ♖b1 ♘d4 16. ♕f7±) 14. ♕h3! e6 (14. . . ♘d7 15. ab4 ♕a1 16. ♘d5+–) 15. ab4 ♕a1 16. ♗f4 ♕b2 (16. . . ♕f1 17. ♗f1 ♗g7 18. ♘b5 1 : 0 Adorjan–Sax, Budapest 1973 — 15/316) 17. ♗e5 ♖g8 18. ♕h7 1 : 0 Romanišin–Kuprejčik, SSSR 1971 — 11/272] 13. ♘d4 ♗e2 14. ab4 ♕a1 15. ♗e2 ♗h6 16. ♗h6 ♕b2 17. ♗d2 ♕b4∓; **11. . . d4**! 12. ♘e4 ♗f3 13. gf3 d3! 14. ♗d3 ♘d3 15. ♗d2 ♕a6 16. ♕d3 ♕d3 17. cd3 ♘e5∓ Krnić–Sax, Vrnjačka Banja 1974

41 5. . . a6 6. e5±

42 6. . . dc6 7. ♕d8 ♔d8±

43 8. e6?! ♘f6 9. ef7 ♔f7=

44 Bokučava–Gavašelišvili, SSSR 1974 — 17/346

45 **7. ♖e1** cd4 8. cd4 0–0∞; **7. d5**!? ♘a5 8. ♗d3 c4 9. ♗c2 0–0 10. b4!±

46 8. de5 ♕d1 9. ♖d1 ♘g4 10. e6 ♗e6 11. ♗e6 fe6 12. ♘a3$\overline{\overline{\infty}}$

47 8. . . 0–0 9. ♘c6 bc6 10. dc5 ♕c7 11. ♘d2 ♗f5 12. ♕e2± Dünhaupt–Behnke, corr. 1969 — 8/301

48 6. . . ♘c6 7. h3 ♘h6 8. ♘c3 0–0 9. ♗b5 ♔h8 10. 0–0 f6= Andersson–Dueball, Berlin 1971 — 12/328

49 7. ♗e2 ♘c6 8. 0–0 e6 9. ♘c3 ♘ge7△ ♘f5=

50 7. . . ♘d7 8. ♘bd2 e6 9. 0–0 ♘e7 10. h3 ♗f3 11. ♘f3 0–0 12. ♖e1 a6 13. ♗d3 ♘b8 14. ♗g5 h6 15. ♗e3 ♘f5= Matulović–Parma, Skopje–Ohrid, 1968 — 6/423

51 8. ♘c3 ♘h6 9. 0–0 0–0 10. ♗c6 bc6 11. ♗h6 ♗h6 12. ♘a4 f6!∓

52 12. ♕e2 a6 13. h3 ♗f5 14. ♘f1 ♕e2 15. ♖e2 ♗d3= Matulović–Bellon, Skopje (ol) 1972 — 14/319

53 6. . . ♕d5 7. ♘c3 ♕d8 8. ♗e3 ♘c6 9. ♗b5 e6 [9. . . ♗d7 10. 0–0 a6 11. ♗e2! ♗g4 12. d5 ♗f3 13. ♗f3 ♘e5 14. d6 ♘f3 15. ♕f3 ♕d6 16. ♕b7+– Suetin–Arnaudov, Albena 1970; 11. . . e6 12. d5!±] 10. 0–0 ♘e7 11. d5! ♘d5 12. ♘d5 ♕d5 13. ♕a4±

54 8. ♘c3 0–0 9. d6 [9. 0–0 ♘b6∓] ed6 10. 0–0 ♘b6=

55 12. ♖e1 ♘f6 13. ♗b3 e6 14. ♗f4!± Tukmakov–Semenov, SSSR 1971 — 12/327

B 28 — 1. e4 c5 2. ♘f3 a6[1]

	3	4	5	6	7	8	9	10	11	
1	b4[2] cb4[3]	a3[4] ba3[5]	♗a3[6] d6	d4 ♘f6	♘bd2 g6	♗c4 ♗g7	0–0 0–0	e5 ♘e8	♗a2 ♘c6[7]	∞
2	♘c3 b5[8]	d4 cd4	♘d4 ♗b7	♗d3[9] b4?![10]	♘a4[11] e5[12]	♘f5 g6	♘e3 ♘f6	0–0[13] ♘e4[14]	♘c4	±
3	d4 cd4	♘d4[15] ♘f6[16]	♘c3[17] e5	♘de2[18] ♗c5[19]	♘g3 d6[20]	♗e2 ♗e6[21]	0–0 0–0	♔h1 d5	ed5 ♘d5[22]	=
4	... ...	... ...	... ...	♘b3 ♗b4	♗d2[23] 0–0[24]	♗d3 ♗c3[25]	♗c3 d5	ed5 ♕d5		=
5	... ...	... ...	... ...	♘f3 ♗b4[26]	♗d2[27] d6[28]	♗d3 ♘bd7[29]	a3[30] ♗c3	♗c3 ♘c5	♗b4 ♕c7[31]	∓
6	... ...	... ...	... ...	... ...	♗c4 ♕c7[32]	♗b3 0–0[33]	0–0 ♗c3	bc3 d6[34]	♖e1 ♘bd7[35]	=
7	... ...	... ...	... ...	... ...	... ...	♕d3 b5[36]	♗b3 ♗b7[37]	♗d2[38] ♗c3[39]	♗c3 d6[40]	∞
8	c3 d6[41]	d4 ♘d7[42]	♗d3[43] e6[44]	0–0 ♘gf6[45]	♕e2 b5	a4 c4	♗c2 ♗b7	♗g5 ♗e7	♘a3 ♕b6[46]	±
9	... ♘f6	e5 ♘d5	d4[47] cd4[48]	cd4[49] d6[50]	♗c4[51] ♘c7[52]	ed6 ♕d6	0–0 e6	♘c3 ♗e7	♘e4 ♕d8[53]	±
10	... d5	ed5 ♕d5[54]	d4 e6[55]	♗d3[56] ♘f6	0–0 ♗e7[57]	♘a3[58] 0–0	♘c4 ♕d8	a4 ♘bd7	♘fe5 cd4[59]	±
11	... ...	... ...	... ♘f6	♗e2[60] e6[61]	0–0 ♗e7[62]	♗e3[63] cd4[64]	cd4[65] ♘c6[66]	♘c3 ♕d6[67]	♘d2 ♘b4[68]	±
12	c4 ♘c6[69]	d4 cd4	♘d4 ♘f6[70]	♘c3 e5	♘c2[71] ♗c5	♗e3[72] d6	♗e2 ♗e6	0–0 0–0	♕d2 ♘b4[73]	=
13	... ...	... ...	... ...	... ...	♘f5 d5[74]	cd5 ♗f5	ef5 ♘d4	♗d3[75] ♘d5	0–0[76] ♗b4[77]	±

[1] O'Kelly

[2] **3. b3** ♘c6 4. ♗b2 d6 5. d4 cd4 6. ♘d4 e5 7. ♘c6 bc6 8. c4 ♘f6 9. ♘c3 ♗e7= Čistjakov–Sardarov, SSSR 1962; **3. ♗e2** d6 4. 0–0 ♘f6 5. ♘c3 e5 6. d3 ♗e7= Aronin–Bronštejn, SSSR 1962; **3. d3**; **3. g3**

[3] 3... d6 4. b5?! e6 5. ♘c3 ♗e7 6. ♗e2 ♘d7 7. 0–0 ♘gf6 8. d4 cd4 9. ♘d4 ♕c7∓ Stalda–Szabo, Venezia 1949; 4. ♗b2!?∞

[4] 4. d4 d5 5. ed5 ♘f6 6. a3 [6. ♗d3 b5 7. 0–0 ♕d5 8. a4=∞ Bokučava–Grigorjan, SSSR 1968] ♕d5 7. ab4 ♗g4 8. ♗e2 e6 9. 0–0 ♗b4 10. c4 ♕d7 11. ♕b3=∞ Dementjev–Terentjev, SSSR 1959

[5] **4... d5** 5. ed5 ♘f6 [5... ♕d5?! 6. ab4 ♗g4 7. ♘c3 ♕h5? 8. ♗e2 e6 9. 0–0 ♘f6 10. ♖a5!± Keres–Gauffin 1936] 6. ab4 ♘d5 7. b5=; **4... e6** 5. d4 d5 6. e5 ba3 7. ♗d3 f5 8. ♘a3 ♗b4 9. ♔f1 ♘e7 10. ♘b5 0–0 11. h4∞ Kinnmark–Hamann, Halle 1963; **4... b5**!? 5. d4 [5. ab4 ♗b7 6. c4?! bc4 7. ♗c4 e6 8. 0–0 ♗e4 9. d4 ♘f6 10. ♘c3 ♗b7 11. d5 ♗b4 12. ♖b1 a5∓ Planinc–Ljubojević, Jugoslavija 1970; 6. d3!?] ♗b7 6. ♗d3∞

[6] 5. ♘a3 e6 6. d4 d5 7. e5 ♘c6= Keres

[7] Bokučava–Raškovski, SSSR 1971

[8] **3... g6** 4. d4 cd4 5. ♕d4 ♘f6 6. e5 ♘c6 7. ♕h4 ♘h5 8. ♗c4 ♕a5 9. 0–0 b5 10. ♗b3 ♗b7 11. ♗d2 ♕d8 12. ♘e4± Nežmetdinov–Tarasov, SSSR 1962; **3... ♘c6** 4. d4 cd4 5. ♘d4 e5?! [5... e6 — B 46] 6. ♘c6 [6. ♘f5 d6 (Filipowicz–Heerst, Warszawa 1962) 7. ♗d3!?] bc6 [6... dc6?! 7. ♕d8 ♔d8 8. ♗c4 f6 9. ♗e3 b5 10. ♗b3 ♔c7 11. a4! b4 12. ♘b1 a5 13. ♘d2 ♗a6 14. ♗c4± Rossolimo–H. Steiner, Venezia 1950] 7. ♗c4 ♗b4 8. ♗d2

♘f6 9. ♕f3± Kotov; **3... e6** 4. d4 cd4 5. ♘d4 — B 43; **3... d6** — B 50

9 6. a3 ♘c6 7. ♗e3 ♘f6 8. ♘c6 dc6 9. ♗e2 ♕d1 10. ♖d1 e5= Osmanović–Ugrinović, Jugoslavija 1966

10 △ 6... e6 — B 43

11 7. ♘b1 e5 8. ♘f3 d6 9. c3 ♘f6 10. ♕e2 ♘bd7 11. ♗g5 h6 12. ♗f6 ♘f6 13. 0–0 bc3 14. ♘c3 ♗e7= Suetin–Tajmanov, SSSR (ch) 1965

12 **7... ♕a5**?! 8. b3 ♘f6 9. 0–0! ♘e4 10. ♖e1 ♘d6 11. ♗f4 e6 12. ♖e5 ♕c7 13. ♕g4 ♘c6 14. ♘c6 ♗c6 15. ♘c5± Privorotski–Sardarov, SSSR 1967 — 3/362; **7...** ♘f6!?

13 **10. f3**? ♗e7 11. 0–0 0–0 12. a3 ♘c6 13. ab4 ♘b4 14. ♗e2 a5 15. c3 ♘a6 16. ♘c4 d5!∓ Liberzon–Tajmanov, SSSR (ch) 1967; **10. ♘c4!?**

14 10... ♗e7 11. ♘c4 d5 12. ♘e5 de4 13. ♗c4 ♘d5 14. ♘b6!±

15 **4. ♗c4** e6 5. 0–0 ♕c7 6. ♗b3 ♘c6 7. ♘d4 ♘f6 8. ♘c3 ♗b4 9. ♘de2 ♗e7 10. ♗f4 d6 11. ♕d3 0–0 12. ♖ad1 ♖d8 13. ♘g3 ♘e5= Cortlever–Auer, Helsinki (ol) 1952; **4. c3**!? dc3 5. ♘c3 e6 [5... ♘c6 6. ♗c4 d6 — B 21] 6. ♗c4 ♘f6?! 7. e5 d5 8. ef6 dc4 9. ♕d8 ♔d8 10. ♗g5 ♔e8 11. 0-0-0± Šmatkov–Bebčuk, SSSR 1967 — 4/390; 6... d6 7. 0–0 ♘c6 8. ♕e2 ♘f6 — B 21

16 **4... e5** 5. ♘f3 [5. ♘b3 ♘f6 6. ♗g5 ♗e7 7. ♘c3 0–0 8. ♗f6 ♗f6 9. ♗c4 b5 10. ♗d5 ♘c6 11. 0–0 ♖b8 12. a3 ♕b6 13. ♖e1 ♔h8 14. ♕d3 g6∞ Milić–Tajmanov, Jugoslavija–SSSR 1959] ♘c6 [5... ♘f6 6. ♗c4 ♕c7 7. ♕e2 b5 8. ♗b3 ♗b7 9. ♘g5 ♗b4 (Mihaljev–Solovjev, SSSR 1958) 10. ♗d2 ♗d2 11. ♘bd2=] 6. ♗c4 h6 7. 0–0 ♘f6 8. ♘c3 ♗c5 9. a3 d6∞ Ortega–Letelier, La Habana 1964; **4... e6** — B 41

17 **5. ♘d2** ♘c6 6. ♘c6 dc6 7. ♗d3 e5 8. 0–0 ♗g4 9. ♕e1 ♗c5 10. ♘b3 ♗a7 11. ♗e3 ♕c7= Spielmann–Tartakower (m) 1921; **5. ♗d3** e5 6. ♘b3 ♘c6 7. 0–0 [Winiwarter–Ortega, Tel Aviv (ol) 1964] d5!? 8. ed5 ♘d5=

18 6. ♘f5?! d5 7. ♗g5 [7. ♘g3 d4∓ Kamenjev–Balmazi, SSSR 1964] ♗f5 [7... d4 8. ♗f6 ♕f6 9. ♘d5 ♕d8=] 8. ef5 ♗b4 9. ♗f6 ♕f6 10. ♕d5 0–0=∞

19 **6... ♘c6** 7. ♗g5 ♗c5 8. ♕d2 h6 9. ♗e3 ♗e3 10. fe3 0–0 11. 0-0-0 d6∞ Toluš–Peterson, SSSR 1960; **6... d6** 7. ♗g5 ♗e6 8. ♘d5 ♗d5 9. ed5 ♕a5 10. ♘c3 ♘bd7= Smailbegović–Ugrinović, Jugoslavija (ch) 1962; 7. g3!?

20 7... ♕b6 8. ♕d2 [8. ♕f3?! d6 9. ♘f5 ♗f5 10. ♕f5 ♘c6 11. ♗d3 ♘d4 12. ♕h3 ♗b4 13. 0–0 ♗c3 14. bc3 ♘e6 15. ♗e3 ♕c6∓ Ledić–Tajmanov, Vinkovci 1970] 0–0 [8... ♘g4?! 9. ♘d1 ♕g6 10. b4!± Fletzer–Prins, Venezia 1949; 8... ♘c6 9. ♘f5 0–0 10. ♘g7 ♗f2 11. ♕f2 ♕f2 12. ♔f2 ♔g7= Barczay–Holmov, Pecs 1964] 9. ♘a4 ♕c6 10. ♘c5 ♕c5 11. c4 ♘c6 12. ♗d3 h5= Ujtumen–Tajmanov, Palma de Mallorca (izt) 1970

21 8... h5!? 9. 0–0 ♘g4 10. h3 ♕h4∞

22 12. ♘d5 ♗d5 13. ♗f3 ♗c4 14. ♕d8 ♖d8 [Koch–Euwe, Berlin 1950] 15. ♗g5! f6 16. ♖fd1=⊥

23 **7. ♗d3** d5 8. ed5 [8. ♗g5 d4 9. a3 ♗c3 10. bc3 dc3 11. 0–0 ♘bd7∓ Makarov–Mnacakanjan, SSSR 1961] e4![8... ♘d5?! 9. 0–0!? ♘c3 10. bc3 ♗c3 11. ♗a3 ♘c6∞ Martius–Heinicke, BRD 1967] 9. ♗e2 ♘d5 10. ♕d4 0–0 11. 0–0 ♗c3 12. bc3 ♘c6 13. ♕c5 ♗e6 14. ♖d1 ♖c8 15. ♗a3 ♖fe8 16. c4 b6 17. ♕d6 ♘c3!∓ Poletajev–Fink, corr. 1957; **7. ♕d3** d5 8. ed5 [8. a3?! ♗c3 9. ♕c3 0–0 10. ed5 ♘d5 11. ♕g3 ♗f5!∓ van Steenis–O'Kelly, Beverwijk 1949] ♘d5∓ Platt–O'Kelly, Trenčanske Teplice 1949; **7. ♗g5** h6 [7... ♕c7?! 8. ♕f3 d5?! 10. ed5 e4 10. ♕g3 ♕g3 11. hg3 ♗c3 12. bc3 ♘d5 13. 0-0-0± Timofejeva–Pahomova, SSSR 1960; 7... d6!?] 8. ♗h4 d6 9. f3 ♗e6 10. ♗e2 ♗c3 11. bc3 ♕c7∓; **7. ♗c4** ♕c7 8. ♕d3 b5 9. ♗d5 ♘d5 10. ed5 0–0 11. 0–0∞ Muhin–Mnacakanjan, SSSR 1963

24 7... d6 8. ♗d3 ♘bd7 9. a3!? ♗c3 10. ♗c3∞

25 8... d6 9. 0–0 ♘bd7 10. a3!? [10. ♕f3?! b5 11. ♖ad1 ♗b7∓ Ramačandran–Aaron, India 1971] ♗c3 11. ♗c3∞

26 **6... d6**?! 7. ♗g5 — B 94; **6... ♕c7** 7. ♗d3 [7. a3 d6 8. ♗g5 ♘bd7 9. ♘d2 b5 10. ♗e2 ♗b7 11. ♗f3 h6 12. ♗h4 ♗e7 13. 0–0 ♘c5= Vuruna–Ugrinović, Jugoslavija 1966] d6 8. a4 ♘bd7 [8... ♗e6!? 9. ♗g5 ♘bd7] 9. a5 ♗e7 10. 0–0 ♘c5?! [Janošević–Ugrinović, Italia 1968 — 6/425] 11. ♗g5! ♗e6 12. ♕e2 ♘d3 13. cd3±

27 **7. ♕d3**?! d5∓; **7. ♘e5** 0–0! [7... ♕e7?! 8. ♘c4! ♘e4 9. ♗e2! ♘c3 10. bc3 ♗c3 11. ♔f1 ♗a1 12. ♗a3!→±] 8. ♗d3 d5 9. 0–0 ♗c3 10. bc3 de4 11. ♗e2 ♕c7∓ Keres–Olafsson, Jugoslavija (ct) 1959; **7. ♗g5** d6 8. ♗c4 h6 9. ♗d2 ♘bd7 10. ♘d5 ♘d5 11. ♗d5 ♗c5 12. b4 ♗b6 13. ♕e2 ♘f6 14. ♗b3 ♗e6∓ Smislov–H. Müller, Venezia 1950

28 7... 0–0 8. ♗d3 ♘c6 9. ♘d5 [9. 0–0 ♗e3 10. ♗c3 d5!] ♗d2 10. ♕d2 d6=

29 **8... 0–0** 9. 0–0 ♗g4 10. a3 ♗c5 11. ♗g5 h6 12. ♗f6 ♕f6 13. ♘d5 ♕d8 14. ♗e2 ♘d7 15. ♕d3 ♗a7 16. b4± Vinkelj–Sardarov, SSSR 1962; **8... ♕c7** 9. 0–0 ♗c3 10. ♗c3 ♘bd7 11. ♖e1 0–0 12. ♗d2 b5 13. ♖c1 ♖b8 14. c4 b4∞ Pederssen–Arnlind, corr. 1963

30 **9. 0–0** ♘c5 10. ♕e2 0–0 11. ♖ad1 b5 12. a3 ♗c3 13. ♗c3 ♘a4! 14. ♕d2 ♘c3 15. ♕c3 ♗g4!∓ Snaevarr–Euwe, Reykjavik 1948; **9. ♘e2** ♗d2 10. ♕d2 ♘c5 11. ♘g3 0–0 12.

0–0 ♗g4 13. ♕e3 ♖c8∓ Panov–Žiljin, SSSR 1960

31 12. ♘d2 ♗e6 13. 0–0 0–0∓ P. Schmidt–O'Kelly, Beverwijk 1949

32 7... ♘e4? 8. ♗f7 ♔f7 9. ♕d5±

33 **8... ♘e4?** 9. ♗f7 ♔f7 10. ♕d5 ♔e8 11. ♕e4 ♗c3 12. bc3 ♕c3 13. ♔e2 ♕a1 14. ♘e5+–→; **8... d6** 9. 0–0 ♗c3 10. bc3 ♘bd7 [10... ♘e4? 11. ♗a3! ♘d7?! 12. ♗f7!± N. Hansen–Euwe, Copenhagen 1949; 11... ♗g4 12. ♖e1 ♘c5 13. ♗c5 ♕c5 14. ♗f7± Geler–Holmov, SSSR 1957] 11. ♖e1 0–0 — 8... 0–0; **8... ♗c3** 9. bc3 ♕c3 10. ♗d2 ♕c7? 11. ♘g5 0–0 12. ♗b4±→ Tajmanov; 10... ♕c5!∞

34 10... ♘e4?! 11. ♖e1! d5 [11... ♘c3 12. ♕d2 d6 13. ♗b2 ♘b5 14. a4 ♘a7 15. ♗a3 ♖d8 16. ♖ad1±] 12. ♕d5 ♘c3 [Geler–Tajmanov, SSSR 1957] 13. ♕e5! ♕e5 14. ♘e5±⊥

35 12. ♗g5 h6 13. ♗h4 b6= Gligorić, Sokolov

36 8... d6 9. ♗d2 [9. 0–0!? ♘bd7 10. ♘d5± Rozenberg–Simovič, SSSR 1959] ♘bd7 [9... ♗e6 10. ♗e6 fe6 11. ♘g5 ♕d7 12. ♕h3 ♔e7 13. 0-0-0± Šapošnikov–Kovalev, corr. 1964] 10. ♘d5 ♗d2 11. ♘d2 11. ♘d2 ♘d5 12. ♗d5 ♘c5 13. ♕c3± Ortega–Honfi, Varna (ol) 1962

37 9... ♗c3?! 10. bc3 ♗b7 11. ♘g5 d5 12. ed5 ♕d7 13. ♗a3 ♕g4 14. ♕e3 ♘bd7 15. f3 ♕h4 16. g3 ♕h5 17. 0-0-0+– Bogdanov–Lomaja, SSSR 1959

38 10. 0–0?! ♗c3 11. ♕c3 ♕c3 12. bc3 d6 13. ♗a3 ♘e4∞ Ćirić–Vošpernik, Jugoslavija (ch) 1968

39 10... 0–0?! 11. 0-0-0 ♖c8 12. ♖he1 d6 13. ♘g5 ♖f8 14. ♘d5 ♘d5? 15. ed5 ♗d2 16. ♖d2+–→ Romanov–Štirov, SSSR 1964

40 **12. ♘d2?** ♘bd7 12. f3 0–0 14. 0-0-0?! ♘c5 15. ♕e2 a5! 16. ♕b5 a4 17. ♗c4 ♖fb8 18. ♕b4 a3–+ Strekalovski–Bastrikov, SSSR 1958; **12. ♘g5** 0–0 13. 0-0-0 [13. ♗b4 h6∞] h6 14. h4 ♘c6 15. ♘f3 ♖ad8∞ Alexander–Prins, Bern 1962; **12. 0-0-0**!? Sokolov

41 **3... g6** 4. d4 cd4 5. cd4 ♗g7 6. ♘c3 d6 7. ♗c4 ♘f6 8. ♗g5 b5 9. ♗b3 ♘c6 10. ♕e2± Kuzin–Grišanik, SSSR 1957; **3... e6** 4. d4 d5 [4... ♕c7 5. ♗d3 d6 6. 0–0 ♘d7 7. ♖e1 ♘e7 8. ♘bd2 ♘g6 9. ♘f1± Parma–Ničevski, Zagreb 1970; 5. d5!?] 5. e5 ♘d7 [5... ♘c6 6. ♗d3! cd4 7. cd4 ♘ge7 8. ♘c3 ♘f5 (Ivkov–R. Byrne, Sarajevo 1967) 9. ♗c2± Ivkov; 5... ♗d7!? 6. ♗d3 ♗b5 Haberditz] 6. ♗d3 h6 7. 0–0 ♘e7 8. ♖e1 ♘c6 9. ♘bd2 ♕b6 10. dc5 ♗c5 11. ♕e2 ♕c7 12. c4± Balašov–Szabo, Soči 1973; **3... b5** 4. d4 ♗b7 5. ♗d3 e6 [5... cd4 6. cd4 ♘f6 7. ♘bd2 e6 8. 0–0 ♗e7 9. ♖e1 0–0 10. ♘b3 ♘c6 11. ♗g5 h6 12. ♗h4 ♕b6 13. ♗b1 d6 14. e5± Balašov–Skvorcov, SSSR 1969; 5... c4 6. ♗c2 d5 7. e5 e6 8. 0–0 ♘c6 9. ♘g5 g6 10. f4±→ Korzin–Vasiljčuk, SSSR 1961] 6. 0–0 ♘f6 7. ♘bd2 ♘c6 8. ♖e1 d5 [8... cd4!? Sokolov] 9. e5 ♘d7 10. ♘f1 ♕b6 11. ♗e3± Browne–Ljubojević, Wijk aan Zee 1972

42 **4... cd4** 5. cd4 ♘f6 6. ♘c3 g6 7. ♗g5 [7. ♗e2!?] h6 [Knežević–Popov, Skopje 1967] 8. ♗f6!? ef6 9. ♗c4±; **4... ♕c7** 5. ♗d3 [5. h3!? ♘f6 6. e5 de5 7. de5 ♘fd7 8. e6! fe6 9. ♘g5 ♘f6 10. ♗d3±→ Zaharov–Lepeškin, SSSR 1965; 5... e5!?] g6 [5... ♗g4 6. 0–0 e6 7. h3 ♗h5 8. ♖e1 ♘d7 9. ♘bd2 ♘gf6 10. ♘f1 ♗e7 11. ♘g3 ♗g6 12. d5!± Parma–Korčnoj, Beograd 1964; 6. dc5!? dc5 7. h3 ♗h5 8. e5!? e6 9. ♗f4± Fuchs–Ortega, Tel Aviv (ol) 1964] 6. 0–0 ♗g7 7. ♖e1 ♗g4 8. ♘bd2 cd4 9. cd4 e5 [Glušnjev–Buhtin, SSSR 1961] 10. de5±

43 5. ♗c4 b5 6. ♗b3 c4 7. ♗c2 e5 8. a4 ♗b7= Banik–Kuuskmaa, corr. 1968

44 **5... e5** 6. 0–0 ♗e7 7. ♘bd2 ♘gf6 8. ♘c4 ♕c7 9. de5 de5 10. a4 b6 11. ♘e3 ♗b7 12. ♘f5 ♗f8 13. ♕e2± Govbinder–Suetin, Tallinn 1959; **5... g6** 6. 0–0 ♗g7 7. ♕e2 [△ e5] e5 8. de5 de5± Aronin–Tajmanov, SSSR 1957

45 6... ♗e7 7. ♕e2 ♕c7 8. e5 b5 9. ♗f4 ♗b7 10. ♘bd2 c4 11. ♗c2 d5 12. h4 h5 13. ♗g5 ♘b6 14. ♗e7 ♘e7 15. ♘g5 g6 16. ♕f3 ♘f5 17. ♖fb1!± Klovan–Kuuskmaa, corr. 1974

46 12. e5 de5 13. de5 ♘d5 14. ♗e7 ♘e7 15. ab5 ab5 16. ♖ad1± Parma–Perez, La Habana 1965

47 5. ♗c4!? ♘b6 6. ♗b3 c4 7. ♗c2 d5 8. d4 cd3 9. ♕d3 g6 10. 0–0 ♗g7 11. ♕e2 ♘c6 12. ♗f4 0–0 13. h3 ♕c7 14. ♗g3 ♗e6 15. ♘a3± Boleslavski–Abramson, Stockholm 1964

48 5... e6 6. ♗d3 [6. ♗e2 ♘c6 7. 0–0 cd4 8. cd4 d6 9. ed6 ♗d6 10. ♘c3 ♘c3 11. bc3 0–0 12. ♗d3 ♖e8? 13. ♘g5→ Han–Nazarov, SSSR 1971] cd4 7. cd4 b6 8. 0–0 ♗b7 9. ♗g5 ♕c7 10. ♘bd2 h6 11. ♖c1 ♗c6 12. ♗h4 ♕b7 13. ♗e4 a5 14. a3 ♘a6 15. ♖e1 ♘ac7 16. ♘c4± Schmidt–Prins, Tel Aviv (ol) 1964

49 **6. ♕d4** e6 7. ♗c4 [7. ♘bd2 ♘c6 8. ♕g4 d6 9. ed6 ♘f6 10. ♕g3 ♗d6 11. ♕g7? ♖g8 12. ♕h6 e5! 13. ♘c4 ♗c5 14. ♗e3 ♗f8 15. ♕h4 ♖g4–+ Junejev–Blehcin, SSSR 1972; 11. ♕h4∓] ♘c6 8. ♕e4 f5 [8... ♘b6 9. ♗b3 d6 10. ed6 ♗d6 11. 0–0± Masejev–Fink, corr. 1960] 9. ♕e2 ♘de7 10. h4 [10. 0–0 ♘g6 11. ♘bd2 ♕c7 12. ♖e1 ♗e7 13. ♗b3 0–0= Lapenis–Peterson, SSSR 1961] ♕c7 11. h5 b5 12. ♗b3 ♗b7 13. ♖h3 ♖c8∞ Lejn–Peterson, SSSR 1962; **6. ♗c4**!? ♘b6 7. ♗b3 d6 [7... dc3?! 8. ♘g5 e6 9. ♕f3±⟳] 8. ed6 ♕d6 9. cd4 ♗f5 10. 0–0 e6 11. ♘c3 ♗e7 12. d5!±↑ Simagin–Barcza, Moskva–Budapest 1949; **11... ♘8d7**!?∞

50 6... ♘c6 7. ♘c3 [7. ♗c4 e6 8. 0–0 d6 9. ♕e2 de5 10. de5 ♗c5 11. ♘bd2 ♘f4 12. ♕e4 ♘g6= Kondrjatev–Čerepkov, SSSR 1951] e6 8. ♗d3 d6 9. 0–0 de5 10. de5 ♗e7 11. ♕e2 ♘cb4 12. ♗b1 ♘c3 13. bc3 ♘d5 14. ♗d2± Šijanovski–Baršauskas, SSSR 1957; **6... e6** 7. ♘c3 [7. ♗c4 ♘b6 8. ♗d3 ♗e7 9. 0–0 ♘c6 10. ♘c3 d5 11. ♕d2! ♘d7 12. ♕f4 ♘f8 13. ♕g4 ♘g6 14. ♘e2 ♗d7 15. a3± Suetin–Gurgenidze, SSSR 1967; 7... d6!?] d6 [7... ♘c3 8. bc3 ♕c7 9. ♕c2 d6 10. ed6 ♗d6 11. ♗d3 ♘d7 12. 0–0 b6 13. h3 ♗b7 14. ♘d2 ♘f6 15. ♘c4± Unzicker–Robatsch, Schweiz 1961] 8. ♗d3 [8. ♘d5 ed5 9. ♗d3 ♘c6 10. h3 de5 11. de5 h6 12. 0–0 ♗c5= Albareda–Korčnoj, Oberhausen 1961] ♘c6 [8... de5?! 9. ♘e5 ♘d7 10. 0–0 ♘e5 11. de5 ♘b4 12. ♗e4 ♕d1 13. ♖d1 ♗e7 14. ♘a4!±⊥ Yanofsky–Filips, Canada 1952] 9. ed6 ♗d6 10. 0–0±

51 **7. ed6** ♕d6 8. ♘c3 ♘c6 9. ♗d3 g6 10. 0–0 ♗g7 11. ♖e1 0–0 12. ♗e4 ♗e6 13. ♗g5± Gipslis–Zaborovski, SSSR 1961; **7. ♘c3** ♘c3 [7... e6 — 6... e6] 8. bc3 ♘c6 9. ed6 ed6 10. ♗d3 ♗e7 11. ♕c2 h6 12. ♗f4± Goljak–Bastrikov, SSSR 1959

52 7... ♘b6 8. ♗b3 ♘c6 9. ♘c3 d5 10. h3 ♗f5 11. ♘h4 ♗g6? 12. ♘g6 hg6 13. e6! fe6 14. ♕g4±→ Kulamaja–Heuer, SSSR 1963

53 12. ♗f4 ♘d5 13. ♗g3 0–0 14. ♖c1 ♘c6 15. h3±

54 4... ♘f6?! 5. c4 e6 6. de6 ♗e6 7. ♘c3 ♘c6 8. ♗e2 ♘d4 9. d3 ♘e2 10. ♕e2 ♗e7 11. 0–0 0–0 12. h3 ♕c7 13. ♘g5 ♗f5 14. ♘ge4± Olafsson–Bazan, Mar del Plata 1960

55 **5... ♗g4** 6. ♗e2 e6 7. 0–0 ♘f6 8. c4!? [8. ♗e3 cd4?! 9. cd4 ♘c6 10. ♘c3 ♕d7? 11. ♘e5!± Unzicker–Beni, Dubrovnik (ol) 1950; 8... ♘bd7 9. c4 ♕d6∞ O'Kelly] ♕d6 9. ♕b3± Suetin; **5... cd4** 6. cd4 e6 [6... ♗g4?! 7. ♘c3 ♕d8 8. ♗c4! e6 9. d5 e5 10. d6!± Šilov–Razdobarin, SSSR 1959; 6... ♘f6?! 7. ♘c3 ♕a5 8. ♗c4 e6 9. 0–0 ♘bd7 10. ♖e1 ♘b6 11. ♗b3 ♗e7 12. ♗d2± Quinones–Letelier, Tel Aviv (ol) 1964] 7. ♗e2 [7. ♗d3 ♘f6 8. 0–0 ♗e7 9. ♘c3 ♕d8 10. ♕e2±] ♘f6 8. 0–0 ♗e7 9. ♘c3 ♕d8 10. ♗d3 0–0 11. ♕e2 ♘c6 12. ♖d1 ♘b4?! 13. ♗b1 ♘bd5 14. ♘e5 ♗d7 15. ♖d3!± Velimirović–Roth, Haag 1966; **5... ♘c6** 6. ♗e2 [△ 7. c4; 6. dc5?! ♕d1 7. ♔d1 ♗g4 8. ♗e3 ♘f6∞ Belov–Sergijevski, SSSR 1961] cd4 7. cd4 ♗f5 [7... ♗g4?! 8. ♘c3 ♕d8 9. d5±] 8. ♘c3 ♕a5 9. 0–0 e6 10. ♗f4 [10. a3!?] ♖d8 11. a3 ♘f6 12. b4 ♕b6 13. ♘a4 ♕a7 14. ♗c7 ♖d7 15. ♗b6± Foltys–Prins, Venezia 1949

56 6. ♗e2 ♘f6 — 5... ♘f6

57 **7... ♘c6** 8. ♗e3 c4 9. ♗e2 b5 10. b3 cb3 11. ab3 ♗e7 12. c4 bc4 13. bc4 ♕d7 14. ♘c3 0–0 15. ♖b1± Gipslis–Mosionžik, SSSR 1961; **7... cd4** 8. cd4 ♘c6 9. ♘c3 ♕d8 10. ♗g5 ♗e7 11. ♖e1±

58 8. ♕e2 0–0 [8... cd4 9. cd4 ♘c6 10. ♖d1 0–0 11. ♘c3 ♕a5 12. ♗f4 ♖d8 13. ♖ac1±; 9... ♘bd7!? 10. ♘c3 ♕a5 (Padevski–Blau, Moskva (ol) 1956) 11. ♗f4!?±] 9. dc5 ♕c5 10. ♘bd2 ♘bd7 11. ♘b3 ♕c7 12. ♗g5 [Pachman–Müller, Venezia 1950] b5!? 13. ♘fd4 ♗b7 14. ♘f5 ♗d8= Kotov

59 12. cd4 ♘b6 13. ♘b6 ♕b6 14. a5! ♕d8 15. ♖e1± Stoltz–Carvalho, Helsinki (ol) 1952

60 6. ♗d3?! ♗g4! Suetin

61 6... cd4 7. cd4 [7. ♕d4?! ♘c6 8. ♕d5 ♘d5 9. ♘a3 e5 10. ♘c4 f6 11. ♗e3 ♗e6= Bagirov–Tajmanov, SSSR (ch) 1960] e6 — 6... e6

62 **7... ♘bd7**?! 8. c4! ♕d6 9. ♘c3 cd4 10. ♘d4 ♗e7 11. ♗g5 0–0 12. ♕d2 ♖d8 13. ♖fd1 ♘f8 14. ♕e3± Fuchs–Tajmanov, Leningrad 1967; **7... cd4** 8. ♘d4!? [8. cd4 ♗e7 9. ♘c3 ♕d6 10. ♗e3 ♘c6 — 7... ♗e7; 10. ♗g5!? ♘bd7 11. ♗d3 b5 12. ♘e4 ♕d5 13. ♖e1 ♗b7 14. a4 b4 15. ♖c1 ♖c8 16. ♖c8 ♗c8 17. ♕c2± Matulović–Tajmanov, Jugoslavija–SSSR 1965] ♗e7 9. ♘d2 0–0 10. ♘c4 ♕d8 11. ♗f4 ♘d5 12. ♗g3 b5 13. ♘e5 ♗b7 14. ♗f3± Gipslis–Tajmanov, SSSR (ch) 1967; **7... ♘c6** 8. ♗e3 cd4 9. ♘d4!?± Boleslavski

63 8. ♗f4 0–0 [8... ♘c6?! 9. ♘e5! ♘e5 10. ♗e5 0–0 11. ♗f3 ♕d8 12. ♖e1 ♖a7 13. ♘d2 b5 14. a4 (14. ♗b8 ♖d7 15. ♗c6 cd4 16. ♗d7 dc3! 17. ♗c8 cd2∞) b4 15. dc5 bc3 16. ♗c3 ♗c5 17. ♘b3 ♗e7 18. ♘a5± Štejn–Bolbochan, Stoskholm (izt) 1962] 9. ♘e5 cd4 10. cd4 ♖d8∞ Arsenjev–Kušelman, SSSR 1962

64 8... ♘c6? 9. dc5±; 9. c4±

65 9. ♘d4 e5! [9... ♘bd7 10. ♘d2 ♕d6 11. ♗g5 0–0 (Geler–Tajmanov, SSSR (ch) 1967 — 3/365) 12. ♗h4!?±] 10. c4 ♕d8 11. ♘b3 ♕c7 12. ♘c3 ♗e6 13. ♖c1 ♘bd7 14. ♘d2 ♖c8= Rellstab–O'Kelly, Bled 1950

66 9... 0–0 10. ♘c3 ♕d6 11. ♖c1 ♘bd7 12. ♕d2 ♘b6 13. ♗f4 ♕d8 14. ♘e5 ♘fd5 15. ♗g3± Suetin–Tajmanov, Leningrad 1967

67 10... ♕d8 11. ♘e5! 0–0 [11... ♘e5 12. de5 ♕d1 13. ♖fd1 ♘d7 14. f4±⊥] 12. ♗f3 ♘b4 [12... ♗d7!?] 13. ♕b3!? [13. ♖c1 ♘fd5 14. ♕b3± Poulsen–O'Kelly, Beverwijk 1951] ♘bd5 14. ♗g5 ♖a7 15. ♖fd1 ♘c3 16. bc3 ♕a5 17. a4± Gurgenidze–Ustinov, SSSR 1972

68 **11... ♘d4**?! 12. ♘c4 ♘e2 13. ♕e2△ 14. ♘b6±; **11... ♘b4** 12. ♘c4 [12. ♘de4 ♘e4 13. ♘e4 ♕d8 14. ♗f3± Ćirić–Tajmanov, Rostov 1961] ♕d8 13. ♗f3 ♘bd5 14. ♗g5 0–0 15. ♕b3 ♖b8 16. ♖ad1 b5 17. ♘e5± Gufeljd–Tajmanov, SSSR (ch) 1964

69 **3... e6** 4. d4 cd4 5. ♘d4 — B 41; **3... d6** 4. d4 ♗g4 5. ♗e2 ♘c6 6. d5 ♗f3= Prins–Robatsch, Moskva (ol) 1956; 5. dc5±

70 **5... g6**?! 6. ♘c6 [6. ♗e2 ♗g7 7. ♘c2 ♘f6 8. ♘c3 0–0± Muhitdinov–Karadžajev, SSSR 1959] bc6 7. ♕d4 f6?! 8. c5! ♕c7 9. ♘c3 e5 10. ♕c4 a5 11. ♘a4± Saharov–Levin, SSSR 1968 — 5/346; **5... e5** 6. ♘f5 [6. ♘c2 ♗c5 7. ♗d3 d6 8. 0–0 ♘ge7 9. ♘c3 0–0 10. ♕h5 ♗e6 11. ♘d5 ♘g6 12. ♘ce3 ♕h4=

Wood–Rossolimo, Heidelberg 1949; 7. ♗e3!?] d5 [6... ♘f6 7. ♘c3 — 5... ♘f6] 7. cd5 ♗f5 8. ef5 ♘d4 9. ♘c3 [9. ♗d3!? ♗b4?! 10. ♘c3△ 11. ♕a4± Boleslavski; 9... ♘f6 10. ♘c3 — 5... ♘f6] ♘e7 [9... ♘f6 10. ♗d3 — 5... ♘f6] 10. ♗d3 [10. f6!?] ♘ef5 11. 0–0 ♗d6 [Vaskan–Kirilov, SSSR 1966] 12. f4!?±↑; **5... e6** — B 41

71 **7. ♘f3** ♗c5 8. ♗d3 8. ♗d3 d6=; **7. ♘de2** ♗c5 8. ♘g3 d6=; **7. ♘b3** ♗b4 8. ♕d3 [8. f3 a5!∓; 8. ♗g5 h6 9. ♗f6 ♕f6 10. ♕d3 d6 11. a3 ♗c3 12. ♕c3 0–0 13. ♗e2 ♕g6 14. ♗f3 ♗e6 15. 0–0 ♖ac8∓ Šu–Fink, corr. 1957] d6 9. ♗e2 ♗e6 10. 0–0 ♗c3!? [10... ♖c8? 11. ♘d5 ♗d5 12. ed5 ♘e7 13. a3 ♗c5 14. ♘c5 ♖c5 15. b4!± Schmid–H. Steiner, Dubrovnik (ol) 1950] 11. bc3 ♘a5 12. ♘a5 ♕a5 13. ♕d6 ♘e4 14. ♕b4 ♕b4 15. cb4 ♘c3=

72 8. ♗e2 d6 [8... 0–0 9. 0–0 ♘d4!?= Koch–Porreca, Helsinki (ol) 1952] 9. 0–0 ♗e6 10. ♔h1 ♘d7 11. f4 ef4 12. ♗f4 ♘de5=

73 **11... ♖c8** 12. f3! [12. ♖ab1 ♘b4! 13. ♗c5 dc5 14. ♕d8 ♖fd8 15. ♘e3 ♘c6 16. ♖fd1 ♘d4∓ Pilnik–Euwe, New York 1949; 12. a3 ♘a5∓] ♘b4?! 13. ♗c5 ♘c2 14. ♕c2 dc5 15. ♖fd1 ♕c7 16. ♖ac1± Michel–Müller, Wien 1950; 12... ♕b6!?∞; **11... ♘b4** 12. ♖ac1 ♖c8= Bely–Szabo, Budapest 1954

74 7... d6 8. ♗g5 [8. ♘e3 ♗e6 9. ♗d3 ♗e7 10. 0–0 0–0 11. ♘ed5 ♗d5 12. ed5 ♘b8 13. ♗e3 ♘bd7 14. b4± Ivkov–Saidy, Uppsala 1956; 8. ♗d3!? ♗f5 9. ef5 d5 10. cd5 ♘d5 11. 0–0 ♘c3 12. bc3 ♗e7 13. ♖b1 ♕c7 14. ♕g4± Hasin–Nejelov, SSSR 1970] ♗f5 9. ef5 [9. ♗f6 ♕f6 10. ♘d5 ♕d8 11. ef5 ♗e7 12. ♗d3 ♕a5 13. ♔f1 ♕d8?! 14. ♕h5 ♗f6 15. g4± Bihovski–Smirnov, SSSR 1962] ♘d4 10. ♗d3±

75 **10. ♗g5** ♕b6!? [10... ♘f5?! 11. ♗d3 ♘d4 12. 0–0 ♗d6 13. f4±; 10... ♗e7 11. ♗d3 ♘d5 12. ♗e7 ♘e7 13. 0–0 ♕d7 14. f4!±; 13. ♗e4±] 11. ♕a4 [11. ♗f6? ♕b2!∓] ♘d7 12. ♖b1 ♕b4=; **10. ♗e3** ♗c5! [10... ♘d5? 11. ♗d4 ed4 12. ♕a4! b5 13. ♗b5 ab5 14. ♕b5 ♕d7 15. ♕d5+– Canal–Euwe, Dubrovnik (ol) 1950; 10... ♘f5 11. ♕a4?! b5 12. ♘b5? ab5 13. ♗b5 ♔e7 14. ♗c5 ♘d6∓ O'Kelly; 11. ♗g5 ♗e7=] 11. ♗c4 0–0 12. 0–0 ♖c8= Fuentes–O'Kelly 1949

76 11. ♗e4 ♘b4 12. 0–0 ♖b8∞ Romanovski–Litvinov, SSSR 1959

77 **11... ♘c3** 12. bc3 ♘c6 13. ♖b1 ♖b8 14. ♕f3 ♕c7 15. ♗e4 ♘d8 16. ♖d1± Ravinski–Kljaščicki, SSSR 1966; **11... ♘f6** 12. ♖e1 ♘c6 13. ♕b3 ♗b4 14. ♖d1 ♕e7 15. ♗g5 ♗c3 16. bc3 0-0-0 17. ♗e4± Rogačovski–Konovalov, corr. 1972; **11... ♗e7** 12. ♗e4 ♘c3 13. bc3 ♘c6 14. ♖b1 [14. ♕a4 0–0 15. ♖b1± Günsberger–J. Szabo, Romania 1955] ♕c8 15. ♕g4± Matanović–Perez, Beograd 1961; **11... ♗b4** 12. ♗e4! ♘c3 13. bc3 ♗c3 14. ♖b1 0–0 [14... ♖b8?! 15. ♕g4 g6 16. ♗g5 gf5 17. ♗f5 f6 18. ♕h5+– Altšuler–Fink, corr. 1960] 15. ♕g4 ♕d6 16. ♖d1 ♖ac8!? [16... ♖ad8? 17. ♖d3 ♗b4 18. f6!+– Kupper–Tordion, Schweiz (ch) 1956] 17. ♖d3 ♖c4 18. h4∞ Kets; 15. ♖b7!± Gligorić, Sokolov

B 29

1. e4 c5 2. ♘f3 ♘f6

	3	4	5	6	7	8	9	10	11	
1	♘c3[1]	ed5[3]	♘e5[5]	bc3[7]	♗b5	♕e2	0–0	♖e1	d4	=
	d5[2]	♘d5[4]	♘c3[6]	♕c7[8]	♘d7	e6	♗d6	0–0	cd4[9]	
2	...	...	♗b5	♘e5[10]	♘d7[12]	d4	♗d7	d5	0–0	±
	...	...	♗d7	♘f6[11]	♘bd7	a6	♘d7	g6		
3	...	...	...	♘e5[13]	dc3[14]	♔d1	♗c6	♘c6	c4[16]	±
	...	...	♘c6	♘c3	♕d1[15]	♗d7	♗c6	bc6		
4	...	d4[17]	ed5[19]	dc5[20]	♕d8	bc3	♗b5[23]	♘e5[25]	♗f4[26]	=
	♘c6	d5[18]	♘d5	♘c3	♘d8[21]	g6[22]	♘c6[24]	♗g7	0–0[27]	
5	...	...	...	♘d5	♗e3[28]	♘d4	♕d4	♗d4	♗c4[30]	±
	...	...	...	♕d5	cd4	♘d4[29]	♕d4	♗d7	e6[31]	
6	...	...	...	...	...	...	c3[32]	b4[34]	♕d4	±
	...	...	...	...	...	♕a5	♘d4[33]	♕e5[35]	♕d4[36]	

1. e4 c5 2. ♘f3 ♘f6 3. e5 ♘d5

	4	5	6	7	8	9	10	11	12	
7	c4[37]	d4	♕d4[39]	♕e4	ed6	♘c3	♕g6	♗f4	♗g3	=
	♘c7[38]	cd4	♘c6	d5[40]	♕d6	♕g6[41]	hg6	♘e6	♗d7[42]	

	4	5	6	7	8	9	10	11	12	
8	d4	♕d4[43]	♗c4[44]	♕e4	ed6[47]	♕e2[48]	0—0[49]	♘c3	♖e1	=
	cd4	e6	♘c6[45]	d6[46]	♘f6	♗d6	♕c7[50]	a6	0—0[51]	
9	♘c3	dc3[53]	ed6	♕d6[56]	♗f4	0-0-0[58]	♗c4![60]	gf3	♗d6	±
	♘c3[52]	d5[54]	♕d6[55]	ed6	♗g4[57]	♘d7[59]	♗f3	f6	♗d6[61]	
10	. . .	. . .	♗c4[62]	♗f4[64]	0—0[66]	♖e1	♘d2	ed6	♗d6	±
	. . .	♘c6	e6[63]	♕c7[65]	b6	h6[67]	d5[68]	♗d6	♕d6[69]	
11	. . .	. . .	♗f4	♕d2[71]	0-0-0	h4	♗d3[74]	♕e2	♘d2	±
	. . .	. . .	e6[70]	♕c7[72]	h6[73]	b6	♗b7	0-0-0	d5[75]	
12	. . .	♘e4[76]	♘c3[78]	♘d5	d4	ed6	♗e2[79]	0—0	b3	∞
	e6	f5[77]	♘c6	ed5	d6	♗d6	0—0	c4!?[80]	c3[81]	

1. e4 c5 2. ♘f3 ♘f6 3. e5 ♘d5 4. ♘c3 e6 5. ♘d5 ed5 6. d4

	6	7	8	9	10	11	12	13	14	
13	. . .	ed6[82]	♗e3[83]	♗e2	0—0	♕d2[84]	c3	h3	♖ae1	=
	d6	♗d6	c4	0—0	♘c6	♗f5	♕c7	♖ae8	♗c8[85]	
14	. . .	♗g5	c3[87]	♗d3[89]	0—0	♖e1	bc3	♘e5	♖e5	∞
	. . .	♕a5[86]	cd4[88]	dc3[90]	♘c6[91]	♗e6	de5	♘e5	♗d6[92]	
15	. . .	♗b5	0—0	c4[95]	♗e3	a4	a5[98]	ed6	dc5	±
	. . .	♘c6[93]	♗e7[94]	♗e6[96]	♕b6	a6[97]	♕c7	♕d6	♕d8[99]	
16	. . .	dc5[100]	♕d5[101]	♗c4[102]	♔e2[103]	♖f1[104]	♘g5[105]	♕e5[107]	♕d5[108]	±
	♘c6	♗c5	♕b6	♗f2	0—0	♗c5	♘e5?[106]	d5	♖e8[109]	

1. e4 c5 2. ♘f3 ♘f6 3. e5 ♘d5 4. ♘c3 e6 5. ♘d5 ed5 6. d4 ♘c6 7. dc5 ♗c5 8. ♕d5 ♕b6 9. ♗c4 ♗f2 10. ♔e2 0—0 11. ♖f1 ♗c5 12. ♘g5 ♘d4

	13	14	15	16	17	18	19	20	21	
17	♔d1[110]	♘e4[111]	ed6	♕h5[114]	♗d3	♖f5	♖f1			=
	♘e6	d6[112]	♖d8[113]	♗d6	f5	♕g1!?[115]	♕h2[116]			
18	. . .	c3	b4	♖b1[119]	♘f7[121]	♖f7	ed6	cb4	♗d5	±
	. . .	d6[117]	♗b4[118]	a5[120]	♖f7	♔f7	♕d6	♕d5	♖a6[122]	

1. e4 c5 2. ♘f3 ♘f6 3. e5 ♘d5 4. ♘c3 e6 5. ♘d5 ed5 6. d4 ♘c6 7. dc5 ♗c5 8. ♕d5 d6 9. ed6 ♕b6

	10	11	12	13	14	15	16	17	18	
19	♕e4[123]	d7[124]	♗e3	♖d1	fe3	♕f4	♔f2			∞
	♗e6	♔d7	♗e3	♔c7	♕b2	♔c8	♖d8[125]			
20	♗c4	♔e2[126]	♖d1	♕e4[128]	♔f1	♕d5[131]	♕e4[132]			=
	♗f2	0—0	♗e6[127]	♖ae8[129]	♗d7![130]	♗e6				

1 3. d3 d6 4. g3 g6 5. ♘c3 ♗g7 6. ♗g2 ♘c6 — B 25

2 3. . . d6 4. e5 — B 50; 4. d4 cd4 5. ♘d4

3 **4. e5** ♘fd7 [4. . . ♘e4?! 5. ♘b1! c4 6. b3±; 4. . . d4 5. ♗b5 ♗d7 — 4. ♗b5] 5. e6!? [5. d4 e6 — C 11; 5. ♘d5 ♘e5 6. ♘e3=] fe6 6. d4 cd4 [6. . . ♘c6 7. dc5 ♕a5 8. ♗b5 g6 9. ♗d2 ♕c7 10. ♕e2 ♘c5 11. ♕e3± Thelidze—Koroljev, SSSR 1972] 7. ♘d4 ♘f6 8. ♗b5 ♔f7 9. ♗f4 ♕b6 10. 0—0 g6 11. a4$\overline{\infty}$ Litviško—Čistjakov, SSSR 1959; **4. ♗b5** ♗d7 [4. . . ♘c6?! 5. ed5 — 4. ed5] 5. e5 [5. ♗d7 ♕d7 6. ed5 ♘d5 — 4. ed5] d4 [5. . . ♘g8?! 6. e6 fe6 7. ♕e2 ♘c6 8. 0—0 a6 9. ♗c6 bc6 10. d4± Paoli—Fletzer, Venezia 1949; 5. . . ♗b5 6. ♘b5 a6 7. ♘c3 d4 8. ♘a4 ♘fd7 9. e6 fe6 10. ♘g5 ♕c7 11. 0—0 ♕c6 12. b3 e5! 13. d3 ♘f6 14. f4± Bronštejn—Saidy, Mar del Plata 1960] 6. ef6 dc3 7. fg7 cd2 8. ♕d2 ♗g7 9. ♗d3 [9.

♕g5 ♗f6 10. ♗d7 ♘d7 11. ♕h5 ♕a5 12. ♘d2 ♕a6 13. ♘e4 0-0-0= Fischer–Pomar, Stockholm (izt) 1962] ♕b6!? [9... ♕c7?! 10. 0–0 c4 11. ♗e4 ♘c6 12. ♕e2 c3 13. bc3 ♗c3 14. ♖b1 0-0-0 15. ♕c4± Fischer–Sherwin, USA (ch) 1962/63] 10. 0–0 ♘c6 11. ♕g5 ♗f6 12. ♕h5 ♗e6?! 13. ♗f5 0-0-0 14. ♗e6 fe6 15. c3 e5 16. ♘d2 ♕c7 17. ♘e4± Zuckerman–Crabbendam, Beverwijk 1968; 12... ♖g8!?∞ Zuckerman–Pomar, Malaga 1968

4 4... a6?! 5. b3 ♘d5 6. ♘d5 ♕d5 7. ♗c4 ♕h5 8. ♗b2±

5 **5. ♗c4** e6 6. 0–0 ♗e7 7. d4 ♘c3 8. bc3 0–0 [8... ♕c7 9. ♗d3 ♘d7?! 10. ♖e1 ♘f6 11. ♘e5 0–0 12. ♖e3±→⟫ Kagan–Sardinha, Lugano (ol) 1968] 9. ♘e5 ♕c7 10. ♗d3 ♘c6 11. ♗f4 ♗d6 12. ♖e1 cd4 13. cd4 ♘b4= Spielmann–Nimzowitsch, San Sebastian 1911; **5. ♘d5** ♕d5 6. d4 ♗g4!? 7. ♗e2 cd4=; **5. d4** ♘c3!? [5... e6 6. ♘d5 ♕d5 7. ♗e3 cd4 8. ♘d4 a6?! 9. ♗e2 ♕g2? 10. ♗f3±→ Nimzowitsch–Alapin, Riga 1912; 6... ed5!? 7. c3 ♘c6 8. ♗e3!±] 6. bc3 e6 [6... g6 7. ♗e3 ♗g7 8. ♗b5 ♗d7 9. ♗d7 (Bogatirčuk–Levenfiš, SSSR 1934) ♕d7△ ♘c6∞] 7. ♗d3 ♗e7 8. 0–0 0–0= Reti–Rubinstein, Göteborg 1920; **5. ♘e4** e6 6. d4 cd4 7. ♘d4 ♗e7 8. ♗b5 ♗d7 9. c4 ♘f6 10. ♘c3 0–0 11. 0–0 ♕c7= P. Johner–Tartakower, Berlin 1928

6 5... ♕c7!? 6. ♗b5 ♘d7 7. ♘d7 ♗d7 8. ♘d5 ♕e5= Levenfiš

7 6. ♕f3 f6 7. ♕h5 g6 8. ♘g6 hg6 9. ♕h8 ♘d5 10. d4∞ Levenfiš

8 6... ♕d5?! 7. ♗b5 ♘d7 8. ♕e2! [8. ♕h5? a6 9. ♘d7 ♕g2!∓ Yates–Tartakower, Kecskemet 1927] a6 [8... ♕g2? 9. ♕d3!! ♕h1 10. ♔e2+– L. Steiner–Csabay, corr. 1922] 9. ♗d7 ♗d7 10. 0–0 ♗a4!? [10... ♗f5?! 11. d3 e6 12. ♖b1 b5 13. c4+–→ L. Steiner–Kmoch, Hastings 1927/28; 10... ♗c6 11. ♘c6 ♕c6 12. c4 e6 13. ♗b2 ♗e7 14. f4 ♗f6 15. ♗f6 gf6 16. ♖ab1± Reti–Kostić, Trenčanske Teplice 1928] 11. d3±; 7... ♘c6!? Kmoch

9 12. cd4 ♘e5= Tarrasch–Tartakower, Berlin 1928

10 **6. ♗c4** ♘b6 7. ♗e2 ♘c6 8. 0–0 ♗f5 9. ♖e1 a6 10. d3 e6= Schlage–Nimzowitsch, Berlin 1928; **6. ♗d7** ♕d7 7. ♘d5 [7. 0–0 ♘c6=] ♕d5 8. d4 e6! [8... cd4?! 9. ♕d4 ♕d4 10. ♘d4± Rossolimo–Tartakower, Venezia 1949] 9. 0–0 ♘c6 10. dc5 ♕d1 11. ♖d1 ♗c5= Schlage–Reti, Berlin 1928; **6. ♕e2**!? ♘c3 7. dc3 [7. bc3 a6=] a6 8. ♗d7 ♕d7 9. 0–0 ♘c6 10. ♗f4± Sokolov

11 **6... ♘c6**? 7. ♗c6 ♗c6 8. ♕f3+–; **6... ♘c3**? 7. ♕f3! ♕c7 [7... f6? 8. ♕h5 g6 9. ♘g6 ♔f7 10. ♘e5 1 : 0 Thomas–Sapiro, Antwerpen 1932] 8. ♗d7 ♘d7 9. ♕f7 ♔d8 10. ♘d7 ♔d7 11. dc3+–; **6... ♗b5** 7. ♕f3 f6 [7... ♘f6? 8. ♕b7 ♗a6 9. ♕a8 ♕c7 10. ♘c6!+–] 8. ♘b5 [8. ♕d5 ♕d5 9. ♘d5 ♘a6=] ♘a6 [8... fe5 9. ♕d5 ♕d5 10. ♘c7 ♔d7 11. ♘d5 ♘c6 12. d3±⊥ Thomas–A. Steiner, Budapest 1929] 9. ♕h5 g6 10. ♘g6 hg6 11. ♕h8 ♕d7 12. ♘c3 ♕e6 13. ♔f1 ♘ab4 14. ♕h3± Sozin–Kirilov, SSSR (ch) 1931; **6... e6** 7. ♕f3 ♕e7 [7... ♕f6? 8. ♘d7 ♘d7 9. ♘d5 ♕f3 10. ♘c7 ♔d8 11. ♘e6 fe6 12. gf3 +–⊥] 8. ♘d7 ♘d7 9. 0–0±

12 7. ♕f3 ♕c8 8. a4 e6 9. d3 ♗e7 10. ♗g5 a6 11. ♗d7 ♘bd7 12. ♘c4 ♕c7!= Balogh–van Scheltinga, corr. 1950; 7... ♕c7!?=

13 **6. 0—0** ♗g4 7. h3 ♗f3!? [7... ♘c3 8. bc3 ♗d7 9. d4 e6 10. d5 ed5 11. ♕d5± Michel–Piazzini, Mar del Plata 1944; 7... ♗h5 8. ♗c6 bc6 9. ♘e4 e6 10. b3 ♗g6 14. d3± Litvinov–Ljubošic, SSSR 1960] 8. ♕f3 e6=; **6. ♘e4**!? e6!? [6... ♕b6? 7. a4 a6 8. ♗c4 e6 9. 0–0 ♗e7 10. ♖e1 0–0 11. b3 ♕d8 12. ♗b2± Haag–Cuibus, Hungary 1973 — 15/319] 7. 0–0 ♗e7=

14 7. bc3?! ♕d5 8. ♘c6 bc6 9. ♗e2 ♕g2 10. ♗f3 ♕g6 11. ♗a3 ♕e6 12. ♗e2 ♗a6 13. ♗c5 g6∓ Pachman

15 **7... ♕b6**? 8. ♗c6 bc6 9. ♕f3+–; **7... ♗d7** 8. ♘d7 ♕d7 9. ♕d7 ♔d7 10. ♗f4±⊥ Rabar

16 ± Rabar

17 **4. e5**? ♘g4 5. ♕e2 ♕c7–+; **4. g3** d5 5. ed5 ♘d5 6. ♗g2 g6 7. 0–0 ♗g7 8. ♘g5 [Lutikov–Szukszta, Warszawa 1969] e6=; **4. ♗b5** e6 [4... ♘d4?! 5. e5 ♘b5 6. ef6?! ♘c3 7. fg7 ♗g7 8. dc3 d6∓ Fletzer–Foltys, Venezia 1949; 6. ♘b5 ♘d5 7. 0–0 ♘c7 8. ♘c7 ♕c7 9. d4 cd4 10. ♕d4 g6 11. ♖e1 ♗g7 12. ♗g5±→ Fuchs–Mnacakanjan, Erevan 1965; 4... a6!? 5. ♗c6 dc6=] 5. 0–0 ♗e7 6. e5 ♘d5 7. ♘e4 f5 8. ♘c3 0–0 9. d4 a6 10. ♘d5 ed5 11. ♗e2 c4 12. b3 b5 14. a4 ♖b8 14. ab5 ab5 15. bc4 1/2 : 1/2 Talj–Přibyl, Lublin 1974

18 4... cd4 5. ♘d4 — B 33

19 **5. ♗b5**? de4! [5... ♘e4 6. ♘e5 ♘c3 7. bc3 ♕a5?! 8. ♖b1!± Cardoso–Mjagmarsuren, Skopje (ol) 1972; 7... ♗d7 8. ♗c6 bc6 9. ♕f3 ♗e6 10. dc5 ♕c8 11. 0–0 f6∞ S. Nedeljković–Kozomara, Jugoslavija (ch) 1957] 6. ♘e5 cd4! 7. ♘c6 bc6 8. ♗c6 ♗d7 9. ♗a8 dc3–+ Breitmann; **5. dc5** d4 6. ♘b5 e5=; **5. e5** ♘e4 6. ♗d3 ♗f5=

20 **6. ♗e2** e6 [6... cd4 7. ♘d4 ♘c3 8. bc3 e5 9. ♘c6 ♕d1 10. ♗d1 bc6 11. ♗f3 ♗d7 12. ♗e3±⊥ Puc–Kozomara, Jugoslavija (ch) 1957] 7. 0–0 ♗e7=; **6. ♗b5** ♘c3 [6... cd4 7. ♕d4 ♘c3 8. ♕c3 ♗d7 9. 0–0 ♕b6 10. a4 a6 11. ♗e3± Šabanov–Naumov, SSSR 1967; 6... e6!?] 7. bc3 e6 [7... cd4 8. ♘d4 ♗d7 9. ♖b1 g6= Janošević–Minić, Beograd 1962; 8. 0–0!? Rovner; 7... ♕a5!?] 8. 0–0 ♗e7 9. ♕e2 [9. ♘e5 ♗d7 10. ♘d7 ♕d7= Rabinovič–Ščipunov, Leningrad 1937] 0–0 10. ♖d1 [Penrose–Szukszta, München (ol) 1958] ♕c7=; **6. ♗c4** ♘c3 [6... ♘b6?! 7. ♗b5 cd4 8. ♘d4 ♗d7 9. ♗e3 a6 10. ♘c6 bc6 11. ♗e2 e6 12. 0–0± Quinones–Mjagmarsuren, Tel Aviv (ol) 1964] 7. bc3 e6 [7... cd4 8. cd4 e6 9. 0–0 ♗e7 10. ♗e3 0–0 11. ♕e2 ♕c7 12. ♗b3 b6

13. c3 ♘a5 14. ♗c2± Kaufman–Semašajev, SSSR 1965] 8. 0–0 ♗e7 9. ♕e2 [9. ♗f4 0–0 10. ♖b1 b6= Quinones–Mjagmarsuren, Skopje (ol) 1972] 0–0 10. ♖d1 ♕c7 [10... ♕a5?! 11. ♖b1 a6 12. d5! ed5 13. ♗d5 ♗f6 14. ♘g5 ♘d8 15. ♘e4 ♗e7 16. c4 ♘e6 17. c3± Janošević–Kozomara, Jugoslavija 1968] 11. ♘e5 ♘e5 12. ♗f4 b6 13. ♗e5 ♗d6 14. ♗d6 ♕d6 15. ♕e5 ♕e5 16. de5 ♗b7=⊥ Milić–Witkowski, Krynica 1956

21 7... ♔d8 8. bc3 f6 9. ♘d4 [9. ♗e3?! e5 10. ♘d2 ♗e6 11. ♗c4 ♗c4 12. ♘c4 ♔c7 13. ♔e2 ♘e7∓⊥ Bogdanović–Kozomara, Jugoslavija 1968] e5 10. ♘b3 ♗e6 11. ♗e3 ♔c7 12. 0-0-0 ♘e7 13. ♖d6 ♗b3 14. cb3 ♘f5 15. ♖d5 ♔c6 16. ♗c4 ♘e3 17. fe3 ♗c5=⊥ Pinčuk–Mnacakanjan, SSSR 1963

22 8... f6?! 9. ♘d4 [9. ♗e3 e5 10. ♘d2 ♗d7 11. ♘e4 ♖c8= Lejn–Vaganjan, SSSR 1973] e5 10. ♘b5± Zak

23 9. ♗e3 ♗g7 10. ♗d4 0–0 11. ♗d3 ♗e6 12. 0–0 ♗d5△ ♘e6=

24 9... ♗d7?! 10. ♗d7 ♔d7 11. ♗e3 ♗g7 12. ♗d4 f6 13. ♗e3! e5 14. ♖d1 ♔c7 15. ♘d2± Zak

25 10. ♗e3 ♗g7 11. ♗d4 0–0 12. ♗c6 bc6 13. ♗g7 ♔g7 14. ♘e5 ♗f5= Zak

26 11. ♘c6 a6 12. ♘d4 ab5 13. ♘b5 ♖a4 14. ♖b1 ♖a2= Zak

27 12. ♗c6 bc6 13. 0–0 ♗e5 14. ♗e5 [Kapengut–Marjasin, SSSR 1970] ♗f5=

28 **7. dc5** ♕d1 [7... ♕c5 8. ♗e3 ♕a5 9. c3 e5=] 8. ♔d1 ♗g4 9. c3 [9. ♗e2 e5 10. ♗e3 f5∓ Dedenly–Antošin, Oslo 1954] e5 10. b4 a5 11. ♗b5 ab4 12. ♗c6 bc6 13. cb4 f6∓ Rusakov–Šestoperov, SSSR 1961; **7. c4** ♕e4 8. ♗e3 cd4 9. ♘d4 e5 10. ♘c6 [10. ♘b5? ♗b4 –+] ♕c6∓ H. Müller

29 **8... e5**? 9. ♘b5! ♕d1 [9... ♕d8 10. ♕d8 ♔d8 11. 0-0-0 ♗d7 12. ♗c4+– Somogyi–Witkowski, Budapest 1956] 10. ♖d1 ♗b4 11. c3 ♗a5 12. ♗c5 ♘e7 13. ♘d6 ♔f8 14. ♗c4 ♗e6 15. ♗e6 fe6 16. ♘b7+– Klovan–Mnacakanjan, Erevan 1959; **8... ♗d7** 9. ♘b5!? [9. ♘c6?! ♕d1 10. ♖d1 ♗c6 11. f3 e6 12. ♔f2 ♗e7 13. a3 0–0 14. ♗e2 ♗h4 15. g3 ♗f6= Matanović–Minić, Jugoslavija 1966] ♕d1 10. ♖d1 ♖c8 11. ♘a7! ♘a7 12. ♗a7 ♖c2 13. ♗d4 ♖c8 14. ♗e2±⊥ Zak; **6... a6** 9. c3!? [9. ♗e2 e5 10. ♘c6 ♕c6 11. ♕d3 ♗e7 12. ♗f3 ♕c7 13. 0–0 ♗e6 14. ♕e4 0-0-0?! 15. ♗a7 ♖d7 16. ♕e3±→ Letzelter–Mjagmarsuren, Lugano (ol) 1968; 14... ♖b8 15. ♗g4 ♗g4 16. ♕g4 0–0= Zuckerman–Mnacakanjan, Budva 1963] e5 10. ♕b3 11. ♘b3± Sokolov

30 **11. 0-0-0** e6 12. g3?! ♗c6 13. ♖g1 a6 14. ♗h3 0-0-0 15. f4 ♖d4 16. ♖d4 ♗c5 17. ♖gd1 ♗d4 18. ♖d4 ♔c7= Ivkov–Antošin, Venezia 1966; **11. ♗e2** ♗c6 12. 0–0± Pachman

31 12. 0–0 ♖g8 [12... ♗c6 13. f4 b6 14. f5± Pogacz–Rejfiř, Oberhausen 1961] 13. c3 ♗e7 14. ♖ad1 a6 15. ♗d3± Čirić–Rejfiř, Oberhausen 1961

32 **9. ♗d2** ♕e5=; **9. ♕d2** ♕d2 10. ♔d2 ♘d4 11. ♗d4 f6 12. f4 [12. ♗b5 ♗d7 13. ♗d7 ♔d7 14. ♖ad1 e5 15. ♗e3 ♔c6= Hort–Kozomara, Sarajevo 1964] ♗f5 13. ♖d1 e6 (= Zak) 14. ♗e2 0-0-0 15. ♔c1 ♗d6 16. g3 a6±⊥ Boleslavski

33 **9... e6** 10. ♘b5± Gligorić, Sokolov; **9... ♗d7** 10. ♗e2 ♘d4 11. ♗d4 e5 12. ♗e3 ♗a4 13. ♕c1 ♗c6 14. 0–0 ♗e7= Llado–Bouwmeester, Leeuwarden 1958; 10. ♘b3!? Gligorić, Sokolov

34 **10. ♗d4** ♗d7 [10... e5? 11. ♕e2! ♗d6 12. f4 f6 13. fe5 fe5 14. ♕h5 g6 15. ♕g5± Robatsch–Kozomara, Sarajevo 1968] 11. ♗c4 ♗c6 12. 0–0 ♕g5 13. g3 e6⇆ Boleslavski; **10. ♕d4** e5 11. ♕d2 [11. ♕e4 ♗e7 12. ♗d3!?] ♗e7 12. ♗c4 0–0 13. 0–0± Boleslavski

35 **10... ♕c7** 11. ♕d4 e5 12. ♗b5±; **10... ♘c2** 11. ♕c2±

36 12. ♗d4 f6 [12... e6!?] 13. f4 ♗d7 [13... e6 14. g3 ♗d6?! 15. 0-0-0 ♔e7 16. ♗g2± Spaski–Přibyl, Tallinn 1973] 14. ♗e2 e6 15. ♗h5 [15. ♗f3!?] ♔d8 16. 0-0-0 ♔c7 17. ♖he1 ♗d6 18. g3± Filipowicz–Přibyl, Polanica Zdroj 1973

37 **4. b3** g6 5. ♗b2 ♗g7 6. c4 ♘c7 7. ♘c3 ♘c6! [7... d6 8. ed6 ed6 9. d4 cd4 10. ♘d4 0–0 11. ♗e2 d5 12. cd5 ♘d5 13. ♘d5 ♕d5= Sozin–Nekrasov, SSSR 1931] 8. ♘d5 [8. ♘e4 ♘e6∓] 0–0 9. h4?! d6!∓ Strobl–Breyer, Wien 1921; **4. ♗c4** ♘b6 5. ♗e2 ♘c6 6. c3 [6. b3 g6 7. ♗a3?! ♗g7! 8. ♗c5 d6 9. ♗a3 de5 10. ♘c3 0–0 11. 0–0 f5∓ Korzin–Švarc, SSSR 1968 — 5/347] d5 7. d4 cd4 8. cd4 ♗f5 9. 0–0 e6= Yates–Nimzowitsch, London 1927; **4. g3** e6 [4... ♘c6 5. ♗g2 g6 6. 0–0 ♗g7 7. ♖e1 0–0 8. ♘c3 ♘c7?! 9. d3 ♘e6 10. ♘d5 d6 11. ed6 ♕d6 12. c4 ♘c7 13. ♘g5!± Pietzsch–Baumbach, DDR 1969] 5. ♗g2 d6 6. 0–0 ♘c6 7. ed6 ♗d6 8. d4= Simagin–Arulaid, SSSR 1960

38 **4... ♘b4**?! 5. a3!? [5. ♘c3 d6 6. ed6 ♕d6 7. d4 cd4 8. ♘b5 ♕d8 9. ♗f4±; 6... ♗f5 7. d3 e6 8. a3 ♘4c6 9. ♗e3 ♗d6 10. ♘e4 b6 11. ♘d6 ♕d6 12. d4±] ♘4c6 6. b4!? [6. ♘c3?! d6 7. ed6 e5!∓] cb4 7. ab4 ♘b4 8. c4±↑ Zak; **4... ♘b6**!? 5. d4 cd4 6. ♕d4 ♘c6 7. ♕e4 d5 8. ed6 ♕d6 9. ♗e2 e5 10. ♘c3 f5∞ Korzin–Tenenbaum, SSSR 1959

39 6. ♘d4 ♘c6 7. ♘c6 [7. ♗f4?! g6 8. ♘c3 ♗g7 9. ♘c6 bc6 10. ♗e2 ♘e6 11. ♗g3 h5 12. h4 ♕b6∓ Uljanov–Klecelj, SSSR 1957; 7. ♘f3 g6!∓] bc6 8. ♘c3 g6 9. ♗e2 ♗g7 10. f4 0–0 11. 0–0 ♖b8 12. ♕c2 d5∓ Miščenko–Mac, SSSR 1966

40 7... g6!?△ ♗g7 Collijn

41 9... e5?! 10. ♗f4 f6 [10... f5? 11. ♕e3 +–] 11. ♖d1± Spielmann–Rubinstein, Göteborg 1920

42 13. 0-0-0 g5= O'Hanlon–Kostić, Hastings 1921

43 **5. ♗c4** ♘c6 [5... ♘b6 6. ♗b3 ♘c6 7. ♗f4 d6 8. ed6 e6 9. ♘d4 ♕f6 10. ♗e3 ♕e5 11. ♘c3 ♕d6 12. ♘db5± Schmidt–Mnacakanjan, Budva 1963; 5... e6 6. 0–0 ♘b6 7. ♗b3 d6 8. ♗g5 ♗e7 9. ♗e7 ♕e7 10. ♕d4 d5 11. a4 ♘c6 12. ♕g4 0–0 13. a5± Estrin–Parr, corr. 1967] 6. ♗d5 [6. 0–0!?] ♕a5 7. ♘c3 dc3 8. 0–0 e6 9. ♗c6 bc6 10. ♖e1 cb2 11. ♗b2 ♖b8∓ H. Müller; **5. ♘d4** e6 6. ♗c4 ♘b6 7. ♗b3 ♘c6 8. ♘f3 d5 9. ed6 ♗d6 10. ♘c3 0–0=

44 **6. c4** ♘c6 7. ♕e4 [7. ♕d1 ♘de7 8. ♗d2 ♘g6 9. ♕e2 ♕c7 10. ♗c3 b6 11. h4 d6!∓ Euwe–Rubinstein, Haag 1921] ♘de7 [7... f5 8. ef6 ♘f6 9. ♕e2∞ Tartakower] 8. ♗d2 ♘g6 9. ♘c3 a6 10. ♘a4 d5 11. ed6 ♗d6 12. c5 ♗c7∓ Matanović–Roessel, Beverwijk 1966; **6. ♗d3**!? ♘c6 7. ♕e4 f5 [7... ♘db4!? Nimzowitsch; 7... d6!?] 8. ♕e2! ♗c5 [8... ♗e7 9. 0–0 0–0 10. ♖d1 ♕c7 11. ♗c4 ♘b6 12. ♗b3 ♘a5 13. ♘c3 a6 14. ♖d4!± Muhin–Přibyl, Luhačovice 1973] 9. 0–0 0–0 10. a3 ♕c7 11. c4 ♘de7 12. b4 ♘d4⇆∞ Nielssen–Nimzowitsch, Copenhagen 1928

45 6... ♘b6?! 7. ♗b3 d6 8. ed6 ♕d6 9. ♕e3 ♗e7 10. ♘c3 0–0 11. 0–0 ♘a6 12. ♖d1 ♕c5 13. ♕f4 ♕h5 14. ♗e3 ♘c5 15. ♕c7± Platonov–Kurganov, SSSR 1961

46 **7... f5** 8. ♕e2! [8. ef6 ♘f6 9. ♕e2=] ♘b6 9. ♗b3 ♗e7 10. 0–0 0–0 11. ♖d1 ♕c7 12. ♘c3 a6 13. ♗f4± Lutikov–Klaman, SSSR 1970; **7... ♘b6** 8. ♗b3 d5 9. ed6 ♗d6 10. 0–0 [10. ♘c3 a6 11. ♗e3 f5 12. ♕d3 ♗c7 13. ♕d8 ♔d8 14. 0-0-0± Liebert–Enevoldsen, Berlin 1962; 10... ♕f6 11. ♗g5 ♕g6 12. 0-0-0 ♗e7 13. ♕g6 hg6 14. ♗e3± Schwarz] 0–0 [10... ♘a5?! 11. ♘c3 ♘b3 12. ab3 0–0 13. ♖d1 ♕e7 14. ♗e3 ♗c5 15. ♖a5! ♗e3 16. ♕e3 ♗d7 17. ♖da1± Zlotnik–Kaganovski, SSSR 1963] 11. ♘g5 g6 12. ♕h4 h5 13. c3±→» Lutikov–Marjasin, SSSR 1972

47 **8. 0–0** de5 9. ♘e5 ♕c7 10. ♘c6 [10. ♗d5? ed5 11. ♕d5 ♘e5 12. ♖e1 ♗d6 13. f4 ♗e6–+] bc6 11. ♘d2 ♗d6 12. ♘f3 0–0= Tukmakov–Vorotnikov, SSSR 1966; **8. ♗d5** ed5 9. ♕d5 de5 10. ♕d8 ♔d8 11. ♘c3 f6 12. ♗e3 ♗f5 13. 0-0-0 ♔e8= Visiljčuk–Čistjakov, SSSR 1956

48 9. ♕h4 ♗d6 10. 0–0 [10. ♘c3 ♘e5! 11. ♘e5 ♗e5 12. 0–0 0–0 13. ♗d3?! ♕d4!∓ Schlechter–Nimzowitsch, San Sebastian 1912; 13. ♖d1!?∞ Tarrasch] a6 [10... ♕c7 11. ♘c3 a6 12. ♗g5 ♘e5?! 13. ♘e5 ♗e5 14. ♖ad1 ♗d7 15. ♖fe1 h6 16. ♗f6 gf6 17. ♘d5! +– Gusakov–Livanov, SSSR 1960; 12... ♗e7∞] 11. ♘c3 b5 12. ♗b3 ♗b7 13. ♗g5 ♗e7 14. ♖ad1 ♕c7= Bakulin–Čistjakov, SSSR 1959

49 10. ♗g5!? ♕a5 11. ♘c3 0–0 12. ♗f6 gf6 13. 0-0-0 ♗e7 14. g4 ♖d8 15. ♖d8 ♕d8 16. ♖d1 ♕f8 17. ♕e3± Matulović–Kozomara, Sarajevo 1968; 10... h6!?∞

50 10... 0–0 11. ♗g5 ♕a5 12. ♖d1 ♗c7 13. ♘c3 ♘e5∞ Gufeljd–Kozomara, Sarajevo 1964

51 13. ♘e4 ♘e4? 14. ♕e4 ♘e5 15. ♘g5! ♘g6 16. h4! b5 17. ♗d3 h6 18. h5+– Savon–Kirov, Suhumi 1972; 13... ♗e7=

52 **4... ♘b4**?! 5. ♗c4 [5. ♘e4 d6 6. c3 ♘4c6 7. d4 cd4 8. cd4 ♗f5 9. ♘g3 ♗g4= Spielmann–Tartakower, Berlin 1928; 5. a3 ♘4c6 6. ♗c4 ♘d4 7. 0–0 ♘bc6 8. ♖e1 e6∞ Koroljev–Šahović, SSSR 1967; 5. d4 cd4 6. ♘d4±] e6 6. 0–0 ♘8c6 7. a3 ♘a6 8. d3±; **4... ♘c7** 5. d4 [5. ♘e4!?] cd4 [5... e6? 6. ♗g5! f6 7. ef6 gf6 8. ♘e5!+–] 6. ♕d4! [6. ♘d4 g6 7. ♗f4 ♗g7 8. ♕d2 ♘c6 (Eliskases–Spielmann (m) 1937) 9. ♘f3± Euwe] ♘c6 7. ♕e4±

53 5. bc3 d5 6. d4 [6. ♗b5 ♘c6 7. h3 ♗f5=; 6. ed6 e6=] ♘c6 7. ♗d3 ♗g4 8. h3 ♗f3 [8... ♗h5? 9. e6!±] 9. ♕f3 [Polugajevski–Šamkovič, SSSR 1955] e6=

54 **5... b6**? 6. e6! [6. ♗d3 ♗b7 7. ♗f4 ♕c7 (Michell–Nimzowitsch, Marianske Lazni 1927) 8. ♕d2±] de6 [6... fe6 7. ♘e5!+–; 6... f6 7. ♘e5!+– Voloček–Pachman, Praha 1944] 7. ♕d8 ♔d8 8. ♘e5 ♔e8 9. ♗b5 ♗d7 10. ♘d7 ♘d7 11. ♗f4+– Rellstab–Schönmann, Hamburg 1932; **5... g6** 6. ♗c4 ♗g7 7. ♗f4 [7. ♕d5?! 0–0 8. ♕c5 d6 9. ed6 ed6 10. ♕d5 ♕c7 11. ♘d4 ♖e8∞ Dubinski–Čistjakov, SSSR 1963] 0–0 8. ♕d2 ♘c6 9. 0-0-0 ♕a5 10. h4 b5 11. ♗d5± Klages–Lloyd, Antwerpen 1955

55 6... ed6 7. ♗c4 ♗e7 8. ♗f4 0–0 9. 0–0 ♘c6 10. ♖e1 ♗g4∞ Unzicker–Penrose, Hastings 1950/51; 9. ♕d2± Spielmann–A. Steiner, Budapest 1928

56 7. ♗e3!? ♘c6 8. ♗d3 e5 9. ♘g5! ♗e7 10. ♕h5 g6 11. ♕h6 ♗f8 12. ♕h4± Parma–Kozomora, Jugoslavija (ch) 1962

57 8... d5 9. 0-0-0 ♗e6 10. ♗b5 [10. ♘g5△ 11. g3± Haberditz] ♘c6 11. ♘e5 ♗d6 12. ♗g3±

58 9. ♗e2!? ♘c6 10. 0-0-0 0-0-0 11. h3±

59 9... ♗f3 10. gf3 ♘d7 11. ♗d6 ♗d6 12. ♖d6± Karaklajić–Enevoldsen, Moskva (ol) 1956

60 10. ♗d6 ♗d6 11. ♖d6 ♗f3 12. gf3 0-0-0±

61 13. ♖d6 0-0-0 14. f4! ♘b6 15. ♗e6 ♔c7 16. ♖d8 ♖d8 17. f5± Rejfiř–Szilagyi, ČSSR–Hungary 1956

62 6. ♗d3 e6 [6... b6 7. 0–0 ♗b7 8. ♗f4 e6 9. ♕e2 d5 10. ed6 ♗d6 11. ♗d6 ♕d6 12. ♖ad1 ♕e7 13. ♗b5 0–0= Jimenez–Bilek, La Habana 1965] 7. 0–0 ♕c7 8. ♖e1 h6 9. c4 b6 10. ♗d2 ♗b7 11. a3 0-0-0∞ Fuchs–Bilek, Varna (ol) 1962

63 6... d6?! 7. ♗f4 de5 8. ♘e5 ♕d1 9. ♖d1 ♘e5 10. ♗e5±⊥ Alapin–Rubinstein, Vilnus 1912

64 7. 0–0 b6 8. ♕e2 ♗b7 9. ♗f4 h6 10. ♗g3 ♕c7 11. ♘d2 ♘a5 12. ♗d3 d5 13. ed6 ♗d6 14. f4 0-0-0 15. ♘e4 f5 16. ♘d6 1/2 : 1/2 Parma–Bronštejn, Hamburg 1965

65 7... ♗e7 8. ♕d2 0—0 9. 0-0-0 ♕a5 10. ♔b1 b5 11. ♗d3 c4 12. ♗e4 ♖b8 13. ♘d4? b4!∓ Barczay—Udovčić, Zagreb 1969; 8. ♕e2!?±

66 8. ♕e2 h6 [8... ♗e7 9. ♗g3 b6 10. 0-0-0 ♗b7 11. h4 a6 12. ♗d3 ♘a5 13. ♗e4± Georgadze—Alburt, SSSR 1969] 9. 0-0-0 a6 10. ♔b1 b5 11. ♗d3 ♖b8 12. h4± 8. ♕d2 h6 9. h4 b6 10. 0-0-0 [10. ♗e2?! ♗b7 11. c4 0-0-0 12. 0-0-0 ♗e7 13. h5 ♘a5∞ Perenyi—Palatnik, SSSR 1973] ♗e7 11. ♗g3± Štejnberg—Palatnik, SSSR 1973; 10... ♗b7∓

67 9... f5?! 10. ♘h4 g6? 11. ♘f5!+— Gurgenidze—Lejn, SSSR 1967 — 3/370; 9... ♗b7 10. ♘g5 h6 11. ♘e4 ♘e5 12. ♕h5 d6 13. ♗e6 g6 14. ♕h3±→⟫ Boleslavski

68 10... ♗b7 11. ♘e4±

69 13. ♕f3 0—0 14. ♘e4 ♕c7=; 13. ♗b5 0—0 14. ♘c4 ♕c7!? [14... ♕d1 15. ♖ad1 ♘e7 16. ♘e5±] 15. ♕d6 ♕d6 16. ♘d6±

70 6... ♕b6 7. b3 e6 8. h4! ♕c7 9. ♕d2 b6 10. 0-0-0 ♗b7 11. ♖h3± Tatai—Estimo, Bauang 1973 — 16/280; 6... ♕c7 7. g3 e6 8. ♗g2 h6 9. h4 b6 10. ♕e2 ♗b7 11. 0-0-0 0-0-0 12. ♕d3± Makaričev—Murej, SSSR 1970

71 7. ♗d3 ♕c7 8. ♗g3 [8. ♕e2 d5 9. c4 d4 10. a3 b6 11. 0-0-0 ♗b7 12. h4± Makaričev—Palatnik, SSSR 1973] b6 9. ♘g5! ♗e7 10. ♕h5 g6 11. ♕h6 ♗f8 12. ♕h4± Popov—Šturm, SSSR 1973; 8... d5!?±; 7. ♕e2 ♗e7 8. 0-0-0 b6 9. g4 ♗b7 10. ♗g2 ♕c7 11. ♖d2 0—0 12. h4 ♖ad8 13. ♘g5 h6 14. ♕d3 g6 15. ♘e4 ♘e5 16. ♕g3±→ Murej—Vasjuhin, SSSR 1967; 7... ♕a5!?±

72 7... b6 8. 0-0-0 [8. g3!? ♗b7 9. ♗g2 h6 10. h4 ♕c7 11. 0-0-0 0-0-0 12. ♖he1± Boleslavski—Vorotnikov, SSSR 1966] h6 9. h4 ♗b7 10. ♕e3 ♕c7 11. ♘d2 ♘e7 12. ♘c4 ♘d5 13. ♕g3 0-0-0 14. ♗d2 ♕c6 15. h5± Knežević—Stanovnik, Jugoslavija 1966 — 2/328; 7... h6 8. g4 h5 9. gh5 ♖h5 10. ♗e2 d5∞ Guljko—Vorotnikov, SSSR 1967; 8. h4!?±

73 8... b6 9. ♗c4!? [9. g4 ♗b7 10. ♗g2 ♗e7 11. ♗g3 h6 12. h4 0-0-0± Bagirov—Mjagmarsuren, Budva 1963] ♗b7 10. ♖he1 h6 11. h4 0-0-0±

74 10. ♕e3 ♗b7 11. ♘d2 ♘e7 12. ♗h2 ♘f5 13. ♕h3 d5 14. ed6 ♗d6 15. ♗b5 ♔e7 16. ♗d3 ♗h2 17. ♖h2 ♘d6∞ Gufeljd—Klaman, SSSR 1968

75 13. ed6 ♗d6 14. ♗d6 ♖d6 15. f4 ♔b8 16. ♖he1 ♖d7 17. g3 h5 18. ♘f3± Carenkov—Kecloh, SSSR 1972

76 5. d4 ♘c3 [5... cd4 6. ♘d5 ♕a5 7. c3 ♕d5 8. ♕d4 ♕d4 9. ♘d4=] 6. bc3 d5 7. ♗d3 ♘c6= Matanović—Trifunović, Jugoslavija (ch) 1949; 5. ♗c4 ♘c3 [5... ♘b6?! 6. ♕e2 ♘c6 7. 0—0 a6?! 8. d3 d5 9. ed6 ♗d6 10. ♘e4 ♗e7 11. c3 ♘c4 12. dc4 0—0 13. ♗f4± Žilin—Mac, SSSR 1962] 6. dc3 d5=; 5. b3 ♘c3 6. dc3 d5 7. ed6 ♗d6?! 8. ♗b5 ♘c6 9. ♗c6 bc6 10. ♕d3±; 7... ♕d6!?=; 5. g3 ♘c6 6. ♗g2 ♘c3 [6... d6 7. ed6 ♗d6 8. ♘d5 ed5 9. d4 0—0 10. 0—0 ♗g4= Barczay—Kozomara, Sombor 1966] 7. bc3 [7. dc3 d5 8. ed6 ♗d6=] d6 8. ed6 ♗d6 9. 0—0 0—0 10. d3= Reti—Rubinstein, Göteborg 1920; 10. d4= Puc—Kozomara, Jugoslavija (ch) 1962

77 5... ♕c7 6. b3 ♘c6 7. c4 ♘f4 8. ♗b2 ♕b8? 9. ♕c2 ♗e7 10. g3 ♘g6 11. ♗g2± Arsenjev—Gosin, SSSR 1960; 5... ♘c6 6. c4 [6. b3 f5 7. ♘g3 ♕c7 8. ♗b2 ♘f4∞ Johansson—Bhend, Lugano (ol) 1968] ♘b6 [6... ♘f4 7. d4 ♘g6 8. d5! ♘ce5 9. ♘e5 ♘e5 10. d6±↑; 6... ♘c7 7. d4±↑ Junke—Vaganjan, Graz 1972; 6... ♘bd4 7. a3 ♘a6 8. d4±] 7. b3! [7. d3 d6 8. ed6 ♗d6= Suetin—Mnacakanjan, SSSR 1960] ♗e7 [7... d6 8. ed6 ♗d6 9. d4±; 7... ♕c7 8. ♗b2 ♘d4 9. ♗d3± Boleslavski] 8. ♗b2 0—0 9. ♗e2 [9. ♗d3 d6 10. ed6 ♗d6 11. ♘d6 ♕d6=] f6 [9... ♕c7 10. 0—0 d6 11. ♘f6! gf6 12. ef6 ♗d8 13. ♘g5 h6 14. ♗d3+—→⟫; 9... d6 10. ed6 ♗d6 11. d4±] 10. ef6 gf6 11. 0—0±→⟫ Boleslavski; 5... d6 6. ed6 ♗d6 7. d4 [7. ♗b5 ♘c6 8. 0—0 0—0 9. ♗c6 bc6 10. d3 e5 11. ♘fd2± Suetin—Kozomara, Sarajevo 1965] ♘c6 8. dc5 ♗c5 9. ♘c5 ♕a5 10. c3 ♕c5 11. ♗d3 0—0 12. 0—0 e5 13. ♖e1 ♖e8 14. ♘g5± Suetin—Mnacakanjan, SSSR 1961

78 6. ♘g3?! ♘c6 7. b3 ♕c7 8. ♗b2 ♘f4∓ Vasjukov—Szukszta, Hungary 1970 — 9/278; 6. ef6 ♘f6=

79 10. dc5 ♗c5 11. ♗e2 0—0 12. 0—0 f4 13. a3 a5 14. b3 ♕d6 15. ♗b2 ♗f5 1/2 : 1/2 Grabczewski—Přibyl, Lublin 1974

80 11... h6 12. b3 ♗e6 13. ♗b2 ♕c7 14. h3 ♖ac8 15. dc5 ♗c5= Vogt—Neckař, Stockholm 1969

81 13. ♕d3 ♕a5 14. a3∞ Tompa—Cuibus, Hungary 1973 — 15/318

82 7. ♗e2 ♘c6 8. 0—0 de5 9. de5 ♗e7 10. ♗f4 0—0 11. c3 ♗e6= Krstić—Mjagmarsuren, Siegen (ol) 1970; 7. ♗d3 ♘c6 8. 0—0 c4 9. ♗e2 a6 10. ♖e1 ♗e7 11. b3 de5 12. de5 b5 13. ♘d4!± Nowak—Szukszta, Warszawa 1969; 8... cd4!?=

83 8. dc5 ♗c5 9. ♗b5 ♘c6 10. ♕e2 ♗e6 11. c3 0—0 12. 0—0 h6 13. ♗e3 ♕b6= Marco—Tartakower, Haag 1921

84 11. b3 c3!? 12. ♕d3 ♘b4 13. ♕c3 ♗f5=∞ Romanovski—Gufeljd, SSSR 1957; 11. c3=

85 15. b3 b5= Rutman—Korčnoj, SSSR 1957

86 7... ♗e7? 8. ♗e7 ♕e7 9. dc5+—; 7... ♕b6 8. dc5 dc5 9. ♕d5 ♗e6 [9... h6? 10. 0-0-0 hg5 11. ♗b5!+— Arulaid—Geler, SSSR 1949] 10. ♗b5 ♘c6 11. ♕d3! [11. ♗c6?! bc6 12. ♕d2 h6= Foltys—Seitz, Lodz 1938] c4 12. ♗c4 ♕b4 13. ♘d2 ♘e5 [13... ♕b2 14. 0—0± Secula—H. Müller, corr. 1958] 14. ♗b5 ♘c6 15. 0—0 h6 16. c3! ♕g4 [16... ♕b2? 17. a3! hg5 18. ♖fb1+— Maximovič—Brychta, Praha 1953] 17. ♗e3±

87 8. ♗d2 ♕b6 9. ♗c3 de5 [9... ♘c6 10. ed6 ♗d6 11. ♕d2 c4 12. 0-0-0 0—0 13. ♘e5

♗e6= Boleslavski] 10. ♘e5 ♘c6 [10... ♗e6 11. ♗e2 ♘c6 12. ♘c6 bc6 13. 0–0 c4? 14. ♗g4 f5 15. ♖e1 ♔f7 16. ♖e6!+– Janošević–Kozomara, Jugoslavija (ch) 1957] 11. ♘c6 [11. dc5 ♗c5 12. ♘d3 0–0 13. ♗e2 ♗f5 14. 0–0 d4 15. ♗d2 ♗d6 16. b3 ♖ac8∓ Parma–Damjanović, Jugoslavija (ch) 1963] bc6=

88 **8... de5** 9. ♘e5±→; **8... h6** 9. ♗f4 de5 10. ♘e5 cd4 11. ♗d3 ♗e7 12. 0–0 0–0 13. cd4± Čerepkov–Vorotnikov, SSSR 1964

89 9. ♕d4 ♘c6 10. ♕e3 ♗e6 11. ♗d3 [11. ♘d4!? de5 12. ♘e6 fe6 18. ♕h3∞ Kelečević–Kozomara, Sarajevo 1968] de5 12. ♘e5 ♗d6 13. ♘f3 0–0= Udovčić–Kozomara, Jugoslavija (ch) 1957

90 **9... de5** 10. ♘e5 ♕c7 [10... ♗e6 11. 0–0 dc3 12. ♕e2 ♗d6 13. ♘f7+–→》 Melihov–Nogovicin, SSSR 1956] 11. 0–0 ♗d6 12. cd4± Keres; **9... ♘c6** 10. 0–0 de5 11. ♘e5 ♘e5 12. ♖e1 ♗e6! [12... ♗d6?! 13. cd4±] 13. ♖e5 ♗d6 14. ♖e1 [14. ♖e6?! fe6 15. ♕h5 ♔f8 16. ♕f3 ♔g8 17. ♕g4 ♖e8 18. ♗f6 ♕c7 19. ♗b5 h5! 20. ♕h3 ♖f8 21. ♕e6 ♕f7 22. ♕d6 ♖h6!–+ Czerniak–Trifunović, Mar del Plata 1950] dc3 15. bc3 0–0 — 9... dc3

91 10... cb2? 11. ♖b1 de5?! 12. ♘e5 ♗d6 13. ♘f7! ♔f7 14. ♕h5 g6 15. ♗g6! hg6 16. ♕h8 ♗f5 17. ♖be1+– Keres–Winter, Warszawa (ol) 1935

92 **15. ♖e3**? d4! 16. ♖e6 fe6 17. ♕h5 g6 18. ♗g6 ♔d7–+ Keller–Witkowski, Beograd 1956; **15. ♖e6** fe6 16. ♕h5 g6!? [16... ♔f8 17. ♖e1 Sokolski] 17. ♗g6 ♔d7 18. ♗d3 ♖af8 19. ♖b1 ♕a2 20. ♗e3 ♔c8∓ Seifert–Szukszta, Moskva 1964; **15. ♖e1** 0–0 16. ♕h5 [16. ♖e6? fe6 17. ♕h5 g6 18. ♗g6 ♕c7 –+] g6 17. ♕h6 ♕c3∓; 16. ♖e3!?∞

93 7... ♗d7 8. ♗d7 ♕d7 [8... ♘d7? 9. dc5+–] 9. 0–0 ♘c6 10. ed6 ♗d6 [10... ♕d6 11. dc5 ♕c5 12. ♗e3 ♕d6 13. ♘d4± Bradvarević–Kozomara, Jugoslavija (ch) 1957] 11. ♖e1 ♘e7 12. dc5 ♗c5 13. ♗g5!? [13. ♗e3 (K. Treybal–Podgorny, Praha 1940) ♗d6 14. ♕d3 0–0 15. ♖ad1± Pachman; 13. b3 0–0 14. ♗b2±] 0–0 14. ♕d3 f6 [14... h6 15. ♗e7 ♗e7 16. ♖ad1 ♖ad8 17. c4 ♗f6 18. cd5 ♗b2 19. d6±] 15. ♗e3± Boleslavski

94 8... ♗e6 9. c4 ♕b6 10. dc5 dc5 11. cd5 ♕b5 12. de6 fe6 13. ♘g5 ♘d4 14. ♗e3 0-0-0 15. ♕g4!± Koch–Zirngibl, DDR (ch) 1950; 9... ♗e7 — 8... ♗e7

95 9. ed6 ♕d6 10. c4 [10. dc5 ♕c5 11. ♕d3 a6? 12. ♗a4 b5 13. ♗b3 d4 14. ♗f4 ♗f5 15. ♕d2 0–0 16. ♖fe1 ♗f6 17. ♗g5!± Günsberger–Witkowski, Romania–Polska 1958; 11... 0–0 12. ♗e3±] a6 11. dc5 ♕c5 12. ♗e3 ♕d6 13. ♗c6 bc6± Osnos–Ljavdanski, SSSR (ch) 1962

96 **9... dc4** 10. ed6 ♕d6 11. d5 a6 12. ♗c4±; **9... a6** 10. ♗c6 bc6 11. cd5 cd5 12. ed6 ♕d6 13. dc5 ♕c5 14. ♗e3 ♕a5 15. ♘d4± Boleslavski

97 11... 0-0-0?! 12. a5 ♕c7 13. ed6 ♗d6 14. dc5 ♗e5 15. a6 ♗b2 16. ab7 ♔b8 17. ♖a2 dc4 18. ♕a4+– Bouwmeester–Pomar, Bern 1962

98 12. ed6 ab5 13. dc5±; 12... ♗d6 13. cd5 ab5 14. de6 fe6 15. ab5 ♖a1 16. ♕a1± Fichtl–Kopriva, ČSSR (ch) 1957

99 15. ♗c6 bc6 16. ♘e5 ♕c7 17. ♕a4± Unzicker–Pomar, Bad Aibling 1968 — 5/350

100 **7. c3** d6 8. ♗d3 cd4 9. cd4 de5 10. ♘e5 ♗b4 11. ♗d2 ♕b6= Marjasin–Vaganjan, SSSR 1972; **7. ♗d3** cd4 [7... c4 8. ♗e2 (8. ♗f5?! d6 9. ♗c8 ♖c8 10. 0–0 de5 11. ♘e5 ♗e7= German–Mjagmarsuren, Lugano (ol) 1968) d6 9. 0–0 h6 10. b3 b5 11. a4± Vasiljev–Ustinov, SSSR 1960; 7... d6 8. ed6 ♗d6 9. dc5 ♗c5 10. 0–0 ♕d6 11. ♖e1 ♗e6 12. ♗g5 0–0 13. ♕d2± Gufeljd–Ustinov, SSSR 1960] 8. 0–0 ♗e7 9. ♖e1 0–0 10. ♗f4 d6=

101 8. **♗e2 d6** 9. ♕d5 [9. ed6 ♕d6 10. 0–0 0–0 11. c3 ♖e8 12. ♗g5 h6 13. ♗h4 ♗f5= Estrin–Přibyl, Olomouc 1972] ♗e6 10. ♕e4 de5 11. ♘e5 ♘e5 [11... ♕a5 12. ♗d2 ♗b4 13. ♗b4 ♕b4 14. ♕b4 ♘b4 15. ♔d2± Estrin –Šmit, SSSR 1960] 12. ♕e5 ♕a5 13. ♔f1 ♕b6 14. ♗e3 ♗e3 15. fe3 0–0 16. ♔f2 ♖fe8= Suetin–Boleslavski, Debrecen 1961; **8... d4**!? 9. 0–0 d6 [9... 0–0 10. ♗d3 d6= Gasporjanc–Vasiljčuk, SSSR 1963] 10. ♗g5 ♕c7 11. ed6 ♕d6 12. ♕d2 0–0 13. ♖fe1 ♗f5= Boleslavski

102 9. ♕d2?! 0–0 10. ♗c4 d6!⩱

103 **10. ♔f1**?! 0–0 11. ♘g5 d6! 12. ed6 ♗h4∓; **10. ♔d1**?! 0–0 11. ♘g5 [11. c3 d6 12. ed6 ♗e6 13. ♕d3 ♗c4 14. ♕c4 ♖ad8 15. ♔c2 ♖d6 16. ♗f4 ♖c8 17. ♕b3 ♘d4 18. ♘d4 ♕d4 19. ♗d6 ♕e4!–+ Kuijpers–Minić, Marianske Lazni 1962] ♕d4 12. ♕d4 ♗d4∓

104 **11. ♘g5**? d6 12. ♕e4 [12. ♘f7? ♗e6! –+] ♗f5 13. ♕f4 ♗c5 14. ♖d1 ♖ae8–+ Zelevinski–Tenenbaum, SSSR 1959; **11. ♗d2** d6 12. ♖af1 ♗e6 13. ♕e4 ♗c4 14. ♕c4 ♗d4 15. ed6 ♖ad8∓ Aronin–Tenenbaum, SSSR 1961; **11. ♖d1** d6! [11... ♘b4? 12. ♕e4 d5 13. ed6 ♗d7 14. ♗g5 ♔h8 15. ♘e5± Aronin–Krasnov, SSSR 1961] 12. ed6 ♗e6 — 8... d6

105 **12. c3** ♘e7 [12... d6!?] 13. ♕e4 d5 14. ed6 ♗f5! [14... ♕d6? 15. ♘g5 ♕h2 16. ♖f7 ♖f7 17. ♗f7 ♔h8 18. ♗f4 ♗g4 19. ♔d3 ♕h6 20. ♗e6± Sarapu–Mjagmarsuren, Sousse (izt) 1967] 15. ♕e7 ♕c6 16. ♘e5 ♕g2 17. ♔d1 ♕c2 18. ♔e1 ♕e4 19. ♗e2 ♖ae8 20. ♖f4 ♕c2 21. ♘c4 ♗d6!–+ Šaljnev–Berger, SSSR 1963; **12. ♕e4** d5! 13. ♗d5 [13. ♕d5 ♗f5△ ♖ad8∓; 13. ed6 ♗d7∓] g6 14. g4 [14. ♗h6 ♗f5 15. ♕c4 (Čeremisin–Tenenbaum, SSSR 1959) ♘a5△ ♖fe8∓] ♗e6 15. ♗e6 fe6 16. ♗h6 ♖fd8 17. b3 ♘d4 18. ♘d4 ♖d4= Čeremisin–Kofman, SSSR 1960

106 12... d6? 13. ♖f7! [13. ♘f7? ♗e6!] ♘d4 14. ♔d1 ♗g4 13. ♖f3 ♔h8 16. ♕g8!+–

107 13. ♘f7 ♘f7 14. ♖f7 ♕e6 15. ♕e6 de6 16. ♖f8 ♔f8 17. ♗e3±⊥

108 14. ♗d5?! ♗g4 15. ♔d2 ♖ad8∓→» Spiridonov–Mjagmarsuren, Marianske Lazni 1962

109 **14... ♗g4** 15. ♖f3 ♗g1 16. ♔f1! ♖ad8 17. ♕e4 ♖d1 18. ♔e2± Prokopčuk–Kuznjecov, SSSR 1972 — 14/322; **14... ♖e8** 15. ♔f3 ♕f6 16. ♔g3 ♗d6 17. ♖f4!± Spaski–Ćirić, Marianske Lazni 1962

110 **13. ♔d3**?! ♕g6! [13... ♘e6?! 14. ♕e4 ♘g5 15. ♗g5 d6!∞ Cehonski–Verner, SSSR 1974] 14. ♕e4 d5! 15. ♗d5 ♗f5 16. ♖f5 ♘f5 17. e6 ♖ad8 18. ef7 ♔h8 19. c4 b5!∓ Gligorić–Larsen, Zürich 1959; **13. ♔e1** d6! [13... ♘c2 14. ♔d1 ♘a1 15. ♖f7+–; 13... ♘e6 14. ♘e4 ♗e7? 15. c3 ♕c7 16. ♗f4 ♕c6 17. ♕d3± Baumgartner–Pytlakowski, Halle 1960] 14. ed6 ♗d7!∞

111 **14. ♕e4**? ♘g5 15. ♗g5 d5 16. ♗d5 ♕b2 17 ♔e2 ♗g4!–+ Pavlov–Radulescu, Romania 1959; **14. ♘h7**? ♔h7 13. ♕e4 ♔g8 16. ♗d3 g6 17. ♖f6 ♗e7 18. ♗e3 ♕c6! 19. ♖g6 fg6 20. ♕g6 ♘g7 21. ♕h7 ♔f7 22. ♔d2 [Vobořil–Maton, corr. 1960] d5 [22... ♕g2 23. ♔c3 ♕c6 24. ♔d2 d5∓ Pachman] 23. ♗h6 ♔e8 24. ♕g7 ♖f2 25. ♔e1 ♖g2!–+ Boleslavski; **14. ♗d3** ♘g5 15. ♗g5 d6!? [15... ♕c6? 16. ♗e4 h6 17. ♗h4 ♕e6 18. ♕e6 de6 19. c3±⊥ Averbah–Kudrjašov, SSSR 1959; 15... ♕b2 16. ♕c5 ♕a1 17. ♔d2 (Mnacakanjan–Ustinov, SSSR 1959) ♕b2!? 18. ♗e7 d6∞ Euwe; 16. ♔d2!? d6 17. ed6 ♕b4 18. c3 ♗e6 19. ♗h7 ♔h8 20. ♕f3 ♕g4= Minić–Kozomara, Jugoslavija (ch) 1960] 16. ♕e4 g6 17. ♗h6 ♗e6! 18. ♗f8 ♖f8 19. ♔c1 [19. ed6? ♕b2 20. ♔e2 ♖e8! 21. ♔f3 ♗g4!–+ Röhrig–P. Schmidt, corr. 1966 — 2/329] ♗d4 20. c3 ♗e5∓; **14. ♘e6** fe6 15. ♖f8 ♗f8 16. ♕e4 ♕g1=

112 14... ♗e7?! 15. c3 d6 16. ed6 ♖d8 17. ♔c2± Savkin–Cejtlin, corr. 1972 — 13/339

113 15... ♗d6? 16. ♘d6 ♖d8 17. ♗f4! ♘f4 18. ♕f7 ♔h8 19. ♕g8! 1 : 0 Unzicker–Sarapu, Siegen (ol) 1970 — 10/394

114 **16. ♕f5** ♗d6 17. ♕f7 ♔h8∞ Euwe; **16. ♗f4** ♘f4 17. ♕f7 ♔h8 18. ♕f4 ♗d6 19. ♘d6 ♖d6 20. ♔c1 ♖f6 21. ♕e5 ♖f1 22. ♗f1 ♕h6 23. ♔b1 ♗d7= Boleslavski

115 18... ♘f8 19. ♖f1!? [19. ♘d6?! ♗f5 20. ♕f7 ♔h8 21. ♘f5 ♕g1= Čeremisin–Tenenbaum, SSSR 1961] ♕d4 20. ♗d2 ♗b4 21. ♗b4 ♕b4 22. a3± Planinc–Dobrev, Varna 1970

116 Muhin–Tenenbaum, SSSR 1969

117 **14... ♗e7** 15. ♘e4±; **14... ♕c6** 15. ♘e4 b5 16. ♕c6 dc6 17. ♗e6 fe6 18. ♖f8 ♗f8 19. ♗e3 ♗b7 20. ♗c5±⊥ Kupper–Krivec, Schweiz (ch) 1962

118 **15... ♘g5**?! 16. bc5 dc5 17. ♗g5 ♗e6 18. ♕e4 ♗c4 19. ♕c4 ♕b2 20. ♖c1 ♕g2 21. ♗e7!+– Gligorić–Matanović, Beograd 1961; **15... ♗e3** 16. ♖f7! ♗g5 [16... ♖f7 17. ♘f7 ♗c1 18. ♘d6!+–] 17. ♖f8 ♔f8 18. ♗g5± Gligorić, Sokolov

119 16. cb4? de5 17. ♘f7 ♖f7 18. ♖f7 ♔f7 19. ♗b2 ♔e7 20. ♗e5 ♗d7∓

120 16... ♘g5?! 17. ♖b4! [17. ♗g5 ♗e6 18. ♕d3 d5! 19. ♖b4 dc4 20. ♕g3 ♕c5 21. ♗f6 g6 22. ♕g5 ♖fd8! 23. ♗d8 ♕d5= Buljovčić–Minić, Jugoslavija (ch) 1962] ♕d8 18. ♗g5 ♕g5 19. ed6 ♗g4 20. ♔c2 ♕g6 21. ♗d3 ♕e6 22. ♕e4± Đurašević–Kozomara, Jugoslavija 1962

121 17. cb4 de5∞

122 22. ba5 ♖d6 23. ♖b5 ♔e8 24. ♔e1 ♘c7 25. ♖c5 ♖d5 26. ♖c7 ♗d7 27. ♖b7 ♖a5± Boleslavski

123 **10. ♕d2**?! 0–0 11. ♗d3 ♖e8 12. ♔f1 ♗g4∓; **10. ♗e3** ♕b2! [10... ♗e3 11. fe3 ♕e3 12. ♗e2 ♗e6 13. ♕g5± Arulajd–Vetohin, SSSR 1960] 11. ♕e4 [11. ♗c4 ♕a1 12. ♔e2 ♕f6 13. ♕c5 0–0∓] ♗e6 12. d7 ♔d7 13. ♖d1 ♔c8 14. ♗c5 ♕c3= Boleslavski; **10. ♗d3**!? ♗f2 11. ♔e2 0–0? 12. d7! ♘b4 13. dc8♕ ♖ac8 14. ♕b3+– Furman–Vaganjan, SSSR 1973 — 16/281; 11... ♗e6∞

124 **11. ♕h4** ♗d6 12. c3 ♗e7 13. ♕g3 0-0-0∓ Lebedev–Mnacakanjan, SSSR 1964; **11. ♗c4** ♗f2 12. ♔f1 0–0! 13. ♗e6 fe6 14. ♕e6 ♔h8∓

125 ∞ Toluš

126 11. ♔f1?! 0–0 12. ♕e4 [12. d7? ♗d7 13. ♕d7 ♖ad8 14. ♕g4 ♖d1 15. ♔e2 ♖h1 16. ♗h6 ♖e8 17. ♔d3 ♖e3–+] ♗d7 13. ♗g5 ♗c5 14. ♗d3 g6 15. ♗f6 ♘b4 16. ♕h4 [Talj–Gipslis, SSSR (ch) 1959] ♘d5∓

127 **12... ♗g4**?! 13. ♔f1! ♖ad8 [13... ♘a5 14. ♗d3 ♗g1? 15. ♘g1 ♗d1 16. ♕e4 g6 17. ♗e3 ♕d6 18. ♖d1+– Buskenström–Soeby, Varna (ol) 1962] 14. ♗f4± Boleslavski; **12... ♗c5** 13. ♔f1 ♘d4? 14. ♖d4! ♗e6 15. ♕e4 ♗d4 16. ♗d3! g6 17. ♕d4+– Kurajica–Pijoan, Olot 1973; 13... ♗e6!?±

128 13. ♕b5 ♘d4 14. ♘d4 ♗d4 15. ♔f3 ♗c4 16. ♕c4 ♗e5∞ Pokros–Rožkov, corr. 1964

129 13... ♖fe8 14. ♔f1 ♗d4 [14... ♘d4? 15. ♔f2! ♘c2 16. ♔g3 ♘a1 17. ♘g5 g6 18. ♘e6 fe6 19. ♗e6+–] 15. ♗d3 f5 16. ♕f4±

130 **14... ♗c4** 15. ♕c4 ♖e6 16. ♗f4± Tatai–Gerusel, Solingen 1968 — 6/426; **14... ♗c5** 15. ♗d3 f5 16. ♕h4 h6 17. ♕g3 ♖f6 18. b3± Planinc–Bojković, Jugoslavija 1962; **14... ♘e5** 15. ♘e5 ♗c4 16. ♘c4 ♖e4 17. ♘b6 ♗b6 18. g3± Levy–Bhend, Lugano (ol) 1968; **14... ♗d4** 15. ♗d3 f5 16. ♕f4 ♗d5 17. ♘d4 ♖e4 18. ♗e4 fe4 19. ♘f5 ♗c4 20. ♔e1 ♖f5 21. ♕f5 1/2 : 1/2 Levy–Cordovil, Siegen (ol) 1970

131 15. ♕f4? ♖e6 16. ♕g5 ♖f6 17. ♕b5 ♖e8–+ Parma–Přibyl, ČSSR 1974

132 = Parma

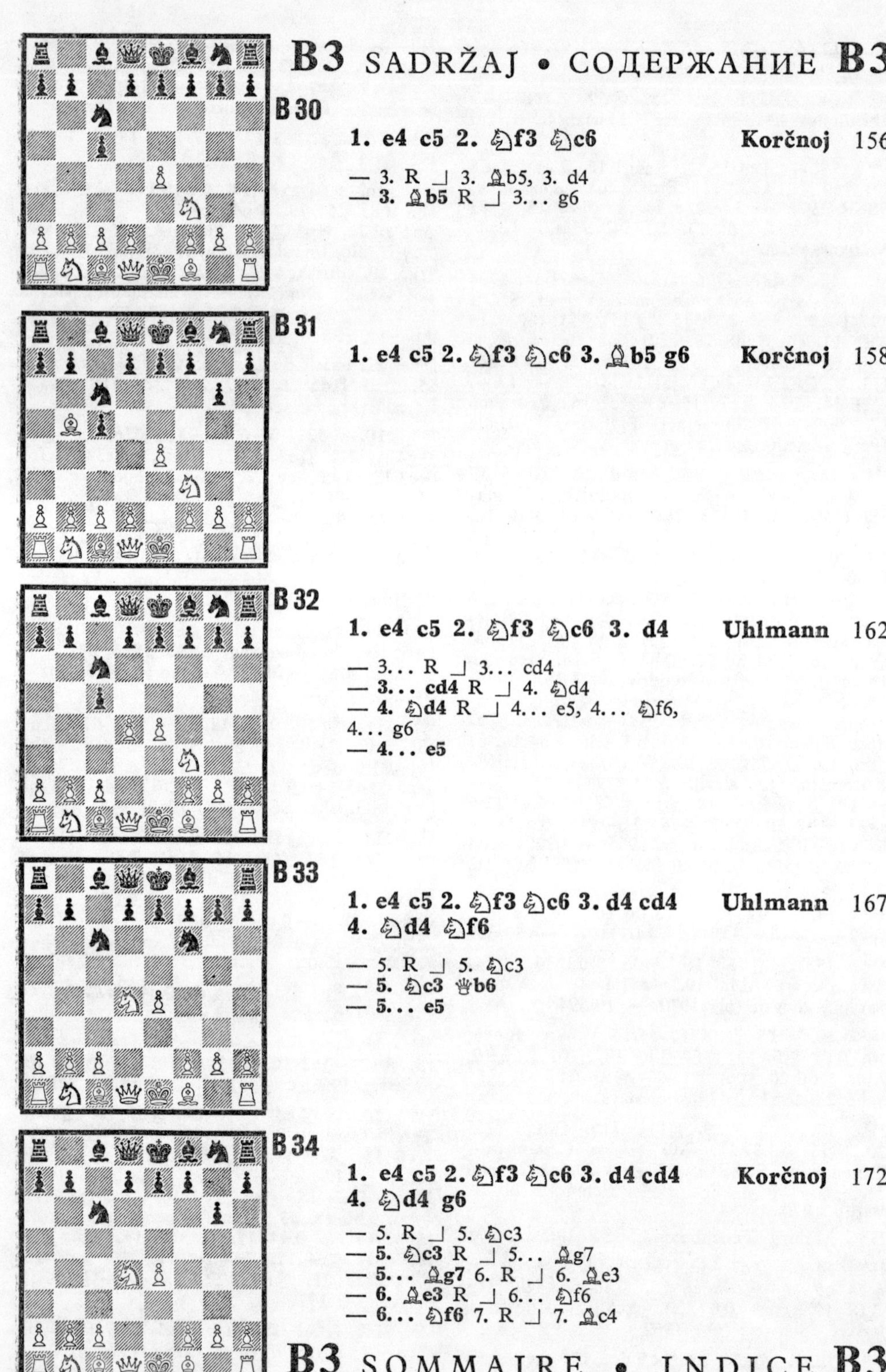

B3 SADRŽAJ • СОДЕРЖАНИЕ B3

B3 SOMMAIRE • INDICE B3

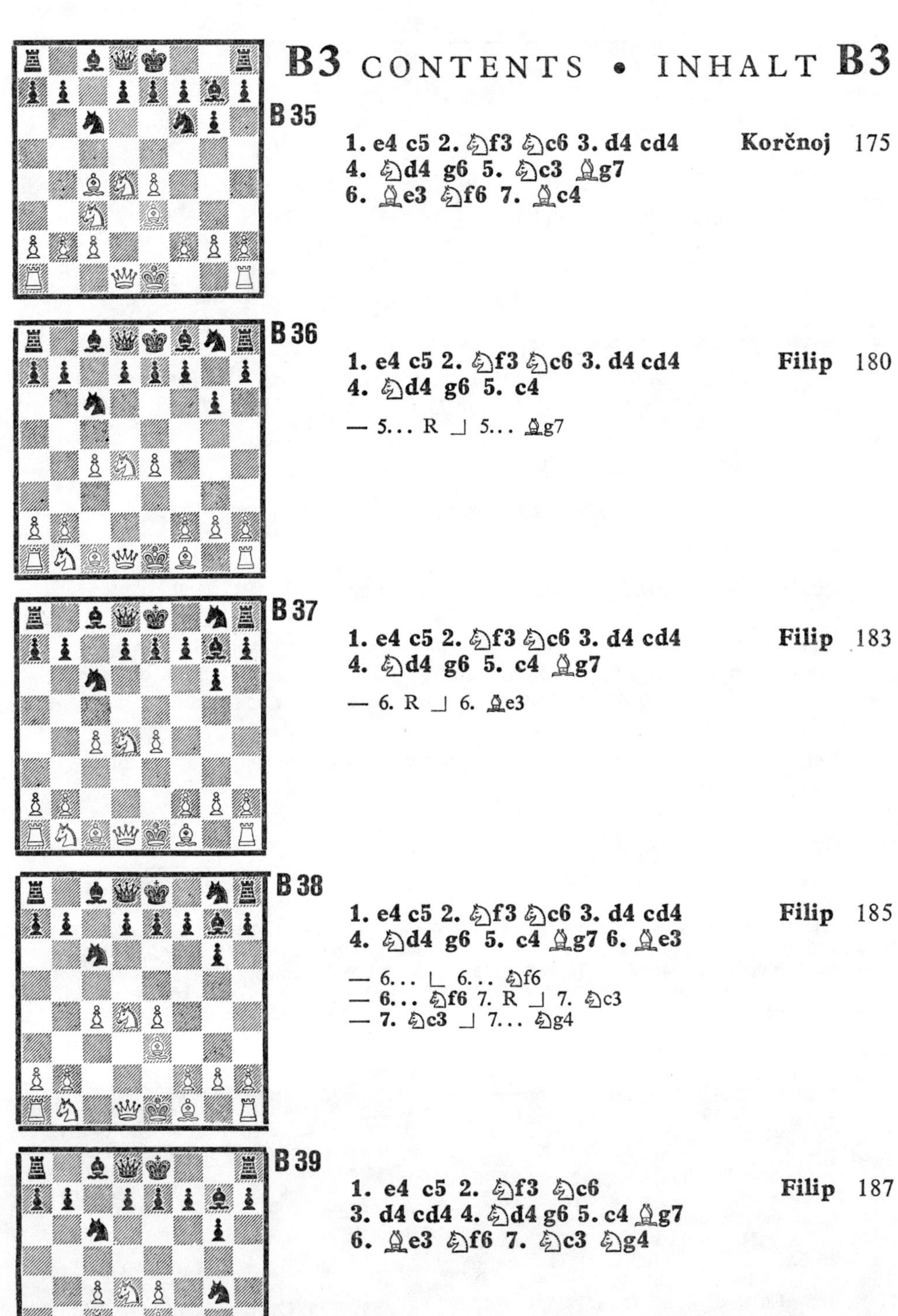

B3 CONTENTS • INHALT B3

B3 INDICE • INNEHÅLL B3

B 30 — 1. e4 c5 2. ♘f3 ♘c6

	3	4	5	6	7	8	9	10	11	
1	♗b5[1]	0–0[3]	♘c3[5]	♖e1	d4	♘d5	ed5	♘d4	♘c6	±
	♕c7[2]	♘f6[4]	e6	d6	cd4	ed5[6]	♗e7	♘d5	bc6[7]	
2	...	♗c6	h3[9]	d3[10]	a4	♘bd2	♘c4	♘h4	g4	±
	a6	dc6[8]	e5	♗d6	a5	♘e7	f6	0–0	♗c7[11]	
3	...	♘c3[12]	0–0	♖e1	♗c4	d3	♘d4	♘e2	c3	±
	♕b6	e6	♘ge7[13]	♘d4	♘ec6	d6	cd4[14]	♘a5[15]	♘c4[16]	
4	...	e5	♘c3[18]	a4	0–0	♖e1	d3	♗c4	ed6	=
	♘f6	♘d5[17]	♘c7[19]	g6[20]	♗g7	0–0	♘d4	d5	♕d6[21]	
5	...	♘c3	e5[23]	♘b5[24]	0–0	♘c3	dc3	ed6	♕d6	=
	...	♘d4![22]	♘b5	♘d5	a6[25]	♘c3	d5	♕d6	ed6[26]	
6	...	♕e2!?	♗c6	d3	♗d2	♗c3	♘bd2			±
	...	a6	dc6	g6	♗g7	♗g4	0–0[27]			

1. e4 c5 2. ♘f3 ♘c6 3. ♗b5 e6

	4	5	6	7	8	9	10	11	12	
7	♘c3[28]	♗c6	e5	d3	♘e5	♗g5	0–0[30]	♕e2		=
	a6[29]	bc6	f6	fe5	♘f6	♗e7	0–0	♘d5		
8	...	0–0	♗c6	d4[31]	♘d4	♘c6	♕g4	e5	♗g5	=
	♘ge7	a6	♘c6	cd4	d6![32]	bc6	g6[33]	d5![34]	♗e7[35]	
9	...	0–0[36]	♗d3	♘d4	♘e2	♗c4	f4			=
	♘d4	a6[37]	d6[38]	cd4	e5	♘f6	♗e7[39]			
10	♗c6	0–0[40]	d3[42]	♘c3	♘e2	b3	c4	ef5	d4![43]	±
	bc6	♘e7[41]	♘g6	♗e7	0–0	d6	f5	ef5		
11	0–0	b3[45]	♗c6[46]	♗b2	d4	♘d4	c4	♕d2	♘c3	±
	♘ge7[44]	a6	♘c6	d6	cd4	♕f6!?[47]	♗e7	♕g6	0–0[48]	

[1] **3. ♗e2**?! ♘f6! [3... e6 4. 0–0 d6?! 5. d4 cd4 6. ♘d4 ♘f6 7. ♗f3 ♘e5 8. c4! ♘f3 9. ♕f3 ♗e7 10. ♘c3 0–0 11. b3± Aljehin–Sämisch, Berlin 1923] 4. ♘c3 [4. e5 ♘d5 5. ♘c3 ♘f4!? 6. d4 ♘g2! 7. ♔f1 cd4 8. ♘e4 d6 9. ♔g2 de5∓; 4... ♘g4 5. d4 cd4 6. ♗f4 ♘ge5∓] e5 5. 0–0 ♗e7 6. d3 d5=; **3. b3** ♘f6?! 4. e5 ♘d5 5. ♗b2 d6 6. ♗b5 ♘c7 7. ♗c6 bc6 8. ed6 ed6 9. 0–0 ♘e6 10. d4 ♗e7 11. ♘c3 0–0 12. d5 ed5 13. ♘d5± Simagin–Boleslavski, SSSR 1956; 3... d6 4. ♗b2 e5 5. ♘c3 ♘f6 — B 50; **3. c3** e6 4. d4 d5 — B 22; **3. c4** ♘f6 4. ♘c3 e6 5. d4 cd4 6. ♘d4 ♗b4 — B 44; **3. g3** ♘f6 4. d3 d6 5. ♗g2 e5 6. 0–0 ♗e7 7. c3 0–0 8. ♕e2 ♖e8 9. ♘bd2 ♗f8△ d5= Žuravljev–Peterson, SSSR 1962; **3. d3** g6 4. g3 ♗g7 [4... e6 5. d4!±] 5. ♗g2 e5 [5... e6 6. 0–0 ♘ge7 7. c3 0–0 (Radulov–Tajmanov, Leningrad (izt) 1973 — 15/334) 8. ♖e1 e5=] 6. ♘c3 ♘ge7 7. ♗e3 d6 8. ♕d2 ♘d4!△ ♗h3= Ajanski–Svešnikov, Plovdiv 1973

[2] **3... ♕a5**? 4. ♘a3 ♘f6 5. e5 ♘d5 6. 0–0 a6 7. ♗c6 dc6 8. ♘c4±; **3... d5**?! 4. ed5 ♕d5 5. ♘c3 ♕h5?! 6. d4 cd4 7. ♗c6 bc6 8. ♕d4 f6 9. ♗e3±; 5... ♕d6!?; **3... ♘d4** 4. ♘d4 cd4 5. c3 a6 6. ♗e2 d5 7. ♕a4 ♗d7 8. ♕d4 de4 9. ♕e4 ♗c6 10. ♕g4 h5 11. ♕h3 e5 12. 0–0 ♕f6 13. d4 ed4 14. cd4 ♗d6 15. ♘c3 ♕d4 16. ♖e1 ♘e7 17. ♗g5± Gipslis–Koblenc, SSSR 1956; **3... d6**!? — B 51

[3] **4. ♗c6**?! dc6 5. d3 ♘f6 6. ♕e2 g6 7. 0–0 ♗g7 8. ♖e1 0–0= Henneberger–Flor, Zürich 1934; **4. c3** a6 5. ♗a4 ♘f6 6. ♕e2 e5 7. 0–0 d6! [7... ♗e7? 8. d4 cd4 9. cd4 ♘d4 10. ♘d4 ed4 11. e5 d3 12. ♕e3 ♘d5 13. ♕g3 g6 14. ♗b3 ♘b4 15. ♗f7 ♔d8 16. ♗h6+– Nimzowitsch–Gilg, Kecskemet 1927] 8. d4 b5=

[4] **4... a6** 5. ♗c6 ♕c6 6. d4 cd4 7. ♘d4 ♕c7 8. ♘c3 e6!? 9. e5 ♘e7? 10. ♘db5 ab5 11. ♘b5 ♕a5 12. ♘d6 ♔d8 13. ♘f7 ♔e8 14. ♘d6 ♔d8 15. ♗d2+– Lutikov–Romanišin, SSSR 1968 — 6/440; 9... d6±; **4... e6** 5. c3 [5. ♘c3 ♘ge7△ a6=] ♘f6 6. ♖e1 a6 7. ♗c6±

5 5. ♖e1 g6 6. e5 ♘d5 7. d4 cd4 8. c4 ♘db4 9. a3 ♘a6∞

6 8... ♕d8 9. ♘d4 ♗d7 10. ♗g5 ♗e7 [10... ed5 11. ♗c6 bc6 12. ed5 ♗e7 13. dc6 +−] 11. ♘e7 ♘d4 12. ♗d7 ♕d7 13. ♗f6 gf6 14. ♘d5+− K. Richter—Grohmann, Berlin 1950

7 12. ♕d5± Simagin—Florian, Moskva—Budapest 1949

8 4... bc6 5. d3 d6 6. 0—0 [6. b3?! e5 7. ♗b2 f5?! 8. 0—0 ♘f6 9. ♖e1 ♗e7 10. ♘bd2 0—0 11. a4 f4 12. c3△ d4±; 7... ♘e7!?△ ♘g6∞] ♗g4∞; 6. c3!?△ d4±

9 5. d3 ♘f6 [5... ♗g4? 6. h3 ♗h5 7. ♘bd2 e6 8. a4 b5 9. ♕e2 ♘f6 10. g4 ♗g6 11. ♘e5 ♘d7 12. ♘d7 ♕d7 13. f4± Nežmetdinov—Šamkovič, SSSR 1954] 6. 0—0 ♗g4 7. ♘bd2 e6 8. ♘c4 ♕c7 9. ♗g5 b5 10. ♘e3 ♗h5 11. ♗h4 ♗d6 12. ♗g3± Rossolimo—Lundin, Bad Gastein 1948; 5... ♕c7!?△ e5

10 6. 0—0 f6 7. d3 ♗e6 8. a4 ♕d7 9. a5 0-0-0 10. b3 g5 11. ♗e3 [11. ♘a3 h5? 12. ♘c4 ♕g7 13. ♗e3 g4? 14. ♘h4 gh3 15. g3± Simagin—Benkö, Moskva—Budapest 1949; 13... h4 14. ♘b6 ♔b8 15. ♘h2±; 11... ♘e7 12. ♘c4 ♕e8∓] ♘e7! 12. ♗c5 ♘g6=∞ Boleslavski

11 12. ♗e3 b6 13. ♕e2 ♗e6 14. b3 ♕d7 15. ♖g1 ♔h8 16. 0-0-0 ♕e8 [Vasjukov—Željandinov, La Habana II 1967 — 4/411] 17. ♘f5±

12 **4. ♘a3** ♘f6 5. ♕e2 a6=; **4. a4** e6 5. 0—0 ♘f6 [5... a6 6. ♗c6 ♕c6 7. ♘c3±] 6. e5 ♘d5 7. ♘c3 [7. c4?! ♘c7 8. ♗c6 ♕c6 9. ♘c3 b6 10. d3 ♗b7 11. ♘e4 d5 12. ed6 ♗d6 13. ♘fg5 ♗e7 14. ♕h5 g6 15. ♕h6 ♗f8 16. ♕h4 ♗g7 17. ♘f3 f6 18. ♗h6 0—0∓ Kramer—Lombardy, Zürich 1961] ♗e7 8. ♘d5?! ed5 9. d4 cd4 10. ♗g5 ♗g5 11. ♘g5 h6 12. ♘f3 0—0∓ Gufeljd—Korčnoj, SSSR (ch) 1961; 8. ♗c4!±; **4. ♗a4** d6?! 5. 0—0 ♗d7 6. c3 ♘f6 7. ♖e1 e5 8. d4!± Sax—Sanz, Nice (ol) 1974 — 17/369; 4... g6!?±; **4. ♕e2** e6 5. 0—0 ♘ge7 6. c3 a6 7. ♗a4 ♘g6 8. ♖d1 [8. d4 cd4 9. cd4 ♘d4!? 10. ♘d4 ♕d4 11. ♘c3 b5∞] ♗e7 9. d4 0—0 10. ♗e3 [10. d5!?] d5 11. ed5 ed5 12. dc5 ♗c5 13. ♗c5 ♕c5 14. ♘bd2± Gufeljd—Radev, Tbilisi 1971 — 12/343

13 **5... ♘d4**?! 6. ♗a4 [6. ♗c4 ♘e7 7. ♖e1 ♘g6 8. d3 ♗e7 9. ♘d4 cd4 10. ♘e2 0—0 11. c3± Holmov—Korčnoj, SSSR (ch) 1964] ♕a5?! 7. a3! b5 8. b4 ♕b6 9. bc5 ♗c5 10. ♖b1± Talj—Ćirić, Sarajevo 1966 — 1/255; 6... ♘e7!?; **5... ♘f6** 6. ♖e1 d6 [6... ♘d4 7. a4?! a6 8. ♗d3 ♘f3 9. ♕f3 d6 10. b3 ♗e7 11. ♗b2 0—0 12. e5 de5 13. ♖e5±↑» Vasjukov—Korčnoj, SSSR (ch) 1965; 7. ♗a4!±; 6... ♗e7 7. ♗c6 ♕c6 8. d4 d6 9. d5 ♕c7 10. ♕d3 0—0 11. ♘d2 e5 12. ♘c4 ♘h5 13. f4 ef4 14. e5± Janata—Jakobi, Solingen 1965] 7. e5 de5 [7... ♘d5!?] 8. ♘e5±

14 9... ♘d4 10. ♖b1 ♗e7 11. b4 cb4 12. ♗e3!± Boleslavski

15 **10... ♗e7**!?; **10... g6**!?

16 12. dc4 dc3 13. ♘c3 ♗e7 14. b3 0—0 15. ♗e3 ♕c6 16. ♕d3 b6 17. ♖ad1 ♖d8 18. ♗d4±○ Kudrjašov—Korčnoj, SSSR 1965

17 4... ♘g4 5. ♗c6 [5. ♕e2 g6 6. h3 ♘h6 7. 0—0 ♗g7 8. c3 0—0 9. d4 cd4 10. cd4 ♘f5 11. ♖d1± Gurgenidze—Lutikov, SSSR 1959; 5... ♕c7!] dc6 6. 0—0 g6 7. ♖e1 ♗g7 8. h3 ♘h6 9. ♘c3 b6 [9... 0—0!?±] 10. d4 cd4 11. ♘d4 ♗b7 [11... c5? 12. ♘c6! ♕d7 13. ♘e7!+− Holmov—Keres, SSSR (ch) 1960] 12. ♗h6! [12. e6 ♕d4 13. ♕d4 ♗d4 14. ♗h6 f5∓] ♗h6 13. ♕g4 0—0 14. ♖ad1± Euwe

18 5. 0—0 **e6** 6. b3 [6. ♗c6 bc6 7. c4 ♘b4? 8. d4 cd4 9. a3 ♘a6 10. ♕d4 c5 11. ♕f4 ♗e7 12. ♕g4! ♔f8 13. ♘c3 ♗b7 14. h4 ♘c7 15. ♖d1+− Bronštejn—Saharov, SSSR 1959; 7... ♘e7!?△ ♘f5=] ♗e7 7. ♗b2 0—0 8. ♗c6 dc6 9. d3 b5 10. ♘bd2 a5 11. ♘e4 ± Matulović—Schöneberg, Skopje (ol) 1972 — 14/342; **5... ♕c7** 6. ♖e1 e6 7. b3 [7. ♘c3!? Larsen] b6 [Kuzmin—Larsen, Leningrad (izt) 1973 — 15/338] 8. ♗c4△ ♗d5, ♘c3=; **5... g6** 6. ♕e2 [6. ♘c3 ♘c7 7. ♗c6 dc6 8. ♘e4 ♘e6 9. b4!? cb4 10. a3 ba3 11. ♗a3 ♗g7 12. d4 0—0 13. c4=∞ Oppenrider—Mohrlok, corr. 1956] ♘c7 7. ♗c6 dc6 8. h3 ♗g7 9. d3 0—0 10. ♖e1 ♘e6=; **5... ♘c7**! 6. ♗c6 dc6=

19 **5... ♘c3** 6. dc3 [6. bc3!?] d5 7. ed6 ♕d6 8. ♕d6 ed6 9. ♗f4 ♗f5 10. 0-0-0 0-0-0 11. ♖he1±○; **5... e6** 6. 0—0 ♗e7 7. ♘d5 ed5 8. d4 a6 9. ♗e2± Cejtlin—Osnos, SSSR 1972 — 13/349

20 6... d5 7. ed6 ed6 8. d4 ♗e7 9. dc5 dc5 10. ♕d8 ♗d8 11. ♗c6 bc6 12. ♗e3± Haag—Pachman, La Habana 1962

21 12. ♘d4 cd4 13. ♘e4 ♕c6 14. ♘g5 h6 15. ♘f3 ♗e6= Haag—Padevski 1958

22 **4... a6** 5. ♗c6 dc6 6. 0—0± Dueball—Schiffer, Berlin 1971 — 12/342; **4... e6** — 3... e6

23 5. ♗a4 ♕a5 6. e5 ♘e4 7. ♘e4 ♕a4 8. 0—0 ♕c2 9. ♘d4 ♕d1 10. ♖d1 cd4 11. b3=∞

24 6. ef6!? ♘c3 7. fg7 ♗g7∞

25 7... ♘c7? 8. ♘c7 ♕c7 9. d4! cd4 10. ♕d4 g6 11. ♖e1 ♗g7 12. ♗g5 d6 13. ♗e7+−

26 12. ♖e1 ♗e6 13. ♘g5 ♔d7 14. ♘e6 fe6= Parma—Tajmanov, Jugoslavija—SSSR 1973

27 Bronštejn—Banik, SSSR 1957

28 4. c3 **g6**?! 5. d4 cd4 6. cd4 ♗g7 7. 0—0 d5 [7... ♕b6? 8. ♘a3 ♘d4?! 9. ♘c4! ♘f3 10. ♕f3 ♕c7 11. ♗f4 e5 (Rossolimo—O'Kelly, Oldenburg 1949) 12. ♖fd1! ef4 13. ♘d6+−; 8... d5!?] 8. ed5 ed5 9. ♖e1±; **4... d5**! 5. ed5 ed5 6. d4 ♗d6 7. 0—0 ♘e7 8. dc5 ♗c5 9. ♘bd2 0—0 10. ♘b3 ♗b6 — C 09

29 **4... d6** 5. e5! d5 6. ♗c6 bc6 7. d3±; **4... ♕c7** 5. 0—0 [5. ♗c6 ♕c6 6. d4 cd4

7. ♕d4 d6 8. 0–0 ♘f6 9. ♗g5± Čistjakov–Platonov, SSSR 1964; 7. ♘d4!?] d6 6. ♖e1 ♗e7 7. d4 cd4 8. ♕d4 ♘f6 9. e5 de5 10. ♘e5 ♗d7! [10... 0–0 11. ♗c6 bc6 12. ♗g5 ♗b7 13. ♕h4 c5 14. ♘g4 ♕c6 15. f3+–] 11. ♗c6 ♗c6 12. ♗f4 ♕b6±; **4... ♘f6** 5. 0–0 ♗e7 6. ♗c6 [6. e5 ♘d5 7. ♘d5 ed5 8. d4 a6 9. ♗e2 d6 10. ed6 ♕d6 11. dc5 ♕c5 12. ♗e3±; 8... cd4!? 9. ♘d4 ♕b6!=] bc6 7. d3 d5 8. ♗g5± Lejn–Lengyel, Cienfuegos 1972 — 13/350

30 10. ♗f6 ♗f6 11. ♘e4 0—0 12. ♘f6 gf6∓ Balašov–Reshevsky, Skopje 1970 — 10/404

31 7. b3 ♗e7 8. ♗b2 0–0 9. d4 cd4 10. ♘d4 d5?! 11. ed5 ed5 12. ♖e1± Ciocaltea–Darga, Skopje (ol) 1972 — 14/343; 10... d6=

32 **8... ♗e7** 9. ♘c6! bc6 10. e5 ♕c7 [10... 0–0 11. ♘e4 f6 12. ef6 ♗f6 13. ♕d6 ♗e7 14. ♕g3 d5 15. ♗h6 ♖f7 16. ♘g5 ♗g5 17. ♗g5 ♕c7 18. ♕c7 ♖c7 19. ♗f4 ♖b7 20. ♗e5±⊥ Gufeljd–Furman, SSSR 1970 — 9/292] 11 ♗f4 ♗b7 12. ♘e4 c5 13. ♖e1 ♗e4 14. ♖e4 ♕b7 15. ♖a4!± Gurgenidze–Radev, Tbilisi 1971 — 12/345; **8... ♕c7** 9. ♖e1 d6 [9... ♗d6 10. ♘c6 dc6?! 11. f4 ♗f4 12. ♗f4 ♕f4 13. e5!±; 10... bc6!? 11. f4 e5 12. ♕g4 0–0 13. f5 f6∞] 10. ♗g5 h6 [10... ♗d7? 11. ♘d5 ed5 12. ♘c6 bc6 13. ed5 ♗e6 14. de6 f6 15. ♗f4+–] 11. ♗h4 ♕b6 12. ♘b3 g5 13. ♗g3 ♘e5 14. ♗e5 de5 15. ♕f3 ♗e7 16. ♖ad1 ♗d7 17. ♖e3 h5 18. ♖ed3 0-0-0∞ Torre–Kurajica, Olot 1973; **8... ♗b4!?** 9. ♘c6 dc6 10. ♕g4 ♗c3 11. bc3 ♕f6 12. ♗a3 ♕c3 13. ♗d6 h5 14. ♕g5 ♕f6 15. ♕c5 ♕g6 16. ♖ad1 f6 [Gurgenidze–Buslaev, SSSR 1971] 17. ♖fe1=∞; 9 ♘de2!?

33 10... ♕f6∞ Hecht–Jansa, Skopje (ol) 1972 — 14/341

34 11... de5? 12. ♗g5 ♗e7 13. ♖ad1 ♗d7 14. ♗e7 ♕e7 15. ♕e2 f6 16. ♖d3 0–0 17. ♖fd1±

35 Gurgenidze–Osnos, SSSR 1969

36 5. ♗d3 ♘f3 6. ♕f3 ♗d6?! 7. ♕e3± Bronštejn–A. Zajcev, Berlin 1968 — 6/399; 5... ♘e7=

37 **5... ♘e7!?** 6. ♘d4 cd4 7. ♘e2 a6 8. ♗a4 b5 9. ♗b3 ♘c6 10. d3 [Gurgenidze–Furman, Gori 1971 — 11/280] ♗e7=; **5... g6!?**

38 6... ♘e7 7. ♘d4 cd4 8. ♘e2 ♘c6 9. c3 ♗c5 10. b4± Gurgenidze–Džindžihašvili, SSSR 1971 — 11/281

39 **10... ♗e6?** 11. ♗e6 fe6 12. d3 ♗e7 13. c3 dc3 14. ♕b3± Cejtlin–Feršter, SSSR 1973; **10... ♗e7**=

40 **5. c4** ♕c7 6. d4?! cd4 7. ♕d4 c5 8. ♕d3 ♗b7 9. ♘c3 a6 10. 0–0 ♘e7 11. ♖e1 d6! [11... ♘g6? 12. ♘d5 ♗d5 13. ed5 ♗e7 14. ♗g5 ♗g5 15. ♘g5 0–0 16. ♖ad1±○ Vasjukov–Haag, Polanica Zdroj 1972] 12. e5 de5 13. ♘e5 ♘g6∓; 6. d3!?; **5. d3** ♘e7 [5... d5 6. c4 d4 7. e5±; 6... ♘f6 7. ♘c3 d4 8. ♘a4 ♘d7△ ♘b6∓; 6. b3!±] 6. 0–0 ♘g6 7. e5 ♗e7 8. ♘bd2 0–0 9. ♖e1 ♕c7 10. c3 ♗a6 11. c4 ♗c8 12. ♘b3 f6∓ Euwe

41 **5... d5** 6. d3 ♘f6 [6... ♘e7 7. ♘c3 ♘g6 8. ♖e1 ♗e7 9. ♘a4 0–0 (Hecht–Krnić, Vršac 1973 — 16/304) 10. b3!△ ♗a3±] 7. ♘c3 ♗e7 8. b3±; **5... ♕c7** 6. d3 d6 7. ♘c3 ♘f6 8. ♕e2 e5? 9. ♘h4 g6 10. f4 ef4 [Vasjukov–Velimirović, SSSR–Jugoslavija 1973 — 16/303] 11. ♗f4±⟳; 8... ♘d7!±

42 6. b3 ♘g6 7. ♗b2 f6 8. e5 ♗e7 9. ♘a3? fe5 10. ♘e5 ♘e5 11. ♗e5 0–0 12. f4 d6 13. ♗c3 d5∓ Matulović–Adorjan, Bath 1973 — 16/301; 9. d3!?

43 Winawer–Steinitz, Paris 1867

44 4... ♘f6 5. ♖e1 d5 6. ed5 ♘d5 7. d4 [7. ♘e5 ♕c7 8. ♕f3 ♗d6 9. ♘c6 (Rossolimo–Kotnauer, Bad Gastein 1948) 0–0∞] ♕b6 8. c4 ♘c7 9. ♗c6 bc6 10. ♘e5± Milić–Bogdanović, Jugoslavija (ch) 1952

45 **5. c3** a6 6. ♗c6 [6. ♗a4 (Timman–Damjanović, Banja Luka 1974 — 18/344) d5=] ♘c6 7. d4 d5 8. e5 ♗e7= Ruban–Lavdanski, SSSR 1970 — 9/290; **5. ♖e1** a6 6. ♗c6 [6. ♗f1 (Diez del Corral–R. Byrne, Skopje (ol) 1972 — 14/340) d5!= Keres] bc6 [6... ♘c6!?] 7. e5 ♘g6 8. b3 ♗e7 9. ♗a3 0–0 10. d4± Talj–R. Byrne, Moskva 1971 — 12/346

46 6. ♗e2 d5 7. ed5 ed5 8. d4 cd4 [8... ♘f5 9. dc5 ♗c5 10. ♗b2 0–0 11. ♘c3 ♘fd4 12. ♘d4 ♗d4 13. ♘a4± Hübner–Mašić, Sombor 1970 — 10/405] 9. ♘d4 ♘d4 10. ♕d4 ♘c6△ ♗e7=

47 9... ♘d4 10. ♕d4 e5 11. ♕d3 ♗e7 12. c4±

48 **13. ♖ad1**?! ♘d4 14. ♕d4 b5=; **13. ♖fd1**±

B 31 — 1. e4 c5 2. ♘f3 ♘c6 3. ♗b5 g6

	4	5	6	7	8	9	10	11	12	
1	c3[1]	d4	a4	cd4[4]	♘c3	ab5	bc3	♕d4	c4	=∞
	♗g7[2]	♕b6[3]	cd4	♘d4	♘b5	♗c3	♕b5!?[5]	f6	♕b4[6]	
2	...	♕e2[7]	0–0[8]	d4[9]	cd4[10]	e5	♘c3[13]	bc3	h3	=
	♘f6	♗g7	0–0	cd4	d5[11]	♘e4[12]	♘c3	♘a5	a6[14]	

1. e4 c5 2. ♘f3 ♘c6 3. ♗b5 g6 4. 0—0 ♗g7

	5	6	7	8	9	10	11	12	13	
3	d3[15] ♕b6	♘c3 ♗c3	♗c6 ♗g7[16]	♗a4 ♘f6	♗b3 0–0	h3 d6	c3 ♗d7	♖e1 ♗c6	e5 ♗f3[17]	=
4	♖e1 ♘f6[18]	♘c3[19] 0–0[20]	♗c6 bc6	h3 d6	e5 ♘d7	ed6 ed6	d3 ♖b8!	♗g5 f6	♗f4 ♘e5[21]	=
5	... e5	b4!?[22] cb4	a3[23] ♘ge7[24]	ab4 0–0	♗b2[25] d6	♗c6 ♘c6	b5 ♕b6[26]	♘a3 ♘a5	♗c3 ♕c7[27]	∞
6	... ...	... ♘b4!	♗b2[28] ♕c7[29]	c3 ♘c6	d4 d6	dc5 dc5	♕d5 ♘e7	♕c5 0–0	♘bd2 ♗h6![30]	∓
7	... ...	c3 ♘ge7	d3[31] 0–0[32]	♗e3[33] d6	a4 f5	♗c4 ♔h8	♘g5 f4	♗c1 d5	ed5 ♘d5[34]	=
8	... ...	♗c6 bc6	c3[35] ♕b6[36]	d4 cd4	cd4 ed4	♘bd2 ♘e7[37]	♘c4 ♕c7	♗g5! ♗a6	♖c1 ♘c8[38]	±
9	... ...	... dc6	d3 ♕e7	a4[39] ♘h6	♗d2 f6	♘a3 ♘f7	♖b1 ♗e6	b4 cb4	♗b4 c5[40]	=
10	c3 ♕b6?[41]	♘a3 ♘f6[42]	e5 ♘d5	♗c4 ♘c7	♖e1 0–0	♗b3 ♘a5	d4 cd4	♘d4 ♘b3	ab3 d5[43]	±
11	... d5?!	♕a4 de4[44]	♗c6 bc6	♕c6 ♗d7	♕e4 ♘f6	♕h4 0–0[45]	d4 cd4	♕d4[46]		±
12	... e5	d3 ♘ge7[47]	♗e3[48] d6	d4[49] ed4[50]	cd4 0–0	♘c3 b6![56]	h3 a6	♗e2 ♗b7	♕d2[52] d5[53]	∓
13	... ...	d4 cd4[54]	cd4 ed4[55]	♗f4 a6[56]	♗a4[57] b5[58]	♗b3 d6	a4![59] b4[60]	♘bd2 ♗e6	♖c1 ♘ge7[61]	±
14	... ♘f6	e5[62] ♘d5	d4 cd4	cd4 0–0	♘c3 ♘c7[63]	♗c4[64] d6!	♕e2 ♗g4	♖e1 de5	de5 ♕c8[65]	=
15	... ...	♖e1 0–0[66]	d4[67] cd4[68]	cd4 d5[69]	e5 ♘e4[70]	♘c3[71] ♘c3	bc3 ♘a5[72]	♕a4[73] a6	♗f1 ♗g4[74]	±
16	... a6	♗a4[75] b5[76]	♗c2 d5[77]	d4 cd4	ed5 ♕d5	cd4 ♘d4	♘d4 ♕d4	♕f3 ♖b8	♖d1 ♗b7[78]	=∞

[1] 4. ♕e2!? ♗g7 5. 0–0 ♘f6 [5... d6?! 6. e5 ♘h6 7. ♗c6 bc6 8. ed6 ♕d6 9. d3 0–0 10. ♘bd2 ♗g4 11. h3 ♗f3 12. ♕f3 ♘f5 13. c3 ♖ad8 14. g4!± Čistjakov–Judovič, SSSR 1969 — 7/328; 5... e5!?] 6. e5 ♘g4 7. ♗c6 dc6 8. d3±; 4... e5=

[2] **4... ♕b6** 5. ♘a3 [5. ♗a4 ♗g7 6. 0–0 e5? 7. ♘a3 ♘ge7 8. b4!± Bronštejn–Tomić, Vinkovci 1970 — 10/406; 6... ♘f6 7. e5 ♘d5 8. d4 cd4 9. cd4 0–0= Bronštejn] ♗g7 9. 0–0 ♘f6 [6... e5 7. d4! cd4 8. ♘c4 ♕c7 9. cd4+– Lutikov–Stefanov, Kislovodsk 1966 — 2/342] 7. e5 ♘d5 8. ♖e1±; **4... a6** 5. ♗c6 dc6 6. d3 ♘f6 7. 0–0 ♗g7 8. ♕e2 0–0 9. ♖d1 ♕c7 10. e5 [10. a4 a5 11. ♘bd2 ♖d8= Averbah–Tajmanov, SSSR 1956] ♘e8 11. ♘bd2 f6 12. h3! fe5 13. ♘c4± Bronštejn–Ree, Amsterdam 1968 — 6/442; **4... d5** 5. ♕a4 de4 6. ♘e5 [6. ♗c6 bc6 7. ♕c6 ♗d7 8. ♕e4 ♘f6=∞] ♗d7 7. ♗c6 [7. ♘d7 ♕d7 8. ♕e4 ♘f6 9. ♕f3 ♖c8 10. 0–0 ♗g7∓ Nežmetdinov–Boleslavski, SSSR 1956] ♗c6 8. ♘c6 ♕d7 9. ♕e4 ♘f6 10. ♕f3 ♕e6 11. ♔d1 bc6 12. ♖e1=

[3] **5... cd4**? 6. cd4 ♕b6 7. ♘c3 ♗d4 [7... ♘d4 8. ♘d5 ♘f3 9. ♕f3 ♕d6 10. ♗d2 e6 11. ♗b4 ♕b8 12. 0–0!±→ Sulejmanov–Komozin, SSSR 1972 — 13/354] 8. ♘d4 ♕d4 9. ♕e2 a6 [9... ♘f6 10. ♗h6 ♖g8 11. 0–0 g5 12. ♖ad1 ♕e5 13. f4 gf4 14. ♗f4 ♕h5 15. e5 ♕e2 16. ♗e2 ♘g4 17. ♘b5 ♔d8 18. e6+– Lutikov–Sazonov, SSSR 1972] 10. ♗e3 ♕b4 11. a3 ♕a5 12. ♗c4 ♘f6 13. 0–0 d6 14. ♘d5 ♘d5 15. ♗d5±→ Bohosjan–P. Popov, Bulgaria 1969 — 7/323; **5... ♕a5** 6. a4 [6. ♗c6 dc6

7. dc5 ♕c5 8. ♗e3 ♕a5∓ Winiwarter–Pirc, Wien 1957] ♘d4 [6... cd4? 7. 0–0 dc3 8. ♘c3 ♗c3 9. bc3 ♕c3 10. ♗d2±→] 7. ♘d4 cd4 8. 0–0 a6 9. ♗c4 ♘f6 10. ♖e1 [10. ♕d4 d6∓] d5!=; 10. ♕f3⩱

4 7. 0–0 d3! [7... a6 8. ♗c6 ♕c6? 9. cd4 ♕e4 10. ♘c3 ♕f5 11. ♖e1 d5 12. a5 ♗d7 13. ♕b3±→ Geler–Bronštejn, Göteborg (izt) 1955; 8... bc6 9. cd4 ♘f6 10. ♘c3 0–0=; 8... dc6!?] 8. ♘a3 ♘f6 9. ♘c4 ♕c7 10. ♕d3 0–0 11. h3 d6 12. a5 ♖d8 13. ♗f4 e5 14. ♗g5 ♗e6∓ Pietzsch–Furman, Harrachov 1966; 9. ♗d3=

5 10... ♘f6 11. e5 ♘e4 12. 0–0 0–0 13. ♕d5 ♘c5 14. ♗e3 d6 15. ed6 ed6 16. ♗h6 +– Štejn–Lavdanski, SSSR (ch) 1964

6 13. ♗d2 ♕d6 14. ♕c3⩱

7 5. e5 ♘d5 6. 0–0 ♗g7 7. d4 — 5. c3

8 6. e5 ♘d5 7. ♕c4?! ♘c7 [7... ♕b6? 8. ♕d5 ♕b5 9. ♘a3±] 8. ♗c6 dc6 9. ♕c5 ♕d3 10. ♕e3 ♗f5 11. ♕d3 ♗d3 12. ♔d1 ♘e6 13. ♘e1 ♘f4∓ Fischer–Matulović, Palma de Mallorca (izt) 1970 — 10/407

9 7. e5 ♘e8 [7... ♘g4 8. d4 cd4 9. cd4 d6 10. h3 ♘h6 11. ♖d1±; 7... ♘d5 8. ♕c4 ♘c7! 9. ♗c6 dc6 10. ♕c5 ♕d3⩱] 8. d4 ♘c7 9. ♗a4 [9. ♗c6 bc6 10. dc5 ♗a6 11. c4 d5 12. cd6 ed6⩱] cd4 10. cd4 d5 [10... d6 11. ♖d1 ♗g4 12. h3 ♗f3 13. ♕f3 de5 14. ♗c6 bc6 15. de5 ♘d5 16. ♘c3 e6=] 11. h3 ♖b8 12. ♗c2 b6 13. ♗d2= Nežmetdinov–Spaski, SSSR (ch) 1957

10 8. ♘d4 ♕c7= Szabo–Boleslavski, Bucuresti 1953

11 8... d6 9. ♖d1 ♗g4 10. ♘c3 a6 11. ♗c6 bc6 12. h3 ♗f3 13. ♕f3 ♕b6 14. ♕e2 ♖ab8 15. ♖b1 ♘d7 16. ♗e3 ♕b7 17. f4 c5∞ Teschner–Stahlberg, Helsinki (ol) 1952

12 9... ♘e8 10. ♘c3 [10. ♗e3 ♘c7 11. ♗c6 bc6 12. ♖c1 ♗b7 13. ♘bd2 f6 14. ♘b3 ♘e6 15. ef6 ef6 16. ♕d2 a5 17. ♗h6 ♗h6 18. ♕h6 a4= Bilek–Larsen, Amsterdam 1964] ♗g4 11. ♗e3 f6 12. ef6 ♘f6 13. h3 ♗f3 14. ♕f3 ♖c8 15. ♕e2 e6 16. ♖ad1 a6 17. ♗d3 ♘h5= Prins–Matulović, Tel Aviv (ol) 1964

13 10. ♗e3 ♕b6 [10... f6 11. ef6 ef6 12. ♘c3 a6 13. ♗d3 ♘c3 14. bc3 ♘e7 15. a4 ♗f5 16. ♖fb1 ♕d7 17. ♘e1 ♖f7 18. ♗d2± Bronštejn–Bilek, Gotha 1957] 11. ♘c3 ♘c3 12. bc3 ♗g4 13. ♖fb1 ♕c7= Bilek–Szilagyi, Hungary (ch) 1964

14 **12... ♗d7**!?; **12... a6** 13. ♗d3 ♗d7=

15 **5. ♘c3** a6 6. ♗c6 bc6 7. d3 d6 8. ♕e2 e5 9. ♘d2 g5 10. ♘c4 h6 11. ♗d2 ♗e6 12. ♖ae1 ♘e7∓ Henneberger–Aljehin, Zürich 1934; **5. ♗c6** dc6 6. d3 ♘f6 7. h3 0–0 8. ♘c3 ♘e8 9. ♗e3 b6 10. a4 ♘c7 11. a5 ♗a6 12. ♘d2 ♘e6 13. f4 ♘d4 14. ♘a4 ♕c7 15. ♖f2 ♖fd8 16. ♕b1 f5 17. e5 ♔h8 18. ♘c4 ♖ab8∓ Hecht–Kunsztowicz, Dortmund 1973

16 7... ♗b2 8. ♗d7 ♗d7 9. ♖b1± Gligorić

17 **13... de5** 14. ♘e5 ♖ad8 15. ♘c6 ♕c6= Lombardy–Forintos, Monte Carlo 1967 — 3/390; **13... ♗f3** 14. ♕f3 de5 15. ♖e5 e6=

18 **5... e6** 6. c3 [6. ♗c6 bc6 7. d3 ♘e7 8. e5±] ♘ge7 7. d4 cd4 8. cd4 ♕b6 9. ♗c6! [9. ♘a3! ♘d4? 10. ♘c4 ♘f3 11. ♕f3 ♕c7 12. ♕a3 0–0 13. ♕e7 a6 14. ♗e3 ab5 15. ♘b6 ♖b8 16. ♖ac1+–; 9... ♗d4? 10. ♘d4 ♕d4 12. ♕f3 0–0 12. ♗h6+–; 9... d5! 10. e5 ♗d7 11. ♗f1 ♘f5 12. ♘c2 f6!∞] bc6 10. b3 d5 [Kuzmin–Kurajica, SSSR–Jugoslavija 1971] 11. e5! c5 12. ♗a3±; **5... a6** 6. ♗c6 bc6 7. d3 ♘f6 8. e5 ♘d5±○ Gurgenidze–Tajmanov, SSSR (ch) 1961; **5... ♕b6** 6. ♘a3 d6 7. h3 ♗d7 8. c3 ♘f6 9. d4 cd4 10. cd4 d5 11. ed5 ♘d5 12. ♕b3 ♗e6 13. ♘g5! [13. ♖e6?! fe6 14. ♘g5 ♔d7∞ Haag–Karanyi, Hungary 1954] ♘c7 14. ♘e6 fe6±

19 **6. e5** ♘d5 7. ♘c3 ♘c7 [7... ♘c3 8. dc3 0–0 9. ♕d5!± Čistjakov–Fajbisovič, SSSR 1962] 8. ♗c6 dc6 9. ♘e4 ♘e6 10. d3 [Biyiasas–Kagan, Petropolis (izt) 1973] 0–0 11. a4 b6 12. a5 ♖b8=; **6. c3**! — 5. c3

20 6... ♘d4? 7. e5 ♘g8 8. d3 ♘b5 9. ♘b5 a6 10. ♘d6! ed6 11. ♗g5 ♕a5 12. ed6 ♔f8 13. ♖e8 ♔e8 14. ♕e2 ♔f8 15. ♗e7 ♔e8 16. ♗d8 ♔d8 17. ♘g5 1 : 0 Rossolimo–Romanenko 1948

21 Hecht–Spaski, Dortmund 1973 — 15/337

22 **6. a3** ♘ge7 7. b4 b6 8. ♗c6 ♘c6 9. b5 ♘e7 10. d3 0–0 11. a4 d5∓ Gurgenidze–Furman, SSSR (ch) 1967 — 5/357; **6. ♘c3** ♘ge7 7. d3 0–0 8. ♗c4 d6 9. ♘d5 [9. ♗g5 h6 10. ♗h4 ♗e6 11. ♘d2 ♕d7 12. ♗e6 ♕e6 13. ♗e7 ♘e7 14. ♘b5 ♕d7 15. c4 h5!∓↑; 10. ♗e7!?] h6 10. c3 ♔h7 11. a3 ♘d5 12. ♗d5 ♘e7 13. ♗a2 f5 14. b4 b6 15. bc5 bc5 16. ♖b1 ♗a6 17. d4 ed4 18. cd4 fe4∓↑⊞ Bisguier–Talj, Tallinn 1971 — 11/286

23 7. ♗b2 ♘ge7 8. a3 0–0 [8... ba3? 9. ♘a3 0–0 10. ♘c4± Maljutin–Hermlin, SSSR 1970 — 10/411] 9. ab4 d6∞

24 7... ba3? 8. ♗a3 [8. ♘a3 ♘ge7 9. ♘c4 0–0 10. ♘d6 ♕c7 11. ♗a3 a6 12. ♗f1 b5 13. c3 h6 14. ♗c5 ♖b8 15. ♕c1 ♗b7 16. ♕a3± Schweber–Mecking, Mar del Plata 1971] ♘ge7 9. ♗d6 0–0 10. ♘c3 ♖e8 11. ♗c4 a6 12. ♕b1 ♗f6 13. ♕a2+– Kapengut–Paoli, Kecskemet 1972

25 **9. ♗a3** a6 10. ♗f1 d6 11. b5 ab5 12. ♗b5 h6 13. d3 ♔h7 14. ♘bd2 f5 15. ♘c4 ♖f6 16. h3 g5∞ Mestel–Radulov, Hastings 1972/73 — 15/335; **9. c3** d5 10. d3 ♗e6 11. ♘bd2 a6 12. ♗a4 h6 13. ♗b3 ♕c7= Lutikov–Petersen, SSSR (ch) 1964

26 11... ♘d4 12. ♘d4 ed4 13. d3 ♕b6 14. c4 a6 15. ♘d2 ♗d7 16. ♕a4 ♖ac8 17. ♕b4 ±↑ Lejn–Reško, SSSR 1964

27 14. ♗b4 ♖d8 15. d3 d5 16. ♕d2∞ Timoščenko–Arsenjev, SSSR 1972 — 13/352

28 7. c3 ♘c6 8. d4 ed4 [8... d6? 9. dc5 dc5 10. ♗c6 bc6 11. ♕d8 ♔d8 12. ♗e3±] 9. e5 ♘ge7 10. cd4 a6! [10... ♘d4 11. ♘d4 cd4 12. ♗a3 0–0 13. ♘d2 a6 14. ♗c4 d5 15. ed6 ♘f5± Lejn–Tajmanov, SSSR (ch) 1961] 11. ♗c6 dc6 12. dc5 ♕d1 13. ♖d1 ♗g4 14. ♗b2 ♗f3 [Rubinetti–Matulović, Palma de Mallorca (izt) 1970] 15. gf3 ♘d5 16. ♘c3 ♘c3∓

29 **7... ♕b6**?! 8. ♘a3 a6 9. ♗f1 d6 10. ♘c4 ♕c7 11. c3 ♘c6 12. d4 b5 13. ♘e3 ♘ge7 14. ♘d5 ♕b7 15. dc5 dc5 16. a4!±↑ Gurgenidze–Katalimov, SSSR 1968 — 6/441; **7... a6** 8. a3 ab5 9. ab4 ♖a1 10. ♗a1 d6 11. bc5 ♘e7 12. d4 dc5 13. dc5 ♕d1 14. ♖d1 ♘c6 15. ♘a3 b4 16. ♘c4 f6= Kapengut–Zaleman, SSSR 1973

30 14. ♘c4 b6∓↑ Sarbaj–Veremejčik, SSSR 1972 — 13/351

31 **7. d4**?! cd4 8. cd4 ed4 9. ♗f4 a6! 10. ♗c4 d6 11. ♘g5 0–0 12. ♕b3 d5 13. ♗d5 [13. ed5 ♘a5 14. d6 ♘d5!! 15. ♕f3 ♘f4 16. ♗f7 ♖f7 17. ♘f7 ♕f6–+ Vasjukov–Radulov, Varna 1971 — 12/341; 15. ♗d5 ♘b3 16. ab3 ♗e6 17. ♘e6 fe6 18. ♗e6 ♔h8 19. ♗g3∞ Seret–Giffard, France 1973 — 16/302; 16... ♗f6–+] ♘d5 14. ed5 ♘a5 15. ♕g3 ♕d5 16. ♗d6 ♗f5! 17. ♗f8 ♖f8 18. ♘d2 d3∓↑; **7. a3** 0–0 8. b4 cb4 9. ab4 d5 10. d3 ♕c7 11. ♘bd2 ♗e6 12. ♗b2 ♖ad8= Botvinik–Veresov, SSSR 1963

32 7... a6 8. ♗a4 0–0 9. ♗e3 d6 10. ♕d2 b5 11. ♗c2 ♖b8 12. ♗h6 ♗g4= Szabo–Ivkov, La Habana (ol) 1966 — 2/339

33 8. ♘bd2 a6 9. ♗a4 b5 10. ♗b3 ♗b7 11. ♘f1 ♘a4 12. ♗c2 ♕c7 13. ♘e3 d5= Simagin–Krogius, SSSR 1960

34 14. ♕f3 ♕g5= Golovko–Reško, SSSR 1964

35 7. d3 ♘e7 8. ♘a3 0–0 9. ♘c4 d6 10. a3 ♗e6 11. b4 cb4 12. ab4 ♗c4 13. dc4 ♕c7 14. ♗e3± Goldenov–Aleksijev, SSSR 1963

36 **7... d6** 8. d4 cd4 9. cd4 ♗g4 10. de5 de5 11. ♘bd2 ♘e7 12. h3 ♗e6 13. ♘g5± Hecht–Damjanović, Bad Pyrmont 1970 — 10/412; **7... ♘e7** 8. d4 cd4 9. cd4 ed4 10. ♘d4 0–0 11. ♘c3 ♗b7 12. ♘b3 d5 13. ♘c5 d4 14. ♘3a4!± Hecht–Radulov, Raach 1969

37 10... ♗a6 11. b3 ♘e7 12. ♗a3 c5 13. e5△ ♘e4± Euwe

38 14. ♕d2 ♗c4! [14... ♘b6 15. ♗f4 ♘c4 16. ♖c4 d6 17. e5!±→ Adorjan–Velimirović, Sombor 1972 — 14/344] 15. ♖c4 ♘b6 16. ♖d4! ♗d4 17. ♕d4 0–0 18. ♗h6± Euwe

39 8. ♗e3 ♘h6 9. h3 f6 10. ♘bd2 0–0 11. ♘b3 b6 12. a4 ♘f7 13. a5 ♗e6=

40 14. ♗c3= Lejn–Ermenkov, Slnčev Brjag 1974 — 18/347

41 5... ♕c7? 6. d4 cd4 7. cd4 ♕b6 8. ♘c3 ♘d4 9. ♘d5+– Darga–Musmann, BRD 1951

42 6... a6 7. ♗a4 [7. ♗e2 d6 8. ♘c4 ♕d8 9. d4 cd4?! 10. cd4 ♘f6 11. d5 ♘b8± Sokolov–Milić, Beograd 1967 — 4/410; 9... b5 10. ♘e3 ♘f6±] ♕c7 [7... ♘f6 8. e5 ♘g4 9. d4 cd4 10. cd4 0–0 11. h3 ♘h6 12. d5!+– Ciocaltea–Pedersen, Siegen (ol) 1970 — 10/409; 8... ♘d5!?] 8. d4 b5 9. ♗b3 d6 10. ♖e1 c4 11. ♗c2 e5 12. h3!± Ciocaltea–Ungureanu, Bucuresti 1971 — 11/287

43 Nimzowitsch–Stoltz (m) 1934; 14. ♗e3!±

44 6... e6? 7. d4! [7. ♗c6? bc6 8. ♕c6 ♗d7 9. ♕c5 de4 10. ♘e5 ♖c8 11. ♕d4 ♗b5∓ Perec–Donner, La Habana 1965] cd4 8. ♘d4 ♘e7 9. ed5 ♕d5 10. ♖d1+– Cordovil–Bellon, Palma de Mallorca 1971

45 Tartakower–Boleslavski, Groningen 1946

46 **12. ♖e1** dc3 13. ♘c3 ♖b8∓⊡; **12. cd4** ♗g4!=; **12. ♘d4** ♖b8= Konstantinopoljski; **12. ♕d4**±

47 6... ♕c7?! 7. ♗e3 a6 8. ♗a4 d6 9. d4± Padevski–Korčnoj, Lugano (ol) 1968 — 6/443

48 **7. ♗g5** 0–0 8. ♘a3 h6 9. ♗e3 d6 10. d4 [Calvo–Mititelu, Siegen (ol) 1970 — 10/410] ed4 11. cd4 ♗g4∓; **7. a3**!? Boleslavski

49 8. ♕c1?! 0–0 9. ♗h6 a6 10. ♗c6 ♘c6 11. ♗g7 ♔g7 12. ♕e3 f5∓ Kurajica–Drimer, Bognor Regis 1967 — 3/391

50 8... cd4 9. cd4 0–0 10. d5 ♘b8 11. ♘fd2 f5 12. f3 ♘d7 13. g4 ♘f6 14. h3 h5 15. g5 ♘h7 16. h4 ♖f7±○ Gurgenidze–Soos, Tbilisi 1965

51 10... cd4 11. ♘d4 ♘e5 12. ♗e2 d5 13. ♕b3 de4 14. ♖fd1 ♕a5 15. ♘e4 ♘g4 16. ♗f4 ♕d5 17. ♗f3 ♕b3 18. ab4 ♘e5±⊥ Nežmetdinov–Gufeljd, SSSR 1964

52 13. d5!?

53 14. ed5 ♘d5 15. ♘d5 cd4 16. ♘d4 ♘d4 17. ♗d4 ♕d5∓ Fajbisovič–Korčnoj, SSSR 1970

54 6... ed4 7. cd4 ♘d4 8. ♘d4 ♗d4 9. ♘c3±↑

55 7... ♘d4?! 8. ♘d4 ed4 9. e5 [9. f4 ♘e7 10. f5 ♕b6 11. f6±→ Kagan–Kapengut, SSSR 1966] a6 10. ♗a4 b5 11. ♗b3 ♗b7 12. ♕d4 ♘e7 13. ♗g5!± Barczay–Gasztonyi, Hungary 1974 — 17/363

56 8... ♘ge7 9. ♗d6 0–0 [Gufeljd–Geler, SSSR (ch) 1961] 10. ♖e1±↑

57 **9. ♗c4**!? d6 10. ♕b3? ♘a5∓ Hort; **9. ♗d3** d6 10. ♘bd2 ♘e5 11. ♕a4 ♗d7 12. ♕a3 ♘e7 13. ♘d4 0–0= Meduna–Hort, ČSSR 1972 — 13/348

58 9... ♘ge7 10. ♗d6 0–0 11. ♘bd2±↑ Jansa

59 11. ♘g5 ♖a7 12. a4 h6 13. ♘f3 b4 14. ♘bd2 ♘ge7! [14... g5?! 15. ♗g3 ♗g4 16. h3 ♗h5 17. ♘c4 ♗f3 18. ♕f3 ♘e5 19. ♗e5 ♗e5 20. a5± Ciocaltea—Radulov, Vršac 1971 — 12/344] 15. ♘c4 ♖d7 16. a5 0—0= Ciocaltea

60 **11... ♗b7** 12. ab5 ab5 13. ♖a8 ♗a8 14. ♘a3±; **11... ♖b8** 12. ab5 ab5 13. ♘a3 ♘ge7 14. ♘c2±

61 **13... ♗b3**? 14. ♕b3 ♘ge7 15. ♘c4 0—0 16. ♗d6± Jansa—Mednis, Houston 1974 — 18/345; **13... ♘ge7** 14. ♗e6 fe6 15. ♘g5 ♕d7 16. ♕b3±↑ Jansa

62 **6. d4**!? ♘e4 7. d5 ♘b8 8. ♖e1 ♘d6 9. ♗d3 0—0 [Keres—Smejkal, Luhačovice 1969 — 8/316] 10. ♗f4!$\overline{\overline{\infty}}$; **6. d3** 0—0 7. ♗g5 ♘e8 8. ♘bd2 ♘c7 9. a4 d6 10. ♗c4 ♗e6= Bronštejn—Furman, SSSR 1959; **6. ♕e2** — 4. c3

63 9... ♘c3 10. bc3 d6 11. ed6 ed6!? [11... ♕d6 12. a4 ♗f5 13. ♗a3 ♕c7 14. ♖e1 ♗f6 15. ♕d2± Bronštejn—Boleslavski, SSSR (ch) 1957; 12... ♘a5 13. ♗a3 ♕c7 14. ♕e2 a6 15. ♗d3 ♖e8∓ Bialas—Schweber, Leipzig (ol) 1960; 13. ♖e1±] 12. ♗f4 ♘e7 13. ♗c4 ♗g4 14. h3 ♖c8 15. ♗b3 ♗e6= Matanović—Bouaziz, Sousse (izt) 1967

64 10. ♗a4 d6 11. h3 [11. ♗f4 ♗g4 12. ♗c6 bc6 13. h3 ♘e6 14. hg4 ♘f4 15. g3 ♘e6 16. ♘e4 ♕a5 17. ed6 ed6 18. g5 ♔h8 19. b3 ♕d5 20. ♖e1 f6∓ Mjagmarsuren—Korčnoj, Sousse (izt) 1967] de5 12. de5 ♕d1 13. ♖d1 ♘e5 14. ♘e5 ♗e5 15. ♗g5 ♗f6 16. ♗f6 ♗f6 17. ♖ac1 ♘a6 18. ♘e4 f5 19. ♘d6$\overline{\overline{\infty}}$ Nežmetdinov—Polugajevski, SSSR (ch) 1959

65 14. ♘d5 ♘d5 15. ♗d5 ♘e5 16. ♗f4 ♗f3 17. gf3 ♕f5 18. ♗g3 ♖ac8 19. ♗e4 ♕f6 20. ♗b7 ♖b8 21. ♕e4 ♕f5= Nežmetdinov—Boleslavski, SSSR (ch) 1959

66 **6... ♕b6**?! 7. ♗c6 ♕c6 8. d4 cd4 9. cd4 ♘e4? 10. d5 ♕c4 11. ♘a3+— Euwe; **6... a6**?! 7. ♗c6 bc6 8. e5 ♘d5 9. d4 cd4 10. c4! ♘c7 11. ♘d4 c5 12. ♘b3 ♘e6 13. ♘c3 ♗b7 14. ♘d5 d6 15. ♘f4 0—0 16. ♘e6 fe6 17. ♕g4 ♖f5 18. ♗f4±○ Gurgenidze—Štejn, SSSR 1971 — 11/283

67 **7. a3**?! a6 8. ♗f1 e5 9. d3?! d5 10. ♘bd2 d4 11. cd4 cd4 12. b4 ♘e8 13. a4 ♘d6 14. ♗a3 ♖e8 15. ♕b1 [Vasjukov—Balašov, SSSR (ch) 1972] b5∓; **7. e5** ♘e8 [7... ♘d5!=] 8. d4 cd4 9. cd4 d6 10. ♗g5± Kupper—Nievergelt Zürich 1959; 9... ♘c7!=; **7. h3** a6 [7... d5?! 8. e5 ♘e8 9. d4 cd4 10. cd4 ♘c7 11. ♗f1±○ Jansa—Lanč, ČSSR (ch) 1974 — 17/365; 7... d6 8. d4 cd4 9. cd4 a6 10. ♗f1 e5 11. ♘c3± Nežmetdinov—Radulov, Varna 1967 — 4/413; 10... d5!?; 7... ♕c7 8. d4 cd4 9. ♗c6 ♕c6 10. e5 ♘d5 11. ♘d4 ♕a6 12. ♕b3 ♘c7 13. ♗g5 ♖e8 14. ♘d2±○ Cejtlin—Matulović, Kragujevac 1974 — 18/348; 7... ♕b6=; 7... ♘e8!?] 8. ♗f1 e5 9. d4 ed4 10. cd4 d5 11. e5 ♘e4 12. dc5 ♗e6 13. ♘a3 ♕a5= Ljubojević—Janošević, Jugoslavija (ch) 1971

68 7... ♕b6 8. ♗c6 bc6 9. e5 ♘d5 10. dc5 ♕c5 11. ♘bd2 f5 12. ♕a4 e6 13. ♘b3 ♕e7 14. ♗g5± Gurgenidze—Suetin, Tbilisi 1967 — 3/389; 8... dc6!?

69 8... a6 9. ♗d3 d5 10. e5 ♘e4 11. ♘c3 ♗g4 12. ♘e4 ♗f3 13. ♕f3! ♘d4 14. ♕g4 de4 15. ♕e4± Hort—Timman, Nice (ol) 1974 — 17/367

70 9... ♘e8!? 10. h3 ♕b6 11. ♘c3 ♘c7 12. ♗f1 a6 13. b3 ♖d8 14. ♘a4 ♕a7 15. ♗a3 ♘e6 16. ♖c1± Minev—Pietrusiak, Halle 1967

71 10. ♗c6 bc6 11. ♘c3 ♘c3 12. bc3 ♕a5! 13. ♕b3 ♗g4 14. ♕a3= Benkö—Štejn, La Habana (ol) 1966 — 2/340

72 **11... ♗d7** 12. ♗d3 ♖c8 13. ♘g5! e6 14. ♕g4 ♘e7? 15. ♘h7!! ♔h7 16. ♕h4 ♔g8 17. ♗g5 ♖e8 18. ♖e3+—→ Barendregt—Szilagyi, Amsterdam 1966 — 2/341; 14... f5!?; **11... ♕a5**?! 12. a4 ♗g4 13. ♖e3 ♖fc8 14. h3 ♗f3 15. ♖f3 a6 16. ♗f1 e6 17. ♗g5 ♕c7 18. h4!± Torre—Gheorghiu, Skopje (ol) 1972 — 14/339

73 **12. ♗a3** ♗d7 13. ♗d3 ♖c8 14. e6!? fe6 15. ♘g5 ♖f6 16. ♖e3 ♖c3 17. ♗b4 ♖d3! 18. ♕d3 ♘c4∓ Barendregt—Szilagyi, Amsterdam 1969; **12. a4** ♗g4 [12... ♗f5?! 13. ♗a3 a6 14. ♗d3 ♗g4 15. ♖b1 ♖c8 16. ♗c5± Hug—Hort, Las Palmas 1973 — 15/336] 13. ♗a3 a6=

74 14. ♘d2 ♖c8 15. ♘b3 ♘b3 16. ♕b3 ♕c7 17. ♗d2 ♖fd8 18. ♖ab1± Sax—Janošević, Madonna di Campiglio 1974 — 17/366

75 6. ♗c6 dc6 7. d4 [7. d3 ♘f6 8. ♕e2 ♗g4 9. h3 ♗f3 10. ♕f3 0—0 11. ♖d1 ♘d7 12. ♗e3 e5= Radovici—Szily, Kecskemet 1962] ♘f6 8. ♖e1 cd4 [8... a5 9. e5 ♘d5 10. a4 cd4 11. ♘d4 0—0 12. ♘a3 ♕c7 13. ♕e2 b6 14. h4±↑ Gufeljd—Tajmanov, SSSR (ch) 1960] 9. cd4 ♗g4 10. ♘c3 0—0 11. ♗e3 e5! 12. de5 ♘d7 13. h3 ♗f3 14. ♕f3 ♘e5 15. ♕e2 ♕d3=

76 6... e5 7. ♗b3 d6 [7... ♘ge7!?] 8. d4 cd4 [8... ed4!? Euwe] 9. cd4 ♘d4 10. ♘d4 ed4 11. f4 ♘e7 12. f5 gf5 13. ♗g5!±→ Bilek—Szily, Budapest 1954

77 7... e5!?

78 Robatsch—Sokolov, Varna 1957; 14. ♕g3$\overline{\overline{\infty}}$

B 32 — 1. e4 c5 2. ♘f3 ♘c6 3. d4

	3	4	5	6	7	8	9	10	11	
1	... cd4[1]	♗c4 ♘f6[2]	♘d4 ♘e4[3]	♗f7 ♔f7	♕h5 g6	♕d5 e6	♕e4 d5	♕f4 ♕f6	♕c7	=

1. e4 c5 2. ♘f3 ♘c6 3. d4 cd4

	4	5	6	7	8	9	10	11	12	
2	♘d4[4] d5[5]	♘c3[6] de4	♘c6 ♕d1	♔d1 bc6	♘e4 ♗f5	♗d3 0-0-0	♔e2 e6	♗f4 ♔b7	♖ad1 ♗e7[7]	±
3	. . . ♕b6	♘b3[8] ♘f6	♗d3[9] d5![10]	ed5 ♘d5	0—0[11] g6	♕f3[12] ♗e6	c4 ♘f6	♗f4 ♗g7	♘c3 0—0[13]	∞
4	. . . ♕c7	c4[14] ♘f6[15]	♘c3 ♘e4	♘e4[16] ♕e5	♘b5 ♕e4	♗e2 ♕e5	f4 ♕b8	0—0![17] e6[18]	f5! a6[19]	∞
5	. . . . . .	♘b5 ♕b8	c4 ♘f6	♘5c3[20] e6	f4[21] d6[22]	♗d3[23] ♗e7	♘d2 0—0	♘f3 a6[24]	0—0 b6[25]	±

1. e4 c5 2. ♘f3 ♘c6 3. d4 cd4 4. ♘d4 e5[26]

	5	6	7	8	9	10	11	12	13	
6	♘c6[27] bc6	♗c4 ♘f6[28]	♗g5[29] ♗c5[30]	0—0 h6	♗f6 ♕f6	♘c3 a5	♔h1 d6	♕d2 g5	♖ad1 ♔e7[31]	∞
7	♘b5 d6[32]	♘1c3[33] a6[34]	♘a3 ♗e6[35]	♘c4 ♖c8	♘d5!? ♗d5	ed5 ♘b8	♗e2 ♘d7	0—0 ♘gf6	a4 ♗e7[36]	±
8	. . . a6	♘5c3 ♗e7[37]	♗c4 ♘f6	0—0 0—0	♗e3[38] d6	h3 b5	♗d5 ♗d7	♘d2 ♖e8	♘b3 b4[39]	∞

1. e4 c5 2. ♘f3 ♘c6 3. d4 cd4 4. ♘d4 e5 5. ♘b5 a6
6. ♘d6 ♗d6 7. ♕d6 ♕f6

	8	9	10	11	12	13	14	15	16	
9	♕d2 ♘ge7[40]	♘c3 d6![41]	♕g5 ♘b4	♗d3 ♗e6	♕f6 gf6	f4 d5	fe5 fe5	ed5 ♘d3	cd3 ♘d5[42]	∓
10	♕d3 ♘ge7	♘c3[43] d5![44]	♘d5 ♘d5	♕d5[45] ♗e6	♕d1 ♖d8	♗d2 ♕g6![46]	f3 0—0	c3 f5	ef5 ♕f5[47]	=∞
11	♕f6 ♘f6	♘c3 ♘b4![48]	♗d3[49] ♘d3	cd3 h6![50]	♗e3 d6	d4 ♗e6	0-0-0 ♖c8	♔b1 0—0	f3 ♖c7	=
12	♕a3 ♕g6[51]	♗e3[52] ♕e4	♘c3! ♕b4	♕b4 ♘b4	0-0-0 ♘e7[53]	♗c5 ♘bc6	f4[54] d5	fe5 ♗e6	♗d6 d4[55]	±
13	. . . ♘ge7	♘c3 ♖b8![56]	♗e3[57] b5	♘d5 ♘d5	ed5 b4![58]	♕d3[59] ♘e7	d6 ♘f5	0-0-0 ♗b7	♗c5 0—0[60]	=
14	♕c7 ♘ge7[61]	♘c3 ♘b4[62]	♗d3[63] d5	0—0 d4[64]	♘e2[65] 0—0[66]	♗d2![67] ♘d3[68]	cd3 ♘c6	♕b6[69] ♕d8	♕c5 ♗e6[70]	±
15	♕d1 ♕g6[71]	♘c3 ♘ge7	h4[72] h5[73]	♗g5[74] d5	♗e7 d4!	♗g5[75] dc3	bc3 ♕e4	♗e2 f6	♗e3 ♗g4[76]	=

1. e4 c5 2. ♘f3 ♘c6 3. d4 cd4 4. ♘d4 e5 5. ♘b5 a6 6. ♘d6 ♗d6
7. ♕d6 ♕f6 8. ♕d1 ♕g6 9. ♘c3 ♘ge7 10. h4 h5
11. ♗g5 d5 12. ed5

	12	13	14	15	16	17	18	19	20	
16	. . . ♘b4[77]	♖c1[78] f6![79]	a3[80] fg5	hg5!?[81] ♗g4!	♕d2 ♘bd5	♘d5 ♘d5	♕d5 ♕g5	♕d2 ♕d2	♔d2 ♔e7[82]	=
17	. . . . . .	♗e7! ♔e7	d6![83] ♔d8[84]	♗d3[85] ♘d3	♕d3 ♕d3	cd3 ♗f5	0-0-0 ♔d7	d4 e4	♖he1	±

1 3... d5 4. ed5 ♕d5 5. ♘c3 ♕e6 [5... ♕h5 6. d5+−] 6. ♗e3! cd4 7. ♘d4 ♕d7 [7... ♘d4 8. ♕d4 ♗d7 9. 0-0-0△ ♗c4+−] 8. ♘db5! ♖b8 9. ♕e2 f6 10. ♖d1 ♕g4 11. f3 ♕h5 12. ♗a7 ♘a7 13. ♘d6+− Boleslavski−Gurgenidze, SSSR 1960

2 **4... e5** 5. c3 dc3 6. ♘c3 ♗b4 [6... d6 7. ♘g5 ♘h6 8. 0−0 ♗g4? 9. ♗f7+− Bondarevski−Kasparjan, SSSR 1937] 7. 0−0 ♗c3 8. bc3 d6 9. ♗a3 ♗g4 10. ♖b1 ♕d7 11. ♕d6 ♕d6 12. ♗d6 ♗f3 13. gf3 0-0-0 14. ♖fd1±; **4... ♕a5** 5. ♘bd2 [5. c3 dc3 6. ♘c3 e6 7. 0−0 a6 8. ♗f4= Sapi−Szabados, Hungary 1954] e6 6. 0−0 ♕b6 7. a3 a5 8. ♘b3 ♗c5 9. ♕e2 ♘ge7 10. ♘c5 ♕c5 11. b4 ♕b6 12. b5 ♘a7 13. ♗b2±⟳; 9... d6!?

3 5... e6 6. ♘c3 ♗b4 7. 0−0 0−0!=

4 4. c3 ♘f6 [4... dc3 5. ♘c3 — B 21; 4... d3 5. c4! — B 21; 4... d5 5. ed5 ♕d5 6. cd4 — B 22] 5. e5 ♘d5 6. cd4 — B 22

5 **4... ♘d4**?! 5. ♕d4 e6 6. ♘c3 d6 [6... ♘ge7 7. ♗e3 ♘c6 8. ♕d2 ♗e7 9. 0-0-0±⟳] 7. ♗e3 ♘f6 8. f3 ♗e7 9. 0-0-0 0−0 10. g4 a6 11. g5 ♘d7 12. h4±; **4... a6** 5. c4 — B 28; 5. ♘c3 e6 — B 46; 5. ♘c6 bc6 6. ♘c3 e6 — B 46

6 **5. ♘c6** bc6 6. ed5 ♕d5 7. ♘d2! [7. ♕e2?! ♗f5!=] ♘f6 8. ♗e2 e6 [8... e5 9. ♗f3 ♕d7 10. ♕e2 ♗d6 11. ♘c4±] 9. 0−0 ♗e7 10. ♗f3 ♕d7 11. ♕e2 0−0 12. ♘b3 a5 13. ♗e3±; **5. ed5** ♕d5 6. ♗e3 e6 [6... ♘d4 7. ♘c3! ♘f3 8. gf3+−] 7. ♘c3 ♗b4 8. ♘db5 ♕e5 9. a3 ♗c3 [9... ♗e7 10. ♗e2 a6 11. ♘d4 ♘f6 12. ♘c6 bc6 13. ♕d2±↑«] 10. ♘c3 ♘f6 11. ♗e2 0−0 12. 0−0 ♖d8 13. ♕c1±; **5. ♗b5** de4 6. ♘c6 ♕d1 7. ♔d1 a6 8. ♗a4 [8. ♘d4?! ab5 9. ♘b5 ♗g4 10. ♔e1 0-0-0∓; 9. ♗d2 f5! 10. ♘b5 ♔f7∓] ♗d7 9. ♘c3! ♗c6 [9... bc6 10. ♘e4 e5 11. ♗e3 f5 12. ♘c5 ♘f6 13. ♔e2 ♘d5 14. ♖hd1!± Unzicker−Steiner, Krems 1967 — 4/414] 10. ♗c6 bc6 11. ♘e4 e5 12. ♔e2 f5 13. ♘d2 ♘f6 14. ♘c4 ♘d7 15. ♖d1 ♖b8 16. b3±

7 13. f3±

8 5. ♘b5 ♘f6 6. ♘1c3 — B 33

9 6. ♘c3 — B 33

10 **6... e6** 7. ♘c3 — B 33; **6... g6**!? Geler

11 8. ♗h7 ♖h7 9. ♕d5 ♗e6≅ Gufeljd

12 9. ♗g6 hg6 10. ♕d5 ♗f5≅

13 13. ♘b5! ♗g4!? 14. ♕g3 e5 15. ♗g5!∞

14 5. ♘c3 e6 6. ♗e2 — B 47; 6. ♗e3 — B 48

15 5... ♕e5 6. ♘f3 ♕e4 7. ♗e2 d6 8. ♘c3 ♕f5 9. 0−0 ♘f6 10. ♘d5± Matanović−Benkö, Portorož (izt) 1958

16 7. ♘db5 ♕a5! 8. b4 ♕b4 9. ♗d2 ♘d2 10. ♘c7 ♔d8 11. ♕d2 ♖b8 12. ♘7d5 ♕c5 13. ♗e2 e6∞

17 11. ♗e3?! g6 12. ♕d2 ♗g7 13. h4 h5 14. g4∞ Nikitin−Furman, SSSR (ch) 1959

18 11... f5!?

19 13. ♘c3 ♗d6 14. ♘e4 ♗h2 15. ♔h1 ef5?! 16. ♖f5 d5 17. ♖f7!+− Mišta−Matulović, Reggio Emilia 1967/68 — 5/359; 15... ♗e5!?∞

20 7. ♘1c3 a6 8. ♘a3 e6 9. ♘c2 b5 10. cb5 ab5 11. ♗b5 ♘e4 12. ♗c6 ♘c3 13. bc3 [13. ♗d7 ♗d7 14. bc3 ♕e5∓] dc6 14. 0−0 ♗d6 15. ♕h5 0−0∓; 8. ♘d4 ♘e4∓

21 8. ♗e3 ♗e7 9. ♗e2 b6 [9... d6 10.a3 b6 11. ♘d2 ♗b7 12. f4 0−0 13. 0−0 ♖d8 14. ♗f3 ♗f8 15. ♗f2±→» Karpov−Kurajica, Hastings 1971/72 — 13/356] 9. ♕d2 ♗b4!? 10. ♗d3 ♘e5 11. a3 ♗c5 12. b4 ♗e3 13. ♕e3 a5∞⇆

22 8... ♗c5 9. e5 ♘g8 10. ♘e4±

23 9. ♗e2 ♗e7 [9... b6 10. 0−0 ♗b7 11. f5 ♘e5 12. fe6 fe6 13. ♗h5 ♘g6 14. ♕a4 ♔f7 15. ♗g4→» Boleslavski−Korčnoj, SSSR (ch) 1961] 10. ♗e3 0−0 11. g4 b6∞

24 11... ♘d7? 12. ♗e3 ♘c5 13. ♗c2 a6 14. a3 b5 15. b4±↑« Bronštejn−Tajmanov, SSSR (ch) 1971 — 12/347

25 13. ♔h1±○

26 Labourdonnais

27 **5. ♘e2** ♘f6 6. ♘bc3 — B 33; **5. ♘b3** ♗b4! [5... ♘f6 6. ♘c3 — B 33] 6. c3 ♗e7 7. ♗c4 [7. c4 ♘f6 8. ♗d3 0−0 9. 0−0 d6 10. ♘c3 ♗e6 11. ♗g5= Muhin−Burlajev, SSSR 1963] ♘f6 8. ♕d3 0−0 9. 0−0 d6 10. ♘a3 ♗e6 11. ♖d1 a6 12. ♗g5 ♘e8 13. ♗e7 ♘e7 14. ♗e6 fe6 15. ♘c4 ♘g6!⇆» Banik−Kuzminič, SSSR 1946; **5. ♘f3** ♗e7! 6. ♘c3 ♘f6 — B 33; **5. ♘f5** d5 6. ♕d5 ♕d5 7. ed5 ♗f5 8. dc6 bc6 9. c3 ♖b8 10. ♘d2 ♗c5 11. ♘b3 ♗b6 12. ♗c4 ♘e7 13. 0−0 0−0=

28 6... ♗a6 [Löwenthal] 7. ♕d3=

29 **7. ♘c3** ♗b4 8. ♗g5 h6 [8... ♗c3 9. bc3 ♕a5∞] 9. ♗d2 ♗c3 10. ♗c3 ♘e4 11. ♕g4 0−0 12. ♕e4 d5 13. ♕e2 dc4∞; **7. 0—0** ♗e7! [7... d5? 8. ed5 cd5 9. ♗b5 ♗d7 10. ♗d7 ♕d7 11. ♖e1 ♗d6 12. ♘c3 e4 13. ♗g5 ♘g4 14. ♕d5+− Morphy−Löwenthal, Paris 1858; 7... ♘e4? 8. ♖e1 d5 9. ♖e4!+−] 8. ♘c3 d6=

30 7... ♗e7 8. ♘c3=

31 14. ♘a4 ♗d4 15. ♕d3 h5 16. h4∞ Macdonnell−Labourdonnais (m) 1839

32 **5... ♗c5** 6. ♘1c3 ♘f6 — B 33; **5... ♘f6** 6. ♗g5 [6. ♘1c3 — B 33] ♗c5 [6... d6 7. ♗f6 gf6 8. ♗c4±] 7. ♘d6 [7. ♗f6 ♕f6 8. ♕d2 0−0 9. ♘c7 ♖b8 10. ♘d5 ♕g6 11. ♘1c3±] ♔e7 [7... ♔f8 8. ♗c4+−] 8. ♘f5 ♔f8 9. ♘c3 d6 10. ♘e3 h6 11. ♗f6 ♕f6 12. ♘cd5±; **5... h6** 6. ♘d6 ♗d6 7. ♕d6 ♕e7 8. ♕e7 ♘ge7 9. ♘c3 ♘b4 10. ♗d3 d5 11. ed5

♘d3 12. cd3 ♗f5 13. d6 ♘c6 14. ♗e3 ♗d3 15. 0-0-0±

33 **6. c4** ♗e7 7. ♘1c3 a6 8. ♘a3 ♘f6 9. ♗e2 0–0 10. ♗e3 ♗e6 11. 0–0 ♖c8 12. ♖c1 h6 13. ♕d2 ♘e8± Suetin–Kopajev, SSSR 1952; **6. ♗c4**!? a6 7. ♘5c3 f5 8. ef5 ♗f5 9. ♗d3 ♗d3 10. ♕d3 ♘b4 11. ♕e2 ♘f6 12. 0–0 ♗e7 13. f4 ef4± Averbah–Kuzminič, SSSR 1947

34 6... ♘f6! — B 33

35 7... h6 8. ♘c4 b5 9. ♘e3 ♘f6 10. ♘ed5 ♗e7 11. ♗e3 0–0 12. a4 b4 13. ♗b6 ♕d7 14. ♘f6 ♗f6 15. ♘d5± Aronin–Kuzminič, SSSR 1948; 11... ♖b8!?

36 14. ♗e3 0–0 15. a5!± Matanović–Larsen, Beverwijk 1960

37 **6... ♗b4** 7. a3 ♗a5 8. b4 ♗b6 9. ♗c4 ♘f6 10. 0–0 h6 11. ♘d2 0–0 12. ♘d5± Venkatroman–Rajagapalan, Madras 1952; **6... ♗c5** 7. ♗e3!? ♗e3 8. fe3 ♘f6 9. ♗c4 ♕b6!? 10. 0–0 ♕b2 11. ♕d6!? ♕a1 12. ♖f6 gf6 13. ♕f6 0–0? 14. ♕g5 ♔h8 15. ♕f6 ♔g8 16. h4 d5 17. h5±→ Brazilski–Tarasevič, SSSR 1960; **6... ♘f6** 7. ♗g5 [7. ♗c4 b5 8. ♗d5 b4? 9. ♘e2 ♘d5 10. ed5 ♘b8 11. ♗e3 d6 12. a3± Fajbisovič–A. Zajcev, SSSR 1962; 8... ♗b7∞] ♗e7 [7... ♗c5 8. ♗c4 h6 9. ♗f6 ♕f6 10. 0–0 0–0 11. ♘d2 d6 12. ♘d5 ♕h4 13. c3 ♔h8∞ Foguelman–Rossetto, Mar del Plata 1958] 8. ♗f6 ♗f6 9. ♘d5 ♗g5 10. ♗c4 0–0 11. ♘bc3 b5 12. ♗b3 ♘d4 13. h4 ♗e7 14. ♘e7 ♕e7 15. ♘d5 ♕c5 16. ♖h3 ♗b7!∞ Čistjakov–Utjacki, SSSR 1961; **6... b5** 7. ♘d5 ♘f6 8. ♘1c3 ♘d5 9. ♘d5 ♖b8 10. ♗e3 ♘b4 11. ♕h5! ♗d6 12. 0-0-0 ♘d5 13. ♖d5 ♕c7 14. ♕g4 ♗f8= Bednarski–Minić, Budva 1963

38 9. ♗g5 ♘e4=

39 14. ♘a4 ♖b8 15. c3 ♘d5 16. ed5 ♘a5 ∞⇄«

40 8... ♕g6 9. ♘c3 [9. f3 d6 10. ♘a3 b5 11. ♗d3 ♘ge7 12. 0–0 0–0 13. c3 f5∓⇆» Möhring–Baumbach, DDR (ch) 1963; 9... ♘ge7 10. ♘c3 d5 11. ♘d5 ♘d5 12. ed5 ♘d4 13. ♗d3 ♗f5 14. ♗f5 ♕f5 15. 0–0 ♘c2 16. ♖b1 0–0=] ♘ge7 10. h4 h5 11. ♕g5 ♘b4 12. ♕g6 ♘g6 13. ♔d1! ♘e7 14. b3 f5 15. ♗a3 ♘bc6 16. ♖h3 b5 17. ♘d5 ♔f7 18. ♗d3 ♘d5± Bogdanović–Baumbach, Zinnowitz 1967; 16. ♗d3!±

41 9... ♕g6 10. h4 [10. ♕g5 d5 11. ♕g6 hg6 12. ♗d2 ♗e6 13. ed5 ♘d5 14. ♘d5 ♗d5 15. 0-0-0 0-0-0 16. f3 1/2 : 1/2 Robatsch–Kottnauer, Beverwijk 1962] ♘d4 [10... b5 11. h5 ♕g4 12. ♕g5 ♕g5 13. ♗g5 h6 14. ♗e3 b4 15. ♘a4 ♖b8 16. 0-0-0± Parma–De Roy, Beverwijk 1964] 11. h5 ♕c6 12. b3 0–0 13. ♗a3 d6 14. f4 ♗e6 15. 0-0-0 ♖fc8 16. ♔b2±↑ Bojković–Grigorjan, Jugoslavija–SSSR 1964

42 17. 0–0 ♘c3 18. bc3 0-0-0∓ Buljovčić–Ciocaltea, Reggio Emilia 1966

43 9. c4 0–0 10. ♘c3 d6 11. ♗e2 ♕g6 12. 0–0 ♘d4 13. f3 b5∓⇆ Raag–Agzamov, SSSR 1970

44 **9... ♕g6** 10. ♕g3±; **9... 0–0** 10. ♗e3 [10. a3 ♕g6 11. ♗e3 d5! 12. ed5 ♗f5 13. ♕d2 ♘d4 14. 0-0-0 ♘c2 15. g4?! ♘e3 16. gf5 ♘3f5 17. ♗d3 ♖ac8 18. ♗c2 ♖fd8 19. ♖hg1 ♕f6∓ Baturinski–Antošin, SSSR 1957] d5 11. ♘d5 [11. ed5 ♘b4 12. ♕d2 ♗f5 13. ♖c1 ♕d6! 14. ♗c4 ♖fd8 15. 0–0 ♘bd5 16. ♗d5 ♘d5 17. ♕d5 ♕d5 18. ♘d5 ♖d5= Kolobov–Utjacki, SSSR 1962] ♘d5 12. ♕d5 ♖d8 13. ♕b3 b5 14. ♗d3 ♕g6 15. g3 ♗g4=/∞↑ Macukevič, Utjacki

45 11. ed5 ♗f5 12. ♕d2 ♘d4=/∞

46 13... 0–0 14. ♗d3 ♕g6 15. ♕f3 f5 16. ♕g3 ♕f7∓↑» Vlagsma–Ditt, Beverwijk 1959; 15. 0–0∞

47 17. ♗e2 e4 18. ♕b1 ef3 19. ♕f5 ♖f5 20. ♗f3 ♖e5=/∞

48 **9... ♘e7** 10. ♗g5 h6?! 11. ♗f6 gf6 12. 0-0-0±; **9... d5** 10. ♗g5! [10. ed5 ♘b4 11. ♗d3 ♘d3 12. cd3 ♗f5 13. 0–0 0-0-0 14. ♗g5 ♗d3 15. ♖fe1±] d4 [10... ♘b4 11. ♗f6 gf6 12. ♘d5 ♘c2 13. ♔d2 ♘a1 14. ♘c7 ♔e7 15. ♘a8 ♗e6 16. ♘b6 ♗a2 17. ♔c3 ♗e6 18. ♗c4 ♗c4 19. ♘c4 ♖c8 20. ♖a1 b5 21. b3±⊥ Bihovski–Minić, Beograd 1963; 10... ♘e4 11. ♘d5 0–0 12. ♗e3 ♖d8 13. ♘b6± Toran–Padevski, Moskva (ol) 1956; 11... ♘g5!? 12. ♘c7 ♔d7 13. ♘a8 ♘b4=/∞] 11. ♗f6 dc3 12. ♗g7 ♖g8 13. ♗h6! [13. ♗f6 cb2 14. ♖b1 ♖g6 15. ♗h4 ♖g4!∓ Klein–Rossetto, Santa Fe 1960] ♘b4 14. 0-0-0! ♘a2 15. ♔b1 ♗e6 16. ♖d6 ♖g6 17. ♗e3 ♘b4 18. ♗c5± Gligorić

49 10. ♔d1 ♘g4 [10... d5 11. a3±] 11. ♗e3 ♘e3 12. fe3 d6 13. a3 ♘c6 14. ♘d5 ♖b8= Gligorić

50 11... d5?! 12. ♗g5!±

51 8... ♘d4?! 9. ♗d3 ♕g6 10. 0–0 d5 11. ed5 ♗f5 [11... ♘f3 12. ♔h1 ♕h5 13. ♗b5+–] 12. ♗f5 ♕f5 13. ♘c3! 0-0-0 14. ♗e3 ♔b8 15. ♕c5 ♘f6 16. f4 ♘e4 17. ♕b6 ♖d6? 18. fe5!+– Saharov–Kapengut, SSSR 1963

52 9. ♘c3? ♘d4! 10. ♕a4 ♖b8△ b5∓

53 12... ♘f6 13. ♗c5 ♘c6 14. f4 [14. ♗c4 b5 15. ♘d5± Židkov–Mnacakanjan, SSSR 1964] d6 15. ♗d6 ef4 16. ♗c4 ♗e6 17. ♖he1± Čeremisin–Ivlev, SSSR 1962

54 14. ♗c4!? b5 15. ♘d5!±

55 **16... 0–0** 17. ♗e2 ♖fe8 18. ♗f3 d4 19. ♘a4±; **16... d4** 17. ♘e4 ♗d5 18. ♗d3 ♘g6 19. c4!± Spaski–Utjacki, Kislovodsk 1960

56 **9... ♘d4** [Ilivicki] 10. ♗d3 ♖b8 [10... ♕g6 11. 0–0? ♘f3 12. ♔h1 ♕h5 13. h3 d6 14. ♗e2 ♗h3 15. ♗f3 ♗g4 16. ♔g1 ♗f3 17. gf3 ♕g6 18. ♔h2 ♕h5 1/2 : 1/2 Burlajev–Macukevič, SSSR 1963; 11. ♗e3 ♕g2 12.

0-0-0±→] 11. ♘e2! [11. 0–0 b5 12. ♘d5 ♘d5 13. ed5 b4 14. ♕a5 0–0∓ Zaharov–Strekalovski, SSSR 1963; 11. ♗d2 d6 12. 0-0-0 0–0 13. f4 b5 14. ♘d5 ♘d5 15. ed5 ♗f5 16. fe5 ♕e5 17. ♗c3 ♕f4 18. ♗d2 ♕e5 19. ♗c3 1/2 : 1/2 Kaliničenko–Macukevič, SSSR 1963] ♘e2 11. ♗e2 0–0 13. ♗e3 b5 14. ♗c5 ♖e8 15. 0-0-0 ♘g6 16. g3 ♕c6 17. f3 ♗b7 18. ♖d6± Selivanovski–Macukevič, SSSR 1963; **9... 0—0** 10. ♗e3 d5 11. ♘d5 ♘d5 12. ed5 ♘d4 13. ♗d3 ♗f5 14. ♗d4 ed4 15. 0-0-0 ♖ac8 16. ♕b3± Drimer–Baumbach, Bucuresti 1962

57 10. ♘d5 ♘d5 11. ed5 ♘e7 12. c4 b5!= Szily–Baumbach, Bad Liebenstein 1963

58 12... ♘e7?! 13. 0-0-0! [13. ♗c5 ♘d5! 14. 0-0-0 ♗b7 15. ♗d3 b4! 16. ♗b4 ♘b4 17. ♕b4 ♕e7 18. ♕g4 0–0∞ Bokučava–Grigorjan, SSSR 1964] d6 14. h4 h6 15. ♗e2 ♘f5 [15... ♗b7 16. ♗f3 0–0 17. ♗e4 b4 18. ♕b3 ♗c8 19. f3 ♗f5 20. g4± Honfi–Pietzsch, Kecskemet 1962] 16. g4!±↑» Honfi–Damjanović, Reggio Emilia 1966/67 — 3/393

59 13. ♕b3 ♘d4! 14. ♗d4 ed4 15. 0-0-0 0–0= Macukevič, Utjacki

60 17. ♗b4 ♗g2 18. ♗g2 ♖b4∞ Fichtl–Smejkal, ČSSR (ch) 1963

61 8... ♕g6?! 9. ♘c3 ♘ge7 [9... ♘f6 10. ♕d6±] 10. ♗e3 0–0 11. 0-0-0 b5 12. ♗c5 ♖e8 13. ♔b1 ♖b8 14. ♗e7 ♖b7 15. ♕d6 ♖e7 16. ♕g6 hg6 17. ♘d5 ♖e6 18. g3! ♔f8 [18... ♘e7 19. ♗h3±] 19. h4!± Unzicker–Bazan, Buenos Aires 1960

62 **9... ♕e6**?! 10. ♗g5! [10. ♗e3 d5 11. ♗c5 d4 12. 0-0-0 ♗d7!= Müller] d5 11. ♗e7 ♘e7 12. 0-0-0 d4 13. ♗c4 ♕c6 [13... ♕f6 14. ♘d5 ♘d5 15. ed5 0–0 16. ♖he1±↑⊞] 14. ♘d5 ♘d5 15. ♕c6 [15. ♕e5!? ♘e7 16. ♕g7 ♖f8 17. ♖d4 ♗e6 18. ♗d5 ♕b6± Ravinski] bc6 16. ed5 cd5 17. ♗d5 ♖a7 18. ♖he1±; **9... 0—0** 10. ♗e3 d6 [10... d5?! 11. ed5 ♘d4 12. 0-0-0 ♗f5 13. f4! ♘c2 14. ♗c5 ♖fc8 15. ♕e7 ♖c5 16. ♕c5 ♖c8 17. ♕c8! ♗c8 18. ♔c2 ♕f4 19. d6+– Parma–Ciocaltea, Bucuresti 1968; 11... ♘b4 12. 0-0-0 ♗f5 13. ♕b6 ♕b6 14. ♗b6 ♖ac8 15. d6±↑⊞ Češkovski–Stukaturkin, SSSR 1965] 11. 0-0-0 ♖d8 12. h4 h6 13. ♘d5 ♘d5 14. ed5 ♘d4 15. ♗d4 ed4 16. ♕b6 ♕f4 17. ♖d2 [17. ♔b1 ♖e8!] ♖e8 18. ♗d3±; 12. ♕b6!?△ ♘d5

63 10. ♘a4 b5! 11. a3 ♕h4!∞

64 11... 0–0?! 12. f4 ♘d3 13. cd3 d4 14. ♘a4 ♗g4 15. ♘b6 ♖ad8 16. ♖f2± Lemoine–Visloužil, Budapest 1959

65 12. ♘a4!? ♕c6 [12... ♘d3 13. cd3 ♕c6 14. ♕c6 ♘c6 15. ♘b6 ♖b8 16. ♗d2 0–0 17. b4 f5 18. ♘c8 ♖bc8 19. ef5 ♘e7!± Parma–Bleiman, Netanya 1971 — 11/288; 17. a4!± Parma] 13. ♕c6 [13. ♕a5 ♘d3 14. cd3 b5 15. ♘b6 ♕c7 16. ♗d2 ♖b8 17. ♘c8 ♕a5 18. ♘d6 ♔d7 19. ♗a5 ♔d6 20. f4 ♘c6 21. fe5 ♔e6=] ♘ec6 14. ♘b6 ♖b8 15. f4 ♘d3 16. cd3 f6±

66 12... ♘d3?! 13. cd3 ♘c6 14. f4 ♕e7 15. ♕e7 [15. ♕b6 ♕b4=] ♔e7 16. fe5 ♘e5?! 17. b3!? [17. ♘d4 ♖d8=] ♖d8 18. ♗a3 ♔e8 19. ♘f4 f6 20. ♖ac1 ♘c6 21. ♗c5± Lukin–Ghizdavu, Bucuresti 1968

67 13. f4?! ♗g4! [13... ♘d3?! 14. cd3 ♘c6 15. ♕b6!±] 14. fe5 ♕c6! 15. ♕e7 ♘d3 16. ♘d4 ♕e4 17. ♘f3 ♗f3 18. cd3 ♕d4= Perfors–Baumbach, DDR 1962

68 13... ♘ec6 14. f4 ♗g4 15. fe5 ♕d8 16. ♕d8 ♖ad8 17. ♘f4 ♘d3 18. cd3 ♘e5 19. h3±

69 15. f4 ♕d8!=

70 17. f4±↑»

71 8... ♘ge7 9. ♘c3 0–0 10. ♗e3 b5 [10... d6 11. ♕d2 b5 12. 0-0-0± Gligorić–Rossetto, Santa Fe 1960] 11. ♕d2 ♕g6 12. f3 d6 13. 0-0-0 ♖d8 14. ♔b1 ♗b7 15. g4! f6 16. ♘d5 ♘d5 17. ♕d5± Gligorić–Benkö, Dublin 1957

72 **10. ♗e3** d5! 11. ed5 [11. ♘d5 ♘d5 12. ♕d5 ♗e6!? 13. ♕c5 ♕e4 14. 0-0-0 ♖c8∓ Unzicker–Mandel, BRD (ch) 1959; 12... 0–0 13. ♕d2 ♕e4 14. f3 ♕g6 15. ♗d3 ♗f5 16. ♗f5 ♕f5∓ Ćirić–Szabo, Beograd 1964] ♘b4 12. ♗d3 ♘d3 [12... ♗f5 13. 0–0 ♖c8 14. ♗f5 ♘f5 15. ♖c1 ♖c3! 16. bc3 ♘a2 17. ♖a1 ♘h4 18. g3 ♕e4–+ Luik–Klavin, SSSR 1959; 13. ♗f5 ♘f5 14. ♗c5 ♕g2 15. ♖f1 ♘h4∞ Hennings–Baumbach, DDR (ch) 1963] 13. ♕d3 ♗f5 14. ♕d2 [Janošević–Matulović, Maribor 1967 — 4/416] ♕g2!=; **10. f3**!? 0–0 11. ♗e3 d5 12. ♘d5 ♘d5 13. ♕d5 ♖d8! [13... ♗e6?! 14. ♕d2 ♖ad8 15. ♕f2 f5 16. ef5 ♗f5 17. c3 e4 18. f4 ♗e6 19. ♗e2 ♘e5 20. 0–0 ♘d3 21. ♕h4!± Matulović–Gerusel 1965] 14. ♕c4 ♗e6 16. ♕e2 f5 16. ef5 ♗f5= Bogdanović–Minić, Jugoslavija 1963

73 **10... d5** 11. h5 ♕d6 12. ed5 ♘b4 13. ♗c4 ♗f5 14. ♗b3 ♖d8 15. g4± Szabo–Szily, Hungary (ch) 1964; **10... h6** 11. h5 ♕f6 12. ♗e3 0–0 13. ♕d2 b5 14. 0-0-0 b4 15. ♘a4 a5 16. ♘b6 ♖b8 17. ♕d6 ♕d6 18. ♖d6± Boleslavski–Saharov, SSSR 1957

74 11. ♖h3?! d5 12. ♖g3 ♗g4! 13. f3 [13. ♗e2 de4 14. ♗g4 ♖d8! 15. ♗d2 hg4 16. ♕g4 e3 17. ♗e3 ♕c2∓ Bastrikov–Gufeljd, SSSR (ch) 1958] de4 14. ♘e4 [14. fg4? ♖d8 15. ♗d2 f5!–+ Bošković–Krstev, Jugoslavija 1965] ♖d8 15. ♗d3 f5 16. ♘g5 [16. ♘f2 e4! 17. fg4 ed3 18. ♖d3 fg4 19. ♖d8 ♘d8 20. ♗g5 ♘e6!∓ Željandinov–Levin, SSSR 1962] e4 17. fg4 hg4 18. ♘e4 fe4 19. ♖g4 ♕d6 20. ♖e4 ♕g3 21. ♔d2 0–0=∞ Geler–Bronštejn, Kislovodsk 1968 — 6/445; 19... ♖h4!?

75 **13. ♘e2** ♘e7 14. ♘g3 ♗g4∓ van den Berg–Vlagsma, Nederland 1958; **13. ♗c5** dc3 14. ♕d3 [14. f3 cb2 15. ♖b1 ♕g3 16. ♗f2 ♕g6=] ♗e6! [14... cb2?! 15. ♖b1 f5 16. ♖b2 fe4 17. ♕e3 ♗g4 18. ♖b7+– Muhitdinov–Šahzade, SSSR 1962] 15. ♕c3 ♕e4∞ Gligorić

[76] 17. ♕d3 ♕d3= Fischer—Talj, Curaçao (ct) 1962

[77] 12... ♘d4? 13. ♗d3 ♗f5 14. ♗f5 ♘ef5 15. ♕d3 f6 16. ♗e3 ♕g4 [16... ♕g2 17. 0-0-0 ♕f3 18. ♘e4 0—0 19. c3 ♘e2 20. ♔b1 ♘f4 21. ♗f4 ♕d3 22. ♖d3 ef4 23. ♘c5 ♘d6 24. ♘e6 ♖f7 25. ♘f4+— Saharov—Šija-novski, SSSR 1962] 17. ♗d4 ed4 18. ♘e2 ♕g2 19. 0-0-0!± Vasjukov—Malich, Berlin 1962

[78] **13. ♗d3** ♘d3 14. cd3 f6 15. d6 ♘c6= Konrady—Belkadi, Varna (ol) 1962; **13. d6** ♘ec6 14. ♗d3 ♘d3 15. ♕d3 ♗f5 16. d7 ♔f8 17. ♕d5 f6 18. ♗e3 ♕f7 19. 0-0-0 ♖d8= Nikitin—Gufeljd, SSSR 1959

[79] 13... ♗f5?! 14. d6 f6 [14... ♘c2 15. ♖c2! ♗c2 16. ♕d2 ♘c6 17. d7 ♔f8 18. d8♕ ♘d8 19. ♗d8+— Romanovski—Lenčiner, SSSR 1959] 15. de7 fg5 16. ♕f3 e4 17. ♕e3 gh4 18. ♖h4 ♖c8 19. ♖f4± Bobkov—Balejev, SSSR 1962

[80] 14. ♗e3?! ♗f5 15. d6 ♖d8∓

[81] 15. ab4 gh4 16. ♖h4 ♘f5 17. ♖h2 ♘d4 18. ♗d3 ♗f5 19. ♘e2 0-0-0 20. ♘g3 e4 21. ♗c4 h4 22. ♘f1 ♘c6∓ Jansa—Baumbach, Bad Liebenstein 1963

[82] 21. ♗d3 ♖ad8 22. ♔e3 h4 23. g3 [23. ♖h2 g5 24. ♖g1 ♔f6 25. ♗e4 b6 26. c3 a5= Liebert—Baumbach, DDR (ch) 1963] hg3 24. ♖h8 ♖h8= Fuchs—Baumbach, Bad Liebenstein 1963

[83] 14. ♗d3?! ♘d3 15. ♕d3 ♕d3 16. cd3 b5= Zuckerman—Bleiman, Netanya 1971

[84] 14... ♕d6?! 15. ♕d6 ♔d6 16. 0-0-0 ♔c7 17. a3 ♘c6 18. ♘d5 ♔b8 19. ♘b6 ♖a7 20. ♗c4 ♖f8 21. ♖d7+— Begun—Koroljev, SSSR 1966

[85] 15. ♖c1 ♗g4 [15... ♗f5 16. ♕f3!±] 16. ♕d2 ♖h6 17. a3 ♘c6 18. ♗c4± Kuprejčik—Georgijev, Ybbs 1968

B 33 — 1. e4 c5 2. ♘f3 ♘c6 3. d4 cd4 4. ♘d4 ♘f6

	5	6	7	8	9	10	11	12	13	
1	♘c3[1] ♕b6	♘b3[2] e6	a3[3] ♗e7[4]	g3[5] 0—0	♗g2 a6	0—0 d6	♗e3 ♕c7	g4[6]		±
2	... ...	... ...	♗e3 ♕c7	♗d3[7] ♗e7[8]	f4 d6	0—0[9] 0—0[10]	g4! d5!	e5 ♘d7	♕f3 a6[11]	±
3	... ...	... ...	♗d3 ♗e7	0—0[12] 0—0[13]	♔h1 d6	f4 ♗d7	♕e2 ♘b4	♗e3 ♕c7	a3 ♘d3[14]	±
4	... ...	... ...	... ♗b4	0—0[15] 0—0[16]	♗e3[17] ♕d8!	f4 ♗c3	bc3 d6	c4 b6[18]	♕e1 ♘g4[19]	±
5	... e5[20]	♘f3[21] ♗b4[22]	♗c4[23] 0—0[24]	♗g5[25] ♗c3	bc3 ♕a5	♗f6 ♕c3	♘d2 gf6	♖b1 ♘d4	♕g4[26] ♔h8[27]	=
6	... ...	♘b3 ♗b4	♗g5[28] h6	♗f6 ♗c3	bc3 ♕f6	♗d3[29] ♘e7	♘d2 0—0	c4 d6	♘f1 ♗e6[30]	=
7	... ...	♘de2 ♗c5[31]	♘g3 d6	♗e2 ♗e6[31]	0—0[33] a6[34]	♔h1[35] ♘d4	f4 ♘e2	♕e2 ♘g4	f5 ♕h4[36]	∞
8	... ...	♘db5 h6[37]	♘d5[38] ♘d5	ed5[39] a6!	dc6[40] ab5	cd7[41] ♗d7	♗d3[42] ♗c6	0—0 ♕d5	♕g4 h5[43]	=
9	... ...	... ...	♗c4 a6![44]	♘d6 ♗d6	♕d6 ♕e7	♕e7[45] ♔e7	♗e3 d6	0-0-0 ♗e6	♘d5 ♗d5[46]	∞
10	... ...	... ...	♘d6 ♗d6	♕d6 ♕e7	♕e7[47] ♔e7	♗e3![48] d6	f3 ♗e6[49]	0-0-0 ♖hd8[50]	g4 ♖ac8[51]	±

1. e4 c5 2. ♘f3 ♘c6 3. d4 cd4 4. ♘d4 ♘f6 5. ♘c3 e5 6. ♘db5 d6

	7	8	9	10	11	12	13	14	15	
11	a4[52] ♗e6[53]	♗g5 a6![54]	♘a3 ♖c8	♘c4 ♘d4	♘e3 ♗e7	♗f6 ♗f6	♗d3 ♗g5	♘ed5 0—0[55]		∞

	7	8	9	10	11	12	13	14	15	
12	♗g5	♘a3	♘d5[58]	♗f6[60]	c3[61]	♘c2	a4[63]	♖a4	b4[65]	∞
	a6[56]	b5[57]	♗e7[59]	♗f6	0—0	♗g5[62]	ba4[64]	a5	♗e6[66]	
13	. . .	. . .	♘c4	♗f6[68]	♘b6[70]	♘cb5	c3	♕a4!	♘d5	±
	. . .	♗e6	♘d4[67]	♕f6[69]	♖b8[71]	♕d8	♘c6	♗d5		
14	. . .	. . .	. . .	♘d5[72]	♗f6[73]	ed5[74]	b4[75]			∞
	. . .	. . .	♖c8	♗d5	gf6	♘e7	f5[76]			
15	. . .	♗f6	♘a3	♘d5[77]	ef5[79]	c3[80]	♕f3	h4	♕h3[81]	±
	. . .	gf6	b5	f5[78]	♗f5	♗g7	♗g6	e4		
16	. . .	. . .	. . .	♕h5[82]	ed5[84]	ba3	♔d2	♕e2	♕c4	=
	. . .	. . .	f5	d5![83]	♗a3	♕a5	♘e7	e4[85]	0—0[86]	
17	. . .	. . .	. . .	♗c4!?	g3	ef5	♗d3	♗e4	♗c6	±
	. . .	. . .	. . .	♕g5	♗e6	♕f5	♕h3	0-0-0	bc6[87]	
18	. . .	. . .	. . .	♘d5[88]	ba3	♗c4[89]	♕d2	♔d2	♖ad1[91]	±
	. . .	. . .	d5	♗a3	♗e6	♕a5	♕d2[90]	0-0-0	f5[92]	

[1] **5. ♘c6**? bc6 6. ♗d3 e5 7. 0—0 ♗c5! 8. ♗g5 ♖b8 9. ♗c4 h6 10. ♗h4 d6 11. ♕d3 g5 12. ♗g3 h5 13. h4 ♘g4! 14. ♘c3 gh4 15. ♗h2 ♕f6—+ Hellmann—O'Kelly 1947; 8. ♕e2∓; **5. f3**?! d5 [5. . . e5? 6. ♘b5! d6 7. c4 a6 8. ♘5c3 h6 9. ♗e3 ♗e7 10. ♘a3 0—0 11. ♕d2 ♖b8 12. ♘d5 b6 13. ♖d1±⟳] 6. ♗b5 [6. ♘c6 bc6 7. e5 ♘d7 8. f4 ♘c5 9. ♘c3 ♗f5 10. ♗e3 e6 11. ♗e2 ♖b8 12. ♖b1 ♕a5 13. 0—0 ♘a4∓] ♗d7 [6. . . de4 7. ♘c6 ♕d1 8. ♔d1 a6=] 7. ♗c6 bc6 8. e5 ♘g8 9. ♘c3 e6∓

[2] 6. ♘db5 a6 7. ♘a3 e6 [7. . . ♕c7 8. ♘d5 ♕e5 9. ♗e3 ♘d5 10. ed5 ♘b4 11. ♘c4 ♕d5 12. ♕e2 ♕c6 13. 0-0-0 d5 14. ♘b6 ♗f5∞ Željandinov—Krupski, SSSR 1970] 8. ♗d3 [8. ♘c4 ♕c7 9. ♗e3 b5= Gufeljd] ♕c7 9. ♘c4 b5 10. ♘e3 ♗b7 11. 0—0 ♗e7 12. f4 d6 13. ♕e1 0—0 14. a4? ♘d4!∓ Željandinov—Gufeljd, SSSR 1971 — 12/348; 14. b3∞ Gufeljd

[3] **7. ♗g5** ♗e7 [7. . . ♗b4 8. ♗f6 gf6 9. ♗d3±] 8. ♕d2 [8. ♗d3!?△ ♕e2] a6 9. 0-0-0 d6 10. h4 ♗d7 11. f3 ♕c7 12. h5! h6 13. ♗e3 b5 14. ♔b1 ♘e5 15. ♕f2 b4 16. ♘e2 ♘c4 17. ♗f4∞ Rossolimo—R. Byrne, USA 1967 — 4/415; **7. ♗e2** ♗b4 8. 0—0 0—0 9. ♕d3 ♗c3 10. bc3 d5 11. ed5 ed5 12. ♗f4 ♖e8 13. ♖ab1 [13. ♖ae1 ♘e5 14. ♕d4 ♕d4 15. cd4 ♘g6 16. ♗g5 ♗f5=] ♘e5 14. ♕d4 ♕d4 15. ♘d4 b6± Fischer—Benkö, Stockholm (izt) 1962

[4] 7. . . a6 8. ♗e3 ♕c7 9. f4 d6 10. ♗d3 [10. ♗e2 b5 11. 0—0 ♗b7 12. ♗f3 ♗e7 13. ♕e1 ♖c8 14. ♖d1 0—0 15. ♕f2 ♕b8!= Bakulin—Kernaševski, SSSR 1973] b5 11. 0—0 ♗b7 12. ♕f3± Ghizdavu—Ungureanu, Romania (ch) 1973

[5] 8. ♗e3 ♕c7 [8. . . ♕d8 9. f4 d5± Pogats—Polgar, Hungary (ch) 1966] 9. ♗e2 0—0 10. f4 ♖d8 11. ♗d3 d6 12. ♕f3 a6 13. g4 d5∞ Yanofsky—Benkö, Winnipeg 1967 — 5/361

[6] Lejn—Seleznev, SSSR 1963

[7] 8. f4 ♗b4 9. ♗d3 d5 10. e5 ♘e4 11. ♗e4 de4 12. 0—0 ♗c3 13. bc3 b6 14. ♘d2 ♗a6 15. ♖f2 0-0-0∞ Szabo—Gufeljd, Tallinn 1969

[8] **8. . . a6** 9. f4 d6 10. ♕f3 [10. g4 b5?! 11. g5 ♘d7 12. ♕d2 ♗b7 13. 0-0-0 ♘c5 14. ♕f2! ♘b4? 15. ♘c5± Beljavski—Gufeljd, Suhumi 1972 — 14/345; 14. . . ♘d3!?] ♗e7 11. g4 h6 12. 0-0-0 b5 13. ♖hg1 ♘d7 14. ♕f2± Estrin—Kopilov, SSSR 1973 — 16/307; **8. . . ♗b4** 9. 0—0 0—0 10. ♘b5! ♕b8 11. f4± Gheorghiu—Forintos, Monte Carlo 1968 — 5/360; 9. . . ♗c3!? Portisch

[9] **10. ♕e2** a6 11. g4!? [11. 0—0!? Petrosjan] b5 12. g5 ♘d7 13. a4?! [13. 0-0-0!? Petrosjan] b4 14. ♘b1 h6 15. g6!? ♗h4 16. ♗f2 ♗f2 17. ♕f2 fg6 18. ♕g3 0—0 19. ♖g1∞ Listengarten—Juferov, SSSR 1972 — 13/357; **10. ♕f3**△ g4, g5, 0-0-0±

[10] 10. . . a6 11. ♕f3 ♗d7 [11. . . b5? 12. e5±] 12. a3 [12. ♘a4 0—0 13. ♘b6 ♖ad8= Kostro—Gufeljd, Tbilisi 1969 — 8/320; 12. ♖ae1± Gufeljd] ♖c8 13. ♘a4 b5 14. ♘b6 ♖b8 15. ♘d7= Minev—Olafsson, La Habana (ol) 1966 — 2/343; 13. g4!?± Parma

[11] 14. ♖ae1 b5 15. ♕h3 g6 16. ♖f3 f6 17. ♕h6 ♘de5 18. fe5± Geler—Gufeljd, SSSR (ch) 1969 — 8/317

[12] 8. ♕e2 d6 9. g4!? a6 10. g5 ♘d7 11. h4 ♕c7 12. h5 b5 13. a3 ♗b7 14. ♗d2 ♘c5∞ Gipslis—Štejn, SSSR (ch) 1972

[13] 8. . . a6 9. ♗e3 [9. ♕e2 d5 10. ed5 ed5 11. ♗g5 ♗g4 12. ♕d2 0-0-0= Talj—Gufeljd, SSSR (ch) 1969 — 8/318] ♕c7 10. f4 [10. a4 d5!? 11. ed5 ed5 12. ♗e2 ♗e6 13. a5 0—0 14. ♗b6± Polugajevski—Averkin, SSSR (ch) 1969 — 8/319] d6 11. ♕f3±

[14] 14. cd3 b6 15. ♘d4 ♖fd8 16. f5 e5 17. ♘c2± Darga—Panno, Las Palmas 1973

15 8. ♗d2 0–0 9. a3 ♗e7 10. f4± Suetin–Reško, SSSR 1971 — 12/349

16 8... ♗c3 9. bc3 0–0 10. c4 d6 11. ♗a3 ♖d8 12. ♕e1 ♘e5 13. ♕c3 ♗d7∞ I. Zajcev–Reško, SSSR 1972; 10. ♗g5±

17 9. ♘b5!?±

18 12... e5 13. f5 b6 14. g4 ♗b7 15. g5± Ruban–Reško, SSSR 1967

19 14. ♗c1± Štejn–Forintos, Kecskemet 1968

20 Lasker

21 **6. ♘c6**?! bc6 7. ♗c4 [7. ♗g5 ♖b8! 8. ♗f6 ♕f6 9. ♗c4 ♖b2 10. ♗b3 ♗b4∓ Malmgren–Aljehin, Örebro 1935] ♗b4 8. ♗g5 h6 9. ♗h4 [9. ♗f6 ♕f6 10. ♕d3 0–0 11. 0–0 d6 12. a3 ♗c5∓] g5 10. ♗g3 ♘e4 [10... d6!?] 11. ♗e5 ♕e7 12. 0–0 [12. ♕d4? ♘c3 13. bc3 ♗c5 14. ♕e4 d5–+] ♗c3=; 9... ♕a5∓; **6. ♘f5** d5 7. ed5 ♗f5 8. dc6 ♕d1 9. ♘d1 bc6 10. ♘e3 ♗g6 11. ♗e2 ♗c5 12. ♗f3 ♖c8 13. 0–0 0–0 14. ♖d1 ♗e4=

22 6... ♗e7 7. ♗c4 0–0 8. ♗g5 d6 9. ♗f6 ♗f6 10. h3 ♗e6 11. ♗b3 ♕d7 12. 0–0 ♗d8 13. ♕d3 ♗b3 14. ab3 ♘b4 15. ♕d2 ♕c6= Kopajev–Kuzminič, SSSR 1940

23 7. ♗d3 d5 8. ♘d2 ♗c3 9. bc3 0–0∓ Atanasov–Hübner, Ybbs 1968

24 7... d6 8. 0–0 ♗g4 9. ♘d5 ♘d5 10. ed5 ♘e7! 11. h3 ♗d7 12. ♗e3 f5 13. c3 ♗a5 14. ♘g5 f4 15. ♘e4 ♘f5 16. ♗d2±; 8... ♗e6=

25 **8. ♕d3**? d5∓; **8. 0–0** d6! [8... ♗c3 9. bc3 ♘e4 10. ♗a3 d6 11. ♕e1 ♗f5 12. ♖b1∞̄] 9. ♘d5 h6 [9... ♘e4 10. ♘b4 ♘b4 11. ♕e1] 10. ♘b4 ♘b4 11. c3 ♘c6 12. ♕d3 [12. ♕e2!?△ ♖d1] ♕c7 13. ♗b3 ♘a5 14. ♗c2 d5!= Ortega–Zinn, Berlin 1968 — 6/483

26 13. 0–0 d5!=

27 14. ♕h4 ♔g7=

28 **7. ♗d3** d5! [7... 0–0 8. ♗d2 ♗c3 9. ♗c3 d5 10. ed5 ♕d5 11. 0–0 e4 12. ♗e2 ♕g5 13. ♔h1 ♔h8∞ Reissman–Lhagva, Lugano (ol) 1968] 8. ed5 ♘d5 9. ♗d2 ♗c3! [9... ♘c3 10. bc3 ♗e7?! 11. 0–0 0–0 12. f4± Mitrev–Ilkov, Sofia 1973; 10... ♗d6!= Schlechter–Lasker (m) 1910] 10. bc3 0–0 11. 0–0 f5 12. ♗c4 ♔h8 13. ♗d5 ♕d5 14. ♗e3 ♕c4 15. ♕d3 ♗e6∓⊥ Rezende–Zinn, Siegen (ol) 1970; **7. ♗c4** d6! [7... 0–0 8. ♕d3 d5!=; 8. 0–0 ♗c3 9. bc3 ♘e4 10. ♗a3 d6 11. ♕d3 ♗f5 12. ♖ae1 ♕h4 13. f4! ef4 14. ♖e4+– Kopajev–Korčnoj, SSSR 1952] 8. 0–0 ♗e6=

29 10. ♗e2 0–0 11. 0–0 d6 12. ♕d3 ♖d8 13. ♖fd1 ♗e6 14. ♗f3 ♖ac8∓↑« Košljak–Pančenko, SSSR 1969

30 **13... b5**!? 14. cb5 d5 15. ♘g3 ♗b7∞ Marjanović–Urzica, Groningen 1973; **13... ♗e6**=

31 **6... d5** 7. ed5 ♘b4 8. ♗g5 ♗c5 9. a3?! ♘g4 10. ♗d8 ♗f2=; 9. ♘g3±; **6... ♗b4** 7. ♗d2 [7. a3 ♗a5 8. b4 ♗b6△ ♘g4] 0–0 8. a3? ♗c5 9. ♘g3 ♕b6 10. ♕e2 ♘d4 11. ♕d3 ♕b2 12. ♖a2 ♕b6 13. ♗e2 d6 14. 0–0 ♗e6 –+ Hoyt–Rossetto, Lugano (ol) 1968; 8. ♘g3=; **6... h6** 7. g3 d5 8. ed5 ♘b4 9. a3= Kagan–Ruderfer, SSSR 1966

32 8... h5 9. ♗g5! [9. ♗h5 ♘h5 10. ♘h5 ♕h4 11. ♘g3 ♗g4 12. f3? ♕g3!–+] ♕b6 10. ♗f6! ♗f2 11. ♔f1 ♗g3 12. hg3 gf6 13. ♕d6 ♘d4 14. ♕b6 ab6 15. ♘d5± Teschner–Richter, Berlin 1949

33 9. ♘d5? ♗d5 10. ed5 ♘e7 11. 0–0 ♘fd5 12. ♗b5 ♔f8∓ Kadiri–Zinn, Lugano (ol) 1968

34 9... d5 10. ♘h5=

35 10. ♗g5!? Nikolov–Panteleev, Primorsko 1970

36 14. h3 h5 15. ♖f3 ♗d7 16. ♗d2∞ Fletzer–Benner, 1953

37 **6... ♗c5** 7. ♗e3! ♗e3?! 8. ♘d6 ♔f8 9. fe3 ♕b6 10. ♘c4 ♕c5 11. ♕d6 ♕d6 12. ♘d6 ♘e8 13. ♘cb5 ♘d6 14. ♘d6 ♘b4 15. 0-0-0! ♘a2 16. ♔b1 ♘b4 17. ♗c4+–; **6... ♗b4** 7. a3! ♗c3 [7... ♗e7 8. ♘d6 ♗d6 9. ♕d6 ♕e7 10. ♕d1±] 8. ♘c3 d6 9. ♗g5 [9. ♘b5? ♘e4 10. ♗d3 a6] h6 [9... a6 10. ♘d5 ♗e6 11. ♗f6 gf6 12. ♘e3± ×d5, f5] 10. ♗f6 ♕f6 11. ♘b5 [11. ♘d5 ♕d8 12. ♗c4±] 0–0 12. ♕d6 ♕h4 13. ♕d3 [13. ♗d3 ♕g5!?] ♖d8 14. ♕e3±; **6... a6** 7. ♘d6 ♗d6 8. ♕d6 ♕e7 9. ♕e7 [9. ♕d1 h6! 10. ♘d5 ♘d5 11. ed5 ♘d4 12. c3 ♘f5 13. ♗d3±⊡; 10. ♗c4 d6 11. ♗e3 ♗e6 12. ♘d5!? ♗d5 13. ed5 ♘b8!? 14. 0–0±] ♔e7 [9... ♘e7 10. ♗g5 d5 11. ♗f6 gf6 12. ♘d5 ♘d5 13. ed5 ♗f5 14. 0-0-0+–] 10. ♗g5 ♘b4 11. 0-0-0 h6 12. ♗f6 ♔f6 13. a3±

38 **7. b3** ♗c5 8. ♘d6 ♔e7 9. ♘f5 ♔f8 10. ♗c4 ♗b4! 11. ♗d2 ♕a5 12. ♕f3 d6 [12... d5?! 13. ed5 ♘d4 14. ♘d4 ed4 15. ♘b1 ♗d2 16. ♘d2± Matulović–Bilek, Sousse (izt) 1967 — 4/467] 13. 0–0 ♗f5 14. ef5 d5∞; **7. ♗e3** d6 [7... a6?! 8. ♘d6 ♗d6 9. ♕d6 ♕e7 10. ♗c5±↗ a3-f8] 8. ♗e2 a6 9. ♘a3 b5 10. ♘d5 ♖b8! 11. ♗f3 ♘d5 [11... ♗e6!?] 12. ed5 ♘e7 13. c4 ♘f5 14. cb5 ♘e3= Mesing–Milić, Jugoslavija 1968 — 5/393; **7. ♗e2** d6 8. a4 ♗e7 9. ♗e3 0–0 10. ♕d2 a6 11. ♘a3 ♗e6 12. 0–0 d5 13. ed5 ♘d5 14. ♘d5 ♗d5= Zinser–Ciocaltea, Reggio Emilia 1966/67

39 8. ♕d5 d6 9. ♗e3 ♗e6 10. ♕d2 a6 11. ♘c3 ♕a5=

40 9. ♘c3 ♘d4 10. ♗d3 [10. ♗c4 ♕h4] d6 11. 0–0 g6 12. ♘e4 ♗g7 13. c3 [13. a4!?] ♘f5 14. f4 0–0 15. ♕f3 ♘h4 16. ♕f2 f5= Johansson–Bilek, ČSSR 1968 — 5/394

41 10. cb7 ♗b7 11. ♕e2 ♕c7! 12. ♕b5 ♗c5 13. ♕e2 0–0 14. ♗e3 ♗e3 15. fe3 ♖fb8△ ♗a6∞̄

42 11. ♕d5 ♕c7 12. ♗d2 ♕c5=

43 14. ♕h3 ♗e7 15. ♗e3 ♗d7 16. ♗f5 [16. ♕g3 g5] ♗f5 17. ♕f5 g6 18. ♕d3= Vitolinš—Lutikov, SSSR 1970 — 10/454

44 7... d6 8. ♘d5 ♘d5 9. ♗d5 a6 [9... ♗e7 10. ♕h5! g6 11. ♕f3 ♕a5 12. ♘c3± Cejtlin—Karasev, SSSR 1972 — 13/397] 10. ♘c3 ♗e7 11. ♕h5! g6 [11... 0—0? 12. ♗h6!] 12. ♕f3 ♖h7 13. ♗e3± Bihovski—Milić, Beograd 1967 — 4/465

45 10. ♕c7 d5! 11. ♕e7 ♘e7 12. ed5 ♗f5=

46 14. ed5 b5!? 15. dc6 [15. ♗b3?! ♘a5 16. f3 ♖hc8 17. g4 ♘d7 18. h4 ♘b3 19. ab3 a5∞ Karpov—Hug, Graz 1972] bc4 16. f4! ♔e6!∞ Parma—Milić, Beograd 1967 — 4/464

47 **9. ♕d2** 0—0 10. ♗c4 d6 11. b3 ♗e6 12. ♗e6 fe6 13. ♗a3? ♘d4 14. 0-0-0 ♖ac8 15. ♗b2 [15. f4?? ♖c3—+ Honfi—Bilek, Kecskemet 1966 — 2/344] b5 16. a3 a5∓; 14. f3∓; 13. ♗b2!?=; **9. ♕d1** 0—0 10. ♗e3 ♖d8 11. a3 d6 12. ♗e2 ♗e6 13. ♘d5 ♗d5 14. ed5 ♘d4= Schalk—Haberditz, 1950; **9. ♘b5** ♕d6 10. ♘d6 ♔e7 11. ♘f5 ♔f8 12. b3 d5 13. ♗a3 ♔g8 14. ed5 ♘d5± Spaski—Gheorghiu, Bath 1973

48 10. b3 d6 11. ♗a3 a6 [11... ♖d8 12. 0-0-0 ♗e6 13. ♘d5 ♗d5 14. ed5 ♘b8 15. ♖e1 ♔d7 16. f4± Zuckerman—Sherwin, USA (ch) 1967 — 3/395; 15. ♗d3 a5 16. ♖he1 ♘fd7 17. f4 f6± Holmov—Ciocaltea, Tbilisi 1969 — 9/335; 12... a6 13. ♘d5 ♘d5 14. ed5 ♘b8 15. ♗d3±; 11... ♗e6!?] 12. ♗d3 ♗e6 13. 0—0 b5 14. ♘d1 ♖hb8 15. ♘e3 a5± Lutikov—Vasjukov, SSSR 1968 — 6/482

49 11... a6 12. 0-0-0 b5 13. a4! [13. g4 ♗e6 14. h4 ♘a5 15. b3 ♘b7= Mednis—Lombardy, USA (ch) 1969 — 8/360] b4 14. ♘d5 ♘d5 15. ed5 ♘a5 16. ♗b6 ♘b7 17. a5±↑⟪ R. Byrne

50 **12... a6** 13. ♗e2 ♖ac8 14. ♖d2± Radulov—Drimer, La Habana 1969 — 8/358; **12... ♖he8** 13. g4 a6 14. h4 ♘d7 15. ♖h2!± Tukmakov—Džindžihašvili, SSSR 1968; **12... ♖hc8** 13. ♔b1 a6 14. ♘a4 ♘d7 15. c4 ♘a7± Kavalek—Soos, Polanica Zdroj 1968

51 14. h4 ♘e8 15. ♖h2 a6 16. g5 hg5 17. hg5 b5 18. ♗b6± Štejn—Mjagmarsuren, Sousse (izt) 1967 — 4/466

52 **7. ♘d5** ♘d5 8. ed5 ♘b8 9. c4 a6 10. ♘c3 ♗e7 11. ♗d3 0—0 12. 0—0 ♘d7 13. ♕c2 g6 14. ♗h6 ♖e8 15. ♗e3 f5 16. f3 ♗f6= Lejn—Minev, Novi Sad 1972; **7. ♗e3** a6 8. ♘a3 b5 [8... ♗e6 9. ♘c4 ♗e7 10. ♘b6 ♖b8 11. ♘bd5±] 9. ♘d5 ♖b8! 10. g3 ♘d5 [10... ♘e4!? 11. ♗g2 ♘c5∞] 11. ed5 ♘e7 12. ♗g2 ♘f5 13. ♗d2 ♗e7= Ree—Langeweg, Nederland 1969 — 7/364

53 **7... h6**?! 8. ♗e3 ♗e7 9. ♘d5 ♖b8 [9... ♘d5 10. ed5 ♘b8 11. a5!±] 10. ♘f6 gf6 11. ♗c4 a6 12. ♘c3 ♖g8 13. 0—0 ♕d7 14. ♕h5 ♖g6± M. Kovacs—Gescos, Budapest 1971; **7... ♗e7** 8. ♗e2?! 0—0 9. ♗e3 ♗e6 10. ♘d5? ♘e4 11. ♘e7 ♕e7 12. f3 a6! 13. fe4 ab5 14. ab5 ♖a1 15. ♕a1 ♘b4 16. ♕a4 ♕h4 —+ Grigorjev—Nenarokov, SSSR 1921; 8. ♗c4!?±; **7... a6** 8. ♘a3 d5 [8... ♗e6!? 9. ♗c4 ♗c4? 10. ♘c4 ♘e4 11. ♘e4 d5 12. ♗g5!+— Galia—Grünfeld, Wien 1946; 9... ♗e7 10. ♗g5! 0—0 11. ♗f6 ♗f6 12. 0—0 ♖c8± Hennings—Pavlov, Bucuresti 1971; 9... ♘b4 10. 0—0 ♖c8=; 9... ♖c8 10. 0—0 ♗e7 11. ♗e3 0—0= Reinhardt—Pelikan, Argentina 1961] 9. ♗g5 [9. ed5 ♘d4 10. ♗c4 ♗f5△ ♗a3] d4 10. ♘d5 ♗e6 11. ♗c4 ♗d5 12. ed5 ♗b4 13. ♔f1 ♘a5 14. ♕e2 ♕d6 15. ♗f6 ♕f6 16. ♗b5 ♔f8 17. ♗d3 g6 18. ♘c4= Letelier—Rossetto, Mar del Plata 1958

54 8... ♗e7? 9. ♗f6 gf6 10. ♘d5 ♖c8 11. c3 a6 12. ♘a3 f5 13. ef5 ♗f5± Hennings—Lorenz, Leipzig 1971

55 △ g6, f5∞ M. Kovacs—Zinn, Baja 1971

56 7... ♗e6 8. ♘d5 ♗d5 9. ed5 ♘e7 10. ♗f6 [10. ♘c3 ♘d7 11. ♗e2 h6 12. ♗h4 a6 13. ♕d2 ♕b6 14. f3 ♖c8 15. ♘a4 ♕d4!?∞] gf6 11. c4 f5 12. ♕h5±

57 **8... ♗e7** 9. ♘c4 ♘d4 10. ♗f6 [10. ♘e3 ♗e6 11. ♗d3 0—0 12. 0—0 b5 13. ♗f6 ♗f6 14. ♘cd5 ♗g5= Vogt—Schöneberg, DDR (ch) 1972] ♗f6 11. ♘d5 b5 12. ♘cb6 ♖b8 13. ♘c8 ♖c8 14. c3 ♘c6 15. a4± Boleslavski; **8... d5** 9. ♘d5 ♗a3 10. ba3 ♕a5 11. ♗d2 ♕d8 12. ♘f6 ♕f6 13. ♗d3 0—0 14. 0—0 ♗e6 15. ♗c3 ♕e7±

58 9. ♗f6! ♕f6? 10. ♘d5 ♕d8 11. c4 [11. c3 ♘e7 12. ♘c2 ♘d5 13. ♕d5 ♗e6=] ♘e7 [11... b4 12. ♘c2 ♖b8=; 12. ♕a4! ♗d7 13. ♘b5+— Lerner—Cejtlin, SSSR 1973] 12. cb5 [12. ♗e2?! ♘d5 13. cd5 g6 14. ♘c2 ♗h6 15. 0—0 0—0 16. ♕d3 f5∓ Jocha—Svešnikov, Budapest 1967] ♘d5 13. ed5±; 9... gf6! — 8. ♗f6

59 **9... ♗e6** 10. c4!±; **9... ♕a5** 10. ♗d2 [10. ♕d2 ♕d2 11. ♔d2 ♘e4 12. ♔e3? ♘g5 13. ♘c7 ♔d8 14. ♘a8 d5!∓; 11. ♗d2 ♘d5 12. ed5 ♘e7=] ♕d8 11. ♘f6 ♕f6 12. c4 [12. ♗d3 ♗e6 13. c3 ♕d8! 14. ♘c2 d5=] ♕g6 13. f3 ♗e7 14. g3 [14. ♔f2?! 0—0! 15. cb5 ♘d4 16. ♗e3 f5 17. ♗d4 fe4!∞ Kurajica—Radojević, Sombor 1968 — 6/481; 14. cb5 ♗h4 15. g3 ♗g3 16. hg3 ♕g3 17. ♔e2 ♘d4 18. ♔e3 f5 ♗c3 fe4 20. ♗d4 ed4∞ Radulov—Cobo, La Habana 1969 — 8/359] 0—0 15. cb5 ♘d4 16. ♗e3 f5!∞

60 10. c3 ♗e6 11. ♗f6 ♗f6 12. ♘f6 gf6 13. ♘c2 0—0 14. ♗d3 ♔h8 15. 0—0 ♖g8 16. ♘e3 b4!∞ Olafsson—Larsen, Zürich 1959

61 11. ♗d3 ♗g5 12. 0—0 0—0 13. c4 b4 14. ♘c2 a5 15. a3 b3 16. ♘ce3 ♗e3 17. fe3 a4 18. ♕h5 ♗e6∓ Jakovljevski—Svešnikov, Jugoslavija—SSSR 1969

62 12... ♖b8!? Svešnikov

63 13. ♘e3 ♗e3 14. ♘e3 ♗e6 15. ♗e2 ♘e7=

64 13... ♖b8!?± Kuprejčik–Svešnikov, SSSR 1973

65 15. ♗c4 ♖b8?± Karpov–Svešnikov, SSSR (ch) 1973; 15... ♗d7△ ♕b8, ♗d8, ♗b6∞

66 16. b5 ♘b8 17. ♗e2 ♘d7∞ Estrin–Kimelfeld, SSSR 1967

67 **9... h6**? 10. ♗f6 ♕f6 11. ♘b6 ♖b8 12. ♘cd5 ♕g6 13. ♕d3 ♗d5 14. ♘d5 ♗e7 15. g3 ♗d8 16. 0-0-0 b5 17. f4± Ribli–Zinn, Zalaegerszeg 1969; **9... ♗e7**?! 10. ♗f6 gf6 11. ♘e3 [11. ♘d5!?] ♕d7 12. ♘cd5 ♗d8 13. ♕h5± Blau–Plater, Hilversum 1947; **9... b5** 10. ♗f6 gf6 11. ♘e3 ♗h6 12. ♘cd5 ♗e3 13. ♘e3 ♘e7 14. a4! b4 15. ♕f3± Honfi–Piket, Wijk aan Zee 1970 — 9/336

68 **10. ♘d5** ♗d5 11. ed5 b5 [11... ♗e7? 12. c3 ♘b5 13. ♗e3!± Lukin–Kuprejčik, SSSR 1967] 12. ♘e3 ♕a5 13. c3 ♘e4 14. ♗h4 g5 15. ♗g3 ♘c3 16. ♕d2 b4∞; **10. ♘e3** ♖c8 [10... ♗e7 11. ♗f6 ♗f6 12. ♘cd5 ♗g5 13. c3 ♗e3?! 14. ♘e3 ♘c6 15. ♗c4 0–0 16. 0–0 ♕c7 17. ♕d3 ♘e7± Kavalek–Benkö, Caracas 1970 — 10/457] 11. ♗d3 ♗e7 12. ♗f6 ♗f6 13. 0–0 0–0 14. ♘cd5 ♗g5∞ Karaklajić–Pilnik, Moskva (ol) 1956

69 10... gf6 11. ♘e3 ♖c8 12. ♗d3 h5 13. 0–0 h4 14. ♘cd5 ♗g7 15. c3 ♘c6 16. ♕f3 ♖h6 17. ♘f5+– Bronštejn–Pilnik, Moskva (ol) 1956

70 11. ♗d3 ♕d8! 12. 0–0 ♗e7 13. ♘e3 0–0 14. ♘cd5 ♗g5 15. c3 ♘c6△ ♘e7=

71 11... ♖d8?! 12. ♘bd5!±

72 **10. ♘e3** ♗e7 11. ♗f6 ♗f6 12. ♘cd5 ♗g5 13. ♘f5?! ♗f5 14. ef5 ♘d4 15. c3 ♕a5!∓ Westerinen–Johansson, Halle 1963; 13. c3!?; **10. ♗f6** gf6 11. ♘e3 ♗h6 [11... ♘e7 12. ♗d3 ♕b6 13. 0–0! ♕b2 14. ♘cd5 ♗d5 15. ♘d5 ♘d5 16. ed5 ♕d4 17. ♕f3± Liberzon–Gerusel, Solingen 1974 — 18/376; 15. ed5! ♕d4 16. ♕f3 ♕f4 17. ♕h3!± Lombardy–Markland, Nice (ol) 1974 — 17/410; 11... ♘d4∞] 12. ♗d3 ♘e7 13. ♘ed5?! ♗d5 14. ed5 ♕a5 15. ♗e2 ♖c5 16. ♗f3 f5 17. a3 ♕c7△ b5∓⇆≪; 13. 0–0!∞

73 11. ed5 ♘b8 12. ♗e2 ♗e7 13. 0–0 0–0 14. a4 ♘bd7 15. ♗e3 ♘e8 16. f3 f5 17. b4∞ Sokolov–Trifunović, Jugoslavija (ch) 1956; 11... ♘e7 12. ♗f6 gf6 — 11. ♗f6

74 12. ♕d5 ♘b4! 13. ♕d2 d5 14. ed5 ♘c2 15. ♕c2 ♗b4 16. ♔d1 b5∞ Larsen

75 **13. ♕f3** f5 14. ♕a3 ♖c5!∓; **13. ♗d3** f5 14. 0–0 ♗g7 15. ♕h5 e4 16. ♗e2 0–0 17. c3!? f4 18. ♗g5 b5∞ Robatsch–Larsen, Halle 1963

76 **13... ♕c7**? 14. a4 b5 15. ab5 ab5 16. ♘d6!± Gligorić–Brinck-Claussen, Hastings 1963/64; **13... f5**!∞ Larsen

77 10. ♘ab5?! ab5 11. ♗b5 ♗d7 12. ♕h5 ♘e7 13. ♗c4 ♘g6 14. f4 ef4 15. ♕d5 ♘e5–+

78 10... ♗e6 11. c3! [11. c4 ♘d4 12. ♗d3 ♖g8 13. g3 ♕a5!∓] ♖g8 [11... ♗g7 12. ♘c2 f5 13. ef5 ♗f5 14. ♘ce3 ♗g6 15. a4±↑≪ Barczay–Radojević, Sombor 1966] 12. ♘c2 ♗h6 13. a4! ♗d5 14. ♕d5 ♘e7 15. ♕d3± Bhend–Kinzel, Venezia 1953

79 **11. ♗b5**?! ab5 12. ♘b5 ♖a7! 13. ♘a7 ♘a7 14. ♕f3 [14. ef5!?] ♘c6 15. 0-0-0 ♗h6 16. ♔b1 fe4 17. ♕e4 0–0∓ Peresipkin–Svešnikov, SSSR 1973 — 15/363; **11. c4** ♕a5 12. ♕d2 ♕d2 13. ♔d2 ♔d8 14. cb5 ab5 15. ♘b5 fe4∞ Karasin–Abramov, SSSR 1966; **11. g3** fe4 12. ♗g2 ♗g7 13. ♗e4 ♖a7!∞; **11. ♗d3** ♗e6 12. ♕h5 ♗g7 [12... f4?! 13. g3 f3 14. c3 ♗g7 15. ♘c2 0–0±] 13. 0–0 f4!? [13... h6?! 14. c3! 0–0 15. ♘c2 fe4 16. ♗e4 f5 17. ♘f4!± Spaski–Svešnikov, SSSR (ch) 1973 — 16/357] 14. c3 0–0 15. ♘c2 f5 16. ♘cb4 [16. a4 ♗d5!= Lukin–Timoščenko, SSSR 1973 — 16/306] ♘b4 17. ♘b4 d5 [17... a5 18. ef5? ♗f7 19. ♕h3 ♕d7! 20. ♘c2 d5∓ Klovan–Timoščenko, SSSR 1974 — 18/373; 18. ♘c2 ±] 18. ed5 ♗d7=∞ Zinn–Svešnikov, Dečin 1974 — 18/375

80 **12. ♗d3** e4 [12... ♗g6 13. h4! e4 14. h5 ed3 15. hg6 fg6 16. ♕d3 ♗g7 17. ♕e4 ♔f7 18. ♕f3± Ceškovski–Šestjakov, SSSR 1974] 13. ♕e2 ♕a5 14. c3 b4∞; **12. ♕f3** ♘d4! 13. ♘c7 ♕c7 14. ♕a8 ♔e7 15. c3 b4!=∞ Klokov–Lomov, SSSR 1973 — 15/364

81 Talj–Šamkovič, SSSR 1955

82 10. ♘c4 b5 [10... fe4 11. ♘e4 ♘d4 12. c3 d5∞ Bazan–Pelikan, Argentina 1961] 11. ♘e3 b4 12. ♘b1 [12. ♘cd5 fe4 13. ♕h5 ♗e6 14. ♗c4 ♘d4 15. c3 bc3 16. bc3 ♖b8 17. cd4 ed4∞ Savon–Kuprejčik, SSSR (ch) 1969] fe4 13. ♗c4 ♗e6 14. ♗e6 fe6 15. ♕h5 ♔d7 16. ♘d2 ♕e8 17. ♕h3 ♕g6 18. 0–0 ♗e7 19. a3∞ Geler–Gufeljd, SSSR 1970

83 10... b5?! 11. ef5! [11. ♘ab5? ab5 12. ♗b5 ♗b7 13. ♕f5 ♗g7 14. 0-0-0 0–0–+ Levčenkov–Svešnikov, SSSR 1969 — 8/361] b4 12. ♗c4+–

84 **11. ♘d5**? ♗a3 12. ba3 ♕a5 13. c3 ♗e6 14. ♖c1 [14. 0-0-0 fe4 15. ♘f6 ♔e7 16. ♘e4 ♕a3 17. ♔d2 ♖ad8–+ Kuzmin–Kuprejčik, SSSR 1972 — 13/398; 16. ♕h4 ♕c3 17. ♔b1 ♗a2!–+] 0-0-0 15. ♗c4 ♕c5 16. ♗b3 fe4 17. ♘e3 ♘d4!∓ Schwarz–Virkulov, SSSR 1972; **11. 0-0-0** ♗a3 12. ba3 ♘d4 13. ef5! ♕a5 14. ♖d4! ed4 15. ♗b5! ab5 16. ♖e1 ♗e6?+– Luczak–Szczepaniec, Polska 1973 — 15/365; 16... ♔d8∞ Marić

85 14... ♗e6!? 15. ♕e5 0-0-0∞

86 16. ♕b4 ♕c7= Želјandinov–Kuprejčik, SSSR 1970

87 16. ♕e2 ♔b7 17. 0-0-0± Kirilov–Ilkov, Bulgaria 1973

88 10. ed5? ♗a3 11. ba3 ♕a5 12. ♕d2 ♘d4 13. ♗d3 ♗h3! 14. 0–0 ♘f3–+; **10. ♕d5** ♗e6 11. ♕d8 ♖d8 12. ♘c4 [12. ♗d3 ♗b4!] ♗b4 13. ♘e3 ♔e7 14. ♗d3 ♗c3 15. bc3 ♘a5 16. 0–0 ♖c8 17. f4 ♘c4= Planinc–Benkö, Sarajevo 1970 — 9/337

89 12. ♘e3?! ♕a5 13. ♕d2 ♕a3 14. ♗d3 0-0-0 15. 0–0 ♖d4!∓ Geler–Pilnik, Amsterdam (ct) 1956

90 13... 0-0-0 14. ♖d1 ♕a3 15. 0–0 ♖hg8 16. ♕e3! ♕e3 17. fe3± Fischer–Rossetto, Buenos Aires 1960

91 15. ♗b3 f5 16. ♔c3 ♘d4 17. ♖ad1 fe4= Tukmakov–R. Garcia, Buenos Aires 1970 — 10/456

92 16. f3 fe4 [16... ♖hg8 17. g3 ♔b8 18. ♔e3± Štejn–Benkö, Caracas 1970 — 10/455] fe4 17. fe4 f5 18. ♔e3±

B 34 **1. e4 c5 2. ♘f3 ♘c6 3. d4 cd4 4. ♘d4 g6**

	5	6	7	8	9	10	11	12	13	
1	♘c6[1] bc6	♕d4 f6	c4[2] ♘h6	♗e2 ♗g7	0–0 0–0	c5 f5	♕a4[3] a5[4]	♘c3 ♖b8	a3 ♕c7[5]	±
2	... ...	... ♘f6	e5 ♘d5[6]	c4[7] ♕b6!	♕e4 ♘c7	♘c3 ♗g7	f4 0–0	♗d2 d5[8]	♕f3 ♗f5[9]	∓
3	♘c3 ♘f6[10]	♘c6[11] dc6	♕d8 ♔d8	♗c4 ♔e8[12]	e5[13] ♘g4	f4 h5[14]	♗d2 ♗f5	h3 ♘h6	0-0-0 ♗g7[15]	±
4	... ...	... bc6	e5 ♘g8[16]	♗c4 ♗g7[17]	♕f3 f5[18]	♗f4 ♖b8[19]	0–0 e6	♖ad1 ♕c7	♖fe1 ♘e7[20]	±
5	... ♗g7	♗e3[21] ♘f6[22]	♗e2[23] 0–0	0–0[24] d5	ed5[25] ♘d5[26]	♘d5 ♘d4!	♗d4[27] ♕d5	♗g7 ♕d1	♖fd1 ♔g7[28]	=
6	... ...	... ...	f4 d6[29]	♗e2[30] ♕b6	♕d3 ♕b2	0–0 0–0[31]	♖ab1 ♕a3	♘c6 bc6	♘d5 ♕d3	=

1. e4 c5 2. ♘f3 ♘c6 3. d4 cd4 4. ♘d4 g6 5. ♘c3 ♗g7 6. ♗e3 ♘f6 7. ♘c6 bc6 8. e5 ♘g8

	9	10	11	12	13	14	15	16	17	
7	♗d4 c5[32]	♗c5[33] ♕c7[34]	♗d4 ♗e5	f4[35] ♗d4	♕d4 ♘f6	g4[36] ♗b7	♖g1 0–0	0-0-0 ♖fe8	♖d2 ♖ab8[37]	±
8	... ♕a5	♗c4[38] ♗e5	0–0 ♘f6![39]	♖e1 d6	♗e5 de5	♕e2 ♗f5	♗b3 e4	♕c4 0–0	♕c6 ♖ad8[40]	=
9	f4 ♘h6	♕d2[41] 0–0	0-0-0[42] d5[43]	h4 ♕a5	h5 ♖d8	hg6 hg6	♕d4 ♘f5	♕c5 ♕c5	♗c5 ♘g3[44]	±
10	... f6	♗d4[45] ♕a5[46]	♕d2[47] fe5	fe5 c5[48]	♗e3 ♗e5	♗c4 ♘f6	0–0 ♗b7[49]	♖ae1 ♕b4	♕e2 0-0-0[50]	±

1. e4 c5 2. ♘f3 ♘c6 3. d4 cd4 4. ♘d4 g6 5. ♘c3 ♗g7 6. ♗e3 ♘f6 7. ♘c6 bc6 8. e5 ♘d5 9. ♘d5 cd5 10. ♕d5 ♖b8

	11	12	13	14	15	16	17	18	19	
11	0-0-0 ♗b7	♕d4[51] 0–0	f4 d6	♗c4 ♕c7	♗b3 de5	fe5 ♗g2	♖hg1 ♖bd8	♕a7 ♕e5	♗d4 ♕f4[52]	=
12	♗a7 ♖b2	♗d4[53] ♖c2	♗d3 e6[54]	♕a8[55] ♖c6	0–0[56] ♗a6[57]	♕d8 ♔d8	♗a6 ♖a6	a4 d6	♖d1 ♔d7[58]	=
13	♗c4 0–0[59]	0–0[60] ♕c7[61]	♗f4[62] ♗b7	♕d4 d6!	ed6[63] ed6[64]	♕d3 ♗b2	♖ad1 ♗e5[65]			=

1 5. ♗c4 ♗g7 6. ♘c6 bc6 7. 0—0 e6 8. ♘c3 d5? 9. ed5 cd5 10. ♘d5! ed5 11. ♗d5 ♗e6 12. ♗a8 ♕a8 13. ♕d6 ♘e7 14. ♗g5 ♘f5 15. ♕a3± Liskov—Liberzon, SSSR 1956; 8... ♘e7!∓

2 **7. h4** ♘h6 [7... ♗h6? 8. ♘d2 ♗f4 9. g3 ♗c7 10. h5±→] 8. h5 ♗a6 9. ♗a6 ♕a5 10. ♘c3 ♕a6∓; **7. ♗c4** ♗g7 [7... ♘h6 8. 0—0 ♘f7 9. ♗f7 ♔f7 10. e5 ♕b6 11. ♕c4 d5! 12. ed6 ♗e6 13. ♕c3 ed6∓ ⊡ Kapu—Barcza, Hungary 1951; 7... e6 8. 0—0 ♘h6 9. ♘c3 ♘f7 10. ♗e3 ♗g7 11. ♖ad1 0—0 12. ♕d2 f5 13. ef5 gf5∓ Schlechter—Lasker, Hastings 1895] 8. 0—0 [8. ♘c3 ♘h6 9. h4 ♕b6 10. ♕d3 ♘g4 11. ♕g3 f5 12. 0—0 ♗a6∓ Aleman—Koch 1952] ♘h6 9. ♘c3 ♕b6 10. ♕b6 ab6 11. ♗e3 ♗a6 12. ♗e2 f5 13. ♖fe1 ♗e2∓ Pilnik—Barcza 1952

3 11. e5 ♘f7 12. ♗c4 ♕c7 13. ♗f7 ♖f7 14. ♖e1 ♗a6 15. ♘c3 ♖b8 16. ♖b1 d6 17. cd6 ed6 18. ed6 ♕a5 19. ♕h4 ♗c3 20. bc3 ♖b1 21. ♖e8= Poljak—Simagin, SSSR 1954

4 11... fe4 12. ♘c3 ♘f5 13. ♘e4 ♘d4 14. ♗c4 ♔h8 15. ♗g5±

5 14. ♕c4±

6 **7... ♘g8** 8. ♗c4 ♗g7 9. 0—0 f6 10. ef6 [10. ♗g8?! ♖g8 11. ♕h4 fe5 12. ♕h7 ♔f7 13. ♗h6 e6 14. ♗g7 ♖g7 15. ♕h6 ♕f6 16. ♕e3 ♕f4∓ Akopjan—Fajbisovič, SSSR 1971; 10. ♗f4 ♕b6∓] ♘f6 11. ♗b3 d5 12. ♗f4 0—0 13. ♗e5 e6 14. ♘c3 c5!? 15. ♕c5 ♘d7 16. ♕c6 ♗e5 17. ♕a8 ♗c3 18. bc3 ♕c7 19. ♗d5 ed5 20. ♕d5=; **7... ♘h5** 8. ♗e2 ♘g7 9. ♘c3 ♘e6 10. ♕e3 ♗g7 11. f4 0—0∓ Adams—Bisguier, USA (ch) 1954

7 8. e6 f6 [8... ♘f6 9. ef7 ♔f7 10. ♗e2 ♗g7 11. h4 ♕b6 12. ♕a4 (Bžuska—Gurgenidze, Sofia 1958) e5∓] 9. ed7 ♗d7 10. ♗e2 [10. ♗c4!? e5 11. ♕e4△ ♘c3] e5 11. ♕d1 ♗g7 12. c3 0—0∓ Vestol—Botvinik, Sverige 1956

8 **12... ♕b2**!? 13. ♖b1 ♕a3 14. ♖b3 ♕a6∞; **12... d6**∓

9 Čistjakov—Veresov, SSSR 1953

10 5... d6 6. ♘d5 ♗g7 [6... e6 7. ♘c3 a6∞] 7. ♘b5 ♖b8 [7... ♔f8 8. ♗c4!? ♗d7?! 9. 0—0 a6 10. ♘bc3 b5 11. ♗b3 e6 12. ♗f4 (G. Szilagyi—Pogats, Hungary (ch) 1965) ♘e5∞; 8... a6!?; 8. c4!?] 8. c4 a6 9. ♘bc3 e6 10. ♘e3 ♘ge7 [10... b5? 11. cb5 ab5 12. a4! ba4 13. ♘c4± Vasjukov—S. Garcia, Camaguey 1974] 11. ♗e2 0—0 12. 0—0 f5=

11 6. f4 ♕b6! 7. ♘f3 d6 8. ♗c4 ♗g7 9. ♕d3 0—0 10. ♗b3 ♗g4 11. ♗e3 ♕a5 12. 0—0 ♗f3 13. gf3 (Ljubojević—Bilek, Teesside 1972 — 13/358) ♖ad8 14. ♘d5 e6 15. ♗d2 ♕c5 16. ♗e3=

12 **8... b5**? 9. ♗f7 e6 10. ♗g5 ♗e7 11. 0-0-0+—; **8... ♗g7** 9. ♗f4 ♔e8 10. 0-0-0 ♘d7 11. ♗c7 ♗c3 12. bc3 ♔f8 13. ♖d2 ♔g7 14. ♖hd1± Gligorić—Kristinsson, Reykjavik 1964

13 9. a4 e5! 10 f4 ♗e6! 11. ♗e6 fe6 12. ♖f1 ♗h6!= Smislov—Botvinik (m) 1958

14 10... ♗f5 11. h3 ♘h6 12. g4 ♗c2? 13. ♖h2 ♗a4 14. ♘a4 b5 ♗b3 ba4 16. ♗a4 ♖c8 17. ♖c2 ♔d7 18. ♗e3+—; 12... ♗d7±

15 14. ♖he1± Boleslavski

16 7... ♘d5? 8. ♘d5 cd5 9. ♕d5 ♖b8 10. e6! f6 11. ♗f4 ♖b4 12. ♗d2 ♖b6 13. ♗b5 ♖d6 14. ♕c4+— Grabek—Sajfert, Harrachov 1966

17 **8... d5**?! 9. ed6 ♕d6 [9... ed6 10. ♕f3 d5 11. ♘d5 cd5 12. ♗d5 ♕e7 13. ♗e3 ♖b8 14. 0—0 ♗g7 15. ♗f4 ♖b6 16. ♗c6 ♖c6 17. ♕c6 ♕d7 18. ♖fe1 ♘e7 19. ♖e7+— Jon—Janowski, Mannheim 1914] 10. 0—0 ♕d1 11. ♖d1 ♗h6 12. ♗h6 ♘h6 13. ♖d2 ♘f5 14. ♘e4 a5 15. a4 ♗a6 16. ♗a6 ♖a6 17. ♖ad1±⊥ Geler—Štejn, SSSR (ch) 1966/67 — 3/396; **8... ♕a5** 9. ♗f4 [9. 0—0 ♕e5? 10. ♖e1 ♕a5 11. b4 ♕d8± Karaklajić—Ivanović, Jugoslavija 1974 — 18/350; 9... ♗g7 10. ♖e1 ♗e5 11. ♗f4 f6 12. ♕f3 ♗f4 13. ♕f4 d5 14. ♘b5?! ♔f7 15. ♖ad1 (Matulović—Bilek, Pécs 1968 — 5/363) dc4! 16. ♘c7 ♖b8 17. ♕c4 ♔g7 18. ♕c6 ♗g4∓; 14. ♗b3⩱] ♗g7 10. 0—0 ♗e5 11. b4 [11. ♗e5 ♕e5 12. ♖e1 ♕f4∞ Andersson] ♕c7 12. ♘d5 cd5 13. ♕d5 ♘f6 14. ♕f7 ♔d8 15. ♖fe1 d6 16. ♗e5 de5 17. ♖ad1⩱→ Kurajica—Ostojić, Skopje 1969 — 8/322

18 9... e6 10. ♗f4 ♕a5 [10... ♕c7 11. 0—0 ♗e5 12. ♘b5!+—] 11. 0—0! ♗e5 12. b4! ♕c7 13. ♘b5 ♕b8 14. ♗e5 ♕e5 15. ♖ad1 d5 16. ♖fe1 ♕b8 17. ♗d5 cd5 18. ♕d5 ♔f8 19. ♕d8 ♔g7 20. ♘c7 ♘f6 (Langos—Balla, Hungary 1958) 21. ♕e7+—

19 **10... ♕a5** 11. 0—0 ♗e5 12. b4 ♕c7 13. ♘b5 ♕b8 14. ♗e5 ♕e5 15. ♖fe1 ♕b8 16. ♕c3 1 : 0 Karakas—Polihroniade, Beverwijk 1966; **10... e6** 11. 0-0-0 [11. g4!? fg4 12. ♕g4 ♕a5 13. 0-0-0 ♗e5 14. ♗e5 ♕e5 15. ♖he1⩱ Daskalov—Milev, Bulgaria 1960] ♕c7 12. ♕e2 ♖b8?! 13. h4 ♘e7 14. h5 g5 15. h6+— Boleslavski; 12... ♘h6!?; 12... ♘e7!?

20 14. b3 0—0 15. ♕e3 ♕a5 16. h4± Andersson—Bilek, Teesside 1972 — 13/359

21 **6. ♘c6**? bc6∓; **6. ♘b3**?! ♗c3! 7. bc3 ♘f6 8. ♗d3 d5 9. ed5 ♕d5 10. 0—0 0—0 11. c4 ♕d6 12. ♗b2 ♘g4 13. g3 ♘ge5 14. ♕e2 ♘d3 15. cd3 ♗h3 16. ♖fe1 e5∓ Bokučava—Raškovski, SSSR 1971; **6. ♘de2** ♘f6 7. g3 0—0 [7... d5!? 8. ed5 ♘b4 9. ♗g2 ♗f5 10. ♘d4 ♗g4 11. ♕d2 ♘bd5 12. ♘d5 ♘d5 13. h3 ♗c8 14. ♘b3± Fuchs—Litvinov, SSSR 1968] 8. ♗g2 d6 9. 0—0 — B 70

22 6... ♘h6? 7. f3!△ ♕d2±

23 **7. f3**? 0—0 8. ♘b3 [8. g4? ♕b6! 9. ♘cb5 a6 10. ♘f5 ♕d8 11. ♘g7 ab5 12. g5 ♘e4!—+ Sczepaniec—Gavlikowski, Polska 1954; 8. ♕d2 d5 9. ♘c6 bc6 10. ed5 ♘d5 11. ♗d4 e5 12.

♗c5 ♘c3 13. ♗f8 ♕f8∓→ Krnić–Velimirović, Jugoslavija 1971 — 11/289; 8. ♗c4 — B 35] a5 9. ♗b5 d5 10. ed5 ♘b4 11. d6 ♗f5 12. ♖c1 a4 13. ♘d4 ♕d6 14. ♘f5 ♕d1 15. ♖d1 gf5 16. ♗c5 ♘c2 17. ♔f2 ♖fc8 18. ♗e7 a3∓ Rubelj–Aronson, SSSR 1957; **7. ♘b3** a5 [7... 0–0 8. ♗e2 b6?! 9. f4 ♗b7 10. ♗f3 e5 11. 0–0 ♕e7 12. g3 ♖ad8 13. ♕d2 d5 (Milner-Barry–Wade, England 1955) 14. ♘d5 ♘d5 15. ed5 ♘a5 16. ♘a5 ba5 17. c4 ef4 18. gf4±; 8... d6 — B 72] 8. ♗b5 0–0 9. 0–0 a4 10. ♘a4 ♘e4 11. ♘b6 ♖b8 12. c3 f5 13. f4 e6 14. a4 d5 15. a5 g5 16. ♗c6 bc6 17. fg5 e5=/∞ Šišov–Kotkov, SSSR 1954

24 8. ♕d2? d5 9. ed5 ♘d5 10. ♘d5 ♘d4 11. ♗d4 [11. ♘e7 ♕e7 12. ♗d4 ♗d4 13. ♕d4 ♖e8 14. ♕e3 ♕b4 15. c3 ♕a4 16. ♕d4 ♕a6 –+] ♕d5 12. ♗g7 ♕g2 13. 0-0-0 [13. ♕d4 e5! 14. ♕e5 ♕h1 15. ♔d2 ♖d8–+] ♔g7 14. ♕e3 ♕c6 15. ♗d3 ♗e6 16. h4 h5 17. ♖hg1 ♗g4∓ Crepeaux–Glatmann, Varna 1972 — 14/347

25 9. ♘c6 bc6 10. e5 [10. ed5 cd5 11. ♗d4 e6 12. a4 a5 13. ♘b5 ♗a6 14. c3 ♘e4 15. ♗e3 ♖e8 16. ♖e1 ♕b8 17. ♗d3 ♘d6 18. ♕e2 e5∓↑⊞ Pilnik–Petrosjan 1952] ♘d7 [10... ♘e4!?] 11. f4 e6 12. ♘a4 ♕e7 13. c4 f6∞ Žuhovicki–A. Zajcev, SSSR 1962

26 9... ♘b4 10. d6 [10. ♘b3 ♘fd5 11. ♘d5 ♘d5 12. ♗d4 ♘f4=] ♕d6 11. ♘cb5 [11. ♘db5 ♕b8 12. ♗f3 ♘c6∓] ♕d7!? [11... ♕b8 12. c4 a6 13. ♘c3 e5 14. ♘f3 ♗f5 15. ♗c5 ♖d8 16. ♕b3± Radulov–Deže, Vršac 1971 — 12/352] 12. c4 a6 13. ♕a4 ♘c6 14. ♖ad1 ♖b8 15. ♘f3 ab5 16. cb5 ♕e8 17. bc6 bc6 18. ♗d4 ♗e6= Bartis–Judovič, corr. 1971 — 12/351

27 11. c4 e5=

28 14. ♗f3 ♗f5= Karaklajić–Trifunović, Jugoslavija (ch) 1961

29 7... 0–0 8. ♗e2 [8. e5 ♘e8 9. ♕f3 ♘d4? 10. ♗d4 d6 11. 0-0-0 ♕a5 12. ♕d5! ♕c7 13. ed6 ♘d6 14. ♗g7 ♔g7 15. ♕d4 f6 16. ♘d5± Pilnik–Casas, Mar del Plata 1958; 9... d6! 10. ♘c6 bc6 11. ♕c6 ♗d7=/∞] d5 9. e5 ♘e4 10. ♘c6 bc6 11. ♘e4 de4 12. ♕d8 ♖d8 13. ♗c4 ♔f8 14. 0–0 a5 15. ♗b6± Olafsson–Larsen, Wageningen 1957; 8... d6 9. 0–0 — B 73

30 8. ♘c6 bc6 9. e5 ♘g4 10. ♗g1 de5 11. ♕d8 ♔d8 12. 0-0-0 ♔c7 13. h3 ♘h6 14. ♖e1 ♘f5 15. fe5 ♘g3–+ Vooremaa–Pohla, SSSR 1967 — 3/398

31 **10... ♘b4** 11. ♕c4+–; **10... ♘e4** 11. ♕e4 ♕c3 12. ♘b5 ♕a5 13. ♘d6 ♔f8 14. ♘c4=/∞

32 **9... ♘h6** 10. e6 0–0 [10... ♗d4 11. ♕d4 0–0 12. ed7 ♕d7 13. ♕d7 ♗d7 14. ♗c4 ♖ad8 15. 0-0-0 ♘g4 16. ♖d2 ♗c8 17. ♖hd1± Bisguier–Geler, Helsinki (ol) 1952] 11. ♗g7 ♔g7 12. ♕d4 f6 13. ed7 ♗d7 14. 0-0-0 ♗g4± Platz–Koch, DDR 1954; **9... f6** 10. f4 — 9. f4

33 10. ♗e3!? ♕c7 [10... ♗e5? 11. ♕d5 ♗c3 12. bc3 ♖b8 13. ♕e5+–] 11. ♗c4 ♗b7 12. ♕d3 ♕e5 13. 0-0-0 ♘f6 14. ♖he1±↑ Tukmakov–Weichert, Graz 1972 — 14/351

34 10... ♗e5?! 11. ♕d5 ♗c3 12. bc3 ♕a5 [12... ♖b8 13. ♕e5+–] 13. ♕a8 ♕c3 14. ♔d1 ♕c5 [14... ♕a1? 15. ♔d2+–] 15. ♗a6 ♕d6 16. ♗d3 ♕c5±

35 12. ♗e2 ♘f6 13. ♗e5 ♕e5 14. 0–0 ♗b7! 15. ♗f3 ♗f3 16. ♕f3 0–0= Vukčević–Pirc, Jugoslavija (ch) 1957

36 14. 0-0-0 0–0 15. ♗c4 ♗b7 16. ♖d2 d5 17. ♗b3 ♖fd8 18. ♖hd1 ♖d7± Tringov–Damjanović, Ljubljana 1969 — 7/327; 16... d6!?

37 18. ♖g3 a5 [Dückstein–Štejn, Sarajevo 1967 — 3/399] 19. ♗b5±

38 **10. f4**?! ♖b8! 11. e6 ♘f6 12. ef7 ♔f7 13. ♗c4 d5 14. ♗b3 ♖d8 15. ♗e5 ♘g4 16. ♗g7 ♔g7 17. ♕d4 e5! 18. fe5 c5∓ M. Kovacs –A. Zajcev, Debrecen 1970 — 10/417; **10. e6** ♘f6 11. ef7 ♔f7 12. ♗c4 d5 13. ♗b3 ♖e8 14. f4 c5 15. ♗e5 e6 16. ♕d2 ♗b7 17. 0–0 ♗c6∓ Plater–Vasjukov, Polska–SSSR 1955

39 11... f6 12. ♖e1 ♕b4 [12... ♗d4 13. ♕d4 d5 14. ♗b3 e6 15. ♘d5 cd5 16. ♗d5 ♖b8 17. ♗e6 ♗e6 18. ♖e6+– Hudjakov–Alterman, SSSR 1973] 13. ♗e5 ♕c4 14. ♗d6 ♔f7 15. ♘e4 ♕d5 16. ♕f3 ♕f5 17. ♕b3 ♔g7 [17... ♕d5 18. ♗e7 ♘e7 19. ♘d6 ♔f8 20. ♕a3±→] 18. ♗e7± Haag–Forintos, Hungary 1965

40 18. ♖ad1 ♕e5= Tringov–Štejn, Sarajevo 1967 — 3/400

41 10. ♕f3 0–0 11. ♗c4 d5! 12. ed6 ed6 13. ♕c6 ♗d7 14. ♕f3 ♖c8 15. ♗d3 ♗g4 16. ♕d5 [16. ♕f2 ♖c3!–+] ♖e8 17. ♔d2 ♖e3 18. ♔e3 ♕b6=/∞ Fichtl–Gereben, Warszawa 1956

42 11. h3 d6! 12. 0-0-0 ♘f5 13. ♗f2 c5 14. g4 ♘d4 15. ♗g2 ♖b8 16. ♗d4 cd4 17. ♕d4 ♕a5 18. ♖he1 ♗e6=/∞ Dückstein–Waller, Austria 1969 — 7/329

43 **11... f6**? 12. ♗c4 ♔h8 13. h4 fe5 14. h5±→ Boleslavski; **11... d6** 12. ed6 ♘f5 [12... ed6 13. ♗d4±] 13. ♗f2! ed6 14. g4!±

44 18. ♖h2 ♗g4± Estrin–A. Zajcev, corr. 1965

45 **10. e6**? d5 [10... de6 11. ♕f3 ♗d7 12. 0-0-0 ♕c8 13. ♗c4 ♘h6 14. ♘a4 ♘f7 15. ♖d7!+– Fichtl–Šajtar, ČSSR 1953; 11... ♕c7 12. ♗b5! (12. ♘b5 ♕b7 13. ♘d4 ♘h6 14. ♕c6 ♔f7 15. 0-0-0 ♖d8?? 16. ♘e6!+– Černikov–Sosonko, SSSR 1965; 15... ♘f5!±) ♗b7 (12... ♗d7 13. 0-0-0 ♘h6 14. ♖d7!+– Boleslavski) 13. ♗c4±→] 11. f5 ♕d6 12. g4 ♕e5 13. ♕d3 h5 14. 0-0-0 ♕e3! 15. ♕e3 ♗h6 16. ♕h6 ♘h6 17. fg6 ♘g4–+ Rakić–Carev, Jugoslavija 1966 — 1/257; **10. ♗d3**? fe5 11. f5 d5 12. fg6 ♘f6 13. gh7 e4 14. ♗e2 ♖h7∓ Sapunov–Milev, Bulgaria 1959; **10. f5**?! ♕a5 11. ef6 ♘f6 12. fg6 ♕e5 13. ♕d4 ♘g4 14. ♕e5

♗e5 15. ♗g1 hg6 16. ♗d3 ♔f7 17. 0-0-0 ♔g7 ∓↑⊞ Zaharov–Antošin, SSSR 1964; **10. ef6** ♘f6 11. ♗e2 0–0 12. 0–0 d5 [12... ♗b7!? 13. ♕e1 ♕c7 14. ♖d1 ♖ae8 15. ♕h4 ♘d5=] 13. ♗d4 ♗f5 14. ♗f3 ♖b8= Aronin–Geler, SSSR 1951

46 **10... fe5**? 11. fe5 e6 12. ♗d3 ♕h4 13. g3 ♕e7 14. ♘e4 ♕b4 15. ♗c3 ♕b6 16. ♘d6 ♔e7 17. ♕f3 ♘h6 18. ♕f4 ♔d8 19. ♘c4 ♕c5 20. ♗a5+– Wade–Bilek, Teesside 1972 — 13/362; **10... ♘h6**? 11. ef6 [11. ♗c4?! ♘f5 12. ef6 ef6 13. ♕e2 ♕e7 14. ♕e7 ♔e7 15. ♗f2 ±; 12... ♗f6 13. ♗f6 ef6 14. ♕f3 ♕e7 15. ♔d2 ♕d6 16. ♔c1 ♔f8± Dückstein–Jansson, Lugano (ol) 1968 — 6/447] ef6 12. ♕e2! ♕e7 13. ♘e4 ♔d8 14. ♗c5 ♕e6 15. ♘d6 ♕d5 16. ♕c4 ♕c4 17. ♗c4 ♗f8 18. 0-0-0+– Ostojić–Ree, Wijk aan Zee 1969 — 7/328; **10... d5**? 11. ed6 ♕d6 [11... ed6 12. ♕f3 ♘e7 13. 0-0-0 0–0 14. ♗c5 d5 15. ♗c4 ♖b8 16. ♖he1± Krogius–Buslaev, SSSR 1956] 12. ♕f3 ♕e6 13. ♗e2 ♗a6 14. 0–0 ♗e2 15. ♘e2± Ivkov–Pirc, Zagreb 1955

47 **11. ♗c4**?! fe5 12. fe5 ♗e5 13. ♕d3 ♘f6 14. 0-0-0 ♗d4 15. ♕d4 d5 16. ♕e5 0–0 17. ♘d5 cd5 18. ♖d5 ♕b4 19. ♖d4 ♔h8∓ Masjejev–Baumbach, corr. 1972 — 13/361; **11. ef6** ♘f6 [11... ♗f6 12. ♗f6 ♘f6= Baumbach] 12. ♗c4 ♗a6?! 13. b4 ♕a3 14. ♕d3 ♗c4 15. ♕c4 a5 16. ba5 ♕a5 17. 0–0 e6 18. g4! 0–0 19. f5±→ Meštrović–Pirc, Jugoslavija (ch) 1964; 12... d5=; **11. ♕e2** fe5 12. ♗e5 ♗e5 13. ♕e5 ♕e5 14. fe5 ♘h6± Boleslavski

48 12... ♗e5 13. 0-0-0±

49 Haag–Hennings, Zinnowitz 1966

50 18. a3±↑

51 12. ♕d2? ♗e5 13. ♗d4 ♗d4 14. ♕d4 0–0 15. ♕d7 ♕a5 16. ♗c4 ♗g2 17. ♖hg1 ♗f3 18. ♖d3 ♗e4 19. ♖c3 [19. ♖e3? ♗c2 20. ♔c2 ♖fd8△ ♕d2–+] ♕b6 20. b3 ♕f6∓ Radulov–Forintos, Hungary 1969 — 7/326

52 20. ♗e3 ♕e5= Štejn–Nej, SSSR 1960

53 12. ♗c4? e6 13. ♕c5 ♗f8 14. ♕e3 [14. ♕d4 ♕a5 15. c3 ♖b7–+] ♕a5 15. c3 ♗a6 16. ♗a6 ♕a6∓→ Boleslavski

54 13... ♖c6 14. 0–0±

55 14. ♕b5 ♖c6 15. 0–0 ♗a6 16. ♕b3 ♗d3 17. ♕d3 0–0 18. a4 ♕a5 19. ♖fb1 d6 20. ♖b5 ♕a6 21. ♕b3 ♖fc8= Štejn–Nej, SSSR 1960

56 15. ♗b5? ♖a6! 16. ♗a6 ♕a5 17. ♔f1 0–0 18. ♕e4 [18. ♕c8 ♖c8 19. ♗c8 ♕b5 20. ♔g1 ♕c4–+] ♗a6 19. ♔g1 d6! 20. ♖e1 [20. ed6 ♕a4–+; 20. f4 de5 21. fe5 ♕a4∓→; 20. h4 de5 21. ♗b2 ♖b8 22. ♕c2 ♕b5∓] ♗b7! 21. ♕e3 ♗h6 22. ♕c3 ♕d5 23. f3 ♖c8 24. ♕b2 ♖c4 25. ♗f2 ♗g7∓ Volčok

57 15... 0–0 16. ♗b5 ♗a6 17. ♕d8 ♖d8 18. ♗c6 ♗f1 19. ♔f1 dc6 20. ♗c3 ♖d3 21. ♖c1 ♖d5 22. f4 g5=

58 20. ed6 ♗d4= Boleslavski

59 11... e6 12. ♕c5 ♗b7 13. 0–0 ♖c8 14. ♕b4 ♕c7 15. ♗b5 [15. f4 a5! 16. ♕b5 ♗g2=] ♗e5 16. ♖fd1 ♗c6= Šmit–Gipslis, SSSR 1959

60 12. ♗a7 ♗b7 13. ♕d2 ♕c7! 14. ♗b8 [14. ♗b3 ♗g2 15. ♗b8 ♖b8 16. 0-0-0 ♗h1 17. ♖h1 ♕e5∓] ♕c4 15. ♗a7 ♗g2 16. ♖g1 ♗e5! 17. c3 [17. ♖g2 ♗b2–+] ♗c6∓ Volčok

61 12... ♗b7 13. ♕d3 ♗e5 14. ♗a7 ♖c8 15. ♗d4 ♗d4 16. ♕d4 e5 17. ♕g4 d5 18. ♗b3 d4 19. ♖fe1 ♕f6 20. ♖ad1 h5 21. ♕h3 ♖fd8 22. c3± Langeweg–Geler, Beverwijk 1965

62 13. f4 d6 14. ed6 ed6 15. ♗b3 ♗e6 16. ♕d2 ♗b2 17. ♖ad1 ♖fe8= Evans–Eliskases, Buenos Aires 1960

63 15. ♖fe1 de5 16. ♗e5 ♗e5 17. ♖e5 ♖fd8 18. ♕c3 [18. ♕f4 ♗d5 19. ♗b3 ♗b3 20. cb3 ♖b5 21. ♖e4 ♕f4 22. ♖f4 ♖d2 23. ♖b1 ♖c5∞] ♖bc8 19. b3 ♗d5 20. ♕e3 ♗c4 21. ♖e7=

64 15... ♕c6? 16. ♕d5! ♕d5 17. ♗d5 ♗d5 18. de7 ♖fe8 19. ♗b8 ♖b8 20. ♖ad1+–

65 = Boleslavski

B 35

1. e4 c5 2. ♘f3 ♘c6 3. d4 cd4 4. ♘d4 g6 5. ♘c3 ♗g7 6. ♗e3 ♘f6 7. ♗c4

	7	8	9	10	11	12	13	14	15	
1	...	♗e2[2]	0–0	f4	♘b3	♕d3[4]	♗f3	cb3	♕c2	=
	♘a5?![1]	0–0	d6[3]	♗d7	♗c6	♘d7	♘b3	♘c5	♕d7[5]	
2	...	♗f7!	e5	ef6	♕f3	0-0-0	h4[8]	♗g5[9]		±
	...	♔f7	d5[6]	♗f6	♘c6[7]	e6	h5			
3	...	f3[10]	♗b3[11]	♘d5[13]	♘b6	♘a8	♘e2			∓
	0–0	♕b6	♘g4![12]	♘e3	♘d1	♘b2	♘d3			

	7	8	9	10	11	12	13	14	15	
4	...	♗b3	f3[15]	♕d2	0-0-0[17]	g4[18]	♘c6	♘d5	ed5	±
	...	♕c7[14]	a6	b5[16]	♗b7	b4	♗c6	♘d5	♗b5[19]	
5	...	...	ed5[20]	♕d2[21]	0-0-0	♗h6	♘b3	♕h6	♖d3[24]	±
	...	d5	♘a5	b6	♗b7	♘b3	♗h6[22]	a5[23]		
6	...	...	f3[25]	ed5[26]	♘de2[27]	♘a4	♗f2[28]	♗a4	0—0[30]	±
	...	a5	d5	♘b4	a4	♘fd5	♖a4	♕a5[29]	♖d8[31]	
7	...	...	f3	♕d2[33]	ed5[34]	0-0-0	♔b1	h4	h5	±
	...	♕a5	e6[32]	d5	ed5[35]	♗e6	♖ad8	♗c8	♘h5[36]	
8	...	...	...	ed5	♕d2	♘d5	♗d2[37]	♗d5	0-0-0	±
	...	...	d5	♘b4	♘bd5	♕d2	♘d5	♗d4	♖d8[38]	
9	...	...	♕g4	♕d1[39]	ab3	♗d4[42]	♕d3[44]	0-0-0	h4	±
	...	♘g4	♘d4	♘b3[40]	b6[41]	f6[43]	♗b7	♗c6[45]	♕c7[46]	
10	...	0—0[47]	♘b3[49]	♗f4	♗e5[50]	h3	hg4	f4	♘d5	±
	♕a5	♘g4[48]	♕h5	♗e5	♘ce5	♘c4	♕e5	♕d6	♘b6[51]	

1. e4 c5 2. ♘f3 ♘c6 3. d4 cd4 4. ♘d4 g6 5. ♘c3 ♗g7 6. ♗e3 ♘f6 7. ♗c4 ♕a5 8. 0—0 0—0

	9	10	11	12	13	14	15	16	17	
11	♘b3[52]	f4[54]	♗e2[55]	a4[57]	♖f2[58]	♗f3	♖d2	♔h1	♕g1	±
	♕c7[53]	d6	a5[56]	♘b4	e5[59]	♗d7	♖fd8	♗c6	♘d7[60]	
12	...	...	...	♗f3[61]	♖f2[62]	♘d5	ed5	♗d4	c3	±
	...	...	♖d8	♗e6	♗c4	♗d5	♘a5	♘e8	♘b3[63]	
13	...	...	...	g4[64]	g5	♘d5[66]	♖b1![67]			⩲
	...	...	b6	♗b7[65]	♘d7	♕d8				
14	♗b3	h3[69]	f4[71]	♘f3[73]	♕e1	♖d1	♕h4			±
	d6[68]	♗d7[70]	♖ac8[72]	♖cd8[74]	♗c8	e6	♕h5[75]			
15	...	...	...	♗d4	♕d3[76]	♖ad1[78]	♗g7	♔h1[79]	♕d4	=
	...	...	♘d4	♗c6	♖ad8[77]	♘d7	♔g7	♘c5[80]	e5[81]	
16	...	...	...	...	♘d5	♗f6[83]	♔h2	♗g7	♗c3[84]	±
	...	...	...	...	♖fe8[82]	♕c5	♗d5	♗b3	♗c4[85]	

[1] **7... ♘e4**? 8. ♘e4 d5 9. ♗b5+ −; **7... ♕c7**?! 8. ♗b3 a6 9. f3 ♘e5 10. ♕e2 d6 11. g4 h6 12. 0-0-0 b5 13. g5 hg5 14. ♗g5 ♗b7 15. f4 ♘ed7 16. ♘d5 ♗d5 17. ed5 ♘c5 18. f5± Štejn—Aronin, SSSR (ch) 1962; **7... d6** 8. h3 — B 72; 8. f3 — B 75

[2] **8. ♗b3** ♘b3 9. ab3 0—0 [9... d6 10. f3 ♗d7 11. g4 a6 12. h4 h6 13. ♕d2 ♖c8 14. h5± Fischer—Leopoldi, USA 1963] 10. 0—0 d5 11. ♘db5 ♗d7 12. ed5 ♗b5 13. ♘b5 ♘d5 14. ♗a7 ♗b2= Valvo—Benkö, USA 1962; **8. ♗d3** 0—0 9. ♘d5 ♘c6 10. ♘f6 ♗f6 11. c3 d5= Ćirić—Pirc, Jugoslavija (ch) 1964

[3] 9... d5 10. ed5 ♘d5 11. ♘d5 ♕d5 12. ♘b5! ♕d1 13. ♖ad1 ♘c6 14. c3 a6 15. ♘c7 ♖b8 16. ♗c5± Fischer—Bertok, Bled 1961

[4] 12. ♗d4 a6 13. e5?! ♘e8 14. ♕d3 b5 15. ♘a5 ♕a5 16. ♗f3 ♗f3 17. ♕f3 de5 18. fe5 ♘c7 19. ♕e3 b4∓ ×e5 Štejn—A. Zajcev, SSSR (ch) 1962; 13. ♕d3=

[5] 16. e5 ♖ac8= Keres—Benkö, Curaçao (ct) 1962

[6] **9... ♘e8** 10. ♘e6! ♔e6 11. ♕d5 ♔f5 12. g4+ −; **9... ♘g8** 10. ♘e6 ♕e8 11. ♕f3 ♗f6 12. ♘c7+ −; **9... ♘c4** 10. ef6 ♗f6 11. ♕e2 d5 12. 0-0-0 ♔g7 13. h4 h5 14. ♗g5 ♗g5 15. hg5 ♗g4 16. ♘e6+ − Honfi—A. Zajcev, Hungary 1963; **9... ♘h5** 10. ♕f3 ♔e8 11. g4±

[7] **11... e5** 12. ♘d5 ed4 13. ♗d4 ♖e8 14. ♔f1 ♖e6 15. ♗f6 ♖f6 16. ♘f6 ♕f6 17. ♕d5 + −; **11... e6** 12. 0-0-0 ♔g7 13. h4 ♘c6 14. h5 e5 15. h6 ♔f7 16. ♘db5 d4 17. ♘e4△ ♗g5 + − Šapošnjikov—Altšuler, corr. 1963

[8] 13. ♖he1 ♖e8 14. ♗g5± Ivkov—Soos, Varna (ol) 1962

9 ± Boleslavski

10 8. ♘**b3**?! d6! 9. f3 ♗d7 10. 0—0 ♖c8∓; **8. ♕d2** ♘g4 9. ♘c6 bc6 10. ♗d4 ♗d4 11. ♕d4 ♕b6∓; **8. 0—0** ♘e4 9. ♘e4 d5=

11 9. a3?! d6 [9... ♘e4? 10. ♘d5+−; 9... ♕b2? 10. ♘a4+−] 10. ♘ce2 ♕a5 11. c3 ♘e5 12. ♗a2 ♕a6 13. 0—0 ♗d7∓↑« Keres—Larsen, Beverwijk 1964; 9... ♘g4!∓

12 9... ♘e4 10. ♘d5 ♕a5 11. c3 ♘c5 12. ♘c6 [12. ♗c4? e6 13. ♘c6 dc6 14. ♘e7 ♔h8 15. 0—0 ♘a6 16. ♗a6 ♕a6 17. ♕d6±; 12... ♕d8! 13. ♘c6 dc6 14. ♗c5 cd5 15. ♗d5 ♕c7∓ Kapengut] dc6 13. ♘e7 ♔h8 14. ♘c8 ♖ac8 15. 0—0 ♖cd8= Fischer—Panno, Portorož (izt) 1958

13 10. fg4 ♗d4∓

14 **8... ♘a5**? 9. e5 ♘b3 [9... ♘e8 10. ♗f7!△ ♘e6+− Fischer—Reshevsky, USA (ch) 1958/59] 10. ef6 ♘a1 11. fg7 ♘c2 12. ♕c2 ♔g7 13. f4±→ Bastrikov—Šamkovič, SSSR 1958; **8... a6**?! 9. f3 b5 10. ♕d2 ♘a5 11. e5 ♘b3 12. ♘b3 ♘e8 13. ♗h6 ♕c7 14. ♗g7 ♘g7 15. 0-0-0± Zwaig—Bleiman, Barcelona 1965; **8... e6** 9. ♘c6 [9. ♘db5 d5!∞] dc6 10. e5 ♕d1 11. ♖d1 ♘g4 12. ♗c5 ♖e8 13. f4± Gufeljd, Lazarev

15 **9. 0—0** a6 10. f4 d6 11. h3 ♘a5 12. ♕d3 b5 13. ♖ae1 e5 14. ♘f3= Geszosz—B. Balogh, Hungary (ch) 1972 — 13/367; **9. h3** a6 10. f4 ♘d4 11. ♕d4 ♘h5 [11... ♘g4 12. ♕c5!±] 12. e5 d6 13. ♘d5± Ribli—Dely, Hungary (ch) 1971 — 12/354

16 10... ♘a5 11. g4 ♘b3 12. ab3± Suetin—Aronin, SSSR (ch) 1962

17 11. ♘c6?! dc6 12. 0—0 e6 13. a4 b4 14. ♘a2 c5 15. ♕e2 ♘d7∓ Örtel—B. Balogh, Hungary (ch) 1972 — 13/366

18 12. h4 b4 [12... ♖fc8 13. h5 ♘a5 14. ♔b1 ♘c4 15. ♗c4 ♕c4 16. hg6 fg6 17. ♗h6 e5 18. ♗g7 ♔g7 19. ♘f5+− Sizov—Voroncov, SSSR 1964] 13. ♘c6 ♗c6 14. ♘d5±

19 16. ♕b4 ♗e2 17. d6± Banik—Aronin, SSSR (ch) 1962

20 9. ♗d5 ♘d5 10. ed5 [10. ♘d5 e6 11. ♘c6 bc6 12. ♘c3 ♖b8=∞] ♘b4 11. ♘de2 ♗f5 12. ♖c1 ♕a5=∞⟳

21 **10. 0—0** b6 11. ♘de2 [11. ♘c6 ♘c6 12. dc6 ♕c7∓ Platonov—Čerepkov, SSSR 1962] ♗b7 12. ♘f4 ♕c8 13. d6 ♘b3 14. de7 ♘a1 15. ef8♕ ♗f8=∞⧉; **10. h3** b6 11. ♘c6 ♘c6 12. dc6 ♕c7 13. ♕f3 ♗a6 14. 0-0-0 ♖ac8 15. ♗a4± Židkov—Kondratjev, SSSR 1964

22 13... a5 14. a4 ♕d6 15. ♗g7 ♔g7 16. ♕d4 ♔g8 17. ♖he1± Boleslavski

23 14... ♗d5!?

24 Kondratjev—Čerepkov, SSSR 1962

25 9. a4 ♘g4 10. ♕g4 ♘d4 11. ♕d1 ♘b3 12. cb3 d6∓J. Szabo—Neamtu, Romania 1969 — 8/325

26 10. ♗d5 ♘d5 11. ed5 [11. ♘d5 e6 12. ♘c6 bc6 13. ♘b6 ♖b8 14. ♕d8 ♖d8 15. c3±⊥ Boleslavski] ♘b4 12. ♘de2 e6 13. a3 [13. ♕d2 ♕h4 14. ♗f2 ♕c4 15. a3 ♘d5 16. ♘d5 ed5 17. ♗d4 ♖e8 18. ♗g7 ♔g7 19. ♔f2± Westerinen—Hecht, Raach 1969 — 8/326; 13... ed5 14. a3? d4 15. 0-0-0 ♘c2 16. ♕c2 ♗f5 17. ♕d2 dc3 18. ♘c3 ♕c7∓ Hennings—Szilagyi, Varna 1970 — 9/298; 14. ♗d4± Tringov] ♘d5 14. ♘d5 ed5 15. ♗d4 ♗d4 16. ♕d4 ♖e8 17. ♔f2±

27 11. d6 ♕d6∓ Matulović—Damjanović, Sarajevo 1969 — 7/337

28 13. ♗c5 ♖a4 14. ♗a4 ♕a5 15. ♗b4 ♘b4 16. c3 ♖d8=∞

29 14... ♗b2 15. ♖b1 ♕a5 16. 0—0 ♗f6 17. ♗b3± Planinc—Damjanović, Ljubljana 1969 — 7/338

30 15. c3 ♖d8 16. 0—0 ♘c3 17. bc3 ♖d1 18. ♖fd1 ♕a4 19. ♖d8 ♗f8 20. cb4 ♗e6 21. ♗c5± Boleslavski

31 **15... ♕a4** 16. c3±; **15... ♖d8** 16. a3 ♘a6 17. ♗b3 ♗b2 18. ♕e1±

32 **9... ♖d8** 10. ♕d2 d5 11. ed5 ♘d4 12. ♗d4 b5 13. 0-0-0 ♗b7 14. ♖he1 b4 15. ♖e7 bc3 16. ♗c3 ♕b5 17. a4 ♕a6 18. d6±→ Kadrev—Cvetkov, Bulgaria (ch) 1963; **9... b6** 10. ♕d2 ♗a6 11. 0-0-0 ♘e5 12. ♔b1 ♘c4 13. ♗c4 ♗c4 14. ♘b3 ♗b3 15. ab3 ♖fc8 16. h4 ♖c6 17. ♘d5!±

33 10. 0—0 ♖d8 [10... d5 11. ed5 ed5 12. ♕d2 ♖d8 13. ♖ad1 ♗e6 14. ♘cb5!± Dely—Korčnoj, Budapest 1961] 11. ♕e1 b6 12. ♘db5 d5= Muhin—Kapengut, SSSR 1969

34 11. 0-0-0 ♘d4! [11... de4 12. ♘c6 bc6 13. ♘e4 ♕d2 14. ♖d2 ♘d5 15. ♗c5± ×c5 Nemet—Pirc, Jugoslavija (ch) 1962] 12. ♗d4 de4 13. ♘e4 ♕d2 14. ♘d2 ♗d7 15. ♘c4 ♖fd8 16. ♘e5 ♗e8=

35 11... ♘d5!? Boleslavski

36 16. g4 ♘f6 17. ♗h6±→ Judovič—Sajgin, corr. 1968 — 5/375

37 13. ♔d2 ♘d5 14. ♗d5 ♖d8 15. c4 [15. ♗b3 e5? 16. ♖he1 ♗f5 17. g4 ♗e6 18. ♗e6 fe6 19. ♔d3 ♖d5 20. c4 ♖d7 21. ♖ad1 ♖f8 22. ♖f1 ed4 23. ♗c1 ♖df7 24. ♔e4±⊥; 15... ♗d4 16. ♗d4 ♖d4 17. ♔e3 ♖d8 18. ♖ad1 ♗d7±⊥] e6 16. ♗e4 ♗d4 [16... f5!? 17. ♔c3 fe4 18. fe4 b6±] 17. ♗d4 ♖d4 18. ♔c3 ♖d7 19. ♖hd1 ♖b8 20. ♖d7 ♗d7 21. ♖d1 ♗e8 22. c5± Talj—Korčnoj (m) 1968 — 5/(7)

38 15. ♗b3 ♗f6 [16... ♗d7? 17. ♗g5 ♗c5 18. ♖he1 ♔f8 19. ♖d5+−] 17. ♗f4 ♗f5 18. g4 g5 [Suetin—Štejn, SSSR (ch) 1963] 19. ♖d8! ♖d8 20. ♗e3 ♗e6 21. ♗e6 fe6 22. c3 a6 23. ♔c2±⊥

39 10. ♕h4?! ♕a5 [10... d6 11. 0–0 ♗e6 12. ♖fd1 ♘c6?! 13. ♗h6 ♖c8 14. ♗g7 ♔g7 15. ♘d5 f6 16. c3 ♕d7 17. f4 b5 18. ♖d3± Kuindži–Grohotov, SSSR 1973; 12... ♗b3!?] 11. 0–0 ♗f6 12. ♕h6 [12. ♕g3? ♕c3–+; 12. ♕f6?! ♘e2 13. ♘e2 ef6 14. ♘c3 ♖e8 15. ♘d5 ♖e6 16. ♗d4 ♔g7 17. ♖ad1 d6 18. ♖d3 ♗d7 19. ♖f3±→ Nežmetdinov–Černikov, SSSR 1962; 14... d5 15. ♘d5 ♖d8 16. ♗d4 ♖d5 17. ed5 ♔g7 18. ♖ae1 ♗f5∓ Šerwinsky–Grabczewski, Polska (ch) 1963; 15... ♗e6 16. ♘f6 ♔g7 17. ♗d4 ♔h6∓ Pietzsch–Mödler, DDR (ch) 1963; 12. ♕g4!?] ♗g7 13. ♕h4 ♗f6=

40 **10... e5**?! 11. h4 d6 12. h5 ♗e6 13. hg6 hg6 14. ♘d5±→ Muhin–Voronkov, SSSR 1969; **10... ♘c6**?! 11. ♕d2 ♕a5 12. ♗h6 d6 13. h4! ♕h5 14. ♗g5 h6 15. ♗e3 ♗e6 16. f3± Dely–Tabor, Kecskemet 1972 — 13/364

41 **11... f5** 12. ♗d4 ♗h6 13. h4 fe4 14. h5 ♕e8 15. ♘d5 e5 16. ♗c5+– Lujk–Westerinen, SSSR 1965; **11... d6** 12. ♗d4 ♗d4 13. ♕d4 b6 14. h4 ♗b7 15. 0-0-0 f6 16. f4±→ Kotkov–Krogius, SSSR 1959; **11... ♗c3** 12. bc3 a6 13. ♕d4 d6 [Browne–Huguet, Malaga 1970 — 9/301] 14. ♗h6 e5 15. ♕d3 ♖e8 16. 0–0 ♗e6 17. ♖fd1± Kurajica

42 **12. ♕d2** ♗b7 13. ♗h6 ♗h6 14. ♕h6 f5 15. f3 fe4 16. fe4 b5 17. h4 b4 18. h5 ♕b6 19. hg6 ♕g6∓ Matanović–Eliskases, Leipzig (ol) 1960; **12. ♕d5** ♗c3 13. bc3 ♕c7 14. 0-0-0 ♕c3 15. ♗d4 ♕c6 16. ♕e5 f6 17. ♕e7 ♗b7= Fischer–Reshevsky (m) 1961

43 12... e5 13. ♗e3 ♗b7 14. 0–0! [14. ♕d2 ♕h4 15. ♕d7 ♗e4 16. g3 ♕f6 17. ♘e4 ♕f3 18. 0–0 ♕e4 19. ♖a7± Milić–Tajmanov, Oberhausen 1961] f5 15. f3 fe4 16. fe4 ♖f1 17. ♕f1 ♔h8 18. ♕d3± Šamkovič–Wade, Moskva 1962

44 **13. ♗f6**? ♗f6 14. ♕d5 e6 15. ♕a8 ♗c3 16. bc3 ♕c7 17. ♕a7 [17. 0–0 a5 18. ♖a4 d5 19. ed5 ♗b7 20. ♖c4 ♕d7 21. ♕a7 ed5–+; 20. ♕a7 ed5–+ Kotkov–A. Zajcev, SSSR 1962] ♕c3 18. ♔f1 d5∓→ Boleslavski; **13. h4** ♗b7 14. h5 d5 [14... ♕c7 15. hg6 hg6 16. ♕g4 ♔f7 17. 0-0-0± Nadeždin–Listengarten, SSSR 1962] 15. hg6 hg6 16. ed5 ♗d5 17. ♕d3 e5 18. ♕g6 ed4 19. ♕h7 ♔f7 20. ♕h5±

45 14... ♕e8 15. h4 ♕f7 16. h5 ♖fd8 17. hg6 hg6 18. f4 d5 19. e5± Veresov–A. Zajcev, SSSR 1962

46 16. h5 ♗h6 17. ♔b1 g5 18. ♖he1± Tukmakov–Fajbisovič, SSSR 1962

47 **8. ♕d2**? ♘e4 9. ♘c6 ♕c3!–+; **8. f3**? ♕b4 9. ♗b3 ♘e4 10. fe4 [10. ♘c6 ♗c3 11. bc3 ♕c3 12. ♔e2 dc6 (Gurgenidze–A. Geler, SSSR 1959) 13. ♕g1 ♘f6 14. ♗d4 ♕b4 15. ♕e3 0–0 16. ♖ad1 b6–+ Ravinski] ♗d4 11. ♗d4 ♕d4 12. ♕f3 e6! 13. a4 a6 14. h4 h5 15. ♖d1 ♕e5∓ Matulović–Toran, Palma de Mallorca 1967 — 4/417

48 **8... ♕b4** 9. ♗b3 ♘e4? 10. ♘c6 bc6 11. a3 ♘c3 12. ♕f3+–; **8... d6** 9. ♗b5 ♗d7 10. ♘b3 ♕d8 11. ♗e2 0–0= Suetin–Lehmann, Berlin 1967 — 3/403; 9. h3 0–0 10. ♗b3 — 8... 0–0

49 **9. ♘c6** dc6 10. ♗d4 ♗d4 [10... e5 11. ♗e3 ♘e3 12. fe3△ 12... 0–0? 13. ♖f7+–] 11. ♕d4 ♕e5 12. ♕e5 ♘e5 13. ♗b3 g5= Usov–A. Geler, SSSR 1962; **9. ♘d5**!? ♘e3 10. fe3 ♘e5 [10... e6 11. ♕f3 0–0 12. ♘f6±↑] 11. ♘b5 ♘c4 12. ♘bc7 ♔f8 13. c3 ♖b8 14. b4 ♕a3 15. ♕g4 f6 16. ♕g5 ♔f7 17. e5∞ Litvinov–Litov, corr. 1964; **9. ♕g4** ♘d4 10. ♕h4! [10. ♘d5?! ♕d8? 11. c3 ♘c6 12. ♕h4 h6 13. ♕g3 0–0 14. ♘f4 ♔h7 15. ♖ad1± Ćirić–Ilijevski, Jugoslavija (ch) 1965; 10... e6!∞] ♘c2 11. ♘d5±→ Boleslavski

50 11. ♕f3 ♘f6 [11... g5 12. ♗g3 ♘f6 13. ♕d3± Ivkov–Lehmann, Beverwijk 1965] 12. ♕h5 ♘h5 13. ♗e5 ♘e5= Bradvarević–Ilijevski, Jugoslavija (ch) 1965

51 16. ♕d4 0–0 17. c4 ♘d5 18. cd5 b6 19. e5±○

52 **9. h3** ♕b4 10. ♗b3 ♘e4 11. ♘d5 ♕a5 12. ♕g4 ♘f6 13. ♘c6 bc6 14. ♘e7 ♔h8 15. ♕f4 ♗a6 16. ♖fe1 ♘h5 17. ♕d6± Lepeškin–Demirhanjan, SSSR 1964; **9. ♘d5** ♕d8 10. ♘f6 ♗f6 11. f4 [11. c3 ♕c7 12. ♕e2 d6 13. f4 ♗d7 14. ♖ae1 ♖ac8= Kinzel–Hort, Krems 1967] d6 12. e5!±↑ J. Rodriguez–Kagan, Skopje (ol) 1972 — 14/352

53 9... ♕d8 10. ♗e2 d6 11. f4±

54 10. ♗g5 a5 10. a4 ♘b4 12. ♗e2 ♖d8 13. ♘d4 ♕e5 14. ♘f3 ♕e6 15. e5!?±↑ Kuzmin–Kapengut, SSSR 1972 — 15/339

55 11. h3 ♗d7 12. ♗e2 a5 13. a4 ♘b4 14. ♗f3 ♗c6 15. ♖f2 ♘d7 16. ♘d4 ♖ad8 17. ♖d2 ♖fe8 18. ♕e2± Timoščenko–Andrejev, SSSR 1973

56 11... a6 12. ♗f3 b5 13. ♖f2 ♗b7 14. ♘d5! ♘d5 15. ed5 ♘a5 16. ♗d4 ♘c4 17. ♗g7± Ghizdavu–Ribli, Bucuresti 1971 — 11/290

57 **12. ♘d5** ♘d5 13. ed5 a4=; **12. a3** a4 13. ♘d4 ♘d4! [13... ♕b6?! 14. ♕d3!? ♘g4 15. ♘d5 ♗d4 16. ♘b6 ♗e3 17. ♕e3 ♘e3 18. ♘a8 ♘f1 19. ♗f1 ♗f5 20. ef5 ♖a8 21. fg6 hg6 22. ♖d1±⊥; 14. e5 de5 15. fe5 ♘e5 16. ♘f5 ♕e6 17. ♘g7 ♔g7 18. ♕d2 ♔g8 19. ♖ae1 ♘c6 20. ♗b5±↑ Boleslavski] 14. ♗d4 e5 15. fe5 de5 16. ♗e3 ♗e6 17. ♕e1 ♘d7 18. ♖d1 ♖fd8=

58 **13. ♖c1** ♗d7 14. ♘d4 ♕c8 15. ♕e1 e5 16. ♘db5 ♗b5 17. ♗b5 ef4 18. ♗f4 ♕c5 19. ♔h1 ♘h5 20. ♗e3 ♕e5∓; **13. ♘d4** ♗d7 14. ♘db5 ♗b5 15. ♗b5 ♖fd8 16. ♖f2 e5! [16... d5? 17. e5 ♘e4 18. ♘e4 de4 19. ♕e2 e6 20. c3 ♘d3 21. ♖ff1 ♗f8 22. ♗d4± Dubinin–Rittner, corr. 1968 — 7/331] 17. ♖d2 [17. f5 d5!] ef4 18. ♗f4 ♘h5! 19. ♗d6 ♖d6 20. ♖d6 ♘c2 21. ♖c1 ♘e3∓ Boleslavski; **13. ♗f3** ♗d7 14. g4? ♗g4 15. ♗g4 ♘g4 16. ♕g4 ♘c2

17. ♕e2 [17. ♘d5 ♕c4∓] ♘a1 18. ♖a1 ♗c3 19. ♖c1 ♕c6 20. ♗f2 ♕a4 21. ♖c3 ♖ac8∓ Zlotnik–Vajsman, SSSR 1964; 14. ♖f2 e5 — **13. ♖f2**

59 13... ♗e6 14. ♘d4 ♗c4 15. ♗f3 ♖fd8 16. ♖d2 ♕c8 17. ♘db5 ♘d7 [Westerinen–Jansson, Suomi 1969 — 7/330] 18. ♖b1!± Boleslavski

60 18. f5± Fischer–Olafsson, Bled 1961

61 12. g4 d5 13. e5 d4 14. ♘b5 ♕b6 15. ♗d4 ♘d4 16. ♘5d4 ♘d5 17. ♕d2 a5! [17... g5?! 18. fg5 ♗e5 19. c3 a5 20. ♗d3 a4 21. ♕e1! ♗g7 22. ♕h4±→ Sergijevski–Zurahov, SSSR 1963] 18. a4 g5 19. fg5 ♗e5∞ Boleslavski

62 13. ♕d2 ♗c4 14. ♖fe1 d5?! 15. e5 ♘e4 16. ♗e4 de4 17. ♕f2 f5 18. ef6 ef6 19. ♘d2 ♘b4 20. ♘de4 f5 21. ♘g5 ♘c6± Kuprejčik–Kotkov, SSSR 1973; 14... e5!?

63 18. ab3 ♗d4 19. ♕d4 ♕c5 20. ♕e4±○ Ostojić–Musil, Jugoslavija (ch) 1968 — 5/366

64 **12. ♕d2** ♗b7 13. ♖ad1 ♘a5 14. ♘a5 ba5 15. ♗f3 [Kuprejčik–Kapengut, SSSR 1972 — 13/363] ♗c6!∞ Kapengut; **12. ♗f3** ♗b7 [12... ♗a6?! 13. ♖f2 ♖ab8 14. ♘d5 ♘d5 15. ed5 ♘a5 16. ♗d4± Jansa–Toran, Siegen (ol) 1970 — 10/418] 13. ♕d2 [13. ♘b5?! ♕c8 14. c4 ♘b4 15. ♘d2 ♘d7 16. a3 ♘c6 17. ♖b1 a6 18. ♘c3 ♘d4∓ Muhin–Baumbach, Primorsko 1973 — 16/312; 13. ♘d5 ♘d5 14. ed5 ♘a5 15. ♘a5 ba5=; 13. g4!?; 13. ♔h1!?] ♖ac8 14. ♖ad1 ♗a6 15. ♖fe1 ♘a5±

65 12... ♘e8?! 13. ♕d2 ♗b7 14. g5 ♘a5 15. ♘d5 ♕d8 16. ♗d4 ♘b3 17. ab3 e5 18. ♗c3 ♗d5 19. ed5 ef4 20. ♕f4 ♗c3 21. bc3 ♕c7 22. c4± Osnos–Saharov, SSSR 1967 — 4/418

66 14. ♖f2 ♖fe8 15. h4 ♘a5 16. ♘d4 a6 17. ♘d5 ♕c8 18. f5 ♗d5 19. ed5 ♘c4 20. ♗c1 b5 21. h5 ♕c5 22. ♘b3 ♕a7 23. hg6 fg6= M. Cejtlin–Georgadze, SSSR 1969

67 **15. f5** ♖e8 16. f6 ef6 17. gf6 ♗f8 18. ♕d2 ♘c5 19. ♘c5 dc5 20. ♗h6± Bednarski–Georgadze, Tbilisi 1971 — 12/353; 15... ♗b2∞; **15. ♖b1!**±

68 9... ♘g4 10. ♕g4 ♘d4 11. ♗d4?! ♗d4 12. ♘d5 e6! [12... ♕d8?! 13. c3 ♗g7 14. f4 d6 15. ♕h4 e6 16. ♘e7 ♔h8 17. f5± I. Zajcev–Pavlovičev, SSSR 1965] 13. c3 ♗g7 14. ♘e7 ♔h8 15. ♖ad1 ♕c7=; 11. ♕d1±

69 10. f3 ♗d7 [10... ♘d4 11. ♗d4 ♗e6 12. ♕d2 ♖fc8 13. ♖fd1 ♘d7 14. ♗g7 ♔g7 15. ♕d4 f6 16. h3 ♕c5 17. ♕c5 ♖c5= Gufeljd–Damjanović, Sarajevo 1964] 11. ♕e1 [11. ♕d2 ♖fc8 12. ♖ad1 ♕a6 13. ♕f2 ♘e5 14. ♘d5 ♘d5 15. ♗d5 ♘c4∓ Kosenkov–Osnos, SSSR 1964] ♖ac8 12. ♖d1 ♖fd8= Spaski–Gurgenidze, SSSR (ch) 1960

70 **10... ♘d4** 11. ♗d4 ♗e6 12. f4 a6 13. ♕f3 ♕h5 14. ♕f2 ♖ac8 15. ♖ae1 ♗c4 16. e5 de5 17. ♖e5± Talj–Stefanov, Kislovodsk 1966; **10... ♘h5** 11. ♘de2 ♗e6 12. g4 ♘f6 [Ciocaltea–Bilek, Bucuresti 1968 — 5/377] 13. ♘f4±

71 11. ♖e1 ♖ac8 [11... ♖fc8?! 12. f4 ♕h5 13. ♘f3 ♖d8 14. ♕e2 e6 15. ♖ad1± Pietzsch–Damjanović, Sarajevo 1966 — 1/259] 12. ♘d5 ♕d8 [12... ♘d5 13. ed5 ♘d4 14. ♗d4±] 13. ♘b5 ♘d5 [13... ♘e4? 14. ♘a7 ♘a7 15. ♗b6 ♕e8 16. ♗a7+−; 13... ♕a5?! 14. a4 ♗e6 15. ♗g5 ♗d5 16. ed5 ♘e5 17. ♗d2 ♕a6 18. ♕e2 ♖fe8 19. ♗e3 b6 20. a5+− Vasjukov–Rojzman, SSSR 1972 — 13/369] 14. ed5 ♘a5 15. ♘d4 [15. ♘a7 ♖a8=∞] b5 16. c3 ♖e8 17. ♘c2 ♕c7 18. ♗d4 ♗h6± Hennings–Kapengut, Lublin 1973; 12... ♖fe8!∞

72 11... ♕h5!? 12. ♕d3!? [12. ♕h5 ♘h5 13. ♖ad1 ♖fc8 14. ♘d5 ♔f8= Georgadze] b5! [Grabczewski–Georgadze, Tbilisi 1974 — 18/352] 13. a3!?±

73 **12. ♕d3** ♘b4 13. ♕e2 ♘a6 14. ♕f3 ♘c5 15. ♖ad1 ♘b3 16. ♘b3= Parma–Štejn, Jugoslavija–SSSR 1965; **12. ♕f3** ♕h5 [12... ♘d4 13. ♗d4 ♗c6 14. ♖ad1 b5 15. ♕e3 b4 16. ♘d5 ♗d5 17. ed5± Janošević–Kagan, Netanya 1971 — 11/292] 13. ♕f2 [13. ♖ad1 ♘a5 14. g4 ♘g4 15. hg4 ♗g4 16. ♕h1 ♗d1= Mnacakanjan–Štejn, SSSR 1965] b5 [13... ♘a5? 14. ♘de2 b6 15. f5! g5 16. ♕g3 h6 17. ♕h2!±→ Talj–Gašić, Sarajevo 1966 — 1/258; 13... ♘b4? 14. ♘de2 a5 15. a3 ♘a6 16. e5 de5 17. ♘g3± Saharov–Štejn, SSSR (ch) 1965] 14. ♘db5 ♘e4 15. ♘e4 ♕b5 16. ♘g3 a5 17. a4 ♕b4 18. f5 ♔h8 19. ♖ad1 ♕h4 20. ♖d3= R. Byrne–Štejn, Sarajevo 1967 — 3/407

74 12... ♕h5 13. ♕e1 b5 14. a3 [14. f5 b4 15. ♘e2 ♘e4 16. fg6 hg6 17. ♘f4 ♕h7!∓ Gliksman–Rajković, Jugoslavija 1973 — 16/313] a5 15. ♖d1 a4 [15... ♗e6 16. ♗e6 fe6 17. ♘g5 ♘d8 18. e5±; 15... b4 16. ♘d5±] 16. ♗a2 b4 17. ♘d5 ba3 18. ♘f6 ♗f6 19. ♖d5 e5 20. ♖d6 ef4 [20... ♗e6 21. ♖e6 fe6 22. ♗e6 ♔h8 23. ♗g4+−] 21. ♖f6 [21. ♗f4? ♕c5 22. ♔h1 ♗e6 23. ♖e6 fe6 24. ♗e6 (Klundt–Kapengut, Ybbs 1968 — 6/450) ♔h8 25. ♗c8 ♗b2∓] fe3 22. ♕e3 ab2 23. ♘g5± Boleslavski

75 **15... ♘e8**? 16. f5 ef5 17. ♖d5 ♕c7 18. ♗g5+− Kurajica–Kuijpers, Wijk aan Zee 1970 — 9/299; **15... ♕h5**±

76 **13. ♕f3** ♕b4 14. ♗f6 [14. ♖ad1 ♘e4 −+] ♗f6 15. ♖fe1 ♕c5 16. ♔h1 ♗c3 17. ♕c3 ♕c3 18. bc3 ♖ac8∓ Ciocaltea–Furman, Harrachov 1966; **13. ♕e2** ♕b4 14. ♖fd1 ♘e4 15. ♗g7 ♔g7 16. ♘d5 ♕c5 17. ♔h2 ♘f6 18. ♘c7 ♗g2!= Hort–Furman, Polanica Zdroj 1967 — 4/426; **13. ♕e1** ♕b4 14. ♖d1 ♘e4 15. ♗g7 ♔g7 16. ♘d5 [16. ♘e4 ♕e4 17. ♕c3 ♔g8 18. ♖f2 e6 19. ♖d6 ♖ad8= Jakobsson–Kapengut, Örebro 1966; 18... ♕f5!∓] ♕c5 17. ♔h2 ♘f6 [17... e6? 18. ♕e4 ed5 19. ♕d4 ♕d4 20. ♖d4±⊥ Janošević–Parma, Jugoslavija (ch) 1964] 18. ♘c7 ♗g2 19. ♕e7 ♗h3 20. f5?!

♗f5 21. ♖de1 ♘g8∓ Janošević–Soos, Skopje 1967; 20. ♔h3=

77 13... ♘d7?! 14. ♗g7 ♔g7 15. ♔h1 [15. ♖ae1 ♕c5 16. ♔h2 b5 17. ♗d5 ♖ac8 18. ♗c6 ♖c6 19. ♘b5 ♕c2 20. ♕d4 e5 21. ♕a7± Matulović–Rajković, Vrnjačka Banja 1974; 15... ♖ac8 16. ♕d4 ♔g8 17. ♘d5±] ♘c5 16. ♕d4 f6 17. ♖ae1 [17. ♗d5 ♕b6 18. ♖ab1± Židkov–Pavlenko, SSSR 1967] ♘b3 18. ab3 ♕c5 19. ♕d2 e6 20. ♖f3 ♖fe8 21. ♖d3± Matanović–Simagin, Jugoslavija–SSSR 1963

78 **14. ♖ae1** e5 [14... ♘d7 15. ♗g7 ♔g7 16. ♘d5 ♗d5 17. ed5 ♖fe8 18. ♖e3± Juarez–Bellon, Siegen (ol) 1970 — 10/421] 15. ♗e3 ef4 16. ♗f4 d5 17. e5 ♘e4=; **14. f5** ♘d7 15. ♗g7 [15. ♘d5 ♗d5 16. ♗g7 ♔g7 17. ♗d5 ♘f6 18. ♖f2 ♕c5 19. c3 e6 20. b4 ♕b6 21. ♗b3 d5 22. ed5 ♘d5 23. ♗d5 ♖d5 24. f6 ♔g8 25. ♕c4 ♖f5 26. ♕d4 ♕d4 27. cd4 ♖d5∓⊥ Janošević–Furman, Harrachov 1966] ♔g7 16. ♕d4 ♕e5= Ekblom–Pytel, corr. 1969 — 7/332; **14. ♘d5** ♘d5 15. ed5 ♗d4 16. ♕d4 ♗d7 17. ♖ae1 ♖fe8 18. ♔h1 ♕c5 19. ♕d2 a5= Klovan–Kapengut, SSSR 1965; 14... ♖fe8!?; **14. ♕e3** ♘d7 [14... b6?! 15. f5 ♘d7 16. ♗d5 ♗d4 17. ♕d4 ♘e5 18. b4 ♕a6 19. a4 ♕b7 20. b5 ♗d5 21. ♘d5 f6 22. a5± Klovski–Averbah, SSSR 1966 — 2/351] 15. ♗g7 ♔g7 16. ♔h2 ♕c5 17. ♕d3 b5 [Matanović–Bilek, La Habana (ol) 1966 — 2/352] 18. ♘d5!?=

79 16. ♘d5 e6 17. ♕d4 e5 18. fe5 de5 19. ♕d3 ♘c5 20. ♕e3 ♘b3 21. ♕b3 ♕c5= Matanović–Talj, Palma de Mallorca 1966 — 2/353

80 16... ♕c5!? 17. ♖d2 [17. ♘d5!?△ 17... e6 18. c4] b5 18. ♖e1 ♘b6= Buljovčić–Bukić, Jugoslavija 1967

81 **18. fe5** ♘b3 19. ab3 de5 20. ♕f2 f5 21. b4 ♕b4 22. ♖d8 ♖d8 23. ef5 g5! [23... ♕f4? 24. ♕e1!± Šagalovič–Baumbach, SSSR 1968] 24. f6 ♔f7 25. ♕e3∞ Martin–Bellon, Olot 1974 — 17/371; **18. ♕e3** ♘b3 19. ab3 ef4 20. ♖f4 ♕e5 [20... f6 21. b4 ♕b6 22. ♕b6 ab6 23. b5 ♗e8 24. ♖f2 g5 25. ♖fd2+− Ćirić–Ree, Amsterdam 1967 — 4/427] 21. ♖df1 a6 22. ♖h4 [22. ♕f2 f6 23. h4 ♖f7 24. ♔g1 ♖df8 ∓ ×e5 Jansa–Furman, Harrachov 1966] ♔g8 23. ♕h6 1/2 : 1/2 Ćirić–Gheorghiu, Wijk aan Zee 1968 — 5/365

82 **13... ♘d5** 14. ed5 ♗d4 15. ♕d4 ♗d7 16. ♖ae1 ♖fe8±; **13... ♗d5** 14. ed5 ♘d7 15. ♗g7 ♔g7 16. ♕d4 ♔g8 17. ♖ae1 ♖ae8 18. ♔h2± Vasjukov–Ciocaltea, Bucuresti 1967 — 3/402

83 **14. ♘f6** ef6 15. f5 ♗e4 16. fg6 hg6 17. ♗f6 ♕c5 18. ♔h1 d5∓ Karker–Judovič, corr. 1968 — 6/451; **14. f5** ♗d5 15. ed5 ♘d7 16. c3 ♗d4 17. ♕d4 ♘f6∓ Browne–Bellon, Malaga 1970 — 9/300; 16. ♔h1!?

84 17. ♗d4? ♗c2! 18. ♕d2 ♕c4 19. ♖ac1 ♕d3∓

85 18. ♖f3±

B 36 **1. e4 c5 2. ♘f3 ♘c6 3. d4 cd4 4. ♘d4 g6 5. c4**[1]

	5	6	7	8	9	10	11	12	13	
1	...	♘c3	♕d4	c5[4]	♗b5[6]	cd6[7]	0–0[8]	♘b5	♘c3[10]	=
	♘f6[2]	♘d4[3]	d6	♗g7[5]	♗d7	0–0	♗b5	a6[9]	♘e8[11]	

1. e4 c5 2. ♘f3 ♘c6 3. d4 cd4 4. ♘d4 g6 5. c4 ♘f6 6. ♘c3 ♘d4 7. ♕d4 d6 8. ♗e2 ♗g7

	9	10	11	12	13	14	15	16	17	
2	♗d2	♕e3	h4	ef5	♘d5	♕a3	♗g5	0-0-0[14]	♕e3	±
	0–0	♘d7[12]	f5	gf5	e5	♘c5[13]	♕d7	♘e4	h6[15]	
3	♗g5	♗e3	♕d2	0–0	f4[17]	b3	a3	f5	b4	±
	h6[16]	0–0	♔h7	♗e6	♖c8	♕a5	a6	♗d7	♕e5[18]	
4	♗e3	♕d2[19]	♖c1[21]	b3	f3	a4[24]	♘d5	ed5	♔d2[25]	±
	0–0	♗e6[20]	♕a5	a6[22]	♖fc8[23]	♕b4	♘d5	♕d2		
5	0–0	♕d3[26]	♗d2[28]	♕e3	♖ac1[31]	f3	♖fd1	ef5	b3	∓
	0–0	♘d7[27]	♘c5[29]	♗d7[30]	♗c6	a5	f5	gf5	f4[32]	
6	...	♗g5	♕d3[34]	b3	♖ac1	♗d2	♘d5	♗g5	♕d2[37]	±
	...	♗e6[33]	♖c8[35]	a6[36]	♕a5	♘d7	♕d8	♖e8		
7	...	♕e3	♗d2[39]	♖fd1	a4[40]	♖ac1[41]	b3	♘d5	ed5	±
	...	♗d7[38]	a6	♕b8	a5	♗c6	♘d7	♗d5	♘c5[42]	

1. e4 c5 2. ♘f3 ♘c6 3. d4 cd4 4. ♘d4 g6 5. c4 ♘f6 6. ♘c3 ♘d4 7. ♕d4 d6 8. ♗e3 ♗g7 9. f3[43] 0—0 10. ♕d2 ♕a5[44]

	11	12	13	14	15	16	17	18	19	
8	♖c1[45] ♗e6	♘d5[46] ♕d2	♔d2 ♗d5[47]	cd5 ♖fc8	♖c8[48] ♖c8	g3 ♖c7[49]	♗h3 ♘d7	♖c1[50] ♖c1	♔c1 ♘c5[51]	±
9	. . . . . .	. . . ♕a2	♘e7 ♔h8	♗d4 ♖ae8[52]	♘d5[53] ♗d5![54]	cd5 ♖c8[55]	♗e2 ♖c1	♕c1 ♘d7	♗g7 ♔g7[56]	=
10	. . . . . .	. . . . . .	. . . . . .	♗e2 ♘g8[57]	♘d5[58] ♗d5	cd5 ♖fc8	0—0 a5[59]	♗d4 ♕a4	♗c3 ♕b3[60]	±
11	. . . ♗d7	♗e2[61] ♖fc8[62]	0—0 a6[63]	b3 ♗c6[64]	♗d4 ♘d7	♗g7 ♔g7	♔h1 ♔g8	f4 b5	♕b2 bc4[65]	±

¹ Maroczy

² 5... d6 6. ♘c3 ♘d4 7. ♕d4 ♘f6 — 5... ♘f6

³ 6... ♗g7 7. ♗e3 — B 38

⁴ **8. f3** ♗g7 9. ♕f2 [9. ♗e3 — 8. ♗e3] 0—0 10. ♗e2 ♗e6 11. ♗d2 ♘d7 12. 0—0 ♕b6 13. ♕b6 ♘b6 14. b3 a5= Klavin—Banik, SSSR 1963; **8. ♕d2** ♗g7 9. ♗d3 0—0 10. 0—0 ♘d7 [10... ♗e6 11. b3 a6 12. ♗b2 ♕a5 13. ♖ad1 ♖fc8 14. ♖fe1 b5 15. ♘d5 ♕d2 16. ♖d2 ♗d5 17. ed5± Rusakov—Aleksejev, SSSR 1962] 11. b3 ♘c5 12. ♗c2 ♗d7 13. ♗b2 ♗c6=; **8. b3** ♗g7 9. ♗b2 0—0 10. ♗e2 ♕a5 [10... b5!? 11. ♘b5 ♗b7 12. f3 a6 13. ♘a3 ♕a5 14. ♕c3 ♕g5 15. g3 ♘h5 16. ♕c2 ♕a5∞ Honfi—Forintos, Hungary 1968 — 7/344; 11. cb5 ♗b7 12. ♘d5!?] 11. 0—0 ♗e6 [11... ♘e4? 12. ♕e4 ♗c3 13. ♗c3 ♕c3 14. ♕e7 ♕e5 15. ♕e5 de5 16. ♗f3±] 12. ♖ac1 ♖fc8 13. ♕d3 a6 14. ♗a1 ♖ab8= Korčnoj—Benkö, Buenos Aires 1960; **8. ♗g5** ♗g7 9. ♕d2 0—0 10. ♗d3 a5 11. 0—0 a4?! 12. ♖ac1 ♗e6 [12... ♕a5 13. ♘d5 ♘d5 14. ♕a5 ♖a5 15. cd5 ♗b2 16. ♗e7 ♖e8 17. ♖c7 ♗a3 18. ♖b1△ ♗b5±; 15... e6 16. ♗e7 ♖e8 17. ♗d6 ed5 18. ♗b4±⊥ Csom] 13. ♕c2±○ Portisch—Reshevsky, Petropolis (izt) 1973 — 16/327; 11... ♗e6=

⁵ **8... a6**? 9. cd6±; **8... dc5**!? 9. ♕d8 [9. ♕c5 ♗g7 10. ♗g5 0—0 11. ♖d1 ♕b6= Boleslavski] ♔d8 10. ♗f4 ♗e6 11. 0-0-0 ♔c8 12. ♗e3 c4 13. ♖d4 ♘g4 14. ♗c4 ♘e3 15. ♗e6 fe6= O'Kelly—Toran, Malaga 1967

⁶ 9. cd6? 0—0 10. e5 ♘g4 11. ♗f4 ed6 12. ♕d6 ♘e5 13. ♗e5 ♗e5∓ Gufeljd

⁷ 10. ♗d7 ♕d7 11. cd6 0—0 12. ♕b4 [12. 0—0 ♘e8 13. ♕d5 e6 14. ♕b5 ♕b5 15. ♘b5 a6= Keres—Gurgenidze, SSSR (ch) 1959; 12. ♗g5 ♘e8 13. ♕b4?! ♘d6∓ Keres—Petrosjan, Curaçao (ct) 1962; 13. ♕d5 ♗c3 14. bc3 ♘d6 15. e5 ♕f5 16. ♗e7 ♘e4 17. 0—0 ♖fe8 18. ♕b7 ♕e5= Boleslavski] a5 13. ♕b5 ♕b5 14. ♘b5 ed6 15. f3 [15. ♘d6 ♘e4!] d5 16. e5 ♘d7 17. f4 f6 18. e6 ♖ae8 19. ♘c7 ♖e7 20. f5 gf5 21. 0—0 ♘c5 22. ♘d5 ♖e6= Boleslavski

⁸ **11. e5**? ♗b5 12. ♘b5 ♘d7 13. f4 ♕a5 14. ♘c3 ed6 15. ♕d6 ♘e5! 16. fe5 ♗e5 17. ♕d3 ♖ad8 18. ♕f3 ♗d4—+ Šijanovski—Gufeljd, SSSR 1966; **11. de7** ♕e7 12. ♗d3 [12. ♗d7 ♘e4 13. ♕e3 ♗c3 14. bc3 ♕d7∓↑] ♘e4!=

⁹ 12... ed6 13. ♘c3 ♖e8 14. ♕d3 ♕a5 [14... ♕b6 15. ♗e3! ♕b2 16. ♖ab1 ♕a3 17. ♗d4 ♖ab8 18. ♖fd1±↑ Szabo—Portisch (m) 1961] 15. ♗d2 ♕b4 [15... ♕h5?! 16. f3 a6 17. ♖ad1 ♖ad8 18. ♗e3± Portisch—Parma, Amsterdam 1963] 16. ♖fe1 ♕b2 17. ♖ab1∞ Balašov—Kuprejčik, SSSR 1967

¹⁰ 13. de7?! ♕e7 14. ♘c3 ♖fe8 15. ♖e1 ♖ad8 16. ♕a4? ♘e4 17. ♘e4 ♕e4∓ Ciocaltea—Parma, Athens 1968 — 7/347; 16. ♕c4!=

¹¹ 14. ♕b4 ♘d6 15. ♖d1 ♖c8 16. ♗f4 ♖c4 17. ♕b3 b5 18. a4 [18. ♘d5 ♘e4!=] ♗c3 19. bc3 ♖e4 20. ♗d6 ed6 21. ab5 ab5= Boleslavski

¹² 10... e6 11. 0—0 d5 12. cd5 ed5 13. ed5 ♖e8 14. ♕g3 ♘d5 15. ♗b5!± Keres—Barczay, Budapest 1970 — 9/312

¹³ 14... ♘f6? 15. ♗g5 ♗e6 16. 0-0-0!±

¹⁴ 16. ♘b6 ab6 17. ♕a8 f4!∞

¹⁵ 18. g4 hg5 19. hg5 ♕d8 20. ♖h5 ♘c5 21. ♖dh1 fg4 22. b4 ♗f5! [22... ♘a4? 23. c5!+— Keres—Dely, Kapfenberg 1970 — 9/311] 23. bc5 ♖c8±

¹⁶ **9... 0—0** 10. ♕d2 ♗e6 11. ♖c1! [11. f3 ♖c8 12. ♘d5 ♗d5 13. ed5 b5! 14. ♖c1 bc4 15. ♗c4 ♘d7 16. b3 ♘e5∓ Suetin—Gurgenidze, SSSR (ch) 1960; 11. 0—0 — 9. 0—0] ♕a5 12. f3 ♖fc8 13. b3 a6 14. ♘a4 ♕d2 15. ♔d2 ♖c6 16. ♘c3 ♖ac8 17. ♘d5± Karpov—Kavalek, Nice (ol) 1974 — 17/385; **9... ♗d7** 10. ♕d2 h6 11. ♗f4 a6 12. 0—0 ♗c6 13. f3 0—0 14. a4 [14. ♗h6?! ♗h6 15. ♕h6 ♕b6 16. ♔h1 ♕b2=] ♘d7 15. a5! ♘c5 16. ♖a3± Pomar—Cordovil, Malaga 1972 — 13/380

¹⁷ **13. f3** ♕a5 14. ♖ac1 a6 15. b3 ♖fc8 16. a4 ♘d7 17. ♘d5 ♕d2= Karasev—Talj, SSSR 1971; **13. ♗d4** ♖c8 14. b3 a6 15. ♕e3 ♘d7

16. ♗g7 ♔g7 17. f4 ♕b6 18. ♕b6 ♘b6 19. f5 ♗d7 20. ♖ad1± Timman–Ribli, Amsterdam 1973 — 17/383

18 **18. ♖ae1** ♗c6! 19. ♗f4 ♘e4 20. ♘e4 ♕e4 21. ♗d3 ♕d4 22. ♔h1 ♖ce8 23. ♗e3 ♕c3 24. ♗h6= Larsen–Fischer, Denver (mct) 1971 — 11/2; **18. ♖ad1**! ♗c6 [18... ♘e4 19. ♘e4 ♕e4 20. ♖f4 ♕c6 21. ♗f3 ♕c7 22. ♖h4 ±→] 19. ♗d4 ♘e4 20. ♕e3 ♘c3 21. ♗e5 ♘d1 22. ♖d1± Rabar

19 10. ♕d3 ♘g4! [10... ♘d7 11. ♗d4 ♘c5 12. ♕e3 ♗d4 13. ♕d4 e5 14. ♕d2 ♘e6 15. ♘b5 ♗d7 16. ♘d6± Gipslis–Georgadze, SSSR 1972 — 14/364] 11. ♗g4 ♗g4 12. ♗d4 ♗d4 13. ♕d4 ♗e6 14. 0–0 ♕a5 15. ♖fe1 ♖fe8 16. b3± Keene–Schmid, Bath 1973 — 16/332

20 10... ♘g4 11. ♗g4 [11. ♗d4 e5 12. ♗e3 ♘e3 13. ♕e3 f5 14. ♖d1 ♗f6= Talj–Ghitescu, Leipzig (ol) 1960; 11... ♗h6 12. ♕d1 ♘e5 13. ♗e5? de5 14. ♕d8 ♖d8 15. 0–0 ♗d7∓ Cardoso–Talj, Portorož (izt) 1958; 13. ♘d5 e6 14. ♘e3 ♘c6 15. ♘g4 ♗g7 16. ♗g7 ♔g7 17. ♕d2 e5= Talj–Gurgenidze, SSSR (ch) 1959] ♗g4 12. ♗d4 [12. 0–0 ♖c8 13. b3 b5 14. ♘b5 ♗a1 15. ♖a1 a6 16. ♘c3 f6 17. f4 ♖f7= Spaski–Petrosjan, Moskva 1967 — 3/416; 12. ♖c1!?] ♗e6 [12... ♗d4 — 10. ♕d3] 13. ♗g7 ♔g7 14. 0–0 ♔g8 15. b3 ♕a5 16. f4 f6 17. ♖f3 ♔h8± Botvinik–Toran, Palma de Mallorca 1967

21 **11. f3** ♖c8 [11... ♕a5 12. ♘b5 ♕d2 13. ♔d2 ♘d7! 14. ♖ab1 ♘e5= Botvinik–Matulović, Beograd 1970 — 9/313] 12. ♘d5 ♘d7 13. 0–0 ♘c5 14. ♖ac1 a5 15. b3 ♗d5 16. cd5 ♕b6∓ Damjanović–Fischer, Buenos Aires 1970; 12. b3!?; **11. 0—0** ♕a5 12. ♖ad1 ♖fc8 13. b3 b5! 14. ♘d5 ♕d2 15. ♖d2 ♗d5 16. ed5 ♘e4=

22 12... ♖fc8? 13. 0–0 a6 14. f4 b5 15. f5 ♗d7! 16. fg6 hg6 17. c5! [17. e5? b4 18. ef6 bc3 19. ♖c3 ♗f6 20. ♖f6! ef6 21. ♗f3=∞ Spaski–Panno, Palma de Mallorca 1969 — 8/330] ♗e6 18. ♗f3 dc5 19. e5± Talj–Parma, Bled 1961

23 13... b5 14. ♘d5 ♕d2 15. ♔d2±

24 **14. 0—0** b5 15. ♘b1 b4! [15... ♕d2 16. ♘d2 ♗d7 17. ♗d3 e5 18. ♖c2± Padevski–Osnos, Budapest 1969] 16. a3 ♖ab8 17. ♗f2 ♘d7 18. ♔h1 ♘e5 19. ♗e1 ♘c6∓ Boleslavski; 15. ♘d5=; **14. ♘d5** ♕d2 15. ♔d2 ♘d5 16. cd5 ♗d7= Spaski–Petrosjan (m) 1969 — 7/345; **14. ♘a4** ♕d2 15. ♔d2 ♘d7 16. ♖c2 ♖c6= Panno–Reshevsky, Siegen (ol) 1970

25 ±○ Hort–Mecking, Petropolis (izt) 1973 — 16/330

26 **10. ♗d2** ♗d7 [10... ♗e6 11. ♕e3 — 10. ♕e3] 11. ♕e3 — 10. ♕e3; **10. ♕d1** ♗e6 11. ♗e3 ♕a5 12. ♖c1 a6! 13. f4 b5=

27 10... ♗e6 11. ♗e3! ♘d7 [11... a6 12. b3 ♘d7 13. ♗d4 ♘e5 14. ♕d2 f6 15. ♘d5± Holmov–Saharov, SSSR (ch) 1964; 11... ♕a5 12. ♗d4! ♖fc8 13. b3 a6 14. f4± Gipslis–Damjanović, Tallinn 1969 — 7/346] 12. ♗d4 ♗d4 13. ♕d4 ♕a5 14. f4± Adorjan–Jansa, Luhačovice 1973

28 **11. ♗e3** ♘c5 12. ♕c2 ♗c3!?∓; **11. ♕g3** ♘c5 12. ♕h4 ♗c3!? 13. bc3 f5 14. ♗g5 ♖f7∓ Schmidt–Parma, Beograd 1961

29 11... ♘e5 12. ♕g3 ♗e6 13. b3 f5 14. ♖ad1 a6 15. ef5 ♗f5 16. ♗g5± Kapengut–Litvinov, SSSR 1971 — 11/298

30 12... a6 13. ♖ac1 ♘e6 14. b3 ♗d7 15. ♘d5 ♘d4 16. ♗c3 ♘e2 17. ♕e2 ♗c3 18. ♘c3± Filip–Deže, Vršac 1971 — 12/365

31 **13. b3** ♗c6 14. f3 a5! 15. ♖ad1 f5 16. ef5 gf5∓↑; **13. ♔h1** ♗c6! [13... ♘a4? 14. b3 ♗c3 15. ♗c3± Osnos–Spiridonov, Debrecen 1969 — 8/332] 14. f3 a5△ f5∓

32 18. ♕f2 e6∓ Gufeljd–Forintos, Debrecen 1969

33 10... h6 11. ♗h4 [11. ♗e3 ♘g4∓] g5 12. ♗g3 ♘h5 13. ♕d2 ♘g3 14. hg3 ♗d7 15. ♖ad1 ♗c6 16. ♗d3± Aronson–Gurgenidze, SSSR 1957

34 11. ♕d2 ♖c8 12. b3 b5? 13. e5! de5 14. ♕d8 ♖fd8 15. ♘b5 a6 16. ♘c3± Bojatincev–Alterman, SSSR 1964

35 11... ♘d7 12. ♕d2 ♖c8 13. ♘d5 ♘f6 14. ♕e3 ♗d5 15. ed5 b5 16. cb5 ♖c2 17. ♗f3 ♖b2 18. a4± Schmid–Toran, Bamberg 1968

36 12... ♘d7 13. ♖ac1 a6 14. f4 ♘c5 15. ♕e3 ♗d7 16. ♘d5 f6 17. ♗h4± Schmid–Brinck-Claussen, Lugano (ol) 1968 — 6/457

37 Unzicker–Parma, Ljubljana 1969

38 **10... ♘d7** 11. ♗d2 ♘c5 12. ♖ad1 ♗d7 13. ♗e1 b6 14. f4 ♘a4 15. b3± Geler–Ostojić Beograd 1969 — 8/331; **10... ♗e6** 11. ♗d2 ♕b6 [11... ♘d7 12. ♖ac1 ♕b6 13. b3 ♖fc8 14. ♕g3± Geler–Matanović, SSSR–Jugoslavija 1964; 11... a6 12. b3 ♘d7 13. f4 ♕b6 14. ♕b6 ♘b6 15. ♖ac1 ♗d4 16. ♔h1 ♘d7 17. ♗f3± Uhlmann–Browne, Amsterdam 1971] 12. b3 [12. ♕b6 ab6 13. a4 ♖fc8 14. b3± Geler] ♕e3 13. ♗e3 ♗d7 [13... ♖fc8 14. ♖ac1 a6?! 15. f3 ♘d7? 16. f4!± Keres–Hug, Petropolis (izt) 1973 — 16/329; 15... ♗d7±; 15. ♘a4! ♘d7 16. f4± Keres] 14. ♖ac1 ♖fc8 15. ♖fd1 ♗c6 16. f3 a5 17. ♔f2 ♘d7 18. ♖c2± Petrosjan–Browne, Nice (ol) 1974 — 17/386

39 11. ♖d1 a6 [11... ♕a5 12. ♗d2 ♖fc8 13. ♘b5 ♕b6 14. ♕b6 ab6 15. ♘c3 ♗e6 16. b3 b5!= Smislov–Browne, Amsterdam 1971 — 12/364; 13. ♖ac1±] 12. c5 ♕a5 13. cd6 ed6 14. ♗d2 ♗c6= Boleslavski; 12. ♗d2 — 11. ♗d2

40 13. ♖ac1 b5 14. b3 bc4 15. ♗c4 ♘g4= Saharov–Kapengut, SSSR 1967

41 **14. ♖a3** ♗c6 15. ♘d5 ♖e8 16. ♗c3 ♘d7= Ničevski–Kapengut, Vilnus 1969 —

8/333; **14. b3** ♗c6 15. ♗e1 ♘d7 16. ♖ab1 ♘c5 17. ♘d5 ♖e8 18. f3 b6= Boleslavski–Averbah, SSSR 1966; **14. h3** ♗c6 15. ♘d5 ♖e8 16. ♗c3 ♘d7 17. ♗g7 ♔g7 18. b3 e5= Uhlmann–Kapengut, Schweiz 1969

42 18. ♖e1± Ivkov–Browne, Wijk aan Zee 1972 — 13/379

43 9. ♖c1? 0–0 10. ♕d2 ♘g4 11. ♗g5 f6 12. ♗f4 e5 13. ♗e3 [13. ♗g3 ♗h6∓] ♘e3 14. ♕e3 f5∓ Holmov–Adorjan, Budapest 1970 — 9/309

44 10... ♗e6 11. ♖c1 ♖c8 12. b3 ♕a5 13. ♗e2 a6 14. 0–0± Kurajica–Toran, Malaga 1970 — 9/307

45 11. a3!? ♗e6 12. b4 ♕d8 13. ♖c1 ♖c8 14. ♘b5 a6 15. ♘d4± Savon–Talj, Suhumi 1972 — 14/363

46 12. b3 ♖fc8 13. ♗d3 a6 14. ♘a4!? ♕d2 15. ♔d2 ♘d7 16. f4 f5 17. ♖he1 ♔f8 18. ef5 ♗f5± Polugajevski–Timman, Hilversum 1973 — 15/348

47 13... ♘d5? 14. cd5 ♗d7 15. ♖c7±

48 15. ♗e2 e5! [15... a6? 16. b4 ♔f8 17. a4 ♘d7 18. a5± Polugajevski–Ivkov, Beograd 1969] 16. de6 fe6△ d5∞ Holmov

49 16... b6 17. ♗h3 ♖c7 18. ♖c1 ♘e8 19. b4 ♖c1 20. ♔c1 ♘c7 21. ♗d7!+– Gheorghiu–Szilagyi, Varna 1971 — 12/361

50 18. ♗d7 ♖d7 19. b3 a6 20. ♖c1± Ree–Cornelis, Siegen (ol) 1970 — 10/430

51 **19... ♘b6**? 20. ♔c2 ♔f8 21. b3 ♔e8 22. a4 ♔d8 23. a5+– Polugajevski–Ostojić, Beograd 1969 — 8/329; **19... ♘e5** 20. ♗a7 ♘d3 21. ♔c2 ♘b2 22. ♗c8 b5 23. ♗a6± Kurajica; **19... ♘c5** 20. ♔c2± Kurajica–Huguet, Malaga 1970 — 9/308

52 14... ♖fe8 15. ♘d5! [15. ♕c3 ♘h5 16. ♗g7 ♘g7 17. b4 a5 18. b5 a4 19. ♗e2 a3 20. ♔f2 ♕b2 21. ♘d5 ♗d5 22. cd5 f5∓ Vajsman–Volčok, corr. 1973 — 16/328; 16. g4 ♗g4 17. ♘d5 ♗f3 18. ♗g7 ♘g7 19. ♕f3 ♕b2 20. ♔d1∞ Andersson] ♗d5 16. cd5 ♖ac8 17. ♗e2 ♖c1 18. ♕c1 ♕a5= Polugajevski–Bednarski, Varna 1972 — 14/360

53 15. ♕c3 ♘h5 16. ♗g7 ♘g7 17. b3 ♕a6! 18. ♘d5 ♗d5 19. cd5 ♕b6∓ Svešnikov–Beljavski, SSSR (ch) 1973 — 16/325

54 15... ♘d5 16. cd5 ♗d5 17. ♗b5 ♗c6 18. ♗c4 ♕a4 19. ♗g7 ♔g7 20. 0–0± Timman–Andersson, Forssa–Helsinki 1972 — 14/362

55 16... ♕d5 17. ♗c4±

56 20. ♕c3 ♔g8 21. 0–0 1/2 : 1/2 Polugajevski–Andersson, Hilversum 1973

57 **14... ♖fe8** 15. ♘d5 ♗d5 16. cd5± Jansa–Gašić, Sarajevo 1972 — 13/377; **14... ♘d7** 15. ♗d4 ♖fe8 16. 0–0 ♕b3 17. ♗d1 ♕a2 18. ♕c3 ♗d4 13. ♕d4 f6 20. ♘d5± Andersson–Reshevsky, Palma de Mallorca 1971 — 12/363

58 15. ♘g8 ♔g8 16. ♗d4 ♗d4 17. ♕d4 ♕a5 18. ♔f2 ♕e5 19. ♖cd1 ♖fc8 [19... ♖fd8 20. ♖d2 ♕d4 21. ♖d4 ♔f8 22. f4 a5 23. g4 f6 24. h4± Ribli–Ghitescu, Kecskemet 1972 — 13/375] 20. b3 ♖c6 21. ♕e3 ♖b6 22. ♖d3 [Andersson–Ree, Teesside 1972 — 13/378] ♕c5!=

59 17... ♕a4? 18. b4 a6 19. ♗d4 ♕d7 20. ♕b2± Ghitescu–Bednarski, Wijk aan Zee 1973

60 **19... ♗c3**? 20. bc3± Schmidt–Hug, Bath 1973 — 16/326; **19... ♕b3**!?±

61 12. ♗d3 a6 13. 0–0 ♖fc8 14. b3 b5 15. ♖c2 b4 [15... ♖ab8 16. ♖fc1 b4 17. ♘e2 ♘e8?! 18. c5± Smejkal–Bobocov, Varna 1971 — 12/362; 15... ♗e6 16. cb5 ab5 17. ♖fc1 ♗d7? 18. ♘b5 ♖c2 19. ♖c2 ♗b5 20. ♖c8! ♖c8 21. ♕a5 ♗d3 22. b4± Portisch–Gheorghiu, Siegen (ol) 1970 — 10/429; 17... b4 18. ♘a4 ♖c2 19. ♖c2 ♖b8 20. ♖c6 ♘d7± Alburt–Georgadze, SSSR 1971 — 11/297] 16. ♘e2 ♗e8 17. ♖fc1 ♘d7= Ghitescu–Deže, Kecskemet 1972 — 13/376

62 12... a6 13. 0–0 ♖fd8?! 14. a3 ♖ac8 15. b4± Ivkov–Ree, Wijk aan Zee 1970 — 9/306

63 13... ♗e6 14. b3 a6 15. ♖c2 b5 16. cb5 ab5 17. ♖fc1 ♗d7? 18. ♘b5! ♖c2 19. ♖c2 ♗b5 20. ♕a5 ♖a5 21. b4+– Polugajevski–Matulović, Kapfenberg 1970 — 10/427

64 14... b5 15. c5! ♖c6 16. cd6 ed6 [16... ♖d6 17. ♕e1±] 17. ♖c2 ♖ac8 18. ♘d5± Polugajevski–Bednarski, Siegen (ol) 1970 — 10/428

65 20. ♗c4± Suetin–Forintos, Budapest 1970 — 9/310

B 37 — 1. e4 c5 2. ♘f3 ♘c6 3. d4 cd4 4. ♘d4 g6 5. c4 ♗g7

	6	7	8	9	10	11	12	13	14	
1	♘b3[1] d6[2]	♗e2 a5[3]	a4[4] ♘f6	♘c3 0–0	♗e3 ♘d7	0–0[5] b6	♘d4 ♗b7	♘c6 ♗c6	♕c2	=
2	♘c2 d6[6]	♗e2[7] ♘h6	g4[8] ♕a5[9]	♗d2[10] ♕e5[11]	♘c3 f5	f4 ♕e6	ef5[12] gf5	g5 ♘f7	♘d5	±

1. e4 c5 2. ♘f3 ♘c6 3. d4 cd4 4. ♘d4 g6 5. c4 ♗g7 6. ♘c2 d6 7. ♗e2										
	7	8	9	10	11	12	13	14	15	
3	...	♘c3	♗e3	bc3	♕d2	f3	0–0	♘b4		∓
	♘f6	♘d7[13]	♗c3[14]	♕a5	♘c5	f6[15]	♘a4[16]	♘c3[17]		
4	...	...	0–0	♕d2[18]	b3[19]	ef5	♘e3	♘f5	♖b1	±
	...	...	0–0	♘c5	f5[20]	♗f5	♘d4[21]	♘f5	e6[22]	
5	...	...	...	f3	♗e3[23]	bc3	♕d2[26]	♖ad1	♘b4	∞
	...	...	♘c5	0–0	♗c3[24]	b6[25]	♗b7	♕c7	♖ac8[27]	
6	...	...	♗d2	0–0	f3[29]	♔h1	ef5	♗e3[31]	♘d4	±
	...	...	0–0[28]	♘c5	a5[30]	f5	♗f5	♔h8[32]		
7	...	ef5	0–0	♘d2[33]	♘f3	♘fd4	♗f3			=
	f5	♗f5	♘h6	0–0	♔h8[34]	♗d7	♘f5[35]			

1 6. ♘b5 d6 7. ♗e2 ♘f6 8. ♘1c3 0–0 9. ♗e3 a6 10. ♘d4 ♘d4 11. ♗d4 b5 12. cb5 ab5 13. ♗b5 ♗b7 14. 0–0 e5∓ Bronštejn–Simagin, SSSR 1951

2 6... ♘f6 7. ♘c3 0–0 8. ♗e2 d6 [8... b6 9. ♗e3 ♗b7 10. f3 ♖c8 11. 0–0 d6 12. ♘d4±] 9. ♗e3 ♗e6 10. 0–0 ♘d7 11. ♕d2 ♘de5 12. ♘d5± Tartakower–Rosselli, Baden Baden 1925

3 **7... ♗e6** 8. 0–0 ♖c8 9. f4 ♘a5 10. ♘a5 ♕a5 11. ♘a3 f5 12. ef5 gf5± Zagorovski–Bernstein, corr. 1968; **7... f5** 8. ef5 ♗f5 9. 0–0 ♘h6 10. ♘c3 0–0 11. ♗e3 ♗e6 12. f3 ♔h8 13. ♘d4± Unzicker–Biebinger, Bielefeld 1959

4 8. ♘a3 a4 9. ♘d2 ♘f6 10. 0–0 0–0 11. ♘c2 ♘d7∓ Kieninger–Gereben, Zürich 1960

5 11. ♕d2 b6 12. ♘d4 [12. 0–0 ♘c5∓] ♗b7 13. ♗d1 ♘c5∓ Schmid–Larsen, La Habana 1967 — 4/430

6 **6... b6** 7. ♗e2 ♗a6 8. 0–0 ♖c8 9. ♘e3 [9. ♘d2 ♘f6 10. b3 ♕c7 11. f4 0–0 12. ♗b2 d6=; 9. ♘ba3 ♘f6 10. f3 0–0 11. b3 ♕c7 12. ♖b1 e6 13. b4 ♘e7 14. ♗b2 ♘h5 15. ♗g7 ♔g7= Nej–Larsen, Beverwijk 1964] ♘a5 [9... ♘f6 10. ♘c3 ♘a5 11. ♕a4 0–0 12. ♖b1±] 10. ♘d2± Boleslavski; **6... ♘h6** 7. ♘c3 [7. ♗d2 f5 8. ♕c1 ♘f7∞] d6 8. ♗e2 [8. h4? f5 9. h5 fe4 10. hg6 hg6 11. ♘e4 ♗f5 12. ♘c3 ♕a5 13. ♗d2 ♕e5∓ Szabo–Botvinik, Amsterdam 1966 — 2/355; 12. ♗d3 ♘e5 13. ♘e3 ♕a5 14. ♔f1 ♘d3 15. ♕d3 0-0-0∓ Malich–Adorjan, Luhačovice 1973] f5 9. ef5 ♘f5 [9... ♗f5 10. 0–0 — 6... d6] 10. 0–0 0–0 11. ♗d2 [11. ♘d5 ♗d7! 12. ♖b1 a6 13. b3 b5∓↑ Flohr–Szilagyi, Amsterdam 1966 — 2/354] ♔h8 12. ♖c1 ♗d7 13. b3 a6 14. ♘e4 b5= Lengyel–Kluger, Budapest 1970; 7. g4!? ♕a5 [7... d6 8. ♗e2 — 6... d6] 8. ♗d2 ♕e5 9. ♘c3 f5 [9... d6 10. ♗e2 — 6... d6] 10. g5 ♘f7 11. f4 ♕e6 12. e5±; **6... ♘f6** 7. ♘c3 d6 8. ♗e2 — 7... ♘f6

7 **7. ♘c3** ♗c3 [7... f5 8. ef5 ♗f5 9. ♘e3 ♘h6 10. g3! 0–0 11. ♗g2 ♕d7 12. ♘f5± Štejn–Honfi, Kecskemet 1968] 8. bc3 ♘f6 9. ♗d3!? [9. f3?! ♕a5 10. ♗d2 ♗d7 11. ♗e2 ♖c8 12. ♘e3 ♗e6 13. ♘d5 ♘d7 14. 0–0 ♘ce5 15. ♗e3 ♘c4 16. ♕d4 ♘de5 17. ♗f2 g5∓ Polugajevski–Averbah, SSSR (ch) 1959] ♘d7∓; **7. ♗d3** ♘f6 8. ♘c3 0–0 9. 0–0 a6 10. ♘e3 ♘d7 11. ♘cd5?! ♘c5 12. ♖b1 e6 13. ♘c3 b6 14. ♕d2 ♗b7 15. f3 ♘d3 16. ♕d3 ♘e5 17. ♕e2 b5∓ Estrin–Vasjukov, SSSR 1955; 10. b3=

8 8. ♗d2 f5! 9. ♕c1 ♘f7 10. ♗c3 e5 11. ♘d2 ♕g5∓

9 **8... f6**? 9. h4 0–0 10. h5 g5 11. ♘c3 e6 12. ♖g1 ♘f7 13. ♗e3± Suetin–Simagin, SSSR 1950; **8... ♗e6**!?

10 **9. ♘c3**? ♘g4 10. ♗g4 ♗g4 11. ♕g4 ♗c3–+ Suetin–Simagin, SSSR 1951; **9. ♔f1** f6∓

11 9... ♕b6 10. g5 [10. ♘c3 ♘g4? 11. c5±] ♘g4 11. ♗g4 ♗g4 12. ♕g4 ♗b2 13. ♕d1±

12 12. gf5 gf5 13. ♗h5 ♔d8 14. ♕e2 fe4∞ Nej–Vasjukov, SSSR 1956

13 **8... ♗e6** 9. 0–0 0–0 [9... a6 10. ♘e3 ♘d7 11. ♘ed5 0–0 12. ♗g5 ♘c5 13. ♖c1 a5 14. ♖e1± Keres–Letelier, Buenos Aires 1964] 10. ♗e3 ♘d7 11. ♕d2± Tajmanov–Ghitescu, Bucuresti 1973 — 16/318; 9... ♘d7!?; **8... ♗d7** 9. 0–0 0–0 10. ♗g5 ♕a5 11. ♕d2 ♖fc8

12. ♖ad1 ♗e6 13. ♔h1 a6 14. a3 ♖ab8 15. b4± Korčnoj—Lepeškin, SSSR 1965

14 9... ♘c5 10. ♘d4! [10. ♕d2 ♕a5 11. f3 ♗e6 12. 0—0 0—0 13. ♖ab1 ♗c3 14. bc3 ♘e5 15. ♗h6 ♖fe8 16. ♘e3 f6∓ Uhlmann—Ivkov, Amsterdam 1972] 0—0 11. 0—0 ♗d7 12. ♕d2 ♘d4 13. ♗d4± Portisch—Reshevsky, Palma de Mallorca 1971 — 12/356

15 12... ♕a4? 13. 0—0 ♗e6 14. ♘b4 ♖c8 15. ♘d5 ♘d7 [15... ♘e5!?] 16. ♕b2 b6 17. c5! bc5 18. ♗b5+— Portisch—Deže, Vršac 1971 — 13/370

16 13... 0—0 14. ♖fb1 ♖d8 15. a4 ♗e6 16. ♘b4 ♖d7 17. ♘d5 ♕d8∞ Polgar—Forintos, Kecskemet 1972 — 13/372

17 ∓ Florian

18 **10. ♘d5** ♘c5 11. f3 ♘a4 [11... f5!?] 12. ♖b1± Šehtman—Kremenecki, SSSR 1972 — 13/371; **10. ♖e1** ♘c5 11. ♗f1 f5 [11... ♗c3!?] 12. ef5 ♗f5 13. ♘e3± Portisch—Gheorghiu, Budapest 1970 — 9/302; **10. ♔h1** ♘c5 11. f3 f5 [11... ♗c3!?] 12. ef5 ♗f5 13. ♘e3 ♘d4 14. ♘f5 ♘f5 [Korčnoj—Benkö, Palma de Mallorca 1969 — 6/452] 15. ♗d3!±

19 11. f3 f5! 12. b4 ♘e6 13. ef5 ♘f4! 14. ♘d5!? [14. ♗b2 ♘e2 15. ♕e2 ♗f5∓ Benkö—Barcza, Budapest 1955] ♘e2 15. ♕e2 ♗f5 16. ♗g5 ♗c2 17. ♕c2 ♖f5 18. ♕d2 ♖g5 19. ♕g5 e6!∓ Pogats—Barcza, Budapest 1955

20 11... ♗c3!?

21 13... ♘e4 14. ♘e4 ♗a1 15. ♘f5 gf5 [15... ♖f5 16. ♗g4±] 16. ♕d5 ♔h8 17. ♗h6 ♗g7 18. ♗g7 ♔g7 19. ♘g5± Ivkov

22 Karpov—Kaplan, San Antonio 1972 — 14/354

23 **11. ♗d2** — 9. ♗d2; **11. ♗g5** a5 12. ♕d2 a4 13. ♖ab1 ♕a5 14. ♔h1? a3!∓ Cvetković—Šahović, Jugoslavija (ch) 1974 — 17/374; 14. ♘d5∞

24 **11... a5** 12. ♕d2 a4 13. ♔h1 ♗e6 14. ♗h6 f6 15. ♗e3! f5 16. ef5 ♗f5 17. ♘d4± Geler—Simagin, Kislovodsk 1969; **11... f5** 12. ef5! gf5 [12... ♗f5 13. ♘d4±] 13. ♕d2 ♗e6 14. ♖ad1± Štejn—Janošević, Vrnjačka Banja 1971 — 11/293

25 12... ♕a5 13. ♕d2 ♘a4 [13... ♗e6 14. ♘d4 ♖ac8 15. ♖ab1 b6 16. ♗h6 ♖fe8∞ Štejn—Kapengut, SSSR (ch) 1971 — 12/355] 14. ♗h6 ♖e8 15. ♘b4 ♗e6∞ Štejn—Kozma, Kislovodsk 1972 — 14/353

26 13. ♕e1!?△ ♕h4

27 Adamski—Jansa, Budapest 1970 — 9/303

28 9... ♘c5 10. b4 ♘e6 11. ♖c1 0—0 12. ♘d5 ♘ed4 13. ♘d4 ♘d4 14. ♗g5 ♖e8 15. 0—0± Korčnoj—Hübner, Leningrad (izt) 1973 — 15/656

29 **11. b3** ♗c3! [11... a5 12. ♖b1 f5 13. ef5 ♗f5 14. ♗g4 ♗d3 15. ♗e2 ♗f5= Korčnoj—Matulović, Sarajevo 1969 — 7/340; 12... ♘b4!?] 12. ♗c3 ♘e4 13. ♗b2 a5∓ Goldštejn—Buslajev, Suhumi 1973; **11. b4**!?

30 **11... ♗c3** 12. ♗c3 ♘a4 13. ♕d2 a5 14. ♔h1 ♗e6 15. f4± Filip—Spiridonov, Soči 1973 — 16/317; **11... f5**!? 12. b4 ♘e6 13. ef5 gf5 14. ♔h1 ♘ed4 15. ♘d4 ♘d4 16. ♗d3 ♔h8= Kestler—Markland, Nice (ol) 1974; 13. ♖b1±

31 14. ♘e3 ♘d4! 15. ♘f5 ♘f5 16. ♖b1 e6∓ Portisch—Tukmakov, Madrid 1973 — 16/316

32 **14... ♘b4** 15. ♘d4±; **14... ♗c2** 15. ♕c2 ♘d4 16. ♕d2±

33 **10. ♘e3** 0—0 11. ♘f5?! ♘f5∓; **10. ♘c3** 0—0 11. ♘e3 [11. ♗e3 ♗c2 12. ♕c2 ♘f5∓ Dückstein—Filip, Zagreb 1955; 11. ♘d5 ♔h8 12. ♘ce3 ♘d4 13. ♘f5 ♘hf5 14. ♗d3 e6∓ Teschner—Smiltiner, Moskva (ol) 1956] ♘d4 12. ♗d3 ♗d3 13. ♕d3 e6 14. ♘c2 ♘c2 15. ♕c2 ♘f5= Averbah—Adorjan, Budapest 1970

34 11... ♕d7 12. ♘e3 ♔h8 13. ♘f5 ♘f5 14. ♖b1 e6 15. b3± Alexander—Botvinik, Amsterdam (ol) 1954

35 = Botvinik

B 38

1. e4 c5 2. ♘f3 ♘c6 3. d4 cd4 4. ♘d4 g6 5. c4 ♗g7 6. ♗e3

	6	7	8	9	10	11	12	13	14	
1	...	♘c3	♗e2	ef5[3]	♗h6[5]	0—0[6]	♕d2	♔h1	f4	±
	♘h6[1]	0—0[2]	f5	♗d4[4]	♖f5	d6[7]	♕a5	♖f7	♗e6[8]	
2	...	...	...	0—0	ef5	f4	♕d2[10]	♗g4	♘d5	±
	...	...	d6	f5	gf5[9]	♗d7	♘g4	fg4	♖c8[11]	

	6	7	8	9	10	11	12	13	14	
3	...	♗e2	♕d2	♗g4	♘c3	0–0	f4[16]	♗d4	fe5	±
	...	d6[12]	♘g4[13]	♗g4	0–0[14]	♕a5[15]	♘d4	e5[17]	de5[18]	
4	...	♘c3[19]	♗e2	0–0	f3[20]	♕d2	♖ad1[22]	♖fe1	♗f1	±
	b6	♗b7	♘f6	0–0	d6[21]	♕d7	♖ad8	♘e8	♕c8[23]	
5	...	♘c3[24]	h3	♗e2[26]	0–0	♕d2	cb5	♗d4	♖fd1[28]	∞
	♘f6	0–0[25]	d6	♗d7[27]	a6	b5	♘d4	ab5	♗c6[29]	
6	...	...	♗e2	0–0	♗d4	f4	b3	♕d3[34]	♖ad1[35]	±
	...	...	d6[30]	♘d4[31]	♗e6[32]	♕c8[33]	♖d8	♗g4		
7	...	...	...	...	♕d2[36]	♖ac1	f3	♗d4	b3	±
	...	...	...	♗d7	♖c8[37]	a6	♘d4	♗e6	♕a5[38]	
8	...	...	...	...	...	♗d4	f3	♗g7	♖f2	±
	...	...	...	...	♘d4	♗c6[39]	♘d7	♔g7	a5[40]	

1 **6... ♕b6** 7. ♘b3 ♕c7 [7... ♕d8 8. ♘c3 ♘f6 9. ♗e2 b6 10. 0–0 0–0 11. ♘d4± Petrosjan–Gipslis, SSSR 1965] 8. ♘c3 ♘f6 9. ♗e2 0–0 10. 0–0 b6 11. ♘d4 ♗b7 12. ♘db5 ♕b8 13. ♖c1 ♖d8 14. f4± Reško–Gipslis, SSSR 1966; **6... e6** 7. ♘c3 ♘ge7 8. ♕d2 d5 9. cd5 ed5 10. ♘c6 bc6 11. ed5 cd5 12. ♗b5 ♗d7 13. ♗e2 ♗e6 14. ♖d1±; 8. ♘db5!?; **6... d6** 7. ♘c3 ♘f6 8. ♗e2 0–0 — 6... ♘f6

2 **7... d6** 8. ♗e2 f5 9. ef5 [9. ♗h6 ♗d4=] ♘f5 10. ♘f5 ♗f5 11. 0–0 0–0 12. c5!± Kovačević–Barcza, Zagreb 1972 — 14/355; 11... ♕a5!?; **7... ♘g4** — B 39

3 9. ♕d2? f4 10. ♗f4 ♗d4 11. ♗h6 ♗f2 12. ♔d1 ♖f7∓ Martin–Gurgenidze, München 1958

4 9... ♘f5 10. ♘f5 gf5 11. f4±

5 10. ♗d4? ♘f5 11. ♗c5 d6 12. ♗a3 ♘fd4 13. 0–0 ♗f5∓↑ Furman–Spaski, SSSR (ch) 1957

6 11. ♗e3 ♗e3 12. fe3 d6 13. ♕d2= Pachman–Sanguinetti, Portorož (izt) 1958

7 11... ♕b6 12. ♘d5! ♗f2 13. ♔h1 ♕d4 14. ♗g4 ♕d1 15. ♖ad1 ♖f7 16. ♘e7± Gruševski–Veresov, SSSR 1959

8 15. ♖ac1± Šamkovič–Vasjukov, SSSR 1965

9 10... ♘d4 11. ♗d4 ♗d4 12. ♕d4 ♘f5 13. ♕d2 ♗d7 14. ♗f3 ♗c6 15. ♗d5± Talj–Kuprejčik, Soči 1970 — 10/424

10 12. h3 ♕b6 13. ♘f5 ♕b2 14. ♘h6 ♗h6 15. ♖c1 ♗g7 16. ♘d5 ♕a2∞ Kavalek–Larsen, Sousse (izt) 1967; 15. ♘d5!? Boleslavski

11 **14... ♖f7**? 15. f5! ♔h8 [15... ♗d4 16. ♗d4 ♗f5±] 16. ♘e6± Szabo–Larsen, Vinkovci 1970 — 10/425; **14... ♖c8**±

12 **7... 0–0** 8. ♕d2 ♕a5 9. ♘c3 ♘d4 10. ♗d4 ♗d4 11. ♕d4 f5 12. ef5 ♘f5 13. ♕d2±; **7... f5** 8. ef5 ♘f5 9. ♘f5 ♕a5 [9... ♗b2 10. ♘d2 gf5 11. ♗h5 ♔f8 12. ♕c2±→ Unzicker–Filip, Baden-Baden 1957] 10. ♘c3 ♕f5 11. c5!±

13 8... ♘d4 9. ♗d4±

14 10... ♕a5 11. ♖c1 ♖c8 12. b3 0–0 13. 0–0 ♖fe8 14. ♔h1 ♗d7 15. f4± Barczay–Szabo, Budapest 1970 — 9/305

15 **11... ♖c8** 12. b3 a6 13. ♖ac1 ♕a5 14. h3 ♗d7? 15. ♘c6 bc6?! 16. c5± Bhend–Keres, Zürich 1959; 14... ♘d4!?; **11... ♗d7** 12. f4 ♖c8?! 13. b3 ♕a5 14. ♖ac1 f5 15. ef5 gf5 16. ♘de2!± Langeweg–Velimirović, Amsterdam 1974 — 18/353; 12... a6!?

16 **12. h3** ♗d7 13. ♖fd1 ♖ac8 14. b3 a6 15. ♖ac1 ♘d4 16. ♗d4 ♗d4 17. ♕d4 ♗e6= Jansa–Kuprejčik, Soči 1970; **12. ♖ac1** ♖fc8 13. b3 a6 14. ♖c2 b5= Geler–Larsen, Monte Carlo 1967 — 3/409; 14. f4±

17 13... ♗d4 14. ♕d4 ♕c5 15. ♕c5 dc5 16. f5 gf5 17. h3±

18 **14... ♗e5** 15. ♗e5 de5 16. ♕e3 ♗e6 17. ♘d5 ♗d5 18. ed5±; **14... de5** 15. ♗e3± Petrosjan–Heinicke, Wien 1957

19 7. ♘c6 dc6 8. ♕c2 ♘h6 9. f3 f5∞

20 **10. ♖c1**? ♘d4 11. ♗d4 ♗h6∓ Smejkal–Bellon, Palma de Mallorca 1972 — 14/357; **10. f4** ♘d4 11. ♗d4 d6 12. ♗f3 ♕c7 13. ♖c1 e5 14. fe5 de5 15. ♘d5 ♘d5 16. cd5 ♕d6= Korzin–Abramov, SSSR 1968

21 **10... ♘d4** 11. ♗d4 d6 12. ♕d2 [12. ♕d3 ♖c8 13. ♖ac1 ♕d7 14. ♖fd1± Honfi–

Puc, Jugoslavija 1962] ♘d7 13. ♗g7 ♔g7 14. f4 [14. ♖ac1 a5 15. f4 ♘c5 16. ♕e3 e5 17. ♖cd1± Boleslavski–Pirc, SSSR–Jugoslavija 1956] a5 15. ♖ad1 ♘c5 16. ♕e3±; **10... ♘e8** 11. ♕d2 f5 12. ef5 gf5 13. ♖ad1△ f4±

22 12. ♖fd1 ♖fd8 [12... ♘e8 13. f4?! ♘f6 14. ♗f3 ♖ad8 15. e5?! ♘d4 16. ♗d4 de5 17. fe5 ♗f3 18. gf3 ♘h5 19. ♕e3 ♕f5!∓ Browne–Bellon, Madrid 1973 — 16/319; 13. ♖ac1±] 13. ♘d5 ♘d5 14. cd5 ♘d4= Ciocaltea–Toran, Nice (ol) 1974

23 15. ♘d5 ♖d7 16. ♘c6 ♗c6 17. ♗g5 ♕b7 18. b4± Tukmakov–Bellon, Madrid 1973

24 7. f3? ♕b6 8. ♘f5 [8. ♕d2 ♘e4–+] ♕b2 9. ♘g7 ♔f8 10. ♘d2 ♔g7∓

25 7... ♘g4 — B 39

26 9. ♖c1!? ♘d4 10. ♗d4 ♕a5 11. ♗d3 ♗e6 12. 0–0 ♖fc8! [12... a6 13. a3 ♖fc8 14. b4± Jansson–Dueball, Grossenbrode 1972 — 14/356] 13. b3 a6△ b5=

27 9... ♘d4 10. ♗d4 ♗d7 11. 0–0 ♗c6 12. ♗d3± Osnos–Ciocaltea, Romania 1968 — 5/378

28 14. ♗f6 ♗f6 15. ♘b5 ♕a5 16. ♘c3 ♖fc8 17. ♖fc1 ♗c3 18. ♖c3 ♖c3 19. ♕c3 ♕c3 20. bc3 ♖a3 21. c4 ♗a4= Larsen

29 15. ♗b5 ♘e4 16. ♘e4 ♗b5 17. ♗g7 ♔g7∞ Larsen–Kavalek (m) 1970 — 9/304

30 8... ♘e8 9. ♕d2 f5 10. ef5 gf5 11. f4 ♘c7 12. 0-0-0 d6 13. ♗f3 ♗d7 14. h3± Aronin–Bronštejn, SSSR 1951

31 9... ♘d7 10. ♕d2 [10. ♔h1 ♘c5 11. f4 ♗d7 12. ♗f3 ♖c8 13. ♕d2 a6 14. ♖ad1± Honfi–Gasztonyi, Hungary 1964] ♘c5 11. ♖ad1 [11. ♖fd1 ♗d7 12. f3 a5 13. b3 ♘d4 14. ♗d4 ♗e6 15. ♗g7 ♔g7 16. ♕e3 ♕b6= Parma–Velimirović, Vršac 1973] ♗d7 12. f3 a5 13. b3 ♘d4 14. ♗d4 [Hecht–Forintos, Vršac 1973 — 16/321] ♗d4 15. ♕d4 ♗c6=; 12. f4±

32 **10... ♕a5** 11. ♕d3 ♗e6 12. f4 ♖ac8 13. b3±; **10... ♘d7** 11. ♗g7 ♔g7 12. ♕d4 f6 13. ♖ad1 ♕a5 14. ♘d5 ♖f7 15. b4± Petrosjan–Tatai, Venezia 1967 — 4/431; **10... ♗d7** 11. ♕d3 [11. ♖e1?! ♗c6 12. ♗f1? e5∓ Geler–Bobocov, Kiev 1966 — 2/358; 12. ♕d3=] ♗c6 12. ♖ac1 [12. ♖fe1 ♘d7 13. ♗g7 ♔g7 14. b4 b6 15. ♖ac1 ♖e8 16. ♗f1± Smislov–Pirc, SSSR–Jugoslavija 1956; 12... a5!±] ♘d7 13. ♗g7 ♔g7 14. b4 ♘f6 15. ♔h1 a5 16. b5± Smislov–Golz, Polanica Zdroj 1969 — 6/455; 12... a5!±

33 11... ♕d7 12. ♕d3 ♖fc8 13. b3 ♗g4 14. ♖ad1 ♗e2 15. ♕e2 ♕e6 16. f5± Gheorghiu–Benkö, Orense 1973 — 16/320

34 h3!?±

35 **14. ♗g4** ♕g4 15. f5 ♕h4= Panno–Najdorf, Buenos Aires 1969 — 6/454; **14. ♖ad1**±

36 10. ♖c1 a6 11. ♘b3 ♘e5 [11... ♖b8 12. f3 b6 13. ♕d2± Smejkal–Andersson, Soči 1973] 12. ♘d5 ♘d5 13. ed5= Darga–Tajmanov, La Habana 1964

37 **10... ♘g4** 11. ♗g4 ♗g4 12. ♖ac1 ♘d4 13. ♗d4 ♗e6 14. f4± Pachman–Gunarsson, Vrnjačka Banja 1967 — 3/412; **10... a6** 11. f3 ♖c8 [11... ♕a5 12. ♘b3 ♕d8 13. ♖fd1 b6 14. ♖ac1 ♖b8 15. ♔h1± Petrosjan–Venalainen, Nice (ol) 1974 — 17/375] 12. ♖fd1± Petrosjan–Pilnik, Göteborg (izt) 1955

38 15. ♖c2 ♘d7 16. ♗g7 ♔g7± Smejkal–Diez del Corral, Skopje (ol) 1972

39 **11... a6** 12. f3 ♗c6 13. b4 ♘e8 14. ♖ac1 ♗d4 15. ♕d4± Lengyel–Wade, Solingen 1968 — 6/453; **11... ♕a5** 12. ♖fd1 ♖fc8 13. ♗f6 ♗f6 14. ♘d5 ♕d2 15. ♘f6 ♔g7 16. ♘h5 gh5 17. ♖d2± Botvinik–Lombardy, Wijk aan Zee 1969 — 7/342

40 15. ♖e1± Robatsch–Kelečević, Sarajevo 1968

B 39

1. e4 c5 2. ♘f3 ♘c6 3. d4 cd4 4. ♘d4 g6 5. c4 ♗g7 6. ♗e3 ♘f6 7. ♘c3 ♘g4

	8	9	10	11	12	13	14	15	16	
1	♕g4[1]	♕d1[3]	♕d2	♖c1	♗e2	0–0	b3	f4	ef5	±
	♘d4[2]	♘c6	♕a5	0–0[4]	d6	♗e6[5]	♖ac8	f5	♗f5[6]	
2	...	...	♗e2[8]	0–0	♕d2	♖ad1	♖fe1	ef5	♗g4	∞
	...	e5[7]	0–0	b6[9]	♗b7	♖c8	f5	♖f5	♖f7[10]	

	8	9	10	11	12	13	14	15	16	
3	...	...	♗d3	0–0	♕d2[13]	♖ac1	♖fd1	b3[15]	♘e2	±
	...	...	0–0[11]	d6[12]	♗e6	a6[14]	♕a5	b5		
4	...	...	♘b5!	♕d2[17]	♗d3	cd5[19]	♗b5	0–0[20]	d6[22]	±
	...	...	0–0[16]	♕h4[18]	d5	♘b5	♕e4	♖d8[21]	♗e6[23]	

1. e4 c5 2. ♘f3 ♘c6 3. d4 cd4 4. ♘d4 g6 5. c4 ♗g7 6. ♗e3 ♘f6 7. ♘c3 ♘g4 8. ♕g4 ♘d4 9. ♕d1 ♘e6

	10	11	12	13	14	15	16	17	18	
5	♗e2	bc3	0–0[26]	f3	♖b1	♕d2	ef5			∓
	♗c3[24]	b6[25]	♗b7	♕c7	0–0	f5	gf5			
6	♕d2	♖c1[28]	♗d3	0–0	♗b1	f4[30]	e5	ed6	♕d6	±
	d6[27]	♗d7	a5[29]	♘c5	♗c6	0–0	b6	♕d6	ed6[31]	
7	...	♗e2	0–0	♖ad1[34]	♘d5	f3[36]	♗g5[37]	b3		±
	...	♗d7[32]	0–0[33]	♗c6	♘c5[35]	a5	♖e8			
8	...	♖c1[38]	♗d3[40]	♗b1[41]	b3	ef5	♘d5	♔d2		±
	♕a5	b6[39]	♗b7	♖c8	f5	gf5	♕d2	♘c5[42]		
9	...	...	♗e2	0–0[43]	♗h6[45]	♗g7	b3	♖fe1	♕b2[48]	∞
	...	d6	♗d7	♘c5[44]	0–0[46]	♔g7	♗c6	♖ad8[47]	e5[49]	
10	♖c1	♗d3[51]	0–0	♗b1	f4	♕e2[54]	f5[55]	♘d5[56]		±
	d6[50]	0–0[52]	a5[53]	♗d7	♗c6	b6	♘c5			
11	...	b4!	♗e2	a3	ab4	0–0	♕d2	♘d5	♗b6	±
	...	0–0	a5	ab4	♗d7	♗c6	♖a3[57]	♔h8	♕d7[58]	
12	...	♗d3[59]	♗b1	0–0	b4[62]	♖c3	a3	ab4	♕d2[64]	±
	b6	♗b7	0–0[60]	d6[61]	♗c3[63]	a5	ab4	♖a1		
13	...	b4	♗d3	0–0	a3	ab4	♕d2			±
	0–0	b6	♗b7	a5[65]	ab4	♖a3	♗d4[66]			

[1] 8. ♘c6? ♘e3 9. ♘d8 ♘d1 10. ♘d1 ♔d8 11. ♖c1 b6 12. ♗d3 ♗b7∓ Cardoso–Talj, Moskva (ol) 1956

[2] 8... ♗d4 9. ♗d4 ♘d4 10. 0-0-0 [10. ♕d1 e5 11. ♗d3 d6 12. 0–0 ♕h4 13. ♘e2 ♘e6 14. ♗c2± Tartakower–Pirc, England 1951] d6 11. ♕g3 e5 12. f4 f6 13. c5!±Pachman

[3] 9. 0-0-0 e5 [9... ♘c6!?△ ♗c3] 10. h4 d5 11. ♕g3 de4 12. h5 ♗f5 13. ♗g5 f6 14. h6 ♗f8 15. ♘d5 ♗e7 16. ♗e3 ♖c8∓ Čerepkov–Gufeljd, SSSR (ch) 1961; 10. ♕g3∞

[4] 11... b6 12. ♗e2 ♗b7 13. 0–0 d6 14. ♖fd1?! 0–0 15. ♗h6 ♕e5= Trifunović–Stoltz, Praha 1946; 14. f4!±

[5] 13... f5 14. ef5 ♗f5 15. f4 e5 16. ♗f3! ♖ad8 17. ♖fd1± Pachman–Gawlikowski, Warszawa 1956

[6] 17. ♗f3 ♔h8 18. ♖fd1 ♖fe8 19. ♘b5 ♕d2 20. ♖d2 a6 21. ♘c3± Polugajevski–Suetin, Kislovodsk 1972

[7] Bronštejn

[8] **10. ♗d4** ed4 11. ♘d5 [11. ♘b5 0–0 12. ♘d4 ♕f6∓] 0–0 12. ♗d3 d6 13. 0–0 ♗e6△ ♗d5∓; **10. g3** d6 11. ♗g2 ♗e6 12. b3 ♕a5 13. ♗d2 ♕c5 14. 0–0 0–0= Keres–Benkö, Moskva (ol) 1956; **10. ♕d2** 0–0 11. 0-0-0 [11. ♗d3 d6 12. 0–0 — 10. ♗d3; 11. ♘b5 — 10. ♘b5] d6 12. ♔b1 ♕a5?! 13. ♘b5 ♕d2 14. ♖d2 ♘b5 15. cb5± Damjanović–Peretz, Netanya 1971 — 11/296; 12... a6!△ b5∞

[9] 11... a6 12. ♕d2 d6 [12... ♖b8 13. ♖fd1 d6 14. ♖ac1 ♗e6 15. ♗f1 b5 16. cb5 ab5 17. ♗d4 ed4 18. ♘b5 ♗a2 19. ♘d4 ♕h4 20. b4± Udovčić–Gipslis, Zagreb 1965] 13. ♖fd1 ♗e6 14. ♗f1 ♖c8 15. b3 ♗g4 16. ♗e2

♗e6 17. ♖ac1 ♕a5 18. ♗f1 ♖c7 [18... ♗g4 19. ♖e1△ ♘e2±] 19. ♘e2± Geler—Uhlmann, La Habana 1963

10 17. b3 a6 18. ♗g5 ♕f8∞ Korn—Vasjukov, SSSR 1954

11 10... a6!?△ ♖b8, b5 Botvinik

12 11... b6 12. ♖c1 ♗b7 13. ♕d2 d6 [13... f5 14. f3±; 14. ef5 ♕h4 15. ♘d5±] 14. ♘e2 ♘e6 15. ♗b1±

13 12. ♖c1 ♗e6 [12... a6!?] 13. b3 a6 14. ♗b1 ♕d7! [14... ♖b8 15. ♔h1?! b5 16. cb5 ab5 17. ♕d3 b4 18. ♘d5 ♗d5 19. ed5 ♕a5∓ Smislov—Botvinik, Moskva 1956; 15. ♘e2! ♘e2 16. ♕e2 f5 17. f3±] 15. ♘e2 ♘e2 16. ♕e2 ♖fc8 17. ♖fd1 ♕e7±

14 13... ♖c8 14. b3 a6 15. f3 ♕a5 16. ♖fd1 f5 [16... ♖c6 17. ♔h1 ♖fc8 18. h3 ♕d8 19. ♗f1± Vasjukov—Cuesta, La Habana 1967] 17. ef5 ♘f5 18. ♗e4± Talj—Partos, Nice (ol) 1974 — 17/382

15 15. ♗f1 b5! 16. cb5 ab5 17. ♘b5 ♘b5 18. ♕a5 ♖a5 19. b4 ♖a2 20. ♗b5 ♖b8= Polugajevski—Bagirov, SSSR 1963

16 **10... ♕b6**? 11. c5 ♕c5 12. ♖c1+−; **10... ♕a5**? 11. ♗d2 ♕b6 12. c5+−; **10... ♘b5** 11. cb5 ♕e7 [11... d6 12. ♗c4! ♗e6 13. ♕b3± Pachman] 12. ♕d2 0—0 13. ♖d1 ♖d8 14. b6 a6 15. ♗c4± Nejkirh—Szilagyi, Sofia 1957

17 **11. ♘d4**? ed4 12. ♗d4 ♕a5! [12... ♕h4? 13. ♗g7 ♕e4 14. ♕e2 ♕e2 15. ♗e2 ♔g7 16. 0-0-0±] 13. ♔e2 ♖e8 14. f3 d5! 15. ♗g7 [15. cd5 ♖e4 16. fe4 ♗g4—+] ♖e4 16. ♔f2 ♕c5 17. ♔g3 ♕e3—+; **11. ♗e2** ♘b5! [11... ♕h4 12. ♘d4 ed4 13. ♗d4 ♕e4 14. ♗g7 ♕g2 15. ♕d4 ♕h1 16. ♔d2 ♕a1?? 17. ♕f6! 1 : 0 Gaprindašvili—Szervaty, Dortmund 1974 — 17/381; 16... ♕h2!? Pytel] 12. cb5 d6 13. ♗c4 ♗e6 14. ♖c1 ♕d7△ ♖fd8±

18 **11... ♕e7** 12. 0-0-0 ♘b5 13. cb5 d5 14. ed5 ♗f5 15. ♗d3± Smislov—Jimenez, La Habana 1963; **11... ♘b5** 12. cb5 d6 13. ♗c4 ♗e6 14. b3 ♖c8 15. ♖c1 ♕h4 16. ♕d3 ♗h6 17. 0—0± Boleslavski

19 **13. ♘c7**? de4 14. ♘a8 ed3∓; **13. ♘d4** de4 14. ♗g5 ♕g4 15. f3 ef3 16. ♘f3 e4 17. 0—0 ed3 18. ♕d3 ♗e6∓; **13. ed5** ♗h3 14. ♗d4 ed4 15. gh3 [15. 0—0 ♗g2=] a6 16. ♘a3 ♗h6 17. ♕c2 ♖fe8 18. ♔d1 [18. ♗e2? d3 19. ♕d3 ♖e3 20. ♕d1 ♖ae8 21. 0—0 ♖e2∓ Željandinov—Šahov, SSSR 1959] ♖e5⩱ Nejštadt; **13. ♗g5** ♕g4 14. f3 ♕d7 15. ♘d4 dc4! 16. ♗c4 ed4 [Bisguier—Štejn, Tel Aviv (ol) 1964] 17. 0—0 b5 18. ♗d5=

20 15. f3 ♕h4 16. ♗f2 ♕f6 17. 0—0±

21 15... ♕f5 16. ♖ac1 e4 17. ♖fd1 ♕e5 18. b3 ♖d8 19. ♗f4 ♕h5 20. h3± Gufeljd—Listengarten, SSSR 1964

22 16. ♖fd1 ♗e6 [16... ♕f5 17. ♖ac1 ♗d7 18. ♗e2 e4 19. ♖c7± Gufeljd—Espig, Suhumi 1972 — 14/358] 17. de6 ♖d2 18. ef7 ♔f7 19. ♖d2 a6! [19... ♕b4? 20. ♖d7 ♔f6 21. ♖b7± Janata—Kraus, Praha 1968 — 5/379] 20. ♗e2 ♖e8 21. ♗f3 ♕b4 22. a3⩱

23 17. ♖ad1± Diez del Corral—Jimenez, Palma de Mallorca 1967

24 **10... b6** 11. ♕d5 ♖b8 12. ♖d1 ♗b7 13. ♕d2 ♘c5 14. f3 0—0 15. 0—0 f5 16. b4 ♘e6 17. ♘d5± Mangini—Barcza, Helsinki (ol) 1952; 11... ♗c3!?; **10... 0—0** 11. 0—0 d6 12. f4 ♗d7 [12... ♘c5 13. ♗f3 ♗e6 14. ♗d4 ♗d4 15. ♕d4 ♕b6 16. ♖ad1± Kapengut] 13. f5 ♘c5 14. ♗d4 a5 15. ♗g7! [15. ♘d5 ♗d4 16. ♕d4= K. Grigorjan—Štejn, SSSR 1972 — 13/374] ♔g7 16. f6 ef6 17. ♕d6 ♘e6 18. ♘d5± Averbah

25 11... ♕a5 12. 0—0 ♕c3 13. c5 0—0 14. ♖c1 ♕e5 15. ♗d3 ♘f4 16. ♗b1⩱ Žilin—Bastrikov, SSSR 1960

26 12. f4? ♗b7 13. ♗f3 ♕c7∓ Kapengut

27 10... b6 11. ♗e2 ♗b7 12. 0—0 [12. ♖d1 d6 13. ♗h6±] 0—0 13. f3 d6 14. ♖ac1 ♖c8 [14... f5 15. ef5 gf5 16. ♘d5 f4 17. ♗f2±] 15. ♘d5 ♖e8 16. ♖fd1 ♘c5 17. b4± Iserman—Rojzman, SSSR 1972

28 11. g3 ♗d7 12. ♖c1 a5 13. ♗g2 ♗c6 14. 0—0 0—0 15. f4 ♖c8 16. ♖fd1 ♘c5 17. ♕f2 ♕e8 (Olafsson—Simagin, Moskva 1959) 18. ♘d5±↑

29 **12... 0—0** 13. 0—0 ♘c5 14. b4 ♘d3 15. ♕d3 ♗e6 16. ♘d5 ♕d7 17. ♖fd1 ♖fc8 18. ♕b3 ♗d5 19. ♖d5± Vitolinš—Romanišin, SSSR 1972 — 13/373; **12... ♘c5** 13. ♗b1?! ♘a4 14. ♗d4 ♗d4 15. ♕d4 0—0= Kapengut; 13. b4!±

30 15. b3 0—0 16. ♖fe1 ♖e8 17. ♗g5 ♘e6 18. ♗e3= Matanović—Kapengut, Jugoslavija—SSSR 1971

31 19. ♖fd1± Polugajevski—Kapengut, SSSR (ch) 1971 — 12/357

32 11... ♘c5 12. ♖d1! ♗d7 13. b4 ♘a4 14. ♘a4 ♗a4 15. ♖b1± Kapengut

33 **12... ♕a5** 13. ♖fc1 [13. ♖ac1 — 10... ♕a5] ♘c5 14. ♗f3 ♘a4 15. ♗d4 ♗d4 16. ♕d4 ♕e5 17. ♕e5± Gufeljd—Georgadze

SSSR (ch) 1973 — 16/322; **12... a5** 13. ♘d5 ♘c5 14. ♗d4 0–0 15. ♗g7 ♔g7 16. ♕e3 ♗c6 17. ♖ad1± Robatsch–Kagan, Skopje (ol) 1972 — 14/359

34 **13. f4** ♗c6 14. ♗f3 [14. f5 ♘c5 15. ♗f3 a5 16. ♗h6 ♕b6 17. ♗g7 ♔g7 18. ♔h1 f6 19. ♘d5?! ♗d5 20. ed5 ♘d7∓ Spaski–Savon, SSSR (ch) 1973 — 16/323; 19. ♖ae1=] ♕a5! [14... b6? 15. b4 ♖c8 16. ♖ac1 f5? 17. ♘d5± Flor–Larsen, Noordwijk 1965] 15. ♖ac1 ♘c5∞ Kapengut; **13. ♖ac1** a5! [13... ♗c6 14. ♘d5 ♘c5 15. f3 ♗d5 16. ed5 a5 17. ♖fe1 ♕b6= Šamkovič–Nevidniči, SSSR 1964; 14. b4! ♗c3 15. ♕c3 ♗e4 16. ♗h6 ♖e8 17. ♖fe1± Schneider–Rittner, corr. 1967] 14. ♖fd1 ♗c6 15. f3 ♘c5 16. b3 ♕b6= Keres–Petrosjan, Jugoslavija (ct) 1959

35 14... ♖e8? 15. f4 ♘c7 16. f5 ♘a6 [Larsen–Petrosjan, Santa Monica 1966 — 2/359] 17. b4!±

36 15. ♕c2 a5! [15... ♘e4 16. ♕e4 e6=] 16. ♗c5 dc5 17. ♘f6 ♗f6 18. ♖d8 ♖ad8=∞ Boleslavski

37 16. ♗d4? ♗d4 17. ♕d4 e5 18. ♕d2 ♘e6 19. ♘e3 ♕b6∓ Porath–Larsen, Amsterdam (izt) 1964

38 11. ♗e2 ♗c3 12. bc3 d6 13. ♖b1 [13. 0–0 ♗d7 14. f4 ♗c6! 15. ♗d4 f6∞] ♗d7 14. ♗d4 0–0 15. h4 ♗c6 16. f3 f6∞ Kapengut

39 11... g5?! 12. h4 [12. ♗e2 ♗e5 13. g3 ♖g8 14. 0–0 d6 15. ♔h1 ♗d7= Kapengut] h6 13. a3 [13. ♕d5 ♕b4 14. ♖c2 d6 15. hg5 hg5 16. ♖h8 ♗h8= Portisch–Reshevsky, Amsterdam (izt) 1964] d6 14. ♕d5±

40 12. ♗e2 ♗b7 13. f3 f5!? [13... g5 14. 0–0 ♗e5 15. ♖fd1 d6 16. ♘d5! (16. b3 ♗f4 17. ♘d5 ♕d2 18. ♗d2± Gligorić–Larsen, Dallas 1957) ♕d2 (16... ♕a2 17. ♖c2 ♕a4 18. b4 f6 19. c5±) 17. ♖d2 ♖c8 18. b4 ♘f4 19. ♘f4 ♗f4 20. ♗f4 gf4 21. c5 0–0 22. ♖dc2± Gufeljd–Kapengut, SSSR 1965] 14. ef5 gf5 15. 0–0 ♖g8 16. ♖fd1 d6 17. a3 f4! 18. ♗f4 ♗d4 19. ♔h1 ♕f5 20. ♗e3 ♖g2!=∞→ Kapengut

41 13. 0–0 g5 14. a3 ♕e5 15. b4 ♖c8 16. ♘d5± Rogoff–Levy, Haifa 1970 — 10/426

42 Talj–Raškovski, SSSR 1973

43 13. b3!? ♗c6 14. f3 Boleslavski

44 13... ♗c6 14. f3 f5! [14... g5 15. b3 ♗e5 16. ♕b2 ♘d4 17. ♗d3 b5 18. ♕d2 bc4 19. ♗c4± Cejtlin–Buhman, SSSR 1970] 15. ef5 gf5 16. f4 ♘c5!= Kapengut

45 **14. f3** ♘a4 15. ♘a4 ♕d2 16. ♗d2 ♗a4= Mikenas–Averbah, SSSR (ch) 1970; **14. ♗f3** ♗c6 15. ♗d4 0–0 16. ♗g7 ♔g7 17. ♕e3 ♖ad8 18. ♖fd1 ♕b6 19. ♖d2 ♘a4= Holmov–Averbah, SSSR 1970

46 14... ♗c3 15. ♖c3 ♘e4 16. ♕d4 ♕e5 17. ♕e5 de5 18. ♖e3±⊡ Korčnoj

47 17... ♘e6 18. ♗g4±○ Korčnoj–Petrosjan, Odesa (mct) 1974 — 17/380

48 18. ♗g4 ♕b4 19. ♖e3 ♖h8= Geler

49 19. b4 ♕b6 20. ♗f1 f5 21. ♘d5 ♗d5 22. ed5 ♖c8∞

50 10... ♕a5 11. ♗d3 d6 [11... ♗c3 12. ♖c3 ♕a2 13. ♕c1 ♕a5 14. c5± Honfi–Szilagyi, Kecskemet 1971] 12. 0–0 0–0 13. ♗b1 ♗d7 14. f4 ♘c5 15. ♘d5± Mednis–D. Byrne, USA (ch) 1973 — 17/376

51 11. ♗e2 ♗d7 12. 0–0 ♗c6 13. f3 0–0 14. ♖c2 f5 15. ef5 ♖f5 16. f4 ♖f7 17. ♗g4± Korčnoj–Averbah, SSSR (ch) 1965; 14... ♘c5±

52 11... ♗d7 12. 0–0 a5 [12... ♗c6 13. b4 b6 14. ♗b1 a5 15. a3 ♕b8 16. ♕d2 ab4 17. ab4 b5 18. cb5 ♗b5 19. ♖fe1± Polugajevski–Zaharov, SSSR 1972] 13. f4 ♗c6 14. ♗b1 ♘c5 15. ♕e2 0–0 16. e5 ♘a4 17. ♘a4 ♗a4 18. b3 ♗c6 19. ♖cd1 ♕c7 20. ed6 ed6 21. f5± Portisch–Larsen, Lugano (ol) 1968 — 6/456

53 12... ♘c5 13. ♗b1 [13. b4 ♘d3 14. ♕d3 ♗e6 15. ♗d4 ♗d4 16. ♕d4 ♕b6= Zajcev] a5 14. ♕d2 [14. f4 b6 15. ♗d4 e5! 16. fe5 ♘e6! 17. ♘d5 ♘d4∓ Kapengut] ♗d7 15. ♗d4 ♗d4 16. ♕d4 ♗c6 17. ♕d2± Portisch–Petrosjan, Palma de Mallorca (mct) 1974 — 17/378

54 15. ♖f2 ♘c5!? 16. e5 [16. f5±] b6 17. ♖d2±; 15... b6!?

55 16. ♖cd1!? ♗c3 17. bc3 ♕c7 18. f5 ♘c5 19. ♗h6±↑ Balašov

56 17. ♕f2 ♘d7!= Portisch–Petrosjan, Palma de Mallorca (mct) 1974 — 17/379; **17. ♘d5±**

57 16... ♗c3 17. ♕c3 ♗e4 18. ♗h6 ♖e8 19. ♖ce1△ ♗g4+−

58 19. f4± Portisch–Pfleger, Manila 1974 — 18/354

59 11. ♗e2 ♗b7 12. f3 ♗e5 13. ♕d2 ♕b8 14. g3 h5 15. f4? ♗c3 16. ♕c3 f6 17. ♗f3 ♗c6∓

Levčenkov—Kapengut, SSSR 1971 — 11/295; 12. ♘d5=

60 12... ♕b8 13. 0—0! ♗e5 14. g3△ f4± Kapengut

61 **13... ♘c5**? 14. b4! ♗c3 15. ♖c3 ♘e4 16. ♗e4 ♗e4 17. ♗h6+—; **13... a6** 14. b3 ♗c6 15. ♕d2 b5 16. c5± Kušnir—Gaprindašvili, Tbilisi (m) 1969 — 7/343; 14. b4±

62 14. f4 ♘c5 15. f5! ♘d7 16. b3 ♘e5 [16... ♗e5!? 17. ♕f3 e6 Kapengut] 17. ♘d5 e6 18. f6 ed5 19. fg7 ♖e8 20. cd5± Olafsson—Hübner, Wijk aan Zee 1971 — 11/294; 17. ♗g5!?

63 13... a5? 14. ♘d5±

64 Bukić—Joksić, Jugoslavija (ch) 1974 — 17/377

65 15... d6 16. ♗b1 — 10... b6

66 **16... f5**?! 17. ♘d5 ♗d5 18. ed5± Csom—Planinc, Banja Luka 1974 — 18/355; **16... ♗d4**!?±

B4 SADRŽAJ • СОДЕРЖАНИЕ B4

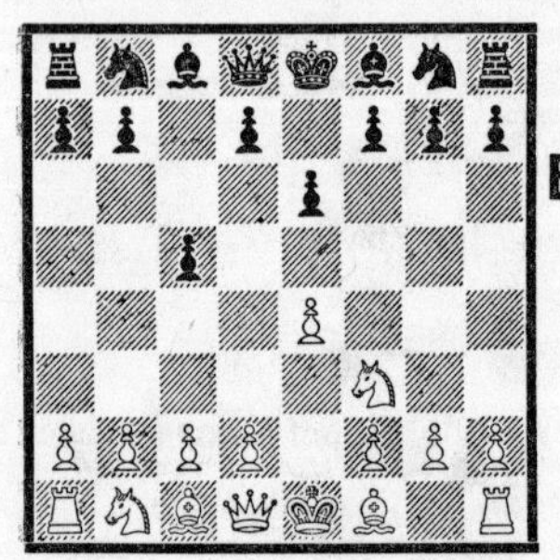

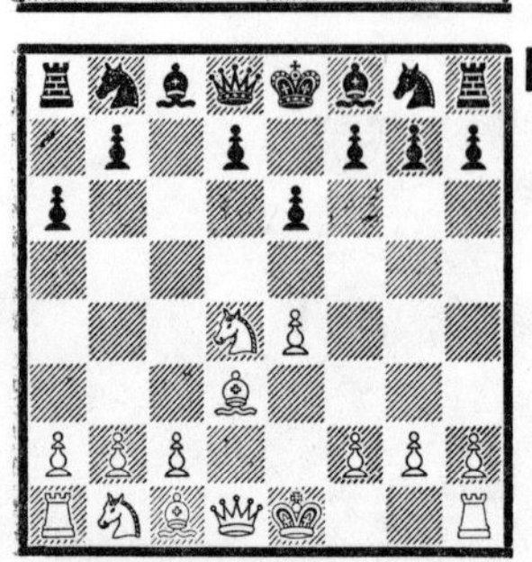

B4 SOMMAIRE • INDICE B4

B4 CONTENTS • INHALT B4

B 45

1. e4 c5 2. ♘f3 e6 3. d4 cd4 4. ♘d4 ♘c6 5. ♘c3 — **Tajmanov** 210

— 5... R ⌋ 5... ♘f6, 5... a6, 5... ♕c7
— **5... ♘f6**

B 46

1. e4 c5 2. ♘f3 e6 3. d4 cd4 4. ♘d4 ♘c6 5. ♘c3 a6 — **Tajmanov** 213

B 47

1. e4 c5 2. ♘f3 e6 3. d4 cd4 4. ♘d4 ♘c6 5. ♘c3 ♕c7 — **Tajmanov** 215

— 6. R ⌋ 6. ♗e2, 6. g3, 6. ♗e3
— **6. ♗e2**
— **6. g3**

B 48

1. e4 c5 2. ♘f3 e7 3. d4 cd4 4. ♘d4 ♘c6 5. ♘c3 ♕c7 6. ♗e3 — **Tajmanov** 220

— 6... R ⌋ 6... a6
— **6... a6** 7. R ⌋ 7. ♗d3, 7. ♗e2
— **7. ♗d3**

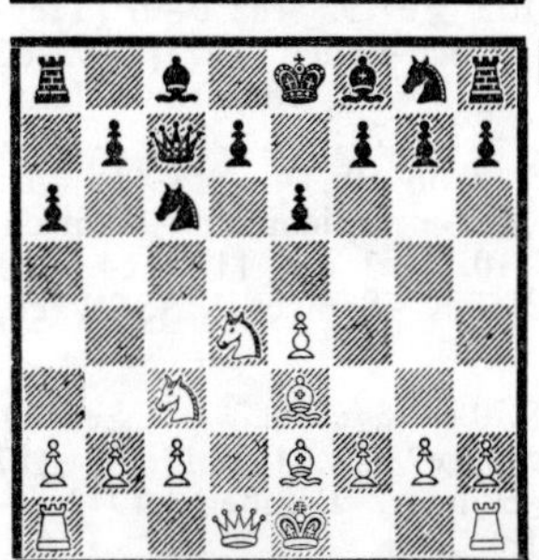

B 49

1. e4 c5 2. ♘f3 e6 3. d4 cd4 4. ♘d4 ♘c6 5. ♘c3 ♕c7 6. ♗e3 a6 7. ♗e2 — **Tajmanov** 224

B4 INDICE • INNEHÅLL B4

B 40	**1. e4 c5 2. ♘f3 e6**								
	3	4	5	6	7	8	9	10	11	
1	d4[1] cd4[2]	♘d4 ♗b4[3]	♗d2[4] ♗e7	♘c3 ♘c6	♘b3[5] ♘f6	♗d3 0–0[6]	f4 ♘b4	0–0 ♘d3	cd3 d6[7]	∞

1. e4 c5 2. ♘f3 e6 3. d4 cd4 4. ♘d4 ♘f6

	5	6	7	8	9	10	11	12	13	
2	♗d3[8] ♘c6[9]	♘c6[10] dc6[11]	♗f4[12] ♘d7	♘d2 e5	♗g3 ♗d6	♘c4 ♗c7	♕f3 0–0	0–0 ♕e7	c3 ♘c5[13]	=
3	♘c3 ♗b4	♗d3[14] e5[15]	♘f5[16] 0–0	♘e3[17] d6![18]	0–0 ♗e6	♗d2 ♗c5				=
4	. . . . . .	e5 ♘e4[19]	♕g4 ♕a5	♕e4 ♗c3	bc3 ♕c3	♔d1 ♕a1	♘b5 d5[20]	♕b4[21] ♘a6[22]	♘d6 ♔d7[23]	±
5	. . . . . .	. . . . . .	. . . . . .	♕g7 ♗c3	bc3 ♕c3	♔e2 ♘c6[24]	♘b5 ♘d4[25]	♘d4 b6	♗e3 ♕a1[26]	+–
6	. . . . . .	. . . . . .	. . . ♘c3	♕g7 ♖f8	a3 ♘b5[27]	ab4 ♘d4	♗g5 ♕b6	♗h6 ♕b4	c3 ♘f5[28]	±
7	. . . . . .	. . . ♘d5	♕g4[29] ♔f8[30]	a3[31] ♗a5	♗d2 ♘c3	bc3 ♕c7	♕g3 ♘c6	f4 ♘d4	cd4 ♗d2[32]	±

[1] **3. b4** cb4 4. d4 d5 5. e5 ♘c6 6. a3 ba3 7. c3 a6 8. ♘a3 ♗d7 9. ♗d3 b5∓ Boleslavski; **3. ♘c3** ♘c6 4. g3 — B 23; 4. ♗b5 — B 30; 4. d4 cd4 5. ♘d4 — B 45; **3. d3** d5 4. ♘bd2 — A; **3. ♕e2** ♘c6 4. g3 — C 00; **3. ♗e2** ♘c6 [3. . . ♘f6!? Tartakower] 4. d4 cd4 5. ♘d4 ♘f6 6. ♘c3! ♗b4 7. 0–0 0–0= Tarrasch–Sämisch, Wien 1922; 6. . . ♗e7!? Maroczy; **3. b3** — B 20; **3. c3** ♘f6 4. ♗d3 [4. e5 ♘d5 5. d4 — B 22] d6 5. ♗c2 ♕c7 6. d4 ♘c6 7. dc5 dc5 8. 0–0± Makaričev–Georgadze, Tbilisi 1973; 3. . . d5 4. ed5 ♕d5 [4. . . ed5 5. d4 — B 22] 5. d4 — B 22

[2] 3. . . d5?! [Marshall] 4. ed5 ed5 5. ♗b5 [5. ♗e2 ♘f6 6. 0–0 ♗e7 7. dc5 0–0 8. ♘bd2!± Reti–Kostić, Trenčanske Teplice 1922] ♘c6 6. ♘c3± ×d5; 6. 0–0±

[3] 4. . . ♗c5?! 5. ♘b3 ♗b6 6. ♘c3 [6. ♗d3 ♘e7 7. ♘c3∞ Bellin–Basman, England 1974 — 17/348] ♘e7 7. ♗f4 0–0 8. ♗d6 f5 9. e5± Timman–Basman, Hastings 1973/74

[4] **5. c3** ♗e7 6. c4!?; **5. ♘c3** ♘f6 6. e5 — 5. . . ♗b4; 5. . . ♘c6 6. ♘db5 ♘f6 7. a3 — B 46

[5] 7. ♗e3!?

[6] △ d5

[7] 11. . . d6 [Földi–Bilek, Hungary 1970 — 9/281] 12. g4!?△ g5, ♕h5, ♖f3∞ Florian

[8] **5. e5**? ♕a5–+; **5. ♗g5**? ♕a5 6. ♗d2 ♕e5–+; 6. ♕d2 ♗b4 7. c3 ♘e4 8. cb4 ♕g5 –+; **5. ♘d2** d5! [5. . . ♘c6 6. ♘c6 bc6 7. e5 ♘d5 8. c4 ♘b4 9. ♘f3 c5 10. a3 ♘c6 11. ♗d3 ♕c7 12. 0–0!?∞ Spielmann–Reti, Karlovy Vary 1923] 6. e5 ♘fd7 7. ♗b5 [7. f4? ♘e5!–+; 7. ♘2f3!?] a6 8. ♗d7 ♗d7 9. f4 ♘c6 10. ♘2b3 a5 11. a4 ♘d4 12. ♘d4 ♕b6= Padevski–Malich, Bulgaria 1967 — 4/394

[9] 5. . . d5!? 6. e5 [6. ed5 ♕d5 7. 0–0 ♗d7 8. ♘f3 ♗e7 9. ♘c3 ♕h5=] ♘d7 7. ♗f4 ♘c6 8. ♘f3 ♕b6∞ Tartakower

[10] **6. c3**? ♕b6!∓ Marshall; **6. ♗e3**?! d5 7. ♘d2 e5 8. ♘c6 [8. ♘f3 h6!? 9. c3 ♗e7 10. 0–0 0–0 11. ♕e2 ♗e6∓↑⊞ Aljehin] bc6 9. 0–0 ♗e7 10. h3 0–0∓ Fajbisovič–Gendler, SSSR 1971

[11] 6. . . bc6 7. 0–0 d5 [7. . . ♗e7?! 8. e5 ♘d5 9. ♕g4 g6 10. ♘d2± Lasker–Bogoljubov, New York 1924; 7. . . e5 8. ♘d2 ♗e7 9. ♘c4 d6 10. f4±] 8. ♘d2 ♗e7 9. ♕e2 0–0 [Treybal–Bogoljubov, Baden-Baden 1925] 10. b3 ♘d7 11. ♗b2 ♘c5= Lechtynsky–Honfi, Luhačovice 1971 — 11/273; 10. c4!?; 8. ed5! cd5 9. c4 [9. ♘c3 ♗d6 10. f4 ♗c5 11. ♔h1 0–0 12. ♘a4 ♗e7= Spielmann–Sämisch, Wien 1922] ♗b7 10. ♘c3 dc4 11. ♗c4 ♕d1 12. ♖d1 a6±⊥ Židkov–Šamkovič, SSSR (ch) 1972

[12] 7. ♘d2 e5 8. 0–0 ♕c7 9. ♘c4 ♗e6 10. ♕e2 ♘d7?! 11. c3 ♗e7 12. f4 f6 13. f5 ♗f7 14. b4± Hort–Hübner, Bamberg 1972 — 13/341; 12. . . b5!?

[13] 14. ♗c2 a5= Smislov–Spaski, SSSR (ch) 1973 — 16/286

[14] **6. ♗g5**? ♗c3 7. bc3 ♕a5∓ Tartakower; **6. ♘db5** 0–0 [6... ♘c6 — B 45] 7. a3 ♗c3 8. ♘c3 d5 9. e5 ♘fd7 10. f4 b6 11. ♗e3 ♗a6 12. ♘b5 ♘c5= Boleslavski

[15] **6... ♘c6** 7. ♘c6! [7. ♗e3?! d5 8. ed5 ♘d5 9. 0–0 ♘e3 10. fe3 ♘d4 11. ed4 ♕d4 12. ♔h1 ♗c3 13. bc3 ♕c5!∓ Tartakower] dc6 [7... bc6 8. e5 ♘d5 9. ♕g4 ♕a5 10. 0–0! →] 8. e5 ♘d7 9. ♕g4 ♕a5 10. 0–0! ♗c3 11. bc3 ♕e5 12. ♗f4 ♕f6 13. ♖ae1 ±→ Spielmann–Tartakower, Moravska Ostrava 1923; **6... d5** 7. ed5 ♘d5 8. ♘e2 ♘c6 9. 0–0 e5 10. ♘d5 ♕d5 [Euwe–Aljehin, Pistyan 1922] 11. ♘g3∞

[16] 7. ♘e2 d5 8. ed5 ♘d5 9. 0–0 ♘c6 10. ♘d5 ♕d5 11. a3 ♗a5 12. b4 ♗c7 13. ♖e1 f5∞ Yates–Aljehin, Haag 1921

[17] 8. ♗g5 d5! 9. ed5? e4!∓

[18] 10... ♗c3 11. bc3 b6 [△ ♗b7 Tartakower] 12. ♗a3 ♖e8 13. c4±

[19] 6... ♕a5? 7. ef6! ♗c3 8. bc3 ♕c3 9. ♕d2 ♕a1 10. c3 ♕b1 11. ♗d3 ♕b6 12. ♗a3 [12. fg7 ♖g8 13. ♕h6+–] gf6 13. ♘b5+– Oskam–Mühring, Nederland 1933

[20] 11... ♔d8 12. c3!±

[21] 12. ed6 ♘a6 [12... 0–0 13. ♘c7 ♖d8 14. ♗d3 f5 15. ♕c4 ♘c6 16. ♘a8 ♖d6 17. ♖e1+–] 13. d7! ♔d7 [13... ♗d7 14. ♘d6 ♔e7 15. ♗a6 ♗c6 16. ♘f5! ♔e8 17. ♕b4+– Ćirić–Kelečević, Sarajevo 1968 — 5/353] 14. ♗c4 ♖d8 15. ♔e2±

[22] 12... ♕e5 13. f4! ♘c6 14. fe5 ♘b4 15. ♘c7 ♔d8 16. ♘a8 b6 17. ♗a3+– Primavera–Palmiotto, Italia 1967 — 3/371

[23] 14. ♗a6 ba6 15. ♘f7 ♖g8 16. ♔d2 d4 17. ♗b2 ♕a2 18. ♖a1 ♕d5 19. ♖a5±→ Euwe

[24] 10... b6 11. ♕h8 ♔e7 12. ♗a3! d6 13. ♘c6! [13. ed6? ♔d7–+] ♕c6 14. ed6 ♔d7 15. ♕b2 ♘c3 16. ♔d2 ♕d5 17. ♔c3 ♘c6 18. ♗d3 ♕a5 19. ♗b4 ♕e5 20. ♔b3 ♘d4 21. ♔a3 a5 22. ♗c3 ♕c5 23. ♔a4+– Fuchs–Kander, Leipzig 1950

[25] 11... ♕c2 12. ♔e1 ♕f2 13. ♔d1 ♖f8 14. ♗d3+–

[26] 14. ♕h8 ♔e7 15. ♕g7+–

[27] **9... ♗a5** 10. ♗h6 ♕e7 11. ♘b3+–; **9... ♕a5** 10. ♘b3 ♕d5 11. ♗d3+– Koch–Elsner, Berlin 1922

[28] 14. cb4 ♘g7 15. ♗g7 ♖g8 16. ♗f6±⊞↑ Szabo–Mikenas, Kemeri 1939

[29] 7. ♗d2 ♘c3 8. bc3 ♗a5 [8... ♗e7? 9. ♕g4 ♔f8 10. ♗d3 d6 11. f4±→] 9. ♗d3 [9. ♕g4 0–0 10. ♗h6? ♗c3 11. ♔d1 g6!∓] d6 10. ed6 ♕d6 11. ♕h5 ♕d5 12. ♕d5 ed5= Adorjan–Bednarski, Polanica Zdroj 1971 — 12/329

[30] **7... g6**? 8. ♘db5!±; **7... g5**!? 8. a3 ♗c3 9. bc3 ♕c7 10. ♕g3 ♕c3 11. ♕c3 ♘c3 12. ♗g5± Čerepkov–Jankov, Primorsko 1973; 10... ♘f4!?

[31] 8. ♗d2 ♘c6= Rellstab

[32] 14. ♔d2± Boleslavski

B 41 — 1. e4 c5 2. ♘f3 e6 3. d4 cd4 4. ♘d4 a6

	5	6	7	8	9	10	11	12	13	
1	g3 d5[1]	♘f3[2] ♘f6[3]	ed5 ed5[4]	♗g2 ♘c6[5]	0–0 ♗e7	♘c3 0–0	♘d4[6]			=
2	♗e2 ♘f6	♘c3[7] ♗b4[8]	♕d3[9] d5	e5 ♘e4	0–0 ♗c3	bc3 ♘d7	c4[10] 0–0	♕e3 ♖e8	♗a3 ♕a5[11]	∞
3	♘d2 ♘e7[12]	♗d3[13] b5?![14]	0–0 ♗b7	a4 ba4	♖a4 ♘g6	♘2b3 ♘c6	♖e1 ♘d4	♘d4 ♗d6	♕h5 ♘f4[15]	±
4	... d6	♗d3 ♘f6	0–0 ♗e7[16]	c4 0–0	b3 ♘bd7[17]	♗b2 ♕c7[18]	♖c1 b6	♕e2 ♗b7	♗b1 ♖fe8[19]	±
5	... ♘f6	e5[20] ♘d5	♗c4[21] d6	ed6 ♘f6!	0–0 ♗d6	♘2f3 0–0	♕e2 ♕c7	♗g5 ♘g4	h3 ♘e5[22]	=
6	c4 ♘f6[23]	♘c3[24] ♕c7[25]	a3!?[26] b6!?[27]	♗d3[28] ♗b7	0–0 ♘c6	♘c6 ♕c6[29]	♕e2 ♗e7	f4 ♗c5	♔h1 ♗d4[30]	±

1. e4 c5 2. ♘f3 e6 3. d4 cd4 4. ♘d4 a6 5. c4 ♘f6 6. ♘c3 ♗b4

	7	8	9	10	11	12	13	14	15	
7	♘c2[31]	bc3	♕d3[33]	f3	♗a3	♕e3	f4	♗e2	0–0	=∞
	♗c3	♕a5[32]	♕e5	d5	de4	♘c6	♕a5	e5	ef4[34]	
8	e5	♕g4	a3	bc3	♕g3	ed6[39]	♕d6	♗d2![40]	♔e2	=
	♘e4[35]	♘c3[36]	♗f8[37]	♕a5[38]	d6	♗d6!	♕c3	♕a1	♕b2[41]	
9	♗d2	e5	♗c3	♕c2[44]	ed6	♕c3	0-0-0[46]	♕e3	fe3	=
	0–0[42]	♗c3[43]	♘e4	d5[45]	♘c3	♕d6	♕f4[47]	♕e3[48]	e5[49]	
10	♗d3	♗c2[50]	0–0	♕d4	e5!?	♗f4	♘e4	♗g3	♖ad1	∞
	♘c6	♕c7[51]	♘d4[52]	♘g4	♘e5[53]	f6!	b6	♗b7	0-0-0	
11	. . .	♘c2	bc3	ed5[55]	♗a3!	♕e2	0–0[57]	c5	♘d4[59]	=
	. . .	♗c3[54]	d5	ed5	♗e6	♕c7[56]	0-0-0[58]	♖he8	♘e4[60]	
12	. . .	♘c6	e5[62]	f4	♗c2	♔d1	♘e4	♗e4	♗e3	±
	. . .	dc6[61]	♘d7[63]	♘c5[64]	♕d1	b5[65]	♘e4	♗b7	0-0-0[66]	
13	. . .	. . .	. . .	ef6	bc3	♗d2[67]	fg7	♗h6	♔f1	=∞
	. . .	. . .	♕a5	♗c3	♕c3	♕d3	♖g8[68]	♕c3	♕c4[69]	

[1] 5... ♘f6 6. ♗g2 ♕c7 7. 0–0 ♘c6 [7... d6 8. b3 ♗d7 9. ♗b2 ♘c6 10. c4 ♗e7 11. ♘c3 0–0 12. ♕d2∞ Rubinstein–Sämisch, Berlin 1922] 8. b3?! ♘d4 9. ♕d4 ♗c5 10. ♕c3 d6 11. ♗e3 e5∓ Dely–Polugajevski, Sarajevo 1964; 8. c4!?; 8. ♘c3 — B 47

[2] **6. e5** ♘c6 7. ♘c6 bc6 8. ♗g2 ♕c7 9. ♕e2 a5!∓ Koc–Polugajevski, SSSR (ch) 1962; **6. ♘d2** de4 7. ♘e4 e5 8. ♘b3 ♕d1 9. ♔d1 ♘c6 10. ♗e3 ♗g4 11. ♗e2 0-0-0 12. ♘bd2 ♗f5 13. ♗d3 ♗g6 14. a3= Averbah–Kan, SSSR 1955; **6. ♘e2**!? de4 7. ♕d8 ♔d8 8. ♘bc3 f5 9. ♗e3 b5!? [9... ♗d7? 10. 0-0-0 ♔e8 11. ♘f4 b5 12. g4!± Klavin–Koblenc, SSSR 1956] 10. 0-0-0 ♔e8∞

[3] 6... ♗c5 7. ed5 ed5 8. ♗g2 ♕e7 9. ♕e2 ♕e2 10. ♔e2 ♗f5 11. ♘c3 ♘f6 12. ♗e3 ♗e3 13. fe3 1/2 : 1/2 Ivkov–Talj, Wien 1957

[4] **7... ♕d5** 8. ♕d5 ♘d5 9. a3±; **7... ♘d5** 8. ♗g2 ♗e7 9. 0–0 0–0 10. c4 ♘b4 11. ♘c3 ♘8c6 12. ♗e3± Krutjanski–K. Grigorjan SSSR 1965

[5] 8... ♗c5!? 9. ♕e2 ♘e4 10. ♗e3 0–0 11. ♗c5 ♘c5 12. 0–0 ♘c6 13. ♘bd2 ♖e8 14. ♕d1 ♕f6 15. c3 ♗g4 16. h3 ♗f5 17. ♘b3 ♘b3 18. ab3 ♗e4= Dely–Kavalek, Szombathely 1966

[6] **11. ♗g5**?! d4 12. ♘e2 h6 13. ♗f4 ♗c5 14. ♘e5 ♘d5∓↑ Czerniak–Gheorghiu, Bucuresti 1966

[7] **6. ♗f3** ♕c7 7. 0–0 d6 8. ♗e3 [Schlechter–Mieses, Berlin 1918] ♘c6=; **6. ♘d2** d5 [6... ♕c7 7. 0–0 ♗c5 8. ♘4b3 ♗a7 9. ♔h1 d5= Padevski–Nejkirh, Bulgaria 1964] 7. e5 ♘fd7=; **6. ♕d3** e5 7. ♘b3 d5 8. ed5 ♕d5= Averbah–Osnos, SSSR (ch) 1965

[8] 6... ♕c7 — B 43

[9] 7. 0–0?! ♗c3 8. bc3 ♘e4 9. ♗f3 ♘c5 10. ♗a3 [Solovjev–Mojsejev, SSSR 1956] ♕c7 11. ♘b3 d6 12. ♕d4 e5∓

[10] 11. f3 ♘ec5 12. ♕e3 ♕c7 13. f4 b6 14. ♗a3 ♗b7∞ Suetin–Livšin, SSSR 1954

[11] 14. cd5 ed5∞ Evans–Portisch, Stockholm (izt) 1962

[12] **5... ♗c5** 6. ♘4b3 ♗a7 [6... ♗e7 7. e5] 7. e5 d6 8. ♘c4± Konstantinopoljski; **5... ♕c7** 6. ♗d3 ♘c6 7. ♘c6 bc6 8. 0–0 ♘f6 9. ♕e2 d5 10. ♖e1 a5 11. c4± Vasjukov–Banik, SSSR 1964; **5... ♘c6** 6. ♘c6 bc6 [6... dc6 7. ♗d3 — B 42] 7. e5 [7. ♗d3 e5 — B 42] d5 [7... ♕a5 8. f4 d5 9. ed6 ♗d6 10. c3 ♗f4? 11. ♘c4 ♕c7 12. ♕d4 ♗h2 13. ♖h2 ♕h2 14. ♗f4±→ Pogacs–Popov, Varna 1965] 8. ed6 ♗d6 9. ♘c4 ♗b4 [Dely–Hajtun, Hungary 1965] 10. c3±⊥

[13] 6. g3 e5?! 7. ♘4b3 d5 8. ed5 ♕d5 9. ♘c4!! ♕d1 [9... ♕h1 10. ♘d6 ♔d7 11. ♘e4 ♔e8 12. ♘d6 ♔d7 13. ♘f7 ♔e8 14. ♘d6 ♔d7 15. ♗e3 ♘d5 16. ♕g4 ♔d6 17. ♕c8 ♘e3 18. fe3 ♔e7 19. 0-0-0+– Savon–Krogius, SSSR 1964] 10. ♔d1 ♗g4 11. ♗e2 ♗e2 12. ♔e2 ♘ec6 13. ♘b6±; 6... ♘ec6!?

[14] 6... ♘bc6!?

[15] 14. ♗f4 ♗f4 15. ♘b3± Vasjukov–Savon, SSSR 1965

[16] 7... ♘c6 8. ♘c6 bc6 9. c4 ♗e7 10. ♕a4 ♕c7 11. c5 ♘d7 12. cd6 ♗d6 13. ♘f3 ♘c5 14. ♕c2 ♘d3 15. ♕d3 0–0 16. ♖d1± Saharov–Banik, SSSR (ch) 1964

[17] 9... ♘c6 10. ♗b2 ♗d7 11. ♕e2 [11. ♔h1 b5 12. f4 ♘d4?! 13. ♗d4 ♗c6 14. ♕e2 bc4 15. ♘c4 ♘d7 16. ♖ad1± Bradvarević–Damjanović, Jugoslavija 1965; 12... ♕b6 13.

♘c6 ♗c6 (Balašov—Bikov, SSSR 1965) 14. e5±] ♖e8 [Kapengut—Gipslis, SSSR 1965] 12. ♘c6 ♗c6 13. f4±

18 10... ♖e8 11. ♖c1 ♗f8 12. ♔h1 d5 13. ed5 ed5 14. ♗b1± Bagirov—Gipslis, SSSR (ch) 1963

19 14. ♖fd1±○ Kapengut—K. Grigorjan, SSSR (ch) 1971

20 **6. ♗d3**?! e5 7. ♘4b3 ♘c6 8. 0—0 ♗e7 9. c4 0—0 10. ♕e2 d6 11. ♘f3 a5 12. ♗e3 a4 13. ♘c1 ♘d7∓ Geršman—Suetin, SSSR 1965; **6. c4**?! ♘c6 7. ♘c6 dc6 8. e5 ♘d7∓

21 **7. ♗d3** ♕c7 8. 0—0?! ♕e5 9. ♘f5 ♕c7 10. ♖e1 ♘e7 11. ♕f3 ♘f5 12. ♗f5 ♘c6 13. ♗d3 ♗e7 14. ♘e4 0—0 15. ♗f4 ♕d8 16. ♘d6 f5∞ Sydor—Gipslis, Lublin 1969; **7. c4**!? ♘b4 8. a3 ♘4c6 9. ♘2f3 ♘d4 10. ♘d4 d6=

22 14. ♘e5 ♗e5= Geler—Gipslis, Sousse (izt) 1967 — 4/395

23 **5... d5**?! 6. cd5 ed5 7. e5±; **5... ♘c6**?! 6. ♘c2±; **5... d6** 6. ♘c3 ♘f6 — 5... ♘f6; **5... ♕c7** 6. a3! ♘f6 7. ♘c3 — 5... ♘f6

24 **6. ♕f3**?! ♗c5 7. ♘c2 d6 8. ♗g5 ♘bd7 9. ♘c3 h6 10. ♗h4 ♕c7∓ Keres—Boleslavski, SSSR 1958; **6. ♘d2** ♕c7△ ♘c6=; **6. ♗d3** ♘c6 7. ♘c2 [7. ♘c6 dc6 8. 0—0 e5 9. ♕c2 ♗c5 10. ♘d2 (Benkö—Smislov, Jugoslavija (ct) 1959) 0—0 11. ♘b3 ♘d7 12. ♗d2 a5 13. ♗e2 ♖e8 14. ♗g4 a4!∓ Boleslavski] d5! 8. ed5 ed5 9. 0—0 ♗e7 10. ♗f4 0—0= Olsson—Smislov, Skopje (ol) 1972 — 14/326

25 6... d6 7. ♗e2 ♘c6 [7... ♗e7 8. 0—0 0—0 9. b3 ♕c7 10. ♗b2 b6 11. f4 ♗b7 12. ♗f3 ♘c6 13. ♔h1 ♘d4 14. ♕d4±○ Adorjan—Peev, Varna 1972] 8. 0—0 ♕c7 9. b3 ♗e7 10. ♗b2 0—0 11. ♘c2 ♖d8 12. ♘e3± Aljehin—Erdely, Praha (ol) 1931

26 Aljehin; **7. ♗e3** ♗b4 8. ♗d3 ♗c3! 9. bc3 d6 10. 0—0 ♘bd7∓ Durao—Portisch, Leipzig (ol) 1960; **7. ♗d3** ♘c6 8. ♗e3 [8. ♘f3?! ♗c5 9. 0—0 ♘g4∓ Johannessen—Portisch, Halle 1963; 8. ♘de2 ♗c5 9. h3 d6 10. 0—0 0—0 11. ♗g5 ♘d7= Nej—Holmov, SSSR 1964] ♘e5 9. h3 ♗e7 10. 0—0 0—0 11. f4 ♘d3 12. ♕d3 d6 13. ♘f3 ♖d8= Selivanovski—Tajmanov, SSSR 1965; **7. ♗e2** ♗b4 8. ♘c2 [8. f3 0—0 9. 0—0 d5∓↑ Spielmann—Tartakower, Wien 1923; 8. ♕d3 ♗c3 9. bc3 d6 10. 0—0 ♘bd7∓] ♗c3 9. bc3 ♘c6 [9... ♘e4?! 10. ♕d4 ♘f6 11. ♗f4=∞] 10. f3 0—0 11. ♗a3 ♖d8 12. ♗d6 ♕a5 13. ♘b4 ♘e8 14. 0—0 ♘d6 15. ♕d6 ♕a3! 16. c5 a5 17. ♘c6 bc6 18. ♕d4 d5 19. cd6= Fischer—Portisch, Varna (ol) 1962; **7. ♘c2** b6 [7... ♘c6 8. f4 d6 9. ♗d3 ♗e7 10. 0—0 0—0 11. ♗e3± Ljubojević—Gheorghiu, Athens 1971 — 12/332] 8. ♗d3 d6 9. 0—0 ♘bd7 10. ♘e3 ♗b7 11. f3 ♗e7 12. ♗d2 0—0=

27 **7... ♘c6** 8. ♗e3 ♘d4 [8... ♗d6 9. ♖c1 ♗f4 10. ♗f4 ♕f4 11. g3 ♕c7 12. ♗g2 d6 13. 0—0 0—0 14. b4±] 9. ♗d4 ♗d6 10. ♗d3 b6 [10... ♗h2? 11. g3 ♗g3 12. fg3 ♕g3 13. ♔d2±] 11. ♕e2 ♗e5 12. ♗e5 ♕e5 13. 0—0± Kavalek—D. Byrne, USA (ch) 1973 — 16/288; **7... ♗e7** 8. ♗e2 0—0 9. 0—0 d6 10. ♗e3 ♘bd7 11. ♖c1 b6 12. b4± Spielmann—Tartakower, Marianske Lazni 1923; **7... ♘e4**!?△ ♕e5

28 8. ♗e3 ♗b7 9. f3 ♘c6 10. ♖c1 ♘e5 11. ♗e2 ♘g6 12. ♕d2 ♗e7 13. ♘a4 ♖b8 14. b4± Honfi—Tajmanov, Copenhagen 1965

29 10... ♗c6 11. ♕e2 ♗d6 12. f4 ♗c5 13. ♔h1 ♗d4 14. e5 ♗c3 15. bc3± Žilin—Bastrikov, SSSR 1957

30 **14. e5**?! ♗c3 15. bc3 ♘e4∓ Krnić—Tajmanov, Vrnjačka Banja 1974 — 17/349; **14. ♘d5**!±

31 7. ♕f3 ♘c6! [7... d6?! 8. ♘c2 ♗c5 9. ♗f4± Kuindži—Džindžihašvili, SSSR 1973; 7... ♕c7 8. ♘c2 ♗d6 9. ♗e2 ♘c6 10. ♕e3 b6 11. ♗d2 0—0 12. g4 ♗c5∞ Smislov—Olafsson, Jugoslavija (ct) 1959] 8. ♘c2 d5 9. ed5 ed5 10. cd5 ♘d5= Matanović—van Scheltinga, Beverwijk 1958

32 8... ♘e4? 9. ♕g4↑

33 9. f3 d5 10. cd5 ed5 11. e5 ♕c3 12. ♔f2 ♘fd7 13. ♗a3 ♘c6∓ Hasin—Furman, SSSR 1957

34 16. ♖f4=∞ Kurtesch—Forintos, Hungary 1966 — 1/242

35 7... ♕a5?! 8. ef6 ♗c3 9. bc3 ♕c3 10. ♕d2! ♕a1 11. ♗e2 ♘c6 [11... gf6 12. 0—0 +—] 12. fg7 ♖g8 13. ♘c6 bc6 [13... dc6 14. 0—0 ♕g7 15. g3 ♕e5 16. ♗a3 c5 17. ♖d1 ♔e7 18. ♗b2 ♕c7 19. ♕h6+—→ Nyman—Varada, corr. 1967 — 3/372] 14. 0—0 ♕g7 15. g3 d5 16. ♗a3 ♕g5 17. ♕b4 ♕d8 18. cd5 cd5 19. ♖c1=∞→ Nielsen—Arlauskas, corr. 1959

36 8... ♕a5? 9. ♕g7 ♗c3 10. bc3 ♕c3 11. ♔e2 ♕a1 12. ♕h8 ♔e7 13. ♗a3 d6 14. ♗d6 ♔d7 15. ♘e6!+— Skotorenko—Belomestnih, corr. 1967 — 3/373

37 9... ♕a5? 10. ♕g7 ♖f8 11. ♗d3 ♘e4 [11... ♗e7 12. ♗d2!] 12. ab4 ♕a1 13. 0—0+—

38 10... d6 11. ed6 e5 12. ♘f5 g6 [12... ♗f5 13. ♕f5 ♗d6 14. ♖b1! ♕c7 15. ♕e4 ♘c6 16. ♗d3 g6 17. g4 0-0-0 18. ♗e3±↑ Nyman—Šapiro, corr. 1969] 13. ♕g3 ♘c6 14. ♘h6 [14. ♘e7 ♕d6 15. ♘d5 ♘e7! 16. ♗g5 ♘d5 17. ♖d1 f6 18. ♗c1 ♕c7∓ Koch—Furman, corr. 1961] ♗d6 15. c5 ♗c5 16. ♗c4 ♖f8 17. 0—0=∞ Boleslavski

39 12. ♗f4 ♘d7 13. ♘b3 ♕b6∓ A. Zajcev—Kotkov, SSSR 1958; 12... g5!∓

40 14. ♔d1 ♕a1 15. ♗d3 ♗d7 16. ♔e2 ♘c6 17. ♘c6 ♗c6 18. ♗g5 ♕b2 19. ♔d1! ♗a4 20. ♔e1 f6 21. ♕e6= Liebert—Abrošin, corr. 1955

41 16. ♔e3 ♘c6 17. ♘c6 ♕b6 18. ♕d4! ♕c6 19. ♕g7 ♕c5 20. ♔e2 ♕c4 21. ♔e1 ♕e4 22. ♗e2 ♕b1= Berczy–Nejštadt, corr. 1959

42 **7... ♗c3**?! 8. ♗c3 ♘e4 9. ♕g4 ♘c3 10. ♕g7 ♖f8 11. bc3± Nikitin–Vasjukov, SSSR 1957; **7... ♕b6**?! 8. ♘c2 ♗c5 9. ♕f3!± Boleslavski; **7... ♘c6**?! 8. ♘c2 ♗c3 9. ♗c3 ♘e4 10. ♕g4± Ravinski–Hasin, SSSR 1957

43 8... ♘e8?! 9. ♘c2 ♗e7 10. ♗d3± Stoljar–Talj, SSSR (ch) 1957

44 10. ♗b4 d6 11. ♕e2 [11. ed6?! ♕b6 12. a3 ♘c6∓↑] ♕b6 12. ♘c2 ♘c6 13. a3 d5! 14. f3 [14. ♗f8? ♕b2→] ♘c5 15. ♕e3 d4! 16. ♘d4 ♘b4 17. ab4 ♕b4= Korčnoj–Furman, SSSR 1957

45 10... ♘c3!?△ 11. ♕c3 f6

46 13. ♖d1 e5!? 14. ♘f3 ♕g6 15. ♗d3 e4 16. ♗b1 f5 17. ♘h4 ♕e6= Unzicker–Talj, Zürich 1959

47 **13... ♕c7** 14. ♗d3 e5 15. ♘c2 ♗e6= Boleslavski–Šagalovič, SSSR 1958; **13... e5**!?

48 14... ♕c7?! 15. f4 b5 16. ♔b1± Matanović–Tajmanov, Jugoslavija–SSSR 1957

49 **15... ♘d7**= Boleslavski–Kotov, SSSR (ch) 1957; **15... e5** 16. ♘f3 ♘c6= Kavalek–Portisch, Halle 1963

50 **8. ♗e3** d5! 9. ed5 ed5 10. 0–0 ♗c3 11. bc3 0–0=; **8. ♘e2** d5! [8... ♕c7 9. 0–0 ♘e5 10. f4 ♘c4 11. ♔h1 ♗e7 12. b3⩱↻ Olafsson–Talj, Jugoslavija (ct) 1959; 9... ♘g4!? 10. ♗f4 ♗d6 11. ♗d6 ♕d6 12. ♘g3 h5∓ Mnacakanjan–Talj, SSSR 1963; 9. a3=] 9. ed5 ed5 10. cd5 ♘d5= Grečkin–Abrošin, corr. 1957

51 **8... ♕a5**?! 9. 0–0; **8... d5** 9. ed5 ed5 10. 0–0±; **8... ♘e5** 9. 0–0 ♘c4 10. ♕e2 ♘e5 11. ♔h1⩱

52 9... 0–0 10. ♗g5 ♘d4 11. ♗f6 gf6 12. ♕d4 ♕e5 13. ♕d3± Dimitrov–Popov, Bulgaria (ch) 1961

53 11... h5?! 12. ♗f4 ♗c5 13. ♕d2± Bronštejn–Boleslavski, SSSR 1958

54 8... d5?! 9. ♘b4 ♘b4 10. ♕a4 ♘c6 11. ed5 ed5 12. ♗g5±

55 10. cd5 ed5 11. e5 ♘e4 [11... ♘e5?! 12. ♗a3! ♘e4 13. 0–0 f6 14. c4 ♗g4 15. f3 ♕b6 16. ♔h1 ♗h5 17. ♕e2 0-0-0 18. cd5 ♘d3 19. ♕d3 ♘f2 20. ♖f2 ♕f2 21. ♖f1 ♕h4 22. ♘d4⩱→ Lukin–Mojsejev, SSSR 1968 — 6/429] 12. ♗e4 [12. ♗a3? ♘c3 13. ♕h5 ♘b5! ∓] de4 13. ♕d8 ♔d8 14. ♗g5 ♔c7= Volčok–Ignatjev, SSSR 1969

56 12... ♕a5 13. ♗b4 ♘b4 14. cb4 ♕c7 15. c5±

57 13. ♗f5? 0-0-0 14. ♗e6 fe6 15. ♕e6 ♔b8∓; 13... ♕e5!?

58 13... ♘e5?! 14. ♘d4± Zinn–Polster, DDR 1972

59 15. ♖fb1 ♘g4! 16. g3 ♘ge5 17. ♗a6 ♗g4 18. ♕f1 [18. ♕b5 ♖d7! 19. ♘e3 ba6∓ Oppenrieder–Mojsejev, corr. 1959] ♘f3 19. ♔g2 ♘a5∞ Mojsejev

60 16. ♗e4 de4 17. ♕e4 ♘d4 18. cd4 ♗c4 19. ♕g4 ♕d7= Hačaturov–Kan, SSSR 1955

61 8... bc6?! 9. 0–0! [9. e5?! ♕a5 10. ef6 ♗c3 11. bc3 ♕c3 12. ♗d2 ♕d3 13. fg7 ♖g8∓] e5 10. ♘a4 d6 11. c5 d5 12. ed5 ♘d5 13. ♕h5± Boleslavski

62 9. 0–0 e5 10. h3 [10. ♕c2 0–0 11. ♗g5 ♗c5 12. ♘a4 ♗d4∓ Goljak–Vasjukov, SSSR 1957] 0–0 11. ♗e3 ♗e6 12. ♘a4 ♗a5 13. ♘c5 ♗c8= Konstantinopoljski–Kan, SSSR 1952

63 9... ♕d4 10. ef6 ♗c3 11. bc3 ♕c3 — 9... ♕a5

64 **10... ♕h4**? 11. g3 ♕e7 12. ♗d2 f5 13. ef6± Ravinski–K. Grigorjan, SSSR 1965; **10... b5**?! 11. 0–0 ♘b6 [Lejn–Kotkov, SSSR 1971] 12. cb5 cb5 13. ♗e4±↑

65 12... ♗c3 13. bc3 ♔d8 14. ♗e3 b6 15. ♖b1 ♔c7 16. ♔e2 a5 17. ♖b6! ♔b6 18. ♖b1 ♔c7 19. ♗c5 ♗a6 20. ♗d6 ♔d7 21. ♔d3± Žilin–Bikov, SSSR 1961

66 16. ♔e2 bc4 [16... c5? 17. ♗b7 ♔b7 18. ♖ac1±] 17. ♖hc1 a5 18. a3 ♗e7 19. ♗b6 ♖d7 20. ♗a5? ♖d4 21. ♔f3 c5 22. ♗b7 ♔b7= Gufeljd–Gipslis, SSSR (ch) 1966; 20. ♔e3!±

67 12. ♕d2 ♕a1 13. fg7 [13. 0–0 ♕f6 14. ♗a3 b6 15. ♖b1 ♕d8 16. ♕c3 f6 17. ♗e4 ♗b7 18. ♕e3 ♔f7∓ Tompa–Honfi, Hungary 1973 — 16/289] ♕g7 [13... ♖g8 14. ♗h7 ♕e5 15. ♔f1 ♖g7 16. ♗b2 ♕g5 17. f4= Karlson–K. Grigorjan, SSSR 1974 — 17/350; 14. 0–0!? ♕g7 15. f4⩱] 14. 0–0 e5 15. f4 ♗d7 [15... ♗h3 16. ♗e4 ♖d8 17. ♕e3± Muhin–Honfi, Suhumi 1972 — 14/328] 16. ♗b2 0-0-0 17. ♗e5 f6 18. ♗d6⩱ Nievergelt–Kupper, Schweiz 1957; 15... ♗g4!? Talj

68 13... ♕e4?! 14. ♔f1 ♖g8 15. ♗g5 ♕c4 16. ♔g1 ♕d5 17. ♗f6± Hasin–Sergijevski, SSSR 1965

69 16. ♔g1 ♕d5 17. ♕e1⩱

B 42 — 1. e4 c5 2. ♘f3 e6 3. d4 cd4 4. ♘d4 a6 5. ♗d3

	5	6	7	8	9	10	11	12	13	
1	...	♘c3[2]	♗e3[3]	♕d2	♘b3	♗h6!	h4	♗g7	♘e4	±
	g6[1]	♗g7	♘e7	d5	♘bc6[4]	0–0	de4	♔g7	h5[5]	
2	...	0–0	♘c6[7]	♕g4!?	♕g3	cd3	a4	♗g5	♗e3[8]	±
	♘e7	♘bc6[6]	♘c6	♘e5	♘d3	b5	b4	f6		
3	...	b3[9]	♗b2	0–0	c4	♕e2	♘d2	♗d4	♖ad1	±
	♘f6	d6	♗e7	0–0[10]	♗d7	♘c6	♘d4	♗c6	e5[11]	
4	...	0–0	f4[13]	♔h1[14]	♕f3	♘c3	♗e3	a4	f5	±
	...	d6[12]	♗e7	♘bd7	♘c5	0–0	♕c7	b6	e5[15]	
5	...	...	c4	♘c3	♗e3[17]	♖e1[18]	f3	♗f1	a4	±
	...	...	g6[16]	♗g7	0–0	b6[19]	♗b7	♘bd7	♕c7[20]	
6	...	...	c4[21]	♔h1	♘c6	♗e3	c5	f3	♘d2	±
	...	♕c7	♗d6[22]	♘c6	dc6	e5	♗e7	0–0	a5[23]	
7	...	♗e3[24]	0–0[25]	h3	♘d2	♘e4				∞
	♘c6	♘f6	♘e5!?[26]	d5	de4!?[27]	♘d5				
8	...	♘c6	0–0	f4[29]	♔h1	♕h5	f5	♗f4	f6	±
	...	bc6	e5[28]	♗c5	♘e7[30]	♘g6	♘f4	ef4	♗d4[31]	
9	...	...	...	♘d2[32]	♖e1[33]	c4	a3	cd5	♗b5	±
	...	...	d5	♘f6	a5[34]	♗b4	♗e7[35]	cd5	♗d7[36]	
10	...	...	...	c4	♘c3[37]	cd5	ed5	♕a4[40]	♖e1!	±
	...	...	...	♘f6	♗e7[38]	cd5	ed5[39]	♕d7[41]	♕a4[42]	
11	...	...	0–0[43]	♘d2	a4	♕f3	♘c4	♘e3	♗c4	±
	...	dc6	e5	♕c7[44]	♘f6	♗c5[45]	0–0	♖e8	♗e6[46]	
12	...	...	f4	f5[48]	a4	♗e3[49]	♘d2	♕e2	♕f2	±
	...	...	e5[47]	b5	♗b7	♘f6	♕c7	♘d7	♗e7[50]	
13	...	c3[51]	♗e3	♕b3[54]	♘d2	cd4	♗d4	♘f3	0–0	$\overline{\infty}$
	♗c5	♘c6[52]	♕b6[53]	♕a7	♘d4	♗d4	♕d4	♕a7	♘e7[55]	
14	...	♘b3	0–0[57]	♕e2[58]	♗e3	c4[61]	♕e3	c5!	♕d3	±
	...	♗b6[56]	♘c6	♘ge7[59]	♘e5[60]	♗e3	♕c7	♘d3	b6[62]	
15	...	...	♕g4[63]	♕g3[64]	♘c3[65]	0–0	♔h1[67]	♗g5	♗h4	∓
	...	♗a7	♘f6	d6	♘c6	♘e5[66]	h5![68]	h4	♘h5[69]	
16	...	...	0–0	c4[70]	♘c3	♕e2	♔h1[73]	♗d2	♖ac1	=
	...	...	♘c6	♘ge7[71]	0–0[72]	e5	d6	♗e6	♖c8[74]	
17	...	...	...	♕e2	♗e3	♕e3	c4[75]	♖d1[76]	♘c3	±
	...	...	...	d6	♗e3	♘f6	0–0	♕c7	♘e5[77]	
18	...	...	...	...	♗e3[78]	♕e3	c4[81]	♘c3	♖fd1	=
	...	...	...	♘ge7	♗e3[79]	e5[80]	0–0	d6	♗e6[82]	
19	...	...	♕e2	♘c3[83]	♗e3	♕e3	0-0-0	f4	♖hg1	±
	...	...	♘c6	d6	♗e3	♘f6	♕c7[84]	♖b8	b5[85]	

[1] **5... b5**?! 6. 0–0 ♗b7 7. ♕e2 [7. a4 ♘c6 8. ♗e3 b4 9. ♘c6 ♗c6 10. ♕e2 ♗b7 11. ♘d2 ♘f6 12. ♖fd1 ♗e7 13. ♘c4± Klavin–Barenbaum, SSSR 1959] ♘e7 8. a4 b4 9. ♘d2 ♘bc6 10. ♘4b3 ♘g6 11. f4± Matanović–Tajmanov, Jugoslavija 1965; **5... ♕c7** 6. 0–0 ♘c6 [6... b5?! 7. a4 b4 8. c3±] 7. ♘c6 ♕c6 8. ♘d2± Lutikov–Kikiani, SSSR 1964

[2] 6. 0–0 ♗g7 7. ♗e3 [7. ♗e2?! ♘e7 8. ♘c3 0–0 9. ♗g5 d6= Ivkov–Gipslis, Sousse (izt) 1967] ♘e7 8. c4 d5 9. cd5 ed5 10. ♘c3 0–0 11. ed5 ♘d5 12. ♘d5 ♕d5 [Majgmar-

suren–Gipslis, Sousse (izt) 1967] 13. ♗e2△ ♗f3±

3 **7. ♘de2**!? ♘c6 8. 0–0 d6 9. f4 ♘f6 [9... ♘ge7] 10. f5±↑ Barczay–Vasjukov, Berlin 1968 — 6/432; **7. ♘f3**!? ♘c6 8. ♗f4 d6 9. ♕d2 e5 10. ♗g5 f6 11. ♗e3 ♗e6 12. 0–0 ♘ge7 13. ♖fd1 0–0 14. ♗e2 ♘c8 15. ♘d5 ±↑⊞ Bobolovič–Suetin, SSSR 1966

4 9... de4? 10. ♘e4 f5 11. ♘d6! ♔f8 12. ♗c4 b5 13. ♗e2 ♘bc6 14. ♗f3 ♖b8 15. 0-0-0± Kapengut–K. Grigorjan, SSSR (ch) 1971

5 14. 0-0-0± Suetin–Mojsejev, SSSR 1970 — 9/283

6 6... ♘ec6?! 7. ♘b3 ♗e7 8. f4 [8. ♘c3 d6 9. f4 b5 10. ♔h1 ♘d7 11. ♕g4 0–0 12. ♗d2± Parma–Larsen, Beograd 1964] d6 9. ♘1d2 ♘d7 10. ♘f3±↑» Kurajica–Popov, Batumi 1966 — 2/330

7 **7. ♗e3** ♘d4 [7... ♘g6 8. ♘c3 (Lejn–Bronštejn, SSSR (ch) 1966/67) d6±] 8. ♗d4 ♘c6 9. ♗e3 ♗e7 10. c4 b6 11. ♘c3 0–0 12. f4 ♗c5 13. ♗c5 bc5= Pogacs–Haag, Hungary (ch) 1964; **7. ♘b3**!?

8 Bednarski–Bañas, ČSSR 1972

9 6. ♗e3 e5 7. ♘f3 [7. ♘b3 d5 8. ♘1d2 ♘c6= Suetin–Korčnoj, SSSR 1964] d5 8. ♘bd2 ♘c6 9. ♗g5 ♗e7= Talj–Vladimirov, SSSR 1963

10 8... ♘bd7 9. ♘d2 ♘c5 10. ♕f3 0–0 11. ♖ad1± Wade–Gligorić, Reykjavik 1964

11 14. ♗c3 ♘d7 15. ♗c2 b5 16. f4±↑ Kapengut–Džindžihašvili, SSSR (ch) 1971

12 6... d5? 7. e5 [7. ed5 ♘d5 8. c3 ♗c5 9. ♘f3± Capablanca–Tartakower, Wien 1914] ♘fd7? 8. ♘e6+–

13 7. ♕e2 ♕c7 — 6... ♕c7

14 8. ♘f3!? e5 9. ♔h1 ef4 10. ♗f4 ♘c6 11. c4 ♗g4 12. ♘c3 0–0 13. ♗e2± Kurajica–L. Popov, Wijk aan Zee 1974 — 17/351

15 14. ♘b3 [Tukmakov–Šamkovič, SSSR (ch) 1972 — 14/330] ♘d3 15. cd3 ♗b7 16. ♖ac1 ♕d8 17. d4 ed4 18. ♘d4± Tukmakov

16 7... ♗e7 8. ♘c3 0–0 9. ♕e2 ♗d7 10. f4 ♘c6 11. ♘c2 [11. ♘f3 e5 12. ♘d5 ♗g4∞ Suetin–Džindžihašvili, SSSR 1972; 12. f5!?] e5 12. f5± Murej–Bikov, SSSR 1967

17 **9. ♕e2** 0–0 10. ♗g5 b6 11. ♖ad1 ♕c7 12. ♔h1 ♗b7 13. f4 ♘bd7 14. f5 ♖ae8∞ Holmov–Gipslis, SSSR (ch) 1967 — 3/377; **9. ♖e1** 0–0 10. ♗f1 ♘c6 11. ♗e3 ♘g4 12. ♘c6 ♘e3 13. ♘d8 ♘d1 14. ♖ad1 ♖d8 15. e5± Geler–Savon, SSSR 1966; 11... ♕c7!?±

18 10. ♗e2 b6 11. ♕d2 ♗b7 12. f3 ♕c7 13. ♖fd1 ♖d8 14. ♘c2 ♘e8 15. ♗d4±○ Matulović–Ćirić, Jugoslavija (ch) 1967 — 3/378

19 10... ♘bd7 11. ♗f1 d5?! 12. ed5 ed5 13. cd5 ♘b6 14. d6!± Gheorghiu–Gipslis, Moskva 1967 — 3/379

20 14. a5±○ Geler–Gipslis, SSSR (ch) 1967 — 3/375

21 **7. ♘d2** ♗c5 8. ♘2b3 ♗a7 9. c4 d6 10. ♗g5 ♘bd7= S. Garcia–Suetin, La Habana 1968; **7. ♕e2** d6 [7... ♗d6 8. ♔h1 ♘c6 9. ♘c6 dc6 10. f4 e5 11. a4±] 8. c4 [8. f4 ♘bd7 9. c4 ♗e7 10. ♘c3 0–0 11. ♔h1± Penrose–Darga, Enschede 1963] g6 9. ♘c3 ♗g7 10. ♗e3 0–0 11. ♖ac1 ♘c6 12. ♘c6 bc6 13. f4± Karpov–Hübner, Leningrad (izt) 1973 — 15/324

22 **7... ♘c6** 8. ♘c6 dc6 9. f4 e5 10. ♔h1 ♗g4 11. ♕c2 0-0-0= Murej–Talj, Suhumi 1972 — 14/331; 10. f5!?±; **7... d6** 8. ♖e1 ♘c6 9. ♘c6 bc6 10. b3 ♗e7 11. ♗b2 e5 12. c5±↑ Mecking–Juarez, Sao Paulo 1972 — 13/343

23 14. ♕c2± Beljavski–Smislov, SSSR (ch) 1973 — 16/291

24 6. ♘b3 ♘f6 7. ♘c3 d5=

25 7. ♘c3 e5! 8. ♘de2 d5= Ragozin–Kotov, SSSR 1959

26 **7... d5** 8. ed5 ♘d5 9. ♘c6 bc6 10. ♗d4±; **7... ♕c7** 8. ♘d2 [8. ♘c6 bc6 9. c4 c5 10. ♘c3 ♗b7 11. f4 d6 12. ♕e2 ♗e7= Korčnoj–Panno, Siegen (ol) 1970] ♗d6 [8... ♘d4 9. ♗d4 ♗c5 10. ♗f6 gf6 11. ♕g4±→] 9. ♔h1 ♗f4 10. ♗f4 ♕f4 11. g3 ♕c7 12. ♘c6 bc6 13. f4 d5 14. ♕e2±↑

27 9... b5 10. a4 b4 11. f4⇆ Dückstein–Schmid, Bamberg 1968

28 7... d6 8. ♕e2 ♘f6 9. ♘d2 ♕c7 10. b3 ♗e7 11. ♗b2 e5 12. f4±↑ Geler–Hort, Sousse (izt) 1967 — 4/400

29 **8. ♘d2** d6 9. b3 ♗e7 10. ♗b2 ♘f6 11. ♘c4± Jimenez–Korčnoj, La Habana 1969; **8. c4** ♘f6 9. ♘c3 ♗e7 10. b3 0–0 11. ♗b2 d6 12. ♕d2 ♗e6 13. ♖ad1 ♘d7 14. ♗e2± Bronštejn–Vasjukov, SSSR 1971

30 9... ef4?! 10. ♗f4 ♘e7 11. ♕h5±

31 14. fg7 ♗g7 15. ♖f4 ♕e7 16. ♘c3± Ravinski–Vorotnikov, SSSR 1963

32 **8. ed5** cd5 9. c4 ♘f6 [9... dc4?! 10. ♗e4!±] 10. cd5 — 8. c4; **8. ♕e2** ♘f6 9. ♗g5 ♗e7 10. ♘d2 0–0 11. f4 [11. ♖ad1 ♘d7= Holmov–Vladimirov, Leningrad 1967 — 4/399] ♖e8 [11... ♘d7 12. ♗e7 ♕e7 13. c4 ♘c5 14. ♗c2 a5 15. ♖ae1 ♗a6 16. ed5 cd5 17. f5 ±→» Holmov–Mojsejev, SSSR (ch) 1970] 12. ♔h1 h6 13. ♗h4 ♗b7 14. c4 de4 15. ♘e4 ♘e4 16. ♗e7 ♘g3= Boleslavski

33 **9. ♕e2** a5!? [9... ♗e7 10. ♖e1 0–0 11. b3 a5?! 12. ♗b2 a4 13. a3! ab3 14. cb3 ♕b6 15. ed5 cd5 16. b4± Smislov–Talj, Jugoslavija (ct) 1959; 11... ♘d7!? 12. ♗b2 ♘c5] 10. ♖e1 [10. b3 ♗b4!?] ♗e7 11. b3 a4 12. a3 ♕b6 13. ♗b2 ab3 14. cb3 ♗a6!= Boleslavski; **9. b3** ♗b4 10. ♗b2 [10. ed5?! ♗c3 11. ♖b1 cd5 12. ♗b2 ♕c7∓ Robatsch–Portisch, Varna (ol)

1962] a5 [10... ♗d2 11. ♕d2 de4 12. ♕g5!±] 11. c3 ♗e7 12. c4 0–0 13. ♕c2 h6∞ Spaski–Petrosjan (m) 1967 — 7/318

34 9... ♗e7 10. e5 ♘d7 11. ♕g4± Geler

35 11... ♗d2 12. ♗d2 de4 13. ♗e4 ♘e4 14. ♖e4±

36 14. ♗d7 ♕d7 15. e5 ♘g8 16. ♕g4± Geler–Vasjukov, SSSR (ch) 1969 — 8/307

37 9. cd5 cd5 10. ed5 ♘d5 [10... ♕d5 11. ♘c3 ♕d7 12. ♗g5 ♗e7 13. ♕e2 ♗b7 14. ♖ac1 0–0 15. ♖fd1± A. Mihaljčišin–Gorčakov, SSSR 1972] 11. ♗e4 ♖a7 [11... ♗e7 12. ♘c3 ♗b7 13. ♕a4 ♕d7 14. ♕d7 ♔d7 15. ♖d1 ♖ad8 16. ♘d5 ♗d5 17. ♗d5 ed5 18. ♖d5 ♔e6 19. ♖d8 ♖d8 20. ♗e3 ♗f6 21. ♖e1± Matanović–Roos, Le Havre 1966 — 1/244; 15... ♗f6 16. ♘d5 ♗d5 17. ♗d5 ed5 18. ♖d5 ♔e6 19. ♖d2 ♖hd8 20. ♖e2 ♔f5 21. ♗e3± Averbah–Tajmanov, SSSR (ch) 1960] 12. ♗d5 ♕d5 13. ♕d5 ed5= Parma–Pachman, Mar del Plata 1962

38 **9... d4** 10. ♘e2 e5 11. f4±; **9... dc4** 10. ♗c4 ♕d1 11. ♖d1 ♖b8 12. ♖b1 e5 13. ♗e3 ♗b4 14. f3 ♔e7 15. ♘a4 ♘d7 16. ♖bc1± Parma–Udovčić, Amsterdam 1963

39 11... ♘d5 12. ♗e4 — 9. cd5

40 12. ♗e3 0–0 13. ♗d4 ♕d6 [13... ♗e6 14. ♖e1 ♕a5 15. a3 ♖ab8 16. ♕e2 ♖b3 17. ♗c2 ♖b7 18. b4± Matanović–Ree, Titovo Užice 1966] 14. h3 ♗e6 15. ♖e1 ♘d7± Parma –Suetin, La Habana 1969

41 12... ♗d7 13. ♕d4 0–0 14. ♗g5±↑⊞

42 14. ♘a4 ♗e6 15. ♗e3±⊥ Fischer–Petrosjan (m) 1971 — 12/335

43 7. ♘d2 e5 8. ♘c4 [8. ♕h5 ♗d6 9. ♘c4 ♘f6 10. ♕g5 0–0 11. 0–0 ♗c7= Larsen–Kavalek (m) 1970 — 9/284] ♘f6 [8... ♘e7 9. ♗e3 ♘g6 10. ♘b6 ♖b8 11. ♘c8 ♖c8 12 g3± Gipslis–Mojsejev, SSSR 1971] 9. ♗e3 ♗e6∞⇆

44 **8... ♗c5**?! 9. ♘c4 ♕c7 10. ♕h5 ♗d4 11. c3 g6 12. ♕f3 ♗a7 13. a4 b5 14. ♘e3± Szabo–Forintos, Hungary 1959; **8... ♘e7** 9. ♘c4 ♘g6 10. ♕h5 ♕c7 11. ♗e3 ♗e7 12. a4± Atanasov–Spasov, Bulgaria 1971; **8... ♗d6** 9. a4 [9. ♘c4 ♗c7 10. ♗e3 ♗e6 11. ♕e1 b5 12. ♘d2 ♘f6 13. ♘b3 ♗b3 14. ab3± Kaplan–Bobocov, Skopje (ol) 1972 — 14/333] ♘e7 10. ♘c4 [10. ♗c4 ♘g6 11. ♘b3 0–0 12. ♗e3 ♘f4 13. f3 ♗e6 14. ♗e6 ♘e6= Geler–Polugajevski, SSSR 1959] ♗c7 11. a5 ♗e6 12. ♗d2±

45 10... h5 11. ♘c4 ♗e6 12. a5 ♗c5 13. ♗e3 ♗e3 14. ♕e3 ♗c4 15. ♗c4 0-0-0± Parma –Damjanović, Jugoslavija (ch) 1960

46 14. ♗e6± Keres–Talj, Jugoslavija (ct) 1959

47 7... ♗c5?! 8. ♕e2 ♘e7 9. ♘d2 ♘g6 10. g3 0–0 11. e5± Kavalek–Kuijpers, Amsterdam 1968 — 6/433

48 8. 0–0 ♗c5 9. ♔h1 ♘f6 10. f5± Bednarski–Doda, Lublin 1972

49 10. ♕e2 ♕c7 11. ♗e3 ♖c8 12. ♘d2 ♘f6 13. 0–0 ♘d7 14. ♕f2± Ciocaltea–L. Popov, Wijk aan Zee 1974 — 17/355

50 14. 0–0± Matulović–L. Popov, Zagreb 1973 — 15/325

51 6. ♗e3 d6 7. 0–0 [7. ♘c3 ♘e7 8. 0–0 ♘d7 9. ♕e2 b5 10. a4 ♕b6= Geler–Filip, Curaçao (ct) 1962] ♘d7 8. ♘d2 ♘gf6 9. f4 0–0 10. ♔h1 e5 11. ♘f5 ♗e3 12. ♘e3 ef4= Keres–Vladimirov, SSSR (ch) 1964

52 **6... ♘e7** 7. 0–0 0–0 8. ♕h5 d6 9. ♘d2 ♘d7 10. ♘2b3± Geler–Tajmanov, SSSR (ch) 1969 — 8/308; **6... d5**!? 7. ♘d2 ♗d4 [7... ♘f6? 8. e5 ♘fd7 9. ♘2f3± Haag–Capelan, Budapest 1972] 8. cd4 de4 9. ♘e4 ♘c6∞

53 7... ♗a7 8. ♘d2 ♘f6 9. 0–0 0–0 10. ♘2f3± Kurajica–Gerusel, Wijk aan Zee 1973 — 15/326

54 8. ♘d2?! ♕b2 9. 0–0 ♕c3 10. ♘2b3 ♗a7∓

55 14. ♕a3=∞

56 6... ♗e7 7. 0–0 d6 8. c4 ♘f6 9. ♘c3 0–0 10. ♗e3 ♘bd7 11. f4 b6 12. ♕f3 e5 13. f5± Bednarski–Matanović, Kecskemet 1964

57 7. ♘c3 ♘c6 8. 0–0 [8. ♕e2 ♘ge7 9. ♗e3 0–0 10. 0-0-0 a5 11. a4 ♗e3 12. ♕e3 d5 13. e5 ♘b4 14. ♘d4 ♘ec6∞ Campos–Portisch, San Antonio 1972] ♘f6 9. ♕e2 d6 10. ♔h1 0–0 [Andersson–Portisch, Raach 1969 — 8/309] 11. f4△ ♗d2±

58 **8. ♗f4**?! d6 9. c4 e5! 10. ♗d2 ♕h4 11. ♘c3 ♘f6 12. ♕f3 ♗g4 13. ♕g3 ♕g3= Biyiasas–Smislov, Petropolis (izt) 1973; **8. c4** d6 9. ♘c3 ♘f6 10. ♔h1△ f4±

59 8... d6 9. ♗e3 [9. ♘1d2?! ♘f6 10. ♘c4 ♗c7△ b5=] ♘f6 10. c4 [10. ♗b6 ♕b6 11. ♘1d2 0–0 12. ♔h1 e5 13. f4 ♗g4 14. ♕e1 ef4 15. ♖f4 ♘e5= Ostojić–Portisch, Wijk aan Zee 1969 — 7/320] 0–0 11. ♘c3 ♗e3 12. ♕e3 b6 13. ♖fd1± Parma–Benkö, Reggio Emilia 1971 — 11/276

60 9... 0–0 10. c4 ♗e3 11. ♕e3 e5 — 6... ♗a7

61 10. f4 ♘g4!? [10... ♘d3 11. cd3 d5= Petrosjan] 11. ♗b6 ♕b6 12. ♔h1 h5∞

62 14. cb6 ♕b6 15. ♘1d2 d5 16. e5±↑ Karpov–Tajmanov, SSSR 1972 — 13/344

63 7. c4 ♘c6 8. 0–0 ♕h4? 9. ♘1d2 ♘ge7 10. c5 ♘e5 11. ♗e2 b6 12. f4± Calvo–Korčnoj, La Habana (ol) 1966 — 2/333; 8... ♘ge7∞

64 **8. ♕g7**?! ♖g8 9. ♕h6 ♗f2∓; **8. ♕h4** ♘c6 9. 0–0 d6 10. ♘c3 ♘e5=

65 **9. ♘1d2** 0–0 10. ♘f3 e5∓ Gipslis–Tajmanov, SSSR (ch) 1964; **9. 0–0** ♘c6 10. ♔h1 0–0 11. f4 [11. ♗g5 ♘h5 12. ♕h4 f6

13. ♗d2 g6 14. f4 f5∓ Matanović–Vladimirov, Jugoslavija–SSSR 1964] ♔h8 12. ♘c3 b5 13. f5 h6 14. ♕h4 ♘e5∓↑ Parma–Vladimirov, Jugoslavija–SSSR 1964

66 **10... b5** 11. ♔h1 ♗b7 12. f4 b4 [12... 0–0 13. ♗d2 ♔h8 14. ♖ae1± van der Weide–Smejkal, Amsterdam 1971 — 12/336] 13. ♘e2 0–0 14. f5 ♘e5 15. ♗g5± Ivkov–Polugajevski La Habana 1962; **10... 0–0** 11. ♗g5 [11. ♔h1 ♕c7 12. f4 ♔h8 13. ♕h4 ♘g8 14. ♗d2 b5 15. a4 b4 16. ♘d5 ed5 17. ed5 f5∞ Bednarski–Benkö, Tel Aviv (ol) 1964] ♘h5 [11... ♘e5 12. ♗e2!] 12. ♕h4 f6 13. ♗d2 g6 14. ♖ad1± Boleslavski–Liberzon, SSSR 1968; **10... h5**!? 11. ♗e3 h4 12. ♕g7 ♖h7= Parma–Forintos, Tel Aviv (ol) 1964

67 11. ♗e3 ♘h5 12. ♕h3 ♗e3 13. ♕h5 g6 14. ♕e2 ♗h6= Jimenez–Gligorić, Moskva 1963

68 11... 0–0?! 12. ♗g5 ♔h8 13. f4 ♘d3 14. cd3± Bednarski–Bukić, Krakow 1964

69 14. ♗d8 ♘g3 15. fg3 ♔d8∓

70 **8. ♕g4** ♘f6 9. ♕g7?! ♖g8 10. ♕h6 ♘e5$\overset{=}{\infty}$→; **8. ♔h1** ♘f6 [8... ♘ge7?! 9. f4 0–0?! 10. e5± Lechtynsky–Pachman, ČSSR 1968 — 6/434] 9. f4 h5∞; **8. ♘c3** ♘ge7 9. ♕h5 ♘g6 10. ♗g5 ♕c7 11. ♖ae1 0–0 12. ♔h1 ♘f4= Portisch–Teschner, Stockholm 1968; 9. ♕e2 — 8. ♕e2; **8. ♘1d2** ♘ge7 [8... ♘f6 9. ♘c4 d5 10. ed5 ed5 11. ♕e2 ♗e6 12. ♘e5 ♘e5 13. ♕e5 0–0 14. ♘d4 (Larsen–Ivkov, Amsterdam (izt) 1964) ♖e8!=] 9. ♘f3 ♘g6 10. ♕e2 0–0 11. ♗e3 d6 12. ♗a7 ♖a7 13. ♕e3 ♖a8 14. ♖fd1 ♕f6 15. c3 e5= Ivkov–Polugajevski, Jugoslavija–SSSR 1964

71 8... d6 9. ♘c3 ♘f6 10. ♕e2 0–0 11. ♗g5 h6 12. ♗h4 ♘e5∞ Kovacs–Polugajevski, Budapest 1965; 11. ♗e3±

72 9... ♘e5 10. ♔h1 ♕c7 11. ♕e2 0–0 12. f4 ♘d3 13. ♕d3 f5 14. ♗d2±

73 11. ♘d5 a5!=

74 14. ♘d5 ♘d4= Tukmakov–Liberzon, SSSR (ch) 1969 — 8/310

75 **11. f4** ♕c7=; **11. ♘c3** 0–0 12. ♖ad1 ♕c7 13. ♔h1 b5 14. f4 ♗b7= Padevski–Smislov, Monte Carlo 1968 — 5/354; **11. ♘1d2** e5 12. ♖fd1 0–0 13. ♗f1 d5 14. ed5 ♘d5 15. ♕c5 ♘f4 16. ♘e4 ♕h4∞ Štejn–Polugajevski, SSSR (ch) 1963

76 12. ♘c3 ♘e5 [12... e5 13. ♖fd1 ♗e6 14. ♗e2±] 13. ♗e2 ♕c7 14. ♖fd1 ♘c4?! 15. ♗c4 ♕c4 16. ♖d6± Parma–Capelan, Solingen 1968 — 7/319; 14... b6±

77 14. ♖ac1 b6 15. ♗e2 ♗b7 16. f4 ♘g6 17. g3± Karpov–Hübner, Graz 1972 — 14/334

78 **9. ♘1d2** 0–0 10. e5?! ♘g6 11. ♘f3 ♕c7 12. ♗g6 fg6 13. c3 b5 14. ♘bd4 ♗b7∓ Štejn–Tajmanov, SSSR (ch) 1964; **9. ♘c3** 0–0 10. ♗e3 ♗e3 11. ♕e3 f6!? 12. ♖ad1 b6 13. ♖d2 ♕c7 14. ♖fd1 ♘e5 15. ♘e2 g5∓ Barczay–Mašić, Sombor 1968 — 6/435

79 9... d6?! 10. c4 0–0 11. ♘c3 ♗d7 12. ♖fd1± Matulović – Korčnoj, Jugoslavija – SSSR 1966 — 1/245

80 10... d5?! 11. e5 ♕c7 12. ♖e1 ♗d7 13. ♘1d2± Parma–Korčnoj, Jugoslavija–SSSR 1964

81 11. ♘1d2 0–0 12. ♖fd1 d6 13. ♘c4 ♗e6 14. ♗f1 ♗c4 15. ♗c4 ♕c7= Vasjukov–Liberzon SSSR (ch) 1969

82 14. ♗f1 ♖c8 15. ♖d2 ♘a5= Boleslavski

83 8. ♗e3 ♗e3 9. ♕e3 ♘ge7 10. ♘1d2 0–0 11. 0-0-0 d6 12. f4 b5 13. e5 ♘d5 14. ♕g3 ♘cb4 15. ♘e4 de5 16. fe5 ♘a2 17. ♔b1 ♘ab4 18. ♖hf1 ♕c7 19. ♘g5 h6 20. ♗h7 ♔h8 21. c3 ♘c6 22. ♗e4 ♘e5 23. ♘f7 ♖f7 24. ♖f7 ♕f7 25. ♕e5$\overset{=}{\infty}$ Gurgenidze–Zurahov, SSSR 1964

84 11... 0–0 12. f4 ♕c7 [12... e5 13. f5 b5 14. ♗e2± Christoph–Hollis, Hastings 1965/66 — 1/246] 13. ♖hg1 b5 [13... ♘b4 14. g4 e5 15. ♗e2 d5 16. ed5 ef4 17. ♕c5+– Spaski–Gerusel, Dortmund 1973 — 15/327] 14. g4 ♗b7 15. g5± Gerusel

85 14. g4±

B 43 — 1. e4 c5 2. ♘f3 e6 3. d4 cd4 4. ♘d4 a6 5. ♘c3

	5	6	7	8	9	10	11	12	13	
1	...	♗e2[2]	♗f3[3]	0–0[5]	♘b3	♗h5	♗e3	f4	♗g4	=
	b5[1]	♗b7	♘c6[4]	♘ge7	♘g6	♗e7	d6	0–0	♖e8[6]	
2	...	♗d3	0–0	♘c6	♕g4[9]	♕e2	f4	♗e3	♖ad1	±
	...	♘e7[7]	♘bc6[8]	♘c6	h5[10]	d6	♗e7	♗d7	g6[11]	
3	...	...	0–0[12]	♘a4[14]	♖e1	e5	c4	♘c5	♗e3	±
	...	♗b7	b4[13]	♘f6	d5	♘e4	♘c5	♗c5	♘d7[15]	
4	...	...	...	♗g5[16]	♗e3!	♘c6[18]	e5[20]	f4	♗c5	±
	...	...	♘e7	h6[17]	♘ec6	dc6[19]	♘d7[21]	♘c5	♗c5[22]	

	5	6	7	8	9	10	11	12	13	
5	... ...	... ...	... ...	♕h5 ♘bc6[23]	♘c6[24] ♗c6[25]	♗f4 ♘g6	♗g3 ♕b6	a4 b4	♘d5 ♗d5[26]	±
6	... ...	... ...	... d6	♖e1[27] ♘f6[28]	a4 b4	♘a2 ♗e7	♗g5[29] a5	c3 bc3	♘c3[30]	±

1. e4 c5 2. ♘f3 e6 3. d4 cd4 4. ♘d4 a6 5. ♘c3 ♕c7

	6	7	8	9	10	11	12	13	14	
7	g3[31] b5[32]	♗g2 ♗b7[33]	0—0 ♘f6[34]	♖e1[35] d6	a4[36] b4[37]	♘d5 ed5	ed5 ♔d8	♗g5 ♗c8[38]	♗f6 gf6[39]	±
8	... ♘f6	♗g2 ♗e7	0—0 0—0	f4[40] d6	g4 ♘c6[41]	♘c6[42] bc6	g5 ♘e8[43]	f5 ef5	ef5 d5[44]	∞
9	♗e2 ♘f6[45]	f4[46] ♗b4[47]	e5 ♘e4[48]	0—0 ♘c3	bc3 ♕c3	♘b3 ♕c7	♗b2[49] ♘c6	f5! ♗e7!?	f6 gf6[50]	∞
10	... ...	0—0 ♗b4[51]	♕d3[52] ♘c6[53]	♘c6[54] dc6[55]	f4 0—0	e5 ♖d8	♕h3 ♗c3	bc3 ♘d7	♗e3 c5[56]	±
11	... b5	♗f3[57] ♗b7	0—0 ♘c6[58]	♘c6[59] dc6	a4[60] ♗d6	ab5 cb5	e5 ♗e5	♘b5 ab5	♖a8 ♗a8[61]	=
12	f4 b5[62]	a3 ♗b7	♗d3[63] ♘c6[64]	♘b3[65] d6	0—0 ♘f6	♕e2 ♗e7	♗e3[66]			±
13	♗d3 b5[67]	f4[68] ♗b7	♕e2 d6[69]	♘b3 ♘d7	♗d2 ♗e7	0—0 ♘gf6	♖ae1 e5[70]	f5 ♘b6	g4 h6	∞
14	... ...	0—0 ♗b7	♕e2[71] ♘f6[72]	a4[73] b4	♘a2 ♘c6	c3 d5	♘c6 de4	♘cb4 ed3	♘d3 ♗d6[74]	=∞
15	... ...	... ...	♖e1 ♘c6[75]	♘c6 ♕c6	a4 b4	♘d5! ♘f6	♗d2 ♘d5	ed5 ♕c5	♗e4 f5[76]	±
16	... ...	... ...	... d6	♗g5![77] ♘f6[78]	♗f6 gf6	♘d5 ed5	ed5 ♔d8	♕f3 ♗e7[79]	♘f5 ♖e8[80]	±
17	... ♘c6	♘c6[81] bc6	0—0 ♘f6	♕e2[82] d5[83]	♗g5[84] ♗b7	f4[85] ♗e7	e5 ♘d7	♗e7 ♔e7	♘a4[86] c5[87]	±

[1] 5... **♗c5** 6. ♗e3 ♗a7 7. ♗e2 ♘e7 8. 0—0± Trajković—Ristić, corr. 1968 — 3/380; **5... ♘e7** 6. ♗g5 f6?! 7. ♗e3 ♘bc6 8. ♘b3± Kavalek—Cvetkov, Polanica Zdroj 1964; **5... ♗b4** 6. ♗d3 [6. ♗d2 (Averbah—Usačij, SSSR 1955) ♘c6=] ♘c6 7. ♗e3±; **5... d6** 6. ♗e2 ♘f6 — B 84

[2] **6. f4** ♗b7 7. a3 ♘f6 8. ♗d3 [Kirpičnikov—Gipslis, SSSR 1966] ♗c5∓; **6. g3** b4 7. ♘a4 [7. ♘ce2? ♗b7 8. ♗g2 f5!?; 7. ♘b1 ♗b7 8. ♗g2 ♘f6= S. Nikolić—Suetin, Titovo Užice, 1966 — 2/334] ♗b7 8. ♗g2 ♘f6 9. ♕e2 ♘c6= Zinn—Portisch, Halle 1967 — 3/381; **6. a3** ♗b7 7. g3 ♘f6 8. ♗g2 d6 [8... ♗e7 9. 0—0 d5 10. ed5 ♘d5 11. ♘d5 ♗d5 12. ♘f5∞ Goldenov—Ilivicki, SSSR 1963] 9. 0—0 ♘bd7 10. ♖e1 ♕c7= Keres—Reshevsky, Amsterdam (izt) 1964

[3] 7. a3 ♕c7 8. 0—0 ♘f6 9. ♕d3 d6 10. ♗g5 ♘bd7= Evans—Talj, Amsterdam (izt) 1964

[4] 7... ♕c7 — 5... ♕c7

[5] **8. ♘c6** ♗c6 9. 0—0 ♘e7 10. a4 ♘g6= Haag—Szabo, Hungary 1964; **8. ♗f4** d6 9. ♘c6 ♗c6 10. 0—0 [Steiner—Glauser, Schweiz 1966 — 1/247] ♗e7=

[6] Štejn—Gipslis, SSSR 1965

[7] **6... b4**?! 7. ♘a4 ♗b7 8. 0—0 — 6... ♗b7; **6... ♗c5** 7. ♘b3 ♗a7 8. ♕f3 ♘c6 9. ♕g3 ♔f8 10. ♗f4± Bogdanović—Flesch, Pécs 1964; **6... d6** 7. 0—0 ♘f6 8. ♖e1 [8. ♗d2 ♗b7 9. ♕e1± Minić—Kavalek, Bucuresti 1966 — 1/248] ♗e7 9. a4 b4 10. ♘a2 e5 11. ♘f3 ♘c6 12. c3 bc3 13. ♘c3 ♗e6 14. ♘g5± Hort—Portisch, Sousse (izt) 1967

8 7... ♘ec6 8. ♘b3 d6 9. ♗e3 ♘d7 10. f4 ♗e7 11. ♕f3 ♕c7 12. ♖ae1± Hecht—L. Popov, Dortmund 1973 — 15/328

9 9. ♖e1 ♗e7 10. ♘d5 ♗d6 11. ♕g4 0—0 12. e5?! ♗e5 13. ♗g5 f5!∓ Mosionžik—Polugajevski, SSSR 1966 — 2/336; 12. ♗f4=

10 9... d6 10. f4 h5 11. ♕f3 ♗d7 12. ♗d2± Pavlov—Korčnoj, Bucuresti 1966 — 1/250

11 14. ♔h1±↑» Gheorghiu—Vaisman, Romania 1971

12 **7. a3** ♗c5 [7... d6 8. ♗e3 ♘d7 9. 0—0 ♘gf6 10. f4 g6 11. ♕f3± S. Nikolić—Kavalek, Sarajevo 1967 — 3/383] 8. ♘b3 ♗a7=; **7. ♗e3** ♘e7 8. f4 [8. 0—0 — 7. 0—0] ♘ec6 9. ♘f3 ♗e7 10. ♕e2 d6 11. 0-0-0∞ Tukmakov—Hübner, Barcelona 1965

13 **7... ♗c5** 8. ♘b3 ♗a7 9. a4 b4 10. ♘a2 ♘c6 11. a5± Zuidema—Szabo, Beograd 1964; **7... ♘c6** 8. ♘c6 [8. ♘b3 ♘f6 9. f4 d6 10. ♗e3 ♗e7 11. ♕f3 ♕c7 12. ♖ae1± Ghizdavu—Ljubojević, Bucuresti 1970 — 9/288] ♗c6 9. ♕e2 d6 10. a4 b4 11. ♘d5± Karklins—Evans, USA 1973 — 16/296

14 8. ♘d5!? ed5 9. ed5 ♗d5 10. ♖e1 ♗e7 11. ♘f5 ♘c6 12. ♘g7 ♔f8 [Estrin—Šackes, SSSR 1967 — 3/386] 13. ♘h5⩱

15 14. ♕g4 ♕b6 15. ♖ac1 0—0 16. ♕h4 g6 17. ♘f3± Bihovski—Suetin, SSSR 1966

16 **8. f4**?! ♕b6 9. ♗e3 ♘ec6 10. ♘ce2 ♗c5 11. c3 b4∓↑; **8. e5** ♘g6 [8... ♘ec6 9. ♘f3 d6 10. ed6 ♗d6 11. ♘e4± Eisinger—Hübner, BRD 1965] 9. ♖e1 ♘c6 10. ♘c6 ♗c6 11. ♕h5 ♕h4 [11... ♕c7 12. a3 ♗e7 13. ♗d2± Boleslavski—Liebert, Hamburg 1965] 12. ♕h4 ♘h4 = Kotkov—Gipslis, SSSR 1966; **8. a4** b4 9. ♘ce2 ♘ec6 10. ♘c6 ♘c6 11. f4 ♗e7= I. Szabo—Damjanović, Hamburg 1965; **8. ♗e3** ♘bc6 [8... ♘ec6 9. ♔h1 d6 10. f4 ♘d7 11. ♕f3± Kinnmark—Gerusel, Halle 1967 — 3/382] 9. ♘b3 [9. ♔h1 ♘d4 10. ♗d4 ♘c6=] ♘a5 10. ♘a5 ♕a5= Padevski—Tajmanov, Budapest 1965; **8. ♖e1** ♘g6 [8... ♘bc6 9. ♘c6 ♘c6 10. ♗f4 d6= Gufeljd—Tajmanov, SSSR (ch) 1965] 9. a4 b4 10. ♘d5 ♗c5 [10... ♗d6 11. ♕h5± Gligorić—Szabo, Beograd 1964] 11. ♘b3 ♗d6 12. ♘e3 ♕c7= Bihovski—Polugajevski, SSSR 1965; **8. ♔h1** ♘ec6 9. ♘c6 ♘c6 10. f4 ♕c7 11. ♗d2 ♘a5 12. b3± Haag—Szilagyi, Pécs 1964

17 8... b4 9. ♘ce2 ♕a5 10. f4 ♘bc6 11. ♔h1 f6 12. ♘b3± Liberzon—Čerepkov, SSSR 1965

18 10. ♘b3 ♗e7 [10... d6 11. f4 ♗e7 12. f5± Bokučava—Gipslis, SSSR 1965] 11. f4 0—0∞

19 10... ♘c6 11. f4 ♕c7 12. e5±

20 11. ♕g4 ♘d7= Meštrović—Ćirić, Sarajevo 1967 — 3/385

21 11... c5?! 12. ♗e4±⊥ Hübner—Gligorić, Oberhausen 1965

22 14. ♔h1±

23 8... ♘g6 9. ♘f3 ♘c6 10. ♗e3 ♕c7 11. ♘g5± Novopašin—Ruderfer, SSSR 1966

24 9. ♘f3!?△ ♘g5

25 9... ♘c6 10. ♗g5 ♗e7 11. ♗e7 ♘e7 12. f4 0—0 13. f5± Dückstein—Polugajevski, Le Havre 1966 — 1/249; 10. ♗f4△ ♖ad1± ×d6

26 **13... ed5** 14. ed5 ♗b7 15. ♖fe1 ♔d8 16. ♗g6 fg6 17. ♕e5±; **13... ♗d5** 14. ed5 ♗e7 [Suetin—Gipslis, SSSR 1966] 15. a5 ♕c5 16. ♕e2± Boleslavski

27 **8. ♗d2** ♘f6 9. ♕e1 ♘bd7 10. a4 b4 11. ♘d1 ♘c5 12. f3± Minić—Perez, Varna 1967 — 4/402; **8. a4** b4 9. ♘a2 ♘f6 10. ♖e1 e5 11. ♘f5 ♘c6 [Fichtl—Kavalek, ČSSR 1962] 12. ♗g5±

28 8... ♘d7 9. a4 ba4 10. ♘a4 ♘gf6 11. ♗d2 ♗e7 12. ♘b3± Keres—Najdorf, Los Angeles 1963

29 11. ♘b4?! d5!

30 Tarve—L. Popov, Bulgaria 1969 — 8/312

31 **6. ♗e3**?! ♗b4 [6... ♘f6 7. ♗d3 ♗a3?! 8. ♘a4 ♗b2 9. ♘b2 ♕c3 10. ♕d2 ♕b2 11. 0—0±↻ Aghili—Mamula, Graz 1972; 7... ♘c6 — B 48] 7. ♕d3 ♘f6 8. ♗d2 ♘c6 9. ♘c6 bc6 10. a3 ♗e7 11. ♗e2 d5 12. 0—0 0—0= Kelvigs—Portisch, Varna (ol) 1962; **6. a3** ♘f6?! 7. f4 d6 8. g4 h6 9. ♗g2 ♘c6 10. h3 ♗d7 11. ♘de2 ♗e7 12. ♕d3 ♖c8 13. ♗e3 g5∞ Olafsson—Bilek, Stockholm (izt) 1962; 6... b5 7. g3 ♗b7 8. ♗g2 — 6. g3

32 **6... ♗b4**?! 7. ♘e2 ♘f6 [7... h5 8. h3 ♘f6 9. ♗g2 ♘c6 10. ♗f4 e5 11. ♗g5± Donner—Keres, Zürich 1959] 8. ♗g2 0—0 [8... ♗e7 9. 0—0 ♘c6 (Ghinda—Honfi, Timisoara 1972 — 13/347) 10. h3±; 8... d6 9. 0—0 ♘bd7 (Medina—Smislov, Las Palmas 1972) 10. h3±; 8... ♘c6 9. ♗f4±; 8... h6 9. 0—0 ♘c6 10. ♗f4 e5 11. ♗e3 d6 12. a3 ♗c5 13. ♗c5 dc5 14. ♘d5± Unzicker—Mohrlok, BRD 1959] 9. 0—0 ♗e7 [9... ♘c6?! 10. ♗f4] 10. b3 ♘c6 11. ♗b2±○; **6... ♘c6** — B 47

33 7... b4?! 8. ♘a4 e5 9. ♘e2 d6 10. ♗e3 ♘d7 11. c3 a5 12. ♖c1 ♕b8 13. 0—0± Estrin—Koblenc, corr. 1960

34 **8... b4**?! 9. ♘d5 [9. ♘a4 ♘f6 10. ♖e1 ♗e7 11. e5 ♘d5 12. ♘f5 ef5 13. ♗d5± M. Levin—Makarov, SSSR 1957] ed5 10. ed5 ♔d8 11. ♖e1 ♘f6 12. ♗g5 ♕b6 13. c3 h6 14. ♗f6 ♕f6 15. ♕e2 ♗d6 16. ♖ad1±→∓ Dimitriev—Šišov, SSSR 1971; **8... d6** 9. ♖e1 ♗e7 [9... ♘d7 10. a4 ba4 11. ♖a4 ♘gf6 12. ♘d5! ed5 13. ed5 ♘e5 14. f4 0-0-0 15. fe5 de5 16. ♖e5!± Dely—Donner, Budapest 1961] 10. a4 b4 11. ♘a2 ♘f6 12. ♗d2 a5 13. ♘b5 ♕c6 14. c3 bc3 15. ♗c3± Šmit—Mnacakanjan, SSSR 1965; **8... ♘c6** 9. ♘c6 ♗c6 [9... dc6 10. e5!?] 10. ♖e1±; **8... ♗c5**!?△ 9. ♘b3 ♗e7

35 9. a3 ♗e7 [9... ♘c6?! 10. ♘c6 ♗c6 11. ♖e1 △ ♘d5± Robatsch—Hamann, Halle 1963] 10. ♖e1 d6=

36 10. ♘d5 ed5 11. ed5 ♔d8 12. ♗g5 ♘d7 13. c4±→⊞ Hörberg—Kotov 1959

37 10... ba4 11. ♘d5 ed5 [11... ♘d5 12. ed5 e5 13. ♖a4 g6 14. ♗d2 ♗g7 15. ♗a5 ♕d7 16. ♖c4± Gligorić—Vranešić, Amsterdam (izt) 1964] 12. ed5 ♔d8 13. ♖a4 ♕d7 14. c4 ♗e7 15. ♗d2 ♔e8 16. ♖b4± Jocha—Kurajica, Jugoslavija 1967 — 4/406

38 13... ♘d7 14. ♕e2 ♔c8 15. c3 b3 16. ♘c6 ♗c6 17. dc6 ♘e5 18. ♖a3 d5 19. ♖b3 ♗d6 20. ♗f6 gf6 21. ♗d5+— Štejn—Furman, SSSR (ch) 1969

39 15. ♕h5± Quinones—Higashi, Siegen (ol) 1970 — 10/403

40 **9. ♘ce2**?! ♖d8!△ d5∓; **9. g4** ♘c6 10. ♘c6 bc6 11. g5 ♘e8 12. f4 d5 [12... d6 13. ♗e3 ♖b8 14. b3± S. Garcia—Gheorghiu, Bucuresti 1971 — 12/339] 13. ♗e3 ♖b8 14. b3 f6 15. h4∞ Timman—Enklaar, Nederland 1972 — 13/345

41 10... d5!? 11. ed5 ♗c5$\overline{\overline{\infty}}$

42 **11. g5**? ♘d4 12. ♕d4 d5!→; **11. ♘b3** b5 12. g5 ♘d7 13. a3 ♗b7 14. ♕h5 ♖fe8∞ Padevski—Nejkirh, Varna 1972 — 13/346

43 12... ♘d7 13. f5± Zuckerman—Hennings, Harrachov 1967 — 4/405

44 Browne—Quinteros, Mar del Plata 1971 — 11/277

45 **6... ♗b4**?! 7. ♕d3 ♘f6 8. ♗d2± Sanakojev—Aarset, corr. 1969 — 8/314; **6... ♘c6** — B 47

46 **7. ♗e3**?! ♗b4∓↑; **7. a3** b5 8. 0—0 ♗b7 9. ♕d3 d6 10. f4 ♘bd7= Ivkov—Portisch, Halle 1963; 7... ♘c6 — B 47

47 7... d6 8. 0—0 — B 84

48 **8... ♗c3** 9. bc3 ♕c3 10. ♕d2 ♕a1 11. ef6 ♘c6 12. fg7 ♖g8 13. c3 ♘d4 14. cd4 ♕b1 15. 0—0 ♖g7 16. f5∞ Janošević—Jansa, Sarajevo 1966 — 1/252; **8... ♘d5** 9. 0—0 ♘c3 — 8... ♘e4

49 12. ♗d3 ♘c6 13. ♗b2 b6 14. ♕e2 ♗b7 15. ♖ab1$\overline{\overline{\infty}}$ Jansa—Ree, Örebro 1966 — 2/337

50 15. ef6 ♗f8 16. ♗h5 d6∞ Jansa—Castro, Lugano (ol) 1968 — 6/438

51 **7... b5** 8. ♗f3 b4 [8... ♗b7 9. e5!] 9. e5 ♗b7 10. ♘cb5 ab5 11. ef6 gf6 12. ♘b5±→ Bachtiar—Cardoso, Skopje (ol) 1972; **7... ♘c6** 8. ♗e3 — B 49; **7... d6** — B 84

52 **8. ♗d2** ♘c6 9. ♘c6 bc6 10. ♗d3 a5= Nežmetdinov—Vladimirov, SSSR 1957; **8. ♗g5** ♘c6 [8... ♗c3 9. ♗f6 gf6 10. bc3 ♕c3 11. ♖b1 ♘c6 12. ♘c6 dc6 13. ♖b3 ♕e5 14. ♕d2$\overline{\overline{\infty}}$ Talj—Hamann, Kislovodsk 1966 — 2/338] 9. ♔h1 ♕d6= Aronin—Tajmanov, SSSR 1962

53 8... 0—0 9. ♗g5 ♘c6 10. ♘c6 bc6 11. ♗f6 gf6 12. f4 ♔h8∞ Mihaljčišin—Suetin, Sarajevo 1965; 9. ♗d2±

54 **9. a3** ♗c3 10. bc3 0—0 11. f4 d5 12. e5 ♘e4 13. ♗f3 ♘c5= Keres—Hasin, SSSR (ch) 1957; **9. ♗d2** ♕d6!=

55 9... ♕c6 10. e5 ♗c3 11. bc3 ♘d5 12. c4±

56 15. ♖f3± Olafsson—Pilnik (m) 1957

57 7. 0—0 ♗b7 8. a3 ♘f6 9. ♕d3 d6 10. f4 ♘bd7= Gheorghiu—Forintos, Soči 1964

58 8... d6 9. a4 b4 10. ♘a2 ♘f6 11. ♖e1 e5 12. ♘f5 g6 13. ♗g5 ♘bd7 14. ♘h6 ♕b6 15. c3± Boleslavski—Getman, SSSR 1965

59 9. ♖e1 ♘e5 10. ♗f4 d6=

60 10. ♗e3 ♘f6 11. a4 ♗d6 12. g3 0—0 [Tatai—Portisch, Amsterdam 1969 — 9/289] 13. ♗g2=

61 15. ♗a8 ♗h2 16. ♔h1 ♗d6= Estrin—Polugajevski, SSSR 1964

62 **6... ♗b4** 7. ♕f3 ♘f6 8. ♗d2 d6 9. a3± Madan—Cagan, Tel Aviv (ol) 1964; **6... ♘c6** 7. ♗e2 — B 47; 7. ♗e3 — B 48

63 8. ♕f3 ♘f6 9. ♗d3 ♗c5 10. ♘b3 ♗e7 11. 0—0 0—0 12. ♗d2± Talj—Filip, Curaçao (ct) 1962

64 8... ♗c5 9. ♘b3 ♗a7 10. ♕g4 ♔f8 [Haag—Liptay, Hungary 1963] 11. ♕e2±

65 **9. ♘f3** ♗c5! 10. ♕e2 ♘d4 11. ♘d4 ♗d4 12. ♗d2 ♘f6∓; **9. ♘c6** dc6 10. 0—0 c5 11. e5 ♖d8 12. ♕e2 ♘e7 13. a4 c4 14. ♗e4 ♘f5= Walther—Gligorić, Zürich 1959

66 **12. g4**?! d5! 13. e5 ♘d7 14. ♗e3 g5!?∞ Pietzsch—Portisch, Lugano (ol) 1968 — 6/437; **12. ♗e3**±

67 6... ♘f6 7. 0—0 ♗c5 [7... b5 8. a4 b4 9. ♘a2 ♗b7 10. ♖e1 ♗c5 11. ♘b3 ♗d6 12. h3 ♘c6 13. ♗e3 ♘a5 14. ♘a5 ♕a5 15. ♗d2 ♕e5∞ Zinn—Hort, Polanica Zdroj, 1964; 10. ♕e2±] 8. ♘b3 [8. ♗e3 d6 9. ♕e2 b5 10. ♘b3 ♗e3 11. ♕e3 0—0 12. ♖ad1 ♗b7 13. ♖d2 ♘bd7 14. ♖fd1 b4 15. ♘e2 d5= Bisguier—Bilek, Stockholm (izt) 1962] ♗a7 9. ♗g5 ♘c6 [9... ♕e5?! 10. ♕d2 ♘h5 11. ♔h1 h6 12. ♗e3 g5 13. ♘a4! ♕c7 14. c4± Radulov—Quinteros, Leningrad (izt) 1973 — 15/ 332] 10. ♔h1 b5 11. f4 d6∞; 9. ♕e2△ ♗e3±

68 7. a3?! ♗c5=

69 **8... b4** 9. ♘d1 ♘f6 10. ♘f2 ♗c5 11. ♘b3 ♗f2 12. ♔f2 d5= Matanović—Vladimirov, Moskva 1963; **8... ♗c5** 9. ♘b3 ♗a7 [9... ♗e7 10. ♗d2 ♘c6 11. a4 b4 12. ♘d1 ♘f6 13. ♘f2 0—0 14. g4± Minić—Kurajica, Batumi 1966] 10. e5 f5 11. ♗e3 ♗e3 12. ♕e3 ♘e7∞ Kavalek—Flesch, Beograd 1965

70 12... 0–0?! 13. e5!±

71 **8. ♔h1** d6 9. f4 ♘d7 10. ♕e2 [Palermo–Cuasnicu, Buenos Aires 1968 — 6/439] ♘gf6 =; **8. ♗e3** ♘f6 9. ♘b3 ♘c6 — B 48

72 **8... ♘c6** 9. ♘c6 ♕c6 [9... dc6 10. a4 b4 11. ♘d1 c5 12. ♘e3± Krogius–Korčnoj, SSSR 1958] 10. ♘d5 [10. a4 b4 11. ♘d5 ♘f6 12. c4 bc3 13. ♘c3 ♗b4= Gipslis–Kotov, SSSR (ch) 1958] ♘f6 11. c4±; **8... d6** 9. a4 b4 10. ♘a2 ♘f6 11. ♗d2 d5 12. ed5 ♘d5= Lejn–Kotkov, Soči 1965

73 **9. ♗d2** ♘c6 10. ♘c6 ♕c6 11. a3 ♗c5= Boleslavski–Kotov, SSSR 1958; **9. ♗g5** ♘c6 10. ♘c6 ♕c6 11. ♗f6 gf6 12. ♘d5 f5∞

74 Boleslavski

75 **8... ♗c5** 9. ♗e3 ♘e7 [9... ♘f6 10. ♘db5! ab5 11. ♘b5 ♕c6 12. ♗c5 ♕c5 13. e5± Keres–Benkö, Curaçao (ct) 1962] 10. ♕h5 e5 11. ♘db5 ab5 12. ♘b5 ♕b6 13. ♗c5 ♕c5 14. b4 ♕c6 15. ♕e5± Keres–Ojanen, Helsinki 1960; **8... ♗d6** 9. ♕h5 ♘f6 [9... ♕c5 10. ♕c5 ♗c5 11. ♘b3 ♗b6 12. a4±⊥ Aronin–Koblenc, corr. 1961] 10. ♕h4± ♘c6? 11. ♘db5 ab5 12. ♘b5 ♕b8 13. ♘d6 ♕d6 14. e5 ♘e5 15. ♕g3 ♖a5 16. ♗f4+– Nikitin–Šofman, SSSR 1966; **8... ♘f6** 9. e5 ♘d5 10. ♗d2 ♘c3 11. ♗c3 ♘c6 12. ♘c6 ♗c6 [Đurašević–Tajmanov, Jugoslavija–SSSR 1958] 13. ♕g4±; 9. ♗g5±

76 15. ♗f3 ♗d5 16. ♗b4 ♗f3 17. ♕f3 ♕c8 18. ♗c3 ♔f7 19. ♖ad1± Talj–Gipslis, SSSR (ch) 1958

77 9. a4 ba4 10. ♖a4± Nilsson–Napolitano, corr. 1969 — 7/322

78 **9... ♗e7** 10. ♗e7 ♘e7 [10... ♕e7 11. ♘f5!] 11. ♗b5! ab5 12. ♘db5 ♕b6 13. ♘d6 ♔f8 14. ♘b7+–; **9... h6** 10. ♗h4 g5 11. ♗g3 ♗g7 12. ♗b5!+– Dünnhaupt–Keller, corr. 1966 — 1/254

79 **13... ♘d7** 14. ♘c6+–; **13... f5** 14. ♕f5 ♗g7 15. ♕g5 f6 16. ♘e6 ♔c8 17. ♕g4 h5 18. ♕h3+– Ghizdavu–Covaci, Romania 1970 — 9/287

80 15. ♘e7 ♖e7 16. ♕f6 ♗d5 17. ♗e4 ♗e4 18. ♖e4 d5 19. ♖d1 ♖a7 20. ♖e3!±→ Rogoff–Fuler, Bognor Regis 1969

81 **7. ♘de2** ♘f6 8. 0–0 ♗e7 [8... b5 9. a3 ♗b7 10. ♗f4 d6= Blau–Gligorić, Zürich 1959] 9. f4 d6 10. ♔h1 0–0 11. ♕e1 b5 12. a4 b4= Keres–Tajmanov, SSSR 1957; **7. ♗e3** ♘f6 — B 48; **7. ♘b3** ♘f6 8. f4 d6 9. ♗e3 ♗e7 — B 82

82 **9. f4** d5 10. ♕f3 ♗b7= Walter–Talj, Zürich 1959; **9. ♗g5** ♗e7 10. ♔h1 d5 11. f4 h6 12. ♗h4 de4 13. ♘e4 ♘e4 14. ♗e7 ♘g3 15. hg3± Ceškovski–Anikajev, SSSR 1967 — 3/387; 11... ♗b7∞

83 9... e5 10. f4 d6 11. ♘d1 ♗e7 12. fe5 de5 13. ♘e3± Lutikov–Hamann, Kislovodsk 1966; 10... ♗d6!? Mikenas–Kotov, SSSR 1958

84 10. f4 ♗e7 11. ♗d2 0–0 12. ♖ae1 ♖e8 13. ♔h1 ♗f8= Spaski–Liptay, Marianske Lazni 1962

85 11. ♗f6 gf6∞

86 14. ♖ae1 g6∞

87 15. c4± Spaski—Petrosjan, Palma de Mallorca 1969 — 8/315

B 44

1. e4 c5 2. ♘f3 e6 3. d4 cd4 4. ♘d4 ♘c6

	5	6	7	8	9	10	11	12	13	
1	c4[1] ♘f6	♘c3 ♗b4	♘c6[2] bc6[3]	♗d3 e5[4]	0–0 0–0	♗d2 ♗e7	♕e2 d6[5]			=
2	♘b5 d6[6]	c4 a6	♘5c3 ♘f6	♗e2 ♗e7	0–0[7] 0–0	b3!?[8] ♕a5[9]	♗b2 ♖d8	a3 ♗d7	♕d3[10]	±
3	... ...	... ♘f6	♘5c3 ♗e7	♗e2 0–0	0–0 b6	♗f4[11] ♗b7	♘d2 ♖c8[12]	♖e1 a6[13]	♖c1 ♖e8!?[14]	∞
4	... ...	... ...	♘1c3 a6[15]	♘d4 ♗e7	♗e2 0–0	0–0 ♗d7	♗e3[16] ♘d4[17]	♕d4 ♗c6	f3 ♕b8![18]	=

1. e4 c5 2. ♘f3 e6 3. d4 cd4 4. ♘d4 ♘c6 5. ♘b5 d6 6. c4 ♘f6 7. ♘1c3 a6 8. ♘a3 ♗e7 9. ♗e2 0—0 10. 0—0

	10	11	12	13	14	15	16	17	18	
5	... ♗d7[19]	♗e3 ♖b8[20]	f4[21] ♕a5	♘c2 b5	cb5 ab5	a3[22]				±
6	... b6	f4[23] ♗b7	♗f3[24] ♖c8	♗e3 ♘a5	♕d3 ♕c7	♖ac1 ♘d7	♕d2 ♖fd8	♘d5 ed5	cd5 ♕b8[25]	=

	10	11	12	13	14	15	16	17	18	
7	...	♗e3	f3[26]	♖f2[27]	♘c2	a4	♗f1	♖d2[28]		±
	...	♗d7	♕b8	♖a7	♖b7	♖d8	♗e8			
8	...	...	♖c1	f3[29]	♕e1	cd5	♘d5	ed5	d6	=
	...	♕c7	♕b7	♖d8	d5	ed5	♘d5	♘b4	♗d6[30]	
9	...	...	♕d2[31]	f3[32]	♖fd1	♖ac1	♕e1	♕f2		=
	...	♗b7	♘e5	♖b8[33]	♕c7	♖fc8[34]	♗a8	♕d8[35]		
10	...	...	♕b3	♖fd1	♕c2[36]	♖ab1[37]	♕d2	bc3	♕b2	=
	...	...	♘d7	♘c5!	♗f6	♘b4!?	♗c3[38]	♘e4	♘a2[39]	
11	...	...	f3	♕b3[41]	♖fd1	♕c2	♖ab1[42]	♕d2	♘c2	=
	...	...	♖e8[40]	♘d7	♘c5	♗f6	♘b4	d5	♘c2[43]	
12	...	...	♖c1	♕d4[45]	♖fd1[47]	♘c2	f3	cd5	ed5[50]	=∞
	...	...	♘e5[44]	♘ed7[46]	♖e8[48]	♖c8[49]	d5!	ed5	♗d6[51]	
13	...	...	...	f3	♗d4	♕d2	♖fd1	♗f1	♗e3	±
	...	...	...	♖c8[52]	♘g6	♕c7	♘d7	♕b8	♖fd8[53]	
14	...	...	...	♕d2	♕d4	♖fd1	♘c2	♔h1	f3	=
	...	...	♖c8	♘e5	♘ed7	♖e8	♕c7	h6[54]	d5[55]	

1. e4 c5 2. ♘f3 e6 3. d4 cd4 4. ♘d4 ♘c6 5. ♘b5 d6 6. ♗f4 e5[56]

	7	8	9	10	11	12	13	14	15	
15	♗e3[57]	♗g5[58]	♗f6[59]	♘5c3	♕h5[61]	♗c4	♘d2	♔e2	♖a1![63]	±
	♘f6	a6?!	gf6	f5[60]	♘d4[62]	♕c7	♘c2	♘a1	b5[64]	
16	...	...	♕d2[65]	♕a5	♗e3	♘1c3[67]	♘c3	♘d5[69]	0-0-0	±
	...	♕a5	♘e4	♘a5	♔d7[66]	♘c3	♔c7[68]	♔b8	♗e6[70]	
17	...	...	♘1c3[71]	♗f6[72]	♘a3	♘d5[74]	ba3	♕d2	♔d2	=∞
	...	♗e6	a6	gf6	d5![73]	♗a3	♕a5	♕d2	0-0-0[75]	
18	...	...	♘d2	♗f6	♘c4	♕d6	c3	♗c4	♘a3	±
	...	...	♗e7[76]	♗f6	0—0	♕c8	♗c4	a6	♕g4[77]	
19	...	♘5a3	♘c3	♘d5	♘f6[81]	♘b1	♘c3	♗d4[83]	♘d5	=
	a6	♘f6[78]	b5[79]	♖b8[80]	♕f6	♗b7![82]	♘d4	ed4	♗d5[84]	
20	...	♘5c3	♗c4[85]	♘d5[86]	♗d5	♘a3	♘c4	ef5	c3	∞
	...	♘f6	♗e7	♘d5	0—0	♔h8[87]	f5	♗f5	♕e8[88]	

1 **5. a3** ♘f6 6. ♘c3 d6=; **5. ♗e2** ♘f6 6. ♘c3 ♗b4=; **5. g3** d5 6. ♗g2 de4=; **5. ♗e3** ♘f6 6. ♗d3 [6. ♘c3 ♗b4=] d5 7. ♘c6 bc6 8. e5 ♘d7 9. f4 ♗a6= Keres—Vladimirov, SSSR (ch) 1961; **5. ♘c6** bc6 6. ♗d3 d5=

2 7. f3 d5 8. cd5 ed5 9. ♗g5 ♕a5 10. ♘c6 bc6 11. ♗f6 gf6= Teller—Tartakower, Hastings 1926/27

3 7... dc6 8. ♕d8 ♔d8 9. ♗d2 e5=

4 8... d5 9. ed5 ed5 10. ♗g5 0—0=

5 Czerniak—Najdorf, Mar del Plata 1942

6 5... ♘f6 6. ♘1c3 d6 7. ♗f4 e5 8. ♗g5 a6 — B 33; 6... ♗b4 — B 45

7 9. ♗e3 0—0 10. f4?! d5!? 11. e5 d4 12. ef6 ♗f6 13. ♗f2 dc3 14. ♘c3 ♕c7 15. 0—0 ♖d8∓ Filipowicz—Hort, Polska 1971 — 11/304

8 10. ♗e3 ♖b8 [10... ♕c7?! 11. ♘a3 b6 12. ♕e1 ♗b7 (Dieks—Marjanović, Manila 1974 — 18/360) 13. ♖c1!△ f3, ♕f2± Marjanović; 10... ♗d7 11. f4 ♕b8 12. ♘d2 ♗d8?! 13. c5± Stanciu—Tajmanov, Bucuresti 1973; 11. ♘d2 ♕b8 12. ♘a4! ♗d8 13. ♘b6± Boleslavski; 10... ♕a5 11. a3 ♖d8 12. ♖a2! ♗d7 13. b4 ♕c7 14. f4±↑ Čabrilo—Krnić, Jugoslavija 1973 — 15/351] 11. ♘d2 [11. ♕d2 b5! 12. cb5 ab5 13. ♘b5 ♘e4=; 11. f3 ♖e8 12. ♕d2 d5! 13. cd5 ed5 14. ♘d5 ♘d5 15. ed5 ♗f6= Nikitin] ♖e8 12. a3 ♘d7 13. b4 b6= Honfi—Korčnoj, Gyula 1965

9 10... ♗d7 11. ♗b2 ♖b8 12. ♕d3 b5 13. ♘d2± Ljubojević

10 Ljubojević—Janošević, Vršac 1971 — 12/378

11 **10. f4** ♗b7 11. ♗f3 ♖c8 [11... a6 12. ♗e3 ♖b8 13. ♘a3 ♘d7 14. ♖c1 ♗a8 15. ♕e2 ♖e8 16. ♖fd1 ♗f8 17. ♘c2± Ljubojević–Hartoch, Wijk aan Zee 1973 — 16/337] 12. b3 ♕c7 13. ♔h1 ♖fd8∞ Tatai–Jansa, Madonna di Campiglio 1973 — 15/352; **10. b3** ♗b7 11. ♗b2 a6 [11... ♖c8 12. ♘d2 ♘d7 13. f4 ♗f6 14. ♘f3 ♘c5 15. ♕d2 ♗c3 16. ♕c3± Krogius–Spaski, SSSR (ch) 1962] 12. ♕d3 [12. ♘d2 ♘d7=] d5!= Ljubojević–Polugajevski, Petropolis (izt) 1973 — 16/335

12 **11... d5** 12. cd5 ed5 13. e5 ♘e4 14. ♘de4 de4 15. ♗c4 ♘d4 16. ♗e3± Ljubojević–Castro, Manila 1973 — 17/389; **11... a6**!? 12. a3 [12. ♖c1 ♘d4 13. ♗d3 b5! 14. cb5 ♘b5 15. ♘b5 ab5 16. ♕b3 ♘d7 17. ♗b5 ♘c5 18. ♕c4 d5! 19. ed5 ed5 20. ♕c2 ♖a2∓↑« Diez del Corral–Kavalek, Montilla 1973] ♘d4 13. ♗d3 ♘d7 14. ♗e3 ♗f6= Ljubojević–Karpov, Madrid 1973 — 16/308

13 12... ♕c7 13. ♖c1±

14 **13... ♘e5** 14. a3 ♖e8 15. b4± Ljubojević–Polugajevski, Las Palmas 1974 — 17/390; **13... ♖e8**!?∞

15 7... ♗e7 8. ♗f4±

16 **11. ♘c2** ♕c7 12. b3 b5 13. cb5 ♘a7 14. ♗b2 ♘b5 15. ♘b5 ab5 16. ♗d3 ♕b7= Pelitov–Liebert, Albena 1973; **11. ♘b3** ♖c8 12. ♗f4 ♘e5 13. ♘d2 ♗c6 14. ♖e1 ♘g6 15. ♗g3 ♕b6= Savon–Tajmanov, SSSR (ch) 1973

17 **11... ♖b8** 12. a4 ♕c7 13. ♖c1 ♖fd8 14. g4 ♗e8 15. g5 ♘d7 16. ♘c2 ♕a5 17. f4± Kuindži–Furman, SSSR 1972; **11... ♕b8** 12. ♘b3 b6 13. ♘d2 ♖a7 14. a3 ♖d8 15. b4 ♘e5 16. f4 ♘g6 17. ♕e1± Kuzmin–Hartston, Hastings 1973/74 — 17/388

18 **13... d5**?! 14. cd5 ed5 15. e5± Bronštejn–Talj, SSSR 1973 — 15/350; **13... ♕b8**! 14. a4 [14. ♕d3 b5 15. cb5 ab5 16. ♘b5 d5= Korčnoj–Krogius, SSSR (ch) 1962] d5 15. ed5 [15. cd5 ed5 16. e5 ♘d7 17. f4 ♗c5 18. ♕d2 ♕a7 19. ♗c5 ♕c5 20. ♔h1 d4∞; 16. ed5 ♖d8 17. ♗c4 b5=] ed5 16. c5 ♘d7 17. b4 ♗f6 18. ♕d2 ♕e5=

19 10... ♖b8 11. ♗f4 [11. ♗e3 ♕a5 12. ♖c1 ♖d8 13. ♕b3 ♘d7 14. ♖fd1 ♘c5 15. ♕c2 ♗d7 16. ♕b1 ♗e8= Vasjukov–Korčnoj, SSSR (ch) 1966/67 — 3/421; 12. ♕e1 ♖d8 13. ♖d1 ♗d7 14. f3 ♗e8 15. ♔h1 ♘d7 16. ♗f4 ♘c5 17. ♖d2± Adorjan–Langeweg, Wijk aan Zee 1972] b6 12. ♕d2 ♗b7 13. ♖fd1 ♘e5 14. f3 ♕c7 15. ♖ac1 ♖fd8 16. ♔h1 [Štejn–Tajmanov, SSSR 1969 — 9/314] ♗c8! △ ♗d7±

20 **11... ♘a7** 13. ♗d3 ♕b8 13. ♕e2 ♖e8 14. ♖ac1 ♗d8 15. ♔h1 ♗c6 16. f4 e5 17. f5± Vasjukov–Tajmanov, SSSR (ch) 1967 — 5/382; **11... ♕b8** 12. f3 b6 [12... ♗d8 13. ♕d2 ♗c7 14. ♔h1 b6 15. ♖fd1 ♘e8 16. ♘c2± Ivkov–Petrosjan, Palma de Mallorca 1968 — 6/463] 13. ♕e1 ♖a7 14. ♕f2 ♖b7 15. ♖fd1 ♘b4 16. ♖d2 ♖d8 17. ♖ad1 ♗e8 18. f4 ♘d7 19. ♘ab1 ♘c6 20. a3 ♘f6 21. g4!± Kapengut–Balašov, SSSR (ch) 1971 — 12/377; 15... ♘e5!? Boleslavski; **11... ♕a5** 12. ♕b3 [12. ♕e1 ♖fe8 13. ♖d1 ♖ad8 14. f3 ♗c8= Karpov–Kuzmin, SSSR 1972] ♖fc8 13. ♖fd1 ♗e8 14. c5 dc5 15. ♘c4 ♕b4 16. ♘b6 ♘a5 17. ♕b4 cb4 18. ♘b1 ♘e4 19. ♘d2 ♘d2 20. ♖d2± Štejn–Bobocov, Moskva 1967 — 3/420; **11... ♘e5** 12. f3 ♗c6 13. ♗d4 ♘g6 14. ♕d2 ♕a5 15. ♖fd1± Geler–Bukić, Skopje 1968 — 6/464; **11... b6** — 10... b6

21 **12. ♕d2** ♕a5 13. ♖fd1 ♖fd8 14. ♖ac1 ♗e8 15. ♔h1 ♘d7 16. f3 ♘c5 17. ♗f1 ♗f6= Vasjukov–Polugajevski, SSSR 1966 — 2/365; **12. ♖c1** ♕a5 13. f4 [13. ♕c2 ♖fc8 14. ♕b1 ♘e5 15. ♗d2 ♘g6 16. ♘c2 b5 17. b4 ♕b6 18. cb5 ab5 19. ♗e3 ♕b7 20. ♘d4 d5= Savon–Averkin, SSSR (ch) 1973] ♖fd8 14. ♕d2 ♗e8 15. ♖fd1 ♘b4 16. ♕e1 b5 17. ♔h1 ♖dc8∞ Spaski–Averkin, SSSR (ch) 1973 — 16/333

22 ± ×b5 Boleslavski

23 11. ♘c2 ♗b7 12. b3 ♕c7 [12... ♖c8 13. ♗b2 ♖e8 14. ♔h1 ♘d7= Muhin–Boleslavski, SSSR 1965] 13. ♗b2 ♖fd8 14. ♖c1 ♖ac8 15. ♕d2 ♘e5= Bogdanović–Pachman, Titovo Užice 1966

24 12. ♗e3 d5 13. cd5 ed5 14. ed5 [14. e5 d4] ♘b4 15. d6 ♗d6 16. ♘c4 ♗c5 17. ♗c5 bc5 18. ♘d6 ♗d5= Kudrjašov–Boleslavski, SSSR 1963

25 19. b4 ♘c6 20. dc6 ♗c6= Suetin–Spaski, SSSR (ch) 1962

26 **12. ♖c1** ♕b8 13. g4 [13. f3 ♖a7 14. ♘c2 ♖d8 15. ♕e1 ♗e8 16. ♕f2 ♖b7= Fischer–Tajmanov, Palma de Mallorca (izt) 1970 — 10/434; 14. g4!?△ g5, f4 Nikitin] ♖c8 14. g5 ♘e8 15. f4 ♖a7∞ Karpov–Hartston, Hastings 1971/72 — 13/381; **12. f4** ♕b8 13. ♗f3 ♖a7 14. ♕e2 ♖c8 15. ♖ac1 ♗e8 16. ♔h1 ♘d7 17. ♖fd1 ♖ac7= Beljavski–Tajmanov, SSSR (ch) 1973

27 13. ♕e1 ♖a7 14. ♕f2 ♖b7 15. ♖fd1 ♘e5∞ Boleslavski

28 Evans–Hartoch, Amsterdam 1971

29 13. f4!?△ ♗f3

30 Matulović–Tajmanov, Skopje 1970 — 9/317

31 **12. f4** d5!= Nikitin; **12. ♖e1** ♖c8 13. ♗f1 ♖e8?! 14. ♘a4 ♘d7 15. ♘b6 ♘b6 16. ♕b3 ♘c4 17. ♘c4 ♖b8 18. ♖ed1± Beljavski–Kupper, Teesside 1973; 13... ♘e5!?=

32 13. ♕d4?! ♘ed7 14. ♖fd1 ♖e8 15. ♘c2 ♕c7 16. ♖ac1 ♖ac8∓ Adorjan–Portisch, Wijk aan Zee 1972 — 13/382

33 13... d5!? 14. cd5 ed5 15. ed5 ♘d5 16. ♘d5 ♗d5 17. ♖fd1 ♗e6= Browne–R. Byrne, San Juan 1969 — 8/335

34 △ ♕d8, ♕f8

35 Matulović—Cvetković, Jugoslavija 1973 — 16/334

36 14. ♗c5 bc5 15. ♕b7?? ♘a5—+

37 15. f3 ♗e5!∓

38 16... ♗e5!?

39 **18... ♘c6**? 19. f3±; **18... ♘a2**! 19. ♗b6 ♕g5 20. ♗e3 ♕a5= Averbah—Polugajevski, Palma de Mallorca 1972 — 14/369

40 **12... ♘b4** 13. ♘c2 d5 14. cd5 ed5 15. e5±; **12... ♘e5** 13. ♕b3 [13. ♕d2 ♕c7 14. ♖fd1 ♖fd8 15. ♖ac1 ♖ac8 16. ♗f1± Boleslavski] ♘ed7 14. ♖fd1 ♕b8 15. ♖d2 ♗d8 16. ♔h1 ♖e8 17. ♖ad1 ♗c7 18. ♗g1 ♖e7 19. ♗f1 ♕a7 20. ♘c2± Suetin—Kuzmin, SSSR 1970 — 10/433; **12... ♘d7** 13. ♕d2 ♖c8 14. ♖ac1! ♘c5 [14... ♘a5 15. ♖fd1 ♘e5 16. b3 d5 17. ♕b2!±] 15. ♖fd1 ♕c7 16. ♘d5± Boleslavski; **12... ♖b8** 13. ♖c1 [13. ♕e1 ♘d7 14. ♕f2 ♘c5= Saren—Karpov, Skopje (ol) 1972 — 14/357] ♖e8∞ Mecking—Kaplan, San Antonio 1972 — 14/370

41 13. ♘c2 ♖c8 14. ♕d2 d5 15. cd5 ed5 16. ed5 ♘b4=

42 16. ♗f1 ♗e5 17. ♕f2 ♕c7 18. ♔h1 ♖f8 19. ♘c2 f5∓ Gufeljd—Furman, SSSR (ch) 1963

43 19. ♕c2 ♖c8= Mecking—Geler, Petropolis (izt) 1973 — 16/336

44 **12... ♘d7** 13. ♘c2 [13. ♕d2 ♘c5 14. ♖fd1 ♖e8 15. f3 ♕c7 16. ♘c2 ♖ac8 17. b4 ♘d7 18. c5 bc5 19. b5± Željandinov—Bobocov, Praha 1966] ♖c8 14. ♘d4 ♘c5 15. f3 ♗g5 16. ♗g5 ♕g5 17. ♘c6 ♕e3 18. ♔h1 ♗c6 19. b4± Honfi—Šamkovič, SSSR 1971; **12... ♖b8** 13. f3! [13. ♕d2 ♘e5 14. f3 d5! 15. cd5 ed5 16. ♘d5 ♗d5 17. ed5 ♘d5 18. ♖fd1 ♘e3= Karpov—Olafsson, Moskva 1971] ♘e5 14. ♕d4± Furman; **12... ♖e8** 13. ♔h1 ♖b8 14. ♕d2 ♘e5 15. f3± Gufeljd—Andersson, Camaguey 1974 — 17/393

45 13. f4!? ♘ed7 14. ♗f3 ♖b8 15. ♕e2± Spaski—Langeweg, Amsterdam 1973

46 13... ♘fd7 14. f3 ♗c6 15. ♖fd1 ♕b8 16. ♕d2 ♖d8 17. ♘c2 ♘f6 18. ♘d4 ♗e8 19. ♕e1± Gipslis—Averkin, SSSR (ch) 1969

47 **14. f3** ♖e8 [14... d5?! 15. ed5 ♗c5 16. ♕d2 ♗e3 17. ♕e3 ed5 18. ♖fd1 ♖e8 19. ♕f2± Karpov—Tukmakov, SSSR (ch) 1971] 15. ♕d2 [15. ♗f2 d5= Reshevsky—Matulović, Sousse (izt) 1967 — 4/436] ♕c7 16. ♖fd1 ♖ac8 17. ♗f1 ♕b8= Muhin—Jansa, Luhačovice 1973; **14. ♖fe1** e5 15. ♕d3 ♘c5 16. ♗c5 bc5 17. ♘c2 ♘e8 18. ♘e3 ♘c7=; **14. ♘c2** ♕b8!? 15. ♖fd1 ♖e8 16. f3 d5!= Estevez—Larsen, Leningrad (izt) 1973 — 15/353; 16. ♔h1!?

48 14... ♕c7 15. f3 ♖fe8 16. b4! ♖ab8 17. ♘ab1 ♗a8 18. a3 ♗f8 19. ♘d2 h6 20. f4± Karpov—Jansa, Skopje (ol) 1972 — 14/368

49 15... ♕c7 16. f3 d5 17. cd5 ed5 18. ♘d5! ♗d5 19. ed5 ♗c5 20. ♕d2 ♕e5 21. ♗c5 ♘c5 22. ♗c4 b5 23. ♗f1 ♕b2 24. ♘b4±

50 18. ♘d5 ♘d5 19. ed5 ♗f6 20. ♕d2 ♗b2∓

51 **18... ♗c5** 19. ♕d2 ♖e3 20. ♘e3 ♘g4 21. fg4 ♕g5 22. ♔f2 ♖e8 23. ♘e4 ♖e4 24. ♖c5 ♘c5 25. ♘f5±; **18... ♗d6**! 19. ♕d2 b5 20. a3 ♕c7! 21. f4 [21. ♔h1 ♕b8 22. g3 ♕a8 23. ♔g2 ♘e5 24. ♗g5 ♖c3—+] ♘c5 22. ♗c5 ♕c5 23. ♔h1 ♘e4 24. ♘e4 ♖e4⩱ Boleslavski

52 **13... ♗c6** 14. ♘c2 ♖c8 15. ♕d2 ♕c7 16. ♖fd1 ♖fd8 17. ♕e1± Židkov—Osnos, SSSR 1974 — 18/361; **13... ♖e8**!?

53 19. ♕f2± Matulović—Langeweg, Novi Sad 1973 — 17/392

54 17... ♕b8!?

55 Karpov—Tajmanov, SSSR 1973

56 6... ♘e5 7. ♘1a3! [7. ♗e5 de5 8. ♕d8 ♔d8 9. ♘1a3 ♗c5 10. ♘c4 f6 11. ♘bd6 ♔e7 12. ♖d1 ♘h6 13. ♗e2 ♖d8= Karaklajić—Langeweg, Beverwijk 1968] ♘f6 [7... a6 8. ♗e5 de5 9. ♕d8 ♔d8 10. 0-0-0 ♗d7? 11. ♘c4!+— Nikitin] 8. ♗e5 de5 9. ♕d8 ♔d8 10. ♖d1 ♔e7 11. ♘d6± Boleslavski

57 7. ♗g3 a6 8. ♘5c3 ♘f6 9. ♗h4 ♗e7 10. ♗f6 ♗f6= Bitman—Mojsejev, SSSR 1972

58 **8. f3** a6 9. ♘5c3 ♗e7=; **8. ♘5c3** ♗e7=; **8. ♘1c3** a6 9. ♘a3 — 7... a6

59 **9. ♘5a3** ♕a5 10. ♗d2 ♕c7 11. ♘c3 b5 12. ♘d5 ♘d5 13. ed5 [Gufeljd—Džindžihašvili, SSSR 1971 — 12/375] ♘e7=; **9. ♘5c3** ♗e7 10. ♘d2 [10. ♗f6 ♗f6 11. ♘d5 ♗g5= Kapengut—Furman, SSSR 1967 — 3/419; 11. ♗c4!?] 0—0 11. ♗f6 ♗f6 12. ♘c4 ♗e7 13. ♘d5 ♗e6 14. c3 b5= Estrin—Judovič, corr. 1965

60 **10... ♗g7** 11. ♘d2! b5 12. a4 b4 13. ♘d5 f5 14. ♗c4 0—0 15. ♕h5 ♘d4 16. 0—0 fe4 17. c3± Sanguinetti—Polugajevski, La Habana 1966 — 2/363; **10... ♗e6** 11. ♘d5 ♗g7 12. ♘bc3 0—0 13. ♗d3 ♘d4 [Peresipkin—Suetin, SSSR 1972 — 14/365] 14. ♕h5!± Suetin

61 11. ♗c4 ♕g5 [11... ♘d4 12. ♘d2 ♕g5 13. g3 ♗h6∓ Balinas—Korčnoj, Lugano (ol) 1968 — 6/459] 12. g3 fe4 13. ♘e4 ♕g6 14. ♘bc3 ♘d4 15. 0—0 ♗h3 16. ♖e1 0-0-0 17. f3 [Štejn—Tajmanov SSSR 1971 — 12/373] d5!∓

62 11... ♗g7 12. ♘d2 [12. ♗c4 0—0 13. ef5 ♘d4 14. ♗d3 ♖e8 15. f6 ♗f6 16. ♕h7 ♔f8 17. ♘d2 d5∓ Estrin—Čerepkov, SSSR 1964] 0—0 13. ef5! [13. 0-0-0 ♘d4 14. ♗d3 fe4 15. ♗e4 h6∞] ♘d4 14. ♗d3 d5 15. f6 e4 16. ♘de4+— Nikitin

63 15. ♘d5 ♕c6 16. ♖c1 ♗e6 17. ♘f6 ♔d8 18. ♖c3 ♗e7∞ Bronštejn—Polugajevski, SSSR (ch) 1963

64 16. ♘d5 ♕d8 17. ♗b3±

65 9. ♗d2 ♕d8 10. ♗g5 ♕a5 11. ♕d2 — 9. ♕d2

66 11... ♔d8 12. f3 ♘f6 13. ♗a7 ♘d5 14. c4+− Mikenas

67 **12. ♘a7**=; **12. ♗a7**= Talj

68 **13... ♗e7** 14. 0-0-0 ♖d8 15. ♘d5 ♘c6 16. ♗b5± Adorjan–Bobocov, Amsterdam 1971 — 12/370; **13... ♔d8** 14. ♘b5 ♗e6 15. 0-0-0 b6 16. f4!± Fischer–Tajmanov (m) 1971 — 11/302

69 14. ♘b5 ♔b8 15. 0-0-0 ♗e6 16. ♘d6 ♗d6 17. ♖d6 ♔c7 18. ♖d3 ♘c6= Zuckerman–Janošević, Netanya 1971 — 11/301

70 16. f4±

71 **9. c4** ♖c8 10. ♘1c3 a6 11. ♘a3 ♗e7 12. ♕d2 0–0 13. ♖d1 h6 [Mac–Boleslavski, SSSR 1963] 14. ♗f6 ♗f6 15. ♕d6 ♕a5=∞; **9. ♗f6** gf6 10. ♘d2 [10. ♘5c3 ♕b6 11. ♘d5 ♗d5 12. ed5 ♘e7 13. ♗c4 ♕b4 14. ♘d2 ♗h6∓ Karaklajić–Ivkov, Beverwijk 1968] d5 [10... a6 11. ♘c3 f5 12. ♗c4±; 11... b5 12. a4 b4 13. ♘d5±] 11. ed5 ♗d5 12. ♘c4 ♗e6!?∞

72 10. ♘a3 ♗e7 11. ♘c4 ♘d4 12. ♘e3 0–0 13. ♗f6 ♗f6 13. ♘cd5 ♗g5 15. c3 ♘c6 16. ♗e2 ♘e7 17. ♘e7 ♕e7 18. ♘d5 ♕d8= Estrin–Boleslavski, SSSR 1964

73 Čebanenko; **11... ♕b6** 12. ♘c4 ♕d4 13. ♘e3 0-0-0 14. ♕f3± Nikitin; **11... ♘e7** 12. ♘c4 d5 13. ed5 ♘d5 14. ♘d5 ♗d5 15. ♘e3 ♗c6 16. ♗c4 ♕d1 17. ♖d1 ♖c8 18. ♗d5± Karpov–Tajmanov, SSSR (ch) 1971 — 12/374; **11... ♘d4** 12. ♘c4 [12. ♗c4 b5 13. ♗e6 fe6 14. ♘e2± Fischer–Najdorf, Santa Monica 1966 — 2/364] f5 [12... ♖c8 13. ♘e3 ♕a5 14. ♗d3± Estrin–Obuhovski, SSSR 1971 — 12/372] 13. ef5 ♘f5 14. ♗d3 ♘d4 [14... ♖c8 15. ♗f5 ♖c4 16. ♗e6 fe6 17. ♕e2 ♖d4 18. 0–0 ♕g5 19. ♖ad1± Fischer–Tajmanov (m) 1971 — 11/303] 15. 0–0 [15. ♘e3 d5 16. ♕h5 ♗g7∞] ♕c7 16. ♘e3 f5 17. f4 [17. ♘cd5 ♕f7 18. ♘b6 ♖d8 19. c3 ♘c6 20. ♕a4 f4 21. ♘ec4 ♕c7∞] 0-0-0± Boleslavski

74 12. ed5 ♗a3 13. ba3 ♕a5 14. ♕d2 0-0-0 15. ♗c4 ♖hg8 16. ♖d1 [16. f3 ♖g2!−+; 16. ♔f1 ♕a3∓; 16. 0-0-0 ♕a3 17. ♔b1 ♗f5 18. ♖hg1 ♘d4∓] ♖g2 [16... ♗f5∓ Fischer–Petrosjan (m) 1971 — 12/376] 17. ♘e4 [17. ♕e3 ♘d4 18. ♔f1 ♘c2 19. ♕f3 ♖f2!−+] ♕b6 18. ♕e3 ♕e3 19. fe3 ♗g4 20. ♖c1 ♗f3 21. ♘f6 ♘e7 22. ♗d3 ♘d5∓

75 16. c4 f5=∞

76 9... ♖c8 10. ♘c4 ♘d4 11. ♗f6 gf6 12. ♘d4 ♗c4 13. ♘f5 ♕a5 14. c3 ♗e6 15. ♕f3± Petrušin–Zaharov, SSSR 1972

77 16. 0–0 ♖ad8? 17. ♕c7 ♖d7 18. h3 ♕g2 19. ♔g2 ♖c7 20. ♖ad1± Peresipkin–Timoščenko, SSSR 1973 — 15/359; 16... ♕e4±

78 8... b5 9. c4 b4 10. ♘c2 ♘f6 11. ♗e2 ♗e7 12. 0–0 0–0 13. ♘d2 ♖b8 14. ♖e1 ♗e6 15. f3 ♘d7= Fischer–Reshevsky, Buenos Aires 1960

79 **9... ♗e6** 10. ♘c4 ♗e7 11. ♘b6 ♖b8 12. ♗e2± Radulov–Liberzon, Nice (ol) 1974 — 17/387; 10... b5!?; **9... ♖b8**!? 10. ♘c4 [10. ♗g5 b5 11. ♘d5 ♕a5] ♘e4?! 11. ♘e4 d5 12. ♗b6 ♕d7 13. ♘e5 ♘e5 14. ♘c3 ♗b4 15. ♕d4 ♕e6 16. 0-0-0±; 10... b5!=

80 10... ♘d5 11. ed5 ♘e7 12. c4 ♘f5 [12... b4 13. ♕a4 ♗d7 14. ♕b4 ♘f5 15. ♕c3 ♗e7 16. ♘c2 0–0 17. ♗e2 ♘e3 18. fe3 ♕b6 19. 0–0 ♖ab8=∞ Konstantinopoljski, Estrin] 13. ♗d2 ♗e7 14. cb5 ♗f6 15. ♗e2 e4 16. b6 0–0 17. ♘c4 ♗d4 18. 0–0 ♗b6 19. ♘b6 ♕b6 20. ♗c3 ♗b7 21. ♗c4 ♖ac8= Fischer–Pachman, Buenos Aires 1960

81 11. ♗e2 ♘e4 12. ♗f3 ♘c5∓

82 12... ♗e7 13. ♘c3 ♕g6 13. f3 0–0 14. ♕d2± Gufeljd–Boleslavski, SSSR (ch) 1961

83 14. a3 g6 15. ♕d2 ♗g7 16. 0-0-0 0–0=

84 16. ed5= Šijanovski–Polugajevski, SSSR (ch) 1962

85 **9. ♗e2** ♗e7 10. 0–0 0–0 11. ♘d2 b5= Hamann–Antošin, Venezia 1966 — 1/264

86 **10. ♘d2** ♗e6!=; **10. 0–0** 0–0 11. ♗b3 ♘a5= Lutikov–Darga, Beverwijk 1967

87 12... ♗e6 13. c3 ♖b8 14. 0–0± Bronštejn–Furman, Tallinn 1971 — 11/299

88 16. f3 ♕g6 17. 0–0 ♗d3 18. ♖f2 ♗h4 19. ♖d2 e4∞ Quinteros–Krnić, Vršac 1973

B 45 — 1. e4 c5 2. ♘f3 e6 3. d4 cd4 4. ♘d4 ♘c6 5. ♘c3

	5	6	7	8	9	10	11	12	13	
1	...	♗e3[2]	♗d3	♘c6[4]	e5	♕g4	f4	♘d1		=
	♘f6[1]	♗b4[3]	d5	bc6	♘d7	♗f8	♖b8	♗a6[5]		

1. e4 c5 2. ♘f3 e6 3. d4 cd4 4. ♘d4 ♘c6 5. ♘c3 ♘f6

	6	7	8	9	10	11	12	13	14	
2	♗f4 d6[6]	♗g3 ♘d4!?	♕d4 ♘h5!?	♗b5 ♗d7	0—0[7] ♘g3	hg3 a6	♗d7 ♕d7	♖ad1 ♕c6		=
3	g3 d5	♗g2[8] ♗b4	ed5 ♘d5[9]	0—0 ♘c3	bc3 ♗c3	♘c6 ♕d1	♖d1 ♗d7	♖b1 ♗c6	♗c6 bc6[10]	=
4	♗e2 ♗b4	0—0[11] ♗c3	bc3 ♘e4	♗d3[12] d5[13]	♗a3 ♘d4	cd4 ♕a5	♕c1 ♗d7	♖b1 ♗c6	♗b4 ♕c7[14]	=
5	♘c6 bc6[15]	e5[16] ♘d5	♘e4 f5[17]	ef6 ♘f6	♘d6 ♗d6	♕d6 ♕b6[18]	♗d3 c5	♗f4[19] ♗b7	0—0 ♖c8[20]	=
6	♘db5 ♗b4[21]	♗f4[22] ♘e4[23]	♕f3[24] d5[25]	♘c7 ♔e7	0-0-0[26] ♗c3	bc3 g5[27]	♗g3[28] f5	♗c4![29] ♗d7[30]	♖he1[31] ♖c8[32]	±
7	. . . . . .	. . . . . .	. . . . . .	. . . ♔f8!	0-0-0[33] ♗c3[34]	bc3 g5![35]	♕e4[36] ♕c7!	♗c7 de4	♗b5 ♔g7[37]	∞

1. e4 c5 2. ♘f3 e6 3. d4 cd4 4. ♘d4 ♘c6 5. ♘c3 ♘f6 6. ♘db5 ♗b4 7. a3 ♗c3 8. ♘c3 d5

	9	10	11	12	13	14	15	16	17	
8	ed5[38] ♘d5	♘d5 ed5[39]	♗d3[40] ♘e5[41]	♗e3 ♘d3	♕d3 0—0	♖d1 ♕f6	c3 ♗f5[42]			=
9	. . . . . .	♗d2 ♘c3[43]	♗c3 ♕d1	♖d1 f6[44]	f4 ♗d7	♗c4 0-0-0	0—0 ♔c7	♖de1 ♖he8	♖f3 ♗c8[45]	±
10	. . . . . .	. . . ♕h4	♕f3[46] 0—0[47]	0-0-0[48] ♘c3	♗c3 e5	♗d3 ♗g4[49]	♕e4 ♕h6	♗d2 ♕g6	f3 ♗e6[50]	±
11	. . . ed5	♗d3[51] 0—0[52]	0—0 ♗g4	f3 ♗e6	♗g5[53] h6[54]	♗h4 g5	♗f2 ♘h5	♘b5		±
12	. . . . . .	. . . . . .	. . . h6	♗f4[55] d4	♘e2[56] ♕d5[57]	♘g3[58] ♗g4	f3 ♗e6	♖e1[59]		±
13	. . . . . .	. . . . . .	. . . . . .	. . . . . .	♘b5 ♘d5	♕f3![60] ♗e6	♖ad1 ♕d7	h3 ♖ad8	♗h2 ♕e7[61]	±
14	. . . . . .	. . . . . .	. . . d4!?	♘e2[62] ♗g4	f3[63] ♗e6	♗g5				±

1 5... ♗b4 6. ♘b5 a6?! 7. ♘d6 ♗d6 [7... ♔e7 8. ♗f4±] 8. ♕d6 ♕e7 9. ♕g3±; 6... ♘f6 — 5... ♘f6

2 **6. ♗g5** h6 [6... ♕b6!? 7. ♗f6 gf6 8. ♘b3 a5 9. a4 ♖g8∞] 7. ♗h4 ♗e7 [7... g5?! 8. ♗g3 ♗b4 9. ♘c6 bc6 10. a3 ♗c3 11. bc3± Savon—Bobocov, Albena 1973 — 16/359] 8. ♘c6 [8. ♕d2? ♘e4!; 8. ♘db5 0—0 9. ♘d6 ♘e4!] bc6 9. ♗d3 d5=; **6. a3** ♗e7 7. ♗e2 0—0 8. 0—0 d5 9. ed5 ♘d5 10. ♘c6 bc6 11. ♘e4 ♕c7=

3 6... d5?! 7. ♗b5 ♗d7 8. ed5±

4 8. ed5 ♘d5 9. ♘c6 bc6=

5 Spielmann—Janowski, Semmering 1926

6 6... ♗b4!? 7. ♘b5 — 6. ♘db5

7 10. ♗d6?! ♗b5 11. ♘b5 ♕a5 12. ♘c3 ♗d6 13. ♕d6 ♖d8 14. ♕a3 ♕a3 15. ba3 ♖c8∓

8 7. ed5 ♘d5 8. ♘c6 bc6=

9 8... ed5 9. 0—0 ♗c3 10. bc3 0—0= Spielmann—Kopa, Barmen 1905

10 15. ♗a3 [Denker—Mieses, Hastings 1945/46] a5! 16. ♖b7 ♗b4 17. ♗b4 ab4 18. ♖dd7 0—0 19. ♖b4 ♖a2 20. ♖c4=

11 7. ♘c6?! bc6 8. 0—0 d5!∓

12 9. ♗f3 d5 [9... ♘c3 10. ♕d3±⟳↑] 10. ♘c6 bc6 11. ♗e4 de4 12. ♕d8 ♔d8 13. ♖e1 f5 14. ♗g5 ♔e8 15. ♖ad1∞

13 9... ♘c3? 10. ♕g4+—→

14 15. ♕a3 a5 16. ♗e4 de4 17. c4 f6 18. ♗d6 ♕d7= Geler—Hasin, SSSR (ch) 1958

15 6... dc6?! 7. ♕d8 ♔d8 8. e5 [8. ♗g5 ♗e7 9. 0-0-0±] ♘d7 9. f4 ♗b4 10. ♗d2± Opočensky—Hasenfuss, Folkestone (ol) 1933

16 7. ♗d3 d5 8. 0—0 ♗b4 [8... ♗e7 9. ♔h1 0—0 10. f4 ♘d7= Tan—Rossolimo, Skopje (ol) 1972] 9. e5?! ♘d7 10. ♕g4 ♗f8 11. ♖e1 g6 12. ♗g5 ♕c7 13. ♕g3 ♗g7∓ Yates—Canal, Trieste 1923; 9. ♕e2=

17 **8... ♕a5**?! 9. ♗d2 ♘b4 10. f4 ♕d5 11. ♘c3 ♕d4 [Schmidt—Butenschön, corr. 1956] 12. ♖c1 ♗c5 13. ♕f3±; **8... ♕c7**?! 9. f4 f5 10. ef6 [10. ♘d6? ♗d6 11. ed6 ♕b6∓] ♘f6 11. ♘f6 gf6 12. ♕h5 ♔d8 13. ♗d2 d5 14. 0-0-0 ♖b8 15. ♕h4 ♗e7 16. ♗c3 ♖f8 17. g3± Kurajica—Rossolimo, Montilla 1972

18 11... ♕a5 12. ♗d2 ♕d5 [Yates—Lasker, New York 1924] 13. ♗b4 ♕d6 14. ♗d6 ♘e4 15. ♗a3± Tartakower

19 13. ♕g3 0—0 14. 0—0∞ Pachman—Konradi, Dublin 1957

20 Cobo—Gonzales, La Habana 1962

21 **6... d5**? 7. ed5 ed5 8. ♗f4+—; 8. ♘d5 +—; **6... a6** 7. ♘d6 ♗d6 8. ♕d6±; **6... ♗c5** 7. ♗f4 0—0 8. ♗d6 [8. ♗c7!? ♕e7 9. ♗d6 ♗d6 10. ♕d6±] ♗d6 9. ♘d6±; **6... d6** 7. ♗f4 e5 8. ♗g5 — B 33

22 **7. ♗g5** h6 [7... a6 8. a3! ab5 9. ab4 ♖a1 10. ♕a1 ♘b4 11. ♕d1∞] 8. ♗h4 g5?! 9. ♗g3 ♘e4 10. ♘c7 ♔f8 11. ♘a8 ♕f6 12. ♕d3 ♘c3 13. ♗d6± Parma—Prahov, Jugoslavija 1962; 8... ♕a5!?=; **7. ♘d6** ♔e7 8. ♘c8 [8. ♗f4 e5 9. ♘f5 ♔f8 10. ♗g5? d5 11. ♗f6 ♕f6 12. ♕d5 ♗f5 13. ef5 ♖d8 14. ♕e4 ♖d4∓; 10. ♗d2 d5 11. ed5 ♘d5 12. ♘d5 ♕d5 13. ♗b4 ♘b4 14. ♘e3= Euwe] ♖c8 9. ♗d3 d5 10. ed5 ♕d5 11. 0—0 ♕h5 12. ♕h5 ♘h5 13. ♗d2= Keres—Trifunović, Moskva 1947

23 7... 0—0?! 8. ♗d6 [8. ♗c7!? ♕e7 9. ♗d6 ♗d6 10. ♕d6±] ♗d6 9. ♘d6 a6 10. ♕d2 b5 11. 0-0-0± Haag—Mjagmarsuren, Polanica Zdroj 1972

24 8. ♘c7 ♔f8 [8... ♔e7 9. ♘a8? ♘c3 10. bc3 ♗c3 11. ♗d2 ♗a1 12. ♕a1 f6△ b6, ♗b7∓; 9. ♕f3 d5 — 8. ♕f3] 9. ♕f3 [9. ♘a8? ♕f6 10. ♕f3 ♘c3 11. ♗d2 ♘d4 12. ♕d3 ♕e5 13. ♗e3 ♘a4 14. c3 ♘b2 0 : 1 Reggio—Tarrasch 1902] d5 — 8. ♕f3

25 8... ♘c3? 9. bc3 ♗a5 10. ♘d6 ♔f8 11. 0-0-0±→ Klovski—Antošin, SSSR 1969 — 8/362

26 10. ♘a8? ♕a5 11. ♗d2 [11. ♗c7 b6] ♘d2 12. ♔d2 d4—+

27 11... ♗d7? (Svenonius) 12. ♘a8? ♕a5 13. ♔b2 ♖a8∞; 12. c4!+—

28 12. ♕e4? de4 13. ♗g5 f6 14. ♖d8 [14. ♗f6 ♔f6 15. ♖d8 ♖d8 16. ♘a8 ♗d7 17. ♘c7 a6—+ Euwe] ♖d8 15. ♘a8 fg5 16. ♘c7 ♖f8∓ Euwe

29 **13. ♘a8**? ♕a5 14. ♔b2 f4∓; **13. c4 f4** 14. ♘d5 ed5 15. cd5 [15. ♖d5 ♕g8! 16. ♕e4 ♕e6 17. ♕e6 ♗e6 18. ♖g5 fg3 19. hg3 ♖af8∓; 17. ♕f3 ♕e1 18. ♖d1 ♕a5∓] ♗f5! 16. dc6 ♕a5 17. ♕b3 fg3∓ Havski—Derviz, SSSR 1970 — 9/338

30 **13... f4** 14. ♘d5 ed5 15. ♗d5±; **13... ♔f7**!?

31 **14. ♘a8**? ♕a5 15. ♗b3 ♖a8∓ Boleslavski; **14. ♘d5** ed5 15. ♖d5 ♕e8 [△ 16. ♖f5 ♗f5 17. ♕f5 ♕g6!; 15... ♕c8 16. ♖e1 ♗e6 17. ♖e4 fe4 18. ♕e4+—→ Schendstock—Mertens, Ybbs 1968 — 6/484] 16. ♖e1 ♕g6 17. ♕d3 ♗e6 18. f3±→ Boleslavski

32 **14... dc4** 15. ♖e4 fe4 16. ♗d6#; **14... ♘g3** 15. ♕g3 dc4 16. ♕d6+—; **14... ♖c8** 15. ♘d5 ed5 16. ♗d5±→

33 10. ♘a8 e5! 11. ♗g3 ♘d4!—+

34 10... ♘c3 11. bc3 ♗a3 12. ♔b1 e5 13. ♘a8 ef4 14. ♕d5 ♕f6 15. ♕b3 ♗d6 16. ♗b5± Ravinski

35 11... ♖b8 12. ♘d5 ed5 13. ♕e4 de4 14. ♖d8 ♘d8 15. ♗b8± Becker—Asztalos 1929

36 **12. ♘a8**? ♕a5!∓; **12. ♗g3** ♘g3 13. ♕g3 ♖b8∓

37 Kapengut—Kuzmin, SSSR 1972

38 9. ♗d3 de4 10. ♘e4 ♘e4 11. ♗e4 ♕d1 12. ♔d1 f5 [12... ♗d7 13. ♗e3 f5 14. ♗f3 e5 15. b4 0—0 16. ♔c1 ♘d4 17. ♗d4 ed4 18. ♖e1± Fischer—Bolbochan, Mar del Plata 1960] 13. ♗c6 bc6 14. ♖e1 ♔f7= Schmid—Bolbochan, Helsinki (ol) 1952; 9... ♘e5! 10. ♗e2?! ♘e4∓ Nežmetdinov—Ilivicki, SSSR 1952; 10. 0—0=

39 10... ♕d5 11. ♕d5 ed5 12. ♗d3 [12. ♗f4 ♗f5 13. ♔d2±] ♘e5 13. ♗e2 ♗f5 14. ♗f4 ♘g6 15. ♗g3 ♗c2 16. ♖c1 ♗a4 17. ♖c7 ♗c6 18. ♗d6 ♖d8 19. ♗c5 ♖d7 20. ♖c8 ♖d8 [Boleslavski—Banik, SSSR 1960] 21. ♖d8±

40 11. ♗e2 0—0 12. 0—0 ♗f5 13. ♗e3 [13. ♗f3 d4 14. b4 d3= Najdorf—Trifunović (m) 1949] d4 14. ♗f4 ♕f6= Boleslavski—Kuznjecov, SSSR 1960

41 **11... ♕e7** 12. ♕e2 ♕e2 13. ♔e2 ♗f5 14. ♗f5± Matanović—Janošević, Jugoslavija (ch) 1953; **11... 0—0** 12. 0—0±⊡

42 1/2 : 1/2 Ivkov—Trifunović, Jugoslavija (ch) 1957

43 **10... ♕b6** 11. ♘b5 ♘d4 12. ♘d4 ♕d4 13. ♗b5 ♗d7 14. ♗d7 ♔d7 15. 0—0± Kaplan—Siaperas, Siegen (ol) 1970 — 10/460; **10... ♕f6** 11. ♕h5 0—0 12. 0-0-0 ♘c3 [12... ♕f2 13. ♘d5 ed5 14. ♗d3±↑] 13. ♗c3 ♕f4 14. ♖d2 e5 15. ♗b5± Matulović—Kokkoris, Athens 1969 — 8/365; **10... 0—0** 11. ♕h5 ♘f6 12. ♕h4 ♕d4 13. ♗g5 ♖d8 14. ♕d4 ♖d4 15. ♗d3 b6 16. 0-0-0± Gufeljd—Hasin, SSSR (ch) 1966

44 12... e5 13. ♗d3 ♗e6 14. 0–0 f6 15. f4±⊞↑ Ivkov–Gligorić, Amsterdam (izt) 1964

45 18. ♖g3± Fischer–Addison, USA (ch) 1962/63

46 11. ♗d3 0–0 12. 0–0 ♘e5= Keres–Matulović, SSSR–Jugoslavija 1966 — 1/276

47 **11... ♘e5** 12. ♕g3±; **11... ♘d4** 12. ♕d3±

48 12. ♘d5? ♘d4!

49 14... ♕g4 15. ♗e4 ♕f3 16. ♗f3± Minić–Gerusel, Halle 1967 — 3/430

50 18. ♕g6 hg6 19. ♗e3 b6 [Talj–Matulović, Kislovodsk 1966 — 2/378] 20. b3±

51 10. ♗g5 0–0 [10... d4?! 11. ♕e2 ♗e6 12. 0-0-0 h6 13. ♗h4 ♕c7 14. ♗f6 ♕f4 15. ♔b1 ♕f6 16. ♘d5 ♕d8 17. ♘f4± Radulov–Rossolimo, Novi Sad 1972 — 14/394] 11. ♗e2 ♗e6 12. 0–0 h6 13. ♗h4 d4 14. ♘e4 g5 15. ♘f6 ♕f6 16. ♗g3 ♖ad8=

52 **10... d4** 11. ♕e2 ♗e6 12. ♘e4 ♘e4 13. ♕e4 ♕d5 14. ♗f4±; **10... ♕e7** 11. ♕e2 ♕e2 12. ♘e2 ♘e5 13. ♗b5 ♗d7 14. ♗d7 ♔d7 [Liberzon–Bronštejn, SSSR 1972] 15. ♗e3! ♖he8 16. ♗d4±

53 **13. ♔h1**?! ♘d7 14. ♗f4 ♕b6 15. b4 ♘ce5= Parma–Benkö, Malaga 1973; **13. ♖e1** h6 [13... d4 14. ♘e2 ♘d5 15. ♘g3 ♕c7 16. ♕d2 ♖ae8 17. ♕f2± Boleslavski–Trifunović, Stockholm (izt) 1948] 14. ♕e2 ♕d7 15. ♕f2 ♗f5= Plater–Trifunović, Hilversum 1947

54 **13... ♖e8**? 14. ♕d2 d4 15. ♘e2 a6 16. ♘g3± Planinc–Andersson, Sombor 1970 — 10/495; **13... ♕b6**?! 14. ♔h1 ♘d7 [14... ♕b2? 15. ♗f6 gf6 16. ♕d2+–] 15. f4! f5 16. ♕f3± Matulović–Benkö, Vrnjačka Banja 1973 — 15/366

55 12. ♖e1 d4 13. ♘e4 ♘e4 [13... ♗f5 14. ♘f6 ♕f6 15. ♕f3 ♗d3 16. ♕f6 gf6 17. cd3± Keres–Buhman, SSSR (ch) 1962] 14. ♗e4 ♕d6±

56 13. ♘e4 ♗f5? 14. ♗c7! ♕c7 15. ♘f6 gf6 16. ♗f5±; 13... ♘d5=

57 13... ♘d5? 14. ♗g3 ♕b6 [14... f5? 15. c4!] 15. ♕d2 ♖d8 16. ♖fe1 ♗e6 17. ♘f4± Rabinovič–Rovner, SSSR 1940

58 14. ♗g3 ♗g4 15. ♖e1 [15. f3 ♗f5=] ♖ad8 16. h3 ♗e2 17. ♖e2 ♖fe8= Kondratjev–Kan, SSSR 1954

59 **16. ♕d2** g5 17. ♘e4 ♘h5 18. c4 [18. g4?! f5!] dc3 19. ♘c3 ♕d7= Euwe; **16. ♖e1**±

60 **14. ♗d6**? a6 [14... ♖e8 15. ♗g3±] 15. ♗f8 ♔f8∓; **14. ♗g3** ♗e6 15. ♖e1 ♕d7 16. h3 ♖ad8 [16... a6 17. ♘d6± Talj–Olafsson, Zürich 1959] 17. ♕f3 ♘de7= Krogius–Talj, SSSR 1958

61 18. ♕g3± Ćirić–Rossolimo, Vršac 1969 — 8/364

62 12. ♘e4 ♗f5 13. ♗g5 ♗e4 14. ♗e4 h6 15. ♗f6 [15. ♗h4 g5 16. ♗c6 bc6 17. ♗g3 ♕d5∞] ♕f6 16. ♕f3 ♕f3 17. ♗f3 ♘e5 18. ♗e4 ♖ac8= Stean–Tompa, Graz 1972

63 13. ♗g5 h6 14. ♗h4 g5 15. f3 gh4 16. fg4 ♘g4 17. ♕e1 ♘e3 18. ♖f4 ♕g5 19. ♕f2 h3 20. ♖f3 ♕g2 21. ♕g2 hg2 22. ♘d4 ♘d4 23. ♖e3 ♖ae8 24. ♖g3 ♔h8 25. ♖g2 ♘f3= Kostro–Szapokowski, Polska 1959; 24. ♖e8!? ♖e8 25. ♔f2

B 46 — 1. e4 c5 2. ♘f3 e6 3. d4 cd4 4. ♘d4 ♘c6 5. ♘c3 a6

	6	7	8	9	10	11	12	13	14	
1	♘c6?![1]	♗d3	0–0	♖e1[3]	e5	♕g4	♗h6	♖ab1	♕e2	=
	bc6	d5[2]	♘f6	♗e7	♘d7	g6	♖b8	♖b4!	♗g5[4]	
2	♗e3	♗d3	ed5	0–0	♘c6	♗d4	♕f3	♖fe1	♗f6	=
	♘f6	d5!?[5]	ed5	♗d6	bc6	0–0	♗e6[6]	c5	♕f6[7]	
3	♗f4	♗g3	♗e2[10]	♘b3	f4	♗f3	♕e2	0-0-0[12]		∞
	d6[8]	♘f6[9]	♗d7[11]	♕c7	♖d8	♗e7	♗c8			
4	♗e2	♘b3[14]	0–0	♗f4	♗d6[16]	♕d6	♖fd1	♖d6	♖ad1	±
	♘ge7[13]	♘a5[15]	♘ec6	b5	♗d6	♕e7	♕d6	♔e7	♘b7[17]	
5	...	...	♗e3	f4	g3[18]	h4	♕d2	h5	h6	∞
	...	b5	♘g6	♗e7	0–0	♖e8	♘a5!?	♘f8	g6[19]	
6	...	♗e3	♕d4	0-0-0[22]	♕d2	♗f4	♖he1	♗d6	♕d6	±
	...	♘d4[20]	b5[21]	♘c6	♗e7[23]	f6	0–0	♗d6	♕e7	
7	g3	♘de2?!	♗g2	0–0	♘f4	♘d3	a4	♘a2		∓
	♘ge7[24]	♘g6[25]	♗c5	b5	♗b7	♗b6	b4	a5[26]		

	6	7	8	9	10	11	12	13	14	
8	...	♗g2	♕d4	♕d1[27]	0—0	♗e3	♘d5!?	ed5	dc6	=
	...	♘d4	♘c6	♗e7	0—0	b5	ed5	♗b7	♗c6[28]	
9	...	♘b3	♕h5![29]	♗g5	♗f4	♘a5	0-0-0	♕c5!	♗c7	±
	...	♘a5?!	♘ec6[30]	♕c7	d6	♘a5	♘c6	dc5	b5[31]	
10	...	...	♗g2	♗e3	0—0	f4	e5!?[33]	♕d8	♖ad1	±
	...	b5	d6	♖b8[32]	g6	♗g7	de5	♔d8	♔c7[34]	
11	...	...	♗g2	0—0[35]	a4[36]	♗e3[38]	f4	♕d2	♖ad1	±
	...	d6	♗d7!?	♘c8	♗e7[37]	b6	0—0	♕c7	♖d8[39]	
12	...	♗g2	0—0	♖e1[40]	♘c6	a4	a5	♗e3	♕d2	±
	d6	♗d7	♘f6	♗e7	♗c6	0—0	♘d7	♕b8	♖d8[41]	

[1] 6. f4 d5?! 7. ♗e3 ♘ge7 [7... ♘f6] 8. ♘f3!± Bronštejn—Razuvajev, Tbilisi 1973 — 17/396; 6... d6 7. ♗e3 ♘f6 — B 82

[2] 7... d6 8. b3 ♘f6 9. ♗b2 ♗e7 10. 0—0 0—0 11. e5? de5 12. ♕f3 ♕c7 13. ♕h3 a5∓ Gurgenidze—Korčnoj, SSSR 1963; 11. f4±

[3] 9. ♗g5?! ♗e7 10. ♕e2 ♘e4! 11. ♗e7 ♘c3 12. ♕e5 ♔e7! 13. ♕c3 f6 14. ♕c6 ♖b8 15. ♗a6 ♕d6 16. ♕d6 ♔d6 17. ♗d3 [17. ♗c8 ♖hc8∓] ♖b2∓ Janošević—Tajmanov, Skopje 1970 — 9/318; **9. ♗f4** ♗e7 10. ♕f3 0—0 11. ♘a4 ♘d7 12. ed5 cd5 13. ♖ad1 ♗b7 14. c4 ♕a5 15. ♘c3 ♘f6 16. cd5 ♘d5 17. ♗e5 ♘c3 18. ♕g3 g6 19. ♗c3 ♕g5= Nežmetdinov—Suetin, Kislovodsk 1972

[4] 15. a3 ♖b8 16. ♗g5 ♕g5= Kajumov—Tajmanov, SSSR 1972

[5] 7... ♕c7 — B 48

[6] 12... ♘g4? 13. h3 ♘h2? 14. ♕h5 g6 15. ♕h6+—

[7] 15. ♕f6 gf6 16. ♖ad1 ♖fd8= Spaski—Fischer (m) 1972 — 14/374

[8] 6... ♕f6?! 7. ♗e3 ♗c5 8. ♘f5 ♗e3 9. ♘e3±

[9] **7... e5**?! 8. ♘b3 ♘f6 9. ♗c4 ♗e7 10. 0—0 0—0 11. a4± Janošević—Hartoch, Amsterdam 1970 — 10/435; **7... ♗e7** 8. ♗e2 ♕c7 9. 0—0 ♘f6 10. ♔h1 0—0 11. f4 ♖d8= Korenski—Sergin, SSSR 1974

[10] 8. ♕d2 ♘h5=

[11] 8... ♗e7?! 9. ♘c6 bc6 10. e5! ♘d5 11. ed6 ♗d6 12. ♘a4 ♗g3 13. hg3± Cejtlin—Mišučkov, SSSR 1972

[12] **13. e5**?! de5 14. fe5 ♘d7 15. 0-0-0 0—0 16. ♔b1 b5 17. ♗c6 ♕c6 18. ♘d4 ♕b7∓ Vasjukov—Furman, SSSR 1972 — 14/372; **13. 0—0**!?; **13. 0-0-0**!?∞

[13] 6... ♘d4 7. ♕d4 ♘e7 8. ♗f4 ♘c6 9. ♕d2 b5 [9... ♕a5 10. 0—0 ♘e5 11. a3 ♗e7 12. ♗e3 ♕c7 13. ♕d4 0—0 14. ♕b6± Krogius—Čukajev, SSSR 1963] 10. 0—0 ♗e7 11. ♖ad1± Boleslavski—Tajmanov, SSSR 1967

[14] **7. ♗f4** ♘g6 8. ♘c6 bc6 9. ♗d6 ♗d6 10. ♕d6 ♕e7 11. 0-0-0 ♕d6 12. ♖d6 ♔e7= Jansa—Flesch, Tel Aviv (ol) 1964; **7. f4** ♘d4 8. ♕d4 b5 9. 0—0 ♕c7 10. ♔h1 ♘c6 11. ♕f2 ♗e7 12. ♗e3 0—0 13. ♖ad1 d6 14. ♕g3 [Talj—Tajmanov, SSSR (ch) 1974 — 18/362] ♗f6∞

[15] 7... ♘g6 8. ♗e3 ♗e7 9. 0—0 0—0 10. f4 ♕c7 [10... d6!?] 11. ♗d3 b5 12. ♕h5 b4 13. ♘e2 [13. ♘a4!?] f6 14. ♖f3±↑ Jansa—Tajmanov, Suhumi 1972 — 14/371; 8. a4!?△ a5

[16] 10. e5!? ♗b7 11. ♘a5 ♘a5 12. ♗f3±↑

[17] 15. ♖6d2± Šibarević—Tajmanov, Vrnjačka Banja 1974 — 17/398

[18] 10. 0—0 d6 [10... 0—0!?] 11. f5 ♘ge5 12. fe6 ♗e6 13. ♘d5 0—0 14. a4 ♘c4 15. ♗c4 bc4 16. ♘d4 ♗d5 17. ed5 ♘e5= Mesing—Jansa, Vrnjačka Banja 1973 — 15/354

[19] Tukmakov—Tajmanov, SSSR (ch) 1973 — 16/339

[20] 7... b5 8. a3 ♘d4 9. ♕d4 ♘c6 10. ♕d2 ♗e7 11. 0—0 0—0 12. ♖ad1 d6 13. ♗f4 ♘e5= Arulajd—Tajmanov, SSSR 1974; 8. ♘b3 — 7. ♘b3

[21] 8... ♘c6?! 9. ♕b6±

[22] 9. 0—0 ♘c6 10. ♕d2 ♗e7 11. f4 0—0 12. ♖ad1 d6 13. a3 ♗b7 14. ♕e1 ♕c7= Radovici—Popov, Tel Aviv (ol) 1964

[23] **10... ♗b7**?! [Velimirović—Krnić, Vršac 1973 — 16/338] 11. ♗b6! ♕c8 12. ♖he1±; **10... ♗b4**!? 11. a3 ♗e7△ b4→

[24] △ 7... ♘d4 8. ♕d4 ♘c6; 6... ♕c7 — B 47

[25] 7... b5!? 8. a3 ♗b7 9. ♗g2 ♘c8 10. 0—0 ♗e7 11. ♗e3 0—0 12. f4 ♘d6 13. b3 ♖c8∞ Beluczik—Doda, Polska 1972

[26] Kapengut—Tajmanov, SSSR (ch) 1971 — 12/380

[27] **9. ♕d2** ♗e7 10. b3 ♕c7 11. ♗b2 0—0 12. 0—0 d6 13. ♘d1 b5 14. ♘e3 ♗b7 15. f4± Sznapik—Schmidt, Polska (ch) 1972 — 13/385; 10... ♕a5!?=; **9. ♕e3** d6 10. b3 ♗e7 11.

♗b2 0–0 12. 0–0 ♖b8 [12... ♗f6 13. ♖fd1 ♕c7 14. ♘a4 ♗b2 15. ♘b2 e5= Keres–Jansa, Sarajevo 1972 — 13/386; 14. ♖d2!? Keres] 13. ♘e2 b5 14. ♖ac1 ♕a5= Hort–Karpov, San Antonio 1972

28 15. ♗d4 ♖c8 16. c3 ♖e8 17. ♖e1 ♗f8 18. ♖e8 ♕e8= Fajbisovič–Tajmanov, SSSR 1973

29 8. **♗g2**?! ♘ec6 9. 0–0 [9. ♕h5 ♗e7 10. 0–0 d6= Browne–Grefe, USA 1973] ♗e7 [9... d6 10. ♘a5 ♕a5 11. ♘e2 ♗e7 12. b3 0–0 13. ♗b2± Keene–Karpov, Hastings 1971/72 — 13/384] 10. ♗f4 d6 11. ♘a5 ♘a5 12. ♕e2 ♘c6 13. ♖fd1 ♕c7= Romanišin–Podgajec, SSSR 1973; **8. ♗f4** ♘ec6 9. ♗d6 ♗d6 10. ♕d6 ♕e7= Andersson–Jakobsen, Forssa–Helsinki 1972

30 8... **♘b3** 9. ab3 ♘c6 10. ♗g5 ♗e7 11. ♗e7 ♕e7 12. ♗g2 0–0 13. 0-0-0± Timman–Radev, Tbilisi 1971 — 12/381; **8... b5** 9. ♘a5 ♕a5 10. ♗g2±

31 15. ♗g2 ♗b7 16. e5 ♖c8 17. ♗b6 ♘a5 18. ♗b7 ♘b7 19. a4± Timman–Andersson, Tallinn 1973 — 15/355

32 9... ♗b7 10. f4 g6 11. ♕d2 ♕c7 [R. Byrne–Tajmanov, Leningrad (izt) 1973 — 15/330] 12. 0-0-0!±

33 12. ♕d2!±

34 15. ♗c5 f5! 16. ♗d6 ♔b6 17. ♗b8 ♘b8 19. de5 ♗e5± Estrin–Tajmanov, Albena 1974 — 18/363

35 9. ♕d6?? ♘d5–+

36 10. f4 ♗e7 11. ♗e3 0–0 12. ♕e2 b5 13. a4 b4 14. ♘d1 ♕c7= Romanišin–Hartoch, Amsterdam 1973

37 10... ♘a5!?

38 11. ♕e2 0–0 [11... b6!?] 12. a5 ♗f6 13. ♗e3 ♗c3 14. bc3± Hort–S. Garcia, Madrid 1973 — 16/340

39 15. g4± Rajna–Tajmanov, Budapest 1973

40 **9. ♗e3** b5!? 10. ♖e1 [10. e5 ♘e5 11. ♗a8 ♕a8∞̄] ♖c8 11. a4 ♘d4 12. ♕d4 ♗e7 13. ab5 ab5∞ Klovan–Vasjukov, SSSR 1972 — 14/373; **9. ♘b3** ♗e7 11. f4 b5! 11. ♗e3 0–0 12. e5 de5! 13. fe5 ♘e5 14. ♗a8 ♕a8∞̄ Izvozčikov–Liberzon, SSSR 1972; **9. ♘de2** b5 10. a3 ♗e7 11. h3 0–0 12. g4 ♘e8 13. f4 a5 14. ♘g3± Gufeljd–Petrosjan, SSSR 1972 — 13/513; **9. ♘ce2** ♗e7 10. b3 ♕c7 11. ♗b2 — B 47

41 Andersson–Petrosjan, Skopje (ol) 1972

B 47 1. e4 c5 2. ♘f3 e6 3. d4 cd4 4. ♘d4 ♘c6 5. ♘c3 ♕c7

	6	7	8	9	10	11	12	13	14	
1	f4[1]	♘c6[2]	♗d3	♕e2	♗d2	a3[3]				=
	a6	♕c6	b5	♗b7	♗c5					
2	♗e2	a3	0–0[5]	g3[6]	♕d4	♕d3	bc3	♗f3	♖d1	∞
	a6[4]	♘f6	♗d6!?	♘d4	♗e5	♗c3	0–0	d6[7]	♗d7[8]	
3	...	...	♘c6	0–0[10]	♗f3	e5	♗b7	♗f4	♕e2	=
	...	b5	♕c6[9]	♗b7	♕c7	♖c8[11]	♕b7	♘e7	♖c4[12]	
4	...	0–0	♘c6	♗f3![15]	♗f4!	♖e1	a4![18]			±
	...	b5[13]	♕c6[14]	♗b7[16]	d6[17]	e5	ba4!?[19]			
5	...	...	♔h1[20]	♕d4	♕d3	f4	♗f3	e5	♘e4	±
	...	♘f6	♘d4[21]	♗c5	b5[22]	♗b7	0–0	♘e8	♗e7[23]	
6	...	...	...	♘c6[24]	♕d4	♕e3	♕g3	♕c3	f3	=
	...	...	♗b4	bc6	c5	d6[25]	♗c3	0–0	♗b7[26]	

1. e4 c5 2. ♘f3 e6 3. d4 cd4 4. ♘d4 ♘c6 5. ♘c3 ♕c7 6. ♗e2 a6 7. f4

	7	8	9	10	11	12	13	14	15	
7	...	♘c6[27]	♕d4	e5	ed6	♕d6	♗f3	♘e4	♗e3[30]	±
	♗b4?!	bc6[28]	♗f8	d5[29]	♕d6	♗d6	♗b7	♗e7		
8	...	♗e3![31]	♕d3[32]	0-0-0[33]	♘c6	♕e3	g4	f5	f6	±
	♗c5	d6	♘ge7	0–0	♗e3	bc6[34]	c5[35]	♘c6	gf6[36]	
9	...	♕d4	♗e3	0–0[38]	♕d2[39]	♖ad1	a4[41]	♘d5	ed5	=
	♘d4	♘e7	b5[37]	♘c6	♗b7[40]	♗e7	b4	ed5	♕d6![42]	

	7	8	9	10	11	12	13	14	15	
10	...	...	♕f2!?	♗e3	0–0	e5[46]	♘e4	♗b6	♗c5[48]	±
	...	...	♘c6[43]	b5[44]	♗e7[45]	0–0[47]	♗b7	♕b8		
11	...	f5[49]	fe6	♘e6	0–0	♗g4	♗h3	♔h1	♕e2[51]	±
	d6	♘f6	♗e6[50]	fe6	♗e7	♘d8	♕b6	0–0		
12	...	♘c6	♗f3[53]	e5[54]	♘e4[55]	♕e2	♘g3[57]	♗e3	♕d3	∞
	b5	♕c6[52]	♗b7	♕c7	♖d8!	d5[56]	g6	h5	♘e7[58]	

1. e4 c5 2. ♘f3 e6 3. d4 cd4 4. ♘d4 ♘c6 5. ♘c3 ♕c7 6. g3 a6[59]

	7	8	9	10	11	12	13	14	15	
13	♗g2	0–0	♖e1	♘c6	♘a4[63]	c4	♘c3[64]	♗f4[65]		∞
	d6[60]	♗d7[61]	♗e7	bc6[62]	♖b8	c5	♗f6	♗e5		

1. e4 c5 2. ♘f3 e6 3. d4 cd4 4. ♘d4 ♘c6 5. ♘c3 ♕c7 6. g3 a6 7. ♗g2 ♘f6 8. 0–0 ♘d4[66] 9. ♕d4 ♗c5 10. ♗f4[67] d6[68]

	11	12	13	14	15	16	17	18	19	
14	♕d3	♘a4	♗d2	♘c5[71]	♕a3	♗a5	♖ad1[73]	♖d5	♖d6	=
	♘d7[69]	e5[70]	b5	♘c5	♗b7	♕c6[72]	0–0[74]	♕c8[75]	♗e4![76]	
15	♕d2	♖ad1[78]	♗e3	♗c5	f3	f4!	♘d5[81]	ed5	fe5	±
	h6[77]	e5	♗g4[79]	dc5	♗e6	0–0[80]	♗d5	♕d6[82]	♕e5[83]	

1. e4 c5 2. ♘f3 e6 3. d4 cd4 4. ♘d4 ♘c6 5. ♘c3 ♕c7 6. g3 a6 7. ♗g2 ♘f6 8. 0–0 ♗e7

	9	10	11	12	13	14	15	16	17	
16	♘b3[84]	f4	e5[86]	♘e2	♘ed4	♘c6	♘d4	♗e3	♕d2	=
	0–0	d5[85]	♘d7	b5	b4	♕c6	♕b6	a5	♗c5[87]	
17	♔h1	f4	♗e3[89]	♘b3	g4	a3	♕d2	ab4	♖f3	∞
	0–0	d6[88]	♗d7	♖ab8	b5	♘e8	b4	♘b4	d5[90]	
18	b3	♗b2	♘ce2	♘d4	♘f5	ef5				=
	0–0	d6[91]	♘d4!?[92]	e5	♗f5	d5[93]				
19	♘ce2	c4	♕d4	♕d3[96]	cb5	♗g5	♖fc1			=
	0–0	♘d4[94]	e5[95]	b5!	ab5	b4	♕b8[97]			
20	♖e1	♘c6	e5	♕e2[101]	♘e4!?	c4	♗g5	f4	♗h4[103]	±
	0–0[98]	dc6[99]	♖d8[100]	♘d5	♕e5[102]	♘f6	♕f5	h6		
21	...	♕d4	♕d1[104]	♗e3[105]	♕d2	♗c5[106]	♖ad1	♖e3		∞
	♘d4	♗c5	d6	e5	♗e6	♕c5	♔e7[107]	♖hd8!?[108]		

1 **6. ♘c6?!** ♕c6 7. ♗b5 ♕c7 8. 0–0 a6 9. ♗d3±; 6... dc6 7. f4±; 6... bc6△ d5=; **6. ♘b3** ♘f6 7. ♗d3 a6 8. f4 d6 9. g4 h6∞ Velimirović–Damjanović, Skopje 1971 — 12/382

2 **7. ♘f3** b5 8. ♗d3 ♘f6 9. ♕e2 ♘b4 10. 0–0 ♗b7= Parma–Janošević, Skopje 1968; **7. ♗e2** — 6. ♗e2; **7. ♗e3** — B 48

3 **11. ♕g4** g6 12. ♕h4 [12. a3 f5! 13. ef5?! ef5 14. ♕e2 ♔f7!∓ Planinc–Karpov, Madrid 1973 — 16/287; 13. ♕h4 ♗e7∓] b4 13. ♘d1 ♗e7 14. ♕h3 ♘f6 15. ♘f2 d5∓ Planinc–Suetin, Ljubljana–Portorož 1973 — 15/356; **11. a3**= Suetin

4 6... ♘f6 7. f4 d6 8. ♗e3 ♗e7 9. 0–0 0–0 — B 83

5 **8. ♗e3** — B 49

6 9. ♘c6!? bc6 10. f4 e5 11. f5 ♗c5∞

7 13... d5!?

8 15. ♗g5 ♗b5∞ Kostro–Suetin, Tbilisi 1969 — 8/339

9 8... dc6?! 9. 0–0 e5 10. ♕d3! ♘e7 [10... ♘f6 11. ♕g3!±↑] 11. a4! b4 12. ♘b1 ♘g6 13. ♕b3 ♗c5 14. ♗c4 0–0 15. ♗e3 ♕e7 16. ♘d2± Holmov–Suetin, SSSR (ch) 1963

10 9. ♗e3 — B 49

11 11... ♖d8!?

12 **14... ♘f5** 15. a4 b4 16. ♘e4 ♗e7 17. ♖ad1 0–0 18. g4! ♘h4 19. ♗g3± Holmov–Suetin, SSSR (ch) 1962; **14... ♖c4** 15. ♗g3 ♕c6=

13 7... ♗b4 8. ♘c6 [8. ♗e3 ♘f6 — B 49; 8. ♔h1 ♘f6 — 7... ♘f6] bc6 [8... ♕c6?! 9. ♕d4±; 8... dc6 9. f4±↑] 9. f4 [9. ♕d4 ♗d6∞] d5 10. ♕d4 ♕a7 11. ♕a7 ♖a7 12. ♗e3±

14 8... dc6 9. f4 ♗b7 — 7. f4

15 9. e5 ♗b7 10. ♗f3 ♕c7 11. ♗b7 [11. ♗f4 ♘e7 12. ♖e1 ♘g6 13. ♗g3 ♖c8 14. ♗b7 ♕b7 15. ♕d3 ♗b4 16. ♘e4 0–0 17. c3 ♗e7 18. ♖ad1 ♖fd8 19. h4± Filep–Somogyi, Hungary 1963] ♕b7 12. ♕d3 ♘e7 13. ♗f4 ♘g6 14. ♗g3 ♗e7±

16 9... ♕c7 10. ♖e1±

17 10... ♘e7 11. ♗d6! ♘g6 12. e5± Parma–Krnić, Vršac 1973

18 12. ♗d2 ♘f6 13. a4 ba4 14. ♖a4 ♗e7 15. ♗g5 0–0= Geler–Tajmanov, Palma de Mallorca (izt) 1970 — 10/440

19 **12... ef4**? 13. e5!+–→; **12... b4**?! 13. ♘d5 ef4 14. c3! b3 15. e5! 0-0-0 16. ♕b3 ♔b8 17. ♘b4!+–→ Velimirović–Vasjukov, Jugoslavija–SSSR 1973 — 16/341; **12... ba4**!?± Cvetković

20 △ f4; 8. ♗e3 — B 49

21 **8... b5**?! 9. ♘c6 dc6 10. f4 b4 11. e5 bc3 12. ef6 gf6 13. ♕e1!± Velimirović–Damjanović, Sombor 1972 — 14/378; **8... ♗e7** 9. f4 d6 — B 85

22 10... h5?! 11. f4 d6 12. ♗e3 ♘g4 13. ♗c5 ♕c5 14. ♗g4 hg4 15. ♖ad1± Velimirović–Christoph, Bath 1973

23 **15. ♗e3** ♖d8 16. a4 d6!= Liebert–Furman, Polanica Zdroj 1967 — 4/441; **15. a4**!±

24 9. ♗g5 ♗c3 [9... ♕d6!? 10. ♘c6 ♕d1?! 11. ♘d1± Smislov–Razuvajev, SSSR 1974 — 18/365; 10... bc6 11. ♗d3 ♕c5∞; 11. ♕d6 ♗d6 12. ♖ad1 ♗e5∞; 9... d6 10. f4 ♗c3 11. ♗f6 ♗d4 12. ♗d4 ♘d4 13. ♕d4 e5= Velimirović–Matulović, Jugoslavija (ch) 1975] 10. ♗f6 gf6 11. bc3 b5!? 12. ♘c6 ♕c6= Parma–Suetin, Ljubljana–Portorož 1973

25 11... ♗b7 12. e5 ♗c3 13. bc3?! ♘d5 14. ♕g3 ♘e7! 15. f4 0–0∓ Ostojić–Suetin, La Habana 1968 — 6/466; 13. ♕c3=

26 Kaplan–Karpov, Madrid 1973 — 17/406

27 8. ♗f3 ♗c3 [8... ♘e5? 9. fe5! ♗c3 10. bc3 ♕c3 11. ♕d2 ♕a1 12. 0–0 ♕a2 13. ♕b4 +–→ Vasiljev–Klavin, SSSR 1962] 9. bc3 ♘a5∓

28 8... ♕c6 9. ♕d4 ♗c3 [9... ♗f8±] 10. bc3 ♘f6 11. e5 [11. ♗f3 d5 12. e5±] ♘d5 12. ♗d2 b5 13. a4 ♗b7 14. ♖b1 ♘b6 15. ab5 ab5 16. ♗b5 ♕g2 17. ♖g1 ♕e4 18. ♕e4 ♗e4 19. ♗d3± Parma–Tan, Beverwijk 1963

29 10... ♘e7 11. ♗d3 ♘f5 12. ♗f5 ef5 13. ♗e3 ♖b8 14. 0-0-0± Unzicker–Tajmanov, Buenos Aires 1960

30 Dely–Navarovszky, Hungary (ch) 1965

31 8. ♘c6 ♕c6 9. ♗f3 d6 10. ♕d3 ♕b6 11. ♗d2 ♗d7 12. 0-0-0 ♘e7 13. ♖he1 ♗b5! [13... 0–0 14. ♗e3 ♖fd8 15. ♗c5 dc5 16. ♕e3 ♗c6= Ivkov–Gipslis, Jugoslavija–SSSR 1962] 14. ♘b5 ab5∓ Gipslis

32 9. ♕d2 ♘ge7 10. 0-0-0 0–0 [10... ♘d4 11. ♗d4 0–0 12. ♗c5 dc5 13. ♕d6±; 10... b5 11. ♘c6 ♗e3 12. ♕e3 ♘c6 13. e5 d5 14. ♕c5±] 11. ♘c6 ♘c6 12. ♗c5 dc5 13. e5 ♖d8 14. ♕e3 ♘d4 [van den Berg–Langeweg, Beverwijk 1963] 15. ♗f3±

33 10. ♘c6 ♘c6 11. 0-0-0 0–0 12. ♗f3 ♖b8 13. ♗c5 dc5 14. e5 ♖d8 15. ♕c4 ♘d4 16. ♘e4 b6 17. ♘d6± Parma–Langeweg, Beverwijk 1963

34 12... ♕c6? 13. ♖d3 ♖d8 14. ♖hd1 ♕c7 15. ♕d2+– Minić–Tajmanov, Jugoslavija–SSSR 1962

35 13... d5 14. f5 ♖e8 15. ♖hf1 f6 [15... de4 16. f6±→] 16. ed5 ed5 17. ♗f3±

36 16. g5 ♕e7 17. gf6 ♕f6 18. ♖df1 ♕d4 19. ♖hg1 ♔h8 20. ♕h6±→ Šamkovič

37 9... ♘c6?! 10. ♕b6 ♕b6 11. ♗b6 ♗b4 12. 0-0-0 ♗a5 13. ♘a4 ♗b6 14. ♘b6 ♖b8 15. ♖d6±

38 10. 0-0-0 ♘c6 11. ♕d2 ♗b4 [11... ♗b7 12. ♗f3 ♖c8?? 13. ♗b6+–; 12... ♖d8±] 12. ♔b1 0–0 13. ♗f3 ♖b8 14. e5 ♘a5 15. ♗d4 ♗b7 16. ♗b7 ♕b7 17. ♕e2 ♗c3 18. ♗c3 b4 19. ♗d4 ♖fc8= Alexander–Judovič, corr. 1965

39 11. ♕d3 ♗e7 12. ♖ad1 ♗b7 13. e5 ♖d8= Bertok–Polugajevski, Jugoslavija–SSSR 1962

40 11... ♘a5 12. a3 ♘c4 13. ♗c4 ♕c4 14. ♖ad1 ♗e7 15. f5 f6= Boleslavski–Dely, Hamburg 1965

41 13. e5 ♖d8 14. ♕e1 ♘a5 15. ♕f2 ♘c4 16. ♗c4 ♕c4 17. f5 ef5 18. ♕f5 0–0= Boleslavski

42 16. dc6 ♕d2 17. ♖d2 ♗c6= Hecht–Matulović, Hamburg 1965

43 9... d5 10. ed5 ♘d5 11. ♘d5 ed5 12. 0–0 ♗e7 13. ♗d3 0–0 14. ♗e3 ♗f6 15. ♗d4 ♕c6 16. ♖fe1± Bajkov–Mojsejev, SSSR 1972

44 10... ♗e7 11. ♗b6 ♕b8 12. e5 d6 13. ed6 ♗d6 14. ♘e4! ♗e7 15. 0-0-0± Kuprejčik–Babev, Dresden 1969 — 8/336

45 11... ♗b7 12. ♗b6 ♕c8 13. f5±→

46 12. ♖ad1 ♗b7 13. ♗b6 ♕c8 14. ♗c5 ♗c5 15. ♕c5 ♘a5= Minić–Matulović, Jugoslavija (ch) 1968

47 **12... f6** 13. ♗h5 g6 14. ef6 gh5 15. fe7 +–→; **12... d6** 13. ♕g3 0–0 14. f5±→ Boleslavski

48 Boleslavski

49 8. ♗e3 ♗e7 [8... ♘f6 9. 0–0 — B 85] 9. ♕d2 ♘f6 10. 0-0-0 0–0 [10... ♘d4?! 11. ♗d4 e5 12. ♗e3 b5 13. fe5 de5 14. ♘d5± Honfi–Talj, Suhumi 1972 — 14/462] 11. g4 b5 12. g5 ♘d7∞

50 9... fe6 10. 0–0 ♗e7 11. ♘c6 ♕c6 12. ♔h1 0–0 13. e5±↑

51 **15. e5** de5 16. ♕e2 ♘c6!= Robatsch–Matulović, Sarajevo 1968 — 5/388; **15. ♕e2**±

52 8... dc6 9. 0–0 ♗b7 [9... ♗b4 10. ♕d4 ♕a7 11. ♗e3 ♕d4 12. ♗d4 ♘f6 13. e5 ♗c3 14. ♗c3 ♘d5 15. ♗d4± Dely–Hajtun, Hungary 1966 — 2/367] 10. ♗e3 ♘f6 11. e5 ♘d5 [11... b4 12. ef6 bc3 13. ♕d4 cb2 14. ♕b2 gf6 15. ♖b1 ♗c8 16. ♕f6± Unzicker–Mikenas, Leningrad 1960] 12. ♘d5 cd5 13. ♗d3±

53 **9. 0—0**?! b4! 10. ♘b1 ♘f6 11. e5 ♗b7 12. ♗f3 ♘d5 13. a3 [13. c3 bc3 14. ♘c3 ♕b6] a5∓ Fućak–Matulović, Jugoslavija 1968 — 7/355; **9. ♗e3** — B 49

54 10. ♗e3 — B 49

55 **11. 0—0** ♘h6 [11... ♖d8?! 12. f5 ♘e7 13. f6 ♘g6 14. ♗b7 ♕b7 15. ♗g5 ♖c8 16. ♕e2±↑ Kuprejčik–Suetin, Soči 1970 — 10/439; 11... ♗c5?! 12. ♔h1 ♘e7 13. ♘e4±; 11... ♖c8 12. ♗b7 ♕b7 13. ♕d3 ♘e7 14. ♗e3 ♘f5 15. ♗f2 ♗c5 16. g4! ♘h4 17. ♘e4 0–0 18. ♖ae1 ♗b6 19. ♕g3 ♖c4 20. ♗b6 ♕b6 21. ♖f2± Kuprejčik–Vujaković, Dresden 1969 — 8/337; 15... h5!? 16. ♘e4 ♗e7 17. ♖ad1 ♕c6 18. ♖fe1 0–0 19. c3 ♖fd8± Ribli–Schmidt, Skopje (ol) 1972] 12. ♗e3 [12. ♗b7 ♕b7 13. ♕d3 ♘f5 14. a4?! ♗c5 15. ♔h1 h5△ ♘g3∓→; 14. ♘e4 ♖d8!∓] ♖d8! 13. ♗f2 d6 14. ♕e2 ♗f3 15. ♕f3 de5 16. fe5 ♗c5 17. ♖ae1 0–0∓ Janošević–Tajmanov, Wijk aan Zee 1970; **11. ♗e3** ♖c8 — B 49

56 12... ♘h6!?

57 13. ed6=

58 Parma–Soos, Titovo Užice 1966 — 2/368

59 **6... ♘f6**? 7. ♗f4 ♘e5 [7... e5 8. ♘db5±] 8. ♘db5 ♕b8 9. ♗e2 ♗c5 10. ♗e5 ♕e5 11. f4± Fischer–Talj, Bled 1961; **6... d6** 7. ♗g2 ♗d7?! [7... a6 — 6... a6] 8. ♘db5 ♕b8 9. ♗f4 ♘e5 10. ♕d4 g5 [10... a6 11. ♘d6! ♗d6 12. 0-0-0+–] 11. ♗g5 a6 12. ♘a3 b5 13. f4?! h6! 14. ♗h4 b4∞ Romanišin–Hort, Göteborg 1971 — 12/382; 13. ♘e2!±

60 **7... b5**?! 8. 0–0 ♗b7 9. ♖e1 ♖c8 [9... d6 10. a4 b4 11. ♘d5!±] 10. ♘d5! ♕b8 11. a4! ♘d4 12. ♕d4 ♖c4 13. ♕d3±→ Čirić–Janošević, Titovo Užice 1966 — 2/370; **7... ♘d4** 8. ♕d4 d6 9. 0–0 ♗e7 10. ♘a4± Barczay–Mecking, Sousse (izt) 1967

61 **8... ♗e7** 9. ♖e1 [9. ♘c6 bc6 10. ♘a4 ♗b7 11. c4 c5= Janošević–Gufeljd, Skopje 1971 — 12/388] ♘f6 — B 80; **8... ♘f6** — B 80

62 10... ♗c6 11. ♕g4! [11. a4△ a5] h5 12. ♕e2 h4 13. b3 [13. ♗e3 ♘f6 14. ♗d4 e5 15. ♗e3 ♕d7∞ Džindžihašvili–Suetin, Tbilisi 1969 — 9/319] hg3 14. hg3 ♘f6 15. ♗b2 b5 16. a3 ♖c8 17. ♖ad1± Honfi–Gufeljd, Suhumi 1972 — 14/379; 11. ♗f4!?

63 11. ♕g4?! h5 12. ♕e2 h4 13. g4?! h3 14. ♗f1 e5∓ Bilek–Doda, Polanica Zdroj 1968 — 6/469

64 13. ♗f4!?

65 **14. ♕c2**?! ♘e7 15. ♗e3 ♘c6∓ Ludolf–Dvorecki, SSSR 1972; **14. f4**!?∞ Dvorecki–Cejtlin, SSSR 1972 — 13/388

66 **8... ♗c5**?! 9. ♗f4 [9. ♘c6 dc6 10. ♘a4 ♗a7 11. c4 b5 12. e5∞ Kuzmin–Averkin, SSSR (ch) 1973 — 16/344; 9. ♘b3 ♗e7 10. f4 d6 11. ♗e3 0–0 12. g4±↑ Muhin–Tajmanov, Suhumi 1972 — 14/380] ♘e5 [9... d6? 10. ♘b3±; 9... e5 10. ♘b3±] 10. ♘a4 ♗e7 11. c4 d6 12. ♖c1 b6 13. b4± Browne–Langeweg, Wijk aan Zee 1974 — 17/401; **8... d6** — B 80

67 **10. ♕d1** d6 11. ♘a4 ♗a7 12. ♗f4 e5 13. ♗g5 ♗d4!? 14. ♗f6 gf6 15. ♕f3 ♔e7 16. c3 ♗a7 17. b3 ♗e6 18. c4 ♗d4∓ Goldenov–Suetin, SSSR (ch) 1963; **10. ♕d3** ♘g4 [10... d6 11. ♘a4 ♗d7=; 11. ♗f4 — 10. ♗f4] 11. ♕e2 ♘e5 12. ♔h1 [12. ♘d1 0–0 13. b3 b5 14. ♗b2 ♗b7 15. ♘e3 d6 16. ♖ac1 ♖ac8 17. ♔h1 ♕b6∓ Estrin–Gipslis, SSSR 1960] d6 13. f4 ♘c6 14. b3 b5 15. ♗b2 ♗b7= Bilek–Tajmanov, Budapest 1961; **10. ♕d2**!? 0–0 11. b3 ♗e7 [11... e5?! 12. ♘a4 ♗e7 13. c4 b5 cb5 ab5 15. ♘c3 b4 16. ♘d5 ♘d5 17. ed5 ♗d6 18. ♗b2± I. Zajcev–Liberzon, SSSR (ch) 1969] 12. ♗b2±

68 10... ♗d4 11. ♗c7 d5 12. ed5 ♗c3 13. bc3 ♘d5 14. ♗e5 f6 15. c4! [15. ♗d4 b5 16. a4 ♗d7=] ♘b4 16. ♗c3 ♘c6 17. ♖ab1±⊥ Honfi–Kozma, Wijk aan Zee 1969 — 7/357

69 **11... ♘g4**?! 12. ♘a4 e5 13. ♗d2 [13. ♘c5?! ef4 14. ♘b3 ♘e5∓↑ Schmid–Hamann, Venezia 1966 — 1/268] ♗e6 14. ♘c5 dc5 15. a4 0–0 16. ♕c3 b5 17. b4 ♗c4 18. ♖fb1± Tringov–Honfi, Čačak 1971 — 11/305; **11... h6**?! 12. ♘a4 e5 13. ♘c5 ef4? 14. ♘b3 fg3 15. hg3 0–0 16. ♖ad1± Podgajec–Vaganjan, SSSR 1971 — 11/306; 13... dc5±

70 12... ♘e5 13. ♗e5 de5 14. ♘c5 ♕c5 15. ♖fd1±

71 14. ♘c3?! ♗b7 15. ♘d5 ♗d5 16. ♕d5 0–0∓ Hübner–Petrosjan, Wijk aan Zee 1971 — 11/308

72 16... ♕e7!? 17. ♕e3 0–0 18. ♖ad1 f5 19. ef5 ♗g2 20. ♔g2 ♖f5= Holmov–Mojsejev, SSSR 1971 — 11/309

73 17. ♖fd1 ♘e4! [17... 0–0?! 18. ♖d5 ♕c8 19. ♖d6 ♘e4 20. ♖b6!± Reshevsky–Vasjukov, Skopje 1970 — 9/324] 18. ♖e1 f5 19. g4 ♕c5 20. ♕c5 ♘c5 21. b4 ♗g2 22. bc5 ♗f3 23. cd6 fg4=

74 17... ♘e4 18. ♖fe1 f5 19. f3±

75 18... f5?! 19. ♖fd1 ♘e4 20. ♕b3 ♔h8 21. ♖d6! [21. ♗e4? fe4 22. ♖d6 ♕e8!∓ Matulović–Vasjukov, Skopje 1970 — 9/325] ♕c8 22. ♖d7 ♘c5 23. ♗b7 ♘b3 24. ♗c8? ♘a5= Adorjan–Timman, Wijk aan Zee II 1971 — 11/307; 24. cb3!+– Adorjan

76 **20. f3**? ♘b7! 21. fe4 ♘a5∓ Matulović –Cvetković, Jugoslavija (ch) 1972 — 13/391; **20. ♗b4**?! ♗g2 21. ♔g2 ♘e4 22. ♖dd1 ♖e8∓ Adorjan–Cvetković, Jugoslavija 1971 — 11/310; **20. ♖e1**! ♗g2 21. ♔g2 ♘b7 22. ♖d2 ♘a5 23. ♕a5 ♕c6 24. f3= Adorjan

77 11... ♘d7?! 12. ♖ad1 ♘e5 13. ♘a4±

78 12. ♘a4?! e5 13. ♘c5 dc5 14. ♗e3 ♘g4= Janošević–Vasjukov, Skopje 1970 — 9/323

79 **13... ♗e3**? 14. fe3±; **13... b5** 14. ♗c5 dc5 15. ♘d5 ♘d5 16. ed5 ♕d6 17. f4 0–0 18. fe5 ♕e5 19. d6± R. Byrne–Lengyel, Moskva 1971 — 13/389; **13... 0–0** 14. ♗c5 dc5 15. ♕d6 ♕d6 16. ♖d6 ♗e6 17. ♖fd1 b5 18. f4 ♖a7 19. f5±↑; **13... ♗e6** 14. ♗c5 dc5 15. ♘d5 ♗d5 16. ed5 ♕d6 17. f4 0–0 18. fe5 ♕e5 19. c4±

80 16... ♖d8 17. ♘d5 ♗d5 18. ed5 e4 19. c4 [19. ♖fe1 ♖d5 20. ♖e4 ♔d8 21. ♕e2 ♖d1 22. ♕d1 ♕d7 23. ♕d7 ♔d7 24. ♖e5±⊥ Fischer–Tajmanov (m) 1971 — 11/311] 0–0 20. ♖fe1 ♖fe8 21. ♕c2± Kurajica–Franklin, Hastings 1971/72 — 13/390

81 **17. f5** ♗c4 18. ♖fe1 b5 19. b3 b4 20. bc4 bc3 21. ♕c3 ♖fd8=∞ Talj; **17. ♕d6** ♖ac8 18. f5 ♗c4 19. ♖fe1 b5 20. b3 b4 21. ♕c7 ♖c7 22. ♘d5 ♗d5 23. ed5 ♘d7 24. d6± Balašov

82 18... e4?! 19. c4 ♕d6 20. ♖fe1 ♖fe8 21. ♖e2?! ♖e7 22. ♖de1 ♖ae8 23. ♖e3 h5∞ Ostojić–Cvetković, Jugoslavija 1973; 21. ♖e3!± Cvetković

83 20. c4±

84 **9. ♘c6**?! bc6 10. b3 d5 11. ♗b2 0–0= Sarapu–Matulović, Skopje 1967; **9. h3** 0–0 10. ♔h2 d6 [10... ♖d8!? 11. f4 d5∞] 11. f4 ♗d7= Pogats–Talj, Palma de Mallorca 1966; **9. ♘de2** 0–0 10. h3 ♖d8 [10... b5 11. a4 b4 12. ♘d5! ed5 13. ed5 ♗b7 14. dc6 dc6 15. ♗f4± Unzicker–Kuijpers, Tel Aviv (ol) 1964] 11. g4 d5 12. ed5 ♘b4 13. ♗f4 ♗d6 14. ♗g5 ♗e7= Foguelman–Lengyel, Amsterdam 1964; **9. ♗e3** 0–0 [9... d6 — B 80] 10. ♕e2 [10. f4 d6 — B 80; 10... d5!?] d6 — B 80

85 10... d6 11. a4 b6 12. g4 ♖b8 13. g5 ♘d7 14. f5±↑ Janošević–Matulović, Vrnjačka Banja 1973 — 15/358; 12... d5!?

86 11. ed5 ed5 12. ♘d5 ♘d5 13. ♕d5 ♗e6 14. ♕f3 ♖ad8=∞ Ljubojević–Janošević, Vrnjačka Banja 1971 — 12/391

87 Barden–Korčnoj, Leipzig (ol) 1960

88 **10... ♖d8** 11. e5 ♘e8 12. ♘c6 bc6 13. ♕f3 ♗b7 14. ♗e3 d5 15. f5!± Bronštejn–Filip, Moskva 1959; **10... d5** 11. e5 ♘d4 12. ♕d4 ♘d7 13. ♕d1 ♗c5 14. b3 b5 15. ♗b2 ♖e8 16. ♘e2 ♗b7 17. ♘d4± Konstantinopoljski–Judovič, corr. 1966 — 2/369

89 11. ♘c6?! bc6 12. g4 [12. e5 de5 13. fe5 ♘d7 14. ♗f4 ♖b8 15. ♖e1 c5∓ Neukirch –Ostojić, Marianske Lazni 1962] d5 13. g5 ♘e4 14. ♘e4 de4 15. ♗e4 ♗b7∓ Rossetto–Tajmanov, La Habana 1964

90 Hübner–Rubinetti, Lugano (ol) 1968 — 6/470

91 **10... ♖d8** 11. ♘ce2 d5 12. ed5 ♘d5 13. c4 ♘db4 14. ♕b1 ♘d4 15. ♘d4 ♗d7 16. ♕e4 ♘c6 17. ♘f3± Korčnoj–Gipslis, Leningrad 1962; **10... ♘d4** 11. ♕d4 d6 12. ♖ac1 ♗d7 [12... b5 13. ♘d1 ♗b7 14. c4±↑ Matanović–Janošević, Maribor 1967] 13. ♘d1 ♘e8 14. c4 ♗f6 15. ♕d2 ♗b2 16. ♕b2 ♘f6 17. ♘e3± Letelier–Pachman, La Habana 1963

92 11... e5 12. ♘c6 bc6 13. c4 ♘d7 14. f4 [14. ♕c2 a5 15. ♖ad1 ♘c5 16. f4 a4∞ Honfi–Talj 1963] a5 15. ♘c1 ♗f6 16. ♘d3 ♖e8 17. ♕c2± Robatsch–Portisch, Palma de Mallorca 1966

93 Parma–Matanović, Zagreb 1965

94 10... ♖d8 11. ♘c3 [11. b3 d5!= Unzicker–Ilivicki, Soči 1965] d6 12. b3 ♗d7 13. ♗b2 ♘d4 [13... ♖ac8 14. ♖c1 ♕b8 15. a4±○ Osmanović–Matulović, Jugoslavija (ch) 1968] 14. ♕d4 b5 15. cb5 ab5 16. a3 ♗c6 17. b4 ♕b7= Joksić–Mihaljčišin, Jugoslavija 1963

95 11... d6 18. ♗d2 [12. b3 ♗d7 13. ♗b2 ♗c6 14. ♖ac1±○ Damjanović–Langeweg, Beverwijk 1966 — 1/269] ♗d7 13. ♖ac1± Tajmanov–Vladimirov, Leningrad 1967 — 3/425

96 12. ♕c3 d6 13. ♗d2 ♗g4 14. ♕d3 ♖fc8 15. ♖fc1 ♗e6 16. b3 ♘d7 17. ♘c3± Ćirić –Janošević, Sarajevo 1968 — 5/390; 12... b5!?∞

97 Tringov–Damjanović, Skopje 1971 — 12/394

98 9... d6 — B 80

99 10... bc6 11. e5 ♘d5 [11... ♘e8 12. ♗f4± Tringov–Doda, Leningrad 1967 —

3/424] 12. ♘a4 [12. ♘e4!? f6 13. c4 ♘b6 14. ef6 gf6 15. ♗f4 e5 16. ♗h6 ♖f7 17. ♕g4 ♔h8 18. ♕h5±→ Boleslavski; 12... ♕e5 13. c4 ♘f6 14. ♗f4?! ♕b2 15. ♘d6 ♕a3!∓ Ćirić – Janošević, Vršac 1969 — 8/343; 14. ♗g5 ♕a5?! 15. ♘f6 ♗f6 16. ♗f6 gf6 17. ♖e4 ♔h8 18. ♕d4 ♕d8 19. ♖h4+−→ Matulović–Janošević, Jugoslavija 1970 — 9/321; 14... ♕f5!?∞] ♖b8 [12... f6? 13. c4 ♘b6 14. ♗f4± Kurajica–Janošević, Skopje 1969 — 8/342] 13. c4 ♘b6 14. ♘b6 ♖b6 15. ♕c2±

[100] 11... ♘d5 12. ♕g4 ♔h8 13. ♗d2± Lukin–Cvetković, Jugoslavija 1965

[101] 12. ♕f3!? ♘d5 13. h4±↑» Vasjukov–Damjanović, Varna 1971 — 12/393

[102] 13... b5 14. ♘g5 h6 15. ♘h3 ♗b7 16. g4 c5 17. g5±↑» Browne–Damjanović, Venezia 1971 — 12/395

[103] Boleslavski

[104] 11. ♕d3 ♘g4 12. ♖e2 d6=

[105] ♗g5 ♗d7=

[106] ♖ad1 ♖d8 15. h3 ♔e7 16. f4 ♗b4 17. ♕f2 ♖c8 18. ♖e2 [Planinc–Matulović, Jugoslavija (ch) 1975] ♗c3∞

[107] 15... ♖d8 16. ♖e3 b5 17. a3∞ Timman–Matulović, Skopje (ol) 1972 — 14/382

[108] **16... ♖ac8** 17. ♘a4 ♕c7 18. ♖c3 ♕b8 19. ♘b6 ♖c6 20. ♖c6 bc6 21. ♕a5± Zuidema–Langeweg, Wijk aan Zee I 1973; **16... ♖hd8**∞

B 48

1. e4 c5 2. ♘f3 e6 3. d4 cd4 4. ♘d4 ♘c6 5. ♘c3 ♕c7 6. ♗e3

	6	7	8	9	10	11	12	13	14	
1	...	f4[2]	♘c6[4]	♕d4	bc3	♗d3[5]	a4[6]	♖b1	♖b4	=
	a6[1]	♗b4[3]	♕c6	♗c3	♘f6	b5	♗b7	0–0	d5![7]	
2	...	a3	f4[9]	♕f3[11]	♗d3	0–0[13]	♗d4	♗e3[15]	♘d5	=
	...	♘f6[8]	d6[10]	♗e7[12]	0–0	♘d4[14]	e5	b5	♘d5[16]	
3	...	♗d3	♘c6[18]	0–0[20]	a3[22]	♕g4[24]	f4	♗c5	♔h1	=
	...	b5[17]	♕c6[19]	♗b7[21]	♘e7[23]	♘g6	♗c5	♕c5	0–0[25]	

1. e4 c5 2. ♘f3 e6 3. d4 cd4 4. ♘d4 ♘c6 5. ♘c3 ♕c7 6. ♗e3 a6 7. ♗d3 ♘f6

	8	9	10	11	12	13	14	15	16	
4	♕e2[26]	g3[28]	♘c6[29]	bc3	♗d4	0–0	♖fe1	♗f6		=
	♗d6[27]	♗e5	♗c3[30]	♕c6	b5	♗b7	0–0	gf6[31]		
5	0–0	♗d4	♗c5[33]	♘a4[34]	c4	cb5	♘c3	♘b5	e5	±
	♘d4[32]	♗c5	♕c5	♕a5[35]	b5	ab5	b4	0–0	♘d5[36]	
6	...	...	♗f6	♕g4	♔h1![38]	♕e2[39]	g3	f4	♕d2	±
	...	...	gf6	♕e5[37]	♕g5	♗d6	h5	♕g4	♗c7[40]	
7	...	♕e2[41]	♖ad1[42]	♗f4	♘b3	♘b1	♗g3	h3	♗f4	=
	b5	♗b7	♘e5[43]	♗c5	♗b4	♗d6	h5!?	h4	♘f3[44]	
8	...	♘c6	a3[46]	♕e2[48]	f4	e5	♘d5	c4	♗c4	±
	...	♕c6[45]	♗b7[47]	♗e7[49]	0–0	♘d5[50]	♕d5	bc4	♕c6[51]	
9	...	h3[52]	♗f4[54]	♘c6[55]	a4	a5				=
	♗d6	♗f4[53]	♕f4	dc6[56]	e5[57]	♗e6				
10	...	♘c6	f4	f5	♕f3	♘a4[61]	♗b6	c4!?[62]		±
	...	bc6[58]	e5	♗b7[59]	♗e7[60]	d5	♕b8			
11	...	h3[63]	f4[64]	♗c4	♕d3	e5[66]	♕c4	f5!?	fe6	$\overline{\infty}$
	♘e5	b5	♘c4	♕c4	d5[65]	♘d7	dc4	♘e5[67]	♗e6[68]	
12	...	...	...	...	e5	♘d5	♕e2[70]	♘b3	c3[71]	±
	...	...	...	...	♘d5[69]	♕d5	♗b7	♖c8	♕c4[72]	

	8	9	10	11	12	13	14	15	16	
13	...	...	♘a4[73]	c4	♖c1	♘c3	b3[75]	♗b1	a4	=
	...	♗c5	♗a7	d6[74]	♗d7	0–0	♖ac8	♕b8	h6[76]	
14	...	...	♕e2	f4	♘b3[79]	♕e3	♖ae1[81]	e5[82]	♗g6	=
	...	...	d6[77]	♘g6[78]	♗e3	0–0[80]	b5	de5	hg6[83]	

[1] 6... ♘f6 7. ♗d3 [7. ♘db5?! ♕b8 8. ♕d2 a6 9. ♗b6? ab5 10. ♘b5 ♗b4! 11. c3 ♗a5∓ Novopašin–Gufeljd, SSSR (ch) 1963; 9. ♘d4=; 7. f4 ♗b4?! 8. ♘b5 ♕a5 9. e5!± Beljavski–Matulović, Sombor 1972 — 14/385; 7... ♘d4 8. ♕d4 ♘g4∞; 7. ♗e2 a6 — B 49] ♘d4 8. ♗d4 ♗c5 9. ♗c5 ♕c5 10. ♕e2 d6 11. ♗b5 ♗d7 12. ♗d7 ♘d7 13. 0–0 ♖c8 14. ♖fd1 a6= Geler–Talj, Curaçao (ct) 1962

[2] 7. ♘b3 ♘f6 8. f4 ♗b4 [8... d6 9. ♗d3 b5 10. ♕f3 ♗b7 11. g4 ♗e7 12. 0-0-0± Fischer–Soos, Skopje 1967 — 4/407] 9. ♗d3 ♗c3 10. bc3 d6 11. 0–0 0–0 12. ♖f3 e5 13. f5 ♘e7 [13... d5 14. ♖g3! ♔h8 15. ed5 ♘e7 16. ♗c5 ♘fd5 17. ♕g4 ♖g8 18. ♖h3± Spaski–Suetin, SSSR 1967 — 4/447] 14. ♖g3 ♔h8 15. ♗g5 d5! 16. ♘d2 [16. ♗f6?! ♕b6!∓] ♘eg8∞ Listengarten–Suetin, SSSR 1973 — 16/345

[3] **7... d6** 8. ♕f3 ♘f6 9. 0-0-0 ♗d7 10. g4 [10. ♗e2 ♖c8 11. g4 ♘d4 12. ♖d4±↑ Šahović–Marangunić, Jugoslavija 1966 — 1/270] ♘d4 11. ♖d4!±↑ Meštrović–Janošević, Sarajevo 1966 — 1/271; **7... b5** 8. ♘c6 [8. ♗e2?! ♗b7 9. ♘c6 ♗c6 10. ♗f3 b4 11. ♘e2 ♘f6 12. ♘g3 d5∓↑ Robatsch–Janošević, Maribor 1967 — 4/444; 8. ♘b3 d6 9. ♗d3 ♘f6 10. ♕f3 — 7. ♘b3] ♕c6 9. ♗e2 — B 49; **7... ♘d4** 8. ♕d4 b5 9. ♗e2 ♘e7 — B 47; **7... ♘a5**!? 8. ♘b3 [8. ♕f3?! b5∓↑ van der Weide–Kurajica, Wijk aan Zee 1973] b5!?∞

[4] **8. ♗d3** ♘f6 9. 0–0 ♗c5 10. ♘f5 ♗e3 11. ♘e3 d6= Schmid–Panno, Lugano (ol) 1968 — 6/472; **8. ♕g4** ♘ce7! [8... g6?! 9. ♕h4 ♗e7 10. ♕f2 ♘f6 11. ♗e2± Planinc–Matulović, Jugoslavija 1965] 9. ♗d3 ♘g6 10. 0–0 ♘f6 11. ♕f3 d6 12. ♕g3 h5∞ Bogdanović–Matulović, Jugoslavija 1965

[5] 11. e5 ♘d5 12. ♗d2 b5 13. c4 bc4 14. ♕c4 ♕b6 15. ♕d3 a5= Matanović–Matulović, Jugoslavija 1964

[6] 12. e5 ♘d5 13. ♗e4 ♗b7∓ Meštrović–Parma, Jugoslavija 1964

[7] Fischer–Matulović, Skopje 1967 — 4/445

[8] 7... b5 8. ♗e2 — B 49; 8. ♘c6 ♕c6 9. ♗e2 — B 49

[9] 8. ♗e2 — B 49

[10] **8... ♘d4** 9. ♗d4! [9. ♕d4 ♘g4 10. ♗d2 ♕c5 11. ♕c5 ♗c5 12. ♘d1 d6 13. ♗e2 ♘f6 14. ♘c3 ♗d4= Yanofsky–Olafsson, Stockholm (izt) 1962] ♕f4 10. g3 ♕c7 11. e5±↑ Vasjukov–Estrin, SSSR 1960; **8... d5** 9. e5 ♘d7 10. ♕f3 ♘d4 11. ♗d4 ♗c5 12. ♗c5 ♘c5 13. ♗d3± Ilijevski–Janošević, Skopje 1967 — 4/446

[11] 9. ♗d3 ♘d4 10. ♗d4 e5 11. ♗e3 ♗e7 12. ♕f3 0–0 [12... b5 13. ♘d5 ♘d5 14. ed5 ♗f6 (Talj–Korčnoj, Curaçao (ct) 1962) 15. f5! ♕e7 16. ♕e4 ♗h4 17. g3 ♗g5 18. ♗g5 ♕g5 19. a4± Filip] 13. 0–0 [13. f5!?] b5 — 9. ♕f3

[12] **9... ♘d4** 10. ♗d4 b5 13. 0-0-0± Talj–Gufeljd, Tbilisi 1970 — 9/326; **9... e5**!? 10. ♘f5 [10. ♘c6 bc6 11. fe5 ♘g4 12. ed6 ♗d6 13. g3 ♘e3 14. ♕e3 ♗e6 15. ♗g2 ♖b8 16. 0-0-0 0–0 17. ♖he1 ♗e5=∞ Šijanovski–Tajmanov, SSSR (ch) 1962; 15. ♗d3!?] ♗f5 11. ef5 ♘d4= Gufeljd

[13] 11. ♘b3 b5 12. 0–0 — B 82

[14] 11... ♗d7 12. ♖ae1 — B 82

[15] 13. fe5 de5 14. ♕g3 ♗c5=

[16] 15. ed5 ef4 16. ♕f4 f5! 17. ♗d4 ♗f6 18. ♖ae1 g5 19. ♕f2 ♗d4 20. ♕d4 ♕a7= Česnauskas–Krogius, SSSR 1963

[17] 7... ♘d4 8. ♗d4 ♘e7 9. 0–0 ♘c6 10. ♗e3 b5 11. f4 ♗b7 12. ♕h5±↑ Estrin–Goldin, SSSR 1966

[18] **8. a3** ♗b7 [8... ♗d6!? 9. ♕g4 ♗e5= Dahlin–Garcia 1964] 9. 0–0 ♖c8= Listengarten–Akopjan, SSSR 1963; **8. 0–0** ♗b7 9. ♘b3 [9. ♔h1 ♘f6 10. a3 h5!∓↑ Antunac–Kurajica, Jugoslavija 1967 — 4/448; 9. a4 ♘d4 10. ♗d4 b4 11. ♘e2 e5 12. ♗e3 ♘f6= Iščenko–Petkevič, SSSR 1964; 9. ♕e2 ♘f6 — 7... ♘f6] ♘f6 [9... ♘e5 10. f4 ♘c4 11. ♗c1?! ♘f6 12. ♕e2 ♗b4∓ Levy–Portisch, Hastings 1970/71 — 10/442; 10. ♕e2 ♘f6 11. f4 ♘c4 12. ♗d4 ♖c8 13. e5 ♘d5 14. ♘e4± Gheorghiu–Soos, Bucuresti 1967 — 3/427] 10. f4 d6 11. ♕f3 ♗e7 — B 82

[19] 8... dc6 9. 0–0 ♗b7 10. a4±

[20] **9. ♕f3** ♗b7 10. ♗d4 ♕d6 [10... ♘f6!? 11. ♗f6 gf6 12. ♕f6 ♖g8=∞ Zajcev–Rošalj, SSSR 1964] 11. ♕e3 e5 12. ♗b6 ♘f6= G. Petrosjan–Rošalj, SSSR 1964; **9. ♕e2** b4 10. ♘d1 ♗b7 11. 0–0 ♘f6 12. f3 d5= Ree–Mecking, Wijk aan Zee 1971 — 11/315; 10. ♘b1!?

[21] **9... ♗c5**? 10. ♕g4± Boleslavski; **9... ♘f6** — 7... ♘f6

[22] **10. ♕e2** ♘f6 11. f3 b4 12. ♘b1 d5?! 13. ♘d2 ♗e7 14. ♔h1± Troianescu–Aloni,

Netanya 1968 — 6/473; 12... ♗c5!= Nej—Suetin, SSSR (ch) 1963; **10. ♖e1** ♘f6 11. ♗g5 ♗e7 12. ♕f3 b4 13. ♘e2 ♕c5= Ghizdavu—Bukić, Athens 1971 — 12/399

23 10... ♘f6 — 7... ♘f6

24 11. f4 ♘f5! 12. ♗f2 ♗c5 13. ♕f3 [13. ♗c5 ♕c5 14. ♖f2 ♘e3 15. ♕e2 ♖c8 16. ♖e1 ♘c4∓ Mesing—Krnić, Jugoslavija 1973] ♘d6 14. ♕g3 g6= Martinović—Krnić, Jugoslavija 1973 — 16/349

25 15. ♖ae1 f6= Minić—Tajmanov, Palma de Mallorca (izt) 1970 — 10/443

26 **8. ♕d2** ♘g4 9. ♗f4 e5 [9... d6 10. ♘c6 bc6 11. 0—0 ♗e7 12. h3 ♘e5 13. ♗h2 0—0 14. ♗e2± Tribuševski—Averkin, SSSR 1969 — 7/361] 10. ♘c6 dc6 11. ♗g3 ♗d6=; **8. ♘b3** b5 [8... ♘e5 9. ♕e2 ♗d6?! 10. g3 b5 11. f4 ♘c4 12. ♗c4 bc4 13. ♘d2 ♗b4 14. ♗d4± Ciocaltea—Kupper, Lugano (ol) 1968 — 6/475; 9... b5!?; 8... ♗b4 9. f4 ♗c3 10. bc3 — 7. ♘b3] 9. f4 [9. 0—0 ♗b7 — 7... b5] ♘b4 [9... ♗b4 10. 0—0 ♗b7 11. a4 ♗c3 12. bc3 b4 13. c4 d6 14. a5 ♖c8 15. ♕e2 0—0± Židkov—Vasjukov, SSSR (ch) 1972; 9... d6 10. ♕e2 ♗e7 11. g4 ♘d7 12. 0—0 ♘c5∞ Bellin—Schmidt, Lublin 1973] 10. 0—0 ♗b7∞ Kurajica—Janošević, Jugoslavija 1968

27 **8... ♗b4**!? 9. 0—0 ♗c3 10. bc3 d6 [10... d5 11. ed5 ♘d5 12. ♘c6 ♕c6 13. c4 ♘e3 14. ♕e3±↑ Mučnik—Hasin, SSSR 1959] 11. f4 0—0 12. ♘c6!± Nikitin; **8... ♗e7** 9. 0—0 0—0 10. f4 d6 — B 82

28 **9. h3** ♗e5 [9... b5 10. ♘b3 0—0 11. 0—0 ♗f4= Đurašević—Tajmanov, Jugoslavija—SSSR 1959] 10. ♘b3 0—0 11. 0—0 ♗c3 12. bc3 d5 13. ed5 ♘d5= Capelan—Matulović, Bath 1973; **9. 0-0-0** ♗e5 [9... 0—0 10. g3 ♗e7 11. f4±] 10. ♘c6 bc6 [10... dc6 11. ♕d2 ♕a5=] 11. ♘a4 ♖b8 12. g3 ♖b4∞ Gipslis—Tajmanov, SSSR 1959

29 10. ♘b3 d5 11. ♗d2 de4 12. ♗e4 ♘e4 13. ♕e4 0—0= Pelitov—Lengyel, Hungary 1966

30 **10... ♕c6** 11. ♗d2 b5 12. f4 ♗d4= Đurašević—Damjanović, Jugoslavija 1962; **10... bc6**!?

31 Lejn—Suetin, SSSR (ch) 1965

32 **8... ♗b4** 9. ♘c6 [9. f4?? ♗c5—+ Zinn—Matulović, Maribor 1967 — 4/455; 9. ♘a4!?] bc6 10. ♘a4!± Pavlov—Matulović, Bucuresti 1966 — 1/273; **8... b6**!?△ ♗c5

33 10. ♗e2 d6 11. ♗c5 [11. ♕d3 b5 12. ♖ad1 ♗b7 13. a3 ♖d8= Ravinski—Tajmanov, SSSR 1958] ♕c5 12. ♕d3 b5 13. ♖ad1 ♔e7= Spaski—Korčnoj, SSSR 1961

34 **11. ♕f3** d6 12. ♕g3 0—0 13. ♔h1 e5 14. ♕h4 b5 15. ♖ae1 ♗b7 16. ♖e3 h6 17. ♖g3 ♔h8= Szabo—Korčnoj, Budapest 1961; **11. ♔h1** d6 [11... b5 12. f4 b4 13. ♘b1 ♗b7 14. ♘d2 d5 15. e5 ♘e4 16. ♕e2± Nežmetdinov—Tajmanov, SSSR 1960] 12. f4 e5 13. ♕e1 0—0 14. ♕h4 ef4 15. ♘d5 ♘d5 16. ed5 g6= Banik—Šamkovič, SSSR 1960; **11. ♕e2** d6 12. ♔h1 [12. ♖fe1 ♗d7 13. ♖ad1 ♗c6 14. e5 ♕e5 15. ♕e5 de5 16. ♖e5= Ivkov—Korčnoj, Jugoslavija—SSSR 1958] b5 13. f4 b4 14. ♘b1 [14. ♘d1 ♗b7 15. a3 0—0 16. ab4 ♕b4 17. ♘f2 e5!= Kupper—Gligorić, Zürich 1959] e5= Gufeljd—Tajmanov, SSSR (ch) 1959

35 11... ♕c7 12. c4 d6 13. ♖c1 [13. ♕b3] 0—0 14. ♕e2 ♗d7 15. ♘c3±○ Minić—Damjanović, Jugoslavija 1961

36 17. a4 ♗b7 18. ♕h5 f5 19. ♕h4 b3 20. ♖fd1± ×b3 Spaski—Polugajevski, SSSR 1963

37 **11... ♗f8**?! 12. ♖ae1 h5 13. ♕h4 ♗e7 14. ♖e2!± Hennings—Hamann, Harrachov 1967 — 4/452; **11... ♔f8** 12. ♔h1! [12. ♕h4 ♕e5 13. ♔h1 ♕g5 14. ♕g5 fg5 15. e5 d5=] h5 13. ♕h4 ♗e7 14. f4 f5 [14... b5 15. f5 ♗b7 16. ♘e2 ♕e5 17. ♘f4±→ Mojsejev] 15. ♕h3 fe4 16. ♘e4 d5 17. ♘g5±→ Toluš—Matulović, SSSR—Jugoslavija 1965

38 12. ♕g7 ♖f8 13. ♔h1 ♕g5 14. ♕h7 ♖g8 15. ♕h3 b5 16. f4 ♕g7 17. ♖f3 ♖h8 18. ♖g3 ♕f8 19. ♕g4 ♗b7 20. ♕e2 [20. ♕g7?! ♕g7 21. ♖g7 ♔e7 22. ♖g3 ♖h4∓ Stanciu—Cvetković, Romania—Jugoslavija 1969] ♔e7 21. ♖f1 ♖h4=∞ Ničevski—Cvetković, Jugoslavija (ch) 1969

39 13. ♕g5 fg5 14. e5 ♗d4 15. ♖ae1 b5 16. ♘d1 ♗b7∓⊥ Uzman—Cvetković, Jugoslavija 1971

40 18. ♗e2 ♕g7 19. ♗f3± Suetin—Cvetković, SSSR — Jugoslavija 1969 — 7/363

41 **9. a4**?! b4 10. ♘a2 ♘d4 11. ♗d4 e5 12. ♗e3 ♗b7∓; **9. h3** ♗b7 10. a3 ♗e7 11. ♔h1 0—0 12. f4 d6 13. ♕f3 ♘d4 14. ♗d4 e5= Popov—Peev, Bulgaria 1967 — 4/456; **9. ♖e1** ♗d6!? [9... ♗b7 10. ♘c6 ♕c6 — 7... b5] 10. g3 ♗e5=; **9. ♕f3** ♗b7 10. ♖ae1 ♗e7= Sydor—Jansa, Polanica Zdroj 1969 — 8/349; **9. ♘b3** ♗e7 10. f4 d6 11. ♕f3 [11. ♔h1 ♖b8 12. ♕e2 0—0 13. a4 ba4! 14. ♖a4 ♘b4= Matanović—Matulović, Sousse (izt) 1967 — 4/443] 0—0!? 12. a4 [12. ♖ae1 ♗b7 13. ♕h3 ♖fd8 14. g4 b4 15. g5 bc3?! 16. gf6 gf6 17. bc3± Ciocaltea—Talj, La Habana 1966 — 2/371; 15... ♘d7 16. ♘e2 ♘f8∞] b4 13. ♘e2 e5 14. f5 d5!?⇆∞ Spaski—Talj, Tbilisi (ct) 1965; **9. a3** ♗b7 [9... ♘d4 10. ♗d4 ♗c5 11. ♗f6!? gf6 12. ♕g4±↑; 9... ♗d6!?] 10. ♔h1 ♘e5 [10... b4 11. ab4 ♗b4 12. ♖a4± Novopašin—Vladimirov, SSSR 1963] 11. f4 ♘c4 12. ♗c1 ♕b6 13. ♗c4 bc4 14. e5 ♘d5=

42 **10. a3** ♘e5 11. h3 ♖c8 12. f4 ♘c4 13. ♘db5 ab5 14. ♘b5 ♕c6 15. ♘a7 ♘e3! 16. ♘c6 ♗c5 17. ♔h2 ♘f1 18. ♖f1 ♗c6∓ Kristinsson—Talj, Reykjavik 1964; 17. ♘a5!?; **10. f4** ♗c5 11. ♘b3 ♗e3 12. ♕e3 d6= Bebčuk—Zwaig, Budva 1963

43 **10... ♗e7** 11. f4 0–0?! 12. e5 ♘e8 13. ♕h5 f5 14. ♗f5!± Geler–Gipslis, Moskva 1969 — 8/348; **10... ♗b4**!?

44 17. ♕f3 ♗f4= Geler–Talj, Curaçao (ct) 1962

45 9... dc6?! 10. f4±

46 10. e5 ♗b7 11. ♕f3 [11. f3 ♘d5 12. ♗e4 ♘c3 13. ♗c6 ♘d1 14. ♗b7 ♘e3 15. ♗a8 ♘f1 16. ♔f1 ♗c5= Zuidema–Matulović, Hamburg 1965] ♕f3 12. gf3 b4 [12... ♘d5 13. ♘e4 ♘e3 14. fe3± Spaski–Talj, SSSR 1968] 13. ♘e4 ♘e4 14. fe4 d6 15. ed6 ♗d6= Pavlov–Smislov, Bath 1973

47 10... ♗c5 11. ♕e2 [11. e5 ♗b7 12. ♕f3 ♕f3 13. gf3 ♗e3 14. fe3 ♘d5 15. ♘e4 ♔e7 16. ♔f2 (Spaski–Talj, Tbilisi (ct) 1965) f6!=] ♗e3 12. ♕e3 ♗b7 13. ♕g3 [13. ♕h3 ♕c5= Cejtlin–Šmit, SSSR 1970 — 10/447] 0–0 14. e5 ♘h5 15. ♕h3 f5 16. f4±

48 11. f4 ♗e7 12. ♕f3 0–0 13. ♕h3 d5 14. e5 ♘e4 15. ♘e2 ♗c5 16. ♘d4 ♕c7 17. c3± Cejtlin–Talj, SSSR (ch) 1971 — 12/404; 11... ♗c5=

49 **11... d6**? 12. ♘b5 ♘e4 13. ♗e4 ♕e4 14. ♘c7 ♔d7 15. f3+– Boleslavski; **11... b4** 12. ab4 ♗b4 13. ♖a4! a5 [13... ♗c3 14. ♖c4!] 14. ♗b5 ♕c7 15. ♗d4± Boleslavski; **11... ♗c5** 12. ♗c5 ♕c5 13. e5 ♕c6 14. f4 ♘d5 15. ♘e4±; **11... ♕c7** 12. f4 d6 13. ♗d4 ♗e7 14. e5 de5 15. fe5 ♗c5 16. ♗c5 ♕c5 17. ♖f2 ♘d7 18. ♗e4 ♗e4 19. ♘e4 ♕e5 20. ♖d1 f6 21. ♘d6 ♔e7 22. ♕g4±→ Kostro–Bednarski, Polska 1972; **11... ♖c8** 12. f4 h5!? 13. h3 h4 14. ♖f2 b4 15. ab4 ♗b4 16. ♖a4 ♗c3 17. ♖c4 ♗b2 18. ♖c6 ♗c6 19. c4 ♗a3 20. ♗d4± Penrose–Mecking, Lugano (ol) 1968 — 6/479; **11... d5**!?

50 13... ♘e8 14. f5 ef5 15. ♗f5±→ Scholl–Langeweg, Nederland 1970 — 9/330

51 17. ♖ac1± Vogt–Mišta, Havirov 1971 — 12/401

52 **9. g3** ♘d4 10. ♗d4 ♗e5 11. ♗e5 ♕e5 12. f4 ♕c5 13. ♔g2 d6 14. ♕e2 b5=; **9. ♔h1** ♗f4 [9... b5 10. ♘c6 ♕c6 11. f4 b4 (11... ♗b7 12. a3 0–0 13. ♗d4±) 12. ♘e2 ♘e4 13. ♗e4 ♕e4 14. ♕d6 ♕e3 15. ♘d4±→; 9... h5 10. f4 (10. ♗e2 ♗h2! 11. g3 h4∓→) ♘g4 11. ♕f3 ♘e3 12. ♕e3 ♕b6 13. ♘ce2 e5 14. ♕g3!?∞ Talj–Vooremaa, Tallinn 1971 — 11/316] 10. ♗f4 ♕f4 11. ♘de2 ♕h4 12. ♕d2 b5 13. a3 ♗b7= Marjanović–Benkö, Vrnjačka Banja 1973

53 **9... ♘d4** 10. ♗d4 ♗e5 11. ♗e5 ♕e5 12. f4 ♕c5 13. ♔h1 d6 14. ♕e2 e5 15. ♘d5! ♘d5 16. ed5±↑ Jurkov–Ignatjev, SSSR 1963; **9... 0–0** 10. ♘de2!± Espig–Kovačević, Ybbs 1968 — 6/476; **9... b5**!? 10. ♘c6 ♕c6 11. a3 [11. f4 b4 12. ♘e2 ♘e4 13. ♗e4 ♕e4 14. ♕d6 ♕e3 15. ♖f2 a5 16. ♘d4 ♖a6 17. ♕c5 ♖c6∓] ♗b7 12. f4 0–0 13. ♕e2 e5= Boleslavski

54 10. ♕d2 ♗e3 11. ♕e3 ♕b6 [11... d6 12. ♘b3 0–0 13. f4 b5∞ A. Zajcev–Suetin, SSSR 1970 — 9/331] 12. ♘f5 ♕e3 13. ♘e3 b5= Radulov–Andersson, Hastings 1972/73 — 15/360

55 11. ♘ce2 ♕c7 12. ♕d2 d6 13. ♖ae1 0–0= Cejtlin–Suetin, SSSR 1971 — 12/403

56 11... bc6 12. ♖e1 d6 13. g3 ♕e5 14. ♗f1 0–0 15. ♕d2±

57 12... a5?! 13. ♖e1 e5 14. ♗c4 0–0 15. ♖e3 ♖e8 16. ♕d6± Andersson–Franklin, Hastings 1971/72 — 13/394

58 9... dc6 10. f4 e5 11. f5±

59 11... ♖b8 12. ♗c4± Kupper–A. Garcia, Lugano (ol) 1968 — 6/478

60 12... ♗b4 13. ♕g3! ♔f8 [13... 0–0 14. ♗h6] 14. ♘a4 d5 15. a3 ♗d6 16. ♘c5± Janošević–Matulović, Sarajevo 1968

61 13. ♗c4 d5 14. ed5 cd5 15. ♘d5 ♕c4 16. ♘f6 ♗f6 17. ♕b7 0–0 18. ♕b3 ♕e4 19. c4 ♖ab8 20. ♕c3 ♖fd8$\overline{\overline{\infty}}$ Grabczewski–Doda, Polanica Zdroj 1968 — 6/477

62 **15. ♕g3** 0–0 16. ♗e3 ♔h8 17. ♕h4 ♕d8 18. ♗b6 ♕e8 19. ♗c5 a5!∓ Dückstein–Portisch, Raach 1969 — 8/347; **15. ♗c5** ♗c5 16. ♘c5 ♕a7 17. b4± Glauser–Honfi, Bath 1973 — 16/347; 16... ♗c8!=; **15. c4**!?±

63 **9. ♗f4** d6 10. ♗g3 b5= Suhanov–Averkin, SSSR 1964; **9. ♗e2** b5 10. f4 ♘c4 11. ♗c4 [11. ♗c1 ♗b4!∓ Hennings–Hamann, Aarhus 1971 — 12/402] ♕c4 12. e5 ♘d5 13. ♘d5 ♕d5= Penrose–Najdorf, Palma de Mallorca 1969 — 8/352

64 10. ♕e2 b4 11. ♘b1 d5 12. ♘d2 de4 13. ♘e4 ♘d5!?∞ Dückstein–Tajmanov, Copenhagen 1965; 12.. ♗b7= Johansson–Portisch, Halle 1963

65 12... ♗b7 13. a4! ♕d3 14. cd3 b4 15. ♘ce2±⊥ Milić–Forintos, Jugoslavija–Hungary 1959; Ujtumen–Reshevsky, Palma de Mallorca (izt) 1970 — 10/451

66 13. ed5 ♕d3 14. cd3 b4 15. ♘e4 ♘d5= Nežmetdinov–Talj, SSSR 1959

67 15... ♘c5 16. b4! cb3 17. ab3± I. Zajcev

68 17. ♖ae1 ♘d7 18. ♘e6 fe6 19. ♗d4 0-0-0 20. ♖e6 ♘c5! 21. ♖c6 ♔b7 22. ♖c5 ♖d4 23. ♖cf5 ♗d6 24. ♖f7 ♔c6 25. ♖g7 b4$\overline{\overline{\infty}}$ Fischer–Petrosjan, Santa Monica 1966 — 2/373

69 12... b4 13. ♕f3! ♖b8 14. ef6 bc3 15. b3 ♕c7 16. f5!± Ivkov–Portisch, Amsterdam 1964

70 14. a4 ♗b7 15. ♕e2 ♗c5 16. ♕f2 ♖c8= Pietzsch–Ivkov, La Habana 1965

71 16. ♖ad1 ♕c4 17. ♕d2 ♗d5 18. ♖f2 ♗e7= Jansson–Zichichi, Siegen (ol) 1970 — 10/450

72 17. ♕f2 ♗d5 18. ♖ad1 [18. ♗d4 ♗e7 19. ♕g3 0–0 20. f5 ef5 21. e6 f6 22. ed7 ♖cd8=

Vasjukov–Suetin, SSSR (ch) 1965] ♗e7 19. ♖d4 ♕c7 20. ♕g3 0–0 21. f5± Boleslavski

73 **10. f4**?! ♘c6 11. ♘ce2 ♕b6∓; **10. a4** d6 11. a5 0–0∓; **10. ♔h1** d6 11. f4 ♘ed7 12. ♕f3 b5∞ Talj–Najdorf, Beograd 1970 — 9/332

74 **11... ♘c4**?! 12. ♗c4 ♕c4 13. ♖c1 ♕b4 14. ♘e6! de6 [14... ♗e3 15. ♘c7 ♔d8 16. fe3 ♖b8 17. e5+–] 15. ♗a7 ♘d7 16. ♘c5±→ Fajbisovič–Litzberger, Harrachov 1967 — 4/453; **11... 0–0** 12. ♖c1 d6 13. ♘c3 b6 14. b3 ♘d3 15. ♕d3± Vogt–Timoščenko, Stary Smokovec 1972 — 14/388

75 14. ♗e2 ♖fc8 15. ♔h1 ♕b8!=

76 Vogt–Schmidt, Leipzig 1973

77 **10... b5** 11. ♘b3 ♗e3 12. ♕e3 d6 13. f4 ♘ed7 14. ♖ae1± O'Kelly–Panno, La Habana 1969 — 8/354; **10... ♘g6** 11. ♘b3 ♗e3 12. ♕e3 d6 13. ♖ad1 0–0 14. ♖d2 b5 15. a4?!∞ Kaplan–Suetin, Hastings 1967/68 — 5/391; 15. a3!±

78 11... ♘ed7 12. ♘b3 ♗e3 13. ♕e3 b6 14. ♖ae1 ♗b7 15. e5 de5 16. fe5 ♘d5 17. ♘d5 ♗d5 18. ♖f4±↑ Spaski–Petrosjan (m) 1969 — 7/362

79 **12. ♕f2**!? 0–0?! 13. e5 de5 14. ♘e6 ♗e6 15. ♗c5 ♘f4!? 16. ♗f8 ♖f8± Petrušin–Suetin, SSSR 1974 — 17/404; 12... ♗d7△ ♖c8∞ Suetin; **12. ♖ae1**!?△ ♘d1, c3, ♘f3 Boleslavski

80 13... b5 14. a3 ♗b7 15. ♖ae1 0–0= Mecking–Juarez, Mar del Plata 1971 — 12/400; 14. ♖ae1!?

81 **14. e5** de5 15. ♗g6 hg6 [15... ef4?! 16. ♗f7 ♖f7 17. ♖f4± Radulov–Barcza, Hastings 1972/73] 16. fe5 ♘d7 17. ♖ae1 b5 18. ♘d4 ♗b7= Radulov–Suetin, Budapest 1970 — 9/329; **14. a4** b6 15. ♖ae1 ♗b7 16. ♔h1 [16. f5?! ef5 17. ♖f5 ♖ae8 18. ♕g3 ♖e5∓ Olsson–Liebert, Skopje (ol) 1972 — 14/389] ♖ad8 17. f5 ef5 18. ♖f5= Kupper–Cvetković, Schweiz–Jugoslavija 1972

82 15. ♘d4 b4! 16. ♘d1 e5∓ van den Berg–Langeweg, Wijk aan Zee 1971 — 11/318

83 **17. fe5** ♘d7=; **17. ♕e5** ♕a7 [17... ♕e5 18. fe5 ♘d7 19. ♘a5±] 18. ♔h2 ♗b7= Hennings–Hort, La Habana 1971 — 11/319

B 49

1. e4 c5 2. ♘f3 e6 3. d4 cd4 4. ♘d4 ♘c6 5. ♘c3 ♕c7 6. ♗e3 a6 7. ♗e2

	7	8	9	10	11	12	13	14	15	
1	...	0–0[2]	♕d2	♗f4	♗g3	♕g5	♘f5	♘h6	♘f5	∞
	♘a5!?[1]	b5	♗b7[3]	e5	♘f6	d6	♖g8!?	♖h8	♖g8[4]	
2	...	♘c6[5]	a3[7]	♕d4[9]	0-0-0	♖d2[11]	♕c5	♗c5	f3[12]	=
	b5	♕c6[6]	♗b7[8]	♖c8[10]	♘f6	♗c5	♕c5	♖c5	♔e7	
3	...	...	0–0	♗f3	e5	♗b7[15]	♗g5[16]	♗e7	♕d3	=
	...	...	♗b7[13]	♖d8[14]	♕c7	♕b7	♗e7	♘e7	♕b8![17]	

1. e4 c5 2. ♘f3 e6 3. d4 cd4 4. ♘d4 ♘c6 5. ♘c3 ♕c7 6. ♗e3 a6 7. ♗e2 b5 8. ♘c6 ♕c6 9. f4

	9	10	11	12	13	14	15	16	17	
4	...	♗f3	e5	♖b1[19]	♔f2	♗a8	♗e4!	ef6	♕h5	±
	b4	bc3[18]	cb2	♗b4[20]	♕c3	f6	♘h6[21]	♕f6	♘f7[22]	
5	...	♗d4	♗f3[23]	0–0	♗c3	♖e1	♕d6	♕c5	♖e2	±
	♗b4	♘f6	♗b7	♗c3	♖c8[24]	♕c4	♕c5	♖c5	♖c4[25]	
6	...	♗d4[26]	♘b5	♗a1	♗g7	♗f6[29]	0–0	♗b5	♔h1	∓
	♗a3!?	♗b2	♗a1[27]	ab5	♘f6![28]	♖g8	♗b7	♕c5	♗c6[30]	
7	...	ba3!?	♔f2	♗f3	♗d4	♕d3	cd3	♖hc1	♗b6[32]	∞̅
	...	♕c3	♘f6	♗b7	♕a3[31]	♕d3	0–0	♖fc8		
8	...	♗f3	e5[33]	0–0	♗b7	♕d3	♗f2			∞
	♗b7	♖c8	♕c7	♘e7[34]	♕b7	♘f5	h5[35]			

1. e4 c5 2. ♘f3 e6 3. d4 cd4 4. ♘d4 ♘c6 5. ♘c3 ♕c7 6. ♗e3 a6 7. ♗e2 ♘f6

	8	9	10	11	12	13	14	15	16	
9	a3 ♗d6[36]	♕d2[37] ♘d4[38]	♗d4 ♗f4	♕d3 e5	♗e3 ♗e3	fe3!?[39] d6	0-0-0 ♔e7	g4 h6	h4 ♗e6[40]	±
10	0—0 ♗b4[41]	♘c6[42] bc6[43]	♘a4[44] ♖b8[45]	c4[46] ♗d6[47]	g3[48] c5	♕d3 ♗b7	♖ad1 ♗e7	♘c3 d6	f4 0—0[49]	=
11	. . . . . .	♘a4 b5[50]	♘c6[51] dc6[52]	♗c5![53] ♗c5	♘c5 0—0[54]	♕d4 e5	♕c3 a5	♖fd1[55]		±
12	. . . . . .	. . . ♗d6	♘b6![56] ♖b8[57]	g3 ♘e4[58]	♘c6 ♕c6[59]	♗f3 f5	♗e4 fe4	♕h5 g6	♕h6 ♗e5[60]	±
13	. . . . . .	. . . ♗e7	♘c6 bc6	♘b6[61] ♖b8	♘c8 ♕c8	e5 ♘d5	♗c1[62] ♗c5	c4 ♘e7	b3 ♕c7[63]	±
14	. . . . . .	. . . ♘e7	c4[64] ♘e4[65]	♕c2[66] f5[67]	♗f3[68] ♗d6	♗e4 fe4	♕e4 ♗h2	♔h1 ♗e5	♘f3 ♗f6[69]	±

1. e4 c5 2. ♘f3 e6 3. d4 cd4 4. ♘d4 ♘c6 5. ♘c3 ♕c7 6. ♗e3 a6 7. ♗e2 ♘f6 8. 0—0 ♗b4 9. ♘a4 0—0

	10	11	12	13	14	15	16	17	18	
15	♘c6[70] dc6	c4[71] ♗d6[72]	f4[73] ♘e4	c5 ♗e7	♕c2 f5	♘b6 ♖b8	g4[74] ♗d7	♗d3 ♗e8!?	♗e4 fe4[75]	±
16	. . . bc6	c4[76] ♗e7[77]	♕c2 c5	f4[78] d6	♗f3 ♖b8	♖ad1 ♗b7	♖d2 ♗c6	♘c3 ♘d7	♖fd1 ♘b6[79]	=
17	. . . . . .	♘b6 ♖b8	♘c8 ♖fc8[80]	♗a6 ♖d8[81]	♗d3 ♗d6	♔h1[82] ♗e5	c3 ♖b2	♕c1 ♘g4!?	f4[83] ♘e3[84]	=

1 **7...** ♘**d4**?! 8. ♕d4 b5 9. a4!? [9. 0—0 ♘e7△ ♘c6±] b4 10. ♘a2±; **7...** ♗**b4**?! 8. ♘c6 ♕c6 [8... dc6 9. ♕d4 ♗f8 10. 0—0± Nežmetdinov—Sergijevski, SSSR 1963] 9. ♕d4 ♗c3 10. bc3 ♘f6 11. ♗g5 ♕e4 12. ♗f6 ♕g2 13. 0-0-0± Dubovik—Kantorin, corr. 1964; 11. ♗f3!?

2 8. ♕d3 b5 9. ♖d1 ♘f6 10. f4 ♘c4 11. ♗c1 ♗b7= Kudrjašov—Šmit, SSSR 1970 — 9/333

3 9... ♘c4!?

4 Sax—Tajmanov, Vrnjačka Banja 1974 — 17/405

5 **8. a3** ♗b7 9. f4 ♖c8 [9... ♘d4 10. ♕d4 ♘e7 △ ♘c6=] 10. ♗f3 [10. ♘c6 ♗c6!? 11. 0—0 ♘f6 12. ♗f3 ♕b7= Mejić—Cebalo, Jugoslavija (ch) 1968] ♘a5 11. 0—0 ♘c4= Klavin—Koblenc, SSSR 1963; **8. f4** ♗b7 9. ♗f3 ♘a5 10. 0—0 ♘c4 11. ♗c1 ♗c5= Littlewood—Penrose, England 1962

6 8... dc6 9. f4 c5 [9... e5 10. fe5 ♕e5 11. ♕d2±↑; 9... ♘f6 10. e5 ♘d5 11. ♘d5 cd5 12. c3± Matanović—Cebalo, Jugoslavija 1964] 10. 0—0 ♗b7 11. f5! ♖d8 [11... ♘f6 12. fe6 fe6 13. ♗h5 ♘h5 14. ♕h5 g6 15. ♕g4± Štejn—Tajmanov, SSSR (ch) 1962] 12. ♕e1 e5 13. a4 b4 14. ♘d5±

7 9. e5 ♗b7 10. ♗f3 ♕c7 11. 0—0 ♖d8 — 9. 0—0

8 9... ♗c5?! 10. ♗d4! ♘f6 [10... f6? 11. ♗b5 ab5 12. ♕h5 g6 13. ♕c5+— Bronštejn—Tajmanov, SSSR (ch) 1961] 11. e5 ♘d5 12. ♗f3±

9 **10.** ♗**f3** ♕c7 [10... e5 11. 0—0 ♗c5 12. ♗c5 ♕c5= Paoli—Brzozka, Miskolc 1963] 11. 0—0 [11. e5 ♖c8 12. 0—0 ♗f3 13. ♕f3 d6? 14. ed6 ♗d6 15. ♗d4! ♗h2 16. ♔h1 ♗e5 17. ♘d5! ♕d6 18. ♗e5 ♕e5 19. ♘b6+— Lutikov—Klavin, SSSR 1961; 13... ♘e7!∓] ♖c8 12. ♖e1 ♘e7 13. ♗d4 d6= Ofstad—Doda, Halle 1967; **10. 0—0** ♘e7! [10... ♕c7?! 11. ♕d3 ♘f6 12. ♖fd1 ♗e7 13. ♗f3± Vasjukov—Boleslavski, SSSR (ch) 1961; 10... ♖c8 11. ♗d4 ♕c7 12. ♕d2 e5 13. ♗e3 ♘f6 14. f3 ♗c5= Polugajevski—Gipslis, SSSR (ch)

1961] 11. ♕d3 [11. f4 ♘f5! 12. ♗f2 ♗c5=] ♘g6 12. f4 ♗e7= O'Kelly–Talj, La Habana 1963

10 **10... ♘e7** 11. 0-0-0 ♕c8 [11... ♕c7? 12. ♗b5] 12. ♕b6 ♗c6 13. ♗c5 [13. ♗f4 ♕b7 14. ♕d4 ♘g6 15. ♗d6 ♕a7= Bronštejn–Ivkov, SSSR–Jugoslavija 1962] ♕b7 14. ♕a5 ♘g6 15. ♗f8±; **10... ♕d6** 11. ♕d6 ♗d6 12. 0-0-0 ♗e5 13. ♗d4 f6= Gurgenidze–Suetin, SSSR 1963

11 12. e5 ♘d5 13. ♗f3 ♗a3! 14. ♗d5 ed5 15. ♖d3 [15. ba3 ♕c3 16. ♕c3 ♖c3 17. ♔b2 ♖c4∓ Sigurjonsson – Tajmanov, Reykjavik 1968] ♗e7 16. ♖d2 ♕e6 17. ♖hd1 ♗c5 18. ♕f4 0–0 19. ♘d5 ♖fe8 20. ♕g3 ♗e3 21. ♕e3 ♕e5= Liebert–Gipslis 1963

12 15. ♗f3?! g5!∓ I. Zajcev–Tajmanov, SSSR (ch) 1962

13 9... b4 10. ♗f3 ♗b7 11. e5 ♕c7 12. ♘a4±

14 **10... ♘e7**?! 11. e5 ♕c7 12. ♗c5! [12. a4 b4 13. ♘e4 ♘d5 14. ♕d4± Mikenas–Popov, Sofia 1962] ♘g6 [12... ♘d5 13. ♘d5 ed5 14. ♗f8 ♔f8 15. ♗d5+– Liberzon–Neukirch, Zinnowitz 1967 — 4/458] 13. ♗f8 ♔f8 [13... ♘f8 14. ♗b7 ♕b7 15. ♕d4± Ivkov–Darga, La Habana 1963] 14. ♗b7 ♕b7 15. ♕d6 ♔g8 16. ♖ad1± Parma–Damjanović, San Juan 1969 — 8/356; **10... ♖c8** 11. e5 ♕c7 13. ♗b7 [12. a4 b4 13. ♘e4 ♕e5 14. ♘f6 ♘f6 15. ♗b7 ♖b8 16. ♗a6 ♗c5= Čerepkov–Bajkov, SSSR 1963] ♕b7 13. ♕d3 ♘e7 14. ♖ad1 ♘g6 15. f4 ♘h4 16. ♘e4 ♖c4 17. ♗d4 ♘f5 18. c3± Pachman–Garcia, La Habana 1964

15 12. ♗f4 d5!? [12... d6? 13. ♗b7 de5 14. ♗e5± Bradvarević] 13. ed6 ♗d6 14. ♗b7 ♗f4 [14... ♕b7? 15. ♗d6 ♕c6 16. ♕d4 ♘e7 17. ♘e4 ♘f5 18. ♕g7!+– Bradvarević–Krnić, Jugoslavija 1970 — 10/452] 15. ♕f3 ♗h2 16. ♔h1 ♗e5= Bradvarević; 12... ♘e7!=

16 **13. ♕d4** ♘e7 14. ♖fd1 ♘f5 15. ♕b6 ♕b6 16. ♗b6 ♖b8 17. ♗d4 ♖c8= Eley–Hartston, England 1962; **13. ♖e1** d6 14. ♗g5 ♗e7!? [14... ♖d7 15. ed6 ♖d6 16. ♕h5±↑ Eley–Hartston, Hastings 1972/73] 15. ♗e7 ♘e7 16. ed6 ♘f5 17. ♘e4 ♕b6=; **13. ♕d3**!? d6?! 14. ♖ad1±↑; 13... d5!=

17 Petrosjan–Tajmanov, SSSR (ch) 1969

18 10... ♗b7 11. e5 ♕c7 12. ♘a4±

19 12. ♗c6?! ba1♕ 13. ♕a1 dc6∓

20 12... ♕c3 13. ♗d2 ♕a3 14. ♗a8 ♗c5 15. ♕f3 ♕a2 16. ♔e2 a5 17. ♕b3 ♗a6 18. ♔f3 ♕b3 19. cb3 ♗a3 20. ♗c3! ♗d3 21. ♗b2 ♗b1 22. ♗a3 ♗a2 23. b4 ab4 24. ♗b4± Ivkov–Szabo, Sarajevo 1963

21 15... fe5? 16. ♕h5 g6 17. ♗g6 hg6 18. ♕h8 ♕c2 19. ♔g3 ef4 20. ♗f4 ♕d3 21. ♔h4 ♗e7 22. ♗g5 ♗g5 23. ♔g5 ♕f5 24. ♔h4 ♕f4 25. g4 ♕f2 26. ♔g5 ♕e3 27. ♔g6+– Boleslavski

22 18. c4 g6 19. ♕e2 ♗c3 20. ♗f3 0–0 21. ♖hd1± Spaski–Suetin, SSSR 1964

23 11. 0–0 ♗c3 12. ♗c3 ♘e4 13. ♗g7 ♖g8 14. ♕d4 ♗b7 15. ♗f3 ♖c8 16. c3 d5∞ Bogdanović–Damjanović, Jugoslavija (ch) 1965

24 13... ♘e4 14. ♗g7 ♖g8 15. ♗d4 ♕c7 16. ♕e2 f5 17. c3± Unzicker–Doda, Tel Aviv (ol) 1964

25 18. ♖ae1±⊥ Boleslavski–Buslajev, SSSR 1968

26 **10. ♘b5**?! ab5 11. ba3 ♕e4 12. ♔f2 ♖a3 13. ♕d4 ♘f6∓ Meštrović–Minić, Jugoslavija (ch) 1967 — 3/426; **10. ♖b1** ♗b2∓; **10. ♕c1** ♕c3∓; **10. ♗c1** ♗c5 11. ♗f3 ♗b7= Dukarev–Bokučava, SSSR 1965

27 **11... ab5** 12. ♗b2±; **11... ♗d4** 12. ♕d4 ab5 13. ♕g7 ♔e7 14. ♕h8 ♘f6 15. 0–0 ♗b7 16. ♕g7 ♕c5 17. ♔h1 ♗e4 18. ♗f3 ♗f3 19. gf3 ♖g8 20. ♕h6 ♕c2 21. ♕h3± Minić–Schmidt, Varna 1967 — 4/404

28 13... ♕e4 14. 0–0 ♖a2 15. ♗d3 ♕e3 16. ♖f2! [16. ♔h1?! ♗b7 17. ♗h8 ♘h6 18. ♗b5 (18. ♗g7? ♕h3! 19. ♕e2 ♘g4–+; 18. ♕h5? ♗g2 19. ♔g2 ♕d3–+) ♗d5 19. ♖f3 (19. ♗g7 ♘f5 20. ♗f6 ♕e4 21. ♕g4 ♘h6!∓ Planinc–Schmidt, Čačak 1969 — 8/357) ♕c5 20. c4 ♗c6∓ Bogdanović–Suetin, Budva 1967 — 4/459; 19... ♕a7∓] ♗b7 17. ♗b5 ♗d5 18. ♗h8 ♘h6 19. h3± Kavalek–Štejn, Sousse (izt) 1967

29 14. ♗h8 ♘e4 15. ♗d3? ♗b7–+ Fichtl–Jansa, ČSSR 1970 — 9/334; 15. 0–0∓

30 Hort

31 13... ♕c7!?

32 Matanović–Vasjukov, Jugoslavija–SSSR 1966 — 1/274

33 **11. 0—0** ♗c5 12. ♗f2 [12. ♗c5 ♕c5 13. ♖f2 ♘e7 14. e5 ♗f3 15. ♕f3 d5= Kuprejčik–Krnić, Sombor 1970 — 10/437] ♕c7 13. e5 f5 14. ♗b7 ♕b7 15. a3 ♘e7= Unzicker–Hartston, Gstaad 1973; **11. ♕d4** ♕d6 12. ♕a7 ♕b8 13. ♕b8 ♖b8= Kupper–Penrose 1963; **11. ♕d3** ♕c7 [11... ♕c4 12. 0-0-0 ♘f6!?] 12. 0-0-0 ♗b4 13. ♗d4 ♘f6 14. ♗e5 ♕c4∞ Plachetka–Hort, ČSSR (ch) 1972; **11. a3** ♕c7 12. 0–0 ♘e7 13. ♕d2 [13. ♕e1 ♘g6 14. g3 ♗c5 15. ♖d1 d6 16. ♗c5 ♕c5 17. ♕f2± Matulović–Damjanović, Jugoslavija 1972 — 14/377] ♘g6 14. g3 ♗c5 15. ♖ad1 ♗e3 16. ♕e3 0–0 17. ♖f2± Unzicker–Damjanović, Palma de Mallorca 1969 — 8/338; 11... ♕c4!? ∞ Parma

34 12... ♗f3 13. ♕f3 d5 14. f5±↑

35 15... ♗c5 16. ♘e4 ♗f2 17. ♖f2± Musil–Janošević, Maribor 1967; 15... ♖c4!? △ 16. g4?! ♖f4 17. gf5 ♖g4 18. ♗g3 ♗c5 19. ♖f2 h5∞; 15... h5∞ Minić–Janošević, Jugoslavija 1966 — 1/275

36 8... b5?! 9. ♘c6 dc6 [9... ♕c6? 10. e5] 10. f4±; 8... ♘d4 9. ♕d4 ♗d6 10. ♕d2! ♗e5 11. ♗d4 ♗f4 [11... ♗d4 12. ♕d4 e5 13. ♕b4 b6 14. 0-0-0± Talj–Tajmanov, SSSR (ch) 1962] 12. ♕d3 e5 13. ♗e3 ♗e3 14. ♕e3 d6 15. 0–0 0–0± Johansson–Doda, Halle 1963; 14. fe3!?; 8... ♗e7 9. f4 d6 10. 0–0 0–0 11. ♕e1 — B 85

37 9. h3 0–0 10. 0–0 ♗f4 [10... ♗h2 11. ♔h1 ♗f4] 11. ♕d2 ♗e3 12. ♕e3 d6 13. ♖ad1 ♖d8= Kuijpers–Langeweg, Amsterdam 1963; 9. g3 ♗e5 10. f4 ♗d4 11. ♗d4 ♘d4 12. ♕d4 b5 13. e5 ♗b7 14. ♖f1 ♘d5 15. ♘e4 0–0 16. 0-0-0 ♗c6 17. ♗f3 a5∞ Keres–Rubinetti, Buenos Aires 1964

38 9... ♗e5 10. f4 ♗d4 11. ♗d4 ♘d4 12. ♕d4±↑ Nežmetdinov–Talj, SSSR (ch) 1959

39 13. ♕e3 d6 14. 0–0 0–0± Keres–Talj, Curaçao (ct) 1962

40 17. g5 hg5 18. hg5 ♘d7 19. g6 [19. ♗g4 ♖ad8± Ivkov–Wade, La Habana 1963] ♖h1 [19... fg6? 20. ♗g4±→] 20. ♖h1 ♘f6± Olafsson–Benkö, Los Angeles 1963

41 8... b5?! 9. ♘c6! dc6 10. f4 ♗b7 [10... b4 11. ♘a4 ♖b8 (11... ♘e4 12. ♗b6±→; 11... c5 12. ♗f3 ♗b7 13. c3 a5 14. ♖c1 ♗e4 15. cb4 ♖d8 16. ♕e1 ♗f3 17. ♖f3 ab4 18. ♘c5± Antošin–Barski, SSSR 1961) 12. ♗f3 c5 13. c3 bc3 14. b3 ♗b7 15. ♘c3 c4 16. bc4 ♕c4 17. ♖c1 ♗a3 18. ♖c2 ♗c5 19. ♘d5± Unzicker–Korčnoj, Buenos Aires 1960] 11. e5 ♘d5 [11... b4 12. ef6 bc3 13. ♕d4 cb2 14. ♕b2 gf6 15. ♖ab1± Matulović–Cebalo, Zagreb 1973 — 15/359] 12. ♘d5 cd5 [12... ed5 13. f5±→] 13. c3±; 13. f5!?; 8... d6 9. f4 — B 85

42 9. f4?! ♗c3 10. bc3 ♘e4 11. ♗d3 ♘f6 12. ♕e1 [Lutikov–Koblenc, Pärnu 1964] ♘e7 =; 9. f3 0–0 10. ♔h1 ♖d8= Bouaziz–Matulović, Sousse (izt) 1967; 9. ♘f3 ♘e5 10. ♗f4 d6= Domnitz–Yanofsky, La Habana (ol) 1966; 9. ♖e1 ♗c3?! 10. bc3 ♘e4?! 11. ♗d3 ♘f6 12. ♘f5! 0–0 13. ♘g7! ♔g7 14. ♗h6!+– Hennings–Kaulitz, DDR 1965; 9... ♘e7!=

43 9... dc6 10. ♘a4±; 9... ♕c6 10. e5 ♗c3 11. bc3 ♘d5 12. ♕d4 [12. c4?! ♘c3 13. ♕d2 ♘e2 14. ♕e2 ♕e4 15. ♖ad1 b5 16. ♖d4 ♕e5 17. f4 ♕f5 18. g4 ♕c5 19. f5 ♕c6∓ Čerepkov–Spaski, SSSR 1963] b5 [12... ♕c3 13. ♕c3 ♘c3 14. ♗f3±] 13. c4 bc4 14. ♕g4 ♔f8 15. ♖ab1$\overline{\overline{\infty}}$ Heuer–Spaski, SSSR 1963; 9... ♗c3 10. bc3 ♕c6 11. ♗d4 [11. ♕d4 ♕e4 12. ♕d6 ♕c6 13. ♕a3$\overline{\overline{\infty}}$; 11... 0–0 12. ♗f3 d5= Stean–Christiansen, Teesside 1973; 11. e5!?] ♘e4 12. ♗f3 0–0 13. ♗g7 ♔g7 14. ♕d4 f6 15. ♗e4 d5 16. ♗f3 ♗d7 17. c4 ♕c4 18. ♕c4 dc4 19. ♗b7 ♖a7 20. ♖ab1 ♗b5= Klovan–Suetin, SSSR (ch) 1963

44 10. ♕d4 c5 [10... ♗d6?! 11. f4 e5 12. ♕d2 ef4 13. ♗f4 ♗f4 14. ♖f4 d6 15. ♖d1 ♔e7± Nežmetdinov–Sergijevski, SSSR 1966 — 2/376] 11. ♕c4 ♗b7 12. ♗f3 ♕e5!∓ Gligorić–Tajmanov, Buenos Aires 1960; 10. ♗d3 d5= O'Kelly–Penrose, Varna (ol) 1962; 10. ♕d3 d5 11. a3 ♗e7 12. f4 0–0= Jimenez–Filip, Leipzig (ol) 1960

45 10... ♗b7 11. c4 ♗d6 12. f4?! ♘e4 13. c5 ♗e7 14. ♗d4± Kuzmin–Furman, SSSR (ch) 1972

46 11. ♕d3 d5 12. ed5 cd5 13. c4 ♗d7 14. ♘c3 dc4 15. ♕c4 ♕c4 16. ♗c4 a5= Židkov–Liberzon, SSSR 1967 — 4/460

47 11... ♗e7?! 12. c5 d5 [12... ♘e4? 13. ♕d4] 13. cd6 ♗d6 14. ♗b6! ♕e7 15. ♕c2± Sznapik–Schmidt, Polska 1973

48 12. ♗b6 ♗h2 13. ♔h1 ♖b6 14. ♘b6 ♕b6 15. ♔h2 ♘e4∞; 12. f4 ♘e4 13. ♗d3 ♘f6 [13... ♘c5 14. ♘c5 ♕a7 15. ♕h5! g6 16. ♕e5$\overline{\overline{\infty}}$ Hort] 14. c5 ♗e7 15. ♗d4∞ Torre–Hort, Nice (ol) 1974 — 17/409

49 Minić–Suetin, Ljubljana–Portorož 1973 — 15/361

50 9... ♘e4?! 10. ♘c6 ♕c6 11. ♘b6 ♖b8 12. ♕d4 ♗f8 13. ♗f3 f5 [13... d5 14. c4] 14. ♖ad1±; 14. g4!? Boleslavski; 9... d5 10. c3! [10. ♘b6 ♕b6 11. ♘e6 d4 12. ♘g7 ♔e7 13. ♗g5 ♖g8 14. ♗f6 ♔f6 15. ♘h5∞ Klovan–Šmit, SSSR 1970 — 10/453] ♗e7 [10... ♗d6 11. ♘b6! ♕b6 12. ♘e6 ♕b2 13. ♘g7 ♔e7 14. ed5 ♘e5 15. ♗d4 ♖g8 16. f4±→] 11. ♘c6 bc6 12. ed5 cd5 13. ♘b6±

51 10. ♘b6!? ♖b8 [10... ♕b6 11. ♘e6 ♕b8 12. ♘g7±→] 11. ♘c8 ♖c8 12. a4± Spektor–Hodos, SSSR 1960

52 10... ♕c6 11. ♘b6 ♖b8 13. e5±

53 11. ♘b6 ♖b8 12. ♘c8 ♖c8 13. f4 0–0 14. ♗d3 c5 15. c3 c4 16. ♗c2 ♖fd8= Lomaja–Banik, SSSR 1963; 11. ♘c5!? ♗c5 12. ♗c5 ♘e4 13. ♕d4 ♘c5 14. ♕c5 ♗b7 15. ♗f3 0-0-0 16. c4$\overline{\overline{\infty}}$ Havski–Usov, SSSR 1961

54 12... ♘d7 13. ♕d4 e5 14. ♕c3 0–0 15. ♖fd1 ♘f6 16. a4 ♗b7 17. f3 ♖fe8 18. ♖d2 ♖e7 19. ♖ad1± Klovan–Abrosimov, SSSR 1966

55 Suetin–Furman, SSSR (ch) 1963

56 **10. ♘c6** bc6 [10... dc6?! 11. ♗b6 ♕e7 12. ♕d3 ♘d7 13. ♖ad1 ♗b8 14. ♗e3± Spektor–Antošin, SSSR 1961] 11. ♘b6 ♖b8 12. ♘c8 ♖c8 13. ♗a6 ♖a8 14. ♗d3 [14. ♗e2?! ♗h2 15. ♔h1 ♗f4 16. ♕c1 ♗e3 17. ♕e3 ♕e5∓ Matanović–Doda, Varna (ol) 1962] ♗h2 15. ♔h1 ♗f4 16. ♕d2 ♗e3 17. ♕e3 ♕e5= Koc–Tajmanov, SSSR (ch) 1961; **10. g3** b5 [10... ♘d4 11. ♕d4 b5 12. ♘b6 ♖b8 13. ♘c8 ♖c8 14. a4 ♗e5 15. ♕d3?! ♕c2 16. ♖fc1 ♕d3 17. ♖c8 ♔e7 18. ♗c5 ♗d6= Gipslis–Buslajev, SSSR 1963; 15. ♕b4!± Mojsejev] 11. ♘b6!? ♖b8 12. ♘c8 ♖c8 13. a4 ♘d4 14. ♗d4 e5 15. ♗e3 ♗c5 16. ♗c5 ♕c5 17. ab5 ab5 18. ♗d3± Suetin–Tajmanov, SSSR 1968 — 6/480

57 10... ♗h2 11. ♔h1 ♕b6 12. ♘e6 ♕b2 13. ♘g7 ♔f8 14. ♘f5±→

58 11... ♗e7 12. ♘c6 bc6 13. ♘c8 ♕c8 14. e5 ♘d5 15. ♗c1±

59 12... bc6 13. ♘c4±→

60 17. ♗f4 ♗f4 [17... ♕c7 18. ♕g7! ♗g7 19. ♗c7+– Szabo–Lengyel, Kecskemet 1964] 18. ♕f4 d6 19. ♘c8 ♖c8 20. ♕f6 ♖f8 21. ♕e6 ♔d8 22. ♖ad1 ♔c7 23. ♕e7 ♔b8 24. c3± Smejkal–Spasov, Örebro 1966

61 11. ♕d4 ♖b8 12. c4 c5 13. ♕d3 [13. ♘c5? e5] d6= Holaszek–Pachman, ČSSR 1968 — 5/392

62 14. ♗d4 c5 15. c4 cd4 16. cd5 ♕c5 17. ♗f3 ♗g5= Mecking–Portisch, Sousse (izt) 1967

63 17. ♗b2± Matulović–Portisch, Sousse (izt) 1967 — 4/461

64 **10. ♘f3** b5 11. ♘b6 ♖b8 12. ♘c8 ♖c8 13. ♗d3 ♘g4= Dely–Janošević, Budapest 1965; **10. ♘b3** b5 [10... ♗d6? 11. ♘b6 ♖b8 12. g3 ♘e4 13. ♕d4 ♘f6 14. ♘c4 ♘f5 15. ♘d6 ♕d6 16. ♕d6 ♘d6 17. ♗f4+– Postler–Liberzon, SSSR 1972] 11. ♘b6 ♖b8 12. ♘c8 ♖c8=

65 10... ♗d6 11. g3 [11. ♘f3 ♘g6∞] ♘e4 12. c5 ♗e5 [12... ♘c5 13. ♖c1 ♘d5 14. b4! ♘b4 15. ♘c5 ♗c5 16. ♖c5! ♕c5 17. ♘e6 ♕e5 18. ♘g7 ♕g7 19. ♗d4+–→] 13. f4 ♗f6 [13... ♘d5 14. fe5! ♘e3 17. ♕d3 ♘f1 16. ♕e4+–] 14. ♘b6 ♖b8 15. ♖c1± Boleslavski

66 **11. ♗f3**?! ♘c5 [11... ♘f6? 12. c5 ♗a5 13. ♘b3+– Matulović–Ostojić, Jugoslavija (ch) 1972 — 13/396] 12. a3 ♘a4 13. ♕a4 [13. ab4 ♘b2∓] ♗d6 14. g3 ♗e5 15. c5 0–0∓ Klovan–Titenko, SSSR 1966 — 2/374; **11. c5** ♘d5 12. ♘b3 0–0 [12... ♘e3 13. fe3 ♕c6 14. ♗f3±] 13. ♕d4 f5 14. ♗c4 ♘e3 15. fe3 d6!∓ Boleslavski

67 11... ♘c5? 12. a3 ♘a4 13. ab4 ♘b6 14. ♘b5!+–

68 12. c5!?

69 17. ♘b6 [Kapengut–Furman, SSSR (ch) 1972] ♖b8 18. c5!±

70 10. c4!? ♗d6 11. ♘f3 ♘g4 12. ♗b6 ♗h2 13. ♔h1 ♕f4 14. g3 ♗g3 15. fg3 ♕g3=∞ Nej–Furman, Tallinn 1971 — 11/323

71 **11. ♘b6** ♖b8 12. ♗d3 ♗d6 13. g3 ♘d7 14. ♘c8 ♖fc8± Boleslavski–Gipslis, SSSR 1967; **11. ♗b6**!? ♕f4 [11... ♕e5?! 12. ♗d3 ♘d7 13. f4 ♕b8 14. ♔h1± Gufeljd–Džindžihašvili, SSSR 1971 — 11/322] 12. f3±

72 11... ♘e4? 12. c5+–

73 12. ♗b6? ♗h2 13. ♔h1 ♕f4 14. g3 ♕h6 15. ♔g2 e5–+ Garcia–Evans, La Habana 1966

74 **16. ♖ad1** ♔h8 17. ♗f3 e5 18. fe5 ♘g5 19. ♗e2 ♗e6 20. ♖d6∞ Balašov–Liberzon, SSSR 1971 — 12/406; 16... e5!?; **16. ♗d3**!? ♘f6 17. ♗d4±↑

75 19. ♕e4 ♖d8 20. ♗d4 e5! 21. fe5 ♗g6 22. ♕e3 h6± Talj–Suetin, Soči 1973

76 11. f4 ♗e7 [11... ♖b8 12. ♗d3 ♗e7 13. c4 d6 14. ♖c1 c5 15. b3 ♗b7 16. ♘c3 ♖bd8= Geler–Talj, SSSR (ch) 1973; 14. c5!± Talj] 12. ♘b6 [12. ♗d3 d6 13. ♘b6 ♖b8 14. ♘c8 ♕c8 15. b3± Lejn–Matulović, Novi Sad 1973 — 16/354; 12... c5= Talj] ♖b8 13. ♘c8 ♕c8 14. e5 ♘d5 15. ♗c1 f6 16. c4 ♗c5 17. ♔h1 [Talj–Kirov, Novi Sad 1974 — 18/371] ♘e3 18. ♗e3 ♗e3 19. ♕d3 ♗c5=

77 **11... ♘e4**? 12. c5 ♕e5 13. ♗d4 ♕f4 14. ♗g7!±; **11... ♗d6**!? 12. f4 ♘e4 13. ♗d3 ♘f6 14. c5 ♗e7 15. ♗d4±○ Kuzmin–Svešnikov, SSSR (ch) 1973

78 13. ♗f3 ♖b8 14. g3 d6= Kuzmin–Matulović, SSSR–Jugoslavija 1973 — 16/356

79 Radulov–Matulović, Vrnjačka Banja 1974

80 12... ♕c8 13. e5 ♘d5 14. ♗a7 ♖a8 15. ♗d4 c5 16. c4 cd4 17. cd5±; 14. ♗c1!?

81 13... ♖e8 14. ♗d3 ♗d6 15. ♔h1 [15. f4 e5 16. f5 ♖b2 17. g4 h6 18. h4 ♘d5!? 19. ed5 e4 20. ♗e2 ♗c5= Šamkovič–Doda, Polanica Zdroj 1970; 15. g4 h5 16. gh5 ♗h2 17. ♔g2 ♗f4=] ♗e5 [15... ♗h2 16. f4 h5 17. ♕f3 ♘g4 18. b3±; 15... ♖b2 16. ♗d4 ♖bb8 17. ♗f6 gf6 18. f4±] 16. c3 ♖b2 17. ♕c1 ♕b7 18. f4 ♗c7 19. e5 ♘d5 20. ♗c5± Kočijev–Ruderfer, SSSR 1972 — 14/392

82 15. f4 e5 16. f5 [16. b3 ef4 17. ♗d4 ♗e5 18. ♗e5 ♕e5 19. ♕f3 d5 20. ♕f4 ♕d4 21. ♔h1

de4 22. ♗c4 ♖b7∞] ♖b2 17. g4 h6 18. h4 ♗f8 19. g5 ♘d5! 20. ed5 e4= Klovan—Vasjukov, SSSR 1973 — 16/351

83 18. ♕b2?? ♗c3!−+

84 19. ♕b2 ♗f4 20. ♕f2 ♘f1 21. ♖f1 g5!? [21... e5 22. g3 ♕d6 23. ♗e2 ♗g5 24. ♕f7 ♔h8 25. a4 ♗e7 26. a5 ♖f8 27. ♕c4± Smejkal—Karpov, Leningrad (izt) 1973 — 15/362; 25. ♗g4!? ♗f6 26. ♔g2± Adorjan—Matulović, Novi Sad 1973 — 16/352] 22. g3 ♕d6 23. ♗e2 [23. ♗c2!? ♗e5 24. ♕f7 ♔h8 25. ♔g2 ♕c5 (25... ♗g7? 26. ♖d1 ♕e5 27. ♖d7 ♖f8 28. ♕e7± Tringov— Ögaard, Reykjavik 1974 — 17/408) 26. ♔h3 ♗g7? 27. ♖d1!± Tringov—Babev, Bulgaria (ch) 1974 — 18/370; 26... ♕c3!?∞] ♗e5 24. ♕f7 ♔h8 25. ♖d1 ♕c7 26. ♕e7 ♗c3 27. ♗g4 ♕c8! 28. ♗e6 ♖e8= Razuvajev—Matulović, SSSR—Jugoslavija 1973 — 16/355

B5 SADRŽAJ • СОДЕРЖАНИЕ B5

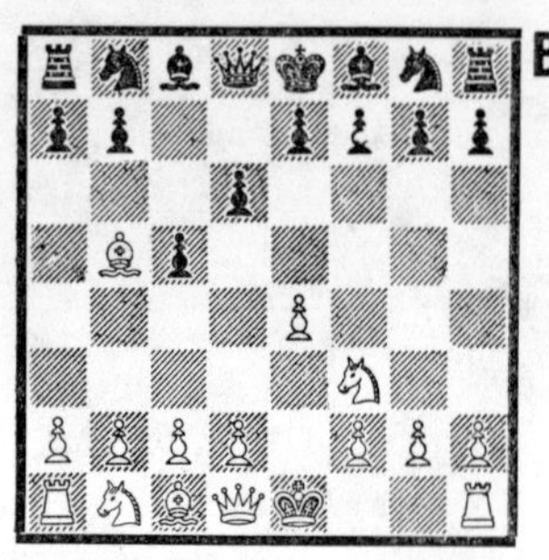

B5 SOMMAIRE • INDICE B5

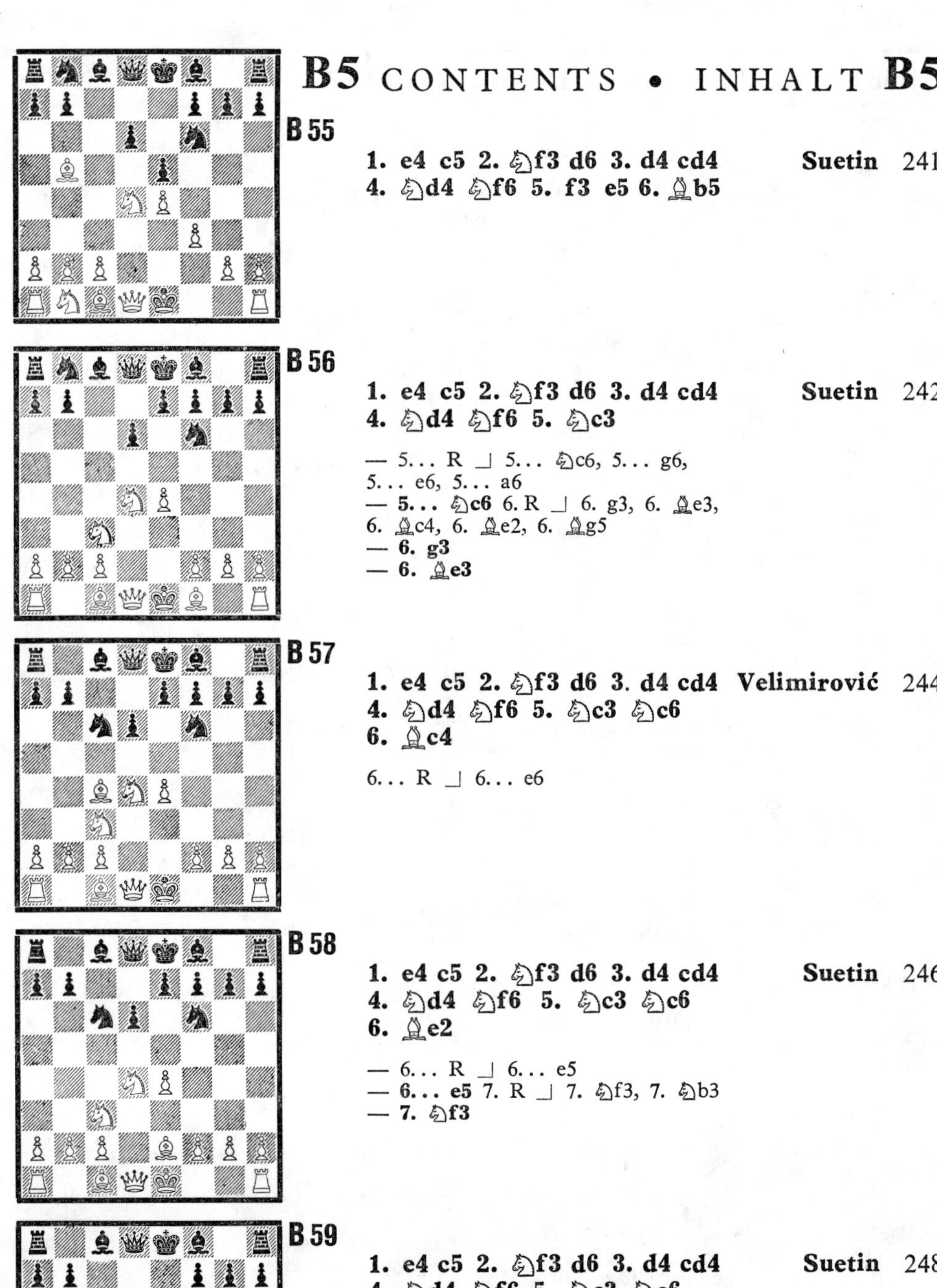

B5 CONTENTS • INHALT B5

B5 INDICE • INNEHÅLL B5

B 50 — 1. e4 c5 2. ♘f3 d6

	3	4	5	6	7	8	9	10	11	
1	b4[1]	bc5	cd6	♗b5[4]	♗d7	♕e2	♘e5			=
	♘f6[2]	♘e4	e6![3]	♗d7	♘d7	♘df6	♘d6[5]			
2	. . .	d4[6]	♗d3	0–0	♘bd2	e5	♘e1	♕g4	♘df3	∓
	cb4	♘f6[7]	e6[8]	♗e7	d5	♘fd7	♘c6	0–0	f5[9]	
3	d3	g3	♗g2	0–0	♘bd2	c3	♖e1	♘f1	d4	=
	♘c6[10]	g6	♗g7	e6	♘ge7	0–0	b6	♗a6	cd4[11]	
4	c3	♕c2[13]	♗b5[15]	0–0	♖e1	♘a3	d4	♗f1	♗g5	∓
	♘f6[12]	♕c7[14]	♘bd7	g6	♗g7	0–0	a6	b5	♗b7[16]	
5	. . .	♗d3	♗c2	d3	♘bd2	h3	0–0	♘h2	f4	∓
	. . .	♘c6[17]	♗g4	g6[18]	♗g7	♗d7	0–0	b5	b4[19]	
6	. . .	♗b5	♕e2[21]	♕b5	♕e2	0–0	d4	cd4	e5	=
	. . .	♗d7[20]	♗b5	♕d7	♘c6	e6	cd4	d5	♘e4[22]	
7	♘c3	h3	♕f3	♗b5![24]	0–0	♖b1!	b4	♖b4	♗a4	±
	♗g4?![23]	♗f3	♘c6	♖c8	g6	♗g7	cb4	♘f6	0–0[25]	
8	. . .	g3	♗g2	d3	0–0	♘h4	♘e2	f4	h3	∞
	a6	b5[26]	♗b7	g6	♗g7	b4	♘c6	♘f6	e5[27]	
9	. . .	♗c4	d3	0–0	♘g5	f4	a4	♘f3![28]		=
	e5	♘c6	♗e7	♘f6	0–0	a6	♖b8			

1. e4 c5 2. ♘f3 d6 3. ♘c3 ♘f6 4. e5[29] de5 5. ♘e5

	5	6	7	8	9	10	11	12	13	
10	. . .	♘c4[30]	b3[32]	♗b2	♕f3	a4	♗d3	♕h3	0–0[33]	±
	♘bd7	e6[31]	♗e7	0–0	♖b8	b6	♗b7	a6		
11	. . .	♗b5[34]	♘d7[36]	0–0	d4	♕d4	♗f4	♗e5[37]	♗d4	=
	e6	♗d7[35]	♘bd7	♗e7	cd4	0–0	♘b6	♕d4	♖fc8[38]	
12	. . .	♗e2	0–0	♗f3	♘c4	b3[40]	♗b2	♗c3	♗b2	±
	. . .	♗e7[39]	0–0	♘bd7	♘b6	♘bd5	♘c3	♘d5	♗f6[41]	
13	. . .	a4	♘c4	♗e2	b3	♗b2	0–0	♘e3	♗c4	=
	a6	♕c7[42]	♘c6	♗e6!	g6	♗g7	0–0	♘d4	♗d7[43]	

[1] **3. b3** ♘c6 4. ♗b2 ♘f6 5. ♘c3 g6 [5... e5!? 6. ♗e2 ♗e7 7. 0–0 0–0 8. ♖e1 ♘d4 9. ♘d4 cd4 10. ♘d5 ♘d5 11. ed5 ♗f5∓ Perfiljev–Rabinovič, SSSR 1928] 6. ♗b5 ♗d7 7. 0–0 ♗g7 8. ♘d5 e5 9. ♘f6 ♕f6 10. c3 0–0∓ Havin–Aronin, SSSR 1949; **3. c4** e5 4. ♘c3 f5 5. d3 ♘f6 6. ♗e2 ♘c6 7. ef5 ♗f5 8. ♘h4 ♗e6 9. ef4 10. ♗f4 ♗e7= Grob–Rossolimo 1939; **3. ♗c4** ♘c6 [3... e6 4. d4 cd4 5. ♘d4 ♘f6 6. ♘c3 — B 86] 4. 0–0 ♘f6 5. ♖e1 ♗g4=; **3. ♗e2** ♘f6 [3... ♘c6 4. c3 ♘f6 — 3. c3] 4. ♘c3 ♗g4 5. d4 cd4 6. ♘d4 ♗e2 7. ♕e2 g6 8. ♗e3 ♗g7 9. ♖d1 ♕c8 10. 0–0 ♘g4= Unzicker–Euwe, Schweiz 1958

[2] 3... b6 4. bc5 dc5 5. ♗c4 ♘c6 6. 0–0 e6 7. ♗b2 ♘f6 8. d4±↻

[3] **5... ed6** 6. ♗b2±↻; **5... ♘d6** 6. ♗b2 e6 [6... ♗g4 7. ♗e2 e6 8. 0–0 ♘c6 9. ♘e5 ♘e5 10. ♗e5 ♘c4 11. ♗c3 ♗e2 12. ♕e2 ♕c7 13. d3 ♘b6 14. g3!± Spielmann–Landau, Noordwijk 1938] 7. ♗d3 ♘d7 8. 0–0 ♘f6 9. ♖e1±

[4] 6. ♗b2 ♕b6 [6... ♘f6 7. ♗d3 ♗d6=] 7. ♗d4 ♕d6=

[5] = Pachman

[6] 4. a3? ♘f6∓

[7] 4... g6 5. ♗c4 ♗g7 6. 0–0 e6 7. a3 ba3 8. ♘a3 a6 9. ♗f4 ♘c6 10. d5 ♘e5 11. de6 ♗e6? 12. ♗e6 fe6 13. ♘g5± Bronštejn–Levin, SSSR 1969 — 8/396; 11... fe6!?

[8] **5... ♗g4**? 6. 0–0 ♘c6 7. e5! de5 8. de5 ♘d7 9. ♗b2 ♕c7 10. e6 ♗e6 11. ♘g5+–

Lehmann–Mross, BRD 1949; **5... d5** 6. e5 [6. ♘bd2 e6 7. e5 ♘fd7 8. ♘f1 h6 9. ♘g3 ♘c6 10. ♘h5 ♘b6 11. ♕d2 ♗d7 12. ♕f4 ♕e7 13. a3 ♘c4!∓ Littlewood–Rohlin, corr. 1970 — 9/371; 6... de4 7. ♘e4 ♘bd7 8. ♘eg5 ♕c7 9. c4 h6 10. ♘h3 g5 11. ♘hg1 ♗g7 12. ♘e2 e5 13. ♘g3 0–0? 14. 0–0 e4 15. ♘e4 ♘e4 16. ♗e4 ♕c4 17. ♗d3± Keres–Eliskases, Semmering Baden 1937; 13... e4 14. ♕e2 0–0 15. ♘e4 ♖e8 16. ♘f6 ♘f6 17. ♗e3 ♘g4∓ Medina–Pomar, España 1947] ♘e4 7. ♘g5 ♘g5 8. ♗g5 ♘c6 9. ♗e3 e6 10. 0–0 ♗d7 11. ♘d2 ♕b6∓

9 Corden–Gligorić, Hastings 1969/70 — 9/370

10 3... ♘f6 4. g3 ♘c6 [4... b6 5. ♗g2 ♗b7 6. 0–0 g6=] 5. ♗g2 g6 6. 0–0 ♗g7 7. c3 [7. ♘bd2 0–0 8. a4 ♗d7= Averbah–Geler, SSSR (ch) 1954] 0–0 8. ♘bd2 ♖b8 9. a4 a6 10. ♖e1 ♘g4 11. ♘b3 e5 12. h3 ♘f6= Keres–Averbah, SSSR (ch) 1955

11 12. ♘d4 ♘e5 13. ♗g5 h6 14. ♕a4 ♗b7 15. ♗e7 ♕e7 16. ♖ad1 ♖fc8 17. ♘e3 ♖c5= Troianescu–Petrosjan, Bucuresti 1953

12 3... e5 4. ♗b5 ♗d7 5. ♗d7 ♘d7 6. 0–0 ♘gf6 7. d4 ♗e7 [7... ♘e4 8. de5 de5 9. ♕a4! ♘d6 10. ♘e5 b5 11. ♕f4±] 8. de5 de5 9. ♕e2 h6 10. ♘bd2 ♕c7 11. ♘c4± Kurajica–Geler, Bognor Regis 1967

13 **4. ♗e2** ♘c6?! 5. d4!? cd4 6. cd4 ♘e4 7. d5 ♕a5 8. ♘c3 ♘e5 9. ♘e5 de5 [9... ♘c3 10. bc3 ♕c3 11. ♗d2 ♕e5 12. 0–0 ♕d5 13. ♖b1± Basman–Stean, Hastings 1973/74 — 17/439] 10. 0–0 [Palatnik–Ljubojević, Beograd 1974 — 18/408] ♘c3 11. bc3 e6 12. ♗f3 ed5 13. ♗d5 ♗c5 14. ♖e1 0–0 15. ♖e5 ♗e6!= Palatnik; 4... g6∓; **4. e5** ♘d5 [4... de5 5. ♘e5 ♘c6? 6. ♘c6 bc6 7. ♗c4 ♗f5 8. d3 e6 9. ♕f3 ♕d7 10. h3 ♗e7 11. 0–0 ♖d8 12. ♖d1± Aljehin–Cvetkov, Buenos Aires (ol) 1939; 5... ♘bd7=] 5. d4 cd4 6. cd4 — B 22

14 **4... ♗g4** 5. d4 ♘bd7 6. d5 ♗f3 7. gf3 g6 8. ♗e3 ♗g7 9. ♗e2 0–0 10. ♘d2 ♖e8 11. f4 e6 12. de6 ♖e6∞ Suetin–S. Garcia, Polanica Zdroj 1974 — 18/407; **4... ♘c6** 5. d4 e6 6. dc5 dc5 7. ♗b5 ♕c7 8. ♗g5 ♗d7 9. ♘bd2 ♗e7 10. 0–0 0–0 = Stoltz–Rabar, Helsinki (ol) 1952; **4... e6** 5. d4 ♗e7 [5... ♕c7 6. dc5 dc5 7. ♗g5 ♗e7 8. ♗h4 0–0 9. ♗g3±] 6. dc5 dc5 7. ♗d3 ♘c6 8. 0–0 ♕c7 9. ♖e1 a6 10. ♗g5 ♘d7 11. ♗e7 ♘e7= Stoltz–Stahlberg, Sverige 1952

15 5. d3 ♗g4 6. ♗e2 e6 7. ♗g5 ♘bd7 8. ♘bd2 ♗e7= Stoltz–Geler, Helsinki (ol) 1952; 5... e6!?

16 Radovici–Polugajevski, Marianske Lazni 1959

17 **4... e5** 5. 0–0 ♗e7 6. ♗b5 ♘bd7 7. ♖e1 a6 8. ♗f1 b5=; 6... ♘c6!?; **4... d5** 5. e5 ♘fd7 6. ♗c2 [6. e6 fe6 7. ♘g5 ♘f6 8. ♗h7 ♘h7 9. ♕h5 ♔d7 10. ♘f7 ♕e8 11. ♘e5 ♔d8–+; 10. ♘h7 ♕e8! 11. ♘f6 ef6 12. ♕h8 ♘c6∓] e6 7. d4 ♘c6 8. 0–0 ♕b6=

18 6... e6 7. h3 ♗h5 8. ♕e2 [8. 0–0 d5 9. ♕e2 ♗e7 10. ♘bd2 ♕c7 11. ♖e1 0–0 12. ♘f1 b5 13. ♘g3 ♗g6 14. ♘h4 ♗d6∓] d5 9. ♘bd2 ♗e7 10. ♘f1 0–0 11. g4 ♗g6 12. ♘g3 b5= Gilg–Aronin, Wien 1952

19 12. ♘c4 d5 13. ♘e5 bc3 14. bc3 de4 15. de4 ♘e5 16. fe5 ♘e8∓ Bisguier–Fischer, USA (ch) 1967 — 3/466

20 4... ♘c6 5. ♕e2 a6 6. ♗a4 b5 7. ♗c2 e5=

21 5. ♗d7 ♕d7 — B 52

22 Mariotti–Minić, Praia da Rocha 1969 — 8/397

23 3... g6 4. d4 cd4 5. ♕d4 f6 6. ♗e3 ♘h6 7. ♗c4 ♘c6 8. ♕d2 ♘f7 9. ♘d4 ♘d4 10. ♗d4 ♗g7 11. f4 0–0 12. 0–0± Keres–Bilek, Moskva 1967 — 3/464

24 6. g3 g6 7. ♗g2 ♗g7 8. 0–0 h5?! 9. d3 h4 10. g4 e5 11. ♘d5!± Keres–Ivkov, Beograd 1970 — 9/373; 8... ♘f6!?= Keres

25 **11... ♖c7**? 12. ♖b7! ♖b7 13. ♗c6+–; **11... ♕d7** 12. d4± Adorjan, Florian; **11... 0–0** 12. ♖b7 ♘d7 13. ♗c6 ♘e5 14. ♕e2 ♘c6 15. ♕a6 ♗d4 16. ♘a4 ♕a5 17. ♕a5 ♘a5 18. ♖b5 ♘c6 19. c3 ♗f6 20. ♗a3± Sax–Bukić, Bath 1973 — 16/385

26 **4... g6** 5. ♗g2 ♗g7 6. d4 cd4 7. ♘d4 ♘f6 8. 0–0 0–0 9. b3± Keres–Kavalek, Wijk aan Zee 1969 — 7/388; **4... ♘c6** 5. ♗g2 ♗g4 [5... g6 6. d4 ♗g4 7. dc5 dc5 8. ♗e3 ♕a5 9. 0–0 ♗g7 10. ♗d2 ♖d8 11. ♘d5 ♕a4 12. ♕c1 ♕e4 13. ♘g5 ♕e5 14. ♗f4± Kurajica–Fischer, Rovinj–Zagreb 1970 — 9/374] 6. h3 ♗f3 7. ♕f3 g6 8. d3 ♗g7 9. 0–0 ♘f6 10. g4 ♖c8 11. ♘e2 b5 12. ♗d2 ♘d7 13. c3? b4∓ Balašov–Saidy, Tallinn 1973 — 16/386; 13. ♖ab1= Saidy

27 12. f5 d5 13. ♗g5 de4 14. ♗e4 c4? 15. ♗g2 cd3 16. ♕d3!± Mecking–Ljubojević, Vršac 1971 — 12/430; 14... ♕d6∞ Mecking

28 **10. ♕e1**?! ♘d4 11. fe5 de5 12. ♕f2 b5 13. ab5 ab5 14. ♗f7 ♖f7 15. ♘f7 ♔f7 16. ♘d5 ♗b7 17. ♘e7 ♕e7 18. ♗g5 ♖f8 19. ♕h4 ♔g8∓ Svešnikov–Raškovski, SSSR (ch) 1973; **10. ♘f3**!=

29 **4. b3** g6 5. ♗b2 ♗g7 6. ♗e2 0–0 7. 0–0 ♘c6=; **4. g3** g6 5. ♗g2 ♗g7 6. 0–0 0–0 7. d3 ♘c6=

30 6. d4 ♘e5 7. de5 ♕d1 8. ♔d1! ♘g4 9. ♗b5 ♔d8 10. ♔e2± Vasjukov–Ree, Amsterdam 1969; 6... e6!=

31 6... a6 7. a4 ♘b6 8. b3 [8. a5 ♘c4 9. ♗c4 ♗g4?! 10. f3 ♗f5 11. g4!? ♗d7 12. g5 ♘h5 13. d4± Benkö–Bogdanović, Sarajevo 1967 — 3/465] e6 9. ♘b6 ♕b6 10. ♗d3 ♗d6 11. ♕e2± Sanguinetti–Ćirić, La Habana (ol) 1966 — 2/409

32 7. d4 ♗e7 8. dc5 0–0 9. ♕f3 ♘c5 10. ♗f4 ♗d7 11. 0-0-0± Keres–Bobocov, Sofia 1969 — 8/395

33 Larsen–Geler, Copenhagen 1966 — 1/290

34 **6. b3** ♗d6 7. ♘c4 ♗e7 8. ♗b2 ♘c6 9. g3 0–0 10. ♗g2 ♕d7 11. 0–0 ♖b8 12. ♘e4 ♘d4= Keres–Bobocov, Moskva 1967 — 4/504; **6. g3** ♘bd7 7. ♘c4 ♘b6 8. ♕e2 ♘c4 9. ♕c4 ♗d7 10. ♗g2 ♕c8 11. a4 ♗c6= Hübner–Petrosjan, Sevilla (mct) 1971 — 11/353; 9... a6!? Petrosjan

35 6... ♘bd7 7. d4 a6 8. ♗d7 ♘d7 9. ♕h5 ♘e5 10. de5 b6 11. ♗g5 ♕c7 12. 0-0-0 ♗b7 13. ♖d2 h6 14. ♖hd1 hg5 15. ♕h8 ♕e5 16. f3 b5 17. ♘e4± Ljubojević–Rogoff, Malaga 1971 — 11/352

36 7. ♕f3 ♕c7= Geler

37 12. ♖ad1 ♕d4 13. ♖d4 ♖fc8=

38 14. ♖fd1 ♘c4 15. ♘e2 a6= Holmov–Geler, SSSR 1973 — 15/390

39 6... ♘bd7 7. ♘c4 ♗e7 8. 0–0 0–0 9. d3 ♘b6 10. ♘b6 ♕b6 11. a4! a6 12. a5 ♕c7 13. ♗f3 ♖d8 14. ♕e2 ♗d7 15. ♘a4!± Neukirch–Dely, Varna (Usic) 1972 — 13/438

40 10. ♘e3 ♘bd7? 11. d4! cd4 12. ♕d4± Keres–Ree, Wijk aan Zee 1969 — 8/394; 10... ♘bd5!= Kurajica–Tringov, Sarajevo 1970 — 9/372

41 14. ♘e5± Keres–Bobocov, SSSR 1970 — 10/483

42 6... ♘bd7 7. ♘c4±

43 Ljubojević–Kaplan, Madrid 1973 — 16/387

B 51 1. e4 c5 2. ♘f3 d6 3. ♗b5

	3	4	5	6	7	8	9	10	11	
1	...	d4[1]	♕d4	♗g5[2]	♘c3	0–0[4]	♗d7	♖ad1	♖fe1[5]	±
	♘d7	cd4	♘f6	e6[3]	♗e7	a6	♗d7	♗c6		
2	...	...	♘c3[6]	♗d7	0–0	dc5[7]	♗g5	♖b1	b4	±
	...	♘f6	a6	♘d7	e6	♘c5	♕b6	♗d7	♘a4[8]	
3	...	...	...	♕d4	e5	♘e5	♗g5	0-0-0	♘c4[10]	±
	...	...	cd4	g6[9]	de5	♗g7	0–0	♕a5		
4	...	0–0[11]	♗c6	d4[13]	♕d4	♕d3	♖d1	♗g5	♗f6[16]	±
	♘c6	a6[12]	bc6	cd4	e5	♗e7[14]	♘f6[15]	0–0	gf6[17]	
5	...	...	h3[18]	♖e1[19]	c3[21]	♗c6	d4	cd4	♘c3	=
	...	♗g4	♗h5	e6[20]	a6	bc6	cd4	♘f6	♗e7[22]	
6	...	...	♖e1[23]	c3	d4	♗g5	♗f6	dc5	♗c6	=
	...	♘f6	e5	♗d7	♕c7	♗e7	♗f6	dc5	bc6[24]	
7	...	...	c3	♖e1	♗a4	♗c2	h3	d4	d5	=
	...	♗d7	♘f6	a6	b5[25]	e5	♗e7	0–0	♘b8[26]	
8	...	...	...	...	♗f1	d4	cd4	e5	♘c3	∞
	...	...	...	...	g6[27]	cd4	d5	♘e4	♘c3[28]	

1 4. c3 ♘f6 5. ♕e2 a6 6. ♗a4 b5 7. ♗c2 e5 8. 0–0 ♗e7 9. d4 0–0 10. ♘bd2 ♖e8= Siaperas–Tatai, Siegen (ol) 1970 — 10/486

2 6. 0–0 e6 [6... a6 7. ♗d7 ♗d7 8. ♗g5 h6 9. ♗f6 gf6 10. ♘c3 e6 11. ♘d2 ♗c6 12. ♖fe1 b5? 13. a4 ♖g8 14. ab5 ab5 15. ♖a8 ♕a8 16. ♘d5! ♗d5 17. ed5 ♗e7 18. ♘e4± Šmit–Petkevič, SSSR 1969 — 9/376; 12... ♗e7] 7. e5 de5 8. ♘e5 a6 9. ♗d7 ♘d7=

3 6... ♕a5? 7. ♘c3 a6 8. b4! ♕d8 9. ♗f6 gf6 10. ♗d7 ♗d7 11. ♘d5±⊞ Liliental–Kotov, SSSR (ch) 1944

4 8. 0-0-0 a6? 9. ♗d7 ♗d7 10. e5!+– Gurgenidze–Gufeljd, Tbilisi 1969 — 9/375; 8... 0–0=

5 ↑⊞ Boleslavski

6 5. e5?! ♕a5 6. ♘c3 ♘e4 7. ♗d2 ♘c3 8. ♗d7 ♗d7 9. ♗c3 ♕a6 10. ed6 ed6 11. ♕e2 ♕e2 12. ♔e2 f6 13. a4 ♔f7∓⊡ Krnić–Tringov, Vršac 1973

7 **8. d5** e5 9. a4 ♗e7 10. ♘d2 0–0 11. ♘c4 ♘b6 [Hutchings–Pytel, Nice (ol) 1974 — 17/440] 12. ♘e3!?±; **8. ♗g5** ♕c7 9. ♖e1 [9. d5!?] cd4 [Gufeljd–Ljubojević, Beograd 1974 — 18/411] 10. ♘d4 h6 11. ♗b4 g5 12. ♗g3 ♘e5∞

8 12. ♘a4 ♗a4 13. ♕d3 h6 14. ♗e3 ♕c7 15. c4 ♗e7 16. ♖fc1 0–0 17. ♘d4 ♖fc8 18. h3 ♗e8 19. ♘e2± Keres–Ljubojević, Petropolis (izt) 1973 — 16/388

9 **6... e5** 7. ♕d3 h6 8. ♘d2! [8. 0–0 a6 9. ♗c4 b5 10. ♗d5 ♖b8 11. ♗e3± Sznapik–Ribli, Skopje (ol) 1972 — 14/430] ♗e7 9. ♘c4 0–0 10. 10. ♗d7 ♕d7 11. ♘e3 ♕c6 12. g4! ±→» Torre–O'Kelly, Malaga 1973 — 16/398; **6... e6 7.** ♗g5 ♗e7 8. 0-0-0 0–0 9. h4 ♕a5 10. ♗d7 ♗d711. ♗f6 gf6 12. g4 ♗c6 13. ♕e3 ♖ac8 14. ♔b1 ♖fe8 16. g5±→ Kuzmin–Kuprejčik, SSSR (ch) 1974 — 18/409

10 **11. ♘d7** ♗d7! [11... ♘d7?! 12. ♕a4! ♗c3 13. ♕a5 ♗a5 14. ♗d7 f6 15. ♗e3 ♔f7 16. ♖d5 ♗c7 17. ♗c8 ♖fc8 18. ♖d7 ♔e6 19. ♖hd1± Larsen–Csom, Palma de Mallorca 1971 — 13/439] 12. ♗f6 ♗f6 13. ♕d7 ♗c3 14. bc3 ♖ad8! 15. ♕e7 ♖d1 16. ♖d1 ♕b5 17. ♖d8 ♕f1= Radulov–Ljubojević, Poiana Brašov 1973 — 16/399; **11. ♘c4**±○

11 **4. b4**?! cb4 5. d4 ♗d7 6. 0–0 e6 7. d5 ♘b8 8. ♗d7=∞; 5... d5∓; **4. d4** cd4 5. ♘d4 ♗d7 6. 0–0 ♘f6 7. ♘c3 e6=; **4. ♘c3** ♗d7 5. 0–0 ♘f6 6. d3 [6. ♗c6 ♗c6 7. e5 de5 8. ♘e5 ♕c7= Velimirović] e6 7. a3 ♗e7 8. ♗c6 ♗c6 9. b4 0–0 10. bc5 dc5 11. ♘e5 ♗e8= Matulović–Velimirović, Vrnjačka Banja 1973 — 15/393; 9... b6!?

12 4... e6 5. c3 ♗d7 6. d4±

13 6. c3 g6 7. d4 cd4 8. cd4 ♗g7 9. ♘c3 ♘f6 10. e5 ♘d5 11. ♕a4 ♕d7 12. ed6 ♕d6= Boleslavski

14 8... ♘e7 9. ♖d1 ♘g6 10. ♘a3±↑ Boleslavski

15 9... ♕c7 10. ♗g5! [10. ♘a3 ♗e6 11. ♘c4 ♖d8 12. ♗e3 ♘f6 13. ♗b6 ♗c4 14. ♗c7 ♗d3= Sokolski–Holmov, SSSR 1960] f6 [10... ♘f6 11. ♗f6 gf6 12. c4±] 11. ♗e3 f5 12. ef5 ♘f6 13. ♘g5 d5 14. f3 0–0 15. ♘d2± Boleslavski

16 **11. ♘a3** d5! 12. ♘e5 [12. ♗f6 ♗f6 13. ed5 e4 14. ♕e4 ♗b2∓ Sokolski–Botvinik, Moskva 1947] ♕c7!∓; **11. ♘bd2** ♗e6 [11... ♕c7 12. ♘c4 ♖d8 13. ♘e3 ♗e6 14. c4± Sokolski–Kotov, SSSR (ch) 1949] 12. ♘c4 ♕b8 13. ♘e3 d5 14. ♗f6 ♗f6 15. ed5 cd5 16. ♘d5 ♗d5 17. ♕d5 ♕b2∓

17 **12. ♘h4** ♔h8 13. ♘d2 ♗g4 14. ♖e1 d5 15. ♘f1 ♖g8 16. ♘e3 ♗e6 17. c3 ♕a5 18. ♘hf5± Szabo–Kotov, Budapest (ct) 1950; **12. c4**!?

18 5. c3 ♘f6 6. ♖e1 a6 [6... ♕b6 7. ♘a3 e6 8. ♗a4 ♗e7 9. ♘c4 ♕c7 10. d3 0–0 11. ♗f4 ♖ad8 12. h3± Sokolski–Aronin, SSSR (ch) 1949] 7. ♗c6 bc6 8. d3 e6 9. ♘bd2 ♘d7 10. ♕a4 ♕b6 11. h3 ♗h5 12. ♘h2 ♗e7 13. ♘c4 ♕b5 14. ♕c2 d5∞⇆ Boleslavski–Aronin, SSSR (ch) 1949

19 6. c3 ♕b6 [6... ♘f6 7. d4 a6 8. ♗c6 bc6 9. ♕a4 ♕b6 10. dc5± Boleslavski–Petrosjan, SSSR 1953; 7... cd4 8. cd4 a6 9. ♗a4 b5 10. ♗b3±] 7. ♘a3 e5 8. d4 cd4 9. cd4 0-0-0∞

20 6... ♕b6 7. ♘c3 e6 8. a4 a6 9. a5 ♕c7 10. ♗c6 ♕c6 11. ♘d5!± Damjanović–Sofrevski, Skopje 1971 — 12/434

21 **7. ♗c6** bc6 8. d3 ♘f6 9. e5!? de5 10. ♖e5 c4 11. ♖h5?! ♘h5 12. ♘e5 ♘f6 13. ♘c4 ♗e7 14. ♘bd2 0–0∓ Damjanović–Larsen, Monte Carlo 1968 — 5/421; 11. ♗g5!?; 9. ♘bd2; **7. c4** ♗f3 [7... ♘e7 8. g4! ♗g6 9. d4 a6 10. ♗a4 cd4 11. ♘d4 h5 12. ♘c3± Katalimov–Borisenko, SSSR 1970 — 10/484] 8. ♕f3 ♘e7 9. ♘c3 a6 10. ♗a4 ♕c7 11. d3 ♘g6= Kotov

22 Andersson–Larsen, Hastings 1972/73 — 15/391; 12. ♕a4 ♕d7 13. e5 ♘d5 14. ed6 ♗d6 15. ♘e5 ♗e5 16. de5 0–0= Bukić

23 **5. ♕e2** e5 6. d3 ♗e7 7. ♘bd2 0–0 8. ♗c6 bc6 9. ♘c4 ♘e8= Lublinski–Tajmanov, SSSR 1948; **5. e5** de5 6. ♘e5 ♕c7 7. d4 e6 8. ♗f4 ♗d6 9. ♘d2 0–0 10. ♗c6 bc6 11. ♘dc4 ♗a6 12. dc5 ♗c5 13. ♕f3 ♘d5= Schwarz

24 **11... ♗c6** 12. c4!±; **11... bc6**= O'Kelly–Najdorf, Amsterdam 1950

25 7... c4?! 8. ♗c2 ♗g4 9. h3 ♗h5 10. b3 cb3 11. ab3 e5 12. d3± Suetin–Balašov, SSSR 1969 — 9/377

26 12. a4 ba4 13. ♘a3 ♘e8 14. ♗a4 f5= Buhtin–Gik, SSSR 1968 — 6/517

27 7... e5 8. h3 h6 [8... ♗e7 9. d4 ♕c7 10. ♘a3 b5 11. ♘c2 ♘a5?! 12. ♗g5± Ciocaltea–Kertesz, Romania 1970 — 10/485] 9. d4 ♕c7 10. a4 ♗e7 [10... g6 11. ♘a3 ♗g7 12. dc5 dc5 13. ♘c4 ♖b8 14. b4 cb4 15. cb4 ♗e6 16. ♘d6+–→⊞ Andersson–Portisch, Skopje (ol) 1972 — 14/431; 13... 0–0 14. ♕d6 ♕d6 15. ♘d6±] 11. ♘a3 0–0 12. dc5 dc5 13. ♘c4± Andersson

28 12. bc3 ♗g7 13. ♖e3∞ Andersson

B 52 — 1. e4 c5 2. ♘f3 d6 3. ♗b5 ♗d7

	4	5	6	7	8	9	10	11	12	
1	a4[1]	0–0	d3[3]	♘bd2	♘c4	♖e1	♗c6	a5	♗g5	=
	♘c6[2]	♘f6	g6	♗g7	0–0	a6	♗c6	♘d7	f6[4]	
2	♗d7	0–0[5]	♕e2[6]	c3	d4	♖d1	♘a3[8]			±
	♘d7	♘gf6	g6	♗g7	e6[7]	♕c7				

	4	5	6	7	8	9	10	11	12	
3	... ♕d7	c3 ♘f6[9]	d3[10] e6	0–0 ♗e7	♕e2 0–0	d4 ♘c6	♖d1 cd4	cd4 d5	e5 ♘e4[11]	=
4	... ...	0–0 ♘f6	e5[12] de5	♘e5 ♕c8[13]	♕f3 e6	♘c3 ♗e7	d3 ♘bd7	♗f4 ♘e5	♗e5 0–0[14]	±
5	... ...	... ♘c6	d3[15] e6	♘bd2 ♘f6	a3[16] ♗e7	♖b1 0–0	b4 cb4	ab4 b5	♖e1 ♖fc8[17]	=
6	... ...	... ...	c3 ♘f6	♖e1[18] e6	d4 cd4	cd4 d5	e5 ♘e4	♘bd2[19] ♘d2	♗d2 ♗e7[20]	=
7	... ...	... ...	... ...	d4 ♘e4[21]	d5 ♘b8[22]	♖e1 ♘f6	♗g5[23] ♘a6	c4 ♘c7[24]	♘c3 e6[25]	=
8	... ...	c4 ♘c6[26]	0–0[27] g6[28]	d4 cd4	♘d4 ♗g7	♗e3 ♘h6[29]	f3 f5	♘c3 fe4	♕d2 ♘f7[30]	±
9	... ...	... e5	♘c3 ♘c6[31]	d3[32] g6[33]	a3[34] ♗g7	♖b1 ♘ge7	b4 b6[35]	0–0[36] 0–0	♘d5 ♘d5[37]	±

1 **4. c4** ♘f6 5. ♘c3 ♗b5 6. cb5 e6 7. d4 cd4 8. ♕d4 ♗e7 9. 0–0 0–0 10. ♖d1 ♘bd7 11. ♗g5 ♕b6 12. ♕d2 ♖fd8 13. ♗e3± Fajbisovič–Ioffe, SSSR 1969 — 7/390; 6... e5!=; 5... ♘c6=; **4. ♕e2** ♘c6 [4... a6? 5. ♗d7 ♕d7 6. 0–0 ♘c6 7. ♖d1! g6 8. d4± Rossolimo–Szabados, Venezia 1949; 4... ♗b5 5. ♕b5 ♕d7 6. ♕e2 ♘f6 7. 0–0 e6 8. d4 cd4 9. ♘d4 ♘c6 10. ♖d1 ♘d4 11. ♖d4 ♕c6= Rossolimo–Kramer, Amsterdam 1950] 5. 0–0 ♘f6 6. ♖d1 e6 7. ♘c3 ♘d4 8. ♘d4 cd4 9. ♗d7 ♕d7 10. ♘b5 ♘e4= Cosulich–Browne, Venezia 1971 — 12/433; 6. c3!?

2 4... ♘f6 5. d3 [5. e5 de5 6. ♘e5 ♗b5 7. ab5 ♕d5! 8. ♘f3 ♕e4 9. ♕e2 ♕c2 10. ♘c3 e6 11. 0–0 ♘bd7 12. ♘e5 ♘e5 13. ♕e5 ♖d8 14. ♖a7 1/2 : 1/2 Larsen–Geler, Sousse (izt) 1967] e6 6. 0–0 ♗e7 7. e5 de5 8. ♘e5 a6!? 9. ♗d7 ♘bd7 10. ♘d7 ♕d7 11. ♘d2 0–0 12. ♘c4 ♘d5 13. a5± Larsen–Bednarski, La Habana 1967 — 4/505

3 6. ♖e1 e6 7. c3 a6 8. ♗f1 ♗e7 9. d4 cd4 10. cd4 d5 11. e5 ♘e4= Siaperas–Robatsch, Skopje (ol) 1972

4 13. ♗d2 d5 14. ed5 ♗d5 15. ♘e3 ♗f7 16. ♘g4 g5= Larsen–Olafsson, Dundee 1967 — 4/506

5 5. d4 cd4 6. ♘d4 ♘gf6 7. ♘c3 g6 8. 0–0 ♗g7 9. ♗e3 0–0 10. f4 ♖c8 11. ♕f3 a6 12. ♖ad1±↑ Korčnoj–Mojsejev, SSSR (ch) 1952

6 6. ♖e1 e6 7. c4 [7. d3△ ♘bd2, ♘f1] ♗e7 8. ♘c3 0–0 9. d4 cd4 10. ♘d4 ♖c8 11. b3 a6 12. ♗b2 ♕a5 13. ♕d2 ♕h5 14. ♖ad1 ♗d8!∞ Zaharov–Petrušin, SSSR 1973 — 16/394

7 8... e5 9. ♘a3 0–0 10. de5 de5 11. ♘c4± Roth–Thorvaldsson, Varna (ol) 1962

8 ± Schwarz

9 5... d5?! 6. ed5 [6. e5 d4!=] ♕d5 7. d4±

10 6. ♕e2 ♕c6 7. d3 c4 8. ♘bd2 cd3=

11 Bronštejn–Kottnauer, Praha 1946

12 **6. ♕e2** ♘c6 7. c3 e6 8. d4 cd4 9. cd4 d5 10 e5 ♘e4 11. ♘bd2 [11. ♖d1 ♗e7 12. ♘e1 h6 13. f3 ♘g5=] ♘d2 12. ♗d2 ♗e7=; **6. ♘c3** ♘c6 7. d4 cd4 8. ♘d4 g6=; **6. ♖e1** ♘c6 — 5... ♘c6

13 **7... ♕c7**? 8. d4 e6 9. ♗f4 ♗d6 10. ♘a3 ±; **7... ♕d8** 8. ♘c3 ♘bd7 9. d4 e6 10. ♗g5 ♗e7 11. ♘d7 ♕d7 12. dc5 ♕d1 13. ♖fd1 ♗c5 14. ♗f6 gf6 15. ♘e4 ♗e7 16. ♘d6 ♗d6 17. ♖d6±⊥

14 13. ♖fe1 ♕d7 14. ♖ad1 ♖ac8 15. h4 ♕c6 16. ♘e4 ♘e4 17. de4± Hug–Savon, Petropolis (izt) 1973

15 **6. ♖e1** ♘f6 7. d4 cd4 8. ♗g5 d5! 9. ♗f6 gf6 10. ed5 ♕d5 11. ♘c3 ♕d7 12. ♘e4 0-0-0∓↑ Tajmanov–Gligorić, Zürich (ct) 1953; 7. c3 — 6. c3; **6. b3** ♘f6 7. ♖e1 g6 8. ♗b2 ♗g7 9. c4 e5 10. ♘c3 0–0 11. d3 ♘h5 12. ♘d5 ♘e7∓ Biyiasas– Geler, Petropolis (izt) 1973 — 16/397; **6. ♕e2** g6! [6... e6 7. ♖d1 d5 8. ed5 ♕d5 9. ♘c3 ♕d7 10. d4 ♘d4 11. ♘d4 cd4 12. ♗e3 ♕c6 13. ♖d4±→ Rossolimo–Müller, Venezia 1948] 7. c3 ♗g7 8. ♖d1 e5 9. d4 ed4 10. cd4 ♘d4 11. ♘d4 cd4 12. ♘a3 ♘e7 13. ♘b5 ♘c6= Rossolimo–Fischer, USA (ch) 1962

16 8. ♖e1 ♗e7 9. ♘f1 0–0 10. ♘g3=

17 13. ♘f1 ♖c7 14. ♗d2 ♖ac8 15. ♕e2 g6= Gurgenidze–Geler, SSSR (ch) 1967 — 3/468

18 7. ♕e2 e6 8. a3 ♘a5! [8... ♗e7 9. b4 0–0 10. d3 b5 11. ♖d1 cb4 12. ab4 a5 13. ba5 ♘a5 14. ♘bd2 ♖fc8 15. ♗b2± Larsen–Olafsson, Lugano 1970 — 9/378] 9. b4 ♘b3 10. ♖a2 ♘c1 11. ♖c1∞

19 11. ♘c3?! ♘c3 12. bc3 ♗e7 13. ♘g5 h6 14. ♘h3 0-0-0∓

20 13. ♗g5 0–0 14. ♗e7 ♕e7 15. ♖e3 ♖ac8 16. ♕d2 ♘b4= Hecht–Polugajevski, Büsum 1969 — 7/391

21 7... cd4 8. cd4 d5 9. e5 ♘g8 [9... ♘e4 10. ♘e1!±] 10. a3 e6 11. b4 a6 12. ♘bd2 ♘ge7 13. ♘b3 ♘c8 14. ♘g5± Fedorov–Zajčik, SSSR 1974

22 **8... ♘d8** 9. ♖e1 ♘f6 10. ♗g5 e6 [10... e5 11. ♗f6 gf6 12. ♕d3 ♖g8 13. ♘bd2 ♕h3 14. g3 ♗e7 15. ♘c4 b5 16. ♘e3 c4 17. ♕e2 ♘b7 18. b4!± Hug–Szabo, Bath 1973] 11. ♗f6 gf6 12. ♘bd2 ♗g7 13. de6 [13. ♘e4 e5 14. ♘g3 f5 13. ♘h4± Gufeljd] fe6 14. ♘e4 ♘f7 15. b4!±→ Ubilava–Babadžanov, SSSR 1972 — 13/441; **8... ♘e5** 9. ♘e5 [9. ♖e1 ♘f3 10. ♕f3 ♘f6 11. c4 ♔d8?! 12. b4 cb4 13. a3 b3 14. ♕b3 ♕c7 15. ♗e3=∞ Vorotnikov–Osnos, SSSR 1971 — 11/354; 11... 0-0-0!?] de5 10. ♖e1 ♘d6 [10... ♘f6 11. ♖e5 e6 12. c4 0-0-0 13. ♘c3± Malich] 11. ♖e5 g6 12. ♖e2 [12. ♗g5?! h6 13. ♗f6 ♖g8 14. ♖e1 0-0-0 15. ♗e5 ♘c4∓ Ljubojević–Csom, Palma de Mallorca 1971 — 12/435] ♗g7 13. ♗e3 b6= Parma

23 10. ♘a3 g6 11. ♗g5 ♗g7 12. ♕e2 ♘a6 13. ♖ad1 ♘c7 14. ♘c4 0–0 [14... ♔f8?! 15. ♘e3± Csom–Malich, Vrnjačka Banja 1972 — 13/442] 15. ♕e7 ♕e7 16. ♖e7 ♘fd5 17. ♖d7 f6!= Malich

24 **11... h6** 12. ♗f6 gf6 13. ♘c3 h5 14. ♘h4 0-0-0 15. h3 ♘c7 16. ♕f3±↑ Makaričev–Pinter, Hungary 1973 — 16/396; 13... ♖g8!?; 13... ♘c7!?; **11... 0-0-0** 12. ♘c3 ♔b8 13. a4 ♖c8 14. ♕e2 h6 15. ♗d2 ♖e8 16. b4 e6 17. de6 ♖e6 18. ♗e3 ♘g4∞ Bronštejn–Mašić, Tbilisi 1969 — 8/398; 15. ♗f6± Suetin

25 Ivkov–Mecking, Vršac 1971 — 12/431

26 **5... ♕g4**?! 6. 0–0 ♕e4 7. d4 cd4 8. ♘d4 [8. ♖e1 ♕c6 9. ♘d4 ♕d7 10. ♘b5 e6 11. ♗f4+– Sokolski–Sučinski, SSSR 1948; 9... ♕c4 10. ♘a3 ♕c8 11. ♗f4 ♕d7 12. ♘ab5 e5 13. ♗e5!+– Browne–Quinteros, Wijk aan Zee 1974 — 17/442] ♘f6 [8... ♘c6 9. ♘b5 0-0-0 10. ♗e3 a6 11. ♘1c3 ♕c4 12. b3 ♕e6 13. ♘d4 ♕d7 14. ♘d5 ♔b8 15. ♖c1+– Kajkamdžozov–Nejkirh, Bulgaria 1958] 9. ♘c3 ♕g4 10. ♕a4 ♕d7 11. ♘db5+– Hort–Rajković, Sarajevo 1972 — 14/427; 7... ♘f6 8. ♘c3 ♕f5 9. ♕b3 b6 10. dc5 ♕c5 11. ♗e3 ♕c8 12. ♖fe1± Ostojić–Quinteros, Torremolinos 1974 — 17/443; **5... e6** 6. 0–0 ♘f6 7. ♘c3 ♘c6 8. d4 cd4 9. ♘d4 ♗e7 10. ♗e3 0–0 11. ♕e2 a6 13. ♖fd1±; **5... ♘f6** 6. ♘c3 ♘c6 7. d4 — 5... ♘c6

27 6. ♘c3 g6 7. d4 cd4 8. ♘d4 ♗g7 9. ♗e3 ♘h6 [9... ♘f6 10. f3 0–0 11. 0–0 — 6. 0–0] 10. f3 f5 11. ♕d2 ♘f7 12. ef5 gf5 13. f4 ♗d4 14. ♗d4 ♕e6 15. ♔d1! [15. ♔f2 ♖g8 16. b3 ♕g6 17. g3 ♘h6∓ Minić–Štejn, Zagreb 1972 — 14/428] 0–0 [15... ♖g8?! 16. ♘d5± Hort–Jansson, Skopje (ol) 1972 — 14/432] 16. b3 ♕g6∞ Hort

28 6... ♘e5!? 7. d3 e6 [7... g6? 8. ♘e5 de5 9. ♗e3 e6 10. ♕a4±; 7... ♘f3 8. ♕f3 g6± Hecht] 8. ♘c3 ♘e7 9. a3 ♘7c6 10. ♖b1 ♗e7 [Šabanov – Raškovski, SSSR 1974 — 18/412] 11. ♘e1△ f4±

29 9... ♘f6 10. f3 0–0 11. ♘c3 ♖ac8 [11... ♖fc8 12. b3 ♕c7 13. ♕d2 ♕a5 14. ♖ac1 a6 15. ♘c6!± Hecht–Sosonko, Amsterdam 1973 — 16/390] 12. b3 e6 13. ♖c1 ♖fd8 14. ♕d2 ♕e8 [14... d5 15. ed5 ed5 16. c5± Blau–Fischer, Zürich 1959] 15. ♖fd1 a6 16. ♕f2 ♘e5 17. ♕h4±○ Jansa–Tukmakov, Amsterdam 1974 — 18/414

30 **12... ♘f5** 13. ♘f5 gf5 14. fe4±; **12... ♘f7** 13. ♘e4 0–0 14. ♖ad1± Nej–Spaski, Tallinn 1973 — 15/394

31 6... ♘e7 7. d3 ♘bc6 — 6... ♘c6

32 7. 0–0 ♘ge7 8. ♘d5 ♘d5 9. cd5 ♘b4 10. d3 ♗e7 11. ♘e1 0–0 12. ♗d2 [12. f4 ef4 13. ♗f4 f5∓ Torre–Kavalek, Bauang 1973 — 16/393] f5∓ Radulov–Smejkal, Leningrad (izt) 1973 — 15/395; 11. a3±

33 **7... ♘ge7** 8. a3 [8. ♘d5 ♘d5 9. cd5 ♘b4 10. 0–0 ♗e7 11. a3 ♘a6 12. ♘d2 0–0 13. ♘c4 f5 14. ♗d2± Unzicker–Štejn, Kislovodsk 1972 — 14/429] h6 9. ♖b1 a5 10. 0–0 g6 11. b4 ab4 12. ♘d5 ♘d5 13. cd5 ♘d4 17. ♘d4 ed4 15. ab4±○ Keres–K. Grigorjan, SSSR (ch) 1973 — 16/391; **7... ♘f6** 8. ♗g5 ♗e7 9. ♗f6 ♗f6 10. ♘d5 ♗d8 11. 0–0 0–0 12. a3 ♘e7 13. ♘e7 ♗e7 14. ♘d2± Szmetan–De la Vega, Argentina (ch) 1974

34 8. ♘d5 ♗g7 [8... ♘ce7 9. 0–0 ♗g7 10. ♖b1 ♘d5 11. cd5 ♘e7 12. b4± Keres–Panno, Petropolis (izt) 1973 — 16/392; 9... ♘d5 10. cd5 ♗g7 11. a4 ♘e7 12. ♘d2 0–0 13. ♘c4 f5 14. f4!±↑ Stoica–Ghitescu, Romania (ch) 1972] 9. a3 ♘ge7 10. ♖b1 ♘d5 11. cd5 ♘d4 12. b4?! ♘f3 13. ♕f3 cb4 14. ♖b4 0–0 15. 0–0 ♖fc8∓ Karaklajić–Gheorghiu, Casablanca 1974 — 17/447; 12. ♘d4=

35 10... 0–0 11. ♘d5 [11. bc5?! dc5 12. 0–0 h6! 13. ♘d5 f5∓ Torre–Radulov, Leningrad (izt) 1973 — 15/396] f5 12. ♗g5±

36 11. ♗g5 f6! [11... 0–0 12. ♗e7± Gheorghiu] 12. ♗d2 ♘d4= Torre–Gheorghiu, Malaga 1973

37 13. cd5 ♘d4 14. ♘d4 cd4 15. ♗d2 ♖ac8 16. ♕b3±○ Spaski–R. Byrne (mct) 1974 — 17/446

B 53 — 1. e4 c5 2. ♘f3 d6 3. d4 cd4 4. ♕d4

	4	5	6	7	8	9	10	11	12	
1	...	c4[2]	♕d2[4]	♘c3[5]	♕d1[6]	h3	♗d3	0–0	♖e1	=
	a6[1]	♘c6[3]	g6	♗h6	♗g7	♘f6[7]	0–0	♘d7	♘de5[8]	
2	...	♗g5	♕d2	♗h4	♗g3	c3	♗d3	♘a3	♘c4	±
	...	♘c6	h6	g5[9]	♗g7	♘f6	♘h5	♗d7	♘g3[10]	
3	...	c4[11]	♕d2[12]	b3[13]	♗b2	♘c3	♗e2[15]	♖b1	a3[18]	=
	♗d7	♘c6	g6	♗g7	♘f6[14]	0–0	♕a5[16]	a6[17]	♖fc8[19]	
4	...	♗b5	♘c3	♗c6	e5[23]	0–0	♖d1	b4	♘e4	±
	♘c6	♕a5?![20]	♗d7[21]	bc6[22]	d5	e6	♘e7	♕a6	♘f5[24]	
5	...	...	♗c6	c4	♕d3	0–0	♘c3	♗g5	♖ab1	±
	...	♗d7	bc6	e5	♕c7	♗e7[25]	♘f6	♖b8[26]	h6[27]	
6	...	...	...	c4[28]	♘c3	0–0	♕d3	♘d4[30]	b3	±
	...	...	♗c6	♘f6	g6[29]	♗g7	0–0	♖c8	♘d7[31]	
7	...	...	...	♘c3	♗g5	0-0-0[32]	♖he1[33]	♕d2[35]	♘d4!	±
	...	...	...	♘f6	e6	♗e7	0–0[34]	♕c7	♖fd8[36]	
8	...	...	♗c6[38]	0–0	♕d3[40]	c4	♖d1	♗g5	♘bd2	=
	...	♕d7!?[37]	bc6[39]	e5	♗e7	♗a6	♘f6	♖d8	0–0[41]	

[1] 4... ♘f6?! 5. e5 ♘c6 [5... de5 6. ♕d8 ♔d8 7. ♘e5±] 6. ♗b5 ♕a5 7. ♘c3 ♕b5 8. ♘b5 ♘d4 9. ♘fd4 de5 10. ♘c7 ♔d8 11. ♘a8 ed4 12. ♗f4± Szabo–Toran, Hastings 1957/58

[2] 5. ♗e3 ♘c6 6. ♕d2 ♘f6 7. ♘c3 e6 8. 0-0-0 ♕c7 9. ♗f4 ♘g4 10. ♗g3 ♗e7 11. ♗e2 ♘ge5 12. ♘e5 de5 13. f4± Schweber–Quinteros, Argentina 1969 — 8/400; 8... ♗e7!?± Sokolov

[3] 5... ♘f6 6. ♘c3 ♘c6 7. ♕d2 g6 [7... e6 8. ♗e2 ♗e7 9. 0–0 0–0 10. b3 b6 11. ♗a3 ±↑ Gerenski–Padevski, Bulgaria 1969 — 9/380] 8. b3 ♗g7 9. ♗b2 ♗g4 10. ♗e2 0–0 11. 0–0 ♕a5 [11... ♖b8 12. h3 ♗f3 13. ♗f3 b5 14. cb5 ab5 (Minev–Ničevski, Albena 1973 — 16/402) 15. ♘d5 ♘d5 16. ♗g7 ♔g7 17. ed5 ♘e5 18. ♗e2±] 12. ♖ad1 b5 13. cb5 ab5 14. h3= Minev

[4] **6. ♕e3** g6 7. ♘c3 ♗h6!? 8. ♕d3 ♗c1 9. ♖c1 ♗g4 10. ♗e2 [10. ♘d4 ♘f6 11. ♘c2 0–0 12. ♕e3 ♕a5 13. a3 ♖ac8 14. f4 ♕h5 15. b4 e5! 16. h3 ♗e6 17. g3 ef4 18. ♕f4 ♕e5∓ Ljubojević–Browne, Madrid 1973 — 16/401] ♗f3= Ćirić; **6. ♕d1** g6 7. ♗d3 ♗g4 8. h3 ♗f3 9. ♕f3 ♗g7 10. ♕d1 ♘f6 11. 0–0 0–0 12. ♘c3 ♘d7= Damjanović–Kuzmin, Cienfuegos 1973 — 15/399

[5] **7. h3** ♗g7 8. ♘c3 ♘f6 9. ♗d3 0–0 10. 0–0 ♕a5 11. a3 ♕h5 12. ♗e2 h6! 13. b4 ♗h3 14. gh3 ♕h3 15. ♗b2 [Ciocaltea–Sax, Budapest 1973 — 15/402] ♘g4! 16. ♕f4! f5∞; **7. b3** ♗g7 8. ♘c3 [Fuller–Cardoso, Penang 1974 — 18/416] ♗g4 9. ♗e2 ♘f6 10. ♗b2 ♗f3 11. ♗f3 ♘d7= Ciocaltea

[6] 8. ♕c2 ♗g7 9. h3 ♘f6 10. ♗e2 0–0 1. 0–0 ♗e6 12. ♖d1 ♕a5 13. ♘d5 ♖fc8 14. ♗d2 ♕d8 15. ♗c3 ♗d5 16. ed5 ♘a5 17. ♕a4 [Radulov–Browne, Wijk aan Zee 1974 — 17/450] ♘c4 18. ♗c4 b5 19. ♗b5 ab5 20. ♕b5 ♖c5 21. ♕e2 ♘d5∓⊞ Minev

[7] 9... ♗c3 10. bc3 [Ciocaltea–Pytel, Skopje (ol) 1972 — 14/437] ♕a5!∞

[8] 13. ♘e5 de5= Tringov–Bilek, Skopje (ol) 1972

[9] 7... ♘f6 8. ♘c3 [8. ♗f6 gf6 9. c4 ♖g8 10. ♘c3 f5 11. 0-0-0 (Meštrović–Grefe, Albena 1974 — 18/415) ♗g7!? 12. ef5! ♗f5 13. ♘h4 ♗h7 14. ♗d3± Minev] ♗d7 9. ♗c4 e6 10. ♖d1 ♕c7 11. ♗b3 ♗e7 12. 0–0± Kajkamdžozov–Bobekov, Bulgaria 1952

[10] 13. hg3 b5 14. ♘e3 ♘e5 15. ♘d4 e6 16. f4 ♘g6= Tan–Savon, Petropolis (izt) 1973; 16. ♗e2±

[11] 5. ♗g5 ♘c6 6. ♕d2 h6 7. ♗h4 g5 8. ♗g3 ♗g7 9. c3 ♘f6 10. ♗d3 ♘h5 11. ♘a3 ♘g3 12. hg3 ♕c7 13. ♘c2 0-0-0= Bialas–Petrosjan, Hamburg 1960

[12] 6. ♕d1 g6 7. ♗d2 ♗g7 8. ♗c3 ♘f6 9. ♗e2 0–0 10. ♘fd2 ♕b6= Damjanović–Kavalek, Netanya 1971 — 11/355

[13] 7. ♘c3 ♗h6! 8. ♕c2 ♗g7 9. b3 ♘f6 10. ♗b2 ♕a5= Packroff–Schöneberg, DDR 1973 — 15/398

[14] 8... ♗b2 9. ♕b2 ♘f6 10. ♘bd2 0–0 11. ♗e2 ♘h5 12. 0–0 ♘f4= Banik–Spaski, SSSR 1957; 12. g3± Aronin

[15] **10. ♗d3** ♕a5 11. 0–0! ♗g4 12. ♘e1± Holmov; 10... ♗g4=; **10. h3** ♕a5 [10... a6

11. ♗d3 ♕a5 12. a3 ♖fc8 13. 0—0 ♕d8 14. b4 ♗e6 15. ♖fe1 ♘d7 16. ♘d5± Estevez—Savon, Skopje (ol) 1972] 11. ♗d3 ♘h5 [11... ♖fc8 12. 0—0 a6 13. ♖fe1 ♗e8 14. ♗f1 ♖ab8 15. a3 ♘d7 (Holmov—Jakobsen, Kislovodsk 1972 — 14/435) 16. ♖ac1±] 12. 0—0 ♘f4! [Bednarski—Saidy, Polanica Zdroj 1969 — 8/401] 13. ♕f4 ♗c3 14. ♕h6 f6!∓ Litmanowitz; 14. ♕c1=

16 10... a6 11. ♖b1 ♕b8 12. a3 b5! 13. cb5 ab5 14. b4 ♕b7= Schaufelberger—Mariotti, Praia da Rocha 1969 — 8/402; 11. ♖c1!± Minić

17 11... ♖fc8 12. 0—0 ♖ab8?! 13. h3! a6 14. a3± Ciocaltea—Csom, Vrnjačka Banja 1972 — 13/444; 12... a6 13. a3 — 11... a6

18 12. 0—0?! b5 13. a3 b4! 14. ab4 [14. ♘d5?! ♘e4 15. ♕e3 ♗b2 16. ab4 ♕a2 17. ♗d3 ♘c3 18. ♘b6 ♘b1 19. ♗b1 ♕a3 20. ♘d7 ♘b4! 21. ♘f8 ♖f8 22. ♕e7 ♕b3 23. ♕c7 d5 24. cd5 ♕d5—+ Andersson—Najdorf, Hastings 1971/72 — 13/443] ♕b4 15. ♗a1 ♖fb8∓ Andersson

19 **12... b5** 13. b4 ♕b6 14. cb5 ab5 15. 0—0 ♕b7 16. ♖e1= Vasjukov—Željandinov, SSSR (ch) 1967 — 5/422; **12... ♖fc8** 13. 0—0 ♗g4 [13... ♖ab8 14. h3 ♗e6 15. b4 ♕d8 16. ♕e3 ♘d7 17. ♘d5 ♗b2 18. ♖b2 ♘ce5 19. ♘e5 ♘e5 20. ♖c1 ♗d5 21. ed5± Vasjukov—Pytel, Polanica Zdroj 1972 — 14/433; 13... b5 15. b4 ♕d8 16. cb5 ab5 17. ♖fe1± Andersson] 14. ♖fe1 [14. b4 ♕h5 15. h3 ♗f3 16. ♗f3 ♕h4 17. ♘d5 ♘d5 18. ed5 ♘e5 19. ♗e5 ♗e5 20. ♗e2 ♕f4= Ciocaltea] ♗f3 15. ♗f3 ♖ab8= Talj—Jakobsen, Skopje (ol) 1972 — 14/438

20 **5... a6**?! 6. ♗c6 bc6 7. 0—0 e5 8. ♕d3 ♗e7 9. c4 ♘f6 10. ♘c3 ♘d7 11. b4 0—0 12. ♗e3 a5 13. b5 ♗b7 14. a4 c5 15. ♘d2±↑ Karpov—Szabo, Budapest 1973 — 15/401; **5... e5**?! 6. ♕d3 ♘f6 [Vasjukov—Balašov, SSSR (ch) 1969 — 8/403] 7. 0—0 ♗e7 8. c4 0—0 9. ♘c3±

21 6... a6 7. ♗c6 bc6 8. 0—0 e5 9. ♕c4 ♕c7 10. ♘g5 ♘h6 11. f4 a5 12. ♖f3 ♗a6 13. ♕a4±↑ Szabo—Steiner, Hungary 1940

22 7... ♗c6 8. 0—0 ♕c5 [8... ♘f6 9. ♗g5 h6 10. ♗f6 gf6 11. ♘d5±] 9. ♕d3 ♘f6 10. ♗g5 e6 11. ♗f6! gf6 12. ♘d4 a6 13. ♔h1 ♖g8 14. f4 f5 15. ♘c6 ♕c6 16. ♕h3± Štejnberg—Šamis, SSSR 1967 — 5/423

23 8. 0—0 c5 9. ♕d3±; 8... e5!?

24 13. ♘c5 ♘d4 14. ♘a6 ♘f3 15. gf3± Krnić—Joksić, Jugoslavija 1973

25 9... ♘e7 10. ♖d1 ♘g6 11. b3 ♖d8 12. ♗g5 f6 13. ♗e3± Bagirov—Rumjancev, SSSR 1969 — 8/404

26 11... ♖d8 12. ♖fd1 ♗e6 13. b4 0—0 14. ♖ac1 h6 15. ♗f6 ♗f6 16. b5±→《

27 13. ♗f6 gf6 14. b4 0—0 15. b5± Štejn—Saharov, SSSR 1960

28 7. ♗g5 f5!? Vasjukov

29 8... e6 9. 0—0 [9. ♗g5 ♗e7 10. 0—0 0—0 11. ♖fe1 h6 12. ♗h4 a6 13. ♖ad1±↑⊞ Schweber—Najdorf, Buenos Aires 1970 — 10/488] ♗e7 10. b3 0—0 11. ♗b2 a6 [11... ♕a5 12. ♖fe1 ♖fd8 13. ♕d2 ♔f8 14. ♘d4 ♕h5 15. a4 a6 16. ♗a3± Ciocaltea—Minić, Varna 1969 — 8/405] 12. a4 ♖b8 13. ♖fd1± Dobrev—Spasov, Bulgaria 1972 — 14/436

30 11. ♗e3 a6 12. ♖fd1 ♖c8 13. ♗d4 b5 14. cb5 ab5 15. a3 ♕d7= Damjanović—Gligorić, Ljubljana 1969 — 7/393

31 13. ♗b2± Padevski—Ghitescu, Reykjavik 1969 — 9/379

32 9. 0—0 ♗e7 10. ♖ad1 0—0 11. ♖fe1 ♕a5 12. h3 [12. ♗h4 ♖fd8 13. ♕d3 ♕h5 14. ♖e3 ♖ac8= Dückstein—Fischer, Zürich 1959] a6 13. a3 ♖ac8 14. ♕d2 ♕b6 15. ♕c1 ♕c7 16. ♘d4 h6 17. ♗h4 b5 18. f4± Čistjakov—Titenko, SSSR 1961

33 10. e5 de5 11. ♕e5 ♕c8 [11... ♕b8 12. ♕e3 ♕c7 13. ♘e5 0—0 14. ♘c6 ♕c6 15. f3 ♖fc8 16. ♕e2 ♔f8∓ Juhtman—Aronin, SSSR 1958] 12. ♘d4 0—0 13. h4 h6 14. ♔b1 ♖d8 15. f3 hg5 16. hg5 ♗d6∓ Perez—Fischer, Leipzig (ol) 1960

34 **10... ♕c7**?! 11. ♗f6 gf6 12. ♘d5 ♕d8 13. ♘e7 ♔e7 14. e5± Hasidovski—Luik, SSSR 1963; **10... h6**!? 11. ♗h4 0—0 12. g4?! ♘g4 13. ♗e7 ♕e7 14. ♖g1 f5 15. ♕d6 ♕d6 16. ♖d6 ♘f2 17. ♘e5 ♘e4 18. ♘e4 ♗e4 19. ♖d7 g5∓ Gheorghiu—Mecking, Petropolis (izt) 1973; 12. ♔b1!?△ ♕d2, ♘d4, f3, g4±↑》 Šašin

35 **11. e5** de5 [11... ♗f3 12. ef6 gf6 13. ♖d3! fg5 14. ♖f3 d5 15. ♖h3!△ ♕d3±; 14... h6 15. ♘e4! ♕a5 16. ♖d1 g4 17. ♖b3± I. Zajcev] 12. ♕h4 ♕c7 13. ♘e5 (△ ♘g4) h6!? [13... ♘d5 14. ♗e7 ♘e7 15. ♖d7! ♗d7 16. ♕e7 ♖ad8 17. ♖e3! ♕c8 18. ♘e4 ♗a4 19. ♘f6! ♔h8 20. ♖c3+— Vasjukov; 16... ♕d8 17. ♕d7 ♕g5 18. ♕d2 ♕g2 19. f4! ♕d2 20. ♔d2 ♖fd8 21. ♘d3± Vasjukov—Dementjev, SSSR (ch) 1972 — 14/434; 15... ♕e5 16. ♖e5 ♘g6 17. ♕g3 ♗d7 18. ♖e1± I. Zajcev; 15... ♘g6 16. ♖c7 ♘h4 17. ♘c6 bc6 18. ♖c6 ♘g2 19. ♖e4± Vasjukov] 14. ♗h6 ♘e4! 15. ♕h5 ♘c3 16. ♗g7 ♘a2 17. ♔b1 ♘c3= Gipslis—Tukmakov, SSSR 1972; **11. ♔b1** ♕a5 [11... ♕c7 12. ♕d2 b5 13. ♘d4 ♕b7?! 14. ♗f6 (Ciocaltea—Dieks, Wijk aan Zee 1974 — 17/451) ♗f6!? 15. ♘c6 ♕c6 16. ♕d6 ♕d6 17. ♖d6 ♗c3± Ciocaltea; 13... b4!?] 12. ♕d2 ♕b6 [12... ♕c7 13. ♘d4 ♖fd8 14. f4 h6 15. ♗f6 ♗f6 16. f5 ♗d4 17. ♕d4 e5 18. ♕e3± Kavalek—Huguet, Las Palmas 1973 — 15/400; 12... ♖fd8 13. ♘d4∞; 12... ♔h8!? 13. ♘d4 ♖ac8 14. f3 ♖fd8 15. g4 a6 16. h4 b5 17. ♗f6 ♗f6 18. g5 ♗d4 19. ♕d4 b4 20. ♘e2 ♗a4∞ Estevez—Cuellar, Leningrad (izt) 1973] 13. ♘d4 ♖fd8 14. f3 ♗e8 [14... ♖ac8 15. g4 ♗e8!= Vasjukov—Platonov, SSSR (ch) 1969 — 7/392] 15. h4 ♕c7! [15... ♖ac8?! 16. g4± Gipslis—Polugajevski, SSSR (ch) 1969 — 8/407] 16. g4

b5!∞ Platonov–Averkin, SSSR (ch) 1969 — 8/406

[36] 13. ♖e3 ♗e8? 14. ♖g3± Wach–Gralka, Polska 1970 — 10/487; 13... ♔h8!?±

[37] I. Zajcev

[38] **6. ♘c3** ♘d4 7. ♘d4 ♘f6 8. ♗g5 e6=; **6. c4** ♘d4 7. ♘d4 ♘f6 8. ♘c3 e6=; 6. ♕e3 a6 7. ♗a4 b5 8. ♗b3 ♘a5?!± Karpov–Csom, Budapest 1973; 8... e6∞ Kurajica–Csom, Olot 1973

[39] 6... ♕c6?! 7. ♘c3 ♗g4 8. ♗g5!? a6 9. ♘d2 ♖c8 10. f4 f6 11. ♗h4 e5 12. ♕e3 ♗e6 13. ♗f2± Krnić–Buljovčić, Vršac 1973

[40] 8. ♕a4!?

[41] **13. b4** h6 14. ♗f6 ♗f6 15. a4 ♗b7 16. b5 ♕c7 17. ♘f1 d5∓↑⊞ Tan–Portisch, Petropolis (izt) 1973 — 16/400; **13. ♘f1**= Mojsejev

B 54

1. e4 c5 2. ♘f3 d6 3. d4 cd4 4. ♘d4

	4	5	6	7	8	9	10	11	12	
1	...	c4[2]	♘b5[3]	♘5c3	♗e2	♗e3	0–0	♘a3	♕d2[4]	±
	♘c6[1]	e5	a6	♘f6	♗e7	0–0	♗e6	♖c8		
2	...	♘c3	♘d5!?	♘c3	♗e2	0–0	♗g5	♘b3	a4	±
	...	g6	e6[5]	♘f6	a6	♗g7	♕c7	0–0	b6[6]	
3	...	♗b5[7]	♗d7	♘c3	0–0	♗e3	f4[10]	♕f3	♖ad1	∓
	♘f6	♗d7[8]	♘bd7[9]	g6	♗g7	0–0	♖c8	a6	b5[11]	
4	...	f3	c4	♘c3	♗e3[15]	♘c2[16]	cd5	♘d5[18]	♕d5	=∞
	...	e6[12]	♘c6[13]	♗e7[14]	0–0	d5[17]	ed5	♘d5	♕c7[19]	

1. e4 c5 2. ♘f3 d6 3. d4 cd4 4. ♘d4 ♘f6 5. f3 e5

	6	7	8	9	10	11	12	13	14	
5	♘b5	♘5c3	♘d5[20]	ed5	♗d3	0–0	c4	♘c3	♗e3	=
	a6	♗e6	♘d5[21]	♗f5[22]	♗g6	♗e7	♘d7	0–0	♗g5[23]	
6	♘b3	c4	♗e3	♘c3	♕d2	♘d5	♘c5[26]	♗e2	0–0	=
	♗e7[24]	0–0	♗e6	♘bd7	♖c8	♘c5[25]	dc5	b6	♘d7[27]	
7	...	♗g5[28]	ed5	♘c3[30]	♗d2	♗b5[33]	♕e2	♗c6	0-0-0	=
	d5	♗e6[29]	♕d5	♗b4[31]	♕d8[32]	♘c6	0–0	bc6	♕c7[34]	

[1] **4... e6** 5. c4±; **4... g6** 5. ♘c3 ♘f6 — B 70

[2] **5. ♗e3**? ♘f6 6. ♘c3 ♘g4!∓; **5. ♗b5** ♗d7 6. c4 [6. 0–0!?] g6 [6... ♘d4?! 7. ♗d7 ♕d7 8. ♕d4±; 6... ♘f6 7. ♘c3 e6 8. 0–0 ♗e7 9. ♗e3±] 7. ♘c3 [7. 0–0 ♗g7 8. ♗e3 ♘h6 9. f3 f5 10. ♕d2 ♘f7=; 8... ♘f6 9. ♘c3 ♘g4∓ Vasjukov–Furman, SSSR (ch) 1965] ♗g7 8. ♗e3 ♘f6 9. f3=; **5. f4** e5!? 6. ♘c6 bc6 7. fe5 ♕a5 8. ♘c3 ♕e5=

[3] 6. ♘c2±

[4] Suetin–Kopajev, SSSR 1952

[5] **6... ♗g7**? 7. ♘b5!+–; **6... a6** 7. ♗e3±

[6] 13. ♕d2 ♗b7 14. ♖ad1 ♘e8 15. f4± Talj–Parma, Moskva 1971 — 12/436

[7] 5. ♗d3 ♘c6=; 5... e5 6. ♘e2 d5=

[8] 5... ♘bd7 6. ♘c3 e6=; 6... g6=

[9] 6... ♕d7 7. ♘c3 ♘c6 8. 0–0 g6 9. h3 ♗g7 10. ♗e3 0–0=

[10] 10. f3 a6 11. ♕d2 b5 12. ♗h6=; 11... ♘e5!∓

[11] 13. a3 ♕c7 14. g4?! ♘b6 15. g5 ♘fd7 16. f5 ♕b7 17. ♕f4 ♗e5 18. ♕h4 ♖c3!∓ Korčnoj–Mojsejev, SSSR 1950

[12] **5... d5**? 6. e5 ♘fd7 7. e6!±; **5... a6** 6. c4±; **5... g6** 6. c4 ♗g7 7. ♘c3±

[13] 6... ♗e7 7. ♘c3 0–0 8. ♗e2 b6 9. 0–0 ♗b7 10. ♗e3±

[14] 7... a6 8. ♘c2! ♕c7 9. ♗e2 b6 10. 0–0 ♗b7 11. b3± Pachman–Hoffman, ČSSR (ch) 1952

[15] 8. ♘c2 0–0 9. ♘e3 [9. ♗e2 d5 10. cd5 ed5 11. ♘d5 ♘d5 12. ed5 ♘b4 13. ♘b4 ♗b4 14. ♔f1 ♖e8=∞ Saharov–Čukajev, SSSR 1956] d5!? 10. cd5 ed5 11. ed5 ♘e5 12. ♕b3 ♗c5 13. ♗d2 ♖e8=∞ Foguelman–Fischer, Mar del Plata 1960

[16] 9. ♕d2 d5 10. cd5 ed5 11. ♘c6 bc6 12. e5? ♘e8 13. ♗e2 ♘c7 14. 0–0 ♘e6 15. ♗f2

♗g5!∓ Bagin–Furman, SSSR 1953; 12. ed5=; **9. ♗e2** d5 10. ♘c6 [10. cd5 ed5 11. ed5 ♘b4!∓] bc6 11. cd5 [11. e5 ♘d7 12. f4 ♗c5∓] cd5 12. ed5 ♘d5 13. ♘d5 ed5 14. 0–0 a5!∞ Korčnoj–Averbah, SSSR 1954

17 9... b6 10. ♗e2 ♗b7 11. 0–0 ♘e5∞

18 11. ed5 ♘b4 12. ♘b4 ♗b4 13. ♔f2 ♖e8∓ Judovič–Simagin, SSSR 1952

19 Lombardy–Fischer, USA (ch) 1961

20 8. ♗g5 ♗e7 [8... ♕b6!? 9. ♗f6 gf6 10. b3 ♘c6∓] 9. ♗f6 ♗f6 10. ♘d5 ♗g5 11. c4 ♘c6 12. ♘1c3 0–0 13. ♗d3 ♘d4∓ Spielmann–Landau, Amsterdam 1938

21 8... ♗d5 9. ed5 ♗e7 10. c4 0–0 11. ♘c3 ♘bd7=

22 9... ♗c8 10. ♗e3 ♗e7 11. ♕d2 f5 [Smislov–Bondarevski, SSSR 1941] 12. c4

23 Fine–Eliskases, Semmering-Baden 1937

24 6... ♗e6 7. c4 ♘c6 [7... ♘bd7? 8. ♗e3 a5? 9. ♘c3 a4 10. ♘d2 ♕a5 11. ♖c1 ♗e7 12. ♗e2 0–0 13. 0–0 ♖fc8 14. ♘b5 ♖c6 15. ♘b1 ♘e8 16. ♘1a3± Prins–Paoli, Bad Pyrmont 1951] 8. ♘c3 ♗e7 9. ♗e3 0–0∞

25 **11... ♗d5** 12. cd5±; **11... ♘b6**!? 12. ♘b6 [12. ♖c1 ♘bd5 13. cd5 ♖c1 14. ♘c1 ♗d7=] ab6 13. ♖c1 b5! 14. cb5 ♖c1 15. ♘c1 d5$\overline{\infty}$

26 12. ♗e2 ♗d5 13. cd5 ♘b3 14. ab3 a6∞

27 15. a3 ♘b8 16. b4 ♘c6= Goldenov–Ilivicki, SSSR (ch) 1952

28 7. ed5 ♕d5 8. ♗d2 ♗e7 [8... ♘c6 9. ♘c3 ♕d8 10. ♗b5 h6 11. ♕e2 ♗d6 12. 0-0-0 ♕c7 13. ♘e4± Montiel–Eliskases, Argentina (ch) 1953] 9. ♘c3 ♕d8 10. ♕e2 ♘c6 11. 0-0-0 ♕c7 12. ♗e3 0–0 13. ♕f2 b6= Hamann–Gelfer, Siegen (ol) 1970; 10. ♗d3!?; 7... ♘d5!?

29 **7... de4** 8. ♕d8 ♔d8 9. ♗f6 gf6 10. fe4±; **7... d4**!? 8. c3 ♘c6 9. ♗c4 [9. ♗b5 ♗e6 10. cd4 ♗b4 11. ♘1d2 ♕b6 12. ♗c6 bc6 13. 0–0 ed4 14. ♖c1 ♘d7= B. Koch–van Scheltinga, Helsinki (ol) 1952] ♗e6 10. ♗e6 fe6 11. 0–0 ♗e7 12. cd4 ed4 13. ♘bd2 0–0= Goldenov–Veresov, SSSR 1953

30 9. ♘1d2 ♗e7 10. ♗c4 ♕c6 11. ♕e2 0–0 12. 0–0 h6 13. ♗h4 ♘bd7 14. ♗e6 ♕e6 15. ♕c4 ♕c4 16. ♘c4 ♖fc8 17. ♘e3 ♘b6= Lombardy–Evans, USA 1959

31 9... ♕d1 10. ♖d1 ♗b4 11. ♗d2 a6 12. ♘a4 ♗d2 13. ♖d2 ♘bd7 14. ♘ac5 ♘c5 15. ♘c5 ♔e7= Prins–Kottnauer, Venezia 1949

32 10... ♗c3 11. ♗c3 ♘c6 12. ♗d3 0–0 [12... e4? 13. fe4 ♘e4 14. ♗g7 ♖g8 15. ♕f3! +– Prins–Pirc, Bad Pyrmont 1951] 13. 0–0 ♕d8 14. f4 e4 15. ♗f6 ♕f6 16. ♗e4 ♗b3 17. ab3 ♖ad8 18. ♕f3 ♕b2= Pachman–Eliskases, Helsinki (ol) 1952

33 11. ♘b5 ♘c6 12. ♗b4 ♘b4 13. c3 ♘bd5 14. c4 ♘e3 15. ♕d8 ♖d8 16. ♔f2 ♘d1 17. ♔e1 ♘b2∓ Šapošnikov–Suetin, SSSR 1952

34 15. ♘e4 [Evans, Prins–Reshevsky, Horowitz, USA 1951] ♗d2 16. ♖d2 ♘e4 17. ♕e4 c5!=

B 55

1. e4 c5 2. ♘f3 d6 3. d4 cd4 4. ♘d4 ♘f6 5. f3 e5 6. ♗b5

	6	7	8	9	10	11	12	13	14	
1	...	♗d7	♘f5	ed5	♘c3	♕e2	0–0	♘d5		∞
	♗d7	♘bd7[1]	d5[2]	♕a5[3]	♘b6	0-0-0	♘bd5	♖d5[4]		
2	...	♘f5[5]	♗d7	♗g5	♗f6	♘e3![8]	♘d5	fe4	0–0	±
	♘bd7	a6[6]	♕d7	d5[7]	gf6	de4	♕c6	♖g8	♖g6[9]	
3	...	...	ed5	♗a4[10]	♗b3	♘e3	♘c3	♕d3[12]		$\overline{\infty}$
	...	d5!	a6	b5	♘b6[11]	♗c5	♗b7	0–0		

1. e4 c5 2. ♘f3 d6 3. d4 cd4 4. ♘d4 ♘f6 5. f3 e5 6. ♗b5 ♘bd7 7. ♘f5 d5 8. ed5 a6 9. ♗d7 ♕d7 10. ♘e3 b5

	11	12	13	14	15	16	17	18	19	
4	a4[13]	ab5	♖a8	♕e2	♘c3	♘e4[15]	fe4	♘g4[17]	ef5	=
	♗b7	ab5	♗a8	♗c5[14]	0–0	♘e4[16]	g6	f5	♕d5[18]	
5	c4	♘c3	♘e4!	♘f6	♗e3	0–0[20]	♕e1	♖d1	♕a5	=
	♗c5	♗b7	♗e3[19]	gf6	bc4	♗d5[21]	♖g8	♕b7	♖d8[22]	
6	...	...	cb5[23]	0–0	♔h1	♘e4	♘d5	♗e3	♗d4	=
	...	0–0!	ab5	♗d4[24]	♗a6	♘d5	♕d5	♗b7	ed4[25]	

1 7... ♕d7? 8. ♘f5 d5 9. ♗g5! d4 [9... ♘c6 10. ♗f6 gf6 11. ♘c3 ♗b4 12. 0–0±; 9... de4 10. ♗f6 ♕d1 11. ♔d1 gf6 12. fe4 ♘c6 13. c3 ♖g8 14. g3 ♖g4 15. ♘d2± Aljehin–Rellstab, Salzburg 1943] 10. ♗f6 [10. c3 ♘c6 11. 0–0 0-0-0 12. cd4 ed4 13. ♔h1 ♕e6 14. ♘d2 h6 15. ♗h4± Keller–Fuderer, Zürich 1960] gf6 11. c3! ♘c6 12. ♕a4 a6 13. 0–0 ♗c5 14. b4 b5 15. ♕b3 ♗a7 16. c4± Koch–Meyer, corr. 1949

2 8... ♘b6 9. ♗g5 d5 10. ♕d3! a6 11. ♗f6 gf6±

3 9... ♘b6 10. ♗g5 ♕d7 11. ♗f6 ♕f5 12. ♗h4 ♖c8 13. c3± Saharov–Geler, SSSR 1949

4 **13... ♕d5** 14. ♗e3 g6 15. ♖fd1 ♕e6 16. ♖d8 ♔d8 17. ♘g3 a6 18. c4 ♘d7 19. ♘e4± Böök–Solmanis, Kemeri–Riga 1947; **13... ♖d5**∞

5 7. ♘b3 a6 8. ♗e2 b5 9. 0–0 [9. a4 ba4 10. ♖a4 ♘b6∓ Karaklajić–Janošević, Sarajevo 1951] ♗b7 10. c4 bc4 11. ♗c4 ♘b6 12. ♘a5 ♘c4 13. ♘c4 ♕c7 14. b3 d5!∓ Nonnemacher–Weiss, BRD 1947

6 **7... ♕b6** 8. ♘c3 a6 9. ♗a4 h6 10. ♘e3 ♕d4 11. 0–0 b5 12. ♗b3 ♘c5 13. ♘cd5+– Habedien–Meyer, corr. 1942; **7... ♕a5** 8. ♘c3 d5 9. ed5 a6 10. ♗a4 b5 11. ♗b3 ♘c5 12. ♘e3 ♘b3 13. cb3 ♗b7 14. 0–0 ♗c5 [14... ♖d8? 15. ♕e2! ♗c5 16. ♔h1 0–0 17. ♘f5! ♘d5 18. ♗h6!!± Aljehin–Bogoljubov, Krakow 1941] 15. ♔h1±

7 9... ♕c6 10. ♗f6 ♗f5 11. ef5! gf6 12. ♘c3± v.d. Bosch–Landau, Delft 1940

8 11. ♘c3 ♗b4!=

9 15. ♕f3 ♗e7 16. ♘bc3 ♗g4 17. ♕d3 ♗c5 18. ♔h1 0-0-0 19. b4!± Saharov–Urgujmanov, SSSR 1949

10 9. ♗e2?! ♘b6 10. ♘e3 ♘bd5 11. ♘d5 ♘d5∓

11 10... ♘c5 11. ♘e3 ♘b3 12. ab3 ♗b7 13. c4 ♗c5 14. 0–0 0–0 15. ♘c3 ♕b6= Hult–Danielson, Sverige 1946

12 13. ♘f5? g6 [13... 0–0 14. ♗g5∞] 14. ♘g7 ♔f8 15. ♗h6 ♔g8 16. ♕d2 b4∓ Foguelman–Reshevsky, Buenos Aires 1960

13 **11. b3** ♗c5 12. a4 ♖b8 13. ab5 ab5 14. ♕d3 0–0 15. ♘c3 ♘h5 16. g3 f5∓ Tartakower–Najdorf, Amsterdam 1950; **11. ♘c3** ♗b7 12. ♕e2 [12. ♘e4? ♘d5 13. ♘d5 ♗d5 14. ♕e2? ♗e7 15. ♗e3 ♕c6–+ Kupper–Sämisch, BRD 1948; 14. 0–0!?] b4 13. ♘e4 ♘d5 14. ♘d5 ♕d5 15. 0–0 ♗e7 16. ♖d1 ♕c6∓

14 14... ♗b4? 15. ♘c3 ♗c3 16. bc3 0–0 17. 0–0 ♘d5 18. ♘d5 ♕d5 19. ♖d1 ♕c5 20. ♕e3 ♕c7 21. ♗a3 ♖e8 22. ♕c5!±

15 16. 0–0 ♘d5! 17. ♘d5 [17. ♖d1 ♘c3!] ♕d5∓

16 16... ♗e3? 17. ♘f6 gf6 18. ♗e3±

17 18. 0–0 f5 19. ♔h1 fe4∓

18 20. fg6 ♕g2 21. ♖f1! ♖f1 22. ♕f1 ♕f1 23. ♔f1 fg6= Böök–Lundin, Suomi–Sverige 1946

19 13... ♗d4 14. ♘c2 bc4 15. ♘d4 ed4 16. ♘f6 gf6 17. ♕d4=

20 16. d6!?∞

21 16... ♕d5 17. ♕e1 ♖g8 18. ♕h4±

22 20. ♖d2 ♖d7= Andrić–Rabar, Jugoslavija 1951

23 **13. ♘e4?** ♘e4! 14. fe4 f5! [14... ♕a7 15. ♕f3 f5 16. ef5 e4!∓ Bely–Gereben, Hungary 1954] 15. ef5 ♕a7! 16. ♕e2 ♗f5 17. cb5 ♗d7 18. a4 ♖f4 19. ♖f1 ♖e4–+ Kläger–Kottnauer, Beverwijk 1954; **13. 0—0** ♘h5 14. ♔h1 f5$\overline{\infty}$↑ Böök–Szabo, Helsinki (ol) 1952

24 **14... ♗b7**=; **14... b4** 15. ♘e4 ♗e3 16. ♗e3 ♘d5=

25 20. ♕d3 ♖fd8 21. ♖fc1 ♖a2= Bely–Navarovszky, Hungary 1954

B 56 1. e4 c5 2. ♘f3 d6 3. d4 cd4 4. ♘d4 ♘f6 5. ♘c3

	5	6	7	8	9	10	11	12	13	
1	...	♗b5	♘f5	♗d7	♗g5[3]	♗f6	ef5	♘d5	0–0	±
	e5[1]	♘bd7[2]	a6	♕d7	♕c6[4]	♗f5	gf6[5]	♗e7		
2	...	♗c4[6]	♗b3	♘de2[8]	♗g5	♗f6[9]	♘d5	♗d5	♗b3	±
	♘bd7	♘b6[7]	e5	♗e6	♗e7	♗f6	♘d5	♕b6	0–0[10]	
3	...	h3[11]	g4	♕d4	♕d3	♗g2	f4[14]	f5	♕f3	$\overline{\infty}$
	♘c6	a6[12]	♘d4[13]	e5	♗e6	♗e7	♖c8	♗c4	d5!?[15]	
4	...	f4	♕d3	♘c6[17]	h3	♗e2	0–0	♔h1	♖b1	±
	...	♗g4[16]	g6	bc6	♗e6	♗g7	♕b6	♘d7	a5[18]	

	5	6	7	8	9	10	11	12	13	
5	... ...	g3 e5[19]	♘de2 ♗e7[20]	♗g2 0–0[21]	0–0 a6[22]	h3 b5	♗e3 b4[23]	♘d5 ♘d5	ed5 ♘a5[24]	±
6	... ...	... ♗g4	f3 ♗d7[25]	♗g2[26] a6[27]	♘b3 e6	♗e3 b5[28]	f4 ♖c8	0–0 ♗e7	♔h1 ♕c7[29]	=
7	... ...	♗e3 ♘g4[30]	♗b5 ♘e3	fe3[31] ♗d7	0–0 e6[32]	♗c6 bc6[33]	♕f3[34] ♕f6[35]	♕e2 ♕g5	♖f3 ♕c5[36]	∞

1 5... ♗d7?! 6. ♗g5 [6. ♗c4 e6 7. 0–0 ♗e7 8. a3 0–0 9. ♗a2 ♕b6?! 10. ♗e3 ♕b2 11. ♕d3! ♖c8 12. ♘de2 ♘a6 13. ♖fb1 ♕a3 14. ♗e6± Sergijevski–Lejn, SSSR 1968 — 6/518; 9... ♘c6!?; 6... ♘c6 — B 57] e6 [6... a6 7. ♕d2 e6 8. 0-0-0 h6 9. ♗f6 ♕f6 10. f4 ♘c6 — B 67] 7. ♕d2 ♗e7 8. 0-0-0 0–0 9. ♕e1 a6 10. f4 ♘c6 11. ♘f3 ♖c8 12. ♔b1± Bagirov–Lejn, SSSR (ch) 1969 — 7/394

2 6... ♗d7? 7. ♗d7 ♕d7 8. ♘f3±

3 9. ♘e3±

4 9... ♘e4 10. ♘g7 ♗g7 11. ♘e4 d5 12. ♘f6 ♗f6 13. ♗f6 ♖g8 14. 0–0 e4 15. f3 ♕c6 16. ♕d4 ♗h6 17. ♖f2± Shocron–Carvalho 1953

5 11... ♕g2? 12. ♕d5!+−

6 **6. ♗e3** a6 7. f3 d5!? 8. ♘d5 ♘d5 9. ed5 ♕a5 10. ♕d2 ♕d5 11. c4 ♕d6 12. 0-0-0∞ Damjanović–Szabo, Salgotarjan 1967 — 4/508; 7... e6!?; **6. g3** g6 7. ♗g2 ♗g7 8. 0–0 0–0 9. ♖e1 a6 10. h3?! e5! 11. ♘de2 ♕c7 12. ♗e3 b5 13. a4 b4 14. ♘a2 ♖b8∓ Fuchs–Tajmanov, Kislovodsk 1966 — 2/411; 10. ♘d5 e6=

7 **6... ♕c7** 7. ♕e2 a6 8. ♗g5 b5 9. ♗d5! ♘d5 10. ♘d5 ♕b7 11. 0-0-0 e6 12. f4 ♘c5 13. ♖he1 ♖a7 14. ♘f5± Talj–Tajmanov, SSSR 1968; **6... g6** 7. f3 ♗g7 8. ♗e3 0–0 9. ♕d2 ♘b6 10. ♗b3 ♗d7 11. a4 ♖c8 12. ♕d3 ♗e8 13. a5 ♘bd7 14. 0–0± Milić–Petrosjan, Jugoslavija–SSSR 1956

8 8. ♘f3 ♗e7 9. ♗g5±

9 10. ♕d3 0–0 11. ♖d1 ♘e8 12. ♗c1 ♖c8 [12... ♘c7 13. 0–0 ♕d7 14. f4 ♕c6 15. ♘d5!± Matulović–Cuellar, Siegen (ol) 1970; 14... ♖ad8 15. ♕g3 f6 16. ♗e3 ♗b3 17. ab3 ♕c6 18. ♗b6 ♕b6 19. ♔h1 ♕c6 20. ♕d3± Suetin–Tajmanov, SSSR (ch) 1967 — 3/470] 13. 0–0 ♘f6 14. ♗e6 fe6 15. ♕h3 ♕d7 16. f4± Gipslis–Tajmanov, Budva 1967 — 4/507

10 **14. ♕d3** a5 15. 0–0 a4 16. ♗e6 fe6 17. ♖ab1 ♖ac8 18. b3 ♕c5 19. c4 ab3 20. ab3 ♖a8 21. ♘c3± Ribli–Přibyl, Siegen (ol) 1970; **14. ♘c3** ♖ac8 15. 0–0 ♕c5 16. ♕e2± R. Byrne–Cuellar, Siegen (ol) 1970

11 **6. f3** e5 [6... e6△ d5=] 7. ♘b3 h6 8. ♗c4 ♗e7 9. ♗e3 0–0 10. ♕d2 ♗e6 11. ♗d5 ♗d5 12. ♘d5 ♘d5 13. ♕d5 a5∓ Matanović–Kostić, Jugoslavija 1948; **6. ♘de2** e6 7. g3 d5 8. ed5 ♘d5 9. ♗g2 ♘c3 10. ♕d8 ♘d8 11. ♘c3 ♗d7 12. ♗e3 ♗b4 13. ♗d4 ♗c6= Euwe–Pirc (m) 1949; **6. ♘b3** a6 7. a4 g6 8. ♗e2 ♗g7 9. 0–0 0–0 10. f4 ♗e6 11. ♗e3 [11. ♗f3 ♘a5 12. ♘a5 ♕a5 13. ♘d5 ♘d5 14. ed5 ♗d7 15. ♖e1 ♖fe8 16. c3 b5∓ Westerinen–Suetin, Soči 1974] ♘a5 12. f5 ♗c4 13. ♗d3∞

12 **6... e6** 7. g4 a6 [7... d5!? 8. ♗g2 ♗b4 9. ed5 ♘d5 10. 0–0=] 8. ♗g2 ♕c7 9. 0–0 ♗e7=; **6... g6** 7. ♗e3 ♗g7 8. ♗c4 0–0 9. ♗b3 ♗d7=

13 7... e5 8. ♘de2 ♗e7 9. ♗e3 0–0 10. ♘g3△ ♘f5±

14 11. b3? 0–0 12. ♗b2 b5 13. 0-0-0? b4 14. ♘e2 a5 15. f4 ♘d7 16. f5 ♘c5∓ Gereben–Geler, Budapest 1952

15 14. ed5 e4 15. ♘e4 ♘e4 16. ♕e4 0–0=∞

16 **6... e5** 7. ♘f3 [7. ♘c6 bc6 8. fe5 de5 9. ♕d8 ♔d8 10. ♗c4±; 8... ♘g4!? 9. ed6 ♗d6=∞] ♗e7 8. ♗c4 0–0 9. f5 ♕b6 10. ♗b3 h6 11. g4?! d5 [11... ♘g4? 12. ♕e2 ♘d4 13. ♘d4 ♗h4 14. ♔f1 ♕d4 15. ♖g1! ♕f2 16. ♕f2 ♘f2 17. ♗h6+− Bronštejn–Barczay, Szombathely 1966 — 2/380] 12. ed5 e4 13. dc6 ef3 14. ♕f3 ♗b4= Marić; 11. ♕d3±; **6... e6** — B 82; **6... g6** — B 71

17 8. ♗e3!?

18 14. ♗e3 ♕c7 15. ♗d4± Parma–Ničevski, Jugoslavija (ch) 1975

19 **6... ♕b6** 7. ♘b3 e6 8. ♗e3 ♕c7 9. f4 a6 10. a4 b6 11. ♗g2 ♖b8 12. 0–0 ♗e7 13. g4± Enevoldsen–Barcza, Berlin 1962; **6... ♘d4** 7. ♕d4 g6 8. ♗g2 ♗g7 — B 70

20 7... ♗g4 8. ♗g2 ♘d4 9. 0–0 ♖c8 10. h3 ♗e2 [10... ♘e2 11. ♘e2 ♗e6±] 11. ♘e2 ♘c2 12. ♖b1 ♗e7 13. ♗d2 0–0 14. ♗c3 b5 15. ♖c1± Boleslavski–Šagalovič, SSSR 1955

21 8... h6 9. h3 ♖b8 10. 0–0 b5 11. ♗e3 ♕d7 12. a3 ♗d8?! 13. ♕d2± Milić–Puc, Jugoslavija (ch) 1951

22 9... ♗e6 10. ♘d5±

23 11... ♘a5 12. b3 ♕c7 13. ♕d2 ♗b7 14. g4 ♖ac8 15. ♖ac1 ♖fd8 16. ♘d5± Keller–Gromek, Moskva (ol) 1956

24 14. b3 ♘b7 15. ♕d2 a5 16. a3± Boleslavski–Bondarevski, SSSR 1953

25 7... ♘d4? 8. ♕d4 ♗f3? 9. ♗b5 ♘d7 10. 0–0± Matanović–Beni, Wien 1951

26 8. ♗e3 e6 9. ♗g2 a6 — B 91

27 8... g6 9. ♘ce2 ♘d4 10. ♘d4 ♗g7 11. c3 0–0= Kieninger–Rellstab, Elster 1938

28 10... ♗e7 11. ♘a4 0–0 12. ♘b6 ♖b8 13. ♘d7 ♕d7 14. 0–0 ♕c7 15. ♕e2 d5= Aitken–Gligorić, Bad Pyrmont 1951

29 Pfeiffer–Ivkov, BRD–Jugoslavija 1960

30 6... e5 7. ♘b3 [7. ♘de2 ♗e7 8. g3 ♘g4 9. ♘d5 ♘e5 10. fe3 ♗g4 11. ♕d3= Velimirović; 7. ♘db5 — B 44] ♗e6 8. ♗e2 ♗e7 9. 0–0 0–0 10. f4 ef4 11. ♗f4 d5!= Ostojić–Gufeljd, Jugoslavija–SSSR 1969 — 7/365

31 8. ♘c6 ♘d1 9. ♘d8 ♔d8 10. ♖d1=

32 **9... ♘e5?** 10. ♘f3! ♗b5 [10... ♘f3 11. ♕f3 f6 12. e5!±] 11. ♘b5 ♕d7 12. ♘e5 de5 13. ♕d7 ♔d7 14. ♖f7±⊥ Ivkov–Tajmanov, Hastings 1955/56; **9... g6?** 10. ♗c6 bc6 11. ♕f3! f6 12. e5± Ćirić–Klages, Anvers 1955

33 10... ♗c6 11. ♕f3 ♕e7 12. ♖ad1 f6 13. ♘c6 bc6 14. e5± Bihovski–Bobolovič, SSSR 1964

34 11. e5!? ♗e7! [11... d5 12. ♕f3 ♕e7 13. b4! g6 14. b5 c5 15. e4!± Karaklajić–Averbah, Jugoslavija–SSSR 1956; 11... de5 12. ♕h5 ♕e7 13. ♕e5±] 12. ed6 ♗d6 13. ♕h5 0–0 14. ♘e4 ♗e7 15. ♖ad1∞ Karaklajić–Tajmanov, Jugoslavija–SSSR 1956

35 11... ♕e7? 12. e5 d5 13. b4 g6 14. b5 c5 15. e4 ♗g7 16. ed5 0–0 17. ♘c6± Gliksman–Bradvarević, Jugoslavija (ch) 1967 — 3/431

36 14. ♖af1 f6 15. ♖g3 ♔e7 16. e5? ♕e5 17. ♕a6 c5 18. ♘fe ♕e3 19. ♔h1 ♕f4 20. ♕b7 ♖c8∓ Kapengut–Georgadze, SSSR 1970 — 9/339; 16. ♕a6∞

B 57

1. e4 c5 2. ♘f3 d6 3. d4 cd4 4. ♘d4 ♘f6 5. ♘c3 ♘c6 6. ♗c4

	6	7	8	9	10	11	12	13	14	
1	... e5?![1]	♘de2[2] h6	f3 ♗e7	♗e3 a6	♕d2 b5	♗d5 ♕c7	g4![3]			±
2	... ♗d7	♗b3[4] g6[5]	f3![6] ♘d4	♕d4 ♗g7	♗g5[7] 0–0	0-0-0[8] h6[9]	♗h4 ♗c6	♕e3 ♕a5[10]		±
3	... ...	... ...	... ♘a5	♗g5 ♗g7	♕d2 h6	♗e3 ♖c8	0-0-0 ♘c4	♕e2 ♘e3	♕e3 ♕a5[11]	=
4	... ...	0–0 g6[12]	♘c6[13] ♗c6[14]	♘d5 ♗g7	♗g5 ♗d5[15]	ed5 0–0	♖e1[16] ♖c8	♗b3 ♖c7	♕d2 ♕d7[17]	±
5	... ♕b6	♘c6[18] bc6	0–0 g6[19]	b3[20] ♗g7	♗b2 0–0	♕d3 a5	♖ae1[21] ♗a6	e5 de5	♘a4 ♗c4[22]	=
6	... ...	♘de2 e6	♗b3[23] ♗e7[24]	0–0[25] 0–0	♗g5[26] ♘a5	♘g3[27] ♕c7	♕d2 a6	♖ad1 ♖d8	♖fe1 b5[28]	=∞
7	... ...	♘db5 ♗g4[29]	f3 ♗d7	♕e2 a6	♗e3 ♕a5	♘d4 b5	♗b3 e6	a3![30] ♘d4[31]	♗d4 b4[32]	±

1. e4 c5 2. ♘f3 d6 3. d4 cd4 4. ♘d4 ♘f6 5. ♘c3 ♘c6 6. ♗c4 ♕b6 7. ♘b3 e6

	8	9	10	11	12	13	14	15	16	
8	♗g5[33] ♗d7[34]	♕e2[35] ♖c8	f4 ♘d4	♘d4 ♕b2	♔d2 ♕b4	♖ab1 ♕c4	♕c4 ♖c4	♗f6 gf6	♔d3 ♖c7[36]	=∞
9	0–0 ♗e7[37]	♔h1 a6[38]	♗g5[39] ♕c7	♗d3 0–0[40]	f4 h6!	♗h4[41] ♘e4	♗e7 ♘c3	♗d6 ♘d1	♗c7 ♘b2[42]	∞
10	... ...	♗e3 ♕c7	f4 a6[43]	a4![44] b6	♗d3 ♘b4[45]	♕d2 e5	f5 ♗b7	a5 ba5	♘a5 ♗c8[46]	±

1 6. . . g6?! 7. ♘c6 bc6 8. e5! ♘g4 9. ♗f4! [9. e6?! f5 10. 0–0 ♗g7 11. ♗f4 ♕b6 12. ♗b3 ♗a6∞ Schlechter–Em. Lasker (m) 1910] ♕b6 [9. . . d5 10. ♘d5 ♗g7 11. ♘c3±] 10. ♕f3 ♗f5 11. ed6 ed6 12. 0–0 0-0-0 13. ♖fe1 d5 14. h3± Lipnicki

2 7. ♘f5 ♗e6 [7. . . ♗f5?! 8. ef5 ♗e7 9. 0–0 ♕d7 10. g4 h6 11. f4 ef4 12. ♗f4± Sokolski–Makovkin, corr. 1954] 8. ♗b3 ♕d7 9. ♗g5 [9. ♘e3!?] ♘e4 10. ♘g7 ♗g7 11. ♘e4 ♗b3 12. ab3 [12. ♘d6 ♔f8 13. ab3 ♘d4∓ Platonov–Kuzmin, SSSR 1970 — 9/340] d5 13. ♘f6 ♗f6 14. ♗f6 ♖g8∓ Saharov

3 Panov–Tarasov, SSSR 1949

4 **7. f4** g6!? [7. . . ♕a5 8. ♕d3 ♘b4 9. ♕e2 ♖c8 10. ♗d3 a6 11. e5± Planinc–Čudina, Sombor 1970 — 10/466] 8. ♘c6 ♗c6 9. e5?! de5 10. ♕d8 ♖d8 11. fe5 ♘g4 12. e6 f5 13. h3 ♘e5 14. ♗b5 ♖d6∓ Lipnicki–Boleslavski, SSSR (ch) 1950; **7. ♗g5** e6 [7. . . ♕a5 8. ♗f6 gf6 9. ♘b3 ♕g5! 10. 0–0 ♖g8 11. g3 h5 12. ♘d5 ♖c8 13. f4 ♕g7 14. ♕d2 h4∞ Geler–Averbah, Zürich (ct) 1953; 12. . . 0-0-0!△ e6, d5 Bronštejn] 8. ♘db5 [8. ♗f6 ♕f6 9. ♘db5 0-0-0! 10. ♘d6 ♔b8∓] ♕b8 9. ♗f6 gf6 10. f4 a6 11. ♘d4 ♕a7 12. ♘ce2 ♖g8 13. g3 ♕c5 14. ♗b3 ♘d4 15. ♘d4 0-0-0 16. ♕d3 [Szabo–Fuderer, München 1954] ♗h6!∓

5 **7. . . ♖c8** 8. f3 [8. 0–0 g6 9. ♗g5 ♗g7 10. ♘c6 ♗c6 11. ♘d5 ♗d5 12. ed5 ♘e4 13. ♗a4 ♔f8 14. ♗c1± Gereben–Kottnauer, Budapest 1952; 8. . . e6 9. f4 ♗e7 10. f5± Gligorić; 8. ♗g5 a6 9. ♗f6 gf6 10. ♕h5 ♘e5 11. f4 ♘c4 12. 0-0-0 e6 13. ♖he1 ♗g7 14. ♘f5! ef5 15. ef5 ♔f8 16. ♘e4 ♕c7 17. ♔b1!± Matulović–Bertok, Jugoslavija 1966 — 1/282] a6 9. ♗e3 ♕a5 [9. . . ♘a5 10. ♕d3 b5 11. g4± Nikitin] 10. ♕d2 e6 11. 0-0-0 ♗e7 12. ♔b1± Bednarski–Emma, Skopje (ol) 1972 — 14/399; **7. . . a6** 8. ♗e3 [8. ♗g5 ♕a5 9. ♗f6 gf6 10. ♕d2 ♖g8 11. g3 ♕c5 12. ♘c6 bc6 13. f4 ♕h5∞ Gipslis–Tajmanov, Tallinn 1967 — 3/432; 8. . . e6 9. 0–0 ♗e7 10. ♘de2 ♕c7 11. ♕d2 h6= Hasin–Simagin, Kislovodsk 1968 — 6/497] ♘g4 [8. . . ♘a5 9. f4 ♘b3 10. ab3 e5 11. ♘f5 ♗c6 12. 0–0± Bogdanović–Tajmanov, Budva 1967 — 4/471] 9. ♘c6 bc6 10. ♕f3 ♘f6 11. h3±; 11. e5!? △ ♘e4

6 **8. 0–0** ♗g7 9. ♗g5 h6 10. ♗h4 0–0 11. ♘c6 ♗c6 12. ♕e2 e6= Šofman–Štejn, SSSR 1969 — 7/369; **8. ♗e3** ♘g4!? 9. ♘c6 bc6 10. ♕f3 ♘f6 [Dely–Meštrović, Varna 1972 — 13/401] 11. ♗g5!? ♗g7 12. e5 de5 13. ♗f6 ef6 14. 0-0-0 0–0 15. ♖d6 ♕e7 16. ♖hd1=∞ Minev

7 10. ♗e3 0–0 11. ♕d2 b5 12. 0–0 [12. ♗h6 a5 13. ♗g7 ♔g7 14. a4 b4 15. ♘d5 ♘d5 16. ♗d5 ♖c8 17. 0–0 ♕b6∓ Pogats–Pietzsch, Kecskemet 1962] a5 13. a4 b4 14. ♘b5 ♕b8∓ Holmov–Averbah, Budapest 1970 — 9/341

8 11. ♕e3 b5 12. h4 a5 [12. . . b4 13. ♘e2 a5 14. ♗h6 ♖c8 15. h5 ♗h6 16. ♕h6± Saren–Robatsch, Helsinki 1972] 13. a4 ba4 14. ♘a4 ♖b8 15. h5 ♘h5 16. g4 ♘f6 17. ♗h6 ♗a4= Ciocaltea–Štejn, Caracas 1970 — 10/465

9 11. . . ♗e6 12. ♕d2 ♕a5 13. ♔b1 ♖fc8 14. h4 b5 15. h5! ♗b3 16. cb3 b4 17. ♘d5 ♘d5 18. ed5± Parma–Averbah, Titovo Užice 1966 — 2/386

10 **13. . . ♘d7**?! 14. ♖d6! g5 15. ♖g6 e6 16. ♖g7 ♔g7 17. ♗f2± Talj–Štejn, SSSR (ch) 1969 — 8/369; **13. . . ♕a5**±

11 **14. . . ♕b6** 15. ♕d2 ♕c5 16. f4 [Fischer–Merini, Mar del Plata 1960] b5 17. ♘f3 ♗c6 18. e5!± Fischer; **14. . . 0–0** 15. g4 ♕a5 16. h4 e6 17. ♘de2 ♖c6 18. g5 hg5 19. hg5 ♘h5 20. f4 ♖fc8 21. ♔b1 ♕b6 22. ♕f3 ♖c5 23. ♕d3!±→» Fischer–Gligorić, Jugoslavija (ct) 1959; **14. . . ♕a5** 15. f4! 0–0 16. h3 e6= Fischer

12 **7. . . ♖c8** 8. ♗g5 ♘a5 9. ♗e2 a6 10. ♗f6 gf6 11. ♗h5± Bialas–Niephaus, Hamburg 1955; **7. . . e6** 8. ♔h1 ♗e7 9. f4 0–0 10. f5± Gufeljd–Štejn, Gori 1971 — 11/341

13 **8. a3** ♗g7 9. ♘de2 [9. ♔h1? ♘e4∓] 0–0 10. ♘f4 ♖c8 11. ♗a2 ♔h8 12. ♖e1 ♘e5 13. ♕e2 ♘g8 14. ♗e3± Pietzsch–Paoli, Kecskemet 1962; **8. ♗g5** ♗g7 9. ♘c6 ♗c6 [9. . . bc6?! 10. ♕d2±] 10. ♕e2 0–0 11. ♖ad1±

14 8. . . bc6 9. f4± Fischer

15 10. . . 0–0 11. ♗f6 [11. ♖e1 e6= Kurajica–Ljubojević, Sarajevo 1970 — 9/343] ef6 12. c3± Boleslavski

16 12. ♕e2!? a6 13. ♖ae1 ♖e8 14. f4± Honfi–Mednis, Varna (ol) 1962

17 15. ♖e2± Cejtlin–Štejn, SSSR (ch) 1970 — 11/324

18 **7. ♗e3**?! ♕b2! 8. ♘db5 ♕b4 9. ♗d3 ♕a5 10. ♗d2 ♕d8 11. ♘d5 ♘d5 12. ed5 ♘e5 13. ♗e2 a6 14. ♘d4 ♕c7 15. 0–0 g6∓ Velimirović–Volvo, Krakow 1964; **7. ♗b5** a6 8. ♗a4 ♗d7 9. ♗e3 ♕c7 [9. . . ♕b2!? 10. ♘de2 ♕a3△ ♘e4∞] 10. 0–0 e6 11. f4 b5 12. ♗b3= Mišta–Paoli, Reggio Emilia 1969 — 7/366

19 **8. . . e6** 9. b3 [9. ♗g5?! ♕c5 10. ♗f6 gf6 11. ♕e2 ♗e7 12. ♔h1 h5∞ Stanciu–Mititelu, Romania 1966 — 1/280; 9. ♗f4 ♕b2?! 10. ♕d3 ♕b4 11. ♖ab1 ♕c5 12. ♖fd1 e5 13. ♗g5±; 9. . . ♕c5 10. ♗b3 ♗e7 11. ♘a4 ♕b4 12. c3 ♕b8 13. ♖e1± Honfi–Csom, Hungary (ch) 1973] ♗e7 10. ♗b2 0–0 11. ♕e2 e5 [11. . . ♘d7 12. ♘a4 ♕c7 13. f4± Krnić–Radulov, Vršac 1973 — 16/363] 12. ♔h1 ♕c7 13. ♖ae1 ♘d7 14. ♘a4± Karpov–Štejn, SSSR (ch) 1971; **8. . . ♘d7** 9. ♗b3 e6 10. ♗e3 ♕a5 11. f4± Molnar–Lörincz, Hungary 1972 — 13/404; **8. . . e5** 9. b3± Haag

20 **9. ♗b3** ♗g7 10. ♗e3 ♕c7 11. h3 0–0 12. f4 e6 13. ♕d2 ♗a6 14. ♖f2 d5 15. e5 ♘d7∓ Nestler–Bouwmeester, Siegen (ol) 1970;

9. ♕e2 ♘g4! 10. ♗b3 ♗g7 11. h3 ♘e5 12. ♗e3 ♕a5 13. f4 ♗a6 14. ♕f2 ♘c4∓ Vasjukov–Mititelu, Budapest 1967; 9. ♕e1 ♘g4 10. h3 ♘e5 11. ♘a4?! [11. ♗e2!?] ♕c7 12. ♕c3 ♖g8∞ Scheipl–Kestler, BRD 1972 — 14/398

21 12. ♖fe1!? Haag

22 Honfi–Cobo, Timisoara 1972

23 8. 0–0 a6 [8... ♗e7 9. a3 0–0 10. ♗a2 ♘e5 11. h3 ♗d7 12. ♗e3 ♕c7 13. f4 ♘c4 14. ♗c4 ♕c4 15. e5 ♘e4∞ Honfi–Drimer, Wijk aan Zee 1970 — 9/351] 9. ♗g5?! ♕c5 10. ♗f6 ♕c4 11. ♗h4 ♘e5 12. a4 b6 13. f4 ♘g4∞ Ljubojević–Ribli, Las Palmas 1974 — 17/413

24 8... a6?! 9. ♗g5 ♗e7 10. ♗f6 gf6 11. 0–0 ♗d7 12. ♔h1 0-0-0 13. f4 ♔b8 14. f5 ♕c5 15. ♘f4± Velimirović–Radulov, Vršac 1973 — 16/365

25 9. ♗e3 ♕c7 10. f4 a6 11. ♘g3 b5 12. ♘h5?! 0–0∓ Wijngaarden–Ostojić, Beverwijk 1967 — 3/433; 12. ♕e2!?=

26 **10. ♘g3** ♖d8?! 11. ♗g5 ♕a5 12. ♗d2± S. Garcia–Hennings, La Habana 1967 — 4/474; 10... a6=; **10. ♗e3** ♕c7 11. ♘g3 a6 12. f4 ♘a5 13. ♕e2 b5= Espig–Pietzsch, Zinnowitz 1967 — 4/472; **10. ♔h1** ♘a5 [10... ♘g4!? 11. ♕e1 ♗h4] 11. ♗g5 ♕c5 12. f4 b5 13. ♘g3 ♘b3 [13... b4? 14. e5!± Fischer–Benkö, Jugoslavija (ct) 1959; 13... ♗b7!? Gligorić] 14. ab3 ♗b7 15. ♘h5 ♔h8= Fischer

27 12. ♔h1!?△ f4, ♘g3∞ Ribli

28 15. ♘f5!? ef5 16. ♗f6 ♘b3! 17. ab3 ♗f6 18. ♘d5 ♕d7! 19. ♘f6 gf6 20. ♕h6≅ Ljubojević–Ribli, Skopje (ol) 1972 — 14/400

29 7... a6 8. ♗e3 ♕a5 9. ♘d4 e6 [9... ♘g4 10. ♘c6 bc6 11. ♗d2± Sax–Radulov, Vrnjačka Banja 1974 — 17/412; 9... ♘e5 10. ♗d3±; 9... ♘e4 10. ♕f3 ♘e5 11. ♗f7±] 10. 0–0 ♗e7 11. ♗b3 0–0 12. f4 ♘d4 13. ♗d4 ♗d7 14. f5!± Bilek–Hort, Göteborg 1971

30 13. 0-0-0?! ♗e7?! 14. a3!± Velimirović–Csom, Sombor 1972 — 14/401; 13... b4!∓

31 13... ♗e7 14. 0–0 ♘d4 15. ♗d4 b4 16. ab4 ♕b4 17. ♖fd1! a5 18. f4±

32 15. ♘b1 ba3 16. ♘d2±

33 **8. a4** ♗e7 [8... a6 9. ♗g5 ♗e7 10. 0–0 ♕c7 11. a5 0–0 12. ♗e2 ♗d7 13. ♗e3±] 9. a5 ♕c7 10. 0–0 0–0= Velimirović–Bradvarević, Jugoslavija 1966 — 1/283; **8. ♕e2** a6 9. f4 ♕c7 10. a4 ♗e7∞ Romanišin–Guljko, SSSR (ch) 1974 — 18/380; **8. ♗e3** ♕c7 9. f4 [9. 0–0 a6 10. a4!? ♘e5 11. ♗e2 ♘c4 12. ♗c1 ♗d7 13. ♕d3 ♖c8 14. ♕g3∞ Butnoris–Aleksejev, SSSR 1968] a6 10. ♗d3 b5 11. 0–0 ♗b7 12. ♕f3 d5!? 13. ed5 ♘b4 14. f5 ♘bd5 15. ♘d5 ♗d5 16. ♕h3 ♗d6 17. ♖ae1 [Hecht–Radulov, Wijk aan Zee 1974 — 17/414] e5∞; 12... ♗e7 — B 82

34 8... ♗e7 9. 0–0 a6 10. ♔h1 ♕c7 11. ♗d3 b5 12. f4 ♗b7 13. ♕e2 b4∞ Drimer–Csom, Lugano (ol) 1968 — 6/487

35 9. 0–0 ♗e7 10. ♔h1 h6 11. ♗f6 gf6 12. ♗e2 h5! 13. f4 h4∞ Cejtlin–Štejn, SSSR (ch) 1971 — 12/412; 11. ♗e3!?

36 17. ♘cb5≅ Savon–Štejn, SSSR (ch) 1971

37 8... a6 9. a4! ♕c7 10. a5! ♘a5?! 11. ♘a5 b6 12. e5! ba5 13. ef6 ♕c4 14. fg7 ♗g7 15. ♕d6 ♗b7 16. ♗g5!± Dončenko–Židkov, SSSR 1974

38 9... 0–0 10. f4 a6 [10... ♖fd8?! 11. ♗d3 a6 12. ♕f3 ♕c7 13. ♗d2± Ćirić–Langeweg, Amsterdam 1970 — 10/464] 11. ♗e2 ♕c7 12. a4 b6 13. ♗f3± Ćirić–Bradvarević, Jugoslavija 1966

39 10. f4 ♕c7 11. ♗d3 b5 12. ♕e2 ♗b7 13. a4?! b4 14. ♘d1 d5∓ Damjanović–Larsen, Palma de Mallorca 1969

40 11... b5 12. f4 h6 13. ♗f6 ♗f6 14. ♗b5 ♗c3 15. ♗c6 ♕c6 16. bc3∞ Polugajevski

41 13. ♗f6?! ♗f6 14. ♕h5 b5∞ Ostojić–Polugajevski, Skopje 1971 — 12/413

42 17. ♗e4 ♘a4∞ Polugajevski

43 10... 0–0 11. ♗d3 a6 12. g4 d5 [12... b5?! 13. g5± Fischer–Saidy, USA (ch) 1966/67 — 3/434] 13. ed5 ♘d5 14. ♘d5 ed5 15. c3±

44 11. ♗d3 — B 82

45 12... ♖b8 13. ♕e2 ♘b4 14. ♗f2! 0–0 15. e5 ♘fd5 16. ♘d5 ♘d5 17. ♗d4 ♖d8 18. c3± Ciocaltea–Csom, Nice (ol) 1974 — 17/415

46 17. ♗c4± Ghizdavu–Csom, Bath 1973

B 58

1. e4 c5 2. ♘f3 d6 3. d4 cd4 4. ♘d4 ♘f6 5. ♘c3 ♘c6 6. ♗e2

	6	7	8	9	10	11	12	13	14	
1	...	♘c6[2]	0–0[3]	f4[4]	f5	♕d3	♕g3	♗h6[7]	♖ad1	∓
	e5[1]	bc6	♗e7	♘d7[5]	0–0	♗b7[6]	d5!	♗f6	♔h8[8]	
2	...	...	...	♕d3	♕g3[10]	f4[11]	♗f4	♗e5	♕e5	=
	...	...	...	♘d7[9]	0–0	ef4[12]	♘e5	de5	♗d6[13]	

	1. e4 c5 2. ♘f3 d6 3. d4 cd4 4. ♘d4 ♘f6 5. ♘c3 ♘c6 6. ♗e2 e5 7. ♘f3									
	7	8	9	10	11	12	13	14	15	
3	... ♗e7	♗g5[14] 0–0	♕d2[15] ♗e6	♖d1 ♕a5	0–0 ♖fd8[16]	♗f6 ♗f6	♘d5 ♕d2	♖d2 ♗d5	♖d5 ♘b4[17]	=
4	... h6	♗c4[18] ♗e7	h3[19] 0–0	0–0 ♗e6	♗b3[20] ♘a5	♖e1 ♘b3[21]	ab3 ♕d7	♗e3 a6	♕d3 b5[22]	∓
5	... ...	0–0 ♗e6	b3[23] ♗e7[24]	♗b2 0–0	♕d2 a6	h3 ♕a5	♖ad1[25] ♖ac8	a3 ♖fd8	♖fe1 ♗f8[26]	=
6	... ...	... ♗e7	b3[27] 0–0	♗b2 ♗e6[28]	♕d2 ♖c8	♖ad1 ♕a5	h3 ♖fd8	♕e3 a6	a3 b5[29]	∞
7	... ...	... ...	♗e3 0–0[30]	♕d2[31] ♗e6	♖ad1 ♕d7[32]	♕e1[33] ♖fd8	♗c1[34] ♗f8	b3 ♕c8		=

[1] Boleslavski; 6... ♘d4!? 7. ♕d4 g6 [7... e6 8. ♗g5 ♗e7 9. 0-0-0±] 8. ♗g5 ♗g7 9. ♘d5±

[2] **7. ♘f5**? ♗f5 8. ef5 d5 9. ♗g5 ♗b4∓; **7. ♘db5** a6 8. ♘a3 ♗e6 9. ♘c4 b5 10. ♘e3 ♘d4∓

[3] **8. f4** ♕b6?! 9. ♕d3 ♗e7 10. ♗e3 ♕b2? 11. ♖b1 ♕a3 12. 0–0 ♘d7 13. ♕c4±; 8... ♘d7!=; **8. ♕d3** ♗e7 9. ♕g3 0–0 10. 0–0 ♔h8 [10... ♗e6 11. f4 ef4 12. ♗f4 ♘e8 13. ♖ad1± Hort–Šamkovič, Moskva 1962; 10... ♖b8 11. b3 ♘d7 12. ♖d1 ♘c5 13. f4 ♕b6 14. ♔h1 ♔h8= Pytlakowski–Tajmanov, Sczawno Zdroj 1950] 11. f4 ♕b6 12. ♔h1 ef4= Unzicker–Rabar, Luzern 1949

[4] **9. ♗c4** 0–0 10. ♕e2 ♕c7 11. h3 ♗b7 12. ♗g5 h6 13. ♗f6 ♗f6 14. ♖ad1 ♖ab8∓⌓; **9. ♔h1** 0–0 11. f4 ♘d7 11. f5 ♗b7 12. ♕d3 ♘b6 13. a4 [13. ♗e3 d5!] a5 14. ♗e3=

[5] 9... ef4 10. ♗f4 ♕b6 11. ♔h1 [Bergquist–Poulsen, Stockholm–Copenhagen 1952] 0–0 12. ♕d3 ♗e6 13. ♕g3± Euwe

[6] 11... ♘b6 12. ♕g3 ♗h4 [12... d5? 13. ♗h6 ♗f6 14. ♗g7? ♗h4 15. ♗f6 ♗g3 16. ♗d8 ♗h2 17. ♔h2 ♖d8=; 13. ♕e5!±] 13. ♕g4 ♔h8 14. ♖f3 g6 15. ♖h3 ♗f6 16. ♗d2 d5 17. ♖f1 ♖g8 18. ♖1f3 ♖g7= Donner–Trott, Nederland 1953

[7] **13. ♔h1** d4! 14. ♘d1 c5∓; **13. ♗d3** ♗f6△ c5!∓

[8] 15. ♗c1 d4 16. ♘b1 c5∓ Fuller–Tajmanov, Hastings 1955/56

[9] **9... ♗e6?** 10. f4 ef4 11. ♗f4 0–0 12. ♖ad1±; **9... 0–0** 10. f4 ♘d7 11. ♗g4! ♕b6 12. ♗e3 ♘c5 13. ♗c8 ♘d3 14. ♗b6 ♖fc8 15. cd3 ab6 16. f5 b5 17. a4± Janošević–Rabar, Jugoslavija (ch) 1949

[10] 10. ♖d1 0–0 11. ♗e3= Louma–Foltys, ČSSR 1948

[11] 11. ♗h6 ♗f6 12. ♖ad1 ♘c5 13. ♗c4 ♘e6∓ Bogoljubov–Gligorić, England 1951

[12] 11... ♔h8 12. ♔h1! ef4 13. ♗f4 ♘e5 14. ♖ad1±

[13] 15. ♕h5 ♕b6 16. ♔h1 ♕b2= Gligorić, Sokolov

[14] 8. 0–0 0–0 9. b3?! ♗g4 10. ♗b2 ♖c8 11. h3 ♗f3 12. ♗f3 ♘d4 13. ♕d3 ♕a5 14. ♗d1 ♘e6 15. a3 a6 16. ♖c1 b5 17. b4 ♕b6∓ Yanofsky–Pirc, Saltsjöbaden (izt) 1948

[15] 9. ♗f6!? △ ♘d5

[16] 11... a6? 12. ♗f6 ♗f6 13. ♘d5 ♗d5 14. ♕a5 ♘a5 15. ♖d5 ♘c6 16. ♖d6± L. Steiner–Pirc, Saltsjöbaden (izt) 1948

[17] **16. ♖d2** d5!=; **16. ♖b5** ♘c2 17. ♖b7 ♖db8=

[18] **8. h3** ♗e7 9. ♘h2 ♗e6 10. ♘g4 0–0 11. ♗e3 ♕d7 12. ♘f6 ♗f6 13. ♘d5 ♗d5 14. ♕d5 ♘e7= Letzelter–Benkö, Lugano (ol) 1968 — 6/486; **8. ♘d2** d5 9. ♘d5 ♘d5 10. ed5 ♕d5 11. 0–0 ♗e6 12. c3 ♗e7 13. ♗c4 ♕d7 14. ♕b3 ♗c4 15. ♘c4= Puc–Ivkov, Jugoslavija (ch) 1958

[19] 9. 0–0 ♗g4! 10. ♗e3 ♖c8 11. ♗b3 0–0∓

[20] 11. ♕e2 ♖c8 12. ♗b3 ♘a5 13. ♖d1 ♕c7 14. g4? ♘b3 15. ab3 a6 16. ♔h1 b5 17. b4 ♕c4∓ Stoltz–Boleslavski, Groningen 1946

[21] 12... ♖c8 13. ♗e3 ♘c4 14. ♗c4 ♖c4∓

[22] L. Steiner–Bronštejn, Saltsjöbaden (izt) 1948

[23] 9. ♗e3 d5! 10. ed5 [10. ♗b5? d4 11. ♘e5 de3 12. ♘c6 bc6 13. ♗c6 ♗d7 14. ♗a8 ef2 15. ♔h1 ♕a8∓] ♘d5=

[24] 9... d5? 10. ♗b5±

[25] 13. ♖fd1 ♖ac8 14. a3 ♖fd8 15. ♖ac1 ♗f8 16. ♕e3 b5= Yanofsky–Šajtar, Karlovy Vary 1948

26 16. ♗f1 b5=

27 **9. ♖e1** 0–0 [9... ♗e6 10. ♗f1 0–0 11. h3 ♕c7 12. ♘d5 ♗d5 13. ed5 ♘b8 14. c4 a5=] 10. ♗f1 ♗g4 11. h3 ♗f3 12. ♕f3 ♘d4=; **9. ♕d3!?** 0–0 10. ♖d1 ♗e6=

28 10... ♗g4 11. ♖e1 ♖c8 12. h3 ♗f3 12. ♗f3 ♘d4 14. ♕d3 b5 15. ♗d1!± Smislov–Ciocaltea, Moskva 1956

29 16. ♘d5∞

30 9... ♗e6 10. ♕d2 d5? 11. ed5 ♘d5 12. ♗b5! f6 13. ♖ad1 ♘e3 14. ♕e3 ♕b6 15. ♕d3 ♖d8? [⌓ 15... 0–0 16. ♘d5±] 16. ♕g6+– Paoli–Kottnauer, Trenčanske Teplice 1949

31 10. ♘e1 ♗e6 11. ♘d3 d5! 12. ed5 ♘d5 13. ♘d5 ♗d5 14. ♗c5? ♗c5 15. ♘c5 ♘d4!∓ Radulescu–Foltys, Budapest 1948

32 **11... a6** 12. h3 b5 13. a3 ♕b8 14. ♘h2 ♕b7 15. ♘g4!± Unzicker–Bogoljubov 1951; **11... ♘a5** 12. ♘d5! ♗d5 13. ed5 b6 [13... ♖c8 14. ♗a7 b6 15. ♕b4 ♘d7 16. ♗b5 ♘c5 17. ♗d3 ♘d7 18. ♗f5 ♘c4 19. b3 ♕c7 20. ♕c4 ♕a7 21. ♕b5± Bronštejn–Boleslavski, SSSR (ch) 1947] 14. b4 ♘b7 15. c4±

33 12. h3 ♖fd8 13. ♘h2? d5!∓

34 13. ♘d2 ♘d4!=

B 59

1. e4 c5 2. ♘f3 d6 3. d4 cd4 4. ♘d4 ♘f6 5. ♘c3 ♘c6 6. ♗e2 e5 7. ♘b3

	7	8	9	10	11	12	13	14	15	
1	...	a4[2]	♗g5	♗f6	♘d5	♗g4	c3	♘e7	0–0[5]	±
	a5[1]	♗e6[3]	♗e7	♗f6	0–0[4]	♗g5	♘e7	♕e7		
2	...	♗e3[6]	f3	♘d5[8]	♕d5	♕d2	♗d3	0–0	♘c1	=
	♗e7	0–0	d5![7]	♘d5	♕c7[9]	♖d8	♘b4	♗e6	♖ac8[10]	

1. e4 c5 2. ♘f3 d6 3. d4 cd4 4. ♘d4 ♘f6 5. ♘c3 ♘c6 6. ♗e2 e5 7. ♘b3 ♗e7 8. 0–0 0–0

	9	10	11	12	13	14	15	16	17	
3	f4	a4[12]	♗f3	♔h1[14]	f5	♖e1	♘d2	♘f1	♖f1	∓
	a5[11]	♘b4	♗e6[13]	♖c8	♗c4	♘d7	♗a6	♗f1!	♘b6[15]	
4	♗f3	a4	♗e3	♕d2	♖fd1[18]	♖ac1				=
	a6[16]	♘b4[17]	♗e6	♖c8	♕d7	♖fd8				
5	f3	♗e3[20]	♘c1	♕d2	♗d3[22]	a3	♔h1	♗g5		=
	a5[19]	a4	♕a5	♘d4[21]	♗e6	♗d8	♗b6	♗d8[23]		
6	♗e3	f3[24]	♘c1	♖b1	♘d5	ed5	c4	ba3	♕d2[28]	∓
	a5	a4[25]	a3[26]	♗e6[27]	♗d5	♘b4	♘d7	♖a3	♘a6[29]	
7	...	♘d2	♘d5	ed5	♘c4	♖fd1	c3[32]	♘d6	♗d4[33]	=
	...	d5[30]	♘d5	♕d5	♕d1	♗e6[31]	f5	♘d4	♗d6[34]	
8	...	♗f3	♘d2[35]	b3[37]	♘c4	♘b6	♘ca4	ed5	♘d5	±
	...	a4	a3[36]	♘b4	♗e6	♖a6	d5	♘bd5	♘d5[38]	
9	...	f4[39]	f5[40]	fe6	♗c4	♗e6	bc3	♖ad1		=
	♗e6	d5	d4	fe6	dc3	♔h8	♕d1	♘e4		
10	...	♗f3	♘a5[42]	♕d2	♖fd1[43]	♖ab1	a3	♖bc1	♗e2	=
	...	♘a5[41]	♕a5	♖fc8	♕b4	h6![44]	♕c4	a6	♕c7[45]	

1 7... ♗e6 8. ♗g5 ♗e7 9. 0–0 0–0 [9... ♘e4 10. ♘e4 ♗g5 11. ♘d6 ♔e7 12. ♘b7+–] 10. ♗f6 ♗f6 11. ♘d5 ♗d5 12. ♕d5 ♕c7 13. c3 ♖fd8 14. ♗c4! ♖ac8 15. ♘d2 ♘a5 16. ♗b3±

2 **8. 0–0** a4 9. ♘d2 d5 10. ed5 ♘d5 11. ♘d5 ♕d5 12. ♗f3±; **8. ♗b5!?** ♗e7 9. 0–0 0–0 10. ♕e2 d5 11. ed5 ♘d5 12. ♘d5 ♕d5 13. ♗e3 ♗f5 14. ♖fd1 ♕e6 15. ♘c5 ♗c5 16. ♗c5±

3 8... ♗e7 9. ♗g5 0–0 10. ♗f6 ♗f6 11. ♘d5 ♗g5 12. c3±

4 11... ♘b4? 11. ♗b5!±

5 O'Kelly—Tartakower, London 1946

6 **8. g4**? 0—0 9. g5 ♘e8 10. ♗e3 ♗e6 11. ♕d2 f5∓; **8. h4**?! 0—0!∓; **8. f3?!** d5!∓; **8. ♗g5** 0—0!? [8... ♘e4 9. ♘e4 ♗g5 10. ♘g5 ♕g5 11. ♕d6 ♕e7=; 9. ♗e7 ♘c3 10. ♗d8 ♘d1 11. ♖d1 ♔d8 12. ♖d6 ♔e7= Böök—Bronštejn, Saltsjöbaden (izt) 1948] 9. ♕d2 [9. ♗f6 ♗f6 10. ♘d5 ♗g5! 11. ♗c4 ♗e6 12. h4 ♗h6 13. g4 ♗f4 14. ♕e2 ♖c8 15. c3 ♘e7∓ Reicher—Boleslavski, Bucuresti 1953] a5 10. a3 a4 11. ♘c1 ♗e6 12. 0—0 ♘d4 13. ♖d1 ♖c8∓ Kasparjan—Geler, SSSR 1952

7 9... ♗e6 10. ♘d5 ♗d5 11. ed5 ♘b4 12. c4 b5? 13. a3 bc4 14. ♗c4 ♖c8 15. ♖c1±; 12... a5!?

8 10. ed5 ♘b4 11. ♗c4 ♗f5 12. ♖c1 ♖c8∓

9 11... ♕d5 12. ed5 ♘b4 13. 0-0-0 ♗f5 14. c3 ♘a2 15. ♔d2 ♘b4 16. d6! ♗d6 17. ♔e1 ♘c2 18. ♔f2± Foltys—Plater, Trenčanske Teplice 1949

10 16. ♖f2 ♕d7 17. ♕e2 ♕a4 18. a3 ♘c2 19. ♗c2 ♖c2 20. ♕c2 ♖d1= Rabar—Gligorić, Opatija 1949

11 9... ef4 10. ♗f4 ♗e6 [10... ♘e5 11. ♘d4 ♗d7 12. ♔h1±] 11. ♔h1! d5 12. e5 ♘e4 13. ♗d3 f5 14. ef6 ♘f6 15. ♕e1 ♕d7 16. ♘a4 ♗f7 17. ♘ac5± Bronštejn—Levenfiš, SSSR (ch) 1949

12 10. ♗e3 a4 11. ♘d2 [11. ♘c1 a3 12. b3 ♕a5!] ef4 12. ♖f4 ♘e5 13. ♘c4 ♘c4 14. ♗c4 ♗e6 15. ♗e6 fe6 16. a3 ♕a5 17. ♕e2 ♕a6∓ Ragozin—Rejfiř, Praha 1956

13 11... ♕c7 12. ♔h1? ♗e6 13. ♗e3 ♖fd8 14. ♕c1 ♗c4 15. ♖d1 ♖ac8∓ Horowitz—Geler, USA—SSSR 1954; 12. ♗e3=

14 12. ♗e3? ef4 13. ♗f4 ♘c2! 14. ♕c2 ♕b6∓

15 18. ♕e2 ♗g5∓ Goldin—Boleslavski, SSSR 1949

16 9... ♗e6 10. ♘d5 ♗d5 11. ed5 ♘b4 12. c4 ♖c8 13. a3 ♘a6 14. ♗e2±

17 10... ♘a5 11. ♘a5 ♕a5 12. ♗e3 ♗e6 13. ♕d2 ♖fc8 14. ♖fd1= Smislov—Holmov, SSSR (ch) 1949

18 13. a5!?=

19 9... ♗e6 10. ♘d5 ♗d5 11. ed5 ♘b4 12. c4 a5 13. ♗e3 ♘h5 14. ♕d2 ♘f4 15. ♗d1!± Geler—Barcza, Stockholm (izt) 1952

20 **10. a4** ♘b4 11. ♗g5 ♗e6 12. ♗f6 ♗f6 13. ♘d5 ♗d5 14. ed5 ♗g5=; **10. ♘d5**!?

21 12... a3!?

22 13. ♗d4 ed4 14. ♕d4 d5!∓

23 Pachman—Bronštejn, Helsinki (ol) 1952

24 **10. a4** ♘b4 11. ♗f3 ♗e6 12. ♕e2 ♕c8 13. ♖fc1 ♗c4 14. ♕d1 ♕e6∓ S. Nedeljković—Milić, Jugoslavija (ch) 1951; **10. a3** a4 11. ♘d2 ♘d4! 12. ♘c4 b5∓ Borisenko—Golovej, SSSR 1966; **10. ♔h1** a4 11. ♘d2 a3 12. ♘c4 ab2 13. ♖b1 ♗e6 14. ♖b2 d5∓ Alexander—Janošević, Beograd 1952

25 10... ♗e6 11. ♘d5 ♗d5 12. ed5 ♘b4 13. c4 ♘d7 14. ♕d2 b6 15. ♘c1 ♘a6 16. ♗d1 ♘ac5 17. ♘e2 h6 18. ♘c3 ♗g5 19. ♗g5 hg5 20. ♗c2 ♕f6= Lombardy—Panno, Mar del Plata 1958

26 11... ♕a5 12. ♕d2 ♗e6 13. ♖d1 ♖ac8 14. ♗b5 a3 15. ♘b3 ♕c7 16. ♘d5 ♗d5 17. ed5 ab2 18. ♖ab1 ♘d4= Janošević—Bajec, Jugoslavija (ch) 1951

27 12... ab2=

28 17. ♖b4? ♖e3∓

29 18. ♖b7 ♘ac5 19. ♖b2 ♕c7 20. ♘b3 ♖fa8 21. ♖fb1 ♕a7!∓ Janošević—Matulović, Beograd 1955

30 **10... ♘d4**?! 11. ♗d4!? [11. ♘c4 b5 12. ♗d4 bc4 13. ♗e3 ♗e6=] ed4 12. ♘b5 ♕b6 13. a4±; **10... ♗e6** 11. ♘c4 b5?! 12. ♘b5 ♘e4 13. f3 d5 14. fe4 dc4 15. ♕d8 ♖ad8 16. c3±

31 14... ♗f5!? 15. c3 ♖fd8 16. ♖d8 ♖d8 17. ♗b6 ♖d7 18. ♖d1 ♖d1 19. ♗d1 ♗e6= Pilnik—Schweber, Mar del Plata 1966 — 1/278; 16. ♗b6!±

32 15. ♘b6 ♖ad8=

33 15. cd4 ♗d6 16. de5 ♗e5=

34 18. ♗b6 ♗e7 19. ♗b5 ♔f7= Paoli—Liptay, Debrecen 1970 — 10/462

35 11. ♘c1 a3 12. b3 ♕a5∓

36 11... ♗e6!?

37 12. ba3 ♕a5! 13. ♘d5 ♘d5 14. ed5 ♘d4 15. ♗d4 ed4 16. ♘b3 ♕a3∓ Matanović—Gligorić, Stockholm (izt) 1952

38 18. ♗c5 ♕c7 19. ♗d5 ♗c5 20. ♘c5 ♕c5 21. ♗b7 ♖d6 22. ♕e2 ♕c3± Karaklajić—Gligorić, Opatija 1949

39 10. ♕d2 a5 11. a4 ♘b4 12. ♖fd1 d5 13. ed5 ♘fd5 14. ♘d5 ♘d5=

40 **11. fe5** ♘e5=; **11. ed5** ♘d5 12. ♘d5 ♗d5=

41 10... a5 11. ♘d5 ♗d5 12. ed5 ♘b8 13. ♕d3 [13. a4 ♘bd7 14. ♗e2 ♘b6 15. c4 ♘bd7!= Pilnik—Petrosjan, Buenos Aires 1954] ♘fd7 14. ♗g4 ♕c7 15. a4 ♘b6 16. ♘d2 ♘8d7 [Pilnik—Smislov, Amsterdam (ct) 1956] 17. c3△ ♕b5±

42 11. ♘d2 d5!=

43 13. ♘d5? ♕d2 14. ♘e7 ♔f8 15. ♗d2 ♖c2! 16. ♗c3 ♔e7 17. ♗d1 ♖c3! 18. bc3 ♘e4∓

44 14... a6 15. a3 ♕c4 16. ♗g5 ♖d8 17. b3 ♕c7 18. a4 ♘e8 [18... ♖ac8 19. ♗f6 ♗f6 20. ♘d5 ♕c2 21. ♘f6 gf6 22. ♕h6± Unzicker—Pachman, Stockholm (izt) 1952] 19. ♗e7 ♕e7 20. a5± Pilnik—Tajmanov, Stockholm (izt) 1952

45 18. f3 ♘d7 19. ♗f1 b5 20. a4 b4 21. ♘d5 ♗d5 22. ♕d5 ♘c5 23. b3 ♗g5= Boleslavski—Euwe, Zürich (ct) 1953

B6 SADRŽAJ • СОДЕРЖАНИЕ B6

B6 SOMMAIRE • INDICE B6

B6 CONTENTS • INHALT B6

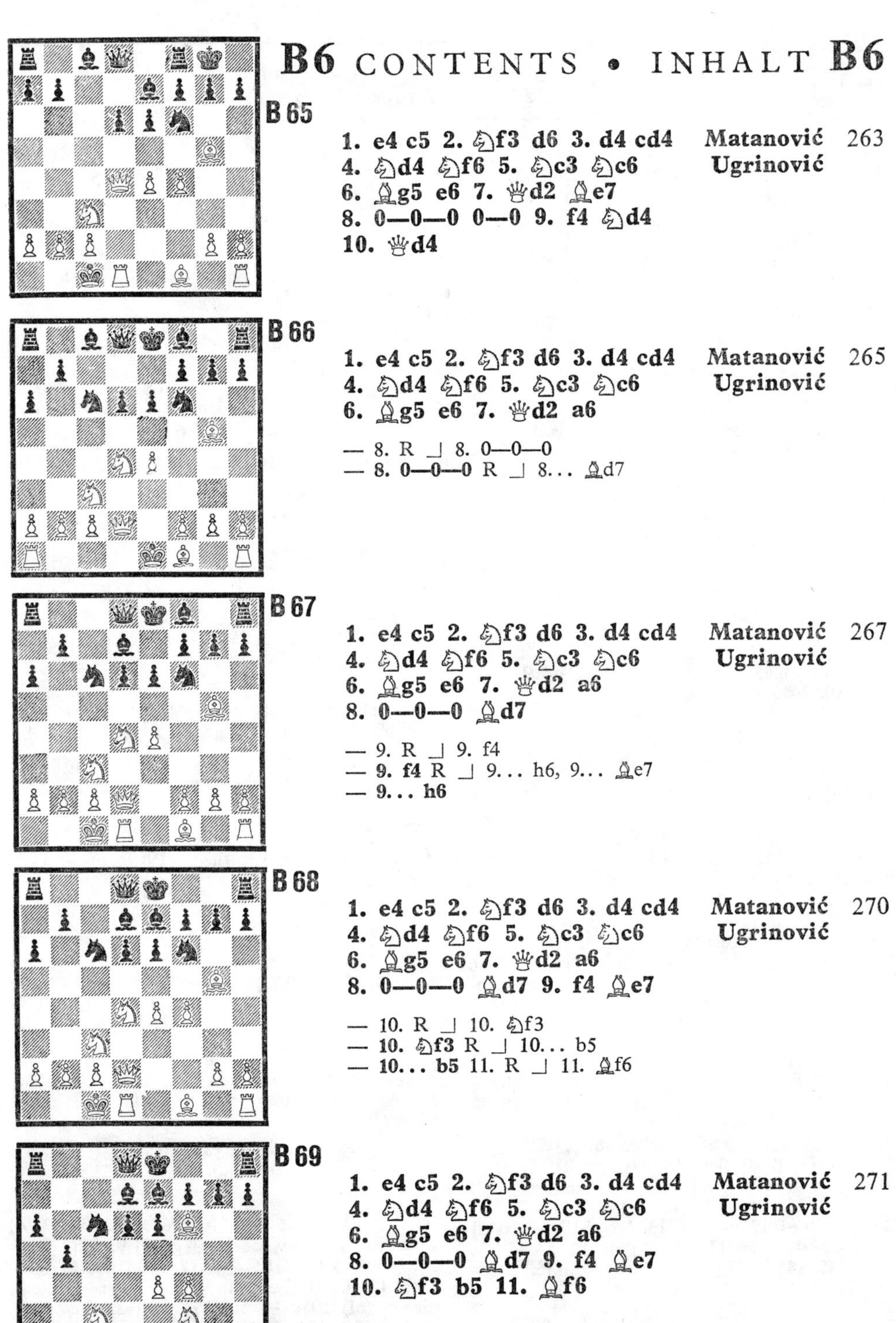

B6 INDICE • INNEHÅLL B6

B 60

1. e4 c5 2. ♘f3 d6 3. d4 cd4 4. ♘d4 ♘f6 5. ♘c3 ♘c6 6. ♗g5[1]

	6	7	8	9	10	11	12	13	14	
1	. . . g6[2]	♗f6 gf6	♗c4![3] ♗g7	♘db5 0–0	♕d6[4] f5	0-0-0 ♕a5[5]	♕c7 fe4[6]	♕a5 ♘a5	♗d5 ♗h6[7]	±
2	. . . ♕a5	♗f6[8] gf6	♗b5[9] ♗d7	♘b3[10] ♕c7	♘d5 ♕d8	♕h5 e6	♘e3 a6	♗e2 ♕c7	0-0-0 ♗e7[11]	±
3	. . . ♕b6	♘b3[12] e6[13]	♗d3[14] ♗e7	0–0 0–0[15]	♔h1 ♗d7[16]	♕e2[17]				±
4	. . . ♗d7	f4[18] ♕b6[19]	♘b3 ♘g4[20]	♕e2[21] ♘d4	♕d2[22] ♘b3	ab3 ♕e3	♕e3 ♘e3	♔d2 ♘f1	♖hf1 e6[23]	∓
5	. . . . . .	♘b3 a6[24]	♗f6 gf6	♕h5 ♖c8	♗d3 ♘e5	0–0 ♖g8	f4 ♘g4[25]	h3 ♕b6	♔h1 ♘f2[26]	∞
6	. . . . . .	♗f6 gf6	♘f5[27] ♕a5	♗b5 a6	♗c6 ♗c6[28]	♕h5 ♕e5	0-0-0 e6	♖he1 0-0-0	♘g3 ♕g5[29]	=
7	. . . . . .	♗e2 e6[30]	♘db5[31] ♕b8	a4 ♗e7	♕d2 a6	♘a3 ♕c7	♖d1 ♖d8	♘c4 ♗c8	♗e3 ♕b8[32]	±

[1] Richter, Rauzer

[2] **6. . . ♘g4**?! 7. ♗e2 [7. ♗b5!? Gligorić, Sokolov] ♘ge5 8. f4 [8. 0–0!?] ♘d4 9. ♕d4 ♘c6 10. ♕d2±; **6. . . ♘d7** 7. ♕d2±; 7. ♗e2±; **6. . . e5** 7. ♗f6 [7. ♘db5 — B 33] gf6 [7. . . ♕f6? 8. ♘d5 ♕d8 9. ♘b5+−] 8. ♘f5±; **6. . . h6** 7. ♗f6 gf6 8. ♕d2 [8. ♘b3 f5 9. ♗b5 ♗g7 10. ♕d5 (Barczay–Pederssen, La Habana (ol) 1966 — 2/395) ♗e6 11. ♗c6 bc6 12. ♕c6 ♗d7∞] ♕b6 9. ♘b3 f5 10. ♘d5 ♕d8 [Matanović–Holm, Lugano (ol) 1968 — 6/500] 11. ♗b5!? ♗g7 12. ♘d4± Matanović; **6. . . a6** 7. ♕d2 [7. ♗f6!?; 7. f4!?] h6 [7. . . ♗d7 — B 61; 7. . . e6 — B 66] 8. ♗f6 gf6 9. 0-0-0 [9. ♖d1 e6 10. ♗e2 h5 11. 0–0 ♗d7 12. ♔h1 (Larsen–Botvinik, Moskva (ol) 1956) ♘d4 13. ♕d4 ♗e7= Gligorić] e6 10. f4 ♗d7 11. ♔b1 [11. g3 ♕b6 12. ♘b3 h5 13. ♔b1 0-0-0 14. ♗e2 (Velimirović–Ničevski, Skopje 1971) ♔b8∞ Gligorić; 14. ♗g2!?] h5 12. ♗e2 — B 63

[3] **8. ♗e2** ♗g7 9. ♘db5 0–0 10. ♕d6 f5 11. 0–0 fe4 12. ♕d8 ♖d8 13. ♘e4 ♗b2∓ Gromek–Bondarevski, Polska 1955; **8. ♕d2** ♗g7 9. ♘db5 0–0 10. ♘d6 f5 11. 0-0-0 ♕a5⩱ Kärner–Černikov, SSSR 1965; **8. ♗b5**!? ♗d7 9. ♘b3 [9. 0–0 ♗g7 10. ♕d2 0–0 11. ♘b3 f5!= Suetin–Gurgenidze, Tbilisi 1969 — 8/379; 10. ♘b3!± Suetin; 9. ♘de2 ♗e6 10. ♕d2 ♗g7 11. ♖d1 0–0 12. 0–0 f5 13. ♘f4± Boleslavski] ♗e6 10. 0–0 a6 11. ♗e2 ♗g7 12. f4 f5 13. ef5 ♗f5 14. ♗d3± Matulović–Minić, Jugoslavija (ch) 1965

[4] 10. 0–0 a6!? [10. . . f5 11. ef5 ♘e5? 12. ♗b3 ♗f5 13. ♘d6 ♗g4 14. f3 ♕b6 15. ♔h1 ♖ad8 16. fg4 ♖d6 17. ♕e2± Štejn–Bokučava, SSSR 1971 — 11/345; 11. . . ♗f5!? 12. ♘d6 ♗c3 13. ♘f5 ♗b2 14. ♖b1± Gufeljd] 11. ♘d6 ♕c7 12. ♗d5 ♗d7 13. ♘c4 f5∞ Matulović–S. Nikolić, Jugoslavija (ch) 1965

[5] **11. . . ♕d6**? 12. ♘d6 ♗c3 13. bc3 fe4 14. ♘e4 ♖b8 15. ♖he1+−⊥ Milić–Gromek, Krynica 1956; **11. . . ♕g5** 12. f4 ♕g2 13. e5±

[6] **12. . . ♗c3** 13. bc3 ♕a4 14. ♘d6±; **12. . . ♕b4** 13. ♘d6 ♗c3 14. bc3 ♕c3 15. ♗f7 ♔h8 16. ♔b1±

[7] 15. ♔b1 e3 16. fe3 ♗e3 17. ♖hf1±⊥ Sušić–Udžvarlić, Jugoslavija 1960; 17. ♘d6△ ♘f7±⊥

[8] 7. ♗b5 ♗d7 8. ♘b3 ♕b6 9. a4 [9. ♗f6!?△ ♘d5] e6 10. 0–0± Georgadze–Beljavski, SSSR 1972 — 13/424

[9] 8. ♘b3 ♕c7 [8. . . ♕e5?! 9. ♕d2 f5 10. f4 ♕e6 11. ♘d4! ♘d4 12. ♕d4 ♖g8 13. 0-0-0 fe4 14. ♘d5± Ruderfer–Štejn, SSSR 1972 — 14/413] 9. ♗b5±

[10] 9. 0–0 0-0-0?! 10. ♘b3 ♕b6 11. a4! a5 12. ♘d5± Aljehin–Frents, Paris 1933; 9. . . e6!?±

[11] 15. ♔b1 0-0-0 16. f4 ♖df8 17. ♖d3 ♔b8 18. ♖hd1±↑ S. Nikolić–Gufeljd, Kislovodsk 1968 — 6/499

[12] 7. ♘db5 a6 8. ♗f6 gf6! [8. . . ab5? 9. ♘d5 ♕a5 10. b4 ♕d8 11. ♗g5±] 9. ♘d5 ♕a5 10. ♘bc3 f5 11. ♕h5 ♗g7 12. 0-0-0!? [12. ♗c4 ♗e6 13. 0–0 ♗c3 14. bc3± Tatai–Larsen, Siegen (ol) 1970 — 10/477] fe4 13. ♗c4 [13. ♗e2 ♗e6 14. a3 ♗e5∓ Šijanovski–Koc, SSSR (ch) 1961] ♗c3 14. bc3 ♗e6 15. ♖he1 ♕a3 16. ♔b1 0-0-0 17. ♖e4± Ceškovski–Anikajev, Soči 1974

13 7... a5?! 8. a4 ♗e6 9. ♗b5 ♘d7 10. 0–0 g6 11. ♘d5 ♕d8 12. ♘d4 ♗d5 13. ed5 ♘d4 14. ♕d4 f6 15. ♖ae1± Holmov–Tomović, Beograd 1963

14 **8. ♗f6** gf6 9. ♕h5 [9. ♗e2 a6 10. 0–0 ♗e7 11. ♔h1 0–0 12. f4 ♔h8 13. ♗h5 ♗d7∞ Tarjan–Ostojić, Venezia 1974 — 18/390; 9. ♕f3!? ♗e7 10. ♕g3 Minić] ♖g8!? [9... ♗d7 10. ♗e2 ♖g8 11. 0–0 ♖g6 12. ♔h1 ♖h6 13. ♕b5 ♕c7 14. f4± Schmid–Larsen, San Juan 1969 — 8/380] 10. ♕h7 ♖g6 11. ♕h5 ♗d7 12. ♕b5 ♕c7 13. ♕e2 a6 14. f4 b5=∞ Suetin–Guljko, SSSR 1972 — 13/425; **8. g4** a6 [8... h6] 9. ♗e3 ♕c7 10. g5 ♘d7 11. f4 b5 12. a3 ♗e7 13. ♕d2 ♘b6 14. 0-0-0 0–0? 15. h4 ♗d7 16. h5± Vasjukov–Guljko, SSSR (ch) 1974 — 18/391; 14... ♘c4!?∞; **8. ♕d2** ♗e7 9. h4 [9. f3 a6 10. 0-0-0 ♗d7 11. g4 ♕c7 12. ♗e3 0–0 13. g5 ♘e8 14. f4 b5 15. h4± Gaprindašvili–Martinović, Vrnjačka Banja 1975] a6 10. h5 h6 11. ♗f6 gf6 12. 0-0-0 ♗d7 13. ♖h3 0-0-0 14. ♔b1 ♔b8 15. ♖d3±↑ S. Garcia–Smislov, Soči 1974 — 18/393; **8. f4** h6 9. ♗f6 gf6 10. ♕f3 ♗d7 11. 0-0-0 0-0-0 12. ♔b1 a6 13. ♕h5 ♗e8 14. g3 ♔b8 15. ♗h3 ♗e7 16. ♖he1± Matanović–Štejn, Jugoslavija–SSSR 1961

15 9... a6 10. ♔h1 ♕c7 11. f4± Mednis–Guljko, Sombor 1974 — 18/392

16 10... h6?! 11. ♗e3 ♕c7 12. f4 a6 13. ♕f3 b5 14. ♖ae1 b4 15. ♘d1 ♗b7 16. ♘f2 e5 17. f5 ♘a5 18. ♘d2 d5 19. ♘g4!±→» Gligorić–Littlewood, Hastings 1964/65

17 **11. f4**?! h6 12. ♗h4 ♘e4 13. ♘e4 ♗h4 14. ♘d6 ♘b4 15. ♘c4 ♕c7 16. ♘e5 ♘d3 17. ♕d3 ♖fd8∓↑ Tringov–Spasov, Bulgaria 1973 — 16/372; **11. ♕e2**±↑ Minev

18 **7. ♗c4**?! ♕a5 8. ♗f6 gf6 9. ♗b3 ♗g7 10. 0–0 0–0 11. ♘d5 ♖ae8 [Huguet–Benkö, Malaga 1970 — 9/359] 12. ♘f5! ♗f5 13. ef5±; 9... ♖g8!∞ Kurajica; **7. ♕d3** ♖c8?! 8. ♘c6 ♗c6 9. 0-0-0 ♕a5 10. ♗f6 gf6 11. ♔b1 ♗g7 12. ♘d5± Muhin–Čečeljan, SSSR 1972 — 13/427; 7... a6!?; 7... e6!?; 7... ♘d4 8. ♕d4 — B 61

19 **7... ♖c8** 8. ♘b3 a5?! 9. ♗b5 ♘g4?! 10. h3 ♘e3 11. ♕e2 ♘b4 12. ♗d3 h6 13. ♗h4 g5 [Damjanović–Štejn, La Habana 1968 — 6/503] 14. ♗g3!± Ivkov; **7... ♘g4** 8. ♘db5! ♕b6 [8... f6 9. f5!±] 9. ♕d2 e6 10. 0-0-0!± Murej

20 8... e6 9. ♕d2 ♗e7 10. 0-0-0± Matanović–Polugajevski, Skopje 1968 — 6/504

21 9. ♕d2 ♕e3 10. ♕e3 ♘e3 11. ♖c1 ♘f1 12. ♔f1 [12. ♖f1 h6 13. ♗h4 g5 14. fg5 hg5 15. ♗g5 ♖h2∓] ♖c8∓ Boleslavski

22 10. ♘d5?! ♘e2 11. ♘b6 ab6 12. ♔e2 h6 13. ♗h4 g5!∓ Matulović–Mašić, Sombor 1968 — 6/505

23 Polugajevski–Štejn, SSSR (ch) 1968 — 6/506

24 **7... h6** 8. ♗f6 [8. ♗h4? ♖c8 9. ♗e2 g5 10. ♗g3 h5 11. h4 g4 12. ♗f4 ♘e5 13. ♕d4 ♘g6 14. ♗g5 ♗g7 15. 0-0-0 a5∓ Damjanović–Štejn, Tallinn 1969] gf6 9. ♕h5±↑; **7... e6** 8. ♘b5 ♕b8 9. ♗f6 gf6 10. ♗e2 ♗e7 11. 0–0 a6 12. ♘5d4 0–0 13. ♕d2 ♔h8= Spaski–Averbah, Kislovodsk 1960

25 12... ♗g4? 13. ♕h4± Suetin–Radulov, Ljubljana–Portorož 1973 — 15/383

26 15. ♔h2 ♕e3! 16. ♕h4!∞

27 **8. ♗e2** ♕b6 [8... ♕a5 9. f4?! e6?! 10. ♘b3 ♕b6 11. ♕d2 0-0-0 12. ♗h5±; 9... ♘d4 10. ♕d4 ♖c8∓ Boleslavski; 9. ♘b3=] 9. ♘b3 f5 10. ef5 ♗f5 11. ♘d5 ♕d8 12. 0–0 e6= Wade–Averbah, Moskva 1962; **8. ♘b3** f5 [8... ♗g7!?] 9. ef5 ♗f5 10. ♗d3 ♕d7 11. ♘d5 0-0-0 12. ♗f5 ♕f5 13. ♘e3 ♕g6 14. ♕e2∞ Bagirov–Furman, SSSR (ch) 1973 — 16/373

28 10... bc6 11. ♕d3 ♖g8 12. 0–0± Adorjan–Radulov, Budapest 1970 — 9/360

29 Ribli–Oegaard, Athens 1971 — 13/426

30 **7... ♕a5** 8. ♗f6 gf6 9. ♘b3 ♕g5 10. g3 h5 11. f4 ♕g6 12. ♕d2 h4 13. ♖g1 hg3 14. gh3 ♖h3∞ Tatai–Diaz, Camaguey 1974 — 17/432; 10. ♘d5± Željandinov–Cerateli, SSSR 1967; **7... a6** 8. ♗f6 gf6 9. 0–0 e6 10. ♔h1 ♗e7 11. f4 ♘d4 12. ♕d4 ♕a5 13. ♖ad1± Geler–Hort, Palma de Mallorca (izt) 1970 — 10/480

31 8. 0–0 ♗e7 9. ♘b3 0–0 10. ♔h1 ♘a5 11. ♘a5 ♕a5 12. f4 ♗c6= Marić–Bertok, Jugoslavija (ch) 1965

32 15. ♘b6 ♘d7 16. 0–0 0–0 17. f4± Spaski–Hort, Moskva 1971 — 12/422

B 61

1. e4 c5 2. ♘f3 d6 3. d4 cd4 4. ♘d4 ♘f6 5. ♘c3 ♘c6 6. ♗g5 ♗d7 7. ♕d2

	7	8	9	10	11	12	13	14	15	
1	...	0-0-0[2]	♘c6[4]	♕e3[5]	♔b1	♗f6	♘d5	♗e2![6]	ed5	±
	a6[1]	b5[3]	♗c6	♕a5	e6	gf6	♗e7	ed5	♗d7[7]	

	7	8	9	10	11	12	13	14	15	
2	...	0-0-0[8]	♗f6	♔b1	♕d4	f4	♕d2	♗e2	f5	±
	♖c8	h6[9]	gf6	♘d4	♕a5	♕c5	e6	♗e7	h5[10]	
3	...	♕d4	0-0-0	f4[12]	♗f6	♗c4	♕d2	♗b3	f5	±
	♘d4	♗c6[11]	♕a5	h6	gf6	♖g8	♕c5	e6	♕e5[13]	

1. e4 c5 2. ♘f3 d6 3. d4 cd4 4. ♘d4 ♘f6 5. ♘c3 ♘c6 6. ♗g5 ♗d7 7. ♕d2 ♘d4 8. ♕d4 ♕a5

	9	10	11	12	13	14	15	16	17	
4	♗d2[14]	♕d3[16]	♗e2[18]	0—0	♘d5	♗g5	♗f6	♕d5	♗c4	±
	e5[15]	♖c8[17]	a6	♗e6	♕d8	♗d5	♕f6	♖c7	♗e7[19]	
5	...	0-0-0[20]	♕d3	♔b1	f3	♗g5	h4	g3	♗e7	±
	♖c8	e5[21]	a6	♕d8	♗e7	♖c6	0—0	♘h5	♕e7[22]	
6	f4	e5	fe5	0-0-0	♗f6[26]	♕g4	♕g7	ef6[28]		±
	♖c8[23]	de5[24]	e6[25]	♗c6	♗c5[27]	gf6	♖f8			
7	...	...	...	...	♗d2[29]	♗c3	♔d2	♕c4[30]	♗c4	=∞
	...	...	...	♖c3	♕a2	g6	♗c5	♕c4	♘e4[31]	
8	...	0-0-0	♗h4	e5![33]	ef6	♗e2	♖he1	♗f3	♖e5	±
	...	h6[32]	g5	gh4[34]	e6	♗c6[35]	♖g8[36]	♔d7	♕b6[37]	
9	...	...	bc3[38]	♕b4[39]	cb4	♗h4[40]	fg5	♖e1	♗d3	±
	...	♖c3	e5	♕b4	♘e4	g5![41]	♗e7	d5	h6[42]	

1 7... ♕b6 8. ♘b3 a5 9. ♗e3 ♕d8 10. ♘d5 ♘d5 11. ed5 ♘e5 12. a4 g6 13. ♗d4± Gufeljd—Damjanović, Tallinn 1969 — 7/376

2 8. ♗f6 gf6 9. 0-0-0 e6 10. f4 ♕b6 11. ♘b3 0-0-0 12. ♗e2 h5 13. ♔b1 ♔b8 14. ♗f3 ♘a5 15. ♘a5 ♕a5 16. ♕d4± Matulović—Sokolov, Jugoslavija (ch) 1965

3 8... ♖c8 9. f4 h6 10. ♗f6 gf6 11. ♗e2 h5 12. ♔b1 e6 13. ♖hf1 b5 14. ♘c6 ♖c6 15. ♗f3 ♖c5 16. f5± Spaski—Bilek, Moskva 1967

4 9. ♗f6 gf6 10. ♔b1 e6 11. f4 ♕b6 12. g3 b4 13. ♘ce2 ♘a5 14. ♘b3 ♘b3 15. cb3 ♗c6 16. ♗g2 e5 17. g4± Tarjan—Larsen, USA 1968 — 6/501

5 10. ♕e1 ♕a5 11. ♔b1 h6 [11... e6 12. f4 ♖c8 13. f5± Vitolinš—Liberzon, SSSR 1967] 12. ♗f6 gf6 13. f4 0-0-0= Planinc—Gheorghiu, Ljubljana 1969 — 7/425

6 14. ♘e7? ♔e7 15. ♗e2 ♕b4 16. ♗f3 ♕c5= Adorjan—Gheorghiu, Budapest 1970 — 9/361

7 **15... ♗b7** 16. ♖he1 ♕c7 17. ♗h5 ♗c8 18. ♖d3 ♗f5 19. ♖c3 ♕b7 20. ♕h6±; **15... ♗d7** 16. ♖he1 ♕c7 17. ♗d3 ♗g4 18. f3 ♗h5 19. ♕h6 ♗g6 20. ♗g6 fg6 21. ♕g7±→ Adorjan

8 **8. ♘b3** e6 9. 0-0-0 a6 10. f4 ♗e7 11. ♔b1 b5 12. ♗f6 gf6 13. ♗d3 ♘a5 14. ♘a5 ♕a5= Matanović—Bobocov, Wijk aan Zee 1968; **8. f4** h6 9. ♗f6 [9. ♗h4 g5!? 10. fg5 hg5 11. ♗g5 ♗g7=∞ Litvinov—Veremejčik, SSSR 1972 — 13/428] gf6 10. 0-0-0 ♘d4 11. ♕d4 ♕a5 12. ♗c4 ♕c5 13. ♗b3 ♕d4 14. ♖d4 e6= Platonov—Štejn, SSSR (ch) 1969

9 8... ♘d4 — 7... ♘d4

10 16. ♗f3 ♕a5 17. ♖he1 ♖c5 18. ♕f4± Radulov—Robatsch, Forssa—Helsinki 1972 — 14/416

11 **8... h6**?! 9. ♗f6 gf6 10. ♗b5 ♗c6 11. f4 h5 12. 0—0 ♕a5 13. ♗c4!± Kostro—Ermenkov, Polanica Zdroj 1972 — 14/415; 10. ♗c4!?; **8... e6** 9. 0-0-0 ♕a5 10. f4 ♗e7 11. ♗c4 ♖d8 12. ♖hf1± Dueball—Csom, Skopje (ol) 1972; **8... ♖c8** 9. 0-0-0 ♖c3 10. bc3!? [10. ♕c3?! ♘e4 11. ♕e3 ♘g5 12. ♕g5 ♕b6 13. ♗c4 e6 14. ♕g3 g6=∞ Bednarski—Simagin, Polanica Zdroj 1968 — 6/509] ♕a5 11. ♗f6 gf6 12. ♗c4± Boleslavski

12 10. h4 h6 11. ♗f6 gf6 12. ♖h3 ♕e5 13. ♕e3 e6 14. ♗b5± Unzicker—Larsen, Santa Monica 1966 — 2/397

13 16. ♕f2± Lukin—Ivanov, SSSR 1974

14 **9. ♗h4** ♖c8 10. ♗e2 [10. 0-0-0?! g5! 11. ♗g3 ♗g7 12. e5 ♘h5∓] e5 11. ♕d3 [Keres—Rojahu, Buenos Aires (ol) 1939] ♘e4! 12. ♕e4 ♖c3!∓; **9. ♗e3** ♘g4 [9... e6 10. 0-0-0 a6∞] 10. ♗c4 ♘e3 11. fe3 ♕c5=; **9. ♗f6** gf6 10. f4 ♖g8 11. 0-0-0 ♖c8 12. ♔b1 f5 13. e5 e6 14. ♕d2 d5 15. ♘e4 ♗b4 16. ♘f6 ♔d8 17. ♕f2 ♖g6 18. ♘d7 ♔d7 19. c4 ♔e8∞ Željandinov—Gufeljd, SSSR 1972; 12. g3!?; **9. h4**!?

15 **9... a6**?! 10. ♘d5 ♕d8 12. ♘b6 e5 [11... ♖b8!?] 12. ♕e3 ♖b8 13. f3 ♗e7 14. ♗c4 0–0 15. 0-0-0± Browne–Radulov, Hastings 1972/73 — 15/380; **9... ♕c7** 10. ♗c4 [10. ♘d5 ♘d5 11. ed5 ♕c2 12. ♖c1 ♕f5 13. ♗d3 ♕e5 14. ♕e5 de5 (Gufeljd–Savon, SSSR 1969) 15. ♖c7 ♖b8 16. 0–0± Gligorić] e6 11. ♗b3 ♗e7 [R. Byrne–Benkö, USA 1970 — 9/364] 12. 0–0±

16 **10. ♘d5**?! ♕d5! 11. ♕d5 ♘d5 12. ed5 ♗e7 13. c4 f5 14. ♗e2 ♗f6 15. ♗f3 ♔e7 16. 0–0 ♖he8∓ Tatai–Štejn, Amsterdam 1969; **10. ♕e3**!? ♕c7 [10... ♕c5?! 11. ♕c5 dc5 12. f3 a6 13. a4 b6 14. ♗c4 ♗c6 15. ♗g5 ♗e7 16. ♗f6 ♗f6 17. ♗d5± Joppen–Kopetzky 1953] 11. f3 a6 12. 0-0-0 ♖c8 13. ♗d3 ♗e6 14. g4 g6 15. h4 h5 16. g5 ♘d7 17. ♘d5± Hübner–Csom, Athens 1969

17 **10... ♕c7** 11. ♗g5 ♗e7 12. ♗f6 ♗f6 13. 0-0-0 ♗e7 14. ♘b5 ♗b5 15. ♕b5 ♕c6 16. ♕d5 ♕d5 17. ♖d5± Bronštejn–Štejn, SSSR 1969; **10... ♕b6** 11. ♗e3 ♕a5 12. ♗g5± Štejn–Kuzmin, SSSR 1970; **10... h6** 11. ♘d5 [11. 0-0-0 a6 12. ♔b1 ♕c7 13. f3 ♗c6 14. g4 0-0-0= Gipslis–Liptay, Budapest 1970] ♕d8 12. ♘f6 ♕f6 13. ♕b3 ♗c6 14. ♗b5 ♕e7 15. 0–0 ♗b5 16. ♕b5 ♕d7 [Vasjukov–Tajmanov, Skopje 1970] 17. a4!?±

18 **11. ♘d5** ♕d8 12. ♗g5 ♗e7 13. ♘e7 ♕e7 14. 0-0-0± Štejn–I. Zajcev, SSSR (ch) 1970; 11... ♕c5!?; **11. f3** a6 12. g4 [12. ♘d5 ♕c5 13. ♘f6 gf6 14. 0-0-0 ♗e6= Tukmakov–Talj, SSSR (ch) 1973 — 15/379] ♗c6 13. h4 ♕b6 14. 0-0-0 ♗e7 15. ♗h3 ♘d7 16. ♔b1± Scholl–Torre, Amsterdam 1973; **11. 0-0-0** a6 12. ♔b1 ♕c7 13. ♗g5± Radulov–Csom, Kecskemet 1972 — 14/414; 12... h6!?

19 18. ♕d3 0–0 19. ♗d5± Talj–Radulov, Skopje (ol) 1972

20 **10. ♘b5** ♕b6 11. ♕b6 ab6 12. ♘c3 ♗c6 13. f3 e6 14. 0-0-0 d5 15. e5 ♘d7 16. f4± Vasjukov–Židkov, SSSR 1972; **10. ♗d3** e5 11. ♕e3 a6 12. 0–0± Tringov–Gufeljd, Skopje 1972

21 **10... ♕c5**? 11. ♕c5 dc5 12. f3 e6 13. ♗f4± Matulović–Schaufelberger, Siegen (ol) 1970; **10... a6** 11. f3 e5 [11... ♕c5?! 12. ♕c5 ♖c5 13. ♗e3± Mecking–Radulov, Vršac 1971 — 12/424; 12. ♕d3!? g6 13. g4 ♗g7 14. h4 h6 15. ♔b1 ♗e6 16. ♗e3 ♕a5 17. ♗d4± Karpov–Markland, Graz 1972 — 15/378] 12. ♕e3 [12. ♕a7?! ♕c7 13. ♗e3 ♗e6 14. ♕b6 ♕b6 15. ♗b6 ♗e7 16. ♗e2 0–0= Gruzman–Lejn, SSSR 1972 — 13/430] ♗e6 13. a3 ♗e7 14. g4 [Kuzmin–Markland, Nice (ol) 1974 — 17/434] ♕c7△ b5∞ Kuzmin; 11. ♔b1 ♕c5 12. ♕c5 ♖c5 13. f3± Kuzmin; 11. ♗c4!? ♕c5 12. ♕c5 ♖c5 13. ♗b3 e6 14. f3 ♗e7 15. ♗f4 ♖c6 16. ♖d3!± Gipslis–Ubilava, Tbilisi 1974 — 18/395; **10... g6**!?

22 18. ♘d5 ♕d8 19. f4± Radulov–Ungureanu, Skopje (ol) 1972 — 14/417

23 **9... h6** 10. b4 ♕d8 11. ♗f6! [11. ♗h4? g5!∓ Platonov–Polugajevski, SSSR (ch) 1969 — 8/388] gf6 12. ♘d5 ♗g7 13. ♗c4 0–0 14. f5 e6 15. ♘e3 b5 16. ♗b3 a5 17. ♕d6 a4 18. fe6 ♗e6 19. ♕d8 ♖ad8 20. ♗d5± Tukmakov–Radulov, Hastings 1972/73 — 15/381; **9... e5** 10. ♕d3 ♗e7 11. 0-0-0 ♗c6 12. ♔b1 ef4 13. ♗f4 0–0 14. ♗e2± Liberzon–Štejn, Moskva 1969 — 8/389; **9... e6** 10. 0-0-0 ♗e7 11. ♗c4 [11. e5?! de5 12. fe5 0-0-0 13. ♗e3 ♗c6 14. ♕a7 ♕a7 15. ♗a7 ♖d1 16. ♘d1 ♘g4∓ Tabor–Csom, Hungary 1971; 13. ♗c4 ♗c6 14. ♕f4 h6= Barczay–Csom, Hungary 1971] ♗c6 12. ♖he1 h6 13. ♗h4 ♕h5? 14. ♗g3 0–0 15. e5 de5 16. ♖e5 ♖fd8 17. ♘d5! ed5 18. ♗d3 ♕g4 19. ♖e7± Janošević–Csom, Amsterdam 1970 — 10/478; 13... 0–0± Gligorić

24 **10... ♖c3** 11. bc3! [11. ♕c3 ♕c3 12. bc3 ♘e4$\overline{\overline{\infty}}$ Parma–Sofrevski, Skopje 1969] ♘e4 12. ♕e4 ♕c3 13. ♔f2 ♕a1 14. ♗b5! ♕c3 15. ♗d7 ♔d7 16. ♕b7 ♕c7 17. ♖b1±; **10... h6** 11. ♗h4± Tatai–Radulov, Venezia 1971 — 12/426

25 11... ♗e6? 12. b4+– Baretić–Radulov, Vršac 1971

26 13. ♗b5 ♘d5 14. ♘d5 [14. ♗c6 bc6 15. a3 h6 16. ♗d2 ♕b6 17. ♕b6 ab6= Karpov–Balašov, Moskva 1971] ♗b5 15. ♕a7!? [15. ♖hf1? ♗c5! 16. ♕f4 ♖f8 17. ♘c3 h6∓ Cordovil–Bilek, Praia da Rocha 1969 — 8/390] ♗b4! [15... ♗a6? 16. ♕b6 ♕b6 17. ♘b6 ♖b8 18. ♖d2+–] 16. ♕a5 ♗a5 17. b4 ed5 18. ba5 ♗c4= Hort–Panno, Palma de Mallorca (izt) 1970

27 13... gf6? 14. ♘e4! fe5 15. ♘f6 ♔e7 16. ♕h4 ♗g7 [16... ♕a2 17. ♘d5 ♔e8 18. ♘c7!+–] 17. ♘h5 ♔f8 18. ♗c4+– Saharov–Kudrjašov, SSSR 1966 — 2/396

28 ±→ Boleslavski

29 **13. ♕c3** ♕c3 14. bc3 ♘e4∞; **13. ♗f6** ♖c7∞

30 16. ♕h4 ♘d5$\overline{\overline{\infty}}$

31 18. ♔e2 ♘c3 19. bc3 ♗c6$\overline{\overline{\infty}}$

32 **10... ♕c5**?! 11. e5! [11. ♕d2 ♘g4 12. ♗h4± Schmidt–Drimer, Lugano (ol) 1968] ♕d4 12. ♖d4 de5 13. fe5 ♖c5? [13... ♘g4? 14. e6!+–] 14. ♗b5! ♖e5 [14... ♗b5 15. ♖hd1 ♘d5 16. ♘d5+–] 15. ♗f6 ♖b5 16. ♖hd1 ef6 [Palermo–R. Garcia, Mar del Plata 1968 — 6/508] 17. ♖d7+–; 13... ♘g8±; **10... e6** 11. ♔b1 ♕c5!? [11... ♗c6?! 12. ♗f6 gf6 13. ♗c4 ♖g8 14. f5 ♗d7 15. ♗b3 ♗e7 16. ♕e3±↑ Jansa–Simagin, Polanica Zdroj 1968 — 6/510] 12. ♗f6 gf6 13. ♕f6 ♖g8$\overline{\overline{\infty}}$ Unzicker–Dueball, Berlin 1971

33 12. ♗e1 ♗g7 13. g3? [R. Byrne–Meštrović, Hastings 1970/71 — 11/347] ♘h5!? 14. e5 ♗c6△ de5∓; 13. e5!?∞ Gligorić

34 12... ♗g7 13. ♗e1 ♘h5 14. ♘d5! ♕a2 15. ♘e7 ♕a1 16. ♔d2 ♖c2 17. ♔c2 ♗a4 18.

b3 ♕a2 19. ♔c1 ♗b3 20. ♖d2 ♕a3 21. ♖b2 +− Gligorić

35 14... ♕c5 15. ♕d3 ♗c6 16. ♗f3 ♗f3 17. ♕f3± Mecking—Belmonte, Sao Paulo 1972

36 15... ♗g2?! 16. ♗g4△ 17. ♗e6; △ 17. f5+− Gligorić

37 18. ♕b6 ab6 19. ♗h5 ♖g2 20. ♗f7 ♖h2 21. ♗e6 ♔c7 22. ♖e3± Karpov—R. Byrne, Hastings 1971/72 — 13/429

38 11. ♕c3?! ♕c3 12. bc3 ♘e4 13. ♗h4 g6 14. ♗e1 ♗g7 15. ♔b2 0—0 16. ♗d3 ♘c5 17. ♔a3 ♖c8∓ O'Kelly—Radulov, La Habana 1969

39 12. ♕e3? ♘g4 13. ♕f3 h6 14. ♗h4 ef4 15. e5 g5 16. ♗c4 ♘e5 17. ♖he1 ♗g7∓ Daskalov—Tringov, Bulgaria 1969

40 **14. ♖e1** ♘g5 15. fg5 ♗e7 16. h4 h6 17. gh6 ♖h6= Zuidema—Picket, Nederland (ch) 1969; **14. ♗c4** ♘g5 [14... ♘f2?! 15. fe5 ♘h1 16. ed6 f6 17. ♗e3±; 14... b5 15. ♗d5 ♘c3 16. fe5 h6 (Janošević—Larsen, Beograd 1964) 17. ♗e3!? ♘d1 18. ♖d1 a6 19. ♗f4 de5 20. ♗e5± Boleslavski] 15. fg5 ♗e7 16. h4 ♗c6 17. ♖hf1 f6 18. gf6 gf6= Pioch—Lorenge, SSSR 1974

41 **14... ef4**?! 15. ♖d4 f5 16. ♗d3±; **14... ♘c3**?! 15. ♖d3! [15. ♖e1 ♘a2 16. ♔b2 ♘b4 17. fe5 d5= Gheorghiu—Hort, Monte Carlo 1968] ♘a2 16. ♔b2 ♘b4 17. ♖b3 ♘c6 18. ♖b7±; **14... f5** 15. fe5 [15. ♗c4 ef4 16. ♖he1 ♗e7 17. ♗e7 ♔e7 18. ♗d5 ♗c6= Bagirov—Talj, SSSR 1969] g5 [15... de5 16. ♖d5±] 16. ♗e1 de5 17. ♗c4±

42 **18. c4** hg5 19. cd5 ♖h4 20. ♖e4 ♖e4 21. ♗e4 f5⩱ Unzicker—Gheorghiu, Ljubljana 1969 — 7/382; **18. ♗e4** de4 19. ♖e4 hg5 20. ♗g3 f6 21. c3± Boleslavski

B 62

1. e4 c5 2. ♘f3 d6 3. d4 cd4 4. ♘d4 ♘f6 5. ♘c3 ♘c6 6. ♗g5 e6

	7	8	9	10	11	12	13	14	15	
1	♘c6[1]	e5[2]	♗f6[3]	ed6	♕e2	0-0-0	♕e5	♘a4	b3	∓
	bc6	♕a5	gf6	♕e5	♗d6	♖b8	♗e5	♖b4	♖f4[4]	
2	...	...	♕f3	♗f6[6]	♕c6[7]	♕f3	♖d1	♗d3		∓
	...	de5	♗e7[5]	♗f6	♗d7	0—0	♕c7	♖b8		
3	♗b5	0—0[8]	♘b3[10]	♗e2	♕e1	f4	♗h4	♗f3	♖d1	=
	♗d7	♗e7[9]	a6	♕c7[11]	0—0	h6	b5	♖ab8	b4[12]	
4	♗e2	0—0[14]	♕d2[15]	♘e4	♘g5	♕d4	♕d6	♖ad1	♖d6	=
	♗e7[13]	0—0	♘e4!?	♗g5	♘d4	♕g5	♕d8[16]	♕d6	e5[17]	
5	♕d3[18]	♖d1[19]	♗e2	0—0	♕g3[21]	♘b3	♗f4[22]	♗c1	f4	=
	a6	♗d7	♗e7	0—0[20]	♕c7	♔h8	♘e5	♗b5!	♘c6[23]	
6	...	0-0-0	f4[24]	♘c6[26]	h4[27]	fe5	♕g3	♗c4[28]	♕f3	∞
	♗e7	0—0	h6[25]	bc6	e5	de5	♕c7	♘h5	♘f4[29]	
7	...	♗e2	0—0	♗f6[32]	♘db5	ed5	♕d5	♘d5		=
	...	0—0[30]	h6[31]	♗f6	d5	ed5	♕d5	♗b2[33]		
8	...	...	♖d1	0—0	♕d4	♔h1[36]	f4	♖d3	♗h4	=
	...	...	♗d7[34]	♘d4	♗c6[35]	♕a5	♖fd8[37]	h6	♕c5[38]	

1 **7. ♗c4**?! ♕b6 8. ♗f6 gf6 9. ♘db5?! ♘e5 10. ♗b3 ♖g8∓ Sursok—Larsen, Siegen (ol) 1970 — 10/481; 9. ♘b3∓; **7. g3** ♗e7 8. ♗g2 0—0 9. 0—0 ♘d4 10. ♕d4 h6=; **7. ♘b3** ♗e7 8. ♕d2 [8. ♕f3 a6 9. ♖d1 h6 10. ♗c1 0—0 11. ♗e2 ♕c7 12. 0—0 b5 13. ♕g3 ♔h8∞ Korčnoj—Suetin, SSSR 1950; 8... 0—0 9. ♗e2 a6 10. ♕g3 b5∓] h6 9. ♗e3 0—0= Aljehin

2 8. ♕f3 ♖b8 9. e5 de5 — 8. e5

3 9. ♗b5? cb5 10. ef6 b4 [10... gf6 11. ♗f6 ♖g8 12. ♕d3 ♖g6 13. ♗h4 ♗a6∓] 11. ♘e4 [11. ♕f3 ♕e5! 12. ♗e3 d5∓] ♕e5 12. f3 d5 13. ♕d2 h6 14. ♗h4 g5 15. ♗g3 ♕b2 16. ♖d1 ♗a6∓ Nilsson—Geler, Sverige—SSSR 1954; 13. 0—0!? Geler

4 16. f3 ♖h4∓ Dahlquist—Lundin, Stockholm 1934

5 **9... ♕b6** 10. ♗f6 gf6 11. ♕f6 ♕b2 12. ♖d1 ♕c3 13. ♖d2 ♕a1=; **9... ♖b8** 10. ♖d1 [10. ♗c4 ♗e7 11. ♗f6 gf6 12. 0—0 ♕c7 13. ♕h5 h6 14. ♖ad1 ♔f8 15. b3 f5∓ Estrin—Ilivicki, SSSR 1946] ♕c7 11. ♘e4 [Richter—Wagner 1932] ♘d5∞

6 10. ♕c6?! ♗d7 11. ♕f3 e4! 12. ♘e4 ♘e4 13. ♗e7 ♕a5 [Troianescu—Samarian, Romania 1940] 14. c3 ♘c3∓

7 11. ♖d1 ♕b6 12. ♗d3 0—0 13. 0—0 ♗b7∓ Fedorov—Čistjakov, SSSR 1940

8 **8. ♗a4** a6 [8... h6 9. ♗h4 (Canal—Gligorić, Venezia 1949) a6=] 9. ♘c6 ♗c6 10. ♗c6 bc6 11. e5 ♕a5 12. ♗f6 gf6 13. ed6 ♕e5= Troianescu—Rejfiř 1956; 11. ♕f3!?; **8. ♕d2** ♗e7 9. 0-0-0 ♕c7 10. ♘f3 a6 11. ♗e2 ♘e5 12. ♘d4 h6= Puc—Pirc, Jugoslavija (ch) 1948

9 8... h6 9. ♗h4 [8. ♗e3!? a6 9. ♗e2 ♗e7 10. ♘b3 ♕c7=] a6 10. ♗e2 ♗e7 11. ♘b3 ♕c7 12. f4 g5! 13. ♗g3! [13. fg5? hg5 14. ♗g5 d5 15. h3 ♖h3∓] gf4 14. ♖f4 ♘e5∞ Aljehin—Foltys, Margate 1937

10 9. ♔h1 h6 10. ♗e3 a6 11. ♗e2 e5 12. ♘b3 0—0 13. ♘d5 [Romanovski—Botvinik, SSSR 1945] ♘e4 14. ♗b6 ♕c8 15. f3 ♘f6 16. ♘e7 ♘e7 17. ♕d6 ♕c2 18. ♗d3=

11 10... b5 11. ♗f6 gf6 12. a4± Aljehin—Napolitano, München 1942

12 16. ♘e2 e5 17. f5 g5= Gligorić—Boleslavski, Moskva 1947

13 **7... ♕b6**?! 8. ♘b3 a6 9. 0—0 ♗e7 [9... ♕c7 10. f4 ♗e7 11. ♗f3 h6 12. ♗h4 g5?! 13. fg5 hg5 14. ♗g5 d5 15. h3± Honfi—Barcza, Hungary 1958] 10. ♔h1 ♕c7 11. f4 0—0 12. ♕e1 ♘e8 13. ♗e7 ♘e7 14. ♗d3± Rätsch—Barcza, Berlin 1962; **7... a6** 8. 0—0 ♗d7 9. ♔h1 ♗e7 10. f4 ♘d4 [10... ♕b6 11. ♘b3 0—0 12. ♕e1 ♘e8 13. ♗e7 ♘e7 14. ♖d1 ♖c8 15. ♗d3± Marić—Paoli, Le Havre 1966 — 1/286] 11. ♕d4 ♗c6 12. ♖ad1 [Paoli—Nievergelt, Zürich 1960] 0—0±; **7... h6** 8. ♗e3 e5 9. ♘b3 ♗e7 10. 0—0 0—0 11. ♕d2 a5 12. ♖ad1 a4 13. ♘c1 ♗e6 14. f3 ♖a5△ d5= Paoli—Korčnoj, Bucuresti 1954

14 **8. ♘b3** a6 9. ♕d2 b5 10. a3 ♗b7 11. ♖d1 ♘a5? 12. ♘a5 ♕a5 13. e5! b4 14. ab4 ♕e5 15. f4 ♕f5 16. g4!+— Gurgenidze—Džindžihašvili, SSSR 1965; 11... ♕c7=; **8. ♕d3** — 7. ♕d3

15 9. ♘db5 a6 10. ♗f6 gf6 11. ♘d4 ♔h8 12. ♔h1 ♗d7 [12... ♖g8 13. f4 ♗d7∞ Smislov—Botvinik, Moskva (mct) 1948] 13. f4 b5 14. ♗f3 ♕b6 15. ♘ce2 ♖ac8∞ Tajmanov—Žuhovicki, SSSR 1949

16 13... ♖d8 14. ♕c7 ♖d7 15. ♕c3 b6 16. ♗f3 ♗b7 17. ♗b7 ♖b7 18. ♖ad1±

17 16. ♗f3 ♗e6 17. b3 ♖ac8= Holmov—Džindžihašvili, SSSR 1965

18 Keres

19 **8. 0-0-0** ♗d7 9. ♗e2 [9. f4 ♕c7 10. ♗f6 gf6 11. ♔b1 0-0-0 12. ♗e2 ♖g8 13. ♘c6 ♗c6 14. ♗f3 ♔b8 15. f5 ♗h6∞ Vasjukov—Simagin, SSSR (ch) 1965; 9... h6 10. ♗h4 g5 11. ♘c6 ♗c6 12. fg5 ♘g4 13. ♕d2 ♗e7 14. ♗e2 ♘e5= Kljavin—Koblenc, SSSR 1952] ♖c8 10. f4 ♗e7 11. ♘b3 [11. ♘f3 ♕b6 12. h3 0—0 13. e5 de5 14. fe5 ♘b4 15. ♕d2 ♖c3!∓ Karaklajić—Matulović, Jugoslavija (ch) 1955] ♘b4 12. ♕d4 a5∞ Milić—Pirc, Beograd 1952; **8. ♗e2** ♗e7 9. 0—0 0—0 10. ♖ad1 ♘e5 [10... ♕b6 11. ♘c6 bc6 12. ♕g3 ♖a7 13. ♖d3 ♖d7 14. ♕h4 ♖e8 15. ♖g3±→ Geler—Ilivicki, SSSR 1947; 10... ♘d4 11. ♕d4 ♕a5 12. ♕d2 ♕c5 13. ♗f6± Kan—Fridštejn, SSSR 1948; 10... ♕c7 11. ♔h1 ♘d4 12. ♕d4 (Kan—Ščerbakov, SSSR (ch) 1955) ♖d8△ b5=] 11. ♕g3 ♘h5 12. ♗e7 ♘g3 13. ♗d8 ♘e2 14. ♘de2 ♖d8= Keres—Boleslavski, SSSR 1947; 11. ♕h3!? Keres

20 **10... ♕c7** 11. ♘b3 ♘e5?! 12. ♕d2 0—0 13. f4 ♘c6 14. e5 de5 15. fe5 ♘d5 16. ♘d5 ed5 17. ♗f6!±→ Platz—Szily, Helsinki (ol) 1952; 11... 0—0!?; **10... ♖c8** 11. ♘b3 0—0 12. ♕g3 ♔h8 13. f4± Marić—Matulović, Jugoslavija (ch) 1956

21 11. ♘b3 b5 12. a3 ♘e5 13. ♕g3 ♘c4 14. ♗c4 bc4 15. ♘d4 ♕c7∞ Marić—Ivkov, Jugoslavija (ch) 1957

22 13. f4!?

23 16. ♖fe1 ♗e2 17. ♖e2 d5= Keres—Stahlberg, Budapest (ct) 1950

24 9. ♘b3 a5! 10. a3 [10. ♗f6? ♗f6 11. ♕d6 ♕d6 12. ♖d6 a4△ a3∓; 10. a4!?] a4 11. ♘d4 h6 12. ♗h4 ♕b6! [12... ♗d7? 13. ♘db5 ♘e5 14. ♕d2 ♗b5 15. ♗b5 ♕a5 16. ♕e2 ♖fc8 17. ♖d4!± Keres—Boleslavski, SSSR 1950] 13. ♘db5?! ♘g4! 14. ♗e7 ♘e7 15. ♕d6 ♘c6 16. ♕c7 ♕f2∓ Toluš—Geler, SSSR 1950; 13. ♗e2 ♘e5!∓; 13. ♕d5∞

25 **9... d5** 10. e5 ♘d7 11. h4 ♘c5 12. ♕e3 a6 13. g4± Dimc—Barden, Bognor Regis 1958; **9... ♗d7** 10. ♘b3 ♕b6 11. a3 ♖fd8 12. ♕g3 a5 13. ♗d3 a4 14. ♘d2± Janošević—Bradvarević, Jugoslavija (ch) 1957; **9... e5**!?

26 **10. h4**?! ♘d4 11. ♕d4 hg5 — B 65; **10. ♗h4** ♘d4 11. ♕d4± — B 65

27 11. ♗f6 ♗f6 12. ♕d6 — B 64

28 14. ♗h6 ♘h5 15. ♕f3 ♘f6=

29 Janošević—Ivkov, Jugoslavija (ch) 1957

30 8... h6 9. ♗h4 [9. ♗f6 ♗f6 10. ♘db5 0—0 11. ♕d6 a6 12. ♕d8 ♖d8 13. ♘a3 b5∓ Troianescu—Geler, Sczawno Zdroj 1950] 0—0 10. ♖d1 ♕b6 11. 0—0 ♘e5 12. ♕b5 ♕c7 13. f4 a6 14. ♕b3 ♘c6 15. ♕c4 d5= Mnacakanjan—Liberzon, SSSR 1965

31 9... ♘d4 10. ♕d4 ♘e4 11. ♘e4 [11. ♗e7 ♘c3 12. ♕h4 ♘e2 13. ♔h1 ♕b6∓] ♗g5 12. ♘g5 — 6. ♗e2

32 **10. ♗h4** ♘d4 11. ♕d4 ♘e4∓; **10. ♗c1** ♔h8 11. a3 ♘d4 12. ♕d4 ♗d7= Keres—Bronštejn, Budapest (ct) 1950

33 Toluš—Tajmanov, SSSR 1950

34 9... d5 10. ed5 ♘b4 11. ♕g3 ♘bd5 12. ♘d5 [12. ♗h6 ♘e8 13. ♘f5 ♗f6∞] ♘d5 13.

♗e7 ♕e7 14. 0—0 e5= Keres—Aronin, SSSR (ch) 1951

35 11... ♘e4? 12. ♘e4 ♗g5 13. ♕d6 ♗c6 14. ♕g3±

36 **12. f4**? h6 13. ♗h4 ♘e4 14. ♘e4 ♗h4 15. ♘d6 ♗f6 16. ♕f2 ♕c7 17. b3 ♗e7 18. ♘c4 ♗e4∓ Barda—Boleslavski, Bucuresti 1953; **12. e5** de5 13. ♕e5 ♘d7 14. ♗e7 ♘e5 15. ♗d8 ♖fd8= Randvir—Bondarevski, SSSR 1949

37 13... h6 14. ♗h4 e5 15. fe5 de5 16. ♕e3 ♖ad8 17. ♗c4± Holmov—Boleslavski, SSSR (ch) 1949

38 Averbah—Fridštejn, SSSR 1949

B 63

1. e4 c5 2. ♘f3 d6 3. d4 cd4 4. ♘d4 ♘f6 5. ♘c3 ♘c6 6. ♗g5 e6 7. ♕d2

	7	8	9	10	11	12	13	14	15	
1	...	♗f6[1]	♖d1[2]	♗e2	0—0	♘b3[3]	♔h1	f4		±
	h6	gf6	a6	h5	♗d7	♕c7[4]	0-0-0			
2	...	...	0-0-0	f4[5]	♗e2[6]	♔b1	♖hf1[9]	♘b3	♖f3	±
	...	...	a6	♗d7	h5[7]	♕c7[8]	0-0-0[10]	♔b8	♗e7[11]	
3	...	♖d1[12]	♗e2	♕d4	♗d2[15]	0—0	♗e3	f4	♗f3	=
	♗e7	0—0[13]	♘d4	♕a5[14]	♕c7	♖d8	♗d7	♗c6	b5[16]	
4	...	0-0-0	♕d4	e5[18]	♕e5	h4[20]	♖h3	♕c7	♘b5	±
	...	♘d4[17]	0—0	de5	♗d7[19]	♖c8	♕c7[21]	♖c7	♗b5[22]	

1. e4 c5 2. ♘f3 d6 3. d4 cd4 4. ♘d4 ♘f6 5. ♘c3 ♘c6 6. ♗g5 e6 7. ♕d2 ♗e7 8. 0-0-0 0—0

	9	10	11	12	13	14	15	16	17	
5	♗e2[23]	♕d4	♗d2[25]	f4	♕f2	♗f3	♖he1			∓
	♘d4[24]	♕a5	♕c7	♖d8	♗d7	♗c6	b5[26]			
6	♘db5	♗f6	♘d6[27]	f4[28]	♕d5	f5	♘db5	♕c4[32]	ef5[34]	=
	♕a5	♗f6	♖d8	e5![29]	♕c7[30]	♘d4[31]	♕a5	♗f5![33]	♖ac8[35]	
7	♘b3	♗f6[37]	♗e2[39]	♗h5	f4	♔b1	f5	♖hf1	♘e2	∞
	a6[36]	gf6[38]	♔h8	♗d7	b5	♕b6	♖ac8	a5	b4[40]	
8	...	f3[41]	♗e3[42]	♕f2![43]	♘b5[45]	g4	♘5d4	♘d4		±
	♕b6	♖d8	♕c7	♘d7[44]	♕b8	a6	♘d4[46]			
9	...	...	g4	♗e3	g5	h4	g6!?[47]	h5	♖h5	=∞
	...	a6	♖d8	♕c7	♘d7	b5	fg6[48]	gh5	♘f6[49]	
10	...	...	...	♗e3[50]	g5[51]	f4[52]	♕f2[53]	♗d2[55]		∞
	...	...	♕c7	b5	♘d7	♘b6	♘a4[54]			

1 8. ♗e3?! ♘g4∓

2 9. ♗e2 a6? 10. ♗h5 ♗e7 11. f4 ♕a5 12. g4!△ f5±; 9... h5±

3 12. ♔h1 ♕c7 [12... ♕b6 13. ♘b3 ♗e7 14. f4 h4 15. ♘a4± Larsen—Botvinik, Moskva (ol) 1956] 13. f4 0-0-0±

4 12... ♕b6 13. ♘a4 ♕a7 [13... ♕c7 14. ♕e3 0-0-0 15. ♘b6 ♔b8 16. ♘d7 ♖d7 17. f4± Ivkov—Petrosjan, Beograd 1954] 14. c4 0-0-0 15. ♕c3 ♘e5 16. ♕a5 ♗a4 17. ♕a4 ♗e7 18. ♘d4± Dückstein—Nievergelt, Zürich 1959

5 **10. ♘c6**?! bc6 11. f4 ♕a5 12. ♗c4 ♗e7 13. ♖he1 ♖b8∞ Simagin—Petrosjan, SSSR (ch) 1955; **10. ♗e2** h5 11. ♔b1 ♕b6 12. h4 ♗d7 13. f4 ♕d4 14. ♕d4 ♘d4 15. ♖d4 0-0-0 16. ♗f3 ♗e7 17. ♘e2 ♖dg8 18. ♖hd1± Keres—R. Byrne, SSSR—USA 1955

6 11. ♗c4 h5 [11... ♕b6 12. f5?! ♕d4 13. ♕d4 ♘d4 14. ♖d4 h5 15. ♗e2 ♗h6= Seidman—R. Byrne, USA (ch) 1961; 12. ♔b1±] 12. ♔b1 ♕b6 [12... b5 13. ♗b3 ♘a5 14. f5 ♘b3 15. ab3 b4 16. fe6 fe6 17. ♘ce2± Aronin—Sohor, SSSR 1956] 13. ♖hf1 ♕d4 14. ♕d4 ♘d4 15. ♖d4 ♖c8 16. ♗b3 ♖g8 17. ♖d2± Suetin—Botvinik, SSSR (ch) 1952

7 11... ♕b6 12. ♗h5 ♕d4 13. ♕d4 ♘d4 14. ♖d4 ♖g8 15. g3 ♗e7 16. ♖f1 ♗c6 17.

f5 ♖g5 18. ♗e2±⊥ Bondarevski—Botvinik, SSSR (ch) 1951

8 12... ♕b6 13. ♘b3 [13. ♖hf1 ♕d4 14. ♕d4 ♘d4 15. ♖d4 h4 16. f5 ♖c8 17. ♖d3± Keres—Petrosjan, Amsterdam (ct) 1956] 0-0-0 14. ♖hf1 [14. h4 ♔b8 15. ♗f3 ♘a5 16. ♘a5 ♕a5 17. ♖he1 ♗e7 18. f5± Vasjukov—Livšin, SSSR 1956] ♘a5 [14... ♗e7 15. ♖f3 ♖dg8 16. ♗f1 ♔b8 17. ♖d3 ♗c8 18. a3 h4 19. ♘a4 ♕c7 (Talj—Nievergelt, Zürich 1959) 20. ♕e3±] 15. ♖f3 ♘b3 16. ab3 ♔b8 17. ♘a4± Keres—Botvinik, Moskva 1956

9 13. ♘b3 0-0-0 14. h4!? ♘e7 15. f5 ef5?! 16. ♘d5 ♘d5 17. ed5 ♖e8 18. ♖h3 ♔b8 19. ♘d4± Cobo—R. Byrne, USA 1958; 15... ♗c6!?±

10 13... ♗e7 14. ♖f3 ♘d4 15. ♕d4 ♕c5 16. ♕d2 ♗c6 17. ♖e3 ♕a5 [17... 0-0-0 18. ♘d5±; 17... h4!?] 18. a3 [18. ♗f3= Bronštejn—Botvinik (m) 1951; 18. f5!±] ♖d8 19. ♗c4 ♗d7 20. ♕e2 ♖c8 21. ♗a2 ♔f8 22. f5± Liberzon—Botvinik, SSSR 1967 — 3/451

11 16. ♖h3 h4 17. ♕e1 f5!? 18. ef5 d5 19. ♕f1± Vasjukov—Šamkovič, Dubna 1973 — 16/374

12 **8. ♗f6** ♗f6 [8... gf6 9. 0-0-0 a6 10. f4 ♗d7 11. g3 ♕b6 12. ♘b3 0-0-0∞ Kozomara—Simonović, Jugoslavija (ch) 1951] 9. ♘db5 0—0 10. ♘d6 ♕a5 11. ♘c4 ♕c5 12. ♕d6 ♕g5 13. ♕g3 [15. f4?! ♕h6 16. ♕d2 ♖d8 17. ♗d3 ♗h4∓] ♕c5 14. ♕d6= Fuderer—Gligorić, Jugoslavija (ch) 1951; 10. 0-0-0 ♕a5 — 8. 0-0-0; **8. f4** ♕b6 9. ♘c6 [9. ♘b3 h6 10. ♗h4 ♘e4=] bc6 10. e5 de5 11. fe5 ♘d5 12. ♘d5 cd5 13. ♗e7 ♕b2? 14. ♗d6 ♕a1 15. ♔f2 ♕b2 16. ♕g5!+— Gusev—Petkevič, SSSR 1965; 13... ♔e7!?∞; 8... ♘d4 9. ♕d4 0—0 10. 0-0-0 — B 65

13 8... a6 9. ♗e2 0—0 10. 0—0 ♕b6 11. ♘b3 [11. ♗e3 ♕c7 12. f4 ♘a5 13. ♘b3 ♘c4 14. ♗c4 ♕c4 15. ♕d4 ♕c7 16. ♕b6 ♕b8△ ♘d7∞ Lublinski—Boleslavski, SSSR (ch) 1949] ♖d8 12. a3 ♕c7 13. ♕e3 b5 14. ♕g3 b4 15. ab4 ♘b4 ♖d2= Lublinski—Bronštejn, SSSR (ch) 1949

14 10... ♗d7 11. ♗f6 ♗f6 12. ♕d6 ♗c6=∞

15 11. ♕d2 ♖d8 12. 0—0 ♕c7 13. ♘b5?! ♕c6 14. e5 ♘e4 15. ♗e7 ♘d2 16. ♖d2 ♖d7 17. ed6 a6 18. ♘c7 ♖a7 19. ♖fd1 b5∓ Trajković—Dünnhaupt, corr. 1963; 13. ♗d3=

16 16. a3 d5 17. ed5 ♘d5= Bihovski—Bradvarević, Kislovodsk 1964

17 8... a6 9. ♗f6 [9. f4 ♕c7 10. ♘f3?! b5 11. ♗d3 ♗b7 12. e5 de5 13. fe5 ♘e5 14. ♘e5 ♕e5 15. ♗b5 ab5 16. ♗f6 ♗f6 17. ♕d7 ♔f8 18. ♕b7 ♖b8∓ Suetin—Mojsejev, SSSR (ch) 1951; 10. ♗e2 0—0 11. ♗f3 ♖d8 12. g4 ♖b8 13. ♕g2 ♗d7 14. ♗h4 ♘d4 15. ♖d4 b5 16. g5 ♘e8 17. f5 b4∞ Gruzman—Belinkov, SSSR 1963] gf6 11. ♗e2 h5 12. ♔b1± Milić—Stahlberg, Beverwijk 1963

18 **10. ♗f6?** ♗f6 11. ♕d6 ♕a5∓; **10. f4** — B 65

19 **11... ♘d7?** 12. ♗e7 ♔e7 13. ♕c7±; **11... ♕b6** 12. ♗e3 ♘g4 [12... ♕b4? 13. a3 ♕h4 14. g3 ♕h5 15. ♕c7+—] 13. ♗b6 ♘e5 14. ♗c7 ♘g4 15. ♗g3 ♘f6 16. ♗b5! a6 17. ♗e2 b5 18. ♗f3 ♖a7 19. ♗d6±⊥ Vasjukov—Boleslavski, SSSR 1957; **11... ♕e8** 12. ♗b5 ♗d7 13. ♗d7 [13. ♘e4 ♗b5 14. ♘f6 ♗f6 15. ♗f6 gf6 16. ♕f6 e5 17. ♕g5=] ♘d7 14. ♕g3 ♗g5 15. ♕g5 ♘f6 16. ♖d3 h6 17. ♕g3 ♖d8 18. ♖d8 ♕d8 19. ♖d1 ♕e7 20. ♕d6 ♕d6 21. ♖d6 ♖c8= Šamkovič—Henkin, SSSR 1962; 12. ♗d3±

20 12. ♗d3 ♘g4 13. ♗e7 ♘e5 14. ♗d8 ♖fd8 15. ♗e4 ♗c6= Gufeljd—Osnos, SSSR (ch) 1963

21 13... ♖c5?! 14. ♕e3 ♕c8 15. ♖g3 [15. ♖d7!? ♕d7 16. ♗f6 gf6 17. ♘e4 ♖e5 18. ♗d3 ♔h8 19. ♕h6 ♖e4 20. ♗e4 f5= Korčnoj—Furman, SSSR (ch) 1958] ♔h8 16. ♔b1 ♕c6 17. h5 ♖g8 18. h6± Žilin—Furman, SSSR 1958

22 16. ♗b5±

23 **9. ♔b1** h6 10. ♗f6 ♗f6 11. ♘b3 ♕b6 12. f4 a5 13. ♘a4 ♕c7 14. g4 [14. ♕d6? ♖d8 15. ♕c7 ♖d1△ ♗d8—+] ♘b4 [14... ♖d8 15. h4 d5 16. e5 ♗e7 (Bivšev—Boleslavski, SSSR (ch) 1952) 17. g5±] 15. c3 [15. a3 ♗d7 16. ab4 ♗a4 17. ♘a5 ♖fc8∓→] ♗d7 16. cb4 ♗a4 17. ♖c1 ♗c6!∓; **9. ♗f6** ♗f6 10. ♘c6 bc6 11. ♕d6 ♕b6! [11... ♕a5 12. ♗c4 ♗a6 13. ♗a6 ♗c3 14. bc3 ♕a6 15. ♖d4 ♕a2 16. ♖hd1 ♕a5∓ Keres—Heinicke 1936; 12. ♕g3 ♗c3 13. ♕c3 ♕a2 14. ♗c4 ♕a4 15. ♔b1 ♖b8 16. ♖d3 ♕b4 17. ♕b4 ♖b4 18. b3 a5∓] 12. ♕g3 ♖b8 13. b3 ♗c3 [13... ♗d4 14. f4 ♕c5 15. ♘b1!∞ Euwe] 14. ♕c3 ♕f2∓; **9. f3** ♕b6 10. ♘b3 — 9. ♘b3

24 9... a6 10. ♘b3 ♕b6 11. ♗e3 ♕c7 12. f4 b5 13. ♗f3 ♘d7 14. ♕f2 ♖b8 15. ♔b1 ♘b6∓ Konstantinopoljski—Boleslavski, SSSR (ch) 1945

25 **11. f4** h6 12. h4 e5 13. ♕f2 ef4 14. ♗f4 ♗e6 15. ♕g3 ♔h8 16. ♖d4 b5!∓→ Bivšev—Liskov, SSSR 1951; **11. ♕d2** h6 12. ♗e3 b5 13. ♗b5 ♘e4 14. ♘e4 ♕b5 15. ♘d6 ♕a4∓→; **11. h4** ♗d7 12. ♗d2 ♕e5 13. ♕e3 ♗c6= Tajmanov—Averbah, Stockholm 1952; 12... ♕c7∓

26 Hooper—Gligorić, Hastings 1951/52

27 11. ♕d6? ♗g5 12. ♔b1 ♖d8 13. ♕a3 ♖d1 14. ♘d1 ♕d2—+

28 **12. ♕e3?** ♗d4! 13. ♖d4 ♘d4 14. ♕d4 e5△ ♕c5∓; **12. ♕e1?** ♘b4! 13. ♘c4 ♘a2 14. ♘a2 ♖d1 15. ♕d1 ♕a2∓

29 12... ♗e7 13. e5 ♘e5 14. fe5 ♖d6 15. ed6 ♗g5 16. ♗b5 ♕d8 17. d7 ♗d7 18. ♗d7± Mendes—Pietzsch, Helsinki (ol) 1952

30 13... ♕d5 14. ed5 ♖d6 15. ♘e4 ♖d8 16. dc6 ♖d1 17. ♔d1 ♗g4 18. ♗e2 ♖d8 19. ♔e1 ♗e2 20. ♔e2±

31 14... a6? 15. ♗c4 ♖d7 16. ♕c5! (△ ♘e8) ♗e7 17. ♘d5 ♕d6 18. ♕d6 ♗d6 19. ♘b6+− Gligorić, Sokolov

32 16. ♕c5 (Flor) a6! 17. b4 b6 18. ♕d4 ed4 19. ba5 ab5 20. ♘d5 ♖a5 21. ♘f6 gf6 22. ♔b2 ♗b7 23. ♗d3 ♖da8∓

33 1/2 : 1/2 Korčnoj–Boleslavski, SSSR (ch) 1952

34 17. b4 ♕b6! [17... ♕a6 18. ♘d4 ♕c4 19. ♗c4 ed4 20. ef5 dc3=] 18. ♘d4 ed4 19. ♘d5 ♖d5 20. ♕d5 ♗g4 21. ♕b5 ♕c7 22. ♗d3 ♗d1 23. ♖d1 ♖c8∓ Sadomski–Dubinin, corr. 1955

35 18. ♕a4 ♕a4 19. ♘a4 ♘b3 20. ab3 ♗g5 21. ♖d2! [21. ♔b1 ♖d1 22. ♔a2 ♖c2∓] a6 [21... ♖d2 22. ♘bc3∞] 22. ♘bc3 ♗d2 23. ♔b1 ♗c3 [23... b5 24. ♘b6 ♖c3! 25. bc3 ♗e3=] 24. ♘c3 ♖c3 25. bc3 ♖d1 26. ♔b2 e4 27. h4=

36 **9... ♘a5**? 10. ♔b1 ♘b3 11. ab3 ♘e8 12. ♗e7 ♕e7 13. ♘b5± Aljehin–Friedmann, Podebrady 1936; **9... a5** 10. a4! ♕b6 11. ♕e3 ♕b4 12. f3 h6 13. h4!± Alexander–Gligorić, England 1951

37 10. f4? ♕c7 11. ♗d3 b5 12. ♖he1 b4 13. ♘e2 e5 14. f5 a5∓ Kondratjev–Bondarevski, SSSR 1952

38 10... ♗f6 11. ♕d6 ♕b6 12. f4 [12. ♕c5 ♕c7 13. ♕d6= Aronin–Boleslavski, SSSR 1949] ♗e7 [12... ♗c3 13. bc3 ♕e3 14. ♔b2 ♕e4? 15. ♗d3△ ♗h7, ♕f8+−] 13. **♕d2** a5 14. a4 ♖d8 15. ♗d3± Šapošnikov–Boleslavski, SSSR 1950

39 **11. ♕h6** ♔h8 12. ♖d3 ♖g8 13. ♖h3 ♖g7∞; **11. ♔b1** ♔h8 12. f4 b5 13. g3 ♕b6 14. ♗g2 b4 15. ♘e2 e5∞ Jovčić–Ostojić, Jugoslavija 1961

40 18. ♘f4 a4 19. ♘c1 ♘e5∞ Talj–Larsen (m) 1969 — 7/383

41 **10. ♗f6**? ♗f6 11. ♘a4 [11. ♕d6 ♕f2∓] ♕c7 12. f4 [12. ♕d6?? ♗g5 13. ♔b1 ♖d8−+] ♖d8 13. g4 a6 14. g5 ♗e7 15. h4 b5 16. ♘c3 b4 17. ♘e2 a5∓ Suetin–Tajmanov, SSSR 1951; **10. f4** ♖d8 11. ♕e1 a6 [11... ♘g4 12. ♗e7 ♘e7 13. h3 ♘f2 14. ♘a4 ♕c6 15. ♕f2 ♕a4 16. ♔b1!± Goldin–Ilivicki, SSSR 1951] 12. ♗d3 ♕c7 13. ♖g1 b5 14. g4 b4 15. ♘e2 a5 16. ♘bd4 ♘d4 17. ♘d4 ♕c5 18. ♘f3 ♗a6∓ Goldin–Tajmanov, SSSR 1951; **10. ♗e3** ♕c7 11. f3 [11. ♘b5 ♕d8 12. f3 a6 13. ♘5d4 e5 14. ♘e2 a5 15. ♔b1 a4∓] a6 12. g4 — 10. f3

42 **11. ♘b5** ♖d7! 12. ♗e3 [12. c4 d5!∓ Suetin–Ilivicki, SSSR 1952] ♕d8 13. ♘5d4 ♘d4 14. ♘d4 e5 15. ♘f5 d5= Simagin–Gurvič, SSSR 1965; **11. g4** d5! 12. ed5 [12. ♗f6 de4∓] ♘d5 13. ♗e7 ♘de7 14. ♗d3 e5= Holmov–Tajmanov, SSSR (ch) 1959; **11. ♕e1** a6 12. h4 [12. ♗e3 ♕c7 13. g4 b5 14. g5 ♘e8 15. f4 ♗f8 16. ♕f2 ♖b8 17. h4 ♘a5∓ Milić–Kupper, Opatija 1953] ♕c7 13. h5 h6 14. ♗e3 b5 15. ♕f2 ♖b8 16. g4 ♘e5∞ Reshevsky–Saidy, USA (ch) 1967 — 3/453

43 12. ♘b5 ♕b8 13. c4 a6 14. ♘c3 ♕c7△ ♘e5∞

44 12... d5 13. ed5 ♘d5 [13... ed5 14. ♘b5 ♕b8 15. ♕g3! ♕g3 16. hg3 a6 17. ♘5d4 ♘e5 18. g4± Milić–Bogdanović, Jugoslavija (ch) 1953] 14. ♘d5 ♖d5 [14... ed5 15. g4 ♗e6 16. ♘d4 ♘d4 17. ♗d4 ♖ac8 18. c3± Spaski–Kozma, Lyon 1955; 16... ♖ac8 17. ♔b1 ♕a5 18. g5 ♘d4 19. ♗d4 ♗f5 20. ♗d3 ♗d3 21. ♖d3± Talj–Savon, SSSR (ch) 1962] 15. ♖d5 ed5 16. g4 ♗e6 17. ♘d4 ♖c8 18. ♔b1 ♗f6 19. ♘e6?! fe6 20. g5? ♗b2! 21. ♔b2 ♘b4! ∓→ Jimenez–Pomar, La Habana (ol) 1966; 19. c3±

45 **13. ♔b1** a6 14. g4 [14. ♘a4 b5 15. ♘b6 ♖b8 16. ♘c8 ♖dc8= Đurašević–Ivkov, Jugoslavija (ch) 1958] b5 15. g5 b4 16. ♘a4 ♘ce5= Tarasov–Ilivicki, SSSR 1963; **13. g4** a6 14. g5 ♘ce5 [14... b5 15. f4 ♘c5 16. ♘c5 dc5 17. ♖d8 ♘d8 18. e5± Spaski–Klages, Anvers 1955] 15. h4 b5 16. ♔b1 b4 17. ♘e2 ♘c4 18. ♗c1 e5∞ Altšuler–Sadomski, corr. 1965

46 15... ♘de5 16. g5 d5 17. ed5 ed5 18. h4 ♘c4 19. ♘c6 bc6 20. ♗c5± Fischer–Benkö, USA (ch) 1959/60

47 15. f4 ♘c5 16. ♗g2 b4 17. ♘e2 a5 18. ♘bd4 ♗b7∞ Đurašević–Bogdanović, Jugoslavija (ch) 1952

48 **15... ♘c5** 16. gf7 ♔f7 17. ♗h3 ♘a4 [17... ♘b4!?△ 18. f4? ♘a2!∓] 18. f4 ♘b4 19. f5± Talj–Stoltz, 1959; **15... hg6** 16. h5 gh5 17. ♖h5 ♘f6 18. ♖h1 d5 19. e5 ♘e5 20. ♕h2$\overline{\infty}$ Talj–Koblenc, SSSR 1957

49 18. ♖g5 ♘e5 19. ♕g2 ♗f8 20. ♗e2 [20. f4 ♘c4 21. ♗c4 bc4 22. ♘d4 ♖b8 23. ♖g1 ♖b7∞ Spaski–Boleslavski, SSSR (ch) 1958; 23. ♖h1!?; 20... ♘f7!?] ♘c4 21. ♗c4 bc4 23. ♘d4 ♖b8 24. ♖h1△ ♖h6$\overline{\infty}$ Talj–Mohrlock, Varna (ol) 1962

50 12. ♗f6 ♗f6 13. ♕d6 ♕b6$\overline{\infty}$

51 13. ♕f2 b4 14. ♘e2 a5 15. ♔b1 a4 16. ♘bd4 ♗a6 17. ♘c6 ♕c6 18. ♘d4 ♕b7 19. h4 d5!∓ Fichtl–Vasjukov, Berlin 1962

52 14. h4 ♘b6 15. a3 ♘e5 16. ♗b6 ♕b6 17. f4 ♘c4 18. ♕d4 ♕d4 19. ♘d4 [Vasjukov–Filipowicz, Budapest 1965] ♗d7=

53 15. f5 b4 16. ♘b1 ♘e5 17. f6 gf6 18. gf6 ♗f6 19. ♗g5 ♗g7 20. ♖g1 ♘g6 21. ♗h6 ♗e5! 22. h4 [22. ♗f8 ♔f8 23. ♕h6 ♔g8 24. h4 ♗b7 25. h5 ♖c8 26. ♗d3 d5 27. ♖df1 ♗g7 28. ♕e3 de4∓] ♗b7 23. h5 ♖fc8 24. hg6 hg6

25. ♕e2 ♘a4∓ Polugajevski–Boleslavski, SSSR (ch) 1958

[54] 15... ♖b8 16. h4 ♘a4 17. ♗d2 ♘c3 18. ♗c3 b4 19. ♗d2 a5∞ Nežmetdinov–Tajmanov, SSSR 1951

[55] **16. ♘a4?!** ba4 17. ♗b6 ♕b7 18. ♘a5 ♘a5 19. ♗a5 ♗d7 20. ♗c3 ♖fc8 21. ♕d4 ♖c3!∓ Milev–Boleslavski, Bucuresti 1953; **16. ♗d2**∞

B 64

1. e4 c5 2. ♘f3 d6 3. d4 cd4 4. ♘d4 ♘f6 5. ♘c3 ♘c6 6. ♗g5 e6 7. ♕d2 ♗e7 8. 0-0-0 0—0 9. f4

	9	10	11	12	13	14	15	16	17	
1	...	e5[1]	♘c6	fe5	h4	♕e3	♖h3	♗e7	♖g3	±
	a6	de5	bc6[2]	♘d7	♖b8	♖e8	♕a5	♖e7	♖e8[3]	
2	...	e5	h4	♗e2[5]	♔b1	♘cb5	♘d6	♗e7	♕e3	=
	d5	♘d7	♘b6[4]	♗d7	♖c8	a6	♖c7	♕e7	♘c8[6]	
3	...	...	♗e7	♘f3[7]	♕e1[8]	♗d3	ef6	g3	♕d2	±
	...	...	♕e7	♘b6	♗d7	f5[9]	♕f6	♖ae8[10]	e5[11]	
4	...	...	♘f3	♗d3	♔b1	♘e2	♗e7	♘ed4	♖he1[13]	±
	...	...	♘b6[12]	♗d7	♖c8	♘a4	♕e7	a6		
5	...	♘f3[14]	h3[16]	gf3	fe5[17]	f4[18]	fe5	ef6	♖d2	=
	e5	♗g4[15]	♗f3	♘d4	de5	♘e6[19]	♘g5	♕d2	♗f6	
6	...	♘f5	ef5	♔b1	♗f6	♘d5	♘f6	♖d2	g4	±
	...	♗f5	♖c8[20]	♕a5[21]	♗f6	♕d2	gf6	♖fd8		

1. e4 c5 2. ♘f3 d6 3. d4 cd4 4. ♘d4 ♘f6 5. ♘c3 ♘c6 6. ♗g5 e6 7. ♕d2 ♗e7 8. 0-0-0 0—0 9. f4 h6

	10	11	12	13	14	15	16	17	18	
7	♗h4[22]	♗e7[24]	♗d8	♘c6	♗e7	♖hf1	♖d6	g3[25]	♖fd1	±
	♘e4[23]	♘d2	♘f1	bc6	♖e8	♖e7	♗b7	c5	g5[26]	
8	...	♘f5	ef5	♔b1[28]	♗f6	♘d5	♖d2[29]	♘f6	♗e2[30]	±
	e5	♗f5	♕a5[27]	♖ad8	♗f6	♕d2	ef4	gf6	♖fe8[31]	

[1] 10. ♗f6?! ♗f6 11. ♘c6 bc6 12. ♕d6 ♕b6 13. ♕d2 [13. e5 ♖d8 14. ♕a3 ♕e3 15. ♔b1 ♖d1△ ♕a3, ♗e7=] ♖b8 14. b3 ♕a5 15. ♔b2 ♖d8 16. ♗d3 ♗d4 17. ♗c4 [Fuderer–Heinicke, Jugoslavija–BRD 1954] c5=∞

[2] 11... ♕d2 12. ♖d2 bc6 13. fe5 ♘d5 14. ♗e7 ♘e7 15. ♗d3±

[3] 18. ♖d7 ♗d7 19. ♗d3± Keres–Szabo, SSSR–Hungary 1955

[4] 11... a6 12. ♘f3 f6 13. ef6 ♘f6 14. ♗d3± Štejn–Tajmanov, Sarajevo 1967 — 3/455

[5] **12. g4** ♗d7 13. ♘cb5 [13. ♗e7 ♕e7 14. g5 ♖ac8 15. h5 ♘a5 16. ♘d5 ♘d5 17. ♕a5 ♘f4∓ Diez del Corral–Korčnoj, Hastings 1955/56] f6 14. ef6 ♗f6 15. ♖e1 ♘a4! 16. ♗f6 ♕f6 17. g5 ♕f4 18. ♕f4 ♖f4 19. ♘e6 ♖f2∓ Bivšev–Talj, SSSR 1956; **12. ♕e1** ♗d7 13. g4 ♖c8 14. ♖h3 [Bivšev–Fajbisovič, SSSR 1972 — 14/419] a6!△ ♘a5∞; **12. ♕e3** ♗d7 13. ♗e7 ♕e7 14. h5 ♘a5∓ Kuijpers–Minev, Halle 1967 — 3/456; 14. ♘b3=

[6] 18. ♘c8 ♖fc8 19. ♗d3 ♘d4 20. ♕d4 ♗b5= Kashdan–Tajmanov, USA–SSSR 1955

[7] **12. ♗b5** ♘d4 13. ♕d4 ♘b6?! 14. ♖he1 ♗d7 [Santacruz–Korčnoj, La Habana (ol) 1966 — 2/398] 15. ♗d3±; 13... ♕c5=; **12. g3** ♘b6 13. ♕e1 ♗d7 14. ♔b1 ♖ac8 15. ♗e2∞ Unzicker–Szabo, Bamberg 1968 — 5/415; **12. g4** ♘d4 [12... ♘b6 13. g5 ♗d7 14. ♖g1 ♖ac8 15. ♖g3 ♘a5 16. ♕f2 g6 17. ♖h3± Söderberg–Olafsson 1957] 13. ♕d4 ♕c5=

[8] 13. ♗d3 ♗d7 14. ♕e2?! h6 15. ♔b1 ♘a5 16. ♖de1 ♖fc8 17. ♘d1 ♘ac4∓ Suetin–Lejn, SSSR (ch) 1967 — 3/457; 14. ♕e1!?

9 14... h6 15. g4 f6 16. h4 ♕b4 17. ♘e2 ♕e1 18. ♖de1 fe5 19. ♘e5 ♘e5 20. fe5 [Suetin—Vasjukov, SSSR (ch) 1967 — 3/452] ♘c4=; 15. h4±

10 16... h6 17. h4 ♖ae8 [O'Kelly—Talj, Palma de Mallorca 1966 — 2/399] 18. ♘g5!±

11 18. ♘e5 ♘e5 19. fe5 ♖e5 20. ♖hf1 ♕e7 21. ♖f8 ♕f8 22. ♖f1 ♕e7 23. ♕f4± Matanović—Minev, Maribor 1967 — 4/497

12 11... ♗g5!?

13 Matulović—Radulov, Wijk aan Zee 1974 — 18/397

14 **10. ♘db5** ♗g4 11. ♗e2 ♗e2 12. ♕e2 a6 13. ♗f6 ab5 14. ♗e7 ♕e7∓; **10. ♘b3** a5!?; **10. ♘c6** bc6 11. fe5 de5 12. ♕d8 ♖d8 13. ♖d8 ♗d8 14. ♗c4 ♗e7 15. h3 ♗d7 16. ♖d1 ♗e8= Kotov—Geler, Zürich (ct) 1953

15 10... ef4 11. ♗f4 ♗e6 12. ♗d6 ♗d6 13. ♕d6 ♕b6 14. ♗d3 ♖ac8 15. ♖he1 ♖fd8 16. ♕a3 ♘b4∞̅ Kagan—Burnevski, SSSR 1964

16 11. ♗e2 ♖c8 12. ♔b1 ♗f3 13. gf3 ♘d4 14. ♖hg1 [14. ♖dg1 ♘e6 15. ♗f6 ♗f6 16. fe5 de5 17. ♘d5 ♘f4= Štejn—Kestler, SSSR—BRD 1965] ♔h8 15. ♖g2 ♘h5= Stoljar—Ilivicki, SSSR 1954

17 13. ♕g2 ♖c8 14. ♖g1 g6 15. ♗d3 ♘e6 16. fe5 de5 17. f4 ♖c3∓

18 14. ♖g1 ♖c8 [14... ♘f3 15. ♕f2 ♕b6 16. ♗e3 ♘d4 17. ♖d4 ed4 18. ♗d4 ♕d8 19. ♘d5 ♘e8 20. ♕g3± Korčnoj—Geler, SSSR (ch) 1954] 15. ♗h6 [15. ♗e2 ♖c3 16. ♗f6 ♗f6 17. bc3 ♗e7 18. ♔b1 ♕b6 19. ♔a1 ♘e2 20. ♕e2 ♗a3 21. ♖b1 ♗b2∓ Karaklajić—Joppen, Beograd 1954] g6 16. f4 [16. ♗f8 ♕f8∓→《] ♕a5∓ Jovčić—Kažić, corr. 1954

19 **14... ♕a5** 15. fe5 ♘f3 16. ef6 ♗f6 17. ♗f6 ♘d2 18. ♖g1±; **14... ♘c6** 15. ♕g2 ♕a5 16. ♗h6±

20 11... ♕a5 12. ♔b1 ♖ad8 [12... ♖ac8 — 11... ♖c8] 13. ♗c4! h6 14. ♗f6 ♗f6 15. ♘d5± Talj—Calvo, La Habana (ol) 1966 — 2/400

21 **12... ♖e8** 13. ♗d3 [13. ♗e2 e4 14. ♖he1 ♕b6 15. ♗c4± Radulov—Diez del Corral, Montilla 1974 — 18/396] d5 14. fe5 ♘e5 15. ♗f6 ♗f6 16. ♗b5 ♕b6 17. ♕d5± Matanović—Diez del Corral, Palma de Mallorca 1968 — 6/511; **12... ♘d4** 13. ♗d3 ♕a5 [13... ♕d7 14. ♖hf1 ♔h8 15. ♗f6 ♗f6 16. ♘d5 ♖fe8 17. c3± Unzicker—Ghitescu, Leipzig (ol) 1960] 14. g4 [14. ♖he1 ♔h8 15. ♘b5 ♕d2 16. ♖d2 ♘c6 17. ♗f6± Milić—Joppen, Jugoslavija—BRD 1954] ef4 15. ♗f4 d5 16. g5 ♘h5 17. ♗e3 ♘c6 18. f6 ♗b4 19. fg7 ♖fd8 20. ♕f2± Hastings—Dordrecht, corr. 1955; **12... h6** 13. ♗f6 ♗f6 14. ♘d5 ef4 15. ♘f6 ♕f6 16. ♕f4 ♕e5 17. g3 ♖fe8= Matanović—Milić, Beograd 1954; 13. ♗h4! — 9... h6

22 **10. h4**?! hg5 11. hg5 ♘h7 [11... ♘g4!?] 12. g4 ♗g5 13. ♘f3±; 10... ♘d4! 11. ♕d4 hg5 — B 65; **10. ♗f6** ♗f6 11. ♘db5 [11. ♘b3 a5 12. a4 ♕b6∓; 11. ♘c6 bc6 12. ♕d6 ♕b6 13. e5 ♖d8 14. ♕a3 ♕e3 15. ♔b1 ♖d1 16. ♘d1 ♕a3=; 13. ♕d3 ♖b8 14. b3 ♕b4 15. ♔b2 (Korzin—Makaričev, SSSR 1968 — 5/416) ♗a6∞̅] e5 [11... ♕a5 12. ♘d6 ♖d8 13. e5 ♘e5 14. ♘ce4 ♕a2 15. c3 ♘d7 16. ♗c4± Pomar—Panno, München (ol) 1958] 12. g3 a6?! 13. ♘d6 ♘d4 [Janošević—O'Kelly, Bognor Regis 1956] 14. ♘c8 ♖c8 15. ♗d3±; 12... ♗g4∞

23 10... ♘d4 11. ♕d4 — B 65

24 11. ♘e4 ♗h4 12. ♘c6 bc6 13. ♕d6 ♕b6 14. ♗d3 ♖b8∓

25 17. ♖e1 c5 [17... ♔f8 18. ♘e4 c5 19. c4 ♖c7 20. g3 ♔e7= Đurašević—Bogdanović, Jugoslavija (ch) 1953] 18. g3 ♖c8 19. b3 ♔f8 20. ♔b2 ♔e8= Szabo—Geler, Amsterdam (ct) 1956

26 **18... ♔f8** 19. ♖d8 ♖d8 20. ♖d8 ♖e8 21. ♖e8△ ♘b5±; **18... g6** 19. ♘a4 ♖c7 20. c4±; **18... g5** 19. ♖e1 gf4 20. gf4 ♔f8 21. ♖e5 ♖c7 22. ♘b5 ♖cc8 23. f5± Unzicker—Stahlberg, Moskva (ol) 1956

27 **12... ♖c8** 13. ♔b1 ♔h8 14. ♖g1 ef4 [14... ♕a5 15. ♗f6 ♗f6 16. ♘e4±] 15. ♕f4 ♕a5 16. ♗e2 ♖fe8 17. ♖ge1 d5 18. ♗f3± Rabar—Geler, Göteborg (izt) 1955; **12... ef4** 13. ♔b1 [13. ♕f4? d5∞] ♕b6 [13... ♘a5 14. ♗e2 ♖c8 15. ♖hf1± Kondratjev—Rovner, SSSR 1956] 14. ♕f4 d5 15. ♘d5 ♘d5 16. ♖d5 ♖ad8 17. ♗c4± Matanović—Geler, Zagreb 1955

28 13. g4 ef4 14. ♕f4 d5 15. ♔b1 d4 16. ♗f6 ♗f6 17. ♘e4 ♗e5= Suetin—Krogius, SSSR (ch) 1967 — 3/454

29 16. ♘f6 gf6 17. ♖d2 ♘e7 18. g4 ♖d7 19. fe5 fe5 20. ♗g2± Suetin—Paoli, Kecskemet 1972 — 14/418

30 18. ♗d3 f3?! 19. gf3 d5 20. ♖hd1 ♖fe8 21. c3± Liberzon—Mititelu, Luhačovice 1971 — 12/428; 18... ♖fe8!∞

31 19. ♖f1 ♖e4 20. ♗f3 ♖e7 21. b3! [21. a3 ♘e5 22. ♗e2?! f3! 23. gf3 ♘c6= Spaski—Gheorghiu, La Habana (ol) 1966 — 2/401; 22. ♗d5 ♘g4 23. ♖f4 ♘e3 24. ♗b3 ♖e5 25. ♖d3 ♔f8 26. g4 b5 27. a4 a6 28. ♖c3 d5 29. ♖d4 ♔e7 30. h3 ♘c4= Spaski—Larsen, Santa Monica 1966 — 2/402] ♘e5 22. ♗d5 ♔g7 23. ♖f4 ♖ed7 24. ♖fd4± Parma—Paoli, Reggio Emilia 1971 — 12/427

B 65 **1. e4 c5 2. ♘f3 d6 3. d4 cd4 4. ♘d4 ♘f6 5. ♘c3 ♘c6 6. ♗g5 e6 7. ♕d2 ♗e7 8. 0-0-0 0—0 9. f4 ♘d4 10. ♕d4**

	10	11	12	13	14	15	16	17	18	
1	. . .	♗e2[1]	♗h4[2]	fe5	♕d3	♕b5	♗b5	♗e2	♗g3	=
	♕a5	h6	e5	de5	♗e6	♕b5	♖fd8	♔f8	♗d6[3]	
2	. . .	♔b1	h4[5]	♕f2	♘d5	♖d5	♗e7	♕f4	♗d3	=
	. . .	h6[4]	e5[6]	ef4	♘d5	♕c7	♕e7	♖d8	♗e6	
3	. . .	e5	♕e5[7]	fe5	♗e7	♗d3[9]	♗e4[11]	♖he1	♖d7	=
	. . .	fe5	♕e5[8]	♘d5	♘e7	b6[10]	♖b8	♗b7[12]	♗e4	
4	. . .	♗c4	h4[14]	♕g1	♗f4	♖d3	♗d6	♖d6	♕d4	±
	. . .	h6[13]	e5[15]	ef4[16]	♗g4	♘h5	♗d6	♘g3	♕h5[17]	
5	. . .	. . .	e5[18]	fe5	♗d2[19]	♘d5	♘e7	♖he1	♕g4[22]	±
	. . .	♗d7	de5	♗c6	♘d7[20]	♕d8	♕e7	♖fc8[21]	♕c5[23]	

1. e4 c5 2. ♘f3 d6 3. d4 cd4 4. ♘d4 ♘f6 5. ♘c3 ♘c6 6. ♗g5 e6 7. ♕d2 ♗e7 8. 0-0-0 0—0 9. f4 ♘d4 10. ♕d4 h6

	11	12	13	14	15	16	17	18	19	
6	h4[24]	hg5	♗e2[26]	♕g1	♗g4	♕h2	♗f3			∓
	hg5[25]	♘g4	e5	ef4	♗g5	♗h6	♕f6			
7	♗h4	♕d3[27]	♗e2[29]	♕g3	♗f3[30]	f5	♔b1	♗f6	♘d5	=
	♕a5	♖d8[28]	♗d7	♗c6	e5	b5	b4	♗f6	♗d5[31]	
8	. . .	e5	♕e5	fe5	♗e7	♗d3[33]	♗e4	♖he1	♖d7	=
	. . .	de5	♕e5[32]	♘d5	♘e7	b6[34]	♖b8	♗b7	♗e4[35]	
9	. . .	♗c4	♖hf1[37]	g3	f5	ef5[39]	♖de1	♖e7	♕f2	±
	. . .	♖d8[36]	♕h5[38]	♗d7	ef5	♗f5	d5	dc4	♗h3[40]	
10	. . .	. . .	fe5[41]	♕d3	♗f6[43]	♖df1	♖f6[44]	♘d5	♕g3	±
	. . .	e5	de5	♗g4[42]	♗f6	♖ac8	gf6	♔g7	f5[45]	
11	. . .	. . .	. . .	. . .	♗f6[46]	♕e2[47]	♔b1	♗b3	♘d5	±
	. . .	. . .	. . .	♕c5	♗f6	a6	b5	♗e6	♗d8[48]	

[1] **11. ♗d3** h6 12. h4 e5 13. ♕g1 ef4 14. ♗f4 ♗e6 15. g4 ♘g4 16. ♘d5 ♗d5 17. ♕g4 ♗e6 18. ♕g3 ♕a2 19. e5 ♖fc8∓ Joppen—Unzicker, BRD 1954; **11. ♕d2** h6 12. ♗h4 ♘e4 13. ♘e4 ♕d2=; **11. ♕d3** b6 [11... ♖d8 12. ♕h3 ♗d7 13. ♗d3 ♖ac8 14. ♖he1 e5 15. f5 ♖c3 16. bc3 ♕c3= Keres—Tajmanov, SSSR (ch) 1952] 12. ♗e2 ♗b7 13. ♗f3 ♖ad8 14. ♗h4 ♗a6 15. ♕d2 b5 16. a3 ♖c8= Spaski—Bronštejn, SSSR (ch) 1959

[2] **12. ♗f6** ♗f6 13. ♕d6 ♗c3 14. bc3 ♕a2 15. ♕b4 b5 16. ♕b5 ♕a3 17. ♕b2 ♕c5 18. ♖d4 e5∓ Dubinin—Veresov, SSSR (ch) 1940; **12. h4** e5 13. ♕f2 ef4 14. ♗f4 ♗e6 15. ♖d4 ♖fc8 16. ♕g3 ♖c3 17. ♕c3 ♕a2 18. ♕a3 ♕a3 19. ba3 d5=∞ Vasjukov—Boleslavski, SSSR 1957

[3] Rossetto—Benkö, Portorož (izt) 1958

[4] 11... ♖d8 12. ♕d2 ♗d7 [12... ♕c7 13. ♕e1 ♘e8 14. ♗e7△ ♗d3± Kamišov—Ilivicki, SSSR 1949] 13. ♗f6 ♗f6 14. ♘d5 ♕d2=

[5] **12. ♗h4** e5 13. fe5 de5=; **12. ♗f6** ♗f6 13. ♕d2 ♗c3 14. ♕c3 ♕c3 15. bc3 ♖d8 16. e5 b6! [16... d5 17. c4 ♗d7 18. cd5 ed5 19. ♖d4±⊥ Lublinski—Liskov, SSSR 1949] 17. ed6 ♗b7 18. ♖g1 ♖ac8=∞ Talj—Slucman, SSSR 1952

[6] **12... hg5** 13. hg5 ♘g4 14. ♗e2=∞→»; **12... ♖d8** 13. g4 e5 14. ♕g1 ef4 15. ♗f6 ♗f6 16. ♘d5 ♗e5 17. g5 h5 [Bivšev—Tajmanov, SSSR (ch) 1952] 18. g6∞

[7] 12. fe5 ♖d8 13. ♕f4 ♖d1△ ♘d5∓ Murski—Judovič, SSSR 1936

[8] **12... ♕b6**? 13. ♘a4 ♕c6 14. ♗b5 ♕g2 15. ♖hg1+—; **12... b6** 13. ♕a5 ba5 14. ♗d3 ♗b7 15. ♖hg1±

[9] 15. ♗b5!?

[10] 15... ♘c6 16. ♖he1 ♖d8 17. b4 ♗d7 [17... a6 18. ♗e4 ♔f8 19. ♘a4 ♔e7 20. ♗c6± Aronin—Suetin, SSSR 1953] 18. b5

♘a5 19. ♘e4 ♖ac8 20. ♘d6 ♖c5 21. ♗e4 ♔f8 22. ♘b7± Talj–Ilivicki, SSSR 1953

11 16. ♖he1!? ♗b7 17. ♗h7

12 17... ♘g6 18. ♗g6±

13 **11... a6** 12. ♔b1 b5 13. ♗b3 ♖d8 14. a3 ♕c7 15. f5± Toluš–Rejfiř, Baden 1957; **11... e5** 12. fe5 de5 13. ♕d3 ♖d8 14. ♕g3 ♗e6 15. ♗f6 ♗f6 16. ♗d5 ♗d5 17. ♘d5± O'Kelly–Lopez, Torremolinos 1961; **11... ♖d8** 12. ♖hf1 [12. f5 b5 13. ♗b5 ef5 14. ef5 ♗f5 15. ♖hf1△ ♖de1± Šamkovič–Saharov, SSSR 1960] ♗d7 [12... h6 13. ♗h4 e5 14. ♕d3 ef4 15. ♖f4 ♗e6 16. ♗e6△ ♕c4± Suetin–Pomar, La Habana 1969 — 8/391] 13. f5 b5 [13... ♖ac8 14. ♗b3 ef5 15. ef5 ♗f5 16. ♘d5+– Šamkovič–Sajgin, SSSR 1959] 14. fe6 bc4 15. ♖f5 ♕b4 16. ef7 [16. ♗f6 ♗f6 17. ef7± Štejn–Osnos, SSSR 1959] ♔f7 17. ♗f6 ♗f5 18. ♗e7± Zuidema–Mohrlock, Beverwijk 1963

14 12. ♗h4 — 10... h6

15 12... hg5 13. hg5 ♘g4 14. ♖d3 f5 15. ♖dh3±

16 13... ♗e6 14. ♗f6 ♗f6 15. ♗e6△ f5±

17 **18... ♘h1** 19. ♖g6+–; **18... ♕h5** 19. ♖d5 ♕g6 20. ♖e1± Pachman–Barcza, Stockholm (izt) 1952

18 **12. ♖he1** ♖fd8 13. ♗b3 b5 14. e5 de5 15. fe5 b4 16. ♗f6 gf6 17. ef6 ♕g5∓ Keres–Geler, Curaçao (ct) 1962; **12. ♔b1** ♗c6 13. ♖hf1 h6 14. ♗h4 ♕h5 15. g3 g5 16. fg5 hg5 17. ♖f6 ♗f6 18. ♕f6 gh4 19. gh4 ♔h7∓ Talj–Larsen (m) 1969 — 7/385; **12. ♗b3** ♗c6 13. ♖hf1 [Polugajevski–Osnos, SSSR (ch) 1969 — 7/384] h6 14. ♗h4 e5 15. fe5 de5=

19 **14. ♗f6**?! gf6 15. ♖de1 f5∓ Dely–Sofrevski, Skopje 1967 — 4/499; **14. ♕f4** ♘d5 15. ♗d5 ♗g5 16. ♕g5 ed5 17. ♖d4 [17. ♖d3 d4 18. ♖d4 ♖ae8 19. ♖e1 f6= Talj–Bradvarević, Kislovodsk 1964] ♖fe8 18. ♖f1 ♕c7 19. ♖f5 ♖e5 20. ♖e5 f6= Bronštejn–Averbah, Beverwijk 1963; **14. h4** ♖ad8 [14... ♗c5?! 15. ♕f4± Spaski–Korenski, Soči 1973 — 16/376] 15. ♕f4 [Matanović–Musil, Ljubljana 1968 — 7/387] ♘h5!? 16. ♕g4 ♗g5 17. ♕g5 g6∞

20 14... ♖fd8? 15. ♘d5 ♖d5 16. ♗a5+–

21 17... ♕c5 18. ♕c5 [18. ♕f4 ♗b5?! 19. ♗b3 a5 20. a4 ♗c6 21. ♖e3± Kavalek–Benkö, Netanya 1969 — 7/386; 18... a5∞] ♘c5 19. ♗b4 b6 20. ♖e2! ♖fd8 21. ♖ed2 ♖d2 22. ♖d2 ♔f8 23. g3± Savon–Paoli, Cienfuegos 1973 — 15/385

22 18. ♕f4 a5 19. ♔b1 ♘b6 20. ♗d3 ♘d5 21. ♕g4 [Karpov–Ungureanu, Skopje (ol) 1972 — 14/421] ♘b4 22. ♗h6 ♕f8±

23 19. ♗h6 g6 20. ♖e2± Ceškovski–Korenski, SSSR 1973 — 16/375

24 11. ♗f6 ♗f6 12. ♕d6 ♕a5 13. e5 ♖d8 14. ♕a3 ♖d1 15. ♔d1 ♕a3=

25 **11... e5** 12. fe5 hg5 13. ed6 ♗d6 14. ♕d6 ♗g4 15. ♕d8 ♖ad8 16. ♖d3± Karanjac–Bajec, Jugoslavija 1958; **11... ♕a5** 12. ♕d2?! b5 [12... ♘e4 14. ♘e4 ♕d2 14. ♖d2 hg5 15. hg5± Averbah–Fridštejn, SSSR 1951; 12... ♖d8 13. g4±→»] 13. ♗b5 ♖b8 14. a4 ♗a6 15. ♔b1 ♗b5 16. ab5 ♘e4 17. ♘e4 ♕b5 18. c4 ♕c4 19. ♗e7 ♕e4 20. ♕c2 ♖b2 21. ♔b2 ♖b8 22. ♔c1 ♕e3∞̄ Zagorovski–Ilivicki, SSSR 1951; 12. ♗c4!± — 10... ♕a5

26 13. e5 de5 [13... ♗g5?! 14. fg5 ♕g5 15. ♔b1 de5 16. ♕d6 ♘h6 17. ♗b5∞̄ Sokolski–Livšin, SSSR (ch) 1954] 14. ♕e4 f5 15. gf6 ♘f6 16. ♕e2 ♕b6 17. fe5 ♘d5∓

27 12. ♕g1 ♗d7 13. g4 ♗c6 [13... ♖fc8 14. ♗e1 ♖c3 15. ♗c3 ♕a2 16. ♗d3 e5∞̄; 14... b5 15. g5 hg5 16. fg5 b4∞; 15. ♘d5 ♕d8=] 14. ♗e1 ♕c7 15. ♗d3 d5 16. e5 ♘e4 17. ♗e4 de4 18. h4 b5 19. ♗g3 b4 20. ♘e2 ♗d5 21. ♖d5 ed5 22. ♕d1∞ Toluš–Tajmanov, SSSR (ch) 1958; 17. h4!?

28 **12... ♖e8** 13. ♗f6 ♗f6 14. ♕b5± Havski–Ilivicki, SSSR 1956; **12... a6** 13. ♔b1 b5 14. e5 de5 15. fe5 ♘d5 16. ♘d5 ♗h4 [Gipslis–Osnos, SSSR 1958] 17. ♘f6±

29 13. g4 ♗d7 14. ♖g1 [14. g5 ♘h5 15. ♕f3 ♘f4∓ Hasin–Banik, SSSR 1958] g5 15. fg5 hg5 16. ♗f2 b5∞

30 15. e5 de5 16. fe5 ♘e4 17. ♘e4 ♗e4 18. ♗e7 ♕c7=

31 20. ♖d5 ♕c7 21. h4 a5= Spaski–Boleslavski, SSSR (ch) 1957

32 13... b6 14. ♕a5 ba5 15. ♗d3 ♗b7 16. ♖hg1 ♖fe8 17. h3 ♗c5 18. ♖ge1 ♗b4 19. f5 e5 20. ♗b5± Boleslavski–Gligorić, Zürich (ct) 1953; 16... ♔h8!= Boleslavski; 15. a3△ ♖d2± H. Müller

33 16. ♗b5 a6 [16... ♖b8 17. ♖he1 b6 18. g3 ♖b7 19. ♘e4 ♖c7 20. ♘d6± Keres–Boleslavski, SSSR (ch) 1957] 17. ♗d3 b5 18. ♗e4 ♖b8 [18... ♖a7 19. b4 ♗d7= Matanović–Boleslavski, Jugoslavija–SSSR 1957] 19. a3 [19. ♖d6 b4 20. ♘a4 a5 21. ♖e1 ♗b7= Matanović–Panno, Portorož (izt) 1958] a5 20. b4 ab4 21. ab4 ♗b7= Schmid–Eliskases, München (ol) 1958

34 **16... ♗d7** 17. ♗h7 ♔h7 18. ♖d7 ♘c6 19. ♖b7 ♘e5 20. ♖e1 [20. ♘b5 ♖fd8= Boleslavski–Geler, SSSR 1954] f6 21. ♖e3 ♖fd8 22. ♖c7 ♖dc8 23. ♘b5± Ivkov–Tajmanov, Jugoslavija–SSSR 1956; **16... ♘c6** 17. ♖he1 ♖d8 18. ♗e4 ♗d7 19. ♘b5±

35 20. ♖e4 ♘c6 21. ♘b5 ♖fd8 22. ♖c7 ♖bc8= Gligorić–Benkö, Jugoslavija (ct) 1959

36 12... a6 13. e5 de5 14. fe5 ♗c5 15. ♕f4± Koch–Müller, corr. 1952

37 **13. ♔b1** ♗d7 14. ♗b3 ♕h5 15. ♗g3 ♗c6= Solovjev—Boleslavski, SSSR 1955; **13. e5** de5 14. ♕e5 ♕b4=

38 13... ♗d7 14. f5 b5 15. fe6 fe6 16. e5±

39 16. ♖de1 f4 17. e5 de5 18. ♖e5± Nejštadt—Osnos, SSSR 1961

40 Schmid—Boleslavski, BRD—SSSR 1960; 20. g4±

41 13. ♕d3 ef4 14. ♘b5 ♗g4 15. ♖df1 a6∓ Canal—Barcza, Venezia 1948

42 **14... ♖b8** 15. ♗f6 ♗f6 16. ♘d5 ♗g5 17. ♔b1 ♗g4 18. h4± Koch—Johansson, corr. 1954; **14... ♔h8** 15. ♗f6 ♗f6 16. ♘d5 ♗h4 17. g3 ♗g5 18. ♔b1 ♗h3= Koch—Gligorić, Helsinki (ol) 1952; 15. h3△ g4±; **14... a6** 15. ♗f6 ♗f6 16. ♘d5 ♗d8 17. h4 ♗e6 18. ♘e3±; 16... ♗g5!?; **14... ♖d8** 15. ♘d5 ♔f8 16. ♗f6 ♗f6 17. b4 ♕a4 18. ♗b3 ♕a3 19. ♔b1 ♗g4 20. ♖df1 ♖ac8 21. ♖f6 gf6 22. ♕e3± van den Berg—Eliskases, Beverwijk 1959; **14... ♗e6** 15. ♗f6 ♗c4 [15... ♗f6 16. ♗e6 fe6 17. ♕d7±] 16. ♕c4 ♗f6 17. ♘d5 ♗d8 18. ♔b1± Stoljar—Ilivicki, SSSR (ch) 1953; **14... b5** 15. ♗b3 [15. ♗b5 ♗g4 16. ♗f6 ♗f6 17. ♖df1 ♖fd8⩱] ♗b7 16. ♗f6 ♗f6 17. ♖df1 ♖ab8 18. ♘d5±

43 15. ♖df1 ♗e6 16. ♗e6 fe6 17. ♕c4 ♕b6 18. ♗f2 ♕d6 19. ♖d1 ♖ac8= Unzicker—Pomar 1962

44 17. ♗b3 ♖fd8 [Hofmann—Pachman, ČSSR (ch) 1953] 18. ♘d5±

45 20. ♗b3 ♔h7 21. h3 ♗e2 22. ♕e5±

46 15. ♗b3 ♗e6 16. ♗e6 [16. ♗f6 ♗f6 17. ♗e6 fe6 18. ♕d7 ♕e7=] fe6 17. ♕h3 ♕c4 18. ♗g3 b5 19. ♗e5 b4⩱ Tringov—Schmid, Tel Aviv (ol) 1964

47 **16. h3** ♗e6 17. ♘d5 ♗d8 18. ♔b1± Đurašević—Gligorić, Jugoslavija (ch) 1952; **16. ♔b1** ♗e6 17. ♗e6 fe6 18. ♕d6 ♕c4 19. ♕d3 ♕d3 20. ♖d3 ♖ad8 1/2 : 1/2 Gligorić—Tajmanov, Stockholm (izt) 1952; 17. ♗d5±

48 20. h4 ♕c8 21. ♖df1 ♖b8 22. ♘e3 ♗b6 23. ♘f5± Parma—Bradvarević, Jugoslavija 1965

B 66

1. e4 c5 2. ♘f3 d6 3. d4 cd4 4. ♘d4 ♘f6 5. ♘c3 ♘c6 6. ♗g5 e6 7. ♕d2 a6

	8	9	10	11	12	13	14	15	16	
1	♖d1[1]	♗e2	0—0	♘b3	♗f6	♕h6[6]	♖d3	♖h3	f4	=
	♗d7[2]	♗e7[3]	0—0[4]	♕c7[5]	gf6	♔h8	♖g8	♖g7	b5[7]	
2	0-0-0	♗h4[9]	♕f4	♘c6[12]	♕a4[13]	f4[15]	f5	fe6	♗c4	⩱
	h6[8]	♘e4[10]	♘g5[11]	bc6	♕b6[14]	♘h7	♖b8[16]	♗e6	♗e7[17]	
3	...	♗e3	f3[19]	g4[21]	♘c6	♗d3	e5	♗d4	f4	±
	...	♗d7[18]	♗e7[20]	b5	♗c6	d5	♘d7[22]	♘b6[23]	♕c7[24]	
4	...	...	...	g4[25]	♘c6	♘e2	♘d4	e5	f4	±
	...	...	b5	b4	♗c6	d5	♗b7	♘d7	♘c5[26]	

1. e4 c5 2. ♘f3 d6 3. d4 cd4 4. ♘d4 ♘f6 5. ♘c3 ♘c6 6. ♗g5 e6 7. ♕d2 a6 8. 0-0-0 h6 9. ♗f4 ♗d7

	10	11	12	13	14	15	16	17	18	
5	♘b3[27]	♗d6	♘d5	ed5	♖e1[29]	dc6	♗d3[30]	f3	fe4	∞
	b5[28]	b4	ed5	♘e4	♗d6	♗c6	f5	0—0	fe4[31]	
6	♘c6	f3[32]	♕e1[34]	a3	b4[37]	ed5	♗e5			±
	♗c6	d5[33]	♗b4[35]	♗a5[36]	♗b6	♗d5[38]				
7	...	...	♗c4[39]	♗e3[40]	♕f2	f4	♗e2	a3[41]		±
	...	♕b6	0-0-0	♕c7	♘d7	b5	♕b7			

1 8. ♗e2 ♗d7 [8... ♗e7 9. ♘b3 0—0△ b5=] 9. ♘b3 b5 10. a3 h6 11. ♗e3 ♘a5 12. ♘a5 ♕a5 13. 0—0 ♗c6= Milić—Malich, Gotha 1957

2 8... ♗e7 9. ♗e2 ♕c7 10. 0—0 0—0 11. ♗f6 gf6 12. ♔h1 ♗d7 13. f4 ♔h8 14. ♗f3 ♖ac8= Janošević—Simonović, Jugoslavija (ch) 1949

3 **9... ♖c8** 10. 0—0 ♗e7 11. ♘b3 0—0 12. ♗f6 gf6 13. ♕h6 ♔h8 14. ♕h5 ♖g8 15. f4 ♖g6 16. ♔h1 ♕b6= Gurgenidze—Bronštejn, SSSR (ch) 1958; **9... h6** 10. ♗e3 ♗e7

[10... ♕c7 11. 0–0 b5 12. a3 ♘e5 13. f4 ♘c4 14. ♗c4 ♕c4 15. ♔h1 ♖d8 16. h3 ♗e7 17. e5± Matanović–Rabar, Jugoslavija (ch) 1949; 10... b5!?] 11. 0–0 0–0 12. f4 ♕c7 13. f5 ♘e5= Fuderer–Janošević, Jugoslavija (ch) 1949

4 **10... ♕c7** 11. ♘b3 ♖d8 12. ♗f6 ♗f6 13. ♕d6 ♕d6 14. ♖d6 ♔e7 15. ♖d2± Drimer–Botvinik, Leipzig (ol) 1960; **10... ♘d4** 11. ♕d4 ♗c6 12. ♔h1 0–0 13. f4 ♕a5= Trajković–Sokolov, Jugoslavija 1951

5 11... ♕b6 12. ♘a4 ♕c7 13. ♗f6 gf6 [Fuderer–Gligorić, Jugoslavija (ch) 1949] 14. ♕e3±

6 13. f4 ♔h8 14. ♗h5 ♘a5= Sokolov

7 17. f5 ♘e5 18. ♖f4 ♕c8= Trajković–S. Nedeljković, Jugoslavija 1950

8 8... ♗e7 9. f4 ♕c7?! 10. ♗f6 [10. ♘f3 b5 11. ♗f6 gf6 12. f5±] gf6 11. ♗e2 ♗d7 12. ♖hf1 ♕b6 13. ♘b3 0-0-0 14. ♗h5± Barczay–Suetin, Polanica Zdroj 1974 — 18/398

9 **9. ♗f6** ♕f6 10. ♘b3 ♕d8 [10... b5 11. f4 ♗e7 12. h4 ♕g6 13. h5± Sokolski–Novotelnov, SSSR 1948] 11. f4 ♗d7 12. ♔b1 ♕c7= Dubinin–Ilivicki, SSSR 1949; **9. ♘c6** bc6 10. ♗h4 ♕a5 12. ♗c4 d5= Panov–Aronin, SSSR 1947

10 9... ♗d7 10. f4 — B 67

11 **10... g5** 11. ♕e4 gh4 12. ♘c6 bc6 13. ♕c6± Krogius–Polugajevski, SSSR 1957; **10... ♘f6** 11. ♘c6 bc6 12. ♘e4 d5 [12... e5 13. ♕f3 ♗e7 14. ♗f6±] 13. ♗f6 gf6 14. ♘f6 ♔e7 15. ♕b4 c5 16. ♕c5 ♕d6 17. ♕d4± Najdorf–Ilivicki, Göteborg (izt) 1955

12 11. ♕e3 ♘d4 12. ♖d4 ♗e7 13. f4 ♘h7 14. ♗e7 ♕e7∓

13 12. ♘e4 d5 13. ♗g5 hg5 14. ♘g5 f6∓

14 12... ♕c7 13. f4 ♘h7 14. f5 ♗e7 15. ♗e7 ♔e7 16. ♕g4∞̅ Feuerstein–R. Byrne, USA (ch) 1972 — 13/432

15 13. ♗c4 ♗d7 14. ♖he1 ♖b8 15. ♗b3 d5 16. ♕g4 ♘h7 17. f4 ♘f6 18. ♗f6 gf6 19. f5 e5 20. ♕g3 [Yanofsky–Mednis 1956] ♗f5∓

16 14... ♗e7 15. ♘e4 ♖b8 16. ♕a3± Polugajevski

17 17. ♗e6 fe6 18. ♗e7 ♔e7 19. ♕g4 ♘g5 [19... ♕b2 20. ♔d2 ♘g5 21. ♖b1 ♕a3 22. h4 ♘f7 23. ♖he1 e5 24. ♖f1± Vasjukov–Zurahov, SSSR 1960] 20. b3 [20. h4?! ♕b2 21. ♔d2 ♖b4∓] ♕b4 21. ♕g3∞̅

18 9... ♘g4 10. ♘c6 bc6 11. ♗c5 ♗b7 [11... ♕c7 12. ♗d6 ♗d6 13. ♕d6 ♕d6 14. ♖d6 ♘f2 15. ♖g1±; 11... ♕g5 12. ♕g5 hg5 13. ♗e2 dc5 14. ♗g4 ♗e7 15. h3 ♗d7 16. ♘a4± Goldenov–Aronin, SSSR (ch) 1947] 12. h3 dc5 13. ♕d8 ♖d8 14. ♖d8 ♔d8 15. hg4± Smislov–Botvinik (m) 1957

19 10. f4 ♗e7 [10... ♖c8 11. ♔b1 b5 12. ♗d3 ♘g4?! 13. ♗g1 ♘d4 14. ♗d4 e5 15. ♗g1 ef4 16. ♘d5± Smislov–Botvinik (m) 1957; 12... ♘a5!?; 10... ♕c7 11. ♗d3 ♘d4 12. ♗d4 ♗c6 13. ♖he1± Geler–Csom, Budapest 1973 — 15/386; 11... b5!?; 11... ♗e7!?] 11. h3 [11. ♗e2 b5 12. ♗f3 b4 13. ♘ce2 ♕a5 14. ♔b1 e5 15. ♘c6 ♗c6 16. ♘g3 g6 17. fe5 de5 18. ♗h6± Gligorić–Olafsson, Dallas 1957; 11... ♘d4△ ♗c6∞] ♘d4 [11... ♕c7 12. g4 b5 13. ♗b5 ab5 14. ♘db5 ♕b8 15. ♘d6± Suetin–Talj, Budva 1967 — 4/501] 12. ♗d4 ♗c6∞

20 10... ♕c7 11. ♕f2 ♗e7 12. g4 b5 13. ♖g1 b4 14. ♘ce2 d5 15. ♘c6 ♗c6 16. e5 ♘d7 17. f4 g5 18. ♘d4± Korčnoj–Saharov, SSSR 1960

21 11. ♔b1 b5 12. g4 ♘e5 13. ♕e1 b4 14. ♘ce2 d5?! 15. ♗f4 ♘c4 16. e5 ♘h7 17. ♘c1± Klovan–Makaričev, SSSR (ch) 1973 — 16/377; 14... ♖c8!? Polugajevski

22 14... d4 15. ef6 ♗f6 16. ♗e4 ♗e4 17. ♘e4±

23 15... ♗c5 16. ♕e3 ♕b6 17. ♘e2±

24 17. ♕f2 ♘c4 18. ♔b1 b4 19. ♘e2 ♗b5 20. f5 a5 21. h4 a4 22. ♘c1 ♕c6 23. g5 0-0-0 [Savon–Talj, Moskva 1971 — 12/429] 24. ♖hg1±

25 11. ♘c6 ♗c6 12. ♕f2 ♕c7 13. ♗d3 ♗e7 [13... b4 14. ♘e2 d5 15. e5 ♘d7 16. f4 ♗b5 17. ♔b1 ♗d3 18. cd3 b3 19. ♖c1 ba2 20. ♔a1 ♕b7 21. ♖c2± Rittner–Simagin, corr. 1966 — 1/287] 14. ♔b1 [14. ♕g3 g6 15. ♔b1 0-0-0 (Smislov–Botvinik (m) 1957) 16. a4∞] ♘d7 15. ♗d4 ♗f6 16. ♗f6 ♘f6 17. ♖he1 0–0 18. g4 ♖fc8 19. ♕e3 ♕a7 20. ♕d2 ♕c5 21. ♖g1 g5= Bihovski–Simagin, SSSR 1968 — 5/418; 15. ♖he1!?

26 **17. ♗d3**± Larsen; **17. ♗g2** ♘e4 18. ♕e2 ♕c7 19. ♔b1 ♗e7 20. ♗e4 [20. ♖hf1 0–0! (Larsen–Gligorić, Manila 1974 — 18/399) 21. f5∞] de4 21. h4 0-0-0 22. h5 ♖d5 23. ♘b3± Matanović–Ničevski, Jugoslavija (ch) 1975

27 **10. ♘f3** b5 11. e5 de5 12. ♘e5 ♘e5 13. ♗e5 ♗e7 14. ♕f4 ♕a5 15. ♗c7 ♕b4 16. ♕f3 ♖c8 17. ♕b7 0–0= Riga–Budapest, corr. 1939; **10. ♗g3** ♗e7 [10... b5 11. ♗d6 ♗d6 12. ♘c6 ♗c6 13. ♕d6 ♕d6 14. ♖d6 ♗e4 15. ♘e4 ♘e4 16. ♖a6+– Tajmanov–Aronin, SSSR 1951; 10... ♘d4 11. ♕d4 ♗c6 12. f3 d5 13. ed5 ♘d5 14. ♗e5± Gligorić, Sokolov] 11. f3 [11. ♗e2 b5?! 12. ♗d6 b4 13. ♘c6 ♗c6 14. e5±; 11... 0–0=] ♘e5 12. f4 ♘h5 13. ♗e2 ♘g3 14. hg3 [Dückstein–Botvinik, München (ol) 1958] ♖c8=

28 **10... e5** 11. ♗e3 ♗e7 [11... b5 12. f3 ♕c7 13. ♘d5 ♘d5 14. ed5 ♘d8 15. ♗d3 a5 16. ♖he1 ♗e7 17. ♘d4 ed4 18. ♗d4 ♔f8 19. ♖e7 ♔e7 20. ♗g7+–; 17... b4 18. ♘f5 ♗f6 19. f4± Ivkov–Ingerslev, Moskva (ol) 1956] 12. f3 ♘a5 13. ♔b1 b5 14. ♘a5 ♕a5

15. g4 [Smailbegović—Bradvarević, Jugoslavija (ch) 1957] ♗e6∞; 10... ♘e5 11. ♗g3 ♘h5 12. f4 ♗e7=

29 14. ♕e3 ♗d6 15. dc6 ♗c6 16. f3 [16. ♗d3 f5 17. ♔b1 0—0 18. ♗e4 fe4 19. ♕d4 ♗b5∓] ♕g5 17. ♕g5 hg5 18. fe4 ♗h2 19. ♔b1 ♔e7∓ Bonč-Osmolovski—Aronin (m) 1950

30 16. f3 ♕c7 17. g3 0—0 18. fe4 ♖ad8=∞

31 19. ♗c4 ♔h8 20. ♔b1∞

32 11. ♕e3 ♕c7 12. ♗e2 ♗e7 [12... 0-0-0 13. ♖d2 ♗e7 14. ♖hd1 ♖d7 15. e5±] 13. ♖d2 b5 14. a3 e5 15. ♗g3 0—0 [15... ♕b7 16. f4 b4 17. ab4 ♕b4 18. ♘d5 ♕a4 19. ♔b1 ♗d5 20. ed5 e4?! 21. ♖d4± Konstantinopoljski —Aronin, SSSR (ch) 1950; 18... ♗d5 19. ed5 ♖b8∞] 16. ♗h4?! b4 17. ab4 ♖fb8 18. ♗c4 ♖b4 19. ♕d3 ♕a5∓ Šapošnikov—Lapin, SSSR 1951; 16. f4∞

33 11... e5 12. ♗e3 b5 13. g4 [13. ♔b1 ♗e7 14. g4 ♖b8 15. h4 b4 16. ♘d5± Unzicker —Johansson, Varna (ol) 1962] ♗e7 [13... ♕c7 14. h4 ♕b7 15. ♗h3 b4 16. ♘d5± Hasin—Yoffie, Beograd 1968 — 6/513] 14. h4 ♕c7 15. ♖h2± Rabar—Đurašević, Jugoslavija (ch) 1957

34 **12. e5** ♘d7 13. ♘e2 ♕c7∓; **12. ♗e5** de4 13. ♕d8 ♖d8 14. ♖d8 ♔d8 15. ♗f6 gf6 16. ♘e4 f5∓ Darga—Ivkov, Moskva (ol) 1956; **12. ed5** ♘d5 13. ♘d5 ♕d5=

35 12... ♗e7 13. ed5 ed5 [13... ♘d5 14. ♘d5 ♗d5 15. ♗c4 0—0 16. ♗d5 ed5 17. ♕e5±] 14. ♘e2 [14. ♗d3 0—0 15. ♘e2 ♖e8 16. ♔b1 ♕b6 17. ♗e5 ♗b4 18. ♗c3 a5 19. a3 ♗c3 20. ♕c3 ♖ac8 (Keres—Tajmanov, SSSR (ch) 1958) 21. ♕d4±] 0—0 15. ♘d4 ♗d6 16. ♕d2 ♖e8 17. g4 ♗f4 18. ♕f4 ♕a5 19. a3 ♖e1 20. ♗d3± Keres—Wexler, Mar del Plata 1957

36 13... ♗c3 14. ♕c3 0—0 15. h4± Gligorić, Sokolov

37 14. ed5 ♘d5 15. b4 ♘f4! 16. ♖d8 ♗d8 17. h4 [17. ♘e4!?] 0—0 18. ♕e3 ♘d5 19. ♘d5 ♗d5 [19... ed5] 20. ♗d3 ♖c8∞ Zagorovski —Rohlin, corr. 1967 — 3/458

38 15... ♘d5? 16. ♘d5 ♗d5 17. c4 ♖c8 [17... ♕f6 18. ♗e5 ♕g6 19. ♗d3+—] 18. ♔b1+— Parma—Mihaljčišin, Athens 1968 — 6/512

39 **12. ♗d6** 0-0-0 13. e5 [13. ♕f4 ♗d6 14. ♖d6 ♖d6 15. ♕d6 ♖d8 16. ♕g3 ♕e3 17. ♔b1 ♘h5—+] ♘e8 14. ♕f4 ♘d6 15. ed6 ♖d7 16. ♕e5 ♕b4 17. ♔b1 ♖g8 18. a3 ♗d6= Janošević—Đurašević, Jugoslavija (ch) 1958; **12. ♔b1** 0-0-0 13. ♗e3 ♕c7 14. ♕f2 ♘d7 15. h4± Liberzon—Saharov, SSSR 1960

40 **13. ♕e2** d5 14. ed5 ed5 15. ♗d3 ♗d6 16. ♗d6 ♖d6 17. ♕e7 ♕c7= Unzicker—Ghitescu, Leipzig (ol) 1960; **13. ♗b3** ♗e7 14. ♗e3 ♕a5 15. ♔b1 ♖he8 16. ♘d5 ♕d2 17. ♘e7± Boleslavski—Averbah, SSSR 1958; **13. ♖he1** ♗e7 14. ♗b3 g5 15. ♗g3 ♔b8 16. ♔b1 ♔a8 17. ♕e3± Hasin—Titenko, SSSR 1962

41 Talj—Đurašević, Varna 1958

B 67

1. e4 c5 2. ♘f3 d6 3. d4 cd4 4. ♘d4 ♘f6 5. ♘c3 ♘c6 6. ♗g5 e6 7. ♕d2 a6 8. 0-0-0 ♗d7

	9	10	11	12	13	14	15	16	17	
1	f3[1]	♕d4	g4	♗e3	♕d2!?[3]	h4	♘e2	♘d4	e5	±
	♘d4[2]	♗e7	♗c6	0—0	b5	b4[4]	d5	♗b7	♘d7[5]	
2	f4	♘f3	♔b1[7]	e5[8]	ef6	fg7	♕d6	♘e5	fe5	±
	♖c8[6]	♕a5	b5	b4	bc3	♗g7[9]	♖c7	♗e5[10]	♖g8[11]	
3	...	♗f6[12]	f5![14]	♘c6	♗d3	♔b1	♖hf1	♘e2		±
	b5	gf6[13]	♕b6[15]	♕c6[16]	h5[17]	♕c5	♗e7			
4	...	♗h4[18]	♘f3	♔b1[20]	e5[21]	ef6	fg7	gh8♕	a3	±
	h6	♖c8[19]	♕a5	b5	b4	bc3	cd2[22]	♘b4	♘c2[23]	

1. e4 c5 2. ♘f3 d6 3. d4 cd4 4. ♘d4 ♘f6 5. ♘c3 ♘c6 6. ♗g5 e6 7. ♕d2 a6 8. 0-0-0 ♗d7 9. f4 h6 10. ♗h4 ♘e4

	11	12	13	14	15	16	17	18	19	
5	♕e1[24]	♘f5	♗f6	♘d5	♕e3[27]	♗e2	♗f3	♖he1	fe5	±
	♘f6[25]	♕c7[26]	gf6	♕d8	b5	h5	♖b8	♘e5	fe5[28]	

	11	12	13	14	15	16	17	18	19	
6	...	...	♘d6	♖d6	♖d2[30]	♕f2[32]	♗d3	f5	♖hd1[33]	±
	...	♕a5	♗d6	♕c7[29]	0-0-0[31]	♘e7	♗c6	e5		
7	...	...	...	...	♖d2[34]	fg5	♗f2[36]	♗g1		=
	...	...	...	0-0-0	g5[35]	hg5	♘g4	♘ge5[37]		
8	...	...	...	...	♖d1!	♕f2	♗d3	f5	♖he1	±
	...	...	...	...	♕c7[38]	♘e7	♗c6	e5	♘ed5[39]	

[1] **9. ♕e1**?! ♕a5 10. f4 ♗e7= Silva–Panno, Sao Paulo 1972 — 13/433; **9. ♗e2** b5 [9... h6?! 10. ♗h4 ♗e7 11. ♗g3±; 9... ♗e7 10. ♘b3 b5 11. ♗f6 gf6 12. ♗h5 ♘e5 13. f4 ♘c4 14. ♕e2± Liliental–Petrosjan, SSSR (ch) 1954] 10. a3 ♖c8 11. f4 ♗e7 12. ♘b3 ♕c7 13. ♖he1 b4 14. ab4 ♘b4 15. e5∞

[2] 9... ♗e7 10. h4 [10. g4 ♕c7?! 11. ♗e3 h6 12. h4 ♘e5 13. ♖g1± Štejn–Bertok, Zagreb 1972 — 14/422; 10... d5!?∞] ♘d4 11. ♕d4 ♕a5 12. g4 ♗c6 13. ♗e3 0-0-0 14. g5 ♘d7 15. ♗h3 ♕c5 [Talj–Mititelu, Bath 1973 — 16/378] 16. ♕d2 ♕a5 17. ♔b1± Talj

[3] 13. g5 ♘d7 14. h4 b5 15. ♕d2!? [15. ♔b1 b4 16. ♘e2 d5 17. ed5?! ♗d5∓ Talj–Balašov, Tallinn 1973 — 16/379] b4 [15... ♘e5? 16. f4 ♘c4 17. ♗c4 bc4 18. h5△ h6± Gipslis–Martinović, Vrnjačka Banja 1975] 16. ♘e2 d5∞

[4] 14... ♕a5?!± Talj–Deže, Novi Sad 1974 — 18/400

[5] 18. f4±

[6] **9... ♕a5** 10. ♘b3 ♕c7 11. ♗f6 gf6 12. ♗e2 h5 13. ♔b1 0-0-0 14. ♖hf1△ ♖f3± Toluš–Kuzminih, SSSR 1951; **9... ♕c7** 10. ♗f6 gf6 11. ♗e2 [11. g3!?] 0-0-0 [11... h5!?] 12. ♗h5± Bivšev–Kuzminih, SSSR 1952

[7] 11. e5?! ♘b4 12. ef6 ♖c3 13. ♘d4 ♖a3∓

[8] 12. ♗f6?! gf6 13. f5 ♘b4 14. a3 ♘c6∞ Talj–Furman, SSSR 1956

[9] **14... cd2** 15. gh8♕ ♘b4 16. a3 ♘c2 17. ♘d2 [17. ♗h6 ♘a3 18. ba3 ♖b8 19. ♔a2 ♕d5 20. ♔a1+–] ♘a3 18. ba3 e5 19. ♘c4!+– Camilleri–Minev, Halle 1967 — 3/459; **14... ♖b8** 15. b3! ♗g7 16. ♕d6 ♖b7 17. ♘d4 ♗d4 18. ♖d4+– Sofrevski–Mihaljčišin, Jugoslavija 1956

[10] 16... ♗f8 17. ♘c4+–

[11] 18. h4± Yanofsky - Olafsson, Dallas 1957

[12] **10. ♗b5** ab5 11. ♘db5 ♘b4 12. a3 ♗b5 13. ♘b5 d5 14. e5 ♕a5∓; **10. a3** b4 [10... ♕b6 11. e5! de5 12. ♘db5 ab5 13. ♗f6 ♕b7 14. ♘e4 b4 15. ♗g7± Romanišin–Zurahov, SSSR 1968 — 5/420] 11. ab4 ♘b4 12. ♔b1∞; **10. ♕e1** ♘d4 11. ♖d4 ♕b6 12. ♕d2 ♗c6∞ Rabar–Malich, Marianske Lazni 1959; **10. ♘c6** ♗c6 11. f5 [11. e5 de5 12. ♕d8 ♖d8 13. ♖d8 ♔d8 14. fe5 h6!∓; 11. ♕e1 ♗e7 12. ♗d3?! ♘d7 13. ♗e7 ♕e7 14. ♕g3 0–0∓ Browne–Tukmakov, Hastings 1972/73 — 15/387; 12. e5 ♘d5 13. ♗e7 ♕e7 14. ♘e4 de5 15. fe5 0–0= Gufeljd–Tukmakov, SSSR (ch) 1972; 12. ♗f6!?; 11. ♗d3 ♕a5! 12. ♖he1 ♗e7 13. ♔b1 h6∞ Milić–Bronštejn, Gotha 1957] b4 12. fe6! [Kozlov–Mojsejev, SSSR 1967 — 3/460] bc3 13. ef7 ♔f7 14. ♕c3∞

[13] 10... ♕f6 11. e5 de5 12. ♘db5 ♕d8 13. ♘d6 ♕d6 14. ♕d6 ef4 15. ♘e4± Kuprejčik–Popov, SSSR 1974 — 18/401

[14] **11. ♔b1** ♕b6 12. ♘c6 ♗c6 13. ♗d3 h5 14. ♖hf1 0-0-0 15. f5± Krogius–Geler, SSSR (ch) 1960; **11. ♘c6** ♗c6 12. ♕e3 ♗e7 13. ♗d3 ♕c7 14. ♔b1 ♕b7 15. ♖he1 b4 16. ♘e2 a5 (Estrin–Anikajev, Lublin 1974 — 18/402) 17. f5±

[15] **11... h5** 12. ♔b1 ♕b6 13. fe6 fe6 14. ♘c6 ♗c6 15. ♕f4± Matanović–Heinicke, Hamburg 1955; **11... ♘e5** 12. ♔b1 b4 13. ♘ce2 ♘c4 14. ♕d3 ♖c8 15. fe6 fe6 16. ♘f4± Lukić–Milić, Jugoslavija 1958; **11... ♘d4** 12. ♕d4 ♗h6 13. ♔b1 ♗f4 14. ♘e2 ♗e5 15. ♕d2 [15. ♕e3!?] ♕c7 [15... ef5!?] 16. g3 ♖c8 17. ♗h3 ♕c4 18. ♘f4 ♔e7 19. fe6± ♗e6 20. ♘d5 ♗d5 21. ed5 ♖c5 22. ♖he1 a5 23. ♗f5± Talj–Malich, Zlatni Pjasci 1958

[16] 12... ♗c6 13. fe6 fe6 14. ♕f4 ♗e7 15. ♕g4±

[17] 13... 0-0-0 14. ♖hf1 ♗e7 15. ♕e2± Jansa–Commons, Houston 1974 — 18/403

[18] 10. ♗f6 ♕f6 11. e5 [11. ♘f3 ♕d8∓; 11. ♘c6 ♗c6 12. g3 (Tringov–Marszalek, Marianske Lazni 1962) ♕d8∓] de5 12. ♘db5 ♕d8 13. ♘d6 ♗d6 14. ♕d6 ef4 [14... ♕e7 15. ♘e4 ♕d6 16. ♘d6 ♔e7 17. ♘f7! ♖hf8 18. ♘e5± Kotkov–Lejn, SSSR 1971 — 11/350] 15. ♘e4 ♕e7 16. ♕d2 [16. ♕c7 ♗c8] ♗c8 17. ♘d6 ♔f8∓ Šamkovič–Jegorov, SSSR 1961

[19] **10... ♘d4** 11. ♕d4 ♗c6 12. ♘d5 ed5 13. ed5 ♗b5 [13... ♗d7 14. ♖e1 ♗e7 15.

♗f6=∞] 14. c4 ♗d7∞; 12. ♗c4±; **10... ♗e7** 11. ♘f3! [11. ♗e2 ♕c7 12. ♘b3 ♖c8 13. ♗f2 b5∞ Szabo–Lundin, Groningen 1946] b5 12. e5! [12. ♗d3 b4 13. ♘e2 0–0 14. ♖hg1 a5∞ O'Kelly–Unzicker Amsterdam (ol) 1954] b4 13. ef6 bc3 14. ♕c3 gf6 15. f5!± Thiemann–Reynolds, corr. 1966

20 **12. e5** ♘b4 13. ef6 ♖c3 14. ♘d4 ♖a3∓; **12. ♗c4** b5 13. ♗b3 b4 14. ♗f6 gf6 15. ♘e2 ♕b6∞ Matanović–Shervin, Portorož (izt) 1958

21 13. ♗d3 b4 14. ♘e2 ♗e7 15. ♘ed4 [15. ♖hg1 (Unzicker–Kupper, Zürich 1959] ♕b6∞] 0–0 16. ♘b3 ♕b6 17. ♗f2 ♕c7∞ 18. ♕e2 e5= Trifunović–Geler, Jugoslavija–SSSR 1957

22 15... ♗g7 16. ♕d6±

23 18. ♘d2 ♘a3 19. ba3 e5 20. ♘c4± Karanjac–Bekavac, Jugoslavija 1958

24 11 ♘e4? ♕h4 12. ♘c6 ♗c6 13. ♘d6 ♗d6 14. ♕d6 ♖d8 15. ♕d8 16. ♖d8 ♔d8∓ Hačaturov–Toluš, SSSR 1940

25 11... g5 12. ♘e4 gh4 13. ♕c3±

26 **12... ♕b8** 13. ♗f6 gf6 14. ♘e4 d5 [14... ef5 15. ♘d6 ♔d8 16. ♘f7 ♔c8 17. ♘h8+–] 15. ♘f6 ♔d8 16. ♕d2±; **12... ♗e7** 13. ♘d6 ♔f8 14. ♘b7 ♕c7 15. ♕d2±

27 15. ♗c4?! ♘a5 16. ♗e2 h5 17. ♗f3 ♗c6 18. ♘g3 ♔d7 19. ♘f6 ♕f6 20. ♕a5 ♕f4 21. ♔b1 d5 22. ♘h5 ♕b4∞ Gheorghiu–Velimirović, Beograd 1965

28 20. ♘d6 ♗d6 21. ♘f6± Bradvarević–Velimirović, Jugoslavija (ch) 1965

29 **14... ♘e7**? 15. ♖d1 ♘g6 16. ♘e4! ♕e1 17. ♘d6 ♔e7 18. ♗e1 ♘d5 19. ♘b7 ♘gf4 20. g3 ♘g6 21. ♗g2+– Talj–Klavin, SSSR (ch) 1958; **14... ♘b4** 15. a3 [15. ♕e5?! ♘a2 16. ♘a2 ♕a2 17. ♗f6 gf6 18. ♕f6 ♖g8 19. f5± Hennings–Neckař, ČSSR 1973 — 16/380] ♘bd5 16. ♕e5 ♗c6 17. f5 ♕c5 18. ♘d5 ♘d5 19. ♕g7 ♖f8 20. ♕e5 ♕e3 21. ♕e3 ♘e3± Karaklajić–S. Nedeljković, Beograd 1954; 17. ♗c4!±

30 **15. ♖d1**?! ♕f4 16. ♔b1 0-0-0 17. ♗d3 ♕e5∓; **15. ♕d2** ♘e7 16. ♗f6 [16. ♗e2 0-0-0 17. ♖d1 ♗c6 18. ♖d8= Bivšev–Klavin, SSSR 1953; 17... ♘f5 18. ♗f6 gf6 19. ♖d3 ♗c6 20. g3= Barden–Tajmanov, England–SSSR 1954] gf6 17. ♘e4 0-0-0 18. ♘f6 ♗c6 19. ♖d3 [19. ♖d8 ♖d8 20. ♕e3 ♘g6= Schmid–Szabo, Amsterdam (ol) 1954] ♘g6 20. ♘h5 ♗e4 [20... ♔b8∞ Koblenc] 21. ♖c3 ♖d2 22. ♖c7 ♔c7 23. ♔d2 ♘h4 24. ♖g1 ♖d8=∞ Averbah–Tajmanov, SSSR 1954

31 15... ♕f4 16. ♗f6 [16. ♗e2 ♘e4 17. ♘e4 ♕e4 18. ♕f2± Gligorić–Barden, Bognor Regis 1957] ♕f6 [16... gf6 17. ♘d5] 17. ♘e4! ♕e5 18. ♘d6 ♔e7 19. ♕f2±→ Berger–Benkö, Budapest 1955

32 **16. ♗f6** gf6 17. ♕h4 [17. ♘e4 ♗e8 18. ♖d8 ♘d8 19. ♕e3 f5 20. ♘c5 ♗c6 21. ♖g1± Talj–Barda, Uppsala 1956] f5 18. ♗e2 ♗e8 19. ♖hd1 ♖d2 20. ♖d2 ♕e7 21. ♕g3 [Ivkov–Smailbegović, Jugoslavija (ch) 1957] f6±; **16. ♗e2**!? Boleslavski

33 **19. ♖e1** ♘ed5 20. ♘d5 ♖d5 21. ♕g3 ♘e8∞ Lukić–Bradvarević, Jugoslavija 1957; **19. ♖hd1**±

34 **15. ♗f6** gf6 16. ♕h4 ♘b4 [16... ♘e7 17. ♖d2 ♕f5 18. ♗d3 ♘g6 19. ♕f2 ♕f4 20. ♗g6 ♕f2 21. ♖f2 fg6 22. ♖f6± Korčnoj–Averbah, SSSR (ch) 1954] 17. a3 ♘c2 18. ♖d7 ♖d7 19. ♔c2 ♖hd8∞; **15. ♗e2** ♘e7 [15... ♕c7 16. ♖d2 ♕f4 17. ♖f1 ♕e5 18. ♕f2 ♕a5 19. ♗f6 gf6 20. ♕f6 ♘e5 21. ♖fd1± Matanović–Matulović, Jugoslavija (ch) 1954] 16. ♗f6 gf6 17. ♕f2 ♗c6 18. ♖d8 ♖d8= Klovan–Vasjukov, SSSR 1973 — 16/381; **15. ♕d2** ♘e7 16. ♗d3 ♗c6 17. ♖d8 ♖d8 18. ♖d1 ♕h5 19. g3 ♘f5 20. ♗f6 gf6= Gligorić–Averbah, Zürich (ct) 1953

35 **15... e5** 16. ♗c4 ef4 17. ♗f6 gf6 18. ♘e4 ♘e5 19. ♘d6 ♔c7 20. ♕e4± Razuvajev–Kasparjan, SSSR 1963; **15... ♕b4** 16. ♗f6 gf6 17. ♘e4 ♗e8 18. a3 ♕e7 19. ♖d8 ♕d8 20. ♕c3 e5 21. ♗c4± Liberzon–Šajtar, Leipzig 1965; **15... ♘e7** 16. ♕e5 [16. ♗d3 ♗c6 17. a3 ♘ed5 18. ♘d5 ♖d5 19. ♕e3 ♖hd8∞ Schmidt–Padevski, Polanica Zdroj 1968 — 6/514] ♕e5 17. fe5 ♘f5 18. ef6! [18. ♗f6? gf6 19. ef6 ♗c6 20. ♗d3 ♖hg8 21. ♘e4 ♖d4=∞ Bertok–Rabar, Jugoslavija (ch) 1954] ♘h4 19. ♘e4 [Tringov–Bilek, Teesside 1972 — 13/434] ♗c6 20. ♘d6 ♔c7 21. ♘f7 ♖d2 22. ♔d2 ♖g8 23. ♘e5 gf6 24. ♘c6±

36 15. ♗g3 ♘d5! 16. ♘d5 [16. ♘e4?! ♕a2 17. ♘d6 ♔b8 18. ♘f7 ♔a8∓] ed5 17. a3 f5⇆∞ Matanović–Rabar, Jugoslavija (ch) 1954

37 Milić–Đurašević, Jugoslavija (ch) 1954

38 **15... ♘e7**? 16. ♘d5!+–; **15... g5** 16. fg5 hg5 17. ♗g3± [17... ♘d5? 18. ♘d5+–]; **15... ♕f5** 16. ♗d3! ♕f4 17. ♔b1±; **15... ♔b8** 16. ♗e2 ♗c8 17. ♕g3 ♕c7 18. ♔b1 ♖dg8 19. ♕e3 ♖d8 20. ♗g3± Toran–Kramer, Beverwijk 1956; **15... e5** 16. fe5 [16. ♗c4 ef4 17. ♘e4 ♗e6 18. ♗e6 fe6 19. ♘d6 (Matanović–Darga, Jugoslavija–BRD 1961) ♔b8 20. ♕e6 ♖hf8∞] ♖he8 17. ♗g3 ♘e5 18. ♘b5! ♗g4 [18... ♘d3? 19. ♗d3 ♖e1 20. ♘a7#] 19. ♖d8 ♖d8 20. ♘a7 ♔b8 21. ♘c6 bc6 22. ♕e5± Levin–Zak, SSSR 1958

39 20. ♘d5 ♖d5 [20... ♗d5 21. ♕a7 ♕a5 22. ♖e5+– Ivkov–Bobekov, Beograd 1955] 21. ♕g3 e4 [21... ♘e8 22. ♗c4 ♖d1 23. ♖d1 **f6** 24. ♕a3±] 22. ♕c7 ♔c7 23. ♗f6 ed3 24. ♗g7 ♖hd8 25. ♗e5± Spaski–Rabar, Göteborg (izt) 1955

B 68 1. e4 c5 2. ♘f3 d6 3. d4 cd4 4. ♘d4 ♘f6 5. ♘c3 ♘c6 6. ♗g5 e6 7. ♕d2 a6 8. 0-0-0 ♗d7 9. f4 ♗e7

	10	11	12	13	14	15	16	17	18	
1	f5[1] ♘e5[2]	fe6 fe6	♘f3 ♕c7	♗e2 0-0-0[3]	♖hf1 ♖hf8	♔b1 ♔b8	♕d4 h6	♗h4 ♗c8[4]		=
2	♗e2 0—0[5]	♗f3 h6[6]	♗h4 ♘e4	♗e7[7] ♘d2	♗d8 ♘f3	♘f3 ♖fd8	♖d6 ♔f8	♖hd1 ♔e7	♘a4 ♗e8[8]	=
3	♕e1 h6[9]	♗h4 g5	fg5 ♘g4	♘c6 ♗c6	♗g3 hg5	♕e2 ♘f6	e5 ♘h5	ed6 ♘g3	♕e5 ♗f6[10]	=/∞
4	♘f3 b5[11]	♗d3[12] ♕a5[13]	♔b1 b4[14]	♘e2 0—0	♖hg1 ♘g4	♗e7 ♘e7	♘ed4 ♘c6	h3 ♘f6	g4 ♘d4[15]	=
5	... ...	... b4	♘e2 0—0[16]	♘g3[17] ♕a5	♔b1 h6	♗h4[18] ♖ab8	♖he1			∞
6	... ...	e5 b4[19]	ed6 bc3	♕c3 ♗f8	f5 ♕a5[20]	♗f6 gf6[21]	♕f6 ♖g8[22]	♗c4 ♗g7	fe6 fe6[23]	∓
7	... ...	... ...	ef6 bc3	♕c3 gf6	♗h4[24] a5[25]	♔b1[26] ♘b4[27]	a3 ♖c8	♕d2[28] ♘d5	c4 ♘b6[29]	±
8	... ...	... ...	... ...	... ...	... d5	♔b1[30] ♘a5[31]	♗e1[32] ♘b7	f5 ♖c8	♕d2	∞

[1] **10. ♗f6** ♗f6 11. ♘b3 ♗e7∓ Castiglioni—S. Nedeljković, Italia—Jugoslavija 1951; **10. ♘c6** ♗c6 11. ♗d3 ♕c7 12. ♖he1 0-0-0 13. e5 ♘e8 [13... de5 14. fe5±] 14. ♗e7 ♕e7 15. ♗e4 d5 16. ♗d3 ♘c7 17. ♕f2± Bronštejn—Ragozin, SSSR (ch) 1949; 11... h6! 12. ♗h4 g5∞; **10. ♔b1** ♘d4 11. ♕d4 ♗c6 12. e5 de5 13. ♕e5 ♕b8 14. ♕d4 ♕c7= Keres—Ciocaltea, Moskva 1956; **10. ♘b3** b5 [10... ♕c7 11. ♗e2 0-0-0 12. ♗f6 gf6 13. ♗h5± van den Berg—Stahlberg, Beverwijk 1963] 11. ♗f6 gf6 12. ♔b1 ♕b6 13. ♗e2 h5 14. ♗f3 0-0-0 15. ♕e2 [Kozlov—Lepeškin, SSSR 1971 — 11/351] h4∞

[2] **10... ♘d4** 11. ♕d4 ef5 12. ♗d3 0—0 13. ef5± Hennings—Korenski, Soči 1973 — 17/435; **10... ♖c8** 11. fe6 fe6 12. ♗c4 ♘d4 13. ♕d4 ♕a5 14. ♗f6± Holmov—Tajmanov, Leningrad 1967 — 3/461

[3] 13... ♖d8!? 14. ♘e5?! de5 15. ♗h5?! g6 16. ♗e2 0—0 17. ♕e1 b5∓ Mecking—Hort, San Antonio 1972 — 14/426; 14. ♖hf1=

[4] Keres—Najdorf, Moskva 1956

[5] **10... b5** 11. ♗f3 b4 12. ♘ce2 ♕c7 13. e5±; **10... ♕c7** 11. ♘b3 [11. ♗f3 0-0-0 12. ♘b3 ♘e8? 13. ♘d5± R. Byrne—Mednis, USA (ch) 1972 — 13/436; 12... ♘a5∞] b5 12. ♗f6 gf6 13. ♗h5± Mnacakanjan—Hellman, Krakow 1964; **10... ♖c8** 11. ♗f3 ♘a5 12. e5 ♘c4 13. ♕e1 ♕b6 14. ♘b3 de5 15. fe5 ♘d5∞ Sokolski—Kopilov, SSSR (ch) 1949

[6] 11... ♖c8!? 12. ♖he1 h6

[7] 13. ♘e4 ♗h4 14. ♘d6 ♕c7=

[8] Fischer—Spaski (m) 1972 — 14/425

[9] **10... 0—0**?! 11. e5 ♘d5 12. ♗e7 ♕e7 13. ♘f5± Gipslis—Rusakov, SSSR 1966 — 2/407; **10... ♕c7** 11. ♘f3 0-0-0 12. ♔b1 ♔b8 13. e5± Judovič—Hasin, SSSR 1959; **10... ♘d4** 11. ♖d4 ♕b6 12. ♖d2△ e5±; 11... ♕a5!?

[10] 19. ♕g3 ♕a5 20. ♗c4 ♖h4 21. ♗b3 ♗e5=/∞ Estrin—Lorens, corr. 1964

[11] **10... ♕c7** 11. e5 de5 12. fe5 ♘d5 13. ♘d5 ed5 14. ♗e7 ♘e7 15. ♗d3 0—0 16. ♕g5 ♘c6 17. ♕h5± Kamišov—Čehover, SSSR 1950; **10... h6** 11. ♗f6 gf6 12. f5 ♕c7 13. ♔b1 0-0-0 14. ♗c4± Spaski—Žuhovicki, SSSR 1958; **10... ♖c8** 11. ♔b1 ♕c7 12. e5 de5 13. fe5 ♘d5 14. ♘d5 ed5 15. ♗e7 ♘e7 16. ♗d3± Spaski—Tajmanov, SSSR 1956

[12] 11. a3 b4 12. ab4 ♘b4 13. ♔b1 [13. e5? ♕a5 14. ♔b1 ♘e4—+; 13. ♗f6 gf6 14. f5 ♖c8 15. ♔b1 e5 16. ♘d5 ♘d5 17. ♕d5 ♕b6 18. ♘d2 0—0 19. h4 ♖c5 20. ♕b3 ♕c7 21. ♖h3 ♖b8 22. ♖g3 ♔f8 23. ♕e3 ♗a4∓ Petro-

sjan–Tihonski, SSSR 1964] ♗c6 14. ♗c4 0–0 15. ♖he1 ♕c7 16. ♘d4 d5 17. ed5 ♗d5 18. ♘d5 ♘bd5= Vasjukov–Wade, Moskva 1962

13 **11... h6** 12. ♗h4 g5 [12... ♕c7 13. h3 b4 14. ♘e2 e5 15. ♔b1 a5 16. g4± Matanović–Toluš, Hastings 1953/54] 13. fg5 ♘g4 14. e5 ♘ge5 15. ♘e5 ♘e5 16. ♘e4 hg5 17. ♗g5 ♗g5 18. ♘g5 ♗c6= Židkov–Šamkovič, SSSR 1973 — 16/383; **11... ♕c7** 12. ♖he1 b4 13. ♘d5 ed5 14. ed5∞ Udovčić–Malich, Gotha 1957

14 12... h6 13. ♗h4 b4 14. ♘e2 e5 15. f5 d5 16. ed5 ♕d5 17. ♘g3± Smailbegović–Ciocaltea, Sarajevo 1957

15 19. ♘d4 ♕b6 20. ♘f3 ♗c6= Olafsson–Toluš, Hastings 1953/54

16 **12... ♕b6** 13. e5 ♘g4 14. ♗e7 ♘e7 15. ed6 ♘d5 16. ♗e4 ♘f2 17. ♗d5 ed5 18. ♘ed4± Šabanov–Arsenjev, SSSR 1965; **12... ♕c7** 13. ♔b1 a5 14. ♘ed4 ♘d4 15. ♘d4 ♕b6 16. ♘f3 ♗c6∞ Medina–Cuellar, Caracas 1961; **12... a5** 13. e5 de5 14. fe5 ♘d5 15. ♗e7 ♘ce7 16. ♘g3 ♕b6∞ Thorsteinsson–Barden, Varna (ol) 1962

17 13. e5 de5 14. ♗f6 ♗f6 15. ♗e4 ♖a7 ♗c6 ♗c6 17. ♕b4 ♕c7= Trifunović–Ivkov, Jugoslavija (ch) 1956

18 15. h4 [Karklins–Jansa, Houston 1974 — 18/406] ♖ab8!? 16. f5 ef5 17. ef5 ♘d5∓

19 11... de5? 13. fe5 b4 13. ef6 bc3 14. ♕d7+– Ivkov–Ciocaltea, Beograd 1956

20 14... ♘e4? 15. ♕e3 ♘g5 16. ♘g5 h6 17. ♘f7 ♔f7 18. ♗c4 ♕g5 19. fe6±

21 15... ♘b4 16. ♗c4 ♖c8 17. a3 ♘a2 18. ♗a2 ♖c3 19. ♗c3±

22 16... ♕a2 17. fe6 fe6 [17... ♗e6 18. d7 ♗d7 19. ♗c4+–] 18. ♕h8 0-0-0 19. ♕f6 ♘b4 20. ♘g5±

23 19. ♕h4 ♖b8 20. ♗b3 ♕f5 [20... ♖b3∓ Larsen–Panno, Mar del Plata 1958] 21. ♖he1 ♗f6 22. ♕f2 ♔d8∓ Burger–Mednis, USA 1970 — 9/369

24 14. f5 d5 15. fe6 fe6 16. ♘d4 ♕a5 17. ♕a5 ♘a5 18. ♗h4 e5 19. ♘b3 ♘b3 20. ab3 ♗e6∓ Beljavski–Spaski, SSSR (ch) 1973 — 16/382

25 14... ♕a5 15. ♗f6 [15. ♕a5 ♘a5 16. ♗e1± Ivkov–Wood, Bognor Regis 1958] ♘b4 16. ♗c4 ♖c8 17. a3±

26 **15. a3** ♖c8 16. ♕e3 ♕c7 17. ♖d2 a4 18. ♘d4 ♘a5 19. ♘b5 ♕b8 20. ♘c3 d5 21. ♖d5 ♖c3∓ Pilnik–Spaanjard, Beverwijk 1957; **15. ♘d4** ♘b4 16. ♔b1 ♖b8 17. ♕d2 ♕b6 18. c3 ♘d5∓ Beni–Tajmanov, Wien 1953; **15. ♗d3** ♖b8 16. ♖he1 ♘b4 17. ♔b1 0–0 18. ♘d2∞ Željandinov–Vistaneckis, SSSR 1954

27 15... ♖b8 16. g4 ♘b4 17. a3 ♖c8 18. ♕b3 ♘d5 19. ♖d5± Gligorić–Conrady, Dublin 1957

28 17. ♕b3!?

29 20. ♕a5± Jimenez–Tajmanov, La Habana 1967 — 4/502

30 15. ♘d4 ♕a5 16. ♕a5 ♘a5= Koch–Bouwmeester, Moskva (ol) 1956

31 **15... ♘b4** 16. ♘d4 ♖c8 [16... ♕a5 17. a3 ♘c6 18. ♕a5 ♘a5 19. ♗e2± S. Nedeljković–Clemens, Oberhausen 1961] 17. ♕b3! [17. ♕e3 ♕b6 18. a3 ♘c6 19. ♖d3 ♘d4= Matanović–Perez, Beverwijk 1958] ♕a5 18. ♗e1! [18. a3?! ♘c2] ♗a4 19. ♕a3!± Matanović–Jansa, Lugano (ol) 1968 — 6/516; **15... a5** 16. ♗b5 ♖c8 17. ♘d4 ♘d4 18. ♗d7 ♕d7 19. ♕d4 ♖g8 20. g3 ♕b5 21. ♖he1 ♖c4 22. ♕a7± Schmid–Kunsztowicz, BRD 1973 — 15/389; 17... ♘b4!?

32 16. f5 ♖c8 17. ♕d2 ♕c7 18. fe6 fe6 19. ♗a6 ♖a8∓ Kestler–Spaski, Dortmund 1973 — 15/388

B 69

1. e4 c5 2. ♘f3 d6 3. d4 cd4 4. ♘d4 ♘f6 5. ♘c3 ♘c6 6. ♗g5 e6 7. ♕d2 a6 8. 0-0-0 ♗d7 9. f4 ♗e7 10. ♘f3 b5 11. ♗f6

	11	12	13	14	15	16	17	18	19	
1	... ♗f6	♕d6 ♗e7[1]	♕d2 ♖a7[2]	♕e3 ♕c8	♗d3 ♖c7	♔b1 0–0	e5 ♘b4	♗e4 ♖d8	♘d4[3]	±
2	... gf6	♗d3[4] ♕a5	♔b1 b4	♘e2 ♕c5[5]	f5 a5	♘f4 a4	♖c1 ♖b8	c3 b3	a3 ♘e5[6]	=

	11	12	13	14	15	16	17	18	19	
3	...	♔b1	g3[7]	♘e2	f5	♘c1	g4	g5		∞
	...	♕b6	b4[8]	a5	e5	♖c8	♘a7[9]	♗c6[10]		

1. e4 c5 2. ♘f3 d6 3. d4 cd4 4. ♘d4 ♘f6 5. ♘c3 ♘c6 6. ♗g5 e6 7. ♕d2 a6 8. 0-0-0 ♗d7 9. f4 ♗e7 10. ♘f3 b5 11. ♗f6 gf6 12. f5

	12	13	14	15	16	17	18	19	20	
4	...	♘e2[11]	♘g3	♗c4	♗d5	♘f1[12]	♘e3	♔b1	♖he1	±
	b4	e5	h5	♘a5	♖b8	♕c7	♗f8	♗h6		
5	...	fe6[13]	g4	♘e2	♔b1	♖g1	♘f4	h4	♘d4	±
	0–0	fe6	b4	♕b6	♔h8	♖g8	♕c5	♘e5	♕c8[14]	
6	...	♔b1	g3[16]	♗h3	fe6	♗f5	♘d5	♖d2	ed5	±
	♕a5	0-0-0[15]	♔b8	♖c8[17]	♗e6	♖c7	♕d2	♗d5	♘e5[18]	
7	...	♔b1[19]	g3	♗h3[20]	♘e2	c3!?[21]				±
	♕b6	0-0-0	♔b8	b4	e5					

[1] **12... b4** 13. ♘a4 ♖a7 14. ♕c5 ♕b8 15. ♕e3± S. Garcia–Polugajevski, La Habana 1967 — 4/503; **12... ♖a7** 13. e5 ♗e7 14. ♕d2± Gaprindašvili–Paoli, Dortmund 1974 — 19/404

[2] 13... b4 14. ♘a4 [14. ♘e2?! ♖a7 15. ♔b1 ♕b6=∞ Parma–Kunsztowicz, Dortmund 1973 — 16/384; 15. ♘ed4 ♕b6 16. ♘c6 ♗c6 17. ♗d3 0–0 18. ♘e5 ♗b5 19. ♔b1 ♖c8=∞ Schmid–R. Byrne, San Juan 1969 — 8/393] ♖a7 [14... ♘b8 15. ♕d4 ♕c7 16. ♘b6 ♖a7 (Gufeljd–Simagin, SSSR (ch) 1956) 17. ♔b1±] 15. ♕f2 ♕c7 16. ♘b6 ♘b8 17. ♘d7 ♕f4∞ Ree–Timman, Wijk aan Zee 1974; 15. ♕e3±

[3] Suetin–Csom, Kecskemet 1972 — 13/437

[4] **12. ♖e1** ♕a5 13. ♔b1 0-0-0 14. g3 [Timman–Deže, Sombor 1974 — 18/405] ♔b8=; **12. g3** ♕b6 13. ♗h3 ♘a5 14. ♘d4 b4= Honfi–Borisenko, Gyula 1965; **12. ♕e3** ♕c7 13. ♗d3 ♘a5 14. ♔b1 ♕c5= Bouwmeester–Gheorghiu, Varna (ol) 1962

[5] 14... ♖g8 15. ♘g3 ♕c5 16. ♖he1 ♖a7 17. e5!± Geler–Larsen (m) 1966 — 1/289

[6] Fischer–Spaski (m) 1972 — 14/424

[7] 13. ♗d3!? 0-0-0 14. ♖he1△ ♘d5 Kurajica

[8] 13... ♘a5 14. ♖e1 ♖c8 15. f5 b4 16. ♘d1= Scholl–Timman, Nederland (ch) 1974 — 17/436

[9] 17... a4!?

[10] **18... fg5** 19. ♘e5± Klovan–Kuprejčik, SSSR 1972 — 14/423; **18... ♗c6**∞

[11] 13. fe6 fe6 14. ♘e2 ♕a5 15. ♔b1 e5 16. ♘g3 ♗e6 17. b3 ♘a7 18. ♗c4 ♘b5 19. ♗e6 ♘c3 20. ♕c3 bc3∓ Golemišev–Panov, SSSR 1964

[12] 17. ♔b1?! ♕c7 18. ♕f2 ♘c4 19. ♘f1 ♘a3 20. ♔c1 ♗f8 21. ♘e3 ♗h6 22. ♖he1 [Nikitin–Malich, Budapest 1959] ♘b5∞

[13] 13. ♔b1 ♔h8 14. g4 ♖g8 15. ♖g1 ♖c8 16. ♘e2± Trifunović–Milić, Jugoslavija (ch) 1956

[14] Petrosjan–Dementjev, SSSR 1964

[15] **13... h5** 14. g3 ♘e5 15. ♘e5 fe5 16. ♗h3± Vasjukov–Partos, Bucuresti 1967 — 3/462; **13... ♖c8** 14. ♗d3 [14. fe6 fe6 15. e5 fe5 16. ♕h6 ♘b4 17. a3 ♘c2∓ Thorvaldsson–Westerinen, Varna (ol) 1962] ♘b4 15. ♘d4 ♘d3 16. ♕d3 b4 17. ♘ce2 e5 18. ♘b3 ♕a4 19. ♕e3 ♗c6 20. ♘g3 h5 21. ♕f3∞ Dückstein–Geler, Zagreb 1955; 14. g3!?±

[16] 14. ♘d4 ♔b7 15. ♘b3 ♕b6 16. ♘e2± Bink–Kramer, Beverwijk 1957

[17] 15... ♗c8 16. ♖he1 h5 17. ♕e3 ♗d7 18. ♘e2± Talj–R. Byrne, La Habana (ol) 1966 — 2/408

[18] 21. ♘d4 h6 22. ♖e1 ♔b7 23. ♖e4± Bihovski–Averbah, SSSR 1967 — 3/463

[19] **13 fe6** fe6 14. ♘e2 ♘e5?! 15. ♘f4 ♘c4 16. ♗c4 bc4 17. ♕c3 0–0 18. ♘d4 d5 19. ed5 e5 20. ♘fe6± Kuzmin–Pytel, Hastings 1973/74 — 17/437; 14... ♕a5=; **13. ♘e2** ♕a5 [13... ♘e5 14. ♘f4 ♖c8 15. fe6 fe6 16. ♘d4 ♘c4 17. ♕e1± Fichtl–Neckař, ČSSR (ch) 1974 — 17/438; 13... ♕f2 14. ♘fd4 ♘d4 15. ♕d4 ♕d4= Kupper–Panno, München (ol) 1958]

14. ♔b1 ♕d2 15. ♖d2 ♘e5 16. ♘ed4 ♗f8= Saharov—Borisenko, SSSR (ch) 1964; **13. g3** 0-0-0 [13... b4 14. fe6 fe6 15. ♘e2 ♕f2 16. ♘h4 ♘e5 17. ♕b4 d5=∞ Zagorovski—Borisenko, corr. 1964] 14. ♗h3 ♕c5 [14... ♔b8?! 15. fe6 fe6 16. ♘e2 ♖he8 17. ♘f4 ♗f8 18. ♘h4± Averbah—Fridštejn, SSSR 1957] 15. ♘e1 ♘e5 16. ♘d3 ♘d3= Clemens—Bielicki, München-stein 1959

20 15. fe6!? fe6 16. ♗h3

21 **17. c4** ♘a5 18. b3 ♗c6 19. ♕d3 ♘b7 20. ♘d2 ♗f8 21. ♕f3 ♗h6 22. ♖he1 1/2 : 1/2 Boleslavski—Tajmanov, SSSR 1970 — 9/368; **17. c3**±

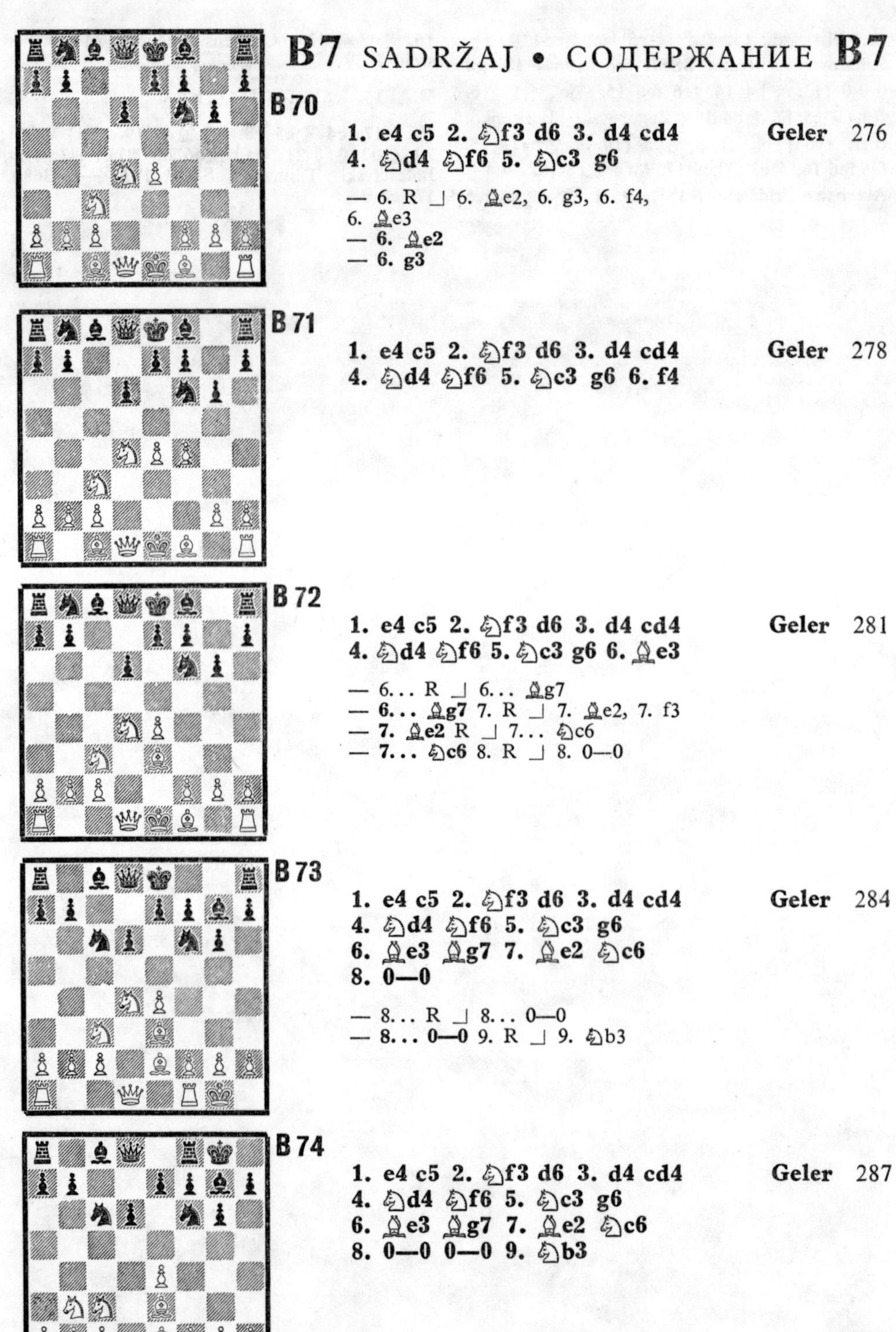

B7 SADRŽAJ • СОДЕРЖАНИЕ B7

B7 SOMMAIRE • INDICE B7

B 75

1. e4 c5 2. ♘f3 d6 3. d4 cd4 4. ♘d4 ♘f6 5. ♘c3 g6 6. ♗e3 ♗g7 7. f3 — **Geler** 290

— 7... R ⌋ 7... 0—0

B 76

1. e4 c5 2. ♘f3 d6 3. d4 cd4 4. ♘d4 ♘f6 5. ♘c3 g6 6. ♗e3 ♗g7 7. f3 0—0 — **Geler** 293

— 8. R ⌋ 8. ♕d2
— **8. ♕d2** R ⌋ 8... ♘c6
— **8... ♘c6** 9. R ⌋ 9. 0—0—0, 9. ♗c4
— **9. 0—0—0**

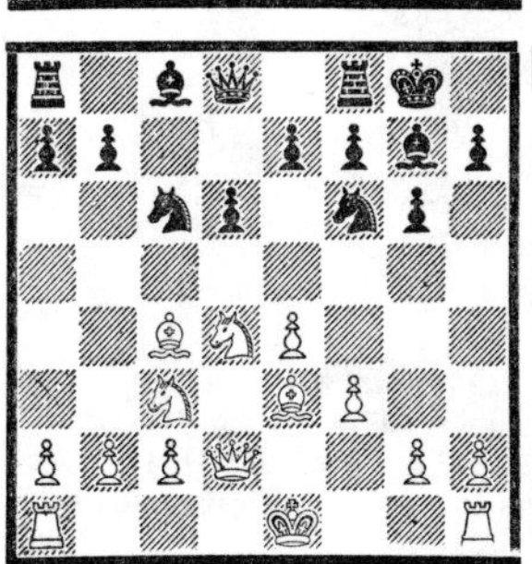

B 77

1. e4 c5 2. ♘f3 d6 3. d4 cd4 4. ♘d4 ♘f6 5. ♘c3 g6 6. ♗e3 ♗g7 7. f3 0—0 8. ♕d2 ♘c6 9. ♗c4 — **Geler** 295

— 9... R ⌋ 9... ♗d7
— **9... ♗d7** 10. R ⌋ 10. 0—0—0

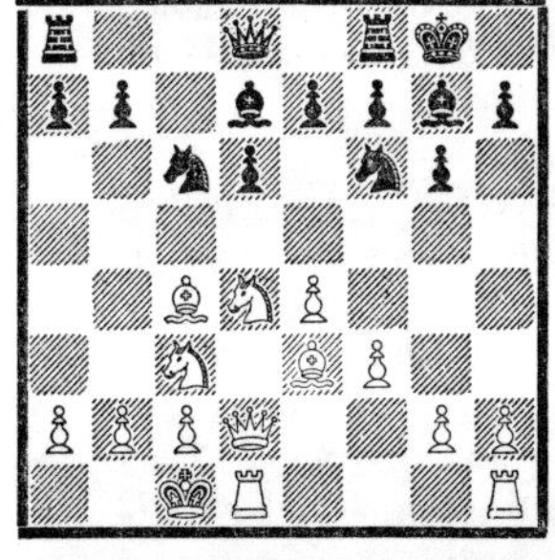

B 78

1. e4 c5 2. ♘f3 d6 3. d4 cd4 4. ♘d4 ♘f6 5. ♘c3 g6 6. ♗e3 ♗g7 7. f3 0—0 8. ♕d2 ♘c6 9. ♗c4 ♗d7 10. 0—0—0 — **Geler** 300

— 10... R ⌋ 10... ♕a5
— **10... ♕a5** 11. R ⌋ 11. ♗b3
— **11. ♗b3 ♖fc8** 12. R ⌋ 12. h4

B 79

1. e4 c5 2. ♘f3 d6 3. d4 cd4 4. ♘d4 ♘f6 5. ♘c3 g6 6. ♗e3 ♗g7 7. f3 0—0 8. ♕d2 ♘c6 9. ♗c4 ♗d7 10. 0—0—0 ♕a5 11. ♗b3 ♖fc8 12. h4 — **Geler** 303

B 70 1. e4 c5 2. ♘f3 d6 3. d4 cd4 4. ♘d4 ♘f6 5. ♘c3 g6

	6	7	8	9	10	11	12	13	14	
1	♘d5[1]	♗b5	0–0	♘b3	♖e1	♗f1	♘f6[3]	c3		=
	♗g7[2]	♗d7	♘c6	0–0	a6	♖c8	♗f6			
2	♗g5	♕d2[5]	0-0-0[6]	♘c6	e5	ed6	♗e7	♕d6	♕d2	$\overline{\infty}$
	♗g7[4]	♘c6	0–0[7]	bc6	♘e8	♘d6	♕e7	♕g5	♕d2[8]	
3	h3[9]	♗e3	g4	g5	h4	f4	♘de2			=
	♗g7[10]	♘c6	0–0[11]	♘e8[12]	♘c7	e5!	♗g4[13]			
4	♗e2	♘b3[14]	g4[15]	f4	♗f3	h4	a4	h5	e5	$\overline{\infty}$
	♗g7	♘c6	b6!	♗b7	0–0	a5	♘b4	d5	♘g4![16]	
5	...	0–0	♘b3[17]	♗g5[19]	f4[20]	♕e1	a4	♖c1	♖c2	$\overline{\infty}$
	...	0–0	♘c6[18]	♗e6	♕c8[21]	a5	♘b4	♘c2	♗b3[22]	
6	...	...	...	♔h1[23]	a4	f4	f5[26]	cb3	♗c4[28]	=
	...	...	...	a5[24]	♗e6	♕b6[25]	♗b3	♕b4![27]		
7	...	...	...	f4	♗f3[30]	♘d5	ed5	♘a5	♖e1	=
	...	...	...	b5[29]	b4[31]	♘d5	♘a5	♕a5	♕c7[32]	
8	g3	♗g2	0–0[34]	♘b3	♘d5	ed5	♘d4	c3	h3	=
	♗g7[33]	0–0	♘c6	♗d7	♘d5	♘e5	♕b6	♖ac8	♕c5[35]	
9	...	...	...	♘de2	h3[37]	♘d5	♘ef4[40]	♘d5	♘e3	=
	...	...	...	♗d7[36]	♖c8[38]	♘e5[39]	♘d5	e6	♗b5[41]	
10	...	♗g2[42]	♕d4	0–0[44]	♕d3[45]	♗d2[46]	b3	♖ac1	♘d5	=
	♘c6	♘d4[43]	♗g7	0–0	♗e6	♕c7	a6	♖fd8	♘d5[47]	

1 **6. f3**?! ♕b6!; **6. ♗b5** ♗d7 7. ♗d7 ♘bd7?! 8. 0–0 ♗g7 9. ♗e3 0–0 10. f4 ♖c8 11. ♕f3± Korčnoj–Mojsejev, SSSR 1950; 7... ♕d7=; **6. ♗d3** ♗g7 7. 0–0 0–0 8. h3 ♘c6 9. ♗e3 ♗d7=; **6. ♘de2** ♗g7 7. ♘f4 ♘c6 8. ♗e2 b6 9. ♘fd5 ♘d5=; **6. ♗c4** ♗g7 [6... ♘c6? 7. ♘c6± — B 57] 7. h3 [7. 0–0 0–0 8. ♗b3 ♘c6 9. ♗g5?! ♕a5 10. ♘d5?! ♘e4 11. ♘c6 bc6 12. ♘e7 ♔h8 13. ♘c8 ♖ac8 14. ♗c1 d5∓ Boleslavski; 9. ♘de2=] 0–0 8. ♗b3 ♘bd7 9. 0–0 ♘c5 10. ♖e1 ♘b3 11. ab3 a6 12. f4 [Bradvarević–Velimirović, Jugoslavija (ch) 1966 — 1/292] e5!?=

2 6... ♘e4? 7. ♗b5 ♗d7 8. ♕e2 f5 9. f3 ♘c6 [9... ♘c5 10. b4 ♘ca6 11. ♘e6 ♗b5 12. ♕b5 ♕d7 13. ♘ec7+−] 10. ♘b3 ♘c5 11. ♘c5 dc5 12. ♗f4 ♖c8 13. 0-0-0 ♔f7 14. ♗c4 e6 15. ♘c7± Estrin–Govbinder, SSSR 1943

3 12. ♗e3 ♘d5 13. ed5 ♘e5 14. ♗d4 ♗f5 15. c3 g5!∓ Estrin–Averbah, SSSR 1939

4 6... ♘c6 7. ♗f6 — B 60

5 **7. ♗b5** ♗d7 8. ♕e2 0–0 9. 0-0-0 ♕a5 10. ♖he1 ♖c8 11. ♘b3 ♗b5 12. ♕b5= Grečkin–Mojsejev, SSSR 1951; **7. ♗e2** — 6. ♗e2

6 8. ♘b3 0–0 9. 0-0-0 ♗e6 10. ♔b1 ♖c8 11. f3?! ♖e8 12. g4 ♘e5 13. ♗e2 ♘fd7 14. ♗h6 ♗h8 15. h4 ♘b6∓ Panov–Kan, SSSR (ch) 1937; 11. ♗h6=

7 8... ♘e4 9. ♘e4 ♗d4 [9... ♘d4? 10. ♘f6! ef6 11. ♕d4± Rauzer–Ragozin, SSSR 1936] 10. ♗b5 ♗g7 11. ♕e3 0–0 12. ♗c6 bc6 13. ♘d6 ♕a5 14. ♗e7 ♕a2 (Ragozin) 15. ♗f8 ♕b2$\overline{\infty}$

8 **14... ♕a5** 15. ♗c4 ♖b8 16. ♗b3 ♗f5∞ Rauzer–Kan, SSSR 1936; **14... ♕d2** 15. ♔d2 ♗h6$\overline{\infty}$ Ragozin

9 Lasker

10 6... a6 — B 90

11 8... a6 9. g5 ♘d7 10. ♗e2 ♕a5 11. ♕d2 ♘c5 12. ♖d1 ♗e6 13. a3 0-0-0 14. ♘c6 bc6 15. ♗d4±→ Henkin–Čistjakov, SSSR 1954

12 9... ♘d7 10. h4 ♕a5 11. f4 ♘d4 12. ♗d4 e5 13. fe5 ♘e5 14. ♗e2 ♕b4 13. a3 ♕d4 16. ♕d4 ♘f3= Reti–Sämisch, Kiel 1921

13 Lasker–Napier, Cambridge Springs 1904

14 **7. h4**?! d5∓↑⊞; **7. ♗g5**?! ♕a5!∓ 8. ♕d2? ♘e4!∓

15 8. 0–0 ♗e6 9. f4 ♖c8 10. f5 ♗d7 11. g4± Gusev–Averbah, SSSR 1951; 8... 0–0 — 7. 0–0

16 15. ♘d4! ♘h6 16. hg6 fg6! [16... hg6 17. f5±] 17. ♘e6 ♕d7 18. ♘f8 ♖f8 19. ♘b5 d4$\overline{\infty}$ Smislov–Korčnoj, Moskva 1960

17 **8. f3** ♘c6 9. ♗e3 d5=; **8. h3** d5 9. ed5 [9. e5?! ♘e4] ♘d5=

18 8... ♘bd7 9. a4 a6 10. ♗e3±; 8... ♗e6 9. f4 b5 10. ♗f3 ♕b6 11. ♕d4! ♗b3 12. ♕b6 ab6 13. cb3 b4 14. e5± Matanović–Castaldi, Jugoslavija–Italia 1951

19 9. f3 (Euwe) ♗e6 10. ♘d5 ♗d5 [10... ♖c8 11. c4 ♘e5 12. ♘d4 b5!=∞] 11. ed5 ♘b4 12. c4 b5! 13. a3 bc4 14. ♗c4 ♖c8∓↑

20 10. ♕d2 ♘a5 11. ♗h6 ♘c4 12. ♗c4 ♗c4 13. ♗g7 ♔g7 14. ♖fe1 ♖c8 15. ♖e3 ♕c7 16. ♘d4 e5 17. ♘f5 gf5= Benkö–Wexler, Buenos Aires 1960

21 **10... a5** 11. a4 ♖c8 12. ♔h1 ♕b6! [12... ♘b4 13. ♘d4! ♗c4 14. ♘db5± Platonov–Buslaev, SSSR 1967] 13. f5 ♗b3 14. cb3 ♕b4∞; **10... b5**! 11. ♗f3 [11. ♗b5? ♘e4] ♖c8= Aljehin–P. Schmidt 1941

22 15. ♖c1 ♕d8 16. ♕h4=∞ Bohosjan–Minev, Bulgaria 1974 — 17/453

23 Aljehin

24 **9... a6** 10. f4 ♕c7 11. g4± Aljehin–Foltys, München 1942; **9... ♗e6** 10. f4 ♕c8! [10... ♘a5 11. ♗f3 ♗c4 12. ♖g1△ g4± König–Thomas, Bournemouth 1939] 11. ♗e3 — B 74

25 11... ♕c8 12. ♗e3 [12. ♗f3?! ♘b4 13. ♘d4 ♗c4 14. ♖f2 ♖d8 15. ♗e3 e5∓ Goljak–Gufeljd, SSSR 1959] ♗g4 13. ♗g1 ♖d8 14. ♘d5 ♗e2 15. ♕e2 ♘d5 16. ed5 ♘b4 17. c4± Aljehin–Golombek, Montevideo 1939

26 12. ♘d5 ♗d5 13. ed5 ♘b4 14. ♗f3 ♕a6 [L. Steiner–Podgorny, Karlovy Vary 1948] 15. ♗e2= Larsen

27 13... ♕d4 14. ♕d4 ♘d4 15. ♗c4± Enevoldsen–Minev, München (ol) 1958

28 **14. ♗e3** ♘d7 15. ♗c4 ♘b6 16. ♘a2 ♘c4 17. ♘b4 ♘e3=∞ van den Berg–Larsen, Beverwijk 1959; **14. ♗c4**!?△ ♘d5=

29 9... ♕b6 10. ♔h1 a5 11. a4 ♗e6 — 9. ♔h1

30 10. ♗b5? ♘e4 11. ♗c6 ♕b6 12. ♔h1 ♕c6 13. ♘d5 ♖e8 14. c3 ♗b7∓ Giusti–Nutrizio, corr. 1949

31 10... ♗b7!? 11. ♗e3 a6 Euwe

32 15. a3 ♗f5 16. ♗e4 ♗e4 17. ♖e4 a5=

33 6... ♗g4 7. ♕d3!? ♕c8 8. ♗g2 ♗g7 [8... ♘bd7!? 9. 0–0 ♘c5] 9. h3! ♗d7 10. ♗e3± Adams–Suesman, Boston 1944; 7. f3 ♗d7 8. ♗e3 ♗g7 9. ♕d2 0–0 10. 0-0-0 ♘c6 11. g4 ♖c8 — B 75

34 8. h3 ♘c6 9. ♘b3 ♗d7 [9... ♗e6?! 10. ♘d5! a5 11. a4 ♘b4 12. c3 ♘bd5 13. ed5 ♗d7 14. ♘d4 ♕c8 15. ♕b3 ♘e8 16. ♗e3 ♘c7 17. h4± Korčnoj–Suetin, SSSR (ch) 1963] 10. ♘d5 ♘d5 14. ed5 ♘e5=

35 15. ♕e2 ♖fe8 16. ♖d1 ♘c4 [Barcza–Pachman, Praha 1954] 17. b3 ♘b6 18. ♗b2 ♘d5 19. c4=

36 9... ♖b8 10. h3 b5 11. ♘f4 b4 12. ♘cd5 a5= Matanović–Gligorić, Jugoslavija (ch) 1951

37 10. ♘f4 ♖c8 11. ♘fd5 ♘d5 12. ♘d5 ♘e5 13. ♖b1 ♗g4 14. f3 ♗e6 15. b3 ♗d5 16. ed5 b5∓↑《

38 **10... ♕a5** 11. ♘d5 ♘d5 12. ed5 ♘e5 13. b3! ♕a6 [13... ♘f3 14. ♗f3 ♗a1 15. ♗d2±] 14. ♘d4 ♘d3 15. ♗e3 ♘c5 16. a4±; **10... a5** 14. ♗e3 a4 12. ♘d5 ♘d5 13. ed5 ♘e5 14. ♗d4 ♕c8 15. ♔h2 ♗b5 16. ♖e1±; **10... a6** 11. ♘d5 [11. ♔h2?! ♘e5?! 12. f4 ♘c4 13. b3 ♘a5 14. ♗e3 ♖c8 15. ♕d2 b5 16. a3 ♕c7 17. ♖ad1± Bronštejn–Šajtar, Moskva–Praha 1946; 11... ♖c8!? 12. ♗e3 ♕c7 13. b3 b5 14. a3 e6!? 15. ♕d2 ♖fd8 16. ♖ad1 ♗e8∞] ♘d5 12. ed5 ♘e5 13. ♘d4=

39 11... ♘d5 12. ed5 ♘e5 13. a4! ♘c4 16. ♖a2 e5 15. de6 ♗e6 16. ♘f4± Korčnoj–Bondarevski, SSSR (ch) 1963

40 12. ♘d4 ♘d5 [12... ♘c6!? Boleslavski–Polugajevski, SSSR 1956] 13. ed5 ♕b6=

41 15. ♖e1 ♕c7 16. f4 ♘c4 17. c3 ♖fd8=

42 7. ♘de2 h5!? 8. h3 ♗d7 9. ♗g2 ♕c8 10. ♘f4 [10. ♗e3 ♗g7 11. f3 ♘e5 12. ♗d4 0–0 13. g4 ♘c4∓ Ćirić–Velimirović, Jugoslavija 1966] ♗g7 11. ♘cd5 ♘d5 12. ♘d5 [12. ed5 ♘e5 13. c3 ♗b5∓] 0–0 13. c3 b5∞

43 **7... ♗d7** 8. 0–0 ♗g7 9. ♗g5 h6 10. ♗e3 ♘g4 11. ♘c6 bc6 [11... ♘e3? 12. ♘d8 ♘d1 13. ♘f7±] 12. ♗d2 0–0 13. h3 ♘e5 14. b3!?∞; **7... ♗g7** 8. ♘c6?! bc6 9. e5 de5 10. ♗c6 ♗d7 11. ♗a8 ♕a8 12. f3 e4! 13. 0–0 ef3 14. ♕f3 ♗c6=∞; 8. 0–0 ♘d4 — 7... ♘d4

44 9. ♗e3 0–0 10. ♕d2 [10. 0–0? ♘g4 11. ♕d2 ♘e3 12. ♕e3 ♗e6∓⊡ Evans–Reshevsky, La Habana 1952] ♘g4 11. ♗f4=

45 **10. ♕d2** ♕c7 11. ♘d5 ♘d5 12. ed5 b5 13. a4 b4! 14. ♕b4 ♖b8 15. ♕h4 ♗b2 16. ♗b2 ♖b2 17. c4 ♗a6 18. ♖ac1 ♖fb8∓ Cuellar–Korčnoj, Stockholm (izt) 1962; **10. ♕d1** ♗g4 11. ♘e2 ♗e6 12. h3 ♘d7 13. ♘f4 ♗c4 14. ♖e1 a5 15. ♘d5 a4 16. a3∞ Sokolski–Furman, SSSR 1954

46 **11. b3**? d5!; **11. ♘d5** ♖c8 12. c3 ♖e8 13. ♗e3 [13. ♗g5!?] ♕a5 14. a4 [14. h3 ♕a4! 15. ♖fe1 b5∓↑ Teschner–Talj, Wien 1957] ♗d5 15. ed5 ♘g4 16. ♕b5 [16. ♗d4!?] ♕b5 17. ab5 ♘e3 18. fe3 ♖c5 19. ♖a7 ♖b5∓⊥

47 15. ed5 ♗f5 16. ♗e4 ♗e4 17. ♕e4 ♗b2! 18. ♖ce1 ♗f6= Keres–Gligorić, Zürich (ct) 1953

B71 1. e4 c5 2. ♘f3 d6 3. d4 cd4 4. ♘d4 ♘f6 5. ♘c3 g6 6. f4[1]

	6	7	8	9	10	11	12	13	14	
1	. . . ♗g7[2]	e5![3] ♗g4[4]	♗b5![5] ♔f8[6]	♕d3 ♘e8	0–0 ♘d7	h3 de5	fe5 ♘e5	hg4! ♘c7[7]	♕e4 ♕d4[8]	±
2	. . . . . .	. . . ♘h5	♗b5[9] ♗d7	e6 fe6[10]	♘e6 ♗c3	bc3 ♕a5	♗d2![11] ♗b5	c4		±
3	. . . . . .	. . . ♘g4	♗b5 ♔f8[12]	h3 ♘h6	♗e3 ♘c6[13]	ed6 ♘d4	♗d4 ♕d6	♗g7 ♔g7	♕d6 ed6[14]	±
4	. . . . . .	. . . de5	fe5 ♘g4[15]	♗b5 ♘c6	♘c6 ♕d1	♔d1[16] ♘f2	♔e2 ♘h1	♘d4 ♗d7	♗f4	±
5	. . . . . .	. . . . . .	. . . ♘fd7	e6 ♘e5[17]	♗b5 ♘bc6	ef7 ♔f7	0–0 ♗f6	♘c6[18] bc6[19]	♕d8[20] ♖d8[21]	⩲
6	. . . ♘bd7[22]	♗e2[23] a6	g4!? ♘c5	♘b3 ♘fd7[24]	♗e3 b6	♗f3 e6	e5 d5	♕e2 ♗b7	0-0-0 ♕c7[25]	∞
7	. . . . . .	. . . ♗g7	♗e3[26] 0–0	♗f3 ♘b6[27]	♕e2 e5	♘b3 ♘g4[28]	♗g4 ♕h4	g3 ♕g4	♕g4 ♗g4[29]	∓
8	. . . . . .	. . . . . .	0–0 a6	♔h1[30] 0–0[31]	♗f3 e5[32]	♘de2 ef4	♘f4[33] ♘e5			∞
9	. . . ♘c6	♘f3[34] ♗g4	h3[35] ♗f3	♕f3 ♗g7	♗e3 0–0	♗e2[36] ♘d7	♖d1 ♕a5	h4 h5	e5 ♘b6[37]	∞
10	. . . . . .	♗b5[38] ♗d7[39]	♘f3 ♗g4![40]	h3 ♗f3	♕f3 ♗g7	♗e3 0–0	♗c6 bc6	0–0 ♕a5		=
11	. . . . . .	. . . . . .	♗c6 bc6	e5 ♘d5[41]	ed6[42] ♘c3	bc3 c5![43]	♘f3[44] ♗g7	♗e5[45] ♗b5	c4[46] ed6[47]	=
12	. . . . . .	. . . . . .	. . . . . .	. . . de5	fe5 ♘g4[48]	e6[49] ♗e6	♕f3[50] ♕d7	♗f4 ♗g7	0-0-0 ♗d5[51]	=
13	. . . . . .	. . . . . .	. . . ♗c6	e5[52] de5	fe5 ♘e4![53]	♘e4[54] ♗e4	0–0 ♗g7	♗f4[55] 0–0	c3 ♕b6	=

1. e4 c5 2. ♘f3 d6 3. d4 cd4 4. ♘d4 ♘f6 5. ♘c3 g6 6. f4 ♘c6 7. ♘c6 bc6

	8	9	10	11	12	13	14	15	16	
14	e5 ♘g4[56]	♕f3[57] ♕b6[58]	ed6[59] ed6	♗d2 ♗g7	0-0-0 0–0	h3 ♘f6	g4 ♖b8	b3[60]		±
15	. . . de5	♕d8 ♔d8	fe5 ♘g4[61]	♗f4 ♗e6[62]	♘e4![63] ♗g7	♘c5 ♗e5	0-0-0 ♔c7	♗e5 ♘e5	♘e6 fe6[64]	±
16	. . . . . .	. . . . . .	. . . . . .	. . . g5!?[65]	♗g5[66] ♘e5	0-0-0 ♔e8	h3			±
17	. . . ♘d7	♕f3[67] ♗g7[68]	♗b5[69] de5[70]	♗c6 ♖b8	♗e3 ♖b2	0-0-0 e4	♕e4 ♗c3	♗d7 ♗d7	♖d7 ♕d7[71]	=
18	. . . . . .	ed6 ed6	♕d4[72] ♘f6[73]	♗e3[74] ♗e7	♗e2 0–0	0–0 c5[75]	♕d2 d5	♗f3 ♗b7	♖ad1 ♖b8[76]	=

	8	9	10	11	12	13	14	15	16	
19	...	...	♗e3	♕d4[78]	♕g7	♗e2[80]	♖f1	♖f3	♗f1	±
	...	...	♕e7?![77]	♗g7[79]	♕e3	♖f8	♗a6[81]	♕g1[82]	♗f1[83]	
20	...	...	...	♕f3[84]	0-0-0	♗d4	h4	♕f2	♗f6	=
	...	...	♗e7	d5	♗f6	0—0	♖b8	♖b4	♘f6[85]	

1 Levenfiš

2 **6... ♗g4**?! 7. ♕d3 ♘c6 8. ♗e3 ♗g7 9. h3 ♗d7 10. ♗e2± Sherwin—D. Byrne, USA (ch) 1955; **6... ♕b6** 7. e5 de5 8. fe5 ♘fd7 9. e6 [9. ♗c4 ♗g7∞] fe6 10. ♗c4 ♘e5 11. ♗b3 ♗g7 12. ♗e3±⟳↑

3 **7. ♗b5** ♘fd7! 8. ♗e3 0—0 9. ♗e2 ♘c6 10. 0—0 [10. ♘b3 ♘b6 11. 0—0 ♗e6∓ Szily—Gereben, Hungary 1948] ♘b6! 11. ♘d5=; **7. ♗e2** 0—0 8. 0—0 ♕b6! [8... d5 9. e5 ♘e4 10. ♘e4 de4 11. ♗e3 f6 12. e6 f5 13. ♗c4±; 8... ♘g4 9. ♗g4 ♗g4 10. ♕d3±] 9. ♗e3 ♕b2? 10. ♕d3 ♕b4 11. e5! de5 12. fe5 ♘g4 13. ♗g4 ♗g4 14. ♖f4!±→ Beljavski—Kuprejčik, SSSR 1973 — 15/405; 9... ♘c6 — B 73; 8. ♘b3 ♘c6 9. ♗e3 — B 72; 7... ♘bd7 — 6... ♘bd7

4 **7... ♘g8** 8. ♗b5 ♔f8 [8... ♗d7 9. e6±] 9. 0—0 d5 10. ♗e3 a6 11. ♗e2 e6 [11... b5 12. ♘d5!] 12. ♘e4! ♘c6 13. ♘c6 bc6 14. ♗c5 ♘e7 15. ♘f6± Rellstab—Wittenberg, Hamburg 1950; **7... ♘fd7** 8. e6 [8. ed6 0—0!? 9. ♗e2 ♘c6!=∞] ♘f6 9. ef7 ♔f7 10. ♗c4 d5 11. ♗b3 ♖f8 12. ♕f3 e6 13. ♗e3 ♔g8 14. 0-0-0±

5 **8. ♕d3** de5 9. fe5 ♘fd7 10. e6 fe6 11. ♕e4 ♘f6! 12. ♕b7 ♕d4 13. ♕a8 0—0∞; **8. ♗e2** ♗e2 9. ♕e2±

6 **8... ♘c6**? 9. ef6! ♗d1 10. fg7 ♖g8 11. ♘c6+—; **8... ♘bd7** 9. ♕d3±

7 13... ♘d3? 14. ♘e6+—

8 15. ♕d4 ♘f3 16. ♖f3 ♗d4 17. ♗e3 ♗c3 18. ♗c4! ♗f6 19. g5± Koch—Nüsken, Grethen 1950

9 8. g4? ♘f4 9. ♗f4 de5∓

10 9... ♗b5 10. ef7 ♔f7 11. ♘cb5 ♘f6 12. 0—0△ f5±→ Levenfiš

11 12. ♕d4±

12 8... ♗d7?? 9. ♕g4+—

13 **10... de5**? 11. ♘e6+—; **10... ♘f5** 11. ♘f5 ♗f5 12. 0—0±

14 15. 0-0-0 ♖d8 16. ♖d2 ♗e6 17. ♖hd1 ♘f5 18. g4 ♘e3 19. ♖e1 a6 20. ♖e3 ab5 21. ♘b5 ♖a2 22. ♖d6±⊥ Levenfiš—Rabinovič, SSSR (ch) 1939

15 **8... ♘h5**?? 9. ♗b5 ♗d7 10. g4+—; **8... ♘g8**? 9. ♗b5 ♗d7 10. e6 ♗b5 11. ♘cb5 ♘f6 12. ♕f3 ♕b6 13. ef7 ♔f7 14. ♕b3 e6 15. ♘c7! ♕c7 16. ♕e6 ♔f8 17. ♕f6! ♗f6 18. ♘e6+— Vlagsma—Wind, Nederland 1946; **8... ♘d5**? 9. ♗b5 ♔f8 10. 0—0 [10. ♗c4!? e6 11. ♘f3±] ♗e5 [10... e6 11. ♕f3+—] 11. ♗h6 ♔g8□ 12. ♘d5 ♕d5 13. ♘f5! ♕c5 14. ♗e3 ♕c7 15. ♘h6 ♔g7 16. ♖f7# Schwarz—Marquardt, Berlin 1950

16 11. ♘d1 a6 12. ♗a4 ♗d7 13. h3 ♘h6 14. ♘e7! ♗a4 [14... ♔e7 15. ♗g5 ♔e8 16. ♗d7 ♔d7 17. 0—0+—] 15. ♘d5 ♖d8 16. c4± Pilnik—Kashdan, New York 1949

17 9... fe6? 10. ♘e6 ♗c3 11. bc3 ♕b6 12. ♗c4 ♘f6 13. ♖b1!+—; 11... ♕a5!?

18 13. ♗c6!? ♘c6 14. ♘c6 ♕d1 15. ♘d1 bc6 16. ♗g5 (Koblenc) ♗f5 17. ♗f6 ef6 18. ♘e3 ♗e6±

19 13... ♘c6 14. ♘d5±

20 14. ♗f4 ♔g7! [14... ♕b6 15. ♔h1± Kamišov—Averbah, SSSR 1948] 15. ♗e5 ♗e5 16. ♕d8 ♖d8 17. ♗c6 ♖b8=∞

21 15. ♗a4± Boleslavski

22 Flor

23 **7. ♗c4** ♕c7 [7... ♗g7 8. ♗e3 0—0 9. h3 a6 10. a4 ♕c7= Rossetto—Najdorf, Mar del Plata 1968 — 6/519] 8. ♗b3 a6 9. 0—0 ♗g7 10. ♗e3 b5 11. ♕f3 ♗b7= Fazekas—Wood, Bognor Regis 1960; **7. ♘f3** ♕c7 8. ♗d3 ♗g7 9. 0—0 0—0 10. ♕e1 a6 — B 93

24 9... ♘fe4? 10. ♘e4 ♘e4 11. ♕d4 ♘f6 12. g5± Gipslis

25 15. ♔b1 0-0-0 16. ♗d4 b5 [Šmit—Vitolinš, SSSR 1973 — 15/404] 17. ♗d5!∞

26 8. ♗f3 0—0 9. g4?! e5! 10. ♘db5 d5 11. ed5 e4 12. ♗e2 ♘b6 13. g5 ♘fd5 14. ♘e4 ♕e7∓→ Tuomainen—Lee, Krakow 1964

27 9... a6 10. 0—0 ♕c7 11. ♔h1 [11. ♕e2 ♘b6 12. ♖ad1 ♘c4 13. ♗c1 e5 14. fe5 de5 15. ♘b3 ♗e6∓ Bihovski—Nikitin, SSSR 1964] e5! [11... ♖b8?! 12. a4 b6? 13. e5! de5 14. ♘c6± Horowitz—Reshevsky, New York 1944] 12. ♘b3 b5∓

28 11... ef4!? 12. ♗f4 ♘h5 13. ♗h5 ♕h4 14. ♗g3 ♕h5 15. ♕h5 gh5 16. 0-0-0 [16. ♗d6 ♖e8=] ♗g4 17. ♖d6 ♘c4 18. ♖d3 f5=∞↑⊞ Keene, Levy

29 ∓ Keene

30 9. a4 0–0 10. ♗f3 [10. ♘b3!? b6!? 11. ♗f3 ♗b7∞] e5! 11. ♘b3 ef4 [11... ♕c7 12. f5!±] 12. ♗f4 ♘e5 13. ♗g5 ♕b6 14. ♔h1 ♗e6∞

31 9... b5 10. e5 de5 11. ♘c6 ♕c7 12. fe5± Gufeljd

32 10... ♘b6 11. a4 e5 [11... ♕c7 12. a5 ♘c4 13. ♘b3 ♖b8 14. ♕e2±] 12. ♘de2 ♖e8?! [Nikitin–Tajmanov, SSSR 1966] 13. a5! ♘c4 14. b3 ♘a5 15. fe5 ♖e5 16. ♗f4 ♖e8 17. e5±; 12... ef4! 13. ♗f4 ♘c4 14. b3 ♘e5 15. ♕d2±

33 **12. ♕d6** g5!∞; **12. ♗f4** ♘e5∞

34 7. ♗e2 ♗g7 8. ♗e3 0–0 9. ♘b3 — B 72

35 **8. ♗e2**!?; **8. ♗e3**!?

36 11. ♖d1 ♕a5 12. a3 ♖ac8 13. ♗e2 ♘d7∓ Evans–Reshevsky, New York 1954

37 15. ed6 ed6 16. 0–0∞ Seidman–Evans, USA (ch open) 1955

38 Botvinik

39 7... ♕c7 **8. ♘d5** ♘d5 9. ed5 a6 10. ♗c6 [10. ♘c6?! ab5 14. ♕d4 e5! 12. de6 ♕c6 13. ♕h8 ♕g2∓; 10. ♗a4 ♕a5 11. c3 ♕d5 12. ♘c6 ♕d1 13. ♔d1 ♗d7∓] bc6 11. ♘c6 ♗g7 12. ♗e3 ♗b7 13. ♗d4 ♗d4 14. ♕d4 0–0 15. 0–0 ♗c6= Schmid–Parma, Malaga 1963; **8. 0–0**!? ♗d7 [8... ♗g7 9. ♘d5±; 8... a6 9. ♗c6 bc6 10. ♘f3±⟳↑ Gufeljd] 9. ♗c6 [9. ♘d5 ♘d5 10. ed5 ♘d4 11. ♗d7 ♔d7 12. ♕d4 ♕c5=] bc6 10. ♘f3±⟳↑

40 8... ♗g7 9. ♕e2± Levenfiš

41 9... ♘g4? 10. e6 fe6 11. ♕g4 e5 12. ♘e6 ♕c8 13. f5+–

42 10. ♘d5 cd5 11. ♕f3 [11. ed6 e6∓] e6 12. ♗d2 de5 13. fe5 ♕h4 14. ♕f2 ♕e4 15. ♕e3 ♕e3 16. ♗e3 ♗g7 17. ♘f3 0–0 18. ♗d4= Čaplinski–Toluš, SSSR 1952

43 11... ed6 12. 0–0 ♗e7 13. f5! 0–0 14. ♗h6 ♖e8 15. ♕f3±→»

44 12. de7? ♕e7 13. ♘e2 ♖d8 14. ♕d3 ♗c6 15. ♕e3 [15. ♕g3? ♗g7 16. 0–0 (Johansson–Nilsson, Stockholm 1960/61) ♕e2! 17. ♖e1 ♖d1–+] ♕e3 16. ♗e3 ♗g2∓

45 13. 0–0 0–0 14. de7 ♕e7 15. ♖e1 ♗e6≅⧉

46 14. ♖b1 ♗a6 15. ♕d5 0–0∓

47 15. cb5 de5= Nilsson

48 10... ♘d5 11. ♘d5 cd5 12. ♕f3±

49 **11. ♘c6**? ♕b6∓; **11. ♗f4** ♗g7 12. ♕e2 ♕a5 [12... ♕b8?! 13. 0-0-0 ♗e5 14. ♗g5 ♗f4 15. ♗f4 ♕f4 16. ♔b1 ♕e5 17. ♕a6 ♕c7 18. ♖he1 ♘e5 19. ♕a3!± Schmid–Gilg, Düsseldorf 1951] 13. ♘f3 ♕b4!⇆= Euwe

50 Nežmetdinov; 12. ♘e6 ♕d1 13. ♘d1 fe6 14. ♘e3 ♘f6 15. ♘c4 ♘d5 =Geler–Pogrebiski, SSSR (ch) 1949

51 **14... ♗d4**? 15. ♖d4±; **14... 0–0** 15. ♘f5 ♕b7 16. ♘g7 ♔g7 17. h3 ♘f6 18. ♗e5±; **14... ♗d5**! 15. ♕e2 ♘f6! [15... 0–0? 16. ♘c6!±] 16. ♗e5 0–0 17. ♗f6 ef6 [17... ♗f6 18. ♘c6! ♕c6 19. ♘d5 ♗g5 20. ♔b1 e6 21. h4!±] 18. ♘c6 ♕c6 19. ♘d5 ♖fe8! 20. ♕f3 ♖ac8 21. c3 f5 22. ♖he1 ♔f8= Euwe

52 9. ♕f3 (Koblenc) ♖**c8** 10. ♗e3 ♗g7 11. 0-0-0 0–0 12. g4 ♕c7 [Klavin–Zajcev, SSSR 1962] 13. ♖d2∞; **9... ♕b6** 10. ♘c6 [10. ♘b3 ♘e4! 11. ♘e4 ♕b4 12. ♘bd2 f5∓] ♕c6! [10... bc6 11. e5 de5 12. fe5 ♘d7 13. e6 fe6 14. ♖f1 0-0-0 15. ♗e3≅↑ Levenfiš] 11. ♗e3 ♗g7 12. 0–0 0–0= Šmit–Kogan, SSSR 1964; **9... ♘d7**! 10. ♘c6 bc6 11. e5 d5∓

53 10... ♘d5 11. e6 f5 12. 0–0 ♘f6 [12... ♗g7? 13. ♘f5!±] 13. ♘c6 ♕d1 14. ♖d1±⊥ Poljak–Tarasov, SSSR 1953

54 11. ♘c6 ♕d1 13. ♘d1 bc6 13. 0–0 ♗g7 14. ♖e1 ♘c5 15. ♗d2 ♘d7? 16. ♗c3± Levenfiš; 15... 0–0!=

55 Penrose; 13. ♖e1?! ♕d5! [13... ♗c6? 14. ♗g5! ♕b6 15. c3 ♖d8 16. ♕e2 ♖d5 17. ♗f6!± Kavalek–Jansa, ČSSR (ch) 1962; 13... ♗d5 14. c3 0–0=] 14. c3 ♕e5 15. ♗f4 ♕f4 16. ♕a4 ♔f8! [16... ♗c6? 17. ♖e7! ♔f8 18. ♘e6 fe6 19. ♕f4 ♔e7 20. ♕c7± Penrose–Barden, Hastings 1957/58] 17. ♘e6 fe6 18. ♖f1 ♕f1 19. ♖f1 ♗f5 20. g4 ♗f6 21. gf5 ef5∓

56 8... ♗g4 9. ♗e2 [9. ♕d4!? de5 10. ♕c4] ♗e2 10. ♕e2 de5 11. fe5 ♘d5 12. e6!? f5 13. ♘d5 ♕d5 14. ♗g5△ ♖d1-d7±→ Euwe

57 **9. ♗e2** h5 10. h3 [10. ♗f3? ♕b6 11. ♕e2 ♗a6 11. ♕e4 d5 12. ♕a4 e6∓ Birstein–Hankin, USA 1959] ♘h6 11. g4 [11. ♗e3 ♘f5 12. ♗f2 h4!∞] hg4 12. hg4 ♗g7 13. ed6 ed6= Seidman–Reshevsky, New York 1956; **9. h3** ♘h6 10. g4 f5 11. ef6 ef6 12. ♗g2 d5 13. ♗e3±

58 **9... de5**? 10. ♗b5!±; **9... d5** 10. ♗d2△ 0-0-0±

59 10. h3!? ♘h6 11. ed6 ed6 12. g4 ♗g7 13. ♗d2 0–0 14. 0-0-0±

60 ± Schwarz

61 **10... ♘d5** 11. ♗d2 [11. ♘d5 cd5 12. ♗g5 ♗e6 13. 0-0-0 ♔c7 14. ♗b5± Penrose–Green, England 1969; 12... h6 13. ♗h4 g5 14. ♗f2 ♗g7 15. 0-0-0± Donner–Spanjaard, Nederland 1953; 15. ♗d4±] ♗g7 12. 0-0-0 ♗e5 [12... ♔c7 13. ♘d5 cd5 14. ♗c3 ♗e6 15. ♗a6 ♔b6 16. ♗e2±] 13. ♘d5 cd5 14. ♗a5 ♔e8 15. ♖d5 ♗f4 16. ♗d2 ♗e6 17. ♖d3± Glass–Steiner, Österreich 1962; **10... ♘d7** 11. ♗f4 ♗g7 12. 0-0-0 ♔e8 13. ♖e1 ♘c5 14. ♗e2 ♗d7 15. ♗f3± Fine

62 **11... ♗d7** 12. ♖d1! ♗g7 13. e6 ♗c3 14. bc3 fe6 15. ♗e2 ♖f8 16. 0–0 ♘f6 17.

♗e5± ; **11...♗g7** 12. 0-0-0 ♔c7 [12... ♔e8? 13. ♘b5!+−; 12... ♗d7 13. e6! fe6 14. ♘e4 e5 15. ♗e2! h5 16. ♗d2! ♔e8 17. h3 ♘f6 18. ♗f3±; 16... ♗f5 17. ♗h6 ♔e8 18. ♗g7 ♖g8 19. ♗f3 ♖g7 20. h3! ♘e3 21. ♖de1 ♘d5 22. ♘g3±⊥] 13. e6 ♗e5 14. ♗e5 ♘e5 15. ef7±⊥; **11... ♗h6** 12. ♗h6 ♘h6 13. 0-0-0 ♔c7 14. ♗c4 ♖f8 15. h3 ♘f5 16. ♖d3 h5± Szily

63 12. h3 ♗h6! 13. ♗h6 ♘h6 14. g4 ♔c7 15. 0-0-0 f5 16. ef6 ef6 17. ♗g2 f5= Keres–Padevski, Moskva 1963

64 17. ♖e1 ♔d6 18. g3 ♘g4 19. ♗c4! [19. ♗h3?? ♘f2 20. ♖e6 ♔c7 21. ♗g2 ♘h1 22. ♖c6 ♔d7 23. ♗h1 ♖af8−+] e5 20. ♖e2! ♘f6 [20... ♖hf8 21. ♖d1 ♔c7 22. ♗e6!±] 21. ♖d1 ♘d5 [21... ♔c5? 22. ♖e5 ♔c4 23. b3+−] 22. ♖de1±⊥ Boleslavski

65 Estrin

66 12. ♗g3 h5 13. h3 ♘e3∓

67 9. ♗c4 ♘b6 [9... d5? 10. ♘d5!±; 9... de5?! 10. 0−0 ♕b6 11. ♔h1 ♗g7 12. ♘e4 0−0 13. ♕e2 ef4 14. ♗f4 h6 15. c3∞̅→ F. Meštrović–Vidmar jr., Jugoslavija 1951] 10. ed6 ♕d6 [10... ♘c4? 11. ♕d4+−] 11. ♕d6 ed6= Averbah–Lisicin, SSSR (ch) 1948

68 **9... ♕b6?** 10. ed6 ed6 11. ♗e3 ♕b2 12. ♗d4 ♕a1 13. ♔d2 ♖g8 14. ♕c6 ♖b8 15. ♗a6 ♕h1 16. ♗c8+−; **9... d5?!** 10. h4 h5 11. ♗e3± Levenfiš

69 10. ♕c6 ♖b8 11. ed6 [11. ♗e3?! 0−0 12. 0-0-0 de5 13. ♗a7 ♖b7 14. ♕a4 ef4 15. ♘b5 ♘b6! 16. ♕b3 ♕e8−+ Šapošnikov–Bonč-Osmolovski, SSSR 1952] 0−0 12. ♗e2 ♗b7 13. ♕c7 ♗g2 14. ♕d8 ♖fd8 15. de7 ♖e8 16. ♖g1 ♗c6∞̅

70 10... 0−0!? 11. ♗c6 [11. ♕c6?! ♖b8 12. ♗e3 a6 13. ♗a4 de5 14. 0-0-0 ♕a5 15. ♗b3 ef4 16. ♗f4 ♖b3 17. ab3 ♕a1 18. ♔d2 ♕b2 19. ♖b1 ♘b8! 20. ♕c8 ♖c8 21. ♖b2 ♗c3∓⊥ Bronštejn–Vasjukov, SSSR (ch) 1959] ♖b8 12. ed6 ed6∞̅

71 17. ♕a8 ♖b8! [17... ♕d8? 18. ♕c6 ♕d7 19. ♕c3+−] 18. ♕b8 ♕d8 19. ♕d8 ♔d8 20. ♗a7 ♔c7= Gragger–Honfi, Österreich–Hungary 1961

72 **10. ♗e2** ♘f6 11. ♗e3 ♗g7 12. ♗f3 0−0! 13. ♗c6 ♖b8∞̅; 13. 0−0=; **10. ♕e2** ♕e7 [10... ♗e7 11. ♗e3 0−0 12. 0-0-0 ♘f6 13. h3 ♗e6 14. g4 ♕a5 15. ♕a6 ♕a6 16. ♗a6± Martsum–Nejštadt, corr. 1959] 11. ♘e4 ♕e6! 12. ♗d2 ♗e7 13. ♗c3 0−0 14. g3 d5 15. ♘f2 ♗f6= Koblenc

73 10... ♕f6 11. ♗e3 ♗g7 12. 0-0-0 d5 13. ♕f6 ♗f6 14. ♘a4±

74 11. b3 ♗g7 12. ♗b2 0−0 13. 0-0-0 ♗g4! 14. ♗e2?! ♘d5 15. ♕g7□ ♔g7 16. ♘d5 f6 17. ♗g4 cd5∓ Timman–Langeweg, Amsterdam 1974

75 13... ♘g4!?∞

76 Szabo–Reshevsky, Helsinki (ol) 1952

77 Eliskases; 10... ♘f6 11. ♕d2 ♗g7 12. 0-0-0 d5 13. ♗c5±

78 11. ♕d2 ♗g7 12. 0-0-0 0−0 13. ♗d4 ♗d4 14. ♕d4 d5 15. ♗d3 [Hubeny–Wentze, corr. 1959] ♖b8=

79 11... ♘f6 12. 0-0-0 ♗g7 13. ♕d6 ♕e3 14. ♔b1± Kmoch

80 **13. ♔d1?** ♖f8 14. ♗b5 ♘e5 15. fe5 cb5∓; **13. ♘e2** ♖f8 14. ♖d1 d5! [14... ♗a6 15. ♕d4 ♕d4 16. ♘d4 ♗f1 17. ♖f1±⊥ Euwe] 15. ♖d3 ♕b6∞

81 14... ♔d8 15. ♖f3! ♕g1 16. ♗f1 [Urzica–Vujačić, Sverige 1969 — 8/408] ♔c7 17. 0-0-0± Ciocaltea

82 15... ♕e7 16. ♔d2±

83 17. 0-0-0 0-0-0 18. ♖df1 ♕g2 19. ♕d4! [19. ♘e4? ♘c5∞ Unzicker–Kottnauer, Leysin 1967 — 4/511] ♘b6 20. h3! g5□ [20... ♖fe8 21. ♕d3 c5 22. ♕d1+− Nicolau–Georgieva, Gori 1970] 21. ♕e4 d5 22. ♕f5 ♔b8 23. ♕g5 ♕g5 24. fg5± Keene

84 11. ♕d2 ♘f6! [11... 0−0 12. 0-0-0 ♘f6? 13. h3 ♗e6 14. g4± Fuderer–Trifunović, Jugoslavija (ch) 1953; 12... ♕a5 13. ♔b1 d5∞ Ščerbakov–Lisicin, SSSR (ch) 1955] 12. 0-0-0 ♗e6 13. ♗d3 ♕a5∞ Honfi–Partos, Bucuresti 1973 — 15/403

85 17. a3 ♕b6?! 18. ♕b6 ♖b6 19. ♘a4± Talj–Lisicin, SSSR (ch) 1956; 17... ♖b7!?=

B 72

1. e4 c5 2. ♘f3 d6 3. d4 cd4 4. ♘d4 ♘f6 5. ♘c3 g6 6. ♗e3

	6	7	8	9	10	11	12	13	14	
1	... a6[1]	f3[2] ♘bd7	♕d2 b5?![3]	a4! ba4[4]	♖a4 ♗g7	♗e2 0−0	0−0 ♘c5	♖a3 ♗b7	♖fa1 ♕c8[5]	±
2	... ♗g7	♗c4[6] ♘g4![7]	♗b5[8] ♔f8	0−0[9] ♘e3[10]	fe3 e6	♗c4 ♕e7	♘cb5 ♗e5![11]			∞

	6	7	8	9	10	11	12	13	14	
3	. . . . . .	h3 ♘c6[12]	♗c4 0—0	♗b3[13] ♘d4[14]	♗d4 b5	0—0[15] ♗b7[16]	♕d3 b4	♘d5 e6	♘f6 ♗f6[17]	±

1. e4 c5 2. ♘f3 d6 3. d4 cd4 4. ♘d4 ♘f6 5. ♘c3 g6 6. ♗e3 ♗g7 7. ♗e2 ♘c6[18]

	8	9	10	11	12	13	14	15	16	
4	h3[19] 0—0	♕d2 d5	ed5[20] ♘d5	♘d5 ♘d4	♘e7[21] ♕e7	♗d4 ♗d4	♕d4 ♖e8	♕e3[22] ♕e3	fe3 ♖e3[23]	=
5	h4 0—0[24]	h5 d5[25]	hg6 hg6[26]	♘c6[27] bc6	e5 ♘e4	♘e4 de4	♗d4 ♕a5[28]	♗c3 ♕d5	♕c1[29]	±
6	. . . h5	f3 0—0	♕d2[30] d5	♘c6 bc6	e5[31] ♘e8[32]	f4[33] f6[34]	g4[35] hg4	0-0-0[36]		∞
7	♕d2 0—0[37]	0-0-0[38] ♘d4[39]	♗d4 ♗e6[40]	♔b1 ♖c8[41]	h4 ♗c4	♗f3[42] ♖e8	h5 ♕a5	a3 ♕a6	hg6 hg6[43]	=
8	♘b3 0—0	g4[44] d5[45]	ed5 ♘b4	♗f3 ♘g4!	♗c5[46] ♘a6	♗d4[47] ♘f6	♗e5 ♗f5	♘d4 ♕d7	♕e2 ♘b4[48]	=

1. e4 c5 2. ♘f3 d6 3. d4 cd4 4. ♘d4 ♘f6 5. ♘c3 g6 6. ♗e3 ♗g7 7. ♗e2 ♘c6 8. ♘b3 0—0 9. f4

	9	10	11	12	13	14	15	16	17	
9	. . . ♗e6[49]	g4[50] d5[51]	f5[52] ♗c8[53]	ed5[54] ♘b4	♗f3[55] gf5	a3![56] fg4[57]	♗g2[58] ♘a6	♕d3![59] e6[60]	0-0-0 ♘d5[61]	±
10	. . . . . .	. . . ♖c8	g5[62] ♘d7	♕d2 ♘b6[63]	0-0-0 ♘b4!	♔b1 ♘c4	♗c4 ♖c4	♗d4 ♗g4	♖c1[64]	=
11	. . . . . .	. . . ♘a5	g5[65] ♘d7[66]	♗d4 f6![67]	h4 fg5[68]	♗g7 ♔g7	♘d4 ♗g8	f5 ♕b6!	hg5 ♘e5[69]	∞
12	. . . a5	a4[70] ♗e6[71]	♗f3[72] ♘b4	0—0 ♘d7	♘d4 ♗c4	♖f2 e5!	♘db5[73] ef4	♗f4 ♗b5	ab5 ♗e5[74]	=

[1] 6... ♘g4?? 7. ♗b5 ♗d7 8. ♕g4+−

[2] 7. ♗c4!? b5 8. ♗b3 ♗b7 9. f3±; 7... ♘g4!?

[3] 8... ♗g7 — B 75

[4] 9... b4 10. ♘d5±

[5] 15. ♘b3 ♘b3 16. ♖b3±↑« Kavalek–Bilek, Sousse (izt) 1967 — 4/513

[6] **7. f4** ♘g4 8. ♗b5 ♔f8∓; **7. ♗b5** ♘fd7=

[7] **7... 0—0** 8. f3 — B 76; **7... ♘bd7** 8. h3 0–0 9. f4 — B 71

[8] 8. 0–0?! ♘e3 9. fe3 0–0∓

[9] **9. ♗c1**? ♕b6∓; **9. ♗g5** h6 10. ♗h4 g5 11. ♗g3 ♕b6∓; **9. ♕d2** a6 10. ♗c4 ♘c6= Sköld–Botvinik, Stockholm 1962

[10] 9... a6!? △ 10. ♗c4 ♘c6

[11] **12... ♔g8**? 13. ♘d6! ♕d6 14. ♘e6! ♕e6 [14... ♕d1 15. ♖d1 ♘c6 16. ♘c7+−] 15. ♕d8 ♗f8 16. ♖f7!+− Zlotnik–Gik, SSSR 1968 — 6/521; **12... ♗e5**!∞

[12] 7... ♘bd7 8. ♗e2 0–0 9. 0–0±

[13] 9. 0–0 ♗d7 10. ♗b3 a5?! 11. a4 ♘b4 12. f4 ♗c6 13. ♕f3 ♘d7 14. ♖ad1± Riemsdyk–Kagan, Sao Paulo 1973 — 16/315; 10... ♕a5 — B 35

[14] **9... ♗d7** 10. 0–0 ♘a5 [10... ♘d4 11. ♗d4 ♗c6 12. ♕d3 ♕a5 13. ♖ae1 ♘h5 14. ♗g7 ♔g7 15. ♘d5± Andersson–Drimer, Wijk aan Zee 1970 — 9/297; 10... ♖c8 11. f4 a6 12. ♕f3 b5 13. a3 ♘a5 14. ♖ad1 ♘b3 15. cb3! ♕c7 16. g4 ♕b7 17. e5!±] 11. f4 [11. ♕d2 ♖c8 12. ♖ad1 a6 13. ♖fe1 b5 14. ♗g5 ♘c4 15. ♗c4 ♖c4 16. e5 de5 17. ♘f3± Radulov–Forintos, Kecskemet 1972 — 13/368] e5 12. ♘de2! ♗c6 13. ♕d3 ♕c7 14. f5 b5 15.

♗g5± Ćirić–Ostojić, Wijk aan Zee 1969 — 7/336; **9... ♕a5** 10. 0–0 — B 35

15 **11. ♘b5** ♘e4 [11... ♕a5 12. ♘c3 ♘e4 13. ♗g7 ♔g7 14. ♕d5 ♘c5 15. ♕a8 ♗b7 16. ♕f8 ♔f8∞ Gufeljd] 12. ♗g7 ♔g7 13. ♕d4 ♘f6 14. 0-0-0 ♗b7 15. ♖hg1 ♕a5= Talj–Gufeljd, SSSR 1972 — 15/340; **11. a3**!?

16 11... e5 12. ♗e3 b4 13. ♘d5 ♘e4 14. ♘b4± Matanović

17 15. ♖ad1 a5 16. ♖fe1 ♕e7 17. c3±

18 **7... a6** 8. 0–0 ♘bd7 9. f4 0–0 10. ♗f3 e5 11. ♘de2 ef4 12. ♘f4± Roland–Polugajevski, Le Havre 1966 — 1/316; **7... 0–0** 8. ♕d2 [8. f4!?] d5 [8... ♘g4?! 9. ♗g4 ♗g4 10. f3△ 0-0-0±] 9. ed5 ♘d5 10. ♘d5 ♕d5=

19 **8. g4**? d5 9. ♘c6 [9. ♗b5 ♗d7 10. ed5 ♘b4!∓; 9. ed5 ♘d5 10. ♘d5 ♕d5 11. ♗f3 ♕c4 12. ♘c6 bc6 13. b3 ♗c3!∓ Euwe] bc6 10. e5 ♘d7 11. f4 e6 12. 0–0 0–0∓ Rödl–Müller, Bad Elster 1940; **8. f3** 0–0 9. ♘b3 — 8. ♘b3

20 10. ♘c6 bc6 11. e5 ♘d7∓

21 12. ♗d4 ♕d5 13. ♗g7 ♕g2∓ Tartakower–Denker, Hastings 1945/46

22 15. ♕d2 ♗f5△ ♖ad8–+

23 = Euwe

24 8... ♘g4 9. ♗g4 ♗g4 10. f3 ♗d7 11. h5±

25 9... ♘d4 10. ♗d4 ♗e6 11. hg6 hg6 12. ♕d2 ♖e8 13. 0-0-0± Salhaazuren–Štejn, Budapest 1959

26 10... fg6 11. ed5 ♘d5 12. ♗c4! [12. ♘d5 ♕d5 13. ♗f3 ♕c4= Smislov–Botvinik (m) 1958] e6 13. ♘d5 ed5 14. ♗b3 ♘d4 15. ♗d4 ♕e7 16. ♔f1± Botvinik

27 11. ed5 ♘d5 12. ♘c6 bc6 13. ♘d5 ♕d5 14. ♕d5 cd5 15. 0-0-0= Smislov–Botvinik (m) 1958

28 14... ♗e6 15. ♕d2 ♕c7 16. ♕f4 ♖fd8 16. ♗c3 ♗d5 17. ♕h4± Bojarinov–Pribilov, SSSR 1963

29 ± Botvinik

30 10. ♘b3 ♗e6△ d5=

31 12. ♗h6? ♗h6 13. ♕h6 de4 14. fe4 [14. ♘e4 ♘e4 15. fe4 ♕d4!∓] ♕d4!∓ Levy

32 12... ♘d7? 13. e6±; 13. f4± [13... f6? 14. e6 ♘b6 15. f5+–] Botvinik

33 13. ♗h6?! ♗e5! 14. ♗f8 ♔f8=∞↑⊞

34 13... e6 14. 0-0-0△ g4±→»

35 14. 0-0-0 fe5 15. fe5 ♗e5 16. g4 ♗g4 17. ♗g4 hg4 18. h5 g5!= Smislov–Botvinik (m) 1958

36 =∞ Botvinik; 15... fe5!? 16. fe5 ♕a5= Levy

37 **8... d5**? 9. ♗b5!±; **8... ♘g4** 9. ♗g4 ♗g4 10. ♘d5 ♖c8! 11. f3 [11. c4? ♕a5 12. ♘c3 0–0 13. b3 ♗d4 14. ♗d4 b5∓] ♗d7 12. c4 ♕a5 13. ♘c3 a6 14. ♖c1 ♘e5 15. b3 b5= Elcov–Čistjakov, SSSR 1936; 10. 0–0! 0–0 — B 73

38 Grigorjev; 9. 0–0 — B 73

39 9... d5 10. ed5 [10. ♘c6 bc6 11. e5 ♘d7 =] ♘d5 11. ♘c6 bc6 12. ♘d5 cd5 13. ♕d5 ♕c7 [13... ♕d5? 14. ♖d5 ♗b7 15. ♖d7 ♗g2 16. ♖g1 ♗h3 17. ♖e7+–] 14. ♕a8 ♗f5 15. ♕f8 ♔f8 16. ♖d2± Wade–Wotkowsky, Heidelberg 1949

40 10... ♕a5!? 11. ♔b1 e5 12. ♗e3 ♗e6=

41 **11... a6** 12. h4 b5 13. h5 b4 14. ♗f6! ♗f6 15. hg6 fg6 16. ♕h6+– Broer–Vlagsma, Nederland 1941; 15... hg6!±; **11... ♕c7** 12. ♗f3! ♖fc8 13. ♖de1 ♘d7 [13... a6 14. e5! de5 15. ♗e5 ♕b6 16. ♕d4±] 14. ♗g7 ♔g7 15. ♘d5!± Fuchs–Liebert, DDR 1961

42 13. h5!?

43 17. ♘d5 e5 18. ♘f6 ♗f6 19. ♗c3 [Smislov–Konstantinopoljski, SSSR 1945] ♗e6 20. ♗e2=

44 9. f3 d5 10. ed5 ♘b4 11. d6 ♕d6= Belavenec–Levenfiš, SSSR 1939

45 **9... ♗e6** 10. g5?! ♘d7 11. h4 ♘b6! 12. h5 ♘c4 13. hg6 fg6 14. ♗c4 ♗c4 15. ♕g4 ♘e5 16. ♕h3 ♕d7! 17. ♕d7 [17. ♕h7? ♔f7 18. ♕h3 ♖h8 19. ♕d7 ♖h1 20. ♔d2 ♘f3#] ♘d7∓ Bronštejn–Goldenov, SSSR 1941; 10. f4 — 9. f4; **9... a5** 10. g5 ♘d7 11. ♘d4 ♘b6 12. f3 [12. f4 d5! 13. ♕d2 (I. Rabinovič–Keres, SSSR 1939) e5∓] d5 13. ♕d2 e5!∞

46 12. ♗g4 ♗g4 13. ♕g4 ♘c2 14. ♔e2 ♘a1 15. ♖a1 ♗c3 16. bc3 ♕d5∓ Ugrinović–Gašić, Jugoslavija 1966 — 2/413

47 13. ♗g4? ♗g4 14. ♕g4 ♘c5 15. ♘c5 ♗c3 16. bc3 ♕d5∓ Lutikov

48 17. ♖d1 ♖fd8 18. 0–0 ♗h3 19. ♖fe1 ♖ac8= Filipowicz–Trapl, Warszawa 1969 — 7/395

49 **9... b6** 10. 0–0 ♗b7 11. ♗f3 ♖c8 12. ♕e2 ♘d7 [Liberzon–Štejn, Tallinn 1969 — 7/396] 13. a3±; **9... e5**!? 10. 0–0 [10. ♕d2? a5! 11. a4 ef4 12. ♗f4 ♖e8 13. 0–0 ♘e4∓] a5 11. a4 ef4 12. ♗f4 ♖e8 13. ♗f3 ♘e5= Pachman; **9... ♘a5** 10. g4?! b6! 11. g5 ♘d7 12. 0–0 ♗b7 13. ♗d3 ♖c8 14. ♘a5 ba5 15. ♕e1 ♘c5∓ van den Berg–Rajković, Örebro 1966 — 2/412; 10. 0–0 ♗e6 — B 74

50 P. Rabinovič; **10. ♕d2** ♖c8 11. 0-0-0 ♘b4∓ Euwe; **10. ♗f3** ♗c4 11. ♕d2 ♖c8 12. ♘e2 [12. ♖d1 ♕c7 13. ♘d5? ♕b8 14. ♘d4 ♖fe8 15. ♔f2 ♘d5 16. ed5 ♘d4 17. ♗d4 ♗d4 18. ♕d4 ♗a2∓ Rauzer–Lisicin, SSSR (ch) 1933; 13. ♔f2!?] d5 13. e5 ♘d7 14. 0–0=; 14. ♖d1!?=; **10. 0–0** — B 74

51 10... ♘d7? 11. h4 f5 12. h5 ♘c5 13. hg6 hg6 14. gf5 gf5 15. ♕d2 fe4 16. 0-0-0 ♘b3 17. cb3 ♖c8 18. ♖dg1± Niephaus—P. Schmidt, Saarbrücken 1950; 11. f5 ♗b3 12. ab3 ♘c5 13. ♗f3 e6 14. 0—0 ♗e5 15. g5± Klavin—Čehover, SSSR 1952

52 11. e5? d4! 12. ♘d4 [12. ef6 ♗f6∓] ♘d4 13. ♗d4 ♘g4∓ Levenfiš—Botvinik, Moskva 1936

53 11... gf5!? Lipnicki

54 12. fg6 hg6 13. ed5 ♘b4 — 12. ed5

55 **13. fg6**?! hg6 14. ♗f3 e6! [14... ♘g4 15. ♗g4 ♗g4 16. ♕g4 ♘c2 17. ♔f2 ♘a1 18. ♖a1 ♖c8! 19. ♗d4 ♖c4 20. ♖d1 b5⇆ Sokolski] 15. ♗c5 ♘fd5 16. ♘d5 ♘d5 17. 0—0 ♖e8 18. c4 ♘f4!∓ Euwe; **13. d6** ♕d6! 14. ♗c5 ♕f4! 15. ♖f1 ♕h2 16. ♗b4 ♘g4! 17. ♗g4 ♕g3 18. ♖f2 ♕g1 19. ♖f1 ♕g3 1/2 : 1/2 Aljehin—Botvinik, Nottingham 1936

56 Pachman; 14. g5 ♘g4 15. ♗c5 ♘a6 16. h3 [16. ♗d4 e5!∓ Bondarevski—Alatorcev, SSSR (ch) 1937] ♘e5 17. ♗d4= Keres

57 14... ♘g4 15. ♗g4 ♗c3 16. bc3 ♘d5 17. ♗h6± Spaski—Listengarten, SSSR 1953

58 15. ab4!? gf3 16. ♕f3 ♗g4 17. ♕g2 ♗h5 18. ♗h6 [18. ♗d4 ♗g6 19. 0-0-0± Pachman] ♗g6 19. ♗g7 ♔g7 20. 0-0-0± Boleslavski

59 **16. ♕d2** (Pachman) ♗f5△ ♗g6±; **16. ♕e2** ♗f5 17. 0-0-0 ♕d7 18. ♘d4 ♗g6 19. h3 [Bastrikov—Rovner, SSSR 1951] g3±

60 **16... ♘d7** 17. h3! [17. ♗d4 ♘e5 18. ♕g3 ♕d6!∓ Louma—Maximović, Praha 1942; 17. 0-0-0 ♘e5 18. ♕e2± Fischer] ♘e5 18. ♕e2 g3 19. 0-0-0±; **16... ♕d6** 17. 0-0-0 ♗d7 18. ♖hf1 ♖ac8 9. ♗d4± Nej—Pitksaar, SSSR 1951

61 **17... ed5** 18. h3 g3 19. ♗d4±; **17... ♘d5** 18. h3 g3 19. ♖hg1 ♕d6 20. ♗d5 ed5 [Fischer—Reshevsky (m) 1961] 21. ♗d4!± Fischer

62 11. f5 ♗b3 12. ab3 d5! [12... e6 13. g5 ♘e4 4. ♘e4 ef5 15. ♘c3 ♖e8 16. ♗f2± Savon—Gufeljd, SSSR (ch) 1972 — 14/440; 12... ♘e5!? 13. g5 ♖c3∞ Gufeljd] 13. ed5 ♘b4 14. ♗f3 ♘fd5∓ Dikarev—Kuprejčik, SSSR 1965

63 12... a6 13. 0-0-0 ♘b4 14. ♔b1 b5 15. ♗d4± Šmit—Bograd, SSSR 1966

64 Estrin—Veresov, SSSR 1962

65 11. f5 ♗c4 [11... ♗c8? 12. ♘a5 ♕a5 13. 0—0±] 12. ♘a5 [12. e5?! ♗e2 13. ♕e2 ♘d7 14. f6 ef6 15. ed6 ♘e5 16. 0-0-0 ♘ac4∓] ♗e2 13. ♕e2 ♕a5 14. 0—0 — B 74

66 11... ♘e8 12. ♗d4! [12. ♕d2 ♖c8 13. ♗d4 ♘c4? 14. ♗c4 ♖c4 15. 0-0-0 ♕d7 16. ♕d3±→ Kan—Botvinik, Moskva 1936; 13... ♗c4! (Botvinik) 14. ♗g7 ♘g7 15. ♗f3 ♗e6! 16. 0-0-0 ♘c4 17. ♕e2 ♕b6 18. ♖d3 (Louma—Alster, Bratislava 1948) ♘a5! 19. ♕g2 ♘c6 20. ♔b1 ♘b4∓ Filip] ♗c4 [12... ♖c8 13. h4! ♘c4 14. ♗c4 ♖c4 15. ♕d3 ♖c8 16. 0-0-0± Foltys—Eliskases, Podebrady 1936] 13. ♗g7 ♗e2 14. ♕e2 ♘g7 [Louma—Prucha, Brno 1944] 15. 0-0-0±

67 **12... ♘b3** 13. ab3 ♗d4 14. ♕d4 ♕b6 15. ♕d2±→⟫; **12... ♗b3** 13. ab3 ♗d4 14. ♕d4±; 13... e5!?±

68 13... ♘c6 14. h5 [14. ♗e3 ♘b6 15. ♘d4 ♘d4 16. ♗d4± Foltys—Pelikan, Podebrady 1936] fg5 15. ♗g7 ♔g7 16. ♘d4 ♗g8 17. hg6±→ Bronštejn—Ragozin, SSSR (ch) 1944

69 18. b3∞

70 **10. 0—0**? a4 11. ♘d2 a3∓ Henderson—Pilnik, Long Beach 1955; **10. a3** a4 11. ♘d4 d5 12. e5 ♘e4∞ Konstantinopoljski—Averbah, SSSR 1950

71 10... ♘b4 11. 0—0 [11. ♗f3? ♗g4! 12. ♗g4 ♘g4 13. ♕g4 ♘c2 14. ♔f2 ♘e3 15. ♔e3 ♕b6—+ Whiteley] ♘d7 12. ♗d4?! e5 13. fe5 ♘e5 14. ♘b5 ♗e6= Fichtl—Foltys, Praha 1943; 12. ♕d2±

72 **11. g4**? d5 12. f5 ♗c8 13. ed5 ♘b4 14. fg6 hg6 15. d6 [15. ♗f3 ♘g4! 16. ♗g4 ♗g4 17. ♕g4 ♗c3 18. bc3 ♘c2 19. ♔f2 ♘a1 20. ♖a1 ♕d5∓ Euwe] ♕d6 16. ♕d6 ed6 17. 0-0-0 ♘g4 18. ♗b6 ♗h6 19. ♔b1 ♘e3∓ Niephaus—Heinicke, BRD (m) 1951; **11. ♘d4** ♕b6! 12. ♘e6 ♕e3 13. ♘f8 ♘g4!∓ Euwe; **11. 0—0** ♕c8 12. ♗f3 ♘b4 13. ♘d4 ♗c4 14. ♖f2 ♖d8 [Janošević—Vasjukov, Beograd 1961] 15. ♖d2=

73 15. fe5 de5 16. ♘db5= Matanović—Dimc, Zagreb 1953

74 18. ♗e5 ♘e5= Bronštejn—Korčnoj, SSSR 1959

B 73

1. e4 c5 2. ♘f3 d6 3. d4 cd4 4. ♘d4 ♘f6 5. ♘c3 g6 6. ♗e3 ♗g7 7. ♗e2 ♘c6 8. 0—0

	8	9	10	11	12	13	14	15	16	
1	...	h3[2]	♕d2	f4	♖ad1	♘c6	e5[3]			±
	h5[1]	♗d7	♕c8	♔f8	h4	bc6				
2	...	h3[4]	f4[6]	♗d4	♗f3	♗g7	♕d4	♖ad1		±
	♗d7	0—0[5]	♘d4[7]	♗c6	♘d7[8]	♔g7	♘f6[9]			

1. e4 c5 2. ♘f3 d6 3. d4 cd4 4. ♘d4 ♘f6 5. ♘c3 g6 6. ♗e3 ♗g7 7. ♗e2 ♘c6 8. 0—0 0—0

	9	10	11	12	13	14	15	16	17	
3	h3[10] d5[11]	ed5[12] ♘d5	♘d5 ♕d5	♗f3 ♕a5	♘c6 bc6	c3[13]				=
4	f4 ♕b6	♕d3[14] ♘g4[15]	♘d5[16] ♗d4[17]	♗g4[18] ♗e3	♕e3 ♕e3	♘e3 ♗g4	♘g4			=
5	. . . . . .	e5 de5	fe5 ♘e5[19]	♘f5 ♕b2[20]	♘e7 ♔h8	♗d4[21] ♕b4[22]	♗e5[23] ♕e7	♕d4[24] ♘h5	♗g7 ♘g7[25]	=∞
6	♕d2 ♗d7[26]	f4[27] a6[28]	♖ad1[29] ♖c8	h3 b5	a3 ♕c7	♘b3 ♖fd8	♗f3[30]			±
7	. . . d5	♖fd1[31] ♘d4[32]	♕d4 ♘e4	♕d5 ♘d6	♕b3 ♗e6	♘d5 ♘f5	c4 ♘e3	♘f6 ♗f6	♖d8 ♖ad8[33]	∓
8	. . . . . .	♘c6 bc6	e5[34] ♘e8[35]	f4 f6	♗f3[36] ♖b8[37]	♗a7 ♖b2	♗d4 ♗f5	♖fc1 fe5	fe5 ♖b4[38]	=
9	. . . . . .	ed5 ♘d5[39]	♘d5[40] ♘d4[41]	c4[42] e5[43]	f4[44] ♗e6	fe5 ♘e2[45]	♕e2 ♗d5[46]	♖ad1[47] ♕e7[48]		=
10	. . . . . .	. . . . . .	♘c6 bc6	♖ad1[49] ♕c7[50]	♗d4 e5	♗c5 ♖d8	♘e4 ♗e6[51]	♕g5[52]		±
11	. . . ♘g4	♗g4[53] ♗g4	♘d5[54] ♗d7[55]	c4 ♘e5	b3 e6![56]	♘c3 ♕a5	h3 a6	a4 f5	f4 ♘f7[57]	=
12	. . . . . .	. . . . . .	f4 ♗d7	♖ad1[58] ♖c8[59]	f5[60] ♘e5	♗h6 ♘c4[61]	♕c1 ♘b2[62]	♗g7 ♘d1	♕h6 ♘c3[63]	±
13	. . . . . .	. . . . . .	. . . ♘d4	♗d4 e5	♗e3[64] ef4	♖f4[65] ♗e6	♖f2 ♗e5	♗d4[66] ♖c8[67]	♖d1 ♕a5[68]	=

1 8. . . d5? 9. ♗b5+−

2 9. f3 h4! [9. . . 0−0 10. ♕d2 ♗d7 11. ♖ad1±] 10. ♕d2 ♘h5 11. ♘d5 e6 12. ♘c3 ♘g3∓ Reti−Breyer 1920

3 Tarrasch−Bird, Hastings 1895

4 9. f4 ♘g4!? 10. ♗g4 ♗g4 11. ♕d2 [11. ♘c6 ♕d7 12. ♕d3 ♕c6=] ♘d4 12. ♗d4 e5 13. ♗e3 ef4 14. ♖f4 ♗e6△ ♗e5=

5 9. . . ♕a5 10. ♘b3±

6 10. ♕d2 a6 11. f4 ♖c8 12. ♖ad1 — 9. ♕d2

7 10. . . ♖c8!?

8 12. . . ♕a5 13. ♕d3△ ♖ad1±

9 14. . . ♔g8!?△ ♕b6

10 **9. f3** d5 [9. . . ♕b6 10. ♘a4△ c4±] 10. ed5 ♘d5 11. ♘d5 ♕d5=; 10. ♘c6 bc6 11. e5 ♘d7 12. f4 ♖b8?! 13. ♖b1 ♕a5 14. ♕d4 f6 15. e6± Norby−Larsen, Copenhagen 1966 — 1/293; 12. . . e6!△ c5, f6=; **9. ♔h1** d5 10. ♘c6 [10. ed5 ♘d5 11. ♘d5 ♕d5 12. ♗f3 ♕a5 13. ♘c6 bc6 14. ♗c6 ♖b8∓; 14. c3=] bc6 11. e5 ♘d7 12. f4=

11 9. . . ♗d7 10. ♘b3 a5 11. a4 ♘b4 12. ♗f3 ♗e6 13. ♘d4= Smislov−Geler, SSSR 1974 — 18/422; 12. f4!?△ ♗f3∞

12 10. ♘c6 bc6 11. e5 ♘d7 12. f4 e6△ c5, f6=

13 **14. ♗c6** ♖b8 15. ♕d5 ♕c7∓ Ravinski−Lisicin, SSSR 1944; **14. c3**=

14 **10. ♘f5**? ♕b2 11. ♘a4 ♕a3 12. c3 ♘e4! [12. . . gf5? 13. ♗c1+−] 13. ♗c1 ♘c3 14. ♗a3 ♘d1 15. ♘g7 ♘e3−+; **10. ♕d2**? ♘e4 −+; **10. ♘a4** ♕b4 11. c3 ♕a5 12. b4 ♕c7 13. ♗f3 ♗d7 14. ♖c1 ♖ab8∓ Postpischl−Alster, Venezia 1949

15 10. . . ♕b2? 11. a3 ♘e4 [11. . . ♕b6 12. ♘e6±] 12. ♘c6 ♘c3 13. ♘e7 ♔h8 14. ♗f3 ♖e8 15. ♘c8 ♖ac8 16. ♗a7± Wach−Oley, Polska 1973 — 16/403

16 11. ♗g4 ♗d4 12. ♗d4 ♕d4 13. ♕d4 ♘d4 14. ♗c8 ♖ac8 15. ♖f2= Meštrović−Hartston, Örebro 1966

17 11... ♕d8? 12. ♗g4 ♗g4 13. f5+−

18 12. ♘b6 ♗e3 13. ♔h1 [13. ♕e3 ♘e3 14. ♘a8 ♘f1 15. ♗f1 f5∓ de Jong−Rogman, Nederland 1933] ♗b6 14. ♗g4 ♗g4 15. f5 [15. c3 ♗e6 16. f5 ♘e5 17. ♕g3 ♗c4∓ Poulson −Weil, München 1936] gf5 [15... ♗h5?! 16. ♖ac1 ♘e5 17. ♕h3 f6 18. ♕h4 ♗g4∓ Horowitz−Reshevsky, New York 1951] 16. ef5 ♘e5 17. ♕g3 ♔h8 18. ♕h4 ♗d8∓ Bosch−Landau, Amsterdam 1939

19 11... ♖d8 12. ef6 ♗f6 13. ♖f6 ef6 14. ♘a4 ♖d4 15. ♘b6 ♖d1 16. ♖d1 ab6 17. a3± Veresov

20 **12... ♕d8** 13. ♕d8 ♖d8 14. ♘e7 ♔f8 [14... ♔h8 15. ♗g5±] 15. ♗c5± Aljehin; **12... ♕e6** 13. ♘g7 ♔g7 14. ♕d2 ♔g8 [14... ♘g8? 15. ♘b5 ♕d7 16. ♕c3± Kramer−Euwe (m) 1940; 14... ♘eg4? 15. ♗d4 ♕d7 16. ♗g4 ♕g4 17. ♖f6± Aljehin] 15. ♖ae1 ♘c6 [15... ♗d7 16. ♗d4 ♗c6 17. ♕f4 ♘fd7 18. b3 ♕d6 19. ♖f2⩱; 17. ♗b5 ♘fd7 18. ♗c6 bc6 19. ♕e3 f6 20. ♗a7± Grečkin−Ivašin, corr. 1952] 16. ♗f3 [16. ♗d3 ♕d7 17. h3 ♘h5 18. ♕f2 ♘g7 19. ♕h4 ♕d8 20. ♘e4 f6∓ Nežmetdinov−Pogrebiski, SSSR 1949] ♕d7 17. ♕f2△ ♕h4⩱

21 **14. ♕d2**? ♗e6 15. ♖ab1 ♕a3 16. ♖b7 ♖fd8 17. ♕e1 ♘e4 18. ♘d1 ♘c4∓ Sanguinetti −Marini, Mar del Plata 1954; **14. ♘c8** ♕c3 15. ♗d4 ♕c8 16. ♗e5 ♖d8 17. ♗d4 ♘e4 18. ♗g7 ♔g7∓

22 14... ♘g8 15. ♘b5 ♕b4 [15... ♘f3? 16. ♖f3 ♗d4 17. ♘d4 ♘e7 18. ♖b3+−] 16. ♘d5 ♕a4 17. ♖f4⩱ Aratovski−Ilivicki, corr. 1948

23 **15. ♘ed5** ♘d5 16. ♘d5 ♕d4 17. ♕d4 ♘f3−+; **15. ♘c8** ♖ac8 [15... ♖d8 16. ♘b5 ♖ac8 17. c3 ♕e7 18. ♘a7 ♖c3∓ Palda−Galia, Wien 1947] 16. ♗e5 ♖fd8 17. ♗f6 ♗f6!∓

24 **16. ♗d6** ♕e3 17. ♔h1 ♕c3−+; **16. ♗f6** ♗f6 17. ♘d5 ♕c5∓

25 18. ♗d3⩱

26 9... a6 10. f4 ♘d4 11. ♗d4 b5 12. ♗e3 ♗b7 13. ♖ad1 ♕c7 14. e5± Unzicker−Spanjaard, Luzern 1948

27 10. ♖ad1 a6 [10... ♘d4 11. ♗d4 ♗c6 12. f3 a6 13. a4 ♕a5 14. ♕e3±] 11. f3 ♖c8 12. ♔h1 ♘a5 13. ♗h6 ♘c4 14. ♗c4 ♖c4 15. ♗g7± Nimzowitsch−Tartakower, Bled 1931; 12... b5!? Pachman

28 10... ♘d4 11. ♗d4 b5 12. e5 de5 13. fe5 ♘g4 14. ♗f3 b4 15. ♗a8± Penrose−Littlewood, Hastings 1961/62

29 11. ♗f3 ♖c8 12. ♘b3 ♗g4 13. h3 [13. ♔h1 ♗f3 14. ♖f3 b5∓] ♗f3 14. ♖f3 b5 15. a3 ♕d7 16. ♖d1 ♕b7 17. ♖e1 ♖fd8∓ Fichtl−Pachman, Teplice Šanov 1953

30 Unzicker−Eliskases, Saltsjöbaden (izt) 1952

31 10. ♖ad1!?

32 10... ♘e4? 11. ♘c6! ♗c3 12. ♕d5 ♕d5 13. ♘e7 ♔g7 14. ♘d5 ♗b2 15. ♖ab1 ♗e5 16. f4 ♗b8 17. ♗d4 ♔h6 18. ♗f3 f6 19. g4+− Gufeljd

33 Vasjukov−Gufeljd, SSSR 1959

34 11. ♖ad1 ♕c7! [11... e6 12. f4 ♕e7=] 12. ed5 cd5 13. ♘d5 ♘d5 14. ♕d5 ♗e6⩱

35 **11... ♘d7** 12. f4 e6 13. ♘a4 f6 14. ♘c5 ♘c5 15. ♗c5 ♖f7 16. ♕e3± Korn−Winter, London 1949; **11... ♘g4** 12. ♗g4 ♗g4 13. f4 f6 14. ♗d4 ♕a5 15. ♕e3 ♗f5 16. ♘e2 c5= Arulajd−Bejlin, SSSR 1946; 16. ♖f2± Evans; **11... ♘e4** 12. ♘e4 de4 13. ♕c3 ♕c7 14. ♗f4! [14. ♗d4? ♖d8 15. f4 ef3 16. ♗c4 ♖d4 17. ♕d4 ♗e5△ ♗e6∓ Ravinski−Rovner, SSSR 1949; 15. ♖ad1 ♗e6 16. f4 ef3 17. ♗f3 ♗d5∓ Boleslavski] ♗e6 15. ♖ad1 [15. ♖fd1? f5∓] a5 16. ♕c5±

36 13. ef6 ef6 14. ♗f3 ♗e6 15. ♘a4 ♘d6 16. ♘c5 ♗f7 17. b3 ♕c7= Bonč-Osmolovski −Kopilov, SSSR 1953

37 13... fe5 14. ♘d5±

38 **18. ♘d5**?! ♖d4 19. ♕d4 cd5 20. ♗d5 ♔h8∓; **18. ♖ab1** ♖c4 19. ♖b7 ♘d6 20. ♗b6 ♕e8= Minev−Gufeljd, Sofia 1967 — 3/471

39 10... ♘b4? 11. d6! ♕d6 12. ♘cb5+−

40 11. ♖fd1 ♘e3 [11... ♘c3 12. ♕c3 ♘d4 13. ♗d4 ♗d4 14. ♖d4 ♕b6 15. h4± Solmanis−Bejlin, SSSR 1946] 12. ♘c6 [12. fe3?! ♘d4?! 13. ed4 ♗f5 14. ♗f3=; 12... ♕b6∓] ♕d2 13. ♘e7 ♔h8 14. ♖d2 ♗c3 15. bc3 ♘f5 16. ♘d5 ♗d7= Solmanis−Renter, SSSR 1946

41 11... ♕d5? 12. ♗f3 ♕c4 13. b3 ♕a6 14. ♘c6 bc6 15. ♗h6±

42 12. ♗c4 ♗e6 [12... ♘f5 13. ♖ad1 ♘e3∓ Schmahl−Carls 1939; 13. ♗g5 ♗e6=; 13. ♗c5 e6 14. ♘e7 ♘e7 15. ♕d8 ♖d8 16. ♗e7 ♖d7= Carls] 13. ♗d4 ♗d5 14. ♗g7 ♗c4 15. ♕h6 ♗f1 16. ♗f8 ♕f8= Honfi−Gufeljd Kecskemet 1968

43 12... ♘e2 13. ♕e2 e6 14. ♘c3 ♗d7 [14... b6 15. ♖fd1 ♕h4 16. c5± Iljin-Ženevski−Kan, Leningrad 1934; 15... ♕e7 16. ♗f4± Kirilov−Terpugov, SSSR 1948] 15. ♖fd1 ♕c7 16. ♖ac1 ♗c6 17. ♘d5± Krogius−Koc, SSSR 1962

44 13. ♖fc1? ♗e6 14. ♗d4 ed4∓ Stoljar−Tajmanov, SSSR 1949

45 14... ♘f5 15. ♘f6 ♗f6 16. ef6±

46 15... ♗e5? 16. ♗c5 ♗d6 17. ♘f6± Gufeljd

47 16. cd5? ♕d5 17. ♗f4 ♖fe8∓

48 **16... ♗c4** 17. ♕c4 ♕c8 18. ♕c8 ♖ac8 19. ♖d7± Geler−Averbah, Szczawno Zdroj 1950; **16... ♕e7**=

49 12. ♘d5? ♕d5 13. ♕b4 ♗e6∓ Engel–Haunolg, Deutschland 1942

50 **12... ♗f5** 13. ♘d5± Smislov–Denker, Groningen 1946; **12... ♗e6** 13. ♗d4△ ♘a4±; **12... ♗c3** 13. bc3±⊞

51 **15... f5** 16. ♘d6±; **15... ♗f5** 16. ♘d6±

52 Gufeljd

53 10. ♘c6 bc6 11. ♗d4 e5 12. ♗e3 ♘e3∓↑⊞

54 **11. f3** ♗d7 [11... ♗e6 12. ♘c6 bc6 13. ♗d4 f6 14. ♘e2 ♕c7=] 12. ♖ad1 ♖c8 13. ♖f2 ♕a5 14. ♘b3 (Euwe–Denker, London 1946) ♗c3∓; **11. h3** ♗e6=

55 **11... ♖c8** 12. c4 ♗e6 [12... ♘d4 13. ♗d4 ♖c4 14. ♗g7 ♔g7 15. ♘e3 ♖e4 16. f3 ♖e3 17. ♕e3± Kok–Spanjaard, Utrecht 1948] 13. b3 ♗d5 14. ed5 ♘d4 15. ♗d4 ♗d4 16. ♕d4± Tajmanov–Ilivicki, SSSR 1948; **11... ♗e6** 12. c4 ♗d5 13. ed5 ♘d4 14. ♘d4 ♗d4 15. ♕d4±

56 Euwe

57 18. ef5 gf5= Boleslavski

58 12. ♘d5 e6 13. ♘c3 ♘a5 14. b3 ♖c8 15. ♖ac1 a6 16. f5 ♘c6= Barden–Pilnik, Helsinki (ol) 1952

59 **12... ♘d4** 13. ♗d4 ♗d4 14. ♕d4 ♗c6 15. b4 ♕b6 16. b5± Richter–Rellstab, Berlin 1938; **12... ♘a5** 13. b3 ♖c8 14. f5 ♘c6 15. ♘d5± **12.. f5** 13. ef5 ♗f5 14. ♘f5 gf5 15. ♖fe1± Pachman

60 **13. ♘d5** ♘d4 14. ♗d4 ♗d4 15. ♕d4 ♖c2 16. f5 ♗c6 17. ♘e3∞̅ Richter–Petrov, Bad Harzburg 1938; **13. ♖f2** ♕a5 14. h3 ♖fd8 15. ♕e2 ♘d4 16. ♗d4 ♗d4 [16... ♗c6!?△ e5] 17. ♖d4 ♗c6 18. ♕d2 ♕c5! [18... ♕b6 19. b4 a5 20. b5 e5 21. ♖d3± Trott–Stuart, Chester 1952] 19. b4 ♕h5=; **13. h3** a6 14. ♖f2 f5?! 15. ef5 gf5 16. ♘d5 ♖f7 17. ♘f3± Radulov–Bobocov Varna 1968 — 7/397; 14... b5!? Sokolov

61 14... f6 15. ♘d5± Levy

62 15... ♗h6 16. ♕h6 ♘b2 17. ♖f3±

63 **18. f6**?! ef6! 19. ♗f6 ♕f6 20. ♖f6 ♘e4 21. ♖f4 f5∓ Unzicker–Giustolisi, Lugano 1959; **18. fg6**!± Euwe

64 13. fe5 de5 14. ♗e3 ♕d2 15. ♗d2 ♖ad8=

65 14. ♗f4!? ♕b6 15. ♔h1 ♕b2 16. ♘d5∞̅

66 16. ♗f4 ♖c8 17. ♗e5 de5 18. ♕e3= Pechan–Marszalek, Praha 1953

67 **16... ♕e7** 17. ♖ad1 ♖fd8= Matanović–Trifunović, Beograd 1952; **16... a6** 17. ♘e2 ♖c8 18. c3 ♗d7 19. ♕h6 ♕e7 20. ♖e1 ♗c6 21. ♘f4 [Jimenez–Larsen, Palma de Mallorca (izt) 1970 — 10/490] f6! 22. ♖e3 ♖f7= Larsen

68 18. a3 ♖c4= Unzicker–Geler, BRD–SSSR 1960

B 74

1. e4 c5 2. ♘f3 d6 3. d4 cd4 4. ♘d4 ♘f6 5. ♘c3 g6 6. ♗e3 ♗g7 7. ♗e2 ♘c6 8. 0–0 0–0 9. ♘b3

	9	10	11	12	13	14	15	16	17	
1	... a5[1]	a4[2] ♗e6[3]	f4 ♖c8[4]	f5 ♗b3[5]	cb3 ♘b4[6]	♗c4 ♘d7[7]	♕e2[8] ♘e5	♗b5 ♘a6	♘d5 ♘c5[9]	±
2	... ...	... ...	♘d4 d5[10]	♘e6[11] fe6	ed5 ♘d5[12]	♗d2[13]				±

1. e4 c5 2. ♘f3 d6 3. d4 cd4 4. ♘d4 ♘f6 5. ♘c3 g6 6. ♗e3 ♗g7 7. ♗e2 ♘c6 8. 0—0 0—0 9. ♘b3 ♗e6

	10	11	12	13	14	15	16	17	18	
3	f4[14] ♘a5[15]	♘a5[16] ♕a5	♗f3[17] ♗c4	♖e1[18] ♖fd8	♕d2 ♕c7	♖ac1[19] e5	fe5[20] de5	♕f2 b6	g4 h6	=
4	... ...	f5 ♗c4[21]	♗d3[22] ♗d3[23]	cd3[24] d5[25]	♘a5[26] ♕a5	e5 d4[27]	♗d4[28] ♘d7	f6 ef6	ef6 ♗f6[29]	=
5	... ...	... ...	♘a5 ♗e2	♕e2[30] ♕a5	g4 ♖ac8[31]	g5[32] ♖c3[33]	gf6[34] ♖e3	♕e3 ♗f6	c3 ♖c8[35]	=
6	... ♕c8[36]	♔h1[37] ♖d8[38]	♗f3 ♗c4[39]	♖e1[40] e5	♕d2 ♕c7	♖ad1 ♖ac8	♕f2 b5	fe5 de5	♗g5 ♖d1[41]	=

	10	11	12	13	14	15	16	17	18	
7	...	♕e1	♘d4	a3	♕e2	♖ad1[43]	♘d5	♕e3	c3	=
	...	♘b4[42]	♗c4	♗e2	♘c6	♘g4[44]	♘e3	♕d8[45]	e6[46]	
8	...	h3	a4[48]	♖c1[49]	♗d4	cb3	♕d4	♖fd1	♖d4	∓
	...	a5[47]	♘b4	♘d7	♗b3	♗d4	♕c5	♕d4	♘c5[50]	
9	...	...	♘d4	♗d4	♗d3	fe5[51]	♗e3[52]	♗g5	♗c4	=
	...	...	♘d4	♗c4	e5	de5	♕c6	♘h5	♕c4[53]	
10	...	...	♘d4[54]	♗d4	f5	e5	f6	ef6	♗c4	=
	...	♖d8	♘d4[55]	♗c4	d5[56]	♘e4	ef6	♗f8	♕c4[57]	
11	...	...	♗f3	♖f2[59]	♖d2[61]	♘d5	♘d4[63]	♗d4	ed5	=∞
	...	...	♗c4[58]	e5[60]	♕e6[62]	ef4	♘d4	♗d5	♕f5[64]	

1 Aljehin; **9... ♗d7** 10. f4 a6 11. g4±; **9... b6** 10. f4 ♗b7 11. ♗f3 ♖c8 [11... ♘d7 12. ♘d4 ♘d4 13. ♗d4±] 12. ♕e2 ♘d7 13. a3! [13. ♖ad1? ♘b4 14. ♕d2 ♗c3! 15. bc3 ♘a2 16. ♗d4 e5 17. fe5 de5 18. ♗f2 ♖c7∓ Liberzon–Štejn, Tallinn 1969 — 7/396] ♘c5 14. ♖ad1±

2 **10. h3**? a4 11. ♘d4 a3 12. b3 ♕a5∓ Mjagmarsuren–Soos, Varna (ol) 1962; **10. ♘d5** ♘e4 11. ♗b6 ♕d7 12. ♘c7 ♖b8 13. ♘a5 ♗b2∓; **10. ♘d2** ♗e6 11. ♘c4 b5 12. ♘b5 ♘e4 13. ♘d4 ♘d4 14. ♗d4 ♖b8 15. ♗g7 ♔g7 16. ♕d4 ♘f6 17. ♖ad1 ♕c7 18. b3 ♖fc8∓ Kopajev–Averbah, SSSR 1952; **10. a3** a4 11. ♘d4 d5 12. ed5 ♘d5 13. ♘d5 ♕d5 14. ♗f3 ♕a5 15. ♘c6 [15. ♗c6? bc6 16. ♘c6 ♕c7∓] bc6 16. ♗c6 ♖a6∓ Berkov–Goldberg, SSSR 1939

3 10... ♘b4 11. f4! ♗d7 12. ♗f3 ♗c6 [12... ♕c8 13. h3±] 13. ♘d5 [13. ♘d4 e5 14. ♘db5 ef4 15. ♗f4 d5∓] ♘d7 14. c3 ♘a6 15. ♘a5 ♗d5! 16. ♕d5 ♘c7 17. ♕b7 ♖a5 18. b4 ♖a8 19. e5!± Zinn–Haag, Zinnowitz 1966 — 2/414

4 **11... ♘d7** 12. ♕d2 [12. f5? ♗b3 13. cb3 ♘c5∓ Denes–Troianescu, Bucuresti 1960] ♗b3 13. cb3± Beni–Trifunović, Helsinki (ol) 1960; **11... ♕c8** 12. ♕d2 [12. h3 ♘b4 13. ♘d4 ♗c4 14. f5?! (14. ♗d3!?) ♘d7 15. ♖f2 ♘e5 16. ♗f3 d5 17. ♘d5 ♘d5 18. ed5 ♖d8∓ Mihaljčišin–Ljubojević, Sarajevo 1970 — 9/381] ♘b4 13. ♘d4 ♗c4 14. f5 ♗e2!? [14... ♘d7 15. ♗c4 ♕c4 16. b3△ ♘d5± Dely–Velimirović, Beograd 1968 — 6/520] 15. ♕e2 ♘d7± Filip

5 12... ♗d7 13. g4 ♘e5 14. g5±

6 13... ♘e5!?

7 14... ♘e4 15. fg6 hg6 16. ♘e4 d5 17. ♘g5△ ♕g4-h4±

8 15. ♘d5 ♘d5 16. ♗d5 ♘f6 17. ♗b7 ♖b8 18. ♗c6 ♖b4∓ Janošević–Averbah, Titovo Užice 1966

9 18. ♗g5± Liberzon–Pavlenko, SSSR 1968

10 Aljehin; 11... ♘d4 12. ♗d4 ♖c8 [12... ♕c7 13. ♖e1± Toluš–Kitajev, corr. 1967 — 4/512] 13. f4 ♗c4 14. ♖f2± Toluš–Rovner, SSSR (ch) 1939; 12... ♘d7!?

11 12. ed5?! ♗d5 13. ♘d5 ♘d5 14. ♘c6 bc6 15. ♗d4 e5 16. ♗c5 ♖e8 17. ♗c4 ♕c7 18. c3 ♖ad8 19. ♕c2 e4!∓↑ Spielmann–Aljehin, Margate 1938

12 13... ed5 14. ♘b5 e5 15. c3 ♖f7 [15... ♔h8 16. ♕b3± Horowitz–Reshevsky, New York 1941; 15... ♕e7 16. ♕b3 ♔h8 17. ♖ad1 ♖ad8 18. ♗b6± Franke–Meyer, corr. 1959] 16. f4 ♕e7 17. ♕b3 ♖d8 18. ♖ae1±; 14. ♗c5!?

13 **14. ♗g4** ♘e3 15. ♗e6 ♔h8 16. fe3 ♕b6∓ Boleslavski; **14. ♗d2**±

14 **10. f3** d5 11. ed5 ♘d5 12. ♘d5 ♗d5 13. c3 e5∓⊞; **10. h3** d5 11. ed5 ♘d5 12. ♘d5 ♗d5 13. ♘d4 e5 14. ♘c6 ♗c6 15. c3=

15 **10... ♕d7**? 11. ♕e1±; **10... d5** 11. f5±; **10... ♖c8** 11. g4 [11. f5?! ♗d7 12. g4 ♘e5 13. g5 ♖c3∓↑ Ravinski–Simagin, SSSR 1957; 11. h3 a6 12. ♕d2 b5= Rauzer–Čehover, SSSR 1933] ♘a5 12. f5 ♗d7 13. e5 de5 14. g5 ♘b3!? 16. gf6 ♘a1 17. fg7 ♔g7∞ Murej; 12... ♗c4!?

16 **11. ♘d4** ♗c4 12. ♗d3 [12. b3 ♗e2 13. ♕e2 ♖c8 14. ♕d3 ♘g4∓] ♖c8 13. ♕f3 e5 14. ♘de2 d5= Pachman; **11. ♗d4** ♖c8!? [11... ♘c4 12. ♖b1±; 11... ♗c4 12. ♘a5 ♗e2 13. ♕e2 ♕a5 14. e5 ♘d5 15. ♘d5 ♕d5 16. ♗c3=] 12. ♗a7 ♖c3 13. bc3 ♘e4 14. ♗d4 ♘c3 15. ♗c3 ♗c3=∞ Iljin-Ženevski, Rabinovič–Levenfiš, Ragozin, SSSR 1933; **11. e5** ♘e8 12. ♘d5! [12. ♗d4 ♗b3! 13. ab3 ♘c6∓↑] ♘b3 [12... ♘c6 13. ed6 ♕d6 14. c4±] 13. ab3 de5 14. ♗f3 ef4 15. ♘f4 ♕d1? 16. ♖fd1 ♗f5 17. ♘d5± Hotchkiss–Dinock, corr. 1934; 15... ♘d6=; **11. g4** ♗c4 12. ♗d3 ♘b3 13. ab3 ♗d3 14. cd3 h5∞ Mangini–Rojahu, Helsinki (ol) 1952; 12... e5!?

17 12. ♗d4 ♖ac8 13. ♔h1 [13. ♕d2? ♘e4 14. ♘e4 ♕d2−+] ♗c4 14. ♗c4 ♖c4 15. ♕d3 ♖fc8 16. ♖ad1 e6∓

18 13. ♖f2 ♖fd8 14. ♕d2 ♕c7 15. b3 ♗a6 16. ♖ad1 ♖ac8∓ Treybal−Foltys, ČSSR 1940

19 15. ♕f2!?

20 16. b3? d5! 17. fe5 [17. ed5 e4∓ Rauzer−Botvinik, SSSR 1933; 17. ♘d5 ♗d5 18. ed5 e4∓] ♘e4!∓

21 **11... gf5**? 12. ef5 ♗c4 13. g4±; **11... ♗d7** 12. e5! de5 13. fg6 ♘b3 14. gf7±

22 Spielmann; 12. g4 ♖c8 13. ♗a7 [13. e5 ♗e2 14. ♕e2 de5 15. ♖ad1 ♕c7 16. g5± Aitken−Winter, England 1950; 13... de5! 14. ♕d8 ♖fd8 15. ♘a5 ♗e2 16. ♘e2 ♖c2 17. ♖fd1 (Aitken−Footner, England 1962) ♖d1 18. ♖d1 ♘g4 19. ♖d8 ♗f8 20. f6 ef6 21. ♗a7 ♔g7∓ Golombek] ♗e2 14. ♕e2 ♘c4=

23 **12... b5**? 13. ♘b5 ♗b5 14. ♗b5 ♘e4 15. ♘a5 ♕a5 16. ♗c6+−; **12... d5** 13. e5 ♘b3 [13... ♗d3 14. ef6 ♗f1 15. fg7+−] 14. ef6 ♗f6 15. ab3± Kashdan−Denker, New York 1941; 13... ♘e8±

24 13. ♕d3 ♘b3 14. ab3 ♘g4∓

25 **13... ♘c6** 14. d4 b5 15. ♕f3 b4 16. ♘e2± Goldberg−Kotlerman, SSSR 1951; **13... ♘b3** 14. ab3 d5 15. ♗d4 de4 16. de4 a6 [16... ♕c7 17. e5 ♖ad8 18. ef6 ♗f6 19. ♖a4! b5 20. ♘b5 ♕d7 21. ♕e2 a6 22. ♗f6 ab5 23. ♗e7 ba4 24. ♗f8± Spielmann] 17. e5 ♘e8 18. b4 ♘c7 19. f6 ef6 ♗h6 21. ♗b6 ♕c8± Spielmann−Landau, Amsterdam 1938

26 **14. e5**? ♘b3 15. ef6 ♗f6 16. ♕b3 d4∓; **14. ♗d4** ♘c6 15. ♗f6 ♗f6 16. ♘d5 ♗b2∓

27 15... ♘d7 16. d4±

28 16. ef6 ♗f6 17. fg6 dc3 18. gh7 ♔h8∞

29 **18... ♘f6**? 19. ♗f6 ♕b6 20. ♔h1 ♗f6 21. ♘d5+−; **18... ♗f6**!=

30 13. ♘b7 ♗d1 14. ♘d8 ♗c2 15. ♘c6 ♖fe8= Lasker−Rjumin, Moskva 1936

31 **14... ♕b4**? 15. g5 [15. ♖ad1 ♖ae8 16. ♗d4 ♘d7 17. ♗g7 ♔g7 18. ♕f3±] ♘h5 [15... ♘e4? 16. ♘d5 ♕b2 17. ♘e7 ♔h8 18. f6+−; 15... ♘d7 16. ♗d2±] 16. a3 ♕b2 17. ♘d5 ♖ae8 18. ♕f2±→ Estrin−Fridštejn, SSSR 1945; **14... ♘d7** 15. ♘d5 ♖ae8 [15... e6 16. ♘e7 ♔h8 17. g5±→ Iljin-Ženevski−Volk, SSSR 1940] 16. g5 [16. b4!? Ragozin] e6 17. ♘e7! [17. ♘f6? ♘f6 18. gf6 ♗f6 19. ♗h6 ef5∓ Nazarov−Žuravljev, SSSR 1951] ♖e7 18. f6± Sokolski; **14... ♖ae8** 15. g5 ♘d7 16. ♘d5 gf5 17. ♖f5 ♕d8 18. ♖f2 e6 19. ♘f6± Pachman

32 15. ♗d4 ♕b4 16. ♖ad1 ♕c4= Boleslavski

33 15... ♘d7 16. ♘d5 ♖fe8 17. ♕f2±

34 16. bc3 ♘e4∓↑

35 **19. ♖f3** b5 20. ♔h1 ♖c4∓ Davie−Whiteley, England 1962; **19. a3** ♖c4 [19... a6 20. ♖ae1 ♕b5 21. ♖e2 ♔g7= Pavlov−Mititelu, Bucuresti 1962] 20. ♖ae1 b5 21. ♖f3 ♕c7= Filipowicz−Hollis, Marianské Lazni 1962

36 Tartakower

37 11. ♕d2 ♖d8 12. ♗f3 ♗c4 13. ♖fd1 e5 14. ♘d5 ♗d5 15. ed5 ♘e7 16. fe5 de5 17. d6 ♘f5 18. ♗c5 e4∓↑ Dunbinin−Aronin, SSSR 1947; 13. ♖fe1 e5 14. ♔h1= — 11. ♔h1

38 11... a5 12. a4 ♗g4 13. ♗g1 [13. ♗g4 ♘g4 14. ♗g1 ♘b4= Holasuran−Mednis, Varna (ol) 1962] ♖e8 [13... ♖d8 14. ♘d5 ♗e2 15. ♕e2± Aljehin−Golombek, Montevideo 1939] 14. ♘d5 ♗e2 15. ♕e2= Kan; 12... ♘b4!=; 12. ♘d4! ♘d4 13. ♗d4 ♗c4 14. ♗d3±

39 **12... ♗g4**?! 13. h3 ♗h3 14. f5± Beni−Busek, Wien 1953; **12... d5** 13. e5 ♘e4 14. ♘e2±

40 13. ♖f2 e5 14. ♖d2 [14. ♕d2 (Ragozin−Aronin, SSSR (ch) 1948) 14... d5=] ef4 15. ♗f4 ♘e5 16. ♖d6 ♖d6 17. ♕d6 ♘f3 18. gf3 ♘h5∞ Rossetto−Panno, Portorož (izt) 1958

41 Holmov−Aronin, SSSR (ch) 1949

42 **11... ♗g4** 12. ♗d3±; **11... ♘g4** 12. ♗g4 ♗g4 13. f5 gf5 14. h3 ♗h3 [14... f4? 15. ♖f4 ♗h5 16. ♘d5± Ragozin−Veresov, SSSR 1947] 15. gh3 fe4 16. ♕h4 f5 17. ♘d5? ♖f7 18. ♖ad1 ♘e5 19. ♗g5 ♕e6∓ Ladbišenski−Lipnicki, SSSR 1948; 17. ♔h1!± Domnitz−Kraidman, Tel Aviv 1964; **11... ♖d8** 12. ♖d1 ♘b4 13. ♘d4 ♗c4 14. a3!±; **11... a5**!? 12. ♖d1 [12. ♘d4? ♘e4! 13. ♘c6 ♕c6−+ Durao−Levy, Praia da Rocha 1969; 12. a4 ♘b4 13. ♘d4 ♗c4 14. f5 ♘d7= Pachman−Gadalinski, Špindlerov Mlyn 1948] ♗g4 13. ♗g4 ♘g4 14. ♘d5 a4 15. ♘d4 ♘e3 16. ♕e3= Richter−Schmidt, Bad Oeyenhausen 1941

43 15. ♘b3 ♘g4 16. ♗d2 a5 17. ♘d5 a4∓ Koblenc

44 15... ♖e8!?

45 17... ♗d4 18. ♖d4 e6 19. ♖c4±

46 Koblenc

47 11... ♘e8 12. ♕d2 [12. g4!? f5 13. ef5 gf5 14. g5 ♗f7 15. ♗h5±] f5 13. ef5 [13. g4!? Aljehin] gf5 14. ♖ae1 ♔h8 15. ♘d4 ♗g8 16. g4± Reti−Tartakower, New York 1924

48 **12. ♘d5**? ♗d5 13. ed5 ♘b4 14. c4 a4 15. a3 [15. ♘d4 a3∓ Cortlever − Fontein, Amsterdam 1939] ♘fd5! 16. cd5 ♘c2 17. ♕d3 ab3∓ Rooze−Kramer, Baarn 1940; **12. ♘a4** ♗b3 13. ab3 [13. ♘b6? ♕e6 14. ♘a8 ♕e4∓; 13. cb3 ♕e6! 14. e5 ♘d5 15. ♗c1 de5∓] ♕e6 14. ♗c4 ♕e4 15. ♖e1 ♘b4∓ Bogoljubov−Hermann, Lüneburg 1947; **12. ♗f3** a4 13. ♘d4 a3 14. b3 ♘e5∓ Koblenc

49 **13. ♗f3** ♘d7 14. ♘d4 ♗c4 15. ♖f2 ♖d8∓ van Hombeck–Nikitin 1960; **13. ♘d4** ♗c4 14. f5 ♘d7 15. fg6 hg6 16. ♔h1 ♘e5∓ Erny–Parma, Basel 1959; **13. ♗d4**!?

50 Momo–Nikitin, SSSR 1960

51 15. ♗e3 ef4 16. ♗f4 d5!∓⊞ O'Hanlon–Cortlever, Buenos Aires 1939

52 16. ♗e5? ♕c5 17. ♔h1 ♗d3–+

53 19. ♕d5 ♕d5 20. ♘d5= Fink–Estrin, corr. 1960

54 **12. ♔h2**? d5 13. e5 ♘e4 14. ♘b5 g5∓ Thomas–Flor, Bournemouth 1939; **12. ♗d3** d5 13. e5 d4∓ Blau–Rabar, Dubrovnik (ol) 1950; **12. g4** d5 13. e5 ♘e4 14. ♘e4 de4 15. ♕e1 f6∓ Koblenc; **12. ♕e1**!? d5 13. e5 d4 14. ef6 ♗f6 15. ♘e4= Eisinger–Rabar, Marianske Lazni 1960

55 12... ♗d7 13. g4 ♘d4 14. ♗d4 ♗c6 [Lehmann–Bogoljubov, Bad Pyrmont 1949] 15. ♗f3±

56 14... ♗e2?! 15. ♕e2 ♘d7 16. ♗g7 ♔g7 17. ♘d5±

57 19. ♕d3= Geler–Lipnicki, SSSR 1950

58 **12... a5** 13. a4 ♗c4 14. ♖f2 e5 15. ♘e2± Nilsson–Engels, München 1936; **12... d5** 13. e5 d4 [13... ♘e4 14. ♘e2 g5 15. fg5 ♗e5 16. ♕c1±] 14. ♘d4 ♘d4 15. ♗d4 ♕c4 16. ♘e2 ♘d5 17. ♗d5±; **12... ♘d7** 13. ♘d5 ♗b2 14. ♖b1 ♗g7 15. c4±

59 13. ♖e1 d5 14. ed5 [14. e5 ♗b3 15. ab3 d4∓] ♘b4 15. ♗d4 ♘bd5∓ Ary–Sentil, Brazil (ch) 1960

60 13... d5 14. ed5 [14. e5? ♗b3 15. ab3 d4∓] ♘d5 15. ♘d5 ♗d5 16. ♗d5 e6 17. ♖d2 ♖d5 18. ♖d5 ed5 19. c3±

61 14. f5 gf5 15. ef5 d5 16. ♗g5 e4∓ Steinmeyer–Benkö, USA (ch) 1962/63

62 **14... ef4**!? 15. ♗f4 ♘e5 16. ♔h2 ♗a6= Matanović–Geler, Jugoslavija–SSSR 1956; **14... ♕c7**!?

63 **16. ♘c7** ♕e5∓; **16. ♗f4** ♘e4 17. ♘c7 ♕f5 18. ♗e4 ♕e4∓

64 19. ♖e2$\overline{\infty}$ Rolland–Larsen, Le Havre 1966

B 75

1. e4 c5 2. ♘f3 d6 3. d4 cd4 4. ♘d4 ♘f6 5. ♘c3 g6 6. ♗e3 ♗g7 7. f3

	7	8	9	10	11	12	13	14	15	
1	...	♗c4	♗b3	♕d2	♗h6[3]	♕h6	0-0-0	cb3	♔b1	±
	a6[1]	b5	♗b7	♘bd7[2]	♗h6	♘c5[4]	♘b3	♕b6[5]	0-0-0[6]	
2	...	♕d2	♗h6[8]	♕h6	0-0-0	♔b1	♘b3	♗d3[9]		±
	...	♘bd7[7]	♗h6	b5	♗b7	♕b6	♖c8			
3	...	♕d2	0-0-0[11]	♔b1[13]	♘b3[14]	h4	♗g5	♗e2	♘b5	=
	♘c6	♗d7[10]	♖c8[12]	♕a5	♕c7	h5	♗e6	♘e5	♕b8[15]	
4	...	♗c4	♗b3[17]	ab3	♕d2	h4	h5	♗h6	♘de2	±
	...	♘a5[16]	♘b3	0–0	a6	♗d7	♖c8	e5	♗e6[18]	
5	...	...	♗b5[19]	♘d5[20]	ed5	♗c6[21]	♘c6	♗d4	♕d4	=
	...	♕b6	♕c7	♘d5	a6	bc6	♗b7	♗d4	0–0[22]	
6	...	...	0–0	♗b3	♘cb5	c4	♔h1	♗c2	b3	=
	...	...	0–0[23]	♕c7[24]	♕d8[25]	♘d7	♘c5	♘e6	a6[26]	
7	...	...	♘f5	♘g7	♘d5	♗d5[28]	♖b1[30]	♔f2	♕c1	$\overline{\infty}$
	...	...	♕b2	♔f8	♘d5[27]	♔g7[29]	♕c3[31]	♕a5[32]	h5[33]	
8	...	...	♕d2[34]	♗b3	0-0-0	♔b1[37]	♗c4	♘b3	g4[39]	±
	...	♗d7	♕a5[35]	♖c8	♘e5[36]	♘c4	♖c4	♕c7[38]	h5[40]	

1. e4 c5 2. ♘f3 d6 3. d4 cd4 4. ♘d4 ♘f6 5. ♘c3 g6 6. ♗e3 ♗g7 7. f3 ♘c6 8. ♗c4 ♗d7 9. ♕d2 ♖c8

	10	11	12	13	14	15	16	17	18	
9	♗b3[41]	♗h6[43]	♕h6	0-0-0	♘d5	ed5	♖he1	♕g7	♔b1[46]	$\overline{\infty}$
	♘e5[42]	♗h6[44]	♘c4[45]	♕a5	♘d5	♕d5	♕h5	♕g5		

	10	11	12	13	14	15	16	17	18	
10	...	h4	a4	♗c4	b3[47]	0-0-0	♘db5	♗d4	♗e3	∞
	...	a5	♘c4	♖c4	♖c8	0—0	h5	e5	d5[48]	
11	...	0-0-0	♗c4[49]	♘b3[50]	♗h6[52]					±
	...	♘c4	♖c4	0—0[51]						

1 **7... h5**?! 8. ♗c4 a6 9. ♗b3 ♘bd7 10. 0—0 ♕c7 11. ♔h1 ♘e5 12. f4 ♘c4 13. ♗c4 ♕c4 14. f5±→ Bitman—Šumakov, SSSR 1964; **7... ♘bd7** 8. ♕d2 0—0 9. ♗c4△ 0-0-0, ♗h6±→»

2 10... h5? 11. 0—0± Bisguier—Reshevsky, Long Beach 1957

3 **11. 0-0-0** ♘c5 12. ♔b1 ♘b3 13. cb3 0—0 14. ♗h6 ♗h6 15. ♕h6 b4∓→ Littlewood—Botvinik, Hastings 1961/62; **11. a4** ba4 [11... b4 12. ♘d5 a5 13. ♗h6± Ree—Bilek, Bad Pyrmont 1970 — 10/491] 12. ♘a4 ♕c7 13. 0—0 0—0 14. c4 ♖fd8 15. ♗a2 ♘c5 16. ♘c3 a5 17. ♘db5 ♕c8 18. ♖ac1 ♗c6?! 19. ♕e2 ♗e8 20. ♖fd1± Ostojić—Ivanović, Jugoslavija 1972 — 14/442; 18... a4=

4 **12... ♕b6** 13. 0-0-0 ♘c5 14. ♔b1 ♘b3 15. ♘b3 0-0-0 16. ♖he1 ♔b8 17. ♘d5 ♘d5 18. ed5± Štejn—Veresov, SSSR 1963; **12... b4** 13. ♘a4 ♕a5 14. ♕d2 0—0 15. a3 ♕e5 16. ab4 d5 17. 0-0-0± Mazzoni—O'Kelly, Paris 1963

5 14... e5 15. ♘c2 ♕e7 16. ♘e3±

6 16. b4!± Krutičin—Botvinik, SSSR 1963

7 8... b5 **9. 0-0-0** ♗b7 10. ♗h6 ♗h6 11. ♕h6 ♘bd7 [11... b4 12. e5±] 12. a3 ♕b6 13. ♕d2 ♘c5 14. ♔b1 e5 15. ♘b3 ♘b3 16. cb3 0-0-0=; **9. ♗h6** ♗h6 [9... 0—0 10. ♗g7 ♔g7 11. 0-0-0 ♗b7 12. e5 ♘e8 13. h4 h5 14. ♘f5 ♔g8 15. ♕g5±→ Konstantinopoljski—Rudakovski, corr. 1937] 10. ♕h6 b4 11. ♘d5 ♘d5 12. ed5 ♗b7 13. ♗c4 ♕c7 14. ♕g7 ♖f8 15. ♗b3 ♘d7 16. 0-0-0! [16. a3? ♘c5 17. ♗c4 ♕b6? 18. 0—0 ♘d7 19. ♗b3 0-0-0 20. ♖fd1± Matanović—Štejn, Sousse (izt) 1967 — 4/514; 17... ♘a4 18. ♗b3 ♘c5=] a5 17. ♗a4±; **9. a4**! ba4 [9... b4 10. ♘a2 a5 11. ♗b5! ♗d7 13. c3 bc3 13. ♘c3△ ♘d5±] 10. ♘a4 [10. ♖a4 ♘bd7 11. ♗e2 0—0 12. 0—0 ♘c5 13. ♖a3 ♗b7 14. ♖fa1 ♕c8 15. ♘b3± Kavalek—Bilek, Sousse (izt) 1967 — 4/513] 0—0 11. ♗e2 ♘bd7 12. 0—0 ♗b7 13. c4 ♕c7 14. b4±↑« Boleslavski—Ufimcev, SSSR (ch) 1947

8 **9. 0-0-0** b5 10. h4 h5 11. ♗d3 ♗b7 12. ♖he1 ♖c8 13. ♔b1= Geler—Furman, SSSR 1961; **9. g4** ♘b6 10. 0-0-0 ♗d7 11. h4 h5 12. g5 ♘h7=; **9. ♗c4** b5 [9... ♘c5 10. ♗b3 ♗d7 11. ♗h6 0—0 12. h4 ♘b3 13. ab3 ♗h6 14. ♕h6 ♔h8 15. h5 ♖g8 16. hg6± Milić—Tajmanov, Oberhausen 1961] 10. ♗d5 ♘d5 11. ♘d5 ♗b7 12. ♗g5!± Vesely—Pachman, ČSSR 1963

9 Bastrikov—Hasin, SSSR 1961

10 8... ♕a5 9. 0-0-0 ♘d4 10. ♗d4 ♗e6 11. ♗b5 ♔f8 12. ♗a4! h5 13. ♔b1 ♖c8 14. ♗b3 ♗b3 15. cb3± Gipslis—Drimer, SSSR 1967 — 4/516

11 **9. g4** h5 10. g5 ♘h7 11. 0-0-0 0—0 12. ♔b1 ♖e8 13. h4= Bednarski—Letelier, La Habana 1967 — 4/515; **9. ♗c4**! — 8. ♗c4

12 9... a6 10. g4 ♖c8 11. ♘c6 ♗c6 12. ♗d4 0—0 13. h4 ♕a5 14. ♔b1± Zuidema—Szabo, Amsterdam 1966 — 2/415

13 10. g4 ♘e5 [10... 0—0 11. h4 ♘d4 12. ♗d4 ♕a5 13. ♔b1 e5 14. ♗e3 ♗e6 15. ♘d5 ♕d2= Judovič—Averbah, SSSR 1964] 11. h4 h5 12. g5 ♘h7 13. ♔b1 0—0 14. ♗e2 ♘c4 15. ♗c4 ♖c4 16. ♕d3 ♖c8∞ Zuidema—Bilek, La Habana (ol) 1966

14 11. g4!?

15 Matanović—Mohrlock, Vrnjačka Banja 1967 — 3/472

16 **8... ♘d7** 9. ♗b5 ♘a5 10. b4 ♘c6 11. ♘d5 ♘db8 12. ♗g5± Gufeljd; **8... ♕a5** 9. 0—0 ♕b4 10. ♗b3 ♘e4? [10... ♘g4? 11. ♗f7+ —] 11. ♘c6 ♘c3 12. bc3 ♕c3 13. ♗d4 + —; 10... ♗d7±; **8... ♘e5** 9. ♗b3 ♕c7 10. ♕e2±

17 9. ♗d3?! 0—0 10. ♕d2 d5=

18 16. g4 ♕c7 17. ♘g3 b5 18. b4 ♕b7 19. ♗g7 ♔g7 20. hg6 fg6 21. ♕d6± Spaski—Geler, SSSR 1965

19 **9. ♕d2**? ♘e4∓; **9. ♘cb5** a6 10. ♘f5 ♕a5 11. ♗d2 gf5 12. ♗a5 ab5 13. ♘b5 ♖a5∓↑

20 **10. ♕d2** ♗d7! [10... a6 11. ♗e2 b5 12. 0-0-0 0—0 13. g4 ♗d7 14. ♘d5 ♘d5 15. ed5 ♘e5=] 11. 0-0-0 0—0 12. g4 ♖fc8 13. ♗e2 b5!∓↑; **10. g4** ♗d7 [10... a6 11. ♗a4 h6 12. ♕d2 b5 13. ♗b3 ♗b7 14. 0-0-0 ♘a5 15. h4 h5 15. g5± Klovan—Rojzman, SSSR 1964; 11... e6 12. ♕d2 0—0 13. ♗b3 b5 14. ♘c6 ♕c6 15. 0-0-0 a5 16. a4 b4 17. ♘e2 ♗a6 18. ♘d4△ ♗h6± Suetin—Geler, SSSR 1964] 11. g5 ♘h5 12. ♘d5 ♕d8 13. f4 [13. ♕d2 0—0 14. ♗e2 e6 15. ♘c3 ♘d4 16. ♗d4 ♗d4 17. ♕d4 ♕g5 18. ♕d6 ♖fd8∓] 0—0 14. ♗e2 e6 15. ♘c3 ♘d4 16. ♗d4 ♗d4 17. ♕d4 ♘f4 18. ♕d6 ♘e2 19. ♘e2 ♗c6∓

21 12. ♗a4 ♕a5 13. c3 ♕d5 14. ♘c6 ♕d1 17. ♖d1 ♗d7∓

22 16. 0-0-0 ♗c6 17. dc6 ♕c6= Bihovski—Štejn, SSSR 1965

23 9... ♘**e4**? 10. ♘f5+−; **9... ♘g4**? ♗f7+−; **9... ♕b2**!? 10. ♘cb5 ♕b4 11. ♘c7 ♔d8 12. ♘c6 bc6 13. ♘a8 ♕c4=∞

24 10... ♘g4 11. fg4 ♗d4 12. ♗d4 ♕d4 13. ♕d4 ♘d4 14. ♘d5±

25 11... ♕b8?! 12. c4 a6 13. ♘c3±

26 16. ♘e6 ♗e6 17. ♘d4 ♘d4 18. ♗d4 ♕a5= Nikitin−Judovič, SSSR 1964

27 11... ♔g7 12. 0−0 [12. ♖b1 ♕a3 13. ♕d2 ♖d8? 14. ♖b3 ♕a5 15. ♗h6 ♔h8 16. ♘f6 ♕d2 17. ♗d2 ef6 18. ♗f7± Bronštejn−Štejn, SSSR (ch) 1965; 13... h5 14. 0−0! ♕a5! 15. c3 ♘d5 16. ed5 ♘e5 17. ♕d4 f6 18. f4=∞] ♕a3 13. ♕d2 ♖d8 14. ♖ab1 ♘d5 15. ed5 ♘e5 16. ♗d4 ♔g8 17. ♖b3 ♘c4 18. ♕h6±→» Boleslavski−Semjonov, SSSR 1966

28 **12. ed5**? ♕c3∓; **12. ♕d5**?! ♕a1 13. ♔f2 ♕g7 14. ♗h6 ♗c6 15. ♗g7 ♔g7 16. ♕b5 ♗c4 17. ♕c4 ♖ac8=∞; 13... ♕f6!?

29 12... ♕c3?! 13. ♗d2 ♕f6 [13... ♕g7 14. ♖b1±] 14. ♕c1 ♔g7 15. ♗h6± Šašin

30 13. 0−0 ♕c3! [13... f6 14. ♕d2±] 14. ♖e1 [14. ♕c1 h5 15. ♖b1 ♕a5 16. f4 f6 17. ♖b3 ♕c7 18. ♕b2 h4 (Haag−Ostojić, Debrecen 1967 — 4/517) 19. f5=∞; 14... h6 15. ♖b1 f6 16. ♖b3 ♕a5 17. ♕b2 ♕c7 18. f4 ♖b8 19. e5 ♗f5! 20. ef6 ef6 21. ♗c6 bc6 22. ♗d4 ♖b3 23. ♗f6 ♔h7 24. ab3 ♖e8=] ♕a5 15. ♕c1 h5 16. ♕b2 f6 17. ♖ad1 ♕c7 18. f4 h4? 19. h3 ♗d7 20. ♖b1 ♖ab8 21. e5± Fischer−Cobo, La Habana 1965; 18... e5!∞

31 13... ♕a3?! 14. ♕d2 h6 [14... h5 15. 0−0 ♕a5 16. ♕d3 ♕c7 17. f4 f6 18. ♕c3 ♗d7 19. e5± Parma−Ostojić, Jugoslavija 1967] 15. 0−0 ♕a5 16. ♕f2±↑

32 **14... ♖d8** 15. h4! e6 16. ♗c6 ♕c6 17. h5 ♗d7 18. hg6 fg6 19. ♕d2±; **14... f6** 15. ♕c1 [15. g4 e6 16. ♗b3 ♖d8=] e6 16. ♖b3 ♕a5 17. ♗e6!? ♗e6 18. ♖b7 ♗f7 19. ♗h6 ♔g8 20. ♕b2±

33 16. ♖d1 ♕c7 17. ♖b3 f6 18. ♕b2 ♖e8 19. f4 e6 20. ♗c6=∞ Dončenko−Telman, SSSR 1966

34 9. ♕e2!?

35 9... ♘e5 10. ♗b3 a5 11. a4±; 10... ♖c8!?

36 11... ♘d4 12. ♗d4 0−0 13. ♔b1 ♔h8 14. h4±→» Matulović−Puc, Jugoslavija 1966 — 1/295

37 **12. ♕e2** a6 13. f4 ♗g4 [13... ♘c6 14. h3 ♘d4 15. ♗d4 ♗e6 16. ♗e6 fe6 17. e5± Estrin−Lohov, SSSR 1966] 14. fe5 [14. ♘f3 ♘f3 15. gf3 ♖c3! 16. fg4 ♖b3! 17. cb3 (17. ab3 ♘e4−+) ♕a2∓ Lohov, Selivanovski] ♗e2 15. ef6 ♗d1 [15... ♗f6? 16. ♘de2 ♗g5 17. ♘f4 e5 18. ♘fd5± Estrin−Litvinov, SSSR 1967] 16. fg7 ♖g8 17. ♖d1 ♖g7∓; **12. ♗h6** ♗h6 13. ♕h6 ♖c3 14. bc3 ♕c3 15. ♔b1 [15. ♘e2? ♘d3−+] a5 [15... b5 16. ♖he1 a5 17. ♖e3 ♕c5 18. ♘e2 a4∓ Altieri−Pelikan, Mar del Plata 1970] 16. a4 [16. ♕d2 ♕c5 17. a4 0−0 18. ♖he1 ♖c8∓ Gruzman−Veresov, SSSR 1964] ♘c4 17. ♕c1 ♘b6 18. ♕a3∓; **12. h4** ♘c4 13. ♗c4 ♖c4 14. g4 b5 15. ♘b3 ♕c7 16. h5 b4 17. ♘d5 ♘d5 18. ed5 a5∓↑

38 14... ♕a6 15. e5! [15. h4 h5 16. ♗g5 ♗e6 17. e5 ♘d7 18. ed6 ♗c3 19. bc3± O'Kelly−Toran, Palma de Malorca 1966; 15... ♗e6 16. ♗h6 ♗h6 17. ♕h6 ♖c3=∞ Dely−Joksić, Beograd 1966; 15. ♗h6!?] de5 16. ♘c5 ♕c6 17. ♘3e4! ♘e4 18. fe4 ♖d4 19. ♗d4 ed4 20. ♘d7 ♕d7 21. c3± Balinas−Sardinha, Lugano (ol) 1968

39 15. h4?! h5 16. ♗g5 ♗e6 17. ♘b5 ♕b6= Gheorghiu−Drimer Bucuresti 1967 — 3/406

40 **15... a6** 16. g5 ♘h5 17. ♘d5 ♕d8 18. ♘a5 ♖a4 19. ♗b6 ♕c8 20. ♘e7+− Bellon−Makropulos, Stockholm 1969; **15... h5** 16. g5 ♘h7 17. ♘d5 ♕b8 18. ♗f4 e5 19. ♗e3 b6 20. ♕d3± Jansa−Gheorghiu, Vrnjačka Banja 1967

41 10. 0-0-0? ♘**d4** 11. ♕**d4** 0−0 12. ♗b3 ♘g4∓↑

42 **10... a6** 11. g4 h6 13. 0-0-0 ♘a5 13. h4 ♘b3 14. cb3! h5 15. g5 ♘h7 16. ♔b1 ♘f8 17. ♘d5± Jurkov−Čistjakov, SSSR 1966; **10... ♘a5** 11. ♗h6 0−0 12. ♗g7 ♔g7 13. h4 e5 14. ♘de2 ♗e6 15. h5 ♕e7? 16. hg6 fg6 17. ♗e6 ♕e6 18. ♘d5± Bihovski−Štejn, SSSR 1964; 15... ♘b3!?; **10... h5** 11. 0-0-0 ♘a5 12. ♖he1 a6 13. ♔b1 0−0 14. ♗h6± Matanović−Simagin, Moskva 1963

43 11. ♕e2 a6 12. f4 ♘eg4! [12... ♘c6 13. ♘f3 ♘a5 14. e5 de5 15. fe5 ♘g4 16. ♗f7 ♔f7 17. e6±→ Hasin−Zotkin, SSSR 1967] 13. ♗g1 [13. ♗d2 ♘h5 14. ♘f3 ♘f4 15. ♗f4 ♖c3∓] ♕a5 14. 0-0-0 ♗h6 15. g3 e5∓

44 11... 0−0 12. ♗g7 ♔g7 13. h4 ♘c4 14. ♗c4 ♖c4 15. h5± Liberzon−Telman, SSSR 1966

45 12... ♕a5!? 13. ♕d2 ♘c4 14. ♗c4 ♖c4 15. ♘b3 ♕c7 [15... ♕e5±] 16. 0−0 b5=

46 Zwaig−Szabo, La Habana (ol) 1966 — 2/345

47 14. 0-0-0 0−0=

48 Gipslis−Bilek, Sousse (izt) 1967 — 4/423

49 12. ♕e2?! ♘e3 13. ♕e3 ♕a5 14. g4 ♕c5 15. ♕d3 h5 16. gh5 ♖h5 17. ♘de2 b5∓ Parma−Bilek, Vrnjačka Banja 1966

50 **13. g4** h5?! 14. g5 ♘h7 15. f4 ♕a5 16. ♕d3 b5 17. e5 ♖c3 18. bc3 de5 19. ♘b3± Barštatis−Alburt, SSSR 1967; 13... ♕a5!?∞; **13. ♔b1** 0−0 [13... a6 14. ♘b3 ♕c7 15. g4 ♗e6 16. ♗h6±] 14. h4 b5 15. h5 b4 16. ♘ce2 e5! [16... ♕b8?! 17. ♗h6 a5 18. hg6 fg6 19. ♗g7 ♔g7 20. ♕h6 ♔f7 21. g4± Dely−Szilagyi, Hungary 1966] 17. ♘b3 d5 18. ♗h6 ♕e7= Lee−Bilek, Haag 1966

51 13... b5? 14. e5! de5 15. ♘c5 ♕c8 16. ♘d7 ♘d7 17. ♘b5 a6 18. b3+− Tringov−Bilek, Lugano (ol) 1968

52 Boleslavski

B 76

1. e4 c5 2. ♘f3 d6 3. d4 cd4 4. ♘d4 ♘f6 5. ♘c3 g6 6. ♗e3 ♗g7 7. f3 0—0

	8	9	10	11	12	13	14	15	16	
1	♗c4[1] ♗d7[2]	♗b3[3] ♘c6	♕d2 ♕a5[4]	0—0[5] ♖fc8[6]	♖ad1 ♘e5	♕e2 ♖ab8	a4 a6	h3 ♕c7[7]	f4 ♘c4	=
2	♕d2 d5[8]	e5 ♘e8	f4 f6[9]	0-0-0[10] fe5[11]	fe5 ♘c6[12]	♘f3 ♗g4[13]	♘d5 ♖f3	gf3 ♗f3	♗g2 ♗d1[14]	±
3	. . . ♘c6	g4[15] ♘d4[16]	♗d4 ♕a5[17]	h4[18] ♖d8	♗c4 e5	♗e3 ♗e6	♗e6 fe6	0-0-0 d5[19]		∞
4	. . . . . .	0-0-0 ♗e6[20]	♔b1[21] ♘e5[22]	♘e6 fe6	f4 ♘eg4	♗c4[23] ♕c8	♗b3 ♘e3	♕e3 ♔h8	♖hf1	⩲
5	. . . . . .	. . . ♘d4	♗d4 ♕a5	♔b1[24] e5	♗e3 ♗e6	a3[25] ♖ad8[26]	g4[27] a6[28]	♕f2		⩲
6	. . . . . .	. . . . . .	. . . ♗e6	♔b1[29] ♕c7[30]	g4[31] ♖fc8	h4 ♕a5	a3 ♖ab8[32]	h5 b5	h6[33] ♗h8[34]	⩲
7	. . . . . .	. . . d5	♘c6[35] bc6	♗h6[36] ♕a5[37]	♗g7[38] ♔g7	e5 ♘g8	♕d4[39] ♖b8	a3 ♕b6	♘a4 ♕d4[40]	=
8	. . . . . .	. . . . . .	. . . . . .	ed5 ♘d5[41]	♘d5 cd5	♕d5 ♕c7[42]	♕c5[43] ♕b7[44]	♕a3[45] ♗f5[46]	♗a6[47] ♕c7[48]	=
9	. . . . . .	. . . . . .	. . . . . .	. . . . . .	♗d4[49] e5[50]	♗c5 ♗e6[51]	♗c4[52] ♘c3[53]	♕c3 ♕g5	♗e3[54] ♕g2[55]	=

[1] **8. g4?!** ♘c6 9. g5 [9. ♕d2 — 8. ♕d2] ♘h5 10. ♗e2 ♕a5∓; **8. ♘b3?!** ♗e6 9. ♕d2 ♘bd7 [9... ♘c6 — 8. ♕d2] 10. 0-0-0 ♘b6 11. g4 ♖c8 12. ♗h6 ♗h8 13. ♗f8 ♕f8 14. ♘d4 ♗c4∞ Panov—Simagin, SSSR 1943; 12... ♗c4!∓

[2] 8... ♘c6 9. ♕e2 [9. ♕d2 — B 77] ♘a5 [9... ♘e4? 10. ♘c6 ♘c3 11. ♘d8 ♘e2 12. ♘f7±; 9... ♗d7 10. 0-0-0 ♘e5 11. ♗b3 ♕b8 12. h4±→ Hartston—Ciocaltea, Vrnjačka Banja 1972 — 13/446; 9... ♘d7!? 10. 0-0-0 ♘de5 11. ♗d5! e6 12. ♗c6 ♘c6 13. ♘db5 ♕a5 14. ♗d2 d5 15. ed5 ed5 16. ♔b1 ♗f5∞ Ciocaltea] 10. ♗d3 [10. ♗b3 e5 11. ♘db5 a6 12. ♘a3 ♘b3 13. ab3 d5∓] e5 [10... ♘c6 11. 0-0-0 ♘d4 12. ♗d4 ♗e6 13. ♗c4± Keres—Lombardy, Wijk aan Zee 1969 — 7/398] 11. ♘b3 ♗e6 12. 0—0 ♖c8 13. ♖fd1 ♘c4 14. ♗c4 ♗c4 15. ♕f2 b6= Talj—Gufeljd, Suhumi 1972 — 14/441

[3] 9. ♕d2 ♘c6 — B 77

[4] 10... ♘d4 — B 77

[5] 11. h4! ♖fc8 12. 0-0-0 — B 79

[6] 11... ♘d4!?△ ♗c6

[7] 15... b5? 16. ab5 ab5 17. ♖a1 ♕b6 18. ♘e6+— M. Kovacs—Szilagyi, Albena 1970 — 10/494

[8] **8... ♗e6** 9. ♘e6 fe6 10. e5 ♘e8 11. ed6 ed6 12. 0-0-0± Gufeljd; **8... ♗d7** 9. 0-0-0 a6 10. g4 b5 11. g5 ♘h5 12. ♘d5± Bronštejn; **8... a6** 9. 0-0-0 b5 10. h4 ♗b7 11. h5 b4 [11... ♕c7 12. ♘f5! gf5 13. h6 ♗h8 14. ♗b6+—] 12. ♘ce2 ♕a5 13. ♔b1 ♘h5 14. g4 ♘f6 15. ♗h6±→ Vasjukov—Čistjakov, SSSR 1953

[9] **10... ♘c6** 11. g3 ♘d4 12. ♗d4 b6 13. ♗g2 ♘c7 14. 0—0 ♗a6 15. ♖fd1± Rauzer—Kasparjan, SSSR 1939; **10... ♘c7** 11. 0-0-0 ♘c6 12. ♘f3! e6 13. h4 b5 14. ♗c5±○; **10... e6** 11. ♗e2 f5 12. ef6 ♘f6 13. ♗f3 ♘c6 14. 0—0±↑⊞ Polugajevski—Čehover, SSSR 1954

[10] 11. h4 fe5 12. fe5 ♗e5 13. 0-0-0 ♘f6 14. ♘f3 ♗c3 15. ♕c3 ♘c6 16. ♗h6 ♖f7 17. h5=∞ →» Ravinski—Zagorovski, SSSR 1952

[11] 11... ♘c6 12. ♘f3±

[12] 12... ♗e5 13. ♘f3 ♗c3 14. ♕c3 e6 15. h4±→

[13] **13... e6** 14. ♗h6 ♕c7 15. ♘b5 ♕b8 16. ♗g7 ♔g7 17. h4±; **13... ♘e5** 14. ♘e5 ♗e5 15. ♕d5 ♕d5 16. ♘d5 ♖f7 17. ♗c4±

[14] 17. ♖d1 ♗e5 18. ♗c5 e6 14. ♘e7 ♔g7 20. ♘c6± Rozinov—Meyer, corr. 1958

15 9. ♘b3 ♗e6 [9... a5 10. a4 ♘b4 11. ♗e2 e5 12. 0–0 ♗e6 13. ♖fd1 ♖c8=; 10. ♘a4 ♗e6 11. ♘b6 ♖b8 12. 0-0-0 ♘d7=] 10. ♘d5 [10. g4 d5! 11. g5 ♘e4 12. fe4 d4∓; 10. 0-0-0 ♖c8 11. g4 ♘b4 12. ♔b1 ♘d7 13. ♗d4 ♘e5 14. ♗e2 a5∓; 10... a5!∓] ♗d5 11. ed5 ♘e5 12. 0-0-0 [12. c4 ♖c8 13. ♖c1 b5! 14. cb5 ♖c1△ ♕a8∓⊞] ♕c7 13. ♔b1 ♖fc8∓ Barcza–Filip, Bucuresti 1953

16 **9... d5**?! 10. g5 ♘h5 11. ed5 ♘d4 [11... ♘b4 12. ♗c4 e6 13. de6± Altšuler–Seleznev, SSSR 1954] 12. ♗d4 ♗d4 13. ♕d4 e5 [13... e6 14. h4 ♘g3 15. ♖g1± Šijanovski–Bivšev, SSSR 1953] 14. ♕d2 f6 15. gf6 ♕f6 16. 0-0-0±; **9... ♘d7** 10. h4 ♘de5 11. ♗e2 ♘d4 12. ♗d4 ♗e6 13. f4± Littlewood–Miles, England 1973 — 15/406; **9... e6**!? 10. ♘db5?! d5 11. ♗c5 a6 12. ♗f8 ♔f8∞ Kočijev–Miles, Manila 1974 — 18/424

17 **10... e5** 11. ♗e3 ♗e6 12. 0-0-0 ♕a5 13. a3 ♖fc8 14. g5 ♘h5 [14... ♘d7 15. ♘d5 ♕d2 16. ♖d2 ♗d5 17. ♖d5 ♗f8 18. ♗h3±] 15. ♘d5 ♕d8 16. ♔b1 ♗d5 17. ♕d5 ♘f4 18. ♕d6 ♕g5 19. ♗h3± Vasjukov–Gufeljd, SSSR 1971 — 12/437; **10... ♗e6** 11. 0-0-0 ♕a5 12. ♔b1 — 9. 0-0-0

18 11. 0-0-0! e5 12. ♗e3 ♗e6 13. ♔b1 ♖ad8 14. a3 — 9. 0-0-0

19 ∞ Filip

20 **9... ♘a5** 10. ♗h6 ♗e6 11. h4 ♗c4 h5±→; **9... a5** 10. a4±; **9... ♗d7** 10. g4 ♖c8 [10... ♘d4 11. ♗d4 ♗e6 12. h4 ♕a5 13. h5±→] 11. h4 ♘e5 12. h5 ♘c4 13. ♗c4 ♖c4 14. hg6 fg6 15. e5! de5 16. ♘e6± Klavin–Heuer, SSSR 1963

21 10. ♘e6 fe6 11. ♗h6 [11. ♗c4 ♕c8 12. ♗h6 ♘a5 13. ♗e2 ♗h6 14. ♕h6 ♕c5∓; 12... ♗h6 13. ♕h6 ♘d8 14. ♗e2 ♕c5∓] ♗h6! [11... ♕a5? 12. ♗c4±; 11... ♖c8 12. ♗c4 ♕d7 13. ♗g7? ♔g7 14. ♗b3 e5! 15. ♘e2 b6 16. h4 ♘a5= Havski–Toluš, SSSR 1961; 13. ♗b3! ♘a5 14. ♗g7 ♘b3 15. ab3 ♔g7 16. e5±] 12. ♕h6 ♘e5 13. ♔b1 ♖c8 14. h4 ♕b6 15. ♔a1 ♕a5= Sherwin–Reshevsky, USA 1955

22 **10... ♕a5**? 11. ♘e6 fe6 12. ♗c4 ♘d8 13. ♘d5 ♕d2 14. ♘f6 ♗f6 15. ♖d2 ♗e5 16. ♖d3 ♖c8 17. ♗b3 b6 18. ♗d2 ♔g7 [18... ♔h8 19. g3 ♖c7 20. f4± Mednis–D. Byrne, USA (ch) 1961/62] 19. g3 ♗f6 20. h4 h6 11. ♖f1 ♖c7 22. f4± Averbah–Larsen, Portorož (izt) 1958; **10... ♘a5** 11. ♘e6 fe6 12. ♘b5 ♘c6 13. ♗c4 ♕c8 14. ♗b3 a6 15. ♘d4 ♘d4 16. ♗d4±; **10... ♖c8** 11. ♘e6! [11. g4 ♕a5 12. ♘e6 fe6 13. ♘b5 ♕d2 14. ♖d2 a6 15. ♘d4 ♘d4 16. ♗d4 ♘d7=; 13. ♗c4 ♘d8 14. ♗e2 ♘g4 15. fg4 ♖c3 16. ♗d4 ♗d4 17. ♕d4 ♖c8∞; 14... ♘d7 15. ♗d4 ♘e5 16. f4 ♘dc6! 17. ♗e5 de5 18. f5 ♘d4 19. fg6 hg6 20. ♖hf1 ♖f4! =; 12. a3 ♘d7 13. ♗e2 ♘d4 14. ♗d4 ♗d4 15. ♕d4 ♘b6= Petrosjan–Panno, Amsterdam (ct) 1956; 12. ♘b3 ♕c7 13. h4 ♘e5=] fe6 12. ♗c4 [12. ♗h6 ♗h6 13. ♕h6 ♘e5 14. ♕h3 ♔f7 15. f4 ♘eg4∓ Fichtl–Toluš, Warszawa 1961] ♕d7 13. ♗b3 ♘e5 [13... b6 14. ♗h6 ♘e5 15. ♗g7 ♔g7 16. h4 b5 17. h5±→ Lepeškin–Vasiljčuk, SSSR 1961] 14. ♕e2 a6 15. f4? ♖c3 16. fe5 ♘e4 17. ed6 ed6 18. ♗d4 ♖b3 19. ab3 d5$\overline{\overline{\infty}}$; 15. ♘a4±

23 13. ♗g1 ♖c8 14. h3 ♘h6 15. g4 ♘f7=

24 11. a3!? Vuković

25 **13. ♕d6** ♗a2 14. ♘a2 ♖fd8–+; **13. ♗e2** ♖fd8 14. g4 b5∞⇆

26 13... ♖fd8 14. ♘b5 ♕d2 15. ♖d2 d5 16. ♘c7 ♖ac8 17. ♘e6 fe6 18. ♗a7±

27 14. ♘b5 ♕d2 15. ♖d2 d5=

28 14... ♔h8 15. ♗g5±

29 **11. a3** ♖b8 12. h4 b5 13. h5 b4∞⇆; **11. g4** ♕a5 12. ♔b1 ♖fc8 13. ♘d5 [13. ♗f6 ♖c3 14. ♕c3 ♕a2 15. ♔c1 ♗f6 16. ♕a3 ♗g5 –+; 13. a3 ♗c4 14. h4 ♗f1 15. ♖hf1 ♖c4∓] ♕d2 14. ♖d2 ♘d5 15. ♗g7 ♘e3= Boleslavski

30 **11... ♖c8** 12. h4 a6 13. h5 b5 14. g4 b4 15. ♘d5 ♗d5 16. ed5 ♕a5 17. hg6 fg6 18. g5 ♘h5 19. ♗h3± Segi–Vošpernik, Jugoslavija 1955; **11... a6** 12. h4 [12. g4 b5 13. h4 ♕c7 14. h5 ♖fc8 15. hg6 fg6 16. ♕h2 ♔f8 17. ♗d3 ♗g8 18. ♘d5±→] h5 [12... b5 13. h5 b4 14. ♘d5 ♗d5 15. ed5 ♕a5 16. hg6 hg6 17. ♗c4 ♖fc8 18. b3±] 13. ♘d5 ♗d5 14. ed5 ♘d7 15. ♗g7 ♔g7 16. ♕d4 f6 17. g4±→; **11... ♕a5** 12. g4 ♖fc8 13. a3 ♖ab8 14. g5 ♘h5 15. ♘d5± Karpov–Dueball, Skopje (ol) 1972 — 14/443

31 12. h4 ♖fc8 13. h5 ♕a5! [13... ♘h5? 14. ♗g7 ♔g7 15. g4 ♘f6 16. ♕h6 ♔g8 17. e5 de5 18. g5 ♘h5 19. ♗d3+– Evans–Zuckerman, USA (ch) 1966/67 — 3/473] 14. hg6 hg6 15. a3 ♖ab8 16. g4 [16. ♗f6 ♗f6 17. ♘d5 ♕d2 18. ♘f6 ♔g7= Karaklajić–Črepinšek, Jugoslavija 1969 — 7/399] b5 17. ♘d5 ♕d2 18. ♖d2 ♘d5= Evans–Zuckerman, USA (ch) 1969 — 8/409

32 14... ♗c4 15. h5 ♗f1 16. ♖hf1 ♖c4 17. h6±

33 16. hg6 hg6 17. ♕g5 ♕c7 18. e5 de5 [18... ♘e4!? 19. fe4 de5 20. ♗f2 b4 21. ab4 ♖b4$\overline{\overline{\infty}}$ Janošević–Bertok, Jugoslavija 1958] 19. ♗e5 ♕b6∞ Šabanov–Kimelfeld, SSSR 1973 — 16/404

34 17. ♗f6 ♗f6 [17... ef6 18. ♘d5 ♕d2 19. ♖d2 ♖c5 20. ♘e3±] 18. ♘d5 ♕d2 19. ♘f6 ef6 20. ♖d2 ♖b6 21. ♗e2 ♔f8 22. ♖hd1 ♔e7 23. f4±

35 10. ed5 ♘b4 11. ♗c4 ♘fd5 12. ♘b3? ♘c3–+ Maeder–Levy, Haifa 1970 — 10/493; 12. ♘d5!? ♘d5 13. ♗h6!? Sokolov; 11. ♔b1!?

36 11. e5 ♘d7 [11... ♘e8 12. f4 f6=] 12. f4 [12. ♘d5? cd5 13. ♕d5 ♖b8 14. ♗b5 ♗e5 15. ♗d7 ♗b2–+] ♕a5 13. g4 e6∓

37 **11... ♗h6** 12. ♕h6 e5 [12... ♖b8 13. e5 ♘d7 14. h4±→] 13. ♕g5 ♕e7 14. f4 ♖e8

15. ed5 ef4 16. ♕f4± Cejtlin–Velimirović, Kragujevac 1974 — 18/425; **11... ♗e6**!? 12. e5 ♘d7 13. ♗g7 ♔g7 14. h4 h5 15. g4 ♖h8=

38 12. e5 ♘e8 13. ♗g7 [13. h4 d4∓] ♔g7 14. h4 h5=

39 14. h4 ♗e6 15. h5 ♖ab8 16. b3 [16. ♗d3 ♖b2 17. ♔b2 ♖b8 18. ♔a1 d4–+ Čenkin–Mašić, SSSR 1957] ♕a3 17. ♔b1 ♖b4 18. ♔a1 ♖fb8∓→

40 Žilin–Lapienis, SSSR 1968

41 11... ♕a5!?

42 13... ♖b8 14. b3 [14. ♕d8? ♗b2 15. ♔b1 ♗d4∓] ♕c7 15. ♕c5! ♕b7 16. ♕a7 ♕c6 17. ♕b8 ♗f5 18. ♕f8 ♗f8 19. ♗c4± Ravinski–Trupan, SSSR 1952

43 14. ♕a8 ♗f5 15. ♕f8 ♔f8 16. ♖d2 h5 [16... ♕b8 17. ♗b5? h5 18. ♖hd1 ♗b2 19. ♔b2 ♕e5∓↑ Smislov–Gufeljd, SSSR (ch) 1961; 17. b3=] 17. ♗e2 [17. ♔b1 ♔g8 18. ♗e2 ♕e5 19. ♗d4 ♕f4 20. ♖hd1 ♗d4 21. ♖d4 ♕h2 22. ♗f1 h4∓; 17. ♗c4 ♗b2∓; 17. ♗d3 ♕e5∓] ♕b8 18. b3 [18. c4∓] ♗c3 19. ♖d5 ♗e6 20. ♖c5 [20. ♖b5 ♕d6 21. ♔b1 a6 22. ♖c5 ♗b4 23. ♖d1 ♕h2–+; 20. ♖d3 ♕b4 21. ♔b1 ♗f5 22. ♖d8 ♔g7 23. ♖hd1 ♗f6 24. ♗d3 ♕c3 25. ♔c1 e5–+ Stoljar–Bejlin, SSSR 1965] ♕b4 21. ♔b1 ♗f6∓↑

44 14... ♕b8 15. b3 [15. c3 a5 16. ♕e7 ♗e6 17. ♕a3 ♖e8∓↑ Dulno–Levy, Örebro 1966; 15. ♕a3 ♗f5 16. ♗d3 ♕e5 17. ♗f5 ♕f5∓→] a5! [15... ♗f5? 16. ♗d3 ♖c8 17. ♕a5 ♗c3 18. ♕b5± Evans–Padevski, La Habana 1965; 15... ♗e6? 16. ♗a6 ♕b6 17. ♗d3 ♖fc8 18. ♕c8 1 : 0 Alexander–Hartston, corr. 1967] 16. ♕b6 ♕e5 17. ♗d4 ♕f4 18. ♗e3 ♕e5=

45 **15. c3**? ♗f5 16. ♕b5 ♕c7 17. ♕c4 ♕e5 18. ♗d2 ♖fd8 19. f4 ♕a5 20. ♗e2 ♖ac8 21. ♕a6 [21. ♕b3 ♖b8 22. ♕c4 ♕a3–+] ♗c3 0 : 1 Bivšev–Bejlin, SSSR 1955; **15. ♗d4** ♗f5 16. ♕b5 ♕c7 17. ♕c5 ♕f4 18. ♗e3 ♕a4 19. ♕c4 ♕a5 20. ♕d5 ♖fc8–+; **15. b3** ♗f5 16. ♗d3 ♗d3 17. ♖d3 ♕a6 18. ♔b1 ♖ac8 19. ♕e7 ♖c2∓ Gufeljd

46 15... a5 16. ♗d4 e5 [16... ♗e6 17. ♗g7 ♔g7 18. ♗c4±] 17. ♗c5 ♗e6∞ Karaklajić–Geler, Dresden 1959

47 **16. ♗d3** ♖fb8 17. b3 a5 18. ♗f5 gf5 19. ♗d4 e5 20. ♗b2 e4∓; **16. c3** ♖fb8 17. ♗a6 ♕c7 18. ♗d3 ♕e5∓; **16. ♗c4** ♖fc8 17. ♗b3 a5 18. ♖d2 a4 19. ♗d5 ♖c2 20. ♖c2 ♕d5=∞ Mikenas

48 **16... ♗b2**? 17. ♕b2 ♕a6 18. ♗h6+–; **16... ♕c6** 17. ♗d3 ♖ab8 18. c3 ♖fc8 19. ♗f5 gf5 20. ♖d3± Karaklajić–Korčnoj, Jugoslavija–SSSR 1956; **16... ♕c7**! 17. ♕c5 ♕b6 [17... ♕c5?! 18. ♗c5±] 18. ♕b6 ab6 19. ♗c4 ♖fc8 20. ♗b3 ♖a2 21. ♖d8 ♖d8 22. ♗a2= Ravinski–Bejlin, SSSR 1955

49 Suetin

50 17... ♗d4 13. ♕d4 ♕b6 14. ♘a4! ♕a5 15. b3 ♖b8 16. ♕c5! ♕c5 17. ♘c5± Suetin–Vasjukov, SSSR 1955

51 Averbah

52 **14. ♗f8** ♕f8 15. ♔b1 ♖b8=∞→; **14. ♘d5** cd5 15. ♗b5 [15. ♗f8 ♕f8 16. ♕a5 ♕e7 17. ♖d3 e4 18. ♖b3 d4=∞ Torbakov–Gufeljd, SSSR 1957] d4 16. ♗f8 ♕f8 17. ♔b1 ♖b8=∞→ Polgar–Dely, Kecskemet 1972 — 13/448; **14. ♘e4** ♖e8 15. ♗a6 [15. g4?! ♘f4 16. ♕c3 ♗d5 17. ♗c4 ♘e6 18. ♗f2 ♘d4 19. ♖he1 ♖b8 20. f4 ♗c4 21. ♕c4 ♕b6 22. b3 ♕a5∓→ Barden] ♕c7 16. g4 ♖ed8 17. ♕e1 ♘f6 18. ♖d8 ♖d8= Keres–Averbah, SSSR 1959

53 **14... ♕h4** 15. ♗d5 cd5 [15... ♖fd8 16. g3!±] 16. ♘d5 ♖fe8!? [16... ♕c4 17. ♕a5 ♖fb8 18. b3 ♕e2 19. ♖d2 ♗h6 20. f4 ♕b5 21. ♘f6 ♔g7 22. ♗f8 ♔f8 23. ♖d8+– Levy] 17. ♕b4 ♕g5 18. ♕d2= Savon–Gufeljd, SSSR 1972 — 13/447; **14... ♖e8** 15. ♘d5 cd5 16. ♗d5 ♗d5 17. ♕d5 ♕g5 [17... ♕f6 18. ♔b1 ♖ad8 19. ♕e4 ♕e6 20. g4± Gligorić–Tajmanov, Jugoslavija–SSSR 1956] 18. ♕d2 ♕f6 19. c3 ♖ec8=∞ Milev–Geler, Moskva (ol) 1956

54 16. ♔b1 e4=

55 17. ♗e6 fe6 18. ♕c6 ♖ac8! 19. ♕e4 ♖f3 20. ♖he1!? [Euwe; 20. ♖hf1 ♖f2!=] ♕h3!=

B77

1. e4 c5 2. ♘f3 d6 3. d4 cd4 4. ♘d4 ♘f6 5. ♘c3 g6 6. ♗e3 ♗g7 7. f3 0–0 8. ♕d2 ♘c6 9. ♗c4

	9	10	11	12	13	14	15	16	17	
1	...	♗b3	ab3[3]	h4	e5	g4	♖g1	0-0-0[6]		±
	♘a5[1]	♘b3[2]	a6[4]	d5[5]	♘h5	♘g3	♗e5			
2	...	0-0-0[7]	a3[9]	♔b1	♗a2	g4	♗d4	♖hf1	♘a2	=
	a5	a4[8]	♕a5[10]	♗d7	♖fc8	♘d4	♗e6	♗a2	♕d2[11]	
3	...	♗b3	a4[13]	♗d4	0-0-0	♔b1	h4[15]	cb3	♔a2	=
	...	♗d7[12]	♘d4[14]	♗e6	♕d7	♖fc8	♗b3	♕e6	h5[16]	

	9	10	11	12	13	14	15	16	17	
4	...	a4	♘d5[18]	ed5	♗d4	♗f2[20]	♖c1	c3	b3	±
	...	♘b4[17]	♘fd5	♗d4[19]	e5	♗f5	♕e8	♘a6	♗d7[21]	
5	...	h4[22]	♗b3[24]	♕d3[25]	h5	hg6	♗h6[27]	♖h6		=
	♘d7	♘b6[23]	♘a5	♗d7[26]	♖c8	hg6	♗h6	♔g7		
6	...	0-0-0	♗b3	♕d3[30]	h4	h5[32]	hg6	♗g5[34]		±
	...	♘b6[28]	♘a5[29]	♗d7[31]	♖c8	♘bc4	hg6[33]			

1. e4 c5 2. ♘f3 d6 3. d4 cd4 4. ♘d4 ♘f6 5. ♘c3 g6 6. ♗e3 ♗g7 7. f3 0—0 8. ♕d2 ♘c6 9. ♗c4 ♘d4 10. ♗d4 ♗e6 11. ♗b3[35] ♕a5[36] 12. 0-0-0[37]

	12	13	14	15	16	17	18	19	20	
7	...	♔b1	♘d5[39]	ed5[41]	♖he1	♕e2	♖e2	♗c4	b3[42]	±
	b5[38]	b4	♗d5[40]	♕b5	a5	♕e2	a4	♖fc8	♔f8[43]	
8	...	...	♖he1[44]	cb3	♗f6[46]	♗c3	bc3	♖e3	♖c3	±
	...	♖fc8	♗b3[45]	b4	bc3	♗c3[47]	♖c3[48]	♖ac8[49]	♕c3[50]	
9	...	cb3	♔b1[52]	g4[53]	♕e2[54]	h4	♗e3	♗g5[56]	♖d7	±
	♗b3	♖fd8[51]	♖d7	♖ad8	♗h8[55]	e5	d5	de4	♖d7[57]	
10	...	♔b1	h4[59]	cb3	a3[61]	b4	e5	♗e5	♘e4	±
	♖fc8	♖c6[58]	♗b3[60]	b5	♖ac8	♕a6	de5	♘e4	♗e5[62]	

1. e4 c5 2. ♘f3 d6 3. d4 cd4 4. ♘d4 ♘f6 5. ♘c3 g6 6. ♗e3 ♗g7 7. f3 0—0 8. ♕d2 ♘c6 9. ♗c4 ♗d7

	10	11	12	13	14	15	16	17	18	
11	♗b3[63]	♗d4	h4[65]	a4[66]	♘a4[68]	♗c3[70]	0-0-0	cb3	♕c2	=
	♘d4[64]	b5	a5	ba4[67]	e5[69]	♗e6	♗b3	♕b8	♖c8[71]	
12	h4	♗b3	h5[73]	g4[74]	0-0-0[76]	♕h2[78]	♕h7	♗h6[79]	♔b1!	±
	♕a5[72]	♖fc8	♘h5	♘f4[75]	♘e6[77]	♘cd4	♔f8	♘b3[80]	♔e8[81]	
13	...	♗b3	h5[83]	g4[85]	♗c4[87]	♕e2	♕e3			$\overline{\infty}$
	♖c8	♘e5[82]	♘h5[84]	♖c4[86]	♘c4	♘e3	♘f6			

[1] **9...** ♖e8? 10. 0-0-0△ h4±→; **9... d5**? 10. ♗d5 ♘d5 11. ed5 ♘b4 12. ♘de2 ♕a5 [Lebedev—Bejlin, SSSR 1956] 13. a3! ♖d8 14. 0-0-0!±; **9... ♕a5** 10. ♗b3! [10. h4?! ♕b4! 11. ♗b3 ♘d4 12. ♕d4=] ♗d7 11. 0-0-0 — B 78; **9... a6** 10. ♗b3 ♕a5 [10... ♕c7 11. 0-0-0 ♘a5 12. ♔b1 ♘c4 13. ♗c4 ♕c4 14. ♗h6 ♘d7 15. h4± Banik—Hanov, SSSR 1955] 11. 0-0-0 ♗d7 12. h4 [12. ♔b1?! ♖ac8 13. g4 ♘e5 14. ♗h6 ♘c4 15. ♗c4 ♖c4 16. ♘b3 ♕e5! 17. h4 ♖cc8! 18. ♗f4 ♕e6∓↑ Fischer—Munoz, Leipzig (ol) 1960] ♖fc8 13. g4 ♘e5 [13... b5? 14. ♘c6 ♗c6 15. h5±→] 14. ♗h6 ♘c4 15. ♗c4 ♖c4 16. ♗g7 ♔g7 17. h5±→

[2] **10... a6** 11. h4 b5 [11... h5 12. 0-0-0 ♗d7 13. g4 hg4 14. h5 ♘h5 15. ♗h6 ♘b3 16. ♘b3±→ Espig—Merino, Kapfenberg 1970 — 9/383] 12. h5 ♘b3 13. ab3 ♗d7 14. ♗h6 ♗h6 15. ♕h6 e6 16. 0-0-0 ♕e7 17. g4 b4 18. g5 ♘h5 19. ♖h5 gh5 20. ♘f5+− Bojković—Adamski 1963; 13... ♗b7!±; **10... ♗d7** 11. h4! ♖c8 [11... ♕c7 12. h5 ♘c4 13. ♗c4 ♕c4 14. 0-0-0 ♖fc8 15. ♗h6± Juferov—Jeropov, SSSR 1967] 12. h5 ♘h5 13. 0-0-0 ♘c4 14. ♗c4 ♖c4 15. g4 ♘f6 16. ♖dg1±→» Vasjukov—Parma, SSSR—Jugoslavija 1963; **10... b6** 11. ♗h6 [11. h4!?] ♗a6 12. 0-0-0 [12. h4 ♗h6 13. ♕h6 e5 14. ♘de2 ♘b3 15. ab3 ♗e2 16. ♔e2 d5∓↑] ♘b3 13. ♘b3 ♗c4? 14. h4 ♗b3 15. ab3 ♖e8 16. ♗g7 ♔g7 17. h5±→ Kupper—Pomar, Enschede 1963; 13... ♖e8!±

[3] **11. cb3**?! d5! 12. e5 ♘e8 13. f4 f6∓↑⊞; **11. ♘b3** ♗e6 12. 0-0-0 a5 [12... ♖e8 13. ♘d4 ♗c4 14. h4±] 13. ♘d4 ♗c4 14. ♗h6 ♗h6 15. ♕h6 e5= Gipslis—Gurgenidze, SSSR (ch) 1961; 11... a5!? Bagirov

4 **11... d5**?! 12. ♘db5 de4 13. ♕d8 ♖d8 14. ♘c7 ♖b8 15. ♗a7±; **11... ♗d7** 12. h4±

5 12... ♗d7? 13. h5 ♖c8 14. ♗h6 e5 15. ♘de2 ♗e6 16. g4 ♕c7 17. ♘g3 b5 18. b4+− Spaski−Geler (m) 1965

6 Sherwin−Seidman, USA (ch) 1960

7 **10. h4**?! ♘e5 11. ♗e2! [11. ♗b3 a4! 12. ♘a4? ♖a4 13. ♗a4 ♘c4 14. ♕d3 ♘e3 15. ♕e3 ♕a5−+; 12. ♗a4 ♘c4 13. ♕c1 ♕b6 14. ♗b3 ♘e3 15. ♕e3 ♘e4∓] d5 12. ♗f4 [12. ed5 ♘d5 13. ♘d5 ♕d5 14. h5 ♘c4∓ Seidman−D. Byrne, USA (ch) 1961; 12. f4 ♘eg4∓] ♘c4?! 13. ♗c4 dc4 14. 0-0-0± Fischer−D. Byrne, USA (ch) 1963; 12... ♘h5!? ∓⊞↑; **10. g4** d5 11. ed5 [11. ♘d5? ♘d5 12. ♗d5 ♘d4 13. ♗d4 ♗d4 14. ♕d4 e6−+; 11. ♗d5 ♘d4 12. ♗d4 e6 13. ♗c4 ♘e4∓] ♘e5 12. ♗b3 a4 13. ♗a4 ♘d5=; **10. 0—0** a4 11. a3 ♕a5 [11... ♘d4 12. ♗d4 ♗e6 13. ♗e6 fe6 14. b3 ♕a5 15. ♖fd1 ab3 16. cb3 ♖ac8 17. b4± Matanović−D. Byrne, Vinkovci 1968 — 6/522] 12. ♖fd1 ♗d7 13. ♘d5 ♘d5 14. ♗d5 ♖fc8= Shapiro−D. Byrne, Varna (ol) 1962

8 10... ♘d7 11. ♗f7 [11. a3 ♘ce5 12. ♗a2 ♘b6 13. g4?! ♗d7 14. ♘d5 ♘bc4 15. ♕e2 b5∓ Đurović−Meštrović, Jugoslavija 1966 — 2/416; 13. ♕e2!?] ♖f7 12. ♘e6 ♕e8 13. ♘c7 ♕f8 14. ♘a8±

9 11. h4 ♕a5 [11... a3 12. b3±] 12. g4 ♗d7 13. ♘c6 bc6 [13... ♗c6!?△ b5] 14. a3 ♖fb8 15. h5 [Dueball−Marović, Dortmund 1973 — 16/405] ♗g4 16. hg6 hg6∞

10 11... ♗d7 12. h4 ♕a5 13. h5 b5 14. h6 ♗h8 15. ♘cb5 ♕d2 16. ♖d2 ♘a5=∞ Kotkov−Rozenberg, SSSR 1972 — 13/449

11 17. ♖d2= Gligorić−Parma, Jugoslavija (ch) 1965

12 **10... ♘d7** 11. h4 h5 12. a4 ♘c5 13. 0-0-0 ♘d4 14. ♗d4 ♘b3 15. cb3 ♗e6 16. ♗g7 ♔g7 17. ♕d4 ♔h7 18. ♘d5± Parma−Rodriguez, La Habana (ol) 1966 — 2/417; **10... ♘d4** 11. ♗d4 ♗e6?! [Sherwin−D. Byrne, USA (ch) 1966/67 — 3/474] 12. h4!?±; 11... ♗d7 12. a4 — 10... ♗d7

13 11. h4 ♘d4 12. ♗d4 a4 13. ♗c4 ♕a5=

14 **11... ♕c8** 12. g4 ♘d4 13. ♗d4 ♗e6 14. g5 ♘h5= Weinstein−D. Byrne, USA (ch) 1960/61; **11... ♖c8** 12. 0−0=

15 15. g4 ♗b3 16. cb3 ♕e6 17. ♔a2 ♘d7 18. ♗g7 ♔g7 19. h4 h6= Matanović−D. Byrne, Palma de Mallorca 1968 — 6/523

16 **17... h6**?! 18. ♘b5 d5 19. e5 ♘d7 20. ♖he1± Matanov'ć−D. Byrne, Vršac 1969 — 8/410; **17... h5**!=

17 **10... ♘d4** 11. ♗d4 ♗e6 12. ♗b5!? [12. ♗b3 ♗b3 13. cb3 ♘d7 14. ♗g7 ♔g7 15. b4! ab4 16. ♕d4 ♔g8 17. ♕b4 ♕a5 18. ♕a5 ♖a5 19. b4±] ♖c8 13. 0-0-0 ♘d7 14. ♗g7 ♔g7 15. f4 ♘f6 16. ♖he1± Karpov−D. Byrne, San Antonio 1972 — 14/444; **10... ♘e5** 11. ♗b3 ♗d7 12. h4 ♖c8 13. ♕e2 ♘h5 14. ♖h2± Levy−Suarez, Örebro 1966

18 **11. ♘db5**!? ♗e6 12. ♗b3 d5 13. e5±; **11. 0—0** d5 12. ed5 ♘fd5 13. ♘d5 ♘d5 14. ♗f2±; **11. ♗b3** ♗d7 12. 0−0 ♗c6 13. ♖ad1± Gufeljd−Lejn, SSSR 1969 — 9/382

19 12... e5 13. de6 fe6 14. c3±

20 14. de6? ♕h4△ ♕d4∓

21 18. ♗b6 ♘c5 19. 0−0 ♕e7 20. ♗c5 dc5 21. ♖fe1± Bogdanović−Meštrović, Sarajevo 1968 — 5/425

22 **10. ♖d1** ♘b6 11. ♗e2 d5 12. 0−0 ♘d4 13. ♗d4 de4 14. ♗g7 ♕d2 15. ♖d2 ♔g7 16. ♘e4 ♗f5= Holmov−Koc, SSSR 1962; **10. ♘c6** bc6 11. ♗h6 ♘b6 12. ♗d3 e5 13. h4 ♗h6 14. ♕h6 ♕f6=; **10. ♗b3** ♘a5 [10... ♘c5 11. 0-0-0 ♘b3 12. cb3 ♗d7 13. h4 f5 14. h5 ♖f7 15. hg6 hg6 16. ef5 gf5 17. ♖h5± Parma−Honfi, Jugoslavija−Hungary 1962] 11. ♗h6 ♘b6 12. ♗g7 ♔g7 13. 0-0-0 [13. h4 ♘bc4 14. ♕e2 ♘b2 15. ♖b1 ♕c7 16. ♘db5 ♕c5 17. ♖b2 a6= Nežmetdinov−Padevski, Bulgaria 1961] a6 14. ♘d5 ♘b3 15. ab3 ♘d5 16. ed5 e5 17. de6 fe6 18. h4±→ Suetin−Plater, SSSR 1958; 10... ♘b6 11. h4 — 10. h4

23 10... ♘de5 11. ♗b3 ♘a5 12. ♕e2 ♗d7 13. 0-0-0 ♖c8 14. h5 ♘ec4 15. hg6 fg6 16. ♗g5 ♖f7 17. ♔b1 ♕b6= Cejtlin−Fedorov, SSSR 1969

24 11. ♗d5? ♘a5 12. ♕e2 e6 13. ♗b3 d5 14. ed5 ♘b3 15. ab3 ♘d5 16. ♘d5 ♕d5⩱ Novopašin−Koc, SSSR (ch) 1962

25 **12. ♕e2** a6!=; **12. h5**!? ♘bc4 13. ♕e2 ♘e3 14. ♕e3 ♘b3 15. ab3 ♗d7 16. 0-0-0 [16. hg6 fg6=] e6 [16... ♕a5 17. ♔b1 ♖fc8 18. ♘d5± Gik−Barhatov, SSSR 1969 — 7/405] 17. ♔b1 ♕b6 18. ♕d3 ♖ad8= Boleslavski

26 12... ♘b3 13. ab3 d5 14. ♘de2! [14. ♘db5 ♗e6 15. 0-0-0 de4?! 16. ♕e4 ♘d7 17. h5 ♕a5 18. hg6 hg6 19. ♔b1±; 15... ♕c8! 16. ed5 ♖d8∓↑ Schmidt−Gufeljd, Marianske Lazni 1962] ♗e6 15. 0-0-0! de4 16. ♕e4 ♕c7 [16... ♕c8 17. ♘d4 ♗d7 18. h5 e5 19. hg6 ed4 20. ♕h4 h6 21. ♗h6 ♕d8 22. ♗g5+−] 17. ♘d4 ♗c8 18. ♘db5 ♕e5 19. ♔b1 ♗f5 20. ♕e5±

27 15. 0-0-0 ♘bc4 — 10. 0-0-0

28 10... ♘de5 11. ♗b3 ♘a5 12. ♕e2 ♗d7 13. f4±

29 11... a5 12. a4 ♘e5 13. ♕e2 ♗d7 14. f4 ♘g4 15. ♗g1 ♗h6 16. g3± Vasjukov−Averbah, SSSR 1956

30 **12. ♗h6** ♘ac4 13. ♕g5 e5 14. ♘de2 ♗f6 0 : 1 Fuchs−Honfi, corr. 1962; **12. ♕e2** a6△ e5∓; **12. h4** ♘bc4 13. ♕e2 ♘e3 14. ♕e3 ♘b3 15. ab3 ♗d7 16. h5 e6 [16. .. a5 17. hg6 hg6 18. ♕g5 a4 19. ba4 ♗a4 20. ♘d5± Fajbi-

sovič–Koginov, SSSR 1967] 17. ♘de2 ♗c6∓⊡ Panov–Šackes, SSSR 1961; 17. ♔b1=

31 12... ♘b3 13. cb3 [13. ab3 a5 14. ♘a4 ♘a4 15. ba4 ♗d7∓ Ivkov–Larsen, Beverwijk 1964] d5 14. ed5 ♘d5 15. ♘c2 e6 16. ♘d5 ed5 17. ♕d5 ♕f6 18. ♗d4± Matanović–Padevski, Moskva 1963

32 14. ♔b1!?△ 14... ♘bc4 15. ♗c1±

33 15... fg6 16. ♔b1! ♘b3 17. ab3 ♘e3 18. ♕e3 ♕e8 19. f4± Gligorić–Haag, La Habana 1962

34 **16. ♗h6** e5! [16... e6 17. f4 e5 18. ♘f5 ♗f5 19. ef5 ♘b2 20. ♔b2 e4 21. ♗g7+– Fischer–Purevzhar, Varna (ol) 1962] 17. ♗g7 ♔g7 18. ♘db5 [18. ♘de2 ♕g5 19. ♔b1 b5∓] ♗b5 19. ♘b5 a6!∞ Savon–Popov, corr. 1963; **16. ♗g5**±

35 11. ♗e6 fe6 12. 0-0-0 [12. e5 de5! 13. ♗e5 ♕d2 14. ♔d2 ♖fd8 15. ♔e2 ♖ac8=] ♕a5 13. h4 b5 [13... e5 14. ♗e3 ♘h5 15. ♗h6 ♖ac8=] 14. ♔b1 b4 15. ♘e2 ♕b5=

36 11... ♕c7 12. 0-0-0 [12. 0–0 ♕a5 13. ♕f2!?±] ♗b3 13. cb3 [13. ab3 ♕a5 14. ♔b1 ♖fc8△ ♖c6=] b5 14. ♔b1±

37 12. 0–0 ♖fc8 [12... ♖fd8 13. ♕f2! b6 14. ♖fe1 ♖ac8 15. ♖ad1 ♗b3 16. ab3 ♕h5 17. ♖a1 ♖d7 18. ♖a4± Pilnik–Milić, Beverwijk 1963] 13. ♖ad1 b5 14. ♗f6 ♗f6 15. ♘d5 ♕d2 16. ♘f6 ♔g7 17. ♘h5 gh5 18. ♖d2 ♗b3 19. ab3 b4= Pilnik–Parma, Mar del Plata 1962

38 12... a6 13. h4! [13. ♔b1 ♖fc8 14. ♖he1 ♗b3 15. cb3 b5 16. ♗f6 ♗f6 17. ♘d5 ♕d2 18. ♘f6 ♔g7 19. ♘h5 gh5 20. ♖d2 ♔f6=] b5 14. ♔b1 ♖fc8 15. ♖he1 ♗b3 16. cb3 b4 17. ♘d5 ♘d5 18. ♗g7 ♘c3 19. bc3 bc3 20. ♗c3 ♖c3 21. ♖e3 ♖ac8 [21... ♖c5 22. ♕a5 ♖a5 23. ♖d5±] 22. ♖c3 ♕c3 23. ♕c3 ♖c3 24. ♖c1 ♖e3 25. ♖c7 a5 26. ♔b2±⊥ Talj–Portisch, Oberhausen 1961

39 **14. ♗f6** ♗f6 15. ♘d5 ♗d5=; **14. ♘e2** ♗b3 15. cb3 e5!=

40 14... ♘d5 15. ♗g7 ♔g7 16. ed5 ♗d7 17. ♖de1 ♖fe8 18. ♖e4 ♖ab8 19. a3±

41 15. ♗d5 ♘d5 16. ♗g7 ♘c3! 17. ♗c3 bc3 18. ♕c3 ♕c3 19. bc3 ♖fc8=

42 20. ♗b5 ♖a5 21. ♗f6 ♗f6 22. ♗c6 a3 22. b3 ♔f8 23. f4 [23. c4 (Talj–Larsen, Zürich 1959) e5!=] e5=

43 **20... ♖c7** 21. g4 ♖b8 22. ♗a6± Hasin–Kovalski, SSSR 1964; **20... ♔f8** 21. g4 [21. ♖d3 ♖cb8 22. c3 ab3 23. ♗b3 bc3 24. ♗c3 h5 1/2 : 1/2 Matanović–Larsen, Sousse (izt) 1967 — 4/519; 21. ♗b5 ab3 22. cb3 (Estrin–Blehcin, SSSR 1959) h5!=; 21. ♖de1!? ♖c7 22. g4±] ♘e8 22. ♗b5 ab3 23. cb3 ♗d4 24. ♖d4 ♘c7 25. ♗c6± Talj–Hasin, SSSR (ch) 1961

44 **14. g4** ♗b3 15. cb3 b4 16. ♘e2 e5 17. ♗f2 ♕b5 18. ♕d3 ♕d3 19. ♖d3 ♗f8= Gufeljd–Novopašin, SSSR 1960; **14. h4** b4 15. ♘e2 ♗b3 [15... ♕b5 16. h5 ♗c4 17. ♗c4 ♕c4 18. hg6 fg6 19. b3 ♕b5 20. ♗b2 a5 21. ♘f4±] 16. cb3 ♖c6 17. a3 e5 18. ♗e3 ♖b8 19. ♖c1±; 16... ♖d8△ e5, d5= Evans

45 **14... ♗c4** 15. ♗f6 ♗f6 16. ♘d5 ♕d2 17. ♘f6 ♔g7 18. ♘h5 ♔h6 19. ♖d2 ♔h5 20. e5±; **14... b4** 15. ♘d5 ♗d5 16. ed5 ♖c7 17. a4 ♗f8 18. h4 ♖ac8 19. ♗f6 ef6 20. ♖e4 ♖b7 21. g4± Bagirov–Gufeljd, SSSR 1960

46 **16. ♘d5** ♘d5 17. ♗g7 ♘e3 18. ♖e3 ♔g7=; **16. ♘e2** e5 17. ♗e3 d5 18. ed5 ♖d8=; **16. ♘a4** ♘d7=

47 17... ♖c3? 18. ♖e2! [18. bc3 ♗c3∓ Matanović–Ivkov, Bled 1961] ♖c5 19. b4+–

48 18... ♕c3 19. ♕c3 ♖c3 20. ♖c1±

49 19... ♖c5 20. ♕a5 ♖a5 21. ♖c3±

50 **20... ♖c3** 21. ♔b2 ♖c5 22. ♕a5 ♖a5 23. ♖c1±; **20... ♕c3** 21. ♕c3 ♖c3 22. ♖c1 ♖c1 23. ♔c1 ♔f8 24. ♔c2 ♔e8 25. ♔c3 ♔d7 26. ♔c4 ♔c6 27. b4 e6 28. g4±

51 13... ♘d7 14. ♗g7 ♔g7 15. ♔b1 ♘f6 16. a3±

52 14. g4 e5 15. ♗e3 d5 16. ed5 ♘d5 17. ♘d5 ♕a2 18. ♘e7 ♔f8 19. ♕b4∞

53 15. h4!? ♖ad8 16. ♕f2 b5 17. h5 e5 18. ♗e3 d5 19. h6 ♗h8 20. ♗g5±

54 **16. g5**? ♘h5 17. ♗g7 ♔g7 18. f4 e6!∓↑ Boleslavski–Ilivicki, SSSR 1945; **16. ♕f2** b5 17. g5 ♘h5 18. ♗g7 ♘g7 19. ♘d5 ♘h5 20. f4= Sajgin–Čukajev, SSSR 1955; **16. h4**!?±

55 **16... ♕a6** 17. ♕f2±; **16... e5** 17. ♗e3 d5 18. g5±

56 19. g5 d4=

57 21. fe4 ♘e8 22. ♘d5± Vesely–Kunz, corr. 1956/57

58 13... ♗c4 14. h4! [14. ♖he1 ♖c6 15. ♘d5 ♕d2 16. ♖d2 ♘d5= Gufeljd–Averbah, SSSR (ch) 1961] b5 15. h5 e5 16. ♗e3 b4 17. ♘e2 ♗b3 18. cb3 ♖c6 19. hg6 fg6 20. ♗g5± Nikitin–Ignatjev, SSSR 1963

59 **14. ♖he1** ♗b3 15. cb3 e6=; **14. ♘d5** ♕d2 15. ♖d2 ♗d5 16. ed5 ♖c7 17. ♖e2± Poutrus–Kapengut, Sinaia 1965

60 14... b5 15. ♗f6! [15. h5 b4? 16. ♘d5 ♘d5 17. ed5 ♗d5 18. hg6+–; 15... ♗b3 16. cb3 b4 17. ♘d5 ♘d5 18. ♗g7 ♖a6 19. ♕d5 ♕a2∓ Gusev–Alterman, SSSR 1967; 15. a3 ♖ac8 16. g4 ♖a6 17. g5 ♘h5 18. ♗g7 ♘g7 19. ♕e1 ♖ac6= Gipslis–Averbah, SSSR (ch) 1963] ♗f6 16. ♘d5 ♕d2 17. ♖d2!±

61 **16. h5** b4 17. ♗f6 bc3 [17... ♗f6 18. ♘d5±] 18. ♗c3 ♗c3 19. bc3 ♕c3 20. hg6 hg6 21. ♕c3 ♖c3 22. ♖c1±; **16. ♗f6** ♗f6 17. ♘d5 ♕d2 18. ♖d2 ♔g7 19. h5±

62 21. h5 ♕b6 22. hg6 hg6 23. ♕g5± Gipslis–Nej, SSSR 1961

63 10. 0–0 ♘d4 [10... a6!?] 11. ♗d4 ♖c8 [11... ♗e6!?] 12. ♗b3 a6 13. a4 ♕a5 14. ♗e3 ♗e6=

64 10... ♕b8 11. 0–0 ♘d4 [11... ♘a5 12. ♘d5±; 11... ♕d8 12. ♖ad1 ♖c8 13. ♘d5 ♘d5 14. ed5 ♘d4 15. ♗d4 ♗d4 16. ♕d4 ±; 11... a5 12. a4±] 12. ♗d4 b5 13. ♖ad1 [13. ♘d5!? Kopilov] b4 15. ♘d5±

65 **12. 0-0-0** a5 13. a3 b4 14. ♘d5 ♘d5∓↑ Damjanović–Musil, Ljubljana 1969; **12. ♘d5** ♘d5 13. ♗g7 ♔g7 14. ♗d5 ♖c8 15. ♕d4 [15. h4 h6=] ♔g8 16. c3 a5 17. a3 ♗e6 18. ♗e6 fe6 19. 0–0 ♖c4= Žuravljev–Lazarev, SSSR 1963; **12. 0–0** a5 [12... b4 13. ♘d5 ♘d5 14. ♗d5 ♗d4 15. ♕d4 ♖c8= Kaplan–Levy, Siegen (ol) 1970] 13. a4 [13. a3 ♖b8 14. ♘e2 ♕c7 15. ♗c3 b4 16. ab4 ab4 17. ♗d4 ♖b7= Smislov–Rabinovič, SSSR 1939] b4 14. ♘b5 ♗c6 15. c3 bc3 16. ♕c3 ♕d7= Ornstein–Forintos, Skopje (ol) 1972 — 14/446; **12. a4** b4 [12... ba4 13. ♘a4 ♗e6=] 13. ♘d5 ♘d5 14. ed5 [14. ♗d5 ♗d4 15. ♕d4 ♖c8 16. ♗b3 ♕a5 17. 0–0 ♕c5=] ♗d4 15. ♕d4 a5 16. 0–0 ♕c7= Romanovski–Nikolajevski, SSSR 1963

66 13. h5 e5 14. ♗e3 a4 15. ♗d5 b4 16. ♘e2 ♘d5 17. ed5 [17. ♕d5 ♗e6 18. ♕d2 b3 19. ♗h6 ♗h6 20. ♕h6 ♕c7∓ Camara–Levy, Lugano (ol) 1968] ♖b8 18. ♗h6 ♗h6 19. ♕h6 ♕e7 20. hg6 fg6 21. ♘g3 ♗f5∓ Kuprejčik–Sarbaj, SSSR 1972 — 13/458

67 13... b4 14. ♘d5 e6 15. ♘f6 ♗f6 16. ♗f6 ♕f6 17. 0-0-0±

68 14. ♗a4 ♖b8 15. ♗b3 e5 16. ♗e3 ♗e6 17. ♗e6 fe6 18. 0-0-0 d5= Nej–A. Geler, SSSR 1963

69 **14... ♗e6**?! 15. ♘b6 [15. ♗e6 fe6 16. 0–0± Zuckerman–D. Byrne, USA 1967] ♖b8 16. ♘d5 ♗d5 17. ed5 ♖b5 18. ♖a4 ♕c7 19. h5 [19. ♗c4 ♖b4 20. ♖b4 ab4 21. ♕b4 ♖b8 22. ♕a4 ♘d7 23. ♗g7 ♘b6=] ♘h5 [19... ♖a8 20. hg6 hg6 21. g4 ♖b4 22. ♕b4± Hort–Forintos, Athens 1969 — 9/384] 20. ♗g7 ♔g7 21. g4±; **14... ♖c8** 15. h5 e5 16. ♗e3△ hg6±

70 **15. ♗b6** ♕b8 16. ♗a5 ♖a6 17. ♗c4 ♗h6! 18. ♕h6 [18. ♕c3 ♖c8 19. b4 ♗e6–+ Techlin–Gheorghescu, Krakow 1964] ♖a5∓; **15. ♗e3** ♗e6 16. ♗b6 [16. ♘b6 ♖b8 17. ♘d5 ♗d5 18. ed5 e4∓ Nagy–Forintos, Hungary 1964; 17. ♘c4 d5 18. ♘a5 d4 19. ♗g5 ♗b3 20. ♘b3 ♕b6=∞ Beljavski–Miles, Teesside 1973 — 16/410; 17. ♕a5 ♗b3 18. cb3 d5 19. ♘d5 ♘d5 20. ed5 ♕d7 21. 0–0 ♖b3 22. ♗c5 ♖c8 23. ♗a3 e4∓ Henao–Miles, Manila 1974 — 18/430; 20. ♕d5 ♕d5 21. ed5 ♖b3= Liberzon–Adorjan, Moskva–Budapest 1971 — 12/440] ♕e8 17. 0–0 [Klovan–Listengarten, SSSR 1973 — 16/411] ♗b3! 18. cb3 ♕e6 19. ♖fd1 ♕b3 20. ♕d3=; 16. 0-0-0 ♗b3 17. cb3 ♕c8 18. ♔b1 ♕e6 19. ♕d3 ♖ab8= Kostro–Forintos, Bath 1973 — 16/409

71 Boleslavski

72 **10... ♕b8**?! 11. h5 d5 [11... ♘h5 12. ♗b3±] 12. ed5 ♕g3 13. ♔f1±; **10... ♕c7** 11. ♗b3 ♘e5 12. h5 ♘c4 13. ♗c4 ♕c4 14. hg6 fg6∞ Damjanović–Rajković, Jugoslavija 1974 — 18/426; **10... h5** 11. 0-0-0 ♖c8 12. ♗b3 — 10... ♖c8

73 12. 0-0-0 — B 79

74 13. 0-0-0 ♘e5 — B 79

75 **13... ♘d4**? 14. ♗d4 ♗d4 15. ♕d4 ♘f4 16. ♗f7! ♔f7 17. ♖h7 ♔e6 18. ♕g7 ♖e8 19. ♕f7 ♔e5 20. 0-0-0+ —→ Šagalovič–Gufeljd, SSSR 1967 — 4/520; **13... ♘f6** 14. 0-0-0 ♘e5 — B 79

76 14. ♘c6 ♖c6 15. ♗f4 ♖c3 16. 0-0-0 ♖ac8 17. ♔b1! [17. bc3? ♗c3 18. ♗f7 ♔h8 19. ♖h7 ♔h7 20. ♕h2 ♔g7 21. ♖d5 ♕a3 22. ♔d1 ♔f7–+] ♖3c5 18. ♕h2∞

77 14... ♘d4 15. ♗d4 ♗d4 16. ♕f4 ♗f6 17. ♘d5±

78 15. ♘f5!? gf5 16. gf5 ♘c5 17. ♖dg1=∞

79 Liliental; 17. ♖d4 ♘g5 18. ♕h2 ♘f3 19. ♕f2 ♗g4 20. e5 ♖c3! 21. ♖g4 ♖b3 22. cb3 ♘e5∓ Jansa–Trapl, ČSSR (ch) 1968 — 6/525

80 17... ♗h6 18. ♕h6 ♔e8 19. ♕h8 ♘f8 20. ♖d4±

81 19. ♗g7 ♗c6 20. ab3±

82 11... h5 (Simagin) 12. 0-0-0 ♘e5 **13. ♗g5** — B 78; **13. ♗h6** ♗h6 [13... ♘c4 14. ♗c4 ♖c4 15. ♗g7 ♔g7 16. g4 a6 17. gh5 ♘h5 18. ♘f5 ♗f5 19. ef5 ♕a5 20. ♕d3± Lazarević–Bruce, Oberhausen (ol) 1966; 13... ♔h7 14. ♗g7 ♔g7 15. g4 hg4 16. h5 ♘h5 17. f4! ♘c4 18. ♗c4 ♖c4 19. f5 e5 20. ♘de2± Bastrikov–Sergijevski, SSSR 1965] 14. ♕h6 ♖c3 15. bc3 ♕a5 16. ♔b2 [16. f4 ♘eg4 17. ♕g5 ♕c3=∞] ♖c8 17. ♕e3 ♕b6 18. ♔a1? ♕c5 19. g4 a5 20. gh5 ♘h5∓ Pritchett–Soltis, Haifa 1970 — 10/498; 18. ♕e2!±; **13. ♔b1** ♘c4 14. ♕d3 ♘e3 15. ♕e3 ♕b6 16. ♖d3±; 14. ♗c4 — B 78

83 12. ♗h6? ♗h6 13. ♕h6 ♖c3! 14. bc3 ♕a5 15. ♕d2 ♖c8 16. 0–0 [16. a4?! b5! 17. c4 b4 18. 0–0 ♘c4 19. ♕f2 ♘e5∓ Bogdanović–Parma, Jugoslavija (ch) 1963] ♖c3 17. ♖ae1 ♕c5 18. ♖e3 ♖e3 19. ♕e3 b5∓ Vasjukov–Parma, SSSR–Jugoslavija 1962; 19... a5∓ Mesing–Velimirović, Jugoslavija 1973 — 15/410

84 12... ♘c4 13. ♗c4 ♖c4 14. 0-0-0 ♕c7 15. hg6 fg6 16. ♗h6 ♘e4 17. ♕e3 ♘c3 18. ♗g7 ♖f7 19. ♖h7 ♘e2 20. ♘e2 ♖c2 21. ♔b1 ♖e2 22. ♖h8 ♔g7 23. ♕h6 ♔f6 24. ♕h4 1/2 : 1/2 Belunović–Starodub, corr. 1972 — 13/457; 15. ♘de2!±

85 **13. ♗h6** ♗h6 14. ♕h6 ♖c3 15. bc3 ♕a5 16. 0-0-0 ♖c8∞ Dueball–Partos, Nice (ol) 1974 — 17/464; **13. 0-0-0** ♘c4 — B 78

86 13... ♘f6 14. ♘d5 ♘d5 15. ed5 ♘f3 16. ♘f3 ♗g4 17. ♘d4 h5 [Ermenkov–Arna-

udov, Bulgaria 1973 — 15/409; 18. c3!△ ♘e2, ♗d4∞; 14. ♗h6 ♗h6 15. ♕h6 ♖c3 16. bc3 ♕a5 17. ♕d2 ♖c8∓ Zederman–Kagan, Israel 1974 — 18/427; 15. ♖h6∞

[87] **14. 0-0-0** ♖d4∓; **14. gh5** ♖d4 15. ♕g2 [15. ♕f2 ♖d3∓] ♕b6! 16. hg6 [16. 0–0 ♘c4 (16... ♗h6? 17. ♗f2±) 17. ♗f2 (17. ♗c4 ♕b2) ♘d2∓; 16. ♕f2 ♖c8 17. 0–0 ♘c4 18. ♗c4 ♖cc4 19. ♘d5 ♕d8 20. b3 ♖c3∓ Levy] ♖e4 17. gf7 ♔h8 18. 0-0-0 ♕e3 19. ♔b1 ♖c4 20. ♖dg1 ♖f7 21. ♗c4 ♘c4 22. ♕g6 ♘a3 23. ba3 ♕b6 1/2 : 1/2 Grefe–Tarjan, USA (ch) 1973 — 17/454

B 78

1. e4 c5 2. ♘f3 d6 3. d4 cd4 4. ♘d4 ♘f6 5. ♘c3 g6 6. ♗e3 ♗g7 7. f3 0–0 8. ♕d2 ♘c6 9. ♗c4 ♗d7 10. 0-0-0

	10	11	12	13	14	15	16	17	18	
1	...	♗b3[2]	♘db5	♘a4	♕e2	ab3	ed5	f4	♔b1	∞
	♕b8[1]	a5[3]	a4[4]	♘a5	♘b3	d5	♕e5	♕f5	♖fc8[5]	
2	...	h4	♘d5[7]	♗d5	♗d4	♕d4	♖d2[9]			±
	...	♖c8[6]	♘d5	♘d4[8]	♗d4	♕c7				

1. e4 c5 2. ♘f3 d6 3. d4 cd4 4. ♘d4 ♘f6 5. ♘c3 g6 6. ♗e3 ♗g7 7. f3 0—0 8. ♕d2 ♘c6 9. ♗c4 ♗d7 10. 0-0-0 ♖c8 11. ♗b3 ♘e5[10]

	12	13	14	15	16	17	18	19	20	
3	♗g5[11]	♕e2	♔b2	♗f6[12]	ab3	c3	f4	♖he1	♕e3	=∞
	♘c4	♘b2	♖c3	♖b3	♗f6	a5	♕c7	♖c8	e5[13]	
4	♔b1	♗c4	♘b3[14]	♘d5[16]	♕d5	♕a5	♘a5	♘b3	a3	=∞
	♘c4	♖c4	a5[15]	♘d5[17]	♗e6	♕a5	♖a4	♖fa8	b5	
5	h4	a4[19]	♗c4[20]	b3	♘db5[21]	♗d4	♗e3	♘d5	ab5	±
	a5[18]	♘c4	♖c4	♖c8	h5	e5	d5	♗b5	♘d5[22]	
6	...	♔b1[23]	♗c4	♘b3[24]	♗d4	g4[26]	gh5	♖dg1	♗g7	±
	h5	♘c4	♖c4	♕c7[25]	♗e6	♖c8[27]	♘h5	♔h7	♔g7[28]	
7	...	♗c4[29]	h5[30]	g4	♘de2[32]	♗h6	♕h6	♖d3[35]	g5	±
	♘c4	♖c4	♘h5[31]	♘f6	♕a5[33]	♗h6[34]	♖fc8	♕d8[36]	♘h5[37]	

1. e4 c5 2. ♘f3 d6 3. d4 cd4 4. ♘d4 ♘f6 5. ♘c3 g6 6. ♗e3 ♗g7 7. f3 0—0 8. ♕d2 ♘c6 9. ♗c4 ♗d7 10. 0-0-0 ♕a5 11. ♗b3[38] ♖fc8

	12	13	14	15	16	17	18	19	20	
8	g4	♔b1[39]	♗c4	♘b3[40]	h4[42]	e5[43]	h5	hg6	♗d4	±
	♘e5	♘c4	♖c4	♕d8[41]	♖ac8	♘e8	♗e5	fg6	♗d4[44]	
9	...	...	g5[45]	♘ce2	h4[47]	♗c4	h5	hg6	♘f4[48]	∞
	...	b5!	b4[46]	♘e8	♘c4	♖c4	♖ac8	hg6	♘c7[49]	
10	...	h4	♗c4[51]	♘b3[52]	h5[54]	bc3[56]	hg6			∞
	...	♘c4[50]	♖c4	♕a6[53]	♖c3[55]	♕a2!?[57]	hg6			
11	♔b1	♕e2[59]	♘cb5[61]	c4[62]	♘a3[64]	♕d2	♖c1	♗a4	♗e8	=∞
	♘e5[58]	b5[60]	♖ab8	a6[63]	♗e8!	♕c7	♘fd7	♘c5	♖e8[65]	
12	...	♗g5!	♗c4	♘b3[67]	♖he1[69]	bc3	♗e3	♗d4		±
	...	♘c4[66]	♖c4	♕e5[68]	♖c3[70]	♗e6	♖c8	♕b5[71]		

1 10... ♕c7 11. ♗b3 [11. ♘db5?! ♕b8△ a6, b5∓] ♖fc8 [11... ♘a5 12. ♔b1!±] 12. h4 ♘e5 13. h5 ♘c4 14. ♕d3 [14. ♗c4!?] ♘e3 15. ♕e3 ♕c5 16. hg6 hg6 17. g4 [Dvojris–Ivonenko, SSSR 1974 — 18/429] a5! 18. a4 b5∞ Baranov; 12. ♔b1±

2 11. ♘d5 ♘d5 12. ♗d5 [12. ed5 ♘e5 13. ♗b3 ♖c8 14. h4 a5 15. a3 a4 16. ♗a2 ♘c4 17. ♗c4 ♖c4△ b5∓] a5 13. h4 ♘b4 14. h5 e6 15. ♗b3 a4 16. ♕b4 ab3 17. ♕b3 e5 18. ♘e2 ♗e6∓ Levy; **11. g4** a5 [11... b5 12. ♗b3! (12. ♘cb5 ♘e5 13. ♗e2 ♘f3!∓; 12. ♘db5 ♘e5 13. ♗e2 ♗b5 14. ♘b5 ♘f3! 15. ♗f3 ♕b5 16. e5 ♖ab8∓; 12. ♗b5 ♘d4 13. ♗d7 ♘f3∓; 12. ♗d5 ♖c8 13. ♗c6 ♗c6 14. h4 b4 15. ♘ce2 ♘e4!∓ Mac–Gufeljd, SSSR 1962) a5 13. ♘d5 a4 (13... ♘d5 14. ♗d5 ♘e5 15. ♗a8 ♘c4 16. ♕e2 ♕a8 17. ♔b1± Suetin–Keene, Hastings 1967/68 — 5/431) 14. ♘f6 ♗f6 15. ♗d5± Suetin] 12. ♘d5 [12. h4 b5!∓; 12. g5 ♘h5 13. ♘d5 ♕d8 14. ♘c6 bc6 14. ♗b6 ♖b8! 16. ♕a5 ♗b2 17. ♔d2 ♖b6 18. ♘b6 ♗d4 19. ♖b1 e5∓ Levy, Keene; 12. a4 ♖c8 13. ♕e2 ♘e5 14. ♗b3 ♖c3! 15. bc3 ♕c7 16. ♗d2 ♖c8 17. ♖hf1 ♕c5=∞ Kurajica–Lee, Vrnjačka Banja 1963] ♘d5 13. ♗d5 ♘b4 14. ♔b1 ♗c6=

3 11... ♖c8 12. h4 [12. g4 a5∞] b5?! 13. h5 ♘a5 14. hg6 ♘b3 15. ♘b3 hg6 16. ♗h6 ♗h8 17. ♗f8!+– Juferov–Gvozdov, SSSR 1966; 12... a5! — 11. h4

4 12... ♖c8 13. ♔b1 ♘e5 14. ♕e2 a4 15. ♘a4 ♖a4 16. ♗a4 ♘c4 17. ♗d4! ♕a8 18. ♘a7 ♗a4 19. ♘c8 ♕c8 20. b3 ♘a3 21. ♔b2 ♘b5 22. ba4 ♘d4 23. ♖d4 ♘d5 24. ♕d2 ♕c4 25. c3± Estrin–I. Zajcev, SSSR 1964

5 19. ♘a7 ♖c7∞ Savon–Štejn, SSSR (ch) 1962

6 **11... a5** 12. ♗h6! [Spaski–Levy, Nice (ol) 1974 — 17/457] ♘d4 13. ♗g7 ♔g7 14. ♕d4 b5 15. ♗e2±; **11... b5** 13. ♘db5 [12. ♗b5 ♘d4 13. ♗d7 ♘f3∓] ♘e5 13. ♕e2?! ♘h5!∓ Zamarajko–Trojnov, corr. 1968/69; 13. ♗e2± Gufeljd

7 12. ♗b3 a5! 13. a4 [13. a3 a4? 14. ♗a2 ♘e5 15. h5 ♘c4 16. ♗c4 ♖c4 17. hg6± Hemmasi–Levy, Siegen (ol) 1970 — 10/503; 13... b5! 14. h5 b4 15. ab4 ab4 16. ♘b1 ♘d4 17. ♗d4 ♗a4!∓] ♘d4 14. ♗d4 b5 15. ♕d3 [15. ♔b1? ba4 16. ♘a4 ♗a4 17. ♗a4 ♖c4 18. ♗b3 ♖d4 19. ♕d4 a4–+ Bouaziz–Levy, Siegen (ol) 1970; 15. ♗f6 ♗f6 16. ♘d5 ba4 17. ♘f6 ef6 18. ♗d5 a3 19. ba3 ♗a4 20. ♗a8 ♕b3–+; 15. ♘d5 e5 16. ♗e3 ♘d5 17. ♗d5 ba4!∓] ba4 16. ♘a4 ♗b5 17. ♕e3 ♗a4 18. ♗a4 ♕b4 19. ♕b3 ♘e4!∓ Petruša–Valejev, SSSR 1963

8 13... e6!? Levy

9 ± Simagin

10 11... ♘d4 12. ♗d4 a5 13. a4 ♕e8 14. ♕d3 ♖b8 15. **e5**!± Kinnmark–Westerinen, Halle 1963

11 **12. ♗h6**?! ♘c4 [12... ♗h6 13. ♕h6 ♖c3 14. bc3 ♕a5 15. ♔b2 ♖c8 16. ♕d2! (16. ♕e3 ♕b6 17. ♔a1 a5∓ Conrady–Velimirović, Haag 1966 — 2/423) ♕b6 17. ♔a1 a5 18. ♗d5 ♘d5 19. ed5 ♘c4∞ Toth–Angantysson, Siegen (ol) 1970 — 10/502; 14... a5! 15. a3 (15. a4? ♕c7 16. ♕e3 ♕c5!∓ Geler–Korčnoj (m) 1971 — 11/360) a4 16. ♗a2 ♕a5 17. ♕d2 ♖c8 18. ♔b2 ♕b6 19. ♔a1 ♕a5= Gufeljd] 13. ♗c4 ♗h6 14. ♕h6 [14. ♗f7?? ♔g7 0 : 1 Zuidema–Lee, Zürich 1964] ♖c4 15. h4 ♖c3! 16. bc3 ♕a5 17. ♔d2 ♖c8∓ Kagan–Lee, Örebro 1966 — 2/421; **12. ♕e2** a6 [12... b5!?] 13. f4 [13. h4 h5? 14. g4 hg4 15. f4!± Moe–Whiteley, Örebro 1966 — 2/419; 13... ♕c7 14. h5 ♘c4=] ♘eg4 14. h3 ♘e3 15. ♕e3 ♘h5= Fridjonsson–Levy, Örebro 1966; **12. g4** a5! 13. h4 a4! — 12. h4

12 15. ♔c3 ♕a5 16. ♔b2 ♕g5=∞

13 21. fe5 ♗e5 22. ♕d3 b5 23. ♖c1 ♕c5=∞ Westerinen–Tarjan, Torremolinos 1974 — 17/458

14 14. h4 — 12. h4

15 14... ♗e6!?

16 15. ♗h6?! ♗h6 16. ♕h6 a4 17. ♘c1 ♖c3! 18. bc3 ♕b6 19. ♔a1 ♖c8 20. ♕d2 ♗e6∓↑

17 15... a4? 16. ♗b6 ab3 17. cb3!+–

18 12... ♕a5 13. ♔b1△ ♘d5±

19 **13. g4** a4! 14. ♘a4 ♘c4 15. ♗c4 ♖c4 16. ♘c3 ♕a8=∞ Nicolau–Nowarra, Romania 1968 — 6/524; **13. h5** a4 [13... ♘h5 14. g4 ♖c3 15. bc3 ♘f6 16. a4? ♕c7=∞ Marjanović–Velimirović, Vrnjačka Banja 1973; 16. ♗h6 a4 17. ♗g7 ♔g7 18. ♗a4 ♗a4 19. ♘f5 +–Drašković–Lazić, corr. 1974] 14. ♘a4 ♗a4 15. ♗a4 ♘c4 16. ♕d3 ♕a5 17. ♗b3 [Klovan–Heuer, SSSR 1963] d5! 18. ed5 [18. hg6 hg6 19. ♗h6? ♗h6 20. ♖h6 de4△ ♕g5–+] ♘d5 19. ♗c4 ♖c4 20. ♕c4 ♘e3 21. ♕b3 ♘d1=∞ Simagin

20 14. ♕e2 ♘e3 15. ♕e3 ♖c5 16. g4 ♕c7 17. h5 ♖fc8 18. hg6 hg6 [Ostojić–Velimirović, Vrnjačka Banja 1973 — 15/412] 19. ♖d3∞ Velimirović

21 16. h5∞

22 21. ♕d5 ♕c7 22. c4 a4 [22... ♖fd8 23. b6!± Larsen] 23. b6 ♕e7 24. ♕d6!± Gipslis–Bilek, Sousse (izt) 1967 — 4/423

23 **13. g4** hg4 [13... ♘c4 14. ♗c4 ♖c4 15. gh5 ♘h5 16. ♘de2 (16. ♖dg1 e6= Bellin–Sosonko, Amsterdam 1973 — 16/407) ♕a5 17. ♗h6 ♗e6 18. ♗g7 ♔g7 19. ♖dg1± Kostro–Rodriguez, Nice (ol) 1974 — 17/463; 15. e5!? de5 16. ♘b3 ♖c6 (Adorjan–Sosonko, Wijk aan Zee 1974 — 17/460) 17. ♗c5!± Sokolov] 14. h5 ♘h5 15. ♗h6 b6 16. ♗g7? ♔g7 17. ♖dg1 ♖h8! 18. fg4 ♘f6 19. g5 ♘h5∓ Calvo–Sosonko, Clare Benedict 1974 — 18/431; 16. ♖dg1∞ Minić; **13. ♗g5** ♘h7 14. ♗h6 ♗h6

15. ♕h6 ♖c3 16. bc3 ♕a5 17. ♘e2± Talj—Mišta, Dubna 1973 — 17/459; **13. ♗h6** — B 77

24 15. ♘de2 b5 16. ♗h6 ♕a5! 17. ♗g5 b4 18. ♘d5 ♘d5 19. ♕d5 ♖c5 20. ♕d3 ♗e6∓ Suetin—Szabo, Leningrad 1967

25 15... b5!? Ivkov

26 17. ♕e3 b6 18. g4 ♖c8 19. gh5 ♘h5 20. ♗g7?! ♔g7 21. ♖hg1 a5 22. f4 a4∞ Musil—Baretić, Jugoslavija (ch) 1968 — 5/427; 20. ♖dg1!±

27 17... hg4 18. h5±→

28 21. ♘d4± Tukmakov—Sosonko, Amsterdam 1974 — 18/428

29 13. ♕d3 (Fischer) ♘e3 14. ♕e3 ♕b6! [14... ♖c5? 15. g4 b5 16. h5 b4 17. hg6 hg6 18. ♘f5!± Westerinen—Tringov, La Habana (ol) 1966] 15. ♕d2 ♕c5 16. h5 b5 17. hg6 hg6 18. a3 a5∞ A. Zajcev—Honfi, SSSR 1963

30 **14. ♔b1** b5 15. h5 b4 16. ♘ce2 e5 17. ♘b3 d5! 18. hg6 fg6∞ Suetin—Kuprejčik, SSSR 1974 — 18/436; **14. g4** ♕a5 15. h5 ♖fc8 16. ♘b3 ♕a6 17. hg6±

31 **14... b5** 15. hg6 [15. ♘db5 ♗b5 16. ♘b5 ♕b8∓] fg6 [15... hg6 16. ♗h6! ♘e4 17. ♕e3±] 16. e5! de5 17. ♘e6± Parma—P. Szilagyi, Reggio Emilia 1966 — 1/294; **14... ♕a5** 15. ♘b3 ♕c7 [15... ♕a6 16. ♗h6 ♖fc8 17. ♗g7 ♔g7 18. hg6 fg6 19. ♔b1 ♗e6 20. g4± Sokolov—Tomović, Beograd 1960] 16. ♗h6 ♗h6 17. ♕h6 ♖c3 18. bc3 ♕c3 19. hg6 fg6 [Đurašević—Averbah, Wien 1957] 20. e5!±; **14... ♕c7** 15. hg6 fg6 16. ♗h6 ♘e4 17. ♕e3 ♘c3 18. ♗g7 ♖f7 19. ♖h7 ♘e2∞; 15. ♘de2!±

32 **16. ♖dg1** ♖e8 [16... e6? 17. ♔b1 ♕a5 18. ♘b3 ♕c7 19. ♗f4± Vasjukov—Parma, SSSR—Jugoslavija 1963; 16... ♗e6 17. ♘f5? ♗f5 18. gf5 ♕a5 19. ♗h6 ♖fc8∓; 17. ♘ce2!± Bergin, Utjacki; 16... ♕a5!? Parma] 17. ♘ce2 [17. g5 ♘h5 18. ♖h5 gh5 19. ♘d5 ♔h8!∓] e5 18. ♘b3 ♗e6 19. ♘g3 d5 20. g5 ♘h5!∓; **16. ♕h2** ♖c3! 17. bc3 ♕a5 18. ♘b3 ♕a3 19. ♔b1 ♗e6 20. ♗d4 ♖c8≅↑« Rantanen—Rodriguez, Nice (ol) 1974; **16. ♗h6** ♘e4 [16... ♗h6? 17. ♕h6 ♖c3 18. g5! ♘h5 19. ♖h5 gh5 20. ♖h1+− Minić—Lee, Krakow 1964] 17. ♕e3 [17. ♘e4 ♖d4 18. ♕h2 ♗e5 19. f4 ♖d1 20. ♖d1 ♗h8! 21. ♗f8 ♕b6!∓ Bergin, Utjacki; 19. ♕h4 ♖e4! 20. fe4 ♕b6 21. c3 ♖c8∓ Bednarski—Szpotanski, Polska 1966] ♖c3 18. bc3 ♘f6 19. ♗g7 ♔g7 20. ♘e2 ♖g8? 21. ♘g3 ♔h8 22. g5± Matanović—Ivkov, Jugoslavija 1974 — 18/432; 20... ♕a5∞ Matanović; 20... ♕b6!?∞ Zuckerman—Velimirović, Vršac 1973 — 16/406; **16. ♘d5** e6 17. ♘f6 ♕f6 18. ♕h2 ♖fc8 19. ♕h7 ♔f8∞ Geler—Ivkov, Amsterdam 1974 — 18/435; 16... ♘d5 17. ed5 ♕c7 18. ♕h2 h5 19. gh5 ♖c8∞ Ivkov; **16. e5**!? ♘g4? 17. fg4 ♗e5 18. ♕g2+− Adorjan—Ostojić, Olot 1974 — 17/462; 16... ♘e8±; **16. ♘b3**!?

33 16... ♖e8 17. e5 [17. ♗h6 ♗h8 18. e5 ♘g4 19. ed6 ♘h6 20. ♕h6 ♗g7 21. ♕h7 ♔f8 22. ♕h2 ♗c6≅ Ostojić—Tarjan, Torremolinos 1974] ♘g4 18. fg4 ♗g4 19. ed6 ♕d6 20. ♕e1± Martin—Tarjan, Torremolinos 1974 — 17/461

34 17... ♗h8!? 18. ♗f8 ♔f8

35 19. ♖d5 ♕d8 20. g5 ♘h5 21. ♘f4 ♕f8 22. ♕f8 ♔f8 23. ♘h5 gh5 24. ♖h5 ♔g7 25. ♖d2±

36 **19... ♖4c5**? 20. g5! ♖g5 21. ♖d5 ♖d5 22. ♘d5+− Karpov—Korčnoj (m) 1974 — 18/433; **19... ♗e6** 20. g5 ♘h5 21. ♘g3 ♕e5 22. ♘h5 gh5 23. ♕h5 ♕g7 24. f4 d5 [24... b5 25. f5 b4 26. ♖dh3! bc3 27. ♕h7 ♕h7 28. ♖h7+−] 25. ♖hd1 b5 [Zambon—Wagman, Italia 1974 — 18/434] 26. ♖1d2! ♕g6 27. ♕h6!±

37 21. ♘f4 ♕f8 22. ♕f8 ♔f8 23. ♘h5 gh5 24. ♖h5 ♔g7 25. ♖d2! ♗e6 26. ♖dh2 ♖h8 27. f4±

38 11. ♔b1!?

39 **13. ♕e2** ♖ab8! 14. g5 ♘h5 15. ♘d5 ♕d8 16. ♖hg1 b5 17. f4 ♘c4 18. f5 ♗e5∓; **13. g5** ♘e8 14. h4 b5 15. h5 ♘c4 16. ♗c4 bc4 17. hg6 hg6∓ Razuvajev—Korjakin, SSSR 1967

40 15. h4 (I. Zajcev) ♖ac8! [15... ♗e6?! 17. ♘b3 ♕a6 17. ♗h6 ♗h8 18. e5!± Damjanović—Haag, Salgotarjan 1967 — 4/529] 16. ♘b3 ♕a6 [16... ♕e5!? Hecht] 17. ♗d4 [17. e5 ♘e8 18. ♘d5 ♖c2! Gufeljd, Lazarev] e5 18. ♗e3 ♗g4 19. fg4 [19. ♖hf1 ♖c3 20. bc3 ♗f3∓ Arbakov—Bihovski, SSSR 1967] ♖c3 20. bc3 ♘e4∓ Jansa—Hindle, Halle 1967

41 15... ♕a6 16. e5 [16. ♗d4 ♖ac8 17. g5 ♘e8 18. h4 e5 19. ♗e3 ♗e6∓ Ceškovski—Dueball, Dresden 1969 — 8/412; 16. h4 ♖ac8 17. h5?! ♗g4! 18. fg4 ♖c3!∓ Curdy—Keene, Örebro 1966 — 2/422; 17. ♗h6 ♗h6 18. ♕h6 ♖c3 19. bc3 ♗g4!∓ I. Zajcev—Barhatov, SSSR 1968] ♘g4 [16... ♘e8 17. ♘d5 ♗e5 18. ♘e7 ♔f8 19. ♘d5 ♖ac8 20. ♗h6 ♘g7 21. c3± Ceškovski—Hartston, Dresden 1969 — 8/414] 17. fg4 ♗g4 18. ed6 ♗c3 19. bc3 ♗d1 20. de7 ♗c2 21. ♕c2 ♖e8 [Tatai—Honfi, Monte Carlo 1967] 22. ♗d2!± Levy

42 **16. ♗d4** ♗e6 17. ♕e3 [Hort—Tatai, Athens 1968 — 6/532] a5!? 18. ♗b6 ♕e8 19. ♘a5 ♖c3≅ Hort; **16. e5**!? ♘e8= Hort

43 **17. ♗d4** e5 18. ♗e3 ♗g4 19. fg4 ♖c3 20. bc3 ♘e4∓ Rodriguez—Garcia, Lugano (ol) 1968; **17. h5** ♗g4! 18. e5 [18. fg4 ♖c3 19. bc3 ♘e4 20. ♕h2 ♘c3 21. ♔c1 ♕c7∓] ♗f3 19. ef6 ♗f6 20. hg6 hg6 21. ♘d4∞

44 21. ♘d4± Minić—Wade, Vinkovci 1968 — 6/528

45 **14. ♘cb5**? ♕d2 15. ♗d2 ♗b5△ ♘f3∓; **14. h4** ♖c4 15. ♗c4 ♘c4 16. ♕d3 ♖c8∓↑

46 14... ♘h5!? Žuravljev

47 16. ♘f4 e6=

48 20. ♖c1 ♕e5! 21. c3 bc3 22. ♖c3 d5!∓ Kozlov–Krasnov, SSSR 1967 — 4/523

49 21. ♕h2 [Rigo–Sapi, Hungary 1967] ♘b5!∞

50 **13... b5** 14. h5 b4 15. ♘ce2 ♘c4 16. ♕d3! ♘e3 17. ♕e3 e5?! 18. hg6 hg6 19. ♘f5! +– Bokor–Sapi, Hungary 1967; 14... ♘c4!? Ljubojević; **13... ♖c4!?** 14. ♗c4 ♘c4 15. ♕d3 b5 16. ♘b3 ♕a6 [Mnacakanjan–Veresov, SSSR 1968 — 6/529] 17. a3!± Judovič

51 14. ♕d3 (Fischer) ♘e3 15. ♕e3 ♕c5 [15... ♖c5!?△ ♖ac8] 16. h5 a5! [16... e5? 17. hg6 hg6 18. ♘f5!± Barczay–Kavalek, Salgotarjan 1967 — 4/528] 17. a4 b5!=

52 15. h5 ♖ac8 16. hg6 fg6 17. ♔b1? ♗g4! 18. fg4 ♖c3! 19. ♘e6 ♕e5 20. ♘g7 ♘e4 21. ♕d4 ♖e3!∓ Litzberger–Whiteley, Harrachov 1967; 17. ♘b3∞

53 **15... ♕c7** 16. e5! ♘e8 17. ♘d5 ♕d8 18. ♗g5!±; **15... ♕d8** 16. h5 ♗e6 17. ♕h2± Ivanović–Đukić, Jugoslavija 1970 — 10/495

54 16. e5 ♘g4! [16... de5 17. g5 ♗f5 18. gf6 ef6 19. ♘c5±] 17. fg4 ♗g4 18. ed6 ♗c3∞

55 16... ♖ac8!? 17. hg6 fg6 18. e5 ♘e8 19. ♕h2 h6 20. ♗h6 ♗e5∞

56 17. ♕c3? ♘g4∓

57 **17... ♗g4** 18. hg6 hg6 19. e5!±; **17... ♗e6** 18. ♔b1 ♖c8 19. ♗d4 ♖c4! 20. hg6 hg6 21. ♕h2 [21. g5 ♘h5 22. ♖h5 gh5 23. ♕h2 ♖c3!∓ Bihovski–Gik, SSSR 1968 — 5/432; 23. ♖h1!? Judovič] g5 [21... ♕a3 22. ♗f6 ♗f6 23. g5 ♗g7 24. ♕h7 ♔f8 25. ♕h8! ♗h8 26. ♖h8 ♔g7 27. ♖dh1+–; 21... ♖a4 22. c4! ♖a2 23. e5!±] 22. f4!±↑ Liliental

58 12... ♖ab8 13. g4 [13. h4 b5 14. h5! ♘h5 15. g4 ♘f6 16. ♘f5!± Kotkov–Krasnov, SSSR 1970 — 9/385; 13... h5 14. g4 hg4 15. f4 ♘d4 16. ♗d4± Suslov–Zelinski, SSSR 1967] b5 14. h4! [14. g5 b4! 15. ♘ce2 ♘h5 16. f4 ♘d4 17. ♗d4 ♗a4 1/2 : 1/2 Gipslis–Bobocov, Moskva 1967] b4 15. ♘d5 ♘d5 16. ed5 ♘d4 17. ♗d4 ♗d4 18. ♕d4 ♕c5 19. ♕d2!± Schmidt–Bobocov, Varna 1967 — 4/531

59 **13. ♗h6?!** ♗h6! [13... ♘c4 14. ♗c4 ♗h6 15. ♕h6 ♖c4 16. ♕d2± Žilin–Alterman, SSSR 1965; 16. ♘b3 ♕e5 17. h4 ♖ac8 18. ♕g5!± Despotović] 14. ♕h6 ♖c3 15. bc3 ♕c3 16. ♕d2! [16. ♘e2?! ♕c5 17. ♘f4 a5∓ Matulović–Despotović, Jugoslavija 1969 — 7/402] ♕c5 17. ♕e2 b5 18. f4 ♘c4∞̅ Sedov–Judovič jr., SSSR 1968; **13. ♘d5** ♕d2 14. ♖d2 [14. ♗d2 ♘d5 15. ♗d5 ♖ab8 16. ♗b3 b5=] ♘d5 15. ♗d5 ♘c4 16. ♗c4 ♖c4 17. ♘b3 a5= Reyes–Berger, Manila 1968; **13. h4** — B 79

60 **13... a6** 14. **g4!** [14. f4 ♗g4 15. ♘f3 ♖c3! 16. fe5 (16. bc3 ♘f3 17. gf3 ♘e4!–+ Liliental; 16. ♗d2!? Marić) ♖b3 17. ab3 (17. ef6 ♖b2 18. ♔b2 ♗f6∓) ♕e5 18. ♗d4 ♕e4∓ Ribli–Adorjan, Hungary 1968 — 6/530] b5 15. g5 ♘h5 16. ♘d5± Kagan–Ujtumen, Singapoore 1970 — 9/386; **13... ♖ab8** 14. f4 ♗g4 15. ♘f3 ♘f3 16. gf3 ♖c3 17. e5! de5 18. fg4± S. Garcia–Letelier, La Habana 1967 — 4/527

61 **14. ♘db5?** ♖ab8 15. ♘d4 ♕b4 16. a3 ♕b7 17. ♗c1 ♖c3 18. bc3 a5 19. a4 ♗a4 20. ♔a1 ♗d7∓→ Šmit–Mnacakanjan, SSSR 1968; **14. h4** ♘c4! [14... a6 15. h5 ♘c4 16. ♘d5!± Najdorf–Pelikan, Mar del Plata 1968 — 6/531] 15. ♕d3 [15. ♗c4 ♖c4∓↑《] ♘e3 16. ♕e3 ♕b6∓

62 15. ♘a3 d5! 16. ed5 ♘d5 17. ♗d5 ♕d5 18. ♘b3 ♕b7= Simagin–Dubinin, corr. 1966

63 15... ♘c4 16. ♗c4 a6 17. ♘a7! ♖c7 18. ♘b3 ♕a4 19. ♖d4!± Jansa–Wostyn, Harrachov 1967

64 16. ♘c3 ♘c4 17. ♗c4 ♕c3!∓

65 Gipslis–Štejn, Moskva 1967 — 3/476

66 **13... ♕d8** 14. ♖he1 ♘c6 15. ♘c6?! ♗c6 16. ♕e2 ♕c8= Kostro–Ostojić, Polanica Zdroj 1970; 15. f4!±; **13... b5** 14. ♘d5! ♕d8 [14... ♕d2 15. ♖d2±] 15. ♗f6 ef6 16. f4 ♘c4 17. ♗c4 bc4 18. f5!± Moles–Green, England 1968; **13... ♖ab8!?**

67 15. ♗f6 ♗f6 16. ♘d5 ♕d2 17. ♘f6 ♔g7!=⊥

68 **15... ♕d8** 16. e5! ♘e8 17. ♘d5±; **15... ♕a6** 16. ♗f6! ♗f6 17. ♘d5 ♔g7 18. ♘f6 ♔f6 19. e5!± Moles, Botterill

69 **16. f4?** ♕c3!!∓; **16. ♗f4** ♕e6 17. ♘d4 ♖d4 18. ♕d4 ♘h5∞̅→ Moles, Botterill

70 **16... ♕h2??** 17. ♗f4 ♕h5 18. ♖h1+–; **16... ♗c6** 17. ♗f4 ♕e6 18. e5 de5 19. ♖e5±

71 ± Talj

B 79

1. e4 c5 2. ♘f3 d6 3. d4 cd4 4. ♘d4 ♘f6 5. ♘c3 g6 6. ♗e3 ♗g7 7. f3 0–0 8. ♕d2 ♘c6 9. ♗c4 ♗d7 10. 0-0-0 ♕a5 11. ♗b3 ♖fc8 12. h4

	12	13	14	15	16	17	18	19	20	
1	... h5	♔b1 ♘e5	♕e2[1] a6[2]	♖dg1 b5	g4 hg4[3]	h5 ♘h5	fg4 ♘f6	♘f5		±

	12	13	14	15	16	17	18	19	20	
2	...	h5	g4[5]	♗h6[6]	bc3[8]	♖h6	♔b2	♕h2[12]	♖h7	=
	♘e5	♘h5[4]	♘f6	♖c3[7]	♗h6[9]	♖c8[10]	♕b6[11]	♕c5	♕c3[13]	
3	...	...	♔b1	♕c3[15]	bc3	♔b2[16]	a3	♗f4	♗g5	=
	...	...	♖c3![14]	♕c3	♖c8	a5	♘f6	♘e8	a4[17]	

1. e4 c5 2. ♘f3 d6 3. d4 cd4 4. ♘d4 ♘f6 5. ♘c3 g6 6. ♗e3 ♗g7 7. f3 0—0 8. ♕d2 ♘c6 9. ♗c4 ♗d7 10. 0-0-0 ♕a5 11. ♗b3 ♖fc8 12. h4 ♘e5 13. h5 ♘h5 14. ♗h6

	14	15	16	17	18	19	20	21	22	
4	...	♕d3	♔b1	bc3[20]	♘f5	f4	♕d4	♘h6	e5	∞
	♘d3[18]	♗h6	♖c3[19]	♖c8	♗g5	♖c3[21]	♗f6	♔f8	♗g7[22]	
5	...	♔b1	♔b2[24]	♕h6	g4[27]	e5[28]	♘e2	ab3	♘c3	±
	...	♘b2[23]	♗h6[25]	♖c3[26]	♘f6	de5	♖b3	♗e6[29]	e4[30]	
6	...	♕h6	bc3	♘e2![32]	g4	g5	♖h5![34]	♖h1	♔b1	±
	♗h6	♖c3	♕c3[31]	♕c5[33]	♘f6	♘h5	gh5	♕e3	♕f3[35]	
7	...	...	...	♘e2[36]	♖d5	♔b1	♘f4	g4		=∞
	...	...	♖c8	♘f6![37]	♕b6[38]	a5	e6	♕e3		

1. e4 c5 2. ♘f3 d6 3. d4 cd4 4. ♘d4 ♘f6 5. ♘c3 g6 6. ♗e3 ♗g7 7. f3 0—0 8. ♕d2 ♘c6 9. ♗c4 ♗d7 10. 0-0-0 ♕a5 11. ♗b3 ♖fc8 12. h4 ♘e5 13. ♔b1

	13	14	15	16	17	18	19	20	21	
8	...	♘cb5[39]	♗d2	♘c3	♘e4	♗g5	♗e7	♖d6	♖d5	±
	b5	♕d2[40]	♘c4	♘e4	♗d4	♗e5	♘b2	♗e8	♗g7[41]	
9	...	♗c4	h5[42]	g4	♘b3	e5[45]	fg4	♕h2[47]	ed6!	±
	♘c4	♖c4	♘h5[43]	♘f6	♕d8[44]	♘g4[46]	♗g4	h5	♗d1[48]	
10	...	...	♘b3	♗h6[49]	h5	hg6	e5![52]	ed6	♗g5	±
	...	...	♕d8	♗h8[50]	♖ac8[51]	fg6	♘e8[53]	e6[54]	♘f6[55]	
11	...	...	...	♗d4[56]	h5[57]	hg6[58]	a4	♖h4![61]	cb3	±
	...	...	♕c7	♗e6	a5	hg6[59]	♖b4[60]	♗b3[62]	e5[63]	
12	...	...	...	♗h6[64]	♕h6	h5	bc3	hg6	♕e3[68]	±
	...	...	♕a6	♗h6[65]	♖ac8	♖c3[66]	♗e6[67]	fg6		

[1] 14. ♗g5!?△ 14... ♘c4 15. ♗c4 ♖c4 16. ♗f6 ♗f6 17. ♘d5 ♕d2 18. ♘f6 ♔g7 19. ♘h5± Boleslavski

[2] 14... b5 15. ♘d5 ♘d5 16. ♗d5! ♖ab8 17. ♖dg1△ g4±

[3] 16... ♘c4 17. gh5 ♘h5 [17... ♘b2 18. hg6 ♕c3 19. gf7 ♔f8 20. ♖g7 ♘c4 21. ♗c4 bc4 (Ristoja–Asplund, Danmark 1968) **22. ♗h6 ♖ab8 23. ♘b3 ♘h5 24. ♖h7 ♘g7** 25. ♖g7 ♕g7 26. ♕g2!+– Liliental] 18. ♘d5!±

[4] **13... gh5** 14. ♔b1! [14. ♗h6?! ♗h6 15. ♕h6 ♖c3 16. bc3 ♕c3 17. ♘e2 ♘d3 18. ♖d3 ♕a1 19. ♔d2 ♕h1∓↑] ♘c4 15. ♗c4 ♖c4 16. ♘b3 ♕c7 17. ♗g5± Gufeljd, Lazarev; **13... ♘c4** 14. ♗c4 ♖c4 15. hg6 fg6 16. ♘b3 [16. ♘b1 ♖ac8 17. ♘b3 ♕a6 18. ♗h6± O'Kelly–Wade, Malaga 1967 — 3/478; 17...

♕d8!?] ♕a6 [16... ♕e5 17. ♗d4 ♕e6 18. ♖he1± Balašov–Agejčenko, SSSR 1967] 17. e5! ♖c3 18. ♕c3 ♖c8 19. ♘c5± Cebalo–Antunac, Jugoslavija 1967 — 4/524; **13... ♖c3** 14. bc3! ♖c8 15. hg6 hg6 16. ♗h6 ♗h8 17. ♗g5 ♗g7 18. g4±

5 14. ♘d5 ♕d2 15. ♖d2 ♔f8 16. g4 ♘f6 [16... ♗g4? 17. fg4 ♘g4 18. ♗g5! ♘hf6 19. ♘f6 ♗f6 20. ♘f3 ♔g7 21. ♗f6 ♘f6 22. e5!+−⊥ Bronštejn–Parma, Moskva 1971 — 12/443] 17. ♘f6 ♗f6 18. ♖h7 ♘c4 19. ♗c4 ♖c4= Hartston

6 15. ♔b1 ♖c3 16. ♕c3 ♕c3 17. bc3 ♖c8 18. ♔b2 a5 19. a3 a4 20. ♗a2 ♗e8 21. ♖h3 ♘fd7 22. ♘e2= Ermakov–Keene, corr. 1970

7 15... ♗h6 16. ♕h6 ♖c3 17. g5 ♘h5 18. bc3 [18. ♖h5? gh5 19. ♖h1 ♖e3!−+] ♖c8 19. ♖h5= Spasov–Keene, Örebro 1966 — 2/425

8 **16. ♕c3** ♕c3 17. bc3 ♗h6 18. ♖h6 ♘h5! 19. gh5 ♔g7∓⊥; **16. ♗g7** ♖c2 17. ♗c2 [17. ♔c2 ♖c8 18. ♔b1 ♕d2 19. ♖d2= Sigurjonsson–Boudy, Harrachov 1967] ♕d2 18. ♖d2 ♔g7 19. g5 ♘h5 20. ♖dh2= Medina–Wade, Malaga 1967

9 16... ♘f3!? 17. ♗f7 ♔f7 18. ♘f3 ♕a3 19. ♔b1 ♘e4 20. ♕f4 ♗f5 [20... ♗f6 21. ♕e4 ♗e6 22. ♖d5+− Keene, Hübner] 21. ♗g7 e5 22. ♘e5 [22. ♗e5 de5 23. ♖h7 ♔g8 24. ♖h8 ♔h8 25. ♕e5 ♔g8∓] ♔g7 23. ♕h6 ♔f6 24. ♘d7 ♔e6! 25. gf5 ♔d7 26. ♕g7 ♔c6∞ Steinhouer

10 17... ♕a3? 18. ♔b1 a5 19. ♖dh1 e6 20. ♖h7 ♘h7 21. ♕h6±→ Scholl–Westerinen, Beverwijk 1967

11 **18... b5**? 19. ♖dh1 ♘c4 20. ♗c4 bc4 21. ♖h7!+− Talj–Wade, Palma de Mallorca 1966 — 2/426; **18... ♘c4** 19. ♗c4 ♖c4 20. ♘b3 ♕e5 21. ♕e3∞ Talj

12 19. ♔c1 ♕c5 20. ♔b2 a5! 21. ♖dh1 a4 22. ♖h7 ♘h7 23. ♕h6 e6 24. g5 ♘g4 25. ♕h7 ♔f8 26. ♘e6! [26. ♘e2? ab3 27. fg4 ♕g5∓ Huguet–Wade, Monte Carlo 1967] ♗e6 27. ♗e6=; 21... e6!∓ Larsen

13 21. ♔b1 ♘h7 22. ♖h1 e6 23. ♕h7 ♔f8 24. ♕h6 ♔e7 25. ♕g5 f6 26. ♖h7 ♘f7 27. ♕g6 ♕e1=

14 **14... ♘c4** 15. ♗c4 ♖c4 16. ♘b3△ 17. ♘d5±; **14... ♘f6**!?△ ♘c4 Keene

15 15. bc3 ♖c8=∞↑«

16 **17. ♗g5** ♗f6! 18. ♗f6 ♘f6 19. ♔b2=; **17. ♘e2** a5 18. a3 a4 19. ♗a2 ♗b5 20. ♖he1 ♘c4= Scholl–Tatai, Beverwijk 1967

17 21. ♗a2 ♘c6! 22. ♖d2 ♘f6 23. ♘c6 ♗c6= Spaski–Štejn, SSSR 1967 — 3/475

18 14... ♖c3!? Gufeljd, Lazarev

19 **16... ♘f4**? 17. ♕d2 ♗g5 18. g3 ♘h5 19. ♕h2 ♖c3 20. bc3 ♕c3 21. g4 ♗f4 22. ♕h4 ♘f6 23. ♘e2!± Gheorghiu–Westerinen, Örebro 1966 — 2/424; **16... e6**!? Kurajica

20 17. ♕c3 ♕c3 18. bc3 ♗g7 19. ♖he1 a5∓ Hartston–Westerinen, La Habana (ol) 1966; 18... ♗f4∓⊥ Levy

21 19... ♘f4 20. ♕g3 ♘e6 21. ♗e6 ♗e6 22. ♕g5 ♕a2 23. ♔c1± Marić

22 **23. ♘f7**? ♖b3!−+ Jansa–Vasjukov, La Habana 1967 — 4/530; **23. g4** ♘g3 24. ♘f7 ♘e2! [24... ♘h1? 25. ♘d6+−] 25. ♕d2 ♖b3 26. cb3 [26. ab3 ♘c3 27. ♔b2 ♘d1−+] ♕d2 27. ♖d2 ♘g3 [Čerepkov–Vasjukov, SSSR 1967 — 4/522] 28. ♖e1 [28. e6!? ♗e6 29. ♘g5] ♔f7 29. ♖g2∞ Judovič

23 **15... ♘f2**? 16. ♕f2 ♗h6 17. g4+−; **15... ♗d4** 16. ♘d5! ♕d2 [16... ♕d8 17. ♖h5! gh5 18. ♕g5 ♔h8 19. ♖d3+−] 17. ♘e7 ♔h8 18. ♖d2±⊥ Dueball–Mišta, Ybbs 1968 — 6/526; **15... ♗h6** 16. ♕h6 ♖c3 [16... ♘b2? 17. ♘d5! ♘d1 18. ♖h5+−] 17. bc3 ♘f2 18. ♖h5 gh5 19. ♖f1 ♕c3 20. ♕g5 ♔h8 21. ♘e2 ♕b4 22. ♕e3± Dueball–Naranja, Bad Pyrmont 1970

24 16. ♘d5? ♕d2 17. ♘e7 ♔f8 18. ♗g7 ♔e7 19. ♖d2 ♘g7 20. ♔b2 [20. ♖h7 ♘c4 21. ♗c4 ♖c4 22. ♖g7 ♖h8−+] h5∓

25 16... ♖c3? 17. ♕c3 ♕c3 18. ♔c3 ♗h6 19. g4+−

26 17... ♕c3? 18. ♔b1 a5 19. ♖d3 [19. ♖h5 gh5 20. ♗f7 ♔f7 21. ♕h7 ♔f8= Hasin; 20. ♕h5 e6 21. e5 de5 22. ♘f5!+− Euwe; 20... d5 21. ♕d5 ♗e8 22. ♕g5 ♔f8 23. ♕e5 ♔g8 24. ♕e7+− Lukjanov] ♕b4 20. a3 ♕b6 21. g4 [21. ♘f5 ♗f5 22. ef5 a4? 23. fg6 ♘f6 24. ♖d6!+−; 22... ♔h8∞ I. Zajcev] a4 22. gh5 ab3 23. ♘b3! d5 24. hg6 ♕g6 25. ♕h2+−

27 18. ♗f7?! ♔f7 19. ♕h7 ♔f6! 20. e5 de5 21. ♖h5 ♖a3∓

28 **19. g5** ♘h5 20. f4 [20. ♗f7 ♔f7 21. ♖h5 ♖h8!−+; 20. ♖h5 ♖b3 21. ab3 gh5 22. f4 ♖c8 23. f5 ♕c3 24. ♔b1 ♕e3!∓ Despotović] ♖ac8 [20... ♗g4 21. f5 ♖b3 22. ab3 ♕e5∓ Terentjev–Štirberg, SSSR 1971 — 11/359] 21. f5 ♖b3 22. ab3 ♕c3 23. ♔b1 ♕e3! 24. ♖he1 [24. ♖h5? gh5 25. f6 ef6 26. ♕f6 ♕e4∓ Segi–Velimirović, Jugoslavija 1970 — 10/496] ♕f4∓↑; **19. ♘e2** ♖c5 20. ♘f4 ♗a4 21. ♘g6 ♕c3 22. ♔b1 ♗b3 23. ♘e7 ♔h8 24. cb3 ♕c2=

29 21... ♗c6 22. g5 ♘h5 23. ♖h5 gh5 24. ♘g3 e4 25. f4!± Grabczewski–Gasiorowski, Polska (ch) 1970 — 9/388

30 **22. . . ♖c8** 23. ♘e4±; **22. . . e4** 23. ♘e4 ♖c8 24. ♔b1± Mecking–Joksić, Vršac 1971 — 13/450

31 16. . . ♘f6!? 17. ♔b1! [17. g4? ♕c3 18. ♘e2 ♕a1 19. ♔d2 ♘f3!–+] b5! [17. . . ♕c3 18. ♘e2 ♕c5 19. ♘f4 e6 20. ♕g5 ♔g7 21. ♘h5 ♘h5 22. ♖h5 ♖h8 22. f4!+–; 19. . . ♗c6 — 16. . . ♕c3] 18. f4 [18. ♘e2 ♘c4!∓; 18. g4 ♕c3 19. ♘e2 ♕f3∓] ♘c4 19. e5 de5= Gufeljd

32 17. ♔b1 ♘c4 [17. . . ♘f6 18. ♘e2! ♕c5 19. ♘f4 ♗c6 20. ♘h3 e6 21. ♘g5± Velimirović–Lee, Haag 1966] 18. ♗c4 ♕c4 19. ♖h5! gh5 20. ♕g5 ♔h8 21. ♕e7± Gaprindašvili–Lee, Hastings 1964/65; 17. . . a5!=

33 **17. . . ♘d3** 18. ♖d3 ♕a1 19. ♔d2 ♕h1 20. g4 ♘g3 21. ♕h1 ♘h1 22. ♔e3!+–; **17. . . ♕a1** 18. ♔d2 ♕b2 19. ♖h5! gh5 20. ♖h1+–→

34 20. ♘g3 ♗g4!∓

35 23. ♖h5 ♘g6! [23. . . e6? 24. g6! ♘g6 25. ♕h7 ♔f8 26. ♖f5!+– Karpov–Gik, SSSR 1968 — 7/404] 24. ♕h7±

36 **17. ♔b1**?! ♘c4 18. ♖d3 ♕a3 19. ♗c4 ♖c4 20. ♘b3 ♗e6∓→ Woodcock–Whiteley, England 1966; **17. ♖h5** gh5 18. ♔b1 [18. ♖h1 ♕c3 19. ♔b1 ♕d4 20. ♖h5 e6!–+; 18. ♘e2 ♘g6 19. ♖h1 ♖c5! 20. ♗d5 e6!–+; 18. g4 ♕c3 19. ♘f5 ♗f5 20. gf5 ♘f3 21. ♔b1 h4∓] ♘c4 19. g4 ♕c3 20. ♗c4 ♕c4 21. gh5 ♔h8! 22. ♕d2 ♗e6 23. ♘e6 fe6∓ Pantazi–Hartston, Örebro 1966 — 2/420; **17. g4** ♘f6 18. g5 ♘h5 19. ♖h5 gh5 20. ♘f5 ♗f5 21. ef5 ♕c3=; **17. ♘f5** ♗f5 18. ef5 ♕c3 19. fg6 hg6 20. ♔b1 ♘c4 21. ♕c1 b5 22. g4= Mazzoni–Lee, Haag 1966

37 **17. . . ♗b5** 18. ♖h5! △ ♖h1+–; **17. . . ♘c4** 18. ♖d5 ♕a3 19. ♔d1 ♘b2 20. ♔e1±

38 18. . . ♕a3 19. ♔b1 a5 20. ♘f4 a4 21. ♖a5!±

39 14. ♗h6 ♘c4 [14. . . ♗h8 15. ♘d5±; 14. . . ♗h6 15. ♕h6 ♖c3 16. bc3 ♕c3 17. ♘e2 ♕c5 18. ♘f4 ♘c4 19. ♘d5 ♘d5 20. ♖d5± Matulović–Korčnoj, Sousse (izt) 1967 — 4/525; 18. . . a5! 19. h5 a4 20. ♘g6 ♘g6 21. ♖d5 ♕a3 22. hg6 fg6 23. ♖g5= Matulović–Jovčić, Jugoslavija 1970 — 10/500] 15. ♗c4 ♗h6 16. ♕h6 bc4 17. h5 ♖ab8 18. ♘d5 ♘d5 19. ed5 ♕a3 20. ♘b3! cb3! 21. ba3 [Janošević–Velimirović, Jugoslavija (ch) 1972 — 13/456] bc2! 22. ♔a1 cd1♕ 23. ♖d1 ♗f5 24. g4!□= Velimirović

40 14. . . ♕d8!?

41 22. h5± Kuzmin–S. Garcia, Hastings 1973/74 — 17/455

42 15. g4 — B 78

43 15. . . ♖c3 16. bc3 [16. hg6? ♖c5 17. gh7 ♔h8 18. b4 ♖b5∓] ♘h5±

44 17. . . ♕a6 18. e5 ♘e8 19. ♕h2+–

45 18. g5 ♘h5 19. ♘d5±

46 **18. . . ♘e8** 19. ♕h2+–; **18. . . de5** 19. g5+–

47 20. ♖dg1 de5 [20. . . h5!?] 21. ♕d8 ♖d8 22. ♘d2 [22. ♘a5? ♖c3 23. bc3 h5 24. ♘b3 e4–+ Bouaziz–Geler, Sousse (izt) 1967 — 4/526] ♖c3 23. bc3 h5 24. ♖h2 b6∓ Janošević–Despotović, Jugoslavija 1969 — 7/401

48 22. ♖d1 ed6 23. ♘d5!±↑ Levy

49 **16. ♗g5** ♗e6 17. e5 ♘e8 18. ♘d5 ♗d5 19. ♕d5 ♖ac8 20. e6 f6 21. ♗e3 ♖c2 22. ♕b7 f5∓ Janošević–Joksić, Jugoslavija 1969; **16. e5**!? ♘e8 17. h5 ♗e5 18. hg6 hg6 19. ♗d4 ♖d4 20. ♘d4 ♗g7 21. g4 ♖c8 22. ♖h3 e6 [22. . . ♘f6 23. ♖dh1 ♕b6 24. ♘f5!+– Simić–Joksić, Jugoslavija 1970 — 10/499] 23. ♖dh1 ♕f6 24. ♘ce2± Kuprejčik–Ribli, Sombor 1970 — 10/497

50 16. . . ♗h6 17. ♕h6 ♕f8 18. ♕e3±

51 17. . . ♘h5 18. ♖h5!+–

52 19. g4?! ♗e6 20. ♕h2 [20. e5 ♖c3! 21. bc3 ♘d5∓ Janošević–Velimirović, Jugoslavija 1970 — 9/389] ♕e8∓

53 19. . . de5 20. ♗g5!±

54 20. . . ♘d6 21. ♕d5+–

55 22. g4 ♕f8 23. ♕h2± Ciocaltea–Drimer, Romania 1968 — 5/430

56 **16. ♗g5**?! ♗e6 17. ♘b5 ♕d7 18. ♘5d4 a5∓ Kaplan–Neuman, Israel 1967; **16. h5** ♖c3 [16. . . ♖ac8 17. hg6 fg6 18. e5!± Ciocaltea–Gufeljd, Kislovodsk 1968 — 6/527] 17. ♕c3 ♕c3 18. bc3 ♘h5 19. ♗d4 ♗e6∞ Ostojić–Honfi, Monte Carlo 1968 — 5/428; 17. bc3=

57 **17. ♖he1** [Moles–Levy, England 1968] a5!∓; **17. g4**!? Bihovski

58 18. a4 b5 19. ♘b5 ♕b7 20. h6± Damjanović–Kaplan, San Juan 1969

59 18. . . fg6 19. ♗f6 ♗f6 20. ♘d5±

60 19. . . ♖c8 20. g4 ♖d4 21. ♘d4 ♕b6 [Hartston–Hollis, England 1967] 22. ♔c1!± Levy

61 20. ♘b5 ♕c4 21. e5± Gheorghiu–Geler, Moskva 1967 — 3/477

62 20. . . ♖c8 21. ♖dh1 ♗b3 22. cb3 e5 23. ♗e3 ♖b3 24. ♘b5±

63 22. ♗e3± Hartston–Kolbaek, Dresden 1969

64 **16. ♗d4** ♖ac8 17. h5 ♗e6 18. hg6 fg6 19. g4 ♗f7 20. ♖h2 [Jacobsen – Keene, Bognor Regis 1967] b5!=; **16. e5** de5! [16... ♘e8 17. ♘d5 ♗e5 18. h5!? e6 19. ♘e7 ♔f8 20. hg6!± Glauser – Purevjav, Lugano (ol) 1968 — 6/533; 18. ♘e7 ♔f8 19. ♘d5 ♖c2 20. ♗h6 ♘g7 21. ♕c2 ♗f5 22. ♕f5 gf5 23. f4!+− Zuckerman – van Scheltinga, Wijk aan Zee 1968 — 5/426; 19... ♗f5 20. ♗h6 ♘g7 21. ♘e3 ♖ac8 22. ♘c4 ♖c4 23. ♖c1 ♖a4 (R. Byrne – Korčnoj, Sousse (izt) 1967 — 4/518) 24. ♖he1!±] 17. ♘c5 ♕d6 18. ♘d7 ♘d7 19. ♕d6 ed6 20. ♖d6 ♘c5= Radovici – Stanciu, Bucuresti 1968 — 5/429

65 16... ♖ac8 17. g4±→

66 18... ♘h5 19. g4 ♘f6 20. ♘d5+−

67 19... ♘h5 20. g4 ♘f6 21. e5!+−

68 Drimer – Levy, Hastings 1969/70

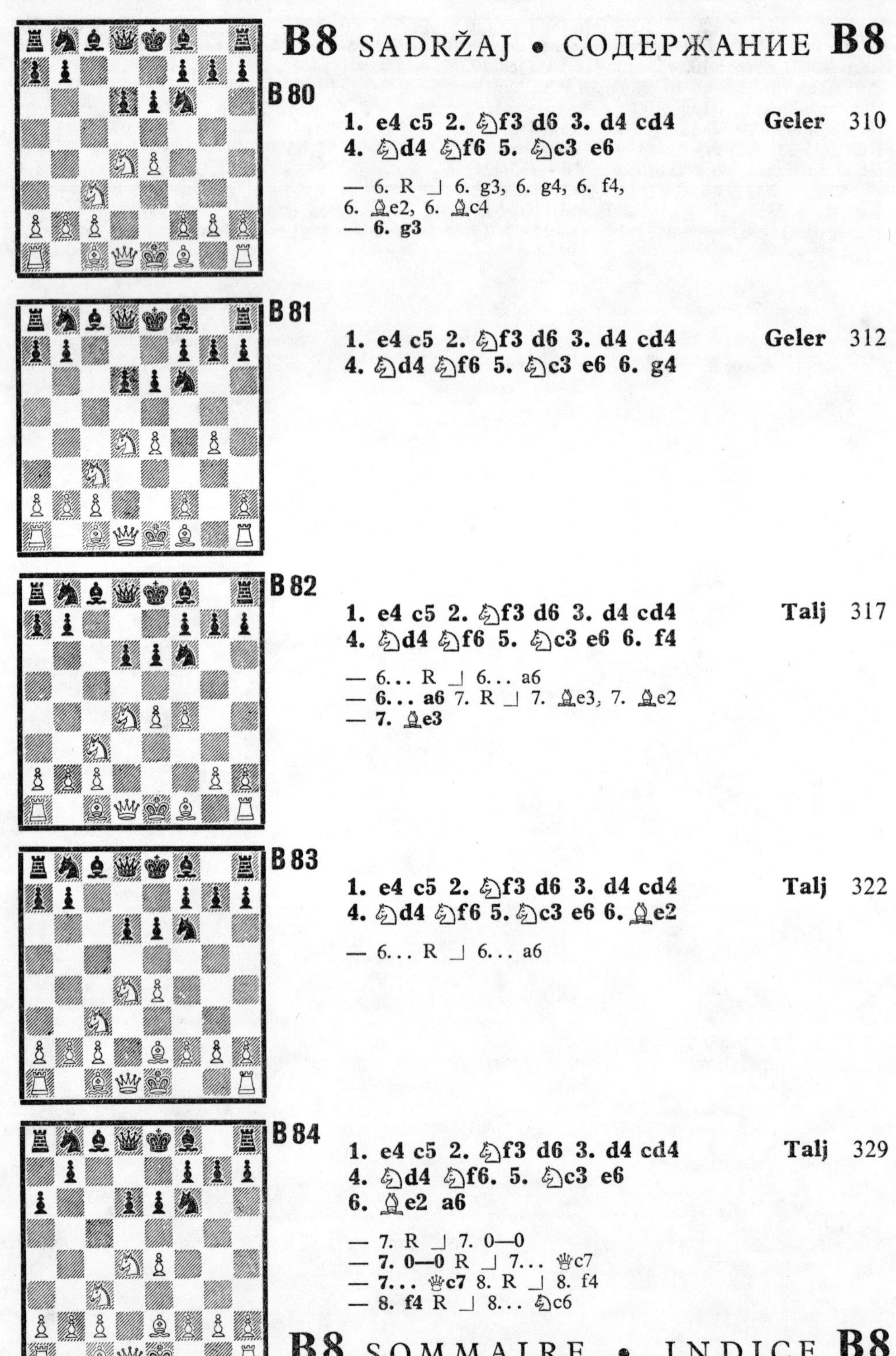

B8 SADRŽAJ • СОДЕРЖАНИЕ B8

B8 SOMMAIRE • INDICE B8

B8 CONTENTS • INHALT B8

B8 INDICE • INNEHÅLL B8

B 80 1. e4 c5 2. ♘f3 d6 3. d4 cd4 4. ♘d4 ♘f6 5. ♘c3 e6[1]

	6	7	8	9	10	11	12	13	14	
1	♗e3[2]	f3[3]	♕d2	g4	♕d4	g5	h4	0-0-0[6]	h5[7]	∞
	♘c6	♗e7[4]	0—0	♘d4[5]	a6	♘d7	b5	♗b7	♗g5[8]	
2	...	♗d3[9]	0—0[10]	♕e1	f3	a4	♘a4			=
	a6	b5	♗b7	♘bd7	♗e7[11]	ba4[12]	0—0[13]			
3	g3	♗g2[15]	0—0[17]	♘ce2[19]	c4	b3	♗b2	cb5	♘d4	=
	♘c6[14]	♗d7[16]	♗e7[18]	♖c8[20]	0—0	a6	b5[21]	♘d4	ab5[22]	
4	...	...	♕d4	e5[24]	♕e5	♗c6	0—0	b3	♕e4	=
	...	♘d4	♗d7[23]	de5	♗c6	bc6	♗e7	♘d7	♗f6[25]	
5	...	♗g2	0—0	f4[27]	♘c6[28]	e5	fe5	♗f4	♘e4[29]	±
	a6	♕c7[26]	♗e7	♘c6	bc6	de5	♘d7	0—0	♗b7[30]	
6	...	...	...	f4	♘b3	♗e3	a3	♕e2	g4	∞
	...	...	♗d7	♘c6[31]	♗e7	b5	♖b8	0—0	♔h8[32]	

1. e4 c5 2. ♘f3 d6 3. d4 cd4 4. ♘d4 ♘f6 5. ♘c3 e6 6. g3 a6 7. ♗g2 ♕c7 8. 0—0 ♘c6

	9	10	11	12	13	14	15	16	17	
7	b3[33]	♗b2	♘ce2	♘c6[35]	c4[36]	f3	♘c3	♔h1		=
	♗e7	0—0[34]	e5	bc6	♗g4	♗h5	♘d7	♘c5[37]		
8	♗e3	♕e2[38]	♖ad1[40]	h3[41]	a3	♗d4	g4	f4		∞
	♗e7	♗d7[39]	0—0	b5[42]	♘d4	♗c6	♖fe8	♕b7[43]		
9	♖e1	♘c6	e5	♖e5	♗f4!?[45]	♖e6[46]	♗d6	♗c5![47]	♖d1	±
	♗e7	bc6	de5	♗b7[44]	♗d6	fe6	♕d7	♕d1	♖d8[48]	
10	...	♘c6[49]	♘a4	c4	♘c3	f4[52]	e5	fe5	♕e2	∞
	♗d7	bc6[50]	♖b8[51]	c5	♗e7	♗c6	de5	♖d8[53]	♘d7[54]	

1 Scheveningen

2 **6. ♗b5** ♗d7=; **6. ♘de2** ♘c6 7. g3 — 6. g3; **6. ♗d3** ♘c6 [6... a6 7. 0—0 ♘bd7 8. ♗e3 b5 9. a3 ♗b7 10. f4 ♗e7 11. ♕f3 — B 82] 7. ♘c6 [7. ♗e3 — 6. ♗e3] bc6 8. 0—0 e5 9. f4 ♗e7 10. ♔h1 0—0 11. ♕f3 ♘d7 12. f5 ♗g5= Padevski—Šamkovič, Moskva 1962

3 7. ♗d3 ♗e7 8. 0—0 0—0 9. h3 ♘d4 10. ♗d4 e5 11. ♗e3 ♗e6= Nej—Polugajevski, Tallinn 1973 — 15/413; 8. f4 — B 82

4 7... d5!?

5 9... d5!? 10. g5 ♘e8 11. ♖g1 de4 12. ♘e4∞

6 13. ♖g1?! b4! 14. ♕b4 ♖b8 15. ♕d4 ♖b2∓

7 14. ♖g1 ♘e5 15. ♗e2 ♖c8∓

8 15. h6 ♗f6∞ Gufeljd—Štejn, SSSR 1973 — 15/414

9 **7. a4** b6 8. ♗d3 [8. g4?! e5 9. ♘f5 g6 10. g5 gf5 11. ef5 ♗b7 12. ♖g1 d5 13. ♗g2 ♘e4∓ Neukirch—Bukić, Zinnowitz 1967] ♗b7 9. 0—0 ♘bd7 10. ♕e2 ♗e7= Tatai—Larsen, Manila 1973 — 16/414; **7. f3** b5 8. ♕d2 ♗b7 9. a4 e5 10. ♘f5 b4 11. ♘d5 ♘d5 12. ed5 ♕a5=; **7. ♕f3**!? ♕c7 8. 0-0-0 ♘c6 9. ♗e2 ♘d4 [9... b5? 10. ♘c6 ♕c6 11. e5+−] 10. ♖d4 b5 11. ♗g5 ♗e7 12. ♖hd1 [Ljubojević—Kavalek, Manila 1974 — 18/437] ♗b7∞; **7. f4** — B 82

10 **8. a4** b4 9. ♘ce2 ♗b7 10. f3 [10. ♘g3 ♘bd7 11. 0—0 (Espig—Bukić, Zinnowitz 1967 — 4/532) h5!△ h4∓] ♘bd7△ d5∓ Aptekman—Tukmakov, SSSR 1973; **8. a3** ♗b7 9. f4 ♘bd7 10. ♕f3 — B 82

11 10... b4!?

12 11... b4 12. ♘a2△ c3±

13 **12... d5**?! 13. ♕g3! de4 14. fe4 0—0 [14... ♘e4 15. ♕g7 ♗f6 16. ♕g4±] 15. e5!± Larsen—R. Byrne, Lugano 1970 — 9/390; **12... 0—0**=

14 **6... b6**?! 7. ♗g2 ♗b7 8. 0—0 a6 9. ♖e1 [9. ♗g5 ♘bd7 10. e5! ♗g2 11. ef6 gf6 12. ♔g2

fg5 13. ♕h5∞ Kan] ♕c7 10. ♘d5! ed5 11. ed5 ♔d8 12. ♗g5 ♘bd7 13. ♕e2± Konstantinopoljski—Gilman, corr. 1949; **6... ♗d7**!? 7. ♗g2 ♗c6 8. 0—0 ♗e7 9. b3 0—0 10. ♗b2 ♕b6 11. ♕d2 ♘bd7 12. ♖fe1 ♘e5 13. f4 ♘eg4 14. h3 e5= Bihovski—Bronštejn, SSSR 1961; 9. ♘c6±⊡

15 **7. ♗g5** ♗e7 8. ♗g2 ♘d4 [8... 0—0 9. 0—0 ♘d4 10. ♕d4 h6= Bronštejn—Geler, Zürich (ct) 1953] 9. ♕d4 ♕a5 10. ♗d2 ♕h5∓; **7. ♘b3** ♗e7 8. ♗g2 0—0 9. 0—0 a6=; **7. ♘de2** ♕c7 8. ♗g2 a6 9. 0—0 — 6... a6

16 7... ♗e7 8. 0—0 0—0 [8... ♘d4 9. ♕d4 — 7... ♘d4] 9. ♘c6 [9. b3 ♘d4 10. ♕d4 ♕a5 11. ♗b2 ♗d7 12. ♘d1 ♖ac8 13. c4 ♗c6 14. ♘c3∞ Goldenov—Kan, SSSR 1946] bc6 10. e5 de5 11. ♕d8 ♖d8 12. ♗c6± Bernstein—Bogoljubov, Zürich 1934

17 **8. ♘db5** ♕b8 9. ♗g5 [9. a4?! a6 10. ♘a3 ♕c7 11. ♗e3 ♖b8 12. h3 ♗e7 13. ♕d2 0—0 14. f4 ♘b4 15. 0—0 ♗c6∓ Olsson—Schmid, Göteborg 1955; 9. ♗f4 ♘e5∓] a6 10. ♗f6 ab5 11. ♗g5 b4 12. ♘e2 ♖a5!? 13. ♗f4 ♗e7 14. 0—0 0—0= Saharov—Vasjukov, SSSR 1961; **8. ♘de2** a6 9. 0—0 [9. b3 ♗e7 10. ♗b2 0—0 11. 0—0 b5 12. ♕d2 ♕c7 13. ♖ac1 ♖fd8 14. ♘d1 d5= Šamkovič—Krogius, SSSR (ch) 1971] ♗e7 [9... b5 10. a3 ♕c7 11. h3 ♗e7 12. ♔h1 0—0 13. g4 ♔h8 14. ♘g3± Toluš—Kotov, SSSR (ch) 1945; 9... ♕c7 10. h3 ♖c8 11. b3 ♗e7 12. ♗e3 0—0 13. ♕d2± Kieninger—Koch, Stuttgart 1939] 10. b3 0—0 11. a4 ♕c7 12. h3 ♖fd8 13. ♗b2 ♗e8= Kluger—Malich, Debrecen 1969

18 8... a6 9. ♗e3 [9. b3 ♖c8 10. ♗b2 ♗e7 11. ♘c6 ♗c6 12. a4!? 0—0 13. a5 ♕c7 14. ♖e1 ♖fd8= Larsen—Panno, Palma de Mallorca (izt) 1970 — 10/505; 10... ♘d4 11. ♕d4 ♕a5 12. ♖fe1 ♗e7 13. e5 de5 14. ♖e5 ♕b4! 15. ♕d3 ♗c6∓ Ragozin—Panov, SSSR 1960; 9. a4 ♖c8 10. ♘de2 ♗e7 11. h3 0—0 12. ♗e3 ♘b4 13. a5 ♕c7 14. ♗b6 ♕b8 15. f4 ♗d8= Kagan—Panno, Petropolis (izt) 1973 — 16/416] ♖c8 10. ♕e2 b5 11. a3 ♘e5 12. ♖ad1 ♘c4 13. ♗c1 ♘a3? 14. e5 de5 15. ♘c6 ♕c7 16. ♘e5 ♘c4 17. ♘d7 ♘d7 18. ♘d5!± Ravinski—Panov, SSSR 1943; 13... ♗e7±

19 **9. ♘de2** ♕b8 10. h3 b5 11. a3 [11. g4 b4∓] a5∓↑«; **9. ♖e1** 0—0 10. ♘c6 ♗c6 11. a4 a6! [11... ♕d7?! 12. ♖e3 ♖fd8 13. ♖d3 b6 14. a5 ♕c7 15. ♗f4 ♖ac8 16. ab6 ab6 17. b3± Browne—Hartston, Las Palmas 1974 — 17/466; 13... ♘e8 14. b3± Browne—Petrosjan, San Antonio 1972] 12. ♖e3 ♕c7= Bukić; **9. ♗e3** 0—0 10. ♕e2 ♘d4 11. ♗d4 ♗c6 12. ♖fd1 ♕a5 13. a3 ♖fd8= Klovan—Kirilov, SSSR 1967 — 3/482

20 9... 0—0 10. c4 a6 11. ♘c3 ♕a5 12. ♘c6 ♗c6 13. ♕e1 ♕h5 14. h4 ♘d7 15. b3 ♗f6= Ivkov—Bronštejn, Beograd 1964

21 12... ♕a5 [Unzicker—Najdorf, Dubrovnik (ol) 1950] 13. ♕e1± Fuderer

22 15. ♕d2 ♕b6 16. ♖ac1 ♖fd8= Gligorić—Boleslavski, Zürich (ct) 1953

23 **8... ♕c7** 9. ♗g5 ♗e7 10. 0-0-0 a6 11. ♗f6 gf6 12. f4±↑; **8... ♗e7** 9. 0—0 [9. e5 de5 10. ♕e5 0—0 11. 0—0 ♕b6 12. ♘a4 ♕a6 13. b3 ♗d7 14. ♘c5= Aronin—Konstantinopoljski, corr. 1960] 0—0 [9... ♗d7?! 10. e5 de5 11. ♕e5 ♗c6 12. ♗c6 bc6 13. ♗e3 0—0 14. ♖ad1± Kan] 10. e5! [10. b3 ♗d7 11. a4 ♗c6 12. ♗a3 ♕c7 13. ♖fe1 ♖fd8 14. ♖ad1 a6 15. ♘e2 b5 16. ab5 ab5 17. ♗b4= Lindrot—Ruđakovski, SSSR 1947] de5 11. ♕e5± Boleslavski

24 9. 0—0 ♗c6 10. ♗g5 ♗e7 11. ♖ad1=

25 15. ♗b2 0—0=

26 **7... ♗e7** 8. 0—0 0—0 9. h3 ♗d7 10. ♔h2 ♘c6 11. ♘de2 b5 12. a3 ♖c8 13. ♗e3 ♘e5 14. b3 ♕c7 15. ♕d2 a5 16. f4± Dubinin—Šestoperov, SSSR 1962; **7... ♘bd7** 8. 0—0 ♗e7 9. ♕e2 [9. g4!?] ♕c7 10. ♘d1 d5 [10... b5 11. e5±] 11. ed5 ♘d5 12. ♗d5±

27 9. h3 ♗d7 [9... 0—0 10. ♗e3 ♘c6 11. g4 ♖b8 12. f4 ♘d4 13. ♕d4 b5= Alexander—Pirc, England 1951] 10. ♘de2 ♘c6 11. b3 b5 12. a3 0—0 13. ♗b2 ♖fe8 14. g4 d5= Klavin—Spaski, SSSR 1960

28 10. ♗e3?! ♘a5!=

29 14. ♕d2±

30 15. ♕h5± Talj—Darga, SSSR—BRD 1960

31 9... ♗e7 10. f5 e5 11. ♘b3±

32 15. g5 ♘g8 16. ♖f3 f6∞ Pilnik—Ivkov, Beograd 1954

33 **9. ♘ce2** ♗d7 11. c3 ♗e7 12. h3 0—0∓; **9. ♘de2** b5 11. a3 ♗b7 11. h3 [11. ♗g5 ♗e7 12. ♕d2 ♘e5∓] ♗e7 12. ♗e3 0—0 13. f4 ♘a5=

34 10... ♘d4 11. ♕d4 b5 12. ♖ac1 ♗b7 13. ♘d1 0—0 14. ♘e3 ♗c6 15. c4 ♕b7=

35 12. ♘f5?! ♗f5 13. ef5 ♕d7∓

36 13. h3?! d5∓

37 Šijanovski—Spaski, SSSR (ch) 1962

38 **10. ♕d2**?! ♘e5∓ Pachman; **10. ♘a4** 0—0 11. c4 ♘e5! 12. ♖c1 ♗d7 13. ♕b3 ♗a4! 14. ♕a4 ♘fg4∓ Adorjan—Suetin, Budapest 1970 — 9/320

39 10... 0—0 11. ♘c6 bc6 12. ♘a4 c5 13. f4 ♖b8 14. c4 ♗b7 15. ♘c3 ♖fd8 16. g4 d5∞ Matanović — Polugajevski, Jugoslavija — SSSR 1962; 16. ♖ad1=

40 11. ♘c6 ♗c6 12. ♖ad1 0—0△ b5, ♖ac8, ♖fd8∓↑

41 **12. ♘b3** b5 13. a3 ♖ab8 14. f4 b4 15. ab4 ♘b4 16. ♖c1 ♖fc8 17. h3 ♗c6 18. ♘d4 ♗a8 19. ♗f2 ♕c4 20. ♕e3 ♗d8!∓ Dubinin—Estrin, corr. 1966; **12. f4** ♖ac8 [12... ♘d4 13.

♗d4 ♗c6 14. f5 e5 15. ♗e3 b5= Sax–Cvetković, Vrnjačka Banja 1974 — 17/465] 13. ♔h1 b5 14. a3 ♘d4 15. ♗d4 e5 16. ♗e3 ♗e6∓ Medina–Talj, Palma de Mallorca 1966; 13. ♘b3=

42 12... ♘a5!?△ ♘c4 Tajmanov

43 Lejn–Jansa, Soči 1965

44 **12... ♗d6** 13. ♕f3 ♗d7 14. ♖g5!±→ Boleslavski; **12... ♘d5** 13. ♘d5 cd5 14. ♗f4±↑ Pietzsch–Janošević, Sarajevo 1968; **12... 0—0** 13. ♗f4 ♕b7 [13... ♗d6 14. ♖e6! ♗f4 15. ♖c6±; 13... ♕d7 14. ♘a4 ♗b7 15. ♕d7 ♘d7 16. ♖e3 ♖ac8 17. ♖d1 ♘f6 18. ♖b3± Pavlov–Vavra, Varna 1972] 14. ♖e3 [14. ♘a4?! ♖d8 15. ♗d2 ♕c7 16. ♖e3 a5∞ Ostojić–Janošević, Jugoslavija (ch) 1968 — 6/468; 14. ♖e2!? ♖d8 15. ♖d2± Padevski–Bobocov, Sofia 1972 — 14/381] ♖d8 [14... ♘d5 15. ♘d5 cd5 16. c4±] 15. ♕e1 ♗d7 16. ♗e5 ♗e8 17. ♘e4± Keres–Vasjukov, SSSR (ch) 1966

45 13. ♖e1 c5 14. ♗f4 ♕c8 15. ♗b7 ♕b7 16. b3 [16. ♘a4 c4 17. ♕e2 ♖c8 18. ♗e5 0–0 19. ♖ad1 ♖fd8 20. b3± Browne–Langeweg, Amsterdam 1971] 0–0 17. ♕e2 c4! 18. ♘e4 ♖fc8 19. ♘d6 ♗d6 20. ♗d6 cb3 [20... ♕c6 21. ♗e5 ♘d5 22. ♗d4 ♘e7 23. ♖ad1± Evans–Portisch, Amsterdam 1971] 21. cb3 ♘d5 22. ♗e5 ♖c6 23. ♖ad1 ♘c3 24. ♗c3 ♖c3 25. ♕e4 ♕e4 26. ♖e4 ♖c7 27. ♖a4±⊥ Westerinen–Bobocov, Venezia 1971 — 12/389

46 14. ♖g5?! ♗f4 15. gf4 ♖d8 16. ♕e2 ♕f4 17. ♖g7 ♖d2 18. ♕f3 ♕f3 19. ♗f3 ♖c2∓ Schmid–Portisch, Adelaide 1971 — 12/390; 16. ♕f3!? Sokolov

47 16. ♕d4?! c5! 17. ♕c5 ♗g2 18. ♗g2 ♖c8 19. ♕e5 ♔f7 20. ♗a3 ♖hd8∓ Timman–Langeweg, Nederland (ch) 1971

48 18. ♖e1 ♔f7 19. ♘e4 ♘e4 20. ♗e4±⊥ Browne–Langeweg, Amsterdam 1972 — 13/392

49 10. ♘d5!? ed5 11. ed5 ♘e5! [11... ♘e7 12. ♗g5! ♗g4 13. ♕d2 0-0-0 14. c4 h6 15. ♗f6 gf6 16. b4±→ Osmanović–Cebalo, Jugoslavija (ch) 1968 — 5/388] 12. f4 ♗e7 13. fe5 de5 14. ♕e2 [14. ♘f3 ♘g4△ ♕b6] ♘g4 15. ♗f3 ♗c5= Boleslavski

50 10... ♗c6? 11. ♘d5±

51 **11... ♗e7** 12. c4 0–0 13. b3 ♖ab8 14. c5!± I. Zajcev–Liberzon, SSSR 1969; **11... e5** 12. c4 ♗e7 13. c5!±↑ Talj–Najdorf, Beograd 1970 — 10/322; 12... c5!?; **11... ♖d8** 12. c4 c5 13. ♗g5 ♗e7 14. f4 h6 15. ♗h4 ♗a4! 16. ♕a4 ♘d7 17. ♗e7 ♔e7∞ Barle–Hug, Athens 1971 — 12/384

52 **14. b3** ♗c6 15. ♗b2 0–0 16. f4∞ Savon–Talj, SSSR (ch) 1970 — 12/386; **14. ♗f4**!?

53 16... ♘d7? 17. ♘d5 ♕b7 18. ♘e7? ♗g2 19. ♕d6 ♘b6!–+ Jansa–Darga, Bamberg 1972 — 13/387; 18. ♕g4!±

54 18. ♘d5 ♕b7∞ Janošević–Matulović, Vršac 1969 — 8/341

B 81 1. e4 c5 2. ♘f3 d6 3. d4 cd4 4. ♘d4 ♘f6 5. ♘c3 e6 6. g4[1]

	6	7	8	9	10	11	12	13	14	
1	...	♘f5[2]	g5[3]	♘g7	♘e4	♘g3	♘h5	♘g7	♕h5[4]	±
	e5?!	h5	♘e4	♗g7	d5	h4	♖h7	♖g7		
2	...	ed5[5]	♗b5	♘d5	♕e2	♘f5	♗d7	♗f4	c3	±
	d5?!	♘d5	♗d7	ed5	♗e7[6]	♔f8	♘d7[7]	♕a5	♖e8[8]	
3	...	g5	♖g1[9]	♗e3	♗b5[11]	♕h5	♕e2[12]			±
	♗e7	♘fd7	♘c6	♘b6[10]	♗d7	g6				
4	...	...	...	♗e3	a3[13]	h4[14]	f3	♘c6[15]	♕d4	=
	...	...	a6	b5	♗b7	♘c5	♘c6	♗c6	0–0[16]	
5	...	♗g2[17]	h3[19]	♗e3[20]	♕e2	f4	♕f2!?[22]	♗d4	♗b6	=
	h6	♘c6[18]	♗d7	a6	♗e7[21]	♕c7	♘d4	e5	♕c4[23]	
6	...	♖g1	♗e3[25]	♕e2[27]	♗d4	♗e3	h4	g5	hg5	±
	...	♘c6[24]	a6[26]	♘d4[28]	e5	♗e6	♘d7	hg5	g6[29]	
7	...	...	♗e3[30]	♕d2	0-0-0	♕d4	♕a4	♕b3[31]		=
	...	♗e7	♘c6	a6	♘d4	e5	♗d7			
8	...	g5	♗g5	♗g2[32]	♕e2	0-0-0	h4[34]	f4	f5	±
	...	hg5	a6	♗d7[33]	♗e7	♕c7	♘c6	0-0-0	♔b8[35]	

	6	7	8	9	10	11	12	13	14	
9	...	...	...	♕d2[36]	0-0-0	h4[38]	♗e2[39]	f4	h5	±
	...	...	♘c6	a6[37]	♗d7	♕c7	0-0-0	♗e7	♔b8[40]	
10	...	g5[41]	♗e3[43]	f4[45]	♕d2	♗d4	♗g2	0-0-0	♕e2	=
	♘c6	♘d7[42]	♗e7[44]	0—0	♘d4	a6	♖e8	♘b6!?	♕c7[46]	
11	...	...	...	h4	♕d2[48]	0-0-0	♕d4	♖g1[50]		±
	...	...	...	a6[47]	0—0	♘d4[49]	b5	♘e5!?[51]		
12	...	...	...	♗g2[52]	f4	h4[55]	b3	♕d2	♗d4[57]	±
	...	...	a6	♗e7[53]	0—0[54]	♘a5[56]	♘c6	♘d4		
13	...	...	...	♕d2	0-0-0	♕d4	h4	♔b1	♘a4	±
	...	...	...	♕c7[58]	♘d4[59]	b5	♖b8	b4	♗b7[60]	
14	...	...	♘db5!	♗f4	♕h5[63]	♗e3[65]	♘d4	♖d1	♕e2	±
	...	...	♘b6[61]	♘e5![62]	♘g6[64]	a6	♘e5	g6	♗d7[66]	
15	...	g5[67]	♗e3[69]	a3[71]	♕d2[72]	f3	♘c6	0-0-0	♗f4[74]	±
	a6	♘fd7[68]	b5[70]	♗b7	♘c5[73]	♘c6	♗c6	♕c7		
16	...	...	...	...	♖g1[75]	f4	f5	♘f5		=
	...	...	...	♘b6!?	♘8d7[76]	♗b7	ef5[77]	♘e5[78]		
17	...	...	♗c4	♗b3[80]	♘c6	♗e3	♕d2	0-0-0	a3	±
	...	...	♘e5[79]	♘bc6[81]	♘c6	♗e7	b5	♗d7	♖b8[82]	
18	...	...	♗g2	f4[84]	h4	hg5	♗h1	♘f3	♕d2!	±
	...	...	♘c6[83]	h6[85]	hg5[86]	♖h1	♕b6	♘c5	♗d7[87]	

1 Keres, Panov

2 7. ♗b5!? ♗d7 8. ♗d7 ♕d7 9. ♘f5 h5 10. f3 [10. g5?! ♘e4 11. ♘g7 ♗g7 12. ♘e4 d5!∓ O'Kelly—Christoffel, Groningen 1946; 10. ♗g5!? ♘g4 11. h3!± Keres] hg4 11. fg4 g6 [11... ♘a6 12. ♕e2± Keller—Rat, Schweiz 1961] 12. ♘e3 ♘c6 13. ♕f3 ♗g7 14. ♘cd5 ♘d5 15. ♘d5 ♘d4 16. ♕g2± Gipslis

3 8. ♗g5 hg4! [8... ♗e6? 9. gh5 ♗f5 10. ef5 ♗e7 11. h6!+— Bagirov—Moršovič, SSSR 1960] 9. ♘e3 ♗e6 10. ♕d2 ♘c6 11. 0-0-0 ♘d4 12. ♗f6 gf6 13. ♘b5 ♕b6! 14. ♘d4 ed4 15. ♕d4 ♕d4 16. ♖d4 ♗h6∓ A. Zajcev—Persitz, corr. 1966 — 3/491

4 Nejelov—Romanov, corr. 1966

5 7. ♗b5 ♗d7 8. ed5 [8. ♗d7? ♕d7 9. e5 ♘e4! 10. ♘ce2 ♘c6 11. ♘c6 ♕c6 12. ♘d4 ♕a6∓ Štejn—De Castro, La Habana 1966 — 2/435] ♗b5 9. ♘db5 a6= Gipslis

6 10... ♕e7 11. ♗e3 g6 [11... a6 12. ♗d7 ♘d7 13. ♘f5 ♕e6 14. 0-0-0 0-0-0 15. ♕d3 ♘f6 16. ♖he1±] 12. ♗d7 ♘d7 13. ♘b5 ♘e5 14. 0-0-0 ♗g7 15. ♖d5 0—0 16. ♖hd1± Fischer—Reshevsky, USA (ch) 1966/67 — 3/488

7 12... ♕d7 13. ♗e3 ♘c6 14. 0-0-0± Bebčuk—Šamkovič, SSSR 1958

8 15. ♘e7 ♕c5 16. ♗e3 ♕e7 17. 0-0-0± Nikitin—Čerepkov, SSSR 1958

9 **8. h4**!? a6 9. ♗h3 [9. ♗e3! ♘c6 — 6... ♘c6] ♘b6 10. f4 d5 11. f5!? e5 [11... de4? 12. fe6 0—0 13. ♘e4± Planinc—S. Garcia, Varna 1970 — 10/513] 12. ♘f3 d4∞; **8. ♗e3**! ♘c6 — 6... ♘c6

10 **9... 0—0** 10. h4 [10. ♕h5!? ♖e8!? 11. 0-0-0± Espig—Adamski, Lublin 1970 — 10/514] ♖e8 11. h5 ♘f8 12. ♕d2 e5 13. ♘b3 ♗e6 14. ♘d5! [14. 0-0-0?!= Matulović—Naranja, Palma de Mallorca (izt) 1970 — 10/515] ♗d5 15. ed5! ♘d4 16. ♗d4 ed4 17. 0-0-0± Matulović; **9... a6** 10. ♕d2 [10. f4 0—0 11. ♕f3 ♘d4 12. ♗d4 e5 13. ♗e3 ef4 14. ♕f4 ♘e5 15. 0-0-0 ♗e6 16. ♘d5 ♗d5 17. ed5 f6= R. Byrne—Padevski, Lugano (ol) 1968] 0—0 11. 0-0-0 ♘d4 [11... ♘de5 12. ♖g3 b5 13. ♘c6 ♘c6 14. f4 ♕a5 15. ♕f2! ♖b8 16. ♔b1 b4 17. ♘e2± Štejn—Ćirić, Sarajevo 1967 — 3/489] 12. ♗d4 b5 13. f4 b4 14. ♘a4 e5 15. ♗e3 ef4 16. ♗f4 ♕a5 17. ♗d6! ♗d6 18. ♕d6 ♕a4 19. ♗c4 ♕a5 20. g6± Schöneberg—Tukmakov, Zinnowitz 1967 — 4/541

11 **10. f4** d5!? 11. ed5 ed5 12. ♕f3 ♗b4! 13. ♘c6 bc6 14. ♗d4 0—0 15. 0-0-0 ♗f5∓ Damjanović—Ree, Bad Pyrmont 1970 — 10/518; **10. ♕h5** g6 [10... 0—0?! 11. f4?! ♘d4 12. ♗d4 e5! 13. fe5 de5 14. ♗e5 ♖e8 15. ♗b5

♗b4 16. ♗e8 ♕e8∓ Kogan–Vitolinš, SSSR 1966; 11. ♖g3!±→»] 11. ♕e2 e5 12. ♘b3 ♗e6=

12 Matulović

13 10. ♕d2 ♗b7 11. ♗d3 ♘c5 12. f3 ♘bd7 13. 0-0-0 b4! 14. ♘ce2 d5∓↑ Neukirch–Malich, Zinnowitz 1967 — 4/540

14 **11. ♕h5** g6 12. ♕h6 ♗f8 13. ♕h4 ♘c5 14. ♗g2 ♘bd7 15. 0-0-0 ♕c7 16. f4 ♘b6= Haag–Bukić, Pécs 1967 — 5/437; 15... ♕a5!? ∓→«; **11. f4** 0–0?! 12. ♕h5! g6 13. ♕h4 ♘c6 14. 0-0-0 ♖e8 15. f5!±→» Ciocaltea–Padevski, Smederevska Palanka 1971 — 12/458; 11... ♘c6!?∞

15 13. ♕d2!? Velimirović

16 15. 0-0-0 ♕b8 16. h5 a5= Matulović–Padevski, Lugano (ol) 1968 — 6/535

17 **7. ♗e3** a6! [7... ♘c6?! 8. ♖g1 e5 9. ♘db5 a6 10. ♘a3 b5 11. ♘d5± Kuprejanov–Benkö, Canada 1971] 8. f3 b5 9. ♕d2 ♗b7 10. 0-0-0 ♘bd7 11. a3 ♖c8∞; **7. ♗e2**!? ♘c6 8. ♗e3 a6 9. ♖g1 ♗e7 10. ♕d2 ♘d4 11. ♕d4 e5 12. ♕d2 ♗e6 13. h4= Radulov–Tukmakov, Leningrad (izt) 1973 — 15/422; 10. h4!?± Radulov; **7. h4** ♗e7!? [7... ♘c6 8. ♖g1 h5 9. gh5 ♘h5 10. ♗g5 ♕c7 11. ♕d2 a6 12. 0-0-0 ♘d4 13. ♕d4 ♗d7 14. ♔b1 ♖c8 15. ♗e2 b5 16. ♖ge1± Vasjukov–Larsen, Manila 1974] 8. ♖g1 — 7. ♖g1

18 7... a6 8. h4 ♘c6 [8... h5?! 9. g5 ♘g4 10. f3 ♘e5 11. f4 ♘g4 12. ♗f3 ♘c6 13. ♗g4 hg4 14. ♘c6 bc6 15. ♕g4± Spaski–Šiškin, SSSR 1960] 9. g5 hg5 10. hg5 ♖h1 11. ♗h1 ♘d7 12. ♘b3 ♘a5 13. ♕e2 ♕c7 14. ♘a5△ ♗d2, f4± Benkö–Clarke, Tel Aviv (ol) 1964

19 **8. ♘b3** a5!? [8... ♗d7 9. h4 d5 10. ed5 ♘d5 11. ♘d5 ed5 12. ♗e3 ♗e6 13. ♘d4± Vasjukov–Tukmakov, SSSR (ch) 1967 — 5/436] 9. a4 d5 10. ed5 ♘b4!=∞ Boleslavski; **8. g5** — 7. g5

20 9. 0–0 a6 10. ♗e3 ♕c7 10. ♕e2 ♗e7 12. ♖ad1 b5 13. a3 ♘d4 14. ♗d4 e5△ ♗e6= Enklaar–Petrosjan, Amsterdam 1973 — 16/417

21 10... ♖c8 11. f4 ♗e7 12. 0–0 ♘d4 13. ♗d4 ♗c6 14. g5∞ R. Byrne–Lombardy, USA (ch) 1972

22 12. 0–0 ♘d4 13. ♗d4 e5 14. ♗e3 ef4 15. ♖f4 ♗e6 16. ♘d5 ♗d5 17. ed5 0–0= R. Byrne–Reshevsky, USA (ch) 1966/67

23 15. 0-0-0 ef4 16. ♖he1 0–0= Lombardy–Larsen, Manila 1973 — 16/418

24 7... g5?! 8. ♗e3 a6 9. ♕d2 ♗d7 10. 0-0-0 ♘c6 11. ♗e2 ♕c7 18. h4!± Radovici–Kluger, Lublin 1971 — 13/463

25 8. ♗e2?! d5! [8... ♗e7?! 9. ♗e3 ♗d7 10. h4 d5 11. ed5 ♘d5 12. ♘d5 ed5 13. g5 hg5 14. hg5± Kurajica–Hort, Wijk aan Zee 1970 — 9/396; 8... ♕a5!? Larsen] 9. ed5 ed5 10. ♗e3 ♗b4!= Ciocaltea–Golombek, Tunis 1971 — 11/369

26 8... ♗d7 9. ♗e2 a6 10. h4 ♘d4 11. ♕d4 h5 12. gh5 ♘h5 13. 0-0-0± Mecking–Najdorf, Hastings 1971/72 — 13/464

27 **9. ♗c4** ♕a5 10. ♘b3 ♕c7 11. ♗e2 b5 12. a3 ♗b7 13. h4 d5= Haag–Šamkovič, Salgotarjan 1967; **9. h4** ♕a5! [9... d5?! 10. ed5 ♘d5 11. ♘d5 ♕d5 12. ♗g2 ♕a5 13. c3± Gheorghiu–R. Garcia, Buenos Aires 1970 — 11/368; 9... h5!? Velimirović] 10. ♘b3 ♕c7 11. ♗e2 d5 12. ed5 ♘d5 13. ♘d5 ed5 14. ♕d5 ♗e6=∞ Krnić–Jansa, Sombor 1970 — 10/511; **9. h3**!? ♗d7 10. f4 ♕c7 11. ♕d2 b5 12. ♗d3 ♘d4 13. ♗d4 ♗c6 14. ♕e2 e5? 15. ♘d5!± Savon–Džindžihašvili, SSSR (ch) 1971 — 12/453; 14... ♗e7!?±

28 9... ♗d7!? Sokolov

29 15. 0-0-0± Matulović–Janošević, Jugoslavija 1972 — 14/449

30 8. h4!? d5 9. ♗b5 ♔f8 10. e5 ♘fd7 11. ♘f3 ♘c6 12. ♗c6 bc6 13. ♗f4 [13. g5? hg5 14. ♗g5 ♗g5 15. hg5 ♖b8∓ Matulović–Tukmakov, Bath 1973 — 16/419] ♖b8∓ Bukić

31 Ghizdavu–Tukmakov, Ybbs 1968

32 **9. f4** ♘bd7 10. ♕e2 ♗e7 11. 0-0-0 ♘h5 12. ♗e7 ♕e7 13. ♕e3 ♘df6 14. ♗e2 e5= Kavalek–Szabo, Salgotarjan 1967; **9. ♕d2** b5?! 10. ♗g2 ♗b7 11. 0-0-0 ♘bd7 12. f4 ♕c7 13. e5 de5 14. fe5 b4 16. ♘e6!± Calvo–Panno, Las Palmas 1973 — 15/419

33 **9... ♕c7** 10. ♕d2 ♘bd7 11. f4 ♖b8 12. 0-0-0 ♘h7 13. ♗h4 ♘b6 14. ♖he1!△ ♘d5± Savon–Bikov, SSSR 1962; **9... ♘bd7** 10. ♕e2! ♕c7 11. 0-0-0± Velimirović

34 12. f4!? ♘c6 13. ♘f3△ e5±

35 15. fe6 fe6 16. ♗h3?! ♘h5!= Geler–Korčnoj, Moskva (mct) 1971 — 11/371; 16. ♖hf1!± Gufeljd

36 **9. ♘b3** a6 10. f4 ♕c7 11. ♕e2 b5 12. 0-0-0 b4∓ Karasev–Krogius, SSSR (ch) 1971 — 12/454; 12. a3!? Korčnoj; **9. ♗g2** ♗d7 [9... ♕a5?! 10. h4 a6 11. ♕d2 ♘g4 12. ♘b3 ♕b6 13. ♕e2 ♘f6 14. 0-0-0 ♗d7 15. ♗e3± Goldenov–Kuzmin, SSSR 1964] 10. h4 ♗e7 11. ♕d2 a6 12. 0-0-0 ♕c7 13. f4 ♘d4 14. ♕d4 ♗c6 15. ♗h3 b5 16. ♖he1 ♕a7 17. ♕d3 b4= Gipslis–Liberzon, SSSR (ch) 1969

37 9... ♕b6!? 10. ♘b3 a6 11. 0-0-0 ♗d7 12. ♗f4! [12. f3?! ♖c8 13. ♔b1 ♕c7 14. f4 b5 15. ♗g2 b4 16. ♘e2 a5∓ Muhin–Estevez, Luhačovice 1973 — 15/421; 12. ♗e3 ♕c7= Štejn–Krogius, SSSR (ch) 1964/65; 12. h4 ♗e7 13. f4 0-0-0 14. ♗g2∞ Dueball–Ribli, Bath 1973 — 16/421; 14. ♗h3!? Adorjan] ♘e5! 13. ♗e3 ♕c7 14. f4± Romanišin–Krogius, SSSR 1971 — 11/370

38 11. f4 ♕b6! [11... ♗e7 12. f5 ♘d4 13. ♕d4 ef5 14. ef5 ♗c6 15. ♖g1 ♖h2∞ Beljavski

— Štejnberg, SSSR 1972] 12. ♗e2 ♘d4 13. ♕d4 ♕d4 14. ♖d4 ♘h5! 15. f5 ♘g3 16. ♖e1 ♘e2 17. ♖e2∓⊥ Bonev — Padevski, Bulgaria (ch) 1972

39 **12. ♗g2** ♗e7 13. ♔b1 ♘d4 14. ♕d4 ♗c6 15. ♖h3 0-0-0 16. ♖hd3 ♔b8 17. ♘d5 ed5 18. ed5 ♘d5! 19. ♗d5 ♗g5= Gipslis — Liberzon, Tallinn 1969; **12. ♗h3** ♗e7 13. f4 ♘d4 14. ♕d4 ♕c5 [14... ♖c8 15. ♖d2± Honfi — Šamkovič, Timisoara 1972 — 13/467; 14... ♗c6 15. ♖he1!± Gipslis — Jansa, Budapest 1970 — 9/399; 14... 0-0-0= Tarjan — Evans, USA (ch) 1973 — 16/420] 15. ♕d3 0-0-0= Browne — Andersson, Las Palmas 1974 — 17/477

40 15. ♔b1 ♗e8 [15... d5 16. e5 ♘e4 17. ♘e4 de4 18. ♗e7 ♘e7 19. ♕e3 ♘f5 20. ♘f5 ef5 21. ♖hg1± Karpov — Štejnberg, SSSR 1971 — 12/452] 16. ♗f3± Karpov — Smith, San Antonio 1972 — 14/457

41 7. ♗e3?! ♘d4 8. ♗d4 e5 9. ♗b5 ♗d7 10. ♗d7 ♕d7∓

42 **7... ♘g8** 8. ♖g1 ♘d4 9. ♕d4 ♘e7 10. ♗e3 ♘c6 11. ♗b5 ♗d7 12. ♗c6 ♗c6 13. f4±; **7... ♘d4** 8. ♕d4 ♘d7 9. ♗e3 a6 10. 0-0-0± Estrin

43 **8. f4** h6!? [8... a6 9. ♗e3 ♗e7 10. ♖g1 ♘d4 11. ♕d4 e5 12. ♕d2 ef4 13. ♗f4 ♘e5 14. ♗e2 ♗e6 15. ♘d5 ♗d5 16. ed5± Karpov — Hort, Moskva 1971 — 12/459] 9. ♘e6 fe6 10. ♕h5∞ Karpov; **8. h4** a6 9. f4 ♗e7 10. ♗e3 0—0? 11. ♗g2 ♘a5 12. ♕e2 b5 13. h5 ♖e8 14. 0-0-0 ♘f8 15. g6!±→» Mecking — Rubinetti, Sao Paulo 1972 — 13/468; 10... ♕c7!?∞ Gipslis; **8. ♗g2**!?=

44 **8... ♘d4**?! 9. ♕d4 a6 10. ♗e2 ♕c7 11. f4 b6 12. f5 ♘e5 13. fe6 fe6 14. a4 ♗e7 15. h4 ♕c5 16. ♕d2 ♕c7 17. ♖f1 ♗b7 18. ♗d4 ♖f8 19. 0-0-0 ♖f1 20. ♖f1± Keres — Bogoljubov, Salzburg 1943; **8... ♘de5** 9. ♗e2 a6 10. f4! [10. h4? b5 11. a3 ♘a5 12. b3 ♗b7 13. ♕d2 ♖c8 14. f4 ♘d7 15. ♗f3 ♕c7 16. ♘de2 g6 17. ♖d1 ♗g7∓ Vitolinš — Razuvajev, SSSR 1964] ♘d4 11. ♕d4 ♘c6 12. ♕d2± Gipslis; **8... ♘b6** 9. h4 [9. a4 ♘a5 10. f4 ♘bc4 11. ♗c1 d5 12. ed5 ♗b4 13. ♗g2! 0—0 14. 0—0 ♗c3 15. bc3 ed5 16. ♕f3± Mišta — Navarovszky, Reggio Emilia 1967/68 — 5/440; 9. ♖g1 a6 10. ♕d2 ♗d7 11. f4 ♖c8 12. ♘b3! d5 13. ed5 ♘d5 14. ♘d5 ed5 15. c3 ♗e6 16. ♗d3 g6 17. ♕f2±↑ R. Byrne — Grefe, USA 1970] d5 10. ♗b5 ♗d7 11. ed5 ♘d5 12. ♘d5 ed5 13. ♕e2 ♗e7 14. 0-0-0±↑» Minić — Navarovszky, Čačak 1969 — 8/425

45 **9. ♕h5**?! g6 10. ♕d1 [10. ♘c6 bc6 11. ♕g4 ♘e5 12. ♕g2!? ♗g5? 13. ♗g5 ♕g5 14. ♕g5 ♘f3 15. ♔e2 ♘g5 16. h4 ♗a6 17. ♔e3 +—; 12... d5!∓] ♗g5 11. ♗g5 ♕g5 12. ♘c6 bc6 13. ♕d6 ♖b8 14. h4 ♕c5 15. 0-0-0 ♕f2!∓ Pietzsch — Ćirić, Sarajevo 1966 — 1/299; **9. ♖g1** — 6... ♗e7

46 15. ♖d3 e5 16. ♗b6 ♕b6 17. ♗h3 ef4 18. ♗c8 ♖ac8 19. h4= Minić — Udovčić, Zagreb 1965

47 9... 0—0 10. ♕d2 [10. ♗c4 ♘b6 11. ♗b3 d5 12. ed5 ed5 13. ♕e2 ♗b4∓ Ivkov — Gligorić, Jugoslavija (ch) 1966; 10. f4 ♘d4 11. ♕d4 e5?! 12. ♕d2 ef4 13. ♗f4 ♘e5 14. 0-0-0 ♕a5 15. ♔b1 ♔h8?! 16. ♘b5! ♕d2 17. ♖d2±⊥ Gipslis — Ćirić, SSSR — Jugoslavija 1967] ♘d4 11. ♗d4 a6 12. 0-0-0 b5 13. f4 b4 14. ♘e2 ♗b7 15. ♗g2 a5 16. ♘g3 ♖e8 17. f5!±↑ Minev — Bobocov, Bulgaria (ch) 1966 — 1/297

48 **10. ♗e2**?!∞; **10. ♖g1** ♕c7=; **10. ♗g2** 0—0 11. ♕d2 ♖b8 12. 0-0-0 ♘d4 13. ♗d4 b5 14. f4 b4 15. ♘e2 ♕a5 16. ♔b1 ♗b7∞; **10. f4** 0—0 11. ♕d2 [11. f5 ♘de5= Boleslavski] ♘d4 12. ♗d4 b5 13. a3 ♗b7 14. 0-0-0 e5 15. ♗e3 ef4 16. ♗f4 ♘e5 17. ♘d5 ♖c8?! 18. ♘e7 ♕e7 19. ♕d6 ♕d6 20. ♖d6 ♗e4 21. ♖h2 ±⊥; 17... ♗d5!?

49 11... ♕c7!? Gufeljd

50 13. f4 ♗b7 14. ♖g1 e5∞ Dubinin — Prjub, corr. 1968 — 5/441

51 **13... ♗b7**?! 14. h5 e5 15. ♕d2 g6 16. hg6 fg6 17. ♘d5± Gufeljd — Dončenko, SSSR 1970 — 10/517; **13... ♘e5**!?±

52 **9. ♗e2** ♗e7 10. h4 ♕c7 11. f4 b5 12. a3 ♘a5 13. h5 ♗b7 14. ♕d2 ♘c5= Rubinetti — Panno, Buenos Aires 1968 — 6/536; **9. f4** h6?! 10. ♘e6 fe6 11. ♕h5 ♔e7 12. ♗c4 ♕e8 13. ♕h3± Platonov — Dončenko, Dubna 1973 — 16/424; 9... ♗e7 — 8. f4; **9. h4** ♗e7 — 8... ♗e7

53 9... ♘de5!?△ b5 Gipslis

54 10... ♕c7 11. 0—0 ♘a5 [11... 0—0± Kurajica — Kuzmin, Jugoslavija — SSSR 1964] 12. ♕e2 ♘c4 13. ♗c1 b5 14. b3 ♘cb6 15. ♗b2 0—0 16. a4± Kuindži — Dončenko, SSSR 1970

55 11. ♕h5? ♘d4 12. ♗d4 e5 13. ♗e3 ef4 14. ♗f4 ♘e5 15. ♘d5 ♗e6∓ Tringov — Lombard, Skopje (ol) 1972 — 14/454

56 **11... ♖e8** 12. 0—0! ♗f8 13. ♕f3? ♕c7 14. ♖ad1 ♖b8 15. h5 ♘d4 16. ♗d4 b5∞ Medina — Tringov, Skopje (ol) 1972 — 14/455; 13. f5!± Matanović; **11... ♘d4** 12. ♕d4 b5 13. a4 ♗b7 14. 0—0 e5 15. ♕d2± Tarasev — Petrosjan, SSSR 1960

57 Padevski — Petrosjan, Zagreb 1965

58 **9... ♕a5** 10. 0-0-0 ♘d4 11. ♕d4 b5 12. ♔b1 ♗b7 13. f4 b4 14. ♘e2 h6 15. gh6 ♖h6 16. ♗g2 ♖h5 17. f5!± Unzicker — Medina, Hastings 1969/70; **9... ♘de5** 10. ♗e2 ♗d7 11. ♘c6 ♗c6 12. f4 ♘d7 13. 0-0-0 b5 14. ♗f3 ♗e7 15. ♔b1 0—0 16. ♕g2 ♖e8 17. h4 ♘b6 18. h5±→» Vasjukov — Đurašević, SSSR — Jugoslavija 1962

59 10... b5?! 11. ♘c6! [11. f4 ♗b7 12. ♖g1 ♘c5 13. ♗b5 ab5 14. ♘db5 ♕d8 15. ♘d6± Darga — Bertok, Bled 1961] ♕c6 12.

♗g2 ♗e7 13. ♖he1 0–0 14. ♗d4 ♖e8 15. f4 ♗b7 16. ♔b1 ♘c5 17. f5! b4 18. ♘e2 ♗f8 19. ♘f4 ♖ac8 20. g6!±→» Gufeljd–Tukmakov, SSSR 1971 — 11/367

60 15. b3± Hort–Andersson, Las Palmas 1973

61 8... ♘c5 9. ♗f4 e5 [9... ♘e5 10. b4 ♘a6 11. a3± Boleslavski] 10. ♗e3 [10. ♘d5!? Nikitin] a6 [10... ♘e6 11. ♘d5 ♘cd4 12. ♗d4 ed4 13. ♘d4 ♘g5 14. ♗b5 ♗d7 15. ♕d3± Gipslis] 11. ♗c5 dc5 12. ♕d8 ♔d8 13. 0-0-0 ♘d4 [13... ♗d7 14. ♘d5 ab5 15. ♘b6 ♖a2 16. ♖d7 ♔e8 17. ♗b5!+– Macukevič–Jakovljev, SSSR 1966] 14. ♘d4 cd4±

62 9... e5 10. ♗e3 ♗e7 11. h4 0–0 12. ♕d2 ♗e6 13. ♘d5± Krasnov–Judovič jr. SSSR 1966 — 3/492; 10... ♗e6!? Hort

63 10. ♗e5? de5 11. ♕d8 ♔d8 12. 0-0-0 ♗d7 13. ♘d6 ♗d6 14. ♖d6 ♔e7 15. ♖d2 h6∓ Meštrović–Ćirić, Beograd 1967

64 **10... a6**? 11. 0-0-0 ♘bc4 12. ♗c4 ♘c4 13. ♘d6! ♗d6 14. ♗d6 ♕b6 15. ♘a4 ♕c6 16. ♗c5!±; **10... g6**!? 11. ♕h3 [11. ♕e2 a6 12. 0-0-0±] ♗d7 12. 0-0-0 ♕b8 13. ♕g3±; **10... ♗d7** 11. ♗e5! de5 [11... g6?! 12. ♗d6!± Tajmanov] 12. g6 a6! 13. gf7 ♔e7 14. ♘a3 ♕c7 15. 0-0-0 g6 16. ♕h4 ♔f7 17. ♘c4! ♘c4 18. ♗c4 ♗e7 19. ♕g3! [19. ♕g4 ♖ad8 20. ♗b3 ♗c8 21. h4 h5 22. ♕g3∞ Plachetka–Hort, Luhačovice 1973 — 15/420] ♖ad8 20. ♗b3 ♗c8 21. h4 ♖d1 22. ♘d1!± Szabo–Ivkov, Hilversum 1973 — 15/423

65 11. ♗d6 ♗d6 12. ♖d1 0–0! 13. ♘d6 ♕e7=∞ Boleslavski

66 15. h4± Fischer–Bukić, Skopje 1967 — 4/538

67 **7. h3** d5; **7. ♗g2** ♘c6! [7... ♗e7 8. ♗e3 0–0 9. g5 ♘fd7 10. f4 ♘c6 11. h4 ♘d4 12. ♕d4± Savon–Espig, Suhumi 1972 — 14/453; 7... ♘fd7 8. 0–0 ♘c6 9. ♔h1 ♗e7 10. f4 0–0 11. g5 ♘d4 12. ♕d4 b5= R. Byrne–Spaski, San Juan (mct) 1974 — 17/475; 7... h6 — 6... h6] 8. ♘c6!? [8. h3!? Radulov] bc6 9. e5 ♘d5 10. ed6 [10. ♘d5 cd5 11. c4 de5 12. cd5 ♗b4 13. ♗d2 ♗d2 14. ♕d2 ♗b7∓] ♕d6! 11. ♘e4 ♕c7 12. c4 ♘f4 13. ♗f4 ♕f4 14. ♘f6!? ♔e7 15. ♘e4 h5!∓ Planinc–Ribli, Wijk aan Zee 1973 — 15/417

68 7... ♘g8 8. ♗g2 ♘c6 9. ♗e3 ♗d7 10. h4 h6 11. f4 hg5 12. hg5 ♖h1 13. ♗h1 ♘d4 14. ♕d4 ♘e7 15. ♕d2± Jakobsen–Sköld, Stockholm 1971/72 — 13/462

69 **8. ♖g1** b5 9. a3! [9. ♗d3 ♗b7 10. f4 ♘b6 11. ♗e3 ♘8d7 12. ♕h5 g6 13. ♕e2 ♘c5= Drimer–Martens, Lidköping 1969 — 8/423] ♗b7 10. ♗e3 ♘c5 11. ♕g4 ♘bd7 12. 0-0-0 ♗e7? 13. f4! ♘e4 14. ♘e4 ♗e4 15. ♗g2!± Vasjukov–Džindžihašvili, SSSR (ch) 1972 — 14/458; **8. a4**!? ♘c6 9. ♗e3 ♘de5 10. ♗e2 [10. ♘b3 ♘a5 11. ♘a5 ♕a5 12. f4 ♘c6 13. h4∞ Bronštejn–Lejn, SSSR 1974] ♘d4 [10... ♗d7 11. ♕d2 ♖c8 12. 0-0-0?! ♘a5∓ Matulović–Cvetković, Vrnjačka Banja 1974 — 17/473; 11. ♘b3!?± Cvetković] 11. ♕d4 ♘c6 12. ♕b6?!∓ R. Byrne–Spaski, San Juan (mct) 1974 — 17/472; 12. ♕d2!△ f4±↑; **8. h4**!?

70 **8... ♗e7** 9. ♕d2 [9. h4!?± Gufeljd] ♕c7 10. f4!± Gufeljd; **8... ♕c7**!?; **8... ♘c6** — 6... ♘c6

71 **9. ♕d2** ♗b7 10. f3 ♘c6 11. 0-0-0 ♗e7= Popović–Benkö, USA 1969; **9. f4** ♗b7 10. f5!? [10. ♗g2!? Kotov] b4 11. fe6 bc3 12. ef7! ♔f7 13. ♗c4! [13. ♕g4? ♕e7 14. ♗g2 ♘e5 15. 0–0 ♔e8∓ Kočijev–Tukmakov, SSSR 1972 — 14/451] ♔e8 14. 0–0 ♘e5 15. ♕e2 [15. ♘e6!? Gufeljd] ♘bc6 16. ♖f5 ♕e7!∞ Beljavski–Talj, Suhumi 1972 — 14/452; **9. ♗g2**!?

72 **10. h4**!? ♘c6 11. ♕e2 ♘de5 12. 0-0-0± Aleksander–Lundholm, corr. 1972; **10. ♖g1** ♘c6 11. ♘c6 ♗c6 12. ♕d4!? ♕c7 13. h4± Liberzon–Lejn, SSSR 1972 — 14/450

73 10... ♗e7 11. h4 ♘c5 [11... ♘b6? 12. ♘e6! fe6 13. ♕d4± Karklins–Commons, USA 1972 — 14/448] 12. f3 ♕c7 13. 0-0-0 ♘bd7 14. ♗b5!± Fischer–Najdorf, Leipzig (ol) 1960

74 Adorjan–Ostojić, Polanica Zdroj 1970 — 10/512

75 10. ♗g2 ♘8d7 11. f4?! e5! 12. ♘f5 g6! 13. ♘d6 ♗d6 14. ♕d6 ♘c4 15. ♕d3 ♘b2 16. ♕d5 ♘c4!∓ Estrin–Espig, Polanica Zdroj 1971 — 12/456

76 10... ♗b7 11. ♕g4!? ♘8d7 12. 0-0-0 g6 13. h4 ♖c8∞ Ničevski–Estrin, Albena 1973 — 16/423

77 12... e5?! 13. ♘b3± Balašov–Malich, Leipzig 1973 — 16/422

78 △ g6= Malich

79 **8... b5**? 9. ♗e6 fe6 10. ♘e6 ♕a5 11. ♗d2±; **8... ♕c7** 9. ♕e2! [9. ♗e6?! fe6 10. ♘e6 ♕c4 11. ♕d5 ♕d5 12. ♘d5 ♔f7 13. ♘ec7 ♖a7 14. ♗e3 b6∞] ♘c6 10. ♗e3± Boleslavski; **8... ♘c5** 9. a4 ♘c6 10. ♗e3 ♕b6 11. ♕d2± Gipslis

80 9. ♗e2 b5 10. a3 ♘bc6 [10... ♗b7 11. f4 ♘c4 12. f5 e5 13. ♘f3± Bronštejn–Korčnoj, Moskva 1963] 11. ♗e3 ♘d4 12. ♕d4 ♘c6 13. ♕d2 ♗e7 14. f4 0–0 15. 0-0-0 ♕a5= Nikitin

81 9... ♕c7 10. f4 ♘ec6 11. ♗e3 ♘d4 12. ♕d4 ♘c6 13. ♕d2 b5 14. f5 ♘a5 15. 0-0-0± Mihaljčišin–Stupica, Jugoslavija (ch) 1961

82 15. f4 0–0 16. h4 ♕a5 17. g6±↑ Day–Amos, USA 1969 — 8/424

83 **8... ♕c7** 9. ♕h5!? [9. 0–0 b5 10. ♖e1 ♘b6 11. ♗f4?! b4? 12. ♘d5! ed5 13. e5 ♔d8 14. g6!± Fajbisovič–Korelov, SSSR 1972 — 15/416; 11... e5! 12. ♗g3 ed4 13. e5 ♗e6∓; 11. f4!? Korčnoj] ♘c5 10. ♗e3 ♘c6 11. 0-0-0

♗d7 12. f4 g6 13. ♕e2 ♗g7? 14. e5± Timman – Röhrl, Madrid 1971 — 11/366; **8... b5** 9. 0–0 [9. f4 ♗b7 10. f5 e5 11. ♘b3 ♘c6 12. ♗e3 ♘a5 13. ♘a5 ♕a5 14. 0–0± Ćirić – Langeweg, Beverwijk 1967] ♗b7 10. ♗e3 ♘b6 11. ♕g4! ♘c4 12. ♗c1 g6 13. b3 ♗g7 14. ♖d1 ♘c6 15. ♘ce2!± Liberzon – Espig, Suhumi 1972; **8... ♗e7** 9. f4 ♘c6 10. ♗e3 — 6... ♘c6

84 **9. 0—0** ♗e7 10. ♘c6?! bc6 11. f4 e5 12. f5 h6!∓ Mednis – Padevski, Orense 1973 — 15/418; **9. ♗e3** ♘de5! 10. f4 ♘c4 11. ♗c1 ♕b6=; 11... h6= Malich

85 9... ♕b6 10. ♘b3 ♗e7 11. ♕e2 ♕c7 12. ♗e3 b5 13. 0-0-0 ♗b7 14. h4 b4 15. ♘d5!?± Andersson – Kuijpers, Wijk aan Zee 1971 — 12/455

86 10... ♘b6 11. ♕d3 ♕c7 12. ♗e3 hg5 13. hg5 ♖h1 14. ♗h1± Ghizdavu – Hübner, Graz 1972

87 15. a3 a5 16. b3!± R. Byrne – Penrose, Nice (ol) 1974 — 17/474

B 82 — 1. e4 c5 2. ♘f3 d6 3. d4 cd4 4. ♘d4 ♘f6 5. ♘c3 e6 6. f4

	6	7	8	9	10	11	12	13	14	
1	... ♗e7[1]	♗d3 ♘c6	♘f3 0–0[2]	0–0 ♘b4[3]	♕e1[4] b6	♕g3 ♗b7	a3 ♘d3	cd3 ♘d7	♗e3 ♘c5[5]	±
2	... ♘c6	♘b3 ♗e7	♗d3 e5[6]	0–0 a5	a4 0–0	♔h1 ♘b4	fe5[7] de5	♗g5		=
3	... ...	♗e3 ♗d7[8]	♕f3 ♘d4	♗d4 ♗c6	0-0-0 ♕a5	♗c4![9] 0-0-0[10]	♗b3 ♗e7	♖he1		±

1. e4 c5 2. ♘f3 d6 3. d4 cd4 4. ♘d4 ♘f6 5. ♘c3 e6 6. f4 ♘c6 7. ♗e3 ♗e7

	8	9	10	11	12	13	14	15	16	
4	♗d3[11] 0–0	0–0[12] ♘d4	♗d4 e5	fe5[13] de5[14]	♗e5 ♘g4	♗f4 ♗c5	♔h1 ♘f2	♖f2 ♗f2	♕f3 ♗b6[15]	∞
5	♕f3 0–0[16]	0-0-0 ♗d7[17]	♗e2 ♘d4[18]	♗d4 ♗c6[19]	g4 ♕a5	g5 ♘d7	♖hg1 b5	f5[20] ef5	♕f5 g6[21]	±
6	... ...	... ...	♖g1! ♘d4	♗d4 ♗c6	g4 ♕a5	g5 ♘d7	♕h5 ♖fd8[22]	f5 ef5	♗c4!	±
7	... ...	... ♕c7	♖d2[23] a6	g4 ♘d4	♗d4 b5	g5 ♘d7	♕h5[24]			±
8	... e5	♘c6[25] bc6	fe5[26] de5[27]	♗c4[28] 0–0	h3[29] ♗e6[30]	♗e6[31] fe6	♕e2[32] ♕b8[33]	0–0[34] ♕b2	♕c4 ♔h8[35]	=

1. e4 c5 2. ♘f3 d6 3. d4 cd4 4. ♘d4 ♘f6 5. ♘c3 e6 6. f4 a6

	7	8	9	10	11	12	13	14	15	
9	♗d3[36] ♘bd7	♕f3[37] ♕c7[38]	a4[39] ♘c5[40]	0–0 b6	♗d2 ♗b7	b4! ♘cd7[41]	♖ae1 ♗e7	♕h3! 0-0-0[42]	♕e3 ♖he8[43]	±
10	... ♘c6	♘f3 ♗e7	0–0 0–0	♕e1 ♕c7	♔h1 b5[44]	e5 de5	fe5 ♘d7	♕e4[45] g6	♗h6 ♗b7![46]	=∞
11	♗e3 ♘c6[47]	♕f3[48] ♕c7[49]	0-0-0 ♗d7[50]	g4 h6[51]	h4[52] h5	g5 ♘g4	♗h3 b5[53]	♖he1 ♘a5[54]	g6! 0-0-0[55]	±
12	... ♕c7	♕f3[56] ♗e7	0-0-0 ♘bd7[57]	g4! ♘c5[58]	g5 ♘fd7	♕h3 b5[59]	g6 b4	gf7[60] ♔f7	♘ce2	±

1. e4 c5 2. ♘f3 d6 3. d4 cd4 4. ♘d4 ♘f6 5. ♘c3 e6 6. f4 a6 7. ♗e3 ♗e7 8. ♗d3[61] ♘c6

	9	10	11	12	13	14	15	16	17	
13	0–0	♕f3[62]	♔h1[63]	♖ae1	a3	♘c6	♕h3	♗d4[65]	fe5	=
	0–0	♕c7	♗d7[64]	b5	♖ab8	♗c6	♖bd8	e5	de5[66]	
14	. . .	. . .	♖ae1	♗d4	fe5[68]	♕g3	♗c5	♔h1	♗c4[70]	±
	. . .	. . .	♘d4[67]	e5	de5	♗c5	♕c5	♕d6![69]	b5[71]	
15	♘b3	0–0[72]	♕f3[73]	♖ae1[74]	♕h3[75]	a3[77]	ab4[78]	e5	ef6	∞
	♕c7	b5	0–0	♗b7	♖ad8[76]	b4	♘b4	♘d3[79]	♘e1[80]	
16	. . .	. . .	. . .	g4!	♘e2	e5	♘g3[81]			±
	. . .	. . .	. . .	b4	d5	♘e4				
17	. . .	. . .	.	♖ae1[82]	a3[84]	cd3	♖c1	♘d4	b4	=
	. . .	. .	♗b7	♘b4[83]	♘d3	0–0[85]	♕d8	♘d7	♖c8[86]	
18	. . .	. . .	. . .	♕h3	♔h1	♗g1	♖ae1[89]	e5	♘c5	±
	. . .	. . .	. . .	h5[87]	♘g4[88]	g6	♗f6	de5	♗c8[90]	

1. e4 c5 2. ♘f3 d6 3. d4 cd4 4. ♘d4 ♘f6 5. ♘c3 e6 6. f4 a6 7. ♗e3 b5

	8	9	10	11	12	13	14	15	16	
19	a3[91]	♕f3	0-0-0	g4	♗d3	e5	♗e4	♘e4	♕f2	=
	♗b7	♕c7	♘bd7	♘c5	d5[92]	♘fe4	♘e4	de4	♗d5!?[93]	
20	. . .	. . .	♗d3[94]	0–0[96]	♖ae1	g4[98]	g5	♕g3	♘f3	=
	. . .	♘bd7	♗e7[95]	♖c8[97]	♘c5	g6	♘fd7	e5	0–0[99]	
21	♕f3	♗d3	g4	g5	0-0-0	f5!?	♕h3	♘ce2	cd3	=
	♗b7	♗e7[100]	g6[101]	♘h5	♘d7	♘e5[102]	b4	♘d3	♗g5[103]	

¹ 6. . . ♕b6 7. ♗e2 ♘c6 8. ♘b3 a6 9. ♗f3 ♗e7 10. ♕e2 0–0 11. ♗e3 ♕c7 13. a4± Timoščenko–Mihaljčišin, SSSR 1973

² 8. . . ♕b6 9. ♕e2 0–0 10. g4 ♘g4 11. ♖g1 ♘f6!? [11. . . f5 12. ef5 ef5 13. ♘d5 ♕d8 14. ♗d2 ♗h4 15. ♔f1 ♗f2!∓; 13. ♗d2 ♗h4 14. ♔f1 ♕f2? 15. ♕f2 ♗f2 16. ♖g2 ♗e3 17. ♗c4 ♔h8 18. ♖e1 ♗d2 19. ♖d2+–; 14. . . ♘d4 15. ♘d4 ♕d4 16. ♘b5±↑ Guljko–Tukmakov, SSSR 1970 — 9/393] 12. ♗d2 ♘b4 13. 0-0-0 ♘d3 14. cd3 g6△ ♗d7, ♖ac8±

³ 9. . . b5!?

⁴ 10. ♔h1 b6 11. ♗e3 ♗b7 12. a3 ♘d3 13. cd3 d5 [13. . . ♕d7!?] 14. e5 d4 [14. . . ♘d7 15. ♗d4±] 15. ♘d4 ♘d5 16. ♗g1 ♘c3 17. bc3 ♖c8± Spaski–Talj, Moskva 1971 — 12/450; 17. . . b5!⩱

⁵ 15. ♖ad1 ♔h8 16. ♘d4 ♗h4 17. ♕h3 ♗f6 18. f5± Kavalek–Timman, Amsterdam 1973

⁶ 8. . . 0–0 9. 0–0 a6 [9. . . e5 10. ♔h1 a6?! 11. f5 b5 12. ♗g5 ♗b7 13. ♗f6 ♗f6 14. ♘d5 ♖c8 15. a4±↑⟪ Matanović–Damjanović, Zagreb 1965] 10. ♕e2 ♕c7 11. a4 b6 12. ♗e3 ♘a5!?∞

⁷ **12. f5** ♗d7 13. ♘d2 ♗c6 [13. . . ♘d3 14. cd3 ♗c6 15. ♘c4 ♖e8 16. ♕b3 ♘d7 17. ♗e3 ♗f8 18. ♗b6±↑ Matanović–Udovčić, Zagreb 1965] 14. ♘c4 ♘d7=; 12. . . d5!=; **12. ♕e2**!?

⁸ 7. . . e5?! 8. ♘f3! [8. fe5 de5 9. ♘db5 ♕a5 10. ♗d2 ♗g4!∞; 9. ♘c6 ♕d1 10. ♘d1 bc6 11. ♘f2 ♗e6=⊥ Suetin–Krogius, Soči 1973 — 16/361; 8. . . ♘g4!?; 8. ♘c6 bc6 9. fe5 ♘g4! 10. ♗f4 ♕b6=] ♘g4 9. ♕d2 [9. ♗d2 ♕b6 10. ♕e2∞ Krogius] ♘e3 10. ♕e3 ef4 11. ♕f4±◯

⁹ 11. ♗f6 gf6 12. f5 0-0-0 13. ♗c4 ♕e5 14. a4 a6 15. ♖he1 ♔b8 16. ♕f2 ♖c8 17. ♕b6 ef5!∓⇆ Fuchs–Štejn, Kislovodsk 1966 — 2/432

¹⁰ 11. . . b5 12. ♗b3 b4 13. ♗f6 gf6 14. ♘e2 f5 15. ♕h5 ♗e4 16. ♗e6± Boleslavski

¹¹ **8. ♕d2** ♘g4 9. ♗g1 ♘d4 10. ♕d4 e5 11. fe5 ♘e5 12. ♘d5 [12. ♗b5 ♗d7 13. ♗d7 ♕d7 14. 0-0-0 ♕g4∞] ♗h4= Lutikov–Tukma-

kov, SSSR (ch) 1969 — 8/421; **8. ♕e2** e5 [8... 0–0 9. 0-0-0 d5 10. e5 ♘d7 11. ♕h5 ♖e8 12. ♗b5±; 11... ♘c5!?; 8... ♘d4 9. ♗d4 0–0 10. 0-0-0 ♕a5 11. ♕e1 b6!= Nikitin] 9. ♘f3 0–0!? [9... a6 10. 0-0-0 ♕a5 11. ♔b1 0–0 12. ♗d2!△ fe5, ♘d5, ♗c3±] 10. 0-0-0 ef4 11. ♗f4 ♖e8=

12 9. ♕f3?! e5! 10. ♘b3 a5 11. a4 ♘b4 12. h3 ♗e6∓ Bahruzi–Kočijev, Manila 1974

13 11. ♗e3 ♘g4 12. ♕f3 ♘e3 13. ♕e3 ef4 14. ♕f4 ♗f6 15. ♕f2 ♗e5∓

14 11... ♘g4!? 12. e6 ♗e6 13. ♗c4 ♘e3! 14. ♗e3 ♗c4 15. ♖f3 ♗f6=

15 17. e5∞ Spaski–Enklaar, Amsterdam 1973 — 16/360

16 8... ♗d7 9. 0-0-0 a6 [9... 0–0 — 8... 0–0] 10. g4 ♘d4 11. ♖d4 [11. ♗d4 e5 12. fe5 ♗g4 13. ♕e3 ♘d7∞] e5 [11... d5 12. ed5 ♘d5 13. ♘d5 ed5 14. ♕d5 ♗c6 15. ♕e5 f6 16. ♖d8 ♖d8 17. ♕c3 ♗h1 18. ♗b6+– Mesing–Barcza, Timisoara 1972 — 13/510; 11... ♘g4 12. ♕g4 e5 13. ♕g1 ed4 14. ♗d4 ♗f6 15. ♗b6 ♕c8 16. ♘d5±→] 12. fe5 ♘g4 13. ed6 ♗f6 14. ♘d5±

17 9... ♘d4 10. ♗d4 ♕a5 11. e5 de5 12. ♗e5 ♘d7 13. ♗d6± Boleslavski

18 10... a6? 11. g4 ♘d4 12. ♗d4 e5 13. fe5 ♗g4 14. ef6 ♗f3 15. fe7 ♕e7 16. ♗f3+–

19 11... ♕a5 12. e5 de5 13. fe5 ♗c6 14. ef6 ♗f3 15. fe7 ♖fe8 16. gf3! ♖e7 [Suetin–Peterson, SSSR 1964] 17. f4±→

20 15. ♕h5 b4 16. ♘d5!? [16. ♖d3 bc3 17. ♗c3 ♕a2? 18. ♖h3 ♗e4 19. g6! ♗g6 20. ♕h7!+–; 17... ♕a4! 18. ♖h3 ♗e4 19. b3 ♕a3 20. ♗b2 ♕c5△ ♗g6–+ Nikitin] ed5 [16... ♗d5 17. ed5 ♕d5 18. ♗f3±] 17. ♕h6! ♘e5 18. fe5!∞ Ostapenko–Kurkin, SSSR 1970 — 10/506

21 **16... ♘c5**? 17. ♗f6! b4 18. ♘d5± Bitman–Gik, SSSR 1965; **16... g6** 17. ♘d5! ♗d5 [17... ♗d8 18. ♘f6±] 18. ♕d5±

22 **14... ♘f6**? 15. gf6+–; **14... b5**? 15. f5 b4 16. ♗g7 ♔g7 17. ♕h6 ♔g8 18. g6+–; **14... ♖fc8** 15. ♖g3 ♘f8 16. f5! ef5 17. ♗c4 +–→; **14... e5** 15. ♗e3 ef4 16. ♗f4 ♘e5 17. ♖g3±

23 **10. ♘db5** ♕b8 11. g4 a6 12. ♘d4 ♘d4 13. ♗d4 b5 [13... e5?! 14. g5 ed4? 15. gf6 dc3 16. fe7△ f5±; 14... ♗g4 15. ♕g3! ed4 16. ♖d4! ♗e6 17. f5!±; 16... ♘e4 17. ♘e4! ♗f5 18. ♘f6 ♔h8 19. ♕h4±] 14. g5 ♘d7 15. ♗d3! [15. a3? b4 16. ab4 ♕b4 17. ♕h5 ♘c5 18. ♖g1 ♖b8 19. b3 ♗b7!∓ Šamkovič] b4 [15... ♗b7 16. ♕h3!± Suetin–Jimenez, La Habana 1969 — 8/420] 16. ♘d5!? ed5 17. ed5 [△ 18. ♗h7 ♔h7 19. ♕h5 ♔g8 20. ♗g7+–] g6! [17... f5 18. ♖de1 ♗d8 19. ♗g7! ♔g7 20. ♕h5△ ♕h6, g6+–; 18... ♖f7 19. h4 ♗b7 20. ♗f5± Talj–Larsen (m) 1965] 18. ♖de1 ♗d8 19. ♕h3 ♘e5 [19... ♗b6? 20. ♗g6+–] 20. ♕h6 ♗b6! 21. fe5 ♗d4 22. ♖e4! ♗f2! 23. ♖f1 ♕a7 24. e6 ♗b7∞⇆ Nikitin; **10. g4** ♘d4 11. ♖d4 e5 12. ♖c4 ♗g4 13. ♕g3 ♕b8 14. ♖g1 g6∞; **10. ♖g1**!? a6 11. g4 ♘d4 12. ♗d4 b5 13. g5 ♘d7 14. f5!±

24 Bednarski–Schmidt, Polanica Zdroj 1971 — 12/448

25 **9. ♘f5**?! ♗f5 10. ef5 ♘d4 [10... e4!? 11. ♘e4 ♘e4 12. ♕e4 d5=/∞ Česnauskas–Vališev, SSSR 1974] 11. ♗d4 ed4=; **9. ♘b3** ef4 10. ♗f4 0–0=; **9. ♘de2** ef4 [9... 0–0?! 10. f5 ♕a5 11. 0-0-0 b5 12. ♔b1 b4 12. ♘d5±; 9... ♗g4 10. ♕f2 ♕a5 11. ♘g3 h5 12. ♗d3±] 10. ♘f4 0–0 11. h3 ♘e5 12. ♕f2 b6 13. ♗d4 ♗b7 14. 0-0-0∞ Bronštejn–Furman, SSSR 1965; **9. fe5** de5 [9... ♘e5 10. ♗b5 ♗d7 11. ♕e2±; 10... ♔f8!? 11. ♕e2 ♘fg4 12. ♘d5 a6 13. ♗d3 ♘e3 14. ♕e3± Boleslavski; 10... ♘fd7 11. ♕e2 0–0 12. 0–0 ♘b6 13. ♘f5 ♗e6 14. ♖ad1 ♕c7 (Ree–Hort, Wijk aan Zee 1971 — 11/364) 15. ♗d4∞] 10. ♘f5!? ♗f5 11. ef5 ♘d4 12. ♗d4 ed4 13. 0-0-0 ♕b6∞

26 10. f5?! ♕a5 [10... 0–0 11. 0-0-0! d5 12. ed5 cd5 13. ♗c4 e4 14. ♕e2 ♕c7 15. ♘d5 +– Ree–Reshevsky, Nice (ol) 1974 — 17/470; 10... ♗b7 11. 0-0-0 ♕a5 12. ♗c4 0–0 13. g4 d5 14. ed5 ♗a3!?∓; 13. ♗b3 ♖ad8 14. g4 d5 15. g5 d4 16. gf6 ♗f6∓ Hulak–Hernandez, Novi Sad 1974] 11. 0-0-0 ♖b8 12. g4 d5 [12... h6!?] 13. ed5 cd5 14. g5 [14. ♘d5 ♗b7 15. ♗c4 e4∓] ♗a3!∓

27 10... ♘g4!? (I. Zajcev) 11. ed6 ♕d6 12. ♗f4 ♘e5 13. ♕g3 ♗f6 14. ♗d3 [14. ♗c4 ♕e7! 15. ♗e5 ♗h4 16. ♗f7 ♔f8∓] ♖b8=/∞

28 11. h3?! ♗e6 12. ♗e2 0–0 13. 0–0 [Mnacakanjan–Boleslavski, SSSR 1967] ♕b8! 14. ♖ab1 ♗b4∓

29 12. 0–0?! ♘g4! 13. ♗f7 ♔h8 14. ♕e2 ♘e3 15. ♕e3 ♗a6! 16. ♖f5 g6 17. ♗g6 ♕d4! 18. ♕d4 ed4 19. ♖h5 dc3 20. bc3 [20. ♖h7 ♔g8 21. ♖e7 cb2 22. ♖b1 ♖f1–+] ♔g8 21. ♗h7 ♔g7 22. ♗f5 ♖h8∓ Džindžihašvili–Polugajevski, SSSR (ch) 1971 — 12/449; 13. ♖ad1 ♘e3! [13... ♕a5?! 14. ♔h1 ♘e3 15. ♗f7 ♔h8 16. ♕e3± Vasjukov–Lavdanski, SSSR (ch) 1965] 14. ♗f7 [14. ♕e3 ♕b6∓ Gufeljd–Furman, SSSR (ch) 1965; 14. ♖d8 ♗d8∓] ♔h8 15. ♕e3 ♕b6 16. ♕b6 ab6=/∞

30 **12... ♘e8** 13. 0–0 ♘d6 14. ♗d3! ♕a5 15. a3 ♗e6 16. b4 ♕c7 17. ♘a4±; **12... ♗b4** 13. 0–0 ♗c3 14. bc3 ♗e6 15. ♗b3 ♕a5 16. ♗g5 ♕c5 17. ♔h2 ♘d7 18. ♕g3± Kuzmin–Furman, SSSR 1966

31 13. ♗b3 c5 14. ♕e2 [14. ♗e6 fe6 15. ♕e2 c4 16. ♕c4 ♘h5! 17. ♕e6 ♔h8 18. ♘d5 ♗h4 19. ♔d2 ♘g3∓ Kogan–Petrjajev, SSSR 1969; 16. 0–0∓] ♖b8 [14... c4 15. ♗c4 ♘h5 16. ♗e6? ♘g3 17. ♕g4 ♘h1 18. ♗d5 ♗h4 19. ♔d2 ♘g3 20. ♗f2 ♘e4–+; 16. ♕h5 ♗c4=/∞] 15. ♗e6 [15. ♖b1 ♗b3 16. ab3 ♖b4 17. ♗g5 c4! 18. ♗f6 ♗f6 19. ♘d5 ♗h4 20. ♔f1 ♖b7 21. ♕c4 f5!∓→; 19. 0–0 cb3 20.

cb3 ♖b3 21. ♘d5 ♗g5∓ Gik—Boleslavski, SSSR 1966] fe6 16. 0—0! [16. b3? c4 17. ♕c4 ♕c8 18. 0—0 ♕c4 19. bc4 ♖b4∓ Talj—Balašov, SSSR 1973 — 15/415] ♖b2 17. ♕c4∞

32 14. 0—0! ♘d5 15. ♕e2 ♘e3 16. ♕e3 ♕b6∓

33 **14... ♘d5** 15. ed5 ♗h4 16. ♔d1 cd5 17. ♗c5±; **14... ♖b8** 15. 0—0! ♖b2 16. ♖ab1 ♖b4 17. ♕a6 ♕c7 18. a3! ♖b1 19. ♖b1 ♖a8 20. a4±↑ Hübner—Petrosjan, (mct) 1971 — 11/365; **14... ♕a5** 15. ♕c4 [15. 0—0 ♗c5!=] ♘d5!? 16. ed5 cd5 17. ♕a4 ♕c7∞

34 **15. 0-0-0** ♕b4 16. a3 ♕a5 17. ♕c4 ♔h8 18. ♖d3 ♖fe8 19. ♘a4 ♘h5∓ Kuindži—Balašov, SSSR 1974 — 17/469; **15. ♖b1** ♘e8 16. ♗f2 ♘d6 17. 0—0 ♕b4 18. a3 ♕c4= Boleslavski

35 17. ♖ab1 ♕a3 18. ♖b3 ♕a5 19. ♕e6 ♖fe8=

36 7. ♕f3 ♕b6?! 8. ♘b3 ♘c6 9. ♗d3 ♗e7 10. ♗e3 ♕c7 11. 0—0 [11. g4!? h6 12. 0-0-0 b5 13. ♖hg1 ♘d7 14. ♕f2 ♗b7 15. ♔b1 (Estrin—Kopilov, SSSR 1973) ♘a5±] 0—0 [Keres—Smislov, Jugoslavija (ct) 1959] 12. a3!?±

37 8. ♘f3 ♗e7 [8... ♕c7 9. 0—0 b5 10. ♕e1 ♗b7 11. ♔h1 ♗e7 12. e5 de5 13. fe5 ♘d5 14. ♘d5 ♗d5 15. ♕g3 0-0-0 16. a4 b4 17. ♗a6 ♔b8 (Lerner—Balašov, SSSR 1974) 18. ♗e3!? ±] 9. 0—0 ♘c5! [9... ♕c7 10. ♕e1! ♘c5 11. e5 ♘fd7 12. ♕g3 g6?! 13. f5 (Janošević—Benkö, Orense 1973) ♘d3 14. fe6 ♘3e5 15. ed7 ♗d7±; 13. ♗e3 b5 14. ♗d4± Karpov—Uddenfeldt, Skopje (ol) 1972 — 14/480] 10. ♔h1 [10. ♕e1!? 0—0 11. ♕g3 b5=] 0—0 11. a4 b6 12. ♗e3 [12. b4?! ♘d3 13. cd3 ♗b7 14. ♗e3 ♖c8 15. ♕b3 d5∓ Sigurjonsson—Štejn, Reykjavik 1972 — 13/507] ♗b7 13. ♗d4∞

38 8... ♘c5 9. 0—0 ♘d3 10. cd3 ♗e7 11. ♗e3 0—0 12. ♖ac1 e5 13. ♘de2 ♗g4 14. ♕f2 ♗e2 15. ♕e2 ♖c8 16. ♔h1 h6 17. d4± Gligorić—Stahlberg 1952; 12. g4!?± Takk—Türke, corr. 1968 — 5/435

39 **9. ♗e3**!?; **9. 0—0**!?; **9. g4**!?

40 9... b6!?

41 12... ♘d3 13. cd3△ ♖ac1±

42 14... 0—0 15. e5? de5 16. fe5 ♘e5 17. ♖f6 ♘d3—+; 15. ♖f3±

43 16. ♕e2± Ghizdavu—Ajanski, Albena 1971

44 **11... ♘d7**?! 12. ♕g3 [12. f5 ♘c5 13. ♕g3 (Janošević—De Castro, Orense 1973) ♗f6!? 14. ♗f4 ♘e5±; 12... ♘ce5! 13. ♕g3 ♗f6±] ♗f6!? [12... ♖d8? 13. f5 ♗f8 14. fe6 fe6 15. e5! ♘de5 16. ♗h7 ♔h7 17. ♘g5 ♔g8 18. ♕h4 g6 19. ♘ce4 1 : 0 Kuzmin—Muhin, SSSR (ch) 1972 — 14/478] 13. e5!? de5 14. ♘e4±; **11... ♘b4**!?

45 14. ♕g3 ♘de5 15. ♗f4 f6 16. ♖ae1±; 16. ♕h3±; 14... f5∞

46 **15... ♖e8**? 16. ♕f4±; **15... ♗b7**! 16. ♗f8 ♖f8=∞

47 7... ♘bd7 8. ♕f3?! ♕c7 9. g4 [9. 0-0-0?! b5! 10. ♗b5? ab5 11. ♘db5 ♕b8 12. e5 ♗b7 13. ♕g3 ♘e4 14. ♘e4 ♗e4 15. ♘d6 ♗d6 16. ♕g7 ♗f8!—+ Bielczyk—Jubicki, Polska 1972; 10. e5 ♗b7 11. ♕h3 de5 12. ♘e6 fe6 13. ♕e6 ♗e7 14. ♗b5 ab5 15. ♘b5 ♕c6 16. ♘d6 ♔d8 17. fe5 (Nej—Darga, Beverwijk 1964) ♘e4!—+; 10. ♗d3 b4 11. ♘b1 ♗b7 12. ♘d2∞] b5 10. g5 b4 11. gf6 bc3 12. fg7 ♗g7 13. b3± Ligterink—Zara, Groningen 1967 — 3/486; 8... e5!? 9. ♘f5 [9. ♘de2!?; 9. ♘b3!?] g6 10. ♘g3 ef4 11. ♗f4 ♘e5 12. ♕f2 ♗e7 13. 0-0-0 ♕a5∓ Grabczewski—Pytel, Polanica Zdroj 1973; 8. a4!?; 8. ♗e2 — B 84

48 8. ♗e2 ♗e7 9. 0—0 — B 84

49 **8... ♗e7**?! 9. 0-0-0 0—0 10. g4 ♕c7 11. g5 ♘d4 12. ♗d4 ♘d7 13. ♖g1 b5 14. f5 ♘e5 15. ♗e5 de5 16. f6 ♗c5 17. fg7 ♖d8 18. ♖g3! +— Andersson—Espig, Raach 1969 — 8/422; **8... e5**?! 9. ♘c6 [9. fe5 ♘e5 10. ♕g3 ♘h5 11. ♕f2 ♘g4 12. ♕f3 ♘e3 13. ♕e3±] bc6 10. fe5 de5 [10... ♘g4!?] 11. ♗c4±

50 9... ♗e7 10. g4?! ♘d4 11. ♖d4 [11. ♗d4?! e5 12. fe5 ♗g4?! 13. ♕g3 de5 14. ♗e5 ♕c8 15. ♖d2±; 12... de5! 13. ♕g3 ♗d6 14. ♗f2 ♗g4 15. ♘d5 ♘d5 16. ♕g4 ♘b4! 17. c3 0—0∓] e5!? [11... b5?! 12. g5 ♘d7 13. h4 ♗b7 14. ♗h3± Mesing—Musil, Jugoslavija 1972 — 13/511] 12. ♖c4 ♗g4 13. ♕g3 ♕d7! 14. fe5 [14. f5 d5? 15. ♘d5 ♘d5 16. ed5 ♗f5 17. ♕g7+—; 14... b5!∓] de5 15. ♕e5 0—0 16. ♖c7 ♗d6 17. ♖d7 ♗e5∓⊥; 10. ♖g1!±

51 10... ♘d4 11. ♖d4 e5 12. ♖c4 ♗g4 13. ♕g3 ♕b8 [13... ♕d7 14. fe5 de5 15. ♘d5! ♘d5 16. ed5 ♗f5 17. ♕e5 ♗e7 18. d6+—; 13... ♕e7 14. fe5 de5 15. ♗c5 ♕e6 16. ♗f8 ♔f8 17. ♖c7±] 14. ♗b6 ♗e6 15. fe5! de5 16. ♗c7±

52 11. ♖g1!?

53 13... ♘e3 14. ♕e3 ♘d4 15. ♕d4 0-0-0 16. f5±

54 **14... b4** 15. ♘d5 ed5 16. ♘c6+—; **14... ♘d4** ♖d4±

55 16. ♗g4 hg4 17. ♕g4 b4 18. ♘ce2 e5 19. ♘f5± Pavlov—Sax, Nice (ol) 1974 — 17/471

56 8. g4!? e5 [8... d5 9. e5 ♘fd7 10. a3 g5?! 11. f5! ♘e5 12. ♕e2!± Keres—Bilek, Leipzig (ol) 1960; 10... ♘c6!?△ ♘c5, ♗d7, 0-0-0 Keres] 9. ♘f5 g6 10. fe5 [10. g5!?] de5 11. ♗g5 ♘bd7 12. ♘e3±

57 9... b5 10. e5 ♗b7 11. ♗b5 — 7... ♗e7

58 **10... h6** 11. h4 b5 12. a3!? ♗b7 13. g5 hg5 14. hg5 ♖h1 15. ♕h1±; **10... ♘b6**!?

59 **12... g6**?! 13. b4 ♘b3 14. ♔b2 ♘d4 15. ♗d4 e5 16. ♘d5 ♕d8 17. ♗c3 ♘b6 18. ♕f3±; **12... 0—0** 13. ♖g1 ♖e8 14. f5 ♘e5

15. ♘f3± Hecht—van der Weide, Amsterdam 1971 — 12/447

60 14. ♕h7 ♖h7 15. gh7 bc3 16. h8♕ ♗f8=∞→

61 8. ♕f3 ♕c7 9. 0-0-0 b5?! [9... ♘c6!?] 10. e5 [10. ♗b5 ab5 11. ♘db5 ♕b7 12. e5 ♘d5 ∞] ♗b7! 11. ♗b5 ab5 13. ♘db5 ♕c3 [12... ♕c8 13. ♕g3 de5 14. fe5 ♘h5 15. ♕h3 g6 16. ♗h6!± Dueball—Ree, Bad Pyrmont 1970 — 10/510] 13. bc3 ♗f3 14. gf3 ♖a2 15. ef6 gf6 16. ♔b1△ ♘d6± Dueball

62 10. ♕e2 ♕c7 11. ♔h1 ♗d7 [11... ♘d4 12. ♗d4 e5 13. ♗e3±] 12. ♘f3!? ♘b4 13. e5 ♘g4!? [13... ♘e8 14. ♖ae1 ♗c6 15. ♗d4± Suetin—Langeweg, Kislovodsk 1972] 14. ed6 ♕d6 15. ♗h7!? ♔h7 16. ♘e4 ♕c6 17. ♘fg5 ♔g8 18. ♕g4 f6 19. ♕h5 fg5 20. ♘g5 ♗g5 21. fg5 ♕b5!∞

63 11. ♕g3?! ♘h5! 12. ♕h3? ♘f4!∓

64 11... b5? 12. e5 ♘d4 13. ♗d4 de5 [13... ♗b7? 14. ♕h3+−] 14. fe5 [14. ♗e5 ♕b7 15. ♕h3±→] ♘d7 15. ♕h3 h6 [15... g6 16. ♘e4 ♘e5 17. ♕g3 f6 18. ♘f6+−] 16. ♘e4 ♗b7 17. ♘f6 ♔h8 18. ♗e3+−

65 16. e5 de5 17. fe5 ♕e5 18. ♗b6 ♖d3! 19. cd3 ♕d6=∞ Nikitin

66 18. ♘d5 ♗d5 19. ♗e5 ♕e5 20. ed5 ♕b2 21. ♖f6 [21. ♖e7 g6 22. ♕h4 ♔g7∓] g6= Novopašin—Korčnoj, SSSR (ch) 1962

67 11... ♗d7 12. ♕g3 [12. a3 ♘d4 13. ♗d4 e5 14. ♗e3 ♗c6 15. f5 ♖ad8!△ d5= Nikitin; 12. ♘de2!? b5 13. g4 b4 14. ♘d1 d5 15. e5 ♘e4 16. ♘g3 ♘c5 17. ♘h5±; 13... ♘b4 14. g5 ♘e8 (Atanasov—Spiridonov, Bulgaria 1974) 15. ♘d4!?±] b5 [12... ♘h5 13. ♕h3 ♘d4 14. ♕h5 ♘c6 15. ♖f3±; 13... ♘f4 14. ♗f4! ♘d4 15. e5 ♘f5 16. g4 ♕b6 17. ♖f2 ♗h4 18. ♗g3+−; 16... de5 17. gf5 ef4 18. f6 ♗c5 19. ♖f2±→] 13. a3 ♔h8 [13... ♖ab8 14. ♘f3!? b4 15. ab4 ♘b4 16. e5 ♘h5 17. ♗h7 ♔h7 18. ♕h3 g6 19. g4±→] 14. ♘c6 ♗c6 15. e5 ♘g8 16. ♕h3 ♘h6 17. f5± Talj—Olafsson, Bled 1961

68 13. ♗e3±

69 **16... ♔h8**? 17. ♘d5 ♘d5 18. ♕e5 ♗e6 19. c4±; **16... ♘e8**?! 17. ♘d5 ♕d6 18. ♗c4± Hennings—S. Garcia, Bucuresti 1971

70 17. ♘d5 ♘d5 18. ed5 f6∞

71 18. ♘d5 ♘d5 19. ♗d5±

72 10. ♕e2 b5 **11. g4** ♗b7 [11... 0—0?! 12. g5 ♘d7 13. 0—0 ♖e8 14. ♖f3! ♘f8 15. ♖af1 ♖b8 16. ♖g3 b4 17. ♘d1 d5 18. e5 g6 19. ♘f2 ±→ Planinc—Gašić, Sarajevo 1970 — 9/342] 12. g5 ♘d7 13. 0—0 [13. h4!?] g6 14. a4 b4 15. ♘d1 ♗f8 16. c3 ♗g7∞ Tringov—Langeweg, Amsterdam 1970; **11. 0—0** ♗b7 12. ♖ae1 ♘b4 13. a3 ♘d3 14. cd3 ♖c8 [14... e5!?] 15. ♘d4 ♕d7 16. ♘d1 ♗d8 17. ♘f2 0—0 18. g4!± I. Zajcev—Ungureanu, Moskva 1969 — 8/368

73 11. a4 b4 12. ♘b1 a5 13. ♘1d2 0—0 14. ♔h1 [14. ♕e2 e5 15. f5 d5 16. g4 (Andersson—Štejn, Reykjavik 1972 — 13/400) ♗b7!?∓⇆] e5 15. f5 d5 16. ♕f3 ♖d8∞ Olafsson—Štejn, Moskva 1971 — 13/399

74 **12. e5**?! de5 13. fe5 ♘e5! 14. ♕a8 ♘eg4 15. ♗f4 [15. ♖f3 ♕h2 16. ♔f1 ♕h1 17. ♗g1 ♘h2—+] ♕b6 16. ♔h1 ♗b7∓; **12. a3** ♗b7 13. ♖ae1 [13. ♕g3 ♖fe8 14. ♖ae1 b4 15. ab4 ♘b4 16. e5 de5 17. fe5 ♘d3 18. cd3 ♘d7∞] ♖ac8 14. g4 [14. ♕h3 b4∓ Kuprejčik—Talj, SSSR 1970 — 10/463] b4 15. ab4 ♘b4 16. g5 ♘d7 17. ♘d4 ♘c5= Kuprejčik—Rojzman, SSSR 1970; **12. a4** b4 13. ♘e2 e5 14. f5 d5 15. ♘g3∞ Spaski—Talj, Tbilisi (mct) 1965

75 **13. ♗f2**?! ♖ac8 14. ♕h3 ♘b4∓ Ciocaltea—Polugajevski, La Habana 1962; **13. g4** b4 14. ♘e2 d5 15. e5 ♘e4 16. ♘g3 ♘g3 17. ♕g3 d4∞ Zajcev—Tukmakov, SSSR 1972

76 **13... b4**?! 14. ♘a4 ♘d7 15. e5 g6 16. ed6 ♗d6 17. ♘ac5± Gheorghiu—Hamann, Harrachov 1967 — 4/449; **13... ♖fd8** 14. g4 ♘e8 15. ♘d5±; **13... ♘b4** 14. a3 ♘d3 15. cd3 ♖ac8 16. ♘d4 ♖fe8 17. g4 ♘d7 18. g5 ♗f8 19. f5 ef5 20. ♘f5 ♘e5=

77 14. g4 ♘b4 15. g5 ♘d7 16. f5 ♘d3 17. cd3 b4 18. ♘e2 ef5= Ciocaltea

78 15. ♘a4 ♘d7 16. e5 g6 17. ed6 ♗d6 18. ♘ac5 ♘c5 19. ♘c5 ♗a8!=

79 16... de5!? 17. fe5 ♕e5 18. ♗b6 [18. ♖f6? ♖d3!∓] ♕g5 19. ♗d8 ♖d8=∞

80 18. fe7 ♗g2 19. ef8♕ ♖f8∞ Nikitin

81 ± Mojsejev

82 12. a4 b4 13. ♘b1 [13. ♘e2 ♘a5 14. ♗d4 e5! 15. ♘a5 ♕a5 16. fe5 de5 17. ♕f5 0—0∓ Bogdanović—Szabo, Sarajevo 1972 — 14/396; 14. ♘a5 ♕a5 15. g4 ♘d7 16. g5 ♘c5 17. ♘d4 g6 18. ♘b3± Ghizdavu—J. Szabo, Romania 1972 — 14/384; 15... d5!? 16. e5 ♘e4=] a5 [13... ♘a5 14. ♘a5 ♕a5 15. ♘d2 ♕h5∞ Hartston—Radulov, Hastings 1972/73 — 15/369] 14. ♘1d2 0—0 15. ♔h1 ♘b8!? 16. ♘d4 ♘bd7 17. ♘b5 ♕b8 18. ♖ae1 ♖c8 19. ♕h3 ♘c5= Parma—Petrosjan, Moskva 1971 — 12/397; 17. ♕h3!?

83 **12... 0-0-0**?! 13. h3 ♘d7 14. ♕f2 ♖dg8 15. a4 b4 16. ♘b5! ab5 17. ab5 ♘cb8 18. c3 bc3 19. ♖c1±→ Ciocaltea—Asmundsson, Reykjavik 1974 — 17/402; **12... ♖c8**!? 13. ♕h3 ♘b4 14. a3 ♘d3 15. cd3 0—0 16. ♕g3 e5= Gheorghiu—Štejn, Moskva 1971 — 12/414

84 **13. ♕g3** 0—0 [13... g6?! 14. a3 ♘d3 15. cd3 h5 16. ♖c1 ♕d8 17. h3 ♖c8 18. ♘e2± Vogt—Hort, Havirov 1971 — 12/410] 14. f5 ♔h8 15. fe6 fe6 16. ♘d4 ♗c8= Espig—Cobo, Timisoara 1972; **13. ♕h3** ♘d7 [13... e5?! 14. a3 ♘d3 15. cd3 ♖c8 16. ♕g3 ef4 17. ♕f4 0—0 18. ♘d4!± Ciocaltea—Mašić, Baja 1971 —

11/328] 14. a3 ♘d3 15. cd3 ♘c5 16. ♘c5 dc5 17. f5 [Ciocaltea – Darga, Romania – BRD 1971 — 11/314] ef5 18. ♖f5 0 – 0 =

85 14. . . ♖c8!? 15. ♖c1 ♕d7 [15. . . ♕b8 16. ♘d4 0 – 0 =] 16. ♕g3 g6 17. ♘d4 ♘h5!? 18. ♕h3 f5∞ Tringov – Gheorghiu, Teesside 1972 — 13/393

86 Ciocaltea – Bobocov, Bucuresti 1971 — 12/396

87 **12. . . ♖d8**?! 13. a4 b4 14. ♘e2 0 – 0 [Locev – Peterson, SSSR 1963] 15. a5 ♖d7 16. g4±↑; **12. . . ♘b4** 13. a3 ♘d3 14. cd3 e5 15. ♖ac1 ♕d8 [Tukmakov – Csom, Zagreb, 1971 — 11/326] 16. fe5 de5 17. ♕g3±; **12. . . ♖c8** 13. a4 b4 14. ♘b1 ♘b8 15. ♘1d2 ♘bd7 16. ♖ac1 e5 17. c3 bc3 18. ♖c3 ♕d8 [Ghizdavu – Židkov, Varna 1973 — 16/346] 19. ♖c8!±

88 13. . . g6 14. f5!? [14. a3?! ♘g4 15. ♗g1 f5 16. ♖ae1 ♔f8∞] ♘g4 15. fe6 fe6 16. ♘d4±

89 15. ♗e2 ♗f6 16. ♖ad1 0-0-0 17. ♗g4 hg4 18. ♕g4 ♖h4 19. ♕e2 ♖dh8⩱↑ Kostro – Schmidt, Polanica Zdroj 1968 — 6/475

90 **17. . . 0—0**?! 18. f5! gf5 19. ♘b7 ♕b7 20. ♕h5+ – Kuzmin – O. Rodriguez, Cienfuegos 1973 — 15/370; **17. . . ♗c8** 18. ♕f3 ♖b8 19. b4±↑ Kuzmin

91 **8. e5**?! (Keres) de5 9. fe5 ♘d5 10. ♘d5 ♕d5 11. ♗e2 ♗b7 12. ♕d2 ♕e5 13. 0-0-0 [13. ♗f4 ♕d5?! 14. 0-0-0 ♕d7 15. ♕c3 ♗d5 16. ♘f5!± Kelvi – Benkö, USA 1966; 13. . . ♕c5 14. 0-0-0 ♗e7 15. ♘b3 ♕c8 16. ♘a5 ♗d5 17. ♕e3 ♘c6∓ van der Weide – Malich, Amsterdam 1971] ♗e7 14. ♘f3∓; **8. ♗d3** ♗e7 [8. . . ♗b7 9. 0 – 0 b4 10. ♘a4 ♘e4?! 11. f5 e5 12. ♘e6! ♕a5 13. ♘b6 fe6 14. ♕h5 ♔d8 15. ♗e4 ♗e4 16. ♕h4+ – Ilijin – Nagy, Romania 1972 — 14/336; 9. . . ♗e7∞] 9. 0 – 0 b4 [9. . . ♕c7 10. ♕f3 ♗b7 11. a4 b4 12. ♘b1 ♘bd7 13. ♘d2 0 – 0 14. g4 Ciocaltea – Lombard, Skopje (ol) 1972 — 14/479; 14. . . ♘c5 15. g5 ♘fd7 16. f5 ef5 17. ♘f5 ♘e5∞] 10. ♘b1 ♗b7 11. ♘d2 ♘bd7 12. ♕f3 ♘c5 [Balašov – Džindžihašvili, SSSR (ch) 1972] 13. ♖ae1 0 – 0 14. ♗f2 =

92 **12. . . ♖c8**!?; **12. . . ♘fd7**!?△ ♘b6

93 **16. . . b4** 17. ab4 ♗b4 18. f5± Džindžihašvili – Dementjev, SSSR 1972 — 13/490; **16. . . ♗d5**!? =

94 10. 0-0-0?! ♖c8△ ♖c3∓

95 **10. . . ♖c8** 11. 0 – 0 [11. g4 ♖c3! 12. bc3 ♘c5∓ Velimirović] ♖c3?! [11. . . g6 12. ♕h3±] 12. bc3 ♘c5 13. ♕h3 [13. ♕e2 ♘fe4 14. c4 bc4 15. ♗c4± Nikitin] ♘fe4 [13. . . ♗e4!?] 14. c4 bc4 15. ♗c4 d5 16. ♗d3± Kovacs – Szabo, Hungary 1972; **10. . . g6**!? 11. 0 – 0 [11. g4 e5 12. g5 ♘h5 13. ♘de2 ef4 14. ♘f4∞] ♗g7 12. ♔h1 [12. ♖ae1 0 – 0 13. ♕h3 ♖c8 14. f5 ef5 15. ef5 ♘e5∞⇆ Nikitin; 12. ♖ad1 0 – 0 13. ♕h3 ♖e8 14. ♘f3 ♕c7 = Amos – Olafsson, Iceland 1971] 0 – 0 13. ♕h3 ♕e7?! 14. ♗f2 e5 15. ♘de2± Vogt – Malich, Zinnowitz 1971

96 11. 0-0-0 ♖c8 12. f5 e5 13. ♘b3?! ♖c3 14. bc3 0 – 0 15. ♔b2 d5!⩱ Bokučava – Džindžihašvili, SSSR 1970 — 9/395; 13. ♘de2!?

97 **11. . . 0—0** 12. ♕h3 ♕c7 13. ♖ae1 ♘c5 14. ♗f2 [Talj – Najdorf, Leipzig (ol) 1960] ♘fd7 = O'Kelly; **11. . . ♕c7** 12. ♖ae1 ♘c5 13. ♘b3 d5 [13. . . 0 – 0!?] 14. ♘c5 ♗c5 15. ed5 0 – 0 16. ♗c5 ♕c5 17. ♔h1 ♗d5 18. ♕h3 [Andersson – Ivkov, Praha 1970 — 9/392] ♗c4 19. ♘e4 ♘e4 20. ♗e4 g6 =

98 13. ♔h1 0 – 0 14. ♕h3 [14. ♗f2 d5 15. e5 ♘fe4∓ Ostojić – Gligorić, Beograd 1969 — 8/419] ♕d7! 15. ♗c1?! ♗d8 16. f5 e5 17. ♘f3 ♖e8∓ Browne – Polugajevski, Las Palmas 1974 — 18/473; 15. ♗f2!?

99 17. f5 ♖e8 18. ♘h4 d5 = Smislov – Tan 1963

100 **9. . . b4**!? 10. ♘ce2 ♘bd7∞; **9. . . ♕c7** 10. g4!? h6 [10. . . ♘c6 11. g5 ♘d7 12. f5! ♘c5 13. fe6 fe6 14. ♕h3! ♕d7 15. 0-0-0 (Sax – Tukmakov, Graz 1973) 0-0-0 16. ♖hf1±] 11. h4!? [11. g5 hg5 12. fg5 ♘fd7 13. g6 ♘f6 14. 0-0-0 ♘bd7 15. gf7 ♔f7 16. h4± Džindžihašvili – Dementjev, SSSR 1972 — 13/491; 13. . . ♘e5! 14. gf7 ♕f7 15. ♕f7 ♔f7 16. 0 – 0 ♔e7 17. ♗g5 ♔d7∓] b4∞

101 10. . . ♘fd7!? 11. g5 ♘c5∞

102 13. . . ef5?! 14. ♘f5±

103 17. fe6 ♗e3 18. ♕e3 [Platonov – Džindžihašvili, SSSR (ch) 1971] 0 – 0 =

B 83

1. e4 c5 2. ♘f3 d6 3. d4 cd4 4. ♘d4 ♘f6 5. ♘c3 e6 6. ♗e2

	6	7	8	9	10	11	12	13	14	
1	. . .	♗e3[2]	f4[4]	♕d2[6]	0-0-0	g4	g5	f5![10]	♗d4	±
	♘c6[1]	♗e7[3]	0 – 0[5]	a6[7]	♕c7[8]	b5[9]	♘d7	♘d4[11]	b4[12]	
2	. . .	. . .	. . .	. . .	♘f3[13]	♗f4	0-0-0	♗c4		=
	. . .	. . .	. . .	e5!?	ef4	♗g4	♖e8	♘e5[14]		

	6	7	8	9	10	11	12	13	14	
3	... ...	... ...	... ♗d7	♕d2[15] a6[16]	g4 ♘d4	♕d4 0–0	g5 ♘e8	0-0-0 b5	♔b1 ♕b8[17]	∞
4	... ...	0–0 ♗e7	♔h1[18] 0–0	f4 ♕c7[19]	♘b3[20] a6	a4 b6[21]	♗f3 ♗b7	♗e3 ♖fd8[22]		=
5	... ...	... ...	♗e3 ♗d7[23]	f4[24] ♘d4[25]	♕d4[26] ♗c6	e5[27] de5	fe5 ♘d5[28]	♘d5 ♕d5	♕d5 ♗d5[29]	=
6	... ...	... ...	... ...	♘db5 ♕b8	a4 0–0	f4 ♖c8!?[30]	♔h1[31] ♘b4	♗f3 a6	♘d4 e5![32]	=

1. e4 c5 2. ♘f3 d6 3. d4 cd4 4. ♘d4 ♘f6 5. ♘c3 e6 6. ♗e2 ♘c6 7. 0—0 ♗e7 8. ♗e3 0—0

	9	10	11	12	13	14	15	16	17	
7	♘b3[33] a6[34]	a4[35] b6[36]	f4 ♗b7[37]	♗f3 ♘b4[38]	a5 b5	♖f2 ♕c7	f5 e5!?[39]	g4 d5	ed5 e4	⩱
8	f4 e5	♘b3[40] a5	a4[41] ♘b4	♗f3[42] ♗e6[43]	♔h1 ♕c7	♖f2[44] ♖fd8	♖d2 ♗c4	♕g1![45] ♘d7[46]	f5! ♘c2[47]	±
9	... ♘d4	♕d4[48] b6	♗f3 ♗b7	♖ad1 ♕c8[49]	e5 de5!?[50]	fe5 ♗c5	♕f4 ♘d5	♘d5 ed5		⩲
10	... ♕c7	♕e1[51] ♘d4[52]	♗d4 e5	fe5[53] de5	♕g3 ♗c5	♗c5 ♕c5	♔h1 ♔h8!	♕h4[54] ♕e7[55]	♖ad1 h6![56]	=
11	... ...	♔h1 ♗d7	♕e1 ♘d4[57]	♗d4 ♗c6	♕g3 ♖ad8	♖ae1[58] b6	♗d3[59] e5[60]	fe5 ♘h5	♕h3![61] de5[62]	⩲
12	... ♗d7	♔h1 ♘d4[63]	♗d4[64] ♗c6	♗d3[65] ♘d7	♕e2[66] a6[67]	♖ad1[68] b5[69]	♖f3[70] e5	♗e3 ♗f6[71]	♘d5[72] ♗d5[73]	=
13	... ...	♕e1 ♘d4	♗d4 ♗c6	♕g3 g6[74]	♗d3[75] ♘h5[76]	♕f2[77] ♘f4	♕f4 e5	♕f2[78] ed4	♕d4 ♕a5[79]	=
14	... ...	... ...	... ...	♗d3 ♘d7[80]	♖d1[81] e5[82]	fe5 de5[83]	♗f2[84] ♗c5	♗c4 ♕b6	♗b3[85] ♘f6[86]	=
15	... ...	♘b3 a5[87]	a4[88] ♘b4[89]	♗f3[90] ♗c6[91]	♘d4[92] g6[93]	♖f2 e5	♘c6! bc6[94]	fe5 de5	♕f1! ♘d7[95]	±
16	... ...	... ♕c7!?	♗f3[96] ♖fd8[97]	g4!?[98] ♘a5	g5 ♘e8	♘a5 ♕a5	♕e1 ♗f8	♖d1 ♘c7	♗g2 ♘b5[99]	⩲
17	... ...	... a6	a4[100] ♘a5[101]	e5![102] ♘e8	♘a5[103] ♕a5	♕d2[104] ♕c7[105]	♗d4[106] f6[107]	♕e3[108] de5	fe5 fe5[109]	±
18	... ...	... ...	... ♘b4	♗f3[110] ♖c8[111]	♖f2[112] e5	♖d2 ♕c7	a5 ♗c6	♕e2 ♕b8	♖ad1[113]	⩲
19	... ...	... ...	... b6	♗f3[114] ♕c7[115]	♕e2[116] ♗e8[117]	g4 ♘d7	g5 ♘c5	♗g2 f6	h4[118]	⩲
20	... ...	... ...	... ...	♔h1 ♕c7	♗f3[119] ♖ab8[120]	♕e2[121] ♘a5	♘d2[122] b5!?	ab5 ab5	e5 ♘e8[123]	⩲

1 6... ♗e7 7. 0–0 ♗d7?! 8. ♘db5! ♗b5 [8... ♗c6 9. ♗f4! e5 10. ♗g5 ♘e4 11. ♗e7 ♔e7 12. ♘e4 ♗e4 13. ♕d2!± Adorjan–Trifunov, Sombor 1972] 9. ♗b5 ♘c6±; **6... ♘bd7** 7. ♘db5 ♘c5 8. ♗g5 a6 9. ♗f6 gf6 10. ♘d4 ♕b6 [10... b5?! 11. b4! ♘d7 12. ♗h5±↑; 10... ♗h6 11. 0–0 0–0=] 11. 0–0 ♕b2 12. ♕d2=∞; 11. ♖b1!?; 7. g4!? ♘c5 8. f3∞; 7. 0–0 a6 — B 84

2 **7. b3**? ♕a5∓; **7. ♘b3** a5 8. a4 ♘b4△ d5=

3 7... ♗d7 8. f4 ♕c7 9. ♕d2!? a6 10. 0-0-0 b5 11. e5!? de5 12. fe5 ♘e5! [12... ♕e5 13. ♗f3 ♕c7 14. ♖he1 ♗e7 15. ♗f4± Espig–Jansa, Stary Smokovec 1972] 13. ♗f4 b4 14. ♕e3 ♗d6∞; 9. 0–0; 8... ♘d4!?△ ♗c6

4 8. ♕d2 ♘d4 9. ♗d4 e5 10. ♗e3 0–0 11. 0-0-0 ♗e6∓; 11. 0–0=

5 8... a6 9. ♕d2 ♕c7 10. 0-0-0 0–0 [10... ♘d4?! 11. ♗d4 e5 12. ♗e3 b5 13. fe5 de5 14. ♘d5! ♘d5 15. ed5± Honfi–Talj, Suhumi 1972 — 14/462] 11. ♔b1 ♘a5 12. ♘b3 ♘c4 13. ♗c4 ♕c4 14. e5 de5 15. fe5 ♘e4 16. ♘e4 ♕e4 17. ♗g5± Klovan–Privorotski, SSSR 1969 — 8/430

6 9. ♗f3 e5!? 10. ♘f5 [10. ♘c6 bc6 11. fe5 de5 12. ♕d8 ♖d8 13. ♘a4 ♘g4 14. ♗c5 ♗h4 15. g3 ♗g5=] ♗f5 11. ef5 e4! 12. ♘e4 ♘e4 13. ♗e4 ♗h4=∞ Kostro–Kuzmin, Nice (ol) 1974 — 17/487

7 **9... ♘d4** 10. ♗d4 ♗d7 11. e5! de5 12. fe5 ♘e8 13. 0–0 ♗c6 14. ♖ad1± Suetin–Korčnoj, Leningrad 1967 — 3/495; **9... ♗d7** 10. ♘db5 ♘e8 11. 0-0-0 a6 12. ♘d4 ♘f6 13. g4 ♘d4 14. ♕d4 ♗c6 15. g5 ♘d7 16. ♖hg1 ♖e8 17. f5± Ujtumen–Spaski, Nice (ol) 1974

8 10... d5!? 11. ♗d3 [11. e5 ♘d7 12. ♘b3?! b5 13. ♗f3 ♘b6∓ Nikitin; 12. g4!?; 12. ♕e1!?△ ♕f2; 11. ed5 ed5 12. ♗f3 ♘a5=] de4 12. ♗e4 ♘e4 13. ♘e4 ♕d5 14. ♘c3 ♕a5 15. ♕e2±; 11... ♗b4!?

9 **11... d5** 12. ed5 [12. e5 ♘d7 13. g5∞] ♘d5 13. ♘d5 ed5 14. ♗f3±; **11... ♘d4** 12. ♗d4 e5 13. ♗e3 [13. fe5 de5 14. ♗e3 ♗g4 15. ♗g4 ♘g4 16. ♘d5 ♕d6 17. ♖hg1 (17. ♗g5 ♗g5 18. ♕g5 ♕h6∓) ♘e3 18. ♕e3=∞] b5 [13... ♗g4? 14. ♗g4 ♘g4 15. ♘d5 ♕d8 16. ♗b6 ♕d7 17. ♖hg1± Nikitin] 14. a3 [14. g5?! b4∞; 14. fe5!?] ♗g4 15. ♗g4 ♘g4 16. ♘d5±

10 13. ♘c6?! ♕c6 14. ♗f3 ♗b7 [14... ♖b8 15. ♔b1 ♘c5 16. ♕f2 ♗b7 17. f5 b4 18. f6∞ Vasjukov–Suetin, Moskva 1966 — 2/441] 15. ♖hf1 ♘b6 16. ♗b6 ♕b6 17. f5 ♔h8 18. ♗h1 b4 19. ♘e2 ♕a5 20. f6 ♗d8∓↑ Osnos–Kirilov, SSSR 1966

11 13... b4 14. f6 gf6 15. ♖hg1 bc3 [15... ♔h8 16. ♘d5! ed5 17. ♘c6 ♕c6 18. ♗d4 +–→] 16. ♕c3! [16. gf6 ♔h8 17. ♕c3 ♗f6∞] ♗d4 [16... ♔h8 17. ♘c6 ♘e5 17. ♘e7 ♕e7 18. gf6+–→] 17. gf6 ♔h8 18. fe7! ♕c3 19. ♗d4+– Cejtlin–Viner, SSSR 1970

12 15. f6 bc3 16. ♗c3 ♘c5 [16... ♗d8 17. fg7 ♖e8 18. ♖hf1 ♗b7 19. ♗h5 ♖e7 20. g6! +– Klovan–Zilberštejn, SSSR 1969] 17. fe7 ♕e7 18. e5 de5 19. ♕e3 ♘d7 20. ♗f3 ♖b8 21. ♗c6±↑

13 10. ♘f5?! ♘e4 11. ♘e7 ♕e7 12. ♘e4 ef4∓

14 **13... ♗h5**∞; **13... ♘e5**= Nikitin

15 **9. ♘db5** ♕b8 10. g4 a6 11. ♘d4 d5 [11... ♘d4? 12. ♕d4 e5 13. ♕d3 Gaprindašvili–Kušnir (m) 1972 — 13/473; 13... ♗g4 14. ♗g4 ♘g4 15. ♘d5 ♗h4 16. ♔e2±↑] 12. ed5 ♘d5 13. ♘d5 ♗h4 14. ♔d2 ed5∓ Gaprindašvili–Kušnir (m) 1972 — 13/474; **9. ♘b3** a6 10. a4 ♘a5!? 11. e5± Gaprindašvili–Kušnir (m) 1972 — 13/475; 10... b6! 11. 0–0 0–0 — 7. 0–0; **9. 0—0** — 7. 0–0

16 **9... ♕b8**?! 10. 0-0-0 a6 11. g4! b5 12. g5 b4 13. ♘c6! [13. gf6 bc3 14. ♕c3 ♘b4! 15. ♔b1 ♗f6 16. a3 a5± Suetin–Cvetković, SSSR–Jugoslavija 1969 — 7/353] bc3 14. ♕c3 ♘e4 15. ♕g7+–; **9... ♘d4** 10. ♗d4 ♗c6 11. ♗f3 0–0 12. 0-0-0 ♘d7 13. ♔b1 ♕c7= Mačuljski–Kočijev, SSSR 1974; 10. ♕d4!?

17 15. ♗f3 b4 16. ♘e2 ♘c7 17. f5 ♖c8∞

18 Maroczy; **8. ♘b3** 0–0 9. f4?! b5 10. ♗f3 [10. ♗b5 ♕b6 11. ♔h1 ♘e4∓] b4 11. ♘e2 ♕b6 12. ♔h1∓ Dementjev–Džindžihašvili, SSSR 1972 — 13/470; 10... ♗b7∓; **8. b3** 0–0 [8... ♕b6 9. ♘f3 a6 10. ♗b2± Bronštejn–Kaminov, SSSR 1945] 9. ♗b2 a6 10. ♔h1 ♗d7 [10... ♕b6!?] 11. f4 ♕a5 12. ♗f3 ♖fd8 13. g4 ♘d4 14. ♕d4± Tajmanov–Panov, SSSR 1944; 9... ♗d7!?△ ♘d4, ♗c6=; **8. f4** ♕b6!? 9. ♗e3 ♕b2 10. ♘db5 ♕b4∞

19 9... ♗d7 10. ♘b3 a5!? [10... ♘a5 11. ♗d2 b6?! 12. ♘a5 ba5 13. e5± Dementjev–Džindžihašvili, SSSR 1972 — 13/471] 11. a4 ♘b4 12. e5?! ♘e8 13. ♘d4 ♗c6! 14. ♘c6 bc6 15. ed6 ♘d6∓ Plachetka–Hort, ČSSR (ch) 1974 — 17/481

20 10. ♗f3 a6 11. g4!? ♘d4 12. ♕d4 ♘d7 [12... e5?! 13. ♕g1 ef4 14. g5±] 13. g5 b5 14. a3 ♗b7 15. ♕f2 f5!∓ Széles–Tompa, Hungary 1973

21 11... ♘a5!? Capablanca

22 **13... ♘b4**?! 14. ♕e2 d5 15. e5 ♘e4 16. ♗e4 de4 17. ♕f2 b5 18. ab5 ab5 19. ♘d4 ♗c6 20. ♕g3!± Maroczy–Euwe, Scheveningen 1923; **13... ♘a5**!?; **13... ♖fd8**= Pachman

23 8... ♕c7?! 9. ♘db5 ♕b8 10. a4 0–0 11. f4 b6 12. ♗f3± Sokolov–Zacrzewski, Polska 1974 — 18/449

24 9. ♘b3 a6 [9... ♘a5?! 10. ♕e1 a6 11. f4 ♗c6 12.e5 de5 13. fe5 ♘d7 14. ♕g3± Žuhovicki–Vasjukov, SSSR (ch) 1969 — 8/426] 10. f4 [10. a4 ♘a5 11. ♘d2 0–0 12. f4 (Westerinen–Liberzon, Solingen 1974 — 18/448) ♕c7 13. ♕e1 b5∓ Liberzon] b5 11. ♗f3 [11. a3 0–0 12. ♗f3 ♖b8 13. ♕d2 ♕c7 14. g4?! ♗e8!

15. g5 ♘d7 16. ♕g2 ♘b6 17. ♖ae1 ♘c4∓ Štejn–Petrosjan, Las Palmas 1973 — 15/425; 14. ♖ad1!?△ ♘d4] b4 12. ♘e2 e5∞

25 9... a6 10. a4 ♘d4 [10... ♕c7 11. ♘b3 b6 12. g4 d5 13. e5?! ♘e4 14. ♘e4 de4 15. c3 ♘a5= Kavalek–Larsen, USA 1970 — 10/525; 13. ed5 ♘d5 14. ♘d5 ed5 15. c3±] 11. ♕d4 ♗c6 12. ♖fd1 0–0 13. a5?! ♖c8 14. ♗f3 d5∓ Tukmakov–Petrosjan, SSSR 1973 — 15/424; 13. b3∞

26 10. ♗d4 ♗c6 11. ♗d3 a6 12. ♔h1 b5 13. a3 0–0 [13... ♕d7 14. ♕e2 0–0 15. ♖ad1 ♕b7 16. e5± Zilberštejn–Kogan, SSSR 1974] 14. ♕e2 ♘d7=

27 11. ♔h1 0–0 12. a4 a6 13. a5 ♖c8 14. ♕d3 ♘d7! 15. ♗d4 e5!∓ Šusterman–Polugajevski, SSSR 1974 — 18/457; 13. ♗f3!?

28 12... ♕d4? 13. ♗d4 ♘e4 [13... ♘d7 14. ♘b5±] 14. ♘b5± Bajkov–Popov, SSSR 1974 — 17/486

29 15. ♗b5 ♗c6 16. ♗c6 bc6 17. ♖ad1 ♖b8=

30 11... ♖d8 12. ♕e1 [12. ♗f3 ♘b4?! 13. ♕e2 ♗c6 14. ♕f2 b6 15. ♘d4 ♗e8 16. ♖ad1± Zaharov–Zilberštejn, SSSR 1974 — 18/456; 12... ♗e8 13. ♕e2 a6 14. ♘d4 ♕c7 15. f5?! d5!∓ Podgajec–Polugajevski, SSSR 1973 — 15/427; 15. ♖ad1 ♘d4 16. ♗d4 e5=; 12. f5!?△ 12... ♘e5 13. ♕e1] ♘b4 13. ♖c1 [13. ♗d1!? e5 14. ♘e2!? d5 15. fe5 ♘g4 16. ♗f4± Ceškovski–Gufeljd, SSSR 1974; 13... d5!? 14. e5 ♘e4∞] ♗c6 14. ♘d4 d5 15. e5 ♘e4 16. ♘e4 de4 17. ♕g3 ♘d5 18. ♗f2± Ljubojević–Calvo, Madrid 1973

31 12. ♗f3!? Larsen

32 Torre–Larsen, Manila 1974 — 18/455

33 **9. ♕d2**?! a6 10. f4 [10. ♖ad1?! ♕c7 11. ♘b3 b5 12. f3 ♖fd8∓ Janowski–Lasker, 1924] ♕c7 11. ♖ad1 [11. ♗f3?! ♘a5! 12. ♕f2 ♘c4 13. ♗c1 e5!∓ Kroone–Euwe, Nederland 1923] ♗d7 12. ♗f3 ♘a5 13. ♕f2 ♘c4 14. ♗c1∓ Michel–Najdorf, Argentina 1944; **9. ♕e1** ♘d4!? 10. ♗d4 e5=; 9... e5!?∞

34 9... a5 10. a4±

35 10. f4 ♗d7 — 9. f4; 10... b5⇆

36 10... ♘a5 11. ♘a5 ♕a5 12. ♕e1 ♔h8±

37 11... ♕c7 12. ♗f3 [12. g4?! d5! 13. ed5 ♘b4! 14. de6 ♗e6 15. f5 ♗b3 16. cb3 ♖ad8 17. ♕c1 ♘d3∓ Leow–Stean, Teesside 1973] ♖b8 13. ♕e2 ♘b4 14. g4 ♘d7 15. g5 ♘c5 16. ♘d4 e5 17. fe5 de5 18. ♘f5 ♘e6= Lublinski–Kotov, SSSR (ch) 1949

38 **12... ♖c8**!?; **12... ♘d7**!?=

39 15... d5 16. ♗b6 ♕b8 17. ed5 ♘bd5 18. ♘d5 ♘d5 19. ♗c5± van Riemsdijk–Talj, Nice (ol) 1974

40 **10. ♘f5**?! ♗f5 11. ef5 ef4 12. ♖f4 d5 13. ♔h1 ♖e8 14. ♗g1 [14. ♗d4 ♗d6!? 15. ♗f6?! ♕f6 16. ♘d5? ♕h6!–+; 14. ♕g1 ♗d6 15. ♖h4 ♗e5 16. ♗f3 ♘e4∓ Torre–Quinteros, Manila 1974] ♗d6 15. ♖f3 ♗e5 16. ♖d3 ♕e7 17. ♗f3 ♗c3 18. ♖c3 ♕e5∓ Mecking–Spaski, Nice (ol) 1974 — 17/484; **10. fe5** de5 11. ♘c6 [11. ♘f5 ♗f5 12. ♖f5 ♕a5! 13. ♔h1 ♖ad8 14. ♕g1 g6 15. ♖ff1 ♘d4∓ Stean–Talj, Nice (ol) 1974 — 17/485; 14. ♗d3 ♘d4 15. ♖f1?! ♘e6 16. a3 a6 17. ♕f3 ♕c7 18. ♕h3 ♘f4!∓ Daskalov–Tringov, Bulgaria 1974 — 18/452; 15. ♗d4 ♖d4 16. ♘e2 ♖d7 17. ♘g3= Minev] bc6 12. ♕d8 [12. ♕e1 ♗e6 13. ♕g3 ♘d7 14. ♗g4 ♗g4 15. ♕g4 ♗c5=] ♖d8 13. ♖ad1± ⊥ Parma–Talj, Nice (ol) 1974

41 **11. ♔h1**?! a4 12. ♘c1 a3∓; **11. a3** a4 12. ♘c1!? ef4 13. ♗f4 ♘e5 14. ♘1a2= Levitina–Kozlovska (m) 1974

42 12. ♔h1 ♕c7 13. ♖c1!? ♗e6 [13... ♗d7!?] 14. ♘d2 ef4 15. ♘b5 ♕d8 16. ♗f4± Geler–Spaski, SSSR 1974 — 18/453; 12... d5!?∞ Gligorić

43 △ 13... ef4 14. ♗f4 ♘c2!

44 △ ♖d2, ♕g1, ♗b6

45 16. ♘b5?! ♗b5 17. ab5 a4 18. ♘c1 d5! 19. fe5 ♘e4 20. c3! ♘d2 21. ♗d2! [21. ♕d2? d4 22. ♗d4 ♘c2!∓] ♕e5 22. g3!? [22. cb4 ♕b2 23. ♘d3 ♕d4 24. ♖a3 ♕b6!∓ Karpov–Spaski, Leningrad (mct) 1974 — 17/483] d4 25. cb4 ♕b5 26. ♕e2=

46 16... ♘c2 17. ♖c2 ♗b3 18. ♗b6 ♕d7 19. ♖d2! ef4 [19... ♖dc8 20. fe5+–] 20. e5± Boleslavski

47 **17... h6** 18. g4 ♗g5 19. ♗g5 hg5 20. h4!± Boleslavski; **17... ♘c2** 18. ♖c2 ♗b3 19. ♖cc1 ♕b8 20. ♗d1 ♗d1 [20... ♗c4 21. b3 ♗a6 22. ♘d5±] 21. ♘d5± Boleslavski

48 10. ♗d4 b6 11. ♕d3 ♗b7 12. ♖ad1 ♖c8 [12... d5 13. ed5 ♘d5 14. ♘d5 ed5 15. ♗f3±; 12... g6!?] 13. ♕g3 d5 [Beljavski–Kavalek, Las Palmas 1974 — 17/482] 14. f5!?±↑

49 12... ♖c8 13. ♕a4±

50 13... ♘e8?! 14. ♕b4! ♗f3 15. ♖f3 ♕b7 16. ♕a4! [16. ed6? ♘d6 17. ♖d6 ♖ad8 18. ♗c5 ♕c7!∓] ♖d8 17. ♗f2 ♘c7 18. ed6 ♖d6 19. ♖d6 ♗d6 20. ♕d7+– Tatai–Kavalek, Bauang 1973 — 16/425

51 **10. ♘b3** b6!? [10... a6 11. a4 b6 — 9. ♘b3] 11. ♗f3 ♗a6!? 12. ♖f2 ♖fd8 13. ♕e1 [13. ♖d2 ♖ac8; 13... ♖ab8!?△ ♘a5] ♖ac8 14. ♖d1 ♗c4 15. ♘d4?! ♘d4 16. ♗d4 e5 17. ♗e3 d5!∓ Ciocaltea–Talj, Halle 1974 — 18/450; 15. ♘d2!?=; **10. f5** ♗d7 11. a4 ♘e5 12. ♔h1 ♘c4 13. ♗c1 ♖ac8 14. ♘db5 ♕b6= Zurahov–Platonov, SSSR 1963

52 **10... e5**?! 11. ♘b3 [11. ♘c6!? bc6 12. fe5 de5 13. ♗c4±] a5 12. a3 a4 13. ♘c1± Keri–Böök, Helsinki (ol) 1952; **10... ♗d7** 11. ♕g3 [11. ♘db5?! ♕b8 12. ♖d1 a6?! 13. ♘d6! ♗d6 14. e5 ♗e5 15. fe5 ♕e5 16. ♗f4 ♕c5 17. ♔h1 ♘d5 18. ♘d5 ed5 19. ♗d3±↑;

12... ♘b4! 13. ♕d2 ♗b5! 14. ♗b5 Sg4!∓↑; 11. ♖d1?! a6 12. ♕g3 ♘d4 13. ♗d4 ♗c6 14. ♗d3 ♖ad8!? 15. ♔h1 b5 16. a3 ♕b7∓ Unzicker—Larsen, Palma de Mallorca 1969 — 8/429] ♘d4 [11... g6?! 12. f5 ♘d4 13. ♗d4 e5 14. ♗e3 ♗c6 15. ♗h6 ♖fd8 16. ♗c4± Klovan—Kozlov, SSSR 1974] 12. ♗d4 ♗c6 13. ♗d3 ♖ad8 14. ♖ad1 b6 15. e5 de5 16. ♗e5 ♕b7 17. f5 ♗c5 18. ♔h1 ♘h5 19. ♕h3 f6! 20. ♗f4 ef5 21. ♗f5 g6 22. ♗e6 ♔g7∞ Vitolinš—Platonov, SSSR 1964; 13. ♔h1! — 10. ♔h1

53 12. ♗e3!? ef4 13. ♖f4 ♗e6 14. ♗d4 ♘d7 15. ♕g3 [15. ♘d5? ♗d5 16. ed5 ♗f6∓] ♘e5 16. ♗d3 [△ ♘d5] ♕a5 17. ♔h1 [17. a3 ♗g5∞] ♖ac8∞

54 **16. ♖f6** gf6 17. ♕h4 ♖g8 18. ♕f6 ♖g7 19. ♖d1 ♗e6=; **16. ♗d3** ♕e7! [16... ♗e6? 17. ♕h4 ♖ae8 (17... ♕e7 19. ♕g5±) 18. ♖f6 ♕e7 19. ♘d5 ♗d5 20. ed5 e4 12. ♗e4± Unzicker—Penrose, Adelboden 1969 — 8/428] 17. ♖ae1 ♗d7 18. ♘d5 ♘d5 19. ed5 ♖ae8=

55 16... ♕b6!? 17. ♗d3 h6 18. ♘d5 ♘d5 19. ed5 ♕d6 20. c4 f5∓ Nikitin; 18. ♖ae1±

56 **17... ♗e6**? 18. ♕g5 ♘d5 19. ♕e7 ♘e7 20. ♘d5± Hennings—Espig, DDR 1973; **17... h6**! 18. ♕g3 b6= Spaski—Talj, SSSR 1974 — 18/451

57 **11... e5**? 12. fe5 de5 13. ♕g3±; **11... a6** — B 85

58 14. e5 de5 15. ♗e5 ♕b6 16. f5 ef5 [16... ♗d6!?] 17. ♖f5 [17. ♗c7? ♕b2 18. ♗d8 ♖d8 19. ♖ab1 ♕c2 20. ♖fc1 ♕d2 21. ♖d1 ♘e4!−+ Jovčić—Estrin, corr. 1965] ♗d6! 18. ♖g5 [18. ♕g7? ♔g7 19. ♗f6 Suetin—Bagirov, SSSR (ch) 1963; 19... ♔g6!−+] g6! 19. ♗d3 ♗e5 20. ♕e5 h6 21. ♖g3 ♖d4= Bojković—Kuzmin, Jugoslavija—SSSR 1964

59 15. e5 de5 16. ♗e5 ♕b7 17. ♗d3 g6 18. ♕h3 b5= Kondratjev—Platonov, SSSR 1962

60 15... ♘e8 16. ♕h3±↑

61 17. ♕f3 de5 18. ♗e3 ♘f6=

62 **18. ♘d5** ♗d5 19. ♗e5 [19. ed5 ed4 20. ♕h5 g6=] ♕e5 20. ed5 ♕g5 21. ♖f5 ♕h4! 22. ♕h4 ♗h4 23. ♖h5 ♗e1 24. ♗h7=; **18. ♗e5**!? ♕e5 19. ♖f5 ♘f4! 20. ♖e5 [20. ♕g4? ♘d3!−+; 20. ♕g3 ♕f5!−+] ♘h3 21. ♖e7 ♘f2 22. ♔g1 ♘d3 23. cd3 ♖d3 24. ♖a7 ♖d2 25. b3 f5 26. ♘d5!±⊥

63 10... ♕b8!? 11. ♗f3 [11. ♘b3 ♖d8 12. a3 ♗e8 13. ♗f3 b5 14. ♕e2 (Ceškovski—Astašin, SSSR 1968 — 6/539) b4!? 15. ab4 ♕b4 16. ♖a4 ♕b8=; 12. ♗f3!?] ♖c8 [11... ♖d8 12. ♘b3 ♗e8 13. ♕e2 ♘d7 14. ♖ad1 a6 15. f5!±↑ Kremenecki—Agejčenko, SSSR 1974; 12... b5!?] 12. ♕e2 ♘d4 13. ♗d4 e5 14. ♗e3 ♗e6= Klovski—Suetin, SSSR 1968 — 6/540

64 11. ♕d4 ♗c6 12. ♖ad1 ♕a5 [12... d5 12. e5 ♘e4±; 12... ♕c7 13. f5 e5 14. ♕d3 ♖fd8 15. ♘d5± Dementjev—Kopilov, SSSR 1972 — 14/459] 13. f5 [13. b4 ♕c7 14. b5 ♗e8△ ♘d7∞] e5 14. ♕d3 h6 [14... b5 15. ♗g5 b4±] 15. ♗f2∞

65 12. ♗f3 ♘d7 [12... ♕c7 13. a4 a6 14. a5 ♖ac8 15. ♕d2 ♕b8 16. ♖fd1 ♖fd8 17. ♕f2 ♘d7 18. ♘a4 ♘c5!∞ Garcia—Holmov, La Habana 1965] 13. a4 e5 14. ♗e3 ef4 15. ♗f4 ♘e5= Ćirić—Krogius, Soči 1965

66 13. ♕h5 ♗f6! [13... g6 14. ♕h3 e5 15. fe5 de5 16. ♗e3 ♗g5 17. ♖ae1 ♗e3 18. ♖e3 ♘b6? 19. ♕h6±→ Kostro—Gasziorowski, Polska 1970 — 9/402; 18... ♘f6!∞] 14. e5 g6! 15. ♕e2 de5 16. fe5 ♗g7 17. ♖ae1 ♕g5 18. ♘e4 ♕h4!= Nikitin

67 **13... ♘c5** 14. ♗c5 dc5 15. e5 ♕b6 [15... ♕e8?! 16. ♘e4 b6 17. ♘f6 ♗f6 18. ef6± I. Szabo—Lehmann, Hamburg 1965] 16. ♖ab1 ♖ad8 17. f5±↑; **13... e5** 14. ♗e3 ef4 15. ♗f4 ♕b6 [15... ♘e5 16. ♗e5 de5 17. ♗c4±] 16. ♖ab1 ♖ac8 17. ♗c4± Nežmetdinov—Jansa, Soči 1965

68 14. a4 ♕c7 [14... e5?! 15. ♗e3 ef4 16. ♗f4 ♕b6? 17. a5 ♕b2 18. ♗d2+−; 16... ♘e5 17. ♗e5 de5 18. ♗c4± Boleslavski; 14... ♖c8?! 15. f5 e5 16. ♗f2! ♗h4 17. ♗g1± Parma—Cvetković, Jugoslavija (ch) 1968 — 5/443] 15. ♘d5!? [15. a5 ♗f6=; 15. ♖ae1 e5 16. ♗e3 ef4 17. ♗f4 ♗f6= Boleslavski] ♗d5! [15... ed5? 16. ed5 ♗f6 17. dc6 bc6 18. ♕e4 g6 19. ♗f6 ♘f6 20. ♕d4±] 16. ed5 e5 17. ♗f5 ♗f6!=

69 14... ♕c7?! 15. ♖f3 e5 [15... b5? 16. ♘d5! ed5 17. ed5 ♗d5 18. ♗h7 ♔h7 19. ♖h3 ♔g8 20. ♗g7+−→; 20. ♕h5+−→] 16. ♗e3 [16. ♘d5 ♗d5 17. ed5 g6=] ef4 17. ♗f4 ♗f6 18. ♖h3 g6 [18... ♗e5 19. ♗g5!△ ♗c4, ♘d5±] 19. ♗c4 ♘e5 20. ♘d5 ♗d5 21. ♗d5 ♖ac8 22. c3± Liberzon—Boleslavski, SSSR 1966

70 **15. a3** e5 16. ♗e3 ef4 17. ♗f4 ♕c7= Banik—Osnos, SSSR (ch) 1966; **15. e5** de5 [15... g6?! 16. ♘e4 ♗e4 17. ♗e4 d5 18. ♗f3± Guljko—Kočijev, SSSR 1974] 16. fe5 ♕c7∞

71 16... ef4?! 17. ♗f4 ♕c7 18. ♘d5 ♗d5 19. ed5±

72 17. ♖h3 ef4 18. e5 g6!=

73 18. ed5 ♖e8= Boleslavski

74 Korčnoj; 12... ♕a5 13. ♗f3 [13. ♗d3 ♕b4! 14. ♕f2 ♘g4!∓; 13. a3 g6 14. ♗d3 ♘h5 15. ♕f2 ♘f4 16. ♕f4 e5 17. ♕f2 ed4 18. ♕d4= Nikitin] ♖fd8 14. ♖ae1 d5 15. ed5 ♗c5 16. ♗c5 ♕c5 17. ♕f2 ♕f2 18. ♔f2 ♘d5=⊥ Parma—Simagin, Jugoslavija—SSSR 1963; 14. ♔h1!?±

75 **13. ♕e3**?! ♕a5 14. e5 de5 15. fe5 ♘d7 16. ♖ad1 ♗c5 17. ♗c5 ♕c5 18. ♕c5 ♘c519. ♗f3 ♖ac8∓ Holmov—Korčnoj, SSSR 1964; **13. ♗f3** b5! 14. a3 [14. ♖ad1 b4 15. e5 ♗f3 16. ♖f3? ♘h5 17. ♕e1 bc3 18. g4 ♘g7 19.

ed6 ♗d6 20. ♖fd3 cb2!∓ Kuprejanov–Spaski, Canada 1971 — 13/476; 16. ♕f3 bc3 17. ef6 ♗f6 18. ♕c3 ♗d4 19. ♕d4 d5 20. ♖f3 ♖c8∓ Pietzsch–Panno, La Habana (ol) 1966 — 2/442] a5! 15. ♖ad1 b4 16. ab4 ab4 17. e5 ♗f3 18. ♕f3 bc3 19. ef6 ♗f6 20. ♕c3 ♗d4 21. ♕d4 ♖a6= Minić–Korčnoj 1964; **13. f5**!? e5 14. ♗e3 ♘e4 [14... ♗e4 15. fg6 ♗g6 16. ♗h6 ♕b6 17. ♔h1 ♖fc8 18. ♖ab1!△ 19. h4, 19. ♗g5±→] 15. ♘e4 ♗e4 16. ♗d3 ♗d3 17. cd3 ♔h8! 18. fg6 fg6 19. ♗h6 ♖f6 20. ♖f3 ♗f8 21. ♖f6⩱ Palatnik–Močalov, SSSR 1974 — 17/491

76 13... b5?! 14. f5! [14. a3 a5 15. ♘b5 ♘e4 16. ♕e3 ♘f6 17. ♖ae1 ♘g4 18. ♕e2 ♗b5 19. ♗b5 ♗f6∓ Barcza–Navarovszky, Hungary (ch) 1965; 14. ♖ae1 b4 15. ♘b1 d5 16. e5 ♘e4= Kirov–Bobocov, Bulgaria 1969 — 7/408; 15. ♘d1!? d5 16. e5 ♘e4 (Suslov–Vaskan, SSSR 1965) 17. ♕h3!?△ ♘e3-g4±] b4 [14... e5 16. ♗e3 b4 17. ♗c4!±] 15. fg6 hg6 [15... bc3 16. gh7 ♔h8 17. e5 de5 18. ♕e5+−] 16. e5! ♘h5 17. ♕g4 de5 18. ♗e5 ♕e8 19. ♘e2± Jurkov–Raškovski, SSSR 1966 — 1/301

77 14. ♕e3 ♘f4 15. ♖f4 e5 16. ♖f3 ed4 17. ♕d4 ♕a5 18. ♖af1 d5 19. ♔h1= Evans–Sherwin, USA (ch) 1967 — 3/498

78 16. ♗e5?! de5!? [16... ♗g5 17. ♕g3 ♗h4 18. ♕f4 ♗g5=] 17. ♕e5 ♗d6 18. ♕f6 ♕f6 19. ♖f6 ♗e5⩱ Lakić–Osmanović, Jugoslavija 1968 — 6/543

79 18. ♔h1 ♕e5= Ždanov–Kapengut, SSSR 1960

80 **12... g6**? 13. ♔h1 a6 14. ♖d1 ♖c8 [14... b5 15. a3 ♕c7 16. e5 ♘d7 17. ed6 ♗d6 18. ♘e4 ♗e4 19. ♗e4± Hennings–Espig, DDR 1973 — 16/427; 15. e5 de5 16. ♗e5! ♘d7 17. ♗e4±↑] 15. ♕g3 b5 [15... ♘h5? 16. ♕e3 ♘f4 17. ♗b6+−] 16. e5 de5 17. fe5 ♘h5 18. ♕g4±↑ Talj–Lavdanski, SSSR (ch) 1964; **12... ♕d7**?! 13. ♖d1 [13. a4 ♘g4 14. ♕g3 f5! 15. ef5 ef5 16. h3 ♗f6 17. ♘e2 ♘h6∞ Matanović–Udovčić, Titovo Užice 1966 — 2/444] b5 [13... ♘g4 14. ♗e2±] 14. ♗f6! ♗f6 15. e5 ♗e7 16. ed6 ♗d6 17. ♘e4 ♗e4 18. ♗e4±; **12... a6** 13. ♔h1 [13. ♖d1 b5 14. a3 ♕d7!? 15. ♕g3 ♖ad8 (Janošević–Hort, Amsterdam 1970 — 10/521) 16. ♗e3△ e5±] b5 14. a3 ♕d7 15. ♖f3?! ♘h5! 16. ♕e3 f5∓ Matanović–Korčnoj, Jugoslavija–SSSR 1965; 15. ♕e2!±

81 **13. ♕g3** e5 14. fe5 ♗h4 15. ♕h3 ♘e5 16. ♘d5 ♗d5 17. ed5 g6 18. c4 ♗f6= Unzicker –Najdorf, Santa Monica 1966 — 2/445; **13. ♔h1** e5 14. fe5 ♘e5 [14... de5 15. ♗f2 a6 16. a3± Matanović–Kuzmin, Jugoslavija–SSSR 1971; 15... ♕c7 16. ♗c4 ♘f6 17. ♗h4± Matanović–Bradvarević, Jugoslavija (ch) 1967 — 3/497] 15. ♖d1 ♗f6 16. ♕g3 [16. ♕e2 ♕e7 17. ♗c4! ♘d7 18. ♕f2± Parma–Polugajevski, Jugoslavija–SSSR 1969 — 7/409; 16... ♖c8 17. ♗c4 ♗d7 18. h3 ♘c4 19. ♗f6 gf6 20. ♘d5∞ Parma] ♕e7 17. ♗e2∞ Matanović–Kurajica, Jugoslavija 1968 — 6/542

82 13... ♕c7 14. ♔h1 ♗f6 15. ♗f6 ♘f6 16. ♕h4 ♖fe8 17. ♖de1 e5± Fuchs–Korčnoj, Erevan 1965

83 14... ♘e5 15. ♔h1 [15. ♘d5 ♗d5 16. ed5 ♗f6 17. ♔h1 g6 18. a4 ♗g7= Browne–Spaski, Siegen (ol) 1970 — 10/522] ♗f6 16. ♕e2 ♘d7 17. ♗c4 [17. ♗f6 ♘f6 18. e5? ♖e8! 19. ♖f6 gf6 20. ♕g4 ♔f8 21. ♗h7 ♖e5∓] ♗d4 18. ♖d4 ♕b6= Matanović–Korčnoj, Hamburg 1965

84 15. ♗e3 ♗c5= Suetin–Polugajevski, SSSR (ch) 1965

85 17. ♘d5? ♕b2 18. ♗c5 ♘c5 19. ♘e7 ♔h8 20. ♘c6 bc6∓ Nikitin

86 18. ♗c5 ♕c5 19. ♕f2 ♕f2=⊥ Parma–Udovčić, Zagreb 1965

87 10... ♘a5 11. e5! ♘e8 12. ♘e4 [12. ♗d3!? de5 13. fe5 ♘b3 14. ab3 ♗c6 15. ♗f4±↑ Nikitin] ♗c6 [12... d5 13. ♘ec5±] 13. ed6 ♘b3 [13... ♘d6 14. ♘d6 ♘b3 15. ♘f7+−] 14. de7 ♕e7 15. ab3 ♗e4 16. ♖a7± Boleslavski

88 11. a3?! a4 12. ♘d4 [12. ♘d2 d5 13. ed5 ed5! 14. ♘f3 ♘g4!∓] ♘d4 13. ♕d4 ♗c6 14. ♗f3 ♘d7= Fichtl–Savon, Halle 1974

89 11... e5 12. ♖f2 [12. ♔h1 ♘b4 13. ♗f3 ♖c8 14. ♖f2 ♖c4? 15. fe5 de5 16. ♖d2 ♕c7 17. ♕g1!+− Geler–Reshevsky, Palma de Mallorca (izt) 1970 — 10/523; 13... ♗c6 14. fe5 de5 15. ♕e2 ♕c7 16. ♕f2!± Kavalek–Naranja, Manila 1974; 13... ♗e6!? 14. ♖f2 ef4 15. ♗f4 ♕b6 16. ♘d4 ♘d7△ ♘e5∞] ♘b4 13. ♗f3 ♕c7 14. ♖d2 ♗c6 15. ♕e2 ♘d7 16. ♕f2 ♗d8 17. ♖ad1!±

90 12. ♘d4!?

91 12... e5 13. ♔h1 ♗e6 [13... ♗c6?! 14. fe5! de5 15. ♕e2 ♕c7 16. ♕f2 ♘d7 17. ♖ad1 ♔h8± Geler– Polugajevski (m) 1973 — 16/428] 14. ♖f2 ef4 15. ♗f4 ♕b6 16. ♘d4 ♘d7△ ♘e5∞ Geler; 13. ♕e2!± Geler; 13. ♖f2!±

92 13. ♕e2 ♕c7 14. ♕f2 ♘d7 15. ♖fd1 ♖fd8 16. ♖d2 b6 17. ♘d4± A. Zajcev–Mjagmarsuren, Tallinn 1971

93 13... ♕b8 14. ♕e2 ♖e8 15. ♖ad1± Klovan–Vasjukov, SSSR 1968 — 6/541

94 15... ♘c6 16. f5!±× d5

95 **17... ♕c8**?! 18. h3 ♘d7 19. ♗g4 h5 20. ♗d7 ♕d7 21. ♕c4± Karpov–Spaski, Leningrad (mct) 1974 — 17/488; **17... ♘d7**!?±

96 **11. g4**!? b6 12. ♗f3 ♖ab8 13. ♕e2 ♕c8± Nikitin; **11. ♔h1** ♖fd8 12. ♕e1 [12. g4?! d5 13. e5 ♘e4 14. ♘b5 ♕b8 15. c3 a6 16. ♘5d4 b5∞ Matulović–Bertok, Jugoslavija 1968 — 5/442; 12. ♗f3 ♖ac8 13. ♕e1 ♗e8 14. ♕f2 ♕b8 15. a4?! b6 16. g4 d5! 17. e5 ♘d7= Pavlov–Kestler, Nice (ol) 1974; 15. g4±] ♘b4?! 13. ♖c1 ♗c6 14. ♘d4! a5 15. ♗f3 d5 16. e5 ♘e4 17. ♘c6 ♕c6 18. ♗e4 de4 19. ♗g1± Geler–Lombardy, Amsterdam 1974 — 18/460; 12... ♗f8±

97 11... ♘a5 12. e5! de5 13. fe5 ♘b3 14. ef6 ♗c5 15. ab3 ♗e3 16. ♔h1 ♖fd8 [16... gf6 17. ♘e4±] 17. ♗e4 ♗c6 18. ♕f3 ♗h6 19. ♗c6 ♕c6 20. ♕h3±→ Klovan–Beljavski, SSSR 1974 — 18/459

98 12. ♕e1 ♗e8 [12... ♗f8 13. a3?! ♘a5 14. ♘a5 ♕a5 15. g4 ♖ac8 16. g5 ♘e8 17. f5 ♘c7∓ Bronštejn–Talj, SSSR 1971 — 12/462; 13. ♔h1±] 13. ♘b5!? ♕b8 14. c4 a6 15. ♘c3 b5? 16. c5! dc5 17. e5 ♘d5 18. ♘d5 ed5 19. ♗c5± Kuijpers–Kestler, Nice (ol) 1974; 15... ♘d7±

99 18. ♘b5 ♕e1 19. ♖fe1 ♗b5 20. ♖d2± Tukmakov–Langeweg, Amsterdam 1974 — 18/458

100 **11. g4** b5 12. g5 ♘e8 13. ♗d3 b4 14. ♘e2 ♘c7∞ Abrasimov–Koblenc, SSSR 1966; 13. a3!?; **11. ♗f3** ♖b8 [11... b5? 12. e5 de5 13. fe5± Makaričev–Mojsejev, SSSR 1968 — 5/444; 11... ♕c7 12. g4! ♖fb8 13. g5 ♘e8 14. a4± Lutikov–Petrjajev, SSSR 1970 — 10/520; 12... b5 13. g5 ♘e8 14. a3 ♖b8 15. ♕e2 ♕c8 16. ♕g2 a5 17. ♖f2± Suetin–Polugajevski, SSSR 1966] 12. g4 [12. a4!?] b5 [12... ♗e8!? (Boleslavski) 13. g5 ♘d7 14. ♗g4 b5 15. h4 ♘b6 16. f5 ♘c4 17. ♕e2 ♗d7!∞] 13. g5 ♘e8 14. ♕d2 ♘c7 15. a4?! ♕c8 [15... ba4 16. ♘a4 ♘b5 17. h4 (Suetin–Polugajevski, SSSR (ch) 1967 — 3/494) f6∞ Boleslavski] 16. ab5 ab5 17. ♖fd1 ♖d8 18. ♕f2 ♗e8 19. ♘a5 ♖a8∓ Smejkal–Tukmakov, Hastings 1968/69 — 7/406; 15. ♕g2!?△ 16. f5, 16. e5∞

101 11... ♕c7 12. ♕e1 ♘b4!? 13. ♗d1 d5 14. e5 ♘e4 15. a5! ♖ac8 16. ♗b6 ♕c4 17. ♖f3± Tukmakov–Beljavski, SSSR (ch) 1973; 12... b6!?

102 **12. ♘d2**?! ♕c7 13. ♕e1 ♖fb8 14. ♗f3 e5 15. f5 b5∓ Ždanov–Koblenc, SSSR 1966; **12. ♘a5** ♕a5 13. ♕d2 ♖fc8=

103 13. ♗d3?! ♘b3 14. cb3 g6 15. ♖f3 ♗c6 16. ♖h3 ♘g7 17. ♕e2 f6!∓ Gerlecki–Pytel, Polska 1972

104 **14. ♗f3**?! ♗c6 15. f5 ef5! [15... ♕e5? 16. ♗d4 ♗f3 17. ♖f3 ♕a5 18. fe6 fe6 19. ♕e2 ♖f3 20. ♕f3∞↑] 16. ♘d5 ♗d5 17. ♕d5 ♕d5 18. ♗d5 de5 19. ♖f5 ♘d6∓⊥ Kapengut–Malich, Sverige 1969; **14. ♘e4**!? ♕c7 15. ♗d4± Nikitin

105 **14... ♗c6**?! 15. b4! ♕c7 16. b5 ♗d7 ♗d4±→ Parma–Spasojević, Jugoslavija 1972; **14... ♖c8** 15. ♗d4 [15. ♔h1?! ♗c6 16. b4 ♕c7 17. b5 ab5 18. ab5 ♗g2 19. ♔g2 ♕c3 20. ♕c3 ♖c3 21. ♗d3 de5 22. fe5 ♘c7 (Tukmakov–Polugajevski, SSSR (ch) 1971) 23. ♗d4 ♖d3 24. cd3 ♘b5=; 15. ♗f3!? ♕c7 16. ♗d4±] ♗c6 16. ♕e3 ♘c7 17. ♗d3 ♘d5 18. ♕h3 h6 19. f5±→ Westerinen–Tukmakov, Hastings 1972/73 — 15/426

106 15. a5 de5 16. ♗b6 ♕d6! 17. ♕d6 [17. ♖ad1 ♗c6 18. ♕d6 ♘d6 19. fe5 ♘f5∓⊥ Hermlin–Liberzon, SSSR 1970] ♗d6!? [17... ♘d6 18. fe5 ♘f5 19. ♗f3 ♗c6 20. ♗c6 bc6 21. ♖ad1 ♘h4! 22. ♖fe1 ♘g6= Tukmakov–Zilberštejn, SSSR 1972 — 14/461] 18. ♘e4 [18. fe5 ♗e5 19. ♗c5 ♗c3 20. bc3 ♘f6∞] ♗b8 19. fe5 ♗c6 20. ♗f3 ♗e5 21. ♗c5 ♗e4 22. ♗e4 ♘d6 23. ♖ae1 f6 24. ♗d6 ♗d6 25. ♗b7 ♖a7= Boleslavski

107 **15... ♗c6** 16. ♕e3 ♖c8 17. ♗d3 g6 18. f5! de5 [18... ef5 19. ♗f5 gf5? 20. ♕g3△ ed6+–] 19. ♗e5 ♗d6 20. ♗d6 ♕d6 21. ♖ad1± Westerinen–Sanz, Torremolinos 1974 — 17/489; **15... de5** 16. fe5 ♗c5 17. ♘e4! ♗d4 18. ♕d4± Parma–Larsen, Teesside 1972 — 13/472

108 16. ♔h1 de5 17. fe5 f5 18. a5± Žuhovicki–Tukmakov, SSSR (ch) 1969 — 8/427

109 **17... f5** 18. ♗b6 ♕c8 19. ♖ad1±↑; **17... fe5** 18. ♗b6! ♕c8 19. ♖f8 ♗f8 20. ♖d1 ♘d6 21. ♕e5± Kapengut–Mihaljčišin, SSSR 1973

110 12. a5!? ♗c6 [12... d5?! 13. e5 ♘e4 14. ♗d3! ♘d3 15. cd3 ♘c3 16. bc3 ♖c8 17. ♕d2 ♕c7 18. ♖fc1± Geler–Bukić, Skopje 1967 — 4/543] 13. ♗f3 d5 14. e5 ♘e4±

111 12... e5 13. ♕d2 ♖c8 14. a5± Suetin–Tukmakov, SSSR 1970 — 10/524

112 13. a5 ♕c7 14. ♗b6 ♕b8 15. ♔h1 ♗c6 16. ♕e2± Masjejev–Persitz, corr. 1966

113 Kapengut–Šamkovič, SSSR (ch) 1972 — 14/460

114 12. g4!? ♗c8 13. g5 [13. ♗f3 ♗b7 14. g5 ♘d7 15. ♗g2 (Gaprindašvili–Kušnir (m) 1972 — 13/478) e5!= Kotov] ♘d7 14. ♕d2 ♖e8?! 15. ♗f3 ♗b7 16. ♗g2 ♗f8 17. ♖f3±↑; 14... ♗b7!?

115 12... ♖b8 13. ♕e2 ♕c8 14. ♗f2 [14. ♔h1 ♘a5 15. ♘d2!? (Adorjan–Pritchett, England 1973) ♗d8!?△ b5∞; 14. ♖ad1 ♘a5 15. e5 ♘e8 16. ♘a5 ba5 17. ♗c1 ♖b4 18. ♗e4 (Gaprindašvili–Kušnir (m) 1972 — 13/477) de5! 19. fe5 ♗c5 20. ♔h1 ♗d4!∞] ♘a5 15. ♗h4 ♘c4 16. e5± Friedgood–McGrilen, Nice (ol) 1974

116 13. g4 ♗e8 14. g5 ♘d7 15. ♗g2 ♘c5 16. f5 ♕d8 17. ♕g4 ♔h8 18. ♕g3± Sigurjonsson– Olafsson, Reykjavik 1974

117 13... ♖fc8!? 14. g4 ♗e8 15. g5!? [15. ♖ad1 ♘d7 16. g5 ♘c5∞ Fichtl–Malich, Halle 1974] ♘d7 16. ♕g2±

118 Spaski–Petrosjan, SSSR (ch) 1973

119 **13. g4**?! d5!? 14. e5 ♘e4 de4 16. c3 ♘a5∞; **13. ♕d2** ♖fd8 14. f5!? ♗c8 15. fe6 fe6 16. ♕e1 ♖b8 17. ♕g3±↑ Dementjev–Tukmakov, SSSR (ch) 1970

120 13... ♖fd8 14. ♕e2 ♗e8 15. ♗f2 [15. ♕c4? ♕b7 16. ♖ad1 ♖ab8 17. ♕e2 ♘d7∓ S. Garcia–Panno, Madrid 1973 — 16/426] ♖dc8 16. ♗g3 [16. g4!? ♘d7 17. g5 ♘c5 18. ♘d4±↑] ♘d7 17. ♖ad1 ♗f6 18. e5!± Geler–Korčnoj (m) 1971 — 11/374

121 14. ♖f2?! ♘a5 15. ♘a5 ba5 16. ♖b1 ♖b4∓↑ Hennings–Unzicker, Kislovodsk 1972; **14. g4**!? ♘a5 [14... ♗c8 15. g5 ♘d7 16. ♗g2 ♖e8 17. ♘c1 ♗f8 18. ♘d3± Geler–Muhin, SSSR 1972; 14... ♖fd8 15. g5 ♘e8 16. ♕d3 ♗c8 17. ♘d4 ♘e5 18. fe5 de5 19. ♘e6 fe6 20. ♕e2 ♘d6± Beljavski–Sax, Teesside 1974] 15. g5 ♘e8 16. ♘d2 b5∞

122 **15. ♕a6**?? ♘c4△ ♖a8–+; **15. ♗d4**?! e5! 16. fe5 de5 17. ♘d5 ♘d5 18. ed5 ♗d6 19. ♗c3 f5∓↑ Torre–Ribli, Athens 1971; **15. ♖ad1** ♘c4 16. ♗c1 b5 17. ab5 ab5 18. e5!? de5 19. fe5 ♕e5! 20. ♕e5 ♘e5 21. ♗f4 ♘c4 22. ♗b8 ♖b8=∞ Timoščenko–Palatnik, SSSR 1974 — 17/492

123 18. ♕f2 d5 [18... b4 19. ♘ce4±↑] 19. ♘e2!? [19. ♗d5? b4–+; 19. ♗a7 ♖b7 20. ♗d4 b4∞ Matanović–Ribli, Forssa–Helsinki 1972] ♘c4 20. ♘c4 bc4 21. ♗d4±

B 84

1. e4 c5 2. ♘f3 d6 3. d4 cd4 4. ♘d4 ♘f6 5. ♘c3 e6 6. ♗e2 a6

	7	8	9	10	11	12	13	14	15	
1	f4[1] ♕c7	♗e3[2] ♗e7[3]	g4[4] b5	g5 ♘fd7	a3 ♘c6	♘c6 ♕c6	h4 ♗b7	♕d4 0–0	0-0-0 ♘c5[5]	±
2	0–0 ♘bd7[6]	f4[7] b5	♗f3 ♗b7	e5[8] ♗f3	♘f3[9] de5[10]	fe5 b4[11]	♘a4 ♘d5	♗g5 ♗e7	♗e7 ♕e7[12]	∞
3	... ...	... ...	... ...	♔h1 ♕c7[13]	a3 ♗e7	♗e3 ♖c8	♕e1 ♗a8	♖d1 0–0	e5![14]	±
4	... ...	... ♕c7	♗f3[15] ♗e7[16]	♔h1[17] ♘f8[18]	♕e1 ♘g6	♗e3 0–0	♖d1 e5	fe5[19] de5	♘f5 ♗b4[20]	∞
5	... ...	a4 b6	f4 ♕c7	♗f3 ♗b7[21]	g4![22] ♘c5	♕e2 ♗e7	♕g2! 0–0	g5 ♘e8	♗e3 e5[23]	±
6	... ♘c6	f4 ♗e7	♗e3 0–0[24]	♕e1 ♘d4	♗d4 b5	♖d1!?[25] ♗b7[26]	♗f3 ♕c7	e5 de5	fe5 ♘d7[27]	±

1. e4 c5 2. ♘f3 d6 3. d4 cd4 4. ♘d4 ♘f6 5. ♘c3 e6 6. ♗e2 a6 7. 0–0 ♕c7 8. f4[28]

	8	9	10	11	12	13	14	15	16	
7	... b5?!	♗f3[29] ♗b7	e5 de5	fe5 ♘fd7	♗f4 ♗e7[30]	♔h1 0–0	♗b7 ♕b7	♕g4 ♔h8	♖f3 ♘c6[31]	±
8	... ♗e7	♗f3[32] ♘c6[33]	♔h1[34] 0–0	g4[35] ♘d4	♕d4 ♘d7	g5 b5	♗e3 ♗b7	f5[36] ♘e5	♗g2[37] ♖fe8[38]	=
9	... ...	♗e3 0–0[39]	g4[40] ♘c6[41]	g5 ♘d7	f5 ♘de5	f6 ♗d8	fg7 ♖e8	♕d2 b5	♗h5[42]	±
10	... ...	... ...	♕e1 b5	♗f3 ♗b7	e5 de5[43]	fe5 ♘fd7	♕g3[44] ♗c5[45]	♗b7 ♕b7	♔h1![46] ♗d4[47]	±
11	... ...	... ...	a4 b6[48]	♗f3 ♗b7	♕e1 ♘bd7[49]	♗f2![50] ♖ac8	g4[51] ♘c5	g5 ♘fd7	♖d1! ♘b8[52]	±

1 7. ♗e3 **b5**? 8. ♗f3 b4 9. ♘a4 e5 10. ♘f5±; **7... ♘bd7** 8. f4 b5 9. ♗f3 ♗b7 10. a3 ♕c7 11. ♕e2 [11. 0–0 ♘c5 12. e5 — 7. 0–0; 11... ♗e7!?] ♗e7 12. g4 ♘b6 13. 0-0-0 ♘c4 14. g5 ♘d7 15. h4± Klovan–Petkevič, SSSR 1970; **7... ♗e7** 8. g4 [8. f4 0–0 9. ♕d2 ♕c7 10. g4 h5∞ Cejtlin–Kuindži, SSSR 1971] ♘c6 [8... d5?! 9. ed5 ♘d5 10. ♘d5 ♕d5

11. ♗f3±; 8... h6!?] 9. g5 ♘d7 10. ♖g1 ♕c7∞ Campos–Mecking, San Antonio 1972; **7... ♕c7** 8. g4 b5 9. g5 ♘fd7 10. a3 [10. h4?! b4 11. ♘a4 ♗b7 12. f3 ♘c5∓] ♘c6 [10... ♘b6 11. f4 ♘8d7 12. 0–0 ♗b7 13. f5 e5 14. ♘b3 ♘a4 15. ♘d5 ♗d5 16. ♕d5 ♘db6∞ R. Byrne–Kavalek, USA (ch) 1972] 11. f4 ♖b8 12. f5 ♘de5 13. fe6 fe6 14. 0–0 ♗e7 15. ♘c6 ♕c6 16. ♗d3 ♗d8!= R. Byrne–Tukmakov, Moskva 1971 — 12/461

2 **8. g4**!? ♘c6!? [8... b5?! 9. g5 ♘fd7 10. a3 ♘b6 11. f5 ♘c6 12. ♘c6 ♕c6 13. 0–0 ♘c4 14. fe6 fe6 15. ♗c4 ♕c4 16. ♕f3± Klovan–Palatnik, SSSR 1973 — 16/431; 8... h6!?] 9. g5 ♘d7∞; **8. ♗f3** ♘c6 9. ♗e3 ♘a5 [9... ♗e7 10. ♕e2 ♘d4 11. ♗d4 e5 12. ♗e3 ♗e6 13. 0-0-0 (Vasjukov–Platonov, Dubna 1973 — 16/430) 0–0!?∞] 10. ♕d3 ♘c4 11. 0-0-0 — 8. ♗e3

3 8... ♘bd7 9. ♗f3 ♗e7 [9... ♘b6 10. ♕d3 ♘c4 11. 0-0-0! ♘e3 12. ♕e3 e5?! 13. ♘f5 h6 14. ♕d2 ♗f5 13. ef5± R. Byrne–Najdorf, Hastings 1971/72 — 13/483; 12... ♗e7 13. g4 — 8... ♗e7] 10. g4 ♘b6 11. ♕d3 ♘fd7 12. 0-0-0 ♘c5 13. ♕e2 ♗d7 14. g5±↑ Hartston–Bukić, Vrnjačka Banja 1973; 11. ♕e2!?

4 9. ♗f3!? ♘bd7 10. ♕e2 ♘b6 11. 0-0-0 ♘c4 12. g4 ♘e3 13. ♕e3 ♕c5 14. ♕e2± Kostro–Janetschek, Nice (ol) 1974 — 17/357

5 16. ♗f3 ♖fc8 17. h5 ♘a4 18. ♖d3 ♕c4 19. h6 ♕d4 20. ♗d4 ♘c5 [Suetin–Polugajevski, SSSR 1971 — 12/460] 21. ♖dd1±

6 7... b5?! 8. ♗f3! [8. f4?! b4? 9. e5 bc3 10. ef6 gf6 11. bc3 d5 12. c4± Timoščenko–Petrušin, SSSR 1973; 8... ♗b7!?; 8... ♕c7!?] ♖a7 [8... ♘fd7 9. e5 d5 10. ♖e1±] 9. ♕e2 ♖c7 [9... ♖d7 10. e5! de5 11. ♘c6± Smislov] 10. ♖d1 ♘bd7 11. a4± Smislov–Kottnauer, Groningen 1946

7 8. ♗e3 b5 9. a4 b4 10. ♘c6 ♕c7 11. ♘b4 d5 12. ♘a6 ♗a6 13. ed5 ♗e7 14. de6 fe6∞ Fajbisovič–Liberzon, SSSR 1970 — 9/403

8 **10. a3** ♕c7 [10... ♗e7? 11. e5±] 11. ♕e2 [11. g4!? h6!? 12. ♖e1 ♘b6∞ Nežmetdinov–Žilin, SSSR 1958; 11. ♕e1 ♗e7 12. ♔h1 ♖b8! 13. b3?! 0–0 14. ♗b2 ♖fe8 15. ♕g3 ♗f8 16. ♖ae1 e5 17. ♘f5 ♔h8= Talj–Smislov, Jugoslavija (ct) 1959] h5 [11... ♗e7 12. e5 de5 13. fe5 ♗c5 14. ♗e3 ♘e5 15. ♗b7 ♕b7 16. ♘e6 ♗e3 17. ♕e3 ♘fg4!? 18. ♘g7 ♔f8 19. ♘e6 ♔e8!= Nikitin; 12. g4!?] 12. e5 [12. ♗e3 ♗e7 13. ♖ad1 ♖c8 14. ♗f2 ♕c4 15. ♕e1 ♘g4∓ Bobkov–Simagin, corr. 1963] ♘g4∞; **10. ♗e3** ♕c7 11. a3 ♘c5 12. e5 de5 13. fe5 [Kirov–Padevski, Bulgaria (ch) 1972] ♕e5!∞; **10. ♕e1** [Aronin–Smislov, Moskva 1961] b4!?∞; **10. ♖e1** ♗e7△ 0–0∞

9 11. ♕f3 de5 12. ♘c6 ♕b6 13. ♔h1 [13. ♗e3 ♗c5∓] e4! 14. ♘e4 ♘e4 15. ♕e4 ♘f6 16. ♕f3 ♖c8= Schwarz–Simagin, SSSR 1964

10 **11... b4** 12. ef6 bc3 13. f5! [13. fg7 ♗g7 14. b3 ♕b6 15. ♔h1 ♘f6 16. f5± Gligorić–Simagin, Moskva 1963] ♕b6 [13... e5 14. fg7 ♕b6 15. ♔h1 ♗g7 16. bc3±] 14. ♔h1 cb2 15. ♗b2 ♕b2 16. fe6 fe6 [16... ♘f6 17. ef7 ♔d7 18. ♖b1 ♕c3 19. ♘d4+– Walker–Bowen, England 1967 — 4/544] 17. f7 [17. ♘d4? ♘f6∓ Lehmann–Benkö, Palma de Mallorca 1968 — 6/545] ♔d8 18. ♘d4 ♘c5 19. ♕g4 e5 20. ♘e6 ♘e6 21. ♕e6 ♕b5 22. ♖ab1 ♕c6 23. c4±→ Matanović; **11... ♘g4** 12. ♕e2 b4!? [12... de5 13. fe5 ♘de5 14. ♘e5 ♕d4 15. ♔h1 ♘e5 16. ♗f4±→] 13. ♘e4 d5 14. ♘g3 [14. ♘eg5!?] ♗c5 15. ♔h1 h5∞ Mednis–Gheorghiu, Los Angelos 1974 — 18/463

11 12... ♘g4 13. ♕e2 [13. ♕e1 b4 14. ♕g3 h5! 15. ♘e4 ♘c5 16. ♘c5 ♗c5 17. ♔h1 ♘f2 18. ♖f2 h4! 19. ♕g7 ♕d1 20. ♘g1 ♗f2 21. ♗e3 ♕a1 22. ♗f2 0-0-0∓; 16. ♘eg5 f6 17. ef6 gf6 18. ♘h3 ♗d6∓; 16. ♕f4 ♘e4 17. ♕e4 ♗c5 18. ♔h1 ♘f2∞ I. Zajcev] b4 [13... ♖c8 14. ♗f4 ♗e7 15. ♖ad1 ♕b6 16. ♔h1 ♘f8 17. ♘g5!+– Jansa–Planinc, Amsterdam 1974 — 18/464; 13... ♕b6 14. ♔h1 b4 15. ♕e4 ♖c8 16. ♕g4 bc3 17. bc3±] 14. ♘a4! [14. ♘e4?! ♘ge5 15. ♘e5 ♘e5 16. ♘g5 ♕b6! 17. ♔h1 ♕b5∓ Lehmann–Fischer, La Habana 1965] ♕a5 [14... ♘de5 15. ♘e5 ♕d4 16. ♔h1 ♘e5 17. ♗f4±] 15. b3 [15. ♕e4!? ♖c8 16. ♕g4 ♕a4 17. c4±] ♖c8 16. ♘g5± Bihovski–Čeremisin, SSSR 1965

12 Nemet–Bukić, Jugoslavija (ch) 1975

13 10... b4? 11. e5! ♗f3 12. ♕f3 de5 13. ♘c6 ♕c8 14. fe5 ♘e5 15. ♘e5 bc3 16. b3 ♗e7 17. ♘c6± Muhin–Gruševski, SSSR 1964

14 Averbah–Spaski, SSSR (ch) 1961

15 9. ♔h1 b5 10. e5?! de5 11. fe5 ♘e5 12. ♗f4 ♗d7! 13. ♗f3 ♖c8∓ Rossetto–Panno, Buenos Aires 1970 — 11/373; 10. ♗f3!?∞

16 **9... g6** 10. ♖e1 [10. ♗e3?! ♗e7 11. ♕e1 e5 12. ♘de2 b5= Nej–Popov, Tallinn 1973; 10. g4!? e5 11. ♘de2±] ♘c5 11. e5 de5 12. fe5 ♘fd7 13. b4 ♘b3 14. ♘d5 ed5 15. e6 ♘f6 16. ef7 ♔f7 17. ab3± Obuhovski–Dončenko, SSSR 1972; **9... ♖b8** 10. ♔h1 [10. a4 g6 11. ♗e3 e5 12. ♘de2 b6 13. ♕e1 ♗b7 14. ♖d1 ♗e7= Ceškovski–Dementjev, SSSR 1972 — 14/465; 11. ♔h1 ♗g7 12. ♘db5 ab5 13. ♘b5 ♕b6 14. ♘d6 ♔e7 15. e5 ♘e8 16. ♘c4 ♕c7 17. b3± Honfi–Ghitescu, Bucuresti 1973 — 15/430] b5 11. e5! de5 13. ♘c6 ♖b6 [12... e4 13. ♘e4 ♖b6 14. ♘e5 ♘e4 15. ♗e4 ♘e5? 16. fe5 ♕e5 19. ♕f3 ♕c7 18. ♗e3+–; 15... ♘f6 16. ♗d3± Klovan–Muhin, SSSR 1969 — 8/432] 13. fe5 ♘g4 [13... ♘e5 14. ♘e5 ♕e5 15. ♗f4 ♕c5 16. ♕e1±↑] 14. ♗g4 ♖c6 15. ♗f4 ♗b7 16. ♘e4 ♖c4 17. ♘g5± Klovan–Dementjev, SSSR 1972 — 14/464

17 10. g4 h6! 11. g5!? [11. h4?! g5! 12. fg5 hg5 13. ♗g5 d5∓↑ Day–Timman, Jerusalem 1967 — 4/545] hg5 12. fg5 d5! 13. ♕e2∞; 11. ♕e2!?

18 10... 0–0 11. g4! [11. ♕e1 ♖e8 12. g4 ♘f8 13. g5 ♘6d7 14. ♗e3± Boleslavski–Kan,

SSSR 1942] ♖d8 12. g5 ♘e8 13. ♗g2 ♘b6 14. f5± Nikitin—Nej, SSSR 1952

19 14. ♘de2 ef4 15. ♘f4 ♘f4 16. ♗f4 ♗e6= Magvik—Bigman, SSSR 1964

20 Darga—Petrosjan, Bled 1961

21 10... ♖b8?! 11. ♖e1 [11. g4!?; 11. ♕e2!?] ♗e7 12. ♔h1 [12. e5 de5 13. fe5 ♘e5 14. ♗f4 ♗d6∞⇆; 13. ♘c6 ♗c5 14. ♔h1 ef4∞] h5 [12... 0—0 13. e5±] 13. ♕e2 ♗b7 14. ♗e3 g6 15. ♖ad1± Timoščenko—Dementjev, SSSR 1973

22 **11. e5**? de5 12. fe5 ♘e5∓; **11. ♔h1** ♗e7 12. e5?! de5 13. fe5 ♘e5 14. ♗f4 ♗f3 [Žuhovicki—Polugajevski, SSSR (ch) 1969 — 8/431] 15. ♘f3 ♗d6 16. ♘d4∓ Boleslavski; **11. f5** e5 12. ♘b3 ♗e7 13. ♕e2 0—0 14. ♔h1 ♖ac8 15. ♗d2 ♖fe8△ d5= Romanovski—Kan, SSSR (ch) 1945; **11. ♕e2** ♗e7 12. ♗e3 ♖b8 [12... 0—0 13. ♔h1?! ♘c5 14. ♗f2 d5= Estevez—Talj, Leningrad (izt) 1973 — 15/429] 13. ♖ad1 g6!? 14. ♘b3 0—0 15. ♖fe1 e5= Rumjancev—Dementjev, SSSR 1973

23 16. ♘de2! ♗c6 17. f5±→ Kopajev—Alatorcev, SSSR 1938

24 9... ♗d7 10. ♕e1 b5 11. ♗f3 ♖c8 12. e5! de5 13. ♘c6 ♗c6 14. fe5 ♘d5 15. ♗d5! ♗d5 16. ♕g3 g6 17. ♖ad1± Adorjan—Doda, Luhačovice 1973; 10... ♕c7 — B 85

25 12. a3 ♗b7 13. ♕g3 g6!? 14. ♗f3 d5!? [14... ♕c7!?; 14... ♘d7!?] 15. ed5 [15. e5 ♘e4=] ♘d5 16. ♗d5 [16. ♖ad1 ♘c3 17. ♗c3 ♕b6 18. ♔h1 ♖fd8=] ♗d5 17. ♖ad1 ♗c4 18. ♖f3 ♖e8=; 14. ♗d3 ♘h5 15. ♕e3 ♕d7 16. ♖ad1 ♘f4 17. ♕f4 e5 18. ♗e5 de5 19. ♕e5 ♕d6!∞ Suetin—Anikajev, SSSR 1974

26 12... b4?! 13. ♘a4 ♘e4 14. ♗f3±

27 16. ♗b7 ♕b7 17. ♘e4±↑ Ceškovski—Petrušin, SSSR 1973

28 **8. ♗e3**?! b5! 9. f3 [9. a3 ♗b7 10. f3 ♗e7 11. ♕e1 ♘bd7 12. ♕g3 0—0∓ Wotulo—Larsen, Manila 1973 — 16/429; 9. f4 b4 10. e5 bc3 11. ef6 gf6 12. bc3 ♗b7∞⇆ Konstannopoljski] ♗b7 10. ♕d2 ♘bd7 11. a4 b4 12. ♘a2 d5!? 13. ♘b4 de4= Lundin—Kotov, Saltsjöbaden (izt) 1948; **8. ♗g5** ♗e7!? 9. ♕d3 ♘bd7 10. ♖ad1 b5 11. a3 ♗b7= Gurgenidze—Zajčik, SSSR 1974; 8... ♘bd7 — B 94

29 9. e5 b4 [9... ♘fd7 10. ♗b5! ab5 11. ♕f3 ♘b6 12. ♘db5± Ibrahimoglu—Bouaziz, Lugano (ol) 1968 — 6/546] 10. ♗f3 bc3 11. ♗a8 cb2 12. ♗b2 de5 13. fe5 ♕e5 14. ♘c6 ♕c7 15. ♘b8 ♕a7 16. ♗d4 ♕a8 17. ♖b1 ♗e7∞ Šah Zade—Muhin, SSSR 1964

30 12... ♘c6 13. ♘c6 ♗c6 14. ♔h1? ♘c5 15. ♕e1 b4 16. ♘e4 ♘e4 17. ♗e4 ♗e4?! [17... ♗e7!?] 18. ♕e4 ♖d8 19. ♖ad1± Tarve—Szabo, Tallinn 1969 — 7/411; 14. ♘e4!±

31 17. ♖h3 ♖fd8 [17... ♘d4 18. ♕h5 h6 19. ♗h6+—] 18. ♘f3 ♘f8 19. ♘e4 ♘d4 20. ♘fg5±→ Klovan—Anikajev, SSSR 1972 — 13/484

32 **9. g4** d5 10. ed5 ♘d5 11. ♘d5 ed5 12. ♗e3∞ Šapošnikov—Kan, SSSR 1950; 9... ♘c6!?; **9. ♕e1** b5?! 10. ♗f3 ♗b7 11. ♕g3 b4 12. e5! de5 13. fe5 bc3 14. ♕g7+— Planinc—Popov 1964; 9... 0—0 10. ♗e3 — 9. ♗e3; **9. ♔h1** 0—0 10. ♕e1 b5?! 11. ♗f3 ♗b7 12. e5 de5 13. fe5 ♘fd7 14. ♗b7 [14. ♕g3 ♔h8 15. ♗f4 ♘c5 16. b4 ♘cd7 17. ♘e4± Šabanov—Palatnik, SSSR 1972; 15... ♘c6!?] ♕b7 15. ♕g3 ♕c7 16. ♗f4 ♔h8 17. ♘e4 ♘c6 18. ♘f3 ♘b4 19. ♘f6!±→ Klovan—Přibyl, Hungary 1970 — 9/404; 10... ♘c6! 11. ♗e3 — B 85; **9. a4** 0—0 10. ♘b3 ♘c6 11. a5?! b6 12. ab6 ♕b6 13. ♔h1 ♖d8 14. ♗f3 a5∓ Tringov—Ornstein, Nice (ol) 1974; 10. ♗e3 — 9. ♗e3

33 9... 0—0 10. ♔h1 ♖e8?! 11. ♕e1 ♘bd7 12. g4! ♘f8 13. g5 ♘6d7 14. a4± Ceškovski—Čeremisin, SSSR 1964; 10... ♘c6 — 9... ♘c6

34 **10. ♘b3** b5 11. e5?! de5 12. fe5 ♘d7 13. ♗f4 ♗b7 14. ♕e1 0—0 15. ♕g3 ♔h8 16. ♖ae1 b4 17. ♘e4 ♘ce5 18. ♔h1 f6∓ Medina—Benkö, Las Palmas 1972; **10. ♘de2** 0—0 11. g4 [11. b3 b5 12. ♗b2 ♗b7 13. ♔h1 ♖fd8 14. a3 d5 15. ed5 b4! 16. ab4 ♘b4∓ Suetin—Spaski, SSSR 1963; 11. ♗e3 — B 85] b5 12. g5 ♘d7 13. ♘g3 b4 14. ♘ce2 ♗b7 15. ♗e3 ♖fd8 16. c4 ♘c5∓ Klovan—Platonov, SSSR 1972; **10. ♘c6** bc6 11. e5 ♘d5 12. ♘e4 de5 13. fe5 ♕e5!? 14. c4 ♘c7 [14... ♘f4? 15. ♗f4 ♕f4 16. ♘f6!±; 14... ♘b6 15. ♗e3 c5 16. ♗f2!△ ♗g3±] 15. ♗d2∞↑

35 11. ♘de2?! b5 12. a3 ♗b7 13. g4 d5 14. ed5 [14. e5 ♘e4! 15. ♘e4 de4 16. ♗e4 ♘e5!∓] ♖ad8∓ Addison—Kristiansson, Reykjavik 1968 — 5/445

36 15. ♖f2?! ♖ae8 16. ♖g1 e5!? 17. ♕d2 ef4 18. ♗f4 ♘e5∓

37 16. f6 gf6 17. gf6 ♗f6 18. ♗h6 ♔h8! 19. ♗f8 ♖f8 20. ♖ad1 ♖d8 21. ♗g2 ♗g7∞ Hasin—Štejn, SSSR 1965

38 **16... ♖fc8**?! 17. fe6 fe6 18. ♗h3 ♕d7 19. ♖ad1 ♗c6 20. ♘d5 ♗d8 21. ♘f4± Nikitin; **16... ♖fe8**! 17. f6 ♗f8=

39 **9... b5**?! 10. e5 [10. ♗f3 ♗b7 11. e5?! de5 12. ♗b7 ed4! 13. ♗a8 de3 14. ♕f3 0—0 15. ♔h1 ♘bd7 16. ♗e4 ♘c5∓ Lujk—Spaski, SSSR 1960; 12. fe5 ♕e5 13. ♖e1 ♕c7∓; 11. a3 ♘c6! 12. ♕e2 0—0=] de5 11. fe5 ♕e5 [11... ♘fd7 12. ♗f3 ♗b7 13. ♗b7 ♕b7 14. ♕g4 g6 15. ♘e6 ♘e5 16. ♕g3 ♘bc6 17. ♘g7 ♔f8 18. ♗h6+— Bradvarević—Sineš, Jugoslavija (ch) 1968 — 5/446; 15... fe6 16. ♕e6 ♕c6 17. ♕f7 ♔d8 18. ♘d5 ♗c5 19. e6! ♗e3 20. ♔h1+—] 12. ♗f4 ♕c5 13. ♗f3±; **9... ♘bd7** 10. a4! [10. ♗f3 0—0 11. ♕e1 ♘b6 12. ♖d1 ♗d7 13. g4!? ♖ac8 14. g5 ♘e8 (Kan—Ragozin, SSSR (ch) 1936) 15. ♕f2! ♘c4 16. ♗c1 ♕b6 17. b3 ♘e5 18. ♗b2 ♘f3 19. ♕f3± Panov] b6 11. ♗f3 ♗b7 12. ♕e1 0—0 — 9... 0—0

40 10. **f5**?! e5 [10... ♘c6?! 11. g4! d5 12. ed5 ♘d4 13. ♕d4± A. Zajcev–Monasterski, Polanica Zdroj 1971] 11. ♘b3 b5 12. a3 ♗b7 13. ♗f3 ♖d8 14. ♘d2 [14. g4 d5! 15. ed5 e4∓] ♘bd7∓ Petrosjan–Smislov, SSSR (ch) 1949; **10. ♔h1** b5!? [10... ♘bd7 11. ♕e1 b5 12. a3 ♗b7 13. ♗f3 ♘b6= Garcia–Petrosjan, Buenos Aires 1964; 11. g4!?] 11. ♗f3 ♗b7 12. e5 de5 13. fe5 ♘fd7 14. ♗b7 ♕b7 15. ♕h5 b4 16. ♘ce2 ♘c6 15. ♘f3 g6 18. ♕h6 ♘ce5 19. ♗d4 ♗f6∞ Kočijev–Palatnik, SSSR 1973

41 10... **h6**?! 11. g5 hg5 12. fg5 ♘e8 13. g6! ♘f6 14. ♗h5± Jansa–Kinnmark, Göteborg 1968 — 5/447; **10... d5**!? 11. ed5 ♘d5 12. ♘d5 ed5 13. ♗f3 ♖d8 14. ♕d2 ♘c6± Sax–Eising 1972; **10... b5** 11. g5 ♘fd7 [Parma–Ribli, Camaguey 1974 — 18/466] 12. f5!±

42 Holmov–Spaski, SSSR 1964

43 12... ♘e8 13. ♕g3 de5 14. fe5 ♘d7 15. ♖ad1 ♖d8 [15... ♗c5 16. ♘e4 ♗e4 17. ♗e4 ♖c8 18. ♗f4 g6 19. ♔h1± Polugajevski–van den Berg, Beverwijk 1966 — 1/303] 16. ♗f4 ♘b6 17. ♘e4 ♘d5 18. ♘f6 ♗f6 19. ♗d5 ♗e7 [19... ♗h4 20. ♕h4 ♗d5 21. ♖d3±] 20. ♗b3± Suetin–Mašić, Tbilisi 1969 — 8/434; 13... ♘d7 14. ♖ad1 b4 [Zuidema–Benkö, Skopje (ol) 1972] 15. ♘a4±

44 14. ♗b7 ♕b7 15. ♘f3?! b4! 16. ♘e2 ♘c6 17. ♕g3 ♗c5 18. ♗c5 ♘c5 19. ♖ae1 ♖ad8= Balašov–Beljavski, SSSR 1974; 15. ♕g3 ♗c5 — 14. ♕g3

45 **14... ♗f3** 15. ♘f3 [15. ♕f3 ♘b6! (Geler–Ivkov, Beograd 1969 — 8/433) 16. ♕g4! ♘8d7? 17. ♘e6+–; 16... ♗c5? 17. ♘e6! ♗e3 18. ♔h1+–; 16... ♘c4 17. ♗h6 ♕e5 18. ♖ae1 f5 19. ♕g7±⊥; 16... ♕e5! 17. ♖ae1 ♗c5 18. ♔h1 f5 19. ♕h4 ♕f6 20. ♕f6 ♖f6 21. ♘f5±⊥ Liliental] ♗c5 16. ♗c5 ♘c5 17. ♖ae1 ♘c6 18. ♘g5 [18. ♘e4?! ♘e4 19. ♖e4 ♖ad8 20. ♖h4 ♘e7∓ Ivkov–Smejkal, Raach 1969] ♖ad8 19. ♖f6!? [19. ♔h1 h6 20. ♘ge4± Geler–Přibyl, Warszawa 1969 — 7/410] ♘d7 [19... ♘d4 20. ♕h4 h6 21. ♖h6 gh6 22. ♕h6 f5 23. ef6 ♖d7 24. ♕g6 ♔h8 25. ♖e3+–] 20. ♖h6! ♘ce5 21. ♖h7 ♕c5 22. ♔h1 ♘g6 23. ♘e6± Liberzon–Adamski, Tbilisi 1972; **14... ♔h8** [Georgadze–Palatnik, SSSR 1973] 15. ♗b7!? ♕b7 16. a3±

46 16. ♖ad1?! ♘c6 [16... ♕c7? 17. ♘e4! ♘c6 18. ♘c5 ♘c5 19. ♘c6 ♕c6 20. ♗h6+– Ivkov–Korčnoj, Jugoslavija–SSSR 1963; 17... ♗d4 18. ♗d4 ♘c6 19. c3±] 17. ♘c6 ♕c6 18. ♔h1 ♗e3 19. ♕e3 ♕c7∓ Unzicker–Korčnoj, Hastings 1971/72 — 13/482

47 17. ♗d4 ♘c6 18. ♖ad1 ♕c7 19. ♖fe1± Nikitin

48 10... ♘c6! — B 85

49 12... ♘c6!?

50 13. ♕g3 ♘c5 14. f5 e5 15. ♘b3 ♖fd8 16. ♘c5 dc5 17. ♘d5 ♘d5 18. ed5 c4= Lejn–Štejn, SSSR (ch) 1971

51 14. e5? de5 15. fe5 ♘e5 16. ♗b7 ♘eg4–+

52 17. ♗e3 ♘c6 18. ♕g3 ♖fe8 19. ♗g2± Smislov–Hort, Petropolis (izt) 1973 — 16/433

B 85

1. e4 c5 2. ♘f3 d6 3. d4 cd4 4. ♘d4 ♘f6 5. ♘c3 e6 6. ♗e2 a6 7. 0–0 ♕c7 8. f4 ♘c6

	9	10	11	12	13	14	15	16	17	
1	♔h1 ♗e7[1]	f5[2] 0–0	fe6 fe6	♗c4 ♘d4	♕d4 ♔h8[3]	♗g5 b5	♗b3 ♗d7	a4[4]		±
2	♗e3 ♗d7	♕e1[5] b5	a3[6] ♗e7	♕g3[7] 0–0	e5 de5	fe5 ♘e5	♗f4 ♗d6	♖ad1 ♘e8[8]	♘e4 f6[9]	±
3	... ♘a5	f5![10] ♗e7[11]	♕e1[12] b5[13]	♕g3 b4	fe6 fe6[14]	♘a4 g6[15]	c3 bc3	♖ac1		±
4	... ♗e7	♗f3[16] 0–0[17]	♔h1[18] ♗d7[19]	♖e1!? ♖ac8[20]	♗g1 ♖fd8	a4 ♗e8[21]	♕e2 ♘a5	e5 de5	fe5 ♘d7[22]	=∞
5	... ...	a4 0–0[23]	♘b3[24] b6	♗f3[25] ♖b8[26]	♕e1[27] ♘a5	♘a5 ba5	b3 ♗b7[28]	♖d1 ♖fc8	♖d3 ♗a8[29]	=
6	... ...	♔h1 0–0[30]	a4[31] ♘a5[32]	♕e1[33] ♘c4	♗c1 ♗d7	b3 ♘a5	♗d3! ♘c6	♘c6 ♗c6	♗b2 e5[34]	±
7	... ...	♕e1 ♗d7[35]	♕g3[36] h5[37]	♗f3[38] h4	♕f2 ♖c8[39]	♖ae1! ♕b8[40]	a4[41]			±

	9	10	11	12	13	14	15	16	17	
8	. . . . . .	. . . ♘d4	♗d4 b5[42]	e5[43] de5	fe5 ♘d7[44]	♘e4 ♗b7	♘d6[45] ♗d6	ed6 ♕d6	♖d1 e5[46]	$\overline{\infty}$

1. e4 c5 2. ♘f3 d6 3. d4 cd4 4. ♘d4 ♘f6 5. ♘c3 e6 6. ♗e2 a6 7. 0—0 ♕c7 8. f4 ♘c6 9. ♗e3 ♗e7 10. ♕e1 0—0

	11	12	13	14	15	16	17	18	19	
9	a4[47] ♘d4[48]	♗d4 e5	♗e3[49] ef4	♖f4 ♗e6	♕g3 ♘d7	♗d4 ♘e5	♗d3[50] ♕a5	♔h1 ♖ac8	♘e2 ♖fe8[51]	=
10	♔h1 ♘d4[52]	♗d4 b5	e5 de5	♗e5[53] ♕b6	♗d3[54] ♗b7[55]	♕h4! h6	♕g3 ♘e8	f5 ef5	♖f5 ♗d6[56]	±
11	♕g3 ♘d4[57]	♗d4 b5[58]	a3[59] ♗b7	♔h1[60] ♖fd8	♗d3 ♘e8	♖ae1[61] ♗f8	♕h3[62] ♗c6	e5 g6	♘e4 ♗e4[63]	±
12	. . . ♗d7	♖ad1[64] ♘d4[65]	♗d4 ♗c6	♗d3 g6[66]	f5!?[67] e5	♗e3 b5	♗h6			±
13	. . . . . .	. . . b5	a3 ♘d4[68]	♗d4 ♗c6	♔h1 ♖ad8	♗d3 ♕b7	♖de1 a5[69]	♕h3!?[70] b4[71]	ab4 ab4[72]	$\overline{\infty}$
14	. . . . . .	♖ae1 b5[73]	a3[74] ♖ab8[75]	♗d3[76] b4	♘c6[77] ♗c6	ab4 ♖b4	♗c1 ♕b7[78]			=
15	. . . . . .	♔h1 b5[79]	a3[80] ♖ab8[81]	e5! ♘e8[82]	♗d3 b4	♘e4 ba3	ba3 de5[83]	fe5 ♘d4	♗d4 ♗b5[84]	±
16	. . . . . .	♘f3 ♘b4[85]	♖ac1![86] d5	ed5[87] ♘bd5	♘d5 ♘d5	♗d4 ♗f6	♘e5			±
17	. . . . . .	♗d3 b5[88]	a3[89] ♔h8[90]	♖ad1[91] ♖ab8	♘f3 b4	ab4 ♖b4	e5 de5	fe5 ♘h5	♕h3 g6[92]	±

[1] 9... ♗d7 **10. ♘b3** b5 [10... ♗e7!?] 11. ♗f3 ♖c8!∞; **10. a4** ♗e7 11. ♗f3 ♖c8 12. ♘b3 ♘b4?! 13. ♗e3 ♗c6 14. ♖f2!? d5 15. e5 ♘e4 16. ♗e4 de4 17. ♘d4 0—0 18. ♕g4± Rjumin—Konstantinopoljski, SSSR 1936; 12... ♘a5!?; **10. f5**!? ♘d4 [10... ♘e5 11. ♗g5 ♗e7 12. fe6 fe6 13. ♗h5!±] 11. ♕d4 ♗e7 12. ♗g5 0—0 13. ♖ad1 ef5?! 14. ef5 ♗c6 15. ♖d3 h6 16. ♗f4± Gruzman—Bebčuk, SSSR 1971; 13... ♔h8!?

[2] **10. ♘b3** 0—0 11. ♗f3 b5 12. a3 ♗b7 13. g4 [Georgadze—Postler, Dresden 1969 — 8/435] d5!∓; **10. ♗f3** 0—0 11. g4 [11. a4 ♖d8 12. ♗e3 ♗d7 13. ♕e1 ♘d4 14. ♗d4 e5 15. ♗e3 b5= Geler—Platonov, SSSR (ch) 1971; 13. ♘b3!?; 11... ♗d7 12. g4 ♘d4 13. ♕d4 ♗c6 14. g5 ♘d7 15. ♘d5 ♗d5 16. ed5 e5 17. ♕f2 f5!∓ Fernandez—Gufeljd, Camaguey 1974; 12. ♗e3!?] ♘d4 [11... ♘d7 12. g5 ♖e8 13. b3 b5! 14. ♘c6 ♕c6 15. e5!? ♕c3 16. ♗d2 ♕d4∞; 14. ♗b2 ♗b7 15. ♗g2 ♗f8∞ Velimirović—Jansa, Sombor 1972] 12. ♕d4 ♘d7 13. g5 b5 14. a4 [14. ♗e3!?; 14. f5!?] ♗b7! 15. ab5 ab5 16. ♗e3 ♗c6∓ Velimirović—Ribli, Nice (ol) 1974 — 17/399

[3] 13... ♗d7 14. ♗g5 h6 15. ♗h4 ♖ac8 16. ♗b3± Velimirović—Jansa, Vrnjačka Banja 1973

[4] Aronin—Kotov, SSSR (ch) 1949

[5] **10. ♘b3** b5 11. a3 ♗e7 12. ♗f3 [12. ♖f2 Petrosjan—Johansson, La Habana (ol) 1966 — 2/447; 12... 0—0∞] 0—0 13. ♕d2 ♖ab8 14. g4 ♖fc8 15. g5 ♘e8 [Fichtl—Jansa, ČSSR 1972 — 13/485] 16. ♕f2∞; **10. a4** ♖c8 [10... ♗e7!?] 11. ♘b3 ♘a5 12. ♘a5 ♕a5 13. ♗d3 ♗e7 [Tringov—Portisch, Teesside 1971] 14. ♕e1 0—0 15. ♘d5±; **10. ♗f3** ♗e7 11. ♔h1 — 9... ♗e7

[6] 11. ♗f3 b4 [11... ♘d4?! 12. ♗d4 e5 13. fe5 de5 14. ♕g3 ♗c5 15. ♗c5 ♕c5 16. ♔h1 0—0 17. ♘d5 ♘d5 18. ♕e5±] 12. ♘ce2 ♗e7 [12... e5?! 13. ♘c6 ♗c6 14. ♘g3 h5 15. ♖d1 h4 16. ♘f5 g6 17. ♘h4 ♗b5 18. fe5 de5 19. ♗e2!+— Geler—Langeweg, Kislovodsk 1972 — 14/467; 14... g6!?] 13. ♕g3 0—0 14.

e5 de5 15. fe5 ♘e5 [15... ♘e8 16. ♗c6 ♗c6 17. ♘f4±] 16. ♗a8 ♖a8 17. ♗h6 [17. ♗f4 ♗d6=∞] ♘h5 18. ♕h3 ♘f6 19. ♕g3 1/2 : 1/2 Unzicker–Portisch, Siegen (ol) 1970 — 10/526

7 12. ♖d1 0–0 13. ♕g3 — 9... ♗e7

8 **16... ♖ad8** 17. ♘b3±; **16... ♘c4** 17. ♗d6 ♕d6 18. ♕d6 ♘d6 19. ♖f6! gf6 20. ♘f3±

9 **17... ♘f3**? 18. ♖f3 ♗f4 19. ♖f4 e5 20. ♖f2!+– Matulović–Janošević, Novi Sad 1973 — 16/435; **17... f6** 18. ♘d6 ♘d6 19. ♗e5 fe5 20. ♕e5± Mašić–Cvetković, Jugoslavija 1973 — 16/434

10 **10. ♕d3**? b5 11. ♖ae1 ♗b7 12. ♗f3 ♘d7∓ Wade–Pachman, Arban 1949; **10. a4** ♗d7!? [10... ♗e7 11. ♘b3 0–0 12. ♘a5 ♕a5 13. ♕e1 ♔h8 14. ♔h1 ♗d7 15. ♗d3 ♖ac8± Bagirov–Furman, SSSR (ch) 1972 — 14/469] 11. ♘b3 ♘b3 12. cb3 ♗c6=

11 **10... ♘c4**? 11. ♗c4 ♕c4 12. fe6 fe6 13. ♖f6! gf6 14. ♕h5 ♔d8 [14... ♔d7 15. ♕f7 ♗e7 16. ♘f ! ♖e8 17. ♖d1 d5 18. ♘d5 +–; 14... ♔e7 15. ♘f5 ef5 16. ♘d5 ♔d8 17. ♗b6 ♔d7 18. ♕f7+–] 15. ♕f7+– Lasker–Pirc, Moskva 1935; **10... e5**!? 11. ♘b3 ♘c4 12. ♗c4 ♕c4 13. ♕f3 ♗e7 14. ♗g5± Pachman

12 11. ♕d3 ♗d7 [11... b5?! 12. fe6 fe6 13. b4 ♘c4 14. ♘db5+–; 12... ♗e6 13. ♘d5±] 12. g4±→» Pachman

13 11... ♘c4 12. ♗c4 ♕c4 13. ♕g3 0–0 14. ♖ad1±

14 13... bc3 14. ♕g7 ♖f8 15. ef7 ♖f7 16. ♗h5+–

15 **14... 0—0** 15. ♘b6! ♖b8 16. ♘c8 ♕c8 17. e5+–; **14... ♗d8** 15. ♘b6 ♖a7 [15... ♕b6 16. ♕g7 ♖g8 17. ♗h5+–] 16. ♘c8 ♕c8 17. ♕d6+– Adorjan–Sax, Hungary (ch) 1972

16 **10. ♗d3** ♘d4 11. ♗d4 e5 12. ♗e3 b5=; **10. g4** ♘d4 11. ♗d4 e5 12. ♗e3 ef4△ ♗e6=

17 **10... ♘a5**?! 11. ♕e2 ♘c4 12. e5! ♘e3 [12... de5 13. ♘db5±] 13. ef6!± Sanakoev–Lundholm, corr. 1967 — 4/546; **10... ♗d7** 11. ♔h1 ♘d4 12. ♗d4 e5 13. ♗e3 ♗c6 14. ♕e1 0–0 15. ♕g3 ef4 16. ♗f4 ♘d7= Koblenc

18 **11. g4**?! ♘d4 12. ♗d4 e5! 13. ♗e3 ef4 14. ♗f4 ♗e6∓ Spasov–Kozma, Zinnowitz 1965; **11. ♘de2** b5 12. ♕e1 ♗b7 13. ♕f2 ♖ab8 14. g4 b4 15. ♘a4 d5∓; **11. a4** ♘a5 12. ♔h1 ♗d7 13. ♕d3 ♘c4 14. ♗c1 ♖ac8 15. b3 ♘a5 16. ♗b2 ♘c6 17. ♖ac1 ♘d4 18. ♕d4 ♗c6= Karpov–Savon, SSSR (ch) 1971

19 11... ♖d8 12. ♕e1 ♘d4 13. ♗d4 e5 14. ♗e3 b5 15. ♕f2 ♖b8 16. fe5 de5 17. ♘d5 ♘d5 18. ed5 ♗d6= Unzicker–R. Byrne, Lugano 1970 — 9/408; 12. ♘b3!?

20 12... ♘d4 13. ♗d4 e5 14. ♗e3 ef4 15. ♗f4 ♗c6 16. e5±

21 14... ♘d4 15. ♗d4 ♗c6 16. a5 ♘d7 17. ♘d5±

22 **18. ♘d5**? ed5 19. e6 ♘f6 20. ef7 ♔f7–+ Beljavski–Muhin, Suhumi 1972 — 14/466; **18. ♘f5** ♗f8 19. ♘d6 ♗d6 20. ed6 ♕d6 21. ♖ad1=∞

23 10... ♗d7 11. ♘b3 ♘b4 12. ♗f3 ♗c6 13. a5± Tringov–Janošević, Vrnjačka Banja 1973 — 15/431

24 11. ♔h1 — 10. ♔h1

25 **12. ♗d3** ♗b7 13. ♕f3 ♘b4 14. ♘d4 [14. ♕h3 e5∓] g6! 15. ♖ad1 e5 16. ♘de2 d5! 17. fe5 [Savon–Polugajevski, SSSR (ch) 1971 — 12/464] ♕e5 18. ♕g3 ♕g3∓; **12. ♔h1** ♖d8 13. ♕e1 ♖b8 14. ♕f2 [Matanović–Palatnik, Beograd 1974] ♘a5=

26 12... ♗b7 13. ♕e1 ♖fe8 14. ♖d1 ♘d7 15. ♕g3! ♗f8 16. ♖f2 ♘c5 17. f5 ♘e5 18. ♘d4!± Levenfiš–Maragonov, SSSR (ch) 1937

27 13. ♕e2 ♘a5 **14. ♘a5** ba5 15. ♖ab1 ♖b4 16. ♖fd1 ♗b7 17. ♗d2 d5 18. ed5 ed5∓ Aljošin–Aramanovič, SSSR 1947; **14. ♖ad1** ♘c4 15. ♗c1 b5 16. ab5 [16. ♔h1 b4 17. ♖d4 ♘a5! 18. ♘a5 ♕a5 19. ♘d1 e5 20. fe5 de5 21. ♖c4 ♕a4∓ Szilágyi–Tompa, Hungary (ch) 1973] ab5 17. ♕f2 b4 18. ♘e2 e5 19. ♘g3 ef4∓ Unzicker–Pachman, München (ol) 1958; **14. ♘d2** ♖d8 15. ♔h1 ♗b7 16. ♕f2 ♘d7 17. ♖ae1 ♘c4 18. ♘c4 ♕c4= Witt–Larsen, Canada 1974; **14. ♔h1** ♘c4 15. ♗c1 ♘d7 16. ♘d4 ♘a5 17. ♗e3 [Sigurjonsson–Enklaar, Oslo 1970] ♘c4=

28 15... ♖b4!?

29 18. ♗d2 ♖b4 19. f5 ♗f8 20. fe6 1/2 : 1/2 Kapengut–Karpov, SSSR (ch) 1971

30 10... ♗d7 11. a4 [11. ♘b3 ♖c8 12. ♗f3 b5! 13. a3 0–0 14. ♕e1 ♖fd8 15. ♕f2 ♖b8 16. ♖ad1 a5∓ Verlinski–Aramanovič, SSSR 1944] ♖c8 12. ♘b3 ♘b4 13. a5 ♗c6 14. ♗f3 e5 15. fe5 de5 16. ♗b6 ♕d6 17. ♕e2 ♕e6 18. ♘c5± Geler–Filipowicz, Hungary 1970 — 9/405

31 11. ♕e1 — 10. ♕e1

32 **11... ♗d7** 12. ♘b3 b6 [12... ♘b4 13. a5 ♗c6 14. ♗b6 ♕b8 15. ♕d2 d5 16. e5 ♘d7 17. ♗d4 b5 18. ♗g4 g6 19. ♖ae1 ♖c8 20. f5!± Karpov–Cobo, Skopje (ol) 1972 — 14/468; 13... ♖ac8 14. ♗b6 ♕b8 15. ♗f3 ♗c6 16. ♕e3±] 13. ♗f3 ♖fd8 14. ♕e2 ♗e8 15. ♗f2 ♖dc8 16. ♗g3 ♘d7 17. ♖ad1± Geler–Korčnoj (mct) 1971 — 11/374; **11... ♔h8** 12. ♕e1 ♗d7 13. ♕g3 b6 14. ♘f3 ♘b4 15. ♗d3 ♘d3 16. cd3 b5 17. e5± Kaplan–Portisch, San Antonio 1972; **11... ♘d4** 12. ♕d4 ♗d7 13. e5 ♘e8 [Rogoff–Evans, USA (ch) 1974 — 18/469] 14. ♗d3±

33 12. ♕d3 e5!? [12... ♗d7?! 13. g4! ♔h8 14. g5 ♘g8 15. ♖f3 ♘c6 16. ♖g1 ♘d4 17. ♗d4+– Tukmakov–Panno, Buenos Aires 1970 — 10/519] 13. ♘f5 ♗f5 14. ef5 ♖ad8∞

34 18. ♕e2± Karpov–Tukmakov, SSSR 1971 — 12/463

35 10... b5? 11. ♘c6 ♕c6 12. e5 ♘d5 [12... ♘d7 13. ed6 ♕d6 14. ♗f3 ♖b8 15. ♗a7±] 13. ♘d5 ed5 14. ed6 ♕d6 15. ♖d1±

36 **11. ♖d1** ♘d4 12. ♗d4 ♗c6 13. ♗d3 [13. ♗f3 0–0 14. ♕g3 Boleslavski–Stahlberg, Saltsjöbaden (izt) 1948; 14... ♖fd8±] 0–0 14. e5 de5 15. fe5 ♘d7 16. ♘e4 ♗e4 17. ♕e4 g6 18. ♕e3 ♗c5 19. c3± Boleslavski–Kotov, SSSR (ch) 1949; 11... b5 12. a3 0–0 13. ♕g3 — 10... 0–0; **11. ♔h1** h5?! 12. ♗f3 [12. ♖d1 ♖c8 13. ♗f3 h4 14. ♕f2± Kuprejčik–Saharov, SSSR 1969 — 7/412] ♘g4 13. ♗g1 g5 14. ♘c6 bc6 15. ♕d2 ♕a5 16. e5± Lombardy–Feuerstein, USA 1972; 11... b5 12. a3 0–0 13. ♕g3 — 10... 0–0

37 **11... g6**?! 12. ♔h1 h5 13. ♕e1 h4 14. ♗f3 ♘h5 15. ♘de2 ♘a5 16. ♗d4 ♖h7 17. b3 ♘c6 18. ♗f2± Krogius–Gheorghiu, Soči 1964; **11... 0–0** — 10... 0–0

38 **12. ♕g7** ♖g8 13. ♕h6 ♖g6=; **12. ♖ad1** h4 13. ♕f2 b5 14. a3 [14. ♗f3?! b4 15. ♘ce2 e5 16. fe5 de5 17. ♘b3 h3 18. g4 ♘d8!∞ Hort–Filipowicz, Polska 1971 — 12/465] ♖c8 15. ♗f3 [15. h3 ♕b8 16. ♘f3 b4 17. ab4 ♘b4 18. e5 ♘fd5∞ Grabczewski–Filipowicz, Polska 1967] ♕b8 16. ♘b3 b4 17. ab4 ♘b4 18. ♘c1 ♗c6 19. ♘d3 0–0 20. ♗d4± Bednarski–Filipowicz, Polska 1970

39 13... b5 14. e5±

40 **14... ♘a5**? 15. ♘e6+–; **14... ♘d4** 15. ♗d4 e5 16. ♗b6 ♕b8 17. fe5 de5 18. ♘d5±

41 Nikitin

42 11... e5? 12. fe5 de5 13. ♕g3 ♗c5 14. ♗c5 ♕c5 15. ♔h1 ♔f8 16. ♘d5+– Boleslavski–Böök, Saltsjöbaden (izt) 1948

43 12. ♕g3 b4 13. e5! de5 14. fe5 bc3 15. ♕g7! ♖f8 [15... ♖g8 16. ef6+–] 16. ef6+– Honfi–Kany, Hungary (ch) 1964; 12... 0–0 — 10... 0–0

44 13... ♗c5? 14. ♕f2 ♗d4 15. ♕d4 ♘d7 16. ♗b5+–

45 **15. ♗h5**? 0–0 16. ♘f6 [16. ♖d1!?] ♔h8! [16... gf6? 17. ♕g3 ♔h8 18. ef6+–] 17. ♘d7 ♕d7 18. c3 ♔g8 19. ♖d1 ♕c6= Aronin–Kotov, SSSR (ch) 1951; **15. ♗d3**!?

46 **17... ♕c7** 18. ♗g7? ♖g8 19. ♗h5 ♕b6 –+; 18. ♕f2!∞̅; **17... e5** 18. ♗c3 ♕g6! [18... ♕c7 19. ♗b4±; 18... ♕c6 19. ♗f3 e4 20. ♗b4 0-0-0 21. ♖d6 ♕c7 22. ♗g4±] 19. ♗f3 e4∞̅

47 **11. ♗f3** ♘d4 [11... ♘a5? 12. ♖d1 ♘c4 13. ♗c1 ♗d7 14. ♕g3 ♖ac8 15. ♔h1 b5 16. b3 ♘b6 17. ♗b2±] 12. ♗d4 e5 13. ♗e3 b5 14. ♖d1 ♗e6 15. a3 ♖ab8∓ Freedgood–Gligorić, Lugano (ol) 1968 — 6/547; **11. g4** ♘d4 12. ♗d4 e5 13. fe5 de5 14. ♕g3 ♗c5! 15. ♗c5 ♕c5 16. ♔h1 ♗e6 17. g5 ♘d7=; **11. ♘b3** b5=; **11. a3** ♘d4 12. ♗d4 e5 13. fe5 [13. ♗e3 b5=] de5 14. ♕g3 ♗c5 15. ♗c5 ♕c5 16. ♔h1 ♔h8 [16... ♕e7 17. ♖f2 b5= Estrin–Liebert, Albena 1973] 17. ♖f6 gf6 18. ♕h4 ♖g8 19. ♘d5 ♖g7 20. ♕f6 [20. ♗d3? ♗e6 21. ♘f6 ♕e3!∓] ♗e6 21. ♕e5= Portisch–Matulović, Palma de Mallorca 1967 — 4/462

48 11... ♗d7 12. ♕g3 [12. ♘b3 ♘b4 13. ♕d2 d5 14. e5 ♘e4 15. ♘e4 de4 16. c3 ♘d5 17. ♗d4 ♗c6 18. a5± Beljavski–Dieks, Teesside 1973] ♖ac8 13. ♘c6 ♗c6 14. ♗d4 g6 15. f5 e5 16. ♗e3 ♔h8 [Karaklajić–Platonov, Cienfuegos 1972 — 13/481] 17. ♗d3±

49 13. fe5 de5 14. ♕g3 ♖e8 [14... ♗c5 15. ♗c5 ♕c5 16. ♔h1 ♔h8 17. ♕h4 ♕e7=] 15. ♔h1 ♗d8 16. ♗e3 ♔h8 [16... ♗e6 17. ♗h6 g6 18. ♖ad1 ♖c8 19. ♖d8? ♕d8 20. ♗g5 ♖c3 21. ♕h4 ♖c2 22. ♗f6 ♕d2–+; 19. ♕f2 ♗e7 20. ♗g5 ♘g4= Ceškovski–S. Garcia, Soči 1974; 19. ♗g5! ♘d7 20. ♗g4 ♗g5 21. ♗e6 ♗f4 22. ♘d5!± Lepeškin] 17. ♗g5 ♗e6 18. ♖ad1 ♗e7= Padevski–Ermenkov, Varna 1973

50 17. ♖af1 ♖ac8 18. b3?! ♕a5 19. ♗d1 ♗d8! 20. ♔h1 ♗b6∓ S. Garcia–Ribli, Camaguey 1974

51 20. ♗c3 ♕d8 21. ♘d4 ♗g5 22. ♘f5 ♗f5 23. ♖f5 ♗h4= Larsen–Andersson, Manila 1974

52 **11... ♔h8** 12. ♗f3?! ♗d7 13. a4 ♖ac8 14. ♖ad1 ♘d4 15. ♗d4 e5 16. ♗e3 b5 17. ab5 ab5 18. ♖d2 b4 19. ♘e2 ♗b5∓ Gligorić–Najdorf, Praha 1946; 12. ♕g3 ♗d7 — 11. ♕g3; **11... ♗d7** 12. ♗f3?! ♖ac8 [12... ♖fd8? 13. ♕f2! ♖ab8 14. ♖ad1 ♗e8 15. g4!± Zaharov–Korčnoj, SSSR (ch) 1963; 12... e5!?] 13. ♕g3 ♔h8 14. ♖ad1 b5 15. a3 ♘d4 16. ♗d4 ♗c6 17. e5 de5 18. fe5 ♘d7 19. ♘e4 ♗e4 20. ♗e4 f5!= Zaharov–Spaski, SSSR (ch) 1963; 12. ♕g3 — 11. ♕g3; **11... ♘a5**!? 12. ♕g3 [12. ♖d1?! b5 13. a3 ♗b7 14. ♗f3 ♘c4 15. ♗c1 ♖ac8 16. ♘de2 e5!∓ Nikitin] ♘c4 13. ♗c1±

53 14. fe5!?

54 15. ♗f3?! ♗b7 16. ♗b7 ♕b7 17. ♖ad1 ♖ac8∓ Kristiansson–Tukmakov, Mayague 1971

55 15... ♘g4!?

56 20. ♖af1±↑ Gufeljd–Platonov, SSSR 1974 — 18/467

57 **11... ♘e8**? 12. ♖ad1 ♗f6 13. ♕f2 ♗d7 14. g4 ♖c8 15. g5 ♗d4 16. ♗d4 ♘d4 17. ♕d4 ♕c5 18. e5!± Averbah–Barcza, Moskva–Budapest 1948; **11... ♘a5**? 12. e5 ♘d7 [12... ♘e8 13. ♘f5 ef5 14. ♘d5 ♕d8 15. ♗b6 ♕d7 16. ♗a5 de5 17. ♖ad1 ef4 18. ♕c3+– Fajbisovič–Černikov, SSSR 1965] 13. ♘d5! ♕d8 14. ♘e7 ♕e7 15. ed6 ♕d6 16. ♖ad1±; **11... ♖d8**?! 12. ♕f2!?±; **11... d5** [O'Kelly] 12. e5 ♘d4 [12... ♘e4 13. ♘e4 ♘d4 14. ♘f6!± Parma–Sax, Teesside 1972 — 13/487] 13. ♗d4 ♗c5 14. ♕e3 ♗d4 15. ♕d4 ♘d7 16. ♗d3? ♕c5 17. ♘e2±; **11... ♔h8** 12. ♖f2 ♗d7 13. ♖af1 b5 14. a3 ♖ac8 15. ♗d3 g6 16. ♘f3 b4

17. ab4 ♘b4 18. ♘g5 ♔g7 19. f5!± Smislov–Barcza, Moskva–Budapest 1949; 15... e5!?

58 **12... d5?** 13. ♔h1 de4 14. ♘e4±→»; **12... ♗d7** 13. e5 de5 14. ♗e5 ♕b6 15. ♔h1 ♘e8 16. ♗d3 f6 17. ♕h4 g6 18. ♘e4±→ Hartston–Ciocaltea, Hastings 1971/72 — 13/486

59 13. e5 de5 14. ♗e5 [14. fe5 ♗c5! 15. ♗c5 ♕c5 16. ♔h1 ♘d7 17. ♖ae1 b4 18. ♘e4 ♕e5 19. ♘f6 ♔h8 20. ♕h4 ♘f6 21. ♗f3 ♕b2 22. ♗a8 ♗d7∓ Altšuler] ♕b6 15. ♔h1 ♗b7 16. ♗d3 ♘h5!? [16... g6?! (Eley–Barcza, Hastings 1972/73) 17. ♕h4! ♕d8 18. ♕h6±; 16... ♘e8 17. ♕h3 g6 18. ♘e4 f5 19. ♘d2 ♘f6= Zagorovski–Zurahov, SSSR 1952; 17. **f5!** ef5 18. ♖f5 ♗f6 19. ♘e4 ♗e5 20. ♖e5!±↑] 17. ♕h3 g6∞

60 **14. ♗d3?!** e5! [14... g6?! 15. f5± Balašov–Andersson, Wijk aan Zee 1973 — 15/433; 14... ♘h5!?] 15. fe5 ♘h5! 16. ♕e3 de5 17. ♗e5 [17. ♗b6 ♕d6 18. ♖ad1 ♘f4 19. ♗e2 ♕g6∓ Bronštejn–Kotov, SSSR 1947] ♕e5 18. ♖f5 ♕e6 19. ♖h5 g6=∞; **14. ♖ae1!?** ♗c6 [14... ♖ad8 15. ♔h1 g6 16. ♗d3 ♘d7 17. f5±→» Williams–Kaplan, New York 1974; 14... ♖ac8!?] 15. ♗d3 ♖ad8 16. ♔h1 ♕b7 17. ♕h3 g6 18. f5±→» Talj–Langeweg, Wijk aan Zee 1973 — 15/432

61 16. ♕h3!?±

62 **17. ♕h4** ♕e7 18. ♕h3 [Szabo–Kotov, Stockholm (izt) 1952] ♗c6± Averbah; **17. e5** g6 18. ♘e4 [18. f5 ef5 19. ♗f5 de5 20. ♗e5 ♗d6 21. ♗d6 ♘d6 22. ♗e4 ♖ac8 23. ♗d5 ♖d7 24. ♖f6 ♖e8!= Evans–Pachman, Amsterdam (izt) 1964] ♗e4 19. ♗e4 ♖b8 20. f5 ef5 21. ♗f5 de5 22. ♗e5 ♗d6 23. ♗d3 ♖d7 24. ♗d6 ♘d6 25. b3± Smislov–Kotov, SSSR (ch) 1951

63 20. ♗e4 ♖ac8 21. c3 ♖d7 22. f5± Smislov–Kotov, Budapest (ct) 1950

64 12. ♖f2 b5 13. a3 ♘d4 [13... ♖fd8?! 14. ♖af1 b4 15. ab4 ♘b4 16. f5 e5 17. ♗h6 ♗f8 18. ♘e6!±→ Levenfiš–Kotov, SSSR (ch) 1940] 14. ♗d4 ♗c6=

65 **12... ♖ac8** 13. e5 ♘e8 [13... de5 14. fe5 ♘d4 15. ♖d4 ♘e8 16. ♘e4±; 14... ♘e5 15. ♗f4 ♗d6 16. ♘b3±] 14. ♔h1 ♔h8 [14... de5 15. fe5 f6? 16. ef6 ♕g3 17. fe7!+−] 15. ♘f3 de5 16. fe5 f5 17. ef6± Geler–Aramanovič, SSSR 1949; **12... ♔h8** 13. a3 [13. ♔h1 ♖ac8 14. ♗d3?! ♘b4 15. e5 de5 16. fe5 ♘h5 17. ♕h3 ♕e5 18. ♗e4 ♖c3 19. bc3 ♕e4 20. ♕h5 ♘d5∓ Mohrlock–Unzicker, BRD (ch) 1965; 14. ♘f3!± Botvinik–Zubarev, SSSR (ch) 1933; 13... b5! — 12... b5] ♖ac8 14. ♘f3± Bronštejn–Gligorić, Saltsjöbaden (izt) 1948

66 **14... e5** 15. fe5 ♘h5 16. ♕e3 de5 17. ♗b6 ♕b8 18. ♘d5±; **14... ♘h5** 15. ♕e3!?±

67 15. ♕h3 e5 16. ♗e3 ef4 17. ♗d4 [17. ♖f4 d5!? 18. ed5 ♘d5 19. ♘d5 ♗d5=] d5 [17... ♘d7 18. ♖f4 ♘e5 19. ♖df1±] 18. ed5 [18. e5 ♘e4 19. ♖f4 ♘g5∞] ♘d5 19. ♘d5 ♗d5 20. ♕h6 ♗f6!= Talj–Espig, Suhumi 1972

68 **13... ♖ac8** 14. ♔h1 ♔h8 15. ♗d3 g6 16. ♘f3 b4 17. ab4 ♘b4 [Klovan–Muhin, SSSR 1973] 18. ♘g5 ♘h5 19. ♕h3±; **13... ♔h8** 14. ♗d3 [14. ♔h1 b4 15. ab4 ♘b4 16. ♖d2 ♗c8! 17. ♘f3 ♗b7 18. e5 de5 19. fe5 ♘e4∓ Talj–Janošević, Sarajevo 1966 — 1/307] ♖ad8 15. ♔h1 g6 16. ♘c6 ♗c6 17. ♗d4 ♔g8 18. f5 e5 19. ♗e3± Matanović–Ćirić, Titovo Užice 1966 — 2/452

69 17... ♘h5 18. ♕h3 ♘f4 19. ♖f4 e5 20. ♘d5! g6 [20... ef4 21. e5+−] 21. ♘e7 ♕e7 22. ♖h4 ed4 23. ♖h7±

70 18. e5 de5 19. ♗e5 g6∓ Unzicker–Larsen, Palma de Mallorca 1969 — 8/429

71 18... h6 19. ♖e3!? b4 20. ♖g3±→

72 20. e5 de5 21. fe5 ♖d4 22. ef6 ♖d3 23. cd3 ♗f6=∞ Larsen

73 **12... e5** 13. fe5 ♘e5 14. ♘f5±; **12... ♘d4** 13. ♗d4 ♗c6 14. ♗d3 e5 15. fe5 ♘h5 16. ♕h3 de5 17. ♗e3 ♘f4 18. ♗f4 ef4 19. e5 g6 20. ♖f4±; **12... ♔h8** 13. ♘f3 [13. a3 ♖ac8 14. ♗d3 ♖fd8 15. ♘f3 b5 16. e5 ♘h5 17. ♕h3± Matulović–Zečević, Jugoslavija (ch) 1968 — 5/448; 13... b5 14. ♔h1 ♖ab8 15. ♗d3 b4=; 14. ♘c6! — 12... b5] ♘b4 14. ♗d3 ♘d3 15. cd3 ♗c6 16. ♕h3 b5 17. ♘g5 h6 18. g4!? e5 [Müller–Malich, DDR (ch) 1973] 19. f5!?±

74 13. e5!? de5 14. fe5 ♘e5 [14... ♘d4 15. ♗d4 ♘e8 16. ♘e4 ♗c6 17. ♗d3 ♖d8 18. c3± Bednarski–Kristinsson, Oslo 1973 — 15/434] 15. ♗h6 ♘e8 16. ♗f4 ♗d6 17. ♘e4=∞

75 13... ♔h8 14. ♘c6! ♗c6 15. ♗d4 ♖ad8 16. ♗d3 ♕b7 17. ♕h3 b4 [Paoli–Jansa, Madonna de Campiglio 1974 — 17/490] 18. ab4 ♕b4 19. ♗f6 gf6 20. ♘d5± Ivkov

76 14. e5!? de5 15. fe5 ♘e5 16. ♗h6 ♘e8 17. ♗f4±

77 15. ♘ce2 ba3 16. ba3 d5! 17. e5 ♘e4 18. ♕h3 g6 19. ♘b3 ♘a5∓ Ničevski–Schmidt, Polanica Zdroj 1973

78 Klovan–Korelov, SSSR 1964

79 **12... g6** 13. ♖ae1 b5 14. e5 ♘e8 15. f5! ♘d4 [15... de5 16. ♘e6! fe6 17. fg6 e4 18. ♖f8 ♗f8 19. gh7 ♔h7 20. ♕h4 ♔g8 21. ♘e4± Adorjan] 16. ♗d4 de5 17. ♗e5± Adorjan–Parr, England 1973; **12... ♔h8** 13. a3 [13. ♖ae1 b5 14. a3 b4 15. ab4 ♘b4∞ Wostyn–Sax, Nice (ol) 1974; 13. ♖ad1 b5 14. a3 b4 15. ab4 ♘b4 16. e5 de5 17. fe5 ♘fd5 18. ♘d5 ♘d5 19. ♗c1 ♗c5 20. ♘f5 ef5 21. ♖d5 ♗e6= O'Kelly–Larsen, Dundee 1967 — 4/548] ♖ac8 14. ♗d3 b5 15. ♖ae1 ♕b8 16. e5! ♘g8 17. ♘c6 ♗c6 18. ♗d4 b4 19. f5± Šamkovič–Damjanović, Soči 1967 — 4/547; **12... ♘d4** 13. ♗d4 ♗c6 14. ♖ae1 b5 15. a3 ♖ac8 16. ♗d3 ♘h5 17. ♕h3 g6 [17... ♘f4? 18. ♖f4 e5 19. ♘d5 ♗d5 20. ed5 g6 21. ♖fe4+−]

18. f5 e5 19. ♗e3 ♔g7 20. ♘d5!? [20. ♗e2 ♘f4 21. ♗f4 ef4 22. ♖f4 ♗f6 23. ♖ef1 g5!=∞ Ravinski—Kan, SSSR 1952] ♗d5 21. ed5 ♘f4 [21... ♗f6 22. ♗e4±] 22. ♖f4 ef4 23. ♗d4±

80 13. e5!? de5 14. fe5 ♘e5 [14... ♘d4?! 15. ♗d4 ♘e8 (Talj—Hartston, Hastings 1973/74 — 17/480) 16. ♘e4 ♗c6 17. ♘g5±] 15. ♗h6! [15. ♗f4 ♗d6 16. ♖ad1 b4! 17. ♘db5 ab5 18. ♖d6 ♘g6!∓] ♘e8 16. ♗f4 ♗d6 17. ♘e4 [17. ♗b5 ab5 18. ♘db5 ♗b5 19. ♘b5 ♕c2 20. ♘d6 ♘g6∞] ♘c4 [17... f6!?] 18. ♘d6 ♘cd6 19. ♗d3=∞ Kostro—Padevski, Polanica Zdroj 1968 — 6/548

81 **13... ♔h8** 14. ♗d3! [14. ♘f3!?] ♖ac8 15. ♖ae1 ♘a5 16. e5 ♘e8 17. f5± Tukmakov—Hesse, Örebro 1966 — 2/451; **13... ♘d4** 14. ♗d4 ♗c6 15. ♖ae1 [15. ♗d3 e5 16. fe5 ♘h5= Hartston—Ribli, Las Palmas 1974; 15. e5 de5 16. ♗e5 ♕b7 17. f5 ef5 18. ♘f5 ♘e8= Polugajevski—Matulović, La Habana (ol) 1966 — 2/449] ♕b7 16. ♗d3 g6 [16... ♖ad8 17. ♕h3! h6 18. ♖e3± Hartston—Larsen, Las Palmas 1974] 17. ♗f6? ♗f6= Parma—Janošević, Jugoslavija (ch) 1972 — 13/489; 17. f5!?±

82 14... de5 15. fe5 ♘e5 16. ♗f4 ♗d6 17. ♖ad1 ♘c4 18. ♗d6 ♕d6 19. ♕d6 ♘d6 20. ♘e6 ♗e6 21. ♖d6±

83 17... g6?! 18. ♘f3± Hartston—Karpov, Nice (ol) 1974 — 17/493

84 20. c4 ♗c6 21. ♘d6±

85 **12... d5** 13. e5 ♘h5 [13... ♘e8 14. f5!±] 14. ♕f2 [14. ♕h3 g6 15. g4 ♘g7 16. ♕h6 f6!∞] g6 15. ♗b6 ♕b8 16. ♘d4 ♘g7 Trifunović—Najdorf, Saltsjöbaden (izt) 1948] 17. ♗d3±; **12... b5** 13 e5 [13. a3?! b4 14. ab4 ♘b4∞ Gipslis—Portisch, Zagreb 1965] de5 [13... ♘e8? 14. ♗d3 de5 15. fe5 f5?! 16. ef6 ♕g3 17. fe7! ♖f3 18. hg3 ♖f1 19. ♖f1 ♘e7 20. ♗c5 ♘f5 21. g4+— Schmidt—Neukirch, 1970] 14. fe5 ♘h5 15. ♕h3 g6 16. g4 ♘g7 17. ♘e4! ♘e5 18. ♘fg5 ♗g5 19. ♘g5 h5 20. gh5 gh5 21. ♗h5 ♘h5 [Hennings—Espig, DDR 1973] 22. ♖f2!±

86 13. e5?! ♘fd5 14. ♘d5 [14. ♗d4? ♘c3 15. bc3 ♘c2 16. ed6 ♘d4—+] ♘d5 15. ♗d4 ♕c2 16. ed6 ♗f6 17. ♗f6 ♘f6 18. ♕f2 ♕b2 19. ♘e5 ♖ac8 20. ♗f3 ♖c2!∓ Gipslis—Bokučava, SSSR 1965

87 14. ♗d4∞

88 **12... ♔h8** 13. ♘c6 ♗c6 14. ♗d4 b5 15. e5 de5 16. ♗e5 ♕b7 17. ♖ae1±; **12... e5** 13. fe5 ♘e5 14. ♘f5± Parma—Bertok, Jugoslavija 1970

89 13. ♘c6 ♗c6 14. e5 de5 15. fe5 ♘h5 16. ♕h3 g6 17. g4 ♘g7 18. ♕g3 ♕b7 19. ♖ae1 b4= Nikitin

90 13... e5 14. fe5 ♘e5 15. ♘f5±

91 14. ♔h1 ♖ab8 15. ♘c6! ♗c6 16. ♗d4 ♖bd8 [16... b4? 17. e5 bc3 18. ef6 ♗f6 19. ♕h3+—] 17. ♖ae1 ♕b7 18. ♕h3± Janošević—Cvetković, Jugoslavija 1972 — 13/488

92 20. ♗h6± Gligorić—Ostojić, Jugoslavija (ch) 1965

B 86

1. e4 c5 2. ♘f3 d6 3. d4 cd4 4. ♘d4 ♘f6 5. ♘c3 e6 6. ♗c4

	6	7	8	9	10	11	12	13	14	
1	... ♗e7	♗b3[1] 0—0	♗e3[2] ♘a6	f4[3] ♘c5	♕f3 a6[4]	f5[5] ♕c7[6]	0—0 b5	fe6 fe6	♕h3 ♘b3[7]	∞
2	... ...	... ...	... ...	f3 ♘c5	♕d2 a6	g4 ♕c7	h4[8] b5	a3 ♘fd7	g5 ♘b6[9]	∞
3	... a6	a3[10] ♗e7[11]	0—0[12] 0—0	♗a2[13] b5	f4[14] ♗b7	f5[15] e5	♘de2 ♘bd7[16]	♘g3 ♖c8[17]	♗g5[18] ♘b6[19]	=
4	... ...	... b5	♗a2 ♗b7	♕e2[20] ♘c6[21]	♗e3 ♗e7[22]	♖d1[23] ♕a5	0—0 0—0	f3		=

1. e4 c5 2. ♘f3 d6 3. d4 cd4 4. ♘d4 ♘f6 5. ♘c3 e6 6. ♗c4 a6 7. ♗b3

	7	8	9	10	11	12	13	14	15	
5	... ♘bd7	♗e3[24] ♘c5[25]	f3 ♕c7[26]	♕d2 ♗e7	0—0[27] 0—0	♖ad1 ♗d7	♔h1 ♖fd8	♗g5 ♗e8[28]		=

	7	8	9	10	11	12	13	14	15	
6	...	f4	♕e2[30]	0–0	f5	♘f3	ab3	g4	♘d5[31]	$\overline{\infty}$
	...	♘c5[29]	♗e7	0–0	e5	♘b3	h6	d5		
7	...	...	♕f3	0–0[33]	e5	♕d1	fe5	♘b3	♖d1	=
	...	...	♕d7[32]	b5	♗b7	de5	♘b3	♕d1	♘e4[34]	
8	...	...	f5!	♕f3	♗e3[36]	ed5	♘de2	♕h3	0–0	±
	...	...	♗e7[35]	0–0	d5	e5[37]	e4	g6	♘b3[38]	
9	...	0–0[39]	f4[40]	f5[41]	♘f5	♖f5	♗g5	♔h1[43]		±
	♗e7	0–0	♕c7	ef5[42]	♗f5	♘bd7	♖ac8			
10	...	f4	f5	ef5[46]	0–0	♗g5	♗h4	♔h1	♕d3[47]	±
	...	0–0[44]	ef5[45]	d5	♘c6	h6	♕c7	♖d8		
11	...	...	♕f3	f5[49]	♗e3	♗d4	a3[53]	ef5	♕h3	±
	...	...	♕c7[48]	♘c6[50]	♘d4[51]	b5[52]	ef5[54]	♗b7		

[1] 7. ♗e3 0–0 8. f4?! [8. ♕e2?! d5 9. ed5 ed5 10. ♗b3 ♖e8 11. 0–0 ♘c6 12. ♕d2 ♗b4∓ Huguet–Hartston, Praja da Rocha 1969] d5 9. ♗d3 de4 10. ♘e4 ♘d5 11. ♕f3 ♘e3 12. ♕e3 ♕b6∓ Hübner–Petrosjan (mct) 1971 — 11/363

[2] **8. 0—0** ♘a6 9. f4 [9. ♕e2 ♘c5 10. ♖d1?! ♗d7 11. ♗g5 a6 12. f4 ♖c8 13. f5 ♔h8∓ Ardijansjah–Larsen, Bauang 1973 — 16/415] ♘c5 10. ♕f3 a6 11. f5 ♕c7 12. g4 [Honfi–Ćirić, Čačak 1969 — 8/418] d5!∞; **8. ♕e2** ♘bd7 9. g4 ♘c5 10. g5 ♘fd7 11. ♖g1 a6 12. f4 ♖e8 13. ♗e3 ♗f8 14. f5± Radulov–Buljovčić, Vršac 1971 — 13/460; 8... ♘c6 9. ♗e3 — B 89

[3] 9. ♕e2?! ♘c5 10. f3 e5! 11. ♘f5 ♗f5 12. ef5 [Minić–Malich, Amsterdam 1971 — 12/445] ♘b3 13. ab3 d5∓

[4] **10... e5** 11. ♘f5 ♗f5 12. ef5 ♘b3 13. ab3 ♕c8 14. g4 ♕c6= Malich; **10... d5** 11. ed5 ed5 12. 0–0 ♖e8 13. h3?! ♘ce4 14. ♘e4 de4 15. ♕e2 ♘d5∓ Novopašin–Talj, SSSR (ch) 1962; 13. f5!?∞

[5] **11. g4** d5!? 12. ed5 [12. e5?! ♘fe4 13. ♘e4 de4 14. ♕h3 ♕a5 15. ♗d2 ♕c7 16. g5 ♖d8∓ Bednarski–Malich, Skopje (ol) 1972 — 14/447] ed5 13. g5 ♘b3 14. ab3 ♘e4 15. ♘e4 de4 16. ♕g2 ♗b4 17. c3 ♗c5∞ Minić–Bogdanović, Jugoslavija 1963; **11. 0—0** ♗d7?! 12. e5 ♘e8 13. ♘e4 de5 14. fe5 ♕c7 15. ♘c5 ♗c5 16. ♕g3 g6 17. ♖ae1±→» Bogdanović–Udovčić, Sarajevo 1960; 11... d5!?∞; 11... e5!?

[6] 11... e5?! 12. ♘de2 b5 13. ♗c5!? [13. ♘d5?! ♘b3 14. ♘f6 ♗f6 15. cb3 d5∞ Bogdanović–Matulović, Sarajevo 1960] dc5 14. ♗d5±

[7] 15. ab3 e5 16. ♘f5 b4 17. ♘a4 ♖b8∞ Bogdanović–Bradvarević, Jugoslavija (ch) 1967

[8] **12. g5** ♘fd7 13. h4 b5 14. g6 ♘e5! 15. gh7 ♔h8 18. a3 ♖b8∞ Reshevsky–Malich, Siegen (ol) 1970; **12. 0-0-0**!? b5 13. g5 ♘fd7 14. g6!?∞ Milić

[9] 15. h5 ♖b8 16. g6 ♘c4! [16... hg6? 17. hg6 fg6 18. ♕g2±→» Minić–van der Weide, Amsterdam 1971] 17. ♗c4 bc4 18. ♖b1 ♗f6∞ Minić

[10] **7. ♗e3**?! b5 8. ♗b3 b4 9. ♘a4 ♘e4 **10.** ♕f3 ♗b7∓; **7. a4** ♗e7 8. 0–0 0–0 9. ♗a2 ♘c6 10. ♗e3 ♘b4 11. ♗b3 b6! 12. f4 ♗b7 13. ♕f3 ♖c8 14. ♕h3 ♔h8∓; **7. ♕e2** ♗e7 8. 0–0 0–0 9. ♖d1 ♕c7 10. ♗g5 h6 11. ♗h4 b5 12. ♗b3 ♗b7= Puc–Ankerst, Jugoslavija (ch) 1965; 7... b5 8. ♗b3 — B 87

[11] **7... ♗d7** 8. 0–0 ♘c6 9. ♗e3 ♗e7 10. f4±↑; **7... ♕c7** 8. ♗a2 ♗e7 9. f4 0–0 10. f5±; **7... ♘bd7** 8. 0–0 b5 9. ♗e6 fe6 10. ♘e6 ♕b6 11. ♗e3 ♕c6 12. ♘d5∞ Paoli–Kolarov, Gyula 1965; 9. ♗a2 ♗b7 — 7... b5

[12] 8. ♗a2 0–0 9. ♗e3 b5 10. g4 ♗b7 11. f3 ♘c6 12. ♖g1 ♘d7 13. g5 ♘de5 14. f4 ♘d4 15. ♗d4 ♘c6 16. ♖g3± Korčnoj–Bobocov, Wijk aan Zee 1969 — 5/450; 11... ♘fd7∞

[13] 9. f4 d5!? [9... ♘e4?! 10. ♘e4 d5 11. f5! ef5 12. ♗d5 ♕d5 13. ♘c3 ♕a5 14. b4± Westerinen–Tatai, Malaga 1967 — 3/503] 10. ed5 ed5 11. ♗a2 ♘c6=

[14] 10. ♕e1 ♗b7 11. f3 [11. f4? ♕b6 12. ♗e3 ♘g4∓] ♘c6 12. ♗e3 ♕c7 13. ♕g3 ♘d4! [13... ♘e5? 14. ♗e6!± Sergijevski–Bobocov, Soči 1966 — 2/453] 14. ♗d4 ♘h5 15. ♕f2 ♗f6=

[15] **11. ♕f3** ♘bd7 12. f5 e5 13. ♘de2 a5! 14. ♗g5 ♖c8 15. ♗f6 ♘f6 16. ♖ac1 b4∓ Sanakojev–Terentjev, SSSR 1962; **11. ♕e2** ♘bd7 12. e5 [12. ♖d1?! ♕b6 13. ♗e3 ♕c7 14. f5 e5 15. ♘f3 ♘e4 16. ♘d5 ♕d8∓ Gufeljd–Polugajevski, SSSR 1959; 12. ♔h1!? Schwarz]

de5 13. fe5 ♗c5 14. ♗e3 ♘e5! 15. ♘e6 ♗e3 16. ♕e3 fe6 17. ♕e5 ♕b6 18. ♔h1 ♖ae8= Ćirić–Polugajevski, Rostov 1961

16 12... ♘e4? 13. ♘e4 ♗e4 14. ♘g3 ♗b7 [14... d5 15. ♘e4 de4 16. ♗d5±] 15. f6! [15. ♘h5 ♗f6 16. ♕g4 ♔h8∞ Ragozin] ♗f6 16. ♘h5 ♔h8 [16... ♘d7? 17. ♕g4 g6 18. ♕d7!+−; 16... ♗e7? 17. ♕g4 g6 18. ♗h6 d5 19. ♗f8 ♔f8 20. ♕e6+−] 17. ♕g4 ♕d7 18. ♘f6 gf6 19. ♕h4 ♕e7 20. ♖f6 ♖g8 21. ♗g5±

17 13... ♘c5 14. ♗d5 ♗d5 15. ed5 a5 16. ♗g5 ♘cd7 17. ♗f6 ♘f6 18. ♘ce4 ♕b6 19. ♔h1 ♘e4 20. ♘e4± Krogius–Polugajevski, SSSR (ch) 1959

18 **14. ♗e3** ♘b6 15. ♗b6 ♕b6 16. ♔h1 ♕e3! 17. ♘d5 ♗d5 18. ♗d5 ♗d8! 10. a4 ♗b6∓ Robatsch–Fischer, La Habana 1965; **14. ♘h5** ♘h5 15. ♕h5 ♖c3! 16. bc3 ♘f6 17. ♕e2 ♘e4 18. c4 bc4 19. ♗c4 d5 20. ♗d3 ♘c5∓

19 **14... ♖c3** 15. bc3 ♘e4 16. ♘e4 ♗e4 17. ♗e7 [17. ♗e3 ♘b6 18. ♕g4 d5 19. ♗h6 ♗f6 20. ♗g7 ♔g7 21. f6 ♗g6 22. fg7 ♔g7∓] ♕e7 18. c4 [18. ♗d5? ♘f6 19. ♗e4 ♘e4 20. ♔h1 ♕h4 21. ♕f3 d5 22. g3 ♕f6 23. ♖fe1 ♕c6 24. ♖e3 f6∓ Ćirić–Gligorić, Jugoslavija (ch) 1965] ♖c8 19. ♕e2 ♘f6 20. ♖ac1 bc4 21. ♗c4 a5 22. ♗d3 d5∞; **14... ♘b6** 15. ♗f6 [15. ♘h5 ♘e4? 16. ♗e7 ♕e7 17. ♘e4 ♗e4 18. f6!+−; 15... ♘h5? 16. ♗e7 ♕e7 17. ♕h5 ♕f6 18. g4! h6 19. h4+−; 15... ♖c3?! 16. bc3 ♘h5 17. ♗e7 ♕e7 18. ♕h5 ♗e4 19. ♕g4 d5 20. f6 ♕c5 21. ♔h1± Olafsson–Fischer, Jugoslavija (ct) 1959; 15... ♘c4! 16. ♗f6 ♗f6 17. ♗c4 ♖c4 18. ♘f6 ♕f6= Rivera–Tringov, Varna (ol) 1962] ♗f6 16. ♖f3 ♘c4 [16... ♘a4? 17. ♘a4 ba4 18. ♔h1 ♕b6 19. ♖b1 ♗g5 20. ♖d3 ♕f2 21. c3± Nikitin–Talj, Kislovodsk 1966] 17. ♗c4 ♖c4 18. ♖d3 ♕b6 19. ♔h1 ♖d4 20. ♘ge2 ♖d3 21. ♕d3 ♖c8 22. ♖ad1 ♗e7= Boleslavski

20 9. 0–0 ♘bd7 [9... ♘e4?! 10. ♘e4 ♗e4 11. ♖e1±; 9... ♗e7!? Keres] 10. f4?! ♘e4 11. f5 ♘c3 12. bc3 e5 13. ♕h5 d5 14. ♘f3 ♗c5 15. ♔h1 0–0∓ Jović–Minić, Jugoslavija (ch) 1962; 10. ♖e1!?

21 9... ♘bd7 10. 0–0 ♖c8 11. ♗g5 [11. f4!? Boleslavski] h6 12. ♗h4 ♕b6 13. ♖ad1 ♗e7 14. ♔h1 g5 15. ♗g3 ♘e5 16. f4 gf4 17. ♖f4± Parma–Velimirović, Jugoslavija (ch) 1963

22 10... ♖c8 11. ♖d1 ♕c7 12. f4 ♘a5 13. ♗c1 ♘c4 14. 0–0 ♗e7 15. ♖d3±→» Ćirić–Mašić, Jugoslavija (ch) 1963

23 11. f4 0–0 12. f5? ♘d4 13. ♗d4 e5 14. ♗f2 ♖c8△ ♖c3∓ Lutovac–Bertok, Jugoslavija (ch) 1963

24 **8. g4** ♘c5 9. ♕e2 d5 [9... ♗e7? 10. g5 ♘fd7 11. f4 ♕c7 12. f5 ♘e5 13. ♗f4 ♗d7 14. 0-0-0± Medina–O'Kelly, Malaga 1967] 10. ed5 ♘b3 11. ab3 ♘d5=; **8. ♗g5** ♘c5 9. ♕e2 ♗e7 10. f4 [10. ♖d1? ♘fe4 11. ♘e4 ♗g5∓ Dely–Ćirić, Hamburg 1965] h6 11. ♗f6 ♗f6 12. 0-0-0 ♕b6 13. e5 de5 14. fe5 ♗e7 15. ♖hf1± Radulov–Ivkov, Budapest 1970 — 9/413

25 8... ♘b6? 9. f4 d5 10. e5 ♘fd7 11. f5 ♘e5 12. fe6 fe6 13. ♕h5 ♘g6 14. 0-0-0± Fajbisovič–Roberts, Harrachov 1967

26 9... ♗d7 10. ♕d2 ♗e7 11. g4 b5 12. 0-0-0 b4 13. ♘ce2 a5∞ Pelitov–Kadrev, Bulgaria (ch) 1966

27 11. g4 b5 12. g5 ♘fd7 13. 0-0-0 ♘b6 14. ♔b1 ♗d7 15. a3 ♖b8∞ Ciocaltea–Bilek, La Habana 1965

28 Paoli–Ciocaltea, Szombathely 1966

29 **8... ♗e7** 9. ♕f3 0–0 10. g4±→ Fischer; **8... b5** — B 87

30 **9. 0–0** ♕c7 10. ♕e2 ♘b3 11. ab3 ♗e7 12. ♔h1 0–0 13. ♖f3 ♗d7 14. ♖g3 ♖fe8 15. ♗d2 ♖ac8∞ Witkowski–Drozd, Polska (ch) 1964; **9. e5** de5 10. fe5 ♘fd7 11. ♗f4= Bednarski–Bogdanović, DDR 1964

31 **15. ♖d1** ♕b6 16. ♔h1 de4 17. ♘e5 1/2 : 1/2 Ćirić–Bogdanović, Sarajevo 1965; **15. ♘d5** ♘d5 16. ed5 ♕d5 17. ♕e5 ♗c5 18. ♔g2 ♕c6 19. ♗e3 ♗e3 20. ♕e3 b5=∞ Ćirić–Bogdanović, Jugoslavija (ch) 1965

32 9... b5 10. f5 e5 11. ♘c6 ♕d7 12. ♘b4 ♘b3 13. ab3 ♗b7 14. ♗e3 [14. ♗g5?! ♘e4 15. ♘e4 d5∞ Bebčuk–Kolinski, SSSR 1965] a5 15. ♘bd5 ♗d5 16. ♘d5 ♘d5 17. ed5 ♗e7 18. 0–0 0–0 19. ♕e4△ c4± Nikitin

33 10. f5 e5 11. ♘de2 ♘b3 12. ab3 d5! 13. ♘d5 ♘d5 14. ed5 ♕f5 15. ♕f5 ♗f5 16. c4 ♗c2∓ ⊥ Jansa–Ćirić, Soči 1956

34 16. ♘e4 ♗e4 17. c3 1/2 : 1/2 Ćirić–Bogdanović, Jugoslavija (ch) 1965

35 **9... ♘fe4**?! 10. fe6! ♗e6 [10... ♕h4? 11. g3 ♘g3 12. ♘f3! ♕h5 13. ef7 ♔d8 14. ♖g1 ♘f5 15. ♘d5+− Fischer–Bednarski, La Habana (ol) 1966; 10... fe6 11. ♘e4 ♘e4 12. 0–0±] 11. ♘e4 ♘e4 12. ♘e6 fe6 13. ♕g4 ♘c5 14. ♗e3!± Fischer; **9... b5**?! 10. fe6 fe6 11. 0–0 ♕d7 12. ♕f3 ♗b7 13. ♕h3± Balašov–Zlotnik, SSSR 1969 — 7/414; **9... e5** 10. ♘de2 h6 [10... ♘b3 11. ab3 h6 12. ♘g3 ♗d7 13. ♘h5 ♘h5 14. ♕h5± R. Byrne–Bogdanović, Sarajevo 1967] 11. ♘g3 ♗d7 12. ♘h5! ♗c6 13. ♘f6 ♕f6 14. ♕e2 ♕h4 15. g3 ♕d8 16. ♗d5± Ćirić–Bogdanović, Jugoslavija (ch) 1967

36 11. 0–0 ♘b3 12. ab3 ♗d7 13. g4 ♘e8 14. ♗e3 ♘c7 15. ♕g3 h6 16. ♖ad1± Darga–Ćirić, Beverwijk 1967

37 12... ♘b3 13. ♘b3 ed5 14. 0-0-0± Fischer

38 16. ab3 ♘d5 17. ♖ad1± Matulović–Bogdanović, Jugoslavija 1967

39 8. **g4** d5! [8... h6 9. ♗e3 ♘c6 10. ♖g1 ♕c7 11. h4 ♘d4 12. ♕d4 ♘d7 13. 0-0-0± Velimirović–Buljovčić, Jugoslavija (ch) 1965] 9. ed5 ♘d5 10. ♗d5 ed5 11. 0–0 ♘c6 12. ♗e3 ♘e5 13. f3 ♘c4∓ Nikitin; **8. ♗e3** 0–0 9. g4 b5 10. g5 ♘fd7 11. ♖g1 ♘c5 12. ♕h5!± Issler–Maeder, Schweiz 1968 — 5/455; 9... d5!?∞

40 9. ♔h1 b5 10. a3 ♗b7 11. ♕e1 ♘bd7 12. f3 ♖c8 13. ♕g3 ♘c5 14. ♗a2 ♔h8= Rocha–Gheorghiu, Hastings 1964/65

41 10. ♗e3 b5 11. ♕f3 ♗b7 12. a3 ♘bd7= Schneider–Aloni, Tel Aviv (ol) 1964

42 10... e5 11. ♘de2 b5 12. ♗g5 [12. ♘d5!? ♘d5 13. ♗d5 ♗b7 14. ♗b7 ♕b7 15. ♘c3± Velimirović] ♘bd7 13. ♘g3 ♗b7 14. ♘h5 ♖ac8 15. ♔h1 ♕d8 16. ♗f6 ♘f6 17. ♘f6 ♗f6 18. ♗d5 ♗d5 19. ♘d5± Gligorić–Attard, Madrid 1960

43 Silva–Aliaga, Skopje (ol) 1972

44 8... ♕c7 9. f5 [9. g4 ♘c6 10. g5 ♘d4 11. ♕d4 ♘h5 12. ♗e3 0–0 13. 0-0-0 b5 14. f5±; 9. ♕f3 b5 10. f5 e5 11. ♘d5 ♘d5 12. ♗d5 ♗b7 13. ♗b7 ♕b7 14. ♘e2 ♘d7 16. ♘c3±] e5 10. ♘de2 ♘bd7 11. ♗g5 0–0 12. g4!± Ree–Kuijpers, Wijk aan Zee 1970 — 10/528

45 9... e5 10. ♘de2 ♘bd7 11. ♘g3 b5 — B 87

46 10. ♘f5?! ♗f5 11. ef5 ♕b6! 12. ♕e2?! d5 [12... ♖e8 13. ♗e3 ♕a5 14. 0–0 ♗d8= Vladimirov] 13. ♗d2 ♘c6 14. 0-0-0 ♖fe8∓ Ledić–Hort, Vinkovci 1968 — 10/532; 12. ♕d3!? ♖e8 13. ♗e3 ♗f8∞ Hort

47 ± Nikitin

48 9... ♘bd7 10. g4!? [10. ♗e3 ♘c5 11. 0-0-0 ♕c7 12. g4 b5∞ V. Popov–Bogdanov, Bulgaria (ch) 1963] ♘c5 11. g5 ♘fd7 12. ♗e3 ♕c7 13. f5 ♘e5 14. ♕h3 ♘b3 16. ab3 ♖e8 16. 0–0±

49 10. g4 ♘c6 11. ♘c6 [11. ♗e3 ♘d4 12. ♗d4 e5] bc6 12. g5 ♘d7 13. ♗e3 c5 14. 0–0 ♖b8∞

50 10... e5 11. ♘de2 b5 12. g4 [12. a3 ♗b7 13. g4± Fischer] b4 13. g5! bc3 14. ♘c3 ♗b7 15. gf6 ♗f6 16. ♗e3 ♗h4 17. ♗f2 ♗f2 18. ♕f2 ♘d7 19. ♖g1±→» Soltis–Maeder, Dresden 1970 — 8/436

51 11... ♘e5!?

52 12... e5 13. ♗e3 b5 14. a3 ♗b7 [Sigurjonsson–Kristjansson, Reykjavik 1968] 15. ♖d1±

53 13. g4 b4 14. g5 ♘e8 15. f6 bc3 16. fe7 ♕e7 17. ♖g1 cb2 18. ♗b2 e5 19. 0-0-0 ♗e6 20. ♗a3 ♖c8 1/2 : 1/2 Minić–Jansa, Budva 1963; 13... ♗b7!? 14. g5? ♘e4!∓

54 13... e5?! 14. ♗f2 ♗b7 15. 0–0 ♖ac8 16. ♖fe1 ♕b8 17. ♔h1 ♕a8 18. ♗h4± Matulović–Bednarski, Polanica Zdroj 1963

B 87

1. e4 c5 2. ♘f3 d6 3. d4 cd4 4. ♘d4 ♘f6 5. ♘c3 e6 6. ♗c4 a6 7. ♗b3 b5

	8	9	10	11	12	13	14	15	16	
1	a3[1]	♕e2[2]	♘c6	♘d5[4]	0–0	♘c3	♗f4	♖ad1	♖d3	=
	♗b7	♘c6[3]	♗c6	♘d7[5]	♗b7	♗e7	0–0	♕c7	♖fd8[6]	
2	♕e2	♗g5	0-0-0	♖he1	♗h4	♗g3	bc3	f3	ed5	=̄∞
	♗b7[7]	♘bd7[8]	♖c8[9]	h6	g5[10]	♖c3	♕a5	d5	♗a3[11]	
3	...	♗e3[12]	f3[13]	0-0-0	g4	h4	h5	♘b1	ab3	∞
	♗e7	0–0	♕c7[14]	♘bd7	♘c5	♗d7	b4	♘b3	♖fc8[15]	
4	...	♗e3	f3	g4	g5	h4	0-0-0	♘b1	ab3	∓
	♕b6	♕b7	♗e7	♘fd7	♘c5	♗d7[16]	b4	♘b3	g6[17]	
5	f3	♗e3	♕d2[19]	g4	0-0-0	h4	g5	♕e2	♗d4	=
	♗e7[18]	0–0	♗b7[20]	♘c6	♘d7[21]	♖c8[22]	♘de5	♘d4	♘c4[23]	
6	f4	♘a4	0–0	f5	♘f5	♘h6[27]	♕h5	♗h6	g3[28]	=̄∞
	b4[24]	♘e4	g6[25]	gf5	♗b7[26]	♗h6	♕e7	♖g8	♘d7[29]	
7	...	...	e5[30]	fe5	0–0	♘f3[33]	♕e1	♗d5	♘b6	=
	...	♗b7	de5[31]	♘d5[32]	♕h4	♕h5	♗e7	♗d5	♗c5[34]	

	8	9	10	11	12	13	14	15	16	
8	. . . ♗b7	f5[35] e5[36]	♘de2[37] ♘bd7[38]	♗g5 ♗e7[39]	♗f6[40] ♘f6	♘g3[41] ♖c8	0—0[42] 0—0[43]	a3 ♕b6	♔h1 ♕e3![44]	=
9	. . . . . .	. . . . . .	. . . . . .	♘g3 ♗e7[45]	♗g5 h5[46]	♗f6 ♘f6	♕d3 h4	♘ge2 b4	♘d5[47]	=
10	. . . . . .	. . . . . .	. . . . . .	. . . . . .	. . . ♖c8	♗f6[48] ♘f6	♕d3[49] ♕c7	0-0-0 0—0	♕e2 b4[50]	=

1. e4 c5 2. ♘f3 d6 3. d4 cd4 4. ♘d4 ♘f6 5. ♘c3 e6 6. ♗c4 a6 7. ♗b3 b5 8. 0—0

	8	9	10	11	12	13	14	15	16	
11	. . . b4?!	♘a4[51] ♘e4[52]	♖e1[53] ♘f6[54]	♗g5[55] ♗e7[56]	♘f5 0—0[57]	♘e7 ♕e7	♘b6 ♗b7[58]	♘a8 ♗a8	♗f6 ♕f6[59]	±
12	. . . ♗e7	♕f3[60] ♕c7[61]	♖e1[62] 0—0[63]	a3 ♘c6	♘c6 ♕c6	♗g5 ♗b7	♖ad1 ♖fd8	♕g3 a5	♗h6 ♗f8[64]	=
13	. . . . . .	f4 ♗b7[65]	e5 de5	fe5 ♗c5[66]	♗e3 ♘c6	ef6 ♗d4	♕e1[67] ♗e3	♕e3 ♕d4	♖ae1 gf6[68]	=
14	. . . . . .	. . . 0—0	a3[69] ♗b7	f5[70] e5	♘de2 ♘bd7[71]	♘g3 ♖c8	♗g5 ♘b6	♘h5 ♖c3	bc3 ♗e4[72]	=
15	. . . . . .	. . . . . .	e5 de5	fe5 ♘fd7[73]	♕h5[74] ♘c5[75]	♗e3 ♘b3[76]	ab3[77] ♗b7	♖f2 ♘c6	♘c6 ♗c6[78]	=
16	. . . . . .	. . . . . .	. . . . . .	. . . . . .	. . . ♘c6	♘c6 ♕b6	♗e3 ♕c6	♔h1 ♗b7	♖f3 ♗c5[79]	=
17	. . . ♗b7	f4[80] b4[81]	♘a4[82] ♗e7[83]	e5 ♘d5	♕g4 0—0	♗d5 ♗d5	f5 ♔h8	fe6 fe6[84]	♘e6 ♖f1[85]	=
18	. . . . . .	♖e1 ♘bd7[86]	♗g5[87] h6[88]	♗f6[89] ♘f6[90]	a4[91] b4	♘a2 ♘e4[92]	♘b4 d5	♘bc6 ♕b6	c4![93]	±
19	. . . . . .	. . . ♘c6!?	a4 b4	♘c6 ♗c6	♘d5 ♗e7[94]	♘e7 ♕e7	♗g5 0—0	♗f6 gf6	a5 ♖fd8	=

[1] **8. ♗e3**?! b4! [8... ♕c7?! 9. f4 b4 10. ♘a4 ♘bd7 11. f5 e5 12. ♘e6!±→ Zajcev—Dementjev, SSSR (ch) 1971] 9. ♘a4 ♗b7 [9... ♘e4?! 10. ♘e6 fe6 10. ♘b6 ♗b7 11. ♘a8 ♗a8 12. ♗e6±↑] 10. f3 ♘bd7∓ Uhlmann; **8. ♗g5** b4 [8... ♗e7 9. ♕f3 ♕b6 10. 0-0-0 0—0 11. g4±→ Kristinssen—Heim 1973; 9... 0—0 10. e5 de5 11. ♘e6±; 9... ♕c7∞] 9. ♘ce2 [9... ♘a4 ♗e7 10. ♕f3 ♗b7∞ Polugajevski] ♗e7 10. ♘g3 0—0 11. 0—0 ♗b7 [Sznapik—Polugajevski, Soči 1974 — 18/474] 12. ♗e6!? fe6 13. ♘e6 ♕a5 14. ♘f5 ♖f7∞; **8. ♕f3** ♗b7 9. ♗g5 b4 10. ♘a4 ♘bd7 11. 0—0 ♕a5 12. ♗f6 ♘f6 13. ♖e1 ♗e7= R. Byrne—Evans, USA (ch) 1966/67

[2] **9. f3** ♗e7 10. ♗e3 0—0 11. 0—0 ♘bd7 12. ♕d2 ♘e5 13. ♕f2 ♕c7 14. ♖ac1 ♔h8!? 15. ♘ce2 ♖g8!? 16. ♔h1 g5∓ Garcia—Fischer, La Habana (ol) 1966; 12. ♗e6!?= Fischer; **9. ♗g5** ♘bd7 10. ♕e2 ♕a5 11. 0—0 b4 12. ♘d5 ed5 13. ed5 ♔d8 14. ab4 ♕b4 15. ♘c6 ♗c6 16. dc6 ♘c5∞ Ibrahimov—Mosionžik, SSSR 1962

[3] 9... ♘bd7 10. ♗g5 ♘c5 11. 0-0-0 ♕b6 12. ♗f6 gf6 13. ♗a2 h5∞ Žugder—Lengyel, Ulan Bator 1956

[4] 11. 0—0 ♗e7 12. f4 0—0 13. f5 ef5 14. ♖f5 ♕b6 15. ♗e3 ♕b7 16. ♗d4 ♖ae8 17. ♖af1 b4∞ Boljoš—Martinović, Jugoslavija 1969

5 11... ♗b7 12. ♘f6 ♕f6 13. 0—0 ♗e7 14. ♖e1 0—0 15. c3 ♖ad8 16. ♗e3 ♕h4 17. f3 d5= Santos—Padilla, Skopje (ol) 1972

6 17. ♖fd1 ♘e5 18. ♖h3 g6 19. ♗c1 ♘c4 20. f4 d5 21. ed5 ed5= Pilnik—Sanguinetti, Mar del Plata 1965

7 **8... ♘bd7** 9. ♗g5 ♘c5 [9... ♗b7?! 10. ♗e6 fe6 11. ♘e6±; 9... ♕a5?! 10. 0-0-0 ♗b7 11. ♗d5 ed5 12. ed5 ♔d8 13. ♘c6 ♗c6 14. dc6 ♘b6 15. ♖he1±→ Timoščenko—Juferov, SSSR 1972] 10. ♗d5 ed5 11. ♘c6 ♕d7 12. ed5 ♗e7 13. ♗f6 gf6 [Velimirović—Bertok, Jugoslavija 1974 — 18/476] 14. 0—0!? ♔f8 15. ♖fe1 ♗d8 16. b4 ♘a4 17. ♘a4 ba4 18. c4±→; **8... b4** 9. ♘a4 ♗b7 10. f3 d5 11. ♗g5 de4 12. 0-0-0 ♘bd7∞; 10. 0—0!?↑ Lepeškin

8 **9... b4** 10. ♘a4 ♕a5 11. ♗f6 gf6 12. 0-0-0 ♘c6 13. ♕e3± Radulov—S. Garcia, Varna 1970 — 9/417; **9... h6** 10. ♗h4 ♘bd7 11. 0-0-0 ♕a5 12. ♖he1 g5?! 13. ♗g3 ♖c8?! 14. e5!± Mariotti—Eppinger, Italia 1969 — 8/440; 10... g5!? 11. ♗g3 ♘bd7 12. 0-0-0 ♕b6△ ♘e5 Gufeljd

9 **10... ♕c7**?! 11. ♖he1 h6 12. ♘d5! ♗d5 13. ed5 e5 14. ♗f6 gf6± Židkov—Lapienis, SSSR 1968; **10... ♕a5** 11. ♘d5?! ed5 12. ed5 ♔d8 13. ♘c6 ♗c6 14. dc6 ♘c5!∓ Gurgenidze—Sorokin, SSSR 1973 — 16/442; 11. ♗f6 ♘f6 12. e5 de5 13. ♘e6!?∞ Gufeljd, 11. ♗d5! — 8... ♘bd7

10 12... ♗e7?! 13. ♗e6! fe6 14. ♘e6 ♕a5 15. ♘g7 ♔f7 16. e5 ♘e5 17. f4 ♖c3 18. fe5 ♖hc8 14. bc3 ♕a2 20. ♖d3± Vadasz—Kluger, Budapest 1968/69

11 17. ♔d2 ♘d5 18. ♗d5 ♗d5=∞ Rossetto—Panno, Buenos Aires 1968 — 6/553

12 **9. g4** b4 10. ♘d1 ♗b7 11. f3 ♘c6 12. ♗a4 ♖c8 13. ♘c6 ♗c6 14. ♕a6 ♕d7 15. ♗c6 ♖c6 16. ♕e2 0—0 17. c3 d5!∓ Ujtumen—Gligorić, Palma de Mallorca (izt) 1970; **9. f3** 0—0 10. g4 b4! 11. ♘a4 ♗d7 12. c3 ♕a5 13. cb4 ♕b4 14. ♕d2 d5!∓ Ćirić—Polugajevski, Amsterdam 1970; **9. ♗g5** 0—0 10. f4 [10. 0-0-0 ♘e4! 11. ♕e4 ♗g5 12. f4 d5 13. ♘d5! ed5 16. ♗d5 ♗f4 15. ♔b1 ♖a7= Radulov—Padevski, Sofia 1970 — 10/533] b4 [10... h6 11. ♗f6 ♗f6 12. 0-0-0 b4 13. ♘a4 ♕a5 14. ♕d2 ♗b7 15. a3 ♗e4 16. ab4 ♕c7 17. ♖he1± Radulov—Jakobsen, Forssa-Helsinki 1972 — 14/473; 12... ♕c7 13. ♖he1 ♘d7∞] 11. ♘a4 ♗b7 12. 0—0 ♘bd7 13. e5 de5 14. fe5 ♘d5 15. ♗e7 ♕e7 16. ♖ad1 g6 17. ♗d5 1/2 : 1/2 Vasjukov—Gligorić, Beograd 1961; 9... b4!? 10. ♘a4 ♗d7∓

13 10. 0-0-0 b4 11. ♘a4 ♕a5 12. ♘f3 ♘bd7 13. ♘d2 ♗b7 14. f3 ♗c6 15. ♘c4 ♕c7 16. ♘ab6 ♖ab8 17. ♘d7 ♗d7∓ Perényi—P. Székely, Hungary 1974 — 18/475

14 **10... ♗b7** 11. 0-0-0 ♘bd7 12. g4 ♘c5 13. g5 ♘fd7 14. h4 ♖c8 15. ♔b1 b4 16. ♘a4 ♘a4 17. ♗a4 ♘c5 18. ♗b3 a5 19. ♗c4!± Bönsch—Talj, Halle 1974 — 18/477; **10... ♗d7**!? Talj

15 Midjard—de Castro, Skopje (ol) 1972

16 13... b4!? 14. ♘d1 [14. ♘a4? ♗d7!—+] ♘b3 15. ♘b3 [15. ab3 e5 16. ♘f5 ♗f5 17. ef5 d5∓] e5∓

17 17. ♕g2 e5 18. ♘e2 a5 19. f4 a4∓ Radulov—Kavalek, Venezia 1971 — 12/469

18 **8... ♘bd7** 9. ♗e3 ♘c5 10. ♕d2 ♗d7 11. g4 b4 12. ♘ce2 e5?! 13. ♘f5 ♗f5 14. ♗c5! dc5 15. ♕d8 ♖d8 16. ef5± Ljubojević—Kubiček, Dresden 1969; **8... ♗b7** 9. 0—0 ♘bd7 10. ♔h1 ♘c5 11. ♗e3 ♗e7 12. ♕e1 0—0= Kuijpers—Gligorić, Moskva 1963

19 10. ♕e2 — 8. ♕e2

20 **10... ♕c7** 11. g4 ♘c6 12. ♘c6 ♕c6 13. g5 ♘d7 14. ♘d5 ♗d8 15. a4 ♘e5∓ Benkö—Talj, Portorož (izt) 1958; 11. a4!?∞; **10... ♗d7** 11. g4 b4 12. ♘ce2 a5 13. g5 ♘e8 14. ♗c4 a4 15. ♘g3 ♘c6 16. ♘c6 ♗c6 17. ♖d1 ♕c7 18. b3 ab3 19. ab3 ♖a2 20. 0—0 d5!∓ Ujtumen—Geler, Palma de Mallorca (izt) 1970 — 10/531; 11. a3=

21 **12... ♘a5** 13. h4 ♘b3 14. ab3 ♖c8 15. h5 [Ivanović—Mesing, Jugoslavija (ch) 1968 — 5/453] b4!? 16. ♘a4 d5∞; **12... b4**!?

22 13... ♘de5 14. ♕e2 ♘a5!=

23 17. f4 ♕c7 18. g6 e5 19. ♗c4 ♕c4 20. gh7 ♔h8 21. ♕c4 ♖c4 22. fe5 de5 23. ♗e5 ♗e4= Ljubojević—Portisch, Palma de Mallorca 1971 — 12/477

24 **8... ♘bd7**?! 9. f5 e5 10. ♘c6 ♕c7 11. ♘b4 ♗b7 12. ♘bd5 ♕a5 13. 0—0 b4 14. ♘f6 ♘f6 15. ♘d5 ♗d5 16. ♗d5 ♘d5 17. ed5± Tringov—Parma, Budva 1963; **8... ♕c7** 9. f5 e5 10. ♘f3 h6 11. a4 b4 12. ♘d5 ♘d5 13. ♗d5± Havski—Vladimirov, SSSR 1963; **8... ♗e7** 9. e5 [9. f5 e5 10. ♘de2 ♘bd7 11. ♘g3 0—0 12. ♗g5 b4 13. ♗f6 bc3 14. ♗e7 ♕e7 15. bc3 ♘f6 16. 0—0 ♗b7 17. ♕f3 a5 18. a4 ♔h8 19. ♖fe1 g6=∞ Bilek—Petrosjan, Moskva 1967 — 4/559; 9. ♗e3 0—0 10. e5 de5 11. fe5 ♘fd7? 12. ♘e6 fe6 13. ♗e6 ♔h8 14. ♗d5 ♘c6 15. ♗c6+—; 9... b4!? Scanavino—Wexler, Buenos Aires 1965] de5 10. fe5 ♘fd7 11. ♗e6 ♘e5 12. ♗f4 fe6 13. ♗e5± Bebčuk—Korzin, SSSR 1964

25 **10... ♗b7**?! 11. f5 e5 12. ♘e6± Vuković; **10... ♘f6** 11. ♕f3 [11. f5 e5 12. ♘e2 ♗b7 13. ♗g5 ♗e7∞] d5 12. f5 ♗d6 [12... e5 13. ♖e1 e4 14. ♕g3±] 13. ♖e1 0—0 14. fe6 fe6 15. ♘e6 ♗e6 16. ♖e6±; **10... d5** 11. f5 ♖a7∞ Kinnmark—Ojanen, Helsinki 1967 — 3/509

26 12... ♖g8 13. ♗d5! ♖a7 14. ♗e3!? [14. ♗e4 ef5 15. ♗f5 ♖e7 16. ♗c8± Fischer—Talj, Jugoslavija (ct) 1959] ♘c5 15. ♕h5 ♖g6 [15... ♘a4 16. ♗a7 ed5 17. ♖ae1] 16. ♖ae1±→» Kevitz

27 **13. ♕h5** ♖g8 14. g3 ♘f6 15. ♕e2 d5=; **13. ♗e6**!? fe6 14. ♕h5 ♔d7 15. ♕f7 ♔c8 16. ♕e6 ♘d7 17. ♗e3 ♔b8 18. a3=∞ Lepeškin

28 **16. ♘b6**? ♖g2!−+; **16. ♖f3**!? ♘f6 17. ♕h3△ ♖af1 Marić

29 17. ♖ae1 ♘e5 18. ♗f4=∞ Szeles−Sax, Hungary 1972 — 13/502; 17... ♖g6!?△ f5 Lepeškin

30 10. 0−0 — 8. 0−0

31 10... ♘e4!?

32 **11... ♘e4**?! 12. 0−0 ♗e7 13. ♗e6! fe6 14. ♘e6 ♕d1 15. ♘g7 ♔d7 16. ♖d1 ♔c6 17. ♘f5± Platonov−Saharov, SSSR 1970; **11... ♘fd7** 12. 0−0 ♘e5 13. ♗e6! ♘bc6 [Kinnmark−Ivkov, Halle 1963] 14. ♗e3! ♘d4 [14... fe6 15. ♘e6 ♕d1 16. ♖ad1 ♖c8 17. ♘b6±] 15. ♗d4 fe6 16. ♗e5 ♕d1 17. ♖ad1±⊥ Velimirović

33 13. ♔h1 ♘d7 14. c4 bc3 15. ♗d5 ♗d5 16. ♘c3 ♗b7 17. ♘f3 ♕c4 18. ♗g5 h6 19. ♗h4 g5 20. ♗g3 ♗g7= Dely−Polugajevski, Budapest 1965

34 17. ♗e3 ♗b6 18. ♗b6 0−0 ♕b4 ♖c8 20. ♕d2 1/2 : 1/2 Ćirić−Polugajevski, Sarajevo 1965

35 9. e5 de5 10. fe5 ♘e4 [10... ♘d5 11. ♕g4 ♘c3 12. bc3±] 11. ♘e4 ♗e4 12. 0−0 ♗c5=

36 **9... b4**?! 10. fe6 bc3 11. ef7±→; **9... ef5**?! 10. ♘f5 g6 11. ♘h6 ♗h6 12. ♗h6 ♘e4 13. ♕d4!± Zuckerman−Velimirović, Marianske Lazni 1967

37 10. ♘f3?! ♗e7 11. ♕e2 ♘bd7 [11... b4!] 12. a4 0−0 13. ab5 ab5 14. ♖a8 ♕a8 15. ♕b5 ♘c5 16. ♘d5 [16. ♗d5?! ♕a1 17. 0−0 ♗a6∓ Tatai−Parma, Reggio Emilia 1966 — 1/311] ♘d5 17. ♗d5 ♗d5 18. ed5 e4! [18... ♕d5? 19. b4 ♕e4 20. ♔d1!±] 19. ♘d4 ♕d5∓

38 **10... ♘e4**?! 11. ♗d5 ♘c5 12. b4 ♕h4 13. g3 ♕b4 14. ♗b7 ♘b7 15. ♕d5 ♖a7 16. ♗e3± **10... b4** 11. ♘d5 ♘e4 12. ♗e3 ♘c5 13. 0−0±

39 11... ♖c8 12. ♘g3 ♗e7 — 11. ♘g3

40 12. 0−0 ♖c8 13. ♘g3 h5 — 11. ♘g3

41 13. ♕d3 ♕b6! [13... ♖c8 14. 0-0-0?! ♕b6!? 15. h3 b4 16. ♘d5 ♗d5 17. ♗d5 ♘d5 18. ed5 ♕b5!∓ Platonov−Polugajevski, SSSR 1971 — 12/474] 14. h3 0−0 15. 0-0-0?! a5 16. ♘d5 ♗d5 17. ♗d5 ♖ac8 18. ♔b1 ♖c5 19. g4 ♖fc8 20. ♘c3 h6 21. ♖d2 a4∓ Suetin−Platonov, SSSR 1971 — 12/475

42 14. ♘h5 — 11. ♘g3

43 14... h5!? — 11. ♘g3

44 **16... a5** 17. ♘h5±; **16... ♕e3**! 17. ♖f3 ♕g5 18. ♕d3 ♕h4 19. ♖e1 ♖c7 20. ♖e3 ♖fc8= Ljubojević−Portisch, Wijk aan Zee 1972 — 13/499

45 11... h5!? 12. ♗g5 [12. ♕f3?! ♗e7 13. ♗g5 h4 14. ♗f6 ♘f6 15. ♘ge2 b4∓ Kristjansson−Tukmakov, Reykjavik 1972 — 13/504] h4 13. ♘ge2=; 12. ♕d3!?

46 **12... ♘c5** 13. ♗f6 ♗f6 14. ♗d5 ♗d5 15. ♘d5 ♗h4 16. ♕f3 0−0 17. 0-0-0± Polugajevski−Donner, Beverwijk 1966 — 1/313; **12... b4** 13. ♗f6 ♘f6 [13... bc3!?] 14. ♘d5 ♘d5 15. ♗d5 ♗d5 16. ♕d5 0−0±; **12... 0—0** 13. ♗f6 ♘f6 14. ♘h5 ♘h5 15. ♕h5 ♖c8 [15... b4 16. ♘d5 ♗d5 17. ♗d5± Liebert−Pietzsch, Leipzig 1965] 16. ♕e2 [16. ♗d5 ♗d5 17. ♘d5 ♖c2 18. 0−0 ♗g5 19. f6 h6 20. ♖f5!± Dely−Simagin, Moskva 1962; 18... ♗f6 19. b3 h6 20. ♖fc1 ♖c1 21. ♖c1=∞ Padevski−Minić, Polanica Zdroj 1963] ♕b6 17. 0-0-0!± Hennings−McCurdy, Harrachov 1967

47 **16. ♗a4**?! ♔f8 17. ♘d5 ♗d5 18. ed5 ♕b6 19. ♗c6 ♖b8∓; **16. ♘d5** ♘d5 17. ♗d5 ♗d5 18. ♕d5 ♖c8 19. ♕d3 0−0=

48 **13. 0—0**?! h5 [13... 0−0 14. ♗f6 ♘f6 15. ♘h5 ♘h5 16. ♕h5 b4 17. ♘d5 ♗d5 18. ♗d5 ♖c2 19. ♔h1 ♗f6∞ Ciocaltea−Minić, Bucuresti 1966 — 1/312] 14. ♗f6 [14. h4?! b4 15. ♗f6 ♗f6 16. ♘d5 ♗h4 17. ♘h5 ♕g5∓ R. Byrne−Fischer, Sousse (izt) 1967 — 4/557] ♘f6 15. ♕f3 [15. ♘d5?! h4 16. ♘f6 gf6 17. ♘e2 ♗e4∓ Ciocaltea−Gheorghiu, Bucuresti 1968; 17. ♘h1 ♗e4∓ Thorstenssen−Ghitescu, Reykjavik 1970 — 9/414; 15. ♕d3 ♖c3!? 16. ♕c3 h4∓] ♖c3! 16. ♕c3 h4 17. ♘e2 ♕b6 18. ♔h1 ♘e4∓ Bednarski−Lehmann, Palma de Mallorca 1967 — 4/555; 15. ♗d5!?∞ **13. ♘h5** ♘h5 14. ♕h5 0−0 15. ♗e7 [15. h4?! b4 16. ♘d5 ♗d5 17. ed5 ♘c5∓ R. Byrne−Bouaziz, Sousse (izt) 1967 — 4/556] ♕e7 16. ♕e2=

49 14. ♘h5 ♖c3!? [14... ♘e4?! 15. ♘e4 ♗e4 16. ♕g4 ♗h4 17. ♔d1 ♕g5 18. ♘g7 ♔f8 19. ♕e4 ♔g7 20. g3±; 14... ♕b6!? 15. ♘f6 ♗f6 16. ♕d3 ♗g5∞] 15. bc3 ♗e4 16. ♘g7 [16. 0−0 ♘h5 17. ♕h5 d5 18. a4 0−0 19. ab5 ♕b6 20. ♔h1 ab5 21. ♖ad1 ♕c6∓ Neukirch−Minić, Krakow 1964] ♔f8 17. ♘h5 ♖g8 18. ♘f6 ♗f6 19. ♕h5 [Cosulich−Minić, Bari 1971 — 11/375] d5!∓ Sokolov

50 17. ♘d5 ♗d5 18. ♗d5 a5 19. ♔b1 a4 20. ♖d3 ♕c5 21. ♖c1 h6= Tringov−Bukić, Skopje 1971 — 12/476

51 9. ♘b1 ♘e4 10. ♕f3 ♗b7 [10... d5 11. c4 bc3 12. ♘c3 ♘c3 13. ♕c3 ♗e7 14. ♘f5! ef5 15. ♕g7 ♗f6 16. ♗a4 ♔e7 17. ♖e1±→》 Henkin−Judovič, SSSR 1954] 11. ♗a4 ♘d7 12. ♘c6 ♘ec5∓

52 **9... ♗e7** 10. f4 — 8... ♗e7; **9... ♗b7** 10. f4 — 8... ♗b7

53 10. ♕f3 d5 11. c4 bc3 12. ♘c3 ♘c5 [12... ♘c3?! 13. ♕c3!±] 13. ♕g4! ♘b3 14. ab3± Estrin–Vasiljev, SSSR 1955

54 **10... ♘c5**? 11. ♘c5 dc5 12. ♗a4 ♗d7 13. ♘e6 fe6 14. ♖e6 ♔f7 15. ♕d5+–; **10... d5** 11. ♗f4 ♗d6 [11... ♗b7 12. ♕h5!] 12. ♗d6 ♕d6 13. ♘f5 ef5 14. ♕d5 ♕d5 15. ♗d5±

55 11. ♕f3 d5 12. ♗f4 ♗d7 13. c4±

56 11... ♘bd7? 12. ♗e6!+–

57 12... ef5 13. ♗f6 gf6 14. ♕d5+–

58 14... ♖a7 15. ♘d5!±

59 17. ♕d6± Jovčić–Slatau, corr. 1957

60 **9. a4** b4 10. ♘a2 ♕b6! [10... 0–0 11. ♘b4 ♕b6 12. c3 ♘e4 13. ♗e3 ♕c7 14. f4 ♘c5? 15. ♗c2 a5 16. f5!± Soltis–Maeder, Haifa 1970 — 10/534; 14... a5!=] 11. c3 [11. ♗e3 ♕b7 12. f3 ♗d7△ ♘c6∓] bc3 12. ♘c3 0–0 13. a5 [13. ♗e3 ♕b7∓] ♕b7 14. f4 [14. f3 ♘c6∓] ♘c6 15. ♘c6 ♕c6 16. ♖a4 ♕c5∓ Sznapik–Pytel, Wroclaw 1972 — 13/503; **9. ♕e2** 0–0 10. a3 ♗b7 11. ♖ad1 ♘bd7 12. ♗g5 ♖c8 13. f3 ♕b6 14. ♔h1 ♘c5 15. ♗a2 ♖fe8∓ Giustolisi–Petrosjan, Lugano (ol) 1968 — 6/552; **9. ♗e3** 0–0 10. a4 [10. a3 ♗b7=] b4 11. ♘a2 ♘e4 12. ♘b4 ♕c7 13. f4 d5 14. ♘d3 ♘d7= Watt–Neumann, Dresden 1970 — 8/438; **9. ♖e1** 0–0 10. ♗g5 h6 [10... ♗b7 11. a4 b4 12. ♘a2 ♘e4 13. ♗e7 ♕e7 14. ♘b4 ♕f6= Nej–Bobocov, Beverwijk 1964] 11. ♗h4 ♗b7 12. a3 ♘c6 13. ♘c6 ♗c6 14. ♕d4 ♕c7 15. ♖ad1 ♖fd8= Vasjukov–Platonov, SSSR 1971 — 12/470

61 **9... ♗b7**?! 10. ♗e6! fe6 11. ♘e6 ♕d7 12. ♘g7 ♔d8 13. ♘f5±→ Holmov–Bobocov, Soči 1963; **9... ♕b6** 10. ♗e3 ♕b7?! 11. a3 [11. ♕g3 g6 (Kuzmin–Bukić, Banja Luka 1974 — 18/480) 12. ♗h6!±] ♘bd7 12. ♗g5 ♘c5 13. ♖fe1 0–0 14. ♗a2 h6 15. ♗h4± Browne–Benkö, Malaga 1972

62 **10. ♕g3** b4 11. ♘ce2 g6 13. c3?! ♘e4 13. ♕e3 ♘f6 14. cb4 0–0∞ Fischer–Olafsson, Buenos Aires 1960; 12. ♗h6!? Fischer; **10. a3** ♘c6 11. ♘c6 ♕c6 12. ♖e1 0–0 13. ♕g3∞ Velimirović–Tukmakov, Amsterdam 1974 — 18/481

63 10... ♗b7?! 11. ♗e6 fe6 12. ♘e6 ♕b6 13. ♗e3±

64 Vasjukov–Polugajevski, SSSR (ch) 1969

65 9... b4 10. ♘a4 ♕c7 11. e5! de5 12. fe5 ♕e5 [Klein–Flesch, Nederland 1968 — 5/449] 13. ♗f4! ♕e4 14. ♕d2 ♗b7 15. ♖ae1±

66 **11... ♘fd7** 12. ♖f7! ♔f7 13. ♘e6 ♕b6 14. ♔h1 ♔e8 15. ♘g7 ♔d8 16. e6+–; **11... ♘d5** 12. ♕f3±

67 14. fg7 ♗e3 15. ♔h1 ♖g8 16. ♕f3 ♖g7 17. ♗e6 [17. ♖ad1 ♕b6 18. ♘e4 ♘e7 19. ♖d3 ♗d4–+; 17. ♘e4 ♗d4 18. ♗e6 fe6 19. ♕f8 ♔d7 20. ♕d6 ♔c8∓] ♕e7! 18. ♗d5 ♘d4 19. ♕h3 ♘c2 20. ♖ad1 ♖d8 21. ♗b7 ♕b7 22. ♖d8 ♔d8 23. ♖d1 ♔e8 24. ♘e4 ♖g6 [Gufeljd–Platonov, SSSR (ch) 1969 — 8/439] 25. ♕h7! ♕c7 26. ♕h8 ♔e7 27. ♕h4= Lepeškin

68 17. ♘e4 0-0-0 [17... ♖d8 18. ♖f6 ♔e7 19. ♕f2 ♕f2 20. ♖f2 ♖g8 21. ♘f6 ♖g5 22. h4 ♖g7 23. ♘d5 ♔d6 1/2 : 1/2 Židkov–Lepeškin, SSSR 1970; 24. ♘f4!± Lepeškin; 18. ♘f6!? ♔e7 19. ♘d5! ♖d5 20. ♗d5 ♕d5 21. ♖d1± Romanišin–Šašin, SSSR 1974 — 18/483] 18. ♖f6 ♕e3 19. ♖e3 ♖d1 20. ♔f2 ♘e5= Štejn–Bobocov, Sofia 1965

69 **10. ♗e3** b4 11. e5 [11. ♘a4 ♗b7 12. f5 e5 13. ♘e2 ♘bd7∓ Gluščević–S. Nedeljković, Jugoslavija 1960] bc3 12. ef6 ♗f6 13. bc3 ♕c7∓ Bronštejn–Korčnoj, Moskva 1971 — 13/496; **10. f5** b4 11. fe6 [11. ♘a4 e5 12. ♘e2 ♗b7 13. ♘g3 ♘bd7 14. ♕f3 ♗c6∓ Janošević–Polugajevski, Skopje 1971 — 12/472; 11. ♘ce2 e5 12. ♘f3 ♗b7∓ Fischer–Smislov, Jugoslavija (ct) 1959] bc3 12. ef7 ♔h8 13. ♕f3 ♘c6 14. ♘c6 ♕b6 15. ♗e3!? [15. ♔h1 ♕c6 16. ♗g5 cb2 17. ♖ae1 ♗g4 18. ♕f4 ♗h5–+ Jansa–Polugajevski, Kapfenberg 1970 — 9/415] ♕c6 16. ♗d4∓; **10. ♕f3** ♕c7 11. f5? b4 12. ♘a4 e5 19. ♘e2 ♗b7 14. ♘g3 ♘bd7 15. ♗e3 ♗c6! 16. ♗f2 ♕b7 17. ♖fe1 d5!∓↑ Fischer–Talj, Jugoslavija (ct) 1959; 11. a3∞

70 11. ♕f3 ♘bd7 12. f5 e5 13. ♘de2 a5! 14. ♖d1 ♘c5∓ Ujtumen–Mecking, Palma de Mallorca 1970 — 10/530

71 12... ♘e4?! 13. ♘e4 ♗e4 14. ♘g3 ♗b7 15. f6! ♗f6 16. ♘h5 ♔h8 17. ♗h6! [17. ♕g4? ♕b6 18. ♔h1 ♕d4∓ Buhtin–Kislov, SSSR 1970] gh6 18. ♘f6 ♘d7 16. ♕d6 ♕b6 20. ♕b6 ♘b6 21. ♖ae1±

72 17. ♘g7!? ♔h8 [17... ♔g7?! 18. ♗f6 ♗f6 19. ♕g4±] 18. ♗f6! ♗f6 19. ♘h5 ♗b7 20. ♘f6 ♕f6 21. ♖f2= Šamroj–Zarjadko, corr. 1972

73 11... ♗c5 12. ♗e3 ♘fd7 13. ♕h5 [13. ♘e4?! ♗d4 14. ♗d4 ♘c6 15. ♗e3 ♘ce5∓ Ostojić–Minić, Vrnjačka Banja 1970] ♗d4 14. ♗d4 ♘c6 15. ♖ad1 ♘d4 16. ♖d4 ♕b6 17. ♖f4 ♕c5 [17... ♗b7!?] 18. ♘d5 ♔h8 [18... ed5? 19. ♗d5 ♗b7 20. ♗f7+– Riemsdyk–Ostojić, Sao Paulo 1973 — 16/439] 19. c3!? [19. ♔f1? ed5 20. ♖h4 h6 21. ♖dg4 ♕e3 22. ♖g5 ♔h7 23. ♗d5 ♕c1–+ Ardijansjah–Quinteros, Nalinas 1973] ed5 [19... ♗b7!?] 20. ♗d5 ♖b8 21. ♗f7 ♖b6 22. e6!±⊥ Levy–Garcia, Nice (ol) 1974

74 **12. ♗f4** ♘c5! [12... ♗b7?! 13. ♕g4± Honfi–Padevski, Čačak 1969 — 8/441] 13. ♘ce2 ♗b7 14. ♕e1 ♕b6!? [14... ♘c6∞ Padevski–Polugajevski, Kapfenberg 1970] 15. ♖d1 a5 16. c3 ♗e4 17. ♕g3 ♘bd7∓ Boleslavski; **12. ♕f3** ♘e5 13. ♕e4 ♗c5 14. ♗e3 ♘bc6 15. ♘c6 ♗e3 16. ♕e3 ♘c6 17. ♖ad1 ♕c7

18. ♘e4 ♕e5 19. ♕f3 ♖a7 20. c3 ♖d8∓ Bronštejn—Talj, Moskva 1971 — 12/473

75 **12... ♘f6** 13. ef6 [13. ♕h4 ♗c5 14. ♗e3 ♘d5 15. ♕d8 ♖d8 16. ♘d5±⊥] ♕d4 14. ♔h1 ♗f6 15. ♕f3 ♕a7 16. ♘e4 ♘d7 17. ♗e3 ♕b8 18. ♖ad1±↑ Bednarski—Zuckerman, Polanica Zdroj 1972; **12... ♕b6** 13. ♗e3 ♗c5 14. ♖f4 ♘c6 15. ♖h4 h6 16. ♖d1∞ Mestel—Wirthensohn, Hastings 1971/72 — 13/498; **12... g6** 13. ♕e2 ♗c5 14. ♗e3 ♗b7 15. ♖f7 ♖f7 [15... ♗d4?! 16. ♗e6 ♗e3 17. ♕e3± Walther—Gereben, Schweiz 1971 — 13/497] 16. ♘e6 ♗e3 17. ♕e3 ♕b6 18. ♕b6 ♘b6 19. ♘d8 ♘c4 20. a4 ♘c6!= Lepeškin

76 13... ♗b7? 14. ♖f7! ♖f7 15. ♘e6 ♘b3 16. ♘d8+— Bednarski—Pytel, Lublin 1972

77 **14. cb3** ♗b7 15. ♖ad1 ♕c7 16. ♗f4 b4∞ Koronghy—Schranz, Budapest 1972 — 14/475; **14. ♘b3**!?

78 Mestel—Browne, Hastings 1972/73 — 15/438

79 **16... f5**? 17. ♘e2±; **16... g6** 17. ♕h6 ♖fd8 [17... ♘e5? 18. ♗d5!+— Bednarski—Ghitescu, Bath 1973] 18. ♕f4 ♖f8 19. ♕h6= Boleslavski; **16... ♗c5** 17. ♖e1 a5 [17... f5? 18. ef6 ♖f6 19. ♗c5± Levy—Savon, Cienfuegos 1973 — 15/442] 18. a4 [18. ♖g3 a4 19. ♗c5 ♘c5 20. ♖g7!=] b4 19. ♘b5 ♗e3 20. ♖ee3 ♘c5 21. ♘d4 ♕a6 22. ♖f4 ♖ad8= Gheorghiu—Polugajevski, Petropolis (izt) 1973 — 16/441; 21. ♗c4!?

80 **9. ♗e6**?! fe6 10. ♘e6 ♕d7 11. ♘d5 ♗d5 12. ed5 ♔f7?! 13. g4 h6 14. f4 ♕a7 15. ♔h1 ♘bd7 16. g5±→» Klundt—Petrosjan, Bamberg 1968 — 5/451; 12... h5!∓; **9. ♗g5** h6 10. ♗h4 ♘c6=; **9. ♗e3** ♘c6 10. f4 ♘a5 11. e5 ♘b3 12. ab3 de5 13. fe5 ♘d7 14. ♕h5 g6∞ Romanišin—Anikajev, SSSR 1973 — 15/439

81 9... ♘bd7 10. ♖e1 ♘c5 11. ♗d5!? [11. e5 de5 12. fe5 ♘b3 13. ab3 ♗c5 14. ♗e3 ♘d5 15. ♘d5 ♕d5= Minić—Bogdanović, Jugoslavija 1960] ♕c8 [11... ed5 12. ed5 ♔d7 13. b4 ♘a4 14. ♘a4 ba4 15. c4=∞ Pinter—Marjanović, Groningen 1974 — 17/497] 12. b4 ♘cd7 13. ♗b7 ♕b7 14. a4 ba4 15. ♖a4 ♗e7= Ćirić—Minić, Jugoslavija 1966

82 10. e5 de5!? [10... bc3?! 11. ef6 ♘d7 12. f5 e5 13. ♗f7!± Dely—Szabo, Hungary 1962] 11. fe5 ♗c5∞

83 **10... ♘bd7**?! 11. f5 e5 12. ♘e6!? fe6 13. fe6 ♘c5 14. ♖f6! ♕f6 15. ♘c5±→ Schran—Kjun, corr. 1966; **10... ♘e4** 11. ♖e1 ♘d7 12. f5 e5 13. ♘e6 fe6 14. ♕h5 ♔e7? 15. fe6± Bañas—Jankovec, ČSSR 1973 — 15/444; 14... g6∞; **10... ♗e4** 11. f5 e5 12. ♗g5 [12. ♘f3 ♗c6! 13. ♕e1 ♗e7 14. ♕b4 0—0∓ Polgar—Lengyel, Hungary 1969 — 7/415] ♗e7 13. ♗f6 ♗f6 14. ♕e1 d5 15. ♘e2 ♘c6 16. ♖d1 0—0 17. c4 bc3 18. ♘ac3 ♕b6 19. ♕f2 ♕f2 20. ♖f2 ♘b4= Browne—Saidy, USA 1967

84 15... de5? 16. ♘f5± Westerinen—Kivipelto, Suomi 1968 — 6/556

85 17. ♔f1 ♗e6 18. ♕e6 de5=

86 **9... ♗e7**?! 10. ♗e6! fe6 11. ♘e6±; **9... h6** 10. f4 ♘c6 11. f5 ♘d4 12. ♕d4 e5 13. ♕d3 ♖c8 14. a4± Mesing—Cvetković, Jugoslavija 1969 — 7/416; **9... b4** 10. ♘d5 ♘bd7 11. ♘b4 ♕b6 12. c3 a5 13. ♘d3 ♘e4 14. ♗e3 d5?! 15. ♘e6!±→» Zinn—Schöneberg, DDR 1973 — 15/443; **9... ♕c7** 10. ♗e6 fe6 11. ♘e6 ♕c8 12. ♘d5 ♗d5 13. ed5 ♔f7 14. ♗g5±→ Witkowski—Jadrijević, Jugoslavija 1960

87 **10. ♗e6**?! fe6 11. ♘e6 ♕c8!? [11... ♕b8 12. ♘d5?! ♔f7 13. ♘dc7 (Gavela—Ilijć, Jugoslavija 1963) ♘c5∓ Sokolov; 12. ♗f4!?∞ Velimirović] 12. ♗f4 ♔f7 13. ♘g5 ♔g6 14. ♘d5 ♗d5 15. ed5 ♕c4!∓ Barden—Kottnauer, Helsinki (ol) 1952; **10. a3** ♖c8 11. f4 ♘c5 12. ♕f3 ♗e7 13. ♗a2 0—0∓ Cebalo—Bogdanović, Jugoslavija (ch) 1968; **10. f4** ♘c5 11. f5?! e5 12. ♘f3 ♗e7 13. ♗d5 ♗d5 14. ♘d5 ♘ce4∓ Janošević—Sokolov, Jugoslavija 1963; **10. ♘d5**!? ♘c5 [10... ♗e7 11. ♘e7 ♕e7 12. c4 b4 13. a3 ba3 14. ♖a3 ♘e4 15. f3±] 11. ♘f6 gf6 12, ♕h5 ♕d7 13. f3± Ždanov—Tukmakov, SSSR 1968 — 6/555

88 **10... ♘c5**?! 11. ♗d5 h6 [11... ed5 12. ed5 ♔d7 13. b4 ♘a4 14. ♘a4 ba4 15. c4±; 11... ♕c7 12. ♗f6 gf6 13. b4 ♘d7 14. ♗b7 ♕b7 15. ♕h5± Palermo—Najdorf, Mar del Plata 1965; 11... b4 12. ♗b7 ♘b7 13. ♘d5!± Zajcev—Savon, SSSR (ch) 1969 — 7/417] 12. ♗b7 ♘b7 13. ♗h4 ♖c8 14. a4 b4 15. ♘d5! ed5 16. ed5 ♔d7 17. ♘c6 ♖c6 18. dc6 ♔c6 19. c3± Honfi—Tatai, Monaco 1968 — 5/452; **10... ♕b6**?! 11. a4 b4 12. ♘d5 ed5 13. ed5 ♘e5 14. a5 ♕c5 15. f4 0-0-0 16. fe5 de5 17. ♖e5 ♗d6 18. ♖f5± Honfi—Barczay, Kecskemét 1968; **10... ♕c7** 11. ♗e6 fe6 12. ♘e6 ♕c4 13. ♘f8 ♖f8 14. ♕d6 0-0-0 15. ♘d5± Nej—Toluš, SSSR 1959

89 11. ♗h4 g5! [11... ♘c5? 12. ♗d5! ed5 13. ed5 ♔d7 14. b4 ♘a4 15. ♘a4 ba4 16. c4 ♔c8 17. ♕a4+— Fischer—Rubinetti, Palma de Mallorca (izt) 1970 — 10/535; 11... ♕b6?! 12. ♘d5± Farkas—Székely, Budapest 1972 — 14/476] 12. ♗g3 ♘e5∞ Velimirović—Parma, Vrnjačka Banja 1963

90 11... ♕f6 12. a4 b4 13. ♘a2 a5 14. c3±

91 12. ♕f3!? ♗e7? 13. ♗e6!±

92 13... d5 14. a5 ♘e4 15. ♗a4±; 14... ♗c5!?

93 Ivkov

94 Vasjukov—Averkin, SSSR (ch) 1969

B 88

1. e4 c5 2. ♘f3 d6 3. d4 cd4 4. ♘d4 ♘f6 5. ♘c3 e6 6. ♗c4 ♘c6

	7	8	9	10	11	12	13	14	15	
1	a3[1] ♗e7[2]	0—0 0—0	♗a2 ♘d4	♕d4 b6![3]	♗g5[4] ♗b7[5]	♖ad1 ♖c8	♖fe1 ♖c5	♗h4 ♕c7	♗b3 ♖d8[6]	∓
2	♗b3 ♗e7	f4[7] ♘d4![8]	♕d4 0—0	0—0[9] b6	♕d3!?[10] ♘d7	♗e3 ♗b7	♖ad1 ♕c8!	♘b5 ♘c5[11]		=
3	. . . . . .	♗e3 0—0[12]	f4 ♘d4[13]	♗d4 b5[14]	e5 de5	fe5 ♘d7	♕g4[15] b4[16]	♘e4 ♗b7	♘d6 ♗d6[17]	∞

1. e4 c5 2. ♘f3 d6 3. d4 cd4 4. ♘d4 ♘f6 5. ♘c3 e6 6. ♗c4 ♘c6 7. ♗b3 ♗e7 8. ♗e3 0—0 9. 0—0

	9	10	11	12	13	14	15	16	17	
4	. . . ♘d4	♗d4[18] b6	f4 ♗b7[19]	♕e1!?[20] d5[21]	ed5 ed5	♖d1 ♕c7	♗e5 ♕c5	♔h1 ♖ad8	♕g3 ♗a6[22]	±
5	. . . . . .	. . . b5	♘b5![23] ♗a6[24]	c4[25] ♗b5	cb5 ♘e4	♕f3 ♘f6	♕e2 ♘d7[26]	♖ac1[27]		±
6	. . . ♘a5	f4[28] b6[29]	e5![30] ♘e8[31]	f5![32] de5	fe6 ♘b3[33]	♘c6! ♕d6!	♕d6[34] ♗d6	ab3 ♗e6	♘b5![35] ♗d7[36]	±
7	. . . ♗d7	f4 ♘d4[37]	♗d4 ♗c6	♕e2[38] b5[39]	♘b5[40] ♗b5[41]	♕b5 ♘e4	f5[42] e5[43]	♗e3 ♗g5![44]	♕e2 ♗e3[45]	=
8	. . . . . .	♕e2 ♘d4[46]	♗d4 ♗c6	♖ad1 ♕a5	f4 e5[47]	fe5[48] de5	♗e3[49]			±

1. e4 c5 2. ♘f3 d6 3. d4 cd4 4. ♘d4 ♘f6 5. ♘c3 e6 6. ♗c4 ♘c6 7. ♗b3 a6

	8	9	10	11	12	13	14	15	16	
9	0—0[50] ♘a5[51]	f4 b5	e5[52] de5	fe5 ♗c5	♗e3 ♘b3[53]	ab3 ♘d5	♕f3 0—0	♘d5 ♕d5[54]	♕d5 ed5[55]	±
10	. . . ♗e7	♗e3 0—0[56]	f4 ♘a5[57]	♕f3 b5![58]	g4[59] b4	♘ce2 ♗b7	♘g3 ♘d7	g5 ♘c5[60]		∞
11	. . . . . .	. . . . . .	. . . ♘d4!	♗d4 b5	e5[61] de5	fe5 ♘d7	♘e4[62] ♗b7	♕g4[63] ♗e4	♕e4 ♘c5[64]	=
12	♗e3 ♘a5[65]	f4 b5	0—0[66] ♘b3[67]	ab3[68] ♗b7[69]	e5 de5[70]	fe5 ♘d7[71]	♕h5 g6	♕h3 ♕e7	♖ae1[72] ♗g7[73]	$\overline{\infty}$

1. e4 c5 2. ♘f3 d6 3. d4 cd4 4. ♘d4 ♘f6 5. ♘c3 e6 6. ♗c4 ♘c6 7. ♗b3 a6 8. ♗e3 ♘a5 9. f4 b5 10. 0—0 ♕c7

	11	12	13	14	15	16	17	18	19	
13	f5 ♘b3	cb3! ♗e7[74]	♖c1 ♕d7[75]	♕f3[76] 0—0[77]	e5!?[78] ♗b7	ef6 ♗f3	fe7 ♕e7	♖f3[79]		±

	11	12	13	14	15	16	17	18	19	
14	...	♘de2	♘d5	♗d5	♕c1	ed5	b3	♕e3		∓
	e5!	♗b7[80]	♘d5	♘c4!	♗d5	♖c8	♘e3	♕c5[81]		
15	♕f3	e5[82]	♕g3	fe5	♕h3[83]	♘b3	♘a5[84]	♘c4	♕h5	=
	♗e7	♗b7	de5	♘h5	♘b3!	♕e5	b4!	♕c7	g6[85]	

1 7. 0–0 ♗e7 8. ♗e3 0–0 9. f4 d5! 10. ed5 ed5 11. ♗e2 ♖e8 12. ♔h1 ♗a3!∓ Grünfeld–Tajmanov 1950; 9. ♗b3 — 7. ♗b3

2 7... a6 8. ♗a2 ♕c7 9. f4 ♗e7 10. ♗e3 0–0 11. ♕f3 ♘d4 12. ♗d4 e5= Vasjukov–Đurašević, Beograd 1961

3 10... ♗d7?! 11. f4 ♗c6 12. f5 e5 13. ♕d3 b5 14. ♗g5 a5 15. ♗f6 ♗f6 16. ♘d5± ×d5 Bogdanović–Puc, Sarajevo 1960

4 **11. f4**?! d5∓; **11. b4** ♗a6 12. ♖e1 ♕c7 13. ♗b2 ♖ac8 14. ♗b3 ♖fd8 15. f4 ♗c4∓ Smirnov–Nikitin, SSSR 1965

5 11... h6 12. ♗h4 ♗b7 13. ♖ad1 ♖c8 14. ♖fe1 [14. ♖d2 ♖c3! 15. bc3 ♘e4 16. ♗e7 ♕e7 17. ♖d3 d5 18. ♕b4 ♕c7⩱ Žuravljev–Suetin, SSSR 1962] ♖c5!= Nikitin

6 16. ♔h1 g5 17. ♗g3 ♘h5 18. ♘a4 ♘g3 19. hg3 ♖e5 20. c4 ♗f8 21. ♘c3 ♕e7∓ Pogats–Bilek, Kecskemet 1962

7 8. 0–0 ♘d4 9. ♕d4 0–0 10. ♔h1 b6 **11. ♗g5** ♗b7 12. f4 ♖c8 13. f5 ♖c5!∞ Ježek–Boleslavski, Baden 1957

8 8... ♕a5!? 9. ♕d3 [9. 0–0?! d5! 10. ♔h1 de4 11. ♘c6 bc6 12. ♕e2 ♗a6 13. ♗c4 ♗c4 14. ♕c4 0–0 15. ♘e4 ♕d5∓ Ničevski–Korčnoj, Rovinj–Zagreb 1970 — 9/354] 0–0 10. ♗d2 ♘d4 11. ♕d4 ♕h5∞ Korčnoj

9 **10. ♗e3** ♘g4 11. 0–0 [11. 0-0-0 e5!∓] b6 12. ♔h1 d5∓; **10. ♗d2**△ 0-0-0=

10 11. ♔h1 ♗a6 12. ♖f3 [12. ♖e1 d5! 13. ed5 ♘g4 14. ♘e4 ♗c5 15. ♕d2 ♕h4 16. g3 ♕h5 17. ♘c5 bc5∓ Klavin–Boleslavski, SSSR 1957] d5 13. ed5 ♗c5 14. ♕a4 ♗b7∓ Fischer–Geler, Curaçao (ct) 1962

11 = Nikitin

12 8... ♕a5?! 9. 0–0 a6 10. ♔h1 ♗d7 11. f4 0–0 12. ♕f3 ♖ac8 13. f5 ♘d4 14. ♗d4 e5 15. ♗f2 ♗c6 16. ♗h4± Tatai–Jimenez, Palma de Mallorca 1967 — 4/492

13 **9... d5** 10. e5 ♘d7 11. 0–0± Bogdanović–Marinković, Sarajevo 1961; **9... e5** 10. fe5 ♘g4 11. ♗g1 ♘d4 12. ♕d4 ♘e5 13. 0-0-0 ♗f6 14. ♘d5±; **9... ♗d7** 10. ♕f3 ♘d4 11. ♗d4 ♗c6 12. f5 ef5 [12... e5 13. ♗f2 b5 14. 0-0-0±] 13. ♕f5 ♘d7 14. 0-0-0 ♗f6 15. ♗f6 ♘f6 16. ♕f4± Bilek–Gheorghiu, Moskva 1967 — 3/439; **9... ♘a5** 10. ♕f3 b6 11. g4 [11. e5!? de5 12. fe5 ♗b7 13. ef6 ♗f3 14. fe7 ♕e7 15. ♘f3 ♘b3 16. ab3± Nikitin] ♗b7 12. g5 ♘b3 14. ab3 ♘e8 15. h4 ♘c7 16. 0-0-0± Fichtl–Wexler, Leipzig (ol) 1960

14 10... ♗d7!? 11. ♕f3 ♗c6 12. g4 b5 13. g5 ♘d7 14. h4 a5 [14... b4 15. ♘e2 e5 16. ♗e3 ef4 17. ♘f4 ♘e5 18. ♕g2 a5 19. ♗d4 ♕d7 20. g6 hg6 21. ♘g6 ♗f6 22. ♗e5 de5 23. ♘f8 ♕d4!⩱ Bronštejn–Averbah, Moskva 1961] 15. a3 ♘c5 16. ♖d1 ♕c8∞ Perez–Ghitescu, Leipzig (ol) 1960

15 **13. ♘b5** ♕a5 14. ♘c3 ♘e5∓; **13. ♕f3** ♖b8 14. 0-0-0 [14. ♘e4 ♗b7 15. ♖d1 ♕c7 16. c3 ♘e5 17. ♕g3 ♕c6 18. 0–0 ♘g6 19. ♗c2∞ Nilsson–Lindblom, Varna (ol) 1962] ♗b7 15. ♕g4 b4 16. ♗a7 [16. ♘b5!?] ♖a8 17. ♘b5 [17. ♗e6? fe6 18. ♕e6 ♔h8 19. ♖d7 ♗c8∓ Tatai–Zuckerman, Wijk aan Zee 1968 — 5/405] ♗a6 18. ♗e6∞; **13. 0–0** ♗c5! [13... b4 14. ♘e4 ♗b7 15. ♘d6 ♗d6 16. ed6 ♕g5 17. ♕e2 ♗d5 18. ♖ad1 ♗b3 19. ab3± Fischer–Olafsson, Stockholm (izt) 1952; 13... a6 — 7... a6] 14. ♗c5 ♘c5 15. ♕d8 ♖d8 16. ♘b5 ♗a6 17. ♗c4 ♖ab8 18. a4 ♘a4= Fischer–Geler, Curaçao (ct) 1962

16 13... ♗c5 14. 0-0-0 ♗d4 [14... ♕b6 15. ♘e4 ♗d4 16. ♖d4 ♘e5 17. ♘f6 ♔h8 18. ♕h3! gf6 19. ♖h4+– Barle–Beljavski, Jugoslavija–SSSR 1971 — 12/415] 15. ♕d4 ♕g5 16. ♔b1 ♕e5 17. ♕e5 ♘e5 18. ♘b5± Alexander–Hollis, Hastings 1962/63

17 16. ed6 ♘f6 17. ♕g3 ♘h5 18. ♕e5 ♗g2∞ Štejn–Gheorghiu, Reykjavik 1972 — 13/416

18 10. ♕d4 b6 11. ♖ad1 ♗b7 12. ♔h1 ♖c8 13. f4 ♘g4 14. ♗g1 ♗f6 15. ♕d3 ♗c3 16. bc3 ♘f6= Aronin–Korzin, SSSR 1961

19 11... ♗a6 12. ♖f3! ♕c7 13. ♖h3 ♖fd8 14. ♔h1 ♗c4 15. ♗f6 ♗f6 16. ♕h5 h6 17. e5!△ ♘e4± Honfi–Sanguinetti, Varna (ol) 1962

20 12. ♕e2 ♕c8 13. ♖f3 ♗a6!? [13... d5 14. ed5 ♗c5 15. ♕e5 ed5 16. ♖g3 ♗d4 17. ♕d4 ♕c5 18. ♖d1 ♖fd8 19. ♖gd3! ♕f8 20. h3± Padevski–Đurašević, Beograd 1961; 13... b5 14. ♕b5 ♘e4 15. ♘e4 ♗e4 16. ♖g3 ♗g6 17. f5! ef5 18. ♖f1 ♗h4 19. ♖c3 ♕d8 20. ♕d5± Gligorić–Larsen, Zürich 1961] 14. ♕e1 ♗c4 15. e5 de5 16. fe5 ♘d7 17. ♘e4± E.

Garcia–Chesca, Harrachov 1967 — 4/490; 16... ♗c5!?

21 12... b5 13. ♖d1△ e5±

22 18. ♗d4 ♕c7 19. ♖fe1± Gheorghiu–Neamtu, Bucuresti 1968 — 5/408

23 11. a3 ♗b7 12. ♕d3 a5! [12... a6 13. ♖ad1 ♕c7 14. f4 e5 15. ♗e3 ♖ac8 16. ♔h1 ♖fd8 17. f5± Nikolajevski–Geler, SSSR 1959] 13. f4 b4 14. ab4 ab4 15. ♖a8 ♕a8∓ Nacht–Pavlov, Romania 1966 — 1/285

24 11... ♘e4?! 12. ♘a7 ♗d7 13. ♕e2 d5 14. ♘b5± Klovan–Saharov, SSSR 1959

25 12. a4 ♘e4 13. ♗a7 ♕d7 14. ♕e2 ♖a7 15. ♕e4 ♗b5=

26 15... d5!? Korčnoj

27 **16. ♕e3**? ♗f6 17. ♗a7 ♕a5 18. b6 ♗d8∓ Fischer–Korčnoj, Rovinj-Zagreb 1970 — 9/356; **16. ♖ac1**± Korčnoj

28 10. ♕e2!? b6 [10... a6 11. f4 b5 12. e5 de5 13. fe5 ♘e8 14. ♖f7! ♖f7 15. ♘e6∞; 12... ♘e8 13. f5 ♘b3 14. ♘c6 ♕c7 15. ♘e7 ♕e7 16. f6±↑ Hasin–Koc, SSSR (ch) 1962; 10... e5!? Gligorić] 11. ♖ad1 ♗b7 12. e5 ♘b3 13. ab3 ♘e8 14. ♕h5 ♕c8 15. ed6 ♗d6 16. ♖fe1±↑ Calvo–Thomson, Amsterdam 1961

29 **10... e5** 11. ♘f5 ♗f5 12. ef5 ef4 13. ♖f4 ♘b3 14. ab3 d5 15. ♗d4 ♗d6 16. ♖f3 ♖e8 17. ♗f6 ♕f6 18. ♕d5± Penrose–Rävissä, Varna (ol) 1962; **10... ♕c7** 11. f5 ♘b3 12. cb3 ♗d7 13. ♖c1 ♕b8 14. g4! h6 15. g5 hg5 16. ♗g5 ♕d8 17. ♖c2± Sokolov–Ivanović, Jugoslavija 1971 — 11/342; 13... ♕d8!? Sokolov; **10... d5** 11. e5 ♘d7 12. ♖f3 [12. ♕h5 ♖e8? 13. ♘d5! ed5 14. ♕f7!!+–; 12... g6 13. ♕h6 ♖e8 14. ♖ad1 ♗f8 15. ♕h3 a6 16. g4 ♕c7 17. ♖f3±↑» Ragozin–Geler, SSSR 1950] ♘b6 13. ♖h3 g6 14. ♘f3 ♘bc4 15. ♗c4 ♘c4 16. ♗d4 f6 [16... ♘b2? 17. ♕c1△ f5±→] 17. b3 fe5 18. fe5 ♘a5 19. ♕d2± Minić–Puc, Jugoslavija (ch) 1960; **10... ♗d7** 11. ♕f3 ♖c8 12. g4 ♘c4 13. g5 ♘e8 14. ♗c4 ♖c4 15. h4 g6 16. f5 gf5 17. ef5 e5∓ Rittner–Simagin, corr. 1968 — 6/495; 11. e5±; **10... ♘b3** 11. ab3 a6 12. ♕f3 ♕c7 13. g4?! d5!∞ Prins–Pilnik, Stockholm (izt) 1952; 12. e5±

30 **11. ♕f3** ♗b7 12. g4 ♖c8 13. g5 ♖c3! 14. gf6 [14. bc3 ♘e4 15. ♕g4 ♕c8 16. ♖f3 ♘b3 17. ab3 f5∓ Padevski–Botvinik, Moskva 1956] ♖e3 15. ♕e3 ♗f6∓ Rubanov–Borisenko, corr. 1960; **11. f5** e5 12. ♘de2 ♘b3 13. ab3 ♗b7 14. ♘g3 d5∓ Milićević–Velimirović, Jugoslavija 1960

31 11... de5 12. fe5 ♘e8 [12... ♘d7 13. ♖f7! ♖f7 14. ♘e6 ♕e8 15. ♘c7±; 12... ♘d5 13. ♗d5 ed5 14. ♕h5±] 13. ♕h5 ♘b3 14. ♘c6 ♕c7 15. ♘e7 ♕e7 16. ab3 ♗b7 17. ♖a4!±↑»

32 **12. ♕f3** ♗b7 13. ♕g3 ♘b3 14. ab3 ♔h8 [14... de5 15. fe5 ♕c7 16. ♖f2△ ♖af1± Nikitin; 15... ♗c5 16. ♖ad1 ♕e7 17. ♘a4±; 14... ♕c8 15. ♖ad1 f5 16. ef6 ♗f6 17. ♖f2 d5 18. ♕h3± Gligorić–Barden, Hastings 1960/61] 15. ♖ad1 ♕b8 16. ♘f3 ♕c7 17. ♗d4 de5 18. fe5 ♖d8 19. ♘g5 ♗g5 20. ♕g5 h6 21. ♕g3 ♕c6∓ Parma–Kuindži, Haag 1961; **12. ♕g4** ♘b3 13. ♘c6 ♕c7 14. ♘e7 ♕e7 15. ab3 ♗b7 16. ♗d4 f6 17. ef6 ♘f6 18. ♕h3 e5= Hort–Marszalek, Marianske Lazni 1962

33 **13... f6**? 14. ♘f5 ♘b3 15. ♘d5! ♗e6 [15... ♘d4 16. ♘de7 ♔h8 17. ♘g6 1 : 0 Geler–Vatnikov, SSSR 1950] 16. ♘fe7 ♔h8 17. ab3 ♖f7 18. ♕f3+– Parma–Bjelicki, Mar del Plata 1962; **13... ed4** 14. ef7 ♔h8 15. fe8♕ ♕e8 16. ♗d4± Nikitin

34 15. ♘d5? ♗h4! 16. ab3 [16. ef7 ♖f7 17. ♖f7 ♘a1! 18. ♕f1 ♗f6 19. ♘f6 ♘f6 0 : 1 Bilek–Petrosjan, Oberhausen 1961; 17. ♕h5 ♕d5 18. ♖ad1 ♖f1 19. ♖f1 ♗b7–+ Bogdanović–Bradvarević, Jugoslavija (ch) 1957] ♗e6 17. ♘db4 ♕c7∓

35 17. ♘a7 ♖b8 [17... ♗c5 18. ♗c5 bc5 19. ♘c6 ♖a1 20. ♖a1 f6 21. ♘e4 c4 22. ♘c5 ♗g4 23. ♘e7 ♔f7 24. ♖a7± Altrock–Hang, corr. 1974] 18. ♖a6 ♘f6 19. ♖b6 ♖b6 20. ♗b6 ♖b8 21. ♗f2 ♘g4 22. ♘ab5± Fischer–Korčnoj, Curaçao (ct) 1962

36 18. ♘ca7 ♗c5 19. ♗c5 bc5 20. ♖a4 ♖b8 21. ♖a5±↑ Gligorić

37 **10... ♕c8**? 11. f5! ♘d4 12. ♗d4 ef5 13. ♕d3! fe4 14. ♘e4 ♘e4 15. ♕e4 ♗e6 16. ♖ae1! [16. ♖f3 ♕c6 17. ♖e1 ♕e4 18. ♖e4 d5= Fischer–Larsen, Denver (mct) 1971 — 11/5] ♕c6 [16... ♕d7 17. ♗g7! ♔g7 18. ♕d4 ♔g8 19. ♖e3!+–→ Sokolov] 17. ♕f4! ♖ae8 18. ♕g3 g6 19. ♖e6 1 : 0 Janošević–Musil, Jugoslavija 1972 — 13/421; **10... a5**? 11. f5 ♘d4 [11... ♕c8? 12. fe6 ♗e6 13. ♘e6 fe6 14. ♘a4+– Fischer–Larsen, Denver (mct) 1971 — 11/3] 12. ♗d4 ef5 13. ef5±

38 **12. ♕e1** b5 13. ♖d1 b4 14. e5 bc3 15. ef6 ♗f6 16. ♕c3 ♗d4 17. ♕d4 d5 18. f5 ♕b6= Neukirch–Hartston 1967; **12. ♕d3** b5 13. e5 [13. a3 a5 14. e5 de5 15. fe5 ♘d7 16. ♕e3 b4 17. ab4 18. ♘e2 ♖a5∓ Keres–Mikenas, SSSR (ch) 1955; 13. ♘b5 ♗e4 14. ♕e2 ♕d7 15. c4 d5 16. ♖ad1 ♕b7 17. cd5 ♗d5 18. ♗d5 ♘d5 19. f5 a6= Szabo–Benkö, Budapest 1951] de5 14. fe5 ♘d7 15. ♘e4 ♗e4 16. ♕e4 ♘c5 17. ♕e3 [17. ♗c5 ♗c5 18. ♔h1 ♕d4!∓] ♕c7 18. c3 ♘b3 19. ab3 a5 20. ♖f3 ♖ac8= Minić–Sofrevski, Jugoslavija (ch) 1965

39 **12... ♕a5**? 13. f5! e5 14. ♗f2 ♖ac8 15. g4 ♘d7 16. h4 h6 17. ♔g2± Zuckerman–Spasov, Harrachov 1967 — 4/489; **12... ♕b8**? 13. f5 e5 14. ♗f2 b5 15. a3 a5 16. ♗h4 a4 17. ♗f6± Margulev–Vooremaa, SSSR 1972

40 13. ♖ad1 b4 14. e5 bc3 15. ef6 ♗f6 16. ♗f6 ♕f6 17. ♖d6 ♖ac8 18. bc3 ♕c3 19. ♖fd1 a5∓ Nežmetdinov – Geler, SSSR 1954; 18. f5!? Simagin; **13. ♖ae1** a5! 14. a3 ♖b8= Nikitin

41 13... e5?! 14. fe5! [14. ♘a7? ♗d7 15. ♗f2 ♕b8 16. ♕a6 ♘e4 17. ♗d5 ♘f2 18. ♗a8 ♘h3!∓→ Witkowski – Sanguinetti, München (ol) 1958] de5 15. ♗e3 a6 16. ♘c3 ♘e4 17. ♖f7! ♖f7 18. ♗f7± Fischer – Nievergelt, Zürich 1959

42 15. ♕e2 d5 16. ♖ad1 ♗f6 [16... ♗c5∓ Ždanov – Šapošnikov, corr. 1961] 17. ♗f6 ♘f6 18. c4 a5! 19. cd5 a4 20. ♗c4 ed5 21. ♔h1 ♕a5∓ Neukirch – Simagin 1965

43 **15... d5**?! 16. fe6 fe6 17. ♕c6! ♕d6 18. ♖f8 ♖f8 19. ♕d6 ♗d6 20. ♗a7± Penrose – Petersen 1962; **15... ♗f6** 16. ♕d3! [16. ♖ad1 ♗d4 17. ♖d4 d5 18. ♖dd1 a5! 19. fe6 fe6 (Neukirch – Möhring, Colditz 1967 — 3/448) 20. ♖f8 ♕f8 21. ♗d5=; 20... ♔f8!?] d5 17. ♗f6 [17. ♖ad1!? ♗d4 18. ♕d4 ♘d6 19. f6!±↑] ♘f6 18. c4! ♕b6 [18... dc4? 19. ♕d8 ♖fd8 20. ♗c4 e5 21. ♖fe1 e4 22. ♖ad1±] 19. ♔h1 dc4 20. ♕c4 ef5 21. ♖f5± Nikitin

44 16... ♘f6 17. ♕e2 d5 [17... a5 18. a4± Prins – Unzicker, Stockholm (izt) 1952] 18. ♖ad1± Matulović – Milić, Sarajevo 1961

45 18. ♕e3 ♘f6 19. ♔h1 ♕b6= Ostojić – Smailbegović, Jugoslavija (ch) 1962

46 10... ♕a5 11. ♖ad1 ♖ac8? 18. ♘db5± Parma – Bradvarević, Jugoslavija (ch) 1963; 11... ♖ad8!?

47 13... b5 14. e5 de5 15. ♕e5± Gligorić

48 14. ♗f2? ef4 15. ♘d5 ♖ae8∓ Koc – Šamkovič, SSSR (ch) 1962

49 **15. ♖f5** ♗c5 16. ♗f2 ♖ad8!? 17. ♖f1 ♖d6 18. ♔h1 ♗f2 19. ♕f2 ♗e4 20. ♘e4 ♘e4 21. ♖f7! 1 : 0 Gligorić – Pomar, Torremolinos 1961; 16... ♕b6!=; **15. ♗f2**±; **15. ♗e3**± Gligorić

50 8. f4 ♕a5 [8... ♘a5 9. f5! ♘b3 10. ab3 ♗e7 11. ♕f3 0–0 12. ♗e3 ♗d7 13. g4 e5 14. ♘de2± Fischer – Bjelicki, Mar del Plata 1960; 8... ♕c7 9. f5 ♘d4 10. ♕d4 ef5 11. ef5 ♗f5 12. 0–0±→ Fischer] 9. 0–0 d5 [9... ♘d4?! 10. ♕d4 ♕c5 11. ♕c5 dc5 12. a4±; 10... d5 11. ♗e3 ♘e4 12. ♘e4 de4 13. f5!±→ Fischer – Dely, Skopje 1967] 10. ♘c6 bc6 11. f5 ♗c5 12. ♔h1 0–0± Fischer; 8... ♗e7 9. ♗e3 — 8. ♗e3

51 8... ♕c7 9. ♔h1 ♘a5 10. f4 b5 11. e5 [11. f5!?] de5 12. fe5 ♕e5! 13. ♗f4 ♕h5 14. ♘d5! ed5 15. ♖e1$\overline{\overline{\infty}}$ Talj – Gurgenidze, SSSR 1970 — 9/358

52 **10. f5** e5 [10... ♘b3 11. ab3 e5 12. ♘db5 ♗b7 13. ♘a3 ♘e4 14. ♘e4 ♗e4 15. ♘c4 ♕c7 16. ♘e3± Nikitin] 11. ♘de2 ♘b3 12. ab3 ♗b7 13. ♗g5 [13. ♕d3 ♕b6 14. ♔h1 ♕c6 15. ♘g3 h5!∓; 13. ♘g3 h5 14. ♗g5 h4∓] ♕b6 14. ♔h1 ♘e4 15. ♘e4 ♗e4 16. ♘c3 ♗b7 17. ♘d5 ♕c5 18. c4 bc4 19. bc4 ♕c4 20. ♘e3± Nikitin; **10. ♗e3** — 8. ♗e3

53 12... ♘c6 13. ♕f3!±

54 15... ed5? 16. ♘c6! ♗e3 17. ♕e3 ♕c7 18. ♘d4± Gheorghiu – Basman, Hastings 1967/68 — 5/409

55 17. b4!±

56 9... ♕c7 10. f4 ♘a5 11. ♕f3 h5!? 12. f5 e5 13. ♘de2 ♗d7 14. ♖fd1 ♘c4 15 ♗c4 ♕c4= Hecht – Cornelis, BRD – Belgique 1967 — 3/449; 11... b5 — 8. ♗e3

57 **10... ♗d7** 11. ♕f3 ♘a5!? [11... ♖c8 12. f5 e5 13. ♘de2 ♘a5 14. g4± Allan – Naranja, Lugano (ol) 1968; 11... ♕c7 12. f5 ♘d4 13. ♗d4 b5 14. a3 a5 15. g4± Nikitin; 12. ♖ad1!? ♖ac8 13. f5! e5 14. ♘de2 ♘a5 15. g4± Keres – Palmason, Amsterdam (ol) 1954] 12. f5 ♘b3 13. cb3 b5 14. b4 ♖c8 15. ♖fd1 ♕c7 16. a3 ♕b8 17. ♖ac1 ♕a8 18. ♗f2 ♖fd8= Smailbegović – Toran, Sarajevo 1960; **10... ♕c7** 11. ♕f3 ♘d4 12. ♗d4 b5 13. e5 de5 14. fe5 ♘d7 15. ♘e4 ♗b7 16. c3 [Sokolov – Janošević, Jugoslavija 1962] ♘c5=

58 11... ♕c7 12. f5 [12. g4 ♘b3 13. ab3 ♗d7 14. g5 ♘e8 15. f5±; 12... ♘c4 13. g5 ♘d7 14. ♘f5! ef5 15. ♘d5±; 13... ♘e8 14. f5 ♘e3 15. ♕e3±; 12... b5 13. g5 ♘d7 14. ♘e6! fe6 15. ♗e6 ♔h8 16. ♘d5 ♕d8 17. ♕h5 ♘c5 18. ♗c8 ♖c8 19. f5±→ Boleslavski – Aronin, SSSR 1949] e5 13. ♘de2 ♘b3 14. ab3 b5 15. g4 b4 16. g5 bc3 17. gf6 ♗f6 18. bc3 ♗b7 19. c4± Fischer – Hamann, Netanya 1968 — 6/496

59 12. e5 ♗b7 13. ♕h3 ♘e8 14. f5 de5 15. fe6 ed4 16. ef7 ♔h8 17. fe8 ♖e8 18. ♖ad1 ♗f6∓

60 ∞ Boleslavski

61 **12. ♕f3**?! ♗b7 13. a3 a5 14. ♖ae1 b4∓ Radulov – Bobocov, Bulgaria 1967 — 4/491; **12. a3** ♗b7 13. ♕d3 a5! 14. e5 de5 15. fe5 ♘d7 16. ♘b5 [16. ♕e3 b4 17. ab4 ab4 18. ♘e4 ♗e4 19. ♕e4 ♖a1 20. ♖a1 ♘c5 21. ♗c5 ♗c5 22. ♔h1 ♕d4!∓ Olafsson] ♘c5 17. ♗c5 ♗c5 18. ♔h1 ♕g5 19. ♕e2 ♖ad8 20. ♖ad1 ♖d1 21. ♖d1 h5∓ Fischer – Spaski (m) 1972 — 14/411; 21... ♗e3!△ ♗f4∓

62 14. ♕g4 ♗b7 15. ♖ad1 [15. ♖f7?! ♔f7 16. ♗e6 ♔e8 17. ♕h5 g6 18. ♕h7 ♕c7 19. ♖d1 ♘e5!∓ Hort] ♘c5 16. ♔h1 ♘b3 17. ab3 ♕c7 18. ♖d3 ♕c6∞ Sikora – Neckař, ČSSR (ch) 1974 — 17/431

63 15. ♘d6 ♗d6 16. ed6 ♕g5 17. ♕e2 e5 18. ♗e3 ♕g6 19. ♖ad1 ♔h8∓ Hamann–Gligorić, Skopje (ol) 1972

64 17. ♗c5?! 18. ♔h1 ♕d4!∓ Jimenez–Lejn, Cienfuegos 1972 — 13/420

65 8... ♗e7 9. f4 0–0 [9... ♗d7 10. ♕f3 ♕c7 11. 0–0 0–0 12. f5 ♘d4 13. ♗d4 e5 14. ♗f2 b5?! 15. ♗h4± Tringov–Kokkoris, Sofia 1967 — 4/480; 14... ♗c6!?] 10. ♕f3 ♘d4! [10... e5 11. ♘c6 bc6 12. fe5 de5 13. 0–0 ♖b8 14. ♔h1 ♕c7 15. ♗g5 (Honfi–Paoli, Timisoara 1972 — 13/418) ♘e8±; 13... ♘g4 14. ♗f7 ♔h8 15. ♕e2± Šamkovič] 11. ♗d4 b5! 12. e5 [12. 0-0-0!?] de5 13. ♗e5 [13. fe5 ♕d4 14. ef6 ♗c5 15. fg7 ♖d8 16. ♖d1 ♕e5 17. ♕e4 ♖d1 18. ♔d1 ♕e4 19. ♘e4 ♗e7∓ Hermlin–Šamkovič, SSSR 1972 — 14/410] ♕b6 14. 0-0-0 [14. ♕a8 ♗b7 15. ♗d4 ♕c6 16. ♕a7 ♘d7 17. ♗e3 ♘c5△ ♖a8∓] ♗b7 15. ♕g3 ♖ad8∓ Šamkovič; 10. 0–0 — 8. 0–0

66 **10. e5** de5 11. fe5 ♘b3 12. ab3 ♘d5 [12... ♘d7 13. ♕f3 ♖b8 14. 0–0±] 13. ♕f3 ♘e3!? [13... ♗b7 14. 0–0 — 10. 0–0] 14. ♕e3 [14. ♕a8 ♘g2 15. ♕g2 ♕d4 16. ♕c6 ♕d7∞] ♗c5 15. 0-0-0 ♗b7 16. ♘e4 ♕b6∞ Minev; **10. f5**!? e5 11. ♘de2 ♘b3 12. ab3 b4 13. ♘d5 ♘d5 14. ♕d5± Parma–Tukmakov, Moskva 1971 — 12/419

67 **10... b4**? 11. e5 de5 12. fe5 ♘b3 13. ab3 bc3 14. ef6 cb2 15. ♖b1! gf6 16. ♕f3 ♗d7 17. ♘c6!+–; **10... e5** 11. ♘f5 g6 12. fe5 ♘b3 13. ab3 de5 14. ♕d8 ♔d8 15. ♗g5+–

68 11. cb3!? ♗b7 12. e5 de5 [12... ♘d5?! 13. ♘d5 ♗d5 14. f5± Feršter–Osnos, SSSR 1972 — 13/422] 13. fe5 ♘d7 14. ♕h5 g6 15. ♕h3 ♕e7 16. ♖ad1 ♗g7 17. ♗g5!? ♕g5 [Damjanović–Krogius, Soči 1967 — 4/493] 18. ♘e6 fe6 19. ♖d7 ♔d7 20. ♖f7 ♔d8 21. ♕d3 ♗d5 22. ♘d5 ♔e8 23. ♘f6!=

69 11... b4?! 12. ♘c6 ♕c7 13. ♘b4 d5 14. ♕d4 ♘e4 15. ♘e4 de4 16. f5±

70 12... b4?! 13. ef6 bc3 14. f5! e5 15. fg7 ♗g7 16. ♕g4 ♗f6 17. ♘e6!±→ Matohin–Karabanov, SSSR 1962

71 13... ♘d5 14. ♕f3 ♕d7 15. ♘d5 ♗d5 16. ♕g3 ♕b7 [16... g6 17. ♖ad1 ♗g7 18. c4! bc4 19. bc4 ♗c4 20. ♘f5+–; 17... ♕b7 18. ♗g5 ♗g7 19. ♗f6±] 17. ♕f2 b4 [17... ♗e4!?△ ♗g6] 18. c4! bc3 19. bc3 ♗e4 20. b4 ♗g6 21. ♘b3 ♗e7 22. ♗c5± Bednarski Mititelu, Varna 1972 — 13/417

72 **16. ♘f3** ♗g7 17. ♘g5 ♘e5 18. ♘ge4 [18. ♗f4 h6 19. ♗e5 hg5!–+] 0–0 19. ♗g5 f6 20. ♗f4 b4∓ Nikitin; **16. ♘db5**!? ab5 17. ♘b5 ♘e5 18. ♖ad1 ♗g7 19. ♘d6 ♔f8 20. ♗c5∞ Krogius; **16. ♖ad1**!?△ ♗g5, ♘e6

73 17. ♗h6 ♗e5! [17... 0–0 18. ♗g7 ♔g7 19. ♘e4 ♗e4 20. ♖e4 ♖ac8 21. c3± Nikitin] 18. ♖e5⩱ Jovčić–Hybl, corr. 1971 — 11/339

74 12... b4 13. ♘a4 ♘e4 14. ♖c1±

75 13... ♕b7 14. fe6 fe6 15. b4 0–0 ♕b3± Toluš–Tajmanov, SSSR (ch) 1952

76 14. fe6 fe6 15. b4 0–0 16. ♕b3 ♔h8 17. h3 e5 18. ♘f5 ♗b7 19. ♘e7 ♕e7 20. ♗g5 h6 21. ♗f6 ♖f6 22. ♖f6 ♕f6 23. ♖f1 ♕g6= Keres–Tajmanov, Zürich (ct) 1953

77 14... ♗b7 15. ♕h3 0–0 16. fe6 fe6 17. ♘e6 ♖fc8 18. ♖cd1 ♘e4 19. ♘d5 ♗d5 20. ♖d5 ♗f6 21. ♖f4 ♕b7 22. ♕f5± Ciocaltea–Padevski, Sofia 1962

78 15. g4 e5 16. ♘c6 ♕c6 17. g5 ♕d7 18. gf6 ♗f6 19. ♘d5 ♗d8 [Geler–Tajmanov, SSSR (ch) 1954] 20. ♖c8! ♖c8 21. f6 ♔h8 22. fg7 ♔g7 23. ♗h6 ♔h6 24. ♘f6 ♗f6 25. ♕f6 ♔h5 26. ♖f5 ♕f5 27. ♕f5± Averbah

79 ± Suetin

80 12... ♘b3 13. cb3!? [13. ab3 ♗b7 14. ♘g3 h5! 15. ♘d5 ♗d5 16. ed5 h4 17. ♘h1 ♗e7 18. ♘f2 ♕b7 19. c4 ♗d8!∓ Ghizdavu–Honfi, Timisoara 1972 — 13/423] ♗b7 14. ♖c1 ♕d8 15. ♘g3 h5 16. ♘d5± Šamkovič

81 Scholl–Polugajevski, Amsterdam 1970 — 10/467

82 12. f5!? e5 [12... ♘b3 13. ab3 b4 14. e5! ♗b7 15. ed6 ♗d6 16. ♘cb5± Marić] 13. ♘d5! ♘d5 14. ♗d5 ed4 15. ♗d4 ♗f6 [15... ♗b7 16. ♗g7 ♖g8 17. ♗d4 ♗d5 18. ed5 0-0-0 19. f6 ♗f8 20. c4 bc4 21. b4⩱ Marić] 16. ♗f6 gf6 17. ♗a8 ♕a7 18. ♖f2! ♕a8 19. ♕c3 ♘c4 20. ♕f6⩱ Adorjan–Ribli, Hungary 1969 — 7/374

83 15. ♗e6 ♘g3! [15... fe6 16. ♕h3 ♕e5 17. ♘e6 ♗c8 18. ♕h5+– Averbah–Tajmanov, Zürich (ct) 1953; 15... 0–0 16. ♖f7!+– Euwe] 16. ♗f7 ♔d7! 17. ♗e6 ♔e8! [17... ♔d8 18. ♖ad1 ♗d6 19. ed6 ♕c5 20. hg3±→ Henkin] 18. ♗f7=

84 17. ♗d4!? ♕g5 18. ♘a5

85 **19... 0—0** 20. ♘b6 bc3 21. ♘a8 ♗a8⩱ Bronštejn; **19... g6** 20. ♕e5 ♕e5 21. ♘e5 bc3 22. ♖f7 cb2= Smailbegović–Đantar, Jugoslavija (ch) 1959

B 89

1. e4 c5 2. ♘f3 d6 3. d4 cd4 4. ♘d4 ♘f6 5. ♘c3 e6 6. ♗c4 ♘c6 7. ♗e3

	7	8	9	10	11	12	13	14	15	
1	. . . a6[1]	♕e2[2] ♗d7[3]	♗b3 ♗e7	0-0-0 ♕a5[4]	f4 b5	a3 b4	ab4 ♘b4	g4 0—0[5]	g5	±
2	. . . . . .	. . . ♕c7	♗b3 ♘a5[6]	g4[7] h6[8]	0-0-0 b5	f3 b4[9]	♘a4 ♘d7	♔b1! ♗e7	h4 g6[10]	±
3	. . . . . .	. . . . . .	. . . . . .	. . . b5!	g5[11] ♘d7	0-0-0[12] b4[13]	♘a4 ♘b3	ab3 ♘c5	♘c5 dc5[14]	∓
4	. . . . . .	. . . . . .	0-0-0 ♘a5[15]	♗d3 b5	g4[16] ♗b7[17]	g5 ♘d7	f4 b4	♘b1 ♘c5	♘d2 d5[18]	±
5	. . . . . .	. . . . . .	. . . ♗e7	♖hg1 ♘a5[19]	♗d3 b5	g4[20] b4	♘a4[21] ♘d7[22]			∞

1. e4 c5 2. ♘f3 d6 3. d4 cd4 4. ♘d4 ♘f6 5. ♘c3 e6 6. ♗c4 ♘c6 7. ♗e3 a6 8. ♕e2 ♕c7 9. 0-0-0 ♗e7 10. ♗b3 ♘a5[23] 11. g4 b5[24] 12. g5[25] ♘b3 13. ab3 ♘d7

	14	15	16	17	18	19	20	21	22	
6	h4[26] b4[27]	♘a4 ♗b7[28]	f3[29] ♕a5	♔b1 ♘c5	h5 ♘a4	ba4 ♕a4	g6 ♖c8	♕g2 ♗f6	♗g5 ♗e5[30]	∞
7	♘f5[31] ef5[32]	♘d5 ♕d8[33]	ef5 ♗b7[34]	f6! gf6[35]	♖he1 ♗d5	♖d5 ♖g8![36]	gf6[37] ♘f6	♖f5 ♖g6[38]	♗b6 ♕d7[39]	±

1. e4 c5 2. ♘f3 d6 3. d4 cd4 4. ♘d4 ♘f6 5. ♘c3 e6 6. ♗c4 ♘c6 7. ♗e3 ♗e7 8. ♕e2 0—0 9. 0-0-0[40]

	9	10	11	12	13	14	15	16	17	
8	. . . d5[41]	♘e6[42] fe6	ed5 ♘a5	de6 ♕c7[43]	♗d5 ♘c6[44]	♗b3[45] ♖e8[46]				∞
9	. . . . . .	♗b3 ♗b4[47]	♗g5 h6	ed5! ♘d4	♖d4 ♗c3	bc3 hg5	de6 ♕a5	ef7 ♔h8	♔b2[48]	±
10	. . . ♕a5	f4[49] ♘d4[50]	♖d4 e5	♖d5![51] ♘d5	♘d5 ♗d8	f5[52]				=∞
11	. . . . . .	♗b3 ♘d4[53]	♗d4 ♗d7	♔b1[54] ♗c6[55]	f4 ♖ad8[56]	♖hf1[57] b5	f5[58] b4	fe6 bc3	ef7 ♔h8[59]	±
12	. . . ♗d7	♗b3[60] ♕b8[61]	g4 ♘d4[62]	♗d4 b5	g5 ♘e8	♕h5[63] b4	♖d3[64] bc3	f4[65]		=∞
13	. . . . . .	f4 ♖c8[66]	♗b3[67] ♘a5[68]	e5 de5	fe5 ♘b3	ab3[69] ♘d5[70]	♘d5 ed5[71]			±
14	. . . ♘d4	♗d4 ♕a5	e5! de5	♗e5[72] b6	♖d4 ♗b7	♖hd1![73]				±

1. e4 c5 2. ♘f3 d6 3. d4 cd4 4. ♘d4 ♘f6 5. ♘c3 e6 6. ♗c4 ♘c6 7. ♗e3 ♗e7 8. ♕e2 0—0 9. 0-0-0 a6 10. ♗b3[74]

	10	11	12	13	14	15	16	17	18	
15	. . .	f4[75]	g4[77]	♔b1	f5	ab3				±
	♕e8	♘d7[76]	♘c5	b5	♘b3[78]	♗d7				
16	. . .	f4	♖d4	♖f1	a3[81]	f5	ef5			∞
	♕c7	♘d4[79]	b5	♖b8![80]	♗d7	ef5	a5[82]			
17	. . .	♖hg1	♔b1[84]	♕h5!	g4	ab3	♖d4[86]	g5		±
	. . .	♘d7[83]	♘c5[85]	♗d7	♘b3	♘d4	b5[87]			
18	. . .	. . .	g4[88]	♘c6[90]	♘d5!	g5	♗d5	♗e4	♗d4	=
	. . .	b5	b4[89]	♕c6[91]	ed5	♘e4![92]	♕a4[93]	♗e6[94]	g6[95]	
19	. . .	g4	♖d4	♖c4[98]	g5	♖g1[100]	♘d5	♗b6	♕g4	±
	. . .	♘d4[96]	e5[97]	♕d8	♘e8[99]	♗d7	♗b5	♕d7	♗d8[101]	
20	. . .	. . .	. . .	g5[102]	f4[103]	♕f2[104]	ef5	♕d2		∞
	. . .	. . .	b5	♘d7	♘c5	f5![105]	♖f5	♗d7![106]		
21	. . .	. . .	♘f5	♘d5	gf5	♘e7[108]	♗d5	♖hg1	♕f3	=∞
	. . .	♘d7	ef5	♕d8	♘a5[107]	♕e7	♔h8	♘f6	♘d5[109]	
22	. . .	. . .	g5	♖hg1[110]	♖g3	♕h5	♕h6	♕h4	♕h6[114]	=
	. . .	. . .	♘c5	♗d7![111]	♖fc8[112]	g6	♗f8	♗e7[113]		

1 7... ♗d7 8. ♕e2 ♘a5 9. ♗d3 ♗e7 10. f4 ♘c6 11. ♘b3! a6 12. g4 0—0 13. g5± Cosulich—Nikolić, Bari 1970 — 10/468

2 △ 0-0-0 Velimirović

3 8... ♗e7 9. ♗b3 ♘a5 10. f4 0—0 11. g4 ♘b3 12. ab3 ♖e8 13. ♖g1 ♗f8 14. g5 ♘d7 15. 0-0-0 b5 16. g6! fg6 [16... hg6 17. f5 ef5 18. ef5 ♘e5 19. fg6 ♘g6 20. ♕g2±] 17. f5 ♘e5 18. fg6 ♘g6 19. ♘f3!± Tan—Hort, Siegen (ol) 1970 — 10/476

4 **10... ♖c8** 11. ♘c6! ♖c6 12. g4 ♖c3 13. bc3 ♘e4 14. ♗d4 d5 15. f3 ♘f6 16. c4!± Ostojić—Sofrevski, Skopje 1969 — 8/371; **10... 0—0** 11. f4! ♘d4 12. ♗d4 e5 13. fe5 ♗g4 14. ef6 ♗e2 15. fe7 ♕e7 16. ♘e2± Velimirović—Ilijevski, Jugoslavija 1969; **10... ♕c7** 11. g4 h6 [11... e5 12. ♘f5 ♗f5 13. ef5± Velimirović—Herzog, corr. 1960] 12. f3 [12. h4 h5! 13. g5 ♘g4 14. ♘f5! ef5 15. ♘d5 ♕b8 16. ♗b6=∞] ♘a5 13. h4 ♘b3 14. ab3 0-0-0 15. ♔b1± Lehmann—Pomar, Palma de Mallorca 1966 — 2/390

5 14... ♖c8?! 15. g5 ♖c3 16. gf6 ♖e3 17. ♕e3 ♗f6 18. ♔b1 0—0 19. e5!+— Velimirović—Pekjun, Sofia 1972 — 14/407

6 **9... b5**?! 10. ♘c6 ♕c6 11. ♗g5△ ♘d5±; **9... ♗e7** 10. f3 ♗d7 11. g4 ♘d4 12. ♗d4 ♗c6 13. 0-0-0 0—0 14. g5 ♘d7 15. f4 ♘c5 [15... e5 16. ♗e3 ef4 17. ♗f4 ♘e5 18. ♘d5 ♗d5 19. ♗d5±] 16. ♖hg1 ♘b3 17. ab3 b5 18. f5 b4 19. ♗g7! ♔g7 20. ♕h5 ♔h8□ 21. f6 bc3 22. ♖g4!±→» Tan—Castro, Hong Kong 1972 — 14/402

7 10. 0-0-0 ♗e7 — 9. 0-0-0

8 10... ♘b3?! 11. ab3 ♗e7 12. g5 ♘d7 13. h4 ♘e5 14. f4 ♘c6 15. f5 ♘e5 16. h5!± Planinc—Ungureanu, Bucuresti 1970 — 9/355

9 12... ♗d7 13. h4 ♘c4 14. g5 ♘h5 15. ♖hg1 g6 16. f4 ♖c8 17. f5 b4 18. fe6 fe6 19. ♘d5! ed5 20. ed5 ♘e5 21. ♘e6 ♗e6 22. de6±→ Gheorghiu—Barczay, Vrnjačka Banja 1966

10 16. h5 g5 17. c3! bc3 18. ♖c1± Velimirović—Štejn, Kapfenberg 1970 — 9/353

11 11. f3 ♗b7 12. 0-0-0 ♘b3 13. ab3 ♗e7 14. h4 ♘d7 15. g5∞ Radulov—Toran, Skopje (ol) 1972 — 14/409; 12... b4!∓

12 **12. ♗e6**?! fe6 13. ♘e6 ♕c4!∓; **12. ♘e6**!? Marić

13 13... ♘c5!?

14 Ribli—Dely, Hungary 1968 — 5/401

15 9... b5?! 10. ♘c6! bc4 11. ♕c4 ♗b7 12. ♘e5 ♕a5 13. ♕b3!± Ghizdavu—Ungureanu, Bucuresti 1971 — 11/337

16 11. a3 ♗b7 [11... ♖b8 12. g4! ♘c4 13. ♗c4 bc4 14. g5 ♘d7 15. f4 ♕b7 16. ♕c4!± Ghizdavu–Ghinda, Bucuresti 1971 — 11/338] 12. f4 ♗e7 13. g4 d5 [13... ♘d7 14. g5 ♘c5 15. ♔b1! ♘c6 16. f5± Cosulich–Ungureanu, Siegen (ol) 1970 — 10/474] 14. ed5 ♘d5 15. ♘d5 ♗d5 16. ♖he1 ♘c4 17. f5± Westerinen–Polugajevski, Tallinn 1973 — 15/375

17 11... ♗e7 12. g5 ♘d7 13. f4 b4 14. ♘b1 ♘c5 15. ♘d2 ♘d3 16. ♕d3 ♗d7 17. ♔b1 ♘b7 18. ♖hf1 ♘c5 19. ♕e2 ♕b7 20. ♕f3 a5 21. f5± Kuprejčik–Kuzmin, SSSR 1972 — 13/410

18 16. e5 ♘d3 17. ♕d3 ♘c4 18. f5!± Ghizdavu–Ungureanu, Romania 1971 — 11/334

19 **10... ♖b8** 11. g4 b5 12. ♗b3 ♘a5 13. g5 ♘b3 14. ab3 ♘d7 15. ♘f5! b4 [15... ef5 16. ♘d5 ♕d8 17. ef5 ♗b7 18. f6 ♗d5 19. ♖d5 gf6 20. ♗d4±] 16. ♘g7 ♔f8 17. ♘e6 fe6 18. ♕h5 ♘e5 19. f4±→ Meštrović–Kelečević, Jugoslavija 1973 — 15/373; **10... b5**!? 11. ♘c6 ♕c6 12. ♘b5 ♘e4∞

20 12. a3 ♖b8?! 13. g4 ♘c4 14. ♗c4 bc4 15. g5 ♘d7 16. f4 ♕b7 17. ♕c4 ♘c5 18. b4!± Holmov–Zurahov, SSSR (ch) 1967; 12... ♗b7△ d5∞

21 13. ♘b1 ♗b7 14. ♘d2 d5 15. f3 de4 16. fe4 ♘d7 17. g5 ♘e5 18. ♔b1 0–0 ∞ Švidenko–Kuras, SSSR 1970 — 9/347; 17... ♘c6!∓

22 **13... ♗d7**?! 14. ♘b6! ♕b6 15. ♘e6 ♕b7 16. ♘g7± Sax–Bellin, Teesside 1972 — 13/415; **13... ♘d7**∞ Dueball–Ree, Nice (ol) 1974

23 10... b5?! 11. ♘c6 ♕c6 12. ♗g5 [12. ♗d4 ♗b7 13. ♖he1 ♖c8 14. f4 0–0 15. ♖d3!± Balinas–Kottnauer, Lugano (ol) 1968] ♗b7 13. ♖he1 ♕c7 14. a3±

24 11... ♘b3 12. ab3 g6?! 13. g5 ♘h5 14. f4 ♗d7 15. f5± Quinteros–Gligorić, Manilla 1974 — 18/386

25 12. ♔b1!? b4 13. ♘a4 ♘b3 14. cb3 ♘e4 15. ♘b6 [15. ♗f4 ♗b7 16. ♖c1? ♕a5 17. f3 ♘f6 18. ♘f5 ef5 19. ♗d6 ♗e4!∓ Ničevski–Anikajev, Vilnus 1969 — 8/375; 16. f3 ♘c5? 17. ♘c5 ♕c5 18. ♘f5!± Kotov; 16... ♘f6!∞] ♖b8 [15... ♕b6 16. ♘e6 ♕b7 17. ♘g7 ♔f8 18. ♗h6 ♔g8 19. ♖he1±] 16. ♘c8△ ♗h6=∞

26 **14. b4**?! [Kristiansen–Tukmakov, Graz 1972 — 14/403] a5! 15. ♘db5 ♕b8 16. ba5 ♖a5∓; **14. ♔b1** ♗b7 [14... ♘c5? 15. ♘f5! ef5 16. ♘d5 ♕b7 17. ♗c5 dc5 18. ef5 ♗f5 19. ♕e5!+– Cejtlin–Zilberštejn, SSSR 1967 — 4/486] 15. ♕h5 g6 16. ♕h6 ♗f8 17. ♕h3∞; **14. ♕h5** ♘f8 [14... ♘c5 15. b4 ♘a4 16. ♖d3± Honfi–Donner, Haag 1966] 15. ♖he1 b4 16. ♘a4 ♗d7 17. f4∞ Ghizdavu–Filipowicz, Bath 1973 — 16/371

27 **14... ♘c5** 15. b4 ♘a4 16. ♖d3 ♗d7 [16... ♕c4?! 17. ♘b1! ♕b4 18. c3 ♕a5 19. ♘c6 ♕c7 20. ♘e7 ♕e7 21. ♖hd1 ♘c5 22. ♗c5! dc5 23. ♖d8 ♕d8 24. ♖d8 ♔d8 25. ♕e3± Radulov–Hamann, Lugano (ol) 1968] 17. ♘f5 ef5 18. ♘d5 ♕d8 19. ♗d4=∞; 16... ♗b7!?; **14... ♗b7** 15. h5 [15. f3 ♕a5 16. ♔b1 b4 17. ♘a2 d5 18. h5! de4 19. g6 ef3 20. gf7 ♔f7 21. ♘f3 ♗f3 22. ♕f3 ♘f6 23. ♖d7± Lerner–Petrušin, SSSR 1971 — 11/332; 15... b4 16. ♘a4 ♘c5 (Weinstein–Larsen, USA 1970 — 10/469) 17. h5! ♘a4 18. ba4 ♕a5∞ Larsen] b4 16. ♘a2 ♕a5 17. ♔b1 ♗e4 18. f3 ♗f5 [Ljubojević–Beljavski, Las Palmas 1974 — 17/418] 19. ♘c6! ♕c7 [19... ♕b5 20. ♕b5 ab5 21. ♘d4±] 20. ♘ab4± Šahović

28 15... ♘c5!? 16. ♘c5 [16. ♕c4 ♗d7 17. ♕b4 0–0=∞; 16. h5!?△ g6] dc5 17. ♘f3 [Hennings–Boleslavski, SSSR 1970 — 9/349] ♗b7∞

29 16. h5!?

30 Platonov–Polugajevski, SSSR (ch) 1967

31 Velimirović

32 14... b4?! 15. ♘g7 ♔f8 16. ♕h5 ♔g7 [16... bc3 17. ♕h6±→] 17. ♗d4 ♘e5 [17... e5? 18. ♕h6 ♔g8 19. ♘d5+–] 18. f4 bc3 [18... ♗d7 19. ♖hg1 bc3 20. fe5 cb2 21. ♗b2 d5 22. ♕h6 1 : 0 Hermlin–Vooremaa, SSSR 1969 — 8/372] 19. ♖hf1! [19. ♗c3 ♗b7? 20. fe5 de5 21. ♖d7!+– Medina–Pomar, Malaga 1969 — 7/371; 19... ♖g8!∞] ♖f8 20. ♖d3±→

33 **15... ♕a5** 16. ef5 ♗b7 17. ♘e7 ♕a1 18. ♔d2 ♕b2 19. ♘c6+–; **15... ♕b7** 16. ♘e7 ♔e7 17. ef5 ♖e8 18. ♗d4 ♔d8 19. ♕h5 ♕c6 ∞ Ceškovski–Petrjajev, SSSR 1968 — 5/404; 18. ♕h5±↑

34 16... 0–0? 17. f6 gf6 18. ♗d4 ♘e5 19. gf6 ♗f6 20. ♖hg1 ♗g7 21. ♗e5+– Velimirović–Sofrevski, Jugoslavija (ch) 1965

35 17... ♗d5?! 18. fg7 ♖g8 19. ♖d5 ♖g7 20. f4 ♔f8 21. ♖e1 ♖c8 [21... ♖g6 22. ♕h5! ♔g8 23. ♗d4△ ♖e3±] 22. ♔b1 ♖c6 23. ♗d4 f6 24. ♕h5± Ceškovski–Petrušin, SSSR 1970 — 9/348

36 **19... 0–0** 20. gf6 ♗f6 [20... ♘f6 21. ♖g5 ♔h8 22. ♗d4 ♖e8 23. ♕e7!+–] 21. ♖g1 ♔h8 22. ♕h5 ♗g7 23. ♖g7 ♔g7 24. ♕h6 ♔g8 25. ♖h5 ♖e8 26. ♗g5!+–; **19... ♘e5** 20. f4 ♘g6 21. gf6 ♗f6 22. ♗b6 ♕e7 23. ♕d2 ♘e5 24. ♖d6±

37 **20. ♗d2** ♔f8!∓ Goljak–Petrušin, SSSR 1971 — 11/331; **20. h4** ♖c8! [20... ♖g6 21. f4 ♔f8 22. ♔b1 ♖c8 23. ♖d3 f5?! 24. ♖d5=∞ Boudy–Kuzmin, Cienfuegos 1973 — 15/372]

21. ♗f4 ♔f8 22. gf6 ♘f6 23. ♖f5 ♖c5−+ Gheorghiu−Hamann, Vrnjačka Banja 1966; **20. ♗f4** ♔f8 21. ♕h5 ♕a5 [21... ♖g7? 22. ♖e7! ♔e7 23. ♗d6 ♔e6 24. c4!± Martinović−Musil, Jugoslavija 1973 — 16/370] 22. ♕e2 ♕d8=

38 21... ♘d7!?

39 23. ♕f3 ♖b8 24. ♖f6 ♖b6 25. ♕a8 ♕d8 26. ♖e7 ♔e7 27. ♖f7 ♔f7 28. ♕d8 [Kuprejčik −Beljavski, SSSR 1974] d5!±

40 9. ♗b3 e5 10. ♘c6?! bc6 11. 0-0-0 ♔h8 12. ♖hg1 ♘g4 13. ♗c5 ♕c7 14. h3 ♘f6 15. ♗e3 a5 16. f4 ef4 17. ♗f4 ♘d7∞ Cobo−Barczay, Salgotarjan 1967; 10. ♘db5!?

41 9... ♕c7 10. ♖hg1 ♘a5 [10... a6 — 9... a6] 11. ♗d3! ♘d7 12. g4 ♘e5 13. ♘f5! ef5 14. ♘d5 ♕d8 15. gf5 f6 16. ♖g3±→» Westerinen−Ribli, Forssa-Helsinki 1972 — 14/404

42 10. ♘f3!? ♘e4! [10... ♘b4 11. ed5 ♘bd5 12. ♗d4± Ostojić−Hartston, Hastings 1968/69 — 6/488] 11. ♘e4 [11. ♘d5 ed5 12. ♗d5 ♘c3!∓] ♕c7 12. ♘eg5 dc4∞

43 12... ♕e8!? 13. ♗b5 ♘c6 14. ♖he1 a6 15. ♗c4 b5 16. ♗b3 ♘a5 17. ♗d5 ♖b8∞ I. Zajcev−Bitman, SSSR 1968

44 13... ♕e5?! 14. f4 ♕f5 15. h3 ♗e6 16. g4+− I. Zajcev−Gik, SSSR 1967 — 3/446

45 **14. ♕c4**∞; **14. ♖he1**∞ Nikitin

46 **14... ♘a5**=; **14... ♖e8**∞ Nikitin

47 10... ♕a5 11. ed5 ed5 12. ♕b5 ♗b4 13. ♘de2 ♗g4 14. **f3** ♖fe8 15. ♕a5 ♘a5 16. ♗g5± Garibjan−Judovič jr., SSSR 1968 — 6/489

48 Astašin−Šestoperov, SSSR 1970 — 10/470

49 10. g4 ♘e5 11. ♗b3 ♘eg4 12. ♖hg1 ♘e3 13. ♕e3 ♕h5 14. ♔b1 ♔h8∓ Šahović−Geler, Beograd 1969 — 8/377

50 10... ♗d7 11. g4! ♘d4 12. ♖d4 e5 13. ♖d5!±

51 12. ♘d5 ed4 13. ♘e7 ♔h8 14. ♗d4=∞

52 Velimirović – Udovčić, Vrnjačka Banja 1963

53 **10... ♗d7** 11. ♘db5 ♘e8 12. ♗f4 e5 13. ♗e3 ♕d8± Tukmakov−Kottnauer, Hastings 1968/69 — 7/370; **10... a6** 11. f4 [11. ♖hg1 ♘d4 12. ♗d4 b5 13. g4 b4 14. g5 ♘e8∞ Hartston−Langeweg, England−Nederland 1967 — 3/443; 11. ♔b1 ♖e8?! 12. ♖hg1 ♗d7 13. g4 ♘d4 14. ♗d4 ♗c6 15. g5 ♘d7 16. ♖d3 g6 17. h4 ♘c5 18. h5!± Talj−Bolbochan, La Habana (ol) 1966 — 2/392] ♗d7 12. g4 ♘d4 13. ♖d4 e5 14. ♖d5! ♘d5 15. ♘d5 ♗d8 16. f5± Martinović−Lejn, Sarajevo 1968 — 5/406

54 12. ♖hg1 b5! 13. g4 b4 14. g5 ♘e8 15. ♘d5?! ed5 16. ♗d5 [Hennings−Navarovszky, Hungary 1970 — 9/350] b3!∓

55 12... ♖ad8 13. ♕e3 b6 14. ♗f6! gf6 15. ♘d5 ♖fe8 [15... ed5 16. ♖d5 ♕a6 17. ♖h5 ♗g4 18. ♕g3+−] 16. ♘e7± Fischer−Sofrevski, Skopje 1967; 16. ♕h6!? Fischer

56 **13... e5** 14. ♗e3! ♗e4 [14... ♘e4? 15. ♘e4 ♗e4 16. ♗d2+−] 15. ♘e4 ♘e4 16. ♕f3±; **13... b5** 14. e5! de5 15. ♕e5± Fischer

57 14. f5 ef5 15. ef5 ♖d7 [15... ♖fe8 16. ♕f2± Trifunović] 16. ♖hf1 ♗d8!= Šamkovič

58 15. e5!? de5 16. fe5 ♘d7 17. ♕g4 b4 18. ♖f7! ♔f7 19. ♕e6 ♔e8 20. ♕c6 bc3 21. e6± Jovčić−Radojčić, Jugoslavija 1969 — 8/376

59 18. ♖f5! ♕b4 [18... ♕c7 19. ♖df1 ♘d7 20. ♖h5!+−] 19. ♕f1! ♘e4 20. ♕f4! [20. a3? ♕b7 21. ♕f4 ♗a4! 22. ♕g4 ♗f6! 23. ♖f6 ♗b3 0 : 1 Fischer−Geler, Skopje 1967 — 4/484] cb2 [20... d5 21. ♕e5 ♘f6 22. ♖f6 ♗f6 23. ♕f6!+−; 20... ♘d2 21. ♖d2 cd2 22. c3! ♕b3 23. ♗g7 ♔g7 24. ♕g4 ♔h8 25. ♕d4+−] 21. ♖h5 ♘c3 [21... ♗f6 22. ♕f5 h6 23. ♖h6 gh6 24. ♕g6+−] 22. ♔b2 ♘d1 [22... ♖f7 23. ♕f7 ♘d1 24. ♔b1! ♕d4 25. ♖h7! ♔h7 26. ♕h5#] 23. ♔c1 ♖f7 24. ♗f7! △ ♖h7+− Fischer

60 10. ♖hg1?! ♖c8! 11. g4 [10. ♗b3 ♘a5 △ ♖c3!] ♘d4 12. ♗d4 e5 13. g5 [Walther−Ortega, Lugano (ol) 1968] ed4 14. gf6 ♗f6∞

61 10... ♘d4 11. ♗d4 a5 [11... ♗c6 12. f4 ♕c7 13. ♖he1±] 12. a4 e5 13. ♗e3 ♗c6 14. f3 ♕d7 15. g4± Minev−Bobekov, Bulgaria 1967 — 4/477

62 11... ♖c8 12. g5 ♘e8 13. h4 ♘a5 14. g6 fg6 15. h5 g5 16. ♘f3 g4 17. ♘e5± Velimirović−Milić, Beograd 1965

63 14. ♖dg1!? △ 14... b4 15. ♘d1± Šamkovič

64 **15. ♘c2**? ♕b5∓; **15. ♘d5**?! ed5 16. ♗d5 ♕c8 17. ♖hg1 ♗e6∓

65 **16. ♖h3**? ♗g5!∓ Espig−Kirov, Timisoara 1972 — 13/407; **16. f4**!?=∞

66 10... ♕c7 11. ♖hf1 ♖fc8 12. ♗b3 ♘d4 13. ♗d4 e5 14. fe5 de5 15. ♘d5! ♘d5 16. ed5 ♗d6 17. ♗e5! ♗e5 18. d6± Kremenecki−Gorškov, SSSR 1967 — 4/485

67 11. f5 ♘a5 12. ♗d3 e5 13. ♘b3 b5 14. ♗b5 ♖c3 15. bc3 ♘e4=∞ Holmov−Talj, SSSR 1968 — 6/494

68 11... a6 12. g4 b5 13. g5 ♘e8 14. h4±

69 14. ♘b3 ♘d5 15. ♘d5 ed5 16. ♖d5 ♕c7=∞

70 14... ♘e8 15. ♘db5! a6 16. ♖d7! ♕d7 17. ♖d1 ♕c6 18. ♘a7 ♕c7 19. ♘c8 ♕c8 20. ♕d3±

71 ± Boleslavski

72 12. ♕e5 ♕e5 13. ♗e5 b6= Velimirović–Dely, Beograd 1965

73 **14. ♗b5** a6 15. ♖a4 [15. ♗d3= Velimirović–Geler, Budapest 1973] ab5 16. ♖a5 ♖a5 =∞; **14. ♖hd1**!±

74 **10. g4** ♘e5 11. f3?! ♘c4 12. ♕c4 b5 13. ♕e2 ♗b7∓ Tatai–Mednis, Madonna di Campiglio 1974 — 17/417; 11. g5!?; **10. f4** d5! 11. ♘b3?! ♘b4 12. ed5 ed5 13. h3 ♖e8 14. ♕f2 ♗f5∓ Meštrović–Talj, Sarajevo 1966 — 1/284; 11. ♘f3!?; **10. ♖hg1** ♕e8 11. g4 b5 12. ♗d3 b4 13. ♘b1 ♘d4 14. ♗d4 e5 15. ♗e3 ♗b7 [Sznapik–Filipowicz, Polska 1972 — 14/408] 16. f3∞

75 **11. f3**?! ♘d7 12. g4 ♘c5 13. h4 b5 14. ♕g2 b4∓ Navojan–Beljavski, SSSR 1972; **11. ♖hg1** ♘d7 12. g4 ♘c5 13. g5 b5 14. ♕h5 [14. ♔b1 ♗d7 15. ♕h5 ♘b3 16. ab3 ♘b4!∞ Ghizdavu–Ostojić, Bucuresti 1973 — 15/374; 16. cb3!? Ciocaltea] b4 15. ♘a4 [15. ♘c6 ♘b3! 16. ab3 ♕c6= Espig–Beljavski, Suhumi 1972 — 14/405] ♘b3 [15... ♘d4 16. ♗d4 ♘a4 17. ♕h6! e5 18. g6! gh6 19. gf7 ♔h8 20. fe8♕±] 16. ab3 ♖b8± Gufeljd

76 11... ♗d8?! 12. ♘c6 ♕c6 13. e5 de5 14. fe5 ♘e4 15. ♕g4± Stean–Beljavski, Teesside 1973

77 12. f5 ♘c5 13. fe6 ♘b3 14. ab3 fe6∓

78 **14... b4**? 15. fe6 fe6 16. ♘c6 ♕c6 17. ♗c5 ♕c5 18. ♘d5 ♗d8 19. ♖hf1±→; **14... ♗f6** 15. fe6 fe6 16. ♘f5! ♘b7 [16... ♘b3 17. ♘d6 ♕e7 18. ab3±] 17. ♘d6 ♘d6 18. ♖d6 ♗e5± Velimirović–Spasov, Poreč 1974 — 18/382

79 **11... b5** 12. ♘c6 [12. g4 b4 13. ♘c6 bc3! 14. ♘e7 ♕e7 15. ♕d3 cb2 16. ♔b2 ♗b7= Radev–Spasov, Albena 1970 — 10/473] ♕c6 13. g4 b4 14. ♘d5 ed5 15. g5!± Suetin; **11... ♗d7** 12. g4 ♘d4 13. ♖d4 e5 14. ♖c4± Planinc–Musil, Ljubljana 1969 — 7/373

80 13... ♗b7?! 14. f5! e5 15. ♖d3± Ljubojević–Ribli, Lanzarote 1973 — 15/445

81 14. f5 b4 15. ♘a4 e5 16. ♖c4 ♕a5 17. ♖c6 ♗d7 18. ♗b6 ♕b5!∓ Nikitin

82 ∞ Nikitin

83 11... ♘d4 12. ♗d4 b5 13. g4 ♘d7 14. g5 ♘c5 15. ♕h5 ♗b7 [15... b4? 16. ♗f6!± Bordonada–Sanz, Nice (ol) 1974 — 17/428] 16. ♗f6 ♖fc8 17. ♖g4!± Bordonada–Pavlov, Nice (ol) 1974 — 17/429; 16. ♖g4!? Bordonada–Haruyama, Penang 1974 — 18/387

84 **12. ♘e6**?! fe6 13. ♗e6 ♔h8 14. ♘d5 [Hramov–Judovič, SSSR 1970 — 10/471] ♕d8! 15. ♗d7 ♗d7 16. ♗b6 ♕e8! 17. ♘c7 ♕f7∓; **12. g4** ♘c5 13. f4 b5 14. f5 ♖e8 15. g5 g6 16. fg6 ♘b3 17. ab3 fg6 18. h4 ♘e5 19. h5 ♗f8∞ Ulker–Tringov, Poiana Brasov 1973 — 16/368; 13. g5 — 11. g4

85 **12... b5**? 13. ♘d5!±; **12... ♘a5** 13. ♘e6!±

86 16. ♗d4?! Velimirović–Tringov, Reykjavik 1974 — 17/425

87 16... f6 17. ♖c1±△ f4

88 12. f3 ♘a5 13. g4 ♘b3 14. ab3 ♘d7 15. g5 ♘b6 16. f4 b4 17. ♘b1 d5∞ Liebert–Möhring, Colditz 1967 — 3/445

89 **12... ♘d4** 13. ♗d4 ♘d7 14. g5 ♘c5 [14... ♗b7 15. ♕h5 g6 16. ♕h6 e5 17. ♖d3 ♖fc8 18. ♗f7!± Žukov–Kudrjašev, SSSR 1971 — 11/333] 15. ♕h5 b4 [15... ♘b3 16. ab3 ♕d8 17. ♖d3 e5 18. ♗e5 b4 19. ♗f6! ♗f6 20. gf6 ♕f6 21. ♘d5+– Kavalek–Polugajevski, La Habana (ol) 1966] 16. ♗f6!± Hennings–Möhring, Colditz 1967 — 3/444; **12... ♘a5** 13. g5 ♘b3 14. ab3 ♘d7 15. ♖g3 [15. h4 b4 16. ♘a4?! ♗b7 17. g6?! hg6 18. h5 e5!–+ Zuckerman–Paoli, Bari 1970 — 10/472; 17. f3!?; 16. ♘d5!? ed5 17. ♘f5∞] ♗b7?! 16. f4!±→» Hübner–Visier, España 1974 — 18/385; 15... ♖e8∞

90 **13. ♘d5**?! ♘d5! 14. ♘c6 ♘e3 15. ♘e7 ♕e7 16. ♕e3 a5∓ Stean–Velimirović, Nice (ol) 1974; **13. g5** bc3 14. gf6 cb2 15. ♔b1 ♗f6 16. ♕f3 ♗e5! [16... ♔h8 17. ♘c6 ♕c6 18. ♗g5 ♗g5 19. ♖g5 f6 20. ♖dg1 ♖a7 21. ♖h5=∞ Davis–Mitroy, Australia 1973] 17. ♗h6 g6∓ Matulović–Nikitin, Kiev 1966

91 13... bc3 14. ♘e7 ♕e7 15. ♗d4±

92 **15... ♕b5**?! 16. ♕b5 ab5 17. gf6 ♗f6 18. ♗d5 ♗e6 19. ♗a8 ♖a8 20. ♗d4! 1 : 0 Bronštejn–Šamkovič, Kislovodsk 1968 — 6/491; **15... de4**?! 16. gf6 ♗f6 17. ♗d5 ♕a4 18. ♕h5! [18. ♗a8?! ♗e6 19. ♗d4 ♗d4 20. ♖d4 ♕a2 21. ♖g3!∞ Damjanović–Langeweg, Amsterdam 1969; 18. ♗d4 ♗d4 19. ♖d4 ♗f5 20. ♖g5 ♗g6 21. h4 ♖ae8∞ Kupper–Paoli, Venezia 1967 — 4/482; 19... ♗e6 20. ♕e4 ♖ac8 21. ♗e6 fe6 22. ♖d6 ♕a2= Gipslis–Talj, Moskva 1967 — 3/436; 21. ♖b4!± Čenrotaj–Judovič, corr. 1969] ♗e6 19. ♖g7! ♗g7 20. ♖g1±→ Ostapenko–Jarcev, SSSR 1969 — 8/373

93 16... ♘c3? 17. bc3 ♕a4 18. ♗b3!±

94 17... b3? 18. ♖d4! ♕a2 19. ♗h7!+−

95 Stean−Dueball, Nice (ol) 1974 — 17/427

96 11... ♘a5 12. g5 ♘b3 13. ab3 ♘d7 14. h4 b5 15. g6 ♘c5 16. b4 ♘a4 17. ♘a4 ba4 [Romanišin−Vajser, SSSR 1972 — 13/408] 18. h5±; 17. ♖d3!?

97 12... ♘d7 13. g5 ♘c5 14. ♕h5 [14. e5 de5 15. ♖h4 g6 16. ♖h6 f5! 17. h4 ♘b3 18. ab3 f4 19. ♘e4? fe3 20. h5 ♖f2!−+ Bronštejn−Lejn, SSSR (ch) 1971 — 12/416; 19. ♗d2!?∓] ♘b3 15. ab3 g6 16. ♕e2 ♗d7 17. h4 ♕a5 18. ♔b1 ♖fc8 19. h5± Suhanov−Kozlov, SSSR 1971 — 11/329

98 13. ♘d5!? ♕d7 [13... ♘d5 14. ♖d5 ♗e6 15. ♖d3 ♖ac8 16. ♗d5±] 16. ♘b6 ♕g4 17. f3 ♕h3 18. ♘a8 ♗e6±

99 14... ♘d7 15. ♘d5 ♘c5 16. h4 b5 17. ♖c3 ♗e6 18. ♖d1 ♘b3 19. ab3 ♗d5 20. ♖d5± Martinović−Stanev, Ybbs 1968 — 6/430

100 **15. ♘d5** ♗g5 16. ♖g1 ♗e3 17. ♕e3 ♗e6 18. ♖c3 ♔h8 19. ♕g3 ♖c8= Glauser−Kupper, Schweiz 1969 — 8/374; **15. h4** b5 16. ♖c8=∞; **15. ♖c8**!? ♖c8 16. h4 ♘c7 17. ♕g4△ h5→» Talj

101 Spasojević−M. Ostojić, Beograd 1966 — 2/387

102 13. f4 ♘d7! 14. f5 ♘c5 15. g5 ♖d8 16. f6? ♗f8∓ Velimirović−Tringov, Vršac 1973 — 16/367; 16. g6∞ Parma

103 **14. e5** de5! [14... d5 15. ♖h4 g6 16. f4 b4 17. ♘a4 ♗b7 18. ♗d4 ♗c6 19. ♕e3! ♖fb8 20. ♖g1 ♕a5 21. f5!±→» Velimirović−Fridjonsson, Reykjavik 1974 — 17/421; 18... ♗c5!?] 15. ♖h4 ♖d8 16. ♕h5 — 14. ♕h5; **14. ♕h5** ♖d8 [14... ♘c5 15. ♖g1 ♘b3 16. ab3 f5? 17. ef5 ♖f5 18. ♖h4+− Tatai−Paoli Monte Carlo 1967 — 3/442; 14... ♘e5 15. f4 ♘c6 16. ♖d3 ♘b4 17. ♖d2 ♖d8 18. f5 g6 19. fg6 hg6 20. ♕h4 ♘c6 21. ♕g3 ♘e5 22. h4± Velimirović−M. Nikolić, Jugoslavija 1967 — 3/441] 15. e5 [Nikitin; 15. ♖g1 g6! 16. ♕h4 ♘c5 17. f4 ♖b8 18. f5 a5∓ Radulov−Ribli, Kecskemet 1972 — 13/413] de5 [15... d5 16. ♗d5±; 15... ♘c5 16. ♖h4 h6 17. ♖g1±] 16. ♖h4 ♘f8 17. ♘e4 ♗b7 18. ♘f6 ♗f6 [18... gf6 19. ♖g1! ♔h8 20. ♕f7 ♗d6 21. g6! ♕f7 22. gf7 ♘d7 23. ♗h6+−; 19... f5 20. g6 fg6 21. ♗e6! ♘e6 22. ♕h7 ♔f8 23. ♕h8 ♔f7 24. ♖h7 ♘g7 23. ♕g7+− Cvetković, Krnić] 19. gf6 ♗h1 20. fg7 ♔g7 21. ♗h6 [21. ♕g5 ♘g6 22. ♕h6 ♔g8 23. ♕h7 ♔f8∓] ♔g8 22. ♕g5 ♘g6 23. ♕f6 ♖d1!△ ♕d8∓; **14. h4** ♘c5 15. h5 f5 [15... ♗b7∞] 16. ef5 ♖f5 17. g6 h6∞ Dely−Paoli, Szombathely 1966 — 2/388; **14. ♖g1** ♘c5!? [14... g6 15. f4 ♘c5 16. f5 ♘b3 17. ab3 ef5 18. ♘d5 ♕b7 19. ♘f6 ♗f6 20. gf6 fe4 21. ♗h6 ♖e8 22. ♕e3± Ćirić−Paoli, Reggio Emilia 1967 — 3/440; 15. h4 ♘c5 16. h5 ♖e8 17. ♖h1 ♗b7 18. ♕g4!± Dueball−Kuzmin, Nice (ol) 1974 — 17/422] 15. e5 ♘b3! 16. ab3 d5∞ Nikitin

104 15. f5 ef5! [15... b4? 16. ♖b4 d5 17. ♗d5! ed5 18. ♘d5+− Gik−Kričevski, SSSR 1968 — 5/402] 16. ef5 [16. ♘d5 ♕d8 17. ef5 ♗f5 18. ♖f1 ♗e6 19. ♕h5 ♘b3 20. ab3 ♗d5 21. ♖d5 ♕d7∓ Planinc−Langeweg, Amsterdam 1974] ♗f5 17. ♖f1 ♕d7 18. ♘d5 ♖ae8∞ Planinc−Kavalek, Amsterdam 1973 — 16/366

105 15... ♖d8?! 16. f5 ♖b8 17. ♖f1 ♗f8 18. g6!± Planinc−Enklaar, Wijk aan Zee 1974 — 17/419

106 **17... a5** 18. ♖e1 a4 19. ♗d5! ed5 [Planinc−Langeweg, Wijk aan Zee 1974 — 17/420] 20. ♘d5± Ćirić; **17... ♗d7**!∞

107 14... ♘f6 15. ♗b6 ♕d7 16. ♖hg1 ♔h8 17. ♖d3=∞→

108 15. ♖hg1!? ♘b3 16. ab3=∞

109 19. ♖d5=∞ Velimirović−Bukal, Jugoslavija 1971 — 11/336

110 **13. ♔b1** ♗d7 14. ♖hg1 ♘b3 15. cb3 b5 [Ceškovski−Šamkovič, SSSR 1972] 16. ♕h5 b4 17. ♘ce2∞; **13. h4** b5 14. h5 [14. f3?! ♗d7! 15. ♕g2 b4 16. ♘ce2 ♘b3 17. ab3 a5∓ Fischer−Larsen, Palma de Mallorca (izt) 1970 — 10/475] b4? 15. ♘a4 ♘e4 16. g6 d5 17. ♘c6 ♕c6 18. ♘b6± Planinc−Subašić, Jugoslavija 1971 — 11/335; 14... ♘b3∞

111 **13... b5**?! 14. ♕h5! b4 15. ♖g3 ♘b3 16. ab3 g6 17. ♕h6 f6! 18. ♘c6! ♕c6 19. ♖dg1 f5 20. ♗d4 e5 21. ♘d5!± Vaisman−Gheorghiu, Romania 1974 — 17/424; **13... ♘b3**?! 14. ab3 ♗d7 15. ♖g3 ♖ad8 16. ♕h5 g6 17. ♕h6 f6 18. f4 ♖f7 [Soltis−Trincardi, Reggio Emilia 1971 — 11/330] 19. f5!± Parma

112 14... ♖fd8 15. ♕h5 g6 16. ♕h4 b5?! 17. ♘f5! ♘b3 18. ab3 ef5 19. ♘d5 ♕a5 20. ♘e7 ♘e7 21. ♗d4!± Davis−Watell, Australia 1973 — 17/423; 16... h5!?

113 17... b5?! 18. ♖h3 ♘b3 19. ab3 ♗g7 20. ♕h7 ♔f8 21. f4 ♘e7 22. ♖d2± Vitomski−Vitolinš, SSSR 1972

114 **18. ♘de2**?! h5! [18. . . b5? 19. ♘f4 h5 20. ♘h5 gh5 21. ♕h5+− Ostapenko] 19. f4 b5 20. f5 ♘b3 21. ab3 b4 [21. . . ♘e5 22. ♖d2→] 22. ♘f4 [22. ♘a4? ♘a5∓; 22. fg6? fg6 23. ♘f4 ♘e5 24. ♘g6 ♘g6 25. ♕h5 ♗e8∓; 22. f6? bc3 23. bc3 e5!∓] bc3 [22. . . ♘e5 23. ♗d4 bc3 24. bc3 ef5 25. ♘h5! gh5 26. ♕h5 ♘g6 27. ♖h3+−; 25. . . ♕d8 26. ♗e5 de5 27. ♘f6 ♗f6 28. gf6 f4 29. ♖h3+−; 25. . . f4 26. ♘f6 ♗f6 27. gf6 ♕d8 28. ♗e5 fg3 29. hg3△ ♖h1+− Ostapenko] 23. bc3 [23. fg6? ♘e5 24. ♕h5 cb2 25. ♔d2 ♕c2 26. ♔e1 ♕d1 27. ♕d1 ♖c1 28. ♗c1 b1♕−+] ♕a5! [23. . . ef5 24. ♘h5! +− Ostapenko] 24. fg6 fg6! 25. ♘g6 ♔g7 26. ♘e7 ♘e7 27. ♗d4 e5 28. g6 ♘g8!∓ Nikitin; **18. ♕h6**=

B9 SADRŽAJ • СОДЕРЖАНИЕ B9

B9 SOMMAIRE • INDICE B9

B9 CONTENTS • INHALT B9

B9 INDICE • INNEHÅLL B9

B 90 1. e4 c5 2. ♘f3 d6 3. d4 cd4 4. ♘d4 ♘f6 5. ♘c3 a6[1]

	6	7	8	9	10	11	12	13	14	
1	h3[2] g6[3]	g4 ♗g7	g5[4] ♘h5[5]	♗e2 e5	♘b3 ♘f4	♘d5[6] ♘d5[7]	♕d5 ♘c6	♗g4 ♗g4	hg4 ♕c8[8]	=
2	. . . e6	g4 d5[9]	ed5 ♘d5	♘de2 ♗b4	♗g2[10] 0–0	♗d2 ♘b6[11]	♘e4 ♗e7	0–0 ♘c6	b3 f5[12]	=
3	♗e3 e5[13]	♘b3[14] ♗e6[15]	♕d2 ♘bd7	f3 ♗e7	g4[16] b5[17]	g5 ♘h5[18]	0-0-0 0–0	♖g1 ♖c8	♘d5 ♗d5[19]	±
4	♗c4 ♘bd7[20]	♗e3[21] g6[22]	f3 ♘b6	♗b3 ♗d7	♘de2 ♗g7	♕d4 ♘c8	♕d2 0–0	h4 b5	♗h6 b4[23]	±
5	. . . g6	0–0[24] ♗g7	♗b3[25] 0–0	f4 ♘bd7	♘f3 ♘c5	♕e1[26]				±

[1] Najdorf

[2] 6. **♘b3** g6 [6. . . ♘c6 7. ♗e2 e5=] 7. ♗e2 ♗g7=; **6. a3** ♘c6 7. ♗e2 e5=; **6. ♗d3** ♘c6 [6. . . b5 7. 0–0 ♗b7=] 7. ♘c6 bc6 8. 0–0 g6 9. ♕e2 ♗g7 10. ♗d2 0–0= Holmov–O'Kelly, La Habana 1968 — 5/549; **6. a4** ♘c6 [6. . . b6?! 7. ♗g5 e6 8. f4 ♗e7?! 9. ♗c4± Kurajica; 8. . . ♕c7 9. ♗f6 gf6 10. ♗e2 ♘c6 11. f5± Westerinen–Ghizdavu, Bucuresti 1974 — 17/494; 6. . . e6 7. ♗e3 — B 80; 6. . . g6!?] 7. ♗e2 e5 8. ♘b3 ♗e7 9. 0–0 0–0 — B 92

[3] **6. . . e5** 7. ♘de2 ♗e6 [7. . . ♗e7 8. g4 0–0 9. ♘g3! g6 10. g5 ♘e8 11. h4±→ Fischer] 8. g4 ♗e7 [8. . . d5 9. ed5 ♘d5 10. ♗g2±; 9. g5! ♘e4 10. ♘e4 de4 11. ♕d8 ♔d8 12. ♗g2± R. Byrne] 9. ♗g2 ♘bd7 10. ♘g3 0–0 11. ♘f5 ♘b6 12. 0–0± R. Byrne–Donner, Lugano 1970; **6. . . ♘c6** 7. g4 ♘d4 8. ♕d4 e5 9. ♕d3 ♗e7 [9. . . ♗e6!? Fischer] 10. g5 ♘d7 11. ♗e3 ♗g5 [11. . . ♘c5? 12. ♕d2 ♗e6 13. 0-0-0 0–0 14. f3 ♖c8 15. ♔b1 ♘d7 16. h4± Fischer–Bolbochan, Stocholm (izt) 1962] 12. ♗g5 ♕g5 13. ♕d6 ♕e7 14. ♕e7 ♔e7 15. ♘d5 ♔f8 16. 0-0-0 g6± Kotov; **6. . . b5** 7. ♘d5 ♗b7 [7. . . ♘fd7 8. ♗g5 h6?? 9. ♘e6+–; 7. . . e6 8. ♘f6 ♕f6 9. c4±; 7. . . ♘e4 8. ♕f3 ♘c5 9. b4 e6 10. bc5 ed5 11. ♕d5 ♖a7= Fischer] 8. ♘f6 gf6 9. c4 ♗e4 [9. . . bc4 10. ♗c4 ♗e4 11. 0–0 d5 12. ♖e1!± Fischer–Najdorf, Varna (ol) 1962] 10. cb5 ♗g7 11. ♕g4 ♗g6 12. ♘f5 0–0∞ Fischer

[4] **8. ♗e3** 0–0 9. g5 [9. ♕d2!?; 9. ♗g2!?] ♘h5 [9. . . ♘e8!?] 10. ♗e2 e5! 11. ♘b3 ♘f4 12. ♗f4 ef4 13. h4 ♘c6 14. ♕d2 ♗e5∞ Damjanović–Zuckerman, Malaga 1968 — 5/550; **8. ♗g2** 0–0 9. 0–0 ♘c6= Fischer

[5] 8. . . ♘fd7 9. ♗e3 ♘c6 10. ♕d2±○ Fischer

[6] 11. ♗g4 ♘c6 12. ♘d5 0–0 13. h4 ♗g4 14. ♕g4 ♘d5 15. ed5 ♘e7 16. ♕e4 ♖c8= Damjanović–Fischer, Skopje 1967 — 4/551

[7] **11. . . ♘h3**?! 12. ♗e3△ ♗b6±; **11. . . 0–0** 12. h4 ♘d7!? 13. ♘f4 ef4 14. ♕d6 ♗e5∞; 12. . . f5∞ Talj; **11. . . ♘e2** 12. ♕e2 ♗e6= Fischer

[8] 15. ♕d1 [15. ♕d6 ♕g4 16. ♕d3 ♖d8 17. ♕e2 ♕g2 18. ♖f1 f6∓↑ Fischer] ♕e6 [15. . . ♘d4? 16. c3 ♘b3 17. ab3 ♕e6 18. ♖a5± Fischer–Reshevsky, USA (ch) 1962/63; 15. . . d5!? 16. ed5 ♘b4 17. c3 ♕c4∞ Fischer] 16. ♗e3 0-0-0= Talj

[9] **7. . . b5**!? 8. g5 ♘fd7 9. a3 ♗b7 10. ♗e3 ♘c6∞; **7. . . ♘c6** 8. g5 ♘fd7 9. ♗e3 ♕c7 10. ♕d2 b5 11. 0-0-0 ♗b7∞ Donoso–Najdorf, Argentina 1971 — 13/493

[10] 10. ♗d2 ♘c3 11. ♘c3 ♗d7 12. ♕e2 ♗c6 13. ♖g1 ♕c7 14. 0-0-0 ♘d7= Gipslis–Geler, Moskva 1967 — 4/550

[11] 11. . . ♘c3 12. ♘c3 ♕c7 13. a3 ♗e7 14. ♕f3! ♘c6 15. 0–0 ♗d7 16. ♖ad1± Kurajica–Bukić, Jugoslavija 1972 — 13/495

[12] 15. gf5 ef5 16. ♘4c3 ♗c5 17. a4 a5 18. ♗f4 ♕e7= Kurajica – Najdorf, Hastings 1971/72 — 13/494

[13] **6. . . ♘g4**?! 7. ♗g5! [7. ♗c4 ♘e3 8. fe3∞] ♘c6 [7. . . h6 8. ♗h4 g5 9. ♗g3 ♗g7 10. ♗e2 h5 11. h4 ♘c6 12. ♘b3 gh4 13. ♗h4 ♘ce5 14. ♕d2 ♘g6 15. ♗g5 ♗e5 16. ♘d5± Romanišin–Muhin, SSSR 1974] 8. ♕d2 h6 [8. . . ♕b6 9. ♘b3 e6 10. h3 ♘ge5 11. f4 ♘g6 12. f5 ♘ge5 13. ♗e2△ 0-0-0± R. Byrne–Browne, USA 1970 — 10/527] 9. ♗h4 ♘d4 10. ♕d4 e5 11. ♕a4 ♗d7 12. ♗d8 ♗a4 13. ♗b6± R. Byrne; **6. . . ♘bd7** 7. g4 [7. ♕d2 e6 8. f3 b5 9. g4 h6 10. 0-0-0 ♗b7 11. ♕g2∞ Buza–Ghitescu, Romania (ch) 1972 — 14/470] d5 8. g5 ♘e4 9. ♘e4 de4 10. ♘b3 b6 11. ♕d4 ♗b7 12. 0-0-0 ♕c7 13. ♗g2 e5 14. ♕d7!? [14. ♕a4 ♖c8 15. ♖d2 ♕c6 16. ♕c6 ♗c6 17. ♖hd1 ♗e7∓ R. Byrne–Korčnoj, Moskva 1971 — 12/466]

♕d7 15. ♖d7 ♔d7 16. ♗b6△ ♘a5∞= Kotov; 7. ♗e2!± — B 92

14 **7. ♘de2** ♘bd7 8. ♘g3 ♕c7 9. a4 b6 10. ♗d3 ♗b7= Dely—Bertok, Vrnjačka Banja 1966 — 1/309; **7. ♘f3** ♕c7 [7... ♗e7 8. ♗g5 ♘c6 9. ♗c4± Westerinen] 8. ♗e2 [8. h3 ♘bd7 9. g4 h6∞ Ćirić] ♗e6 9. 0—0 ♘bd7 10. ♘d5 ♗d5 11. ed5 g6 12. c4 ♗g7 13. ♘d2 0—0 14. ♖c1± Westerinen—Browne, Netanya 1971

15 7... ♗e7 8. ♕d2 ♗e6 9. f3 0—0 [9... d5 10. ed5 ♘d5 11. ♘d5 ♕d5 12. ♕d5 ♗d5 13. 0-0-0± Gufeljd] 10. 0-0-0 ♘bd7 11. g4 b5 12. a3 ♘b6 13. g5 ♘h5 14. ♘d5 ♗d5 15. ed5 ♖c8 16. ♘a5 ♘d5 17. ♕d5 ♕a5 18. ♗d3±↑ Džindžihašvili—Raškovski, SSSR (ch) 1972 — 15/435

16 10. 0-0-0 b5 [10... h5!? 11. ♖g1 b5 12. ♘d5 ♗d5 13. ed5 ♘b6 14. ♗b6 ♕b6 15. ♘a5 ♘d7 16. ♗d3 ♘c5 17. ♘c6 ♗f6= Petrušin—Šašin, SSSR 1973] 11. ♘d5 ♗d5 12. ed5 ♘b6 13. ♗b6 ♕b6 14. ♘a5 0—0 15. ♘c6 ♖fe8 16. c4 bc4 17. ♗c4 ♗f8= Mecking—Evans, San Antonio 1972

17 10... ♖c8 11. 0-0-0 ♘b6 12. g5 ♘fd7 13. ♖g1± R. Byrne—Balašov, Moskva 1971 — 12/467

18 11... b4 12. ♘a4 ♘h5 13. ♕b4 ♗g5 [13... d5 14. ♕a5] 14. ♗g5 ♕g5 15. ♕d6 ♕h4 16. ♔d1 ♕f2 17. ♘d2± Hartston

19 15. ed5 f5 16. h4± Hartston—Smejkal, Vrnjačka Banja 1972

20 **6... e5** 7. ♘f5 ♗f5 8. ef5 ♗e7 9. 0—0 0—0 10. ♗e3 ♘bd7 11. ♘d5 ♖c8 12. ♗b3 ♘c5 13. ♘f6 ♗f6 14. ♗d5± Sudoplatov—Ignatjev, SSSR 1956; **6... b5** 7. ♗b3 ♗b7 8. 0—0 ♘bd7 9. ♕e2 g6 10. f4± Levenfiš—Aronin, SSSR 1950; **6... ♗d7** 7. ♗g5 e6 8. f4 ♘c6 9. ♕d3 h6 10. ♗h4 ♕c7 11. ♗f6 gf6 12. ♗b3± R. Byrne—Rossolimo, USA (ch) 1967 — 3/502

21 **7. 0—0** ♕c7 8. ♕e2 g6 9. f4 ♗g7 10. ♘f3 b5 11. ♗b3± Estrin—Aronin, corr. 1959; **7. a3** g6 8. h4 ♘e5 9. ♗b3 ♗g7 10. ♗g5 ♕a5 11. ♕d2 ♗d7 12. ♗f6 ♗f6 13. ♘d5± Bronštejn—Olafsson, Portorož (izt) 1958

22 7... e6 8. ♗b3 ♘b6 9. f4 d5 10. e5 ♘fd7 11. f5±→》 Fajbisovič—Roberts, Harrachov 1967 — 4/553

23 15. ♘d5± Averbah—Sherwin, Portorož (izt) 1958

24 **7. f4** ♕c7?! 8. ♗b3 ♗g7 9. 0—0 0—0 10. ♘f3 ♘bd7 11. ♕e2 ♘c5 12. e5± Aronin—Mojsejev, SSSR 1951; 7... ♗g7±; **7. ♗b3** ♗g7 8. f3 ♘c6 9. ♗e3 0—0 10. ♕d2±

25 8. ♗g5 ♘c6?! 9. ♘c6 bc6 10. e5 de5 11. ♕d8 ♔d8 12. ♗f7± Ćirić—Matanović, Jugoslavija (ch) 1958; 8... 0—0!?; 8... ♘bd7!?

26 Averbah—Mojsejev, SSSR 1951

B 91

1. e4 c5 2. ♘f3 d6 3. d4 cd4 4. ♘d4 ♘f6 5. ♘c3 a6 6. g3

	6	7	8	9	10	11	12	13	14	
1	... b5[1]	♗g2 ♗b7	0—0[2] e6	♖e1[3] ♕c7[4]	a4 b4	♘a2 a5[5]	c3			±
2	... ♗g4	f3[6] ♗d7[7]	♗e3[8] ♘c6[9]	♗g2[10] g6[11]	0—0 ♗g7	♘d5 0—0	a4[12]			±
3	... e5	♘b3[13] ♗e7[14]	♗g2 0—0	a4 ♘c6	0—0 ♘b4	♗g5 ♗e6	a5 b5	ab6 ♕b6[15]		=

1. e4 c5 2. ♘f3 d6 3. d4 cd4 4. ♘d4 ♘f6 5. ♘c3 a6 6. g3 e5 7. ♘de2

	7	8	9	10	11	12	13	14	15	
4	... ♗e6[16]	♗g2 ♗e7[17]	0—0 ♘bd7	a4[18] ♖c8	h3 ♘b6[19]	♗g5 h6	♗f6 ♗f6	b3 0—0	a5[20]	±
5	... ♘bd7	a4[21] ♗e7	♗g2 0—0[22]	0—0 ♖b8	h3 b5	ab5 ab5	♖a7 ♗b7	♗e3 ♘b6[23]		=
6	... ♗e7	♗g5[24] ♘bd7[25]	♗h3 b5![26]	♗d7[27] ♕d7	♗f6 ♗f6	♘d5 ♗d8[28]				∞
7	... ...	♗g2 0—0[29]	0—0 b5	a4[30] b4	♘d5 ♘d5	♕d5 ♖a7	♗e3 ♗e6	♕d2 ♖b7	f4 b3![31]	∞

1 **6... h5** 7. h3! e6 8. ♗g2 ♕c7 9. 0–0 ♘bd7 10. f4 ♘b6 11. ♕d3 ♗e7 12. b3 ♗d7 13. ♗b2 0-0-0!? 14. a4 ♔b8 15. a5 ♘c8 16. b4 ♘a7 17. ♖fb1 e5 18. ♘f3 ef4 19. gf4 ♗e6 20. ♘d5+ –→ Robatsch–Barczay, Sarajevo 1968 — 5/460; **6... ♘c6** 7. ♗g2 ♗d7 8. 0–0 g6±; **6... g6** 7. ♗g2 ♗g7 8. 0–0 0–0±

2 8. a4 e5 [8... b4 9. ♘d5 ♘bd7 10. 0–0 e6 11. ♘f6 ♘f6 12. ♖e1± Horowitz–Denker, USA 1949] 9. ♘b3 b4 10. ♘d5 ♗d5 11. ed5 a5 12. ♗d2 ♗e7 13. c3 ♘a6 14. cb4 ab4 15. 0–0± Fuderer – Kotov, Jugoslavija – SSSR 1958

3 **9. a3** ♕c7 10. g4 ♘c6 11. g5 ♘d7 12. ♘de2= Fine–Denker, USA 1950; **9. ♕e2** ♘bd7 [9... ♕c7 10. a4 ba4 11. ♖a4 ♘bd7 12. ♖c4 ♕d8 13. ♘c6 ♗c6 14. ♖c6± Vasjukov–Kogan, SSSR 1951] 10. a3 [10. ♖d1 ♕c7? 11. a4 b4 12. ♘d5! ed5 13. ed5 ♔d8 14. 14. ♘c6 ♔c8 15. ♗g5$\overline{\overline{\infty}}$ Dubinin–Suetin, SSSR 1953; 10... b4!?] ♕c7 11. f4 ♖c8 12. h3 ♕c4 13. ♕f2 d5 14. e5 ♘e4= Fine–Najdorf (m) 1949

4 **9... ♘bd7**?! 10. e5! ♗g2 11. ef6 ♗b7 12. fg7 ♗g7 13. ♘f5±; **9... ♕c8** 10. ♗h3?! ♘bd7 11. ♘e6 fe6 12. ♗e6 ♗e7 13. ♘d5 ♗d5 14. ed5 ♕b7∓ Jansa–Padevski, Siegen (ol) 1970 — 10/541; 10. a4±

5 11... d5? 12. ed5 ♘d5 13. ♘e6!+– Estrin–Želnin, SSSR 1973

6 7. ♕d3 ♘c6!? [7... ♘bd7 8. ♗g2 ♘e5 9. ♕e3 ♘c4=; 8. f4 ♘c5 9. ♕e3 e5 10. ♘b3 ♘b3 11. ab3 ♗d7 12. ♗g2 ♗e7 13. 0–0 0–0 14. f5 ♕c7 15. ♕d3 h6 16. h3±] 8. ♘c6! [8. h3 ♘e5=; 8. ♗g2 ♘e5=] bc6 9. ♗g2 e5 10. f4 ♗d7 11. h3 ♗e7 12. g4 0–0 13. f5 d5∞ Reshevsky–Najdorf, Amsterdam 1950

7 7... e5 8. fg4 ed4 9. ♕d4 ♘g4 10. ♗e2 ♘c6 11. ♕d1 ♘ge5 12. ♗e3 ♗e7 13. ♘d5 0–0 14. ♕d2± Beni–Scafarelli, Italia 1952

8 8. g4! h6 9. ♗e3 ♘c6 10. ♕d2 e6 11. h4 ♗e7 12. 0-0-0 ♕c7 13. ♖g1 0-0-0 14. g5 hg5 15. hg5 ♘g8 16. f4± Bertok–Pirc, Jugoslavija 1951

9 8... e5 9. ♘b3 [9. ♘de2 ♗c6 10. ♕d2 ♘bd7 11. ♘d5 ♗d5 12. ed5 ♘b6 13. ♘c3 ♕c7∞ Matanović–Pirc, Bled 1951] ♗e6 10. ♘d5 ♗d5 11. ed5 ♘bd7 12. c4 ♖c8 13. ♗h3!± Matanović–Kübart, Jugoslavija 1951

10 9. ♕d2 ♕a5 [9... g6? 10. ♘d5 ♘d5 11. ed5 ♘e5 12. h3 ♗c8 13. f4 ♘d7 14. ♗g2± Panov–Sorokin, SSSR 1953] 10. ♘b3 ♕c7 11. 0-0-0 b5 12. f4 ♖c8 13. e5 de5 14. fe5 ♘e5 15. ♗f4 g5 16. ♗e5 ♕e5 17. ♖e1 ♕c7∞ Baranov–Šamkovič, SSSR 1953

11 9... e6 10. 0–0 ♗e7 11. ♕e2 ♕c7 12. ♖ad1 b5 13. ♕f2 0–0 14. h3 b4∞ Fuderer–Najdorf, Bled 1950; 11. f4!±

12 **12. c4** b5 13. cb5 ab5 14. ♘c6 [14. ♘b5 ♘d5 15. ed5 ♘a5$\overline{\overline{\infty}}$] ♗c6 15. ♘b4 ♗b7= Sokolski–Terosjan, SSSR 1950; **12. a4**±

13 7. ♘f5 d5 8. ♗g5 d4 9. ♗f6 gf6 10. ♘e2 ♗f5 11. ef5 ♕d5∓↑ Čistjakov–Štejn, SSSR 1957

14 **7... ♘bd7** 8. ♗e3 b5 9. f3 ♗b7 10. a3 ♖c8 11. ♗h3 ♗e7 12. 0–0 0–0 13. ♕d2 ♕c7 14. ♖fd1 ♖fd8 15. ♕f2 ♗c6 16. ♗f1 ♖b8 17. ♘d5 ♘d5?! 18. ed5 ♗a8 19. a4!± Rižkov–Cejtlin, SSSR 1971 — 11/384; 17... ♗d5; **7... ♗e6** 8. ♗g2 ♘bd7 9. 0–0 b5 10. h3 ♗e7 [10... ♖c8 11. g4 ♗c4 12. ♖e1 b4 13. ♘d5 ♘d5 14. ed5 ♗e7= Reshevsky–Najdorf, Dubrovnik (ol) 1950] 11. ♗e3 ♘b6= Koblenc; 9. a4!±

15 Robatsch–Bogdanović, Sarajevo 1968 — 5/462

16 **7... b5** 8. a4! [8. ♗g2 ♗b7 9. 0–0 ♘bd7 10. h3 ♖c8?! 11. g4 b4 12. ♘d5 ♘d5 13. ed5 ♗e7 14. a3± Vasjukov–Littlewood, Hastings 1965/66 — 1/323; 10... ♗e7 11. g4 b4!∓; 11. ♗e3 ♘c5!∓] ♗b7 [8... b4 9. ♘d5 ♘e4 10. ♗g2 f5 11. ♗e3 ♘d7 12. g4!±] 9. ab5 ab5 10. ♖a8 ♗a8 11. ♗g5±; **7... ♕c7** 8. ♗g2 b5 9. a3 ♘bd7 10. 0–0 ♗b7 11. h3 ♘c5 12. ♘d5 ♘d5 13. ed5± Panov–Lebedev, SSSR 1955

17 8... b5 9. 0–0 [9. ♘f4!? ♗g4? 10. f3 ef4 11. fg4△ e5±; 9... ef4 10. e5 ♗g4 11. f3 de5 12. ♕d8 ♔d8 13. fg4 ♖a7 14. g5△ gf4± Euwe] ♘bd7 10. a4 b4 11. ♘d5 ♘d5 12. ed5 ♗g4 [12... ♗f5 13. ♗d2 ♖b8 14. f4 ♗g6 15. h3 f6 (Gligorić–Najdorf, Zürich (ct) 1953) 16. a5±] 13. ♗d2 a5 14. c3 bc3 15. ♗c3± Gligorić–Kotov, Zürich (ct) 1953

18 10. h3 b5 11. a4 b4 12. ♘d5 ♘d5 13. ed5 ♗f5 14. f4 ♕c7 15. c3 bc3 16. ♘c3± Boleslavski–Ciocaltea, Bucuresti 1953

19 11... 0–0 12. ♗e3 ♘b6 13. b3 ♕c7 14. a5± Alexander–Bogoljubov 1951

20 Matanović–Barczay, Vrnjačka Banja 1967 — 3/512

21 8. ♗g2 ♗e7 9. 0–0 b5 10. ♘d5 [10. h3 ♗b7 11. g4 b4 12. ♘d5 ♘d5 13. ed5 0–0∓ Balašov–Polugajevski, Tallinn 1973 — 15/449] ♘d5 11. ♕d5 ♘b6 12. ♕d3 ♗b7! [12... ♗e6?! 13. b3 d5 14. ♗b2 d4 15. f4 f6 16. fe5 fe5 17. c3± Teschner–Szilagyi, Moskva (ol) 1956] 13. ♗e3 ♗e7 14. ♘c3 ♖c8=

22 9... b6!? 10. 0–0 ♗b7 11. ♘d5 ♘d5 12. ed5 ♖c8 13. ♗e3 0–0 14. ♕d2 ♕c7= Lipnicki–Furman, SSSR 1953

23 Kagan–Bronštejn, Petropolis (izt) 1973 — 16/455

24 8. a4 b6 [8... ♘c6 9. ♗g2 0–0 10. 0–0 ♘b4 11. h3 ♗e6 12. f4 ♕c8 13. f5 ♗c4 14. g4 h6∞ Pilnik–Eliskases 1953] 9. ♗g2 ♗b7 10. h3 [10. 0–0 0–0 11. ♗e3 ♘bd7=] ♘bd7 11. g4 ♘c5 12. ♘g3 ♘e6 13. ♗e3 g6 14. ♘d5 ♘d5 15. ed5 ♘c5 16. ♕d2 0–0 17. 0–0 ♗h4=

25 8... ♗e6!? Fischer

26 **9... 0—0** 10. a4!±; **9... ♘b6** 10. ♗c8 ♖c8 11. ♗f6 ♗f6 12. a4± Matulović—Tatai, Reggio Emilia 1968 — 5/461; 10... ♕c8

27 10. a4 b4 11. ♘d5 [11. ♗d7?! ♕d7 12. ♗f6 bc3! 13. ♗g7? ♖g8 14. ♗h6 ♕h3 15. ♗e3 cb2 16. ♖b1 ♕g2 17. ♖g1 ♕e4 18. ♖b2 ♗e6∓ Fischer] ♘d5 12. ♕d5 ♖b8 13. ♗e7 ♔e7 14. ♕d2 ♘f6 [Matulović—Fischer, Vinkovci 1968 — 6/560] 15. ♗c8 ♕c8 16. f3 ♕c5!∓ Fischer

28 Fischer

29 **8... b5?!** 9. a4! [9. 0—0 ♘bd7 — 7... ♘bd7] b4 10. ♘d5±; **8... ♕c7** 9. 0—0 b5 10. h3 ♗b7 11. ♗e3 ♘bd7 12. a4! b4 13. ♘d5 ♗d5 14. ed5 0—0 15. c3 ♖ab8 16. ♖c1 b3!? 17. ♖a1! ♘b6 18. ♗b6 ♖b6 19. ♘c1± Cardoso—Tatai, Bauang 1973 — 16/456

30 10. a3 ♘bd7 11. h3 ♗b7 12. g4 ♘c5!? [12... ♘b6 13. ♘g3 d5?! 14. g5 ♘e4 15. ♘ce4 de4 16. ♘f5± Mejić—Mašić, Jugoslavija 1967 — 4/563] 13. ♘g3 ♘e6=

31 **15... ♘c6?!** 16. b3 ♗g4 17. ♖f2 ♕a5 18. ♖af1± Kagan—Ree, Siegen (ol) 1970 — 10/543; **15... b3!** 16. c3 ♘c6△ ♘a5-c4∞

B 92

1. e4 c5 2. ♘f3 d6 3. d4 cd4 4. ♘d4 ♘f6 5. ♘c3 a6 6. ♗e2

	6	7	8	9	10	11	12	13	14	
1	...	f4[2]	♘b3[4]	♗f3	0—0	♕e2	♖d1	a3	♕f2![5]	
	♘bd7[1]	e5[3]	b5	♗b7	♗e7	0—0	♖e8	♗f8	♕c7	=
2	...	♗e3	f3[7]	a4[8]	0—0	♕d2	♖fd1	b4!	b5![9]	
	...	♘c5[6]	e6	b6	♗b7	♖c8	♗e7	♘cd7		±
3	...	♗e3[10]	0—0	a3[11]	f4	♗f3[13]	♕e1[14]			
	♕c7	e6	b5	♗e7[12]	0—0	♗b7				±
4	...	♘f3[15]	0—0[17]	a4	♖e1	♘d2	♘f1	♘e3	♕d3	
	e5	h6![16]	♗e7	♕c7	0—0	b6[18]	♗b7	♖d8	♘bd7[19]	=

1. e4 c5 2. ♘f3 d6 3. d4 cd4 4. ♘d4 ♘f6 5. ♘c3 a6 6. ♗e2 e5 7. ♘b3 ♗e6

	8	9	10	11	12	13	14	15	16	
5	f4![20]	f5	♗f3	♗g5[22]	♕d2	♗e3	♗e2[23]			
	♕c7	♗c4	♘c6![21]	♗e7	h6	a5				=
6	...	g4	a3[25]	g5	fg5	h4[27]	♕d3	♗d2	0-0-0	
	...	b5[24]	h6[26]	hg5	♘fd7	♘b6	♘8d7	♘c4	♘db6[28]	±
7	...	...	g5[29]	♗f4	♕d2	0-0-0	♘d4[34]	h4[35]	♘e6	
	...	ef4	♘fd7[30]	♘c6[31]	♗e7[32]	♘ce5[33]	g6	♘b6[36]	fe6[37]	±

1. e4 c5 2. ♘f3 d6 3. d4 cd4 4. ♘d4 ♘f6 5. ♘c3 a6 6. ♗e2 e5 7. ♘b3 ♗e7

	8	9	10	11	12	13	14	15	16	
8	♗e3[38]	g4	g5	♕d2[40]	0-0-0	h4	h5	♗c4	♘d5[42]	
	0—0[39]	♗e6	♘fd7	♘b6[41]	♘8d7	♖c8	♘c4	♖c4	♗d5[43]	=
9	0—0	♗g5[45]	♗f6	♕d3[47]	♘d5	♖fd1	c3	♘e7[49]		
	0—0[44]	♗e6[46]	♗f6	♘c6	♗g5	♖c8[48]	♘e7			=
10	...	♗e3	a4	♕d2[51]	f3	♖fd1	♘c1[53]	♘1a2	b3	±
	...	♘bd7[50]	b6	♗b7	♕c7	♖fc8[52]	h6[54]	♘c5	♘e6[55]	

	8	9	10	11	12	13	14	15	16	
11	...	...	a4[56]	a5	f3	♕d2	♖fd1	ed5	♘d5	=
	...	♗e6	♘bd7[57]	♖c8	♕c7[58]	♖fd8	d5[59]	♘d5	♗d5[60]	
12	...	...	f4	♗f4[62]	♔h1	♕e1[65]	♖d1	♘d4	♕g3	±
	...	...	ef4[61]	♘c6[63]	♖c8[64]	♘e5[66]	♘fd7	♕b6	♕b2[67]	
13	...	a4	f4	♗f4	♔h1	♘d5!	ed5	a5	c4	±
	...	♘c6[68]	ef4[69]	♕b6[70]	♗e6	♗d5	♘e5	♕c7	♘g6[71]	

1. e4 c5 2. ♘f3 d6 3. d4 cd4 4. ♘d4 ♘f6 5. ♘c3 a6 6. ♗e2 e5 7. ♘b3 ♗e7 8. 0—0 0—0 9. f4 ♕c7 10. a4 ♗e6 11. f5[72] ♗c4 12. a5 ♘bd7

	13	14	15	16	17	18	19	20	21	
14	♗e3[73]	ab6	♔h1![75]	♗b6[77]	♗c4	♕e2[78]	♖a2!	♖fa1	♖a4[81]	±
	b5[74]	♘b6	♖fc8[76]	♕b6	♖c4	♖b4[79]	h6[80]	♗f8	♖c8[82]	

1. e4 c5 2. ♘f3 d6 3. d4 cd4 4. ♘d4 ♘f6 5. ♘c3 a6 6. ♗e2 e5 7. ♘b3 ♗e7 8. 0—0 0—0 9. f4 ♕c7 10. a4 ♗e6 11. f5 ♗c4 12. a5 ♘bd7 13. ♗e3 b5 14. ab6 ♘b6 15. ♔h1 ♖fc8 16. ♗b6 ♕b6 17. ♗c4 ♖c4 18. ♕e2

	18	19	20	21	22	23	24	25	26	
15	...	♖a2	♖fa1	♖a4	♖a4	♖c4[84]	♕c4	fg6	g3	=
	♖ac8!	♗d8	♕b7	♖a4	a5[83]	♖c4[85]	g6	hg6	♔g7[86]	

1. e4 c5 2. ♘f3 d6 3. d4 cd4 4. ♘d4 ♘f6 5. ♘c3 a6 6. ♗e2 e5 7. ♘b3 ♗e7 8. 0—0 ♗e6 9. a4[87] ♘bd7 10. f4 ♕c7

	11	12	13	14	15	16	17	18	19	
16	♔h1[88]	♗e3	♖f4[91]	a5![92]	♗b6[94]	♖a4	♖d4	bc3	♕e1!?	±
	0—0[89]	ef4[90]	♘e5	♖fe8[93]	♕d7	♖ac8	♖c3[95]	♕c6	♘g6[96]	

[1] 6... b5 7. ♗f3 [7. 0—0 b4 8. ♘d5±] ♖a7 8. ♗e3 ♖d7 9. ♘d5 e5 10. ♘e6! ♕a5 [10... fe6 11. ♗b6 ed5 12. ♗d8 ♔d8 13. ed5±] 11. b4 ♕a4 12. ♘ec7±

[2] 7. 0—0 g6! [7... ♘c5 8. ♗f3 e6 9. ♖e1 ♗e7 10. a4 0—0 11. g4± Hartston—Quinteros, Las Palmas 1974 — 17/501] 8. f4 ♗g7 9. ♗e3 0—0 10. ♗f3 [10. ♔h1 ♕c7 11. ♕e1 b5= Korenski—Polugajevski, SSSR (ch) 1967 — 5/463; 10. a4 ♕c7 11. ♔h1 e5 12. ♘b3 b6 13. ♕d3 ef4= Židkov—Štejn, SSSR 1967 — 3/515; 10. ♘b3!?] e5 11. ♘de2 ef4 12. ♘f4 ♘e5 13. ♘fd5 ♘d5 14. ♘d5 ♗e6= Rolland—Polugajevski, Le Havre 1966 — 1/316

[3] **7... ♕b6**? 8. g4 h6 9. g5 hg5 10. fg5 ♘g8 11. ♘d5 ♕a5 12. b4 ♕a4 13. ♘c7 ♔d8 14. ♘de6+— Šmit—Dementjev, SSSR 1970; **7... ♘c5**? 8. ♗f3 ♕b6 9. ♘b3 ♘b3 10. ab3 g6 11. e5 de5 12. fe5 ♘d7 13. ♘d5 ♕d8 14. ♗g5+— Gipslis—Quinteros, Olot 1973 — 15/451; **7... g6** 8. g4! [8. 0—0 ♗g7 9. a4! 0—0 10. ♔h1 ♕c7 11. a5!± Matanović—Mašić, Jugoslavija (ch) 1969 — 7/421] ♘c5 [8... e5 9. ♘b3 h6 10. g5 ♘g8 11. h4 ef4 12. ♕d4 ♘e5 13. ♗f4 ♘e7 14. ♗e5 ♘c6 15. ♗h8+— Klovan—K. Grigorjan, SSSR 1970; 9... b5 10. g5 b4 11. ♘a4! ♘g8 12. ♕d5 ♖a7 13. ♗c4 ♘b6 14. ♘b6 ♕b6 15. ♕d3±] 9. ♘b3! ♘b3 [9... ♘ce4? 10. ♘e4 ♘e4 11. ♕d4 ♘f6 12. g5+−; 9... ♘fd7 10. ♗e3 e6 11. ♗f3 ♕c7 12. ♕e2 b6 (Šmit—Vitolinš, SSSR 1972) 13. 0-0-0±] 10. ab3 ♗g7 11. g5 ♘d7 12. ♗e3 ♖b8 [Liberzon—Savon, Suhumi 1972 — 14/484] 13. h4±

[4] 8. **♘f5** ♘c5 9. ♘g3 ♕b6! [9... ♗e7? 10. a4 ♗d7 11. 0—0 g6 12. ♗e3 ♗c6 13. fe5! ♘fe4 14. ♘ge4 ♘e4 15. e6!±↑ Kirpičnikov—Petkevič, SSSR 1975] 10. f5 ♗d7 11. a4 [11. ♖b1 ♗c6 12. ♗f3 ♗e7 13. ♗e3 ♕c7 14. 0—0 b5= Olafsson—Quinteros, Lanzarote 1974 — 17/504] ♗c6 12. ♗f3 a5 13. b3 ♗e7 14. ♗e3 ♕b4= Adorjan—Talj, Hastings 1973/74; **8. ♘f3**!?

5 14. ♔h1?! ♖c8 15. ♗e3? d5!−+ Campos Lopez—Quinteros, Nice (ol) 1974 — 17/505; 15. fe5∓

6 **7... g6** (Cvetković) 8. ♕d2 b5?! 9. a4 ba4 10. f3 ♗g7 11. ♖a4 ♕c7 12. ♖c4 ♕b7 13. ♘a4± Ceškovski—Polugajevski, SSSR (ch) 1969 — 7/419; **7... ♕c7**!?

7 8. ♗f3 ♗d7 [8... g6 9. ♕e2 ♗g7 10. 0-0-0 ♕a5 11. e5! de5 12. ♘c6 bc6 13. ♗c6 ♗d7 14. ♗a8 0—0 (Browne—Ljubojević, Las Palmas 1974 — 17/502) 15. ♕c4!?±] 9. g4 h6 10. ♕e2 g6 11. g5 hg5 12. ♗g5 ♗g7 13. 0-0-0 ♕a5 14. h4 ♖c8∞ Hartston—Ljubojević, Skopje (ol) 1972 — 14/471

8 9. ♕d2 b5 10. a3 ♗b7 11. 0-0-0 ♗e7 12. g4 ♘fd7 13. h4 ♘e5 14. g5 ♖b8 15. b4± Ceškovski—Liberzon, SSSR (ch) 1969 — 7/420

9 Kavalek—Quinteros, Nice (ol) 1974 — 17/503

10 **7. f4** ♘bd7 8. ♗f3 g6 9. ♘d5 ♘d5 10. ed5 ♗g7 11. 0—0 0—0 12. ♖e1 ♖e8= Schmid—O'Kelly, La Habana 1967 — 4/564; 8. g4!?→» Gipslis; **7. ♗g5** ♘bd7 8. 0—0 e6 — B 94

11 9. f4?! b4 10. e5 de5 11. fe5 ♘fd7 12. ♘cb5 ab5 13. ♘b5 ♕d8 14. ♗h5 ♘e5 15. ♗f7 ♘f7 16. ♕f3 ♕d7 17. ♖ad1 ♗b7∓

12 **9... ♘c6**?! 10. ♘c6 ♕c6 11. ♗f3±; **9... ♗b7** 10. ♗d3!? ♗e7 11. f4 0—0 12. ♕f3±

13 11. ♗d3!?△ ♕f3±

14 Geler

15 7. ♘f5?! ♗f5 8. ef5 h6!∓

16 7... ♗e7 8. ♗g5 [8. 0—0 0—0 9. ♗c4 ♕c7 10. ♘d5 ♘d5 11. ♗d5± Robatsch—Ardiansjah, Skopje (ol) 1972 — 14/485; 9. ♗g5!? Gufeljd] ♘bd7? 9. a4 b6 10. ♗c4 ♗b7 11. ♕e2 0—0 12. ♖d1 ♕c7 13. 0—0± Westerinen—Stean, Hastings 1972/73 — 15/450; 8... ♗e6!? Bukić

17 8. ♗c4 ♗e6 9. ♗e6 [9. ♗b3 ♗e7 10. 0—0 ♘bd7=] fe6 10. 0—0 ♗e7 11. ♕e2 0—0 12. ♖d1 ♘c6=

18 11... ♗e6 12. ♘f1 ♘bd7 13. ♘d5 ♗d5 14. ed5±

19 Urbanec—Pavlik, ČSSR 1955

20 **8. ♗g5** ♘bd7 9. f3 ♗e7 10. ♕d2 d5= Sköld—Danielson, Sverige 1949; **8. 0—0** ♘bd7 9. f4 ♖c8 [9... ♕c7 10. f5 ♗c4 11. a4 ♗e7 12. ♗g5 0—0 13. a5 ♖fc8 14. ♗c4 ♕c4 15. ♖f2± Karpov—Gheorghiu, Moskva 1971 — 12/485; 13... ♖fd8!?] 10. f5 ♗c4 11. a4 ♗e7 12. a5± Liberzon—Suetin, SSSR (ch) 1967 — 3/514

21 10... a5 11. a4 ♘c6 [11... ♕b6 12. ♗e2 ♕c6 13. ♗g5 ♘bd7 14. ♘d2 ♗e2 15. ♕e2± Talj—Pohla, Pärnu 1971 — 12/483] 12. ♗g5 ♘b4 13. ♗f6 gf6 14. ♗e2! ♗b3 15. ♗b5 ♔d8 16. cb3 ♕c5 17. ♕d2± Smislov—Portisch, Ljubljana—Portorož 1971 — 11/385; 14... ♔e7!? Portisch; 14... d5!?= Keres

22 11. ♘d2?! ♘d4

23 **14. ♘c1**? d5! 15. ♘d5 ♗d5 16. ed5 ♖d8 17. ♕f2 ♘b4! 18. ♗b6 ♕c4 19. c3 ♖d5!∓ Karasev—Bronštejn, SSSR (ch) 1971 — 12/484; **14. ♗e2**!?=

24 9... h6 10. g5! [10. h4 ef4 11. ♗f4 ♘c6=] hg5 11. fg5 ♘fd7 12. ♗g4 ♖h4 13. ♗e6 fe6 14. ♗e3 ♗e7 [14... ♘c6 15. ♕f3 0-0-0 16. ♕g3! ♖h8 17. ♕g4 ♖e8 18. 0-0-0±] 15. ♕f3 ♘c6 16. ♕g3 ♖h8 17. ♕g4± Gurevič—Balašov, SSSR 1973 — 17/507

25 **10. g5** b4! 11. ♘b5 ab5 12. gf6=; **10. f5** ♗c4 11. g5 b4! 12. gf6 bc3 13. bc3 gf6?! 14. ♗c4 ♕c4 15. ♕d3 ♕c6 16. ♘a5!± Zaharčenko—Zlotnik, SSSR 1973; 13... ♘d7!?

26 **10... ef4** 11. g5 ♘fd7 12. ♗f4 ♘e5 13. ♘d5 ♗d5 14. ♕d5 ♘bc6 15. ♘d4 ♖c8 16. ♘f5 g6 17. ♘e3±; **10... ♕b7** 11. f5 ♗c4 [11... ♗b3 12. cb3 ♘bd7 13. g5 ♘e4 14. ♗f3 ♘dc5 15. b4±] 12. ♘a5 ♕c7 13. ♘c4 bc4 14. g5±

27 **13. ♗g4**!?; **13. ♘d5**!?

28 17. g6 0-0-0 18. ♘d5± Gipslis—Kengis, SSSR 1974 — 17/510; 17... ♘a4!?; 17... fg6!?

29 10. ♗f4? h6! 11. ♘d4 ♘bd7 12. ♘e6 fe6 13. ♕d3 g5 14. ♗g3 ♘e5 15. ♕d4 ♗e7 16. ♕a4 ♔f7∓ Kaplan—Saidy, San Antonio 1972

30 10... f3 11. gf6! fe2 12. ♕e2 ♘d7 13. ♘d5!± Adorjan

31 11... ♘e5 12. ♘d5! ♗d5 13. ♕d5 ♘bc6 14. c3±

32 12... ♖d8 13. 0-0-0 ♘de5 14. h4! g6 15. h5 ♗g7 16. ♘d5 ♗d5 17. ed5 ♘b8 18. ♖h3 ♘bd7 19. ♖dh1 ♖g8 20. ♔b1±↑⊞» Olafsson—Kavalek, Las Palmas 1974 — 17/509

33 13... ♘de5 14. ♘d5! ♕d8 15. h4 b5 16. ♘e7 ♔e7 16. ♘d4±↑⊞ Baumstark—Georgieva, Medellin 1974

34 14. h4 0-0-0 15. ♘d5 ♗d5 16. ♕d5 ♔b8 17. ♖h3± Pritchett—Hansson, Hamburg 1974 — 18/490

35 15. ♔b1 0-0-0 16. ♘d5 ♗d5 17. ed5 ♔b8 18. ♕b4!± Tolonen—Petrušin, SSSR 1974

36 15... 0-0-0 16. ♘d5 ♗d5 17. ed5 ♔b8 18. ♖h3 ♖c8 19. ♖c3 ♕d8 20. ♘c6!±↑« Raškovski—Gutman, SSSR 1974 — 18/491

37 17. ♕e3 ♖c8 18. ♕h3± Adorjan—Browne, Wijk aan Zee 1974 — 17/508

38 **8. f4** ef4? 9. ♗f4 ♘c6 10. 0—0 0—0 11. ♔h1 ♕b6? 12. ♗d6 ♖d8 13. ♖f6!±→ Valejev—Aratovski, SSSR 1954; 8... 0—0!?; **8. ♗g5** ♗e6 [8... ♘e4? 9. ♘e4 ♗g5 10. ♘d6 ♔f8 11. ♕d5 ♕c7 12. ♗c4± Pachman; 8... ♘bd7!?] 9. ♗f6 ♗f6 10. ♘d2 [10. ♘d5 ♗g5=]

♘c6 11. ♘c4 ♘d4 12. ♘e3 ♖c8 13. ♗d3 g6 14. 0–0 0–0 15. ♘cd5 ♗g7 16. c3 ♘c6= Fuchs–Evans, La Habana (ol) 1966 — 2/458; 10... ♕c7!?; **8. a4** 0–0 9. ♗e3 ♕c7?! 10. a5 ♗e6 11. ♘d5 ♘d5 12. ed5 ♗f5 13. c4 ♘d7 14. 0–0 ♗g6? 15. ♖c1 ♘c5 16. ♘c5! dc5 17. b4!±; 14... ♖ac8± Ceškovski–Saharov, SSSR (ch) 1967 — 5/465; 14... h6 [J. Szabo–Ghitescu, Romania 1969 — 8/448] 15. ♖c1!±; 9... ♗e6!?

39 8... ♗e6 9. 0–0 [9. g4 d5!] ♘bd7 10. f4 ♖c8 11. h3 b5 12. a3 0–0= Miyasaka–Fischer, Siegen (ol) 1970 — 10/545

40 11. h4 ♘c6 12. ♘d5 a5 13. c3 a4 14. ♘d2 ♘c5∓

41 11... ♘c6 12. ♘d5 a5 13. a4 ♘c5!? [13... ♗d5?! 14. ed5 ♘b4 15. c3 ♘a6 16. ♗d3 ♘ac5 17. ♘c5 ♘c5 18. ♗c2± Zinn–Ghitescu, Sofia 1967 — 4/565] 14. f3 ♘b3 15. cb3 ♗d5 16. ed5 ♘b4=

42 16. g6 ♘f6!

43 17. ♕d5 b5= Röhrl–Kavalek, Skopje (ol) 1972 — 14/486

44 8... ♕c7 9. a4 b6 10. ♗g5! ♘bd7 11. ♘d2 ♗b7 12. ♘c4! 0–0 [12... ♘e4 13. ♘d5 ±] 13. ♘e3 ♖fc8 14. ♗c4 ♕c5 15. ♗f6 ♘f6 16. ♘cd5 ♗d5 17. ♗d5 ♖a7 18. c3± Bogdanović–Buljovčić, Jugoslavija (ch) 1967 — 3/516

45 9. ♕d3 b5 10. ♗e3 ♗b7 11. f3 ♘bd7 12. a3 ♖c8 13. ♖fd1 ♘b6 14. ♘a5 ♗a8 15. a4 b4 16. ♕a6 ♘fd7!=

46 **9... ♘e4** 10. ♗e7 ♘c3 11. ♗d8 ♘d1 12. ♗e7 ♖e8 13. ♖fd1 ♖e7 14. ♖d6±⊥ Larsen; **9... ♘bd7** 10. a4 h6 [10... b6 11. ♗c4 ♗b7 12. ♕e2 ♕c7 13. ♖fd1 ♖fc8 14. ♘d2 h6 15. ♗f6 ♘f6 16. ♗b3 ♗c6 17. ♘c4± Larsen–Gligorić, Moskva (ol) 1956] 11. ♗h4 b6 12. ♗c4 ♗b7 13. ♕e2 ♕c7 14. ♖fd1 ♖fc8 15. ♘d2 g5 16. ♗g3 ♘c5 [Bisguier–Donner, Budapest 1961] 17. ♘d5!±

47 11. ♘d5 ♘d7 12. ♕d3 [12. ♘f6 ♘f6 13. ♗f3 d5!=] ♖c8 13. c3 ♗g5 14. ♖ad1 ♔h8= Averbah–Petrosjan, SSSR (ch) 1959

48 **13... b5**? 14. a4! b4 15. ♕c4±; **13... ♔h8** 14. c3 f5? 15. ♗f3± Talj–Najdorf, Bled 1961

49 **15. ♗f3** ♗d5 16. ed5 f5∓↑; **15. ♘e7**=

50 **9... b5** 10. a4 b4 11. ♘d5±; **9... ♕c7** 10. a4 [10. ♕d2 b5?! 11. ♖fd1 ♗b7 12. ♘d5 ♘d5 13. ed5 ♘d7 14. ♘a5±; 10... ♗e6! 11. f4 ♘bd7 12. f5 ♗c4 13. g4 d5! 14. ♘d5 ♘d5 15. ed5 ♘f6 16. ♖ad1 ♘e4 17. ♕e1 ♗h4!∓ Yanofsky–Gligorić, Stockholm (izt) 1962] b6 11. ♕d2 [11. f3 ♗e6 12. ♕d2 ♘c6 13. ♘d5 ♗d5 14. ed5 ♘a5!= Uusi–Boleslavski, SSSR 1954] ♗e6 12. ♖fd1 ♘bd7 [12... ♘c6? 13. ♘d5 ♗d5 14. ed5 ♘a5 15. ♗b6!±] 13. f3 ♖fd8 [13... ♕b7 14. ♘c1! ♖fd8 15. ♘1a2 ♘c5 16. ♘b4± Geler–Bolbochan, Stockholm (izt) 1962; 13... ♘c5 14. ♘c5 dc5 15. ♕e1 c4! 16. ♕f2 ♕c6 17. ♔h1 b5 18. ♗g5 ♖ad8∓ Bradvarević–Sokolov, Jugoslavija 1962; 14. ♘c1!?±] 14. ♘c1! ♘c5 15. ♘d5 ♘d5 16. ed5 ♗f5 17. a5±

51 11. ♗c4 ♗b7 12. f3 ♕c7 13. ♕d3± Ivkov–Đurašević, Beograd 1954

52 13... ♖fd8 14. ♕e1 d5 15. ed5 ♗b4 16. ♕f2 [16. ♖d3 ♘c5 17. ♘c5 bc5=; 16. ♕h4 ♗c3 17. d6 ♕c6 18. bc3 (Lublinski–Aronin, SSSR 1952) ♕c3∞] ♗c3 17. d6! ♕c6 18. bc3 ♘d5 [18... ♕c3 19. ♗b6±] 19. c4 ♘c3 20. a5! ♘d1 21. ♖d1 b5 22. c5± Geler–Polugajevski, SSSR 1954

53 **14. ♕e1** d5! 15. ed5 ♗b4 16. ♕f2 ♗c3 17. d6 ♕d8 18. bc3 ♖c3∓; **14. ♖ac1** ♗c6 15. ♕e1 ♕b7 16. ♕f1 d5!= Suetin–Šamkovič, SSSR (ch) 1960; **14. ♗f1** d5 15. ed5 ♗b4 16. d6 ♕c6 17. ♕f2 ♗d6 18. ♗d3 ♗e7 19. ♘e4 ♘d5= Geler–Bogdanović, 1965

54 **14... ♗c6** 15. ♕e1 h6 16. ♕f1 ♕b7 17. ♗c4 ♘f8 18. ♖d2 ♘g6 19. ♘1a2± Geler–Fischer, Stockholm (izt) 1962; **14... d5** 15. ed5 ♗b4 16. ♘1a2±

55 17. ♗c4± Tatai–Ciocaltea, Monte Carlo 1969 — 7/423

56 10. ♗f3 ♘bd7 [10... ♘c6 11. ♘d5±] 11. a4 ♘b6 12. ♘d2 [12. a5 ♘c4 13. ♗c1 b5 14. ab6 ♘b6=] a5 13. b3 ♘fd7 14. ♘d5 ♗d5 15. ed5 f5 16. ♗e2 ♘f6= Milev–J. Szabo, Bucuresti 1953

57 10... ♕c7 11. a5 ♕c6 [11... ♘bd7 12. ♘d5 ♘d5 13. ed5 ♗f5 14. c4 ♗g6 15. ♖c1 ♘c5 16. ♘c5 dc5 17. b4± Geler–Fischer, Curaçao (ct) 1962; 12... ♗d5!?] 12. ♕d3 [12. ♕d2 ♘e4? 13. ♘e4 ♕e4 14. ♗f3 ♕g6 15. ♗b7 ♘bd7 16. ♗a8±; 12... ♘bd7 13. ♗f3 ♖fc8 14. ♖fd1 h6 15. ♖ac1 b5∓ Klovan–Saharov, SSSR 1969 — 7/422; 13. f4 ef4 14. ♗f4± Petrosjan; 12. ♗f3 ♘bd7 13. ♘d5 ♗d5 14. ed5 ♕b5 15. ♕d3! ♖fc8 16. ♖fc1 ♕d3±⊥ Smislov–Talj, Jugoslavija (ct) 1959; 16... ♕b4!?; 14... ♕c4 15. ♘d2 ♕b5 16. ♕b1!△ b4, c4± Štejn–Boleslavski, SSSR 1970 — 9/422] ♖d8 13. ♖fd1 ♘bd7 14. ♘d5± Boleslavski

58 12... ♖c3!? 13. bc3 d5 14. ♗d3 ♕c7 15. ♕e1 ♖c8 16. ♔h1 de4 17. fe4 ♕c6=∞ Nej–Bronštejn, SSSR 1971 — 12/488

59 14... ♕c6 15. ♖ac1 ♗c4! 16. ♗c4 ♕c4= Geler–Mučnik, SSSR 1970 — 9/424

60 Geler–Ivkov, Palma de Mallorca (izt) 1971 — 10/544

61 10... ♕c7 11. a4 ♖d8 [11... ef4 12. ♖f4? ♘c6 13. ♗d3 ♘e5 14. ♘d4 ♖ae8∓ Najdorf–Olafsson, Amsterdam (ol) 1954; 12. ♗f4±] 12. ♕e1 ♘bd7 13. ♖d1 ♖ac8=; 12. ♕d3!?±; 11... ♘bd7 12. ♔h1 — 8. 0–0 ♗e6

62 11. ♖f4 d5 12. e5 ♘fd7 13. ♘d5 ♗g5! 14. ♖d4 ♘c6 15. ♖d2 ♗e3 16. ♘e3 ♕b6!∓ Alonso–Walter 1954

63 **11...** **♕c7** 12. ♘d5 ♗d5 13. ed5 ♘bd7 14. ♔h1△ ♘d4±; **11...** **d5** 12. e5 [12. ed5 ♘d5 13. ♘d5 ♗d5 14. ♗f3 ♗f3 15. ♕f3 ♘c6=] ♘e4 13. ♘e4 de4 14. ♘d2!±

64 **12...** **♕b6** 13. ♕d2 ♖ac8 14. ♗e3 ♕c7 15. ♘d4 ♘d4 16. ♗d4 ♘d7 17. ♖ad1 ♘e5 18. ♕e3± Smislov—Panno, Amsterdam (ct) 1956; **12...** **d5** 13. e5 ♘d7 [13... ♘e4 14. ♗d3!] 14. ♘d5±

65 **13.** **♘d5**? ♘e4 14. ♘e7 ♕e7 15. ♗d3 ♗b3! 16. ab3 d5∓ Levy—Reshevsky, USA 1971 — 12/489; **13.** **♘d4** ♘d4 14. ♕d4 [Furman—Žuhovicki, SSSR 1970 — 9/423] ♕a5!?∞

66 13... ♘d7 14. ♖d1 ♘de5 15. ♘d5 ♗g5 16. ♗g3± Smislov—Petrosjan, SSSR (ch) 1960

67 17. ♘d5 ♗d5 18. ♘f5 ♗f6 19. ♖d5±↑ Ardiansjah—Ojanen, Siegen (ol) 1970 — 10/546

68 **9...** **♕c7** 10. a5 ♘bd7 [10... ♗e6 11. f4 ef4 12. ♗f4 ♘bd7 13. ♔h1 ♘e5 14. ♘d4 ♖ac8 15. ♕e1 ♔h8 16. ♕g3±] 11. ♗e3 b5 12. ab6 ♘b6 13. ♘a5 ♗e6 14. ♗b6 ♕b6 15. ♘d5 ♘d5 16. ed5 ♗d7 17. ♖a2± Geler—Štejn, SSSR (ch) 1962; **9...** **♘bd7** 10. f4 ef4 11. ♗f4 ♘e5 12. a5 ♖e8 13. ♔h1 ♕c7 14. ♗g5 ♗e6 15. ♘d4 h6 16. ♗f6 ♗f6 17. ♖f6 gf6 18. ♕d2±→» Karasev—Joffe, SSSR 1969; **9...** **♗e6** 10. f4 ♕c7 — 9. f4

69 10... ♘b4 11. ♔h1 ♗e6 12. f5 ♗d7 13. ♗g5 ♗c6 14. ♗f6 ♗f6 15. ♗c4 ♖c8 16. ♕e2 ♕c7 17. ♖fd1 ♖fd8= Beljavski—Talj, SSSR (ch) 1973; 11. ♗e3±

70 11... ♗e6!?

71 **16...** **♘c4**? 17. ♖c1+−; **16...** **♘g6** 17. ♗e3 ♘d7± Klovan—Gufeljd, SSSR 1967

72 11. ♔h1 ♘bd7 — 8... ♗e6

73 13. ♔h1 — 8... ♗e6

74 13... ♖ac8 14. ♗c4 ♕c4 15. ♖a4 ♕c7 16. ♕e2±

75 15. ♗b6? ♕b6 16. ♔h1 ♗b5! 17. ♗b5 ab5 18. ♘d5 ♘d5 19. ♕d5 ♖a4! 20. c3 ♕a6∓ Talj—Fischer, Curaçao (ct) 1962

76 15... ♗e2? 16. ♕e2 ♘c4 17. ♗g5!± ×d5

77 16. ♖a2!? ♖ab8 17. ♗g5± Minić

78 18. ♕d3 ♖ac8 19. h3 g6?! 20. ♕f3!± Schmid—Pytel, Bath 1973 — 16/459; 19... ♗d8△ ♕b7∞ Pytel

79 18... ♕c7 19. ♖a2 d5 20. ed5 ♗b4 21. d6! ♗d6 22. ♘b5!+− Klovan—Ozol, SSSR 1970

80 **19...** **♗d8** 20. ♖fa1 a5 [20... ♕b7 21. ♖a6 ♖a6 22. ♕a6 ♕a6 23. ♖a6 ♗e7 24. ♖a8 ♗f8 25. g4!±⊥] 21. ♖a5 ♖a5 22. ♘a5 ♔f8 23. ♘b3 ♕b7 24. ♖e1± Klovan—Pohla, SSSR 1970; **19...** **♕b7** 20. ♘a5 ♕c7 21. ♘d5! ♘d5 22. ed5 ♖b5 23. ♕d2 ♕c5 24. c4 ♖b6 [Geler—Fischer, Curaçao (ct) 1962] 25. ♖a4!±; **19...** **♕c6** 20. ♖fa1 ♖b6 21. ♕d3 h6 22. g3 ♕c8 23. ♖a4 ♗d8 24. ♖c4± Schöneberg—Kaufman, DDR 1967

81 21. ♖a6? ♖a6 22. ♖a6 ♕b7 23. ♘a5 ♕c7= Karpov

82 22. ♖b4 ♕b4 23. ♕a6± Karpov—Bronštejn, Moskva 1971 — 12/486

83 22... ♖c6 23. ♖c4! [23. ♕d3 g6 24. fg6 hg6 25. ♖a1 ♔g7 26. h3 ♘h5 27. ♘d5 ♕b5!∓ Scholl—Ivkov, Amsterdam 1971 — 12/487; 24. h3 ♘h5 25. ♖a1 ♘f4 26. ♕f3 ♖c4!= Karpov—Stoica, Graz 1972 — 14/483] h6 [23... g6 24. ♖c6 ♕c6 25. g4! d5 26. ed5 ♘d5 27. ♕e4± Bukić] 24. ♕d3 ♖c4 25. ♕c4 ♕b6= Torre—Bukić, Niš 1972 — 14/487

84 23. h3 g6 24. fg6 hg6 25. ♕d3 [25. ♖c4!?] ♕b6 26. ♕f3 ♕b8∓ Izvozčikov—Gutman, SSSR 1974 — 18/492

85 23... ♗b6 24. h3 ♗d4 25. ♘d5!∞

86 Bajkov—Zilberštejn, SSSR 1974

87 9. f4 ♕c7 [9... ef4 10. ♗f4 ♘c6 11. ♔h1 ♘e5 12. ♘d4±] 13. ♕d3 ef4 [16... b5 11. ♕g3 0—0 12. f5 ♗c4 13. ♗h6 ♘e8 14. ♗c4±] 11. ♗f4 ♘c6 12. ♕g3 0—0 13. ♖ad1± Smislov—Letelier, Mar del Plata 1962; 13... ♘c6!?=

88 11. a5 0—0 12. f5 [12. ♔h1 ♘c5 13. ♘c5 ♕c5 14. f5 ♗c4? 15. ♗c4 ♕c4 16. ♗g5± Spaski—R. Byrne, San Juan (mct) 1974 — 17/506; 12... ef4 13. ♗f4 b5 14. ab6 ♕b6∞] ♗c4 13. ♔h1 ♗b5 [13... b5 14. ab6 ♘b6 15. ♗g5! ♖fd8 16. ♗c4 ♕c4 17. ♘a5 ♕c7 18. ♗f6 ♗f6 19. ♕d3± Klovan—Circenis, SSSR 1974] 14. ♘b5 [14. ♗g5 ♗c6 15. ♗f3∞ Ivkov] ab5 15. ♗g5 b4 16. ♗d3 ♘c5 17. ♕e1 ♘b3 18. cb3 ♖a5 19. ♖a5 ♕a5 20. ♗c4= Ivkov—Mecking, Petropolis (izt) 1973 — 16/457

89 11... ♖c8 12. f5 ♗c4 13. a5 0—0 14. ♗c4! ♕c4 15. ♖a4 ♕c6 16. ♗e3 ♖fd8 17. ♕f3 h6 18. ♖aa1! ♘c5 19. ♘d5! ♘d5 20. ed5 ♕b5 21. ♘c5 dc5 22. ♕g4± Geler—Ivkov, Hilversum 1973 — 15/665

90 **12...** **b5**?! 13. f5 ♗c4 14. ♗g5! ♖fc8 15. ♘d2 ♗e2 16. ♕e2 h6 [16... ♕c6!?] 17. ♗f6 ♗f6 18. ♖fe1 ♕b7 19. ♕d3± Haag—Micheli, Milano 1974; **12...** **♖fc8** 13. a5 ♗c4 14. ♗c4 ♕c4 15. ♕f3 [15. ♖a4 ♕c6 16. ♕d3 ♗d8 17. f5 b5 18. ab6 ♘b6 (Ceškovski—Talj, SSSR 1974 — 18/494) 19. ♘a5!?±; 18... ♗b6∞ Talj] ef4 16. ♕f4 ♘e5 [Matanović—Talj, Beograd 1974] 17. ♘d4±↑» Matanović; **12...** **♖ac8** 13. a5 [13. f5 ♗c4 14. a5 ♖fd8 15. ♖a4!?± Polugajevski] ♗c4 14. ♗c4 ♕c4 15. ♖a4 ♕c6 16. ♕f3 ♗d8 17. ♘d2 b5 18. ab6 ♗b6 [Klovan—Gutman, SSSR 1974 — 17/517] 19. ♖a6! ♕b7 20. ♖a2±

91 13. ♗f4!? Polugajevski

92 14. ♘d4 ♖**fe8** 15. ♘f5 ♗f8 [15... ♘g6? 16. ♖f1 ♗f8 17. ♕d4± Karpov—Polugajevski, Moskva (mct) 1974 — 17/511; 17. ♗d4!± Polugajevski] 16. ♗d4 d5! 17. ♘h6 [17. ed5

♘d5 18. ♘d5 ♗d5∓ Klovan–Vladimirov, SSSR 1974] ♔h8 18. ♕f1 ♘e4 19. ♗h5 gh6∓ Kirpičnikov–Kengis, SSSR 1975; **14... ♖ad8** 15. ♕g1?! [15. a5!? ♖d7∞ Polugajevski] ♖d7 16. ♖d1 ♖e8 17. ♘f5? ♗d8!∓ Karpov–Polugajevski, Moskva (mct) 1974 — 17/512

93 **14... ♘fd7** 15. ♖f1 ♗f6? 16. ♘d5! ♗d5 17. ♕d5± Karpov–Polugajevski, Moskva (mct) 1974 — 17/513; **14... ♖fe8!?**; **14... ♖ac8** 15. ♘d4 ♖fe8 16. ♘f5 ♗f8 17. ♕d2 ♘fd7 18. ♗d4 g6 19. ♖af1∞ Klovan–Tukmakov, SSSR 1974 — 17/516; 18/495

94 15. ♘d4 ♗d8 [15... ♕d7 16. ♖f1 (16. ♘f5!?) ♖ac8 17. ♘f5 ♗f5 18. ♖f5 ♘c4 (18... ♘e4? 19. ♖e5+–) 19. ♗d4 ♘e4 20. ♗g4!↑± Klovan–Kirpičnikov, SSSR 1974 — 17/515] 16. ♘f5 ♘g6 17. ♘d6!? ♘f4 [17... ♖e7!?∞ Polugajevski] 18. ♗f4 ♖f8 19. e5 ♘e8 20. ♗f3 ♘d6 21. ed6=∞ Češkovski–Polugajevski, Soči 1974 — 18/493

95 17... ♕c6? 18. ♖d2!± Karpov–Polugajevski, Moskva (mct) 1974 — 17/514

96 20. ♖f1 d5 21. ed5 ♗d5 22. ♕g3±

B 93

1. e4 c5 2. ♘f3 d6 3. d4 cd4 4. ♘d4 ♘f6 5. ♘c3 a6 6. f4

	6	7	8	9	10	11	12	13	14	
1	...	♘f3[2]	e5	h3	♗c4	g4	♗e3	fe5	♗e6	±
	g6[1]	♗g7	♘g4[3]	♘h6	0–0	♘c6	de5	♗e6	fe6[4]	
2	...	♗e2[5]	g4	♘b3!	ab3	g5	h4[7]			±
	♘bd7	g6[6]	♘c5	♘b3	♗g7	♘d7				
3	...	♘f3[8]	♗c4	♕e2	f5[9]	fg6	♗b3	♗e3	♖d1	⩲
	♕b6	g6	♗g7	e6	0–0	hg6	♘c6	♕c7	b5[10]	
4	...	♘c6[11]	e5	♗c4	♗d3	ed6	0–0	♘e4	♕e2	⩲
	♘c6	bc6	♘d7	♘b6[12]	e6	♗d6	0–0	♗e7	♘d5[13]	
5	...	♗d3[14]	♕e2[16]	♘f5	♘d5	ed5	♗f5	fe5[18]	♗e4	∞
	♕c7	b5[15]	e5[17]	b4	♘d5	♗f5	g6	de5	♗d6[19]	
6	...	...	0–0[20]	♘f3[22]	♕e1[24]	♔h1	♕h4	♗e3	♗d4	=
	...	g6	♗g7[21]	0–0[23]	♘bd7[25]	e6[26]	♘c5[27]	b5	♕d8[28]	
7	...	...	...	...	♕e1[29]	♔h1	e5	fe5	♗f4	∞
	...	...	...	♘bd7	♘c5[30]	b5	de5	♘fd7	♗b7[31]	

1. e4 c5 2. ♘f3 d6 3. d4 cd4 4. ♘d4 ♘f6 5. ♘c3 a6 6. f4 e5 7. ♘f3[32]

	7	8	9	10	11	12	13	14	15	
8	...	♗d3	0–0	♔h1[34]	a3[35]	♕e1[37]	fe5	♗g5	♕h4	=
	♘bd7	♗e7[33]	0–0	b5	♗b7[36]	♖e8[38]	de5	♘h5	♘f4[39]	
9	...	♗c4	♗b3[41]	0–0	fe5	♗g5[43]	♗f6	♘e5		=
	...	b5[40]	♗e7	0–0[42]	de5	♗b7	♘f6	♕c7[44]		
10	...	a4	♗c4[46]	0–0[48]	♕e2	fe5	♗g5	♖ad1	♗b3	⩲
	...	♗e7[45]	0–0[47]	b6	♗b7	de5	♕c7[49]	♖fc8	♘c5[50]	
11	...	♗d3	0–0[51]	♕e1	♔h1[54]	fe5	♗g5	♘d1[55]	♘e3	=
	♕c7	♗e7	0–0[52]	♘bd7[53]	b5	de5	b4	♘c5	♗e6[56]	
12	...	...	0–0[57]	♕e1[58]	♔h1[60]	♘d1[61]	♗d2	a3	♖a3	∞
	...	b5	♘bd7	♗b7[59]	b4	♗e7[62]	a5	ba3	0–0[63]	
13	...	a4	♗d3	0–0	♕e1[66]	♘h4	f5	ed5	♘e4	∞
	...	b6[64]	♘bd7[65]	♗b7	♗e7	g6	d5![67]	♘d5	0-0-0[68]	

1 6... b5? 7. e5 de5 8. fe5 ♘d5 9. ♘db5!+−

2 **7. ♗d3** ♗g7 8. ♘f3 0–0 [8... ♘c6 9. 0–0 ♗g4 10. ♕e1 ♗f3 11. ♖f3 ♖c8 12. ♔h1± Kapengut–Židkov, SSSR 1973 — 16/445] 9. 0–0 ♗g4 10. ♕e1± Tringov–Barczay, La Habana 1971 — 11/378; 10. h3 ♗f3 11. ♕f3±; **7. ♗e2** ♗g7 8. ♗f3 ♕c7 9. 0–0 0–0 10. ♗e3 ♘c6 11. ♘b3± Pitksaar–Aronin, SSSR 1953; **7. e5** de5 8. fe5 ♘g4 [8... ♘d5!? Tukmakov] 9. e6 f5 [9... ♗e6 10. ♗e2!?] 10. h3 [10. ♗c4 ♗g7 11. ♘ce2 ♘c6 12. ♘c6 ♕d1 13. ♔d1 bc6 14. ♔e1 ♖b8∓ Honfi–Barczay, Bari 1970 — 10/536] ♘e5 11. ♗e3 ♘bc6 12. ♘c6 [12. ♘f5? gf5? 13. ♕h5 ♘g6 14. ♕f5 ♘ce5 15. ♖d1+−; 12... ♗e6 13. ♘d4 ♗f7 14. ♘c6 ♘c6 15. ♕d8 ♖d8∓ Bronštejn–Tukmakov, SSSR (ch) 1971 — 12/479] ♘c6 13. ♕d8 ♔d8 14. ♘d5!±↑ Tukmakov

3 8... de5? 9. ♕d8 ♔d8 10. fe5 ♘g4 11. ♗f4△ 0-0-0, ♘d5±→ Šamkovič

4 15. ♕d8 ♘d8 16. 0–0 ♘hf7 17. ♗f4 ♘c6 18. ♖ae1± Ghizdavu–Ghitescu, Timisoara 1972 — 13/509

5 **7. ♘f3** e6 8. ♗d3 — B 82; **7. ♗c4** e6 [7... ♕c7 8. ♕e2 e6 9. f5?! e5 10. ♗f7?! ♔f7 11. ♘e6 ♕a5! 12. ♗d2 ♘c5! 13. ♘d5 ♕b5 14. ♘d8 ♔g8!∓ Stanciu–Gheorghiu, Bucuresti 1973 — 15/447; 9. a4=] 8. a4 ♕a5 9. ♕e2 ♗e7 10. ♘b3 ♕c7 11. 0–0 b6 12. ♔h1 ♗b7∞ Filipowicz–Ribli, Bath 1973 — 16/446; **7. ♗d3** b5 [7... ♕b6!? Štejn] 8. 0–0 ♗b7 9. a3 g6 10. ♕e1 ♗g7 11. ♔h1 ♘c5 12. ♘f3 0–0 13. ♗d2 ♖c8 [13... a5!?] 14. ♖d1 ♕c7= Penrose–Ljubojević, Bath 1973 — 16/444; **7. a4** g6 8. ♗e2! [8. ♗d3 ♗g7 9. ♘f3 0–0 10. 0–0 ♘c5 11. ♕e1 ♖b8 12. ♕h4 b5 13. ab5 ab5 14. e5 ♘d3∓ Ghizdavu–Karpov, Bath 1973 — 16/443] ♗g7 9. 0–0 0–0 10. ♔h1±

6 **7... e5**?! 8. ♘f5!±; **7... e6**!?

7 Adorjan, Florian

8 **7. ♗e2** e5 [7... ♘c6 8. ♘b3 g6 9. ♗f3 ♗g7 10. ♕e2 0–0 11. ♗e3 ♕c7 12. 0–0 ♗e6 13. ♖fd1 ♘d7 14. ♘d5± Ciocaltea–Ostojić, Kragujevac 1974 — 18/485] 8. ♘b3 ♘bd7 9. f5 ♕c7= Suetin–Šamkovič, SSSR 1953; **7. ♗c4** ♘c6 8. ♘c6 bc6= Pitksaar–Šamkovič, SSSR 1953

9 10. ♗b3 0–0 11. ♗e3 ♕c7 12. a4 b6 [12... ♘bd7 13. 0–0 ♘c5 14. ♗d4± Boleslavski] 13. 0–0 ♗b7 14. ♘d2 ♘bd7∞

10 15. a3 ♗b7 16. 0–0 ♘e5 17. ♘g5 [17. ♘e5!?] ♖ae8 18. ♕e1± Savon–K. Grigorjan, SSSR (ch) 1972 — 14/481

11 7. ♗e2 ♕b6 [7... g6 8. ♗e3 ♗g7 9. 0–0 0–0 10. ♕d2±] 8. ♘b3 g6 9. ♗f3 ♗g7 10. ♕e2 e5! 11. ♗e3 ♕c7 12. 0–0 ef4 13. ♗f4 0–0= Olafsson–Aronin, Moskva 1959

12 9... de5 10. 0–0 e6 11. ♘e4 ♗e7 12. ♘d6 ♗d6 13. ♕d6 ♘b6 14. ♕d8 ♔d8 15. ♗b3 ef4 16. ♗f4 ♔e7 17. ♖ad1 ♘d5 18. ♗d2±↑ Geler–Tajmanov, SSSR (ch) 1949

13 Foltys–Reshevsky, Amsterdam 1950

14 **7. ♗e2** e5 8. ♘f3 ♗e6 9. f5 ♗c4 10. ♗g5 ♘bd7 11. ♘d2 ♗e2 12. ♕e2 ♖c8∓ Szabo–Petrosjan, Stockholm (izt) 1952; 8. ♘b3 ♗e6 — B 92; **7. ♘f3** ♗g4 8. h3 ♗f3 9. ♕f3 g6 10. g4 ♗g7 11. ♗d3 ♘c6 12. g5 ♘d7 13. ♘d5 ♕d8 14. c3 b5 15. 0–0 0–0∞ Janošević–Mecking, Vršac 1971 — 12/478; **7. a4** g6 8. ♘f3 ♗g4 9. ♗d3 ♘c6 10. h3 ♗f3 11. ♕f3 ♗g7 12. 0–0 0–0 13. ♗d2 e6 14. ♘e2 ♖ac8 15. ♔h1 e5= Karpov–Kuzmin, SSSR (ch) 1973 — 16/448

15 **7... ♗g4** 8. ♘f3 g6 — 7... g6; **7... ♘c6** 8. ♘f3 ♗g4 9. h3 ♗f3 10. ♕f3 g6= Ostojić–Saharov, Jugoslavija–SSSR 1968 — 5/456; **7... ♘bd7** 8. ♘f3 e5 — 6... e5

16 8. 0–0 ♘bd7 9. ♘f3 [9. ♔h1 ♗b7 10. ♕e1 g6 11. ♘f3 e5∞ Adorjan–Browne, Wijk aan Zee 1972 — 13/505] b4 10. ♘e2 [10. ♘d5 ♘d5 11. ed5 ♕c5] ♗b7 11. ♘g3 h5!?∞ Stean–Rajković, Hastings 1972/73 — 15/446

17 8... ♘bd7 9. ♘f3 e5 10. 0–0 g6 11. ♔h1 ♗g7 12. fe5 de5 13. ♗g5 0–0 14. a4 [14. ♘d2?! ♗b7 15. a4 b4 16. ♘a2± Filipowicz–Ničevski, Polanica Zdroj 1973; 14... h6! 15. ♗h4 ♗b7 16. a4 b4 17. ♘a2 a5 18. c3 ♘h5∓ Ničevski–Rajković, Jugoslavija 1973 — 16/451] b4 15. ♘a2 a5 16. c3 b3 17. ♘c1 ♘c5 18. ♗f6 ♗f6 19. ♘d2 ♗g5∞ Rajković

18 13. ♗d3? ♗g7 14. a3 ba3 15. ♖a3 0–0 16. 0–0 ef4! 17. ♖f4 ♗h6 18. ♖f7 ♕b6!∓ Larsen–Gheorghiu, Siegen (ol) 1970 — 10/539

19 15. g4∞ Ciocaltea

20 **8. a4** ♗g7 9. ♘f3 ♘c6 10. 0–0 0–0 11. ♕e1 ♘b4 12. ♕h4 ♕c5 13. ♔h1 ♕h5= Kuijpers–Gligorić, Wijk aan Zee 1971 — 11/377; **8. ♘f3** ♗g4 [8... ♗g7 9. ♕e2 ♘c6! 10. h3 0–0 11. g4 b5 12. a3 ♗b7 13. h4 b4 14. ab4 ♘b4 15. h5 ♘g4 16. ♗d2 d5!∓ Hecht–Polugajevski, Solingen 1974 — 18/487; 9. 0–0 — 8. 0–0] 9. h3 ♗f3 10. ♕f3 ♗g7 [10... ♘bd7 11. 0–0±↑ Boleslavski–Simagin, SSSR 1952; 10... ♘c6=] 11. g4 0–0 12. g5 ♘fd7 13. ♘d5 ♕d8 14. c3 ♘c6 15. h4!? e6∞ Janošević–Buljovčić, Jugoslavija 1972 — 13/508

21 **8... ♕c5** 9. ♔h1 ♗g4 10. ♘f3 ♗g7 11. ♕e1±; **8... ♘c6** 9. ♘f3 [9. ♘c6 bc6 10. e5 de5 11. fe5 ♕e5 12. ♕f3∞] ♗g4 10. ♕e1±; **8... ♘bd7** 9. ♘f3 ♗g7 — 8... ♗g7

22 9. ♔h1 0–0 [9... b5!? 10. a3 ♗b7 11. ♘f3 ♘bd7 12. ♕e1 ♘c5 13. f5 ♕c6 14. ♘d4 ♕b6= Krogius–Polugajevski, SSSR 1953] 10. ♕e1 b5 [10... ♘c6 11. ♘f3 ♘b4 12. ♗d2 ♘d3 13. cd3 b5? 14. e5!± Balogh–Batik,

corr. 1955; 13... e6!?±] 11. a3 ♗b7 12. ♘f3 ♘bd7 13. ♕h4 e6 14. ♗e3 ♘h5! [14... d5 15. e5 ♘e8 16. ♘g5 h6 17. ♘e6!±→» Najdorf —Reshevsky, (m) 1952] 15. g4 ♗f6 16. ♕h3 ♘g7∞ Ciocaltea

23 **9... ♘c6** 10. ♕e1 [10. ♔h1 0—0 11. ♕e1△ ♕h4±] 0—0 11. ♕h4± **9... b5** 10. ♔h1 ♗b7 [10... ♘bd7 11. ♘d5±] 11. e5 de5 12. fe5 ♘g4 13. ♗f4±

24 **10. a4** ♘bd7 11. ♕e1 b6 12. ♔h1 ♗b7 13. ♕h4±; 10... ♗g4!=; **10. ♔h1** ♘bd7 11. ♕e1 ♘c5 12. ♕h4 ♗g4 13. ♗d2 ♖ad8 14. ♖ae1 ♕d7∞ Krogius—Šamkovič, SSSR 1956; **10. ♕e2** b5 11. e5 de5 12. fe5 ♘g4 13. ♗f4 ♗b7 14. ♗e4 ♗e4 15. ♕e4 ♘d7∞ Klavin —Šamkovič, SSSR 1953

25 10... ♘c6 11. ♕h4 b5∞

26 11... e5 12. ♕h4 b5 13. fe5 de5 14. ♗h6 [14. a3 ♗b7 15. ♗h6 ♖ae8? 16. ♘g5 ♕d6 17. ♗e2 ♕e7 18. ♖ad1±→» Ostojić—Ghitescu, Smederevska Palanka 1971 — 12/480; 15... ♘h5! 16. ♗g7 ♔g7 17. ♘g5 ♘df6 18. ♘h3 ♖ae8 19. ♖f3 h6 20. ♖af1 ♕e7= Calvo —Smejkal, Palma de Mallorca 1972] ♗b7 15. ♘g5 ♖ae8 [15... ♘h5? 16. ♗g7 ♔g7 17. ♖f7!+—] 16. g4! ♕d8 [16... b4 17. ♘e2 ♖e7 18. ♖f3± Buljovčić—Bobocov, Reggio Emilia 1967 — 3/510] 17. a3 ♕e7 18. ♖f3 ♖c8 19. ♖af1!± Mihaljčišin—Bogdanović, Jugoslavija (ch) 1968 — 5/458

27 12... b5 13. ♗d2 b4?! 14. ♘d1 ♗b7 15. ♘f2 a5 16. a3± Minić—Pavlov, Bucuresti 1966 — 1/314; 13... ♘c5!?

28 15. ♖ad1 ♘h5 16. ♕d8 ♖d8= Enklaar —Quinteros, Lanzarote 1974 — 17/499

29 10. a4 b6 11. ♕e1 ♗b7 12. ♕h4 b5!? 13. ab5 ab5 14. ♖a8 ♗a8 15. e5 de5 16. fe5 ♗f3 17. ♖f3 ♕e5 18. ♗b5 0—0= Popovych—Saidy, USA 1968 — 5/457

30 10... e5 11. ♕h4 0—0 [11... h6?! 12. fe5 de5 13. ♔h1 b5 14. ♗d2± Andersson—Tatai, Siegen (ol) 1970 — 10/537] 12. fe5 de5 13. ♗h6 ♖e8∞ Marić

31 **15. ♘g5**?! ♕c6 16. ♖f3 h6 17. ♘ge4 ♘d3 18. cd3 ♘e5∓ Sax—Polugajevski, Hilversum 1973 — 16/447; **15. ♕g3** ♘e6 16. ♖ae1 0—0 17. ♗e4 ♗e4 18. ♖e4 ♕c6∞

32 **7. ♘f5** ♗f5 [7... g6? 8. fe5+—] 8. ef5 ♕c7 9. ♗e2 ♗e7=; **7. ♘b3** ♕c7 8. ♗e2 ♗e6 — B 92

33 **8... b5**!? 9. 0—0 g6 10. ♕e1 ♗g7 11. ♕h4 ♗b7 12. fe5 de5 13. ♗h6 0—0 14. ♘g5 ♘h5 15. ♗g7 ♕b6 [15... ♔g7? 16. ♖f7+—] 16. ♔h1 ♔g7 17. ♘h7 ♔h7 18. g4 ♘df6 19. gh5 ♘h5∞ Diesen—Browne, USA 1973 — 16/450; **8... ♕c7** 9. a4 b6 — 7... ♕c7

34 **10. ♕e2** b5 11. a3 ♗b7=; **10. a4** b6 11. ♕e1 ♗b7 12. ♔h1 ♖e8=; **10. ♕e1** b5 11. fe5 de5 12. ♗g5 b4 13. ♘e2 ♘c5 14. ♖d1= Suetin—Furman, SSSR 1953

35 11. fe5 de5 12. ♘e2?! ♘h5 13. ♘c3 ♗b7 14. ♘d5 ♗d5 15. ed5 ♘hf6 16. d6 ♗d6 17. ♗h7 ♘h7 18. ♕d6 e4 19. ♘d4 ♘df6∓ Pilnik—Gligorić, Stockholm (izt) 1952; 12. ♕e1!? ♗b7 13. a3∞

36 11... ♕c7 12. fe5 de5 13. ♘h4 ♗d8 [13... ♘c5 14. ♗g5 ♕d8 15. ♘f5 ♗f5 16. ♖f5 ♘fd7 17. ♗e7 ♕e7 18. ♘d5 ♕d6 19. ♕g4±↑ Talj—Pasman, SSSR 1967] 14. ♕e1 ♘c5 15. ♗g5 ♗e6 16. ♘f5 ♘h5 17. ♕h4 ♘f4 18. ♘g7 ♘cd3 [18... ♔g7? 19. ♖f4! ef4 20. ♕h6 ♔g8 21. ♗f6 ♗f6 22. e5+— Ravinski —Ilivicki, SSSR 1952] 19. ♘e6 fe6 20. ♗d8 ♕d8= Suetin

37 **12. ♘h4** g6 13. ♘f3 [13. f5 ♘c5 14. ♕e1 ♘fe4!∓] ♘h5 14. fe5 de5 15. ♗h6 ♖e8= Eliskases—Najdorf, Mar del Plata 1953; **12. ♕e2** ♖e8 13. ♗d2 ♕c7 14. ♖ae1 ♘c5 15. ♕f2 ef4 16. ♗f4 ♗f8∞ Krogius—Ilivicki, SSSR 1957; **12. ♗d2** ♕c7 13. ♕e2 ♖ac8?! 14. fe5 de5 15. ♘h4 g6?! [15... ♖fe8!? Sokolov] 16. ♗g5± Andersson—Rogoff, Olot 1971 — 11/382; 13... ♖fe8=

38 12... ef4 13. ♗f4 ♖e8=

39 **15... ♗g5** 16. ♘g5 ♘hf6= Brat—Pachman, ČSSR (ch) 1953; **15... ♘f4** 16. ♗e7 ♖e7 17. ♖ad1 ♘g6 18. ♕h3 ♘f6 19. ♘h4 ♘h4 20. ♕h4 ♖d7= Nej—Ilivicki, SSSR 1959

40 8... ♗e7 9. ♗f7? ♔f7 10. ♘g5 ♔e8! 11. ♘e6 ♕b6 12. ♘g7 ♔f7∓; 9. a4 — 8. a4

41 9. ♗d5 ♖b8 [△ b4, ♘d5]10. ♘g5 ♘d5 11. ♕d5 ♕e7 12. ♕d3 ♘c5 13. ♕e2 ♗b7 14. 0—0 ef4 15. ♗f4 f6 ♘f3 b4∞

42 10... ♗b7 11. fe5 de5 12. ♘h4 0—0 13. ♘f5 ♘c5 14. ♗g5! [14. ♘d5 ♘d5 15. ♗d5 ♗d5 16. ♕d5 ♕c7! 17. ♗e3 ♘a4= Boleslavski —Mojsejev, SSSR (ch) 1952] ♘b3 [14... ♘ce4 15. ♘e4 ♗e4 16. ♘e7 ♕e7 17. ♗f6 gf6 18. ♕g4 ♗g6 19. h4±] 15. ab3 b4 16. ♘e7 ♕e7 17. ♗f6 gf6 18. ♘d5 ♗d5 19. ed5 ♖fd8 20. ♕f3±

43 12. ♘h4 ♘c5= Boleslavski, Suetin

44 = Boleslavski

45 **8... b6** 9. ♗c4 ♗e7 10. 0—0 0—0 11. fe5 de5 [11... ♘e5 12. ♗b3±] 12. ♗g5 ♗b7 13. ♕e2±; **8... ♕c7** 9. ♗d3 b6 — 7... ♕c7

46 9. ♗d3 0—0 10. 0—0 b6 [10... ef4 11. ♗f4 ♕b6 12. ♔h1 ♕b2 13. ♕d2±] 11. ♕e1 ♗b7 12. ♔h1 ♖e8 13. fe5 de5 14. ♗g5 h6 [14... ♕c7!? 15. ♕g3! ♖ac8 16. ♘h4± Penrose—O'Kelly, Madrid 1960] 15. ♗h4 ♕c7 16. ♖ad1 ♖ad8= Euwe

47 9... ♕c7 10. ♕e2 b6 11. 0—0 ♗b7 [11... 0—0 12. ♘h4!? ♘c5 13. fe5 de5 14. ♘f5 ♗f5 15. ef5∞ Sax—Marjanović, Nederland 1972 — 13/512; 12. fe5 de5 13. ♗g5±] 12. fe5 de5 13. ♗g5±↑ Penrose—Fischer, Leipzig (ol) 1960

48 10. f5?! b6 11. ♗e3 ♗b7 12. ♘d2 d5 13. ♘d5 ♘d5 14. ♗d5 ♗d5 15. ed5 ♗c5 16. ♕e2 ♕h4 17. g3 ♕b4∓ Karpov–Wirthensohn, Skopje (ol) 1972 — 14/482

49 **13... ♘e4**? 14. ♘e4 ♗e4 15. ♕e4 ♗g5 16. ♘g5 ♕g5 17. ♖f7+– ; **13... ♘h5**? 14. ♖ad1! ♗c5 15. ♔h1 ♕c7 16. ♖d7 ♕d7 17. ♘e5 ♕c7 18. ♘f7+– Clarke–Toran, Hastings 1956/57; **13... h6** 14. ♗f6 ♘f6 15. ♖ad1 ♕c7 16. ♔h1± Estrin–Rojzman, SSSR 1953

50 16. ♗f6 ♗f6 17. ♘d5 ♗d5 18. ♗d5 ♖a7 19. b3± Wach–Barle, Athens 1971 — 12/481

51 9. a4 — 8. a4

52 9... ♗e6 10. ♕e2 0–0 11. f5 ♗c8 12. a4 b6 13. ♘d5 ♘d5 14. ed5 ♗b7 15. c4 ♘d7 16. ♗e3± Ciocaltea–Šajtar, Bucuresti 1953

53 10... b5 11. ♔h1 ♗b7 [11... ♘bd7] 12. fe5 de5 13. ♘h4 b4 14. ♘d1 ♔h8 15. ♘f5±↑ Tarjan–Gilden, USA (ch) 1973 — 16/449

54 11. ♘h4!? ♘c5 12. fe5 de5 13. ♗g5 ♘e6 [13... ♘d3?! 14. cd3 ♕d8 15. ♔h1!± Medina–Blau, Leysin 1967 — 4/562] 14. ♗f6 ♗f6 15. ♘d5 ♕c5∞ Marić

55 14. ♘d5 ♘d5 15. ed5 ♗d6! 16. ♘h4 [16. ♕h4 f5 17. ♗e7 e4 18. ♘g5 ♘f6 19. ♗f8 ♗f8 20. ♗e2 ♕c2∞] ♘c5 17. ♗f5 f6 18. ♗e3 a5 19. ♗c8 ♖fc8 20. ♘f5 ♗f8= Boleslavski

56 16. ♗f6 ♗f6 17. ♗c4 ♗c4 18. ♘c4 ♕b7 19. ♕e3 ♘a4= Bronštejn–Boleslavski, SSSR 1969

57 **9. a3** ♘bd7 10. 0–0 ♗b7 11. ♔h1 g6=; **9. ♕e2** ♗b7 10. a3 g6 11. 0–0 ♗g7= Herst–Evans, USA 1954

58 **10. a3** ♗b7 11. ♕e1 ♗e7 12. ♘h4 g6 13. fe5 de5 14. ♗h6 ♘g4 15. ♗d2 ♘c5= Martinović–Barczay, Sarajevo 1968 — 5/459; **10. fe5** de5 11. ♘d5 ♘d5 12. ed5 ♗e7 [12... h6 13. ♕e1 g6 14. ♕h4 ♗g7∞] 13. ♘g5 ♗g5 14. ♗g5 0–0∞

59 10... g6?! 11. ♔h1 ♗g7 12. ♕h4 0–0 — 6... ♕c7

60 **11. ♘h4** g6 12. ♘f3 ♗g7 13. ♕h4 0–0 14. fe5 de5= Sanguinetti–Fischer, Portorož (izt) 1958; **11. ♗d2** g6 [11... ♗e7 12. ♔h1 0–0 13. ♘h4 g6 14. f5∞ Janošević–Browne, Skopje 1970 — 9/419] 12. ♔h1 ♗g7 13. fe5 de5 14. b4 ♗c6!? [14... 0–0 15. a4 ba4 16. ♖a4 ♖fc8 17. ♖a5±↑ Janošević–Portisch, Vršac 1971 — 12/482] 15. a4 ba4 16. ♘a4 0–0△ ♕b7∞

61 **12. ♘b1** ♘c5 13. ♘bd2 ♗e7 14. fe5 de5 15. ♕g3 0–0= Boleslavski; **12. ♘d5** ♘d5 13. ed5 ♗d5 14. ♕b4 ♗e7 15. ♗e4 ♖b8 16. ♕e1 ♗e4 17. ♕e4 0–0= Ciocaltea–Kavalek, Athens 1968 — 6/559

62 12... ♘c5 13. ♘f2 ♗e7 14. ♗d2 a5 15. a3 b3 16. fe5 de5 17. ♗e3!± Ghizdavu–Tratatovici, Romania 1970

63 Boleslavski

64 **8... ♗e7** 9. ♗d3 0–0 10. 0–0 ♗e6 11. ♔h1 ♘bd7 12. f5 ♗c4 13. a5 ♖fc8 14. ♗g5± Hohler–Klundt, Berlin 1969 — 7/418; **8... ♘bd7** 9. ♗d3 g6 10. 0–0 ♗g7 [10... b6?! 11. ♕e2 ♗b7 12. ♗c4± Spaski–R. Byrne, San Juan (mct) 1974 — 17/500] 11. ♔h1 0–0 12. ♕e1 b6 13. ♕h4 ♗b7 14. f5! [14. fe5 de5 15. ♗h6 ♘h5= Pogats–Bilek, Hungary (ch) 1971] ♘c5 15. ♗g5±→» Kuzmin–Raškovski, SSSR (ch) 1973

65 **9... g6** 10. ♕e2 ♗g7 11. fe5 de5 12. ♗g5 0–0 13. ♗c4±; **9... ♗e7** 10. 0–0 0–0 11. ♕e1 ♘bd7 12. ♘h4 g6 13. fe5 de5 14. ♗h6 ♖e8 15. ♕e2±↑

66 11. ♔h1 g6 12. fe5 de5 13. ♕e2 ♗g7 14. ♗g5 0–0= Clarke–Darga, Hastings 1958/59

67 13... 0–0 14. ♗h6 ♖fe8 15. fg6 hg6 16. ♘f5 ♗d8 17. ♕g3±→»

68 16. ♘g5 ♗g5 17. ♗g5 f6 18. ♗d2 g5∞ Macukevič

B 94

1. e4 c5 2. ♘f3 d6 3. d4 cd4 4. ♘d4 ♘f6 5. ♘c3 a6 6. ♗g5

	6	7	8	9	10	11	12	13	14	
1	... ♘bd7[1]	f4[2] ♕b6[3]	♘b3[4] h6[5]	♗h4[6] ♕e3	♗e2 ♕f4	♗g3 ♕e3	♘d5 ♘d5	ed5 ♘f6	♗f2 ♕e5[7]	∞
2	... ...	♗e2 e6[8]	0–0 ♕c7	♗h5 g6[9]	♗e2 ♗g7	♕d2 b5	a3 0–0	♖ad1 ♘c5	f3 ♗b7	=
3	... ...	♕f3 h6	♗f6[10] ♘f6	♗c4 e6[11]	0-0-0 ♕c7	♗b3 ♗d7	♖he1 ♗e7	♕g3 0–0	f4 b5[12]	=

1. e4 c5 2. ♘f3 d6 3. d4 cd4 4. ♘d4 ♘f6 5. ♘c3 a6 6. ♗g5 ♘bd7 7. ♗c4

	7	8	9	10	11	12	13	14	15	
4	. . . h6[13]	♗f6[14] ♘f6	♕e2[15] ♕a5[16]	0-0-0 g6	h3 ♗g7	f4 ♘h5	♘b3 ♕c7	♘d5 ♕d8	♕e3 0—0[17]	±
5	. . . ♕a5	♕d2 h6[18]	♗f6 ♘f6	0-0-0 e6[19]	♖he1[20] ♗e7[21]	f4 0—0	♗b3 ♖e8	♔b1 ♗f8	g4 ♘g4[22]	±
6	. . . . . .	. . . e6	0—0[23] h6[24]	♗h4 ♘e5[25]	♗b3 g5	f4 gh4	fe5 ♕e5	♖ae1 ♘g4	♘f3 ♕c5[26]	±
7	. . . . . .	. . . . . .	. . . ♗e7	♖ad1 h6	♗h4 g5[27]	♗g3 ♘e5[28]	♗e2[29] ♗d7[30]	f4 gf4	♖f4 ♘h7[31]	±

1. e4 c5 2. ♘f3 d6 3. d4 cd4 4. ♘d4 ♘f6 5. ♘c3 a6 6. ♗g5 ♘bd7 7. ♗c4 ♕a5 8. ♕d2 e6 9. 0-0-0 b5[32]

	10	11	12	13	14	15	16	17	18	
8	♗d5[33] b4![34]	♗a8 bc3	bc3[35] ♘b6	♘b3[36] ♕b5[37]	♘d4 ♕a5	♘b3[38]				=
9	♗b3 ♗b7[39]	♖he1[40] ♖c8[41]	e5![42] ♘e5[43]	♘e6 fe6	♖e5 de5	♗f6 ♕c7	♗e5 ♕f7	f4 ♗c6	♕e2 ♗e7[44]	+—
10	. . . . . .	. . . 0-0-0	f3[45] h6	♗h4 g5[46]	♗f2 ♘e5	♔b1 ♔b8	a4 ba4	♗a4 ♗e7	♕e3 ♘fd7[47]	±
11	. . . . . .	. . . ♗e7	f4 ♘c5[48]	♗f6[49] gf6[50]	♕e3[51] 0-0-0	a3 ♘b3	♘b3 ♕c7	f5 ♔b8[52]		±

1 **6... h6** 7. ♗f6 gf6 8. ♗c4±; 8. ♕h5±; **6... b5** 7. ♗f6 gf6 8. ♕h5±; **6... g6** 7. ♗f6 ef6 8. ♗c4±⟳; **6... e5** 7. ♗f6 ♕f6 [7... gf6 8. ♘b3 f5 9. ♕h5±] 8. ♘d5 ♕d8 9. ♘f5 ♗f5 [9... ♗e6 10. ♗c4 ♘d7 11. 0—0 ♖c8 12. ♗b3 ♘c5 13. ♕f3 ♘b3 14. ♕b3 ♖c5 15. ♖ad1 ♖b5 16. ♕a4?! ♕a5= Foltys—Opočensky, ČSSR 1949; 16. ♕g3!±] 10. ef5 ♗e7 11. c4±

2 **7. a4** ♕c7 8. ♗e2 e6 9. ♗h4 ♗e7 10. ♗g3 ♘c5 11. f3 0—0 12. ♗f2 d5 13. ed5 ed5 14. 0—0 ♗d6 15. g3 ♗h3 16. ♖e1 ♖ad8∓ Lublinski—Kotov, SSSR 1951; **7. ♗d3** e6 8. ♕e2 b5∞; **7. f3** e6 8. ♕d2 b5∞; **7. ♕e2** e6 8. 0-0-0 ♕c7!? [8... ♗e7 9. f4 0—0 10. h4 ♕c7 11. ♘f3!± Velimirović—Ermenkov, Sombor 1972 — 14/489] 9. f4 b5∞ Velimirović; **7. ♕d2** e6 [7... h6?! 8. ♗f6 ♘f6 9. 0-0-0 e6 10. f4 ♗e7 11. ♗e2 ♕a5 12. ♔b1 ♗d7 13. ♗f3 ♖d8 14. ♖he1± Zinser—Lombardy, Zagreb 1969 — 7/427] 8. ♗c4 b5? 9. ♗e6 fe6 10. ♘e6 ♕b6 11. ♘d5 ♕c6 12. 0—0± Walther—Matanović, München (ol) 1958; 8... ♕a5 — 7. ♗c4

3 **7... ♕c7** 8. ♕f3 g6 9. 0-0-0 ♗g7 10. ♗e2 h6 11. ♗h4 e5 12. ♘db5 ab5 13. ♘b5 ♕a5 14. ♘d6 ♔f8 15. ♗c4+— Spaski—Vladimirov, SSSR 1962; **7... g6** 8. ♕f3 ♗g7 9. 0-0-0 0—0 10. ♗c4±; 10. h3△ g4±; **7... h6** 8. ♗h4 ♕b6 9. ♖b1 e5 10. ♘de2 ♗e7=; 8. ♗f6±; **7... b5** 8. ♗f6 [8. ♗d3 ♗b7 9. ♕e2 e5 10. ♘d5?! ed4 11. e5 ♘d5 12. ♗d8 ♘f4∓ Quinteros—Browne, Las Palmas 1974] ♘f6 [8... gf6 9. ♘d5±] 9. e5 de5 10. fe5 ♘g4 11. ♘db5 ♘e5 12. ♕d5±

4 **8. a3** h6 9. ♗h4 e5 10. fe5 de5 11. ♘b3 ♗e7 12. ♗f2 ♕c7 13. ♗e2 0—0= Kojčev—Filčev, Bulgaria 1960; **8. ♕d2** ♕b2 9. ♖b1∞

5 8... ♕e3 9. ♕e2 ♕e2 10. ♗e2±

6 9. ♗f6 ♘f6 10. e5 de5 11. fe5 ♘g4 [11... ♕e3 12. ♕e2 ♕e2 13. ♗e2 ♘g4 14. ♘d5±] 12. ♕e2 ♘e3=

7 15. c4 g6∞ Boleslavski

8 **7... ♕a5** 8. ♕d2 e6 9. 0—0 ♗e7 10. f4 h6∞; **7... h6** 8. ♗e3 [8. ♗h4 ♕c7 9. 0—0 g5 10. ♗g3 e6 11. ♕d2 b6 12. f3 ♗b7∓ Pietzsch—Đurašević, München (ol) 1958] ♕c7 9. 0—0 e5 10. ♘b3= Suetin—Gurgenidze, SSSR (ch) 1958

9 9. . . ♕c4? 10. ♘e6 ♕e6 11. ♘d5±→ Keres–Kotov, Budapest (ct) 1950

10 8. ♗d2 ♕b6 9. ♘b3 e6=; 8. ♗h4 e6 9. 0-0-0 ♕c7=; 8. ♗e3 e5 9. ♘f5 [9. ♘b3 b5=] g6 10. ♘g3 b5 11. h4 h5= Nežmetdinov–Petrosjan, SSSR (ch) 1954

11 9. . . ♕b6 10. 0-0-0 ♕c5 11. ♕e2 g6 12. h3 ♗g7 13. ♘b3 ♕c7∞ Paoli–Gligorić, Jugoslavija 1954

12 = Boleslavski

13 **7. . . b5** 8. ♗d5 ♘d5 9. ♘d5 ♗b7 10. 0–0±; **7. . . ♕c7** 8. ♗b3 e6 9. ♕e2△ 0-0-0±; **7. . . ♘b6** 8. ♗b3 e6 9. ♕e2 ♗e7 10. 0-0-0±; **7. . . g6** 8. ♕e2 [8. h4 h6 9. ♗e3 ♘e5 10. ♗b3 ♘eg4∞ Bronštejn–Rabar, Beograd 1964; 8. 0–0 ♗g7 9. ♘d5 ♘d5 10. ♗d5 ♕b6 11. ♘e2 ♘c5 12. ♖b1 e6 13. b4∞ Bronštejn–Aronin, SSSR 1967 — 3/517; 8. ♗b3 ♗g7 9. ♕d2 h6 10. ♗h4 ♘c5 11. f3 ♗e6 12. 0-0-0 ♘b3 13. ab3! ♕a5 14. ♔b1± Bitman–Aronin, SSSR 1967 — 4/566; 8. f3 ♗g7 9. ♕d2 h6 10. ♗e3 ♕c7 11. ♗b3 ♘e5 12. 0–0 b5 13. a4±↑; 9. . . 0–0 10. 0-0-0 ♘e5 11. ♗b3 ♗d7 12. h4 ♖c8 13. h5±→] ♗g7 9. 0-0-0 h6 [9. . . ♕a5 10. f4 0–0 11. h4 ♖e8 12. h5 b5 13. ♗b3 ♗b7 14. hg6 hg6 15. e5 ♘c5 16. f5!±→ Omelčenko–Kuncevič, corr. 1972] 10. ♗f6 [10. ♗h4 ♕c7 11. ♔b1 0–0 12. f4 e5∞ Kotkov–Aronin, SSSR 1953] ♗f6 [10. . . ♘f6 11. e5±] 11. f4 e5 12. ♘f3± Zagorovski; **7. . . e6** 8. ♕d2 ♕a5 — 7. . . ♕a5

14 8. ♗h4 g6 9. ♕e2 ♗g7 10. 0-0-0 0–0∞

15 9. ♕d3 g6?! 10. 0-0-0 ♗g7 11. f4±; 9. . . e6± Ivkov

16 9. . . e6 10. 0-0-0 ♕c7 11. f4 [11. ♗b3 ♗d7 12. f4 0-0-0 13. f5 ♖e8 14. ♕f3 ♔b8 15. ♖he1± Parma–Gligorić, Bled 1961] e5 12. ♘d5 ♘d5 13. ed5 ♗e7 14. fe5 de5 15. ♘e6!+– Talj–Bilek, Amsterdam (izt) 1964

17 16. e5!± Judovič jr.–Mojsejev, SSSR 1968

18 **8. . . b5** 9. ♗d5 ♘d5 10. ♘d5 ♕d2 11. ♔d2 ♖a7 12. ♘c6+– Estrin–Rojzman, SSSR 1961; **8. . . g6** 9. 0-0-0±

19 10. . . e5!? 11. ♘f5 ♗f5 12. ef5 ♗e7 13. ♔b1 ♖c8 14. ♗b3 ♖c3 15. ♕c3 ♕c3 16. bc3 ♘e4⩱ Geler; 11. ♘b3±; 11. ♘de2±

20 11. ♗b3 ♗d7 12. f4 ♗e7 13. ♔b1 ♕c7 14. ♖he1 ♖d8 15. g4± Kuijpers–Damjanović, Beverwijk 1966 — 1/317

21 11. . . ♗d7 12. f4 0-0-0 13. ♗b3 ♘e8 14. f5±↑

22 **15. . . ♘d7** 16. h4 ♘c5 17. g5± Geler; **15. . . ♘g4** 16. ♕g2 ♘f6 17. ♖g1 ♗d7 18. f5 ♔h8 19. ♖df1±→» Spaski–Petrosjan (m) 1969 — 7/428

23 9. a4 h6 10. ♗e3 ♘e5 11. ♗a2 ♘eg4 12. 0–0 ♗d7 13. h3 ♘e3 14. ♕e3 ♗e7 15. f4 0–0= Dückstein–Petrosjan, Bamberg 1968 — 5/466

24 9. . . b5 10. ♗d5 ed5 11. ed5 ♕b6 [11. . . ♘c5 12. ♖fe1 ♔d7 13. a3 ♕b6 14. b4 ♘a4 15. ♘a4 ba4 16. c4+–→; 11. . . ♘e5 12. f4 ♘g6 13. ♖ae1 ♗e7 14. ♗f6 gf6 15. ♖e3 0–0 16. f5 ♘e5 17. ♖h3 ♖e8 18. ♕h6 ♗d8 19. ♘c6+– Boleslavski; 11. . . ♗b7 12. ♖ae1 ♔d8 13. ♘c6 ♗c6 14. dc6 ♘c5 15. ♕d4 ♘e6 16. ♗f6 ♔c7 17. ♘d5 ♔c6 18. ♖e6 fe6 19. b4+– Süss–Wocke, Kiel 1962] 12. ♘c6 ♘e5 13. ♖ae1 ♗b7 14. ♗e3 ♕c7 15. f4 ♗c6 16. fe5 de5 17. dc6 ♗e7 18. ♗g5±

25 10. . . g5 11. ♗g3 ♘h5 12. ♗e6 fe6 13. ♘e6 ♘g3 14. fg3 ♘e5 15. ♖f8 ♖f8 16. ♕d6 ♖f6 17. ♕c7! [17. ♘c7 ♔f8 18. ♖f1 ♖f1 19. ♔f1 ♘c4= Talj–Petrosjan, Jugoslavija (ct) 1959] ♕c7 [17. . . b6 18. ♘g7 ♔f8 19. ♘h5 ♘d7 20. ♘f6 ♘f6 21. ♖f1+–] 18. ♘c7 ♔d8 19. ♘a8 ♖c6 20. a4 b6 21. ♖d1 ♔e8 22. ♘d5+–

26 16. ♔h1±

27 11. . . ♘e4 12. ♘e4 ♕d2 13. ♘d6 ♗d6 14. ♖d2±

28 12. . . ♘h5 13. ♘e6! fe6 [13. . . ♘g3? 14. ♘d5+–] 14. ♗d6±→

29 13. ♗b3 ♘h5 14. ♗a4 b5 15. ♗e5 de5 16. ♘c6 ♕c7 17. ♘e7 ♔e7 18. ♗b3 ♘f6 19. ♕e3 ♗b7= Talj–Korčnoj, SSSR (ch) 1959

30 13. . . ♕c7?! 14. f4 gf4 15. ♖f4 ♘c4? 16. ♗c4 ♕c4 17. ♗h4+– Kaplan–Matera, Jerusalem 1967 — 4/567; 15. . . ♗d7±

31 **15. . . ♗c6** 16. ♖df1 ♘fd7 17. ♗h5 ♗g5 18. ♘e6+–→; **15. . . ♘h7** 16. ♗h4 ♗g5 17. ♗g5 hg5 18. ♖f2±

32 **9. . . ♗e7** 10. f4 b5 11. ♗d5! ed5 12. ♘c6±; **9. . . h6** 10. ♗f6 ♘f6 11. ♖he1 ♗e7 12. f4±

33 10. ♗e6 fe6 11. ♘e6 ♔f7 12. ♘f8 [12. ♗f6 ♘f6 13. ♘g5 ♔g8 14. f4 b4 15. ♘d5 h6∓ Šijanovski–Aronin, SSSR 1958] ♖f8 13. ♕d6 b4 14. ♘d5 ♕a2 15. ♖he1 ♔g8 16. ♗f6 ♘f6 [16. . . gf6 17. ♖d3 ♕a1 18. ♔d2 ♕b2 19. f4 b3 20. ♘e7 ♔h8 21. ♖b3±] 17. ♘e7 ♔f7 18. e5 ♗g4 19. ♕c7 [19. ef6 ♖fd8 20. ♕d8 ♕a1–+] ♘e8∓

34 10. . . ed5? 11. ed5 [11. ♘c6 ♕b6 12. ed5±→] ♘c5 12. ♖he1 ♔d7 13. ♘c6 ♕b6 14. b4! ♘a4 15. ♕d3+– Tatai–Hamann, Amsterdam 1970 — 10/547

35 12. ♕e3 ♘g4 13. ♕f4 ♕a2 14. bc3 ♘ge5 15. ♔d2 h6–+

36 13. ♗c6 ♗d7 14. ♗d7 ♔d7 15. ♕f4 [15. ♔b1 ♘a4 16. ♘b3 ♘c3–+] ♘c4 16. ♖d3 ♗e7 17. ♘b3 ♕a2 18. e5 ♕a3 19. ♔d1 ♘b2 20. ♔e2 ♘d3∓ Tukmakov–Petkevič, SSSR 1973

37 13... ♕a3 14. ♔b1 ♘a8 15. ♕d4 e5 16. ♕a7 ♘e4 17. ♗d2 ♗e7 18. ♕a8 ♘d2 19. ♖d2 0–0 20. ♕c6 ♗e6 21. ♕c7 ♖e8 22. ♕a5±

38 Boleslavski

39 **10... b4** 11. ♘d5 ed5 [11... ♘e4 12. ♕b4 ♕b4 13. ♘c7#] 12. ♘c6±→; **10... ♘c5** 11. e5 b4 [11... de5 12. ♘c6+–] 12. ef6 bc3 13. ♕f4 gf6 [13... ♘b3 14. ♘b3 ♕a2 15. bc3±] 14. ♗f6 ♖g8 15. ♔b1 ♖g6 16. ♖he1 ♕b6 17. ♗h4 ♖a7 18. ♘f5 ♖d7 19. ♕d4 cb2 20. ♕h8± Kuprejčik–Danner, Groningen 1966 — 1/318

40 **11. f4** b4∞; **11. f3** b4∞

41 **11... ♘c5** 12. e5! [12. ♗f6 gf6 13. ♕f4 ♗e7 14. ♕g4 (14. ♘d5 e5 15. ♘f6 ♔d8 16. ♕f5 ed4 17. ♘d5 ♗c8 18. ♕f3 ♖a7∓) 0-0-0 15. ♗d5± Štejn–Talj, SSSR 1962; 15. ♘d5±] de5 13. ♗e6 fe6 [13... ♘e6 14. ♘e6 fe6 15. ♗f6+–] 14. ♘e6 ♘cd7 15. ♗f6 ♘f6 16. ♖e5 ♔f7 17. ♕f4 [17. ♕e3 h6 18. ♘f8 ♖hf8 19. ♖e7 ♔g8 20. ♖b7+– Macukevič–Vooremaa, SSSR 1968 — 6/561] ♔g8 18. ♖f5 ♕b4 [18... ♖e8 19. ♖f6 gf6 20. ♕f6 ♕b6 21. ♖d3 +–] 19. ♖f6 gf6 20. ♕g3 ♔f7 21. ♘f8 ♖hf8 22. ♖d7 ♔e8 23. ♖b7+– Boleslavski; **11... b4** 12. ♘d5±→

42 12. ♗f6 gf6 [12... ♘f6? 13. e5 de5 14. ♖e5 ♗b4 15. ♘e6 fe6 16. ♖e6 ♗e7 17. ♖e7+– Gligorić–Sofrevski, Jugoslavija (ch) 1959] 13. ♔b1 [13. ♗e6 fe6 14. ♘e6 ♘e5 15. ♘f8 ♘c4∓] ♘c5 14. ♕f4 ♗e7 15. ♘d5 e5 16. ♘f6∞ Gipslis–Osnos, SSSR 1960; 15. ♕g4±↑ Talj

43 **12... de5** 13. ♗f6 gf6 14. ♘e6!+–; **12... b4** 13. ef6 bc3 14. ♕f4!+–

44 19. g4+– Šamkovič–Titenko, SSSR 1963

45 **12. a3** ♔b8 13. f4 ♖c8 14. e5 [14. ♔b1 ♖c3!] de5 15. fe5 b4 16. ♘a2 ♘e4 17. ab4 ♕e5∞ Vitolinš–Hermlin, SSSR 1971 — 11/386; **12. ♔b1** h6 13. ♗h4 g5 14. ♗g3 ♘h5!= Boleslavski; **12. f4** h6 13. ♗f6 [13. ♗h4 b4 14. ♘a4 g5 15. hg5 hg5 16. ♗g5 ♕g5 17. ♕g5 ♗h6 18. ♕h6 ♖h6∞] ♘f6 14. a3 d5 15. e5 ♘d7 16. f5 ♗e7 17. ♔b1 ♕b6±

46 13... ♗e7!?

47 19. ♘b3 ♕c7 20. ♗d7 ♖d7 21. ♕a7 ♔c8 22. ♘a4± Parma–Saidy, Sarajevo 1971 — 11/387

48 12... b4?! 13. ♘d5±→

49 13. e5 de5 [13... b4 14. ♗a4 ♘a4 15. ♘a4 ♘e4! 16. ♖e4 ♗e4 17. ♗e7 ♕a4 18. ed6 ♖c8 19. ♔b1 ♔d7=] 14. ♗f6 [14. fe5 ♘fe4 15. ♘e4 ♕d2 16. ♗d2 ♗e4=] gf6! 15. fe5 0-0-0=

50 13... ♗f6 14. e5 de5 [14... ♗h4 15. g3 ♗d8 16. ed6 0–0 17. a3 ♗f6 18. ♗a2 ♕b6 19. b4 ♘d7 20. ♘e6 fe6 21. ♗e6 ♔h8 22. ♗d7± Korčnoj–Polugajevski, SSSR 1958] 15. fe5 ♗h4 16. g3 ♗e7 17. ♗e6! 0–0 [17... fe6 18. ♘e6 ♘e6 19. ♕d7+–] 18. ♗b3 ♖ad8 19. ♕f4 b4 20. ♘a4!± Spaski–Polugajevski, SSSR (ch) 1958

51 **14. ♗d5** b4 15. ♗b7 bc3 16. ♗c6 ♔f8∞ Strekalovski–Polugajevski, SSSR 1958; **14. ♔b1** b4?! 15. ♘d5! ♘e4 16. ♖e4 ♗d5 17. ♗d5 ♕d5 18. ♕e2 ♕b7 19. ♖e3+– Talj–Johansson, Stockholm 1961; 14... 0-0-0±

52 Boleslavski

B 95

1. e4 c5 2. ♘f3 d6 3. d4 cd4 4. ♘d4 ♘f6 5. ♘c3 a6 6. ♗g5 e6

	7	8	9	10	11	12	13	14	15	
1	♕d3[1]	♗h4	0-0-0	f4	♗e2	♗f3	♕e2	e5	fe5	∞
	h6[2]	♗e7	♘bd7	♕c7[3]	b5	♘c5[4]	♗b7	de5	♘h7[5]	
2	♕f3	0-0-0	♖g1[8]	g4	♖d4	♗e3	g5	♕h3!?[10]		∞
	♗d7[6]	♘c6[7]	♗e7	♘d4[9]	♕a5	♗c6	♘d7			
3	...	♗h4[11]	0-0-0	♕e2[13]	♗g3	h4	hg5	♘f3	♕e3	=
	h6	♘bd7	♘e5[12]	g5	♗d7	♖g8	hg5	♕c7	♗e7[14]	
4	...	0-0-0	♕g3[16]	♗b5[18]	♘db5	♘d6	♕d6	♖d6	♗f6[20]	±
	♘bd7	♕c7[15]	b5[17]	ab5	♕b8[19]	♗d6	♕d6	h6	♘f6[21]	
5	...	...	h4	♗e2	e5	♘c6	♕c6	♕a8		=∞
	...	♕a5	♗e7	♘c5	de5	bc6[22]	♘cd7	0–0[23]		
6	...	0-0-0[24]	♖g1[26]	g4	a3[28]	♗e3[29]	ed5	♘d5	♕h3	∞
	♗e7	♕c7[25]	0–0[27]	b5!	♗b7	d5	♘d5	♗d5	♘c6[30]	

1 **7. f3** ♗e7 8. ♕d2 b5∞⇆; **7. ♕e2** ♗e7 8. 0-0-0 h6∞; **7. ♕d2** h6 [7... ♘c6 — B 66] 8. ♗f6 [8. ♗h4? ♘e4 9. ♗d8 ♘d2−+] ♕f6= Schmidt−Evans, USA 1959; **7. ♗d3** ♗e7 8. f4 h6 9. ♗f6 [9. ♗h4 ♘e4!] ♗f6∞; **7. ♗c4** ♗e7 8. ♕d2 [8. 0−0 b5=] h6!=; **7. ♗e2** ♘bd7 8. 0−0 ♗e7 9. a4 h6 10. ♗h4 ♘e4 11. ♘e4 ♗h4 12. ♘d6 ♔f8 [12... ♔e7 13. ♘4f5 ef5 14. ♕d5+−→] 13. ♗h5 ♘e5 14. f4±; 7... ♘c6!=; **7. a4** ♗e7 8. ♗c4 0−0 9. 0−0 ♘c6 10. ♖e1 ♕c7 11. ♘b3 b6 12. ♗f1 ♗b7 13. ♖e3 ♖fd8 14. ♕e2 ♖ac8 15. ♖d1 ♘e5 16. ♖h3 h6 17. ♗h4∞ Ljubojević−Tukmakov, Madrid 1973

2 7... ♘bd7 8. f4?! b5 9. 0-0-0 ♗b7= Veselovski−Peresipkin, SSSR 1971 — 12/491; 8. 0-0-0 ♕c7 9. ♕g3 — 7. ♕f3

3 10... g5?! 11. fg5 ♘g4 12. ♗g3 ♘ge5 13. ♕e2 hg5 14. ♘f3 ♕a5 15. ♔b1± Muhin−Kajumov, SSSR 1968 — 6/562

4 12... ♗b7? 13. ♘e6 fe6 14. e5 de5 15. ♕g6 ♔f8 16. ♗f6 ♗f6 17. ♗h5+−→ Muhin−Platonov, SSSR 1969 — 8/449

5 ∞ Korčnoj

6 7... ♘c6 8. ♘c6 bc6 9. 0-0-0 [9. e5 de5 10. ♕c6 ♗d7 11. ♕f3 ♗e7∓] e5∞

7 8... ♗e7 — 7... ♗e7

8 **9. ♕g3** h6 10. ♗e3 ♕c7△ 0-0-0∞; **9. ♗e2** ♕a5 [9... b5 10. ♘c6 ♗c6 11. ♕e3∞ Mnacakanjan−Korčnoj, SSSR (ch) 1963] 10. ♕g3 ♘d4!? [10... b5? 11. ♘c6 ♗c6 12. ♖d6!± Hecht−Schaufelberger, Bath 1973 — 16/464] 11. ♖d4 ♗c6∞

9 10... ♕c7 11. ♗e3 ♘d4 12. ♗d4 e5 13. ♗e3 ♗c6 14. g5 ♘d7 15. ♗h3± Toran−Wexler, Buenos Aires 1955

10 **14. ♕g3**?! b5 15. a3 e5 16. ♖d2 b4∓; **14. ♕h3**!?∞

11 **8. ♗e3** e5 9. ♘b3 [9. ♘f5? g6 10. ♘g3 ♗g4−+] ♗e6=; **8. ♗d2** ♕c7 9. ♗d3 ♘c6 10. ♘de2 b5 11. 0−0 ♗b7 12. ♕h3 ♘e5∞ Lutikov−Krogius, SSSR 1954; **8. ♗f6** ♕f6 9. ♕f6 gf6 10. 0-0-0 [10. ♗e2 h5 11. 0-0-0 ♗d7! 12. ♔b1 ♔d8!∓ Bokučava−Platonov, SSSR 1971 — 11/388] b5 11. a3 ♗b7 12. f4 ♘d7 13. ♗e2 h5 14. ♔b1 ♖c8 15. ♖hf1 ♘b6 16. f5 ♔e7= Sidorov−Polugajevski, SSSR 1953

12 9... ♕c7 10. ♖g1 [10. ♗e2 ♗e7 11. ♖he1 g5 12. ♗g3 ♘e5 13. ♕e3 b5 14. a3 ♖b8= Talj−Platonov, SSSR 1969 — 7/429] ♗e7 11. ♗f6 ♗f6 12. ♔b1 ♖b8 13. ♕e3 b5= Hecht−Kristjansson, Reykajavik 1970 — 9/425

13 10. ♕h3 ♘g6 11. ♗g3 ♗d7 12. f3 b5 13. ♗e1 e5∓ Lapin−Šapošnikov, corr. 1957

14 16. ♗e2 b5= Spaski−Petrosjan, SSSR (ch) 1955

15 8... ♗e7 — 7... ♗e7

16 **9. ♖g1** b5 10. a3 ♗b7 11. g4 ♘e5 [11... h6 12. ♗f6 gf6 13. h4 ♗e7 14. ♕e2 ♘b6 15. ♖g3± Talj−Petrosjan, SSSR 1954] 12. ♕e2 ♖c8 13. f4 ♘c4= Macukevič; **9. g4**!? ♘e5 10. ♕g3 ♘eg4 11. h3 ♘e5 14. f4=∞ Loktev−Kogan, SSSR 1967 — 4/568; **9. ♕h3** ♗e7 10. f4 — B 99

17 **9... h6** 10. ♗f6 ♘f6 [10... gf6 11. ♔b1 ♘b6 12. f4 ♗d7 13. ♕h4± Aronin−Petrosjan, SSSR 1955] 11. f4 b5 12. e5 de5 13. fe5 ♘d7 14. ♘e6! fe6 15. ♗d3±; **9... ♗e7** 10. ♗e2 [10. f4 — B 99] 0−0 11. f4± Pachman−Bogatirčuk, Praha 1944

18 10. ♗d3 ♗b7 11. ♖he1 [Bastrikov−Kogan, SSSR 1971 — 11/389] 0-0-0∞

19 **11... ♕c5**? 12. ♗e3 ♕c6 13. ♘d6 ♗d6 14. ♖d6 ♕b7 15. e5 ♘h5 [15... ♘e4 16. ♕g7 ♖f8 17. ♖d7 ♗d7 18. ♘e4 ♕e4 19. ♗c5+− Konstantinopoljski−Gerstenfeld, SSSR 1940] 16. ♕g4 g6 17. ♖e6! fe6 18. ♕e6 ♔f8 19. ♗h6 ♘g7 20. ♘d5+− Verner−Beljavski, SSSR 1970 — 9/426; **11... ♕a5** 12. ♘d6 [12. ♗f6 ♘f6 13. ♖d6± Grankin−Gutkin, SSSR 1968 — 6/563] ♗d6 13. ♖d6 0−0 14. ♖hd1±

20 15. ♗d2 ♗b7 16. f3 [Bronštejn−Najdorf, SSSR−Argentina 1954] 0-0-0!=

21 16. ♖hd1 ♗b7 17. f3± Fichtl−Doležal, ČSSR (ch) 1954

22 12... ♕c7 13. ♘e7 ♕e7 14. b4 ♘cd7 15. ♘e4±; 14. ♕g3!?

23 Kivioja−Bronštejn, Pärnu 1971 — 12/492

24 **8. ♗e2** ♗d7 9. 0−0 [9. 0-0-0 ♕c7∞] ♘c6 10. ♖fd1 ♖c8 11. ♘c6 ♖c6= S. Nikolić−Milić, Beograd 1966 — 2/460; **8. ♖d1** ♕a5 9. ♗d2 ♕b6 10. ♘b3 ♘c6 11. ♗d3 0−0= Suetin−Šamkovič, SSSR 1953

25 **8... ♗d7** 9. e5! de5 10. ♘e6 fe6 11. ♕b7 ♘c6 12. ♗f6 ♗f6 13. ♖d7!+− Havin−Borisenko, SSSR 1954; **8... ♘bd7** 9. ♖g1 [9. ♕h3 ♕c7 10. f4 — B 99] ♕c7 10. g4 b5 11. a3 ♗b7 12. ♗f6 ♘f6 13. g5 ♘d7 14. ♕h3△ g6± Rossetto−Letelier, Mar del Plata 1955; **8... ♕a5**∞

26 **9. g4** ♘c6 10. ♖g1 ♘d4! [10... ♗d7 11. ♗e3±] 11. ♖d4 b5∞; **9. ♕h3** e5? 10. ♘f5 g6 11. ♗f6 ♗f6 12. ♘d6+−; 9... ♘c6!=; **9. ♔b1** ♘bd7△ b5=; **9. ♕g3** ♘c6 10. ♘c6 bc6 11. f4 h6 12. ♗f6 gf6 [12... ♗f6? 13. e5△ ♘e4±] 13. ♕g7± Spaski−Krogius, SSSR 1954; 9... b5 10. f4 ♘bd7 — B 99; 9... 0−0 10. f4 ♘bd7 — B 99

27 **9... b5**?! 10. ♗f6 [10. a3 ♗b7 11. g4 ♘c6!∞] ♗f6 11. e5 [11. ♗b5!? ab5 12. ♘db5 ♕c6 13. e5!±] de5 [11... ♗b7 12. ed6 ♗f3 13. dc7+−; 11... ♗g5 12. ♔b1 d5 13. ♕g3±] 12. ♘db5 ab5 13. ♕a8±; **9... ♗d7** 10. g4 ♘c6 11. ♗e3 ♘e5 [Ciocaltea−Filip, Bucuresti 1954] 12. ♕h3△ g5±; **9... ♘c6** 10. g4 ♘d4 11. ♖d4 ♗d7 12. ♗e3 ♗c6 13. g5 ♘d7 14.

♕h3±; **9... h6** 10. ♗e3 [10. ♗f6 ♗f6△ ♘c6∓; 10. ♗h4 ♘bd7△ g5∞] ♘bd7 11. ♕g3! [11. g4?! b5 12. a3 ♗b7 13. h4 ♘c5 14. ♗d3 d5! 15. ed5 ♘d5∓] g6!? 12. h4 ♖g8∞

28 11. e5 de5 [11... ♗b7 12. ef6!] 12. ♘db5 ♕c6 13. ♕c6 ♘c6 14. ♘d6 ♘d4∞

29 12. ♗f6 ♗f6 13. g5 ♗e5!△ ♘c6∓

30 16. ♗d3 g6 17. ♘c6 ♗c6 18. ♕h6∞

B 96

1. e4 c5 2. ♘f3 d6 3. d4 cd4 4. ♘d4 ♘f6 5. ♘c3 a6 6. ♗g5 e6 7. f4

	7	8	9	10	11	12	13	14	15	
1	...	♕f3[2]	♗f6[4]	e5[5]	♘e4	fe5	♗d3	♘e6	♗e4	+−
	♕c7[1]	b5?![3]	gf6	♕b7[6]	fe5	de5	f5[7]	fe4	♕b6[8]	
2	...	♕f3	0-0-0	♖d4	♗c4[10]	♖hd1	♕e2	♗h4	♗f6	±
	♗d7	♘c6	♘d4[9]	♗c6	♗e7[11]	♕a5	h6	e5	♗f6[12]	
3	...	♗c4	♗e6	♘e6	♘f8[15]	♕d6	0-0-0	♖d6	♘a4[16]	∞
	♘bd7	b5[13]	fe6	♕a5[14]	♖f8	♕b6	♕d6	b4	h6[17]	
4	...	...	♗b3	f5[18]	fe6	♗e3	0—0	a3[21]	cb3	∞
	...	♕b6	♗e7	♘c5[19]	fe6	♕c7[20]	b5	♘b3	0—0[22]	
5	...	♕e2	0-0-0[23]	f5[25]	fe6	ed7	♕c4	♔b1	♗c4	⩲
	...	♕c7	b5[24]	b4[26]	bc3	♘d7[27]	cb2	♕c4	♘e5[28]	
6	...	♗d3	♕e2!	♘f3	♗h4	0-0-0	e5!	fe5	♘d5	⩲
	...	♕c7	♗e7[29]	h6	♘c5	b5	de5	♘d5	ed5[30]	

1. e4 c5 2. ♘f3 d6 3. d4 cd4 4. ♘d4 ♘f6 5. ♘c3 a6 6. ♗g5 e6 7. f4 ♘bd7 8. ♕f3 ♕c7 9. 0-0-0 b5[31]

	10	11	12	13	14	15	16	17	18	
7	e5[32]	♕h3	♘e6	♕e6	♗f6[33]	♗e2	♘d5[34]	♖d5		=
	♗b7	de5	fe6	♗e7	gf6	h5!	♗d5	♘b6[35]		
8	♗d3	♖he1	♘b3![37]	♘a4	♘d4	♕h3	♘c5	♘e6	♗c4[39]	±
	♗b7	♕b6[36]	b4	♕c7[38]	♗e7	♘c5	dc5	fe6	♖d8[40]	
9	♗b5!?	♘db5	e5[41]	♕e2	♕c4	♗f6	♖d7	♔b1	♖d1	±
	ab5	♕b8	♗b7	de5	♗c5	gf6	♗e3	♔d7	♔e8[42]	

1. e4 c5 2. ♘f3 d6 3. d4 cd4 4. ♘d4 ♘f6 5. ♘c3 a6 6. ♗g5 e6 7. f4 h6 8. ♗h4[43] ♕b6[44]

	9	10	11	12	13	14	15	16	17	
10	♕d3[45]	♖b1	e5[46]	♘d5	♗d3	e6[47]	♗g6	♗f7[49]	♘f5	∞
	♕b2	♕a3	♘d5	♕d3	ed5	fe6[48]	♔d7	e5	d4[50]	
11	...	...	...	fe5	♘d5	e6	ef7	♗d3	♗f5[55]	=
	...	...	de5	♘d5[51]	ed5[52]	♕d3[53]	♔f7	♘d7[54]	♗c5[56]	
12	a3	♗f2	♕f3[57]	♗d3[59]	h3	♘b3	0—0	♘d4	e5	±
	♘c6	♕c7	♗e7[58]	♗d7	0-0-0	♘a5	♗c6[60]	d5	♘d7[61]	
13	...	♗f2[62]	♗d3	0—0[64]	♔h1	♕e2	♗d4	♗e3[65]		±
	♗d7	♕c7[63]	♘c6	♗e7	0—0	♘d4	e5			

1. e4 c5 2. ♘f3 d6 3. d4 cd4 4. ♘d4 ♘f6 5. ♘c3 a6 6. ♗g5 e6 7. f4 b5[66]

	8	9	10	11	12	13	14	15	16	
14	a3[67] ♗b7	♕e2[68] ♗e7	0-0-0 ♘bd7	g4 ♖c8	♗f6 gf6	♕e1 ♕b6	h4 ♘c5	b4 ♘d7	g5[69]	∞
15	♕f3 ♗b7[70]	0-0-0[71] ♘bd7[72]	♗d3 ♖c8[73]	♘d5! ♕a5[74]	♔b1[75] ed5	ed5!?[76]				=∞
16	e5 de5[77]	fe5 ♕c7[78]	♘f3 b4[79]	♘b5[80] ab5	ef6 ♘d7	♗b5 ♖a5	♕d4[81] gf6[82]	♕f6 ♖g8	♘e5 ♖g7	∞

1. e4 c5 2. ♘f3 d6 3. d4 cd4 4. ♘d4 ♘f6 5. ♘c3 a6 6. ♗g5 e6 7. f4 b5 8. e5 de5 9. fe5 ♕c7 10. ♕e2 ♘fd7[83] 11. 0-0-0 ♗b7[84]

	12	13	14	15	16	17	18	19	20	
17	♘e6?! fe6	♕g4 ♕e5[85]	♗b5[86] ab5	♖he1 h5	♕h4 ♕c7[87]	♖e6 ♔f7	♘b5 ♕c5			∓
18	♕h5 g6[88]	♕g4[89] ♕e5	♗b5 h5	♕h4 ♕g5	♕g5 ♗h6	♕h6 ♖h6	♗d7[90] ♘d7[91]			∓
19	♘f5 ef5	e6 ♘f6	♗f6 gf6	♕h5 ♗b4[92]	♗b5 ab5	ef7 ♕f7![93]	♖d8 ♔e7	♖e1 ♗e4	♘d5 ♔e6[94]	=
20	♕g4! ♕e5[95]	♗d3[96] h6[97]	♗h4 g5	♘e6[98] h5[99]	♕g5[100] ♗h6	♖he1 fe6	♗g6 ♔f8	♖f1 ♔g8[101]	♗f7 ♔h7[102]	=

1. e4 c5 2. ♘f3 d6 3. d4 cd4 4. ♘d4 ♘f6 5. ♘c3 a6 6. ♗g5 e6 7. f4 b5 8. e5 de5 9. fe5 ♕c7 10. ef6 ♕e5 11. ♗e2[103] ♕g5

	12	13	14	15	16	17	18	19	20	
21	♕d3 ♖a7[104]	♘e4 ♕e5	♘f3[105] ♕b2	0—0 ♖d7	♕e3 ♗b7	a4 b4	c3 ♕c2	♘fg5 b3	♖ac1[106]	±
22	. . . ♕f6	♖f1 ♕g6[107]	♕e3 ♗c5	♗f3 ♖a7	♘e4 ♗b4![108]	c3 ♗e7	♘e6[109] ♕e6	♕a7 ♘c6	♕c7 f5[110]	=
23	0—0 ♖a7	♕d3 ♖d7	♘e4 ♕e5[111]	♘f3[112] ♕c7[113]	♕e3 g6	c4 b4	♗d1[114] ♗b7	♗a4 ♗c6	♗c6 ♘c6[115]	±
24	. . . ♕e5	♗f3[116] ♖a7	♘c6[117] ♘c6[118]	♗c6 ♗d7	♗d7 ♖d7	♕f3 ♗d6![119]	g3[120] ♕f6	♕a8 ♕d8	♕a6 b4[121]	∞

[1] **7. . . ♕a5** 8. ♘b3 [8. ♕f3△ 0-0-0±] ♕b6 9. ♕f3 ♘bd7 10. 0-0-0±; **7. . . ♘c6** 8. ♘c6 bc6 9. e5 de5 10. ♕d8 ♔d8 11. fe5 h6 12. 0-0-0±↑

[2] **8. ♗f6** gf6 9. f5 ♕c5 10. ♕d3 ♘c6 [10. . . ♗h6 11. ♖d1± Litvinov—Juferov, SSSR 1973] 11. ♘b3 ♕b6 12. ♗e2 h5=; **8. ♕e2** b5 9. e5 [9. 0-0-0 ♘c6? 10. ♗f6 gf6 11. ♘d5 ed5 12. ♘c6+— Murej—Korzin, SSSR 1970 — 9/427; 9. . . ♗e7∞] de5 [9. . . b4? 10. ef6 bc3 11. 0-0-0 ♕b6 12. b3 ♕a5 13. ♖d3 ♕a2 14. ♖c3± Tukmakov—Raškovski, SSSR 1966 — 1/321] 10. fe5 — 7. . . b5; 8. . . ♘bd7 — 7. . . ♘bd7

[3] 8. . . ♘bd7 — 7. . . ♘bd7

[4] **9. 0-0-0** ♗b7 10. ♗f6 gf6 11. ♕h5 ♕c5 12. f5 ♔e7 13. ♕h3 ♘c6= Damjanović—Barczay, Reggio Emilia 1971 — 12/498; **9. a3** ♘bd7 10. ♗d3 ♗b7 11. 0-0-0 ♘b6! 12. ♖he1 ♖c8 13. f5 e5 14. ♘b3 ♗e7= Makarov—Raškovski, SSSR 1973 — 16/460

5 10. ♗d3? ♘d7 11. 0-0-0 ♗b7 12. ♖he1 0-0-0 13. f5 ♘c5∞ Suetin–Balašov, Soči 1973 — 16/478

6 10... ♗b7 11. ♕h5 b4 12. ♘e6+– Peretz–Kavalek, Netanya 1971 — 11/394

7 13... ed4 14. ♘f6 ♔e7 14. ♗e4 ♕c7 16. 0–0! ♖a7 17. ♘d5 ed5 18. ♕f6 ♔e8 19. ♗d5+–

8 16. ♘f8 ♖f8 17. ♕h5 ♖f7 18. ♕e5 ♗e6 19. 0-0-0! ♖a7 20. ♖d6+– Parma–Balašov, Moskva 1971 — 12/500

9 **9... ♗e7**?! 10. e5 de5 [10... ♘d4 11. ♖d4 ♗c6 12. ♕g3 ♕b6 13. ♖d2±] 11. ♘c6 bc6 12. fe5 ♘d5 13. ♗e7 ♕e7 14. ♘e4±; **9... ♕c7** 10. ♘c6 bc6 [10... ♗c6 11. f5±] 11. ♗c4 ♗e7 12. ♖d3 d5 [12... e5 13. ♗f6 ♗f6 14. ♖hd1 0–0 15. ♖d6 ♗c8 16. f5+– Keres–Panno, Amsterdam (ct) 1956; 12... 0–0 13. ♖hd1 d5 14. e5! dc4 15. ♗f6 cd3 16. ♕g4 g6 17. ♕g5±; 12... h6 13. ♗h4 ♖b8 14. e5 de5 15. fe5 ♘d5 16. ♗e7 ♘e7 17. ♘e4±] 13. ♗f6 ♗f6 14. ed5 cd5 15. ♗d5±→

10 **11. f5** ♕a5 12. ♗f6 gf6= Alexander–Larsen, Hastings 1956/57; **11. ♗e2** ♗e7 12. ♖hd1 ♕a5 13. ♕e3 h6 14. ♗h4 e5 15. fe5 de5 16. ♖4d3± Talj–Larsen, Reykjavik 1957

11 11... h6 12. ♗h4 ♗e7 13. ♖hd1 ♕a5 14. ♗e1 ♕c7 15. f5±→

12 16. ♖d6 ef4 17. ♘d5 ♗d5 18. ♖1d5± Panno–Lombardy 1958

13 **8... ♕a5**? 9. ♕e2 h6 10. ♗f6 ♘f6 11. 0-0-0 ♗e7 12. ♗b3 ♗d7 13. e5 de5 14. fe5 ♘h7 15. ♘e6! ♗e6 [15... fe6 16. ♕h5+–] 16. ♗e6 0–0 17. ♗b3+– Jovčić–Prieditis, corr. 1971 — 12/494; **8... ♕c7**? 9. ♕e2 ♘b6 10. ♗b3 ♗e7 11. 0-0-0 h6 12. ♗f6 ♗f6 13. ♘db5! ab5 14. ♘b5 ♕c5 15. ♘d6 ♔f8 16. f5! ♕e5 17. c3 ♗e7 18. ♘f7!△ ♕h5+–→ Kamenshvaran–Aaron, India 1972 — 15/453

14 10... ♕b6 11. ♘d5 ♘d5 12. ♕d5 ♕e3 13. ♔f1 ♘b6 14. ♘c7 ♔d7 15. ♕f7 ♔c6 16. ♘d5! [16. ♘a8 ♘a8 17. ♕d5 ♔c7 18. ♖e1 ♕a7 19. e5± Parma–Szabo, Solingen 1968 — 6/564] ♕e4 17. ♕c7+– Matanović–Gufeljd, Jugoslavija–SSSR 1969 — 7/430

15 11. 0–0 b4 12. ♘d5 ♔f7 13. f5 ♗b7 [13... h5? 14. a3 ♘d5 15. ed5 ♘f6 16. ♗f6 gf6 17. ab4 ♕b4 18. ♖a3!+–→ Vitolinš–Šmit, SSSR 1973 — 15/454] 14. c4 [Zaharov–Juferov, SSSR 1973 — 16/465] ♗d5!∞ Gipslis

16 15. ♘e2 h6?! 16. ♗h4 ♘c5 [16... ♗b7? 17. e5 ♘d5 18. ♖d1 ♘7b6 19. e6+–; 17... ♘e4 18. ♖e6 ♔f7 19. ♖e7+–] 17. ♘g3± Matulović–Tringov, Vrnjačka Banja 1973 — 15/455; 15... ♘c5!∞ Krnić

17 16. ♗h4 a5 17. ♖hd1 ♖a6 18. ♖6d4 ♖c6 19. h3 ♘h5 20. f5 g5!∞ Cejtlin–Polugajevski, SSSR (ch) 1971 — 12/495

18 10. ♕d2 ♘c5=

19 10... e5 11. ♗f6 ♘f6 12. ♘f3±

20 12... ♘fe4 13. ♘e4 ♘e4 14. ♕g4+

21 14. ♕f3 0–0 15. e5 [15. ♕h3 ♘b3 16. ab3? e5 17. ♘f5 ♗f5△ b4∓; 16. cb3 e5! 17. ♘f5 b4 18. ♘a4 ♘e4 19. ♘b6 ♗f5 20. ♖f5 (Matulović–Ljubojević, Jugoslavija 1973 — 15/452) ♖ae8!∓ Marić] de5 16. ♕c6 ♖a7 17. ♕c7 ♖c7 18. ♘f5 ♗d8 19. ♗c5 ♖c5 20. ♘d6 ♗d7= Matulović–Gheorghiu, Forssa-Helsinki 1972 — 14/491

22 16. b4 ♖e8 [16... ♕d7 17. ♕e2 ♗b7 18. ♗f2 ♖ac8= Bronštejn–Savon, SSSR (ch) 1970 — 10/548] 17. h3 ♗d8! 18. ♘b3 ♗b7 19. ♖c1 ♕d7 20. ♕d3 ♖c8∞ Matulović–Ciocaltea, Novi Sad 1973 — 16/466

23 9. g4 b5 10. a3 ♗e7 11. ♗g2 ♗b7 12. 0-0-0 ♖c8 [12... ♘b6 13. ♗h4 h6 14. ♗g3 0-0-0 15. ♗f3 g5 16. fg5 hg5 17. e5± Kuzmin–Stean, Hastings 1973/74 — 17/520] 13. ♗h4 ♕c4 14. ♕c4 ♖c4 15. ♗f3 ♘c5∓ Savon–Mecking, Petropolis (izt) 1973 — 16/470; 13. ♖he1∞

24 9... ♗e7 — B 98

25 **10. a3** ♖b8 [10... ♗b7 11. g4 0-0-0 12. ♗g2 ♔b8 13. e5 de5 14. ♘db5 ab5 15. ♘b5 ♕b6 16. ♗b7 ♕b7 17. fe5 h6 18. ♗f6 gf6 19. ef6 ♖g8∞ Karasev–Balašov, SSSR (ch) 1970] 11. ♘d5! ed5 12. ed5 ♗e7 13. ♘c6 [Bronštejn–Gheorghiu, Petropolis (izt) 1973 — 16/472] ♘f8 14. ♗f6 gf6 15. ♖e1 ♘g6 16. g3△ h4= Bronštejn; **10. g4** ♗b7 [10... b4 11. ♘d5!? ed5 12. ed5 ♗e7 13. ♘f5∞] 11. ♗g2 ♘b6∞ Dementjev–Gutman, SSSR 1972 — 14/492

26 10... e5 11. ♘d5 ♘d5 12. ed5 ♘c5 13. ♕h5 ♗e7 14. ♘c6 ♗g5 15. ♕g5 f6 16. ♕h5 ♕f7 17. ♕f3± Tukmakov–Browne, Madrid 1973 — 16/471

27 12... ♗d7 13. ♗f6 gf6 14. ♕c4 ♕c4 15. ♗c4 ♗h6 16. ♔b1 ♗f4 17. b3 ♔e7 18. ♖d3 ♖hg8 19. g3 ♗e5 20. ♖hd1± Tukmakov–Averkin, SSSR (ch) 1973

28 16. ♗d5 ♖b8 17. ♗f4 f6 18. ♖he1 ♗e7 19. ♖e3 ♗d8 20. h3 ♗d7 21. ♖b3± Tukmakov–Polugajevski, SSSR (ch) 1973

29 9... b5 10. 0-0-0 ♗b7 11. ♖he1 ♗e7 12. e5! [12. ♔b1 ♘c5 13. e5 de5 14. fe5 ♘d5∞ Savon–Raškovski, SSSR (ch) 1973 — 16/473] de5 13. fe5 ♘d5 14. ♗e7 [14. ♘e6!? fe6 15. ♕h5 ♔d8 16. ♘d5 ♗d5 17. ♗e7 ♔e7 18. ♕h4 ♔e8 19. ♗g6+–] ♘c3 15. ♕g4 ♘d1 16. ♘e6 ♕c6 [16... fe6 17. ♗d6 ♕b6 18. ♕g5 ♕d8 19. ♕g6+–] 17. ♘g7 ♔e7 18. ♕g5+– Spaski–Raškovski, SSSR (ch) 1973 — 16/474

30 16. ♗e7 ♕e7 17. h3 [17. ♘d4 ♕g5 18. ♕d2 ♕d2 19. ♔d2±] 0–0 18. ♘d4 ♕g5 19. ♔b1 ♘e6 [Talj–Balašov, SSSR (ch) 1969 — 8/452] 20. ♘f3± Petrosjan

31 **9... ♖b8** 10. f5 [10. ♗f6 ♘f6 11. g4 b5 12. g5 b4 13. ♘cb5±; 12... ♘d7 13. f5 ♘c5∞]

♘e5 [10... e5 11. ♘e6 fe6 12. fe6 ♘b6 13. ♗f6 gf6 14. ♕f6 ♗g7 15. ♕f5 ♕e7 16. ♕f2! ♕c7 17. ♗b5 ♔d8 18. ♖d6 ♕d6 19. ♖d1 ♕d1 20. ♔d1+−] 11. ♕h3 b5 12. ♗f6 gf6 13. ♕h5 b4 14. ♘ce2±; **9... ♗e7**! — B 99

32 **10. g4**?! b4 11. ♘ce2 d5 12. ♗f6 ♘f6 13. e5 ♘e4 14. ♘g3 ♗b7 15. ♗d3 ♘c5 16. f5 0-0-0!∓ Unzicker—Zilberštejn, Kislovodsk 1972 — 14/498; **10. a3** ♖b8! 11. ♗f6 ♘f6 12. e5 [12. g4 b4 13. ab4 ♖b4 14. g5 ♘d7 15. f5 ♘e5 16. ♕h3 ♕b6 17. ♘b3 ♗e7 18. g6 fg6 19. fe6 ♖b3! 20. cb3 ♕b3 21. ♕g3 ♗e6∓ Bronštejn—Polugajevski, Moskva 1967 — 4/571] ♗b7 [12... de5 13. ♕c6±] 13. ♕h3 de5 14. ♘cb5 ♕b6! [14... ab5? 15. ♗b5 ♔e7 16. fe5 ♕e5 17. ♖he1+− Kuprejčik—Gutman, SSSR 1960] 15. fe5 ♘d5 16. ♘c3 ♘c3 17. ♕c3 ♗e7△ 0—0∞

33 **14. ♘b5** ab5 15. ♗b5 ♗e4! [15... ♗d5! 16. ♖d5 ♘d5 17. ♕d5 ♖c8 18. c4 ♗g5 19. fg5 ♔e7∓] 16. c4 0-0-0 17. ♕e7 h6 18. ♗f6 [18. fe5 hg5 19. ef6 ♕f4∓] gf6 19. ♖d7 ♖d7 20. ♗d7 ♕d7 21. ♕c5 ♕c7 22. ♕c7 ♔c7 23. fe5 f5!∓ Željandinov—Gutman, SSSR 1970; **14. ♗b5** ab5 15. ♘b5 ♕c6 16. ♘d6 ♔d8 17. fe5 [17. ♘f7? ♔c7 18. ♕e7 ♘d5 19. ♖d5 ♕d5 20. ♘h8 ♖a2! 21. ♔b1 ♖a8−+ Haag—Kluger, Hungary 1968 — 5/472] ♔c7!? [17... ♖e8 18. ef6 gf6 19. ♘b7 ♔c7 20. ♖d7 ♕d7 21. ♗f4 ♔c8 22. ♕b3 ♕a4 23. ♕f3 ♖a6 24. ♖d1± Bronštejn—Ciocaltea, Kislovodsk 1968] 18. ♕e7 [18. ♔b1 ♘d5 19. ♗e7 ♖a2∞ Espig—Bremeier, DDR 1970] ♖a2 19. ♗f6 [19. ♖d4? ♖a1!−+ Planinc—Minić, Ljubljana—Portorož 1973 — 15/461] gf6 20. ♘b7 [20. c4?! ♔b8 21. ♕g7? ♖c8!−+ Kupka—Cejtlin, ČSSR 1973 — 16/467; 21. ♘b7 ♖a1 22. ♔d2 ♖d1 23. ♖d1 ♕b7 24. ♔c3!∞ Marić] ♖a1 21. ♔d2 ♕g2 22. ♔c3 ♕c6= Minić

34 **16. ♗d3**? ♘f8 17. ♕h3 ef4 18. ♖he1 ♖d8∓ Tringov—Polugajevski, Skopje 1971 — 12/499; **16. fe5**? ♘f8 17. ♕b3 ♖d8 18. ef6 ♕f4 19. ♔b1 ♖d1 20. ♖d1 ♕f6∓ Kuindži—M. Cejtlin, SSSR 1971 — 11/393

35 1/2 : 1/2 Spaski—Polugajevski, Amsterdam 1970 — 10/549

36 **11... 0-0-0**!? 12. ♕e2 h6 13. ♗h4 g5 14. fg5 hg5 15. ♗g5 b4 16. ♘b1 ♕a5∞ Feršter—Zilberštejn, SSSR 1973; 12. ♕h3±; **11... h6** 12. ♕h3 [12. ♗h4 ♗e7 13. ♘d5!? ed5 14. ♘f5!∞; 13... ♘d5 14. ed5 ♗h4 15. ♘e6 fe6 16. ♕h5 ♔d8 17. ♕h4 ♘f6∞ Geler—Polugajevski, Kislovodsk 1972 — 14/497] 0-0-0 13. ♗f6 [13. f5 e5 14. ♘e6?! hg5 15. ♕h8 fe6 16. fe6 ♘c5 17. ♕h3∞⇆ Spaski—Donner, Amsterdam 1973 — 17/522] ♘f6 14. ♘d5 ♘d5 15. ed5 ♗d5 16. a4!±; **11... b4** 12. ♘d5 ed5 13. ed5 ♔d8 14. ♗f5 [14. ♘c6 ♗c6 15. dc6 ♘b6!∓] ♗e7 [14... ♔c8? 15. ♘c6+−; 14... ♕c5 15. ♗e6!+−; 14... ♘c5 15. ♗h3!?△ 16. ♕e2 ♗e7 17. ♘f5 ♖e8 18. ♘g7+−; 14... ♘b6 15. ♗e6!△ 16. ♗f6 gf6 17. ♕h5!±; 14... h6!? Kavalek] 15. ♗e6 ♖f8 16. ♗f7 ♖f7 17. ♘e6± Kavalek—Gheorghiu, Skopje (ol) 1972 — 14/499

37 12. ♘e6? fe6 13. ♕h3 e5!−+ Geler—Polugajevski (mct) 1973 — 16/468

38 13... ♕c6 14. ♘a5! ♕a4 15. ♘b7±

39 18. e5?! ♘d5 19. ♗g6? hg6 20. ♕h8 ♔f7∓

40 19. ♕e6 ♖d1 20. ♖d1 ♖f8 21. ♗f6 ♖f6 22. ♕g8 ♗f8 23. g3±→ Spaski—Tukmakov, SSSR (ch) 1973 — 16/469

41 12. ♖he1 h6 13. ♗h4 ♗b7 14. ♕d3 ♘c5 15. ♕c4 ♘fd7? 16. b4!±→ Vitolinš—Gutman, SSSR 1973 — 16/477; 15... ♗e7!?; 13... ♖a2!? Gipslis

42 **18... ♗d4** 19. fe5 fe5 20. ♘d4 ed4 21. ♕d4 ♔e7 22. ♕c5 ♔f6 23. ♖f1± Talj—Stean, Hastings 1973/74; **18... ♔e8** 19. ♘c7± Vitolinš—Anikajev, SSSR 1973 — 17/523

43 8. ♗f6 ♕f6 9. ♕d2 ♘c6=

44 **8... ♘bd7** 9. ♕f3 ♕c7 10. 0-0-0±; **8... ♗e7** 9. ♕f3 [9. ♗f2?! ♕c7 10. ♕f3 ♘bd7 11. 0-0-0 b5∞ Velimirović—Ostojić, Skopje 1971 — 12/501] ♕c7 10. 0-0-0 — B 98

45 **9. ♕d2** ♕b2 10. ♖b1 [10. ♘b3 ♕a3 11. ♗f6 gf6 12. ♗d3 ♗g7 13. f5 ♘c6 14. 0—0 ♘e5 15. ♘e2 ef5 16. ♘f4 0—0 17. ef5 ♔h7 18. ♖ae1 ♗d7∓ Minić—Cvetković, Jugoslavija (ch) 1968] ♕a3 11. ♗f6 [11. e5 de5 12. fe5 ♘fd7 13. ♗e2 ♗e7 14. ♗g3 ♗g5 15. ♕d3 ♘c5 16. ♕f3 0—0∓ Matanović—Minić, Jugoslavija (ch) 1959] gf6 12. ♗e2 ♗g7 13. 0—0∞; **9. ♖b1** ♘c6 10. ♗f2 ♕c7 11. ♗d3 ♗e7 12. 0—0 b5= Unzicker—Gligorić, Zürich 1959; **9. ♘b3** ♕e3 10. ♗e2 ♕f4 [10... ♘e4 11. ♘e4 ♕e4 12. 0—0=∞→] 11. ♗g3 ♕e3 12. ♗d6 ♘c6 13. ♗f8 [13. ♖f1 ♘e4 14. ♘e4 ♕e4 15. ♗f8 ♖f8 16. ♔f2∞ Talj—Tringov, München (ol) 1958] ♖f8 14. ♕d2 ♕d2 13. ♔d2 ♗d7 16. ♔e3 0-0-0= Fichtl—Talj, München (ol) 1958

46 11. f5 ♗e7 12. fe6 fe6 13. e5 de5 14. ♕g6 ♔f8∓ V. Kuznjecov—Spaski, SSSR 1960

47 **14. ♘f5**?! de5 15. fe5 ♘c6 16. ♗g3 ♗b4 17. ♖b4 ♘b4 18. ♘g7 ♔f8 19. ♘h5 ♘d3 20. cd3 ♗e6∓ Nežmetdinov—Ščerbakov, SSSR 1959; **14. ♔d2** ♘c6 [14... de5 15. fe5 ♗c5 16. ♘f5 (Keres—Olafsson, Zürich 1959) ♗f5 17. ♗f5=∞] 15. ♘c6 bc6 16. ♖he1 de5 17. ♖e5 ♔d7 18. ♗f2= Šamkovič

48 14... ♘c6?! 15. ef7 ♔f7 16. ♘c6 bc6 17. ♖b6 c5 18. c4!± Mikenas—Talj, SSSR 1959

49 16. f5 e5 17. ♘e6 b5 [17... ♗e7 18. ♗e7 ♔e7 19. ♘c7 ♖a7 20. ♘d5±] 18. a4 ♖a7 19. 0—0=∞

50 **17... ♔c6** 18. ♘e3 d4 19. ♘d5=∞; **17... d4** 18. 0—0 ♘c6 19. ♗d5 ♔c7 20. fe5 de5 21. ♗g3∞ Žilin—Ščerbakov, SSSR 1959

51 12... g5?! 13. ef6 gh4 14. ♗e2±

52 13... ♕d3 14. ♘c7 ♔d7 15. ♗d3 ♔c7 16. ♖f1±

53 14... ♗b4 15. ♖b4 [15. ♔d1 0–0? 16. ♖b3 ♕a4 17. ♘f5±→»; 15... ♕d3 16. ♗d3 ♗e7 17. ef7 ♔f7 18. ♖f1 ♗f6 16. ♗f6 gf6 20. ♖b6 ♘d7 21. ♖d6∞] ♕b4 16. c3 ♕c5 [16... ♕d6 17. ef7 ♔f7 18. ♗e2±→] 17. ef7 ♔f7 [Vasiljčuk–Kondratjev, SSSR 1958] 18. ♗e2 ♘c6 19. ♖f1 ♔g8 20. ♗h5±

54 16... ♘c6? 17. ♖f1 ♔g8 18. ♘c6 bc6 19. ♖b6 c5 20. c4!+–

55 17. ♖f1 ♘f6 18. ♗f6 gf6 19. ♖b6 ♗e7 [Bertok–Minić, Jugoslavija 1962] 20. c4 ♖g8∞ Šamkovič

56 **17... ♘c5** 18. 0–0±; **17... ♘f6** 18. ♗c8 ♖c8 19. ♖b7 ♔g6 20. ♗f6 gf6 21. ♔d2± Parma–Minić, Jugoslavija (ch) 1960; **17... ♗c5** 18. ♗e6 [18. ♗d7 ♗d4 19. ♗c8 ♖ac8 20. ♖b7 ♔g6=] ♔g6 19. ♗f5=

57 11. ♗d3 ♗d7 — 9... ♗d7

58 11... e5 12. ♘c6 bc6 13. fe5 de5 14. ♗c4 ♗e7 13. 0–0± Suetin–Štejn, SSSR 1959

59 12. 0-0-0 ♗d7 13. g4 g5 14. ♘c6 ♗c6 15. fg5 [15. h4 gf4 16. ♕f4 0-0-0∞⇆ Smislov–Benkö, Jugoslavija (ct) 1959] hg5 16. ♗d4 ♖h6 17. h4 ♘d7 18. h5± Talj–Olafsson, Jugoslavija (ct) 1959

60 15... ♘c4? 16. ♗c4 ♕c4 17. ♗b6△ ♘a5+–

61 18. b4 ♘c4 19. b5± Nežmetdinov–Toprover, SSSR 1959

62 **10. ♕d3** ♘c6 11. ♘b3 ♗e7 12. ♗e2 ♘e4 13. ♘e4 ♗h4 14. g3 ♗e7 15. ♘d6 ♗d6 16. ♕d6 0-0-0 17. 0-0-0 e5∞ Žilin–Šamkovič, SSSR 1959; **10. ♘b3** ♕e3 11. ♗e2 ♕f4 12. ♗g3 ♕e3 13. ♗d6 ♘c6∓; **10. ♖b1** ♘c6 11. ♗f2 ♕c7 12. ♗e2 ♗e7 13. 0–0 0–0= Mednis–Westerinen, USA 1960; **10. ♕d2** ♘c6 11. ♘b3 [11. ♗f2 ♕c7 12. ♗e2 ♗e7 13. ♗f3 ♖c8 14. ♘b3 ♘a5= Matanović–Đantar, Jugoslavija (ch) 1959] ♗e7 12. ♗f2 ♕c7 13. ♗e2 b5 14. 0–0 0–0 13. ♖ad1 ♖fd8∞ Suetin–Spaski, SSSR (ch) 1960

63 **10... ♕b2**? 11. ♘de2 ♗b5 12. ♖a2 ♗e2 13. ♕d2 ♕a2 [13... ♘e4 14. ♖b2 ♘d2 15. ♗e2+–] 14. ♘a2 ♗f1 15. ♖f1±; 12. ♗d4! +– Boleslavski; **10... ♘c6**? 11. ♘db5 ♕a5 12. b4+–; 11. ♘e6!+–; **10... ♘g4** 11. ♗g1 ♕b2 12. ♘de2 ♗b5 13. ♖a2 [13. ♗d4 ♗e2 14. ♗e2 ♘e3!∞] ♗e2 14. ♕d2 ♕a2 15. ♘a2 ♗f1 16. ♔f1± Kosikov–Vojgel, SSSR 1964; 12. ♔d2!+–

64 12. ♘b3 ♗e7 13. ♕e2 b5 14. 0–0 g5?! 15. e5 de5 16. fe5 ♕e5 17. ♕e5 ♘e5 18. ♗d4± Spaski–Bazan, Mar del Plata 1960; 14... 0–0±

65 Gufeljd–Suetin, SSSR (ch) 1960

66 Polugajevski

67 **8. ♗d3** ♘bd7 9. f5 [9. ♕e2 ♕b6 10. ♘e6? fe6 11. e5 de5 12. fe5 ♕c5!–+ Saharov–Polugajevski, SSSR (ch) 1960; 10. ♘f3 ♗b7 11. ♗h4 b4 12. ♘b1 d5 13. e5 ♘e4∞ Toluš–Hottes, SSSR–BRD 1960] e5 10. ♘c6 ♕b6 11. ♘b4 ♗b7 12. ♕e2 ♗e7 13. 0-0-0 ♖c8 14. ♗f6 ♘f6 15. g4 ♕a5∞⇆« Spaski–Polugajevski, SSSR (ch) 1960; **8. ♗e2** b4 9. ♘a4 ♗e7 10. ♗f3 ♖a7 11. 0–0 ♗d7 12. b3 ♗a4 13. ba4 0–0 14. ♘b3 ♘bd7 15. ♕e2 ♕b6 16. ♔h1 ♖c7∞ Suetin–Polugajevski, SSSR (ch) 1959

68 **9. e5** de5 10. fe5 ♕c7 11. ef6 ♕e5 12. ♕e2 ♕g5∞ Lejn–Nikolajevski, SSSR 1959; **9. ♕f3** ♘bd7 10. 0-0-0 [10. f5 e5 11. ♘b3 ♗e7 12. 0-0-0 ♖c8 13. ♗d3 0–0 14. ♗f6 ♘f6 15. ♘d5 ♗d5 16. ed5 ♕c7 17. ♔b1 ♖fe8∓ Nikitin–Polugajevski, SSSR (ch) 1959] ♗e7 11. ♗d3 ♖c8 12. ♕h3 ♕b6 13. ♘b3 b4 14. ab4 ♕b4∞⇆ Zavernajev–Morozov, SSSR 1960

69 Spaski–Tatarincev, SSSR 1960

70 8... b4 9. 0-0-0 bc3 10. e5 ♕b6 11. ♕c3± Velimirović

71 9. ♗d3 ♗e7 10. 0-0-0 ♕b6 11. ♖he1 ♘bd7 12. ♘ce2 ♘c5 13. ♗f6 ♗f6 14. g4 ♘a4 ∞⇆ Kupper–Talj, Zürich 1959

72 9... b4 10. ♘d5 ed5 11. e5±

73 10... ♕b6!?∞

74 11... ed5 12. e5! de5 13. fe5 ♘e5 14. ♖he1 ♗d6 15. ♕f5±

75 12. ♗f6 gf6 13. ♕h5 ed5 14. ed5 ♕a2 15. ♖he1 ♔d8 16. ♕f7 ♗d5∞

76 **13. ♖he1**∞ Velimirović–Ribli, Budapest 1973 — 15/459; **13. ed5**!? Velimirović

77 8... h6 9. ♗h4 [9. ♗f6 gf6 10. ed6 ♕d6 11. ♕f3 ♕d4 12. ♕a8 ♕f4 13. ♕e4 ♕e4 14. ♘e4 f5=∞⇆ Morozov–Šapošnikov, SSSR 1959] g5 10. ♗g3! [10. fg5 ♘h7∞] de5 [10... gf4 11. ♗h4! de5 12. ♘e6! ♕d1 13. ♖d1 fe6 14. ♗f6 ♖g8 15. ♖d8 ♔f7 16. ♖c8 ♔f6 17. ♗d3 +– Boleslavski] 11. fe5 ♘d5 12. ♘d5 ♕d5 13. ♗e2± Paoli–Primavera, Italia (ch) 1959

78 9... h6 10. ♗h4 g5 11. ef6 gh4 12. ♕f3 ♖a7 13. 0-0-0∞; 11. ♗g3±

79 **10... h6** 11. ♗h4 b4 12. ef6 bc3 13. fg7 ♗g7 14. b3 ♘c6 15. ♗c4 0–0 16. 0–0 ♔h8 17. ♕e2 ♗b7 18. ♖ad1± Bazan–Bielicki, Mar del Plata 1960; **10... ♘fd7** 11. ♘e4 [11. ♕d2 ♘e5 12. 0-0-0∞; 11... ♗b7!?=] ♗b7 12. ♘d6 ♗d6 13. ed6 ♕c6∞; 12... ♕c5∞

80 11. ef6 bc3 12. b3 [12. fg7 ♗g7 13. b3 0–0 14. ♗d3 ♗b7 15. 0–0 ♘c6∞ Radovici–Ader, Leipzig (ol) 1960] ♘d7 13. fg7 ♗g7 14. ♗e2 ♗b7 15. 0–0 ♘c5 16. ♔h1 ♘e4∞ Bouwmeester–Wexler, Leipzig (ol) 1960

81 14. ♕e2 gf6 15. ♗f6 ♖g8 16. ♗e5 [16. ♘e5 ♖b5! 17. ♕b5 ♖g2 18. ♖d1 ♗d6 19. ♘d7 ♗d7 20. ♕d3 ♗e7∓ Kotkov–Šapošnikov, SSSR 1958] ♕b7 17. ♗d7 ♗d7 18. 0-0-0 ♖a2 19. b3 ♗c6 20. ♔b1 ♖a5∓

82 14. . . ♗c5 15. ♕c4 gf6 16. ♗f6 ♖g8 17. ♗d4± Fuderer–Kapić, Jugoslavija 1959

83 10. . . b4 11. ♘cb5 ab5 12. ef6 ♖a5 [12. . . h6 13. ♘b5 ♕c6 14. ♕e5+– Majstorović–Little, corr. 1967 — 3/521; 12. . . b3 13. ♘b5 ♕a5 14. c3 gf6 15. ♗f6 ♖g8 16. ♕c4 1 : 0 Estrin–Buhtin, SSSR 1968 — 5/470] 13. ♘b5 ♕b6 14. ♕e5 gf6 15. ♗f6+–

84 **11. . . ♕e5**? 12. ♕e5 ♘e5 13. ♘db5+–; **11. . . ♗b4**? 12. ♘e4 ♕e5 13. ♘f3 ♕c7 14. a3 ♗f8 15. g4 ♗b7 16. ♗g2 ♕c4 17. ♕c4 bc4 18. ♘e5+– Giterman–Štejn, SSSR 1960; **11. . . ♗e7**? 12. ♗e7 ♔e7 13. ♕g4 ♕e5 14. ♗b5 ♗b7 15. ♖he1 h5 16. ♘f5 ♔d8 17. ♕h4 +– Kupper–Walter, Zürich 1961; **11. . . ♘c6** 12. ♘c6 ♕c6 13. ♕d3 ♗c5 [13. . . ♗b4 14. ♗e2 ♖b8 15. ♘e4 0–0 16. ♘f6! ♘f6 17. ♗f6 ♗b7 18. ♕h3!+–→» Kelečević–Bućan, Jugoslavija (ch) 1971 — 12/496] 14. ♗e2 ♕c7 15. ♘e4 0–0 [15. . . ♕e5 16. ♖f1△ ♗f4+–] 16. ♕g3 ♔h8 17. ♗f4±→» Tomson–Kovačević, SSSR–Jugoslavija 1961

85 **13. . . ♕b6** 14. ♖d6! ♗d6 15. ♕e6 ♔f8 16. ♗c4+–; **13. . . ♘e5** 14. ♕e6 ♗e7 15. ♗b5+–; **13. . . ♘c6** 14. ♕e6 ♘e7 15. ♗b5 ab5 16. ♘b5 ♕c6 17. ♘d6+–; **13. . . ♘c5** 14. ♖d8 ♕d8 15. ♗d8 ♔d8 16. b4 ♘cd7 17. a3 ♘c6 18. ♕e6 ♘ce5 19. ♗e2 ♖c8∞

86 14. ♗d3 ♗e7 15. ♗e7 ♔e7 16. ♖he1 ♕f6 17. ♗e4 ♘c6!–+ Euwe, Boleslavski

87 16. . . ♕f5!∓

88 **12. . . ♕b6** 13. ♗b5 ab5 14. ♘db5 g6 15. ♕h3 ♖a2 16. ♖d6 ♖a1 17. ♔d2 ♗d6 [17. . . ♕f2 18. ♘e2 ♗d6 19. ♘d6 ♔f8 20. ♕h6 ♔g8 21. ♘e8+–] 18. ♘d6 ♕d6 19. ed6 ♖h1 20. ♕h6+–; **12. . . ♕e5** 13. ♗b5 ab5 14. ♘e6△ ♖he1+–

89 13. ♕h4 ♕e5! [13. . . h5? 14. ♔b1! ♘c6 15. ♘c6 ♗c6 16. ♘e4± V. Nikolić–Mihevc, Jugoslavija 1973 — 16/475] 14. ♗b5 ab5 15. ♖he1 ♕c5–+

90 18. ♗f1? h4! 19. ♖g1 ♔e7 20. ♘b3 ♘c6∓ Bojković–Vitolinš, Jugoslavija–SSSR 1963

91 ∓ Euwe, Boleslavski

92 15. . . ♗g7 16. ♗b5 ab5 17. ef7 ♕f7 [17. . . ♔f8 18. ♖he1 ♗e4 19. ♘e4+– Belokurov–Sanakojev, SSSR 1962] 18. ♖he1 ♗e4 19. ♘e4! ♕h5 20. ♘g5+–

93 17. . . ♔f8 18. ♖he1 ♘a6 19. ♖e8 ♔g7 20. ♕f5 ♕f7 21. ♕g4 ♕g6 22. ♖d7 ♔h6 23. ♕h4+–

94 21. ♘f4 ♔e7 22. ♘d5=

95 **12. . . ♘e5** 13. ♘e6 fe6 14. ♕e6 ♗e7 15. ♗b5+–→; **12. . . ♕b6** 13. ♗b5?! ab5 14. ♘db5 ♘e5 15. ♕f4 ♘bc6! [15. . . ♘bd7? 16. ♖d7 f6 17. ♖b7 ♕b7 18. ♗f6 ♘g6 19. ♕c7+– Simovič–Vitolinš, SSSR 1962] 16. ♖he1 h6 17. ♕f2 ♕a5 18. ♗f4 f6∞; 13. ♗f4!?; **12. . . h5**!?

96 13. ♗b5!? ab5 14. ♖he1 h5 15. ♕h4 ♕c5! [15. . . ♕c7? 16. ♘cb5 ♕a5 17. ♘e6 fe6 18. ♖e6 ♔f7 19. ♕c4 1 : 0 Ljiljak–Godard, corr. 1968 — 5/469; 16. . . ♕c4 17. ♘e6+–; 16. . . ♕c8 17. ♕f4+–; 16. . . ♕b6 17. ♕f4 ♘a6 18. ♘e6 fe6 19. ♖f1+–→] 16. ♘cb5 [16. ♘e6?! fe6 17. ♖e6 ♔f7 18. ♖de1 ♕f5 19. g4 ♕g4–+ A. Zajcev–Belov, SSSR 1966 — 2/461] ♗d5!? [16. . . ♖a6 17. b4!+–; 16. . . ♘a6 17. ♘e6 fe6 18. ♖e6 ♔f7 19. ♖d7 ♔e6 20. ♕h3+–; 16. . . ♖a2 17. ♔b1 ♖a5 18. ♕f4+– Veljković–Šahović, Jugoslavija (ch) 1973 — 15/457] 17. ♖d3∞ Ugrinović

97 13. . . ♘f6 14. ♗f6 [14. ♕h4 ♘bd7 15. ♖he1 ♕c5 16. ♗f5∞ Roos–Saharov, corr. 1962] gf6 [14. . . ♕f6 15. ♖he1+–→] 15. ♗f5 ♕e3 [15. . . h5 16. ♕h3 ♗c5 17. ♖he1 ♕f4 18. ♔b1 ♗d4 19. ♗e6 ♗c3 20. bc3 0–0 (Tukmakov–Anikajev, SSSR 1969) 21. ♗f7! ♔f7 22. ♕h5 ♔g8 23. ♕g6 ♔h8 24. ♖e7+–; 21. . . ♖f7 22. ♖e8 ♔g7 23. ♖dd8+– Tukmakov] 16. ♔b1 h5 17. ♘e6 hg4 [17. . . ♕e6 18. ♕d4 ♘c6 19. ♕d7+– Kogan–Kotenko, corr. 1971 — 11/392] 18. ♘c7 ♔e7 19. ♘7d5 ♔e8 20. ♘e3±

98 **15. ♖he1** h5!∓; **15. ♗g3**!? ♕e3 16. ♔b1 h5 17. ♖he1! ♕e1 18. ♕g5 ♗h6 19. ♕h5 ♕e3 20. ♘e6 ♕e6 21. ♖e1 ♕e1 22. ♗e1 ♗g7 23. ♕g4 [Litvinov–Zarenkov, SSSR 1973 — 16/476] ♔f8!∞

99 15. . . fe6 16. ♖he1+–→

100 16. ♕h3 fe6△ ♕f4–+

101 **19. . . ♔g7** 20. ♖f7 ♔g8 21. ♗h7!+–; **19. . . ♘f6** 20. ♕h6 ♖h6 21. ♗f6 ♕e3 22. ♔b1±

102 21. ♗g6= Dueball–Kerr, Skopje (ol) 1972 — 14/495

103 **11. ♕e2** ♕g5 12. ♘e4 ♕e5 13. 0-0-0 ♖a7! [13. . . ♗b7? 14. ♘b5 ab5 15. ♕d2+–→ Reicher–Krogius, Ploesti 1957] 14. ♘f3 ♕f4 15. ♔b1 ♖d7∓ Štejn–Saharov, SSSR 1960; **11. ♘e4** ♕e4 12. ♘e2 [12. ♗e2 ♕g2 13. ♗f3 ♕g5 14. ♗a8 ♕h4 15. ♔f1 ♕f6 16. ♘f3 ♗c5 17. ♕d3 0–0 18. ♔g2 ♖d8∓ Ghitescu–Kavalek, Zwolle 1967] ♘c6! 13. ♕d2 h6 14. ♗e3 ♗b7 15. ♘g3 ♕e5 16. fg7 ♗g7 17. ♗d3 ♘b4 18. 0–0 ♘d3 19. ♕d3 ♖d8∓↑ Nežmetdinov–Polugajevski, SSSR (ch) 1961

104 **12. . . ♘d7** 13. ♕f3 ♖a7 14. ♘e4 ♕e5 [14. . . ♕d5 15. ♖d1 ♗b7 16. fg7 ♗g7 17. ♘f5!+–] 15. ♘c6 ♕b2 16. ♖d1 ♖c7 17. fg7 ♕g7 18. ♖d7+–; **12. . . gf6** 13. ♘e4 ♕e5 14. ♘f3 ♕b2 15. 0–0 f5 16. ♘d6 ♗d6 17. ♕d6 ♕f6 18. ♘d4 [18. a4 ♕e7 19. ♕g3+–] ♘d7 [18. . . ♕e7 19. ♕e5 f6 20. ♗h5 ♔f8 21. ♕e3 ♖g8 22. ♖ae1△ ♘f5+–] 19. ♗f3 ♖a7 20. ♗c6+–→ Matulović–Ermenkov, Sombor 1972 — 14/496; **12. . . ♕h4** 13. g3 ♕f6 14. ♖f1! [14. ♕e4 ♖a7 15. ♖f1 ♕g6 16. ♕f4

♘d7 17. ♘c6 e5 18. ♘e5 ♘e5 19. ♕e5= Bronštejn–Polugajevski, SSSR (ch) 1961] ♕g6 [14... ♕e5 15. 0-0-0 ♗c5 16. ♘e6 ♕e3 17. ♖d2 ♕d3 18. ♘c7 ♔d8 19. ♖d3 ♔c7 20. ♖f7 ♗d7 21. ♗g4 ♖d8 22. ♘e4+– Judovič jr.] 15. ♕e3! [15. ♕f3 ♖a7 16. ♕f4 ♘d7 17. ♘c6 e5 18. ♘e5 ♘e5 19. ♕e5 ♕e6= Nemet–Rajković, Jugoslavija (ch) 1974] ♗c5 16. ♗f3 ♖a7 17. ♘e4 ♖c7? 18. ♕f4 ♗b6 19. ♘d6 ♔e7 20. ♖d1+– Matulović–Rajković, Jugoslavija 1974; 17... ♗b4!△ 18. c3 ♗e7=

105 14. 0-0-0 ♖d7 15. ♕g3 [15. ♕c3 ♗b7 16. ♘b5 ♕c3 17. ♘bc3 ♖d1 18. ♖d1 gf6 19. ♘f6 ♔e7 20. ♘fe4 f5∞] gf6! 16. ♕e5 fe5 17. ♘f6 ♔e7 18. ♘d7 ♗d7∞ Minić–Fischer, Skopje 1967 — 4/569

106 Minić–Rajković, Jugoslavija 1973 — 15/458

107 13... ♕e5 14. 0-0-0 [14. ♖d1 ♖a7 15. ♘f3 ♕c7 16. ♘e5 ♗e7 17. ♘f7 0–0?! 18. ♘d6± Ljubojević–Polugajevski, Hilversum 1973 — 15/460; 17... ♕h2! 18. g3 0–0 19. ♕f3 ♗b7 20. ♕e3 ♖f7∓ Ljubojević] ♖a7 15. ♘f3 ♕f4 16. ♔b1 ♖d7∞

108 16... ♖c7? 17. ♕f4±

109 18. ♘b5 ♖d7∞

110 21. 0-0-0 fe4 22. ♗h5! g6 23. ♗g4 ♕g4 24. ♕c6 ♗d7 25. ♖d7 ♕d7 26. ♕a8= Matulović–Polugajevski, Beograd 1974 — 18/502

111 14... ♕g6 15. ♕e3 ♗b7 16. ♗f3 ♕h6 17. ♕h6 gh6 18. ♘b3 ♗e4 19. ♗e4± Gligorić–Bhend, Zürich 1959

112 15. c3 ♗b7 16. ♕g3 [16. ♗f3 ♗e4 17. ♗e4 ♗d6 18. g3 gf6 19. ♔h1 ♗c5 20. ♖ad1 ♔f8∓ Zagorovski–Polugajevski, SSSR 1959] ♕g3 17. ♘g3 ♘c6! [17... g6 18. ♘b3 ♗d5 19. ♗f3 ♗b3 20. ab3± Zaharjan–Saharov, SSSR 1965] 18. ♘b3 gf6 19. ♘e4 ♗e7 20. ♘f6 ♗f6 21. ♖f6 ♔e7 22. ♖f2 ♘e5= Bagirov–Polugajevski, SSSR (ch) 1960

113 **15... ♖d3** 16. ♘e5 ♖e3 17. ♗d3 ♘d7 18. ♘d7 ♗d7 19. ♔f2+–; **15... ♕b2** 16. ♕e3 ♗b7 17. a4 [17. fg7 ♗g7 18. ♗d3 ♗d4 19. ♘d4 ♕d4 20. ♕d4 ♖d4 21. ♘f6 ♔e7 22. ♖f2 ♘d7∓ Šmit–Kovačević, SSSR–Jugoslavija 1961; 17. ♖ab1 ♕c2 18. ♘fg5 ♕c7 19. fg7 ♗g7 20. ♘e6 fe6 21. ♘g5 ♕e5∞ Parma–Tatai, Athens 1968 — 6/566; 17. c4 ♗e4 18. ♕e4 ♕f6 19. ♘e5 ♗c5 20. ♔h1 ♖d4 21. ♕e3 ♖d5∞ Simovič–Vitolinš, SSSR 1961] b4 18. c3 ♗e4 [18... bc3 19. ♖ab1 ♕a2 20. fg7 ♗g7 21. ♖b7 ♖b7 22. ♘d6+–] 19. ♕e4 ♗c5 20. ♔h1 gf6 21. ♖fc1 0–0 22. ♖ab1 ♕a2 23. cb4+–→ Novopašin–Vitolinš, SSSR 1961

114 18. ♔h1 ♗b7 19. ♖ad1 h5 20. ♘eg5 ♗c5 21. ♕e5 ♗d6 22. ♖d6 ♕d6 23. ♘f7 ♔f7 24. ♘g5= Novopašin–Polugajevski, SSSR 1960

115 21. ♖ad1 h5 22. c5 ♗h6 23. ♕e2± Zagorovski–Kaverin, SSSR 1961

116 **13. ♔h1** ♖a7 14. ♕d3 ♖d7 15. ♘f3 ♕f6 16. ♕e3 ♗d6 17. ♘e4 ♕f4∞ Estrin–Korzin, SSSR 1961; **13. fg7** ♗g7 14. ♘f3 ♕c5 15. ♔h1 ♗b7 16. ♕d3 0–0 17. ♖ad1 ♘c6= Belov–Polugajevski, SSSR 1961

117 14. ♖e1 ♕f6 15. ♗c6 ♘c6 16. ♘c6 ♖d7 17. ♘d5 ♗c5 18. ♔h1 ♕h4 19. ♕f3 0–0∓ Ortega–Polugajevski, La Habana 1962

118 14... ♕c5? 15. ♔h1 ♖d7 [15... ♘c6 16. ♘e4 ♕e5 17. fg7 ♗g7 18. ♘d6 ♔e7 19. ♗c6 ♕d6 20. ♖f7+–; 16... ♕b6 17. fg7 ♗g7 18. ♘d6 ♔e7 19. ♗c6 f5 20. ♘f5 ef5 21. ♖e1 ♔f6 22. ♕d6 ♔g5+–→ Pedersen] 16. ♘b8! ♖d1 17. ♖ad1 gf6 18. ♘e4+– Parr–Klibor, BRD 1967 — 4/570

119 17... ♗c5? 18. ♔h1 0–0 [18... ♗d6 19. ♕h3 b4 20. ♘d5 ♕d5 21. fg7△ ♕h7+– Korčnoj] 19. ♘e4+– Pedersen

120 **18. ♕h3** b4! 19. fg7 [19. ♘d5? ♕d5 20. fg7 ♕d4–+] ♖g8 20. ♕h7 ♕h2 21. ♕h2 ♗h2 22. ♔h2 bc3∓; **18. ♘e4** ♕h2 19. ♔f2 ♕e5! 20. g3 [20. fg7 ♗c5! 21. ♔e2 ♖g8∓] 0–0∞⇆ Fridštejn

121 21. ♘e4 0–0∞⇆

B 97

1. e4 c5 2. ♘f3 d6 3. d4 cd4 4. ♘d4 ♘f6 5. ♘c3 a6 6. ♗g5 e6 7. f4 ♕b6

	8	9	10	11	12	13	14	15	16	
1	♘b3[1]	♕e2	♗e2	♗f3	0-0-0	♘a4[4]	♗f6[5]	♘b6	♘d7	±
	♕e3[2]	♕e2	♘c6[3]	♗d7	♗e7	0-0-0	gf6	♔b8	♖d7[6]	
2	. . .	♕f3[7]	a4[8]	♗d3	♕h3	♗h4[10]	fg5	♗f2	♕e3	=
	♘bd7	♕c7	♗e7[9]	h6	♖g8	g5	hg5	g4[11]	♘e5[12]	
3	. . .	. . .	0-0-0[13]	♗e2[15]	♗f6	e5	♕g3[16]	fe5	♗f3[17]	±
	. . .	♗e7	♕c7[14]	b5	♘f6	♗b7	de5	♘d7		

1. e4 c5 2. ♘f3 d6 3. d4 cd4 4. ♘d4 ♘f6 5. ♘c3 a6 6. ♗g5 e6 7. f4 ♕b6 8. ♕d2 ♕b2[18] 9. ♖b1 ♕a3

	10	11	12	13	14	15	16	17	18	
4	♗f6[19] gf6	♗e2[20] ♘c6[21]	♘c6[22] bc6	0–0 ♕a5[23]	♔h1 ♗e7[24]	f5[25] ef5	ef5 ♗f5	♗a6[26] ♕a6	♖f5 d5[27]	=
5	. . . . . .	. . . ♗g7	0–0[28] f5[29]	♖fd1 ♘c6[30]	♘c6 bc6[31]	♖b3 ♕c5	♔h1 0–0[32]	♘a4[33] ♕f2	♖f3 ♕h4[34]	=
6	f5 ♘c6[35]	fe6[36] fe6	♘c6 bc6	e5![37] ♘d5[38]	♘d5[39] cd5[40]	♗e2[41] de5	0–0[42] ♗c5[43]	♔h1 ♖f8	c4 ♖f1[44]	±
7	. . . . . .	. . . . . .	. . . . . .	. . . de5	♗f6 gf6	♘e4[45] ♗e7[46]	♗e2 h5[47]	♖b3[48] ♕a4	c4 f5[49]	=
8	e5 h6[50]	♗f6[51] gf6	♘e4[52] fe5[53]	♖b3[54] ♕a4[55]	fe5 de5	♘f6 ♔e7	♘f5 ef5[56]	♘d5 ♔e6	♘c7 ♔f6[57]	=
9	. . . de5	fe5 ♘fd7	♘e4[58] h6![59]	♗h4[60] ♕a2	♖b3 ♕a1[61]	♔f2 ♕a4	♗b5[62] ab5	♘b5 ♗c5	♘c5 ♕h4[63]	∓
10	. . . . . .	. . . . . .	♗c4 ♗e7[64]	♗e6[65] 0–0[66]	0–0[67] ♗g5[68]	♕g5 h6[69]	♕h5![70] fe6[71]	♘e6 ♖f1[72]	♖f1 ♕e7[73]	±
11	. . . . . .	. . . . . .	. . . ♕c5	♗e6 fe6[74]	♘e6 ♕e5	♕e3 ♕e3[75]	♗e3 ♗d6	♘d5 ♔f7!?[76]	♘ec7 ♘f6[77]	=

1. e4 c5 2. ♘f3 d6 3. d4 cd4 4. ♘d4 ♘f6 5. ♘c3 a6 6. ♗g5 e6 7. f4 ♕b6 8. ♕d2 ♕b2 9. ♖b1 ♕a3 10. e5 de5 11. fe5 ♘fd7 12. ♗c4 ♗b4 13. ♖b3[78] ♕a5

	14	15	16	17	18	19	20	21	22	
12	a3[79] ♗c5[80]	♘e6 fe6	♗e6 h6[81]	♗f7 ♔f7	♕d5 ♔g6	♕e4 ♔f7	♕d5[82]			=
13	0–0 0–0[83]	♗f6![84] ♘f6[85]	ef6 ♖d8[86]	♖b4 ♕b4	♕g5[87] g6	♖f4[88] ♖d4[89]	♕h6[90] ♕f8[91]	♕f8 ♔f8	♖d4 ♘c6[92]	∞

1. e4 c5 2. ♘f3 d6 3. d4 cd4 4. ♘d4 ♘f6 5. ♘c3 a6 6. ♗g5 e6 7. f4 ♕b6 8. ♕d2 ♕b2 9. ♘b3

	9	10	11	12	13	14	15	16	17	
14	. . . ♘c6[93]	♗d3[94] ♕a3[95]	0–0[96] ♗d7	♖ae1 0-0-0	♗h4[97] ♗e7	♗f2 ♘g4	♗b6 ♕b4	♗d8 ♗d8	♔h1 h5[98]	±
15	. . . ♕a3	♗f6![99] gf6	♗e2 h5[100]	0–0 ♘c6	♔h1[101] ♗d7	♕e3[102] ♖c8[103]	♘b1 ♕a4[104]	c4 ♘a5	♕c3[105] ♘c4[106]	±

[1] 8. a3 ♘c6 [8... ♗d7!? 9. ♕d2 ♘c6 10. ♘f3 ♕b2 11. ♖b1 ♕a3 12. e5 de5∓ Lujk–Banik, SSSR 1960] 9. ♘f3 [9. ♘c6 bc6 10. ♗f6 gf6∓] ♘g4 10. ♕d2 h6 11. ♗h4 g5 [11... ♗e7!?] 12. fg5 hg5 13. ♗g5 ♕b2 14. ♖b1 ♕a3 15. ♗d3 ♗g7 16. ♘d1 ♕c5∓ Szabo–Tringov, Kecskemet 1964

[2] 8... **h6** 9. ♗f6 gf6 10. ♕f3 [10. f5± van den Berg–Olafsson, Beverwijk 1961] ♘c6 11. 0-0-0 ♗d7 12. ♔b1 0-0-0 13. ♕h5 ♗e8 14. g3 ♔b8 15. ♗h3± Matanović–Bertok, Jugoslavija 1966 — 1/322; 8... **♗e7** 9. ♕e2?! h6 10. ♗f6 ♗f6∓ Karklins–Verber, USA 1971 — 11/395; 9. ♕f3 ♘bd7 — 8... ♘bd7

3 10... ♘bd7 11. 0-0-0! [11. a4 ♗e7 12. 0-0-0 h6 13. ♗h4 e5 14. f5 b6= Joppen–Bronštejn, Beograd 1954; 11. ♗f3 ♖a7 12. 0-0-0 b5 13. ♘a5 h6 14. ♗h4 ♖c7 15. e5 de5 16. fe5 b4 17. ♘a4 ♘h7= Tukmakov–Koc, SSSR 1962] b6 12. f5! e5 13. ♗c4 ♗b7 14. ♗f6 ♘f6 15. ♗d5± Keres–van den Berg, München (ol) 1958

4 13. ♖he1 h6 14. ♗f6 [14. ♗h4!?] gf6 15. ♗h5 ♖c8 16. ♖e2 b5 17. ♔b1 ♖c7 18. a3 0–0 19. ♖d3 ♖b8 20. ♘d5± Pedersen–van den Berg, München (ol) 1958

5 14. ♘b6 ♔c7 15. ♘d7 ♘d7 16. ♗e7 ♘e7=

6 17. ♗h5 ♗d8 18. ♖hf1 ♖g8 19. g3± Štejn–Gligorić, Stockholm (izt) 1962

7 **9. ♗d3** ♕e3 10. ♕e2 ♕e2 11. ♗e2 b6 12. ♗f3 ♗b7 13. 0-0-0 ♗e7 14. ♖he1 e5= Tukmakov–Ankerst, SSSR–Jugoslavija 1962; **9. ♕e2**!? ♕c7 10. 0-0-0 b5?! 11. a3 ♗b7 12. g4!? ♖c8 [12... ♗e7!?] 13. ♗h4! ♘b6 14. g5 ♘fd7 15. f5± Grabczewski–Talj, Lublin 1974 — 18/506; 10... ♗e7∞

8 **10. ♗h4** b5 11. a3 ♗b7 12. ♗d3 ♗e7 13. 0-0-0 ♖c8 14. ♔b1 ♘b6 15. ♗e1= Estrin–Banik, SSSR 1962; **10. ♗f6**!? ♘f6 11. g4 g6?! 12. ♗g2 ♗g7 13. 0-0-0 ♘d7 14. h4 h5 15. g5 ♘b6 16. f5 ♗e5 17. ♖hf1 ♘c4 18. ♗h3 b5 19. ♘d4± Dementjev–Peresipkin, SSSR 1972 — 14/500; 11... b5!∞; **10. 0-0-0** b5 11. ♗d3 [11. a3 ♗b7 12. g4 ♖c8 13. ♖d2 d5 14. ♗f6 ♘f6 15. **g5** ♘e4 16. ♘e4 de4∓ Szabo–Štejn, Hamburg 1965; 12. ♗f6 ♘f6 13. f5 e5 14. g4 h6 15. h4 ♕b6 16. ♗g2 ♗e7 17. g5 ♘d7 18. f6! gf6 19. gh6 ♖h6 20. ♗h3± Ciocaltea–Najdorf, Varna (ol) 1962] ♗b7 12. ♖he1 ♗e7 13. a3 ♖c8 14. ♕g3!± Westerinen–O'Kelly, La Habana 1967 — 4/572; 10... ♗e7 — 9... ♗e7

9 Barczay; 10... b6 11. ♗d3 ♗b7 12. 0–0 ♗e7 13. ♕h3 e5 [13... h6 14. ♗h4 ♖g8 15. ♗g3⩲] 14. ♖ae1 0–0 15. ♔h1 ♖fe8 16. ♘d2 ♘f8 17. ♗c4!± Štejn–Parma, SSSR–Jugoslavija 1962

10 13. ♗f6 ♗f6 14. 0–0 ♗c3!? [14... ♘c5 15. ♖ae1 ♗c3 16. bc3 ♗d7 17. e5 0-0-0= Gipslis–Minić, SSSR–Jugoslavija 1962] 15. bc3 ♕c3 16. e5 [16. ♖ad1? ♕c7 17. ♘d2 ♘b6∓ Villun–Sorokin, corr. 1970 — 10/550] de5 17. ♖ae1∞

11 15... b6 16. 0–0 ♘e5 17. ♕e3± Gufeljd–Suetin, SSSR (ch) 1967 — 3/522

12 **17. ♗h4**? ♘d5∓ Kuprejanov–Matanović, Jugoslavija (ch) 1962; **17. 0—0**!?=

13 **10. g4**?! h6 11. ♗f6 ♗f6 12. h4 ♕c7 13. 0-0-0 ♗c3 14. bc3 b6 15. ♕d3 ♗b7 16. ♗g2 0-0-0∓ Bojković–Gligorić, Jugoslavija (ch) 1962; **10. ♗d3** h6 [10... ♕c7 11. ♗h4 ♘e4 12. ♗e7 ♘c3 13. ♕g3 g6 14. ♗g5 ♘d5 15. 0-0-0⩲; 11... b5 12. a3 ♗b7 13. 0–0 0–0= Boleslavski] 11. ♕h3 [11. ♗h4 ♘e4 12. ♗e7 ♘c3 13. ♗h4 ♘d5∓] ♖g8 [11... ♘c5? 12. 0-0-0 ♘d3 13. ♖d3 ♖g8 14. ♗f6 gf6 15. f5 ♗d7 16. fe6 fe6 17. ♕h5±→ Suetin–Saharov, SSSR 1968] 12. ♗h4 g5 13. ♗f2 [13. fg5!?] ♕c7 14. g3 b5∓↑

14 10... h6?! 11. ♗h4 g5 12. ♗f2 ♕c7 13. g3 b5 14. ♗g2 ♖b8 15. ♖he1± Tukmakov–Buhover, SSSR 1963

15 **11. f5**?! ♘e5 12. ♕h3 b5∓↑; **11. ♗d3** h6 12. ♗h4 g5 [12... ♘e4 13. ♘e4 ♗h4 14. ♕g4!⩲] 13. fg5 ♘e5 14. ♕e2 ♘fg4 15. ♘d4 hg5 16. ♗g3 ♗d7= Rajković–Udovčić, Jugoslavija 1963; **11. g4** b5 12. ♗f6 gf6 13. a3 ♖b8 14. ♘e2 b4 [14... ♘c5 15. ♘c5 ♕c5=] 15. ab4 ♖b4 16. ♖d4= Bagirov–van den Berg, Beverwijk 1965

16 14. ef6?! ♗f3 15. ♗f3 ♗f6 16. ♗a8 ♗c3 17. bc3 d5!∓

17 **16. ♖d7**?! ♔d7 17. ♖d1 [17. ♕g7 ♖af8 18. ♗h5 b4 19. ♗f7 bc3∓ Szabo–Quinteros, Amsterdam 1973 — 16/479] ♔c8 18. ♕g7 ♖d8∓; **16. ♗f3**± Petrosjan

18 **8... ♘c6** 9. 0-0-0 ♗d7 [9... ♘d4 10. ♕d4 ♕d4 11. ♖d4± Keres–Panno, Göteborg (izt) 1955] 10. ♗e2 ♘d4 11. ♕d4 ♕d4 12. ♖d4± Hort–Smislov, Moskva 1960; **8... ♘bd7**!?

19 10. ♖b3 ♕a5 11. ♗f6 gf6 12. ♗e2 ♘d7 13. 0–0 ♘c5 14. ♖bb1 b5 15. ♘b3≅ I. Zajcev–Murej, SSSR 1964

20 11. f5 ♗h6 12. ♕h6 ♕c3 13. ♕d2 ♕d2 14. ♔d2 ♔e7= Banik–Toluš, SSSR (ch) 1957

21 11... h5 12. 0–0 ♘d7 [12... ♘c6!?] 13. ♔h1 ♕c5 [13... ♘c5?! 14. e5!± Spasov–Tukmakov, Ybbs 1968 — 6/577; 13... ♗e7!?] 14. ♖f3! ♗e7 15. ♖h3 h4 16. f5 [16. ♘d1 b5 17. a4 b4 18. c3±] ♘b6 17. ♘d1± Simagin–Štejn, SSSR (ch) 1961

22 12. ♘b3 h5!? [12... ♗g7 13. 0–0?! f5 14. ef5 ♕b4 15. ♘d1 ♕d2 16. ♘d2 ♘d4 17. ♗d3 ♘f5∓⊡ Rossetto–Panno, Mar del Plata 1962; 13. f5 0–0 14. 0–0 ♘e5 15. ♘d4 b5 16. ♔h1 ♗d7 17. ♗h5≅ Panno–Fischer, Bled 1961; 15. ♗d3 ♕b4 16. a3 ♕b6 17. ♔h1 ♖d8 18. ♘e2 d5 19. fe6 fe6 20. ed5 ♖d5 21. ♘f4 ♖d6 22. ♘h5±↑ Matulović–Minić, Jugoslavija (ch) 1956] 13. 0–0 ♗d7 14. ♖f3 ♖c8 15. ♔h1 b5 16. ♖e1 ♗e7 17. ♖h3 h4∓ Tukmakov–Platonov, SSSR (ch) 1969

23 **13... ♗h6**?! 14. ♔h1 0–0 15. ♖f3 ♖d8 16. ♕e1! ♕a5 17. ♕h4 ♗g7 18. ♖g3±→ Ghizdavu–Espig, Riga 1967; **13... d5**?! 14. ♔h1 ♕a5 15. f5 ♗b4 16. ♖b3± Minić–Korčnoj, Jugoslavija–SSSR 1963; **13... ♗g7**!? 14. ♔h1 0–0 15. ♖b3 ♕a5 16. ♕d6 ♖a7 17. ♖a3 ♖d8 18. ♖a5 ♖d6 19. ♗d3 [19. ♘a4 ♖d4 20. ♗d3 ♗f8 21. ♘c5 ♖b4= Matanović–Tringov, Kecskemet 1964] f5 20. e5= Matanović–Minić, Jugoslavija 1962

24 14... d5 15. ed5 cd5 16. f5 ♗g7 17. ♖f3 0–0 18. ♖bf1± Parma–Ramirez, Malaga 1963

25 15. ♖f3 ♖a7 16. f5 ♖b7 17. ♖bf1 h5 18. ♗c4 d5= Parma—Bertok, Jugoslavija 1962

26 17. ♗f3? 0—0! [17... ♖c8 18. ♖fe1 ♗e6 19. ♖b7 (Janošević—Ostojić, Kragujevac 1974 — 18/508) h5∓] 18. ♗c6 ♖ac8 19. ♗b7 ♖c3 20. ♖f5 ♖b3!—+ Marić—Gligorić, Beograd 1962

27 19. ♖e1 ♕b7 20. ♖f6 0—0 21. ♕g5= Matanović—Bertok, Jugoslavija 1962

28 **12. f5** 0—0 [12... ♗h6!? 13. ♕d3 ♕c5 14. fe6 fe6 15. ♗g4 ♖g8! 16. ♗e6 ♖g2 17. ♗c8 ♖d2!= Ivkov—Saharov, Jugoslavija—SSSR 1966 — 1/325] 13. ♖b3 ♕a5 14. 0—0 ♘c6 15. ♘c6 bc6 16. ♕d6 ♖a7! 17. ♖a3 ♖d8 18. ♖a5 ♖d6 19. e5! ♖d4!= Balašov—Christoph, Hastings 1965/66 — 1/326; **12. ♖b3** ♕a5 13. f5 [13. 0—0?! f5 14. ♖d1 fe4∓] 0—0 [13... ♕e5 14. ♘f3 ♕a5 15. ♘d4 ♕e5 1/2 : 1/2 Koc—Štejn, SSSR 1962] 14. 0—0 ♘c6 [14... b5 15. fe6 fe6 16. ♗g4±] 15. ♘c6 bc6 16. ♕d6 ef5 17. ♕c6 ♗e6 18. ♘d5 fe4 19. c4 ♕d2 20. ♘e7 ♔h8 21. ♕e4= I. Zajcev—Krogius, SSSR (ch) 1962

29 **12... 0—0** 13. f5! ♘c6 14. ♘c6 bc6 15. ♔h1 ♕a5 16. ♖f3±↑ Zinser—Buljovčić, Reggio Emilia 1967 — 3/531; **12... ♘c6** 13. ♘c6 bc6 14. ♖b3 ♕c5 15. ♔h1 f5 16. ef5 ef5 17. ♘a4 ♕d4 18. ♕d4 ♗d4= Bronštejn—Suetin, SSSR (ch) 1967 — 3/532

30 **13... fe4** 14. ♘e4 d5 15. f5±↑; **13... 0—0** 14. ef5 ef5 [14... ♘c6 15. ♘c6 bc6 16. f6 ♗f6 17. ♘e4 ♗g7 18. ♖b3 ♕a4 19. ♘d6± Parma—Bogdanović, Jugoslavija 1965] 15. ♘d5 ♘c6 16. ♘c6 bc6 17. ♘e7 ♔h8 18. ♘c8 ♖fc8 19. ♕d6! [19. ♕d3? ♕c5 20. ♔h1 ♖e8∓ Parma—Fischer, Rovinj-Zagreb 1970 — 9/433] ♕a2 20. ♕c5±

31 14... ♗c3 15. ♕e3 bc6 16. ♖b3 ♕c5 17. ♕c5 dc5 18. ♖c3 fe4 19. ♖c5 ♗d7 20. ♖e5 f5 21. g4 ♖g8 22. ♔f2 fg4 23. ♔g3! [23. ♖e4 h5 24. ♔g3 ♔e7 25. ♖e5 h4!= Parma—Fischer, La Habana 1965] ♔e7 24. ♗c4 ♖g7 [1/2 : 1/2 Lehmann—O'Kelly, Solingen 1968 — 6/576] 25. f5! ♔f6 26. ♔f4± Matanović, Parma

32 16... d5?! 17. ♘a4△ ed5, c4±

33 17. ♕d6 ♕d6 18. ♖d6 e5= Matanović—Bronštejn, Beverwijk 1963

34 **18... ♕a7**? 19. ♕d6 fe4 20. ♖g3 ♕f2 21. f5!±→ Ankerst—Bogdanović, Jugoslavija 1966 — 2/464; **18... ♕h4** 19. ef5 ef5 20. ♘b6 ♖b8 21. ♘c8 ♖fc8 22. ♗a6 ♖e8= Parma—Barczay, Sarajevo 1969 — 7/432

35 **10... ♕c5**? 11. fe6 fe6 12. ♗f6 gf6 13. ♘a4 ♗h6 14. ♕h6 ♕d4 15. ♘b6 ♕c3 16. ♔d1 ♖a7 17. ♕g7!+—; **10... ♗e7** 11. fe6 fe6 12. ♗c4 d5 13. ed5 ♕c5 14. ♗b3 ♘d5 15. ♘d5 ed5 16. 0—0!+— Fridh—Steiner, Vesely 1967 — 4/577; **10... e5** 11. ♗f6 gf6 12. ♘d5±; **10... b5** 11. fe6 fe6 12. ♗e2 [12. e5? de5 13. ♗b5? ab5 14. ♘db5 ♕a5—+ Wade—O'Kelly, Dundee 1967 — 4/575] ♗e7 13. ♗f3 ♖a7 14. ♗e3±; 12. ♗d3!?

36 11. ♘c6?! bc6 12. fe6 ♗e6!

37 13. ♗f6 gf6 14. ♗e2 ♖g8! [14... ♕a5?! 15. 0—0 ♗e7 16. ♖f3 0—0 17. ♕h6 ♔h8 18. ♖h3 ♖f7 19. ♕g6 e5 20. ♕f7+— Hennings—Kavalek, Sinaia 1965] 15. 0—0 ♕c5 16. ♔h1 ♕g5=

38 13... ♘d7 14. ♗e2!? [14. ed6 ♕d6 15. ♗d3 ♕e5 16. ♔d1±; 15... ♖b8 16. ♖d1 ♕e5 17. ♘e4 ♗c5 18. ♗f4 ♗b4 19. c3 ♗c3 20. ♕c3 ♕f4 21. ♘d6±↑ Vitolinš—Peresipkin, SSSR 1972] d5 15. 0—0 ♗e7 16. ♗e3 ♗c5 17. ♔h1 ♗e3 18. ♕e3 ♕c5 19. ♕h3 ♘f8 20. ♘a4 ♕c2 21. ♗h5±→ Platonov—Kudišev, SSSR 1970

39 **14. ♖b3** ♕a5 15. ♘e4 ♕d2 16. ♔d2 de5 17. c4 h6 18. ♗h4 [Bergin—Zlotnik, SSSR 1964] ♗e7!∓; **14. ♘e4** de5 [14... ♕a2 15. ♖d1 de5 16. ♗e2! ♗b4 17. ♕b4! ♘b4 18. ♖d8 ♔f7 19. 0—0 ♔g6 20. h4!+—] 15. ♗e2 [15. ♖d1!? Geler] ♗b4 16. ♖b4 ♕b4 17. ♕b4 ♘b4 18. 0—0 ♘d5 19. ♘d6 ♔d7 20. ♘c4∞ Jurkov—Astašin, SSSR 1964

40 14... ed5? 15. ♖b3! ♕a2 16. ♕c3 c5 17. ed6 ♔d7 18. ♕c5 ♗d6 19. ♗b5!+— Nikitin—Hajkin, SSSR 1967 — 3/524

41 15. c4 de5!? [15... dc4 16. ♗c4 ♕c5 17. ♗e2 ♕e5 18. 0—0 ♗e7 19. ♗f4± Vogt—Espig, Colditz 1967 — 3/526] 16. cd5 ♗e7±

42 16. ♖f1!? ♗e7 17. ♖b3 ♗g5 18. ♕g5 ♕e7 19. ♕h5 g6 20. ♕e5±↑

43 **16... ♗d6**? 17. c4 ♕c5 18. ♔h1 d4 19. ♕d3!+— Hartston—Moe, Harrachov 1967 — 4/583; **16... ♖a7** 17. c4 d4 [17... ♕c5 18. ♔h1 d4 19. ♕c2 ♗e7 20. ♕a4 ♖d7 21. ♗d2 ♖f8 22. ♗h5 g6 23. ♗f3 ♖f3∞ Bednarski—Saharov, Varna 1968; 19. ♗h5!? g6 20. ♗d1±→ Petrušin—Dementjev, SSSR 1972 — 13/519] 18. ♗h5!? [18. ♗d1 ♗e7 19. ♖f3 ♕c5 20. ♗a4 ♔d8 21. ♖bf1 e4∓ Piotrowski—B. Pytel, corr. 1970 — 9/431] g6 19. ♗d1 ♗e7 20. ♖f3 ♕c5 21. ♗a4 ♔d8 22. ♖f7±

44 19. ♖f1 ♗b7 [19... ♖a7 20. cd5 ♖d7? 21. ♕c2 ♖f7 22. ♗h5 g6 23. ♗g6+— Đukić—Marjanović, Jugoslavija 1970 — 10/551; 20... ♖f7!?±; 19... ♗d4 20. ♕c2! ♕b2 21. ♕h7 ♕e2 22. ♕g8±↑ Sirotkin—Sorokin, SSSR 1967 — 4/580] 20. ♗d1 [20. ♗g4?! dc4 21. ♗e6? ♕d3 22. ♕e1 ♗e4 23. ♗g4 ♖b8—+ Fischer—Geler, Monte Carlo 1967 — 3/523; 21. ♕c2!?; 20. ♕c2 (Talj—Bogdanović, Budva 1967 — 4/581) g6 21. ♗g4 ♗e7 22. ♕f2!±] ♗e7 [20... ♖c8 21. ♕e2! ♗e7 22. ♕h5 g6 23. ♕h7+— Žuravljev—Gutman, SSSR 1967 — 4/579; 20... ♔d7 21. ♖f7 ♔c6 22. cd5 ed5 23. ♗b3 ♗d4 24. ♕c2 ♕c5 25. ♗d5 ♔d5 26. ♕b3+—] 21. ♗e7 ♔e7 [21... ♕e7 22. ♗a4 ♔d8 23. ♕a5 ♔c8 24. c5!±→] 22. ♕g5±→

45 15. ♗e2?! ♕d6! [15... h5?! 16. ♘e4 ♕e7 17. 0—0 f5 18. ♕c3!± Illi—van Herck,

Ybbs 1968 — 6/573] 16. ♗h5 ♔e7 17. ♕e2 ♕d4 18. ♘d1 a5∓ Petrašević—Marjanović, Jugoslavija 1973

46 **15... f5** 16. ♗e2! fe4 17. ♗h5 ♔e7 18. 0—0 ♕d6 19. ♖f7 ♔d8 20. ♖f8!+—; **15... ♕a4**?! 16. ♘f6 ♔f7 17. ♗d3 ♕h4 [17... ♔f6 18. 0—0 ♔e7 19. ♕g5 ♔e8 20. ♕e5 ♖g8 21. ♗h7±] 18. g3 ♗h6 [Kavalek—Barczay, Varna 1967 — 4/576] 19. ♕a5! ♕f6 20. ♖f1±

47 16... 0—0 17. ♖b3 ♕a4 18. c4 ♔h8 [18... ♖f7? 19. 0—0 f5 20. ♖g3 ♔h8 21. ♕c3+— Vitolinš—Gutman, SSSR 1967 — 3/525] 19. 0—0 ♖a7 20. ♕h6± Gipslis—Korčnoj, SSSR (ch) 1963

48 17. 0—0 f5 18. ♗f3 fe4 [18... ♗d7 19. ♖fd1 ♖d8 20. ♖b3 ♕a4 21. ♘d6+— Mrea—Sekely, Hungary 1973] 19. ♗e4 ♗d7 20. ♖f3!? [20. ♗g6? ♔d8 21. ♖b7 ♕d6 22. ♕e2 (Barlov—Sindik, Jugoslavija 1973 — 16/481) ♔c8∓; 20. ♖b7 0-0-0 21. ♖fb1∞̅ Ribli—Barczay, Budapest 1968] ♕a2 21. ♖d1∞̅

49 **18... ♖a7**? 19. ♖b8! ♔f7 [19... 0—0 20. 0—0 ♔g7 21. ♕e3!±] 20. 0—0 f5 21. ♖c8! ♖c8 22. ♕h6±→ Smejkal—Trapl, ČSSR (ch) 1964; **18... f5** 19. ♘d6 [19. 0—0 fe4 20. ♔h1 c5 21. ♕c2 ♕c6 22. ♖fb1 ♗d8 23. ♗f3∞ Lilloni—Butler, corr. 1972 — 14/501; 20. ♕c3 ♕a2∞ Kavalek—Fischer, Sousse (izt) 1967 — 4/573; 20. ♕d1 ♗d7?! 21. ♖b8! ♖b8 22. ♕a4± Nelson—Berg, USA 1968 — 6/570; 20... ♗c5 21. ♔h1 ♗d4 22. ♗h5 ♔d8 23. ♖f7 ♗d7∞] ♗d6 20. ♕d6 ♕a5 [20... ♕a2? (Schöneberg—Barczay, Berlin 1968 — 6/574) 21. ♕e5! ♕b3 22. ♕h8 ♔e7 23. ♕g7 ♔d8 24. ♔f2!±] 21. ♔f2 ♖a7!? [21... ♗d7? 22. ♖d1+— Glauser—Goetgeluck, Ybbs 1968 — 6/572; 21... ♔f7 22. c5 ♔f6 23. ♖e3 e4 24. ♖e4 fe4 25. ♕f4= Cejtlin—Šašin, SSSR 1971 — 11/396] 22. ♕c6 [22. ♖b8 ♔f7∓] ♔f7 1/2 : 1/2 Martin—Marjanović, Groningen 1973

50 **10... ♘d5** 11. ♘d5 ed5 12. ♖b3 ♕a2 [12... ♕a4 13. ♘b5!+—] 13. ♕c3 [13. ♖e3!?] ♘d7 14. ed6 ♗d6 15. ♘f5±→; **10... ♘fd7** 11. f5! ♘e5 [11... de5 12. fe6 ed4 13. ef7 ♔f7 14. ♗c4 ♔e8 15. ♕f4 ♕c3 16. ♔d1+— Keres; 11... ef5 12. e6!±↑] 12. fe6 fe6 13. ♗e2± Keres—Fuderer, Göteborg (izt) 1955

51 **11. ef6**? hg5 12. f5 gf6 13. fe6 fe6 14. ♗d3 ♘c6 15. ♘c6 bc6 16. ♗g6 ♔d8 17. ♘e4 d5!∓; **11. ♗h4** — B 96

52 **12. ed6** ♕d6 13. ♘e4 ♕d8 14. ♕c3 ♗e7 15. g4 ♖g8 16. ♗e2 h5 17. ♔f2 hg4∓ Koc—Bikov, SSSR 1962; **12. ♖b3** ♕a5 13. ed6 ♗d6 14. ♘db5 ♗e7 15. ♘d6 ♗d6 16. ♕d6 ♕d8!∓

53 12... ♘d7 13. ♖b3±

54 13. fe5 de5 14. ♘f6 ♔e7 15. ♘f5 ef5 16. ♘d5 ♔e8 17. ♘c7 ♔e7 18. ♘d5 1/2 : 1/2 Vooremaa—Šmit, SSSR 1961

55 13... ♕a2 14. ♘f6 ♔e7 15. fe5 de5 16. ♘f5 ♔f6 17. ♕d8 ♔g6 18. ♘e7 ♗e7 19. ♕e7 ♕a5 20. ♔e2±↑ Sporiš—Sorokin, corr. 1968 — 6/575; 16... ef5 17. ♘d5=

56 16... ♔f6? 17. ♕d8 ♔f5 18. ♗d3 e4 19. 0—0 ♔g6 20. ♕f6 ♔h7 21. ♖f4!±→» Gubat—Prieditis, corr. 1967 — 3/529

57 **19. ♘a8**?! ♕e4 20. ♔d1 ♗c5!∓→; **19. ♘d5**= Bradvarević—Buljovčić, Jugoslavija 1965

58 12. ♗e2 ♕a5 [12... ♕c5!? 13. ♘e4 ♕e5 14. ♗f3 ♘f6 15. ♘e2 ♘bd7 16. ♘f6 ♘f6∓ Vasjukov—Ščerbakov, SSSR 1955; 13. ♘a4 ♕e5 14. ♘e6 ♕e6 15. ♘b6 ♗c5! 16. ♘a8 0—0∓ Euwe] 13. ♘b3 [13. 0—0 ♗c5 14. ♔h1 ♗d4 15. ♕d4 ♘c6 16. ♕f2 0—0 17. ♘e4 ♕e5 ∓] ♕c7 14. 0—0 ♘e5 15. ♘e4 f5 16. ♗h5 g6 17. ♘f6 ♔f7!∓ Toluš

59 **12... ♘e5**? 13. ♘b5!+—; **12... ♕a4** 13. ♗b5! ab5 14. 0—0 ♗c5 15. ♘c5 ♘c5 16. ♘f5!+— Alexander—Walther, Dublin 1957; **12... ♕a2** 13. ♖b3 ♕a1 [13... ♘c6 14. ♘c6 bc6 15. ♕c3 ♕a4 16. ♗c4 ♘e5 17. 0—0± Ostrovjerhov—Košelj, corr. 1971 — 11/397] 14. ♔f2 ♕a4 [Talj—Toluš, SSSR 1956] 15. ♘e6! fe6 16. ♘d6 ♗d6 17. ♕d6 ♖f8 18. ♔g3±

60 **13. ♗f4** ♘c5 14. ♘d6 ♗d6 15. ed6 ♘e4 ∓; **13. ♖b3** ♕a4 14. ♗e3 ♘e5 15. ♗e2 ♘bc6 ∓; **13. ♗b5**!? ab5! [13... hg5? 14. ♖b3 ♕a2 15. ♕c3! ab5 16. ♕c8 ♔e7 17. 0—0!+—] 14. ♘b5 hg5 15. ♘a3 ♖a3 16. ♖b5 ♘c6 17. 0—0 ♗e7∞̅ Platonov—Minić, Soči 1968 — 5/480

61 14... ♘c6 15. ♘c6 bc6 16. ♕c3! [16. ♘d6? ♗d6 17. ed6 a5! 18. ♗e2 a4 19. ♖c3 ♕a1 20. ♗d1 a3—+ Boey—O'Kelly, Belgique 1957] ♕a4 17. ♗c4±↑

62 16. ♖e3?! ♘c6 17. ♘c6 ♕c6 18. ♘d6 ♗d6 19. ed6 ♕c5 20. ♗e7 ♘e5∓ Tringov

63 19. g3 ♕d8 20. ♕d6 ♘c5! 21. ♘c7 ♕c7 22. ♕c7 ♘ba6∓ Korčnoj—Toluš, SSSR (ch) 1958

64 **12... ♘c6** 13. ♘c6 bc6 14. ♘e4 ♕a4 15. ♕c3±; **12... h6** 13. ♗f4 ♘c6 14. ♘c6 bc6 15. ♘e4±; **12... ♘e5** 13. ♘e6! ♕a5 [13... fe6 14. ♕d8 ♔f7 15. 0—0 ♔g6 16. ♖f6!+—] 14. ♗d8 [14. ♖b6? ♕b6 15. ♘d5 ♘f3 16. gf3 ♕e6 17. ♔d1 ♕c6∓ Bahčevanski—Kadrev, Bulgaria 1957] ♘f3 15. gf3 ♕e5 16. ♔d1 [16. ♘e4!? fe6 17. ♗h4 ♘c6 18. 0—0 b5 19. ♗d3± Bednarski—Tringov, Kecskemet 1964] fe6 17. ♘d5 ♗d6 18. ♗g5±↑ Đorđević—Uzunov, corr. 1968 — 5/475; **12... ♕a5**!? 13. ♗e6 [13. ♘e6 fe6 14. ♗e6 ♕e5 15. ♕e3 ♕e3 16. ♗e3 ♘c6 17. ♘d5 ♗d6 18. 0—0 ♘f6∓ Mazzoni—Fischer, Monte Carlo 1967] fe6 14. ♘e6 ♘e5 15. ♗d8 ♘f3! 16. gf3 ♕e5 17. ♔d1 ♗e6 18. ♖e1 ♕f5∓ Šalamon—Murej, corr. 1970 — 9/432; 13. 0—0!? [Vittoni—Cillo, corr. 1972] ♘e5∞

65 13. ♖b3?! ♕c5 14. ♘d5 ♗g5 15. ♕g5 g6 16. ♖f1 [16. ♖e3 h6! 17. ♘f6 ♘f6 18. ♕f6 ♖f8∓] ed5 17. e6 ♕d4 18. ef7 ♔f8 19. ♖e3 ♔g7∓ Ortega—Ivkov, La Habana 1963

66 **13... fe6** 14. ♘e6 ♗g5 15. ♘c7! ♔d8 16. ♘e6 ♔e8 17. ♘g5±→; **13... ♗g5** 14. ♗f7! ♔f7 15. 0–0 ♔e8 16. ♕g5±→

67 **14. ♗f7** ♖f7 15. e6 ♖f8 16. ♘d5 ♘f6∓; **14. ♘d5** ♗g5! 15. ♕g5 h6 16. ♕d2± Schmidt–Lombardy 1963; 15... ♕a5!? Macukevič

68 **14... fe6**? 15. ♘e6 ♘c6 16. ♘d5! ♗c5 17. ♔h1 ♘ce5 18. ♘f8 ♗f8 19. ♘c7±→ Dückstein–Euwe 1958; **14... ♘e5**?! 15. ♘d5 ♘bc6 16. ♘c6 ♘c6 17. ♘e7 ♘e7 18. ♗f7 ♔h8 19. ♖b3±→ Volčok–Bahmatov, SSSR 1960; **14... ♘c6**!?

69 15... ♕c3? 16. ♘f5!+–

70 **16. ♕h4**? ♕c3 17. ♖f7 ♖f7 18. ♕d8 ♘f8 19. ♗f7 ♔f7 20. ♖f1 ♔g6 21. ♖f8 ♗d7! 22. ♘f3 ♕e3 23. ♔h1 ♕c1–+ Bilek–Fischer, Stockholm (izt) 1962; **16. ♕g3** ♕c5!△ fe6–+; **16. ♕d2** fe6 17. ♘e6 ♖f1 18. ♖f1 ♕e7 19. ♕d5 ♘b6!–+ Schmidt–Minić, Marianske Lazni 1962; **16. ♕e3** fe6 17. ♘e6 ♖f1 18. ♖f1 ♘c6 19. ♕g3 ♕e7 20. ♘c7 ♖b8∓ Volčok–Savon, SSSR 1962

71 **16... ♕c3** 17. ♖f7!+–; **16... ♘e5** 17. ♕e5 ♗e6 18. ♘e6 fe6 19. ♖b7!+–

72 **17... ♘f6** 18. ef6 ♗e6 19. fg7 ♖f1 20. ♖f1 ♕c3 21. ♕h6+–; **17... ♕e7** 18. ♘f8 ♘f8 19. ♘d5! ♕c5 20. ♔h1+–; **17... ♕c3** 18. ♘f8 ♕c5 19. ♔h1 ♘f6 [19... ♘f8 20. ♕f7 ♔h7 21. ♕f8 ♘d7 22. ♕f5 ♔h8 23. ♖bd1 +–] 20. ♖f6! gf6 21. ♘h7!±→

73 19. ♕f5!? ♘b6 20. ♕f8 ♕f8 21. ♖f8 ♔h7 22. ♘c7 ♖a7 23. e6±

74 13... ♗e7 14. ♗f7! ♔f7 15. 0–0 ♔g8 16. ♗e7 ♕e7 17. ♘d5 ♕c5 [17... ♕d8 18. e6 ♘f6 19. e7!+–] 18. ♘c7 ♕c7 19. ♘e6 ♕c6 20. ♕g5+–

75 15... ♗d6 16. ♘e4!±

76 17... ♘f6? 18. ♘g7 ♔f7 19. 0–0 ♔g7 [19... ♘bd7 20. ♘h5 1 : 0 Mikulčić–R. Ivkov, Jugoslavija 1968 — 5/476] 20. ♖f6 ♖d8 21. ♖bf1!+– Matanović–Barcza, Jugoslavija–Hungary 1957

77 19. 0–0 ♔g6 20. ♘f4 ♗f4 21. ♖f4 ♘c6 22. ♘a8 ♘d5 23. ♖f3 ♗g4= Darga

78 13. ♘e6 fe6 14. ♖b4 ♕b4 15. ♗e6 h6!? [15... ♘c6 16. 0–0 ♘de5? 17. ♘d5! ♕c5 18. ♔h1 ♕d6 19. ♘f6 gf6 20. ♕d6+– Smekal–Gutzler, corr. 1967 — 3/530; 16... ♖f8!?] 16. ♗f7! ♔f7 17. e6 ♔e8 18. ed7 ♘d7 19. ♕e2 ♔f7 20. 0–0 ♔g8 21. ♕e6=

79 14. ♗e6 0–0! [14... fe6? 15. ♘e6 ♕e5 16. ♕e3±] 15. ♗f7 ♖f7 16. e6 ♖f8 17. ♖b4 ♕b4 18. e7 ♖e8 19. ♘f5 ♘f6!∓ Kurajica–Tukmakov, Jugoslavija–SSSR 1965

80 **14... ♗f8** 15. ♘e6 fe6 16. ♗e6 ♘c6 17. ♘d5±; **14... ♗a3**!? 15. ♖a3 ♕a3 16. 0–0 0–0 17. ♗f6 gf6 18. ef6 ♖d8!=

81 16... ♘c6 17. ♖b7!

82 1/2 : 1/2 Martinov–Murej, SSSR 1968

83 14... ♘e5 15. ♖b4 ♕b4 16. ♘e6 ♕b6 17. ♗e3 ♘c4 18. ♗b6 ♘d2 19. ♘c7 ♔d7 [19... ♔e7 20. ♖d1=∞] 20. ♖f7 ♔c6 21. ♘a8 ♘d7 22. ♗f2 b5 23. ♖e7 ♘c4 24. ♗g3= Boleslavski

84 **15. a3** ♗c5 16. ♔h1 ♗d4 17. ♕d4 ♘c6 18. ♕f4 ♘ce5∓; **15. ♘e6** fe6 16. ♗e6 ♔h8 17. ♖f8 [17. ♖fb1!?] ♗f8 18. ♕f4 ♘c6 19. ♕f7 ♕c5 20. ♔h1 ♘f6!∓ Tringov–Fischer, La Habana 1965

85 15... gf6?! 16. ♕h6 ♕e5 17. ♘f5 ef5 18. ♘e4 ♖e8 [18... ♗d2 19. ♘d2 ♕d4 20. ♔h1 ♘e5 21. ♖g3± R. Byrne–Evans, USA (ch) 1965] 19. ♖h3 ♘f8 20. ♘f6 ♕f6 21. ♕f6 ♗e6 22. ♗e6± Mazzoni–Bobocov, Le Havre 1966 — 1/324

86 16... gf6 17. ♕h6±↑

87 18. ♕d3!?

88 19. ♘e4 ♕f8 20. ♘f3 b5 21. ♗b3 ♗b7 22. ♗e6? ♗e4∓ Švager–Prieditis, corr. 1968 — 5/479; 22. ♕h4!?△ ♘eg5

89 **19... b6**? 20. ♖h4 ♕f8 21. ♕e3 [21. ♔f1 ♖a7 22. ♘f3 ♘d7 23. ♘e4 ♗b7 24. ♖h7! +– Mazzoni–Lee, La Habana (ol) 1966; 21. ♘ce2 ♗b7? 22. ♘e6!+– Szekely–Toth, Hungary 1968 — 5/477; 21... ♗d7!?] ♖a7 22. ♘e4 ♖ad7 23. ♖h7 1 : 0 Tringov–Palmasson, La Habana (ol) 1966 — 2/463; **19... ♕f8** 20. ♖h4 b5 21. ♗d3 b4∞ Hartston–Mecking, Hastings 1966/67 — 3/528

90 20. ♖d4? ♕b6 21. ♘e2 ♘d7 22. c3 e5 0 : 1 Lukjanenko–Saharov, SSSR 1968 — 5/478

91 20... ♖d1 21. ♘d1 ♕f8 22. ♕g5 ♘d7∞

92 R. Byrne–Zuckerman, USA (ch) 1967 — 3/527

93 9... ♘bd7 10. ♗f6! [10. ♗d3 ♘c5 11. 0–0 ♗d7 12. ♘c5 ♕b6 13. ♕f2 ♕c5 14. ♕c5 dc5 15. e5= Petrušin–Doroškevič, SSSR 1973 — 16/487; 10. ♗e2!?] gf6 11. ♗e2 ♕a3 12. 0–0! [12. ♗h5? ♘c5! 13. f5 ♘b3 14. cb3 ♗g7 Velimirović–Bogdanović, Jugoslavija 1973 — 16/483] h5 13. ♔h1 ♗e7 14. ♖ad1 ♘c5 15. ♗f3 [15. f5 ♗d7 16. fe6 fe6± Kuzmin–Platonov, SSSR (ch) 1967 — 5/474] ♖a7? 16. ♘c5 dc5 17. f5 ♕b4 18. ♕e3± Andersson–Adamski, Raach 1969; 15... ♘b3±

94 **10. ♖b1** ♕a3 11. ♗f6 gf6 12. ♗d3 [12. ♗e2 h5 13. 0–0 ♗d7 14. ♔h1 ♖c8 15. ♖f3= Balašov–Ioffe, SSSR 1970 — 9/429; 14. ♖f3!? Kuprejčik–Muhin, SSSR 1970] ♗g7 13. 0–0 0–0 14. ♖f3 ♔h8 15. ♖h3 ♘e7 16. f5±↑ Matulović–Kavalek, Sousse (izt) 1967 — 4/574; 12... ♗d7!∞; **10. ♗f6** gf6 11. ♗e2 [11. ♘a4 ♕a3 12. ♘b6 ♖b8 13. ♘c4 ♕a4 14. 0-0-0?! d5! 15. ed5 ed5 16. ♕d5 ♗e6 17. ♕e4 ♘b4∓→《 Petrušin–Murej, SSSR 1974 — 17/525; 14. ♗e2 b5!? 15. ♘d6 ♗d6 16. ♕d6 ♕b4 17. ♕b4 ♘b4∞ Mrđa–Marjanović, Jugoslavija 1973] d5 [11... ♕a3 12. 0–0 ♗g7 13. ♖f3

0–0 14. f5 ♘e7 15. ♖af1 ♔h8 16. ♗d3 ♕b4 17. ♖h3±→» Rajković–Tukmakov, Harrachov 1967 — 4/582] 12. ♘a4 ♕a3 13. ♘b6 ♖b8 [13... d4?! 14. 0–0 ♖b8 15. ♘c4 ♕b4 16. ♕d1!± Kuprejčik–Peresipkin, SSSR 1973 — 15/462] 14. ed5 [14. ♘c8? ♖c8 15. ed5 ♗b4 16. c3 ♘a5!∓ Henao–Marjanović, Manila 1974 — 18/507] ♘a5!∞ Mesing–Marjanović, Jugoslavija 1974

95 10... d5 11. ♗f6 [11. ♖b1 ♕c3∓] gf6 12. ♘a4 [12. ♘d1 ♕a3 13. ed5 ♘b4!∞ Ivanović–Marjanović, Vrnjačka Banja 1973] ♕a3 13. ♘b6 d4 [13... ♘d4? 14. ♖b1!+–] 14. 0–0 ♖b8 15. ♘c4! [15. f5 ♕b4 16. ♕b4 ♗b4 17. ♘c8 ♖c8 18. fe6 fe6 19. ♖f6 ♔e7= Minić–Barczay, Varna 1967] ♕b4 16. ♕e2 [16. ♕f2 b5 17. ♘cd2 h5 18. ♘f3 ♗b7 19. ♔h1 ♖d8∓ Anselmo–Marjanović, Groningen 1974] b5 17. ♘cd2 ♗g7 18. ♖f3±↑ Boleslavski; 17... h5!?△ h4, ♗e7 Marjanović

96 11. ♗f6 gf6 12. 0–0 ♗d7 13. ♔h1 ♗e7 14. ♘d5!?∞ Kuprejčik–Muhin, SSSR 1972

97 13. e5 h6 14. ♗h4 de5 15. fe5 g5=

98 18. ♖b1 ♕b6 19. ♘d1± Zaharov–Dementjev, SSSR 1973 — 15/463

99 **10. ♗d3** ♗e7 [10... ♘bd7!? 11. 0–0 ♗e7 12. ♖ae1 h6 13. ♗h4 ♕b4 14. ♗f2 ♘c5 15. a3 ♕b6 16. ♕e2± Šmulenson–Sorokin, corr. 1973 — 16/486; 16. e5 ♘g4 (Guterman–Saharov, SSSR 1967 — 4/578) 17. ♘d5!?±→; 12... e5 13. ♕f2 h6!= Minić] 11. 0–0 h6! 12. ♗f6 [12. ♗h4 ♘e4! 13. ♘e4 ♗h4 14. f5! ef5 15. ♗b5 ab5 16. ♘d6 ♔d8 17. ♘c8 ♘c6∓ Spaski–Fischer (m) 1972 — 14/502] ♗f6 13. e5!? de5 14. ♘e4 ♘d7 15. f5! ef5 [15... ♕e7?! 16. fe6 ♕e6 17. ♗c4!± Muhin–Sorokin, SSSR 1973 — 16/485; 15... 0–0!?] 16. ♖f5∞ Talj–Saidy, SSSR 1973; **10. ♗e2** ♘c6 11. 0–0 ♗e7 12. ♖f3 ♗d7 13. ♖d1 ♖d8 14. ♖h3 ♕b4 15. a3 ♕a3 16. ♕e3 ♕b4 17. e5!± Kotkov–Fridštejn, SSSR 1956

100 **11... ♗d7** 12. 0–0 ♗c6 13. ♗h5 ♘d7 14. ♔h1 ♘c5 15. ♘d4 ♘e4 16. ♘e4 ♗e4 17. ♘e6+– Estrin–Široky, Olomouc 1972; **11... ♗g7** 12. 0–0 ♘c6 13. ♖f3!? [13. f5?! ♘e5= Velimirović–Minić, Jugoslavija 1965] ♗d7 14. f5 ♖c8 [14... h5!?] 15. ♖g3 ♖g8 16. ♖f1± Minić–Buljovčić, Jugoslavija 1966 — 2/462; **11... ♕b4** 12. 0–0 ♗e7 13. ♔h1 ♕b6 [Minić Quinteros, Ljubljana – Portorož 1973 — 15/464] 14. ♗h5!? ♘c6 15. f5 ♘e5 16. ♘d4 ♘c4 17. ♕f2 ♕b4 18. ♕g3±; **11... ♘c6** 12. 0–0 ♗d7 13. ♗h5 [13. ♘b1? ♕a4?! 14. c4 ♗e7 15. ♔h1 ♖c8 16. ♘c3 ♕a3 17. ♖ad1± Kuprejčik–Palatnik, SSSR 1974; 13... ♕b4 14. ♕e3 d5∞] ♗g7 14. ♖f3 0–0 [Talj–Platonov, Dubna 1973 — 16/484] 15. ♔h1!?±; 15. f5!?

101 13. ♘b1 ♕b4 [13... ♕b2 14. a3!+–; 13... ♕a4 14. c4! ♕b4 15. ♕e3 ♗g7 16. a3 ♕a4 17. ♕g3!± Talj–Zilberštejn, SSSR 1973 — 17/524; 15... ♘a5!?] 14. ♕e3 d5!? [14... f5? 15. ef5 d5 16. fe6 fe6 17. c3 ♕e7 18. ♘1d2 ♗d7 19. ♘f3 0-0-0 20. ♖ab1± Robatsch–Korčnoj 1971] 15. ed5 ♘e7 16. c4 ♘f5 17. ♕c3! [17. ♕f2? a5–+; 17. ♕d3?! ♕b6 18. ♔h1 h4 19. ♗g4 ♘e3∓] ♗d7 18. ♕b4 ♗b4 19. a3 ♗e7∓↑ Šamkovič

102 **14. ♘b1** ♕b2! [14... ♕b4 15. ♕e3 d5? 16. ed5 ♘e7 17. c4!± Spaski–Fischer (m) 1972 — 14/503; 15... ♘e7 16. ♘1d2± Gligorić] 15. ♘c3 [15. a4 d5! 16. ed5 ♘b4 17. de6 ♗e6 18. ♘a3 ♖d8 19. ♕c1 ♕c1 20. ♘c1 f5 21. ♗f3 b6∓↑; 15. ♕e3 ♘b4! 16. ♕b6 ♘c2 17. ♕b7 ♖d8 18. ♘1d2 ♘a1 19. ♖a1 ♗h6!∓; 16. c3 ♘c2 17. ♕d2 ♗a4 18. ♗c4 ♗h6! 19. g3 h4! 20. ♖c1 ♗b3∓; 15. a3 ♖c8 16. ♘c3 ♘b4!=] ♖c8?! 16. ♘a4 ♕a3 17. ♘b6±; 15... ♕a3!=; **14. ♖f3**!? ♖c8 15. ♖h3 h4 16. ♕e1 ♘b4 17. ♘d4!±

103 14... ♘a5 15. ♘d5! ed5 16. ed5 ♗e7 17. ♖fe1! ♘b3 18. ♗d3+–

104 **15... ♕b4**? 16. a3+–; **15... ♕b2** 16. ♘1d2 b5 17. a3±

105 17. ♘c3? ♕b4 18. ♖ab1 ♘c4 19. ♕d4 ♕b6! 20. ♕f6 ♖h6∓

106 18. ♕f6 ♖h6 19. ♕d4 ♖h7 20. f5± Talj–R. Byrne, Leningrad (izt) 1973 — 16/482

B 98 **1. e4 c5 2. ♘f3 d6 3. d4 cd4 4. ♘d4 ♘f6 5. ♘c3 a6 6. ♗g5 e6 7. f4 ♗e7**

	8	9	10	11	12	13	14	15	16	
1	♕e2[1] h6[2]	♗f6[3] ♗f6	0-0-0 ♘d7[4]	g3[5] ♕b6	♕d2 0–0	♗g2 ♘c5	♖he1 ♗d7	♔b1 ♖fd8		=

1. e4 c5 2. ♘f3 d6 3. d4 cd4 4. ♘d4 ♘f6 5. ♘c3 a6 6. ♗g5 e6 7. f4 ♗e7 8. ♕f3 h6[6] 9. ♗h4 g5 10. fg5 ♘fd7[7]

	11	12	13	14	15	16	17	18	19	
2	♘e6[8] fe6	♕h5 ♔f8	♗b5 ♔g7[9]	0–0 ♘e5[10]	♗g3! ♘g6	gh6 ♖h6	♖f7 ♔f7	♕h6 ab5[11]	♖f1 ♔e8[12]	±

	11	12	13	14	15	16	17	18	19	
3	...	...	...	♗g3![13]	♗e5	♖d1	g6!	0–0	♗c4	±
	...	...	♘e5	♖h7[14]	de5	♗d7[15]	♖g7	♔g8	♕c8[16]	
4	...	...	...	0–0[17]	g6	♖f7	♕h6	gf7	♖f1[20]	=
	...	...	♖h7!	♔g8	♖g7	♗h4[18]	♖f7[19]	♔f7	♗f6[21]	
5	♕h5	♗g3[23]	♗e2[24]	♗e5	♘f3[26]	♘d1	c3	0–0	♘f2	±
	♘e5[22]	♗g5	♕b6[25]	de5	♕b2[27]	♕b4[28]	♕e7	♖f8	♘d7[29]	

1. e4 c5 2. ♘f3 d6 3. d4 cd4 4. ♘d4 ♘f6 5. ♘c3 a6 6. ♗g5 e6 7. f4 ♗e7 8. ♕f3 ♕c7 9. 0-0-0

	9	10	11	12	13	14	15	16	17	
6	...	♗d3[30]	♘c6	e5[32]	♕h3	♗h6	♕h6	♘e4	♗e4	±
	0–0	♘c6	bc6[31]	de5	h6[33]	gh6	e4[34]	♘e4[35]	f5[36]	
7	...	e5!	fe5	♗e7	♕g3	♘e4!	♘d6	♘c6	♗d3	±
	♗d7	de5	♘d5[37]	♘e7	♘g6[38]	0–0[39]	♘c6	♗c6	♕a5[40]	
8	...	♘c6![41]	♕g3[43]	♗f6	e5!	fe5	♔b1	h4[45]	♗d3	±
	♘c6	♕c6[42]	h6[44]	♗f6	de5	♗g5	0–0	♗e7	♗d7[46]	

1. e4 c5 2. ♘f3 d6 3. d4 cd4 4. ♘d4 ♘f6 5. ♘c3 a6 6. ♗g5 e6 7. f4 ♗e7 8. ♕f3 ♕c7 9. 0-0-0 h6 10. ♗h4 ♘bd7[47]

	11	12	13	14	15	16	17	18	19	
9	♗e2[48]	f5[50]	♘b3[51]	♗f6[52]	h4	g4	♘d5	ed5	g5[53]	⩲
	♖b8[49]	e5	b5	♘f6	♗b7	b4	♗d5	a5		
10	...	♕g3	♖hf1[55]	fg5	♘f3	♗f3	♗g5	♗e7!	♗d6	±
	...	♖g8[54]	g5[56]	♘e5[57]	♘f3[58]	hg5	♘h7	♖g3	♕a5[59]	
11	...	fg5	♕f2[60]	♗g5	♕f4	♕f2	♔b1	h4	g4	=∞
	g5	♘e5	hg5[61]	♘fg4	♘f2[62]	♗g5	♗d7	♗e7	♕c5[63]	
12	♗d3	e5!?[65]	ef6	f5!?[68]	♘de2	♗e4[69]	♘d5	♗d5	♘c3	=∞
	g5[64]	gh4[66]	♘f6[67]	e5	♗d7	♗c6	♗d5	♖c8	♖b8[70]	
13	...	fg5	♕e2[71]	♘f3[73]	gf3	fg4[74]	♖hf1	e5![76]		⩲
	...	♘e5	♘fg4[72]	♘f3	hg5	gh4[75]	♖h6			
14	...	...	...	...	♗g3[77]	h3[78]	hg4![79]	e5	♖h3![80]	±
	...	...	...	hg5	♗d7	♘f3	♘h4	d5		
15	...	...	...	...	...	gf3	f4[81]	♗f4	♖df1[82]	⩲
	...	...	...	...	♘f3	♘e5	gf4	♗d7	♖h7[83]	

[1] 8. ♕d2?! ♘bd7 9. 0-0-0 0–0△ ♘c5 =; 8... h6!?

[2] 8... ♘bd7 9. 0-0-0 ♕c7 10. g4 [10. ♘f3 ♘b6 11. e5 de5 12. fe5 ♘fd5 13. ♘d5 ♗g5 14. ♘g5 ♘d5∞; 12. ♘e5 0–0 13. g3 h6 14. ♗h4 ♗d7 15. ♗g2?! ♗b5!∓ Kavalek–Ljubojević, Las Palmas 1974 — 17/521; 15. ♘d7∞ Šahović] b5 [10... h6 11. ♗h4 g5? 12. fg5 ♘h7 13. ♘f5! ef5 14. ♘d5+– Calvo–Kavalek, Las Palmas 1973 — 15/456; 11... ♘c5!?] 11. ♗g2 ♗b7 12. ♖he1±

[3] 9. ♗h4? ♘e4! 10. ♗e7 ♘c3 11. ♕g4 ♔e7! [11... ♕e7 12. ♕g7 ♕f8=] 12. bc3 ♔f8∓; 12... ♕a5∓

[4] 10... ♕a5!?

[5] **11. e5**? de5 12. ♘e6 [12. fe5 ♗e5 13. ♘e6 fe6 14. ♕h5 ♔e7 15. ♖d7 ♔d7!–+ Savon] fe6 13. ♕h5 ♔f8 14. fe5 ♗g5 15. ♔b1 ♕e8–+ O. Rodriguez–Savon, Cienfuegos 1973 — 15/465; **11. g4**?! g5!∓; **11. f5** ♘e5 12. g3 ♘c6 13. ♘c6 bc6 14. ♕c4 ♕c7∓ Sanguinetti–Kavalek, La Habana (ol) 1966 — 2/465

6 8... ♘bd7?! 9. ♗c4!± Keres–Benkö, Jugoslavija (ct) 1959; **8... ♗d7** 9. 0-0-0 ♘c6 10. e5! de5 11. ♘c6 bc6 12. fe5 ♘d5 13. ♗e7 ♕e7 14. ♘e4±

7 10... hg5 11. ♗g5 ♘bd7 12. ♗d3 ♘e5 13. ♕e2 ♘h5 14. ♗e7 ♕e7 15. 0-0-0 ♕g5 16. ♔b1 ♗d7 17. ♘f3± Balanel–Pilnik, Praha 1956

8 11. ♗g3 ♘e5 12. ♕f2 hg5 13. 0-0-0 ♕b6 14. ♕e1 [14. ♘e6!? ♕f2 15. ♘c7 ♔d7 16. ♗f2 ♔c7 17. ♘d5∞] ♘bc6 15. ♘c6 ♕c6 16. ♗e2 ♗d7 17. ♖f1 ♖h7!△ 0-0-0=

9 13... ab5? 14. ♖f1 ♗f6 15. gf6±→

10 14... ♕g8 15. g6 ♘f6 [15... ♗h4 16. ♗d7 ♘d7 17. ♕h4 ♕d8 18. ♖f7 ♔g6 19. ♖e7+– Vasiljčuk–Suetin, SSSR 1956] 16. ♗f6 ♗f6 17. ♖f6 ♔f6 18. e5 ♔g7 19. ♕h4±→

11 18... ♕h8 19. ♖f1 ♗f6 20. ♗e8! ♔e8 21. ♕g6 ♔e7 22. ♖f6+–

12 20. ♕g6 ♔d7 21. ♖f7 ♔c6 [21... ♘c6 22. ♘d5!+– Keres–Najdorf, Spaski–Pilnik, Göteborg (izt) 1955] 22. ♕h7 ♗g5 23. e5 d5 24. ♕d3±→《

13 14. 0–0 ♔g8!∓

14 **14... ♔g8** 15. ♗e5△ ♕g6+–; **14... ♗g5** 15. 0–0 [15. ♗e5+–] ♔e7 16. ♗e5 ♕b6 17. ♔h1 de5 18. ♕f7 ♔d6 19. ♖ad1+– Geler–Panno, Göteborg (izt) 1955

15 16... ♘d7 17. ♕g6 ♖f7 18. ♕h6 ♔g8 19. g6 ♖g7 20. ♗c4 ♕b6 21. ♖d3 ♘f8 [Minić–Velimirović, Jugoslavija 1963] 22. ♖g3!±→

16 **19... ♕e8** 20. ♘d5! ♗c5 21. ♔h1 ed5 22. ♗d5 ♗e6 23. ♗e6 ♕e6 24. ♖d8+–; **19... ♕c8** 20. ♗b3 ♗e8 [20... ♘c6 21. ♖f7 ±→] 21. ♘d5! ♗c5 [21... ♕c5 22. ♔h1 ♗g6 23. ♕e5!±] 22. ♔h1 ♖g6 23. ♖f6!±→ Blatny–Minić, Jugoslavija 1966 — 2/466

17 14. ♕g6 ♖f7 15. ♕h6 ♔g8 18. ♕g6 ♖g7 17. ♕e6 ♔h8 18. ♗d7 ♘d7 19. 0-0-0 ♘e5 20. ♕d5 ♗g4∓ Gligorić–Fischer, Portorož (izt) 1958

18 16... ♗g5 17. ♗d7 ♘d7 18. ♖af1±→

19 **17... ♗f6** 18. ♖g7 ♗g7 19. ♕h7 ♔f8 20. ♖f1 ♘f6 21. e5! de5 12. ♘e4±; **17... ♕f6**!?

20 19. ♕h7 ♔e8 20. ♕h5 ♔f8 [20... ♔e7 21. ♕h4 ♘f6 22. ♖f1 ♕b6 23. ♔h1 ab5 24. ♖f6⩱] 21. ♖f1 ♗f6 22. e5 de5 23. ♗d7 ♘d7 24. ♘e4∞ Boleslavski

21 20. ♕h7 ♔f8? 21. e5!? [21. ♗d7? ♘d7 22. e5 de5 23. ♘e4 ♕e7 24. ♕h8 ♔f7 25. g4? ♕f8–+ Matulović–Ćirić, Sarajevo 1966 — 1/327; 21. ♗e2!?] de5 22. ♘e4 ♕e7 23. ♕h8 ♔f7 24. ♘g5+– V. Nikolić–Ž. Nikolić, Jugoslavija 1972 — 14/504; 20... ♔e8!=

22 11... ♗g5 12. ♗g5 ♕g5 13. ♘e6!±

23 12. ♗f2 ♗g5 13. h4 ♗e7 [13... ♗f6? 14. 0-0-0 ♘bc6 15. ♗e2 ♘d4 16. ♗d4 ♗d7 17. ♖hf1 ♕e7 18. ♖f4!± Jansa–Milev, Bad Liebenstein 1963] 14. 0-0-0 ♘bc6 15. ♗e2 ♗d7 16. ♖hf1 ♕a5 17. ♘c6 ♗c6 18. ♗g3 ♖h7± Benkö–Minić, Beograd 1960

24 **13. ♖d1** ♕c7?! 14. ♗b5! ♘bc6 [14... ab5 15. ♘db5 ♕a5 16. ♘d6 ♔e7 17. ♗e5+–] 15. 0–0 ♖h7 16. ♔h1 ♗d7 17. ♗c6 bc6 18. ♘f3± Lakić–Halik, Jugoslavija 1968 — 6/578; 13... ♕a5!?∞; 13... ♕e7!?∞; **13. ♗e5** de5 14. ♘f3 ♘c6 15. ♘g5 ♕g5=; **13. h4** ♗f6 14. ♗e2 ♘bc6 15. ♘c6 bc6 16. 0-0-0±

25 13... ♘bc6?! 14. ♘c6 bc6 15. 0–0 ♕e7 16. ♗e5 de5 17. ♖f3±

26 15. ♘b3 ♗d7 16. ♖f1 ♖f8∞

27 15... ♖f8 16. ♘g5 ♕b2 17. ♘d1 ♕a1 18. ♘f7± Parma–Minić, Jugoslavija (ch) 1968 — 5/481

28 16... ♗d2 17. ♔d2 ♕a1 18. ♖f1 ♘c6 19. ♘c3 ♕b2 20. ♘g5±

29 20. ♘g4± Klundt–Kestler, BRD 1970 — 10/552

30 **10. g4** b5 11. ♗f6 ♗f6 12. g5 ♗d4 13. ♖d4 ♘c6 14. ♖d3 b4△ e5=; **10. ♗e2** ♘c6 11. f5?! ♘d4 12. ♖d4 b5 13. a3 ♗b7 14. ♕g3 ♖ac8 15. ♗f3 [Tatai–Kavalek, Manila 1973 — 16/490] e5 16. ♗f6 ♗f6 17. ♖d2 ♕b6∞; 11. ♕g3!± Tatai; **10. ♕g3**!? ♔h8 11. ♗d3 ♘bd7 12. ♔b1 ♘c5 13. e5±

31 11... ♕c6 12. ♕g3△ e5±

32 **12. ♖he1**?! e5! 13. f5 ♗b7 14. ♗c4 ♖ad8 14. g4 h6 16. ♗h4 d5!∓ Dückstein–Matanović, Moskva (ol) 1956; **12. ♕g3** h5 13. e5 de5 14. fe5 ♘g4 15. ♗e7 ♕e7 16. ♘e4± Unzicker–Fischer, Buenos Aires 1960

33 **13... g6**? 14. ♕h4+–; **13... ♖e8**?! 14 ♗f6 ♗f6 15. ♘e4! ♗e7 16. ♘g5 h6 17. ♘f7 ♔f7 18. ♕h5 ♔f8 19. fe5±→; **13... e4** 14. ♘e4 ♘e4 15. ♗e4 g6 16. ♗e7△ ♕c3!±

34 15... ♖d8 16. ♖hf1! [16. g4 e4 (16... ♖d3 17. ♖d3 ♘g4 18. ♖g1±) 17. ♘e4 ♘d5 18. ♖hf1 ♗f8 19. ♕g5 ♗g7∞ Sax–Stean, Groningen 1972 — 13/520] e4 17. ♗e4±→

35 16... ♘g4 17. ♘f6! ♘f6 18. ♖de1! ♖d8 19. ♖e3 ♖d3 20. ♖g3! ♖g3 21. hg3+–

36 **18. ♖d3** ♗f6 19. ♖g3 ♗g7 20. ♗c6 ♖a7 21. ♗a4∞ Paoli–Primavera, Reggio Emilia 1958; **18. ♕g6** ♔h8 19. ♖d3 ♕f4 20. ♔b1 fe4 21. ♕h5 ♔g7 22. ♖g3±→

37 11... ♕e5? 12. ♗f6 ♗f6 13. ♕b7 ♕f4 14. ♔b1 ♗d4 15. ♘e2!±

38 13... 0–0 14. ♗d3 ♘bc6 15. ♘f3 h6 16. ♖he1±

39 14... ♕e5 15. ♘d6 ♔f8 16. ♕a3! ♘e7 17. ♗c4 ♘bc6 18. ♖hf1±→ Waltes–Ways 1956

40 18. ♗g6 fg6 19. ♔b1 ♗d5 20. c4 ♗c6 21. h4±→ Velimirović—Šuvalić, Jugoslavija 1969 — 8/454

41 **10. ♘b3**?! ♗d7 11. ♗h4 0—0 12. g4 ♖fc8 13. ♗g3 b5 14. e5 ♘e8 15. ♕e2 b4∓↑ Rabar—Najdorf, Göteborg (izt) 1955; **10. ♗h4** ♗d7 11. g4 ♘d4 [11... h6 12. f5 ♘e5 13. ♕h3 b5 14. a3 0-0-0 15. ♗e2 ♔b8= Lutikov—Aronin, SSSR 1960] 12. ♖d4 ♗c6 13. ♗g2 ♖c8 14. ♖hd1 0—0 15. g5 ♘d7 16. ♖4d2 ♘c5 17. ♕e3 b5∓ Keres—Stahlberg, Göteborg (izt) 1955; **10. f5** ♗d7 11. ♔b1 b5 12. a3 ♖b8 13. ♕h3 0—0 14. fe6 fe6 15. ♘c6 ♕c6 16. e5! de5 17. ♗d3 g6 18. ♘e4 b4∞ Kotkov—Terentjev, SSSR 1960; 11. ♕h3!?; **10. ♗e2** ♗d7 [10... 0—0?! 11. ♕g3 ♗d7 12. e5!± Abakarov—Aronin, SSSR 1956] 11. ♖he1 ♘d4 12. ♖d4 ♗c6 13. ♖ed1 ♖c8 14. ♕e3 0—0 15. e5 ♘d5= Geler—Najdorf, Göteborg (izt) 1955

42 10... bc6? 11. e5! de5 12. fe5 ♘d5 13. ♗e7 ♘e7 14. ♘e4 [14. ♖e1 ♘d5 15. ♘e4 ♕e5 16. ♕a3 ♕f4 17. ♔b1 f5 18. g3 ♕b8 19. ♘d6 ±→ Havski—Aronson, SSSR 1961] 0—0 15. ♕c3 ♘d5 16. ♕d4± Keres—Stahlberg, Moskva 1956

43 **11. e5** ♕f3 12. gf3 de5 13. fe5 [Vasiljčuk —Aronson, SSSR 1957] ♘h5!?=; **11. ♗e2** ♗d7 [11... ♖b8 12. ♕d3 ♕c7 13. ♖hf1 ♘d7 14. ♗e7 ♔e7 15. ♕g3 ♔f8 16. ♕h4± Vasjukov —Bordell, Uppsala 1956] 12. ♕d3 0-0-0 13. ♗f3 [J. Szabo—Balanel, Romania (ch) 1956] ♕c5!? 14. ♖he1±

44 **11... ♘e4**? 12. ♘e4 ♕e4 13. ♗e7 ♔e7 14. ♕g5±↑; **11... ♘h5** 12. ♕h4 ♗g5 13. ♕g5 g6 14. ♗e2±

45 16. ♗d3!?±

46 18. ♕g4 ♖fd8 19. ♖h3 ♗e8 20. ♖f1± Bagirov—Majzel, SSSR 1961

47 10... ♘c6 11. ♘c6△ e5±

48 **11. g4** g5! 12. fg5 ♘e5 13. ♕g3 [13. ♕g2 ♘fg4∓ Hörberg—Johansson, Stockholm 1960] ♘fg4 14. gh6 ♗h4 15. ♕h4 ♕e7! 16. ♕g3 [16. ♕e7 ♔e7∓⊥] ♕g5! [16... ♗d7?! 17. ♗e2 ♖h6 18. h4! 0-0-0? 19. ♗g4 ♖g6 20. ♘f5!± Malachi—DeFotis, Dresden 1969 — 8/456; 18... ♘f6=] 17. ♔b1 ♖h6!∓ Izvozčikov—Buslajev, SSSR 1959; 13. ♕e2!?; **11. ♗g3** h5 [11... 0—0 12. ♗e2 b5 13. e5 ♗b7 14. ef6!±; 11... b5 12. e5 ♗b7 13. ♕e2 ♘d5 14. ♘e4±; 12. a3 ♗b7 13. ♗d3 0—0 14. ♔b1 ♘c5 15. ♕e2 ♘d3 16. cd3 ♖ac8 17. ♖c1± Matulović—Jansa, Oberhausen 1961] 12. h3 [12. e5 de5 13. fe5 ♘g4 14. ♘f5 ef5 15. e6 ♘de5∓; 12. ♗h4!?; 12. a3!?] h4 13. ♗h2 b5 14. e5 ♗b7 15. ♕e2 [15. ♕f2 de5 16. fe5 ♘e5; 15. ♕e3 de5 16. fe5 ♘d5 17. ♘d5 ♗d5 18. ♘f5 ♖c8∞] de5 16. fe5 ♘d5= Soltis—DeFotis, Chicago 1973

49 **11... ♘f8** 12. e5! de5 13. fe5 ♕e5 14 ♘c6 ♕c7 15. ♘e7 ♕e7 16. ♘e4 ♘8h7 17. ♘d6± Minić—Gligorić, Jugoslavija 1964; **11... ♖g8** 12. ♗g3 b5 13. e5 ♗b7 14. ♕f1! [14. ef6 ♗f3 15. ♗f3 ♗f6 16. ♗a8 ♗d4 17. ♖d4 ♕a7 —+] de5 15. fe5 ♘d5 [15... ♘e5 16. ♗b5 ab5 17. ♕b5±] 16. ♘e6!? [16. ♘d5 ♗d5 17. ♗f3=] fe6 17. ♘d5 ♗d5 18. ♖d5 ♖c8 19. ♖d2? ♗b4∓ Matulović—Ljubojević, Jugoslavija (ch) 1975; 19. ♗d3±→

50 **12. e5** de5 13. fe5 ♘e5 14. ♗g3 0—0 15. ♕e3 ♘fd7 16. ♘f3 f6 17. ♔b1 b5∓↑; **12. ♗g3** b5 13. e5 ♗b7 14. ♕f2 de5 15. fe5 ♘e4 16. ♘e4 ♗e4= **12. ♖he1**!? Hort

51 13. ♘e6?! fe6 14. fe6 ♘b6 15. ♗f6 ♗f6! [15... 0—0? 16. ♗e7! ♖f3 17. ♗d6 ♖c3 18. ♗c7!± Solovjev—Gratvol, SSSR 1968 — 5/482] 16. ♕h5 ♔d8 17. ♖d6 [17. ♗g4 ♖e8∓] ♕d6 18. ♖d1 ♕d1 19. ♗d1 ♗e6∓

52 14. ♔b1?! ♗b7 15. a3 ♗a8 16. ♗f6 ♘f6 17. ♕d3 0—0∓ Jansa—Smejkal, Luhačovice 1969 — 7/436

53 Feldman—Buhman, SSSR 1971 — 11/398

54 **12... g5** 13. fg5 ♖g8 14. ♘e6! fe6 15. gf6! ♖g3 16. ♗h5+—; 13... hg5!?; **12... 0—0** 13. ♗f3 ♘b6 [13... b5? 14. e5 de5 15. fe5 g5 16. ♘c6 ♘e5 17. ♘e7+— Haag—Bednarski, Zinnowitz 1965] 14. ♖he1 ♘c4 [14... ♘h7!?] 15. e5 de5 16. fe5 ♘h7 17. ♗e7± Vasjukov — Najdorf, Wijk aan Zee 1973 — 15/466; 13. ♘d5!?± Vasjukov; **12... b5** 13. f5! [13. ♕g7 ♖h7! 14. ♘e6 fe6 15. ♕g6 ♖f7 16. e5 de5 17. ♖d7 ♕d7 18. ♗f6 ♗f6 19. ♖d1 ♕e7 20. ♗h5 ♗b7 21. ♕g8 ♕f8 22. ♗f7 ♔e7 ∓; 14. ♕g3∞ 13. ♗f6!?] e5 14. ♕g7! ♖g8 15. ♘d5 ♕d8 16. ♗f6 ♖g7 17. ♗e7 ♕e7 18. ♘e7 ed4 19. ♘c8 ♖c8 20. g3± Rubinetti—Wirthensohn, Skopje (ol) 1972 — 14/506

55 13. ♖he1 g5 14. fg5 ♘e5 15. ♘f3 ♘h5 16. ♕f2 ♘g4 [16... hg5 17. ♘e5+—] 17. ♕d4 hg5 18. ♗g5 ♗g5 19. ♘g5 ♖g5 20. ♕h8±↑ Tarjan—Browne, USA (ch) 1973 — 16/488; 15... ♘h7!?

56 **13... b5** 14. ♘e6! [14. f5!? e5 15. ♘e6→] fe6 15. ♕g6 ♔d8 [15... ♔f8 16. e5! de5 17. f5! e4 18. ♗f6 gf6 19. ♕h6 ♖g7 20. fe6+—; 18... ♘f6 19. ♗h5+—] 16. e5 de5 [16... ♘e8 17. ♕e6+—] 17. f5! ef5 18. ♗f6 ♗f6 19. ♘d5 ♕c6 20. ♖f5 ♖f8 21. ♗g4!+— Lombardy—Quinteros, Manila 1973 — 17/526; **13... ♘c5** 14. ♗f6 ♗f6 15. f5 ♗e5 16. ♕h3 b5 17. fe6 ♘e6 18. ♘d5 ♕d8 [Kengis—Zajčik, SSSR 1974 — 18/509] 19. ♘f5!?±

57 **14... b5** 15. ♘e6 fe6 16. gf6! ♖g3 17. ♗h5+—; **14... ♕a5** 15. ♘e6! fe6 16. gf6! ♖g3 17. ♖d5 ♕d5 18. ♘d5 ♘f6 19. ♘f6 ♗f6 20. ♗g3± N. Weinstein—DeFotis, Chicago 1973 — 17/527

58 **15... ♘h7?** 16. ♘e5 de5 17. ♗h5+−; **15... ♘h5** 16. ♕f2 ♘g4 17. ♕d4 hg5 18. ♗g5!± **15... b5** 16. ♘e5! b4 [16... de5 17. gf6 ♖g3 18. fe7 ♖g5 19. ♗h5! ♕c7 20. ♖f7 ♕f7 21. ♗f7 ♔f7 22. ♗g5 hg5 23. ♖d8+−] 17. ♘f7 bc3 18. gf6+− Grefe—Browne, USA (ch) 1973 — 16/492

59 18. ♗g3±

60 **13. ♕g3** ♖g8 14. ♘db5? ab5 15. ♘b5 ♕a5 16. gf6 ♖g3 17. fe7 ♖g5! 0 : 1 Juarez—Bobocov, La Habana (ol) 1966; **13. ♕e3** ♘fg4 14. ♕d2 hg5 15. ♗g5 ♘f2 16. ♘db5!± Pietzsch—Bobocov, Leipzig 1965; 13... ♘h7!∓

61 13... ♘fg4 14. ♗g4! ♘g4 15. ♕d2 ♖g8 [15... hg5 16. ♗g5 ♖h2 17. ♖h2 ♘h2 18. ♗e7 ♕e7 19. ♕f4 e5 20. ♕h2 ed4 21. ♕h8+−] 16. ♘f3 ♕d8 17. ♗g3 hg5 18. ♗d6±

62 15... ♗g5 16. ♕g5 ♘f2? 17. ♘db5!±

63 20. ♕g3 b5=∞

64 **11... b5** 12. e5 [12. a3 ♗b7 13. ♗f2 ♖c8 14. g4? ♘c5 15. h4 d5 16. e5 ♘fe4∓ Klavin—Buslaev, SSSR 1959; 12. ♗f6 gf6 13. e5 ♗b7 14. ♕h5 ♘c5 (Paoli—Unzicker, Schweiz 1958) 15. f5±] ♗b7 13. ♘e6 fe6 14. ♗g6 ♔f8 15. ef6±→⊞ Gligorić—Bobocov, Hastings 1959/60; Unger—Bengston, corr. 1967 — 3/533; **11... ♘c5** 12. e5! de5 13. fe5 ♘d3 14. ♖d3 ♕e5 15. ♘c6!±

65 12. ♗g3 gf4 13. ♗f4 e5 14. ♘f5 ef4 15. ♘e7 ♔e7 16. ♕f4 ♕c5 17. e5! de5 18. ♕h4 ♔f8 19. ♖hf1±→ Jimenez—Bobocov, La Habana 1963; 13... ♘e5=

66 12... de5 13. ♘e6 ♕b6 [13... fe6 14. ♗g6 ♔f8 15. fg5 hg5 16. ♗g5 ♔g7 17. ♕g3! +−; 14... ♔d8 15. fg5 hg5 16. ♗g5 ♖f8 17. ♖hf1±↑] 14. ♘g7 ♔f8 15. fg5 hg5 16. ♗f2±↑ Wagman—Tatai, Reggio Emilia 1966 — 1/329

67 13... ♗f6!?

68 14. ♖he1 ♗d7 15. ♕f2 0-0-0 [15... ♕b6!?] 16. ♘f5 ♗c6 17. ♕a7 ♖he8!∞ Westerinen—Evans, Siegen (ol) 1970 — 10/554

69 16. ♘e4 ♗c6 17. ♘f6 ♗f6 18. ♗e4△ ♘c3=∞

70 Caturla—Goh, Penang 1974 — 18/515

71 13. ♕f2 ♘fg4 14. ♕e1 hg5 15. ♗g3 ♗d7 16. h3 ♘f6 17. ♖f1 ♘h5 18. ♗h2= Matulović—Bednarski, Bucuresti 1966 — 1/330

72 13... ♘h7 14. ♘f3!? [14. ♖hf1 ♘g5? 15. ♗g3 ♗d7 16. ♘f3! ♘gf3 17. gf3 0-0-0 18. f4 ♘c6 19. ♕e1!±↑《 I. Zajcev—Sax, Varna 1972 — 13/521; 14... hg5 15. ♗g3 ♘f8 16. ♕f2±] hg5 15. ♗f2 ♘f8 [15... ♗d7!?] 16. ♗e3 ♖g8 17. ♘e5 de5 18. ♕f2!± Hort—Bobocov, Wijk aan Zee 1970 — 10/553

73 **14. ♕d2** ♘g6 15. g3 ♕c5∓; **14. ♗g3** hg5 15. ♖hf1 [15. ♘f3 ♗d7 16. h3 ♘f3 17. ♕f3 ♘e5∓] ♗d7 16. ♘f3 b5! [Guljko—Savon, SSSR 1973 — 16/496] 17. ♘e5!?=; **14. h3** hg5 15. ♗g3 ♘f6 16. ♖hf1 [16. ♔b1 ♗d7 17. ♗f2 0-0-0 18. ♘b3 (Szabo—Browne, Amsterdam 1972 — 13/524) ♗c6!?=] ♗d7 17. ♔b1 0-0-0 18. ♘f3 ♘h5 19. ♗h2 ♗f6! 20. ♕e3 ♖dg8= Ćetković—Minić, Priština 1973 — 16/489

74 **16. ♗e1** ♘e5 17. ♗d2 ♗d7 18. ♖dg1 f6 19. h4 0-0-0 20. hg5 ♖h1 21. ♖h1 fg5 22. f4 gf4 23. ♗f4 ♗f6= Sigurjonsson—Szabo, Reykjavik 1968 — 5/483; **16. ♗g3** — 14... hg5

75 16... ♖h4 17. ♖hf1 ♖h6 [17... ♗d7 18. ♕f3 f6 19. e5!±] 18. e5!? [18. ♕e3 ♗d7 19. ♖d2 f6= Damjanović—Browne, San Juan 1969 — 8/457; 18. ♖f3 ♗d7 19. e5! de5 20. ♕f1 f6 21. ♖h3 ♖h3 22. ♗g6 ♔d8 23. ♕h3 ♔c8 24. ♕h7±↑ Ivanović—Ostojić, Vrnjačka Banja 1973 — 15/467] de5 19. ♕f3 ♖f6 20. ♕h3±↑ Smejkal—Kavalek, ČSSR (ch) 1963

76 18. e5!△ ♘e4±

77 15. ♗g5?! ♗g5 16. ♘g5 ♕c5 17. ♘h3 [17. ♘f3 ♘f2 18. ♘a4 ♕a7∓] ♗d7 18. ♕d2 [18. ♔b1 ♗c6 19. ♖d2 0-0-0 20. ♘d1 ♖dg8 21. a3 ♔b8 22. ♔a1 ♔a7∓ Pokojowczyk—Pytel, Polska 1972 — 14/505] 0-0-0 19. ♗e2 ♘e3∓ Litvinov—Židkov, SSSR 1973 — 16/491

78 16. ♖hf1 ♘g6! 17. ♔b1 ♘4e5 18. ♘e5 de5 19. ♕f3 ♖h7 20. ♗f2 ♘h4 21. ♕h3 [Damjanović—Minić, Jugoslavija 1974 — 18/518] ♖h8!? 22. ♗e3 f6∓ Minić

79 17. gf3 ♘e5 18. h4? gh4 19. f4 ♘d3 20. ♖d3 0-0-0 21. ♗f2 ♗c6 22. ♗d4 e5∓ Damjanović—Lakić, Banja Luka 1974 — 18/520

80 Ljubojević—Bukić, Jugoslavija (ch) 1975

81 **17. h4**!? gh4 18. f4 ♘g6 19. ♗h2 ♗d7 20. e5=∞ Janošević—Minić, Vinkovci 1974 — 18/513; **17. ♕f2** ♗d7 18. h4 gh4 [18... 0-0-0!? 19. hg5 ♗g5 20. f4 ♘d3 21. cd3 ♗f6=] 19. ♗h4 ♗h4 20. ♖h4 0-0-0=

82 **19. ♔b1** 0-0-0 20. ♕f2 ♖dg8 21. h4 ♗c6!= Evans—Portisch, San Antonio 1972 — 14/511; **19. h4** 0-0-0 [19... ♗h4? 20. ♕f2? ♗f2 21. ♖h8 ♔e7 22. ♖a8 ♕c5 23. ♔b1 ♗e3 24. ♗g3 ♗g5 25. ♗e2 ♕e3∓ Robatsch—Gheorghiu, Palma de Mallorca 1972; 20. ♗e5! de5 21. ♕g4 ♕d8 22. ♖dg1+−] 20. h5 ♖dg8 21. ♔b1 ♗c6 22. ♖h3 ♗g5 23. ♗h2 ♗h6= Westerinen—Browne, Hastings 1972/73 — 15/468

83 20. h4 0-0-0 21. h5± Minić

B 99

1. e4 c5 2. ♘f3 d6 3. d4 cd4 4. ♘d4 ♘f6 5. ♘c3 a6 6. ♗g5 e6 7. f4 ♗e7 8. ♕f3 ♕c7 9. 0-0-0 ♘bd7

	10	11	12	13	14	15	16	17	18	
1	♔b1[1] b5	♗d3[2] b4	♘ce2 ♗b7	♖he1 h6!	♗f6[3] ♗f6	♕e3 ♕c5	♕g1 g5	♘b3 ♕g1	♖g1 ♗d8[4]	∓
2	♕g3 h6[5]	♗h4 g5[6]	fg5 ♘h5![7]	♕e3[8] ♕c5	♔b1 hg5	♗f2 ♘e5	♕d2 ♕c7	♘f3 ♘f3	gf3 ♗d7[9]	=
3	♗e2 b5![10]	♗f6 ♘f6[11]	e5 ♗b7	ef6[12] ♗f3	♗f3 ♗f6[13]	♗a8 ♗d4[14]	♖d4 d5	♗d5! ed5	♖e1![15] ♔f8[16]	=
4	♗d3 b5	♖he1[17] ♗b7	♘d5 ed5[18]	♘f5[19] h6[20]	ed5[21] hg5	♖e7 ♔f8	fg5 ♘d5	♕e2[22]		∞
5	. . . . . .	. . . . . .	♕g3 0-0-0[23]	♗b5![24] ab5	♘db5 ♕b6	e5 d5[25]	f5![26] ♘h5[27]	♕h4 ♗g5	♕g5[28]	±
6	. . . h6	♕h3 ♘b6[29]	♖he1[30] e5	♘f5 ♗f5	ef5 0-0-0!	♗h4[31] ef4	♗f2 ♖he8[32]	♗b6 ♕b6	♗c4 d5![33]	=
7	g4 b5[34]	♗g2[35] ♗b7	♖he1 b4![36]	♘d5 ed5	ed5 ♔f8	♘f5 ♖e8[37]	♕e3 ♗d8	♕d4 ♗c8[38]		∓
8	. . . . . .	♗f6 gf6	f5![39] ♘e5[40]	♕h3 0—0[41]	♕h6![42] ♔h8[43]	g5![44] ♖g8[45]	g6 fg6	fe6[46] ♗b7	♘d5 ♗d5[47]	±
9	. . . . . .	. . . ♘f6	a3 ♖b8	f5 0—0[48]	g5 ♘e8[49]	♖g1 b4	ab4 ♖b4	♖g3 ♕c5	♘b3 ♕e5[50]	=

1. e4 c5 2. ♘f3 d6 3. d4 cd4 4. ♘d4 ♘f6 5. ♘c3 a6 6. ♗g5 e6 7. f4 ♗e7 8. ♕f3 ♕c7 9. 0-0-0 ♘bd7 10. g4 b5 11. ♗f6 ♘f6 12. g5 ♘d7

	13	14	15	16	17	18	19	20	21	
10	f5[51] ♘e5	♕g3 b4[52]	♘ce2 ♗d7[53]	♘f4 ♖c8	♖d2 ♘c4	fe6! fe6	♘fe6 ♗e6	♘e6 ♕a5	♗c4 ♖c4[54]	±
11	. . . ♗g5	♔b1 ♘e5[55]	♕h5 ♕d8[56]	♖g1[57] ♗f6	fe6 0—0[58]	♗h3 g6	♕e2 ♔h8	♘d5![59]		⩲
12	. . . ♘c5	f6[60] gf6[61]	gf6 ♗f8	♗h3[62] b4	♘d5 ed5	ed5 ♗h3	♖he1[63] ♔d8	♕h3[64] ♕d7	♘e6 fe6[65]	=∞
13	. . . . . .	. . . . . .	. . . . . .	♕h5! ♗d7[66]	♗h3[67] b4![68]	♘ce2![69] 0-0-0	♕f7[70] ♗h6	♔b1 ♖df8	♕h5 ♖f6[71]	=
14	a3 ♗b7[72]	♗h3[73] 0-0-0[74]	f5[75] ♗g5[76]	♔b1 e5	♘db5 ab5	♘b5 ♕c5[77]	♘d6 ♔b8	♕b3[78] ♕b6	♕b6 ♘b6[79]	⩲
15	. . . ♖b8	♗h3[80] ♘c5[81]	♖hg1[82] b4	ab4 ♖b4	f5 ♕b6[83]	fe6[84] fe6	♘e6! ♗e6[85]	♗e6 ♘e6	♘d5 ♕a5[86]	=
16	. . . . . .	h4 b4	ab4 ♖b4	♗h3[87] ♘c5[88]	f5[89] ♕b7[90]	♖hf1[91] 0—0[92]	f6 ♗d8	fg7 ♔g7	♕h5! ♔g8[93]	±
17	. . . . . .	. . . . . .	. . . . . .	. . . ♕b6	♘f5![94] ♖b2[95]	♘g7 ♔f8	♘e6! fe6	♗e6 ♔e8![96]	e5![97] de5[98]	∞

	13	14	15	16	17	18	19	20	21	
18	...	...	...	...	♘e6[99]	♗e6	♘d5	♗d7	♘e7	=
	...	...	...	0–0	fe6	♔h8	♕c4!	♗d7	♗a4[100]	
19	...	...	...	...	♘b3[101]	h5	♘c5	g6[104]	gh7	∞
	...	...	...	♕c5	♕b6[102]	♘c5	♕c5[103]	0-0![105]	♔h8[106]	

¹ **10. ♖g1**?! b5! 11. g4 [11. e5?! ♗b7∓] b4 12. ♘ce2 ♗b7 13. ♘g3 ♘c5 14. ♗d3 ♖c8 ∓↑; **10. f5**?! e5 11. ♘de2 [11. ♘b3 b5∓] b5 12. ♘g3 b4? 13. ♗f6 ♘f6 14. ♘d5 ♘d5 15. ed5 0–0 16. ♘e4± Benkö–Olafsson, Jugoslavija (ct) 1959; 12... ♗b7!?= **10. ♕h3** b5 11. a3 ♗b7 12. ♗d3 ♘c5? 13. ♖he1 ♘d3 14. ♖d3 ♖c8 [14... 0-0-0? 15. ♘cb5!+–] 15. ♔b1 ♕c5 16. e5!± Bivšev–Ščerbakov, SSSR 1954; 12... 0-0-0!?=

² 11. a3 ♖b8 12. f5 e5 13. ♘b3 ♗b7 14. ♗d3 ♘b6∓ Sergijevski–Aronin, SSSR 1959

³ 14. ♗h4 g5!?

⁴ 19. g3 ♔e7 20. c3 a5 21. cb4 ab4 22. ♗c2 ♗b6 23. ♖ge1 ♖hg8!∓ Troianescu–Fischer, Netanya 1968 — 7/434

⁵ **10... b5**?! 11. ♗b5! ab5 12. ♘db5 ♕b8 13. e5! de5 14. fe5 ♘e5 15. ♖he1 ♘c4 16. ♕c7!+– Vitolinš–Anetbajev, SSSR 1975; **10... 0—0** 11. ♗d3 b5 [Konstantinov–Fridštejn, SSSR 1953] 12. ♖he1!± **10... ♘c5** 11. ♖e1 h6 12. ♗h4 0–0 13. e5± Keres–Aronin, SSSR 1957

⁶ 11... ♖g8?! 12. ♗f6! ♗f6 13. f5 ♘e5 14. ♕h3 ♕e7 15. fe6 fe6 [15... ♗e6 16. ♘f5±] 16. ♘a4± Hase–Szmetan, Argentina 1974 — 17/528

⁷ 12... ♖g8 13. ♗e2 [13. ♕e1 hg5! 14. ♗g3 ♘e5 15. ♘f3 ♗d7 16. ♗e5 de5 17. ♕g3 ♗c6?! 18. ♗d3 ♘d7 19. h4!± Mnacakanjan–Polugajevski, SSSR 1967 — 4/586; 17... 0-0-0! 18. ♕e5 ♘g4=] ♘e5 14. ♘f3! [14. g6 ♘g6 15. ♖hf1 ♘h4 16. ♕h4 ♖g6 17. ♗d3 ♘g4 18. ♕h5 ♘e5 19. ♘f3 ♕c5 20. ♘e5 ♕e5 21. ♕e5 de5∓⊥ Talj–Fischer, Zürich 1959] hg5 [14... ♘f3 15. ♕f3 hg5 16. ♗g3 e5 17. ♖hf1 ♗g4 18. ♕f6! ♗f6 19. ♘d5 ♕a5 20. ♘f6 ♔f8 21. ♗g4 ♖g6 22. ♔b1±; 15. ♗f3 ♘h7 16. g6 ♖g6 17. ♗e7 ♖g3 18. ♗d6± Bronštejn] 15. ♘g5 ♘g6 16. ♖hf1 ♘h4 [16... ♕a5? 17. ♘f7! ♔f7 18. ♗f6 ♗f6 19. ♖d5!+– Kuprejčik–K. Grigorjan, SSSR (ch) 1974 — 18/514] 17. ♖f6 ♗f6? 18. ♘e6! ♖g3 19. ♘c7±; 17... ♕c5!=; 17. e5!±↑ A. Geler

⁸ 13. ♕e1 hg5 14. ♗f2 ♘e5 15. ♘b3 ♗d7 16. ♗d4= Rubel–Aronson, SSSR 1958

⁹ 19. ♖g1 0-0-0 20. ♗e3 f6= Kuprejčik–Beljavski, SSSR (ch) 1974

¹⁰ **10... h6**?! 11. ♗h4 b5 12. e5! ♗b7 13. ef6 ♗f3 14. ♗f3 d5 15. ♘e6±→; **10... ♖b8** 11. g4 b5 12. ♗f6 ♘f6 13. g5 ♘d7 14. ♗d3 [14. f5±] b4 15. ♘ce2 ♘c5 16. ♖hg1 g6 17. f5 [17. h4!?] e5 18. ♘b3± Mecking–Najdorf, Mar del Plata 1971 — 11/399; 11. ♕g3!? Boleslavski

¹¹ **11... gf6** 12. ♕h5! ♘c5 13. a3 [13. ♗f3 ♗b7 14. f5±] ♖b8 14. f5 e5 15. ♘d5 ♕b7 16. ♘e6!?± Sarapu–Ibrahimoglu, Siegen (ol) 1970 — 10/555; **11... ♗f6**?! 12. ♗b5! ab5 13. ♘db5 ♕a5 14. ♘d6±

¹² 13. ♕g3 de5 14. fe5 ♘d7!? [14... ♘e4? 15. ♘e4 ♗e4 16. ♗f3 ♗f3 17. ♕g7 ♗g5 18. ♔b1 0-0-0 19. ♘f3 ♖dg8∓; 15. ♘e6! fe6 16. ♗h5 ♔f8 17. ♖hf1± Velimirović–Bronštejn, Vinkovci 1970 — 10/556; 14... ♘d5 15. ♘d5 ♗d5 16. ♕g7 0-0-0 17. ♖hf1± Bronštejn] 15. ♗b5!? [15. ♗f3 ♗f3 16. gf3 g6! 17. f4 ♕b7! 18. h4 0-0-0∓ Larsen–Portisch, Manila 1974 — 18/510; 18. ♖he1!?] ab5 16. ♘db5 ♕c5 17. ♕g7 0-0-0 18. ♕f7 ♗g5= Bronštejn

¹³ 14... ♖c8 15. fe7 b4 [15... ♕b6 16. ♖he1 h5 17. f5 e5 18. f6!+– Rantanen–Denman, Skopje (ol) 1972 — 14/509] 16. ♘d5 ed5 17. ♖he1 ♕c4!∞

¹⁴ 15... d5 16. ♗d5! [16. ♘ce2 0–0 17. ♗c6 ♗d4 18. ♘d4 ♕f4 19. ♔b1 ♕c7!∓] ♕f4 17. ♔b1 ♗d4 18. ♗c6△ ♘e2±

¹⁵ 18. ♘d5 ♕c5 19. ♖e1 ♔f8 20. c3 h5 [Keres–Fischer, Jugoslavija (ct) 1959] 21. ♖e5∞

¹⁶ 19. ♖e5!? g6 20. ♘d5 ♕a7 [20... ♕c5 21. c3 ♔g7 22. f5! gf5 23. ♖f5 ♖d8= Dueball–Bjerre, Dresden 1969 — 8/455; 20... ♕b8 21. ♖de4 ♔g7 22. f5 gf5 23. ♖f5 ♖d8= Andersson–Donner, Berlin 1971 — 12/502] 21. c3 ♔g7 22. f5 gf5 23. ♘e3 ♕c7 24. ♖d6 ♖d8= Meštrović–Bukić, Jugoslavija (ch) 1975

¹⁷ 11. ♗f6?! ♘f6 12. e5 [12. ♖he1 ♗b7 13. ♔b1 0-0-0=] ♗b7 13. ♕g3 de5 14. fe5 ♘d7 15. ♕g7 [15. ♖he1 0-0-0 16. ♕g7? ♘c5∓ Paoli–Toluš, Balatonfüred 1958] ♕e5 16. ♕e5 ♘e5 17. ♗e4 0-0-0=⊥ Drimer–Sofrevski, Balatonfüred 1960

¹⁸ 12... ♘d5 13. ed5 ♗g5 [13... ♗d5?! 14. ♕d5! ed5 15. ♖e7 ♔f8 16. ♗f5 ♖d8 17. ♗e6+–] 14. ♖e6?! [14. ♘e6 fe6 15. ♕h5 ♔f8 16. fg5 ♘e5 17. ♗h7 ♕c4 18. b3 ♕f4 19. ♔b1 ♔e7–+ Miščević–Mašić, Vršac 1973] fe6 15. ♘e6 ♕b6! [15... ♕a5? 16. ♕h5 g6 17. ♕g5! ♖g8 18. ♖d2!+– Velimirović–Ljubojević, Jugoslavija (ch) 1972 — 13/523; 17... ♖f8 18. f5 ♗d5 19. ♘f8 ♘f8 20. fg6 ♕a2 21. gh7± Solonec–Balandir, SSSR 1973]

16. ♕h5 g6 17. ♗g6 [17. ♕g5 ♕e3! 18. ♔b1 ♔f7−+] ♔e7∓ Pioch−Pytel, Polska 1973 — 15/470; 15. ♕h5∞ Jacobsen

19 13. ed5!?∞

20 **13... ♗f8** 14. e5!? [14. ♗f6?! gf6 15. ed5 ♔d8 16. ♕e4 ♕c5= Jimenez−Mecking, Palma de Mallorca 1970 — 10/557] de5 [14... ♘e4 15. ♗e4±] 15. fe5 ♘e4 [15... ♘e5 16. ♘g7+− Enevoldsen−Hamann, Danmark 1972 — 13/522] 16. ♗e4 de4 17. ♖e4 ♕c4 18. e6!+− Vitolinš−Zilber, SSSR 1973 — 15/471; **13... ♔f8** 14. ♕g3 [14. ed5!?] de4 15. ♗e4 ♗e4 16. ♖e4 ♕c5!? [16... ♘e4? 17. ♗e7 ♔e8 18. ♕g7 ♖f8 19. ♕d4+− Beljavski−Trifunov, Sombor 1972 — 14/510] 17. ♗f6 ♗f6 18. ♘d6 ♕c7 [18... ♘b6!?∞] 19. ♕e3 g6 20. ♖e8 ♔g7 21. ♘f5 gf5 22. ♕g3= Wibe−Gunnarsson 1973

21 **14. e5** de5 15. fe5 ♘e5 16. ♖e5 ♕e5 17. ♗f4 d4∓ Boey−Hamann, Skopje (ol) 1972 — 14/508; **14. ♗h4**!?

22 ∞ Parma, Marić

23 12... b4 13. ♘d5! ed5 14. ed5 [14. e5 de5 15. fe5 ♘e4?! 16. ♗e4 ♗g5 17. ♕g5 de4 18. e6 ♘e5 19. ♘f5 f6∞; 18. ♘f5 ♕e5 19. ♘d6 ♔f8 20. ♕e5 ♘e5 21. ♘b7±⊥ Čudinovski−Petrušin, SSSR 1973; 15... ♘h5 16. ♕h4 ♗g5 17. ♕g5 g6 18. e6!±⊞] ♔d8 15. ♕e3 [15. ♘f5 ♗f8∓] ♖e8 16. ♘f5 ♘d5 17. ♕e2 ♘7b6 18. ♕h5! ♗g5 [18... g6 19. ♘e7 ♘e7 20. ♕h7± Geler] 19. ♕g5 f6 20. ♖e8±→» Geler−K. Grigorjan, SSSR (ch) 1973 — 16/494

24 13. ♗f6 ♘f6 [13... ♗f6? 14. ♗b5 ab5 15. ♘db5±→; 13... gf6 14. ♕g7!±] 14. ♕g7 ♖df8 15. ♕g3 b4 16. ♘a4 ♖hg8 17. ♕f2 ♘d7 [17... ♕a5 18. b3 ♔b8 19. ♔b1 ♖c8 20. g3 ♘d7 21. ♘f3± Mesing−Čabrilo, Jugoslavija 1973 — 15/473; 21. e5!± Martinović−Mesing, Jugoslavija 1974 — 17/529] 18. ♔b1! [18. c3 ♘c5 19. ♗c2 ♘a4 20. ♗a4 bc3 21. ♖d3 cb2 22. ♔b2 ♕b6∞ Minić−Novoselski, Jugoslavija (ch) 1973 — 15/472; 18. b3!? ♘c5 19. ♘b2 ♔b8 20. ♔b1 ♗f6 21. g3± Mesing−Vujačić, Jugoslavija (ch) 1973] ♔b8 19. c3!± Spaski−Fischer (m) 1972 — 14/507

25 15... de5 15. fe5 ♘d5 17. ♗e7 ♘e7 18. ♘d6 ♔b8 19. ♘f7+−

26 16. ef6 gf6 17. ♗h4 ♗c5!=∞ Minić

27 **16... ♗c5** 17. ef6 gf6 18. fe6 fe6 19. ♖e6+− **16... ♘e4** 17. ♘e4 ♕b5 18. ♗e7 de4 19. ♗d8 ♖d8 20. fe6 fe6 21. ♕g7± Széles−Bartha, Hungary 1974 — 18/511

28 Velimirović−Casas, Nice (ol) 1974 — 18/516

29 **11... b5**?! 12. e5 de5 13. ♘e6 fe6 14. ♗g6 ♔d8 15. ♗f6 ♗f6 [15... gf6 16. ♕e6 ♖b8 17. ♘d5 ♕d6 18. ♕f7 ♖f8 19. ♕g7 ♖b7 20. ♖d2±] 16. ♕e6 ♕c4! 17. ♘d5 ♕a2 18. ♕d6!± Zaharov−Palatnik, SSSR 1973 — 16/495; **11... ♘f8**!? 12. f5? ♘8h7 13. ♗e3 e5 14. ♘b3 b5∓ Savon−Šusterman, SSSR 1974 — 18/517; 12. ♗f6!?±; **11... ♖g8**!?

30 **12. f5** e5 13. ♘f3 [13. ♘b3 ♗d7 14. ♔b1 0-0-0 15. ♗f6?! ♗f6 16. ♘d5 ♘d5 17. ed5 e4!∓ Ciocaltea−Najdorf, Nice (ol) 1974 — 17/531; 15. ♗e3!?] ♗d7 14. ♗f6 ♗f6 15. g4 0-0-0 16. ♕g3 ♗g5! 17. ♘g5 hg5 18. h4= Grefe−Browne, USA (ch) 1974 — 18/512; **12. ♖hf1** ♗d7 [12... e5 13. ♘f5 ♗f5 14. ♕f5 hg5 15. fg5→∞] 13. f5 e5 14. ♘b3 0-0-0 15. ♗e3 ♘a4 15. ♗d2 ♘c3 17. ♗c3 ♔b8= Bronštejn−Tukmakov, SSSR 1974 — 18/519

31 15. ♗f6 ♗f6 16. ♘e4 d5!∓

32 16... ♖d7!? 17. ♗b6 ♕b6 18. ♗c4 ♗d8= Minić

33 **19. ♘d5**? ♘d5 20. ♗d5 ♗f6 21. ♕b3 ♕b3 22. ♗b3 ♖e1! 23. ♖e1 ♗g5∓⊥ Timman−Browne, Wijk aan Zee 1974 — 17/530; **19. ♗d5** ♗b4 20. ♘a4 [20. ♗f7? ♖d1 21. ♖d1 ♖e3−+] ♕f2 [20... ♗d2!?] 21. ♖e8= Planinc−Browne, Madrid 1973 — 16/497

34 10... h6 11. ♗f6 ♘f6 [11... ♗f6 12. h4 g5 13. hg5 hg5 14. e5! ♖h1 15. ♕h1 de5 16. ♘e6! fe6 17. ♕h5±→»] 12. h4 b5 13. g5 ♘d7 14. f5 ♘e5 15. ♕h5±↑ Geler

35 11. a3 ♖b8 [11... ♗b7 12. h4 ♖c8 13. ♗f6 gf6 14. g5 f5 15. ♖h2 ♘c5 16. ♕h5 fe4 (Böök−Uusi, SSSR 1959) 17. f5!±↑; 12... 0-0-0!?=] 12. ♗f6 ♘f6 13. g5 ♘d7 14. f5! ♘c5 15. b4∞

36 12... ♘b6 13. ♗f6 ♗f6 14. g5 [14. ♘db5 ab5 15. ♘b5 ♗b2!∓] ♗e7 15. h4 [15. f5 e5? 16. f6! ed4 17. ♘d5!±; 15... ♗g5 16. ♔b1 e5 17. ♘e6 fe6 18. ♕h5 ♕f7∓] b4 16. ♘ce2 g6 17. ♔b1 d5∓ Saharov−Korčnoj, SSSR 1960; 17. ♗h3!=

37 15... ♖c8 16. ♖e2 ♗d8∓

38 Bernstein−Fischer, USA (ch) 1958

39 **12. h4** b4 13. ♘ce2 [13. ♘d5 ed5 14. ed5 ♘b6 15. ♖e1 ♗b7 16. ♘f5 ♗d5∓] ♗b7 14. ♘g3 d5 15. ♗g2 de4 16. ♘e4 0-0-0∓↑ Holmov−Suetin, SSSR 1964; **12. a3** ♗b7 [12... ♘c5? 13. f5! ♖b8 14. fe6 fe6 15. g5! fg5 16. b4± Toluš−Aronin, SSSR (ch) 1957] 13. f5 e5 14. ♘de2 ♘b6 15. ♘g3 ♖c8 16. ♖d2 ♕c5 17. h4 ♖g8!∓↑; **12. ♗d3** b4 13. ♘ce2 ♗b7 14. ♔b1 ♘c5 15. f5 d5= Padevski−Evans, La Habana (ol) 1966 — 2/467; **12. ♗g2** ♗b7 13. ♖he1 0-0-0 14. a3 ♘b6 15. ♖d3 ♔b8 16. ♖ed1 d5= Gligorić−Fischer, Zürich 1959

40 **12... b4**?! 13. fe6! bc3 14. ed7 ♗d7 15. e5! ♖b8 16. ef6 ♗f8 17. g5!± Estrin−Sergijevski, SSSR 1962; **12... ♘c5** 13. fe6 fe6 14. a3 0−0 15. ♗d3 [15. ♗e2!?±] ♖b8 16. h4 b4 17. ab4 ♖b4 18. ♕e3 ♕b6 19. ♗e2 ♘a4 20. ♘a4 ♖a4 21. b3± Capelan−Donner, Solingen 1968 — 6/579; 14. g5!?± Boleslavski

41 13... b4?! 14. ♘ce2△ ♘f4±→⊞

42 **14. g5** fg5 [14... b4? 15. gf6 ♗f6 16. ♖g1 ♔h8 17. ♕h6 ♕e7 18. ♘c6 ♘c6 19. e5+− Holmov−Bronštejn, SSSR (ch) 1964]

15. fe6 fe6 16. ♘e6 ♕d7 17. ♘d5 ♕e6∓; **14. ♘ce2** ♔h8 [14... ♗b7!?] 15. ♘f4 ♖g8 16. fe6 [16. ♖g1? d5!∓ Gligorić–Fischer, Jugoslavija (ct) 1959; 16. ♗e2 ♗b7! 17. fe6 fe6 18. ♘fe6 ♕a5 19. ♔b1 ♗e4∓ Kotkov–Belinkov, SSSR 1971 — 11/400] fe6 17. ♘fe6 ♗e6 18. ♘e6 ♕d7 19. ♘d4 ♕g4 20. ♕g4 ♘g4= Spaski–Donner, Leiden 1970 — 10/558

43 14... ♕d8 15. g5±; 15. ♘c6 ♘c6 16. ♖d3+–

44 15. ♖g1? ♖g8 16. g5 ♗f8 17. ♕f6? ♗g7–+

45 **15... ♘g4** 16. ♕h4!±; **15... ♕d8** 16. ♘c6! ♘c6 17. g6 fg6 18. fg6± Pjaeren–K. Grigorjan, SSSR 1974 — 18/522

46 17. ♘e6 ♗e6 18. fe6 ♕c8 19. ♗h3 f5 20. ♖hg1 ♕e6 21. ef5 ♕f7 22. ♗g2 ♖ab8 23. ♗d5 ♕f8 24. ♕h3 ♖g7 25. ♖gf1± Boleslavski

47 19. ed5 ♕c5 20. ♗g2 ♖ac8 21. h4 a5 22. h5 g5 23. ♗e4△ ♘f5±

48 13... e5!? 14. ♘de2 b4 15. ab4 ♖b4 16. g5 ♘e4! 17. ♘e4 ♗b7 18. ♘2c3 ♗g5 19. ♔b1 0–0! 20. ♘d5 ♗d5 21. ♖d5 ♖fb8 [21... ♕b7 22. b3!±] 22. ♖b5 [22. b3? ♖b3∓] ab5= Epštejn–Andrejeva, SSSR 1972 — 14/512

49 14... ♘d7 15. f6 gf6 16. gf6 ♘f6 17. e5! de5 18. ♘c6 ♔h8 [18... ♗b7 19. ♕g3 ♔h8 20. ♘e5 ♗d8 21. ♖d8 ♕d8 22. ♖g1 ♘h5 23. ♕g8!+–] 19. ♘b8± Kavalek–Donner, Wijk aan Zee 1969 — 7/435

50 19. ♗d3 a5 20. ♘d2 a4 21. f6 ♗d8 22. ♘c4 ♖c4 [22... ♕c5? 23. e5! g6 24. ♘e4± Šamkovič–K. Grigorjan, SSSR (ch) 1971 — 12/503] 23. ♗c4 a3 24. ba3 gf6= Gufeljd

51 **13. ♗g2**?! b4∓; **13. ♗h3** b4! 14. ♘ce2 ♗b7 15. ♔b1 ♘c5 16. ♘g3 d5∓↑⊞; **13. ♕h3** ♘c5 14. b4 ♘a4 15. ♘a4 ba4 16. g6 ♗f6! 17. gf7 ♕f7 18. e5 de5 19. ♗g2 ed4! [19... ♖b8 20. ♘c6±] 20. ♗a8 0–0 21. ♕d3 ♕c7 22. ♗e4 h6 23. ♔b1 a5 24. ♖hg1? ab4∓ Hort–Gligorić, Wijk aan Zee 1971 — 11/401; 24. b5!?∓; **13. h4** b4! 14. ♘ce2 ♗b7 15. ♘g3 d5 16. e5 g6 17. ♗d3 ♘c5 18. h5 0-0-0= Komljenović–Bukić, Jugoslavija (ch) 1972 — 13/532

52 14... ♗d7!? Geler

53 15... ♗b7 16. fe6 ♗e4 17. ♗g2 ♗g2 18. ♕g2 0–0 19. ♘f4 [19. ef7 ♘f7 20. ♘e6 ♕c4 21. ♘f8 ♖c8 22. ♔b1!± Saharov–Belov, SSSR 1965] ♕c4 20. ♘d5± Pavlov–Minić, Hamburg 1965

54 22. ♔b1±→⊞ Strautinš–Štaerman, SSSR 1966 — 2/468

55 **14... e5** 15. ♘d5 ♕c5 16. ♘e6 fe6 17. ♕h5 ♔f8 18. fe6+–; **14... ♘c5** 15. ♗b5! ab5 16. ♘db5 ♕e7 [16... ♕a5? 17. ♘d6 ♔e7 (17... ♔f8 18. ♘f7! ♔f7 19. fe6 ♔g6 20. ♕f5 ♔h6 21. ♖d5+–) 18. ♕h5! g6 19. ♕g5 f6 20. ♕h6+– Seuss–Beni, Austria 1966 — 1/331] 17. ♘d6 ♔f8 18. ♖hg1 ♗h6 19. e5±→; **14... ♘f6** 15. ♖g1 ♗h6 16. fe6 fe6 17. e5 ♗b7 18. ♕h3 de5 19. ♘c6⊥

56 15... ♕e7 16. ♘e6! [16. fe6 g6 17. ef7 ♔f7 18. ♕e2 ♗g4 19. ♕f2 ♕f6=] ♗e6 17. fe6 g6 18. ef7 ♔f7 19. ♕e2 ♔g7 20. ♘d5±↑⊞ Ervin–Gligorić, USA 1972 — 13/526

57 16. fe6 g6 17. ef7 ♔f7 18. ♕e2 ♔g7? 19. h4!± Asfora–Najdorf, Argentina 1972 — 13/527; 18... ♗g4=

58 17... g6 18. ef7 ♔f7 19. ♕h6±

59 **20. ♖gf1**?! ♗g7 21. ♕g2 ♘c4∓ Matulović–Quinteros, Wijk aan Zee 1974 — 17/532; **20. ♘d5**!↑±

60 **14. a3** ♗g5 [14... ♗d7 15. h4±] 15. ♔b1 ♗f6? 16. fe6 fe6 17. ♗b5 ab5 18. ♘db5 ±→ Pietzsch–Bogdanović, Sarajevo 1966 — 1/332; 15... 0–0∓; **14. g6** hg6 14. fg6 ♗g5 [15... fg6 16. b4 ♘a4 17. ♘a4 ba4 18. ♗h3± Kotkov–Uljanov, SSSR 1965; 15... 0–0 16. gf7 ♖f7 17. ♕g4 b4 18. ♘ce2 ♗b7 19. ♘g3 ♖c8∓ Atanasov–Maeder, Groningen 1969] 16. ♔b1 b4 17. ♘ce2 fg6 18. ♕g4 ♗f6 19. ♕g6 ♕f7∓ Gutman; **14. fe6** fe6 15. ♗h3 [15. h4!?] b4 16. ♘ce2 ♗g5 17. ♔b1 ♕f7?! 18. e5! d5 19. ♕g2 ♗h6 20. ♖hf1 ♕g6 21. ♕f3± Muhin–Danov, SSSR 1966 — 2/469; 17... ♗f6!?∓; **14. ♖g1** b4 15. ♘ce2 e5 16. f6 ed4 17. fe7 d3 18. cd3 b3! 19. ab3 ♘d3 20. ♔b1 ♘e5∓ Boleslavski–Aronin, SSSR (ch) 1956; **14. b4** ♘a4 15. ♘a4 ba4 16. fe6?! ♗g5 17. ♔b1 0–0∓ Matulović–Mašić, Vršac 1969 — 8/459; 16. ♖g1=

61 14... ♗f8?! 15. ♗b5! ♗d7 [15... ab5 16. ♘db5 ♕b8 17. fg7+–] 16. e5 d5 17. ♘f5!± Oechslein–Olsson, corr. 1969 — 8/458

62 **16. ♕e3** ♗b7 [16... ♗d7!?; 16... h5!?] 17. ♗h3! h5 18. ♔b1 ♗h6 19. ♕f3 0-0-0? 20. ♘d5±→ Barczay–Bacso, Hungary 1973 — 16/498; 19... b4!?∞; **16. a3** ♖b8 17. ♗h3 [17. b4 ♘a4 18. ♘a4 ba4 19. ♔b2 ♖g8 20. c3 ♖g6 21. ♗d3 e5 22. ♘f5 ♖f6∞] b4 18. ab4 ♖b4 19. ♖he1 ♕b6 20. ♘d5 ♗h6 21. ♔b1 ♖b2 22. ♔a1 ed5 23. ed5 ♔f8 24. ♕e2 ♖b1=; 16... ♗d7! 17. ♕h5 — 16. ♕h5

63 19. ♕h3!? ♕d7 20. ♖he1 ♔d8 21. ♘c6 ♔c7 22. ♕h4 a5 23. ♔b1 h5 24. ♕c4!=/∞ Poulsson–George, Ybbs 1968 — 6/580

64 20. ♘c6!? ♔c8 21. ♕h3 ♔b7 22. ♖e2! [22. ♘b4? ♕d7! 23. ♕h5 ♖g8 24. ♘c6 a5∓ Ciocaltea–Fischer, Netanya 1968 — 7/437; 24. ♘d3!?; 22. ♖d4 a5 23. ♘b4 ab4? 24. ♖b4 ♔a7 25. ♖e3 ♘a6 26. ♖a3 ♗h6 27. ♔d1 ♖c8 28. ♖a6+– Minić–Tringov, Beograd 1965; 23... ♕d7! 24. ♕c3 ab4∓ Kopilov–Danov, SSSR 1966 — 2/470] h5 [22... ♕d7±↑ Žuravlev–Prieditis, SSSR 1969] 23. ♖de1 ♔b6 24. ♕h4 a5∞ Boersma–Maeder, Nederland 1968 — 5/484

65 22. de6 ♘e6 [22... ♕c6!? Bukić] 23. ♖e6=/∞ Meštrović–Bukić, Jugoslavija 1974 — 17/533

66 16... b4? 17. ♘d5 ed5 18. ed5 ♗d7 [18... ♗b7 19. ♗h3±; 18... ♘d7 19. ♗h3 ♘f6 20. ♕g5 ♗h3? 21. ♕f6 ♖g8 22. ♖he1±; 20... ♗e7 21. ♖he1 ♗h3 22. ♕f6 ♖g8 23. ♕h4!±→⊞ Poselnikov–Kondakov, corr. 1974 — 18/521] 19. ♖e1 ♔d8 20. ♔b1! [20. ♕f7? ♔c8? 21. ♖g1 ♔b7 22. ♘e6!± Scholl–Donner, Amsterdam 1970 — 10/560; 20... ♗h6 20. ♔b1 ♗e8!∓] ♗e8 [20... ♔c8 21. ♕f7 ♔b7 22. ♘e6!± Krnić–Vujović, Jugoslavija 1971 — 13/525] 21. ♗h3△ ♖e3±

67 17. a3 0-0-0 [17... ♖g8 18. ♕h7 ♖g6 19. ♕h4 0-0-0 20. ♔b1 ♗h6 21. ♘f3 ♗c6 22. ♗h3 ♔b7 23. ♖hg1 ♖dg8 24. ♖g6 ♖g6 25. ♖g1± Boleslavski] 18. ♕f7 [18. b4 ♘b7? 19. ♔b2 ♗e8 20. ♗h3 ♔b8 21. ♖hf1 ♕b6 22. ♖f3± Matulović–Bogdanović, Sarajevo 1971 — 11/403; 18... ♘b3! 19. ♔b2 ♘d4 20. ♖d4 ♔b8 21. ♗h3 ♖c8 22. ♖d3 ♗c6∓ Matulović–Zuckerman, Vrnjačka Banja 1971 — 11/404; 19. cb3 ♕c3 20. ♔b1 ♔b8 21. ♖d3 ♕c7 22. ♗h3 ♗e8 23. ♖c1∞ Boleslavski; 18. ♔b1!?] ♗h6 19. ♔b1 ♖hf8 [19... ♖df8? 20. ♕h5 ♖f6 21. ♗b5±↑] 20. ♕h5 [20. ♕h7 ♖f6 21. ♕e7 ♖ff8 22. ♕h4 ♗g7=∞] ♖f6 21. ♗h3 ♖df8= Ribli–Bukić, Debrecen 1970 — 10/559

68 17... 0-0-0?! 18. ♕f7 ♗h6 19. ♔b1 ♖df8 20. ♕h5! ♖f6 21. e5! de5 22. ♘e6± Parma–Bogdanović, Titovo Užice 1966 — 2/472

69 18. ♘d5 ed5 [18... ♕b7 19. ♖he1 0-0-0 20. ♘e7 ♔b8 21. ♔b1 ♗e8 22. e5± Martinović–Buljovčić, Vukovar 1966 — 2/471] 19. ed5 0-0-0 20. ♘c6=∞ Milić

70 19. ♘g3 ♔b8 20. ♔b1 [20. ♕f7!?] ♗c8= Matanović–Bukić, Jugoslavija (ch) 1969 — 7/438

71 22. ♖hf1 ♖hf8 23. ♖f6 ♖f6 24. ♕h4 [24. ♘g3!? Parma] ♖g6 25. ♘f3 [25. ♘b3 ♗g5 26. ♕h7 ♖h6 27. ♕g7 (Tringov–Browne, Sarajevo 1970 — 9/434) ♖h3∞; 25... ♕d8!?] ♗e3 [25... ♗a4?! 26. ♘ed4 ♔b8 27. ♗f5± Nowak–Schmidt, Polska 1971 — 11/402] 26. ♘f4 ♗f4 27. ♕f4± Parma–Zuckerman, Netanya 1971 — 11/405; 25... a5= Browne–Mecking, San Antonio 1972 — 14/513

72 **13... ♘c5** 14. h4 ♗d7 15. f5! ♕b6 [15... ♕a5 16. e5! d5 17. ♘d5! ed5 18. ♕d5 ♖a7 19. f6 gf6 20. ef6 ♗f8 21. ♘c6±; 18... 0–0 19. f6 ♗e6! 20. ♘e6 fe6 21. ♕g2!±] 16. b4! ♖c8 [16... ♘a4 17. ♘a4 ba4 18. fe6±] 17. ♗h3! [17. bc5 ♕c5 18. ♔b2 d5!] 0–0 18. f6!±→ Adorjan–Hamann, Amsterdam 1970 — 10/561; **13... ♘b6** 14. h4 ♗d7 15. f5±

73 **14. h4** d5! 15. ed5 ♘b6 16. f5 ♘d5 17. fe6 0-0-0! 18. ♗g2 ♘c3 19. ♕b7 ♕b7 20. ♗b7 ♔b7 21. bc3 ♗a3 22. ♔b1 fe6 23. ♘e6 ♖c8=⊥ Sherwin–Fischer, USA 1960; **14. ♖g1** ♘c5 [14... 0-0-0!?] 15. ♗h3 g6 16. ♕e3 ♕b6! 17. f5 e5 18. ♘d5 [18. f6 ed4 19. ♕d4 ♗d8! 20. e5 0–0∓] ♗d5 19. ed5 ed4 20. ♕d4 0–0! 21. f6 ♖fe8=

74 **14... ♘c5** 15. ♕e3! [15. f5? e5 16. f6 ed4 17. ♘d5 ♗d5 18. ed5±; 15... ♗g5!?=; 15. ♖hg1 g6 16. ♕e3 e5 17. ♘de2 ♕b6 18. ♘d5 ♗d5 19. ed5± Šmit–Štejn, SSSR 1963; 16... ♕b6!?=] g6 16. f5 gf5 17. ef5 0-0-0 18. fe6 ♔b8 19. ♖hg1± Olafsson–Garcia, Mar del Plata 1960; **14... b4** 15. ab4 ♕c4 16. ♖he1 [16. ♖hg1 ♕b4 17. ♗e6 fe6 18. ♘e6 ♘c5 19. ♘g7 ♔d8 20. ♕e3 ♔c7 21. ♖d4 ♕b6 22. ♘d5 ♗d5 23. ed5± Bazan–Szabo, Buenos Aires 1960] ♖b8 [16... ♕b4? 17. ♘d5! ed5 18. ed5 ♘b6 19. ♖e7! ♔e7 20. ♕e4 ♔d8 21. ♘c6+– Kuindži–Jansa, Lvov 1961] 17. b5 ab5 18. ♘db5±

75 15. ♗e6!? fe6 16. ♘e6 ♕b6 [16... ♕c4 17. ♘d5! ♗d5 18. ed5 ♔b7 19. b3 ♕c8 20. ♖d3 ♘b6 21. ♖c3 ♕d7 22. ♖c7± Talj–Gligorić, Moskva 1963] 17. ♘d5 ♗d5 18. ed5 g6 19. ♖he1 ♔b7 20. ♕c3!±

76 15... e5 16. f6! ed4 [16... gf6 17. ♘f5 ♗f8 18. gf6 ♔b8 19. ♘g7!±] 17. fe7 ♖de8 18. ♖d4 ♖e7 19. ♖hd1 ♔b8 20. ♗d7!±

77 18... ♕b6!?

78 20. ♘f7 ♕e7 21. ♘h8 ♖h8 22. ♖he1 ♗f4 23. ♕b3± Gligorić–Fischer, Jugoslavija (ct) 1959

79 22. ♘f7±

80 14. f5 ♘e5!? [14... b4?! 15. fe6 ♘e5 16. ♘d5! ♘f3 17. ♘c7 ♔d8 18. ♘a6 ba3 19. ♘c6 ♔e8 20. b3 ♗g5 21. ♔b1±; 14... ♗g5 15. ♔b1 ♘e5 16. ♕h5 ♕e7 17. ♖g1 ♗f6 18. fe6 g6 19. ef7 ♕f7 20. ♕h6 ♗g7 21. ♕h4 0–0= Rakitin–Gutkin, SSSR 1971 — 13/529] 15. ♕g3 b4 16. ab4 ♖b4 17. ♗h3 [17. ♘b3 g6 18. h4 gf5 19. ef5 ♗b7∓ Agzamov–Lepeškin, SSSR 1965; 17. h4 g6 18. ♗h3 gf5 19. ef5 ♗b7 =; 17... ♕a5 18. ♔b1 ♗d7 19. fe6 fe6 20. ♘b3 ♕b6 21. ♗d3 a5=] ♕b6 18. fe6!? ♖d4 [18... fe6? 19. ♘e6 ♖b2 20. ♖hf1+–] 19. ef7 ♘f7=

81 14... 0–0 15. g6! hg6 16. ♘e6 fe6 17. ♗e6 ♖f7 18. h4±→

82 **15. ♘f5**?! ef5! [15... 0–0± Parma–Buljovčić, Jugoslavija 1965] 16. ♘d5 ♕d8 17. ef5 ♗b7 18. f6 gf6 19. ♕h5 ♗d5 20. ♖d5 b4 21. a4 b3∓ Uljanov–Lepeškin, SSSR 1965; **15. b4** ♘a4 16. ♘a4 ba4 17. ♔b2 a5 18. c3 e5! 19. ♗c8 ed4∓→ Estrin–Uljanov, SSSR 1966

83 **17... g6**? 18. f6 ♗d8 19. ♖ge1 0–0 20. ♗g4! ♕b7 21. ♕h3 h5 22. ♗h5 e5 23. ♗g4 ♗g4 24. ♕h6±→ **17... ♗d7** 18. fe6 fe6 19. ♘e6±; **17... ♕b7** 18. f6 ♗f8 19. b3 gf6 20. gf6 ♗h6 21. ♔b2 ♕b6 22. ♘ce2± 19... a5!?=

84 18. f6?! gf6 19. gf6 ♗f8 20. ♘b3 [20. b3 ♖d4∓] ♖b3! 21. cb3 ♘b3 22. ♔c2 ♕g1 23. ♔b3 ♕b6 24. ♔a2 ♖g8∓→ Džanojev–Lepeškin, SSSR 1966

85 19... ♘e6 20. ♘d5 ♕c5 21. ♘b4 ♕b4 22. e5 ♗b7 23. ♕f5 ♕f4 24. ♕f4 ♘f4 25. ed6 ♘e2 26. ♔b1 ♘g1= Ivkov–Donner, Beverwijk 1965; 24. ♔b1!?

86 22. ♘b4 ♕b4! [22... ♕a1? 23. ♔d2 ♕b2 24. ♕b3! ♗g5 25. ♔e1 ♕e5 26. ♕a4 ♔f7 27. ♘d3±] 23. e5 ♕f4 24. ♕f4 ♘f4 25. ed6 ♗d6 26. ♖gf1 [Balašov–Danov, SSSR 1965] ♗e7=

87 **16. f5** ♘e5! 17. ♕g3 [17. ♕e2 ♕b6!∓] ♕b6 18. ♘b3 0–0= Geler; **16. h5** ♕b6 17. ♘b3 [Lobigas–Micheli, Skopje (ol) 1972 — 14/515] ♘c5 18. ♘c5 ♕c5 19. g6 fg6 20. hg6 h6 21. ♖h5 ♕b6∞ Parma, Marić; 16... ♘c5!?

88 16... ♘b6 17. f5! [17. b3 d5! 18. ed5 ♗b7⩱] ♘c4 18. fe6 0–0 19. b3 [19. ♘d5? ♕a5∓] fe6 20. ♕g3 ♕a5 21. bc4 ♖c4 22. ♘b1+– Barczay–Tatai, Bari 1970 — 10/566

89 17. ♖hf1!?

90 **17... ♕a5** 18. ♘c6! ♕a1 19. ♔d2 ♕b2 20. ♖b1 ♘b3 21. ♔d1+–; **17... ♕b6** 18. fe6 fe6 19. ♘e6 ♘e6 [19... ♗e6 20. ♗e6 ♘e6 21. ♘d5 ♕c5 22. ♘b4 ♕b4 23. e5 ♕f4 24. ♕f4 ♘f4 25. ed6±⊥] 20. ♘d5 ♕b7 21. ♘b4?! ♕b4 22. e5 ♗b7! 23. ♕f5 ♕f4 24. ♕f4 ♘f4 25. ed6 ♗h1 26. de7 ♗d5!–+; 21. ♕c3!±→

91 18. fe6 fe6 19. b3? ♖f8 20. ♕e3 g6 21. ♗g4 ♕b6∓ Matulović–Bogdanović, Sarajevo 1966 — 1/333; 19. ♖hf1 — 18. ♖hf1

92 **18... ♖b2** 19. fe6 ♗e6 20. ♗e6 fe6 21. ♘e6! ♘e6 33. ♕f7 ♔d7 23. e5!±→⊞; **18... ♖f8** 19. fe6 [19. ♕h5 e5 20. ♘e6 ♗e6 21. fe6 ♖b2 22. ♖f7∞ Levčenkov–Žuravljev, SSSR 1971 — 12/505] fe6 20. ♕e3 [20. ♕h5 g6 21. ♕h7? ♗g5–+; 21. ♖f8 ♗f8∓] ♖f1 21. ♖f1 ♕b6 22. ♕f2!±→⊞ Adorjan–Tatai, Amsterdam 1970 — 10/563; 20... g6!?

93 **21... ♘e4** 22. ♗e6! ♖d4 23. ♕h6 ♔g8 24. g6!+– Gutman–Lapienis, SSSR 1969 — 8/460; **21... ♔g8** 22. ♕h6 ♖c4 [22... ♖e8 23. ♗g4+– Levčenkov–Gutkin, SSSR 1971 — 13/528] 23. ♗f5±→⟫ Tabban–Bouaziz, Tunis 1971 — 11/406

94 **17. ♘e6**? fe6 18. ♗e6 ♖b2! 19. e5 de5! 20. ♕d5 ♗a3! 21. ♗d7 ♔f8!–+ Petruk–Dobocz, Polska 1970 — 10/565; **17. ♘b3**?! a5∓

95 17... ef5? 15. ♘d5 ♕c5 [18... ♕a5 19. ♕c3] 19. ef5 ♗b7 20. ♖he1 [20. f6 gf6 21. ♗d7 ♔d7 22. gf6 ♖a4! 23. c3 ♗d5 24. ♖d5 ♕c4!=] ♗d5 21. ♖d5 ♕c6 22. f6 gf6 23. gf6 ♘f6 24. ♖c5!+– B. Pytel–Hausner, corr. 1971 — 11/407

96 20... ♔g7 21. ♕h5 ♖f8 22. ♕h6 ♔h8 23. g6+–

97 **21. ♘d5** ♖b1 22. ♔d2 ♕d4 23. ♔e2 ♕c4∓; **21. ♕h5** ♔d8 22. ♕f7 ♖f8∓

98 22. ♕h3 ♘f8 23. ♗c8 ♗a3 24. ♖he1? ♖b4∓ Holmov–Savon, SSSR (ch) 1971 — 10/564; 24. ♔d2!?∞ Holmov; 24. ♖d5!?∞ Marić

99 **17. ♘f5** ♘c5! 18. ♘e7 ♕e7 19. ♕e3!? [19. h5?! ♗b7 20. h6 ♗e4 21. ♘e4 ♘e4 22. hg7 ♖c8!∓ Minić–Fischer, Rovinj-Zagreb 1970 — 9/436] ♗b7 20. ♖d4=; **17. g6** ♘c5! [17... hg6? 18. h5±→] 18. gf7 ♖f7 19. ♕e3 ♕b6 20. e5 de5 21. fe5 ♗h4?! 22. ♗f5!±→⟫ Tuczak–Pytel, Polska 1971 — 12/504; 21... ♗b7!?∞; **17. ♖hf1** ♕c5 18. ♕f2 [18. ♘b3 ♕b6 19. f5 ♘c5 20. ♘c5 ♕c5 21. f6 ♗d8 22. fg7 ♔g7 23. ♖d2 ♕e5 24. ♖df2 ♖b7= Timoščenko–K. Grigorjan, SSSR 1971 — 11/408] ♘b6 19. f5 ♘a4 20. f6 ♘c3 21. fe7!? [21. bc3? ♕c3∓ Planinc–Bukić, Jugoslavija (ch) 1972 — 13/531] ♘a2=

100 22. ♕d3 ♕a2 23. ♕a3 ♕a3 24. ba3 ♖e4 =⊥ Kuzmin–K. Grigorjan, SSSR (ch) 1971 — 11/409

101 17. ♕e3?! 0–0

102 17... ♕c7!?

103 19... dc5!? 20. g6 fg6 21. hg6 h6 22. ♘d5 ed5 23. ♗c8 0–0 [23... ♖b2 24. ♖d5∞] 24. ♕g4 [24. e5 ♖c8? 25. ♕d5 ♔h8 26. ♕f7△ ♖h6+–; 24... ♖b2!?] ♖e4 25. ♖de1!? [25. ♗f5? ♗f6!–+ Kaplan–Browne, Madrid 1973 — 16/499] ♗f6 26. c3∞ Bellin–Portisch, Teesside 1972 — 13/530

104 20. ♖hg1? ♕a5 21. ♔b1 ♕a3 22. b3 a5 23. ♖d3 ♗a6! [23... a4?! 24. ♘a2! ♖b8 25. f5 ab3 26. cb3 ♗a6 27. ♖c3 ♗c4 28. ♘c1± Cejtlin–Savon, SSSR (ch) 1971 — 12/507] 24. ♖e3 ♗c4 25. ♘a2 ♖a4–+ Korčnoj

105 20... fg6?! 21. hg6 h6 [21... h5!?] 22. ♗g4! ♕a5 23. b3! ♕a3 [23... ♗f6 24. e5! ♕a3 25. ♔b1 ♗b7 26. ♕d3 ♗e5 27. fe5 ♗h1 28. ♗e6+–; 24... ♖f4 25. ♕f4 ♗g5 26. ♕g5±] 24. ♔d2! ♖d4 25. ♔e2 ♖d1 26. ♖d1 ♕c5 27. ♕e3! ♕c6 28. ♖d3± Planinc–Savon, Mar del Plata 1971 — 11/410; 28. ♕h3!± Armas–Grünberg, Hungary 1973 — 15/474

106 Szmetan–Quinteros, Sao Paulo 1972

AUTORI-SARADNICI · АВТОРЫ-СОТРУДНИКИ · AUTHORS-ASSISTANTS · AUTOREN-MITARBEITER · AUTEURS-COLLABORATEURS · AUTORES-COLABORADORES · AUTORI-COLLABORATORI · FÖRFATTARNA-MEDARBETARE

BOTVINIK MIHAIL	**B 13** (13), **B 14** (13)	26
EUWE MAX	**B 28** (13), **B 29** (20)	33
FILIP MIROSLAV	**B 10** (19), **B 12** (14), **B 15** (14), **B 17** (22), **B 36** (11), **B 37** (7), **B 38** (8), **B 39** (13)	108
GELER EFIM	**B 20** (16), **B 21** (14), **B 22** (17), **B 23** (9), **B 24** (7), **B 25** (12), **B 26** (10), **B 70** (10), **B 71** (20), **B 72** (12), **B 73** (13), **B 74** (11), **B 75** (11), **B 76** (9), **B 77** (13), **B 78** (12), **B 79** (12), **B 80** (10), **B 81** (18), **B 97** (15), **B 98** (15)	266
GIPSLIS AJVAR	**B 92** (16), **B 99** (19)	35
HORT VLASTIMIL	**B 02** (23), **B 03** (22)	45
KERES PAUL	**B 04** (13), **B 05** (20)	33
KORČNOJ VIKTOR	**B 30** (11), **B 31** (16), **B 34** (13), **B 35** (16)	56
LARSEN BENT	**B 00** (10), **B 01** (20), **B 16** (19)	49
MATANOVIĆ ALEKSANDAR —UGRINOVIĆ DRAGAN	**B 62** (8), **B 63** (10), **B 64** (8), **B 65** (11), **B 66** (7), **B 67** (8), **B 68** (8), **B 69** (7)	67
PARMA BRUNO	**B 07** (31), **B 08** (24), **B 09** (32)	87
POLUGAJEVSKI LEV	**B 44** (20), **B 50** (13), **B 51** (8), **B 52** (9), **B 53** (8), **B 60** (7), **B 61** (9), **B 86** (11), **B 90** (5), **B 91** (7), **B 93** (13), **B 94** (11), **B 95** (6), **B 96** (24)	151
SUETIN ALEKSEJ	**B 27** (11), **B 54** (7), **B 55** (6), **B 56** (7), **B 58** (7), **B 59** (10), **B 87** (19)	67
TAJMANOV MARK	**B 40** (7), **B 41** (13), **B 42** (19), **B 43** (17), **B 45** (14), **B 46** (12), **B 47** (21), **B 58** (14), **B 49** (17)	134
TALJ MIHAIL	**B 82** (21), **B 83** (20), **B 84** (11), **B 85** (17)	69
TRIFUNOVIĆ PETAR	**B 06** (30), **B 11** (14), **B 18** (16), **B 19** (12)	72
UHLMANN WOLFGANG	**B 32** (17), **B 33** (18)	35
VELIMIROVIĆ DRAGOLJUB	**B 57** (10), **B 88** (15), **B 89** (22)	47

Tehnički urednik — Техничесский редактор — Tehnical editor — Technischer Redakteur — Rédacteur technique — Redactor técnico — Redattore tecnico — Teknisk redaktör

A. Božić

Korektori — Корректоры — Proof-readers — Korrektoren — Correcteurs — Correctores — Correttori — Korrektorläsare

A. Božić, K. Božić, S. Cvetković, S. Marjanović, D. Šahović

Štampa: Grafičko preduzeće „PROSVETA", Beograd, Đure Đakovića 21